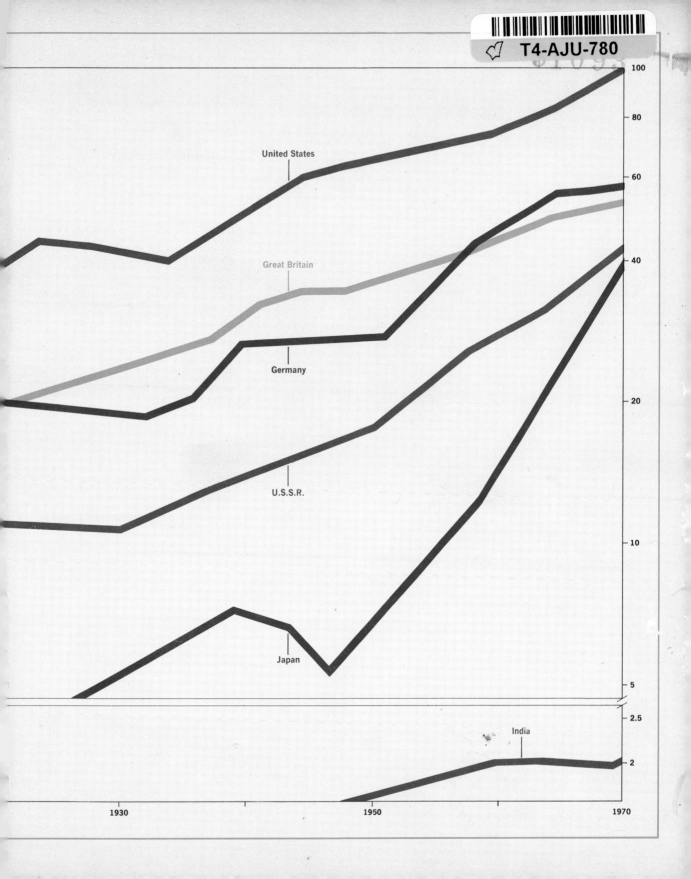

ECONOMICS

ECONOMICS

8 TH EDITION

PAUL A. SAMUELSON

Institute Professor
Massachusetts Institute of Technology

McGRAW-HILL BOOK COMPANY
New York, St. Louis, San Francisco, Düsseldorf
London, Mexico, Panama, Sydney, Toronto

ECONOMICS

Library of Congress Catalog Card Number 78-109688

ISBN 07-054565-0

4 5 6 7 8 9 0 VHVH 7 9 8 7 6 5 4 3 2 1 0

*This book was set in Laurel by Graphic Services, Inc., and bound by
Von Hoffmann Press, Inc. The designer was John Horton; the drawings
were done by Matt Roberts, Roberts, Reinhardt, & Ong, Inc. The copy
editing was done by Beatrice Eckes, the proofreading by Earle Resnick,
and the Index by Delight Ansley. The editors were Gerald C. Spencer
and John M. Morriss. John F. Harte supervised the production.*

Preface

This book is an introduction to economics. It is written for a half-year or full-year beginning course and for students who may or may not go on to further study of economics. This eighth edition is an unusually thorough revision of earlier editions.

Economics is an important subject. And experience shows it can also be an exciting one. It deals with inflation and unemployment, with how some people enjoy great wealth and even more live in deadening poverty. A subject is at its liveliest when it faces challenging problems to be solved; so in a sense—now that our cities are blighted, our environment polluted, inflation melts the value of our cash—political economy takes on a cardinal importance in every person's education. Particularly in this eighth edition, I have tried to use the touchstone of "relevance" for my exclusions and inclusions, knowing from experience that this is also the key to reader motivation and interest.

A rigorous introduction Why does a scholar interested in the frontier of research write a textbook? In my case, for two reasons: I sensed that there was coming to be a widening *gap* between the technicalities of advanced economics and what the intelligent nonprofessional has to know about the subject if he is to be a good citizen, a competent statesman, an effective businessman, or a cogent critic or defender of the modern mixed economy. And like economists here and abroad, I lamented the fact that in our generation we did not have any great introductory treatise like those which have become classics in other subjects—*The Principles of Psychology* by William James, *Differential and Integral Calculus* by Richard Courant or *Pure Mathematics* by G. H. Hardy, and in the present age *Lectures on Physics* by the Nobel laureate Richard Feynman.

Eschewing encyclopedic coverage, I have taken their motto for my motto: Nothing unnecessarily hard, but nothing essential being omitted as beyond the grasp of the serious student; and above all, nothing that later will have to be unlearned as wrong.

The reception of the book seems to have been favorable. It has been extensively used, widely translated, and appears to have left its mark on the present-day curriculum. But a book is like a child, taking on a life of its own. Our knowledge grows, times and problems change, so that no one can embalm and preserve in amber the corpus of a dynamic science.

And like a child, a book makes demands upon its parent and will not take no for an answer. Writing a beginning textbook is hard work (only my wife knows quite how hard). But its rewards have been tremendous—and I do not mean simply pecuniary rewards. Contact with millions of minds of a whole generation of students is an experience like no other that a scholar will ever meet. Writing out what we economists know about economics has been an exciting adventure. I can only hope that some of this excitement will rub off on the reader.

Revisions in this new edition Although the most obvious change has been the addition of two new chapters—Chapter 39, "Economic Inequality: Poverty, Affluence, and the Quality of Life," and Chapter 40, "Economic Problems of Race, Cities, and the Polluted Environment"—all of the book has been thoroughly revised, with no single page going unscathed. And some basic rearrangements of chapter groupings and topics have been introduced in both the macroeconomics and the microeconomics. (E.g., experience suggested that the simple multiplier be brought into

Chapter 12's introduction to income determination rather than be left in the following chapter's applications to fiscal policy and inflationary gaps; and the important Phillips-curve tradeoff between inflation and unemployment has been removed from appendixes and introduced into the main text. Or again, partly through the counsel of various colleagues at MIT and elsewhere, I have drastically changed the chapter groupings of the microeconomic treatment of costs, competitive and otherwise.)

But the biggest change has been a change in the spirit of the book. I have tried to go over every paragraph with a glass to root out complacency and smugness. True, the New Economics has had some great triumphs in scientific content and in successful applications. *But why get rid of one kind of orthodoxy just to replace it by the deadening rule of a new establishment economics?* John Kenneth Galbraith proposes new viewpoints for the new industrial state. Radical economists are knocking at the door, to insist that every facet of our society be subjected to unsparing criticism. Libertarian economists, like Milton Friedman of the University of Chicago, are challenging the consensus of post-Keynesian analysis—not by the naked force of plutocratic intimidation of teachers characteristic of the Joseph McCarthy period—but by deployment of data and the use of logical reasoning. All of these views deserve a dispassionate hearing, and in this eighth edition I try to evaluate cogent criticisms. Equally important, I have hoped to render unto the realm of value judgment that which "neutral, *wertfrei*" scholarship cannot cope with. While it has been toil to update the book and to change its design so that hard things could be made easier, it has been a release and a joy to breathe this new spirit into the work.

To the reader   Experience proves that anyone can learn economics from this book—not to become a professional scholar in the field but to gain genuine basic *literacy* in the subject. Experience also shows that an economics text has to be read with care. Each chapter is carefully planned. Each has a comprehensive summary. The diagrams and tables are defined so that each also tells its own story. With every new edition there has come new knowledge on how to utilize color most functionally—with key concepts flagged here in blue at each chapter's end, with basic principles set out in brown type, and with the diagrams' crucial points marked in gold for emphasis. This functional design is one reason why a modern text can teach, in the same time, far more than we dared cover in the past.

No author can tell you how best to read a textbook. Obviously, this is not like a novel or detective story, hammock reading for a drowsy day. The first time you read a chapter, turn its pages for perspective. Then read and underline, not stopping to overcome every difficulty. You will be pleasantly surprised to find that the final summaries and checklists of key concepts will help synthesize your understanding. And on review and rereading—giving independent attention to the self-contained story of the figures and tables—your understanding will deepen. (I should call to your attention the *Study Guide*, which Professor Romney Robinson has prepared to go along with this edition and which is cited on the next page. Even if your instructor does not assign it, you may find it a great time-saver in the end. Or for self-instruction in the analytical core, you might want to get hold of *Economics: An Introductory Program* which has been prepared by Professor Edward Foster to go along with the book.)

You will discover that harder or less important material—they are not always the same!—has been put in appendixes, or often in footnotes. And in this edition I have introduced the innovation of giving some final "Questions For Discussion" that are marked as "extra-credit problems" which enable the highly trained student to pursue on his own some of the fascinating further developments of the subject. If you are in a fast, brief course, don't be put off by this carefully planned layering of more difficult material: experience has proved that this gives the more intensive course meat to bite into, without really inconveniencing those who work with the severest time limitations. And to the bright honors student, may I say: Don't be put off by the use of color and the attempt to state matters plainly. This book is as challenging as you may care to make it. (Not a few who are now professors have written me to say that they used parts of it in their final review for their Ph.D. oral exams.)

Finally, I've tried to look ahead to what you might still want to know about in 1980. Praise is always sweet to the ears of an author, and it has been pleasant when readers have written to say some kind word about the book. But I must confess that I would have to consider it the highest praise of all if—when the election of 1984 comes around and the issues of tariffs, the public debt, and the environment are under debate—some of you should pull your old economics textbook down from the shelf for a rethinking of the issues. That would be any author's dream of glory!

To the instructor   Since almost half the classes using this book are one-semester courses, I append to the Table of Contents a suggested one-semester outline. And in the *Instructor's Manual*, newly revised in co-authorship with Professor Maureen S. Crandall of Wellesley College, suggestions are given for flexible adaptation.

Forty per cent of the teachers using this book prefer to teach microeconomics before macroeconomics. A good case can be made for either ordering, and experimental programs show each to have advantages. This text has been carefully designed for either program. The instructor who wishes to deal first with microeconomics can skip from Part One to Part Three, knowing that the exposition and cross references have been tailored with his needs in mind. Because college courses in economics are taught both by large-lecture and small-section methods, we have used MIT classrooms as a laboratory, one year trying out lecturing to a large group and another year confining classes to 25 students. A good text must be prepared with both needs in mind.

I have not hesitated to segregate some of the material into appendixes. Often this involves slightly more difficult topics, with which briefer courses can easily dispense. Sometimes, as in the case of the discussion of the stock market in Chapter 4's Appendix or the presentation of cases on supply and demand in Chapter 20's Appendix, the material is not more difficult, but is such as can be conveniently skipped. Occasionally a teacher has written me questioning the advisability of this use of the appendixes. My answer is a pragmatic one based on experimentation: because courses differ in their time span and emphasis, it is incumbent upon an author to give signals as to which sections are organically necessary and which are dispensable. For example, in this edition I have added a brief treatment of von Neumann game theory. The fact that it is put at the end of Chapter 25's Appendix will not inconvenience the reader eager for a terse account of this important subject; but this arrangement will be deemed a blessing by those instructors who lack the time for such a topic.

In this edition, I have particularly emphasized the welfare-economics aspects of competitive and other pricing, putting great stress on "externalities," public goods, and interpersonal-equity considerations. (A term like "Pareto optimality" is named in but one appendix footnote, but the issue of economic efficiency is emphasized as never before.)

Auxiliary teaching aids   To go with this eighth edition a completely revised *Study Guide* has been prepared by Professor Romney Robinson of the University of Toronto. Both as assigned by instructors and bought independently by students for self-study, the *Study Guide* has proved to be an impressive success. Available for the first time, to go with this edition (or for that matter with any similar text), is *Economics: An Introductory Program* by Professor Edward Foster of the University of Minnesota. This program covers the analytical core of macroeconomics and microeconomics: It can be assigned to the student, thereby freeing the instructor to lecture in class on other material; or students may wish, at their own option, to consolidate their understanding by working through the program. Trial tests of the Foster program have been successful at MIT and also with Professor Dennis R. Weidenaar's Purdue students.

Readings in Economics has been revised by me to go with the eighth edition. In its expanded sixth incarnation, just shy of 100 readings are provided. By use of color, editorial subheads, and generous selection from the great names of the past—Smith, Keynes, Ricardo, Marx—and the titans of the present age—Galbraith, Tobin, Friedman, Hayek, Solow, Burns, Kindleberger, Heilbroner—a broad spectrum of opinions is put before the student in a format convenient for assignment along with the text. Reference may be made to the *Instructor's Manual* for information about further teaching aids (such as McGraw-Hill's film strips and transparencies or the 4-minute silent-movie cassettes of the Visual Learning Corporation). Also available to instructors is a *Test Bank* of over 1,000 graded and matched multiple-choice questions that are taken from the Samuelson-Crandall *Manual* and appear on perforated pages convenient for reproducing quizzes in small or large numbers.

Acknowledgments   Again I am a hopeless bankrupt when it comes to indebtedness. Over the years thousands of students and hundreds of economics teachers have written, raising questions and giving me the benefit of unsparing criticisms. My MIT colleagues have helped in innumerable ways, and my conscience requires that I make special mention of Professors E. Cary Brown, Richard Eckaus, Morris Adelman and Paul MacAvoy (particularly in regard to educating me in modern antitrust), Lester Thurow, and Robert Solow, and also my earlier collaborators on the *Readings*, Dean Robert L. Bishop of MIT and President John R. Coleman of Haverford. In earlier editions I carried a growing list of economists from other colleges who have left their mark on this work, but alas that has grown beyond limits. In connection with the present edition I have received particular help from suggestions by my brother Professor Robert Summers (Pennsylvania) and his colleague, Professor Herbert S. Levine (Pennsylvania). I owe thanks also to Professors Charles Maurice (Texas A & M), Lyle Owen (Tulsa), Romney Robinson (Toronto), Richard U. Sherman, Jr. (Ohio State), and Donald J. Yankovic (Toledo). Professor Edward Coen (Minnesota) made valuable suggestions for reorganizing and improving the microeconomics, and my erstwhile collaborator, Felicity Skidmore of the Institute for Research on Poverty (University of Wisconsin), provided valuable criticism for some of the new chapters. I owe her much thanks for my conversion toward making this a thorough revision both in spirit and content. Mrs. Karen Johnson has joined that distinguished group of graduate students of MIT, many of whom have gone on to fame in their own right, who have helped to keep this book up to date. I must record special thanks for the tireless free-lance editorial efforts of Mary Griffin, who is a professional without peer in the publishing trade. My McGraw-Hill collaborators are acknowledged elsewhere. My secretary Joan Thompson helped make the preparation of the manuscript a pleasure rather than a bore, and I owe her thanks.

A textbook should be dedicated to one's children—of whom I have my share—but they will forgive me for naming my longest-time collaborator, Marion.

Paul A. Samuelson

Cambridge, Mass.
February, 1970

Contents

PART 3   THE COMPOSITION AND PRICING OF NATIONAL OUTPUT

of International Trade   Foreign-trade Supply-and-demand Charts   Effects
of Tariffs and Quotas   Qualifications and Conclusions

Summary   Questions for Discussion

APPENDIX: COMPARATIVE ADVANTAGE AMPLIFIED AND QUALIFIED   658

America without Trade   Europe without Trade   The Opening Up of
Trade   Exact Determination of the Final Price Ratio   Many Commodities
Many Countries   Increasing Costs   International Goods Movements as a
Substitute for Factor Movements

Summary to Appendix   Questions for Discussion

35   THE ECONOMICS OF TARIFF PROTECTION AND FREE TRADE   668

Noneconomic Goals   Grossly Fallacious Arguments for Tariffs   Some Less
Obvious Fallacies   The "Foreigner Will Pay" or Terms-of-trade Argument
Arguments for Protection under Dynamic Conditions   Conclusion

Summary   Questions for Discussion

36   CURRENT INTERNATIONAL ECONOMIC PROBLEMS   681

A. Modern Trends and Institutions of International Finance
Trends 1914–1950   Marshall Plan, Military Aid, and Other Programs   The
International Bank and Foreign Lending   The International Monetary Fund
The European Common Market and the Free-trade Area   Freer Multilateral
Trade: GATT

B. Threatened Breakdown of the International System
From Dollar Shortage to Dollar Glut   Reasons for Chronic International
Deficit, 1955–1970   Equilibrium in the 1970s?   Therapy for a Chronic
Deficit

C. Structural Reform of International Finance
Three Major Problems of Structural Reform   The Two-tier Gold System
Alternative Proposals for Reform   The Crawling or Sliding Peg with
Widened "Gold Points"   SDRs and Paper Gold

Summary   Questions for Discussion

PART 6   CURRENT ECONOMIC PROBLEMS

37   THE THEORY OF GROWTH   709

Stages of History   Fact and Fiction   The "Magnificent Dynamics" of
Smith and Malthus   Detailed Economic Analysis of Smith-Malthus   Graph
of Malthusian Development   End of the Labor Theory of Value   Technical
Advance and Classical Growth Theory   Ricardo-Marx-Solow Models of
Capital Accumulation   Deepening of Capital in Diagram Form   Technical
Progress and Wages   The Approximate Facts of Modern Development
Six Basic Trends of Economic Development   Analyzing the Laws of Motion

Defense Expenditure and Prosperity: An Important Digression   Publicly
Determined Thrift   Austere Fiscal Policy Combined with Expansionary
Monetary Policy   A New Cost-push Sellers' Inflation?   The Phillips-curve
Tradeoff between Full Employment and Inflation   Are Growth and Price
Stability Opposing Goals?   Wanted, an "Incomes Policy": Wage-Price
Guideposts?   Conclusion

Summary   Questions for Discussion

Suggested Outline for
a One-semester Course

For courses with institutional emphasis Chapters 6 to 9, 29, and 40, dealing with income distribution, labor, government finance, and race could be included.

*For inclusion in courses with macroeconomic emphasis.
**For inclusion in courses with microeconomic emphasis.
***For inclusion in courses with policy emphasis.

Basic Economic Concepts and National Income 1

Introduction 1

Half a century ago, when the Harvard Business School was founded, President A. Lawrence Lowell described business as "the oldest of the arts, the newest of the professions." Almost the same words can be used to describe economics: the oldest of the arts, the newest of the sciences—indeed the queen of the social sciences.

As a scholarly discipline, economics is not yet two centuries old. Adam Smith wrote his pathbreaking book *The Wealth of Nations* in 1776, a year notable for the Declaration of Independence. And the nearness of timing is hardly a coincidence: political freedom from the tyranny of monarchy was closely related to the emancipation of free-market pricing from the interfering hand of state regulation.

Adam Smith, of course, represented only a beginning. In more than a century and a half that elapsed from the publication of *The Wealth of Nations* to the publication of John Maynard Keynes' *The General Theory of Employment, Interest and Money* (1936), economics—or political economy, as it used to be called—has gone through many stages of development. Almost at the halfway point, there appeared the massive critique of capitalism by Karl Marx: *Das Kapital* (1867, followed by two posthumous volumes). A billion people, almost a third of the world's population, regard *Das Kapital* as economic truth.

And yet, without the disciplined study of economic science, how can anyone form a reasoned opinion about the merits or lack of merits in the classical, traditional economics? Or about the achievements of the "New Economics" that has evolved since 1929? Or about problems yet unsolved?

FOR WHOM THE BELL TOLLS

Few study economics merely to judge the merits in the grand debates concerning historic capitalism, the modern mixed economy, or the collectivist economic systems of the East. One studies economics to answer many and diverse questions. Here are some of the more common ones.

Poverty, development, and affluence   America is a prosperous nation. We grow more prosperous each year, and our present affluence is an outgrowth from the lower standard of productivity prevailing in past generations. In recent years all over the world, men have become preoccupied with economic development.

How can preindustrial economies, teeming with masses of people and poorly endowed with natural resources, break through the vicious circle of poverty and backwardness?
How can policies be formulated and programs be promulgated that will speed the pace of *economic growth and development?*

Look at the front flyleaf: Contrast the Western world's affluence with the poverty of India, whose growth curve barely shows on the chart; and note the success story of Japan in its bare century of contact with the modern world.

Undoubtedly this new interest in development and growth has made economics an exciting and vital subject in the capitals of the world, and on Main Street as well as Wall Street.

Personal stake in economics   An even more immediate reason for studying economics is that it deals with many of the matters that will concern each of us most:

What kinds of jobs are available? What do they pay? How much in goods will a dollar of wages buy now, and how much in a time of galloping inflation?
What are the chances that a time will come when a trained man will not be able to get work? Are the black days of the depressed 1930s likely to return?
Will automation and scientific discovery make man obsolete? How can one make a killing in the stock market? Or best run a business?

Economics is relevant to these questions, but, as will be seen, they are not the prime target of an introductory course.

Economics for the citizen   Beyond personal family matters, economics deals even more importantly with decisions each citizen must face. Here are a dozen vital problems:

Will the government tax me to help unemployed miners, or are there other things it can do to help mitigate the problem of unemployment?
Should I vote to build a new school and road now, or vote to put this aside until business slackens and cement prices come down and jobs are needed? Should I vote to keep married women out of public employment, so there will be more jobs for men?
What about antitrust legislation that purports to fight monopolies?
If you are a humanitarian, deeply concerned to improve the lot of the poor, the disadvantaged black, and the aged, will legislating a good, stiff, high minimum wage serve to help or hinder the good cause for which you fight?
Why not "fair-shares" rationing?
What consequences will follow if the federal budget is not balanced in every year? Is it true, as Moscow no longer claims, that American prosperity is dependent on cold-war military expenditures? If "peace breaks out," are we in for a recession? Can the government wash its hands of the matter, knowing that we can rely on the spontaneous forces of private markets to convert the swords of war into the plowshares of peace?

Is old-fashioned poverty from niggardliness of nature extinct? And what about "poverty midst plenty" as in the post-1929 Great Depression, when factories lay idle and people couldn't find jobs? Has this given way to the modern pockets of poverty in the ghetto and rural slums?

Economics and national interest   As Adam Smith said, security is even more important for a nation than opulence. Survival itself can depend on economics.

Can a modern nation afford expensive military expenditures (as, for example, in Vietnam)? Is it true, as ex-President Hoover once warned, that "inflation is worse than Stalin"?

Important in the minds of people in the more advanced Western civilizations and in the underdeveloped regions of the world are these questions: Two decades from now, will the Soviet Union have overtaken the United States as the most affluent society in the world? Or as the most powerful military power? What is happening to the gap between these different types of economic systems? Uncommitted people all over the world are watching this peaceful competition, deliberating over which economic system to embrace.

An introduction can serve as a preview. A diagram from the last chapter of this book (Fig. 42-1) is reproduced here as Fig. 1-1. It shows in one graphic picture the economic growth prospects for the Soviet Union and the United States. As we shall see, the economist does not have the clairvoyance of the astronomer, who can tell you exactly where all the planets will be in the year 2000 A.D. The economist must give the calculated prudent odds.

Every national issue mentioned requires economic understanding to make any progress in dealing with it. A person who has never made a systematic study of economics is handicapped in even thinking about national issues; he is like a deaf man trying to appreciate a symphony: give him a hearing aid, and he may still lack talent, but at least he has a fighting chance of sensing what music really is. The head of state[1] must be constantly making vital decisions that involve economics. But of course he need not *himself* be a professional student of economics; he need only be an intelligent "consumer" of the (often conflicting) economic information being given him.

Economic graphs throw light on future growth prospects:

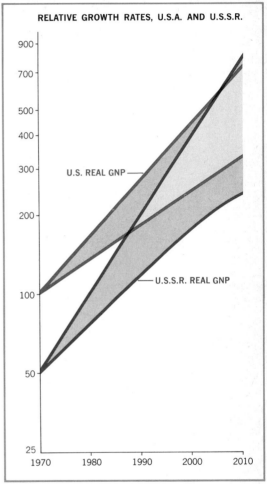

FIG. 1-1. The art of judgment, as well as scientific analysis, is involved in determining reasonable projections of growth rates free of either wishful or paranoid thinking. Not only are Americans and Russians concerned with the outcome of this economic sweepstakes, but so are Asians and Africans interested in choosing that form of economic organization which will move them most rapidly along the road of development. (Source: Fig. 42-1.)

---

[1] As an example, Winston Churchill was a great man—a leader without peer, an orator, a gifted writer, and a shrewd judge of the Hitlerian threat while most around him slept. Yet all his life, Churchill was a babe in the woods when it came to economics. In 1925, as Chancellor of the Exchequer, he put England back on the gold standard at the pre-1914 parity of $4.87 for the British pound. (Chapter 33 will explain

LIGHT AND FRUIT

Of course most students do not expect to specialize in economics. Most will study it for only a term or two, and this book is intended to give an overview of the whole subject. One's view of the world can never be quite the same after even a single semester of economics.

C. P. Snow, scientist and novelist, once called for an end to the separation of "the two cultures." Economics is part of both those cultures, a subject that can combine the attractive features of both the humanities and the sciences. For two centuries, educated men have found in it the human interest of life itself, while at the same time economic principles display some of the logical beauty of Euclid's geometry. To appreciate the charms of quantum physics, sophisticated mathematical techniques must first be mastered; but to sense the aesthetic structure of economic analysis requires only a feeling for logic and a capacity for wonderment that such mental constructs really do have a life-and-death significance for billions of men all over the world. Of course, mere beauty is not enough. We do not study economics for its own sake, but for the light it sheds.

WHAT ECONOMICS IS

Beginners often want a short definition of economics; and in response to this demand, there is no shortage of supply. Here are a few such definitions:

1. Economics is the study of those activities which, with or without money, involve exchange transactions among people.

2. Economics is the study of how men choose to use scarce or limited productive resources (land, labor, capital goods such as machinery, technical knowledge) to produce various commodities (such as wheat, beef, overcoats; concerts, roads, bombers, yachts) and distribute them to various members of society for their consumption.

3. Economics is the study of men in their ordinary business of life, earning and enjoying a living.

4. Economics is the study of how mankind goes about the business of organizing its consumption and production activities.

5. Economics is the study of wealth.

The list is a good one. Yet a scholar can extend it many times over. It is always hard to compress into a few lines an exact description of a subject, one that will differentiate its boundaries from those of other disciplines and convey to the beginner all the things it is. Economics certainly does involve all the elements stressed in these various definitions—and all those implied in the larger list that could be compiled.

Economists today agree on a general definition something like the following:

 Economics is the study of how men and society end up *choosing*, with or without the use of money, to employ *scarce* productive resources which could have alternative uses, to produce various commodities and distribute them for consumption, now or in the future, among various people and groups in society.

what this means.) Experts at the time warned against such folly, and history has recorded that England has never quite recovered from her stagnation of the late 1920s.

THE QUEEN OF THE SOCIAL SCIENCES

Economics borders on other important academic disciplines. *Sociology, political science, psychology,* and *anthropology* are all social sciences whose studies overlap those of economics. Here is just one example.

In impoverished India cows are sacred animals and, numbering millions, are allowed to walk through the streets foraging for food. While a naïve economist might regard these herds as a prime source for protein supplements to an already-inadequate diet, the more profound scholar will take the psychology of custom into account when analyzing Indian economic development.

Economics also draws heavily on the study of *history.* Was it a coincidence that prices rose for centuries in Spain and Europe after Columbus discovered America with all its silver and gold? Why did the age of the steamship and railroad help the Iowa farmer, hurt the farmers of Vermont and Oxfordshire, and help the slum dwellers of London? To the interpretation of recorded history, *analytical* tools must be brought for the reason that facts will never "tell their own story"; yet this need for theorizing does not deny the old Chinese proverb, "One peek is worth a thousand finesses." Facts count.

Among the numerous other subjects relating to economics, the study of *statistics* is of special importance. Governments and businesses issue vast amounts of numerical information. Most of what we know about the actual shapes of the various curves to be seen in turning over the pages of this book has to come from a careful statistical analysis of recorded information. The mathematical methods of probability and statistics find many of their most important applications in the realm of economics.

Although every introductory textbook must contain geometrical diagrams, knowledge of *mathematics* itself is needed only for the higher reaches of economic theory. Logical reasoning is the key to success in the mastery of basic economic principles, and shrewd weighing of empirical evidence is the key to success in applications.

Nobel prize in economics   Since the turn of the century Nobel prizes have been given annually in physics, chemistry, medicine and physiology, literature, and peace. As if to commemorate the coming of age of economics as a science, a new Nobel prize in economics was instituted in 1969.

The first award went jointly to Professors Ragnar Frisch of Norway and Jan Tinbergen of the Netherlands. Both men have been pioneers in the statistical, theoretical, and mathematical advances of the modern generation. Yet each has also been passionately concerned with economic policy, both within his own country and for the world at large. In honoring these men of genius, the Swedish Academy of Science could not have more fittingly summarized the nature of economic scholarship.

ECONOMIC DESCRIPTION AND ANALYSIS

It is the first task of modern economic science to *describe,* to *analyze,* to *explain,* and to *correlate* the behavior of production, unemployment, prices, and similar phenomena. To be significant, descriptions must be more than a series of disconnected narratives. They must be fitted into a systematic pattern—i.e., constitute true analysis.

Because of the complexity of human and social behavior, we cannot hope to attain the precision of the physical sciences. We cannot perform the controlled experiments of the chemist or biologist. Like the astronomer, we must be content largely to "observe." But economic events and statistical data observed are, alas, not so well behaved and orderly as the paths of heavenly satellites. Fortunately, our answers need not be accurate to several decimal places; on the contrary, if the right general *direction* of cause and effect can be determined, we shall have made a tremendous step forward.

ECONOMIC POLICY AND REFORM

This brings us to the important problem of economic policy. Ultimately, understanding should aid in *control and improvement*. How can the vagaries of the business cycle be diminished? How can economic progress and efficiency be furthered? How can adequate standards of living be made more widely available?

At every point of our analysis we shall seek to shed light on these policy problems. To succeed in this, we must try to cultivate an objective and detached ability to see things as they *are*, regardless of our likes or dislikes. The fact must be faced that economic issues are close to everybody emotionally. Blood pressures rise and voices become shrill whenever deep-seated beliefs and prejudices are involved, and some of these prejudices are thinly veiled rationalizations of special economic interests.

We know that a doctor passionately interested in stamping out disease must first train himself to observe things as they are. His bacteriology cannot be different from that of a mad scientist out to destroy mankind by plague. Wishful thinking is bad thinking and leads to little wish fulfillment. "Where it is a duty to worship the sun, the laws of heat will be poorly understood."

"Beauty is in the eye of the beholder" is an aphorism reminding us that judgments of better or worse involve *subjective* valuations. But this does not deny that one girl's nose may be *objectively* shorter than another's. Similarly, there are elements of valid reality in a given economic situation, however hard it may be to recognize and isolate them. There is not one theory of economics for Republicans and one for Democrats, one for workers and one for employers, one for the Russians and still another for the Chinese. On the basic economic principles concerning prices and employment, most economists are in fairly close agreement.

This statement does not mean that economists always agree in the *policy* field. Economist A may be for full employment at any cost. Economist B may not consider it of primary importance. Basic questions concerning right and wrong goals to be pursued cannot be settled by mere science as such. They belong in the realm of ethics and "value judgments." The citizenry must ultimately decide such issues. What the expert can do is point out the feasible alternatives and the true costs that may be involved in the different decisions. But still the mind must render to the heart that which is the heart's domain.

And peculiarly in the social sciences we must realize that we are subjects—even victims—of our preconceptions, prejudices, sentiments, and sordid interests. [2]

---

[2] Which questions we ask, and from what perspective we photograph the "objective reality"—these are themselves at bottom subjective in nature.

METHODOLOGY OF ECONOMICS: BRIEF PREVIEW

No one can understand a complicated subject such as chemistry without long and careful study. This is an advantage and a disadvantage. The man on the street or behind a newspaper desk cannot possibly consider himself a final authority on such a subject—which is all to the good. On the other hand, the new student of chemistry must become familiar with all the basic concepts for the first time, which takes a good deal of effort.

From childhood days on, everyone knows *something* about economics. This acquaintance is both helpful and deceptive: helpful, because much knowledge can be taken for granted; deceptive, because it is natural and human to accept superficially plausible views. A little knowledge may be dangerous. On close examination common sense may prove to be really nonsense.

A union leader who has successfully negotiated several labor contracts may feel that he is an expert on the economics of wages. A businessman who has "met a payroll" may feel that his views on price control are final. A banker who can balance his books may conclude that he knows all there is to know about the creation of money.

Each individual naturally tends to judge an economic event by its immediate effect upon himself. A worker thrown out of employment in the buggy industry cannot be expected to reflect that new jobs may have been created in the automobile industry; but we, as students of economics, must be prepared to investigate whether this is so.

In an introductory survey, the economist is interested in the workings of the economy *as a whole* rather than in the viewpoint of any one group. Social and national policies rather than individual policy are his goals. Too often, "everybody's business is nobody's business." It is just as well, therefore, to reiterate at the beginning that an elementary course in economics does not pretend to teach one how to run a business or bank, how to spend money wisely, or how to get rich quick from the stock market. But this is not to deny that general economics can provide a useful background for many such activities.

Certainly, the economist must know a good deal about how businessmen, consumers, and investors behave and think. This does not mean that those individuals must use the *same language and methods* in approaching their decisions as economists find useful in describing their behavior—any more than the planets need know that they are following the elliptical paths traced by the astronomer. Just as many of us have been "speaking prose" all our lives without knowing it, so too would many businessmen be surprised to learn that their behavior is capable of systematic economic analysis. This lack of awareness is not necessarily to be deprecated. It does not help a baseball pitcher to know the laws of aerodynamics; and if we become self-conscious about how to button our shirts, we may find it harder to do.

Theory versus practice The economic world is extremely complicated. As we noted, it is usually not possible to make economic observations under the controlled experimental conditions characteristic of scientific laboratories. A physiologist who wishes to determine the effects of penicillin on pneumonia may be able to "hold other things equal" by using two test groups that differ only in the fact that they do and do not get penicillin injections. The economist is less fortunately situated. If he wishes to determine the effect of a gasoline tax on fuel consumption, he may be vexed by the fact that, in the same year when the tax was imposed, pipelines were first introduced. Nevertheless, he must try—if only mentally—to isolate the effects of the tax, "other things being equal." Otherwise, he will understand the economic effects neither of taxation nor of transportation improvements, nor of both together.

The difficulty of analyzing causes when controlled experimentation is impossible is well illustrated by the confusion of the savage medicine man who thinks that both witchcraft and a little arsenic are necessary to kill his enemy, or that only after he has put on a green robe in spring will the trees do the same.[3] As a result of this limitation and many others, our quantitative economic knowledge is far from complete. This does not mean that we do not have great amounts of accurate statistical knowledge available. We do. Reams of census data, market information, and financial statistics have been collected by governments, trade associations, and business concerns.

Even if we had more and better data, it would still be necessary—as in every science—to *simplify*, to *abstract* from the infinite mass of detail. No mind can comprehend a bundle of unrelated facts. All analysis involves abstraction. It is always necessary to *idealize*, to omit detail, to set up simple hypotheses and patterns by which the facts can be related, to set up the right questions before going out to look at the world as it is. Every theory, whether in the physical or biological or social sciences, distorts reality in that it over-simplifies. But if it is good theory, what is omitted is outweighed by the beam of illumination and understanding that is thrown over the diverse empirical data.

Properly understood, therefore, theory and observation, deduction and induction, cannot be in conflict. The test of a theory's validity is its usefulness in illuminating observed reality. Its logical elegance and finespun beauty are irrelevant. Consequently, when a student says, "That's all right in theory but not in practice," he really means, "That's not all right in the relevant theory," or else he is talking nonsense.

The tyranny of words   Especially in the social sciences, we must watch out for the "tyranny of words." The world is complicated enough without introducing further confusions and ambiguities as (1) two different names are unknowingly being used for the same thing or (2) the same word is applied to two different things.

Jones may call Robinson a liar for holding that the cause of depression is oversaving, saying, "Underconsumption is really the cause." Schwartz may enter the argument, asserting, "You are both wrong. The real trouble is underinvestment." They may go on arguing; but if they really stopped to analyze their language, they might find that there were no differences in their opinions about the facts and that only a verbal confusion was involved.

Similarly, words may be treacherous because we do not react in a neutral manner to them. Thus a man who approves of a government program to speed growth will call it a program of "sensible planning," while an unsympathetic opponent will describe the same activity as "totalitarian bureaucratic regimentation." Who can object to the former, and who could condone the latter? Yet they refer to the same thing. One does not have

[3] In logic, the *post hoc, ergo propter hoc* fallacy (after this, therefore necessarily because of this).

to be an expert in *semantics*—the study of language and its meaning—to realize that scientific discussion requires us to avoid such emotional terminology wherever possible.

Social versus physical science? Some distortions of thinking that result from emotion and prejudice are so blatant as to be clearly recognizable. But at a deeper level, one can ask:

Since economics deals with man and not with inanimate objects, and since the scientist is himself necessarily a man, can there be any hope of an *objective* science of economics? Can the methods of the physical sciences—observation and quantitative measurements, mathematical model building—ever work in the study of human affairs?

No simple answer can be given to this profound question. In a sense, precisely because we are ourselves men, we have an advantage over the natural scientist. He cannot usefully say, "Suppose I were an H_2O molecule; what might I do in such a situation?" The social scientist often, knowingly or unknowingly, employs such introspective acts of *empathy*.

Still a problem remains. Experienced scholars would put it this way:

Slavish imitation of the physical sciences is a mistake in the study of humans and society. Yet there is no substitute for patient *attendance to the empirical facts* of life, and no substitute for *systematic reasoning* about them. As in the case of modern biology, great advances have resulted from mathematical scientific methods, despite the earlier warnings against imitating the physical sciences. Let experience tell the final story.

Exactitude and subjectivity But recall again this important point. Even in the so-called exact physical sciences, how we *perceive* the observed facts depends on the theoretical spectacles we wear. The light that hits a newborn baby's eyes forms no pattern: the baby sees, but it does not perceive. Modern historians of science have learned the same lesson from gestalt psychology: post-Newtonians perceived the "same facts" differently from pre-Newtonians. To a degree we are all prisoners of our theoretical preconceptions. It is not so much discordant fact that kills off an old false theory as the final emergence of a new theory.

That is why science belongs to the young. The old know too many things that are just not so. To illustrate this we do not have to consider a soft science like economics, in which it is taken for granted that your uncles will believe that what was good enough for Calvin Coolidge ought to be good enough for you. Let us listen to Nobel laureate Max Planck, the physicist renowned for his discovery of the revolutionary quantum theory. In his *Scientific Autobiography*, Planck reports what he observed in the development of physics:

This experience gave me also an opportunity to learn a fact—a remarkable one in my opinion: A new scientific truth does not triumph by convincing its opponents and making them see the light, but rather because its opponents eventually die, and a new generation grows up that is familiar with it.

Just as Galileo, Newton, Einstein, and Planck revolutionized perceptions in physics, so did Smith, Marshall, Keynes—indeed all the names that appear on the family tree of economics shown on the back flyleaf of this book—transform economic understanding.

Facts tell different story to scientists wearing different theoretical spectacles:

(a)   (b)

FIG. 1-2. If you look at problems of depression un-employment through pre-Keynesian glasses, you may think it is due to forces that government tax and expenditure policies cannot change. In (a) is this a picture of a leftward-looking bird? Or is it a rightward-looking antelope (or rabbit)? In the presence of (b)'s *field of birds*, most people think it a bird. But next to the footnote's *field of antelopes*, most will see it as an antelope. [Source: N. R. Hanson, *Patterns of Discovery* (Cambridge University Press, London, 1961).]

Figure 1-2, taken from a philosophic study of physics, illustrates the irreducible subjective element in *any* science. Does the picture show a bird looking to the left? Or an antelope (or rabbit) looking to the right? It is not an optical illusion to say it is one rather than the other. Each is admissible.[4]

So it is with scientific facts and theories in general. When you adopt a new systematic model of economic principles, you comprehend reality in a new and different way. We do not have to be students of physics or gestalt psychology to realize how literally these words apply to the contrasts between new and old economics, or between free-world and Iron Curtain economics. So let us be forewarned.

Probability of errors: normal or not   There is another important difference between an exact science like physics and a less exact science like economics. Our laws may particularly hold only "on the average," with considerable dispersion of exceptions around that average.

Figure 1-3 gives a preview of a vital statistical relationship whereby consumption spending by families can be related to the dollar incomes people have. Note that the observation points do not fall exactly on the line, as they might in chemistry or astronomy. Still, we do see a pattern that is stable in a probability sense—the same sense in which a life-insurance company can *count on* a stable proportion of deaths in a sample of 100,000 policyholders of a given age (even though any one man's living or dying cannot be foretold). And note a further important point, the chance deviations around the expected values will form an especially simple frequency pattern called the "normal curve of error." The normal curve is symmetric and bell-shaped; this is because the addition of *many independent* errors tends to give a resultant error which (through probable cancellation) is more likely to be small than large. When this normal distribution appears in economics, it resembles distributions from gambling dice, genetics, or surveying measurements.[5]

[4]Contrast your gestalt perception of Fig. 1-2's image with its appearance when placed next to this field of antelopes. The bird-antelope ambiguity cannot be dismissed as an optical "illusion": it is unlike the accompanying two lines, which are really the same length even though most people wrongly infer the lower line to be the longer. What Fig. 1-2 portrays is an objectively reproducible shape that looks subjectively different depending on the context in which it appears. But once we see the forelegs of the beast, we are right to perceive it as an antelope.

[5]Gambling houses in Nevada and Monte Carlo know very well from experience that repeated coin tossing (or dice throwing) will generate a sequence with the following two properties: (*a*) If we write down 1 for heads and 0 for tails, a random series of tossing will give sequences—such as 0, 1, 1, 0, 1, 0, 1, 0, 0, 0, 1, 0—which eventually

In economics, "normality" may not always prevail. Figure 1-4 on the next page reproduces a later diagram, Fig. 6-5, showing how abnormally spread out people's incomes are in comparison with the allegedly "normal" distribution of their abilities (IQs, verbal or mathematical aptitudes, etc.). The blue curve of distribution of incomes is asymmetric: unlike the symmetric normal curve, it has a long tail skewed to the right. This reflects the fact that while there are a few multimillionaires with incomes equal to hundreds of times the average income, no one can be that many dollars below the average. Such asymmetric, superextended distributions, alas, appear often in economics. One says "alas" because where such abnormal probability laws occur, they do not lead to the same *precision of average behavior* that the natural sciences can often count on.

Despite the approximative character of economic laws, economics is a field blessed with many important regularities and valid principles.

Economic laws are probability laws, not exact relationships:

FIG. 1-3.   Observed points of consumption spending fail to fall exactly on the brown line. But clustering of the data around the line does confirm the regularity of the relationship between dollar income and spending. (Source: Fig. 11-5.)

THE WHOLE AND THE PART: THE "FALLACY OF COMPOSITION"

A good final warning in economics is this: things are often not what at first they seem. The following true statements provide examples:

1. If all farmers work hard and nature cooperates in producing a bumper crop, total farm income may *fall,* and probably will.

2. *One* man may solve his own unemployment problem by great ingenuity in hunting a job or by a willingness to work for less; but *all* cannot necessarily solve their problems in this way.

3. Higher prices *for one industry* may benefit its firms; but if the prices of *everything* bought and sold increased in the same proportion, no one would be better off.

4. It may pay the United States to *reduce* tariffs charged on goods imported, even if *other* countries refuse to do likewise.

5. It may pay a firm to take on some business at much *less than full costs.*

---

average out close to ½ by the famous "law of large numbers." (*b*) For a long enough sequence of random tosses of a symmetric coin, the fraction of heads appearing will approach a normal-error dispersion around the expected value of ½. This "central limit law" (of approach to a normal distribution) enabled mathematicians like De Moivre, Laplace, and Gauss to predict with great accuracy how often deviations will tend to occur, the expected size of the absolute errors halving when the sequence quadruples in length. [Thus when the number of customers of a firm doubles, it needs only 1.4 (or $\sqrt{2}$) times the amount of inventory.] However, many economic distributions, like that of income, may have tails too dispersed to be subject to this normal distribution.

Abnormal as well as normal probability patterns of errors occur in economics:

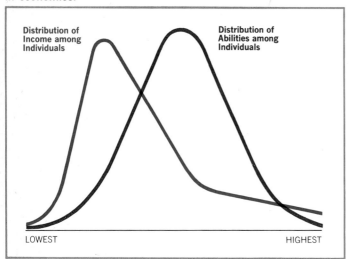

FIG. 1-4. Although behavior on the average is predictable in economics, there are exceptions and deviations around the average. The brown curve depicts the well-behaved case in which the deviations follow the symmetric bell-shaped "normal curve of error." The blue curve of abnormal error, which is skewed off to the right, has relatively more extreme deviations than does the normal curve. Where this occurs in the social sciences, we cannot guarantee laws of average behavior with quite so much accuracy. (Source: Fig. 6-5, where normal distribution of abilities is contrasted with asymmetric distribution of dollar incomes and great income spread.)

6. *Attempts* of individuals to save more in depression *may lessen the total* of the community's savings.

7. What is prudent behavior for an *individual* may at times be folly for a *nation*.

Let us emphasize: Each of the above statements is true; but each is outwardly paradoxical. In the course of this book, the seeming paradoxes will be resolved. There are no magic formulas or hidden tricks. It is typical of economics that anything which is really correct must seem perfectly reasonable once the argument is carefully developed.

At this point it is just as well to note that many of the above paradoxes hinge upon a single confusion or fallacy. It is called by logicians the "fallacy of composition." In books on logic, this is defined as follows:

Fallacy of composition: **a fallacy in which what is true of a part is, on that account alone, alleged to be also necessarily true of the whole.**

Very definitely, in the field of economics, it turns out that what seems to be true for individuals is not always true for society as a whole; and conversely, what seems to be true for all may be quite false for any one individual. For everybody to stand on tiptoe to watch a parade does no good, even though one person may gain a better view by so doing. Countless similar economic examples can be given. You might amuse yourself by checking over these seven examples to see which are probably related to the fallacy of composition. Or better still, find some new ones.

We have come to the end of our introductory survey. Perhaps the best answer to the question, Why study economics, is a famous one given by Lord Keynes. The final lines of his 1936 classic, *The General Theory of Employment, Interest and Money*, consist of a famous passage:

The ideas of economists and political philosophers, both when they are right and when they are wrong, are more powerful than is commonly understood. Indeed the world is ruled by little else. Practical men, who believe themselves to be quite exempt from any intellectual influences, are usually the slaves of some defunct economist. Madmen in authority, who hear voices in the air, are distilling their frenzy from some academic scribbler of a few years back. I am sure that the power of vested interests is vastly exaggerated compared with the gradual encroachment of ideas.

SUMMARY

1   Economics, both a science and an art, is studied for a variety of reasons: to understand problems facing the citizen and family; to help governments in both underdeveloped and advanced nations promote vigorous growth, while avoiding depression and inflation; to analyze fascinating patterns of social behavior.

2   Among many definitions, the leading one today defines economics thus: How do we choose to use scarce productive resources with alternative uses, to meet prescribed ends—what goods to produce, how, and for whom, now or later.

3   Overlapping with other social or behavioral sciences—psychology, sociology, history—economics uses the deductive methods of logic and geometry, and inductive methods of statistical and empirical inference. Because it cannot employ controlled experiments of the physicist, it raises basic problems of methodology: subjective elements of introspection and value judgment; semantic issues of ambiguous and emotional meanings; probability laws of large numbers, both of normal-error and skewed type.

QUESTIONS FOR DISCUSSION

1   Would a major depression like that of the 1930s, or a peacetime inflation, affect you (*a*) seriously, (*b*) moderately, or (*c*) not at all?

2   Discuss the emotional content of the following words: regimentation, planning, usury, monopolist, gambling, speculation, American way of life, free enterprise, cartels, thrift, hoarding.

3   Give examples of the fallacy of composition and of the *post hoc, ergo propter hoc* fallacy. Is the former involved in the debate over cigarettes and longevity? Is the latter involved in this debate?

4   Can you fit into the brief definition of economics many of this chapter's problems?

5   In Fig. 1-3, is income the cause and consumption the effect? Or vice versa? To answer this, economic study is needed. Similarly, does the fact that smoking and cancer are related prove that smoking causes cancer? Is low IQ among the poor genetically caused?

6   "As every insurance company knows, single events may be unpredictable at the same time that large number of events average out to virtual certainty." Show how this same statistical fact can be helpful in economics, as for example in the case where we study how thousands of families choose to spend their incomes on consumption as against saving.

7   Which would you expect to be nearer to the normal curve of error, the incomes of carpenters of different skills or the incomes of different Texas millionaires whose fortunes depend on wildcat drilling for oil?
    Which would you expect to be more regular, the outcome of gambling in Las Vegas or the movements of stock prices on the New York Stock Exchange? Why?

8   "Facts by themselves are dumb; before they will tell us anything we have to arrange them, and the arrangement is a theory." Elucidate.

Review your understanding of the following concepts:

economics as distinct from other
   disciplines
analysis and policy
practice and theory
wishful thinking, semantics
exactitude and probability
normal and skewed errors

subjectivity and theorizing
valuations and so-called "facts"
tyranny of words
controlled experiment
fallacy of composition
post hoc fallacy
definition of economics

A PREVIEW

Here in Part One we deal with the fundamental tools needed to analyze the basic facts and institutions of modern economic life, culminating this survey in the unifying concept of national income.

In Part Two we analyze the causes of prosperity and depression: how the processes of saving and investment interact to determine the level of prices, income, and employment; and how public monetary and fiscal policies can stabilize business activity at a healthy level of progressive growth.

Part Three is concerned with the forces of competition and monopoly, which act through supply and demand to help determine—efficiently or inefficiently—the composition of the national income, in terms of both goods and services to be produced and their prices. (Unlike Part Two's "macroeconomics," this is "microeconomics.")

Part Four treats distribution of income: determination of wages, rent, interest, and profits.

Part Five discusses international trade in both its monetary and real aspects.

The last chapter of Part Five and all of Part Six deal with some of our most vital current economic problems: development of backward countries; poverty, inequality, and the quality of economic life; economics of racial discrimination and problems of urban and environmental blight; promotion of economic growth and control of inflation; comparisons of alternative economic systems.

Central Problems of Every Economic Society

At the foundations of any community there will always be found a few universal economic conditions. Certain background problems are as crucial today as they were in the days of Homer and Caesar, and they will continue to be relevant in the brave new world of the future.

In Section A of this chapter we see that every society must meet a certain trio of *basic problems of economic organization.* Section B shows that technological *knowledge,* together with limited amounts of *land, labor,* and *capital,* defines the available choices between goods and services open to a community and that these *production possibilities* are subject to change and to the law of diminishing returns. Section C develops the point that the basis of any economy is its *population,* or *human element.*

We leave to Chapter 3 those important economic features characteristic of our own mixed economy—a system of private and public enterprise intertwined.

A. PROBLEMS OF ECONOMIC ORGANIZATION

Any society, whether it consists of a totally collectivized communistic state, a tribe of South Sea Islanders, a capitalistic industrial nation, a Swiss Family Robinson, a Robinson Crusoe—or, one might almost add, a colony of bees—must somehow confront three fundamental and interdependent economic problems.

1. WHAT commodities shall be produced and in what quantities? That is, how much and which of alternative goods and services shall be produced? Food or clothing? Much food and little clothing, or vice versa? Bread and butter today, or bread and grape plantings today with bread, butter, and jam next year?

2. How shall goods be produced? That is, by whom and with what resources and in what technological manner are they to be produced? Who hunts, who fishes? Electricity from steam or waterfall or atoms? Large- or small-scale production?

3. For Whom shall goods be produced? That is, who is to enjoy and get the benefit of the goods and services provided? Or, to put the same thing in another way, how is the total of national product to be *distributed*[1] among different individuals and families? A few rich and many poor? Or most people in modest comfort?

These three questions are fundamental and common to all economies, but different economic systems try to solve them differently. In a primitive civilization, custom may rule every facet of behavior. What, How, and For Whom may be decided by reference to traditional ways of doing things. To members of another culture, the practices followed may seem bizarre and unreasonable; the members of the tribe or clan may themselves be so familiar with existing practices as to be surprised, and perhaps offended, if asked the reason for their behavior. Thus, the Kwakiutl Indians consider it desirable not to accumulate wealth but to give it away in the *potlatch*—a roisterous celebration. This deviation from acquisitive behavior will not surprise anthropologists; their studies show that what is correct behavior in one culture is often the greatest crime in another.

In the bee colony, all such problems, even those involving an elaborate cooperative division of labor, are solved automatically by means of so-called "biological instincts." (Fair enough as a description, but not much of an "explanation.")

At the other extreme we can imagine an omnipotent benevolent or malevolent dictator who by arbitrary decree and fiat decides What, How, and For Whom. Or we might imagine economic organization by decree, but with decrees drawn up by democratic vote or by selected legislative authorities.

As Chapter 3 develops at length, the What, How, and For Whom questions in a so-called "capitalist free enterprise economy" are determined primarily[2] by a system of prices (of markets, of profits and losses).

THE LAW OF SCARCITY

What to produce, How, and For Whom would not be problems if resources were unlimited: if an *infinite* amount of every good could be produced, or if human wants were *fully* satisfied, it would not then matter if too much of any particular good were produced. Nor would it then matter if labor and materials were combined unwisely. Since everyone could have as much as he pleased, it would not matter how goods and incomes were distributed among different individuals and families.

There would then be no *economic goods*, i.e., no goods that are relatively *scarce;* and there would hardly be any need for a study of economics or "economizing." All goods would be *free goods*, like air.

In the world as it is, even children learn in growing up that "both" is not an admissible

[1] Warning: Usually when an economist is talking about "distribution," he means the distribution *of incomes*—the principles which determine labor's wage, land's rent, capital's interest, and the whole For Whom process. The man on the street usually means, by distribution, wholesaling and retailing—how goods once produced get into the hands of the consumer. We shall avoid this last confusing usage.
[2] There never was a 100 per cent purely automatic enterprise system, although Victorian England came close. Certainly in our system, the government has an important role in modifying the workings of the price system. This is what is meant by the saying that we live in a "mixed economy."

answer to a choice of "Which one?" Compared with backward nations or previous centuries, modern industrial societies seem very wealthy indeed. But higher production levels seem to bring in their train higher consumption standards. People feel that they want and "need" indoor plumbing, central heating, refrigerators, education, movies, radios, records, television, antibiotics, books, autos, travel, sports and concerts, music, chic clothes, and so forth. The biological scientist tells them that they can be well nourished on a thin porridge for a few cents a day,[3] but that leaves them as cold as the information that the chemicals in their bodies are worth only a couple of dollars. Anyone who has kept a family budget knows that the necessities of life—the absolute musts—have little to do with the minimum *physiological* needs of food, clothing, and shelter.

In *The Affluent Society*, J. Kenneth Galbraith[4] has eloquently pointed out that Americans today have for the most part gone beyond the level of physiological necessity; that often the consumer flits from one purchase to another in response to pressures of fashion and advertising. Without challenging Galbraith's thesis that the time has come to spend more on public needs and less on private needs, one may properly point out that our total product would have to become many times higher than its present level if everyone were to become able to live at the level of a moderately well-off doctor, lawyer, professor, or advertising man—to say nothing of the living standards of the really well-to-do.

Whether or not people would be "genuinely" happier spending twice as much as now, observation suggests that folks in the suburbs now act *as if* they want more income to spend: they take on extra work; they resist tax increases; they end up saving much the same fraction of their incomes as in 1900; and middle-class mothers seem to work harder than their mothers did. Even if the national income were divided up equally between every man, woman, and child—an extreme case—there would be only about $75 per week to go around.

 Therefore, while it recognizes the important germ of truth in the notion that America has become an affluent society, economics must still contend with *scarcity* as a basic fact of life. Abroad, this is even more the case.

B. THE TECHNOLOGICAL CHOICES OPEN TO ANY SOCIETY

SOCIETY'S PRODUCTION-POSSIBILITY FRONTIER

We have discussed the basic economic fact that *limitation* of the total resources capable of producing different commodities necessitates a choice between relatively scarce commodities. This can be illustrated quantitatively by simple arithmetic examples and geometrical diagrams. Diagrams and graphs are indispensable visual aids in many aspects

---

[3] A study suggests that modern standards of adult nutrition could be bought in 1970 for about $110 per year. But what a diet this implies: kidneys, cabbage, buckwheat flour, and not much else! George J. Stigler, "The Cost of Subsistence," *Journal of Farm Economics*, May, 1945, pp. 303–314. This paper achieved fame as a forerunner of an important mathematical technique of economics and national defense called "linear programming." Victor E. Smith of Michigan State University in the same journal (May, 1959, pp. 272–283) reported that a family of three could get a "palatable diet" for about 50 cents per person per day, perhaps 65 cents in the 1970s.
[4] John Kenneth Galbraith, *The Affluent Society* (Houghton Mifflin, Boston, 1958).

Full employment of scarce resources means society must choose between more guns or more butter:

1st, This can be shown by a table:

	ALTERNATIVE PRODUCTION POSSIBILITIES	
POSSI- BILITIES	BUTTER (millions of pounds)	GUNS (thou- sands)
A	0	15
B	1	14
C	2	12
D	3	9
E	4	5
F	5	0

TABLE 2-1. Economic resources can be shifted from butter production to gun production, in effect enabling us to transform butter into guns. The cost of getting extra guns can be reckoned as the extra butter we are forced to sacrifice.

2d, Or shown graphically by plotting points on a grid:

FIG. 2-1. Each marked point is a careful plot of each gun-and-butter numerical combination from Table 2-1. (Guess where the point midway between *B* and *C* might approximately fall. Read off *its* guns-butter numbers, and pencil them into Table 2-1 at about the right place.)

of economics. A little care at the beginning in understanding them will be rewarded manyfold later on.

Consider an economy with only so many people, so much technical knowledge, so many factories and tools, and so much land, water power, and natural resources. In deciding WHAT shall be produced and How, the economy must really decide just how these resources are to be allocated among the thousands of different possible commodities. How much land should go into wheat cultivation? Or into pasturage? How many factories are to produce hairpins? How much skilled labor should go into machine shops?

These problems are complicated even to discuss, much less solve. Therefore we must simplify. So let us assume that only two economic goods (or classes of economic goods) are to be produced. For dramatic purposes, we can choose the pair Adolf Hitler ranted about—guns and butter. These two commodities are commonly used to illustrate the problem of choosing between civilian and war goods, but the same analysis applies to *any* choice of goods. Thus the more resources the government uses to build public roads, the less will be left to produce private houses; the more the public chooses to consume of food, the less it can consume of clothing; the more society decides to consume today, the less can be its production of machines and capital goods to turn out more consumption goods for the next year or decade.

But let us stick to the example of guns and butter. Now, suppose that *all* resources are thrown into the production of civilian goods (butter). There will still be a *maximum* amount of butter that can be produced per year. (The exact amount depends upon the quantitative and qualitative resources of the economy in question and the technological efficiency with which they are used.) Suppose 5 million pounds of butter is the maximum amount that can be produced with the existing technology and resources.

At the other extreme, imagine that 100 per cent of society's resources had been devoted instead to the production of guns. Only some maximum number of guns could then be produced: 15 thousand guns of a certain description can perhaps be produced if we are really willing to produce no butter.

These are two extreme possibilities; in between there are still others. If we are willing to give up *some* butter, we can have *some* guns; if we are willing to give up still more butter, we can have still more guns. A schedule of a number of possibilities is given in Table 2-1, *F* being the extreme where all butter and no guns are produced, and *A* being the opposite extreme where all resources go into guns. In between, at *E*, *D*, *C*, and *B*, butter is being given up increasingly in return for more guns. Butter is "transformed" into guns, not physically, but by diverting resources from one use to the other.

It is even more illuminating to represent this same production-possibility or production-transformation schedule by measuring butter along the horizontal axis and guns along the vertical, as in Fig. 2-1.

The reader should now be able to go directly from the numerical table to the diagram: for *F*, by counting over 5 butter units to the right and going up 0 gun units; for *E*, by going 4 butter units to the right and going up 5 gun units; and finally, for *A*, by going over 0 butter units and up 15 gun units.

We may fill in all intermediate positions, even those involving fractions of a million pounds or fractions of a thousand guns, as in the so-called "production-possibility frontier" shown in Fig. 2-2.

The curve that we now have represents this fundamental fact:

> A full-employment economy must always in producing one good be giving up something of another. *Substitution* is the law of life in a full-employment economy. The *production-possibility frontier* depicts society's menu of choices.

Unemployment and inefficiency But what if there had been widespread unemployment of resources: idle men, idle land, and idle factories? We have already warned that our economic laws may then be quite different. This is one such instance.

With unemployment, we are not on the production-possibility frontier at all, but somewhere *inside* it,

3d, Or we can picture production possibilities by drawing a smooth curve:

THE PRODUCTION-POSSIBILITY FRONTIER

FIG. 2-2. This shows how society can choose to substitute guns for butter, assuming a given state of technology and a given total of resources. Any point *inside* the curve, such as *U*, indicates that resources are not being fully employed in the best-known way. (Source: Table 2-1. A smooth curve has been passed through the previous chart's points.)

say, at U in Fig. 2-2, producing only 2 million pounds of butter and 6 thousand guns. If resources are idle, by putting them to work we can have more butter *and* more guns. We can move from U to D and thereby get *more* butter *and more* guns.

This throws important light on the different experience in World War II of three countries: the United States, Germany, and Russia. After 1940, how was the United States able to become the "arsenal of democracy" and to enjoy civilian living standards higher than ever before? Largely by taking up the slack of unemployment. On the other hand, Hitler's war effort began in 1933, long before any formal declaration. It stemmed from a period of unemployment acute enough to win him the votes to get into power peacefully. Almost all the extra output made possible by utilizing previously unemployed workers and plants was siphoned into German war goods rather than into higher civilian consumption. Still a third case is that of the wartime Soviet Union. The Russians had little unemployment before the war and were already on their rather low production-possibility frontier. They had no choice but to substitute war goods for civilian goods—with consequent privation.

Business-cycle unemployment is not the only way of being inside the *p-p frontier*. If an economy is inefficiently organized, it may also be well short of the frontier—as in China of 1960 when the ideological drive for a "great leap forward" resulted in ousting of experts and a disastrous attempt to make steel in backyard furnaces, or as in an economy riddled with monopoly and subject to arbitrary decrees by corrupt and inept bureaucrats. (We shall analyze all this later.)

SOME USES OF THE PRODUCTION-POSSIBILITY CONCEPT

This concept, represented as a simple curve, can help introduce many of the most basic concepts in economics. For example, Fig. 2-2 illustrates the basic definition of economics given in Chapter 1, namely, the problem of *choosing* among *scarce* or limited resources ("means" capable of *alternative* uses), in order to achieve best *goals* ("ends"). Land, labor, and capital can be used to produce guns or butter along the frontier curve in Fig. 2-2. Where does the society choose to end up? Southeastward in the diagram, with much of civilian goods? Or northwestward, with much of defense goods? Economics is a *quantitative* subject: choice is not a qualitative matter of "either-or," but rather of how many of each good and just where we draw the line of final decision.

The production-possibility frontier provides a rigorous definition of scarcity.

Definition: "Economic scarcity" refers to the basic fact of life that there exists only a finite amount of human and nonhuman resources, which the best technical knowledge is capable of using to produce only a *limited* maximum amount of each and every good, as shown by the *p-p frontier*. And thus far, nowhere on the globe is the supply of goods so plentiful or the tastes so limited that the average man can have more than enough of everything he might fancy.

The production-possibility schedule can also help make clear the three basic problems of economic life: WHAT, HOW, and FOR WHOM.

WHAT goods are produced and consumed can be depicted by the point which we choose on the *p-p frontier.*

How goods are to be produced involves an efficient choice of methods and proper assignment of different amounts and kinds of limited resources to the various industries. What would happen if the men well fitted for machine-tooling of guns ended up on the farms? We would be *inside* the *p-p frontier,* not on it. Or what if government regulations made the land most suitable for corn be used for wheat production, and the land most suitable for wheat be used for corn? We would end up with less of both corn and wheat, inside the *production-possibility frontier* on a diagram whose axes were labeled *C* and *W.* Being inside the frontier is, as we have already seen, a crime of *economic* inefficiency; but it need not involve any *engineering* inefficiency, since, on the wrongly allocated land, production might still be following the latest methods known to science.[5]

FOR WHOM goods are to be produced cannot be discerned from the *p-p* diagram alone. Sometimes, though, you can make a guess from it: if you find a society on its *p-p frontier* with many yachts and few compact cars, you are justified in suspecting that it enjoys considerable inequality of income and wealth among persons.

PICTURES IN AN EXHIBITION

The graphs of Figs. 2-3 to 2-7 are meant to be self-explanatory. They show that the production-possibility frontier can illustrate many familiar, but basic, economic processes. Later chapters will deal with each of these in depth, and it is necessary here only to comprehend the common-sense ideas involved.

Figure 2-3 illustrates how a society consumes much food when it is poor but shifts toward comforts and luxuries as it develops—a topic to be met in Chapter 11.

Figure 2-4 on the next page illustrates how the electorate must choose between private goods bought at a price and public goods paid for largely by taxes, a topic to be met in Chapter 8.

Figure 2-5 illustrates how an economy chooses between (1) current consumption goods and (2) capital goods (machines, etc.), which make possible more of *both* goods in the future. Much of Parts Two,

[5] More difficult is the notion that the economy should often prefer scientifically *less* efficient methods over methods that are allegedly technically more efficient. EXAMPLE: Physics texts teach that converting heat to motion at 2500°F is intrinsically more efficient than converting it at 1200°. Yet if metals that can stand the higher temperature are scarce and dear, it is *economically* better for the engineer and businessman to use the thermodynamically less efficient method!

Production-possibility frontiers illustrate many economic cases:

1st, Choice between luxuries and necessities:

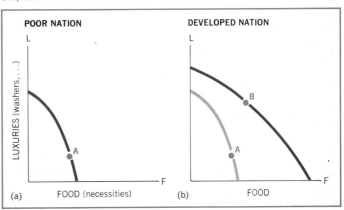

FIG. 2-3(a).   Before development, the nation is so poor it must devote almost all its resources to food, enjoying few comforts.
FIG. 2-3(b).   After development, it goes from *A* to *B*, expanding its food consumption very little compared with its increased consumption of nonnecessities.

2d, Choice between public and private goods:

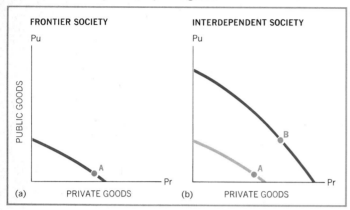

FIG. 2-4(a). The first economy is poor and dispersed as in Daniel Boone's frontier days: the proportion of resources going to government's public sector is low.

FIG. 2-4(b). The second economy is more prosperous and chooses to spend more of its higher income on governmental services (roads, defense, research, education); in dense urban life, it has no choice but to spend on traffic lights, police, antipollution devices, and city planning.

3d, Choice between more consumption today and capital goods for enhancing tomorrow's possibilities:

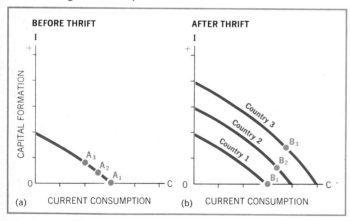

FIG. 2-5(a). Three countries start out even, but Country 1 does no saving for the future at A_1 (merely replacing used-up machines). Country 2 abstains modestly from consumption at A_2. Country 3, by private sacrifice or democratic vote, is at A_3, investing much in new machines and sacrificing much of current consumption.

FIG. 2-5(b). In the next years, Country 3 has forged ahead of Country 2, which has moved ahead of nonprogressing Country 1. Possessing more machines for labor to work with, Country 3 now can have more of *both* goods than can Country 2. Country 1 remains where it started.

Four, and Six will deal with this basic saving and investment problem.

Figure 2-6 shows how Economy B, blessed by scientific and engineering discoveries, might surpass A, which was undergoing more thrift and investing for the future, but with less progressive technology. Growth discussions, in Part Six, will develop this theme.

Finally, turn to Fig. 2-7, which tells its own story and prepares us for the next topic, the law of diminishing returns.

THE LAW OF DIMINISHING RETURNS

Figure 2-7 introduces us to a famous technological economic relationship, the so-called "law of diminishing returns." This law states the relation, *not* between two goods (such as guns and butter), but between an *input* of production (such as labor) and the resulting output of a good it helps produce (such as butter or, in the traditional examples, corn).

More specifically, the law of diminishing returns refers to the amount of *extra output* that we get when we successively add *equal extra* units of a *varying input* to a *fixed* amount of some *other* input. (Note the emphasized words.)

Here is an example to illustrate the law of diminishing returns. We make the following controlled experiment: Given a fixed amount of land, say, 100 acres, we shall first add no labor at all. We note that with zero labor input there is no corn output, and so we record zero output in Table 2-2 on page 24.

Now we make a second related experiment. We add 1 extra unit of labor to the same fixed amount of land. How much output do we now get? Pure reason cannot tell us: we must look to the facts of the experiment. When we do we observe, let us say, that we now have produced positive output of corn equal to 2,000 units (bushels or whatever units you choose for corn). We now summarize the result of this second experiment: Adding 1 extra unit of labor to 100 of fixed land gives us extra output of 2,000 units.

To observe the law of diminishing returns, we must make a third controlled experiment. We still hold land fixed. Once more we vary the labor input and make sure to add again exactly the same extra unit of labor as before; i.e., we now go from 1 unit of labor to 2 units of labor.

4th, Case where technical advance outstrips thrift alone:

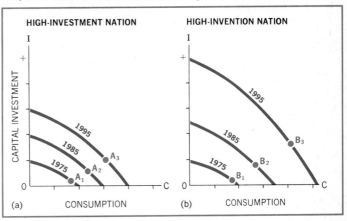

FIG. 2-6(a). Country A, on the left, is thrifty and advances by accumulating capital goods.

FIG. 2-6(b). Country B advances even more from 1975 to 1985 because it spends more on science and technical research. From 1985 to 1995 it grows faster still by using both methods: technical progress *and* much capital formation.

5th, How output on fixed land will not keep pace with population:

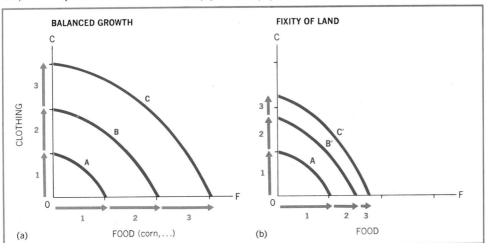

FIG. 2-7(a). We begin initially at the lower curve *A*. But population now doubles and is able to spread over double the previous land, leaving each county and state in the same land-labor balance as before. Hence the new curve *B* depicts exactly twice the scale of food and clothing production. Finally, let labor and land both rise again by the same extra amount as between *A* and *B*. We end up at *C*, gaining fully as much of extra products as we did before from the same balanced additions of labor and land. Note that the arrows 1, 2, and 3 on each axis show no diminishing length.

FIG. 2-7(b). We begin at the same *A* curve as in Fig. 2-7(a). But now *land is held constant* while population doubles. Each laborer has less land to work with than under balanced growth. Hence, the *B'* curve is below the *B* curve of Fig. 2-7(a). Finally, add another equal increment of labor, still holding land constant. The new *extra* product is even lower, as shown by the diminishing lengths of the arrows 1, 2, and 3, which depict extra output. We shall understand the reasons for all this after the "law of diminishing returns" has been mastered.

Diminishing returns is a fundamental law of economics and technology:

MAN-YEARS OF LABOR	TOTAL PRODUCT (bushels)	EXTRA OUTPUT ADDED BY ADDITIONAL UNIT OF LABOR
	LAW OF DIMINISHING RETURNS	
0	0	
		2,000
1	2,000	
		1,000
2	3,000	
		500
3	3,500	
		—
4	3,800	
		100
5	3,900	

TABLE 2-2. Law of diminishing returns refers to successively lower extra outputs (e.g., of corn) gained from adding equal increments of a variable input (e.g., labor) to a constant amount of a fixed input (e.g., 100 acres of land). (Pencil in the extra output of the fourth laborer.)

We breathlessly await the outcome of the experiment in terms of extra corn produced. Shall we now have a total of 4,000 units of corn, which would again represent exactly 2,000 extra units of output produced by the extra unit of the varying labor? Or shall we find *diminishing* returns, with the new extra unit of input adding less than the 2,000 extra units of output which was previously added?

If the law of diminishing returns does in fact hold, our experiment can have but one result: the second extra labor unit will add *less extra output* than did the first. Adding a third extra unit of labor will, if diminishing returns holds, result in *still lower* extra output. And so forth. Table 2-2 gives numerical values to illustrate exactly what diminishing returns means.

The law of diminishing returns is an important, often-observed economic and technical regularity; but it is not universally valid. Often it will hold only *after* you have added a considerable number of equal doses of the varying factor. Beyond that point, we say the law of diminishing returns has set in. (Before such a point the varying factors might be yielding increasing extra returns, since until then we might find that adding extra varying inputs to a fixed input leads to increasing rather than diminishing extra outputs; but ultimately decreasing returns can be expected to prevail.)

Why is the law of diminishing returns plausible? Frequently we feel that by adding land and labor together—no input being fixed and all being varied in the same proportion so that the whole *scale* of operations is getting larger—then output should also increase proportionately and extra outputs need not diminish. For why should the extra outputs diminish if each of the inputs always has as much of the other inputs to work with?

In short, *balanced* scale changes may often be expected to leave inputs and outputs in the same ratios. [Reexamine Fig. 2-7(a).]

On the other hand, when we do hold one input or group of inputs constant and vary the remaining inputs, we see that the varying inputs have *less and less of the fixed inputs to work with.* Consequently, we are not too surprised that such extra varying inputs begin to add less and less extra product. In effect, the fixed factor of production (land) is decreasing in proportion to the variable input (labor). As we crowd the land more and more, we may still get some extra corn by intensive cultivation of the soil; but the amount of extra corn per unit of extra labor will become less and less. We shall see in Part Four that the real wage paid to workers depends upon the extra output a last man adds for his employer. Diminishing returns reveals that living standards in crowded China or India are low because of this basic technical truth, and not *merely* because land happens to be owned by the state or by private landlords.

In conclusion, we may summarize as follows:

The law of diminishing returns: **An increase in some inputs relative to other fixed inputs will, in a given state of technology, cause total output to increase;** *but after a point the extra output resulting from the same additions of extra inputs is likely to become less and less.* **This falling off of extra returns is a consequence of the fact that the new "doses" of the varying resources have less and less of the fixed resources to work with.**

ECONOMIES OF SCALE AND MASS PRODUCTION: AN IMPORTANT COUNTERFORCE

Before leaving this section we ought to take note of a phenomenon that is different from our controlled variation of one thing at a time.

Suppose we merely increase "*scale* of operations," i.e., increase *all* the factors at the same time in the same degree. In many industrial processes, when you double *all* inputs, you may find that your output is more than doubled; this phenomenon is called "*increasing returns to scale.*"

Our previous law of diminishing returns always refers to cases where *some* factors were varied *while some remained fixed.* Hence, this case of increasing returns to scale is not a direct refutation of the law of diminishing returns.

Increasing returns to scale, or so-called "economies of mass production," are often associated with one of the following advances: (1) the use of nonhuman and nonanimal power sources (water and wind power, steam, electricity, turbines and internal-combustion engines, internal nuclear energy); (2) the use of automatic self-adjusting mechanisms (lathes, jigs, servomechanisms); (3) the use of standardized, interchangeable parts; (4) the breakdown of complex processes into simple repetitive operations; (5) the specialization of function and division of labor; and many other technological factors as well. The automobile-production assembly line and the historical development of modern textile spinning and weaving are examples typifying these diverse factors.

Upon thought, it will be evident that *each of these economies or savings comes into full play only if a large enough number of units is being produced to make it worth while to set up a fairly elaborate productive organization.* If only a few guns are to be produced, they might just as well be produced by hand; but if resources are available to produce many thousands, it will pay to make certain elaborate initial preparations that need not be repeated when still more units are to be produced. In such cases, where mere scale matters much, the tendency for land fixity to force diminishing extra returns to labor could be thwarted for a long time by an increase in the total labor scale involved.[6]

Economies of scale are very important in explaining why so many of the goods we buy are produced by large companies. We shall see that they are important in helping explain "the division of labor" and pattern of "specialization." They raise questions to which we shall return again and again in later chapters—as, for example, monopoly.

---

[6]Accordingly, it might come about that, unlike our earlier simplified picture, we should have to pay 2 butter units for our first gun unit; but to get still another gun unit we should have to pay only 1 butter unit because of the efficiency of mass production. This would be a case of *decreasing* rather than increasing extra-costs-for-one-good-in-terms-of-another. When increasing returns to scale predominate, advanced treatises show that you have to redraw Fig. 2-2 to be "bowed in" (convex from below) rather than "bowed out" (concave from below), at least near each axis.

LAW OF INCREASING (RELATIVE) COSTS

We are now in a position to indicate why the *production-possibility frontier* has been drawn as a bowed-out or concave curve in all our diagrams. If the *p-p frontier* were a straight line, the relative costs of getting some extra guns in terms of sacrificed butter would always be the same. Economists call this a case of "constant (relative) costs." But actually it is more common in life to meet the law of increasing (relative) costs.

Definition: **The "law of increasing (relative) costs" prevails when in order to get equal extra amounts of one good, society must sacrifice ever-increasing amounts *of the other good.* A bowed-out or concave curvature of the *production-possibility frontier* depicts the law of increasing (relative) costs—as shown by the fact that when we want more farm goods (butter), their (relative) cost in terms of sacrificed Manufactures (guns) rises.**

Land scarcity for food, plus diminishing returns, entails increasing (relative) costs:

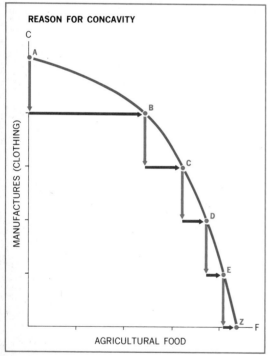

FIG. 2-8.   In going from A to B, B to C, C to D, D to E, and E to Z, we have to give up equal amounts of Manufactures as we transfer equal labor amounts out of the manufacturing industry. Note the equal vertical gold arrows below A, below B, . . ., etc. But, as equal units of varying labor are added to fixed agricultural land, diminishing returns yields less and less of extra food—as measured by the shorter and shorter brown horizontal arrows. This accounts for the curve's bending, or for the law of increasing relative costs.

Why is this reasonable?[7] We shall see that the law of increasing (relative) costs is related to, but definitely not the same thing as, the law of diminishing returns. We shall see that, along with the law of diminishing returns, economists must be able to assume that guns and butter use the factors of production, such as labor and land, in different proportions or intensities to deduce this law of (increasing) relative costs.

To derive the law of increasing (relative) costs, let us use an oversimplified example. In Fig. 2-8, suppose that Manufactures (guns) require *labor alone* and negligible land. But suppose that Agricultural food (butter) requires, along with labor, fertile *land that has grown scarce enough to have become private property.* Now we have the two ingredients to explain the law of increasing (relative) costs shown in the *p-p frontier:* The two industries use land and labor in different proportions; so transferring varying amounts of labor onto fixed Agricultural land will turn out to bring into play the law of diminishing returns. Let us see exactly how.

Begin by using all labor to produce Manufactures, at A in Fig. 2-8. Now sacrifice equal amounts of Manufactures to get more Agriculture, going to B and C. How is this transformation accomplished? By transferring *equal amounts of labor* away from Manufactures. But note that these equal amounts of transferred labor are applied to a *fixed* total of Agricultural land. As equal amounts of varying labor are applied to a fixed land factor, each has less and less acres to work with and hence adds less and less of extra Agriculture

[7] The remainder of this section may be skipped without loss of continuity.

product. We see then why each new Agriculture is procured at higher and higher costs in terms of Manufactures.[8]

THE LABOR THEORY OF VALUE: A DIGRESSION[9]

On reflection, one sees that the law of increasing (relative) costs serves to rebut the so-called "labor theory of value," which was adopted by Karl Marx (1818–1883) from the earlier classical writers Adam Smith (1723–1790) and David Ricardo (1772–1823). According to it, goods should exchange at prices dependent upon their labor requirements alone.

Thus, if food requires 2 labor hours and clothing requires 6 labor hours, clothing should have a value 3 (or $\frac{6}{2}$) times that of food. Marx argued that only "exploitation" keeps these values from actually being realized under capitalism.

What are the merits of this doctrine? As Smith pointed out: "In that early and rude state of society which precedes the accumulation of stock [i.e., capital] and the appropriation of land, . . . the quantities of labour . . . seem to be the only circumstance which can afford any rule for exchanging them for one another. . . ."

But Smith, and Ricardo too, recognized that as soon as land and capital are scarce, goods which require land and capital in especially heavy proportions will, even if their labor hours are the same, have to be valued higher. Marx saw this too in the third (posthumous) volume of his *Das Kapital* (1894); but, particularly in his first, 1867, volume, he thought the disparity from labor value was somehow "exploitative" and would lead to "contradictions" that would cause capitalism to break down.

In later chapters, we shall deal repeatedly with causes of unemployment and of business cycles, and with efficient pricing under both communism and capitalism. A fair-minded reader of 1970—whether in Moscow, Idaho, or Moscow, Russia—will then be in a position to judge whether the "labor theory of value" is of more than historical interest in the twentieth and twenty-first centuries.

Figure 2-8, which is as applicable under capitalism as under communism, under anarchism as under fascism, illustrates that the labor cost to get an extra unit of food, relative to the labor cost to produce a unit of manufactures, is not something that is a constant. If society wants much food—as near Z—limited land (a fact in China, Russia, India, Switzerland, and the United States) will invoke the law of diminishing returns and require that food be valued at a high price relative to clothing. Why this rise in food price attributable to land scarcity? To benefit idle landlords?

---

[8] The common sense of this law of increasing (relative) costs does not depend upon one of the goods using labor alone. It depends only on having the two goods—call them guns and butter—differing in the proportions of factors they require. Thus, note that the first few guns can be produced in part with the kind of resources that are no good for butter anyway. If more guns are wanted, we must use resources that are valuable for butter production; and if we insist upon having all guns, we must be prepared to take farmers and farmlands, which are very efficient in the production of butter, and transform them to the production of guns even though they can produce only very little in this sphere. Thus, increasing (relative) costs are to be expected in such a case. Even if resources could be divided into two uniform classes, such as homogeneous land and homogeneous labor, increasing costs would still result from the fact that guns and butter do not require the same proportion of these resources— butter taking more land, and guns requiring relatively more labor—as in the example above. (An Extra-credit problem, for geometry-inclined readers, returns to this problem at end of Chapter 27's Appendix.)

[9] This section may be skipped in brief courses.

Of course not. In China and Russia, the State owns the land; there is no wealthy landlord class. Still, even in those societies, as Chapter 32 will elucidate, adhering to the labor theory alone will result in *inefficient* production *inside* the *p-p frontier;* aside from distorted answers to the question of How, there will result distorted answers to the WHAT problem, as too much is produced of some goods and too little of others in terms of what the State and the consumers really desire and what technology determines could be available to them to choose from.[10]

In leaving this digression, one may note that abandonment of the labor theory of value to ancient history need not affect one way or the other the passion for social reform or for conservation of the status quo.

C. THE UNDERLYING POPULATION BASIS OF ANY ECONOMY: PAST AND FUTURE POPULATION TRENDS

THE MALTHUS THEORY OF POPULATION

The law of diminishing returns has an important and interesting application in the field of population. Around 1800, Thomas Robert Malthus, a young English clergyman, used to argue at breakfast against his father's perfectionist view that the human race was getting ever better. Finally the younger Malthus became so agitated that he wrote a book, his *Essay on the Principle of Population* (1798), which was an instantaneous best seller. Going through several editions, for a century the book influenced the thinking of people all over the world (including Charles Darwin, the expositor of the famous doctrine of biological evolution). It is still a living influence today. Malthus' views depend directly on the law of diminishing returns, and continue to have relevance.

Malthus first took the observation of Benjamin Franklin that, in the American colonies where resources were abundant, population tended to double every 25 years or so. Malthus postulated, therefore, *a universal tendency for population—unless checked by food supply—to grow at a geometric progression.* Now, anyone with imagination knows how fast geometric progressions grow—how soon 1, 2, 4, 8, 16, 32, 64, 128, 256, 512, 1,024, . . . , becomes so large that there is not space in the world for all the people to stand.[11]

All this left members of the "perfectionist school," such as the elder Malthus and William Godwin, unimpressed. So at this point Malthus in effect unleashed the devil of the law of diminishing returns.

As population doubles and redoubles, it is exactly as if the globe were halving in size, until finally it has shrunk so much that food and subsistence fall below the level necessary for life. Because of the law of diminishing returns, food tends *not* to keep up with the geometric-progression rate of growth of population.

---

[10] If all goods used land and every other input in the *same proportions* as labor, Fig. 2-8's frontier would become a straight line. In this case prices *proportional* to labor hours would involve no distortions.
[11] At 6 per cent compound interest, money doubles in value every 12 years. It has been estimated that the $24 received by the Indians for Manhattan Island would, if deposited at compound interest, be today worth as much as all real property on the island. At 6 per cent, Sir Francis Drake's plunder of Spanish gold would today equal Britain's wealth.

Mind you, Malthus did not say that population *would* increase at these rates. This was only its *tendency* if unchecked. He considered it an important part of his argument to show that, in all places in all times, checks do operate to hold population down. In his first edition he put emphasis on *positive* checks that act to increase the death rate: pestilence, famine, and war. Later he backed down from this gloomy doctrine and held out hope for the human race through *preventive* checks operating on the birth rate. Although the birth-control movement is called neo-Malthusianism, Malthus, himself an early-nineteenth-century clergyman, advocated only *moral restraint* with prudential postponement of early marriages until a family could be supported. In fact, he preached that the struggle for existence was an illustration of the wisdom of Nature, keeping poor people from getting soft and lazy.

This important application of diminishing returns illustrates the profound effects a simple theory can have. Malthus' ideas had widespread repercussions. His book was used to support a stern revision of the English poor laws, whereby destitution was considered a result of laziness and unemployment a state to be made as uncomfortable as possible. His opinions also bolstered the argument that trade-unions could not improve the welfare of workers, since any increase in their wages would only cause workers to reproduce until there was again barely subsistence enough for all.

Despite the statistics covering many countries incorporated in his later editions, it is today recognized that his views were oversimplifications. In his discussion of diminishing returns, Malthus never fully anticipated the miracles of the Industrial Revolution. In the next century technological innovation *shifted* production-possibility frontiers rapidly *outward* and made possible better standards of living for more people, even though at the same time medical advances were prolonging human life and further lessening the positive checks to population. Nor did he anticipate that after 1870 in most Western nations family *fertility* as measured by actual number of children would begin to fall far short of family *fecundity*, or biological reproductive capacity.

Nevertheless, the germs of truth in his doctrines are still important for understanding the population behavior of India, Haiti, China, and other parts of the globe where the balance of numbers and food supply is a vital factor.

Table 2-3 shows how much world population has increased. This increase was made possible mainly through the declining death rate, resulting from scientific advances in medicine and from the improved living standards made possible by the Industrial Revolution. Life expectancy of a Western baby has doubled since 1800 to over seventy years at present, and standards of living far exceed those of any previous century.

Even more dramatic has been the reduction of death rates in low-income regions. Ceylon offers the dramatic case where control of mosquitoes by DDT greatly reduced malaria, cutting the death rate by 34 per cent in a single year! In India alone, one of the fruits of modern science has been a great increase in average

World population has more than tripled since 1800:

POPULATION OF THE WORLD (in millions)			
	1800	1940	1970
Europe (including all of U.S.S.R.)	188	572	710
North, South, and Central America	29	277	510
Asia, Africa, and Oceania	702	1,396	2,400
World	919	2,245	3,620

TABLE 2-3 (Sources: United Nations *Statistical Year Book*; author.)

life expectancy. In the last 20 years India's population grew by at least 120 million, an amount greater than the combined populations of France and England!

Professor Kingsley Davis of California, an expert on population, has warned against the facile belief that it is primarily hunger (or even malnutrition) which makes life so short in poor societies. The role of disease is important as an independent factor: if inexpensive science greatly lengthens life without greatly increasing productivity and greatly changing preindustrial attitudes, the fears of Malthus take on a new relevance.

CONTROLLING POPULATION GROWTH

As we shall see in Part Six, much of the world is in a state of underdevelopment and poverty. If the birth rate were to continue at the high levels typical of the past—when you had to have six or more children in order to ensure that there would be a surviving child to carry on your line—population numbers would explode, and the law of diminishing returns would vitiate the gains from technical progress. Little wonder then that, wherever religious and ethical attitudes permit, there is beginning to be an active birth-control or family-planning movement.

Education is, of course, basic. But nevertheless the new chemical means popular in the advanced Western nations—the so-called "pill"—are often inordinately expensive in poorer lands. A couple of dollars a month may seem like little in New York City; but in Java or El Salvador you could raise a family on that much. The American foreign-aid programs, when foreign nations have requested such aid, and when it is not in conflict with prevalent ethical beliefs, have provided assistance for programs of family planning. No doubt technological changes will vastly alter costs in this as in other areas.

All that needs stressing here is the fact that there is an important relationship between population density and average standards and amenities of life.

DO AMERICA AND EUROPE FACE DEPOPULATION?

At the end of World War I men still feared the Malthusian curse of overpopulation. Books then had such alarming titles as *The World Faces Overpopulation* and *Standing Room Only!* But just as these books were coming off the presses, Western Europe and the United States were undergoing a profound revolution in population. This was understood only a generation later. The pendulum then swung to the other extreme; best sellers had flashy titles like *The Twilight of Parenthood* and *England without People.*

Since 1870—even earlier in France—birth rates began to drop in most countries of Western European civilization. After World War I, and especially after the Great Depression of the 1930s, the drop became precipitous. The crisis in births, however, was hidden for a time.

Observations that there was an excess of births over deaths gave a misleading feeling of security, because they ignored the fact that the United States and Western Europe *temporarily* had an unusually large number of women in the childbearing groups. Why this excess in these age groups? Because people in 1900 had larger families than people in 1935 were having. With so many women of the age to be mothers, prewar birth *totals* temporarily held up; and yet the number of births *per mother* was low—so low that, if the same prewar rates had continued, the future growth of the population would have eventually ended and turned into a decline.

Before World War II there was every reason for the population expert to despair for the future of the population of Western nations. Nor did the problem appear to be directly economic. Everyone knew that the rich had fewer children than the poor. Before 1940, Harvard and Vassar students were not reproducing themselves. Neither were Michigan State and Oberlin students, nor high school graduates and urban groups generally.[12]

OUR AMAZING POPULATION UPSURGE

Just then something remarkable happened to jar the expert. Nobody yet knows quite how to explain it. During and after World War II the pattern of fertility began steadily to climb, reaching new heights. Every year now brings more than $3\frac{1}{2}$ million babies.

Some of the reasons are, of course, obvious. With the war came prosperity, and the backlog of depression-deferred marriages began to melt. The Draft also had something to do with the increase in marriages. The number of bachelors and spinsters shrank; and the age of (first) marriage fell sharply, so that more girls marry at eighteen than at any other age, with half married by shortly after twenty, and with half the men married by age twenty-three!

With many more recent marriages, it was only natural to expect the birth rate to leap upward. But more than that, people stepped up the rate at which they had children. In the 1950s third and fourth children became very fashionable among the middle classes, a dramatic reversion from the pre-World War II situation.

A glance at a college faculty—young, old, and middle-aged—will show the changing trends in this regard: the associate professors have already had more children than retired professors, and the final score is not yet in. Paradoxically, poorer nations such as Japan and Greece, which used to have high birth rates, now restrict family size more than do the rich nations.

Table 2-4 shows that the richer countries of Western Europe had pre-World War II net reproduction rates[13] far below unity and now have rates above the critical level of unity. The United States has come to have a net reproduction rate that is one of the

---

[12] Most authorities believe birth rates are to be explained by social rather than biological factors. Thus, the French Canadians, who long had high birth rates, once came from just those rural regions of France with lowest rates. Second-generation Italian and Jewish city dwellers show greatly reduced rates, as do Negroes who move from the South to the North. Some of the highest net reproduction rates are among the white people in Appalachia. Ironically, the highest rates of all are to be found among—of all peoples—the American Indians, suggesting that we may yet give the country back to the Indians. Physiologists now dispute the notion that modern man is less fecund than his hungry ancestors.

[13] Demographers define the net reproduction rate (NRR) as "the *average* number of girl babies that will be born to a representative newly born girl in her lifetime." Thus, if 1,000 girls born in 1970 will, by A.D. 2020, have produced 1,600 girl babies, the NRR = 1,600/1,000 = 1.6; and were such a fertility rate to be maintained indefinitely, population would ultimately be growing at the rate of 60 per cent per "generation," i.e., about every 25 years, the average age of a mother when giving birth. (Explain exactly what NRR = 0.7 or = 1.0 means, showing why 1.0 is the watershed between decay and growth.)

Net reproduction rates make correction for changing age distribution:

NET REPRODUCTION RATES FOR VARIOUS COUNTRIES					
United States			**Belgium**	0.90	1939
Total	0.98	1930–40		1.28	1965
	1.72	1960	**Netherlands**	1.15	1935–39
	1.38	1965		1.43	1965
White	0.96	1935–40	**Australia**	0.98	1935–39
	1.66	1960		1.40	1965
	1.32	1965	**Palestine**		
Nonwhite	1.14	1935–40	Moslems	2.17	1940
	2.04	1960	Jews	1.61	1945
	1.76	1965	**Israel**		
United Kingdom	0.78	1935–39	Jews	1.57	1963
	1.29	1966	**Japan**	1.49	1935–39
France	0.87	1935–37		1.01	1965
	1.32	1966	**India**	1.25	1931
Sweden	0.78	1935–39		1.31	1941
	1.13	1966	**Soviet Union**	1.72	1926
Germany				1.54	1938
Total	0.71	1933		1.14	1965
West	1.17	1965			

TABLE 2-4. An NRR (net reproduction rate) permanently greater than 1 means ultimate population growth. An NRR less than 1 means ultimate population decline. The NRR for the United States is still above 1, but declining in the 1970s. (Source: *Population Index*, April, 1968, Office of Population Research, Princeton, N.J.; author.)

highest in the world or in recent history, and only recently has begun to show a change in trend.

TURN OF THE TIDE?

Since 1957, however, America has experienced a modest but steady fall in the birth rate. In part this was because of a temporary drop in the ratio of women of childbearing age to total population. More significant for the longer-run trend is the fact that the fertility and net reproduction rates have been dropping slightly among married women of every age. National surveys of the number of children that women say they *want* still report about 3, on the average. Nonetheless, the *actual* number being born to them has been slowly declining.

No doubt economic factors are involved here. Professor Richard Easterlin of the University of Pennsylvania has put forth an interesting hypothesis. He speculates that a young married couple will be less eager to have many children if their current income is falling far below that which their own families had a few years earlier. He points out that in the 1950s, when young people were scarce and their incomes relatively high, they hastened to have many children. In the early 1970s, when the vast crop of war babies has been coming onto the labor market and bidding down incomes, the comparison is less favorable. In Easterlin's view, this helps to explain the decline in NRR.

Finally, though, let us be clear on one thing: Birth rates are still quite high in America compared with what they are in other advanced nations.

ECONOMIC EFFECTS OF POPULATION GROWTH

The economic impact of population changes is already very noticeable. Our suburbs teem with children; our schools are overcrowded. The bulge of postwar births has already hit colleges: by 1980 college enrollment will be double that of 1970! Beer and piano sales reflect the rise in youths.

Figure 2-9 shows the rising proportion of dependent children. For some time people of working age will decline in relative importance: caught between the growth of the dependent old *and* young, they will each have to support more nonworkers.

From the military manpower viewpoint, time may be working against the countries of Western Europe. Table 2-5 shows estimates of future populations for certain countries. Note the high estimate for the Soviet Union, where only recently have net reproduction rates been low; note the low figures for Sweden and the United Kingdom.

Is our population upsurge a good thing? Economics alone cannot answer such a general question. The joys and aches of family life are not to be measured in mere dollars and cents. Yet we can study certain economic aspects of population growth; and when we come to do so in later chapters, we shall find that the answers are rarely simple.

On the one hand, *growing* population makes for high money spending, as homes and factories are being replicated in like numbers. Therefore it may act against unemployment, and by the same reasoning, it could also aggravate inflationary threats. On the other hand, a considerably higher *level* of population threatens us with the law of diminishing returns. It fills our cars with people and fills our roads with cars; it pollutes the air with smog; it pollutes our water with filth; it spoils the countryside and ruins privacy. (Chapter 40 will deal with urban and environmental problems.)

The old and young are gaining on the productive age group:

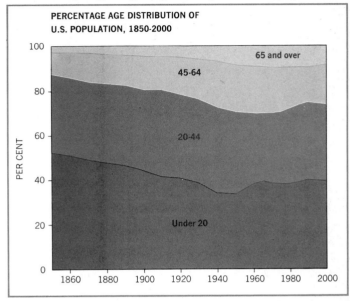

FIG. 2-9. As couples have larger families and length of life increases, each person of working age will have more dependents to support. Note the rising flood of youthful workers, which could bring with it serious unemployment problems. (Source: U.S. Bureau of the Census.)

United States and Soviet populations gain relative to rest of Europe:

ESTIMATED FUTURE POPULATION OF DIFFERENT COUNTRIES IN 1980 (in millions)			
	ANNUAL GROWTH (% per year)	1966	1975	1980
United States	1.3	197	221	236
United Kingdom	0.7	55	58.6	60.6
France	1.1	49	55	57
Soviet Union	1.2	233	260	275
Sweden	0.9	7.8	8.4	8.8
Italy	0.9	52	56	59
Japan	1.0	99	108	114

TABLE 2-5. Note the different rates of growth (1963–1966 average) in the first column, showing the United States and the Soviet growing fastest and the United Kingdom, Sweden, and Italy slowest. (Source: United Nations *Statistical Year Book*.)

SUMMARY

A. PROBLEMS OF ECONOMIC ORGANIZATION

1   Every economy must somehow solve the three fundamental economic problems: WHAT kinds and quantities shall be produced of all possible goods and services; HOW economic resources shall be used in producing these goods; and FOR WHOM the goods shall be produced, i.e., the distribution of income among different individuals and classes.

2   Societies meet these problems in different ways—by custom, instinct, fiat or command and decree, and in our mixed economy, largely by a system of price and markets.

3   The basic problems are important because of the fundamental fact of all economic life: with limited resources and technology, standards of living are limited. Economic goods are *scarce* rather than free; society must choose among them, because not all needs and desires can be fulfilled.

B. THE TECHNOLOGICAL CHOICES OPEN TO ANY SOCIETY

4   With given resources and technology, the production choices open to a nation between two such goods as butter and guns can be summarized in the *production-possibility frontier.* This indicates the way in which one good can be transformed into another by transferring resources from its production to that of the other.

5   Production-possibility frontiers can illustrate many basic economic processes: how we use relatively *less* of our resources for food *necessities* as we develop; how we choose between *private* market goods and *public* governmental goods; between *current consumption* and *capital goods* that enhance *future* capacity to produce. The *p-p frontier* can illustrate *technical progress* and pave the way for diminishing returns.

6   The *law of diminishing returns* asserts that, after a point, as we add more and more equal doses of a variable input (such as labor) to a fixed input (such as land), the amount of extra product will fall off. This law is really a matter of proportions: the varying input has less and less of the fixed input to work with.

7   *Economies of mass production or of scale* are often described as "increasing returns *to scale.*" The word "scale" is a warning that *all* inputs are being varied simultaneously, with none held fixed as in the law of diminishing returns. Many modern processes do pass through an initial stage of increasing returns to scale.

8   The *labor theory of value* can validly predict prices in terms of labor hours alone only in a hypothetical time when land and other nonlabor factors of production are abundant enough to be freely available. Once such factors as land become scarce, true social scarcities depend on the whole mix of labor-wage, land-rent, and capital-interest costs.

The *p-p frontier* then ceases to be a straight line and becomes a bowed-out curve which is concave (from below). *This depicts the law of increasing (relative) costs.* To get equal amounts of one good requires society to sacrifice more and more of the other. All this results when goods use factors of production in different proportions, and hence the proper transfers of productive factors bring the law of diminishing returns into play.

C. THE UNDERLYING POPULATION BASIS OF ANY ECONOMY: PAST AND FUTURE POPULATION TRENDS

9   Malthus' theory of population rests on the law of diminishing returns. He thought that a population, if unchecked, would tend to grow in *geometric* rate, doubling every generation or so. But each member of the growing population would have less natural resources and land to work with. Therefore, because of diminishing returns, income would have a tendency to fall so low as to lead to a stable population at a subsistence level of starvation and pestilence.

10 For a century and a half after Malthus, populations grew by leaps and bounds everywhere. Numbers grew primarily because death rates fell sharply as a result of improved medical and public health technology; yet technological progress in industry more than offset the law of diminishing returns.

11 After 1870 birth rates began to fall. Prior to World War II, advanced nations had net reproduction rates below 1 and faced depopulation. After 1939 the middle classes swung back toward a larger-family pattern, a trend predicted by few and one which has had momentous future consequences. Only recently has the tide been slowly turning.

QUESTIONS FOR DISCUSSION

1   Without looking at the next chapter, can you anticipate how a price system through supply and demand solves the three problems of *economic* organization?

2   Explain what economists mean by *scarcity,* by *free goods,* by *inefficiency.*

3   Draw society's *p-p frontier* if scientific inventions increased the productivity of given resources in butter production only, and not in guns.

4   If land were increased in a number of steps and labor were held constant, would the law of diminishing returns hold? Illustrate and tell why this would indeed happen.

5   Describe and contrast (*a*) the law of diminishing returns; (*b*) the phenomenon of increasing returns to scale. How about (*c*) the law of increasing (relative) costs?

6   How many were there in your great-grandparents' family? In your parents' family? How many do you think there will be in your own family?

7   "Population pressure doesn't cause war, as is commonly believed. Careful study suggests cause and effect are just the reverse. Nations that want to expand try to persuade their

citizens to grow in numbers so the nation will be militarily strong and will have a pretext for expansion." Discuss.

8   *Extra-credit problem* for those mathematically inclined: We can illustrate the "linear programming" technique referred to in footnote 3 on Stigler's least-cost-diet problem. Suppose each unit of milk, beans, and meat has respectively (1, 8, 2) calories and (4, 2, 1) vitamins. Suppose each unit of the 3 goods costs ($1, $2, $3) respectively. Suppose you must buy at least 120 calorie units per month and 180 vitamin units. Can you show by experiment that the least monthly cost is $60 per month, with meat not being bought at all, and with milk at 40 and beans at 10 units? Mathematically the linear programmer writes this as

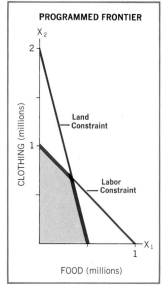

PROGRAMMED FRONTIER

$$\text{Minimize } Z = \$1X_1 + \$2X_2 + \$3X_3, \text{ subject to}$$
$$1X_1 + 8X_2 + 2X_3 \geq 120$$
$$4X_1 + 2X_2 + 1X_3 \geq 180$$
$$X_1 \geq 0, X_2 \geq 0, X_3 \geq 0$$

A similar linear programming problem will define a *p-p frontier* like that shown here. Suppose food and clothing each take 1 unit of labor. But food being land intensive takes 4 acres of land, while clothing takes only 1 acre. If society has 1 (million) men and 2 (million) acres, the frontier is defined by

$$1X_1 + 1X_2 \leq 1$$
$$4X_1 + 1X_2 \leq 2$$

the first giving the heavy blue part and the second the heavy brown part.

Review your understanding of the following concepts:

economic and free goods
substitution and law of scarcity
production-possibility frontier
law of diminishing returns
total versus extra product
productive factors or inputs

increasing returns to scale
law of increasing (relative) costs
labor theory of value
Malthusian population theory
age distribution of population
net reproduction rate (NRR)

Price Functioning of a "Mixed Economy"

THE MIXED ECONOMY

Most of our attention will be devoted to the special features of economic life found in twentieth-century industrial nations (with the exception of the Soviet system). In most of these countries there was a trend in the past few centuries toward less and less direct governmental control of economic activity; gradually feudal and preindustrial conditions were replaced by greater emphasis on what is loosely called "free private enterprise," or "competitive capitalism."

Long before this trend had approached a condition of full laissez faire (i.e., of complete governmental noninterference with business), the tide began to turn the other way. Since late in the nineteenth century, in almost all the countries under consideration there has been a steady increase in the economic functions of government.

Ours is a "mixed economy" in which both public and private institutions exercise economic control.

Section A of this chapter shows how our mixed economy tackles the three problems of economic organization that must be met by any society. Section B describes some fundamental characteristics of the present economic order.

A. HOW A FREE ENTERPRISE SYSTEM SOLVES THE BASIC ECONOMIC PROBLEMS

In a system of free private enterprise, no individual or organization is *consciously* concerned with the triad of economic problems set forth in Chapter 2: WHAT, HOW, and FOR WHOM. This fact is really remarkable.

To paraphrase a famous economic example, let us consider the city of New York. Without a constant flow of goods in and out of the city, it would be on the verge of starvation within a week. A variety of the right kinds and amounts of food is involved. From the surrounding counties, from 50 states, and from the far corners of the world, goods have been traveling for days and months with New York as their destination.

How is it that 10 million people are able to sleep easily at night, without living in mortal terror of a breakdown in the elaborate economic processes upon which the city's existence depends? For all this is undertaken *without coercion or centralized direction* by any conscious body!

Everyone notices how much the government does to control economic activity—tariff legislation, pure-food laws, utility and railroad regulations, minimum-wage regulations, fair-labor-practice acts, social security, price ceilings and floors, public works, national defense, national and local taxation, police protection and judicial redress, zoning ordinances, municipal water or gas works, and so forth. What goes unnoted is how much of economic life proceeds *without* direct government intervention.

Hundreds of thousands of commodities are produced by millions of people more or less of their own volition and without central direction or master plan.

NOT CHAOS BUT ECONOMIC ORDER

This functioning alone is convincing proof that a competitive system of markets and prices—whatever else it may be, however imperfectly it may function—is not a system of chaos and anarchy. There is in it a certain order and orderliness. It works.

A competitive system is an elaborate mechanism for unconscious coordination through a system of prices and markets, a communication device for pooling the knowledge and actions of millions of diverse individuals. Without a central intelligence it solves one of the most complex problems imaginable, involving thousands of unknown variables and relations. Nobody designed it. It just evolved, and like human nature, it is changing; but it does meet the first test of any social organization—it can survive.

A dramatic example of the importance of a pricing system is Germany after World War II. In 1946–1947 production and consumption had dropped to a low level. Neither bombing damage nor postwar reparation payments could account for this breakdown. *Paralysis of the price mechanism* was clearly to blame: Money was worthless; factories closed down for lack of materials; trains could not run for lack of coal; coal could not be mined because miners were hungry; miners were hungry because peasants would not sell food for money and no industrial goods were available to give them in return. Prices were legally fixed, but little could be bought at such prices; a black market characterized by barter or fantastically high prices existed. Then in 1948 a "miracle" happened. A thoroughgoing currency reform set the price mechanism back into effective operation. Immediately production and consumption soared; again the WHAT, HOW, and FOR WHOM were being resolved by markets and prices.

The fact to emphasize is that such so-called miracles are going on all around us all the time—if only we look around and alert ourselves to the everyday functioning of the market. A revolutionist out to destroy the capitalistic system could ask nothing better than a great inflation or deflation that would paralyze the price mechanism.[1]

---

[1] In the 1970s governments in the Soviet Union and Eastern European countries are rediscovering some virtues of a pricing system. Imitation is the sincerest form of flattery.

THE INVISIBLE HAND AND "PERFECT COMPETITION"

Students of economics have to avoid the error of thinking that a price mechanism must work chaotically if it is not controlled by somebody. Having learned this lesson, they must not go to the other extreme and become enamored of the beauty of a pricing mechanism, regarding it as perfection itself, the essence of providential harmony and beyond the touch of human hands.

Adam Smith, whose *The Wealth of Nations* (1776) is the germinal book of modern economics or political economy, was thrilled by the recognition of an order in the economic system. Smith proclaimed the principle of the "Invisible Hand"; every individual in pursuing only his own selfish good, was led, as if by an invisible hand, to achieve the best good for all, so that any interference with free competition by government was almost certain to be injurious. (See this chapter's initial quotation.) While Smith did recognize some of the realistic limitations on this doctrine, it was not until later that economists discovered this truth: The virtues claimed for free enterprise are fully realized only when the complete checks and balances of "perfect competition" are present.

Perfect competition is defined by the economist as a technical term: "Perfect competition" exists only in the case where no farmer, businessman, or laborer is a big enough part of the total market to have any personal influence on market price; on the other hand, when his grain, merchandise, or labor is large enough in size to produce depressing or elevating effects on market prices, some degree of monopolistic imperfection has set in, and the virtues of the Invisible Hand must be that much discounted.

Actually, much of the praise of perfect competition is beside the point. As discussed earlier, ours is a mixed system of government and private enterprise; as will be discussed later, it is also *a mixed system of monopoly and competition*. A cynic might say of perfect competition what Bernard Shaw said of Christianity: The only trouble with it is that it has never been tried.

Historians quarrel over whether there ever was a golden age of free competition. And certainly, competition is not now perfect in the economist's sense. We do not even know whether, because of the fundamental nature of large-scale production and technology, consumers' tastes, and business organization, competition is becoming less or more intense. The statistics suggest at least a slight weakening of monopolistic concentration of power as giant conglomerates coexist in diverse industries.

In any case, society need not accept as inevitable any trend toward big business, mergers, trusts, and cartels such as began to swell in the 1890s. The challenge is to work out laws and customs that help to improve the working of our less-than-perfect competitive system. The polar cases—laissez faire and totalitarian dictatorship of production—dramatize economic principles. Yet the relevant choice for policy today is not a decision between these extremes, but rather the degree to which public policy should do *less* or *more* in modifying the operation of particular private economic activities.

THE PRICE SYSTEM

Just how does the unconscious automatic price mechanism operate? The bare outlines of a *competitive* profit-and-loss system are simple to describe.

Everything has a price—each commodity and each service. Even the different kinds of human labor have prices, namely, wage rates. Everybody receives money for what he sells, and uses this money to buy what he wishes.

If more is wanted of any one good—say, shoes—a flood of new orders will be given for it. This will cause its price to rise and more to be produced.

Similarly, if more of a commodity such as tea becomes available than people want to buy at the last-quoted market price, its price will be marked down by competition. At the lower price people will drink more tea, and producers will no longer produce quite so much. Thus equilibrium of supply and demand will be restored (as the next chapter and Part Three will show).

What is true of the markets for consumers' goods is also true of markets for *factors of production* such as labor, land, and capital inputs. If welders rather than glassblowers are needed, job opportunities will be more favorable in the welding field. The price of welders, their hourly wage, will tend to rise, while that of glassblowers will tend to fall. Other things being equal, this will cause a shift into the desired occupation. Likewise, an acre of land will go into sugar cultivation if sugar producers bid the most for its use. In the same way, machine-tool production will be determined by supply and demand.

The general-equilibrium system   In other words, we have a vast system of trial and error, of successive approximation to an *equilibrium system of prices and production*. We shall see later that the matching of supply and demand and of prices and costs helps solve our three problems simultaneously. Here are the bare outlines:

1. WHAT things will be produced is determined by the *dollar votes* of consumers—not every 2 years at the polls, but every day in their decisions to purchase this item and not that. Of course, the money that they pay into business cash registers ultimately provides the payrolls, rents, and dividends that consumers receive in weekly income. Thus the circle is a complete one.

2. How things are produced is determined by the competition of different producers. The method that is cheapest at any one time, because of both physical efficiency and cost efficiency, will displace a more costly method.

The only way for producers to meet price competition and maximize profits is to keep costs at a minimum by adopting the most efficient methods. For example, synthetic rubber will be made from oil rather than alcohol if the price of the one is in a certain relation to the price of the other; or electric power will be generated by steam rather than atomic power if the price of coal is below some critical level. The large tractor-operated farm will displace the family-size farm if this leads to lower costs of production.

International example: Bob Jones farms *extensively*, with much American land relative to each hour of labor; Pierre Reny farms *intensively*, using much labor to each hectare of French land. Who orders these sensible How decisions, which properly adjust to the fact that France is more densely populated than America? Congress? The National Assembly? The UN? Of course not. The price system is society's signaling device. Like a master who gives carrots and kicks to coax his donkey forward, the pricing system deals out profits and losses to get WHAT, How, and FOR WHOM decided.

3. FOR WHOM things are produced is determined by supply and demand in the markets for productive services: by wage rates, land rents, interest rates, and profits, all of which

go to make up everybody's income—relative to everyone else and relative to the whole. (Of course, the character of the resulting distribution of income is highly dependent upon the *initial* distribution of property ownership, upon acquired or inherited abilities, educational opportunities, and presence or absence of racial and sex discriminations.)

Note this: Consumer votes do not by themselves determine WHAT goods are produced. Demand has to meet with a supply of goods; so business cost and supply decisions, along with consumer demand, do help to determine WHAT. Just as a broker may help arrange a match between buyer and seller, the auctioneer in the commodity market acts as the go-between who reconciles the consumer votes and business supplies that impinge on the market. (The next chapter explains how.) The profit seeker is society's agent to determine How, seeking least factor-costs for producing each good and being punished by ruthless competition if he fails to use best methods.

A PICTURE OF PRICES AND MARKETS

To amplify this highly simplified explanation, turn over to Fig. 3-1. It gives a bird's-eye view of the way market pricing reconciles public demand and supply with business supply and demand. Note that markets serve as the connecting device between the public and business. Fifteen minutes of poring over this diagram may be worth an hour of disconnected musing about economic pricing. (In Chapters 10 and 32, similar circular-flow diagrams will appear, namely, Fig. 10-1 and Fig. 32-1.)

A competitive system is impersonal but not completely so. The consuming families face business enterprises on two fronts, with only prices in between. One front is the widely dispersed one, the retail market on which consumers buy thousands of small items from a score of different retail establishments; grocery, drug, and department stores; movie theaters; gasoline stations; and from electric-power companies, government post offices, landlords, railroad lines, and insurance companies.

On the other front—the market for labor and other productive services—relations are not always so peaceful. To the family breadwinner his wage is not simply another price; it is the difference between luxury and comfort, between comfort and privation. The laborer may feel inferior to the large corporation in bargaining power, and he may turn to collective bargaining through trade-unions. By doing this, he may at times be helping to restore competition, while at other times he may be causing conditions to deviate still further from perfect competition.

ETHICAL ASPECTS OF INCOME DISTRIBUTION

The above picture of competition tending toward ideal efficiency, toward being on the production-possibility frontier and not inside it, is a highly oversimplified one. But even if the system worked perfectly as described above—which all know is not the case—many would not consider it ideal. In the first place, goods go where there are the most votes or dollars. A rich man's dog may receive the milk that a poor child needs to avoid rickets. Why? Because supply and demand are working badly? Quite possibly badly from ethical viewpoints, but not from the standpoint of what the market mechanism is geared to accomplish. Functionally, auction markets are doing what they are designed to do—put-

The competitive price system uses supply-demand markets to solve the basic economic problems—WHAT, HOW, and FOR WHOM:

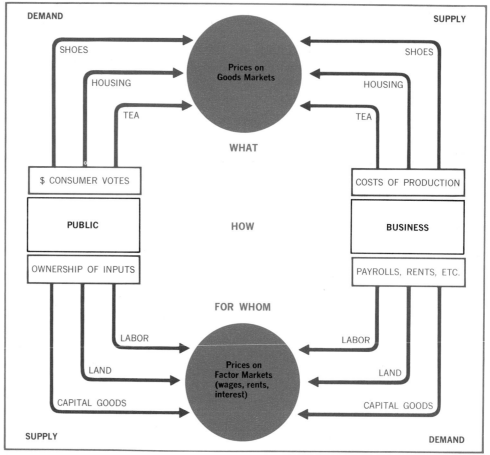

FIG. 3-1.   All demand relations are shown in blue; all the supply relations, in brown. See how consumer dollar votes of demand interact in the upper goods markets with business cost-supply decisions, thus helping determine WHAT is produced. And how business demand for inputs or productive factors meets the public's supply of labor and other inputs in the lower factor markets to help determine wage, rent, and interest income—i.e., FOR WHOM goods are produced. Business competition to buy factor inputs and sell goods most cheaply determines HOW goods are to be produced. (WARNING: All parts of the diagram interact together. WHAT depends on the lower part, just as FOR WHOM depends on the upper part—carpenter wages depend on housing demand, and demand for yachts depends on oil-land royalties.)

ting goods in the hands of those who can pay the most, who have the most money votes. Defenders and critics of the price mechanism should recognize this fact.[2]

Or suppose the invention of automatic machines should cause the competitive price

[2]Cecil Woodham-Smith, *The Great Hunger: Ireland 1845–9* (Harper & Row, New York, 1963), relates the unbelievable details of how a laissez faire Victorian government let millions of Irish children, women, and men literally starve when a fungus destroyed the potato crop.

of labor to fall greatly, thereby reducing incomes of the poor. Would all ethical observers regard that as necessarily right or ideal? Certainly not.

Should the fact that a man inherited 500 square miles of rangeland, for which oil companies offer a million dollars per year, necessarily justify so large an income?

These questions are discussed repeatedly in Congress. Whether incomes should be completely determined by a competitive struggle—the survival of the survivors—is an ethical question that goes beyond the mere mechanics of economics. In the modern mixed economy, the electorate insists on providing minimum standards when the market fails to do so. Economics teaches how interventions can be accomplished at least costs in terms of inefficiency.

IMPERFECTIONS OF COMPETITION

As we said earlier, one drawback to the picture of the price system as described above is the fact that, in the real world, competition is nowhere near "perfect." Firms do not know when consumer tastes will change; therefore they may overproduce in one field and underproduce in another. By the time they are ready to learn from experience, the situation may have changed again. Also, in a competitive system many producers simply do not know the methods of other producers, and costs do not fall to a minimum. In the competitive struggle one can sometimes succeed as much by *keeping knowledge scarce* as by keeping production high.

The most serious deviation from perfect competition comes from *monopoly elements*. These—as we shall see later on—may result in wrong pricing, incorrect and wasteful resource allocation, and monopoly profits. We shall be reminded again and again how strict is the economist's definition of a "perfect competitor." The mere presence of a few rivals is not enough for perfect competition.

Monopoly elements The economic definition of "imperfect competitor" is *anyone who buys or sells a good in large enough quantities to be able to affect the price of that good.* To some degree that means almost all businessmen, except possibly the millions of farmers who individually produce a negligible fraction of the total crop. All economic life is a blend of competitive and monopoly elements. Imperfect (monopolistic) competition is the prevailing mode, not perfect competition. A good approximation of perfect competition may be the most society can strive for.

Of course, as we shall later see, a businessman cannot set his prices completely as he pleases and still make profits. He must take into account the prices of goods that are substitutes for his own. Even if he produces a trademarked coal with unique properties, he must reckon with prices charged for other coals, oil, gas, and insulation.

Businessmen, farmers, and workers both like and dislike competition. We all like it when it enables us to expand our market, but we label it as "chiseling," "unfair," or "ruinous" when the knife cuts the other way. The worker whose livelihood depends on how the market prices his labor may be the first to howl when competition threatens to depress wages. Farm groups, aware of what competition can do to agricultural prices, often bring pressure on the state to restrict production and thereby raise prices.

In the idealized model of an efficiently acting competitive market mechanism, consumers are supposed to be well informed. They recognize low quality and avoid it; they never buy drugs that turn out to be poisonous or ineffective. Most important, their "desires" are supposed to represent genuine "wants" and "needs" and "tastes." But in actual life, as Galbraith never tires of repeating, business firms spend much money on advertising to *shape*—and, some insist, *distort*—consumer demands. We are terrorized into buying deodorants; from childhood on, we are conditioned to desire what business wants to sell. The sequence "consumer demand→corporate price and production" is often inverted to become "corporate advertising→consumer demand→high price and profit."

Some of the basic factors responsible for monopoly-creating bigness in business may be *inherent in the economies of large-scale production.* This is especially true in a dynamic world of technological change. Competition by numerous producers would simply not be efficient in many fields and could not last. Trademarks, patents, and advertising are often responsible for still other market imperfections. It would be humanly impossible, therefore, to attempt to create *perfect* competition by law. The problem is one of achieving reasonably effective "workable competition."

We shall proceed later to a more microscopic examination of supply and demand. After that discussion we shall be in a position to appraise the workings of the price system more judiciously. A competitive price system is one way of organizing an economy, but not the only way. Admiration should not inhibit reform. Still it is of interest that some socialists plan to continue to use a price mechanism as part of their new society. A price system is not perfect, but neither are its alternatives.

ECONOMIC ROLE OF GOVERNMENT

It was said earlier that ours is not a pure price economy but a *mixed economy* in which elements of government control are intermingled with market elements in organizing production and consumption. The economic role of government is now so important that two chapters in Part One are devoted to it. An outline of its influence can be briefly indicated here.

Welfare minima   Democracies are not satisfied with the answers to WHAT, HOW, and FOR WHOM given by a completely unrestrained market system. Such a system, as already said, might dictate that some people starve from lack of income while others get inadequate or excessive incomes.

Therefore the citizenry through their government step in with expenditure to supplement the real or money incomes of some individuals. Thus, governments provide hospital beds for citizens, and the needy with monthly allowances in times of unemployment or old age. Minimum standards of life are widespread modern goals.

Public services and taxes   More than this, government provides certain indispensable *public* services without which community life would be unthinkable and which by their nature cannot appropriately be left to private enterprises. Government came into existence once people realized, "Everybody's business is nobody's business." Obvious examples are the maintenance of national defense and of internal law and order, and the administration of justice and of contracts.[3]

By and large, in its expenditure of money, government is behaving exactly like any other large spender. By *casting sufficient votes in the form of dollar bids* in certain directions, it causes resources to flow there. The price system then takes over and performs much as if these were private rather than public needs.

Actually, most government expenditure is paid for out of taxes collected. It is here that an important element of *coercion* enters. It is true that the citizenry as a whole imposes the tax burden upon itself; also, each citizen is sharing in the collective benefits of government. But there is not the same close connection between benefits and tax payments as holds when the individual citizen puts a nickel into a gum machine or makes an ordinary purchase. I need not smoke Winstons or buy nylon stockings or choose fried eggs, but I must pay my share of the taxes used to finance the various activities of government.

Laws and fiats   Moreover, a second important form of coercion is involved in the universal custom of passing governmental laws: thou shalt not sell false weight, thou shalt not employ child labor, thou shalt not burn houses, thou shalt not pour out smoke from thy factory chimney, thou shalt not sell or smoke opium, thou shalt not charge more than the ceiling price for food, and so forth. This set of rules gives the framework within which private enterprise functions; it also modifies the direction of that functioning. Together with government expenditure and taxation, *the decrees of government* supplement the price system in determining the economic fate of the nation.

It would be fruitless to debate whether public enterprise or private enterprise is the more important—as fruitless as to debate heredity versus environment. Without either, our economic world would be an entirely different one.

Finally, as we shall see in Parts Two and Six, it is part of the government's function to help stabilize acute and chronic cycles of unemployment and inflation and to help achieve and maintain healthy economic growth.

B. CAPITAL, DIVISION OF LABOR, AND MONEY

There are three further important features of modern economic society:

1. Modern advanced industrial technology rests upon the use of vast amounts of *capital:* elaborate machinery, large-scale factories and plants, stores and stocks of finished and unfinished materials. "Capitalism" got its name because this capital, or "wealth," is primarily the *private* property of somebody—the capitalist.

[3]Here is a later example of government service: lighthouses. These save lives and cargoes; but lighthouse keepers cannot reach out to collect fees for skippers. So we have here a divergence between *private* and *social* advantage. Philosophers and statesmen have always recognized the necessary role of government in such cases of "external-economy divergence between private and social advantage." Much more on this subject will come in Chapter 8, Chapter 24, and elsewhere.

2. The present-day economic system is characterized by an almost incredibly elaborate degree of *specialization* and intricate *division of labor.*

3. Ours is a system that makes extensive use of *money.* The flow of money is the lifeblood of our system. It also provides the measuring rod of values.

All these features are interrelated, each with the other and all with the price mechanism described in Section A of this chapter.

Thus we shall see that, without the great facility for trade and exchange which money provides, an elaborate division of labor would be impossible. Money and capital become related through credit activities of the banking system and through the organized capital markets where securities can be transformed into money by sale or vice versa. Of course, the relationship between the price mechanism and money is immediate and obvious.

CAPITAL AND TIME

No one has trouble seeing that production of economic goods can result from use of such inputs as labor and land (including in the latter term natural resources generally). These are often called "*primary* factors of production," for the reason that neither land nor (these days) labor is regarded as a result of the economic process, but instead exists by virtue of physical and biological rather than economic factors.[4]

Capital, which is the word often used to refer to capital goods generally, is a different kind of production factor. A capital good differs from the primary factors in that it is *an input which is itself the output of the economy.*

Capital goods, then, represent *produced* goods that can be used as factor inputs for further production, whereas labor and land are primary factor inputs not usefully thought of as being themselves produced by the economic system.

Part Four will show that, just as wages and rent are the factor-prices of primary labor and land, the 4 or 6 or 10 per cent interest rate per annum can, in a more subtle way, be usefully regarded as the factor-price that rations and rewards society's scarce supply of various capital goods and investment projects.

Because an interest rate is a percentage per unit of time (per year or month or decade), it calls our attention to another way of looking at capital—a way that stresses its special relationship with time. Let us survey this important economic role of capital. If men had to work with their hands on barren soil, productivity and consumption would be very low indeed. Thus, when an anthropologist asked of mourning tribesmen, "Who died?" they replied, "What is death? We have lost the needle!" Over a long time advanced economies have amassed a vast stock of equipment, plant and housing, inventories, and drained land.

[4]Some qualifications will be evident. Land can sometimes be made by drainage or filling in; this is true of much of Chicago's lake front and Boston's Back Bay. Natural resources such as minerals are laid down by nature, but it may take much economic effort to locate, use, and process them. Therefore they come to have some of the properties of capital goods. Even if one abandons in the Western world a Malthusian theory of population, whereby people seem to be given a cost of production not unlike that of machines, one realizes that the process of education consists in *investing in people*, thereby making them more productive factors of production. When you see a medical-school graduate, you are in a certain sense looking at a chunk of capital.

Men learned very early that the simple, direct methods of production can be improved upon by using *time-consuming indirect methods*. We who are inside the economic system are not conscious of *how roundabout* productive processes have become. An outside observer would be struck with the fact that almost no one in our system seems to be producing *finished* goods. Almost everyone is seen to do work of a preparatory nature, with final consumption a distant future goal. The farmer spends his time in fattening hogs, the truck driver in carrying them toward market, and the packer in advancing them further toward the last stage of consumption. A steel worker prepares pig iron, part of which will become a hammer to build a house; another bit will become part of a pig-iron furnace; which in turn will prepare pig iron to be used in making further hammers and more pig-iron furnaces; and so forth, on and on.

THE NEED TO FORGO PRESENT CONSUMPTION

The fact that it takes time to get things started and synchronized is important. It explains why society does not automatically replace all direct processes by more productive indirect ones, and all indirect processes by still more indirect processes. The advantage in doing so is balanced by the initial disadvantage of having *to forgo present consumption goods* by diverting resources from current production to uses that will bear fruit only after some time.

To the extent that people are willing to save—to abstain from present consumption and wait for future consumption—to that extent society can devote resources to new capital formation.[5] And to the extent that people are unconcerned about the future, they may at any time try to "dissave"—to snatch present pleasures at the expense of the future. How? By diverting resources away from the endless task of *replacing and maintaining* capital and to the job of producing extra present-day consumption goods. (Turn back to Fig. 2-5 of Chapter 2, page 22, to review the process of forgoing current consumption in favor of capital formation which adds to future production possibilities.)

We may summarize as follows: Economic activity is future-oriented. By the same token, current economic consumption is largely the consequence of past efforts. Current productive efforts, so to speak, produce for the future, in order to repay the past for present consumption. Also, in progressive societies a fraction of current consumption is sacrificed to production of net capital formation—to increase future production.

CAPITAL AND PRIVATE PROPERTY

Physical capital goods are important in any economy because they help to increase productivity. This is as true of Soviet communism as it is of our own system. But there is one important difference. By and large, private individuals own the tools of production in a mixed economy.

What is the exception in our system—government ownership of the means of produc-

[5] We shall see later, in Chapter 13, that, *sometimes* in our modern monetary economy, the more people try to save, the less capital goods are produced; and paradoxically, the more people spend *on consumption*, the greater will be the incentive for businessmen to build new factories and equipment.

tion—is the rule in a socialized state where productive property is collectively owned. The returns from such real capital goods accrue to the government, not to individuals directly. The government then decides how such income is to be distributed among individuals. The communist government also decides how rapidly resources are to be invested in new capital formation: the government decides by how much *present* consumption should be curtailed in order to add to the total of factories, equipment, and productive stocks of goods that are necessary if *future* output is to rise.

In our system individual capitalists earn interest, dividends, and profits, or rents and royalties on the capital goods that they supply. Every patch of land and every bit of equipment has a deed, or "title of ownership" that belongs to somebody directly—or if it belongs to a corporation, then indirectly it belongs to the individual stockholders who own the corporation. Moreover, each kind of capital good has a money market value; hence each claim or title to ownership of a capital good also has a market value. A share of common stock of General Electric is quoted at a certain price, a Penn Central bond at its price; a mortgage on a house is valued at some amount; the deed to a house is appraised by the real-estate market at some price; and so forth.

It should be pointed out that the government does own a good deal of the national real capital, e.g., Hoover Dam and submarines. In addition, its agencies, such as the Federal Housing Administration (FHA) and the Small Business Administration (SBA), are important sources of capital loans for homeowners and private business.

Also, we note that the *legal property rights of an individual are relative and limited.* Society determines how much of his property a man may bequeath to his heirs and how much must go in inheritance and estate taxes to the government. Society determines how much the owners of public-utility companies—such as electric and gas firms—can earn and how they must run their business.

Even a man's home is not his castle. He must obey zoning laws and, if necessary, make way for a railroad or slum-clearance project. Interestingly enough, most of society's economic income *cannot* be capitalized into private property. Since slavery was abolished, human earning power is forbidden by law to be capitalized. A man is not even free to sell himself: he must rent himself at a wage.

SPECIALIZATION, EXCHANGE, AND DIVISION OF LABOR

Turn now to the second characteristic feature of the present-day economy. The economies of mass production upon which modern standards of living are based would not be possible if production took place in self-sufficient farm households or regions. *Specialization* of function permits each person and region to use to best advantage any peculiar differences in skill and resources. Even in a primitive economy men learn that, rather than have everyone do everything in a mediocre way, it is better to start a *division of labor*—better for fat men to do the fishing, lean men the hunting, and smart men to make the medicine, each exchanging his goods for the goods he needs.

Besides resting on interpersonal differences in ability, specialization accentuates and creates differences. Hunting makes a man thin and good at stalking prey; a region with no resources especially adapted to weaving may still develop through experience skills which give it advantages in weaving. (Specialization may involve some costs, breeding half men—anemic clerks, brutish stokers—and producing social alienation.)

Finally, specialization may pay, even with no natural or acquired differences in skills: often in this way alone can a large enough volume of activity be reached to realize all the economies of large-scale production mentioned in the preceding chapter. Two *identical* Indian twins might find it better for one to make all bows and the other all arrows—even if they had to draw lots to see which would make which—because only in this way could each be making enough to warrant introducing improved techniques.

To illustrate the increased productivity of specialization, Adam Smith provided the classical example of pinmaking. One man could at best make a few dozen imperfect pins per day. But when a small group of men are subdivided with respect to function so that each performs simple repetitive operations, they can turn out hundreds of thousands of perfect pins per day.[6]

Moreover, the simplification of function made possible by specialization lends itself to mechanization and the use of labor-saving capital. At the same time specialization avoids the wasteful duplication of tools that would be necessary if every man had to be a Jack-of-all-trades; and it also saves time lost in going from one job to another. The modern conveyor system of automobile assembly illustrates the efficiency of specialization. Today automation is the watchword.

SPECIALIZATION AND INTERDEPENDENCE

Clearly, however, specialization and division of labor involve one serious problem—that of *interdependence*. A single-celled low form of life such as the amoeba may not be particularly good at doing anything, but it can live alone and like it. In higher animals such as man, every cell will die if once the heart cells fail. When all goes well, the extreme specialization of cells is very efficient—but at the cost of extreme interdependence.

In modern economic society this process is carried to the *n*th degree. No one man makes the smallest fraction of the commodities that he consumes. In medieval times the

---

[6]Smith recognized that specialization and division of labor were limited by the extent of the market, i.e., by the volume that can be sold. Smith would have approved of the European Common Market, which aims to lower the internal tariff barriers to trade and create a market big enough to support fruitful mass production and specialization.

The following passage describing the extent of specialization in meat slaughtering is often quoted: "It would be difficult to find another industry where division of labor has been so ingeniously and microscopically worked out. The animal has been surveyed and laid off like a map; and the men have been classified in over thirty specialties and twenty rates of pay, from 16 cents to 50 cents an hour. The 50-cent man is restricted to using the knife on the most delicate parts of the hide (floorman) or to using the ax in splitting the backbone (splitter); and, wherever a less skilled man can be slipped in at 18 cents, $18\frac{1}{2}$ cents, 20 cents, 21 cents, $22\frac{1}{2}$ cents, 24 cents, and so on, a place is made for him, and an occupation mapped out. In working on the hide alone there are nine positions, at eight different rates of pay. A 20-cent man pulls off the tail, a $22\frac{1}{2}$-cent man pounds off another part where good leather is not found, and the knife of the 40-cent man cuts a different texture and has a different 'feel' from that of the 50-cent man. Skill has become specialized to fit the anatomy. . . .

"The division of labor grew with the industry, following the introduction of the refrigerator car and the marketing of dressed beef, in the decade of the seventies. Before the market was widened by these revolutionizing inventions, the killing gangs were small, since only the local demands were kept at the most exacting work." J. R. Commons, *Quarterly Journal of Economics,* vol. XIX, 1904, pp. 3, 6.

artisan made one article and exchanged it for many others. Today a worker produces not even a single good; he may make only shoe tongues or simply turn bolt 999 on the Ford assembly line. Such may be his whole life work. In exchange for doing this he will receive an income adequate to buy goods from all over the world.

Thus, specialization involves complete mutual dependence. A bank in Austria fails, and the natives in Fiji, who carry water in empty Standard Oil cans and clothe their infants in Pillsbury flour bags, lose their livelihood—yes, and may even starve. In the backwash of a strike or war, a breakdown in transportation and the economic fabric of exchange reveals how perilously modern economic life depends upon exchange. Would we, if we could, turn the clock back to a simpler and poorer life? Or can we keep the advantages of division of labor by finding policies that prevent breakdown?

BARTER VERSUS THE USE OF MONEY

Along with capital and specialization, money is a third aspect of modern economic life. Without the use of money, our present division of labor and exchange would be impossible. To be sure, we could imagine a state of *barter*, where one kind of merchandise is traded directly for another. In primitive cultures it is not uncommon for food to be traded for weapons, or aid in the building of a house exchanged for aid in clearing a field. Even in the most advanced industrial economies, if we strip exchange down to its barest essentials and peel off the obscuring layer of money, we find that trade between individuals or nations largely boils down to barter—transforming one good into another by exchange rather than by physical transmutation.

Barter represents a great improvement over a state of affairs in which every man had to be a Jack-of-all-trades and master of none. A great debt of gratitude is owed to the first two ape-men who suddenly perceived that each could be made better off by giving up some of one good in exchange for some of another. Nevertheless, simple barter operates under grave disadvantages. An elaborate division of labor would be unthinkable without the introduction of a great new improvement—the use of money.

In all but the most primitive cultures men do not directly exchange one good for another. Instead they sell one good for money, and then use money to buy the goods they wish. At first glance this seems to complicate rather than simplify matters, to replace a single transaction by two transactions. Thus, if I have apples and want nuts, would it not be simpler to trade one for the other rather than to sell the apples for money and then use the money to buy nuts?

Actually, the reverse is the case: the two transactions are simpler than one. Ordinarily there are always people ready to buy apples and always some willing to sell—at a price—nuts; but it would be an unusual *coincidence* to find a person with tastes exactly opposite my own, with an eagerness to sell nuts and buy apples. Such a coincidence would be as unlikely as the chance of flipping a dozen "tails" in a row. (Even if the unusual should happen—as occasionally it must—there is no guarantee that the desires of the two parties with respect to the exact *quantities* and terms of the exchange would coincide.)

To use a classical economic phrase: Instead of there being a double coincidence of wants, there is likely to be a want of coincidence; so that, unless a hungry tailor happens to find an undraped farmer, who has both food and a desire for a pair of pants, neither can make a trade.

Money does simplify economic life. But do not suppose that, for society as a whole, a mere increase in the total of money will enable people to consume more than the real products technically producible with existent totals of labor, land, and capital. And, as Part Two shows, money can misbehave and produce recession and inflation.

HISTORICAL STAGES OF MONEY

If we were to reconstruct history along hypothetical, logical lines, we should naturally follow the age of barter by the age of commodity money.

Commodity money   Historically a great variety of commodities has served at one time or another as a medium of exchange: cattle (from which come the Latin stem of "pecuniary" and also the words "capital" and "chattel"), tobacco, leather and hides, furs, olive oil, beer or spirits, slaves or wives, copper, iron, gold, silver, rings, diamonds, wampum beads or shells, huge rocks and landmarks, and cigarette butts.

Each of the above has some advantages and disadvantages. Cattle are not divisible into small change; but while it is being hoarded, such "money" is likely to increase by reproduction, giving the lie to the doctrine of Aristotle that "money is barren." Beer does not improve with keeping, although wives may. Olive oil provides a nice liquid currency that is as minutely divisible as one wishes. Iron will rust and is of so little value that one would need a cart instead of a pocketbook. The value of a diamond is not proportional to weight but varies with its square; if cut into pieces, it loses value.

The yearly additions to (by mining) or subtractions from (by use in teeth, jewelry, and electric relays) the accumulated stock of *precious metals* are small in percentage terms; so their total amounts and value do not fluctuate widely. Silver has luster but will tarnish in air. Gold keeps its attractive sheen but, unless mixed with an alloy, is soft. Gold's high specific gravity makes detection of counterfeiting and admixture easy; but through most of historical time, gold's scarcity value has been so great per ounce as to require inordinately minute coins for ordinary purchases.

Most kinds of money tended once to be of some value or use for their own sake. Thus, even wampum had decorative uses, and paper money began as warehouse or mint receipts for so much metal. But the intrinsic usefulness of the money medium is now the least important thing about it.

Paper money   The age of commodity money gives way to the age of paper money. The essence of money, its intrinsic nature, is typified by paper currency. *Money, as money rather than a commodity, is wanted not for its own sake but for the things it will buy!* We do not wish to use up money directly, but rather to use it by getting rid of it; even when we choose to use it by holding it, its value comes from the fact that we can spend it *later on.*

Money is an artificial, social convention. If for any reason a substance begins to be used as money, all people will begin to value it, even if they happen to be teetotalers or vegetarians or disbelievers in its intrinsic usefulness. As long as things can be bought and sold for a given substance, people will be content to sell and buy with it. Paradox: money is accepted because it is accepted!

The use of paper currency (dollar bills, fives, tens, . . .) has become widespread because it has many conveniences as a medium of exchange. Currency is easily carried and stored away. By the printing of more or fewer zeros on the face value of the bill, a great or small amount of value can be embodied in a light, transportable medium of little bulk. By the use of decimal points it can be made as divisible as we wish. By careful engraving, the value of money can be made easily recognizable and protected from counterfeiting and adulteration. The fact that private individuals cannot create it at will in unlimited amounts keeps it scarce, i.e., an economic, and not, a free good.

Given this limitation in supply, modern currencies have value, i.e., can buy things, independently of any gold, silver, or government backing. The public neither knows nor cares—and need not know or care—whether its currency is in the form of silver certificates, Federal Reserve notes, or copper or silver coin. So long as each form of money can be converted into any other at fixed terms, the best is as good as the worst.[7]

Bank money   Finally, along with the age of paper money, there is the age of bank money, or bank checking deposits. Today at least nine-tenths of all transactions, by value if not number, take place by checks. A professor has his salary paid directly into his bank account, after income taxes have already been withheld by his employer. His rent or dentist bills are paid by check; his gasoline and hotel bills, by a credit card. Except for petty sums for lunches and carfare, he needs little cash.

This completes the discussion of the way in which money performs its essential functions. In Part Two, we shall examine in detail the monetary and credit operations of banks and the government to see how they bear on fluctuations in prices, production, and employment.

SUMMARY

A. HOW A FREE ENTERPRISE SYSTEM SOLVES THE BASIC ECONOMIC PROBLEMS

1   The price mechanism, working through supply and demand in competitive markets, operates to answer the three fundamental problems of economic organization in our mixed private enterprise system. The system is not perfect, but it is one way to solve the WHAT, HOW, and FOR WHOM.

2   The dollar votes of people affect prices of goods; these prices serve as guides for the

[7] A century ago it was the exception rather than the rule for bank notes and coins to exchange for each other at par. Each had different prices which varied from day to day, so that it was necessary for storekeepers to keep daily lists of values; and it became a profession in itself to change money, buying and selling it at a profit.

amounts of the different goods to be produced. When people demand more of a good, a competitive businessman can make a profit by expanding production of that good. Under perfect competition, he must find the cheapest method of production, using labor, land, and other factors that are relatively cheap and economizing on the use of relatively expensive factors; otherwise, he will incur losses and be eliminated.

At the same time that the WHAT and HOW problems are being resolved by prices, so is the problem of FOR WHOM. The distribution of income is determined by competitive bidding up or down of factor-prices—wages of each kind of labor, rents of land, royalties of books, and various returns to capital. Anyone possessing fertile land or widely admired crooning ability will be supplied with many dollar votes for his use in the markets for consumer goods. Anyone without property or education and with skills and color that the market cares little about will receive a low annual income.

3 Our economy is mixed in two senses: Governments modify private initiative; monopolistic elements condition the working of perfect competition.

B. CAPITAL, DIVISION OF LABOR, AND MONEY

4 Capital goods—produced inputs such as machinery, housing, and inventories of goods in process—add much to a nation's output. *Roundabout,* time-consuming methods take time to get started; hence, adding to the stock of capital goods requires a temporary sacrifice of present consumption. The interest rate serves to ration and to coax.

5 Under the mixed economy, capital goods are largely owned as private property; the incomes they produce go to their owners and to taxes. Under communism, the state owns capital goods. In no system are private-property rights unlimited.

6 Specialization and division of labor characterize modern economies. This raises productivity, but at the cost of interdependence.

7 Without exchange, division of labor could not be highly developed. Simple barter is inefficient and tends to be superseded by the use of money. Commodity money is in turn superseded by paper money and bank money. Unlike other economic goods, money is valued because of social convention; we value it indirectly for what it buys rather than for its direct utility. Its misbehavior—in producing depression or inflation—governments can no longer tolerate.

QUESTIONS FOR DISCUSSION

1 During World War II, did we let consumers' dollar demand determine their sugar consumption? Why not? Why recourse to rationing?

2 Could supply and demand work out to give salesmen with a "gift of gab" twice the income of skilled scientists? At other times could it give surgeons about the same income as accountants and plumbers? Five times that of butchers?

3   Do you think that an "instinct of craftsmanship" and a "sense of social responsibility" could ever replace the "profit motive"? Read the chapter head's Invisible Hand quotation aloud. What do you think Smith is trying to say there? And here: "I have never known much good done by those who affected to trade for the public good."

4   List a number of cases where the government modifies the working of an automatic price system. For example: pure food and drug laws; minimum wages; farm supports; rent and interest ceilings.

5   List cases where monopoly elements intervene. How can business by advertising shape, as well as respond to, consumer demands and wants?

6   Assuming it cannot borrow abroad, what must China do if it wishes to become an efficient industrialized nation in the next few generations?

7   "Lincoln freed the slaves. With one pen stroke he destroyed much of the capital the South had been able to accumulate over the years." Comment.

8   Would ice cubes make a good unit of money? Radium? What would?

9   What are some of the advantages of using checks on bank deposits rather than paper currency or metal coins? List any disadvantages.

10   *Extra-credit problem:* Anticipating Chapter 15's discussion of the so-called Quantity Theory of Money and Prices, suppose when we woke up tomorrow each dollar bill became two dollars. Would we all be *twice* as well off? Would we be *any* better off if the change caused *all* prices (including wage rates) to double? Refer to Chapter 1's "fallacy of composition" to demonstrate that one man's increase in money might make *him* better off, but that it is dangerous to extrapolate to all of society.

Review your understanding of the following concepts:

mixed economy
demand-and-supply markets for
   goods and for factors of
   production
profit seeking, cost minimizing
price "rationing"
perfect and imperfect competition
roundaboutness of production

abstinence and waiting, forgoing
dissaving by failure to maintain
   and replace capital goods
specialization, interdependence
division of labor, exchange
barter versus money pricing
commodity, paper, and bank-deposit
   money

Supply and Demand: The Bare Elements

4

Chapters 2 and 3 introduced the three basic problems every economy must face: (1) WHAT shall be produced of the great variety of possible goods and services, and in precisely what quantities? (2) How shall society combine its different productive factors—land, labor, and so forth—to produce each good? (3) FOR WHOM shall goods be produced—that is, how shall the national product be distributed among the different people with their different labor skills and ownerships of land and capital goods?

Chapter 2 showed that a variety of systems can be thought of to solve these three problems. WHAT, HOW, and FOR WHOM might be determined by custom, instinct, or even by centralized, collective fiats. But Chapter 3 indicated that the modern mixed economy relies primarily on none of these to solve its basic problems. Instead, it relies on a system of markets and prices.

The consumer, so it is said, is the king. Or rather, with every man a king, each is a voter who uses his money as votes to get the things done that he wants done. His votes must compete with other men's votes; and the people with the most votes end up with the most influence on what gets produced and on where those goods go.

Now our task is to see just how this spending of money votes—this system of "consumer sovereignty"—takes place.

THE MARKET MECHANISM

Let us take an example. You wake up this morning with an urge for a new pair of shoes. You would not think of saying, "I'll go down to the city hall and vote for the mayor most likely to give me a new pair of shoes. Of course, I mean a new pair of size 9, soft-leather, dark brown shoes."

Or, to take an actual case from history, suppose men begin to get prosperous enough to afford meat every day and do not have to fill up on potatoes. How does their desire to substitute meat for potatoes get translated into action? What politician do they tell? What orders does he in turn give to farmers to move from Maine to Texas? How much extra rent does he decide will be needed to bribe landlords to transfer land from potato production to cattle grazing? And how does he ensure that people get what they want of pork and lamb as well as beef? And who is to get the choice cuts?

Why belabor the obvious? Everyone knows it never works itself out that way at all. What happens is this. Consumers begin to buy fewer potatoes and more meat. That raises the price of meat and cuts the price of potatoes. So there result losses to the potato growers and gains to the ranchers. Ranch labor finds it can hold out for higher wages, and many a potato digger quits his job for a better-paying job elsewhere. In time, the higher meat prices coax out larger productions of beef, pork, and lamb. And the different parts of the cow—its horn, hide, liver, kidneys, choice tenderloin, and tough ribs—get auctioned off for what each part will bring.

To show that it is not some important government official or businessman who sets relative prices, see what actually happened when science discovered that liver was good for anemia. Kidneys, for reasons somewhat obscure, were previously dearer than liver. In fact, according to the records, you could hardly give liver away before this discovery. Now go to the butcher shop: price liver; and, if you can find any, also price kidneys. A veritable revolution has taken place; the price of liver has risen greatly relative to the price of kidneys, so as to *ration* the limited supply of liver among the eager demanders for it—all through the *impersonal* workings of supply and demand.

Similar revolutions are taking place in the economic market place all the time. As people's desires and needs change, as engineering methods change, as supplies of natural resources and other productive factors change, the marketplace registers changes in the prices and the quantities sold of commodities and productive services—of tea, sugar, and beef; of land, labor, and machines. There exists a *system of prices*, a concept that is far from obvious.

The purpose of this chapter is to show how supply and demand work themselves out in the competitive market *for one particular good*. We shall define a demand curve and then a supply curve. Finally, we shall see how the market price reaches its competitive equilibrium, where these two curves intersect—where the forces of demand and supply are just in balance.

THE DEMAND SCHEDULE

Let us start with demand. It is commonly observed: The quantity of a good that people will buy at any one time depends on price; the higher the price charged for an article, the less the quantity of it people will be willing to buy; and, other things being equal, the lower its market price, the more units of it will be demanded.

Thus there exists at any one time a definite relation between the market price of a good (such as wheat) and the quantity demanded of that good. This relationship between price and quantity bought is called the "demand schedule," or "demand curve."

Table 4-1 gives an example of a hypothetical demand schedule. At any price, such

A demand schedule and a downward-sloping curve relate quantity to price:

DEMAND SCHEDULE FOR WHEAT	(1) PRICE ($ per bu.) P	(2) QUANTITY DE-MANDED (million bu. per month) Q
A	$5	9
B	4	10
C	3	12
D	2	15
E	1	20

TABLE 4-1. At each market price, there will be at any time a definite quantity of wheat that people will want to demand.

At a lower price, the quantity demanded will go up—as more people substitute it for other goods and feel they can afford to gratify their less important wants for wheat.

FIG. 4-1. Prices are measured on the vertical axis, and quantities demanded on the horizontal axis. Each pair of Q, P numbers from Table 4-1 is plotted here as a point, and a smooth curve passed through the point, gives us the demand curve.

The fact that dd goes downward and to the right illustrates the very important "law of downward-sloping demand."

as $5 per bushel, there is a definite quantity of wheat that will be demanded by all the consumers in the market—in this case 9 (million) bushels per month. At a lower price, such as $4, the quantity bought is even greater, being 10 (million) units. At still lower P of $3, quantity demanded is even greater—namely 12 (million). By lowering P enough, we could coax out sales of more than 20 (million) units. From Table 4-1 we can determine the *quantity demanded at any price*, by comparing Column (2) with Column (1).

THE DEMAND CURVE

The numerical data of Table 4-1 can be given a graphic interpretation also. The vertical scale in Fig. 4-1 represents the various alternative prices of wheat, measured in dollars per bushel. The horizontal scale measures the quantity of wheat (in terms of bushels) that will be demanded per month.

A city corner is located as soon as we know its street and avenue; a ship's position is located as soon as we know its latitude and longitude. Similarly, to plot a point on this diagram, we must have two coordinate numbers: a price and a quantity. For our first point A, corresponding to $5 and 9 million bushels, we move upward 5 units and then over to the right 9 units. A dot marks the spot *A*. To get the next dot, at *B*, we go up only 4 units and over to the right 10 units. The last dot is shown by *E*. Through the dots we draw a smooth curve, marked *dd*.

This picturization of the demand schedule is called the "demand curve." Note that quantity and price are *inversely* related, *Q* going up when *P* goes down. The curve slopes downward, going from northwest to southeast. This important property is given a name: the *law of downward-sloping demand*. This law is true of practically all commodities: wheat, electric razors, cotton, ethyl gasoline, cornflakes, and theater tickets.

The law of downward-sloping demand: **When the price of a good is raised (at the same time that all other things are held constant), less of it is demanded. Or, what is the same thing: If a greater quantity of a good is put on the market, then—other things being equal—it can be sold only at a lower price.**

REASONS FOR LAW OF DOWNWARD-SLOPING DEMAND

This law is in accordance with common sense and has been known in at least a vague way since the beginning of recorded history. The reasons for it are not hard to identify. When the price of wheat is sky-high, only rich men will be able to afford it; the poor will have to make do with rye bread, just as they still must do in poorer lands. When the price is still high but not quite so high as before, persons of moderate means who also happen to have an especially great liking for white bread will now be coaxed into buying some wheat.

Thus a first reason for the validity of the law of downward-sloping demand comes from the fact that *lowering prices brings in new buyers.*

Not quite so obvious is a second, equally important, reason for the law's validity; namely, each reduction of price may coax out some *extra purchases by each of the good's consumers;* and—what is the same thing—a rise in price may cause any of us to buy less. Why does my quantity demanded tend to fall as price rises? For two main reasons. When the price of a good rises, I naturally try to *substitute* other goods for it (for example, rye for wheat or tea for coffee). Also, when a price goes up, I find myself really poorer than I was before; and I will naturally cut down on my consumption of most normal goods when I feel poorer and have less real *income.*

Here are further examples of cases where I buy more of a good as it becomes more plentiful and its price drops. When water is very dear, I demand only enough of it to drink. Then when its price drops, I buy some to wash with. At still lower prices, I resort to still other uses; finally, when it is really very cheap, I water flowers and use it lavishly for any possible purpose. (Note once again that someone poorer than I will probably begin to use water to wash his car only at a lower price than that at which I buy water for that purpose. Since market demand is the sum of all different people's demands, what does this mean? It means that even after *my* quantity demanded stops expanding very much with price decreases, the *total* bought in the market may still expand as new uses for *new people* come into effect.)

To confirm your understanding of the demand concept, imagine that there is an increase in demand for wheat brought about by a boom in people's incomes or by a great rise in the market price of the competing rye, or simply by an increased desire of people to spend their money on wheat. Show that this *shifts* the whole demand curve in Fig. 4-1 rightward, and hence upward; pencil in such a new curve and label it *d'd'* to distinguish it from the old *dd* curve. Note that such an increase in demand means that more will now be bought at each price—as can be verified by carefully reading off points from the new curve and filling in a new *Q* column for Table 4-1.

THE SUPPLY SCHEDULE

Let us now turn from demand to supply. The demand schedule related market prices and the amounts *consumers* wish to buy. How is the supply schedule defined?

By the *supply schedule*, or *curve*, is meant the relation between market prices and the amounts of the good that *producers* are willing to supply.

Table 4-2 illustrates the supply schedule for wheat, and Fig. 4-2 plots it as a supply curve. Unlike the demand curve, the supply curve for wheat *normally rises upward* and to the right, from southwest to northeast.

At a higher price of wheat, farmers will take acres out of corn cultivation and put them into wheat. In addition, each farmer can now afford the cost of more fertilizer,

The supply schedule, relating price to quantity produced, can also be plotted as a curve:

SUPPLY SCHEDULE FOR WHEAT

	(1) POSSIBLE PRICES ($ per bu.) P	(2) QUANTITY SELLERS WILL SUPPLY (million bu. per month) Q
A	$5	18
B	4	16
C	3	12
D	2	7
E	1	0

TABLE 4-2. At each *P*, there is listed the *Q* that producers will want to bring to market.

FIG. 4-2. Each *Q*, *P* pair of numbers in Table 4-2 is here plotted as a point. A smooth curve passed through them gives the brown upward-sloping supply curve *ss*.

more labor, more machinery, and can now even afford to grow extra wheat on poorer land. All this tends to increase output at the higher prices offered.

As will be seen in Part Three, our old friend the law of diminishing returns provides one strong reason why the supply curve would slope upward. If society wants more wine, more and more labor will have to be added to the same limited hill sites suitable for producing wine grapes. Even if this industry is too small to affect the general wage rate, each new man will—according to the law of diminishing returns—be adding less and less extra product; and hence the necessary cost to coax out additional product will have to rise. (Cost and returns are opposite sides of the same coin, as will be shown later.[1])

How shall we depict an increase in supply? An increase in supply means an increase in the amounts that will be supplied at *each different price*. Now if you pencil the new supply curve into Fig. 4-2, you will see that it has shifted *rightward;* but for an upward-sloping supply curve, this change means the new s's' curve will have shifted rightward and *downward* (not rightward and upward as in the case of a shifted downward-sloping demand curve). To verify that s's' does depict an increase in supply, fill in a new column in Table 4-2 by reading off points from your new diagram carefully.

EQUILIBRIUM OF SUPPLY AND DEMAND

Let us now combine our analysis of demand and supply to see how competitive market price is determined. This combining is done in Table 4-3. Thus far we have been considering all prices as possible. We have said, "If price is so and so, Q sales will be so and so; if price is such and such, sales will be such and such; and so forth." But to which level will price *actually* go? And how much will then be produced and consumed? The supply schedule alone cannot tell us. Neither can the demand schedule alone.

Let us do what an auctioneer would do, i.e., proceed by trial and error. Can situation A in Table 4-3, with wheat selling for $5 per bushel, prevail for any period of time? The answer is a clear No. At $5, the producers will be supplying 18 (million) bushels to the market every month [Column (3)]. But the amount demanded by consumers will be only 9 (million) bushels per month [Column (2)]. As stocks of wheat pile up, competitive sellers will cut the price a little. Thus, as Column (4) shows, price will tend to fall downward. But it will not fall indefinitely to zero.

To understand this better, let us try the point E with price equal to only $1 per bushel. Can that price persist? Again, obviously not—for a comparison of Columns (2) and (3) shows that consumption will exceed production *at that price*. Storehouses will begin to be emptied; disappointed demanders who cannot get wheat will tend to bid the price up. This upward pressure on price is shown by Column (4)'s rising arrow.

[1] While the exceptions to the law of downward-sloping demand are few enough to be unimportant in practice, we shall encounter in Part Three an interesting exception to the upward-sloping supply curve. Thus, suppose that a family farmer produces wheat and its price rises so much as to give him a much higher income. With wheat so lucrative, he is at first tempted to *substitute* some of his leisure time to produce more of it. But might there not reasonably come a time when he feels comfortably enough off at his higher *income* to be able to afford to take things easier and work less?

Equilibrium market price is at the point where supply and demand match:

	(1)	(2) QUANTITY DEMANDED (million bu. per month)	(3) QUANTITY SUPPLIED (million bu. per month)	(4)
	POSSIBLE PRICES ($ per bu.)			PRESSURE ON PRICE
A	$5	9	18	Downward
B	4	10	16	Downward
C	3	12	12	Neutral
D	2	15	7	Upward
E	1	20	0	Upward

SUPPLY AND DEMAND SCHEDULES FOR WHEAT

TABLE 4-3. Only at the equilibrium price of $3 will quantity demanded by consumers equal quantity supplied by producers. At any lower price, amount demanded would exceed amount supplied; at any higher price, amount supplied would exceed amount demanded.

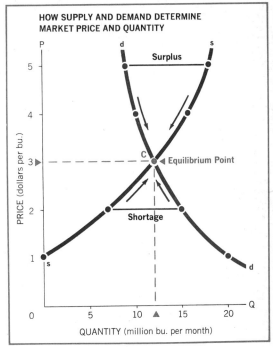

HOW SUPPLY AND DEMAND DETERMINE MARKET PRICE AND QUANTITY

FIG. 4-3. At the *C* equilibrium intersection, the amount supplied just matches the amount demanded.

At any lower *P*, the excess amount demanded will force *P* back up; and at any *P* higher than the equilibrium, the amount supplied will be excessive and *P* will be forced back down to the equilibrium level.

We could go on to try other prices, but by now the answer is obvious:

The equilibrium price, i.e., the only price that can last, is that at which the amount *willingly* supplied and amount *willingly* demanded are equal. Competitive equilibrium must be at the intersection point of supply and demand curves.

Only at *C*, with a price of $3, will the amount demanded by consumers, 12 (million) bushels per month, exactly equal the amount supplied by producers, 12 (million). Price is at equilibrium, just as an olive at the bottom of a cocktail glass is at equilibrium, because there is no tendency for it to rise or fall. (Of course, this stationary price may not be reached at once. There may have to be an initial period of trial and error, of oscillation around the right level, before price finally settles down in balance.)

Figure 4-3 shows the same equilibrium in pictorial form. The supply and demand curves, superimposed on the same diagram, cross at only one intersection point. This golden point *C* represents the equilibrium price and quantity.

At a higher price, the black bar shows the *excess* of amount supplied over amount demanded. The arrows point downward to show the direction in which price will move because of the competition of *sellers*. At a price lower than the $3 equilibrium price, the black bar shows that amount demanded exceeds amount supplied. Consequently, the eager bidding of *buyers* requires us to point the arrow indicators upward to show the pressure that they are exerting on price. Only at the point *C* will there be a balancing of forces and a stationary maintainable price.

Such is the essence of the doctrine of supply and demand.

EFFECT OF A SHIFT IN SUPPLY OR DEMAND

Now we can put the supply-and-demand apparatus to work. Gregory King, an English writer of the seventeenth century, noticed that when the harvest was bad, food rose in price; and when it was plentiful, farmers got a lower price. Let us try to explain what happens by our diagrams.

Figure 4-4(a) shows how a spell of bad weather *reduces* the amount that farmers will supply at each and every market price and thereby displaces the equilibrium point *E*. The *ss* curve has shifted to the left and has become *s's'*. The demand curve has not changed. Where does the new supply curve *s's'* intersect *dd*? Plainly at *E'*, the new equilibrium price where demand and the new reduced supply have again come into balance. Naturally, *P* has risen. And because of the law of downward-sloping demand, *Q* has gone down.

Suppose the supply curve, because of good weather and fertilizers, had *increased* instead. Draw in a new equilibrium *E''* with lower *P* and higher *Q*.

Our apparatus will help us also analyze the effect of an increase in demand. Suppose that rising family incomes make everyone want more wheat. Then at each unchanged

The equilibrium market price is where demand and supply curves intersect:

FIG. 4-4(a).   If supply shifts leftward for any reason, the equilibrium-price intersection will travel up the demand curve, giving higher *P* and lower *Q*.
FIG. 4-4(b).   If demand shifts rightward, the equilibrium will travel up the supply curve.

In peace, market pricing might handle army recruitment:

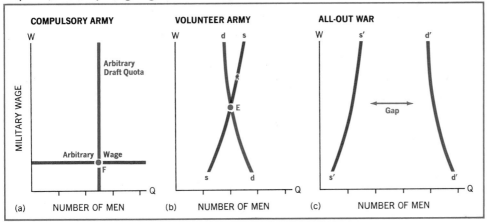

FIG. 4-5(a). By command, wage is set low at *F* and those unlucky enough to be drafted serve at that low wage.

FIG. 4-5(b). Here raising military pay (and improving conditions!) coaxes out the needed supply at the *E* intersection. Those serve who least dislike military life, who have least attractive civilian alternatives, and whose families are least affluent. (Defense forces are of lesser size along *dd* as the authorities use men less wastefully and rely more on nonuniformed civilian employees.)

FIG. 4-5(c). If risk of death rises in shooting war so that no sufficient number of volunteers are forthcoming to meet expanded defense needs, supply-and-demand fail and must be supplemented by some more direct form of coercion.

P, greater *Q* will now be demanded. The demand curve will shift rightward to *d'd'*. Figure 4-4(b) shows the resulting travel up the supply curve as enhanced demand raises competitive price.

A VOLUNTARY ARMY?

Reliance on supply and demand and on market pricing can be a substitute for explicit government directions and controls. A good example is military recruitment. One can rely on a compulsory draft. As in World War II, all able-bodied young men may be compelled to serve in the armed forces. (In actuality some exceptions were granted to those with exceptionally valuable skills, and to a narrow group of conscientious objectors on religious grounds.) Or, in less than all-out war, a lottery may be used to select even-handedly that subset of young men called into the armed services.

An alternative way to recruit a peacetime army of limited size is to *raise wages of the armed services to whatever level is needed to coax out an adequate supply of volunteers.* Figure 4-5 contrasts the case of reliance on supply and demand to the case of a compulsory draft. In Fig. 4-5(a) the coercive intersection, *F*, comes at an arbitrary low wage at which an arbitrary number of young men are compelled to serve in the armed forces. In Fig. 4-5(b), the peacetime army is recruited by raising the wage to the *E* intersection at which supply and demand balance out. Just as the rich have more yachts and tenderloin steaks than the poor, so too do their sons manage better to avoid the tedium and danger that national defense necessitates. Blacks, and other minority groups who face less lucrative alternative occupations in civilian life, will presumably bulk larger in a volunteer army than in an equitably-run draft. And those least eager to serve will presumably be the last to volunteer at each wage.

As Fig. 4-5(c) indicates, during a shooting war of many casualties, perhaps no wage however high would tempt the requisite number of men to volunteer. But even then, raising army pay could somewhat lower the tax that the rest of the community is, in effect, levying on those males who happen to be of prime military age during the war.

The present discussion warns that one must have care in speaking of *dollar* costs as if they necessarily measure *true* costs with accuracy. In the draft case the government was seen to pay out much less in military wages than in the volunteer-army case. But the actual real costs to the community were not less: just as many careers were interrupted and just as much of civilian goods failed to get produced in consequence of manpower's being drained off into the defense forces. (Actually, since the volunteers are probably used more effectively in uniform and probably represent youths with less productive civilian alternatives and with greater tolerance for risk and military discipline, the real costs may be a bit less in the second case.) How then did the true costs get hidden in the compulsory-army case? In effect, a *nonmoney* tax was being put on young, healthy males, and particularly on those whose number happened to be drawn. In the volunteer-army case, part of this cost-burden is shifted to older people and women and to those who get deferred, and it is only this *explicit tax* on them (needed to pay the higher military wages), that shows up in money terms. Yet the economic burden is there in any case.

TWO STUMBLING BLOCKS

It is well to pause here to consider two minor sources of possible confusion concerning supply and demand. These have puzzled students of economics in all generations. The first point deals with the important fact that in drawing up a demand schedule or curve, one always insists that "other things must be equal." The second deals with the exact sense in which demand and supply are equal in equilibrium.

"Other things equal"   To draw up a demand schedule for wheat, we vary the price of wheat and observe what would happen to its quantity bought *at any one period of time in which no other factors are allowed to change so as to becloud our experiment.* Specifically, this means that, as we change wheat's P, we must not at the same time change family income or the price of a competing product such as rye or anything else that would tend to *shift* the demand schedule for wheat. Why? Because, like any scientist who wants to isolate the effects of one causal factor, we must try to vary only one thing at a time. True enough, in economics we cannot perform controlled experiments in a laboratory, and we can rarely hold other things constant in making statistical observations of economic magnitudes. This limitation on our ability to experiment empirically in economics makes it all the more important *to be clear in our logical thinking*, so that we may hope to recognize and evaluate important tendencies—such as the effect of P on Q demanded—when other tendencies are likely to be impinging on the situation at the same time.

The case of demand shift in Fig. 4-4(b) can illustrate this common fallacy based upon a failure to respect the rule that other things must be held equal in defining a demand curve. Suppose that the supply curve shifts little or not at all. But suppose the demand curve shifts up to $d'd'$ in good times when jobs are plentiful and people have the incomes to buy more wheat; and suppose in the more depressed phase of the business cycle, demand always shifts down to dd. Now take a piece of graph paper and plot what would actually be recorded in the statistics of the wheat market.

In good times you would record the equilibrium point E', and in bad times the equilibrium point E. Take a ruler and join the points E and E'. The fallacy to be avoided like the plague is expressed as follows: "I have disproved the law of downward-sloping demand; for note that when P was high, so too was Q—as shown by E'. And when P was lowered, instead of that change increasing Q, it actually lowered Q—as shown by E. My straight line joining E and E' represents an upward-sloping, not a downward-sloping, demand curve; so I have refuted a basic economic law."

Being alerted beforehand, one detects the fallacy in this argument. For at the same time that P went up, other things were *not* held constant; rather, income was also raised. The tendency for a rise in P to choke off purchases was more than masked by the counter-tendency of rising income to raise purchases. Instead of testing our economic law by moving *along* the demand curve, the beginner has measured changes that result from the *shift* of the demand curve.

Why is this bad scientific method? Because it leads to absurd results such as this: "On the basis of my revolutionary refutation of the law of downward-sloping demand, I confidently predict that, in the years when the harvest is especially big, wheat will sell for a higher rather than a lower price." Not only will such reasoning lead to absurd predictions that would lose fortunes for a speculator or a miller, but it also fails to recognize other important economic relationships—such as the fact that, when family incomes go up, demand curves for goods such as wheat tend to shift rightward.

Meaning of equilibrium The second stumbling block is a more subtle one, less likely to arise but not so easy to dispel. It is suggested by the following.

"How can you say that the equality of supply and demand determines a particular equilibrium price? For, after all, *the amount one man sells is precisely what another man buys.* The quantity bought must always equal the quantity sold, no matter what the price; for that matter, whether or not the market is in equilibrium, a statistician who records the Q bought and the Q sold will always find these necessarily identical, each being a different aspect of exactly the same thing."

The answer to this must be phrased something like this:

You are quite right that measured Q bought and measured Q sold must be identical as recorded by a statistician. But the important question is this: At which P will the amount that consumers are *willing to go on buying* be just matched by the amount that producers are *willing to go on selling?* At such a price, where there is equality between the *scheduled* amounts that suppliers and demanders want to go on buying and selling, and only at such an equilibrium P, will there be no tendency for price to rise or fall.

At any other price, such as the case where P is above the intersection of supply and demand, it is a trivial fact that whatever goods change hands will show a statistical identity of measured amount bought and sold. But this measured identity does not in the least deny that suppliers are eager at so high a price to sell more than demanders will continue to buy; and that this excess of scheduled supply over scheduled demand will put downward pressure on price until it has finally reached that equilibrium level where the two curves intersect.

At this equilibrium intersection, and there alone, will everybody be happy: the auctioneer, the suppliers, the demanders—as well as the patient statistician, who always reports an identity between the measured amounts bought and sold.[2]

WHAT SUPPLY AND DEMAND ACCOMPLISHED: GENERAL EQUILIBRIUM

Having seen how supply and demand work, let us take stock of what has been accomplished. The scarce goods of society have been rationed out among the possible users of them. Who did the rationing: a board? a committee? No. The auctioneering mechanism of competitive price did the rationing. It was a case of "rationing by the purse."

FOR WHOM goods are destined was *partially* determined by who was willing to pay for them. If you had the money votes, you got the wheat. If you did not, you went without. Or if you had the money votes, but preferred not to spend them on wheat, you did without. The most important needs or desires for goods—if backed by cash!—got fulfilled.

The WHAT question was being *partially* answered at the same time. The rise in market price was the signal to coax out a higher supply of wheat—the signal for men and other scarce resources to move into the wheat-production industry from alternative uses.

Even the How question was being *partially* decided in the background. For with wheat prices now high, farmers could afford expensive tractors and fertilizers and could bring poorer soils into use.

Why the word "partially" in this description of how the competitive market helped solve the three problems? Because this wheat market is but one market of many. What is happening in the corn and rye markets also counts; and what is happening in the market for fertilizer, men, and tractors obviously matters much.

We must note that the pricing problem is one that involves *interdependent markets*, not just the "partial equilibrium" of a single market.[3]

There are, so to speak, auctioneers operating simultaneously in the many different markets—wheat, rye, corn, fertilizer, and land; labor, wool, cotton, mutton, and rayon; bond, stock, and personal loans. Each ends up at the equilibrium intersection point of

---

[2] A similar question of measured identity versus scheduled intersection can arise in the discussion of income determination in Chapter 12.

[3] The alert reader will not have to be reminded that the competitive market gives goods to those with money votes and does so efficiently. But the distribution of the money votes depends on how much you can sell your labor and property for in competitive and imperfectly competitive factor markets, and it is affected in an important way by (1) how lucky you are, (2) how lucky your parents and in-laws were, and (3) the advantages and disadvantages of your genetic and acquired skills and aptitudes. If a student writes on a final exam, "FOR WHOM is decided (in part) by how people decide to use their money votes," he is not wrong. Indeed, he gets possibly 50 per cent credit. However, he will not get the other 50 per cent unless he adds, "The basic problem of FOR WHOM is the process by which the money votes *themselves* get determined, which is primarily not by supply and demand in a single good's market, but by supply and demand in the labor, land, and other interdependent factor markets of Part Four; and factor supplies depend much on distribution of ownership."

his supply and demand schedules—wheat, rye, corn, fertilizer prices, and land rent; labor wage, wool, cotton, mutton, and rayon prices; bond price and its interest yield, stock prices and dividend yield, interest charges on personal loans.

No market is an island unto itself: when wool P rises (because, say, of sheep disease abroad), it pulls up the Ps of domestic labor, fertilizer, and land needed for expanded wool output; and it raises the Ps of rival goods like cotton that some demanders will now turn to; it might well lower the P of wool spinners and of suit-company stock shares, since the latter must now pay more for their raw materials and may bid less eagerly for spinning labor.

The new "general-equilibrium set of interdependent prices" adjusts to the new situation. The price system meets the problem posed by the basic definition of economics: the study of (1) how *scarce means with alternative uses*—limited land and labor that can be switched from one industry to another—are allocated, and (2) how to *achieve ends or goals*—as prescribed by the tastes for wool, nylon, food, and housing of sovereign consumers, possessed of factors of production that give them money-income votes for the market place. Each separate market, with its supply and demand curves, is doing its bit toward creating the general-equilibrium set of prices, which in our society resolves the basic economic problems of WHAT, HOW, and FOR WHOM.

PERFECTION AND IMPERFECTIONS OF COMPETITION

Our curves of supply and demand strictly apply only to a *perfectly competitive* market where some kind of *standardized* commodity such as wheat is being auctioned by an organized exchange that registers transactions of *numerous* buyers and sellers. The Board of Trade in Chicago is one such example, and the cotton exchanges in New York or Liverpool are others. The New York Stock Exchange, while it does not auction goods and commodities or productive services rendered by factors of production, does provide a market where shares of common stocks such as those of General Motors and Royal Dutch Petroleum are auctioned at each moment of the working day. Many corporate bonds are also bought and sold in the bond division of the Exchange.

The economists' curves of supply and demand are important ways of *idealizing* the behavior of such markets. The curves do not pretend to give an accurate microscopic description of what is going on during each changing moment in such a market place, as various brokers mill around on the trading floor while frantically giving hand and voice signals to the specialist who serves as auctioneer for each grain or company stock. Nonetheless, the tools of supply and demand do summarize the important average relationships resulting over a period of time from such organized trading.

As far as these fundamental tools of supply and demand are concerned, it matters little what kind of exchange the goods are traded on: whether hand signals or slips of paper or modern computers are used; whether the auction is of the familiar kind, where the auctioneer calls out a *minimum* starting price and accepts higher and higher bids until only one high bidder is left to get the Renoir painting in question; whether there is a "Dutch auction," where the price starts high instead of low and moves downward at stated time intervals until an eager buyer, fearing that someone else will get in the bid

Supply-and-demand tools have many applications:

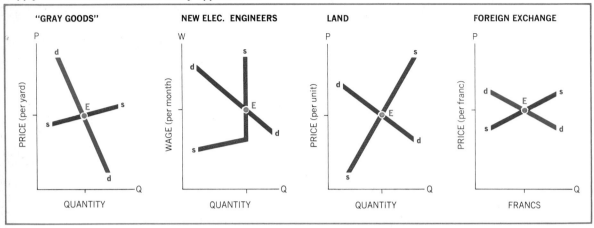

FIG. 4-6.   Here are a few examples of the many uses of supply and demand. Note that these diagrams have straight lines rather than the curved lines of previous figures: in connection with supply and demand and many other diagrams, the economist often makes such simplified drawings merely because the eye takes them in rapidly; usually, this is a tolerably good approximation to the true empirical curves, but when this is not so, it is easy to modify the straight lines. (EXAMPLE: The supply of graduating electrical engineers is a relatively fixed number, and this is depicted in the vertical supply line in the second diagram; however, it is an exaggeration in view of the fact that, as the wage gets low enough, some graduates will take jobs in other fields and some will go to graduate school—which is the reason why the *ss* curve rises from the southwest at low wages.) Can you interpret the four cases?

first, finally gives the first bid and gets the merchandise; or whether the auctioneer asks for written bids and offers in order to be able to make up a table or chart like those of Table 4-3 and Fig. 4-3 and find the equilibrium intersection at one fell swoop.

Indeed, the market need not have a single auctioneer: all the bidding may well take place by telephone calls, as in the case of the market for United States government bonds, which is a much more nearly perfect one than the corporate bond market on the floor of the New York Stock Exchange. The same can be true of stocks listed on the so-called "over-the-counter market," a market which is conducted throughout the country completely by telephone and by daily mailing of price-quotation lists by different brokers; for example, an important stock such as Bank of America, which is listed on this market, may actually behave more nearly like our competitive model than does some stock *inactively* traded on the floor of the New York Stock Exchange.

Needless to say, the requirements for absolutely perfect competition are as hard to meet as the requirements for a perfectly frictionless pendulum in physics. We can approach closer and closer to perfection but can never quite reach it; yet this fact need not do serious damage to the usefulness of our employing the idealized concept. Actually, it matters little to the economic scientist that different grades of wheat will call for slight variations from the quoted market prices. It matters little, too, that dealers in foreign exchange, whose bids and offers determine whether the price of an English pound (or German mark) will be \$2.39 rather than \$2.40 (or 27 cents rather than $27\frac{1}{3}$ cents), use the telephone and cable rather than a trading floor with auctioneer or specialist dealer presiding. Nor does it matter in the case of standardized cotton goods, so-called "gray goods," that they are sold and bought in an informal way by many competing firms:

so long as there are *numerous* buyers and sellers on each side, *well informed* about quality and about each others' prices and having no reason to discriminate in favor of one merchant rather than another and no reason to expect that variations in their *own* bids and offers will have an *appreciable effect* upon the prevailing market price—so long as all this is true, the behavior of price and quantity can be expected to be much like that predicted by our supply and demand curves.

The various diagrams in Fig. 4-6 illustrate how the tools of supply and demand might be used to give a good approximate description of various economic situations other than that of a staple commodity such as wheat: there is pictured a competitive market for cotton gray goods; for a factor of production such as newly graduating electrical engineers, whose price is represented by a wage per month; for a bond or capital asset such as a corner lot of land; and finally, as will be explained later in the discussion of international trade in Part Five, a foreign exchange market in which the dollar price of an English pound, a German mark, or a single unit of any other foreign currency is determined by the bids of those who need foreign currency and by the offers of those who want to sell such currencies to get American dollars.[4]

To be sure, not all today's markets are anywhere near to being perfectly competitive in the economist's sense. We shall see later, in Part Three, that elements of monopoly power or of market imperfection may enter in, and these imperfections will require us to modify the competitive model. After we have learned how to handle such cases, we shall recognize that the world is a blend of competition and imperfections—which means that the competitive analysis, properly qualified, is still an indispensable tool for interpreting reality.

SUMMARY

1   A basic problem of economics is how the mechanism of market pricing grapples with the triad of problems WHAT, HOW, and FOR WHOM.

2   By the *demand schedule* we mean a table showing the different quantities of a good that people will—at any time and with other things held equal—want to buy at each different price. This relationship, when plotted on a diagram, is the *demand curve*.

3   With negligible exceptions, the higher the price the lower will be the quantity demanded, and vice versa. Almost all commodities obey this "law of *downward*-sloping demand."

4   The *supply curve or schedule* gives the relations between the prices and the quantities of a good that producers will—other things equal—be willing to sell. Most usually, supply curves rise *upward* and to the right: diminishing returns implies that higher P is needed to coax out higher-cost extra Q.

[4]Question 10 at the end of this chapter reproduces from a newspaper its financial reports for a single day, showing what might have been the market price quotations for grains, bonds, common stocks, and foreign exchange. After studying economics, one is in a better position to understand the basic forces underlying these price quotations; but only experience and study can make one reasonably expert at the hazardous game of forecasting. The stock market is discussed in this Appendix; Chapter 21's Appendix discusses the economics of speculation in organized commodity markets.

5   Market equilibrium can take place only at a price where the quantities supplied and demanded are *equal*. At any price higher than the equilibrium intersection of the supply and demand curves, the quantity producers will want to go on supplying will exceed the quantity consumers will want to go on demanding; downward pressure on price will result as some sellers undermine the going price. Similarly, the reader can show why a price lower than the equilibrium price will meet irresistible upward pressure.

6   Competitive pricing rations out the limited supply of goods to those with desire or need backed by money votes. Along with helping to decide For Whom, it signals changes in What shall be produced and in How goods shall be produced. But any one market only "partially" helps solve the What, How, and For Whom because of its interdependence with other commodity and factor markets in setting "the general-equilibrium system of prices."

7   To illustrate the allocation function of supply and demand, one can contrast the case of a compulsory draft for the military services with the case where service pay is raised high enough to coax out a voluntary army. Although money costs appear greater, the real cost to the nation may be less if re-enlistments cut out training needs and better use is made of service personnel.

8   Organized trading markets exist for a number of staple commodities such as wheat; they may also exist for some common stocks, bonds, and other financial items. There are still other markets that behave much like an auction market, even if there is no formal auctioneering procedure: so long as there are numerous well-informed suppliers and demanders, each too unimportant to have *by himself* an appreciable effect upon the price of the standardized good in question—so long as such conditions prevail, the tools of supply and demand will give an adequate approximation of the behavior of such markets. Yet, as will be seen later, a good deal of modern economic reality departs from the strict competitive model of the economist, and he must find tools applicable to monopoly and imperfect competition.

QUESTIONS FOR DISCUSSION

1   Although we should all like to escape the hardship implied by higher market price, show that rising market prices may perform some useful functions in time of scarcity. Show how such hardships might work themselves out in some different kind of economy.

2   Define carefully what is meant by a demand schedule or curve. State the law of downward-sloping demand—that there is some kind of *inverse* relation between P and Q, the latter going down when the former goes up.

3   Define the concept of a supply schedule or curve. Show that an increase in supply means a rightward and downward *shift* of the supply curve. Contrast this with the rightward and upward shift implied by an increase in demand. Why the difference? Treat cases of decrease.

4   What factors might increase the demand for wheat? The supply? What would cheap mechanical pickers do to cotton prices? To farm wages?

5 Spell out arguments to show that competitive price must settle down at the equilibrium intersection of supply and demand. Use too high or too low P.

6 "An increase (or decrease) in supply will lower (or raise) price. An increase (decrease) in demand will generally raise (lower) price. While we can predict that an increase in demand accompanied by a decrease in supply will be followed by a rise in price, we cannot guess without further information what will happen if we *simultaneously* increase demand and *increase* supply." Verify. Puzzle out this use of parentheses, common in economics, for alternatives.

7 "A simultaneous increase of demand and decrease of supply, as in question 6 above, is statistically impossible. Demand and supply are identically the same thing." Comment in terms of the section "Two Stumbling Blocks."

8 Give the pros and cons, in peace and war, of a draft, lottery, or high-wage army. Who gets taxed and at whose expense?

9 "If there is only one seller or only a few very large sellers, monopoly and imperfect competition theory will need to be considered rather than the tools of competitive supply and demand. If products are far from being standardized, then each brand-name seller may well have a degree of control over his price not enjoyed by the perfect competitor as defined by the economist." Verify. Make a check list of conditions needed for "perfect competition."

10 *Extra-credit problem*, only for those who know some mathematics: The demand curve is a functional relation between Q and P, namely, $Q = f(P)$. Downward-sloping demand means Q falls as P rises, or in terms of calculus that $df(P)/dP < 0$. Other variables, such as income (X_1) or price of rye (X_2), are being held constant, etc.; hence $f(P)$ is short for $f(P; X_1, X_2, \ldots)$, and a change in any X_i shifts the demand curve. Similarly, denote the supply functional relationship between Q and P by $Q = s(P)$, with $ds(P)/dP > 0$. Then, equilibrium intersection price, P^*, is the root of the equation $f(P) = s(P)$.

11 Try to puzzle out what the following newspaper reports mean.

WHEAT

	Open	High	Low	Close	Change	Season's High	Low
July	127½	127⅞	126⅞	127⅜–¼	−⅜ to ½	142⅛	125¼
Sept.	130¾	130⅞	129¾	130¼	−¾	144¾	128
Dec.	136¾	137⅛	135⅞	136⅜–¼	−¾ to ⅞	143⅞	133¾
Mar.	141½	141⅞	140⅞	131	−¾	145⅝	138½
May	142⅞	143¼	142¼	142¼	−⅞	146¼	140½

CORN

	Open	High	Low	Close	Change	Season's High	Low
July	127⅞	128¼	127¼	127⅝–½	−⅛ to ¼	131½	112¼
Sept.	126¼	126⅜	125¾	126–126⅛	−⅜ to ¼	132⅛	113
Dec.	123¼	123¾	122¾	123⅛–¼	−⅛ to unch	128⅞	112¾
Mar.	128	128⅛	127½	128–128⅛	+⅛ to ½	132⅞	117
May	131	121½	120½	121	+⅛	135¾	129⅞

TREASURY BONDS

Rates	Maturities		Bid	Asked	Yield
6s	1969	Aug.	99.26	99.28	6.61
4s	1969	Oct.	99.3	99.5	7.08
2½s	1969–64	Dec.	98.1	98.3	6.61
4s	1970	Feb.	98.3	98.5	6.96
2½s	1970–65	Mar.	97.3	97.5	6.55
5⅝s	1970	May	98.27	98.29	6.91
6⅜s	1970	May	99.16	99.18	6.89
4s	1970	Aug.	97.1	97.5	6.60
6⅜s	1970	Aug.	99.15	97.17	6.81
5s	1970	Nov.	97.13	97.17	6.89
5⅜s	1971	Feb.	97.25	98.1	6.66

1969 HIGH	1969 LOW	STOCKS AND DIV. IN DOLLARS	SALES IN 100s	FIRST	HIGH	LOW	LAST	NET CHGE.
38½	28½	Abacus .49f	77	30	30¼	29	30	−½
76	64¾	AbbtLab 1.10	10	71½	71½	70½	70½	−½
66¼	47¼	ACF Ind 2.40	19	47¼	47¾	47¼	47¼	...
30⅝	22⅞	AcmeCl 1.40a	22	23	23¼	22⅞	22⅞	−⅝
54¼	41¾	Acme Mkt 2b	22	47⅝	47⅞	47¾	47¾	−⅝
20¾	16⅞	AdamE 1.51g	6	17	17⅞	17	17⅞	+⅞

	THURS-DAY	WEDNES-DAY	WEEK AGO	YEAR AGO
STERLING—$2.40 a pound ($2.376–$2.424)				
Spot	2.3908	2.3895	2.3904	2.3846
90 days'	2.3655	2.3635	2.3649	2.3578
GERMANY (Fed. Rep.)—25.00 cents a mark (24.8148–25.189)				
Spot	25.00⅝	25.02⅞	24.99½	25.02½
90 days'	25.36¼	25.36	25.36¾	25.23½
INDIA—13.33 cents a rupee (13.20–13.46)				
Spot	13.30	13.30	13.30	13.30
JAPAN—2.7777 cents a yen (.279876–.275709)				
Spot	0.2789¾	0.2789	0.2788⅞	0.2766¾

Review your understanding of the following concepts:

demand schedule or curve, *dd*

law of downward-sloping demand

supply schedule or curve, *ss*

diminishing returns and rising *ss*

equilibrium intersection

shifts of schedules

movements along a schedule

how supply and demand in one market "partially" solve WHAT, How, and FOR WHOM

general-equilibrium prices

imperfectly competitive situations

APPENDIX: Stock-market Fluctuations

To the public the most dramatic example of a competitive market is in Wall Street, where supply and demand bid up and bid down the prices of common stocks each second. A man makes a fortune one year; another year he is ruined.

The New York Stock Exchange lists more than 1,000 securities. It started as a private club with rules on its members, but these days it will cost you half a million dollars to buy a seat. The American Stock Exchange began as the Curb: it was literally a case where brokers met *on the street* to buy and sell, giving hand signals to the clerks hanging out the windows to record the transactions; and only in this century did it move indoors.

Every large financial center has its stock exchange. Important ones are in London, Paris, Tokyo, Frankfurt, Toronto, Montreal, and Zurich. Within the United States there are such regional markets as the Pacific Coast, Midwest, Boston, and Philadelphia exchanges. They deal in stocks of local and smaller companies, and to tell the truth much of their reason for existing would disappear if the New York Exchange were to lose its monopoly privileges and have its facilities thrown open more evenhandedly to all.[1]

PEOPLE'S CAPITALISM

The New York Stock Exchange for many years tried to sell the notion of "people's capitalism," in which everyone owns stock and therefore will vote to take account of the interests of property. Few would oppose the notion of a wider and more equal distribution of

[1]In 1968 pressure by the Antitrust Division and SEC caused the Exchange to lower some of its minimum commission rates, and to outlaw "give-ups" (i.e., rebates or fee-splitting).

wealth, but it is a bit of a confidence trick to entice union workers—or their wives—into owning a few shares of a mutual fund so that at the polls they will go easy on corporation tax rates—when, in fact, their own well-being is trivially affected by what happens to the few shares they own in comparison with even a 1 per cent change in wage rates or pension benefits.

In any case only about 27 million out of more than 200 million Americans own any appreciable amount of stocks, and that is a generous estimate. Indirectly, now that private and public pension funds are beginning to invest in equities (i.e., in common stocks), low-income people are beginning to get some protection of their savings against inflation, a privilege that up until recently was enjoyed mostly by the affluent.

THE GREAT CRASH

One traumatic event long kept the general populace fearful to venture into stock ownership—memory of the 1929 panic and crash in Wall Street, which ushered in the long and painful Hoover depression.

In the United States, during the fabulous stock-market boom of the "roaring twenties," housewives, Pullman porters, college students between classes—all bought and sold stocks. Most purchases in this wild "bull" market were "on margin"; i.e., the buyer of $10,000 worth of stocks had to put up only $2,500 or less in cash and borrowed the difference, pledging his newly bought stocks. What matter that he had to pay his broker 6, 10, or 15 per cent per year on his borrowing when in one day Auburn Motors or Bethlehem Steel might jump 10 per cent in value!

The most wonderful thing about a bull market is that it creates its own hopes. If people buy because they think stocks will rise, their act of buying sends up the price of stocks. This causes people to buy still further, and sends the dizzy dance off on another round. And unlike a game of cards or dice, no one loses what the winners gain. Everybody gets a prize! Of course, the prizes are all on paper and would disappear if everyone tried to cash them in. But why should anyone wish to sell such lucrative securities?

When the whole world is mad, 'tis folly to be sane. Suppose one were so wise or so naïve as to believe that the public-utilities holding companies were paper pyramids on cardboard foundations; or that Florida dream real-estate developments were midway between pine thicket and swamp; or that private foreign loans to South America and Europe were being frittered away in roads to nowhere or on public swimming pools? What could such a social misfit do? He would soon learn the first rule of property values: "A thing is worth what people *think* it is worth." But to be successful, this has to be applied in connection with the second rule, which is as hard to follow in practice as belling the cat or catching birds by putting salt on their tails: "Don't be the sucker left holding the bag."

When the black October crash of 1929 came, everyone was caught, the big-league professionals and the piddling amateurs—Andrew Mellon, John D. Rockefeller, the engineer in the White House, and the economics professor from Yale. The bottom fell out of the market. Brokers had to sell out the "margin" accounts of investors who could no longer pony up extra funds to cover the depleted value of their collateral,[2] sending the market down still further. Even those who did not buy on margin lost one-third of their capital by the end of the year, and five-sixths by 1932!

The bull market was over. The bear market had taken its place. And as the former had lived on its dreams, so the latter was consumed by its own nightmares. Billions of dollars of security values were wiped out every month, taking with them not only the capital of gamblers out for speculative gains, but also the widow's mite supposedly invested for steady income. A "blue chip" stock like United States Steel fell from a 1929 high of 261 to a 1932 low of 21! Less respectable securities (Studebaker, for example,) dropped off the board completely, becoming worthless. Even though President Hoover and his administration were friendly toward business, in vain did they try to restore

confidence by predicting "prosperity is just around the corner" and "stocks are excellent buys at their present levels."

Finally, after the great banking crisis of 1933, the stock market began to follow general business recovery.

Figure 4-7, on the next page, shows the movements of stock-market values over the whole period. Although stocks were bullish in 1936–1937 and again during World War II, it was not until the mid-fifties that they returned to anything like the peak levels of 1929. The boom in glamor growth stocks, which ended in the mid-1962, mid-1966, and 1969 collapses, confirmed the fact that human nature never changes much.

FAVORABLE ODDS

Actual historical experience has shown that, even in the face of the great crash, over a lifetime one would have done better in risky common stocks than in safe gilt-edge bonds or savings accounts.

Alfred Cowles III, founder of Yale's Cowles Foundation for Economic Research, showed in the 1930s that equity holders did better than bondholders for most of the years between 1870 and World War II. A Merrill Foundation research study at the University of Chicago Business School found in the 1960s that this had become even more true in the 1925–1960 years.

In an age of inflationary price creep and growth of the mixed economy, you can throw a dart at the financial page to select your portfolio of stocks at *random* and, on the average, come out substantially ahead of your "prudent" brother who stays invested in government bonds and savings deposits!

Again, Fig. 4-7's chart of the 30 Dow-Jones "blue chip" industrial stocks illustrates these facts. But the same story would be told by the more comprehensive 500-stock Standard & Poor's Averages or by the New York Stock Exchange Comprehensive Average, which shows how you would have done if you had spread your money evenly over *every* security listed on the exchange.

THE CULT OF EQUITIES

People, of course, go from one extreme to another. After shunning the stock market for many years, by the 1970s they began to think that you couldn't lose in it. As a result they have bid up common-stock prices to the point where their dividend yields are scarcely 3 per cent, whereas good bonds yield 6 or more per cent. Why this inverted structure when bonds are allegedly safer? Obviously, investors—most of whom are

[2] Frederick Lewis Allen's amusing and interesting chronicle of the 1920s, *Only Yesterday*, gives a detailed account of the role of the stock-market boom in American life. See also John Kenneth Galbraith, *The Great Crash, 1929* (Houghton Mifflin, Boston, 1955).

The only thing sure about stock prices is that they will fluctuate:

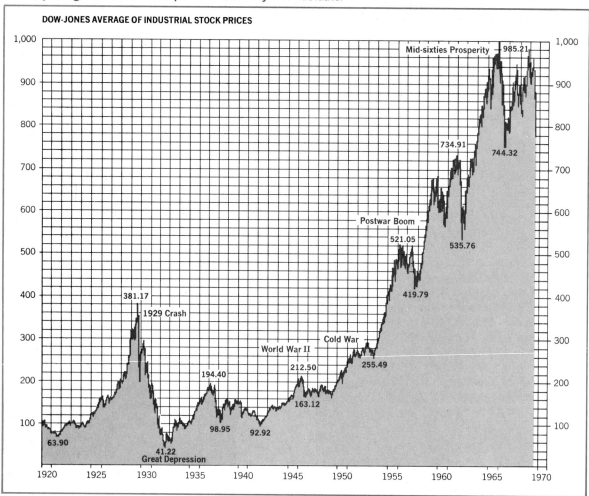

FIG. 4-7. As money national income rises, from output and price-level growth, trend in common-stock prices is upward. But note the severe oscillations. (Source: Dow-Jones and Co., Inc.)

in fairly high tax brackets—are shooting for capital gains rather than heavily taxed dividends.

Experience with the markets abroad shows that all good things come to an end. When American share prices get bid high enough, there will be plenty of room for steep declines, and investing in common stock will cease to be the one-way street it seemed to be from 1942 to 1970.

OUTGUESSING THE MARKET?

To the age-old question, "Does the market follow business activity or business activity the market?" no simple answer can be given. It is reasonably clear that

business activity, national income, and corporate earnings determine stock prices and not vice versa; and also that the psychological effects of market movements no longer have primary importance. But still the market can occasionally *anticipate* changes in national income and total purchasing power. It then appears to be leading them when really it is following what it thinks they will be doing later.

How to invest   There are no simply stated foolproof rules for making money out of the stock market. Anyone who can accurately predict the future course of business activity will prosper; but there is no such person. At least four main classes of investors and speculators can be distinguished:

1. The group who simply *buy and hold*. Because the national economy has a long-term upward trend, they fare reasonably well over the long run. They might do a little better if they followed the statistical advice of investment services as to how to switch to companies of more favorable growth prospects. Surprisingly, though, representative studies show that the best mutual funds and investment counselors rarely do much better than the Dow-Jones average of 30 industrial stocks.

The effect of this holding group is neither to stabilize nor to destabilize prices; to the extent that they freeze shares off the market and limit the number of tradings, they tend to make the market "thinner." In a thin market there are so few transactions that the attempt to buy a few hundred shares of a stock may send its price up a few points because of the absence of ready sellers around the ruling market price. An attempt to sell may depress the price a few points.

2. At the other extreme are the hour-to-hour, day-to-day *ticker watchers*, to be seen in every brokerage office. Generally speaking, they buy and sell, sell and buy. Usually, they make money only for their brokers.

The existence of this trader group has the effect of making the market less thin. Because of this group, any investor can expect to be able to liquidate his market holdings at any time at some price, although not at a price predictable in advance or that he would like. Still, even this restricted "liquidity" enhances the attractiveness of securities traded on organized exchanges over and above the unlisted issues of smaller companies that are bought and sold by brokers over the counter.

3. In between are those *speculators who play intermediate swings* of many months or years. The least successful of these are the amateurs whose entrance into the market at the top when it is too late is supposed to be the signal for the "smart money" to leave. The most successful speculators are those who are able to avoid the extremes of enthusiasm of the mob and to discern underlying business conditions. This does not mean that they buy simply because a stock looks low and sell when it looks high. On the contrary, they buy when stocks look as if they will continue to rise. When a drop seems imminent, they sell short or, more conservatively, they simply go into cash or high-grade bonds. It takes cool nerves to sell short, because on the whole the market is overoptimistic. But if a single individual does it cleverly, he may achieve success in avoiding the losses of a bear market.

The behavior of such speculators is often destabilizing to prices. They "pile on" to a price rise and send it further; they similarly *accentuate* a decline.

Thus, in the mid-1960s certain so-called "performance" mutual investment funds became prominent. They would buy electronic or airline glamor stocks just before these became glamorous. Then as people saw them buying, the public would be attracted to the same stocks. After the prices of these had been bid up, the performance funds would sell out to the public at a nice profit, moving on to new fields to conquer. The evident perils in all this are well illustrated by a modern Wall Street story.

A broker phones me, telling me to buy XYZ at $2 a share. I buy 100 shares. He phones to say: "XYZ has risen to $3, better buy a couple of hundred more." I do. He calls again: "Better buy 300 at $5." Again I do; but when next he calls I finally refuse to buy and ask to sell. "What, sell XYZ," he says, "sell it *to whom?*" (*In joco veritas.*)

4. Finally, there are individuals who study special situations. From public or inside sources, they learn in advance of changes in the fortunes of particular companies: of rumored bankruptcies; of special stock dividends, split-ups, or mergers; of likely earnings and dividend announcements. When combined with the successful characteristics of the third group, members of this group—such as the elder statesman of two wars, Bernard Baruch—make the largest profit from the market. Since World War II some alert operators have been able to run $1,000 up to $10 million or more—at the same time keeping profits in the form of less heavily taxed capital gains.

But the would-be investor must take to heart Baruch's caution:

If you are ready to give up everything else—to study the whole history and background of the market and all the principal companies whose stocks are on the board as carefully as a medical student studies anatomy—if you can do all that, and, in addition, you have the cool nerves of a great gambler, the sixth sense of a kind of clairvoyant, and the courage of a lion, you have a ghost of a chance.

SCIENCE OF STOCKS

Buying common stocks is an art, not a science. No one can draw the line between risky speculation and safe investment. But an art or craft, being science in a still-primitive state, has its general rules of behavior. Here are a few gleaned from scientific study of this unscientific field.

1. You can't compile a good track record by *consulting the stars*. Don't laugh. Financial services have gotten rich—their clients haven't, though—by selling astrological advice, and one man made a fortune purporting to interpret the signals being given in the comic strips!

2. Hunches work out to nothing in the long run.

3. The best brains in Wall Street scarcely do as well as the averages (Standard & Poor's, etc.). At first this seems surprising. They have all the money needed for any kind of research and digging. But remember, they are all competing with each other; and if there is a bargain for one man to see, it is also there for another; and hence it will *already* have been wiped out of existence by competitive bids.

4. Chartists claim to see in plots of stock prices "resistance levels," "gaps," "head-and-shoulder formations," "flags," "pennants," "channels"—all of which are supposed to improve your odds of guessing right. Experienced investors say: "The chartists generally end up with holes in their shoes. So forget it."

5. Are there then no good tricks? Alas, few indeed. Because inflation and growth push the country ahead, a random investment will probably show capital gains in the long run. Not much more can be said. Statisticians have demonstrated that the day-to-day changes in stock prices are very much like a "random-walk" —like the brownian motion you see in a microscope due to the chance impacts of invisible and unpredictable atoms on just-visible huge molecules or colloidal particles. Wall Street doesn't believe this random-walk theory, but the Ph.D's in the business schools laugh at their disbelief.

6. To have unusual performance, you must be able to predict increases in the per share earnings of companies *before* the market place in general is aware of them. *After* is too late. For each stock tends to sell at a certain "price-earnings multiple,"—e.g., stagnant and cyclical U.S. Steel at 12/1, glamorous IBM at 40/1. And if you are correct in foretelling an unanticipated rise in earnings, the market will probably mark up the stock price once those earnings become visible. (As a kicker, if you are early in recognizing an area of glamorous earnings growth, you may find the market putting higher and higher price-earnings multiples on your holdings—and after that has happened, it is a good time to get out.)

7. The above rule is easy to state but practically impossible to put into practice even if you have a vast research staff and inside management contacts. Hence, unless you like the fun of investing your own money—and are willing to pay something for that fun in the form of bad performance—most amateurs would be well advised to buy shares in some mutual fund. A mutual fund buys 30 to 100 stocks deemed best by professional money managers and gives you your prorated share in them. If the market goes up, your mutual fund shares will probably go up; but it works both ways. (WARNING: Most mutual funds are sold by salesmen who get a fat commission for doing so—usually an 8 per cent "load" skimmed off your principal. Through the mail you can buy no-load funds involving *no* sales commission at all, and which experience shows do about the same on the *average* as the heavy-load funds. How do the no-loads manage this? Simply by paying the same management fees to money managers but cutting out the selling expenses—the equivalent in finance of the "discount retail store" that quotes low prices for cash-and-carry. You can recognize no-loads on the financial pages by *equality* of bid and asked.)

For an amusing, but well-informed, account of the modern stock market, the reader might refer to *The Money Game* (Random House, New York, 1967), samplings from which occur in P. A. Samuelson, *Readings in Economics* (McGraw-Hill, New York, 1970, 6*th* ed.).

FOR REVIEW

Review your understanding of the following concepts:

New York and other exchanges	**equities and inflation protection**
common stocks or equities	**price-earnings multiple**
great crash	**random-walk versus chartism**
dividend versus bond yield	**mutual funds: load and no-load**

Business Organization and Income **5**

The business of America is
business.
CALVIN COOLIDGE

To understand our business civilization, we must first understand the organization and functioning of business enterprise. The first part of this chapter leads up to the analysis of the modern corporation, primarily by an extensive case study; the last half deals with the financial structure of corporations, particularly the modern large-scale, or "giant," corporation. The Appendix presents a brief introduction to the fundamentals of accounting. Without some comprehension of accounting, there can be no deep understanding of the economics of enterprise.

The "new industrial state"—to use the name John Kenneth Galbraith has coined for the organization of our large corporate bureaucracy—is something new in the history of mankind. If the corporate structure is not to control man, society must see that it stays subject to control.

BIG, SMALL, AND INFINITESIMAL BUSINESS

There are 8 million American business units in 1970. All but a small fraction of these enterprises are very small-scale units owned by a single person. Most businesses are here today and gone tomorrow, the average life expectancy of a business being only half-a-dozen years. Some will terminate in bankruptcy; many more will be voluntarily brought to a close with sighs of regret for dashed hopes and an expensive lesson learned; others will come to a joyous end when their owner lands a good job.

Faster than old businesses die, new ones are born. The present population of business concerns grew up as a result of the cumulative excess of business births over business deaths during previous years. As an economy grows, we can expect a steady excess of business births over deaths.

By number the tiny, self-owned "individual proprietorship" is overwhelmingly the dominant form of business. But in dollar value, political and economic power, payrolls, and employment, some few hundred "giant corporations" occupy a strategically dominant position.

Let us glance briefly at the role in our economy of "infinitesimal businesses." There are more than 200,000 grocery-store owners in the United States, all trying to make a living. There are nearly a quarter of a million automobile service stations; more than 50,000 drugstores; and so it goes.

Some of these ventures are highly successful; but it is still true to say that most do not earn for their owners much more than they could get with less effort and risk by working for somebody else. Thus, chain stores do about 55 per cent of all the grocery business, the rest being divided among the independents. Most of these independents consist of the so-called "Ma and Pa" stores, doing less than $100 of business every day. These are often started by people who have only a few thousand dollars of initial capital— less than half the amount necessary for an adequate grocery store to do the $150-a-day business necessary if the owner is to earn even minimum wages for his effort. Such small-scale efforts are doomed from their very beginning. When the owners' initial capital is used up, they are finished. They illustrate why one-third to one-half of all retail businesses are discontinued within 3 years. (In these days of brave talk about "black capitalism," it is sobering to read in Chapter 40 that most Negro businesses are small and of low profitability, being confined chiefly to a protected market of service needs for blacks— as e.g., restaurants, undertaking, hairdressing and barber shops, drycleaning, etc.)

Of course, business fields differ in the amount of capital required. To build a modern service station costs more than $100,000, but to lease one from an oil company brings the initial capital down to around $10,000. Occupations with a high "rate of turnover of inventory"—such as vegetable stores—obviously require less initial capital than drugstores, hardware, or jewelry stores, where many items of stock will stay on the shelves for 3 to 5 years and where the average "turnover ratio" of annual sales to stock of inventory may be a good deal less than one.

Aside from the capital necessary to open a business, there is the tremendous amount of personal effort required. Self-employed farmers usually work from 55 to 60 hours per week during the peak summer months. Similarly, it has been estimated that the people who are their own bosses put in more hours per week than wage earners. Who, on his Sunday ride in the country, has not pitied some self-employed drudge, whose own efforts and those of all his family hardly suffice to cause him to break even?

Still, people will always want to start out on their own. *Theirs* may be the successful venture. Even if they never do succeed in earning more than a few thousand a year, there is something attractive about being able to make your own plans and do the variety of tasks that a small enterprise or franchise operation calls for.

THE SINGLE PROPRIETORSHIP

We gain insight into the principal forms of business organization—the single proprietorship, the partnership, and the corporation—by following the history of a particular business venture as it grows from a small beginning into a good-sized corporation.

Let us suppose you decide to start a business to produce toothpaste. You may have hit upon a good preparation in your chemistry class; or perhaps you simply looked up an old formula in the *Encyclopedia Britannica*. To be a single proprietor you need not get anybody's permission; you simply wake up one morning and say, "Today, I am in business!" And you are.

You can hire as few or as many men as you wish, borrow whatever capital you can. At the end of the month whatever is left over as profits—after all costs have been met!—is yours to do with as you like. And there is nothing to stop you from going to the cash register at any time, taking out $800 if you can find it there, and giving it to your wife to buy a fur coat or a Chippendale chair. (Of course, as an individual you must pay personal income taxes on all earnings.)

The losses of the business are all yours, too. If your sales fail to cover the costs you have incurred, your creditors can ask you to dig deeper into your personal assets: the bonds set aside for Junior's education, the old farmstead, and the rest. In legal terms, an individual proprietor has "unlimited liability" for all debts contracted by the business. All his property, with the exception of a small minimum, is legally attachable to meet those debts.

BUSINESS GROWTH AND THE NEED FOR SHORT-TERM CAPITAL

Suppose the business is prospering tremendously—perhaps because your low price has induced a chain of 5-and-10-cent stores to place a large order for tubes of paste to be marketed under its name. You are now making more money than you expected to; but you find yourself harder pressed for cash than ever before. Why? Because you are not *paid in advance* for your sales, whereas you must pay your workers and suppliers promptly on receipt of their services. For the moment you are putting out money and getting nothing for it, i.e., nothing except the certainty of future payment on the sales orders which you have booked, nothing but a miscellaneous batch of "goods in process"— unfinished toothpaste, empty tubing, and so forth.

To some extent, the stringency of cash can be relieved by your not paying for supplies until the end of the month or even longer. However, there is a limit to how far your suppliers will let you run up bills. Also, letting your so-called "accounts payable liabilities" pile up is an expensive way of raising capital, because goods are often billed at 2 per cent discount if paid within 30 days. When you do not take advantage of such discounts, you are, in effect, paying a very high interest rate—up to 24 per cent per year!

Where is such a single proprietor to borrow? A personal finance company will probably charge you something like 3 per cent per month or 40 per cent per year for a small personal loan; and even it will prefer to lend to a man with a steady wage that can be legally "attached" or "garnisheed" in case of nonpayment. If you own a home without a mortgage, a loan at 6 to 8 per cent might be raised upon it. To borrow in this way is clearly to risk your family's future well-being; but probably, if you are hopeful of your business future, you may go ahead and assume the risk.

Why can't the local banker be called upon for a commercial loan at 6 or 7 per cent? Ordinarily, a commercial bank will not provide "venture capital" for an unproven enterprise. The bank's president looks at your checking balance and finds it has always been near the vanishing point; this is natural, since as fast as payments have come in, you have had to write checks to stave off the ever-insistent claims of your creditors. Ordinarily, the bank likes to make 3-month loans to be used for peak-season needs and to be canceled during the rest of the year. It is idle to pretend that 3 months from now your growing business will be more liquid than now. At that time you will be applying for continuous renewal of the loan; you know it, and the banker knows it.

Even if the bank were emancipated from the older prejudice against "term loans" of some years' duration, it could not conscientiously provide capital to a business like yours. To the banker you are only one of numerous would-be entrepreneurs; and most, he knows are destined for failure even in the best of times, and almost all would be wiped out if a really big depression came along. For the bank actually to protect the sums entrusted to it by its depositors, it would have to charge you an extra risk premium of perhaps 10 per cent or more,[1] in addition to, say, 7 per cent interest. Otherwise, the gains from successful ventures would not offset the losses of the unsuccessful.

There is one possibility of your getting a loan from the bank. The Small Business Administration (SBA) might join with the bank to make you a loan, thus coaxing the banker to make it. Or there might be a Small Business Investment Company, set up for tax advantages, that will lend you venture capital in return for eventual partial ownership. In some states, there are development commissions which have limited funds to help bring a business to town or keep it there.

Despite your makeshift attempts to raise capital, the business is still suffering from growing pains. You have exhausted all possibilities of raising further loan capital. Perhaps the time has come to look for a partner.

THE PARTNERSHIP

Any two or more people can get together and form a partnership. Each agrees to provide some fraction of the work and capital, to share some percentage of the profits, and of course to share the losses or debts. A purely oral agreement will do; but it is more businesslike and makes for less misunderstanding if you have a lawyer draw up some sort of formal partnership agreement.

In the case of the toothpaste business, suppose your brother-in-law is given a part ownership in the business in return for putting up $40,000 capital. Like you, he is to work for the company, for, say, $8,000 per year as compared with your $12,000. You are to receive two-thirds of all profits or losses, computed after the partnership withdrawals are treated as costs; he gets one-third.

Your partner has put up $40,000 in cash. What have you brought into the venture? In the first place, you have, of course, some unfinished barrels of toothpaste to contribute, along with some uncollected accounts receivable for goods already delivered. This does not seem like much.

Actually, what you bring to the partnership is an intangible but valuable asset: the

---

[1] Another alternative has been used extensively in Germany but not in the United States or Britain: German banks buy part ownership in business and share in the profits. Such participation in ownership inevitably leads to management responsibilities by the banks and often to monopoly control of business by banking interests. For this reason, and others, such activity is legally forbidden to our banks, which are rarely sources of venture capital.

profitable sales orders and the know-how, or what is called "good will." In short, you are bringing with you a potential profit-earning power over all costs and drawings of, say, $15,000 a year. You are letting your partner have an $8,000-a-year job—which we shall assume is perhaps equal to what he can get elsewhere—and, in addition, for $40,000 he is purchasing a one-third slice of $15,000 every year.

To get this much per year from bond investments would cost him much more than $40,000. He would have to buy $100,000 worth of 5 per cent government bonds to get such a return, or $83,333 worth of 6 per cent private bonds. Aside from the risk element, your partner is getting a good buy for his $40,000, since he will annually collect some $12\frac{1}{2}$ per cent on his investment. So your two-thirds share is justified by the good will that you supply.[2]

"THIS IS THE WAY WE GROW"

And your business continues to prosper and grow. Each year, both partners agree to take out of the business only their stipulated drawings (which are like wages) and about a fifth of their share of profits, plowing the rest of the profits back into the business. Why do you decide to take out any profits from the business at all? Because you need the cash to pay your federal personal income taxes, which are levied not only on your salaries but also *upon your respective shares of the partnership's earnings.*

Why does a business like this grow? Here are some possible reasons: (1) Your toothpaste sales have risen as a result of your trade name's becoming advertised and better known and as a result of your sending out more salesmen. (2) As more toothpaste is produced, economies of large-scale production are realized so that you are able to cut your price. (3) A new factor of growth results from "vertical integration." You decide to buy a chemical factory to produce your own raw materials, and you also become your own wholesaler, thus operating three stages rather than only one "stage of production." (4) The company also grows by "horizontal integration": you take advantage of a profitable opportunity to buy out a number of competitors who produce similar toothpastes. (5) New "complementary products" such as soap and lipstick are added. You feel that bringing in the new lines under the same roof will help to spread the overhead expenses, and your salesmen feel that they might just as well get many orders as few when making a call. (6) You might even become a baby "conglomerate," growing by adding *unrelated* activities to your business (e.g., machine tools, car repairing, fortune-telling). (7) Finally, your business may grow just because you are producing a better toothpaste.

NEW NEEDS AND SOURCES FOR CAPITAL

Once again, the enterprise finds itself in a paradox: the more successful it is and the faster it grows, the harder up it is for capital. The $40,000 of new "equity capital" brought into the business did not stay long in the form of cash. It was quickly transformed into

---

[2]Good will and capitalized earning power are discussed in the accounting appendix to this chapter.

circulating assets such as goods in process and office supplies. In part it went to pay off the most pressing liabilities.

The remainder was used as a down payment on a factory building and equipment. The difference between the down payment and the purchase price of the factory was secured by a mortgage loan on the property. The mortgage money was advanced by a nearby life-insurance company and was to be amortized or paid off in installments over a period of 20 years, along with 7 per cent interest per year on the actual principal still unpaid at any time. In case the loan should not be paid, the holder of the mortgage of course has the right to foreclose the mortgage, i.e., to take over the ownership of the building and sell it for what it will bring. Since the down payment on the factory came to about one-fourth of its price, since this price was a bargain price to begin with, and since each year the insurance company will be getting back part of its principal, the risk it takes is not very great. The only way it could lose would be if there were a disastrous real-estate crash within the first few years.

Despite the continuous plowing of profits back into the business, growth still leaves you needing more capital. But now, having established your reputation, so to speak, new avenues of borrowing are open to you. Your banker will be glad to lend you money to tide you over the busy pre-Christmas period. A company, such as the Commercial Credit Corporation, will lend you money on the basis of your safe, but as yet uncollected, "accounts receivable" (i.e., sums owed you for goods already sold).

Suppose, when all is said and done, you need still more capital than you can raise by any kind of borrowing. The painful necessity arises of getting more "equity" capital by letting some new people share in the profits (and losses) of the business. (As a matter of fact, even if you could still find some institutions to borrow from, it would be unwise to do so. You have already superimposed too many liabilities and fixed charges on a narrow equity base. As long as things go well, it would be nice to earn $12\frac{1}{2}$ per cent profit on capital that costs you only 7. But if losses should occur, they will fall all the more heavily on you, the two partners, who are the residual owners.)

DISADVANTAGES OF THE PARTNERSHIP FORM

One possibility of getting more ownership capital is to admit new partners. There is no limit to the number you can admit; there have been partnerships in the brokerage and banking fields involving more than 100 people. However, every time a new partner is admitted, or one dies or resigns, a whole new partnership must be formed.[3]

---

[3] More weighty is the real disadvantage stemming from the fact that a partnership can be dissolved whenever any party finds the existing arrangement unsatisfactory and wishes to withdraw. The law of partnerships also makes it impossible for any partner to sell his share to a new party without the consent of his partners; if agreement cannot be secured, the partnership may have to be wound up.

The reader may recall that the novelist William Dean Howells has his famous title character Silas Lapham, a rising self-made paint tycoon, present his partner with the ultimatum: "You buy me out or I'll buy you out." Silas' two excuses, that his were the real brains and energy responsible for the success of the business and that the proffered price exceeded his partner's original investment, were cleverly seen through by Mrs. Lapham. She pointed out that, without the partner's money at the critical time, the business could never have succeeded and that Silas' offer to sell was premised upon the knowledge that his partner was not in a position to buy the whole of the business.

As the number of partners increases, there comes to the fore a factor that has been soft-pedaled in our discussion up to now. Each partner is *liable without limit* to the full extent of his personal fortune for all debts contracted by the partnership. If he owns 1 per cent of the partnership and the business fails, then he will be called upon to foot 1 per cent of the bills and the other partners will be assessed their 99 per cent. But suppose they cannot pay any part of their assessment. Then the 1 per cent partner may be called upon to pay *for all*, even if it means selling his fine etchings or auctioning the family home.

This feature of *unlimited liability* reveals why partnerships tend to be confined to small, personal enterprises. According to the doctrine of "mutual agency" involved in the law of partnerships, each partner has broad powers to act as agent to commit the whole partnership. When it becomes a question of placing their personal fortunes in jeopardy, people are reluctant to put their capital into complex ventures over which they can exercise little control.

This explains why agriculture and retail trade are the only sectors of our economy where more than half of the business done is done by single proprietors and partnerships. In the field of investment banking, concerns like J. P. Morgan & Company used to advertise proudly "not incorporated" so that their creditors could have extra assurance. But even these concerns have converted themselves into corporate entities.

Comparatively recently the giant brokerage concern Merrill Lynch, Pierce, Fenner & Smith incorporated. For a long time it had many major partners and scores of junior partners, illustrating that the barriers to running a large enterprise put up by the partnership form are not insuperable. Such giant partnerships now are rare.

Undoubtedly, unlimited liability and the red tape needed to ensure continuity are the main drawbacks to the partnership form.

THE CORPORATION

At this point, therefore—or even long before—you will probably decide to form a corporation rather than a partnership. Usually you will incorporate in the state in which you live and operate. However, if the corporation is sizable, you may prefer to establish token headquarters in some state such as Delaware or New Jersey, which have set up very easy rules in order to attract firms.

Centuries ago, corporation charters were awarded by governments very rarely and only by *special acts* of the king and legislature. Parliament or Congress would graciously permit a public-utility enterprise or railroad to form a corporation to do specific things and perform specific functions. The East India Company was such a privileged corporation. The early railroads here and abroad often had to spend as much money in getting a charter through the legislature as in preparing their roadbeds. Gradually, within the past century, this procedure began to seem unfair, and it became the practice to pass general incorporation laws granting almost anyone the privilege of forming a corporation for almost any purpose, without having to get a special vote of approval from the state legislature or from Congress.

Today, for a small fee a lawyer will draw up the necessary papers and will write into the corporate charter almost as wide powers and purposes as you could wish. Automatically, the state will grant the charter. Let us see how the incorporating procedure works in the case of your toothpaste company. You decide to issue 20,000 shares of common stock in the corporation: 6,600 going to you; 3,300 to your partner; 100 to your wife; and the other 10,000 to be sold to outside interests. Although each share is to have an initial stated value of $10, your lawyer has advised you to make them no-par shares, since "par value" has no longer any particular significance.

The 10,000 shares to be sold to the public are to be marketed through a local *investment banking* firm. These firms are simply merchandisers of securities; and as with any merchant, their profit comes from the difference between their buying and selling prices. Because yours is such a small business, they must drive a hard bargain, especially since they can claim that the costs of selling the securities are likely to be high. Thus the investment brokers may offer you $10 per share and plan to resell at a price of $12.50 per share. Had you been a large company, you might have held out for as much as $12.25—or even in some cases $12.40—out of the $12.50 selling price, because of the eager competitive bidding of the different investment banking syndicates.

For a large company the investment banker would probably have agreed to *underwrite* the new issue of 10,000 shares. This means that he would have guaranteed the purchase of the full 10,000 shares at a set price. If the market then refused to buy all these shares from the investment banker at his announced price, he, not you, would have to absorb the loss. But he probably regards you as too small and untried a business to justify his assuming the risk of underwriting. So he takes your issue on a "best effort" basis; and if he cannot sell all the shares, you end up raising less capital. (Also, as a "sweetener," he may insist upon being given warrants—which we shall see are options to buy stock later at today's low price.)

Corporation structure   Fortunately, all goes well, and he pays you $100,000 in cash for the securities sold. Unlike the case of the partnership, you need not concern yourself with the people to whom he has sold the shares or with the fact that they may resell their shares. The names of the owners of the shares are registered with the company or its bank agent in case they get lost and so that you will know where to send the dividend checks or the announcements of stockholders' meetings.

Ordinarily, each share gives its owner one vote. Shares in the corporate earnings are also in direct proportion to the number of shares owned. Those with 100 shares get 100 votes and correspondingly higher dividends.

The outside owners of 10,000 shares have paid in $100,000 cash to the company. What have you and your partner paid in? Obviously not cash, but rather a sizable amount of earning assets: plant, equipment, goods in process, and perhaps good will, which is, as already seen, the capitalized value of the presumed "excess earning power" of the business, resulting from its trademarks, patents, know-how, and so forth.

Back in the old days before 1929, you and your investment banker might have evaluated the good will as liberally as you wished, possibly giving yourself 20,000 rather than 10,000 shares. This practice has been called "watering the stock." Today, you would have to submit any sizable new issue to the Securities and Exchange Commission (SEC), a regulatory agency set up as part of the New Deal in 1934. It would have to satisfy itself that there are no misleading claims before permitting the new flotation. However, it does nót pretend to pass judgment on or attest to the value of the stock. *Caveat emptor*—let the buyer beware—still prevails as a doctrine!

ADVANTAGES AND DISADVANTAGES OF THE CORPORATE FORM

Private advantage   The corporation has solved most of the problems that bothered you about the partnership. It is an almost perfect device for the raising of large sums of capital. Of first importance, every stockholder now has *limited liability*. After paying $12.50 per share, the investor need not worry about his personal estate's being in jeopardy. If worse comes to worst and the business goes bankrupt, the most each shareholder could lose would be his original $12.50 per share. He cannot be assessed further.

Of secondary importance is the fact that the corporation is a fictitious legal person created by the state. It exists not by "natural right" but only at the pleasure of the state. The corporation, as distinct from its owners, can be sued in court and can sue. Any officer of the company, unlike any partner, is strictly limited in his legal ability to act as agent for the other owners and to commit them financially. Also, the corporation may have "perpetual succession" or existence, regardless of how many times the shares of stock change hands by sale or bequest and regardless of whether there are 10,000 different stockholders. No group of shareholders can force any other group to sell or retain their holdings, and only a majority vote rather than unanimity is needed to reach usual business decisions. Normally, the stockholders will be too many to meet for every decision; they will prefer to elect a board of directors consisting of a dozen or so members to represent them between annual meetings, in much the same way that democratic electorates select legislative representatives to act for them. As we shall see, the problem of keeping large corporations "truly democratic" is a hard one.

You will face one disadvantage to incorporation that has become increasingly serious in recent years. *The federal government taxes corporate income.* Thus, during World War II, a profitable corporation might have had to pay as much as 80 per cent of its income to the government in excess-profit taxation; the Korean conflict also brought an excess-profit tax. Most sizable corporations must pay almost half of each extra dollar of income. (This is *in addition* to the personal income tax that owners pay on dividends they get.)

The corporate tax is a rather high price for a small business to pay for limited liability and greater ease of raising capital. Yet there are also tax *advantages* offered by the corporate form. There is a loophole in our present law: *undistributed* corporate profits escape *personal* income taxes; only paid-out dividends are so taxed. A rich man who is taxed about 70 cents of every dollar of personal income can say, "Why pay such rates on partnership earnings? Let's incorporate, pay the lower corporate tax, and keep dividends low."[4]

[4]To some degree he is only putting off the evil day. For unless his lawyer can work out a lightly taxed "capital-gains deal," his dividends will be taxable *later* when he receives them. But in any case the delay in tax payment is worth money to him. Under new tax revisions, many people can win either way: they are given the option of being taxed as partnerships or as corporations. Doctors and other professional men like the tax-sheltered pension and other benefits they can give themselves through the corporate form.

Another loophole used to avoid the disadvantages of double taxation under the corporate form is where the owners of a closely held corporation vote most of its earnings to themselves and their relatives in the form of high salaries, pensions, and perquisites. The Treasury Department tries to check up on avoidance of taxes by such padding of expenses; but it is always hard to know whether a given in-law is worth $25,000 a year and whether a trip to a Bermuda convention is truly a business rather than a personal expense.

Social advantage   When Prime Minister Gladstone was shown electricity on a visit to Michael Faraday's laboratory, he asked, "What is the use of electricity?" Faraday gave the ironic reply, "I suppose some day, Sir, you may come to put a tax on it." Surely the advantage of the corporate form *to society* is not merely that the state can tax it.

Large-scale production is technically efficient, and a large corporation is an advantageous way for investors to pool the irreducible risks of business life. Without limited liability and the corporation, society could simply not reap the benefit that comes when large supplies of capital can be attracted to competing corporations that produce a variety of complementary products, that pool risks, and that best utilize the economies of sizable research units and managerial know-how.

This is the economic rationale of the legal fiction called the corporation.

HOW A CORPORATION CAN RAISE CAPITAL

Let us suppose your corporation continues to grow as a result of vertical, horizontal, or conglomerate combinations, new products, economies of mass production, advertising promotion, and so forth. Besides borrowing on promissory notes or mortgages, buying on credit, and relying on earnings not paid out in dividends, what new forms of financing are now available to you?

Bonds   First, you may issue bonds. These are nothing but special kinds of promissory notes, nicely printed on gilt paper, issued in $1,000 or other denominations so as to be readily marketable for resale. A bond is a security promising to pay a certain number of dollars every 6 months for a number of years until it matures. At that time the borrowing company promises to pay off the principal of the bond at its face value. (Often the company has the right to call in the bond a few years before its maturity date by paying the bondholders some previously agreed-upon price.)

Ordinarily, payments for interest and principal must be made on time, regardless of whether the company has been making earnings or not. Otherwise the company is in default of its obligations and can be taken to court like any debtor.[5]

Common stocks   Issuing bonds and issuing common stocks are opposite methods of financing. The common stockholder is providing "equity" capital. He shares in profits and in

[5] Income bonds, whose interest is payable only if there are large enough earnings, are not uncommon. Mortgage bonds, secured by property, are often encountered. Convertible bonds, which can be exchanged for a stated number of common shares, are a popular hybrid as will be seen.

control of business decisions, but he must also share in all losses. His is a more risky venture, because he can never receive any dividends until the fixed charges owed to the bondholder are paid off. The bondholder gets a limited but steadier income. Unless the corporation is bankrupt or in danger of being so, the bondholder ordinarily has no legal control over the decisions of the business; but a wise management will take care to stay on good terms with all sources of future capital.

Preferred stocks   Between bonds and common stocks are so-called "preferred stocks." These pay *at most* a stated dividend—say, a stipulated 5 per cent of the face value per share—no matter how profitable the business becomes. The preferred stockholder is more likely to get his dividend even when profit is low than is the common stockholder, because legally he stands next in line after the bondholder and before the common stockholder. The latter gets no dividends if the preferred stock fails to receive its full dividend.

Often "cumulative" preferred stock is issued. This means that, if for four years of hard times there has not been enough in the way of earnings to pay any of the 5 per cent dividends on the preferred stock, when good times come back again the "cumulated" $20 (= 4 × $5) of unpaid preferred stock dividends must be made good before the common stockholders can begin to receive any dividends. Often, too, preferred stock is "callable" and "convertible." The first term means that at some previously stated value, say $103, the company can buy back its outstanding preferred stock. The second term refers to the right given the preferred stockholder of converting each share into shares of common stock at some stipulated ratio.[6]

Hybrid convertibles   After decades of price inflation, investors have become wary of putting their funds in bonds which merely repay the principal in dollars that have deteriorated in purchasing power. To tempt them back into bonds, corporations have increasingly had to resort to *convertible bonds*. Thus the J. C. Penney chain has sold $1,000 bonds that pay $4\frac{1}{4}$ per cent interest and come due in 1993. These could be sold at so low an interest rate only because each bond is made to be convertible at the owner's will into 50 shares of J. C. Penney common stock. The investor can, so to speak, have his cake and eat it too. If prices stay steady, he has a nice safe bond. If inflation or anything else sends Penney stock far upward, he can convert and protect the real purchasing power of his principal. Similarly, we today often meet *convertible preferred stock* (as in the case of American Express pfd., which is convertible into one share of common in addition to paying an annual dividend of $1.50). Finally, some companies issue *warrants*, which are options to buy the common at some stated exercise price until some future date: thus there is a Textron warrant, good until 1984, which permits me to buy a share of its common by paying $8.75 of exercise price. Such warrants are very volatile, often moving in a "leveraged" way in comparison with the common; hence, you can make a lot on them if you are right, but you can also lose your shirt.

[6] Also, some preferred stocks are made more attractive by being "participating." This means that, once profit exceeds some agreed-upon figure, they share with the common stockholder in further profits. But this form is rare. When one corporation owns stock in another, it pays tax on only 15 per cent of the dividends; this explains why corporations are important holders of preferred stocks.

ADVANTAGES OF DIFFERENT SECURITIES

From the standpoint of the investor, bonds, preferred stocks, and common stock usually form a sequence of increasing risk and decreasing security—balanced by an increased chance of making high earnings or capital gains. Today, a "gilt-edge" bond may yield about 6 or 8 per cent, a good preferred stock about the same. Because common stocks may rise in value and give capital gains, they now often have a spread of dividend yields that begins even *lower* than bonds: some "growth stocks" like IBM yield much, much less than the safest government bonds. To test his understanding of these three forms of securities, the reader should make sure that he understands why common stocks tend to be better investments in time of inflation than the other two.

It would be a mistake to leave the reader with the impression that bonds are perfectly safe investments. On the contrary, during depressions many companies went bankrupt and defaulted on their bonds, paying off only a few cents on the dollar. The basic risk in all corporate investment is a possible loss of earning power, which will greatly reduce the value of its assets. Often a company will undergo reorganization in which the stockholders may be squeezed out completely; the courts may appoint a "receiver" or trustee to run the business, and the bondholders may be given bonds (or even stocks!) equal only to some fraction of their original investments. Moreover, certain bondholders may have prior claims over holders of other bonds. Many investors in railroad securities have learned of these possibilities the hard way.

From the corporation's view, bond debt creates low but inflexible fixed charges. These may be embarrassing in bad times. Preferred stock is slightly better with respect to flexibility; equity capital, best of all.[7]

THE GIANT CORPORATION

While one should not infer that all corporations go through these stages, we have now carried our successful toothpaste enterprise far enough up the ladder of success. The rest of this chapter will be concerned with the economic position and power of the very large modern corporation and the problems that it creates for the American economy. It is these which play the dominant role in today's economy.

A list of the 200 largest nonfinancial corporations reads like an honor roll of American business, almost every name being a familiar household word. Among the industrial companies will be United States Steel, Bethlehem Steel, and the Aluminum Company of America; Standard Oil of New Jersey, of California, of Indiana; the Texas Company; General Motors, Chrysler, and Ford; Swift and Armour meat packing; American (Tobacco) Brands (Luckies) and R. J. Reynolds (Camels); The Great Atlantic & Pacific Tea Company, Sears, Montgomery Ward, F. W. Woolworth, and J. C. Penney; Kraftco, Borden; Procter & Gamble, Lever Brothers; IBM, Xerox, Boeing; and many others.

Among the railroads are such old stand-bys as Penn Central, Southern Pacific, and many others. The public-utility list is headed by AT&T. If we go on to add the largest financial

---

[7] Interest charges can also be deducted for tax purposes from the corporation earnings. There is an incentive, therefore, other things being equal, to use debt rather than stock financing.

organizations, we bring in such giants as the Bank of America (California), First National City Bank (New York), the Chase Manhattan Bank, the Continental Illinois National Bank (Chicago), and the First National Bank of Boston; the Metropolitan Life Insurance Company, Prudential Life, Equitable Life; etc. Altogether there are now almost 200 companies with assets above the billion-dollar mark!

The tremendous concentration of economic power involved in giant corporations may be gauged from the following facts: The largest 100 nonfinancial corporations own 45 per cent of the total assets of that group; the 50 largest banks own 40 per cent of all banking assets. The 50 largest insurance companies own 83 per cent of all life-insurance assets. The largest 200 corporations hold about one-fourth of income-producing national wealth. They employ one out of every eight workers. The 500 largest United States industrial corporations have more than half the sales in manufacturing and mining and get more than 70 per cent of the profits. Five industrial corporations each handle more money than any one of our 50 states does.

The power of large corporations did not grow overnight. After 1900 their percentage importance gradually rose. In the 1920s local public utilities were gathered together into vast regional networks, in itself a move toward greater technological efficiency. As the country grew mightily in the recovery from the Great Depression and in World War II, the largest corporations grew too.

In the 1960s there was a speed-up in the merger movement, particularly in connection with take-overs by "conglomerates," which brought under one roof scores of companies belonging to quite unrelated industries. The giants meet on diverse battlefields: Du Pont and Standard Oil compete in petrochemicals and once again in insecticides and fertilizers. Who are Textron's rivals? Textile firms which compete with its synthetics plants? Or Boeing and McDonnell-Douglas, which compete with its helicopter divisions? Or a dozen quite different industries?

Large size breeds success, and success breeds further success. But there are also economic and political barriers to largeness. The statistical evidence on profits suggests that profits increase with size but that the very biggest firms in an industry sometimes seem to show a slight dropping off of relative profits compared with the next to the largest.[8] Statistics suggest that, relatively, the giants have probably lost a little ground since 1900, when the "trust movement" had not yet run afoul of the Sherman Antitrust Act (1890). And just as a hotel may be always full—but with different people—so do we find the list of biggest corporations to be a changing one, but at a very slow rate.

DIVORCE OF OWNERSHIP AND CONTROL IN THE LARGE CORPORATION

Let us examine the internal workings of one of these giant corporations. *The most striking feature is the diversification of ownership among thousands and thousands of small stockholders.* In 1970 more than 3 million different people had shares in AT&T. To be sure, half these people had less than 15 shares each; one-quarter of the shares were held in blocks of less than 100 shares; and no single owner has as much as 1 per cent

[8]A larger percentage of small firms than of large firms falls in the class of firms making losses.

of the total. The Stock Exchange has a goal of "people's capitalism," in which the masses have appreciable ownership of society's capital. While more than 27 million people do own some common stocks, still less than 1 in 10 gets an appreciable return.

In a pathbreaking study,[9] Berle and Means pointed out that this wide diversification of stockholding has resulted in a *separation of ownership and control.* Recent studies show that in the typical giant corporation, all management together—officers and directors—holds only about 3 per cent of the outstanding common stock. The largest single minority ownership groups typically hold only about a fifth of all voting stock. Such a small fraction has been deemed more than enough to maintain "working control."[10]

LEADERSHIP AND CONTROL OF THE LARGE CORPORATION

The problem of keeping a large corporation truly democratic is a difficult one. Until recent years, a few dozen stockholders would turn up for the annual meeting. More recently, many hundreds have been attending some meetings.

Decisions at the annual meeting are really settled by use of "proxies." Each stockholder is asked to mail in a proxy permitting the management to exercise his votes. Some do not reply; but enough usually do to establish a quorum and a comfortable plurality for management. The SEC has tried to improve the democratic structure of corporations by insisting that motions to be decided at the annual meeting be indicated on the proxy statement so that stockholders can indicate their preferences; also, rival groups must be permitted mailing access to the stockholders, and so forth.

Prior to recent years, most managements could be said to be self-perpetuating. Whether the corporation runs well or poorly, whether the managers work efficiently or not, the typical small stockholder could do little about it. He could rubber-stamp approval or relieve his feelings by not voting. In either case management went undisturbed.

Recently there has been a slight change. Thanks to the SEC rules, some challenging minority groups have attempted—and successfully attempted!—to oust the in-group and put themselves in as new managers. Thus, the late Robert Young ran a tremendous campaign—using all the devices of modern publicity—to oust the New York Central railroad officers. And he did succeed in winning majority support. Similar battles have taken place in connection with United Fruit and Montgomery Ward.

In a sense, therefore, we can hope that democratic control of corporations by stock owners has increased. But competent observers still insist that, barring blatant incom-

[9]A. A. Berle, Jr., and Gardner C. Means, *The Modern Corporation and Private Property* (Commerce Clearing House, New York, 1932). See R. A. Gordon, *Business Leadership in the Large Corporation* (Brookings Institution, Washington, 1945), Chap. II. R. J. Larner in a 1966 *American Economic Review* study has shown that the Berle-Means thesis on separation of ownership and control was even truer in the 1960s than in 1929: whereas 6 of the 200 largest corporations were privately owned (80 per cent or more of stock) in 1929, in 1963 there were none; and 84.5 per cent of the firms had no group of stockholders owning as much as 10 per cent!

[10]You can even pyramid control by owning one-fifth of a million-dollar company, which owns one-fifth of a 5-million-dollar company, and so forth. Such a pyramid of so-called "holding companies" can give control over billions to small ownership at the base.

petence, management can often count on remaining in office; and often the proxy battle is fought to determine which minority group shall control.[11]

A MANAGERIAL REVOLUTION?

Who makes corporate decisions? Primarily, the increasingly important class of *professional managers*—what Galbraith calls the "technostructure." The old-time captain of industry, for all his creativeness and ability to calculate the risks necessary to build up a great enterprise, often had something of the buccaneer in his makeup and "the-public-be-damned" attitude. In company after company, the original founder has been replaced by a new type of executive, usually having a different surname. He is less likely to be a self-made man than a graduate of Harvard Business School; he will probably have acquired special training and management skills. The new professional executive is more adept at public relations and in the handling of people. He is necessarily more the "bureaucrat," often interested as much in preserving the status quo as in taking risks.

Typically, the dominant man will be the president of the corporation. As he begins to feel his years, he may be made chairman of the board of directors, who, together with a small executive or steering committee of the board of directors, gives advice and approval to the actions of the president and his many vice-presidents.

The exact role of the board of directors varies from company to company and from group to group. Some directors are simply well-known men selected to give prestige. Others are insiders with special knowledge who take an active part in determining policy. On the whole, it would be going too far to say that most boards of directors act simply as rubber stamps to approve the decisions already taken by the officers of the company. But it is true that, so long as management possesses the confidence of the board, that body will usually not actively intervene to dictate specific policies. This is the same administrative procedure usually followed by the board of trustees of a philanthropic foundation or college, and is not too unlike the parliamentary system of ministerial responsibility in Great Britain and elsewhere.

Generally speaking, there will be no clash of goals between the management and stockholders. Both will be interested in maximizing the profits of the firm—to wit, the growth in earnings and market price per share. But in two important situations there may be a divergence of interests, not infrequently settled in favor of management. First, insiders may vote themselves and friends or relatives large salaries, expense accounts, bonuses, retirement pensions, and stock options at the stockholders' expense.[12]

---

[11] A dissatisfied stockholder can always sell his shares and buy into another company. If enough stockholders do so, the company will find it hard ever to raise capital by selling a new issue; the fall in its share prices may depress the value of "stock options" issued to company executives as a tax-loophole bonus and could galvanize other stockholders into a proxy revolt.

[12] Other conflicts can involve outright cheating: executives may take bribes, throw business to their own companies, or violate SEC rules by using inside knowledge and spreading false rumors to make market profits on the company's stock. A recent president of Chrysler had to resign when it was discovered he had secret ownership in a supplying firm. An insurance executive came under fire for joining privately in a tax deal with a company the insurance company had dealings with. Such cases are rare, but not rare enough.

A second conflict of interest may arise in connection with undistributed profits. The managers of every organization have an understandable tendency to try to make it grow and perpetuate itself. The psychological reasons are subtle and by no means always selfish. In some cases when profits are plowed back into a company, there is reason to suspect that the same capital could better be invested by the stockholders elsewhere or spent upon consumption. Indeed, the case occasionally arises when a company would be well advised to wind itself up and pay back its capital. But a cynic might doubt that management is likely to vote itself out of existence and out of jobs.

THE NEW INDUSTRIAL STATE

Thorstein Veblen, radical son of the Midwest soil at the turn of the century, had looked forward to a time when engineers would run the price system. John Kenneth Galbraith has in our time become the philosopher of the new industrial state. In his words:[13]

. . . the influence of the technostructure of the mature firm extends to *shaping the demand* for its particular product or range of products. . . . [emphasis added]

Paralleling these changes, partly as a result and partly as a cause, has been a profound shift in the locus of economic and political power. The financier and the union leader are dwindling influences in the society. They are honored more for their past eminence than for their present power. The technostructure exercises much less direct political power than did the antecedent entrepreneur. But that is because it has far more influence as an arm of the bureaucracy and in its influence on the larger climate of belief. The scientific, technical, organizational and planning needs of the technostructure have brought into being a large educational and scientific estate.

THE EVIL OF MONOPOLY

In view of all the above facts, it is not surprising to find that most important American industries are characterized by a few large corporations whose share of the output of that particular industry is vastly greater than their numerical importance would warrant. Figure 5-1 gives a list of some large American industries and depicts their degree of concentration by showing the relative proportion of total industry shipments controlled by the first four dominant corporations and by the next four.

In Part Three we shall analyze some of the problems raised by monopoly and imperfect competition. In the past century, particularly since the 1890 Sherman Antitrust Act, there has been great concern over the breaking down of free competitive markets under the encroachment of large-scale enterprise. In recent years officials of General Electric, Westinghouse, and other electric suppliers were even sent to jail for colluding on monopoly price setting.

From an economic point of view it does not much matter which of the following monopolistic devices causes price to be too high: (1) mergers of competing firms, (2) cooperative "pools" or "cartel agreements," (3) so-called "trusts" (involving selected "trustees" who "coordinate" pricing policy), (4) interlocking directorates, (5) "holding-

---

[13]John Kenneth Galbraith, *The New Industrial State* (Houghton Mifflin, Boston, 1967), p. 320.

company" control, (6) tacit collusion and trade-association action, (7) government "fair price" legislation (Robinson-Patman Act, etc.) and government-sponsored "commodity agreements" (wheat, rubber, cotton, etc.).

Too high a price, wastage of resources,[14] and creation of monopoly profits are economic evils, however brought about and whatever the legal technicalities of the matter. This we shall study in Part Three, but a brief preview can be presented here.

THE CURSE OF BIGNESS?

Is bigness itself a bad thing? Undoubtedly there is much popular hostility toward large corporations. Even if they could do so, General Motors or United States Steel would be most reluctant to swallow up competitors until they accounted for, say, nine-tenths of their respective industries. They would fear the effect on public opinion. Is this antagonism toward big business directed toward bigness itself? Or against the alleged evils of monopoly that are often

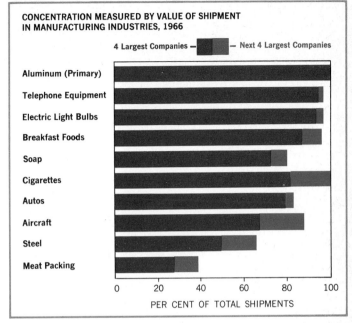

Some industries are dominated by a very few sellers:

CONCENTRATION MEASURED BY VALUE OF SHIPMENT IN MANUFACTURING INDUSTRIES, 1966

4 Largest Companies — ■ ■ — Next 4 Largest Companies

Aluminum (Primary), Telephone Equipment, Electric Light Bulbs, Breakfast Foods, Soap, Cigarettes, Autos, Aircraft, Steel, Meat Packing

PER CENT OF TOTAL SHIPMENTS 0 20 40 60 80 100

FIG. 5-1. In aluminum, autos, steel, and many other industries, a few firms get most of the business. This is in contrast to the notion of perfect competition among innumerable small sellers (e.g., farmers), each too small to affect the market price. But MIT's expert M. A. Adelman thinks industry concentration was probably even greater back in 1900. (Source: U.S. Census.)

supposed to be associated with bigness? What should public policy be toward a "benevolent, well-behaving, efficient" giant corporation?

The so-called "A & P" case provides an example. This chain of food stores was noted for its low prices. Yet the Department of Justice prosecuted it under the antitrust acts. Leaving aside certain minor irregularities that the company may have engaged in, the basic issue was clearly posed: Shall it be a crime to grow large as a result of efficiency and continued maintenance of low, competitive prices? The federal courts seemed almost to answer, Yes. Fortunately, as Chapter 26 shows, this trend is abating.

Another example shows that policy problems are not easy. In the mid-fifties there was a rash of mergers; e.g., in the auto industry Nash combined with Hudson, and Studebaker with Packard. Often there was a "tax angle" to the merger; but in some cases, firms merged in order to try to become more efficient, so as to be able to compete with General Motors and Ford. Do such mergers—even though they undoubtedly increase the size of the merged units—really *reduce* competition rather than increase it? (Was the Attorney General wrong in forbidding a merger between Bethlehem and Youngstown steel com-

[14]Undertakers provide a case in point: People generally, including poor people, pay in some regions an average of $900 per complete funeral! But so many undertaking establishments come into existence that—as in New York—each handles only about one funeral per week, or 56 per year, to be exact!

panies? Was the Interstate Commerce Commission right in permitting the C & O railroad to merge with the B & O? Not easy questions to answer.)

To produce an atomic bomb, the government turned to the Du Pont Company and gave it a cost-plus-one-dollar contract. The scientific know-how of General Electric and Western Electric is invaluable for peace as well as war. In the words of Schumpeter, a world-famous economist who died in 1950:[15]

The modern standard of life of the masses evolved during the period of relatively unfettered "big business." If we list the items that enter the modern workman's budget and from 1899 on observe the course of their prices not in terms of money but in terms of the hours of labor that will buy them—i.e., each year's money prices divided by each year's hourly wage rates, we cannot fail to be struck by the rate of the advance which, considering the spectacular improvement in qualities, seems to have been greater and not smaller than it ever was before. . . . Nor is this all. As soon as we go into details and inquire into the individual items in which progress was most conspicuous, the trail leads not to the doors of those firms that work under conditions of comparatively free competition but precisely to the doors of the large concerns—which, as in the case of agricultural machinery, also account for much of the progress in the competitive sector—and a shocking suspicion dawns upon us that big business may have had more to do with creating that standard of life than keeping it down.

This suggests that the future problem may not be one of choosing between large monopolistic corporations and small-scale competitors, but rather that of devising ways to improve the social and economic performance of large corporate aggregates. To keep the tremendously creative abilities of the modern large-scale corporation working toward the public good—that must be the goal for the years ahead.

The so-called "military-industrial complex" must not be allowed to call the tune. In a system of true voter and consumer sovereignty it must dance to the music the people prescribe.

We shall study the problem of the maintenance of "effective and workable competition" after Part Three's analysis of prices and cost under perfect and imperfect competition.

SUMMARY

1   The present population of American businesses has grown up as a result of a cumulative excess of business births over business deaths. The great majority of businesses consist of infinitesimal single proprietorships, largely in retail and service establishments. Their turnover is rapid.

[15]J. A. Schumpeter, *Capitalism, Socialism and Democracy* (Harper, New York, 1942). Whatever the merits of the Schumpeter thesis, it is still true that there have been great productivity changes in competitive agriculture; that many basic inventions come from independent persons or small companies; and that there is no evidence of an upswing in inventiveness during the 1890s, a decade of monopoly concentration. Reference will be made later to Galbraith's doctrine of "countervailing power" in *American Capitalism* (Houghton Mifflin, Boston, 1952). It is there argued that big units do characterize American life, but that "big labor" checks big business, and vice versa; that big Sears and A & P check their big suppliers, and so a kind of a tolerable equilibrium is achieved, albeit not one of a competitive type. Part Three studies E. H. Chamberlin's imperfect competition.

2   One should understand how an enterprise grows, its needs and avenues for short-term or long-term capital, and the advantages and disadvantages of the corporate form over the single proprietorship and partnership.

3   One should also be acquainted with the fundamental legal rights involved in the corporation and with the general features of bonds and of preferred and common stocks.

4   Problems created by the separation of ownership and control and by the concentration of economic wealth and monopoly power in the modern giant corporation deserve serious study. (Part Three will discuss imperfect competition and antitrust policies.)

Accounting is a great help to the understanding of economics, and its fundamental principles are presented briefly in the Appendix to this chapter.

QUESTIONS FOR DISCUSSION

1   Imagine you are starting a business of your own. Write its case history.

2   Compare the advantages and disadvantages of (a) the single proprietorship, (b) the partnership, and (c) the corporate form of business organization.

3   List ways of raising capital for small, medium, and large businesses.

4   What are the advantages and disadvantages of different securities?

5   Discuss the structure of the large modern corporation. The "military-industrial complex."

6   What is meant by calling ours the age of the "Managerial or Bureaucratic Revolution"? Does this apply outside government?

7   Give examples of conflict of interest between stockholders and management. Of coincident interests. Of problems of democratic control.

8   Defend "bigness as such." Attack it. What evils might accompany it?

9   What are the economic evils of monopoly? Give examples.

Review your understanding of the following concepts:

single proprietorship
partnership
corporation
unlimited and limited liability
investment underwriting
Securities and Exchange Commission (SEC), SBA
corporate, personal income tax

bonds; common, preferred stocks; hybrids
proxy, minority control
director, executive, technostructure
forms of monopoly control
conglomerate mergers, collusion
evils of monopoly
possible dynamic advantages of bigness

APPENDIX: Elements of Accounting

In this "age of accounts" some literacy in accounting has become a prime necessity.

THE BALANCE SHEET

We begin with the two fundamental accounting statements: the Balance Sheet and the Statement of Profit and Loss (or the so-called "Income Statement").

The Balance Sheet is presented in a report, usually annually. It represents an instantaneous "still picture" of the condition of the enterprise on some particular day, usually the last day of the year. Corresponding to the dollar value of every *asset*—tangible or intangible—there must necessarily be an exactly equal total amount of *claims or ownership*. The value of a $40,000 house is exactly matched by somebody's claim to its ownership consisting, say, of $25,000 owed a creditor and $15,000 owned by its owner.

This is the fundamental identity underlying every Balance Sheet:

Value of assets = value of total claims or
                    ownership
              = value of liabilities (owed)
                + value of proprietorship
                  (owned)

or

Assets = Liabilities + Net Worth

Let us illustrate this by considering a simple Balance Sheet, as shown in Table 5-1; this lists Assets on the left and on the right Liabilities and Net Worth for a new company whose operations have just begun.

A blank space has been deliberately left next to the Common Stock Net Worth item because you should realize that the only correct entry compatible with our fundamental Balance-Sheet truism is $200,000. A Balance Sheet must always balance—because Net Worth, i.e., ownership of the "residual claimants," always adjusts itself to make a balance.

To illustrate this, suppose a thief steals all the cash, and a fire burns up one-half the inventory. The accountant will learn of this sad news without turning a hair. "Total Assets are down $60,000 all told; Liabilities remain unchanged. Very well, I must write down total Net Worth by $60,000, to only $190,000." Such is his way of keeping score.

A number of interesting facts are revealed by even this simple Balance Sheet. First, it is customary to divide up Assets according to whether they will be convertible into cash by normal operations within a year or not, the first category being called Current Assets and the second Fixed Assets. The Liabilities can also be subdivided into Current and Long-term Liabilities, depending upon whether they come due in less than a year.

Here is something to be emphasized about a Balance Sheet: Although its two sides must balance *in total*, yet no single item on one side is matched by an item on the other side. Thus, Bonds do not correspond in

A Balance Sheet is a point-of-time picture showing that Assets = Liabilities + Net Worth:

BALANCE SHEET OF PEPTO-GLITTER, INC., (DECEMBER 31, 1975)			
ASSETS		**LIABILITIES AND NET WORTH**	
		Liabilities	
Current Assets:		**Current Liabilities:**	
Cash	$ 20,000	Accounts Payable	$ 20,000
Inventory	80,000	Notes Payable	30,000
Fixed Assets:		**Long-term Liabilities:**	
Equipment	130,000	SBA Note	50,000
Buildings	170,000	Bonds Payable	50,000
		Net Worth	
		Capital:	
		Preferred Stock	50,000
		Common Stock	. . . . . .
Total	$400,000	Total	$400,000

TABLE 5-1.

value to the Equipment or Buildings, nor do Capital items correspond to Cash. The only correct statement about a Balance Sheet is that creditors have a general claim of a definite value against the enterprise, and owners have a residual claim against the rest.

Most of the specific items listed are more or less self-explanatory. Cash consists of coins, currency, and money on deposit in the bank. Cash is the only asset whose value is exact rather than an estimate. All other valuations involve some guesswork, albeit careful guesswork. Moreover, all accounting valuations must be made relative to the actual intended purpose or use of the asset in question. If a business is a going concern and not in the process of liquidation, the accountant will be careful not to value doubtful assets at the low figure they would bring at a forced sale; he rather will value them at their worth to the company in its normal operation.

Inventory, consisting in the case of our toothpaste company of sugar, chemicals, tubing, raw materials, and other goods in process, can be valued in many different ways. Many conservative companies use original cost of the inventories or present market value, whichever is lower. Especially difficult problems arise when the prices of materials vary from month to month. Should we figure the chemical cost of the toothpaste at the original price of the ingredients actually used, which of course were bought some time ago when prices were different? Or should we figure, as our cost, the price that must *now* be paid for the chemicals to replace those being used up? An elementary discussion cannot go into these two possible methods of inventory valuation.[1] Obviously, it will make a great difference in stated profits during a time of inflation or deflation which of these two methods is used. It also will make a difference in income taxes. Therefore the government is compelled to say, "Use whichever method you wish, but having made up your mind, stick to it." So much for inventories.

If we assume that the Equipment and Buildings items were bought just at the end of 1975, the date of the Balance Sheet, then their Balance-Sheet values will be listed equal to their purchase price. This follows a fundamental accounting rule or convention: "At time of purchase a thing is presumed worth what the enterprise pays for it." However, as we shall see in connection with the Income Statement and the next year's Balance Sheet, hard problems are involved in deciding how to evaluate exactly equipment and buildings that have depreciated through use and age.

[1] Accounting texts refer to them as "First-in-first-out" (FIFO) and "Last-in-first-out" (LIFO) and analyze them in detail.

On the Liabilities side, Accounts Payable are, as their name implies, the sums owed for goods bought and charged. Notes Payable are promissory notes owed to the banks or to a finance company. The SBA Note listed under the Long-term Liabilities is a 5-year loan advanced by, or guaranteed by, the federal Small Business Administration. The Bonds Payable are a long-term loan, floated at a 6 per cent coupon rate, and not due for 15 years. (NOTE: What appears as a Liability to this company may show up as an Asset to someone else; thus the creditors who own these bonds will carry them as left-hand–side Assets, "Bonds Receivable.")

Turning now to Net Worth items, we find that 500 shares of $100, 4 per cent, cumulative (nonparticipating) preferred stock have been issued; and 20,000 shares of no-par common stock were issued at $10 each.

This completes our first glance at a simple Balance Sheet.

THE STATEMENT OF PROFIT AND LOSS, OR INCOME STATEMENT

Now let time march on. During the following months, the firm is profitably engaged in producing and selling toothpaste. To show its flow of income over the 12 months of the year, we must turn to its Income Statement, or—as many companies prefer to call it—the Statement of Profit and Loss, Table 5-2, p. 98.

This is a statement which reports the following: (1) Pepto-Glitter's revenues from sales in 1976, (2) the expenses to be charged against those sales, and (3) the profit remaining after expenses have been deducted. That is,

Total Profit = Total Revenue minus Total Costs

(the fundamental identity of the Income Statement).

You will understand it better if at first you disregard the figures in the Manufacturing Cost of Goods Sold section (the indented figures) and look only at those in the right-hand column. Sales were $240,000; and the cost of manufacturing the goods sold came to $170,000. After deducting another $14,000 for Selling and Administrative Costs, $56,000 remained in Net Operating Profit. Out of this, a total of $6,000 + $17,500 in interest and taxes had to be paid, leaving $32,500 in Net Earnings after Taxes. Dividends of $2,000 on the preferred and $10,500 on the common were paid, leaving $20,000 of net profit (Addition to Surplus) retained in the business.

Now turn to the indented Manufacturing Cost of Goods Sold section, which lists the costs incurred in this part of the business. The firm's outlays for

The Income Statement gives flow of income over the year:

INCOME STATEMENT OF PEPTO-GLITTER, INC., (JANUARY 1, 1976, TO DECEMBER 31, 1976)		
Net Sales (after all discounts and rebates)		$240,000
Less: Manufacturing Cost of Goods Sold:		
Materials	$ 50,000	
Labor Cost	100,000	
Depreciation charges	20,000	
Miscellaneous Operating Cost	5,000	
Total Manufacturing Cost	$175,000	
Add: Beginning Inventory	80,000	
	$255,000	
Deduct: Closing Inventory	85,000	
Equals: Manufacturing Cost *of Goods Sold*	$170,000	170,000
Gross Profit (or Gross Margin)		$ 70,000
Less: Selling and Administrative Costs		14,000
Net Operating Profit		$ 56,000
Less: Fixed Interest Charges and State		
and Local Taxes		6,000
Net Earnings before Income Taxes		$ 50,000
Less: Corporation Income Taxes		17,500
Net Earnings after Taxes		$ 32,500
Less: Dividends on Preferred Stock		2,000
Net Profits of Common Stockholders		$ 30,500
Less: Dividends Paid on Common Stock		10,500
Addition to Surplus		$ 20,000

TABLE 5-2.

materials, labor, and miscellaneous expenses are listed, together with an item for Depreciation. (Depreciation is worth a section to itself, and we shall consider it soon.) The sum of these four items ($175,000) is the Total Manufacturing Cost. Then follows what may seem a puzzling adjustment. The value of the inventory on January 1 is added, and that of the year-end inventory is deducted. The result, which differs from Manufacturing Cost by $5,000, is the Manufacturing Cost *of Goods Sold*. What is the difference between these terms, and why this inventory adjustment?

Pepto-Glitter began the year with inventory of $80,000 in raw materials and finished goods. During the year, it built up inventories by an extra $5,000. In this case, it would be false to attribute all the manufacturing cost to *the goods actually sold*. Some of these costs are really attributable to goods to be sold *in the future*. To neglect this fact would be to overstate the Manufacturing Cost of Goods Sold in this year; it would mean subtracting too much from this year's Net Sales and understating this year's Profits.

If there had been no change in inventory, then all would be simple: Manufacturing Cost and Manufacturing Cost of Goods Sold would be identical.

On the other hand, what if we had had less inventory on hand at the year's end than at the beginning? Clearly, we would be fooling ourselves if we did not recognize that the cost of the goods we have sold this year ought really to be *greater* than the money we have paid out to labor and other firms. We would have neglected the cost element of used-up and unreplaced inventory.

Summary: To reach a valid figure for Manufacturing Cost of Goods Sold, we must adjust the Manufacturing Cost figure thus:

If the Closing Inventory shows an increase over the Beginning Inventory, deduct that increase; if the Closing Inventory has decreased, add that decrease.

Instead of subtracting $5,000 directly from the $175,000 total manufacturing expense, the accountant does it in two steps. Rather than working with the difference between the two, he first adds the total

Beginning Inventory, then subtracts the Closing Inventory. This procedure has the advantage of being standardized; it is the same whether inventory is up or down, whereas a single change-in-inventory figure would in some cases be a subtraction, in others an addition. And the accountant's method also reveals the change in inventory relative to the size of the total.

Note that items in Table 5-2 differ from Table 5-1's Balance-Sheet items. Income items refer to *flows* over time: moving-picture action. Balance-Sheet items refer to *stocks* at an instant of time: still pictures.

DEPRECIATION

At first, one may wonder why any Depreciation Charges have been made for 1976. The buildings and equipment were newly bought at the beginning of the year, and surely they will not have worn out already. (It will, of course, be necessary to spend money on men to maintain the equipment and keep the factories painted: but such wages are already included in Labor Cost or Miscellaneous Operating Cost and are not included in Depreciation Charges.)

Here is where the farseeing wisdom of the accountant comes to the fore. He points out that not a cent may have to be spent upon replacement of equipment for 10 years, at which time all the machines may *suddenly* have to be bought anew. It would be nonsense to charge nothing to depreciation for 9 years and fool yourself into thinking you are making a nice profit and then suddenly in the tenth year have to charge off all the value of the machines at once and think you have incurred a great loss in that year.

Actually, he points out, the equipment is *being used up all the time*. A truer, undistorted picture of net income or profit will be reached if the costs of the equipment are spread more evenly over its lifetime. The value of equipment declines as a result of age and use; it depreciates from its price as new to its final scrap value. In recognition of this, the accountant depreciates the value of fixed capital items by some *gradual* formula. Of the various proposed methods, here are two widely used ones.

The first is called "straight-line depreciation." Suppose that you have a truck whose cost new is $10,100 and whose economic life is 10 years; after this its physical life may continue but its economic life will be over, because of its unreliability and high maintenance costs. Suppose that its scrap value at the end of 10 years is $100. According to the straight-line method, you will each year charge off to depreciation one-tenth of the lifetime decline in its total value, $10,000 (new

price minus scrap value). Thus, $1,000 will be entered in Depreciation Charges every year.

A second method of more rapid early depreciation has become fashionable, especially since tax laws now permit generous use of it. Instead of writing off a new asset steadily by the straight-line method, firms can use the "declining-balance method," or—what is somewhat similar in its generosity toward fast early depreciation—the "sum-of-the-digits" method. Only the first will be described in this brief treatment.

Disregarding scrap value as negligible, consider the 10-year $10,000 truck. Instead of taking one-tenth its value for depreciation in the first year, the tax law lets you charge off, under the declining-balance method, twice that amount, or 2×10 per cent = 20 per cent in its first year. So you get a much larger deduction for tax purposes. Evidently you cannot go on charging off that amount for each year of life, since that would leave you with zero value by the halfway point, at the end of 5 years. What the declining-balance method does is to let you take off 20 per cent of *remaining* value or balance each year. In the second year, then, you take off 20 per cent of the $8,000 of remaining value, or $1,600. In the third year you take off 20 per cent of what is left, namely, of $6,400. So the process goes. It can be calculated that by the time the asset has reached half the length of its useful life, you have been permitted to write off for tax purposes almost two-thirds its value—rather than one-half, as under the straight-line method. It is later in life that the declining-balance method begins to be less generous in order to compensate for its early generosity.[2]

Although depreciation is usually figured by some apparently exact formula, every accountant knows that the estimates are really very rough, being subject to large and unpredictable errors and involving arbitrary corrections and assumptions. He comforts himself with two thoughts: (1) A rough method of depreciation, like an imperfect watch, is often better than none at all. (2) Mistakes in depreciation will ultimately "come out in the wash" anyway.

Let us see why a mistake in depreciation ultimately tends to correct itself. Suppose that the truck lasts 15 years rather than the predicted 10. We have then been

---

[2] A quite different method, called the "service-unit method," or "unit-of-production method," can be mentioned only briefly here. According to this we should estimate the number of miles, loads, or service units that the truck will perform in its life. Thus, if the truck goes a million miles in 10 years and its loss of value during that time is $10,000, then each mile used up represents about 1 cent.

overstating our depreciation *expenses* during the first 10 years. But in the eleventh and later years there will be *no* depreciation charged on the truck at all, since it has already been written down to its scrap value by the end of the tenth year. Our profits in these later years tend, therefore, to be overstated by about as much as they were understated in the earlier years. After 15 years, everything is pretty much the same after all. That is, except for taxes. Different methods of depreciation result in a different apparent distribution of earnings over time, and therefore in a different pattern over time of corporation income taxes. Naturally, a businessman prefers a method of depreciation that will make his income average out more steady over time, so as to keep his effective tax rate as low as possible and permit him to cancel off losses against profits; and he also likes a fast method (such as the declining balance) that enables him to *put off* the evil day of taxes as far as possible.

This explains why so many corporations took advantage of the government's emergency offer to let them amortize (or depreciate) their defense plants and equipment over 5 years. They were glad to be able, by charging high depreciation expenses, to reduce their stated profits during the defense emergency when their profits were enormous. They much preferred to take advantage of this "accelerated depreciation" plan so as to shift their profits from those emergency years to later years when it was hoped that corporation tax rates would be lower.

The Treasury will not let a corporation manipulate its Depreciation Charges to avoid taxes. The company may select *any reasonable* method; once having made its choice, it must stick to it.

Many people are today worried about the harmful effects of taxation on "venture capital." They argue, we shall get more investment in new tools and create more jobs if the Treasury is more liberal in letting companies depreciate their equipment rapidly, thereby saving on taxes and enjoying the same advantages that European countries bestow on our competitors. In the 1960s the Kennedy administration introduced an "investment tax credit," which actually gave a subsidy to firms that invest in new equipment. This tax credit could be turned on and off to stabilize investment but was repealed by the Nixon administration during the Vietnam inflation.

THE RELATION BETWEEN THE INCOME STATEMENT AND THE BALANCE SHEET

Now we must relate the description by the Income Statement of what has happened during the year to the Balance Sheets at the beginning and end of the

year. Table 5-3 shows the Balance Sheet of our toothpaste corporation at the end of its first year of operation. It has prospered. Net Worth, the difference between Total Assets and Total Liabilities, has increased between the beginning and end of the accounting period by $20,000—from $250,000 to $270,000. The amount of this increase, as seen by comparing Balance Sheets, just equals the earnings or profits *available* to the common stockholders but not paid out to them in dividends, or as we saw at the bottom of the Income Statement, just equal to $30,500 minus $10,500, or $20,000 of undistributed profits.

Some Net Worth item must be written up by $20,000. It would clearly never do to increase the Preferred Stock Capital Account, because such stockholders are not the residual claimants to the profits of the corporation and no new stock has been sold. Conceivably, one could add the $20,000 to the Common Stock Capital Account. However, this is not done. Instead, the Common Stock Capital Account is left at its original par or issued value.

It is more informative to create a new account called Surplus—or sometimes Earned Surplus or Earnings Retained in the Business—to show how much of the increase in "book value" or Net Worth has resulted from accumulated undistributed earnings plowed back through the years.

In many ways Surplus is a misleading word. It sounds like something extra or unnecessary, or too often like a spare chunk of cash which the company's workers or stockholders might hope to stage a raid against. Actually, Surplus is distinctly not an Assets account, much less a pool of liquid cash. It simply indicates a part of the ownership—over and above Liabilities to creditors and original subscribed capital ownership—in the polyglot Assets of the corporation. A glance at Table 5-3 shows us that the $20,000 of Surplus is not matched by an equivalent amount of cash on the Assets side.

We must again warn against trying to link *specific* items on the two sides of the Balance Sheet. Only the final *totals* correspond. It is not even possible to say exactly how the $20,000 plowed back into the business, or added to Surplus, was used. An addition to Surplus must be associated with an increase in Assets and/or a decrease in Liabilities—that is all we can say.

It would be an equal mistake to think that the profits of a corporation accrue in the form of cash, so that on the last day of the year, just before the board of directors decided upon its dividend rate, there was some $30,500 of cash on hand, available either for the stockholders or to be reinvested in the business. In the case of our toothpaste company, the very hand-

After the year's operations, we get a new Balance Sheet:

BALANCE SHEET OF PEPTO-GLITTER, INC., (DECEMBER 31, 1976)

ASSETS			LIABILITIES AND NET WORTH		
			Liabilities		
Current Assets:			**Current Liabilities:**		
Cash		$ 17,000	Accounts Payable		$ 10,000
Inventory		85,000	Notes Payable		17,000
Sinking Fund to Replace Equipment		5,000	Reserve for Taxes		21,000
(U.S. government bonds)					
Fixed Assets:			**Long-term Liabilities:**		
Equipment	$130,000		SBA Note		50,000
Less: Allowance (or Reserve)			Bonds Payable		50,000
for Depreciation	15,000				
		115,000			
Buildings	$170,000		*Net Worth*		
Less: Allowance (or Reserve)			**Capital Stock:**		
for Depreciation	5,000		Preferred Stock		50,000
		165,000	Common Stock		200,000
Intangible Assets:			**Surplus:**		20,000
Patents		10,000			
Good Will		21,000			
Total		$418,000	Total		$418,000

TABLE 5-3.

some profit earned was largely embodied in the form of new noncash Assets and lowered Liabilities; not very much more than $10,500 could have been paid out as cash dividends without forcing serious changes in the financial decisions of the company—decisions such as to borrow more, to grow more slowly, to sell off some of the equipment and inventory at a loss, or to operate with a ludicrously low cash balance.

SUMMARY OF ELEMENTARY ACCOUNTING RELATIONS

Before taking a last look at the new complexities introduced in the 1976 Balance Sheet over that of 1975, we may briefly summarize the relationship between Balance Sheets and Income Statements:

1. The Balance Sheet indicates an instantaneous financial picture: it is like a measure of the stock of water in a lake.

2. The Income Statement shows the flow of sales, cost, and revenue over the year or accounting period: it measures the flow of water in and out of the lake.

3. The change in total Net Worth between the be-

ginning and the end of the period—as shown by comparing the new and old Balance Sheets—is also to be understood from an examination of the changes in Surplus as appended at the end of Table 5-2's Income Statement: the change in the lake's level over the year we can relate to the flows during this year. (If new common stock is sold, that will be revealed by comparing the two Balance Sheets.)

There do remain, however, certain changes in the Balance-Sheet items from their previous levels in the earlier period to which the intervening Income Statement gives no clue. A closer look at the December 31, 1976 Balance Sheet will therefore prove instructive, although enough has been said already to introduce the reader to the fundamentals of accounting.

RESERVES AND FUNDS

The new Balance Sheet looks much like the old for the most part; but some new items are present for the first time. The last of these new items, Surplus, we have already explained. Among the Liabilities there is a new item called Reserve for Taxes of $21,000. It is not hard to understand. The taxes that the corporation will have to pay the government are as much short-term Liabilities as the Accounts Payable or Notes Payable.

Taxes Payable might have been a better title, since the word "Reserve" suggests a pool of cash, which it decidedly is not. Instead, the Reserve for Taxes is simply an earmarking of part of the Total Assets of the company for a special creditor—a reminder that the owners' Net Worth is less by the amount of owed taxes. We shall soon see there are three main kinds of "Reserves," and no one represents a pool of cash or liquid Assets.

Let us turn to the Assets side for new items.[3] The first stranger, entitled "Sinking Fund to Replace Equipment," is listed midway between the Current and Fixed Assets. It is an asset consisting of, say, 6 per cent government bonds which are to be held for the purpose of ultimately providing part of the money to buy new machines when the old ones are to be replaced. Although the corporation could change its mind and use the Sinking Fund bonds for another purpose, it presumably will not choose to do so. The nature of this Sinking Fund is understandable; it is simply a pool of liquid Assets set aside for a specific future purpose.

Allowance for depreciation   Turning to the Fixed Assets, we find ourselves in for a surprise. From our previous discussion of the Depreciation Charges of the Income Statement, we should have expected the Buildings and Equipment items to total $280,000. Why? Because at the beginning of the year they added up to $300,000, because no new equipment was bought during the year, and because the Income Statement told us that $20,000 of depreciation accrued during the period as part of the necessary costs of production.

Why, then, are these Fixed Assets carried on the new Balance Sheet at the old $130,000 and $170,000 figures? Looking more closely, we see that they really are not. From the $130,000 nominal Equipment valuation, there is subtracted a $15,000 Allowance (or Reserve) for Depreciation, so that really only $115,000 is carried for Equipment. Similarly, from the $170,000 original value of the Buildings, there is subtracted a $5,000 Allowance for Depreciation. Our faith in the accountant's sanity is restored; but we may wonder why he

goes through this roundabout procedure of stating "two" as "four minus two" instead of simply as "two."

Actually, he has his good reasons. An honest accountant knows his Depreciation estimate is only the roughest of guesses. Were he simply to guess and put down the final figure of $115,000 for Equipment, the public would not know how much reliance to place upon the figure. So he puts down $130,000 of original value, which is firmly rooted in the solid fact of original cost; and he then carefully isolates his own guessed-at Allowance for Depreciation. Then the public is in a better position to evaluate the reliability of the final $115,000 figure. The roundabout procedure does no harm, and may do good.

Now we know the precise meaning of Allowances (or Reserves) for Depreciation. They are not sums of money; they are not sinking funds of liquid Assets that can be spent on replacement. They are *subtractions from overstated Assets figures*. Thus, the Allowance for Depreciation of Buildings of $5,000 is an explicit correction of the original value of the Buildings, which would be an overstatement of the value left in them. This correction must be made to keep Assets and Net Worth from both being artificially inflated.

It must be made regardless of whether at the same time any money is or is not being set aside into sinking funds to replace the Depreciation asset. Note that there is no Sinking Fund for Buildings and that the Sinking Fund to Replace Equipment is only one-third as large as the estimated Allowance for Depreciation of Equipment. As a matter of fact, American businesses rarely set aside any considerable sums of money in replacement sinking funds. This is because liquid gilt-edge bonds earn at most only a few per cent interest, whereas capital invested in the firm's own activities usually brings in much more.[4]

We have met two kinds of Reserves: (1) a Liability Reserve, like that for taxes, which is really simply a liability of fairly certain amount, and (2) an Asset Valuation Reserve like that for Depreciation (or allowance for estimated uncollectible bills), which is really

---

[3]Neither this Balance Sheet nor the previous one contains a frequently met Current Assets item, Prepaid Expenses. Often an enterprise will pay its rent or buy some supplies a number of months in advance. Very properly, the enterprise is regarded as possessing on its Balance Sheet an equivalent asset.

[4]Where, then, will the money be coming from to replace any particular machine or building if no sinking funds have been set aside? Ordinarily, the equipment can be purchased with sales dollars earned by *other* equipment that is not currently calling for replacement expenditure. The selling price of the output of such other equipment contains an accounting allowance for depreciation expense, and a corresponding sum of money is available for investment elsewhere in the business. Speaking somewhat loosely, we may say that each asset not needing replacement lends its Depreciation Charges to those which need replacement, knowing that it too will be taken care of when the need arises.

simply a subtraction from an overstated asset. A third so-called "Surplus Reserve," which is also not to be confused with a sum of money, may be mentioned: Sometimes a firm takes part of its Surplus and sets it aside under a different name so that stockholders will not be tempted to lobby for higher dividend payments. For example, our toothpaste company might earmark half of its $20,000 Surplus account into a Reserve for Research and Development. This $10,000 Reserve would no more consist of cash or liquid funds than does Surplus itself, or than does any other kind of Reserve. It should never be confused with a fund.[5]

This completes the *fundamentals* of accounting. The rest of the Appendix deals with further issues.

INTANGIBLE ASSETS

Only one further new category of Assets can still be found on the December 31, 1976, Balance Sheet. To illustrate that an asset need not be a tangible commodity, a piece of equipment, or a sum of money, a patent has been introduced into the picture. Suppose it is a patent on a profitable new chemical process, giving us exclusive production rights for 17 years.

Such a patent is obviously worth money. Of course, as 5, 10, 12, and 16 years pass, the patent will be coming near to the end of its 17-year life and will be declining in value. Therefore, some depreciation formula will be applied to it just as if it were a truck.

Good Will and monopoly earning power   So much for Patents as an illustration of an intangible asset. Let us suppose that, at the same time we bought the patent, we also took over a rival toothpaste company. This horizontal combination will presumably add to our monopoly position and earning power. Therefore we were willing to buy the company for more than its trifling Assets—which happened to consist solely of a little inventory—were worth. Perhaps part of the purchase price went as profits to those who promoted this little monopolistic merger.

An example of the capitalization of earning power is J. P. Morgan's formation of the giant United States Steel Corporation at the turn of the century. He bought out the Andrew Carnegie steel plants and combined them with half a dozen other holdings. But in economics, as in atomic physics, the whole is equal to more than the sum of its parts.

After Morgan had put the pieces together, he found himself with some $130 million of extra capital value!

Who was hurt by this transaction? Certainly not Carnegie or Morgan. Even the people who bought the stock had no right to complain that it had been "watered," since for many years they got more than a fair return on their investments. To have sold them the stock for its actual cost (without water) would be (1) to make them a free gift of the enlarged profits of the concern, and (2) to give them the privilege of reselling the stock at the higher price that its earning power could earn for it in a competitive stock market. (Of course the consumer was not given the full benefit in lower steel prices of the efficiencies achieved by merger; but in terms of standards at the time, there was nothing illegal or unethical about this merger.)

Our practical-minded accountant, however, is not concerned with such matters of public policy and political economy as whether the consumer will or will not now pay higher prices. He will tell our toothpaste company or J. P. Morgan the same thing: "If you paid a certain sum of money for some assets, they must presumably be worth that much to you. If the assets don't exist, they must be created. 'Good Will' is their name." But since this term has come into bad repute in recent years, it is often lumped in with some other assets.

The intangible asset Good Will is thus the difference between what a company pays in buying out another company and what it gets in identifiable Assets.

ACCOUNTING ABUSES

In economics and finance nothing can be measured with the great accuracy of the physical sciences. But approximate measurement will suffice, so long as the method of measurement remains roughly the same over time.

Nowhere is this better illustrated than in accounting. When auditors certify that a company has prepared its accounting reports properly, they are not really able to swear that all measurements are 100 per cent accurate. But it is valuable for anyone who is contemplating buying the stock of the company to know that the usual methods of accounting have been adhered to. For example, when the company reports a rise of 10 per cent in earnings per share over the previous year, then even though there may be some uncertainty in the exact figures for each year, the direction of improvement should be not at all in doubt.

Unfortunately, in the 1960s and 1970s certain abuses crept into the accounting used by some of the "conglomerates." Here are a few examples.

---

[5] The problem of Reserves becomes even more complicated in connection with contingencies that may or may not occur. Thus Reserve for Depression Contingencies or for Renegotiation would fall halfway between true Liability and Surplus Reserves.

1. Manipulation of the way the assets taken over by the conglomerate are treated—good will adjustments and so forth—have been used to permit the conglomerate *to report rising per share earnings every year even though actual operating earnings have fallen.*

2. Conglomerates will issue many securities that are *convertible* into common stock—convertible bonds, convertible preferred stock, warrant options to buy new common at low prices, stock options for executives and underwriters. These really are potential common stock which, in many cases, are sure to become actual common stock. Hence, if we were to restate the earnings per share to allow for this *dilution*—and many accounting committees have recommended that this be done—what looks like a rising profile of earnings per share may actually be a dismally falling one.

3. Sometimes a small conglomerate will take over a larger corporation that is cash-rich, using in the end the money of the company swallowed to do so. Even where this is not illegal or unethical, it may be possible only because the old accounting reports of the giant carried its assets *concealed by undervaluations.*

4. Sometimes conglomerates give the appearance of becoming more profitably efficient in their operations than their predecessor companies, when actually all the improvements in per share earnings have resulted merely from taking advantage of tax loopholes—such as changing convertible preferred stocks into convertible bonds so that their dividend return will now appear in the form of interest, which is deductible under the law from corporation income subject to taxes. There may be nothing illegal or even unethical about this razzle-dazzle, but the alert investor will have to learn how to discern that this is all that is taking place and that further improvement is not possible.

The accounting profession and government agencies are working to reform some of these abuses. But,

alas, the old adage *caveat emptor*—let the buyer beware—must still prevail.

CONCLUSION

Finally, some interesting relations between economics and accounting can be briefly mentioned. (1) All Balance Sheets depend on valuation of Assets, which is one of the basic questions of the capital and interest theory discussed in Part Four. (2) National-income statistics depend on the accounting data of sales, cost, and so forth, as Chapter 10 shows. (3) We shall see in later discussion of how firms set price that accounting cost data play a role in price determination.

The accountant deals with *money* magnitudes; the economist tries to probe deeper to the underlying *real* magnitudes. Especially in periods of great inflation or deflation, the accountant realizes that his ordinary methods may give strange results.

One example is the problem of changing price levels and depreciation. Suppose prices are rising. If I sell my goods for enough to cover labor and other costs and also to cover depreciation, you might think I am breaking even. What would an accountant say who figures depreciation on the basis of the past low prices originally paid for my tools and plant? He, too, would say I am breaking even. But in fact I can be said to have been selling my goods at a *real* loss; for when my machines and buildings have worn out, I shall not have enough money to *reproduce them* at the new higher price level. The same is true of a merchant who sells off inventory at less than replacement cost.

So we must beware of fictitious money overstatements of real profits during rising prices and of fictitious understatements of profits during falling prices. (Later, in national-income statistics, you will note that profits are "adjusted" for inventory revaluations.)

SUMMARY TO APPENDIX

Instead of a lengthy recapitulation, here is a check list of accounting concepts that you should understand:

1   The fundamental Balance-Sheet relationship between Assets, Liabilities, and Net Worth and the breakdown of each of these into Current and Fixed Assets, Current and Long-term Liabilities, Capital and Surplus.

2   The character of the Income Statement (or Profit-and-Loss Statement) and the relationship between undistributed profit and Surplus changes on the new Balance Sheet.

3   The whole problem of Depreciation, both in its income-statement aspect as a necessary expense, which need not be an expenditure, and in its balance-sheet treatment as a deduction

from a purposely overstated asset; also the logic of the principal depreciation methods. Although any errors in calculating depreciation tend to cancel out eventually, recent tax concessions that allow rapid depreciation do improve the cash position of corporations.

4   The difference between a Fund or a pool of liquid Assets and three kinds of so-called "Reserves"; also the meaning of intangible Assets like Patents and Good Will.

QUESTIONS FOR DISCUSSION

1   Describe the Balance Sheet's right-hand side. Its left-hand side. What items must match from the "fundamental identity"?

2   You are a banker deciding whether to lend money to the toothpaste company. Why be especially interested in current items?

3   Write out a list of many different Assets. Give the nature of each in a few lines. Do the same for Liabilities.

4   Is an Income Statement a "still picture" at an instant of time? Why not?

5   A company has $10 million of net sales, $9 million of costs of all kinds (including taxes, interest, etc.), rents its equipment. Its inventory doesn't change in the year. It has no preferred stock. It pays no dividends. Draw up its simplified 1976 Income Statement.

6   The same company as in question 5 owes no money, having been completely equity-financed years ago. Fill in the year-end Balance Sheet below.

ASSETS		LIABILITIES AND NET WORTH		
1975	1976		1975	1976
		Liabilities	0	0
		Net Worth	$50 million	....
Total $50 million	....	Total	....	....

7   Redo problems 5 and 6, making the following changes: In addition to the other expenses, its buildings depreciate by $2 million; also its inventory has fallen off by $3 million. Draw up an Income Statement showing its loss, and adjust its 1976 Balance Sheet accordingly.

8   Describe two methods of calculating Depreciation, and explain tax advantages.

9   Differentiate between three different kinds of Reserves. Which, if any, are "Funds"? Which cash? Describe intangible Assets. Give examples of accounting abuses.

10 Guess how much you would pay for a business that is sure of yielding a net profit of $15,000 per year with little risk of principal. Suppose its Total Assets exclusive of Good Will were valued at $100,000. What would you guess for Good Will?

Review your understanding of the following concepts:

Balance-Sheet identity
Income-Statement identity
Assets, Liabilities, and Net Worth
Current versus Fixed Assets
Surplus, earnings, dividends
Manufacturing Cost of Goods Sold

Manufacturing Cost, inventory change
Depreciation (as expense and reserve)
Intangible Assets—Patents and Good Will
Asset and Liability Reserves versus Sinking Fund

Incomes and Living Standards 6

Everyone realizes the importance of income. The expression "Clothes make the man" would be more nearly right if it were "Income makes the man." That is to say, if you can know but one fact about a man, knowledge of his income will probably reveal most about him. Then you can roughly guess his political opinions, his tastes, and education, his age, and even his life expectancy. Furthermore, unless a family has a steady stream of money coming in every week, month, and year—even though it has saintly endurance—that family is sick. Not only its materialistic activities but its nonmaterialistic activities, the things that convert existence into living, must suffer: education, travel, recreation, and charity, to say nothing of food, warmth, and shelter.

It is a commonplace to state that the American standard of living and level of family income are the highest in all the world. But few people realize just how small the average American income really is, or how great is the range between the highest and the lowest incomes.

This chapter gives some basic facts about incomes and wealth, here and abroad. America has been described by Galbraith as The Affluent Society. And the mixed economies of Western Europe are following hot on our heels. Yet pockets of poverty remain: and as we shall see, this kind of poverty is new in history and different from that found in most other parts of the earth. (More on poverty will come in Chapter 39.)

THE DECLINE OF POVERTY

It is now well over a century since Karl Marx and Friedrich Engels in 1848 issued the Communist Manifesto containing the lines: "Workers of the world unite! You have nothing to lose but your chains." While some of Marx's predictions about the future of industrial capitalism were proved correct in the intervening years, one of his most famous has proved to be quite wrong. His assertion that *the rich will become richer and the poor will become poorer* cannot be sustained by careful historical and statistical research. In Europe and America there has definitely been a steady long-term improvement in minimum standards of living, whether measured by food, clothing, housing, or length of life. This fact about mixed economies is clear from statistics soon to be given.

It used to be fashionable for economic historians to dwell on the evils of the Industrial Revolution and the poverty-ridden condition of the masses in the disease-producing cities. In point of fact, no Dickens novel did full justice to the dismal conditions of child labor, length of the working day, and conditions of safety and sanitation in early nineteenth-century factories. A workweek of 84 hours was the prevailing rule, with time out at the bench for breakfast and sometimes supper, as well as lunch. A good deal of work could be got out of a six-year-old child; and if a man lost two fingers in a machine, he still had eight left.

However true their lurid picture of industrial factory towns, the earlier historians seem to have erred in thinking that conditions were worse than in the preindustrial era. The earlier "putting-out," or domestic, system, in which wool or yarn was provided to workers for them to spin or weave in their homes, brought the worst conditions of the sweatshop into the home. The whole family was figuratively forced to run on the treadmill.

Furthermore, poverty is never so obvious in the country as in the industrial cities, where it forces itself on the observer. The idyllic picture of the healthful, happy countryside peopled by stout yeomen and happy peasantry is a mirage in most parts of the world. Even today, New York's Hell's Kitchen or Harlem, Boston's South or North End, "behind the Yards" in Chicago or its black belt hardly overshadow the poverty and squalor of our rural problem areas: the Tobacco Road of the deep South, hillbilly regions of the Appalachian Plateau, dust bowls, and ghost mining towns.

Modern historians therefore emphasize that the conditions of the industrial present, inadequate as they may seem, are nevertheless great improvements in living standards over the previous periods of commercial enterprise and agrarian feudalism.

TWO WORLDS?

Most of Asia and Africa are even today at lower levels of living than were the Western countries before the Industrial Revolution. Figure 6-1 shows how fortunate the United States growth in output has been. A great economic statistician, Simon Kuznets of Harvard, has recently shown that the leading Western nations have for decades been averaging rapid rates of growth of output per head. Examine the front-leaf charts to see just how fast countries have grown.

What about the progress of the poorer countries? We lack data to give firm answers. Professor Kuznets has made shrewd guesses and inclines to the view that their productivity growth has been lagging behind. He makes the important observation:[1]

. . . the presently developed countries were already in advance of the "rest of the world" when modern industrialization began—and the latter only increased the disparity.

[1] Simon Kuznets, "Quantitative Aspects of the Economic Growth of Nations: I," *Economic Development and Cultural Change*, vol. V, 1956, p. 25. From 1956 to 1970 there have been some success stories: Thailand, Taiwan, Korea, Mexico, for example, have made remarkable sprints of progress.

Higher productivity gives us more output and more leisure:

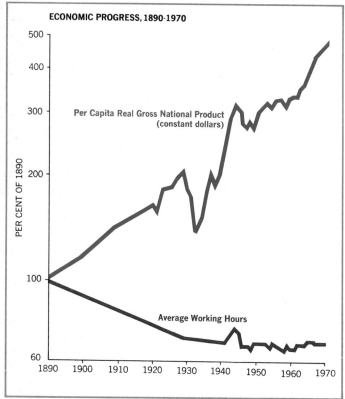

ECONOMIC PROGRESS, 1890-1970

FIG. 6-1. Technological improvements, better capital goods, and more highly trained labor have raised production faster than the growth of population. NOTE: This is a "ratio," or "semilog," chart; the vertical scale is arranged so that equal vertical distances depict equal percentage rather than equal absolute changes. EXAMPLE: Verify that 400 is as far above 200 as 200 is above 100. (Source: U.S. Department of Commerce.)

Table 6-1 shows the wide international spreads of income per head. In the United States itself, the South has much lower incomes than the Northeast and the West Coast. States such as Mississippi have scarcely attained per capita incomes equal to those reached in Pennsylvania and New York back in 1910 or those found in France today. But it is interesting to note that the regional differentials in income are gradually narrowing and changing. The South and West grow faster than the average; and older regions, such as the Middle Atlantic states, are reverting toward the average.

DISTRIBUTION OF INCOME IN THE UNITED STATES

A poll of students will show that they are not very sure what their own family incomes really are. Usually it turns out they have a slightly exaggerated notion of their fathers' earnings. And despite the recent (quite justified) claim of a prominent clubwoman that "women spend 70 per cent of the national income, and we soon hope to get hold of the rest," an astonishing number of wives have no conception of their husbands' paychecks. In addition, there are some people so inept at keeping records and with such variable earnings that they do not themselves know how much they make. Even where income is known within the family, there is a quite natural reticence to reveal it to outsiders; thus investigators who made a survey of the birth-control habits of native white Protestants of Indianapolis often found it harder to get financial data than intimate personal information.

In the absence of statistical knowledge, it is understandable that one should form an impression of the American standard of living from the full-page magazine advertisements portraying a jolly American family in an air-conditioned mansion, with a Mercedes, a station wagon, a motor launch, and all the other good things that go to make up comfortable living. Actually, of course, this sort of life is still beyond the grasp of 90 per cent of the American public and even beyond most families from which the select group of college students comes.

The sober truth   In the early 1970s, at the pinnacle of American prosperity, the per capita income in the United States is about $95 per week. Such an average figure is derived by pretending that all the income in the United States is divided equally among every man, woman, and child. Of course, income is distributed far from equally; and there is no guarantee that an attempt to divide it equally would leave the total unchanged.

If the members of a classroom, or of the whole country, write down their family incomes on cards, these cards may be sorted into different income classes; i.e., some cards will go into the $0-to-$1,999 class, some into the $2,000-to-$3,999 class, and so forth. In this way we get the *statistical frequency* distribution of income. At one extreme will be the very poor, who have drawn a blank in life; at the other, the very rich. The vast majority fall in between.

Table 6-2 summarizes recent statistics on this subject. Column (1) gives the *income class interval*. Column (2) shows the percentage of families and individuals in each income class. Column (3) shows the percentage of the total of all income that goes to the people

Americans still enjoy highest standard of living in world:

PER CAPITA GNPs, 1970			
United States	$4,900	Japan	$1,500
Canada	3,500	Italy	1,490
Sweden	3,300	Soviet Union	1,300
Denmark	3,000	Poland	1,100
West Germany	2,800	Portugal	600
Norway	2,800	Turkey	320
France	2,750	China (Taiwan)	300
United Kingdom	2,400	U.A.R. (Egypt)	190
Israel	1,900	Korea	115
Czechoslovakia	1,600	India	90

TABLE 6-1. All estimates have been converted into 1970 U.S. dollars at exchange rates designed to reflect actual purchasing powers; but all figures should be regarded as rough approximations, particularly in countries at drastically different stages of development. (Source: Center for International Studies, MIT, updated by author.)

Few families in America reach income level of $15,000:

DISTRIBUTION OF INCOMES OF AMERICAN FAMILIES AND INDIVIDUALS, 1967				
(1) INCOME CLASS	(2) PERCENTAGE OF ALL FAMILIES AND INDIVIDUALS IN THIS CLASS	(3) PERCENTAGE OF TOTAL INCOME RECEIVED BY FAMILIES AND INDIVIDUALS IN THIS CLASS	(4) PERCENTAGE OF FAMILIES AND INDIVIDUALS IN THIS CLASS AND LOWER ONES	(5) PERCENTAGE OF INCOME RECEIVED BY THIS CLASS AND LOWER ONES
Under $2,000	13	2	13	2
$ 2,000-$ 3,999	14	6	27	8
4,000- 5,999	14	9	41	17
6,000- 7,999	16	13	57	30
8,000- 9,999	14	15	71	45
10,000- 14,999	19	26	90	71
15,000 and up	10	29	100	100
Total	100	100		

TABLE 6-2. Half of these families and individuals are below the median income of $7,100. The average (or arithmetic mean) income each would get if all income was distributed exactly equally is $8,100. More families and individuals have incomes around the modal $6,000 level than around any other income. (Source: U.S. Department of Commerce. To update these numbers to the early 1970s, increase all money incomes by about 20 per cent.)

in the given income class. Columns (4) and (5) are computed from (2) and (3), respectively. Column (4) shows what percentage of the total number of families and individuals belongs to each income class *or below*. Column (5) shows what percentage of total income goes to the people who belong in the given income class or have still lower incomes.

This table shows it would be a great mistake to think that the poor and the rich are equally distributed around the middle. The Biblical statement, "For the poor ye have always with you," gives no inkling of their vast numbers. Abraham Lincoln pointed up this fact picturesquely in his statement, "The Lord prefers common people. . . . He made so many of them."

A glance at the income distribution in the United States shows how pointed is the income pyramid and how broad its base. "There's always room at the top" is certainly true; this is so because it is hard to get there, not because it is easy. If we made an income pyramid out of a child's blocks, with each layer portraying $1,000 of income, the peak would be far higher than the Eiffel Tower, but almost all of us would be within a yard of the ground.

The middle, or "median," income class (which divides the upper from the lower half of the people) corresponds to a modest income—only about $7,100 in the 1967 table. The median income falls short of the average (or "arithmetic mean") income of $8,100. This is primarily because the distribution of incomes is always a skewed one, with a long tail of incomes stretching out above the mean. (To estimate a typical income in the 1970s, add about $500 for each elapsed year.)

HOW TO MEASURE INEQUALITY AMONG INCOME CLASSES

How great is the spread of incomes, and how shall we measure the degree of inequality of income distribution?

From Table 6-2, we can estimate that roughly half of all Americans fall in the middle-income range of $3,500 to $11,000. This means that one-fourth fall below $3,500 and an approximately equal number have incomes above $11,000. Of course, the fact that there are the same number of individuals and families in the above-$11,000 group as in the below-$3,500 group does not mean that they each receive the same percentage of the total income. Actually, the lowest fourth of the people receives less than *half of one-half* of the income received by the highest fourth (as Fig. 6-2 will show).

This suggests how to go about the task of getting a numerical measure of the degree of inequality of income distribution. We can ask, What per cent *of all income* goes to the lowest 10 per cent *of the population?* What to the lowest 20 per cent? The lowest 50 per cent? The lowest 95 per cent? And so forth. Such data can be derived from Columns (4) and (5) back in Table 6-2.

If incomes were absolutely uniformly distributed, the lowest 20 per cent of the population (which in this case would mean *any* 20 per cent) would receive exactly 20 per cent of the total income; the lowest 80 per cent would receive 80 per cent of the income; and the highest 20 per cent would also get only 20 per cent of the income.

This is depicted by the brown diagonal in the so-called "Lorenz curve" of Fig. 6-2. It plots percentage of people, ranked from the poorest up, on the horizontal axis and percentage of total income they receive on the vertical axis.

The second column of the new table in Fig. 6-2 gives data for this brown diagonal line of absolute equality.

At the other extreme, we have the hypothetical case of absolute *inequality*, where everybody (say, 99 out of 100 people) has no income, except for *one* person who has *all* the income. This is shown in the third column of the table. Why those numbers? Because the lowest 0, 20, 80, and 99 people have no income at all. But the lowest 100 do include the last man; and all the people, of course, have all the income. The lowest curve on the Lorenz diagram—the brown, right-angled line—represents this limiting case of absolute inequality.

Any actual income distribution, such as that of 1967, must fall between these extremes. Its Lorenz curve is given in Fig. 6-2 by the indicated intermediate blue curve, with the shaded area indicating the deviation from absolute equality, and hence giving us a measure of the degree of *inequality* of income distribution.[2] (Since we shall meet Lorenz curves often, Fig. 6-2 repays careful study.)

[2] There are still other ways of measuring the degree of inequality of income. One of the most interesting of these we can mention but not discuss in detail here. The Italian-born Swiss professor of economics Vilfredo Pareto was often called, with somewhat questionable accuracy, the ideological precursor of fascism. By using a certain logarithmic chart called the "Pareto chart," he found that the "upper tail" of the income data of many different countries and many different times fell along straight lines of almost the same slopes. He came to believe this to be a fundamental natural law. According to Pareto's Law, *there is an inevitable tendency for income to be distributed in the same way—regardless of social and political institutions and regardless of taxation.* In the past 70 years, more careful studies have refuted the universality of Pareto's Law, as well as its inevitability. Thus, in Great Britain, in the period just after World War II, income taxation had gone so far as to leave only 70 people with incomes of more than $24,000 after taxes were paid! More on this in Chapter 39's discussion of inequality.

Incomes are distributed with neither absolute equality nor absolute inequality:

INEQUALITY TABLE			
	PERCENTAGE OF INCOME		
PERCENTAGE OF PEOPLE	ABSOLUTE EQUALITY	ABSOLUTE INEQUALITY	ACTUAL 1967
0	0	0	0
20	20	0	5
40	40	0	17
60	60	0	35
80	80	0	59
95	95	0	85
100	100	100	100

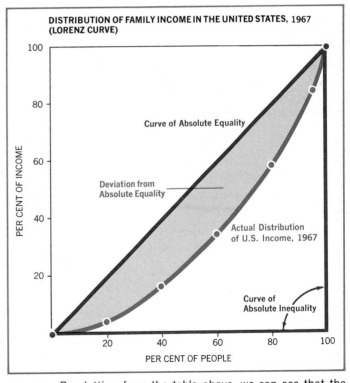

DISTRIBUTION OF FAMILY INCOME IN THE UNITED STATES, 1967 (LORENZ CURVE)

Curve of Absolute Equality

Deviation from Absolute Equality

Actual Distribution of U.S. Income, 1967

Curve of Absolute Inequality

PER CENT OF INCOME

PER CENT OF PEOPLE

FIG. 6-2. By plotting from the table above, we can see that the actual distribution-of-income curve lies between the two extremes of absolute equality and absolute inequality. The shaded area of this Lorenz chart (as a percentage of half the square's area) measures relative inequality of income. (How would the curve have looked back in the roaring 1920s when inequality was greater? In a 1984 welfare state that narrows income differences?)

Inequality differs among nations and is different for income than for wealth:

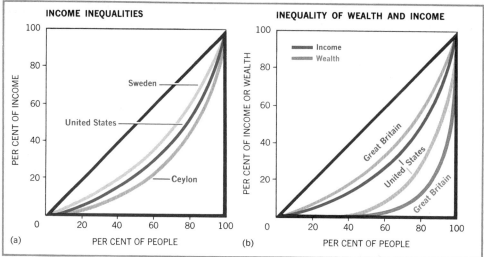

FIG. 6-3(a). Advanced economies show less inequality of income distribution than do pre-industrial economies. Contrary to dire predictions of scientific socialists that the rich get richer and the poor get poorer under capitalism, the mixed economy shows greater equality. FIG. 6-3(b). Holdings of wealth tend to be more concentrated than do incomes earned annually. The United States and the United Kingdom have rather similar equality of incomes; but British wealth is much more concentrated than American.

TRENDS OF INEQUALITY

What is happening to the degree of inequality of incomes in modern nations? Is it getting greater, as pessimists feared? By calculating Lorenz and other curves, scholars find that inequality is definitely less in America than it was back in 1929, but little different today from 1945. A glance at Fig. 6-3(b) will show that the United Kingdom and the United States have rather similar degrees of inequality of incomes, the major difference apparently not being attributable so much to differences in social philosophy as to the fact that there is a larger fraction of subsistence farmers and low-paid Negro workers in the American economy.

Which country today has the greatest equality? No one knows how to compare the inequality in the Soviet Union[3] or China with that in mixed economies. If we confine ourselves to the noncommunist world, it has been suggested that the new state of Israel may lead the list. Sweden and other mixed economies have low inequality, as the comparison in Fig. 6-3(a) shows.

[3] A very careful study of wage inequalities in Russia's communistic economy, Abram Bergson, *The Structure of Soviet Wages* (Harvard University Press, Cambridge, Mass., 1944), showed inequalities and dispersions between the best-paid and the poorest-paid workers astonishingly like those of our own society. Shostakovich, other top Soviet musicians, and top scientists probably make more there than do Stravinsky, Teller, and similar persons in America. The inequality of political privilege among Soviet bureaucrats, military officers, Communist party members, and the Soviet public at large is not susceptible to precise numerical measurement. Employment incomes in mixed economies like Australia and Sweden were found in a 1965 study to be slightly more equal than in Poland.

Before industrialization, was there a golden age of greater equality of distribution? Fragmentary historical data suggest otherwise. Have developed societies generally greater inequality than underdeveloped nations? Casual tourist observation often suggests the reverse; the extremes of poverty and wealth *appear* greater in poor countries than in industrialized ones. The limited statistics available do confirm this view; thus, the Lorenz curve for a country like Ceylon in Fig. 6-3(a) will show greater inequality than will such a curve for the United States, the United Kingdom, or Sweden.

DISTRIBUTION OF WEALTH

A Lorenz curve of distribution of *wealth* ownership shows considerably more inequality than does a curve of *income* distribution. Figure 6-3(b) shows how great is the difference between the wealth and income curves. Whereas the United Kingdom and the United States have similar inequality of incomes, note that the United Kingdom has much greater inequality of wealth than does the United States. In part this is because certain peers and tycoons in Britain own tremendous concentrations of land and other property. But study of the data shows that much of the difference comes from the fact that many Americans of quite modest incomes do have positive net worth (i.e., assets minus liabilities), whereas this is less common among the lower-income British.

Turn back to Fig. 3-1 on p. 42. It shows that the For Whom problem is determined by (1) the price that people can get for the factors they supply—land, labor, machinery, and general capital goods, and (2) the amounts of these factors that they start out with. If labor could be ignored, the distribution of incomes would tend to be that determined by the distribution of wealth: at the same interest return, twice the wealth yields twice the income. Hence, property incomes show great Lorenz inequality.

The earnings from work—wages, salaries, earnings of unincorporated entrepreneurs—are evidently less unequally distributed. But of course they are not uniform, as the following sections show.

INCOME DIFFERENCES AMONG OCCUPATIONS

What single profession seems to make the most money? In recent years it has without question been the doctors. They have forged well ahead of lawyers. Doctors have mean earnings of about $39,000 and median earnings of about $34,000; lawyers have mean and median earnings of $20,000 and $17,000. Why these high doctor earnings? Primarily because the costs of training doctors are so high and the capacities of our medical schools are so low; as a result, we train not very many more doctors than we did in 1910, even though the demand has greatly increased. Medical societies (like the AMA) are also accused of helping to keep doctors' incomes up by various devices, including the insistence on high quality standards.

Dentists, engineers, and schoolteachers are estimated to have median incomes of about $21,000, $15,000, and $7,000, respectively. College teachers as a class have a median salary of about $10,000 for a 9-month academic year ($12,000 if they also teach summer school, but only half have this opportunity). Full professors at the largest universities get twice these amounts; professors of physics and engineering average higher incomes than do professors of Greek and botany. While teachers' salaries have been improving recently, it is ministers who are lowest paid of all professionals. Their median salary is still around $6,000! And even with special perquisites, the figure is unbelievably low.

Do incomes increase with age? Not in the lowest-paid manual jobs. For such work, a man is at his best in his early twenties; after that he goes downhill. In the professions and in business executive jobs, earnings do increase with age: doctors and lawyers reach their prime after fifty; both can hope to work beyond the normal retirement ages. A junior executive with an A.B. or business degree will begin training at $1,000 a month; if he is very successful, he may retire as chairman of the board, earning, say, $150,000 a year and with stock bonuses and retirement provisions.[4]

On the other hand, many corporations and institutions have been fixing inflexible retirement ages of sixty-five. With improvements in life expectancies, this poses a problem of long years of wasteful and unhappy retirement. The ultimate solution seems to be along these lines: Let each man taper off slowly rather than abruptly, with other factors besides chronological age being decisive.

IS COLLEGE WORTH WHILE?

How do education and training affect lifetime income? Are they worth their cost? The evidence answers, Decidedly yes. Men who never finish eight grades of school earn scarcely $5,000 annually; college graduates do three times as well. Unemployment among school dropouts exceeds that of graduates by a growing margin.

Even if you have to borrow at 7 per cent interest, put off years of gainful employment, live away from home, and pay for food and books, your lifetime earnings in the professions that are open only to college graduates will probably turn out to be more than compensatory. (Good grades help: A *Time* study showed, in its own argot, that "greasy grinds" end up with slightly higher pay than do "big men on campus"; both outearn the anonymous face in the college crowd.)

Money is not everything—better to be uneducated, poor, and happy than to be well-off and miserable? The Governmental Commission on Mental Illness and Health reported a 1960 survey of how people with different education compared mentally. Were college graduates worried and depressed in comparison with those of little schooling? Surprisingly, the answer was, Definitely not. College graduates reported greater happiness and less mental illness. True, they were more introspective; but coupled with this went a greater sense of well-being and satisfaction. Their perspectives were broader and aspiration levels higher; and when they worried, their worries tended to be over genuine rather than imagined troubles.

Figure 6-4 shows how professions differ in inequality of earnings. Can you guess why the order of inequality is self-employed lawyer, . . . , salaried army officer?

[4]Salaries of top officers do increase with the size of the firm, but by no means in strict proportion. Statistics suggest that the head of Corporation A, twice the size of Company B, will *not* get twice the salary that the head of B gets, but only about 30 per cent more. Since 1945, the percentage rise in executive salaries seems not to have kept up with the rise in other professional incomes.

Education is one of society's most profitable investments. Human capital yields a return as great as or greater than capital in the form of tools and buildings. That is why economists urge developed and undeveloped countries to spend more on education and training.

DIFFERENCES IN ABILITY AND INCOMES

In Part Four we shall study in detail the economic principles underlying the distribution of income. Our common sense enables us to anticipate part of its analysis and suggests that one factor helping to explain differences in income must be *differences in people.*

These differences in people may be physical, mental, or even temperamental. They may be associated with biological inheritance through the genetic cells or with social and economic environment. They may be permanent—like being blue-eyed—or acquired, like educational advantage or being blond. These differences may even involve such conventionalities as the possession of a union card, or a propensity to drop aitches in speaking or to pronounce "oil" with an "r" and "girl" without one.

Lawyers and doctors show great income inequalities, professors and army officers less:

FIG. 6-4. Why would the curve for *salaried* doctors and lawyers fall in the middle of the four curves shown? Why would you expect dentists to have a curve just above doctors? How might the curve for speculators in common stocks look? (Source: G. J. Stigler, National Bureau of Economic Research, New York, 1956.)

These personal differences provide us with only part of the answer to the puzzle of income dispersion. Physical traits (such as height or hip girth) and measured mental traits (such as intelligence quotient or tone perception) appear to be *not* so different among people as are the differences in income distribution. Often, the scientist who measures individual traits finds that they are "normally" distributed, with most people in the middle and fewer people at each end, as represented by the brown bell-shaped curve of Fig. 6-5 on page 116. (If their IQ scores depart from the normal distribution, psychologists often *rescale* them so as to force agreement!) Incomes—even those from work, but especially those from property ownership—are distributed *skewly*, as shown by the blue curve with a very long tail off in the direction of the highest-paid individuals.

Actually, there is nothing particularly sacred about the so-called "normal curve." If *heights* of cubes (not people) are normally distributed, then their *volumes* will be skewed off to the right. Moreover, careful examination of census data on incomes suggests that *each kind of wage income* may tend to approximate to a bell-shaped distribution curve of modest symmetry. But when we add together the distributions of earnings for women as well as men, for property owners as well as workers, for lucky speculators, and other diverse groups, the great "skewness" of the whole distribution does emerge. Moreover,

Are abilities more normally distributed than market incomes?

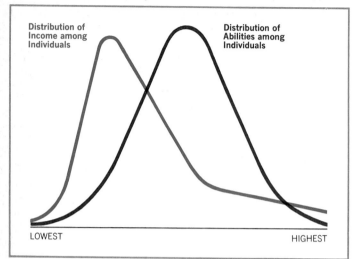

FIG. 6-5.   Heights, intelligence quotients, and many measured human traits seem to follow a so-called "normal" bell-shaped statistical distribution. Market incomes seem to be more skewed, highest incomes being more than a hundred times the lowest (as in blue curve).

if we follow each wage earner over a period of years, a pattern of dispersion will emerge, one of the important factors causing differences among individuals being the different degrees of unemployment they suffer.

Perhaps a warning is in order at this point against jumping to the conclusion that there is something *necessary* and *inevitable* about this dispersion of income. Within the framework of the mixed economy, fundamental changes in education have already made significant changes in inequality. Moreover, as no one knows better than the man at the top, our system of progressive income taxation has already greatly changed the relative take-home and—what is more important—the "keep-at-home" of the high- and low-paid. And presumably this will continue to be an abiding feature of American life and one subject to control by the electorate.

ECONOMIC STRATIFICATION AND OPPORTUNITY

America was always considered the land of opportunity, where anyone with ability might get ahead in the world. The success legend of Horatio Alger, Jr.'s, "poor but proud" hero who worked his way to the top and married the boss's daughter—or vice versa—has no doubt been overdrawn. (Few black, or even Catholic, go-getters went to the altar with those Alger heiresses.) But the notion of an open society did have elements of truth as compared with the situation in older countries, where an aristocratic tradition lingered and where free schooling beyond the primary grades was late in being established.

For example, the "old school tie" and, more important, the Oxford accent were until recently almost indispensable to political and social advancement in Britain; even with the free scholarship system, few members of the lower or middle class could jump this hurdle. In this country, few people even recognize a "prep school" accent, and variations in speech are geographical rather than social. The American secretary is almost indistinguishable in appearance from the blue-blood debutante.

Moreover, ours has been rather a materialistic civilization in which success is interpreted in business terms. Because "money talks," it is easier for outsiders to break into the upper crust than it would be in a culture that puts greater emphasis upon tradition. The *nouveaux riches* of one generation, such as the Vanderbilts a century ago, become the social arbiters of the next.

Recruitment of the elite   Nevertheless, careful questionnaire investigation of the social origins of successful businessmen, namely, the directors and officers of corporations, turns

Anyone can climb the ladder of success, but it helps to start high:

OCCUPATION OF FATHER	PERSONS LISTED IN Who's Who, 1912 (per cent)	AMERICAN MILLIONAIRES, LIVING IN 1925 (per cent)	AMERICAN BUSINESS LEADERS, 1928 (per cent)	AMERICAN BUSINESS LEADERS, 1952 (per cent)	AMERICAN BUSINESS LEADERS UNDER 50, 1952 (per cent)
Businessman	35.3	75.0	60.0	61.8	67.8
Professional man	34.3	10.5	13.4	13.5	14.8
Farmer	23.4	7.3	12.4	12.7	11.1
Laborer	6.7	1.6	12.5	7.8	2.5
Other	0.3	5.6	1.7	4.2	3.8
Total	100.0	100.0	100.0	100.0	100.0

SOCIAL ORIGIN OF SUCCESSFUL LEADERS IN AMERICA

TABLE 6-3. Though laborers far outnumber businessmen in the population at large, most successful businessmen had a businessman father. What trends do you see in this table? How would you explain them? (Sources: F. W. Taussig and C. S. Joslyn, *American Business Leaders*, Macmillan, New York, 1932; *Fortune*.)

up some surprising facts. The typical American business executive does not come off a farm or out of a workingman's home. More likely his father was also a businessman or possibly in one of the professions. Table 6-3 summarizes some typical research studies made by Taussig and Joslyn and others.

Does this mean that American economic society is hardening along caste lines?[5] Taussig and Joslyn are not sure. They point out that two diametrically opposite explanations are possible:

(1) There has long been social mobility in America: all the cream rose to the top some time ago, leaving naturally less-gifted people at the bottom. (2) There are strong, and perhaps growing, barriers to circulation between the economic classes.

Taussig and Joslyn incline rather to the first view, believing that "you can't keep a good man down." Many sociologists would disagree. They would emphasize the thousand

[5] A generation ago, most scholars inclined toward the view that it was becoming increasingly difficult to go from the bottom to the top. Now they are not so sure. Recent careful studies of the origins of business leaders back *before* 1900 suggest that the present may compare favorably with the good old days, which were not so good after all. Increasingly, as organizations become bigger, the elements of nepotism and personal favoritism seem to become less important, and the increasing emphasis upon civil-servant-like quasi-objective tests of performance (and conformity!) suggests greater mobility among the elite. Aristocrats complain that we are becoming a "meritocracy."

The arithmetic of "transition probabilities" can be made to yield the following results. Divide society into two classes, so that I am either a U in the Upper class or a *non-U* in the Lower. If a child's chance to move out of his parents' class is as great as to stay in, then $\frac{1}{2}$ the children, grandchildren, great-grandchildren, and descendants generally of a U parent will be U's. But if there is social stratification so that a child has only $\frac{1}{4}$ chance of moving into a class different from his parents, $\frac{3}{4}$ ($= \frac{1}{2} + \frac{1}{4}$) of the children of U's will be U's. However, it can be deduced that only $\frac{5}{8}$ ($= \frac{1}{2} + \frac{1}{8}$) of grandchildren of U's will be U's; and only $\frac{9}{16}$ ($= \frac{1}{2} + \frac{1}{16}$) of their great-grandchildren. Evidently, the chance of remote descendants of U's being also U's goes ultimately down to $\frac{1}{2}$, with 50 per cent of the excess above the $\frac{1}{2}$ equality level being wiped out at each new generation. Hope for the *non-U's* means despair for the U's only if a fair race is deemed a tragedy. For more on transition probabilities, see W. Feller, *An Introduction to Probability*, Vol. I (Wiley, New York, 1968).

and one subtle psychological, social, economic, and educational disadvantages of the children of less fortunate families from the cradle on; that equal ability is not always able to give rise to equal achievement.

Whichever view is right, the implications for policy are the same. Human beings are a nation's most important form of social capital—a high-yielding form, moreover, in which we have invested too little in the past. Talent, wherever it may be, is worth seeking out and nurturing. And certainly when it comes to Chapter 40's analysis of racial discrimination, no one will argue that nonwhites have enjoyed equality of opportunity.

AFFLUENCE FOR WHOM?

In the 1960s America dropped the complacent notion that it had already become an affluent society with no more economic problems. The last act of President Kennedy, before his tragic 1963 assassination, was to map out a war against poverty. President Johnson carried forward and expanded this gigantic social program. Prior to Chapter 39's extended discussion, here is a brief outline of the fight against poverty.

The Economic Opportunity Act (1964), proposed by Kennedy, established the Office of Economic Opportunity (OEO) under R. Sargent Shriver. The OEO, building upon earlier work by the Ford Foundation, set up Community Action Agencies to coordinate federal, state, and local programs in cities. The Neighborhood Youth Corps, Job Corps, and Work Experience Programs were started by OEO in 1965 to furnish job training in schools and camps and to provide literacy programs for adults. VISTA, the domestic Peace Corps, was initiated, and project Head Start was begun to help underprivileged preschool children break the vicious circle of environmentally inherited poverty.

By 1970 the Nixon administration, under the prodding of Daniel P. Moynihan and Secretary of HEW Robert Finch, was starting family-incentive allowances, manpower training, and preschool education.

DEFINITION OF POVERTY

Let us see how large the group is that is stuck below an adequate income level, and just which minorities are likely to be in this group.

Economists have tried to calculate "minimum-subsistence" incomes in two different ways: First, they have taken over from social-service welfare workers carefully calculated budgets purporting to measure the cost of a minimum-subsistence income. Second, as a check, OEO economists have noted that poor families generally spend about one-third of their income on food; and hence from calculations by the Department of Agriculture of the cost of a subsistence food budget in different places, they can, by multiplying by 3, get estimates of needed minimum-subsistence income.

The two methods agree fairly well, and Fig. 6-6 shows how the cost of such a minimum-subsistence budget for a family of four[6] has risen in half a century. It is to be stressed

---

[6] Statistical budgetary data throw light on the age-old question, Can two live as cheaply as one? According to the Bureau of Labor Statistics, the answer is, No. Even if one person works in the home, it costs

The minimum-subsistence budget moves with the economy:

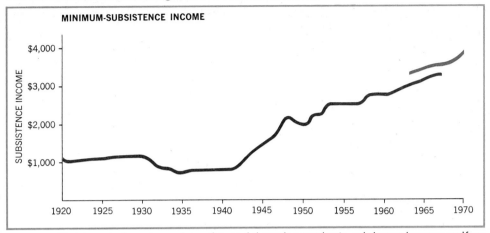

FIG. 6-6. The brown line shows how the social-service worker's minimum-income welfare budget for a family of four has risen with economic growth. The cost-of-subsistence budget, $4,000 in 1970, is shown in blue, and is in close agreement with the welfare budget.

Even after allowing for cyclical price-level changes, society's estimate of "minimum subsistence" income moves up in prosperity, down in recession. World War II and postwar high employment much reduced the percentage of population living in poverty; but since 1945 our standards have risen as fast as our incomes; the challenge remains to reduce numbers in poverty further and raise earning abilities. (Sources: Oscar Ornati, New School of Social Research; U.S. Department of Health, Education, and Welfare; updating by author.)

that most of the rise comes because, *as the nation as a whole gets more prosperous, the definition of minimum requirements is raised.* What Americans consider poverty would be regarded as affluence in Asia, and most families behind the Iron Curtain would be deemed poor if our budget requirements were extrapolated to them.

What do these standards come to? In 1970 the cost of the "subsistence" budget might be about $4,000 for a family of four, and includes only the bare necessities: no movies, little meat, no dental care, no newspapers, little clothing, and so forth. A "minimum-comfort" budget, hardly luxurious, costs about $7,000 and allows for adequate diet, occasional recreation, some tobacco and books, but not much else.

THE POSITION OF MINORITIES

No discussion of the inequality of incomes would be complete without mention of the position of economic minorities. In a real sense this is the concern of everyone, because everyone belongs to some minority, even the Smiths, or for that matter, the Lodges and the Cabots. What are the characteristics of the people who live in families with less than minimum-subsistence income?

---

a married couple about $100/_{70}$ times what it costs a single person to live, on the average. There are advantages, however; and this amount is still less than it costs two to live singly. Each child in the family adds to the cost of living. Thus, if it costs 70 to live alone and 100 to live with a wife, it will cost about 130 with one child, 160 with two, and so forth, for each additional child.

Blacks have less income and education, and more unemployment, than whites:

DISCRIMINATION AND INEQUALITY OF OPPORTUNITY, 1967	WHITE	NONWHITE
Income		
Median income of families	$8,274	$5,141
Per cent of persons in poverty	10.2	35.3
Per cent of families with incomes of $10,000 or more	36.5	16.7
Education		
Median years of school completed by men 25 years or older	12.1	8.9
Per cent of persons 20–24 years old who complete high school	78.8	53.0
Per cent of persons over 25 who are college graduates	10.6	5.2
Unemployment rates (per cent)		
Adult men	2.1	4.4
Adult women	3.9	8.1
Teenagers	13.6	27.0

TABLE 6-4. Because of less education and racial discrimination, nonwhites get fewer good jobs. The resulting lower income makes them less able to afford a good education. The incidence of unemployment compounds the inequality and shows that minorities have a particular interest in full-employment programs. Education is not a cure-all. A black college graduate earns only about the same in a lifetime as does a white high school graduate! (Source: Bureau of the Census; Bureau of Labor Statistics.)

Table 6-4 shows at a glance the relative economic position of the white and nonwhite population. Over one-third of the nonwhite population has less than minimum-subsistence income! The United States population is only 12 per cent nonwhite, but the poor are 32 per cent nonwhite. Other groups with high poverty incidence are farmers (26 per cent in poverty, twice the ratio for nonfarmers), the aged, children, and Southerners. Consider the odds against an aged Negro in the rural South. Many of the poor are untrained, stuck in economically stagnant areas, isolated in city ghettos, and so forth. Yet many are also active job seekers in the urban labor markets.

Surveys show that female-headed households, or those headed by an unemployed male, are most likely to be poor, and there are relatively more fatherless black families than white.

Experienced observers used to insist that outright sexual discrimination, in the sense of paying men higher rates for the *same* kind and volume of work, is not a common practice. Similarly it has often been asserted that racial discrimination in the sense of unequal pay for the *same* work is not common.

How can we reconcile these statements with the economic inequalities which every sophisticated person knows prevail between the sexes and races, as shown in Table 6-4? The answer to the paradox lies partly in the fact that discrimination usually takes the more subtle and more effective form of *not admitting women to the same jobs as men and barring blacks from skilled labor, executive, and sales positions.*

Undoubtedly this explains much of the story. However, other competent observers maintain that women and Negroes on exactly the same job *do* often receive less pay. Women grade school teachers often receive lower pay than men. In a large electrical-goods plant, job-evaluation experts divide all factory work into two parts: women's jobs and men's jobs. The lowest pay of the men begins about where the women's highest pay leaves off; yet both management and the union will admit, off the record, that in many borderline jobs the productivity of the women is greater than that of the men.

Now, it cannot be denied that there are physical and temperamental differences between men and women; for example, a woman could not win the heavyweight wrestling championship or set a record for the 100-yard dash. Still the female sex is the stronger sex in the sense of life expectancy and also, perhaps, in being capable of sustained, painstaking effort. It is equally obvious that there are differences of skin color and hair texture between white, black, and yellow peoples, but there is no logical way to infer how much of observed differences in achievement is due to inequality of opportunity.

Reducing discrimination   Whatever one's views are about the biological and environmental differences between the races and sexes—and the views of the scientists who have studied the question most are quite different from those of the man on the street—it is absolutely clear to any observer that there are numerous good jobs which either sex or either race can do equally well and is prevented from so doing. This is shown by the experience of wartime and boom, when the usual barriers were lowered.

Similarly, the older worker in ordinary times finds himself at a disadvantage in our society. A man may be thrown on the scrap heap by the age of fifty when many of his best years are still ahead. It is not true that an older worker is the first to be fired; usually his experience or seniority helps to protect him. But once he is fired, it is much harder for him to become reemployed. Paradoxically, the humanitarian measures adopted by corporations to aid older workers—such as retirement pension schemes—are one reason for corporations' refusing to hire older men, since it then becomes more expensive to hire them.

From the horror of World War II, a few salutary lessons were learned. Women, Negroes, and older workers showed that they were capable of holding down better jobs and earning more money than was thought possible before the war. The experience of the federal and state Fair Employment Practices Commissions has not been that prejudice can be legislated away overnight, but that steady improvement is possible if the people really want it. Nor can all the blame be placed upon bigoted employers. Organized labor must incur some of the onus for racial discrimination, particularly in the building trades.

The Civil Rights Act (1964) set up the Equal Employment Opportunities Commission, which has been making some steady progress in lessening discrimination—discrimination against women and discrimination against nonwhites. But even the most ardent believer in gradualism will admit that progress has been discouragingly slow in coming.

CONCLUSION

Sargent Shriver [McGovern] prophesied that by 1976, 200 years after the Declaration of Independence, poverty could be finally terminated in the United States. Of course, the millennium will not arrive in 1976 or on any other date. New times define new challenges. Ideas that seem impractical now—such as a guaranteed-minimum-income-incentive plan, implemented through the device of a negative income tax[7] or some other method—will be taken as a matter of course by our posterity. (Chapter 39 analyzes this.)

[7] Diverse economists—such as Yale's New Frontiersman, James Tobin, and Chicago's Milton Friedman, adviser to candidate Barry Goldwater and President Nixon—have advocated a negative income tax.

Some experts in the field have put the challenge bluntly:[8]

The U.S. has arrived at the point where poverty could be abolished easily and simply by a stroke of the pen. To raise every individual and family in the nation now below a subsistence income to the subsistence level would cost about $10 billion a year [perhaps $15 billion in 1970]. This is less than 2 per cent of the gross national product. It is less than 10 per cent of tax revenues. It is about one-fifth of the cost of national defense.

SUMMARY

1   Factual studies of the American distribution of income show that median incomes are lower than popularly believed. Even though incomes today are higher than in any other country or time, they are still not high in comparison with common notions as to what represents comfortable modern living.

2   The view that the poor are becoming poorer in modern industrial nations will not stand up under careful factual examination. Since the Industrial Revolution, average standards of life in Western Europe and America seem definitely to have been showing a rising long-term trend, tending to outstrip most underdeveloped nations. Even within the United States, the regional differentials in living standards are very great; there is a trend, though, toward narrowing the old differentials between North and South.

3   The Lorenz diagram is a convenient device for measuring the spreads or inequalities of income distribution. It shows what percentage of total income goes to the poorest 1 per cent of the population, to the poorest 10 per cent, to the poorest 95 per cent, and so forth. The modern distribution of American income appears to be less unequal than in 1929 or than that in underdeveloped countries, but it still shows a considerable measure of inequality and little change in recent decades. An interesting question is to try to relate the skew distributions of income to the more "normal" differences in human mental and physical abilities.

4   Minority groups—such as the aged, women, nonwhites, and various ethnic groups—pose important economic problems for any democracy. At the borders between economics and sociology, we run into interesting questions concerning the "circulation of the elite." Such popular clichés as "shirt sleeves to shirt sleeves in three generations" appear to have but a partial basis in fact. There is a strong positive correlation between income and social status of a person's parents and grandparents and his own, but the exact direction of causation is hard to establish.

5   Within the affluent society the public war against poverty goes unceasingly on. As each rampart is conquered, higher standards of performance are set by society for itself. The vicious circle by which poverty is environmentally inherited has to be broken if the antipoverty war is to be permanently won.

[8]J. N. Morgan, M. H. David, W. J. Cohen, and H. E. Brazer, *Income and Welfare in the United States* (McGraw-Hill, New York, 1962), pp. 3–4.

QUESTIONS FOR DISCUSSION

1 Let each member of the class write down on a slip of paper an estimate of his own family's income. From these, draw up a frequency table showing the distribution of incomes. What is the median income? The arithmetic mean or average income?

2 How much do you think it takes for a childless married couple to live comfortably in your community? How would the money be spent?

3 Were your parents better off than their parents? What does this suggest with respect to the advantages and disadvantages of capitalism versus the modern mixed economy?

4 Formulate some of your own ethical beliefs concerning how unequal incomes should be for people of different abilities and needs. How do you justify these beliefs? Would a nineteenth-century American agree? A Russian? A Fiji Islander? What is the relevance of the Bureau of Labor Statistics report that those in the under-$1,000 income class give 3.3 per cent of their income to church and charity while those in the over-$10,000 class give 2.6 per cent?

5 Compare the front-endpaper charts with Table 6-1. Note how Japan has come up. What about the United Kingdom? The U.S.S.R.? The United States and Germany?

6 What are your views on the Food Stamp program which channels surplus farm products to the poor? Contrast with cash aids.

7 *Extra-credit problem:* Instead of using the Lorenz curve to measure inequality, why not calculate the "average absolute income difference between *every pair* of families" in society? Such a standardized so-called "Gini coefficient" turns out to be *identical* to the Lorenz measure. Pareto used still a different measure of inequality. He discovered that the upper tail of the distribution became a straight line with negative slope if he used logarithm scales to plot (1) log of percentage of families with income above each income level against (2) log of that income level. When inequality rises, the "average income of those richer than you" becomes a larger constant multiple of your income; but by "Pareto's Law" it has to be the same (new) *common* multiple no matter how rich you become. (Obviously, when you get to Rockefeller or whoever is the richest man in the world, Pareto's Law must finally fail. It also fails at incomes lower than the mode.)

Review your understanding of the following concepts:

income distribution	normal and skew distributions
mean, median, and modal income	social stratification
per capita incomes	minimum budget
Lorenz curve of income and wealth	war against poverty

Labor and Industrial Relations

Almost everybody is at some time in the labor force. Nearly half of our hours awake are spent on the job. Earnings from work—wages, salaries, and unincorporated earnings—constitute fully four-fifths of the total of national income. It is no wonder that the late Sumner Slichter of Harvard said—with pardonable exaggeration—that ours is a *laboristic* rather than a capitalistic society.

This chapter surveys the important role of labor unions in American life, paving the way for the more detailed discussion of wage determination in Part Four.

WHO BELONGS TO UNIONS?

About 20 million Americans belong to a union. Almost one-third of the nonagricultural working force is thus made up of union men. If we excluded white-collar workers, foremen, and executives, the proportion would be higher still. In certain important industries, such as rail and other transportation, basic steel, autos, mining, and clothing, practically all eligible workers belong to unions. Few large firms escape being organized by unions.

Figure 7-1 shows the growth of union membership since 1900: the slow, steady advance up to World War I; the upsurge during that war and immediately thereafter; and the rather sharp decline and leveling off during the 1920s. It shows the explosive acquisition of new members during the New Deal recovery years following the Great Depression; the continued rapid growth during World War II; and finally, the relative stagnation in recent years.

To what unions do workers belong? Here are the eight largest, with size of membership: the Teamsters (TCWH), 1,700,000; the United Auto Workers (UAW), 1,400,000; the United Steel Workers (USA), 1,100,000; the Electrical Workers International Brotherhood (IBEW), 900,000; the Machinists (IAM), 850,000; the Carpenters (CJA), 800,000; the Mine Workers (UMW), 500,000; the Retail Clerks International Association (RCIA), 500,000.

With three exceptions, they all belong to the merged American Federation of Labor and Congress of Industrial Organizations, i.e., the AFL-CIO. The Teamsters, under their leader James R. Hoffa, were expelled from the federation because of corruption. The United Mine Workers, under John L. Lewis and later leaders, have been in and out of the AFL and the CIO; Walter Reuther more recently pulled the Auto Workers out of the AFL-CIO.

Statistics of membership understate the influence of unions. Many nonunion people are covered by union agreements on wages, hours, and working conditions. If you took a solemn oath never to join a union or work under a union agreement, you would have to give up all hope of being a factory worker in many sectors of manufacturing industries. *In every single manufacturing industry*, at least 20 per cent of all wage earners are under union agreements—even if they are not actually union members. You would have to give up a career in mining; in construction; in transportation. Where could you go? You could avoid unions on the farm, in finance, and in trade.

Unionism spurted in the Depression and during World War II, but has been stagnating recently:

FIG. 7-1. Of nonfarm workers, 30 per cent belong to unions, as against but 11 per cent in 1933. The outlook for union growth looks bleak: "Automation" entails a trend toward fewer blue-collar production-line workers, and white-collar workers are hard to organize. The South, a region traditionally hard to organize, grows relatively fast; public and legislative hostility toward unionism, based on suspicions of union power, is on the rise. (Source: U.S. Department of Labor.)

Or go South: attempts to organize workers have met strong resistance there. Fully two-thirds of all union members now live in 10 industrial states.

Besides outright trade-unions, there are many organizations of professional people—like the American Medical Association (AMA), to which 300,000 doctors belong, and the National Education Association (NEA), to which 1,200,000 teachers belong—which in fact are important forces lobbying for higher incomes and specified working conditions. You would be naïve to think that the AMA and the NEA are not important influences on the interplay of supply and demand, even though economic betterment is not primary in their official constitutions. Within government itself is the new frontier for unionization: policemen, clerks, and even atomic-energy workers.

NATIONAL AND LOCAL UNIONS

There are three layers in the structure of American unions: (1) the *local* union, (2) the *national* union,[1] and (3) the *federation* of national unions.

---

[1] Many unions have Canadian chapters and are called "international unions."

To a member, the *local* is the front line of unionism. He joins the local in his plant or town. He pays his dues to it. Usually, the local union signs the collective bargaining agreement determining his wages and work conditions.

But the local is only a single chapter or lodge of the national union. Thus, a linotypist in Chicago belongs to the local union located there, but this is one of hundreds of local chapters of the International Typographical Union, whose headquarters is in Colorado Springs. Part of the local dues—one-half or less, usually—goes to the national union; the bylaws and practice of the local cannot transcend the broad policies laid down at the national level. The president and other officers of the local are probably local workers; but the important office of business agent is a full-time job, the salary for which is often paid by the national union. The trend is increasing for the national unions to lend a hand in collective bargaining by the local.

Altogether there are about 190 autonomous national unions. We have seen that eight of these have more than half a million members. More than half the national unions have between 10,000 and 200,000 members each; and a quarter of the national unions have less than 5,000 members each.

The number of local union chapters or lodges is no less than 76,000. Some have as few as a dozen men. A few giant locals cover thousands of men. For example, the Ford local of the UAW in Detroit is the largest of all. It alone has 30,000 members! The vast majority of locals number from 50 to 1,000 workers.

NATIONAL UNIONS AND THE FEDERATION

The AFL-CIO is a loose federation made up primarily of national unions as members. It is dependent upon these member national unions for financial support. Like the Big Five nations on the Security Council of the United Nations, the national unions have insisted upon their "sovereignty" and right of veto and their right to "exclusive jurisdiction" over workers in their area. Most of the headaches and fights come from such jurisdictional disputes.

The public thinks of the federation as being the most important part of the labor movement; but it is not. It acts as spokesman for labor; yet its own power is strictly limited. Thus I. W. Abel wields more real power in his capacity as head of the United Steel Workers than he does as vice-president of the AFL-CIO. Former Teamsters' boss Dave Beck had more to fear from government action than he did from criticisms of his financial peccadilloes by the AFL-CIO. As a federation the AFL-CIO strongly disapproves of union discrimination against Negroes, but it has no power short of expulsion to act against those member unions which still follow restrictive practices. When the United Electrical Workers and 10 other left-wing unions were expelled for being Communist-infiltrated, this was considered a precedent-breaking action.

The AFL-CIO has been politically quite active, working to elect candidates favorable to labor. Nominally nonpartisan, organized labor has usually supported Democratic candidates; but there have been some notable exceptions. And a few labor leaders do generally support Republican presidential candidates.

Figure 7-2 gives an organization chart for the AFL-CIO. The state and city federations shown thereon lobby at these levels of government and cooperate in producing TV programs, parades, and election or strike solidarity. The chart also shows a few local unions that attach directly to the federation rather than to any national union. Usually, these locals are in new fields just being organized or in fields that fall between the jurisdiction of the constituent national unions. The departments usually are coordinating bodies made up of unions in similar areas, such as the building trades.

THE URGE TO UNIONIZE

Aside from the medieval guilds to which craftsmen and their apprentices belonged, how did present-day unions first begin?

American labor finally reunited in the 1955 AFL-CIO merger:

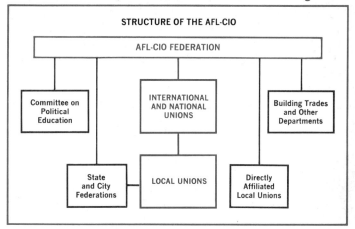

FIG. 7-2. The national and local unions remain the important units in our federated labor structure.

Why were men tempted to join such organizations? What are their general functions?

In past centuries wages were low everywhere. Productivity was then low, so that no way of dividing the social pie could have given the average man an adequate slice. But workers often felt that they were at the particular mercy of the boss; they felt poor, uninformed, and helpless to hold out economically against the employer, with his greater staying power in any conflict. Shops were organized on dictatorial principles, and orders were passed down from on high; the worker was but a cog in the machine, a dehumanized robot. Such was the worker's image of the situation as revealed in historical records.

Men gradually discovered that in numbers there is strength. One hundred men acting in concert seemed to have more bargaining power than all had by acting separately. Workers began to meet in taverns and chapels. They formed fraternal societies for mutual contacts, entertainment, and discussion. Gradually such early unions began to offer mutual death benefits and various other forms of insurance, and promoted self-education. They also began to propose standard wage rates that members were to insist upon getting paid.

Naturally, employers fought back. They, too, learned that strength came from formal cooperation, in which each employer backed up the other and refused to hire men on the "blacklist" of known labor agitators. Not unexpectedly, employers invoked the powers of the law against labor conspiracies and group actions. Later they hired gunmen and spies to fight unions.[2]

This then is the background of the modern American union. In contrast to the labor movements in many foreign countries, American unions exist primarily for *economic* betterment: to try to get higher wages, shorter hours, more vacations, easier work rules,

[2]The chief weapons used by employers to fight unions have been (1) discriminatory discharge of union members, (2) the blacklist, (3) the lockout, (4) the "yellow-dog" contract (requiring agreement in advance not to join a union), (5) the labor spy, (6) the strikebreaker and armed guards, and (7) the "company union." Also, employers have used court injunctions to fight unions.

fringe benefits such as pensions and health insurance, democratic rights for men on the job, and so forth.

While economic goals are the major preoccupation and reason for the existence of unions today, unions do also perform purely social functions. Union men bowl together. Through their union they join in campaigns for blood donations, charity, and civic uplift. Just as man belongs to his lodge, his church, the American Legion, and his boat club, so may he feel the necessity of union affiliation. (This is not to deny that a co-worker down the line may never do more than pay his union dues; or that still another worker, whose wage is also determined by collective bargaining, may detest the whole idea of organized labor.)

BRIEF HISTORY OF THE AMERICAN LABOR MOVEMENT

Although American labor was late in becoming organized, the beginnings go back well into pre–Civil War times. Local craft unions of highly skilled, strategically placed workers (printers and others) were the first to be formed; and periodically, in boom times or in times of industrial unrest, these would combine in city and national federations for political and reform purposes. But not until the 1880s, when the AFL was formed, did the American labor movement assume its characteristic present-day form.

The Knights of Labor   In the last third of the nineteenth century, out of the populist revolt against "big interests," the Knights of Labor emerged. At first it was a secret society which all but "lawyers, bankers, gamblers or liquor dealers, and Pinkerton detectives" could join. Later, secrecy was dropped; and by 1886, the high-water mark, the Knights had some 700,000 members. The Knights represented an attempt to form *one great labor union* to speak for all labor. But it was a heterogeneous collection, throwing together "craft unions" of workers with one skill, "industrial unions" of *all* workers in a given plant or industry, and mixed assemblies of any who cared to join.

The Knights were much interested in political reform and agitation. Some officials were more interested in "uplift" and radical political changes than in day-to-day increases in hourly wages. After a few unsuccessful strikes, the Knights declined in membership as rapidly as they had grown. America did not seem susceptible to such a political labor movement, and the organization of the Knights of Labor was too loose to give it any staying power.[3]

The American Federation of Labor   In 1881, and formally in 1886, the present-day labor movement took its form in the birth of the American Federation of Labor. For almost half a century, until his death in 1924, Samuel Gompers dominated this organization and gave the movement its characteristic pattern. Though early interested in socialistic

[3] Again, around the time of World War I, the IWW (Industrial Workers of the World, or "Wobblies") tried to organize the whole working class for the overthrow of capitalism. It had limited success in its efforts to organize unskilled migratory workers, loggers, and metal-mine workers. It had greater success in inducing panic in Wilson's Attorney General Palmer, who in 1920 threw suspected radicals in jail in defiance of civil liberties. But nothing came of the IWW, and it soon faded away.

uplift movements, he soon realized that no movement opposed to capitalism would flourish on American soil.

Gompers' main principles were simple:

1. He insisted on "business unionism," aiming at day-to-day higher wages and better working conditions rather than engaging in the class struggle to alter the form of society. Labor was to get more and still more by evolution, not by violent revolution.

2. He committed the AFL to the principle of *federalism*, with each national union having autonomous sovereignty and "exclusive jurisdiction" over its craft specialty. This meant that the AFL would not tolerate "dual unionism": two unions could not try to organize the same workers; and a group of workers could not break away from a recognized national union.

3. Finally, he insisted on *voluntarism*, with the government not to interfere in collective bargaining. In politics he favored rewarding labor's friends and punishing its enemies, but he would not commit labor to any one political party.

Thus, the AFL was a polar opposite of the Knights of Labor in almost every respect. As the Knights dwindled in importance, the AFL grew. It has continued to grow. One might say that the philosophy of the AFL turned out to be the dominant philosophy of the American labor movement.

The unfavorable 1920s   After World War I, the AFL had about 5 million members and seemed to be riding high; but during the 1920s, labor met determined opposition from the National Association of Manufacturers (NAM) and other business groups. The "open shop" was declared to be the "American plan." Moreover, the 1920s was a "new era" of eternal prosperity. As John J. Raskob, business executive and Democratic party leader, said, anyone could easily get rich by saving $15 a week and investing it in the stock market. (He added that not only was it possible for people to become rich—it was their *duty* to become rich as well.) Also, the 1920s was one of those rare high-employment periods when prices were not rising; so discontent over the cost of living was not operating to encourage unionization.

Recovery and the formation of the CIO   By the depths of the Depression, the AFL had fallen to less than 3 million members. But with recovery, a new era for unionism was in the offing. The Depression had soured the American public on many of the slogans of the 1920s and had excited class antagonisms. Even before Roosevelt's New Deal, the electorate and the courts began to modify their opposition toward unions.

But within the AFL itself, the old insistence on the exclusive jurisdiction of national unions stood in the way of organization of the great mass-production industries. For example, before Judge Gary of United States Steel crushed the great 1919 steel strike, an unwieldy committee of some two-score craft unions was set up to conduct the strike. To this day the Carpenters' and Machinists' unions have never been able to settle some of their differences.

Astute observers in 1933 saw the handwriting on the wall: industrial unions were to play an important part in the future. John L. Lewis of the UMW, Sidney Hillman of the Amalgamated Clothing Workers Union, and other leaders formed in 1935 the

Congress of Industrial Organizations (CIO) with Lewis as president. Helped by new government attitudes, legislation (especially the Wagner Act of 1935), and court decisions, a whirlwind campaign followed; in it the important mass-production industries, such as automobiles, steel, rubber, and oil, were organized, despite the bitter opposition of the principal companies in these industries.

By this time the AFL had learned the important lesson of industrial unionism. It, too, began to organize on an industrial basis; but its craft unions remained dominant.

Unions in the 1970s   Labor's dream of a united movement was finally realized when the AFL-CIO was formed. The union movement seems now to have settled down, with few new industries left to be organized. A new breed of man seems to be moving to the top. Back in the days when unions were being born and were fighting for their lives, colorful men such as John L. Lewis, Philip Murray, and Dan Tobin were the leaders. The new men who are replacing them are often men with gifts as *administrators*. With millions of members and literally hundreds of millions of dollars in their welfare funds, the unions are in need of men who can administer and who can deal persuasively with Congress, management, and the public.

A new frontier for unionization still exists in the field of agriculture (as e.g., the Mexican grape pickers of California whom Cesar Chavez is trying to organize). Civil servants and teachers also are on the march toward organization.

COMMUNISM AND CORRUPTION IN UNIONS

Boring in by Communists used to be something of a problem for the union movement. Thus, in the 1920s David Dubinsky led a successful effort to purge the communist influence from his union, the International Ladies' Garment Workers. During the 1930s the Communists attempted to influence policy in many unions. Although usually forming only a tiny percentage of membership, they exercised an influence beyond their numbers because they acted as a unit, using Machiavellian tactics to achieve their goals. They provided zealous labor organizers, and Lewis himself in his factional disputes for a time tolerated their help. In the United Electrical Workers (until 1949, CIO), the National Maritime, and the longshoremen's unions, the struggles between the "Commies" and anti-Communists were especially severe; and in the International Fur and Leather Workers (CIO) Communists did get control.

After 1949 there was a showdown. In addition to expelling the UEW and half a dozen other unions, the CIO expelled Harry Bridges' West Coast longshoremen's union as a Communist-infiltrated union. Later laws against Communists became stiffer and stiffer, until the Supreme Court intervened. Except in a dozen or so unions, the Communists never attained any considerable power. Theirs was almost entirely a minority influence resting on their cleverness in strategy and in identifying themselves with popular labor causes. Whatever one may think of the economic wisdom of its policies, American labor is red-white-and-blue, not red.

Corruption   Gangsterism has had only a minor role in the union movement. After the repeal of prohibition, corrupt gunmen did work their way into some urban unions (e.g., the longshoremen around New York). Such union officials were more ready to sell out labor than to fight in labor's interests. Labor had some success in cleaning its own house; in cities with effective law enforcement, labor gangsterism is pretty well under control.

One trouble spot does remain: fraud and mismanagement of the sizable union funds are not yet completely at an end. Teamster Dave Beck got rich speculating with union funds, and other misuses of union welfare funds have been turned up by congressional investigating committees. "Jimmy" Hoffa, Beck's successor, long successfully defied the AFL-CIO, congressional committees, court-appointed monitors, and minorities in the Teamsters Union. Because Teamster members believed that "Jimmy delivers the goods for us," Hoffa remained in control even after courts had found him guilty.

Stirred by public revelations of graft, Congress overcame labor opposition and passed the Labor-Management Reporting and Disclosure (Landrum-Griffin) Act (1959). Among other things, this requires filing of union financial reports, limits union loans to officials to $2,000, and prohibits nonwage payments by employers to union representatives. The Act also provides a "Bill of Rights" for union members, which guards against rigged elections and summary disciplining of members by the union.

HOW DEMOCRATIC ARE UNIONS?

In Chapter 5 we discussed the problems involved in democratic control by stockholders of corporation management. Similar problems arise in connection with unions. It is true that union officials are elected to office and all union members are given equal votes. But officers once elected often stay in power for a considerable time, and between annual conventions the union is usually run by a small executive board. Men such as John L. Lewis and Walter Reuther have on the whole been popular with members; but if a member disagreed with their policies, he might not get very far.

The average union member does not participate very actively in policy formation. However, according to the late Sumner Slichter, who must still be regarded as one of the most astute writers on the American labor movement:[4]

This does not mean the rank and file lack influence. Their influence is great, but influence is not participation. If democracy simply means strong rank and file influence, most unions are democratic. The typical situation in a union is similar to that found in most organizations, churches and clubs of all sorts. There is a minority which is sufficiently interested in the affairs of the organization to attend business meetings and to participate actively in discussing problems. In the case of unions this minority usually asks the officers to press for stiff demands—stiffer than employers would be willing to grant without a long fight, stiff enough to force many employers out of business. In order to avoid trouble, the great majority of the union would settle for much less than the active minority demand.

Quite naturally the professional leader feels on the spot. If he disappoints the active minority too deeply, his leadership will be challenged. If he gets the inactive majority into too much trouble, he may provoke revolt also. He compromises, as, of course, he must. Usually he is more interested in placating the active minority than the inactive majority because he knows that the support or opposition of the active members is more important than the support or opposition of the inactive members. The record shows that union officials lose their jobs, not for being too radical for the majority, but for being too conservative for the minority.

[4] S. H. Slichter, *The Challenge of Industrial Relations* (Cornell, Ithaca, N.Y., 1947), p. 111.

HOW COLLECTIVE BARGAINING WORKS

Let us examine how collective bargaining is carried on.[5] Consider a production-line worker in a factory that has just been organized. An AFL-CIO union has petitioned the National Labor Relations Board (NLRB) for an election to determine the exclusive bargaining agent in this plant. The worker marks a secret ballot in favor of the union, and it wins more votes than an existing so-called "company union" which has no outside affiliations and which management prefers to deal with. The NLRB then certifies the new union as the collective bargaining agent for the plant, limiting any other union from negotiating directly with management.

A day is set for the new union representatives to meet with representatives of management at the bargaining table. Seated at the table will probably be a vice-president in charge of industrial relations; with him will be attorneys from a law firm that specializes in the labor field. On the union side will be the local business agent of the union and a small committee of union officers, and handling the negotiations will be an expert from union headquarters. He may be neither a lawyer nor a professional economist, but the economic research staff of the union helps him prepare an extensive brief backing up the union's demands.

The stakes Hourly wage rates are not the only issue in bargaining. In addition, the union may ask for a dues "checkoff" (whereby union dues are automatically deducted from the payroll of union members). The union may bargain for a "union shop," requiring all employees to become union members *within 30 days after employment*. Pension and health-insurance demands may be discussed at the bargaining table. In many industries where piece rates prevail, the structure of rates is an important subject for negotiation; the exact work load—how many looms each man will attend, and similar matters—may be discussed, and the general problem of how rapidly technological improvements shall be adopted will enter into the final contract. The seniority rights of workers and a grievance procedure for handling cases of discharge—these and many other problems will come into the collective bargaining.

Indeed, management has become worried over the inroads that organized labor has been trying to make into what it regards as its prerogatives. Many employers claim they can no longer run their business the way they feel is best. They find it hard to hire whom they will, fire for just cause, determine work methods, and decide on the order in which people will be laid off. They feel that every new decision occasions a committee meeting; and time that could better be spent on production must be devoted to labor relations. They claim the worker acts as if he has a *right* to any job he has held for some time. Such critics complain that many unions oppose incentive wage schemes, insist upon rigid seniority, discourage efficient work methods, and seriously limit the autonomy of management. A recent casebook on collective bargaining devotes more space to issues arising from workers' rights in jobs than to any other subject.

But at last the contract, covering many pages of fine print, is signed. Everything is set down in black and white, including provisions for grievances that arise during the

---

[5] Chapter 29 includes a more analytical discussion of the collective bargaining process.

life of the contract; often, too, there are provisions for the *arbitration* of issues that arise under it, each side agreeing in advance to accept the decision of an impartial outside arbitrator. The usual life of a contract is one or more years, with provisions made for reopening negotiations for a new contract under specified conditions.

Collective bargaining is a complicated business—a matter of give and take. Many business leaders have learned to agree with the statement by Cyrus S. Ching,[6] formerly vice-president of United States Rubber Company and subsequently head of Federal Mediation and Conciliation:

Where we are dealing with organized labor, we are going to get about the type of leadership that we are ourselves.

And many businessmen recognize the grain of realism in the statement by Philip Murray, who long headed the CIO:[7]

Employers generally get the kind of labor relations they ask for. If the unions indulge in "excesses," then the employer as a rule has no one but himself to blame for it. For instance, if he engages the services of labor espionage agencies such as the Railway Audit, Pinkerton's or others, if he stocks up his plant with tear gas, hand grenades, sub-machine guns, blackjacks, rifles, and other implements of war, if he hires high-priced Wall Street lawyers to harass the union before the Labor Board and in the courts, if he distributes to his foremen anti-union literature and lets it be known to them that any harm they can do to the union would be forgiven by him, if he contributes to anti-labor organizations such as the notorious Johnstown Citizens' Committee, if he quibbles over words, if he refuses to consent to an election or to sign a contract when he knows the union has a majority, if after a contract has been forced from him he delays and hampers the settlements of grievances, if he continues to discriminate against union members, then labor will answer in kind and nine out of ten businessmen, viewing it from afar, will say, "Ah, another excess."

Peaceful coexistence   No one should get a false impression that all management has been antiunion. Violence makes the headlines, while patient cooperation goes unnoticed. In most industries there has long been a successful pattern of fruitful cooperation between labor and management. To highlight this fact, the National Planning Association has published studies describing cases of successful labor relations. These reports describe "how historically hostile groups can co-exist on a basis of reasonable equality of position in the enterprise, and at the same time be participants in a common endeavor from which both seek security, opportunity, and sustenance."[8]

Thus, the West Coast pulp and paper industry, whose leading member is the Crown Zellerbach Corporation, has had 40 years of healthy labor relations. The Nashua Corporation has maintained relations with no less than seven AFL unions for 38 years without strikes. And the Hickey-Freeman Company, a men's-clothing manufacturer, has dealt with unions for 55 years without a strike; for 40 years no grievance ever went as far as arbitration. Many historic problem areas in labor relations, like the West Coast longshoremen, have settled down in recent years to relatively peaceful dealings.

[6] Cyrus S. Ching, "Problems in Collective Bargaining," *Journal of Business*, 1938, Part 2, p. 40.
[7] P. Murray and M. L. Cooke, *Organized Labor and Production* (Harper, New York, 1940), pp. 259–260.
[8] *Fundamentals of Labor Peace*, Case Study 14 (National Planning Association, Washington, 1953).

These are not cases where peace has been maintained because the management or the union was soft. Hard bargaining on both sides is likely to accompany a good management-labor relationship; apathy on both sides or one-sided dominance postpones solutions and ultimately leads to breakdowns. In healthy cases, each side has a respect for the rights of the other. The two sides are not in love, but they are compatible.

ROLE OF GOVERNMENT IN COLLECTIVE BARGAINING

Although unions are relatively free in this country in comparison with their control in collectivist countries, government has played an important role in their historic development. Two hundred years ago, when labor first tried to organize in England and America, the common-law doctrines against "conspiracy in restraint of trade" were used against their members. Well into this century, unions and their members were convicted by courts, assessed for damages, and harassed by various injunctive procedures. Repeatedly the Supreme Court struck down acts designed to improve work conditions for women and children and other reform legislation on hours and wages.

In 1890 the Sherman Antitrust Act made monopolistic restraints of trade illegal. It did not mention labor unions; but in the next 20 years, the Sherman Act was used increasingly by the courts to curb the activities of unions. If a union struck for ends which in a judge's opinion were undesirable, he might rule against it. And many traditional means used by unions were declared illegal even if in pursuit of a legitimate end.

Finally the AFL was forced into the political arena; and in 1914, labor was successful in getting the Clayton Antitrust Act passed. Although hailed as "labor's Magna Carta" and designed to remove labor from prosecution under the Sherman Act, this did not end legislative and judicial opposition to the labor movement.

Prolabor legislation   After 1930 the pendulum swung toward support of union bargaining. Particular landmarks of legislation involved the Railway Labor Act (1926), which accepted the basic premise of collective bargaining; the Norris–La Guardia Act (1932), which virtually wiped out injunctive interference of the federal courts in labor disputes; the Walsh-Healey Act (1935), which provided that minimum wage standards be required on all government contracts; and the Fair Labor Standards Act (1938), which set a minimum wage ($1.60 in 1970) for most nonfarm workers engaged in interstate commerce, barred child labor, and called for time-and-a-half pay for hours in excess of 40 per week.

The biggest landmark of all was the National Labor Relations (Wagner) Act (1935). It stated bluntly:

Employees shall have the right to self-organization, to form, join, or assist labor organizations, to bargain collectively through representatives of their own choosing, and to engage in concerted activities, for the purpose of collective bargaining or other mutual aid or protection [Sec. 7].

Moreover, it set up the National Labor Relations Board (NLRB) to make sure that employers do not engage in "unfair labor practices" against labor.[9] The NLRB also goes

---

[9] The term "unfair labor practices" as used in the Wagner Act refers to employers' activities that interfere with employees' rights to self-organization. Examples of such employer practices are (1) firing

into plants and holds elections to see what organization is to be regarded as the collective bargaining representative for all the workers. It can, and does, issue "cease and desist orders" against employers, enforceable by the courts after appeal; and it often makes employers reinstate with back pay employees unjustly discharged.

Without such favorable governmental attitudes, it is doubtful that the union movement could have grown to its present status.

Antiunion trends After World War II the electorate became fed up with strikes and rising prices. Labor was no longer considered the underdog; and people felt that the Wagner Act had been one-sided, favoring labor and putting all the penalties upon the employer. Congress passed the Labor-Management Relations (Taft-Hartley) Act (1947).[10] This is a *two-edged* labor relations law that—unlike the Wagner Act—prescribes standards of conduct for unions as well as employers. The hand of the worker who does not want to join a union is also strengthened, and so are rights of a member within the union as against the officers. Among its principal features are the following:

Strikes which "imperil the national health or safety" may be suspended by an 80-day court injunction requested by the Attorney General. Unions must give 60-day notice before any strike.

Unfair union labor practices are defined, and unions' behavior limited. Unions can be sued and held responsible for acts of their agents. The "closed shop," which requires all employees to be union members, is limited, and states are given a free hand to pass stronger laws. Secondary boycotts and jurisdictional strikes are made illegal. Political activity and financial contributions by unions are restricted; the free-speech rights of the employer are reaffirmed and strengthened.

CURRENT BARGAINING PROBLEMS

The key issues facing America and other nations in the 1970s are these:

1. Organized labor tries to improve its money wage rates, in the hope that this will not induce a commensurate rise in prices which leaves *real wages* little or no better off. Because the strike is labor's ultimate bargaining weapon, and the right to refuse a wage increase even though this brings on a strike is the employer's ultimate weapon, work stoppages provide the major headlines in labor relations.

2. In an age of rapid technical change and much talk of "automation," union men are often more concerned about *job security* than about mere money wage gains. What good is a raise in pay for a job that no longer exists?

3. Modern mixed economies seem to be subject to a new disease—a tendency for anything like an approach to full employment to lead to "creeping inflation."

Strikes The power to strike is central in present-day collective bargaining. Contrary to common impressions, this power is, as shown in Fig. 7-3, used sparingly: the number

---

men for joining a union, (2) refusing to hire men sympathetic to unions, (3) threatening to close an establishment if employees join a union, (4) interfering with or dominating the administration of a union, or (5) refusing to bargain with the employees' designated representatives. NOTE: Workers always had various rights to organize, but legislation of the 1930s explicitly encouraged and expanded those rights.

[10] The Landrum-Griffin Act (1959), which was set up to cope with corruption, was discussed earlier.

Work stoppages reached their peak just after World War II:

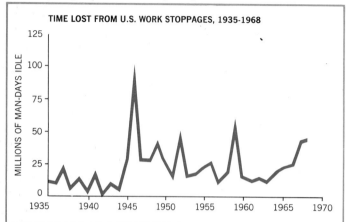

TIME LOST FROM U.S. WORK STOPPAGES, 1935-1968

FIG. 7-3.   While time lost from strikes is measured in millions of man-days, as a per cent of total labor days worked, it never has reached one-and-a-half per cent and has averaged less than half a per cent. (Source: U.S. Department of Labor.)

of days lost from work on account of the common cold is by far greater than that from all work conflicts.

Chapter 29, which discusses wage determination in detail, points out that, without the right to strike, a union's powers to bargain would, for better or worse, be substantially altered. Time and again concessions have been wrung out of an employer only by the realistic threat of forcing upon him the heavy financial losses involved in a prolonged shutdown. And, of course, workers also suffer grievous financial losses and demoralization from a long shutdown. Yet many a time employers have successfully refused union demands by a determined willingness to "take" a painful strike rather than accede.

When strikes involve key industries (such as steel) or key functions (such as the railroads or the docks) or take place on a nation-wide scale in an important sector like autos, at this point the public interest becomes overriding. Two men are not free to engage in a fight if that does harm to other people. Just as the rights of private property and of personal freedoms are not absolute and must be reconciled when they come into conflict with the rights of others and of the public generally, so too must the rights of "free collective bargaining" be subject to limitation and coordination with social necessities.

These are not academic questions. In 1919 Governor Calvin Coolidge said in connection with the Boston police strike, "There is no right to strike against the public safety, by anybody, anywhere, any time." But 1970 is not 1919.

In fact, the government will not today let a crippling strike long persist. Again and again, Presidents Truman, Eisenhower, Kennedy, Johnson, and even Nixon reluctantly, were forced to use Taft-Hartley injunction procedures or other devices to suspend strikes in crucial areas.[11] The President often appoints blue-ribbon committees to help end serious strikes. In the future, unionization among government and quasi-public workers—teachers, air controllers, firefighters, defense and atomic-energy employees—is bound to make the problem of avoiding pivotal work stoppages more acute.

Productivity restraints   Unions become especially concerned when new techniques threaten the job security of their members. The word "sabotage" arose when laborers

---

[11] If anything, the state seems prone to interfere quickly, urging compulsory arbitration proposals: a rail strike, which might reduce the national product by 25 per cent, has to be distinguished from a newspaper strike that hampers the dissemination of news and advertising or from an auto strike that puts off new-car purchases and sends ripples of reduced spending throughout the system. The case of rails is much more fraught with public interest than the others, serious as they may seem to be.

threw their wooden shoes (*sabots*) into the works of the new machines brought in by the Industrial Revolution to replace workers. "Featherbedding" refers to any rules imposed on employers merely for the purpose of keeping up the demand for workers: use of small shovels, limitation on number of bricks laid per day, requirement that use of music recordings be accompanied by a stand-by orchestra that does nothing but draw pay, requirement of a fireman (i.e., coal shoveler) on a diesel engine under the pretense that he is needed for safety reasons.

Entrenched unions have power to enforce uneconomical makeshifts. The railroads have been a flagrant example. As Chapter 29 will show, there are limits on how much unions can raise wages, but their powers are particularly great in keeping wages up within dying industries. Elsewhere, they are sometimes helpful in the orderly introduction of improved production techniques.

Wage-cost creeps   Later (in Chapter 41) we shall be discussing the problems involved in inflation. Few modern countries have been able for long to enjoy simultaneously (1) reasonably full employment and (2) reasonably stable price levels. Part of the difficulty will be found to arise in the realm of monetary and fiscal policy. Part may come from a tendency for wage rates to be sticky against downward adjustments, but to be prone to rise in excess of productivity improvements even before full employment is approached.

Some of this wage pressure seems to be associated with our system of free collective bargaining. In good times workers ask for, and get, steady wage increases. Unsuccessful strikes only slow down the process. Under voluntary or compulsory arbitration the chances are not even that the rate will be raised or be cut; it is almost sure to be raised. Those directly concerned deem it cheaper to buy labor peace by granting wage awards averaging more than is compatible with steady prices.

SUMMARY

1   Labor unions occupy an important but not expanding role in the American economy, in terms of both membership and influence. Their present structure is in three layers: (*a*) local unions, (*b*) national unions, and (*c*) federation of unions (AFL-CIO), the first two being the most important.

2   By the 1880s, the typical American pattern of federated, nonpolitical, gradualistic business unionism had been established. Since 1933, the CIO and finally the AFL have modified the pattern in the direction of *industrial* unionization of whole mass-production industries rather than relying solely upon *craft unionization* of skilled workers.

3   After a union has been recognized by an NLRB election as the exclusive bargaining agent, management and labor representatives meet together to negotiate a contract fixing wage rates, work conditions, productivity standards, degree of union recognition, seniority rights, and grievance procedures.

4   Right up until the middle 1930s there was bitter opposition to unions. But finally, the pendulum of government swung to support of collective bargaining, and since the Wagner Act (1935) most manufacturing industries have become unionized. The result has been less violence, but still vigorous collective bargaining between the opposing groups. After 1947 Congress felt it had become one-sided in favor of labor and passed the Taft-Hartley and Landrum-Griffin Acts to correct the balance. Strike threats in crucial industries always invoke governmental action.

5   Aside from strikes and featherbedding, a major post-World War II problem has been the relation of wage increases to the price level. If patterns of "successive rounds of general wage increases" are established that go far beyond the 3 to $3\frac{1}{2}$ per cent yearly rise in productivity, the price level is almost sure to rise in an inflationary manner and "cost-push" inflation will become a serious problem—as we shall see in Chapter 41.

QUESTIONS FOR DISCUSSION

1   Describe the structure of America's organized labor. Describe the layers of the union movement. Which are the largest unions in your locality?

2   Historically, American unions have followed principles associated with Gompers. What are these? How have they been modified since 1933? How do you explain the fact that American labor has not been more active in politics along the lines of European socialists?

3   Give some contrasting examples of peaceful collective bargaining.

4   Describe the swing of the pendulum in the attitude of legislatures and courts toward organized labor before and after the Wagner Act.

5   Should policemen have the right to strike? Postmen? Milkmen? Anyone?

6   "Wage rates tend to be sticky as far as downward moves are concerned." Why might this be increasingly true? Interpret the phrase "inflationary wage-cost push."

7   Does early company opposition to unions (use of Court injunctions, discharge, etc.) remind you at all of college opposition to student activism?

Review your understanding of the following concepts:

national and local union	strike, lockout, work stoppage
AFL-CIO federation	union corruption, communism
UAW, UMW, NLRB	Wagner, Taft-Hartley Acts
collective bargaining	featherbedding
business versus revolutionary unionism	wage-cost push on prices
craft versus industrial unions	automation and occupational trends

Economic Role of Government: Expenditure, Regulation, Finance

8

Government plays an increasing role in the modern mixed economy. This is reflected in the quantitative growth of government expenditure, of redistribution of income by government, and of direct regulation of economic life. So in this chapter we survey government expenditure. In the next chapter we survey government taxation and local and state finance. Part Six analyzes the war against poverty and inequality, against urban and environmental blight.

THE GROWTH OF GOVERNMENT EXPENDITURE

Before World War I, federal, state, and local government expenditure amounted to little more than one-twelfth of our whole national income. During World War II, it became necessary for the government to consume about half of the nation's greatly expanded total output. In half a century, the cost of all government in the United States rose from a minute $3 billion spent in 1913 to over $250 billion per year in the early 1970s.

For more than a century, national income and production have been rising. At the same time, in almost all countries and cultures, the trend of governmental expenditure has been rising even faster. Each period of emergency—each war, each depression—expands the activity of government. After each emergency is over, expenditures never seem to go back to previous levels.

Nor is the end in sight. Government expenditure receded from its World War II peak, but it did not drop to the prewar levels of less than $10 billion, levels which used to be considered alarmingly high. In the years ahead, regardless of whether the Republican party or the Democratic party holds office, the upward trend seems likely to continue.

Figure 8-1 shows the historical trend of total government expenditure and federal debt relative to the growth of gross national product. And Table 8-1 points up the

Government spending has risen faster than gross national product all this century:

GOVERNMENT EXPENDITURES, GROSS NATIONAL PRODUCT, AND NATIONAL DEBT, 1900-1970

Gross National Product

Total Annual Government Expenditure

National Debt

FIG. 8-1. Government expenditures include federal, state, and local annual expenditures. Note the relative trends. Also note that this is a "ratio," or "semilog," chart, with equal vertical distances arranged to reflect equal percentage changes. (Source: U.S. Departments of Commerce and Treasury.)

fact that rich countries tend, relatively, to spend more on government than do poor countries. (Also refer back to Fig. 2-4, page 22).

Note that mixed economies, such as Sweden, France, and (supposedly laissez faire) Germany spend relatively most on government. And these happen to be the kinds of nations which have shown the greatest growth and progress in recent decades. Contrary to the "law" enunciated by Australia's Colin Clark—that taking more than 25 per cent of GNP is a guarantee of quick disaster—the modern welfare state has been both humane and solvent.[1]

THE GROWTH OF GOVERNMENT CONTROLS AND REGULATION

The increase in collective expenditure is only part of the story. Besides larger direct participation by government in national production, there has been a vast expansion in its laws, regulations, and executive fiats governing economic affairs.

Perhaps nineteenth-century America came as close as any economy ever has to that state of laissez faire which Carlyle called "anarchy plus the constable." The result was a century of rapid material progress and an environment of individual freedom. There were also periodic business crises, wasteful exhaustion of irreplaceable natural resources, extremes of poverty and wealth, corruption of government by vested interest groups, and at times the supplanting of self-regulating competition by monopoly.

No longer does modern man seem to act as if he believed "That government governs best which governs least." Gradually, and in the face of continuing opposition, the methods of Alexander Hamilton were applied to the objectives of Thomas Jefferson. The constitutional powers of government were interpreted broadly and used to "secure the public interest" and to "police" the economic system. Utilities and railroads were brought under state regulation; after 1887, the ICC (Interstate Commerce Commission) was set up to regulate rail traffic across state boundaries. The Sherman Antitrust Act and other laws were invoked after 1890 against monopolistic combinations in "restraint of trade."

[1] When account is taken of high per capita incomes in the United States, our government share is a modest one. Still we raise a larger fraction from personal income taxes than does a country like France. Studying the pattern among scores of countries reveals that share of government tends to be least at low income per capita and where foreign trade—which is an easy object to tax in poor nations—is relatively unimportant. Exceptions remain, e.g., the low portion for the Caribbean countries compared with those of South America.

Regulation of banking became thorough-going: after 1913, the Federal Reserve System was set up to serve as a central bank, controlling member commercial banks; and since 1933 most bank deposits have been insured by the Federal Deposit Insurance Corporation (FDIC). The FPC (Federal Power Commission) and FCC (Federal Communications Commission) regulate power and broadcasting.

Pure food and drug acts were passed following the revelations of the muckraking era of the early 1900s. Loan sharks came under regulation in many states. The abuses of high finance, before and after 1929, gave rise to ever more stringent regulation of financial markets by the Securities and Exchange Commission (SEC) and other bodies.

Government share of national product is biggest in wealthy, developed countries:

TAXES AS PERCENTAGES OF GROSS NATIONAL PRODUCT, 1970

DEVELOPED COUNTRIES	RECENT AVERAGE TAX, PER CENT	LESS-DEVELOPED COUNTRIES	RECENT AVERAGE TAX, PER CENT
Sweden	41	India	13
France	39	Spain	12
West Germany	35	Colombia	11
United Kingdom	33	Philippines	11
Canada	29	Mexico	10
United States	29	Jamaica	9
Switzerland	22	Nigeria	9
Japan	20	Afghanistan	6

TABLE 8-1. Governments of poor, underdeveloped countries show a tendency to tax and spend less, relative to national product, than advanced countries. With affluence come greater interdependence and less need to spend on private necessities. (Sources: First National City Bank of New York; IMF; author.)

Political evolution With the passage of time, the radical doctrines of one era became the accepted and even reactionary beliefs of a later era. State and federal legislation was expanded to include minimum-wage laws; compulsory workmen's accident compensation insurance, compulsory unemployment insurance and old-age pensions; maximum-hour laws for children, women, and men; regulation of factory conditions, compulsory collective bargaining, and fair-labor-relations acts. Private property is never wholly private, free enterprise never wholly free.

To understand the trend toward greater governmental authority one must maintain a sense of historical perspective. Each new step generated strong political feelings on both sides. Thus the "square deal" doctrines of the Republican Theodore Roosevelt, which today would cause no fluttering of pulses, were once considered dangerously radical. Our Republic cannot, and would not if it could, turn the clock back to the conditions of the nineteenth century as represented by Henry Ford's Greenfield Village and McGuffey's *Reader*. Still, it would be wrong to think these historical processes inevitable—to join Omar Khayyám in his mournful chant:

> The Moving Finger writes; and having writ,
> Moves on: nor all your Piety nor Wit
> Shall lure it back to cancel half a Line,
> Nor all your Tears wash out a word of it.

A democracy generally gets—in the end—the kind of government it wants.

Unfortunately, not until long after the event will history tell us—and perhaps not then—whether or not a given expansion of governmental authority was a good or bad policy; whether it deserves the approval of all who are genuinely interested in conserving

Local and state spending has been rising faster than federal nondefense spending:

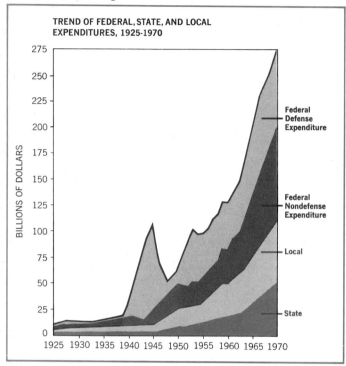

TREND OF FEDERAL, STATE, AND LOCAL EXPENDITURES, 1925-1970

FIG. 8-2. Federal expenditure rose sharply in the Great Depression, and even more during World War II. Defense expenditure has remained high; but it is local and state expenditure on schools, sewers, and roads that shows the steepest civilian trends. (Sources: U.S. Bureau of the Census; U.S. Commerce Department.)

and improving the good elements in the system. And in politics as elsewhere, it is only too true that the road to hell is paved with good intentions.

But past history does seem to suggest this: Unyielding conservatism defeats its own purpose. Steel without "give" will break suddenly under strain. Brittle economic systems without the flexibility to accommodate themselves in an evolutionary manner to accumulating tensions and social changes—however strong such systems may appear in the short run—are in the greatest peril of extinction, as science and technology are constantly changing the natural lines of economic life. If a system is to continue to function well, social institutions and beliefs must be able to adjust themselves to these changes. And without a sense of historical perspective, neither radicals nor conservatives nor middle-of-the-roaders can effectively advance their own true long-run interests.

Before applying economic analysis to the nature of governmental activity, we must get a broad picture of what that activity now is.

FEDERAL, STATE, AND LOCAL FUNCTIONS

Each American is faced with three levels of government: federal, state, and local. It will surprise most people to learn that, of the three, the states have always been the least important with respect to government expenditure. This is still true even though the years after World War II have seen strong expansion at the state level.

Prior to World War I, local government was by far the most important of the three. The federal government did little more than pay for national defense, meet pensions and interest on past wars, finance a few public works, and pay salaries of judges, congressmen, and other government officials. Most of its tax collections came from liquor and tobacco excises and tariff duties levied on imports. Life was simple. Local governments performed most functions and depended primarily on property taxes.

In Fig. 8-2, we see how the picture has changed since World War I. Though nondefense federal spending grows relatively less than the total of state and local, the federal government is still ahead in total spending.

FEDERAL EXPENDITURE

The United States government is the biggest business on earth. It buys more typewriters and more cement, meets a bigger payroll, and handles more money than any other organization anywhere. (The U.S.S.R., if regarded as one vast unit, might provide an exception to this statement.) The numbers involved in federal finance are astronomical: not millions or hundreds of millions, but billions (i.e., thousands of millions). Such magnitudes convey little meaning to the human mind. The magnitude may have more meaning if we remember that each billion dollars amounts to about $5 per American man, woman, and child. A current federal annual budget of about $200 billion would be equivalent, then, to about $1,000 per capita—about $2\frac{1}{2}$ months of the average annual income.

Table 8-2 gives the estimated importance of different categories of federal expenditure in the fiscal year 1970, i.e., from July 1, 1969, to June 30, 1970.

In the main, the first five items represent the costs of past and future wars. Together they account for two-fifths of all federal expenditure, as well as for most of the increase in federal expenditure over prewar levels. Naturally, these are estimates—subject to change when international tension changes.

Much of the sixth item goes to the support of conservation programs, the control of water and air pollution, and so forth. The other items are largely self-explanatory, representing aid to the farmer; welfare aid to the needy, aged, and handicapped under the Poverty program, Medicare, the Family-Assistance program, and other programs; and expenditure on labor, education, and health. The final category includes the costs of running Congress and the courts, as well as the general expenses of the executive branch of the government.

It needs emphasizing that the bulk of federal expenditure and debt is the consequence of hot and cold war, not of welfare and development programs.

THE CHANGING FUNCTIONS OF GOVERNMENT

The last quarter of a century has witnessed great political changes. How great have been the economic changes? How great have been the departures from the traditional capitalistic system? We can tackle these questions by considering government activity under five headings:

Direct controls   As noted, there has been an increase in the amount of government *con-*

Most federal expenditure goes to pay for defense and past wars:

FEDERAL EXPENDITURE IN FISCAL 1970	ESTIMATE (billions of dollars)	PERCENTAGE OF TOTAL
1. National security	$ 81.5	41.7
2. Veterans benefits and services	7.7	3.9
3. Interest on public debt	16.0	8.2
4. International affairs and finance	3.8	1.9
5. Space research and technology	3.9	2.0
6. Natural resources	1.9	1.0
7. Agriculture and agricultural resources	5.2	2.7
8. Health, labor, welfare, and education	62.9	32.2
9. Commerce, transportation, and housing	11.7	6.0
10. General government and other	.7	.4
Total expenditure	$195.3	100.0

TABLE 8-2.   The first five items take about three-fifths of total expenditure. Hence, purely civilian expenditure for domestic peacetime purposes is only two-fifths of the total. In the prewar era the proportions would have been reversed. (These figures are from the *Budget of the U.S. Government, 1970*, and include expenditures of $45.9 billion from social security and retirement trust funds and $5 billion from the highway trust funds.)

trol. Much of this regulation can hardly be dignified by the title of "planning," and market prices still run most activities. Economic analysis of government interventions deserves detailed discussion and will be met in later chapters.

Social consumption of public goods   As we have also seen, the increase in government expenditure means that as a nation we are consuming more of our national product *socially* rather than individually through private money purchases. Rather than pay to ride on the public roads as we do to ride on railroads, we pay for such valuable services by taxes.

Note that socially consumed goods and services are *largely produced by private enterprise.* The government pays for a hospital or typewriter, but these are produced by private industry. And so it is with most government expenditure on productive goods—the post office and armed services being notable exceptions. This is not what the original socialists meant by socialism—government ownership and operation of factories and land.[2]

Stabilizing fiscal and monetary policy   As will be seen in Parts Two and Six, an important function performed by modern governments involves the control of runaway price inflation and the prevention of chronic unemployment and stagnant growth. Two principal weapons are used: monetary and fiscal policy.

A central bank—which is a bank for bankers and which is given the power to issue currency—either is directly in the executive branch of government or, more commonly, is a public not-for-profit organization ultimately responsible to the legislature. We shall study how our version of it, the Federal Reserve Banks and Board, exercises *money and credit policies* designed for high production and price stability.

Since the beginning of recorded history, governments have had constitutional authority over money. But only in the last 40 years has it become widely recognized that *fiscal policy of government*—variations in public expenditure and tax totals, which create a surplus or deficit rather than a balanced budget—has profound effects on unemployment, total production, money and real incomes, and the level of prices.

Bad fiscal policy can make the business cycle worse. Stabilizing fiscal policy can moderate the ups and downs of business. Now that governments are large, claiming to have no fiscal policy is like claiming to be dead: left to themselves, budgets will definitely not balance; a policy of trying to balance the budget in every month, year, decade, or over the whole business cycle—these all involve deliberate social policy choice.

Later chapters will study monetary and fiscal policy in depth.

Government production   There has been little expansion in this direction in recent decades. Historically, our government has performed certain direct productive operations, and not others. The post office and parcel post have long been a function of government, while private management has operated telegraph service and railway express. Airports, but not railway terminal facilities, are usually governmentally owned. Municipalities now

[2]See the discussion of socialism, communism, and fascism in the final chapter of this book.

often provide water, sometimes gas and electric utilities, but rarely telephone service. (Abroad telegraph and telephones are typically publicly operated.)

The reasons for drawing the line at one place rather than another are partly historical and are to some degree changing; but, economically, the distinction is not completely arbitrary. Thus, the courts have held that, in the special case of "public utilities affected with public interest," there is limited possibility of effective competition among many independent producers, so they must be *publicly regulated or owned;* but one would not expect the production of soap or perfume to be natural candidates for governmental operation.

Whatever the merits of the arguments on each side, it is well to examine the facts to see how much government ownership of production has been introduced these last 40 years. Under the New Deal, there was but one direction in which such expansion took place, namely, the power field. (EXAMPLES: Tennessee Valley Authority, Bonneville Dam in the Northwest, Hoover Dam in the Southwest, rural electrification, and so forth.) Unlike Canada, or Sweden, or Britain, we have never had national ownership of railroads, coal mines, steel mills, airlines, or radio and television broadcasting.

If words are used in their traditional meanings, it is not incorrect to call TVA "creeping socialism." The fact to note is how little of that sort of thing has, for better or worse, taken place in recent years.[3]

The atomic-energy program was a post-New Deal development: It shows how poorly traditional "black-and-white" words and concepts are adapted to describe the gray territory of modern life. When the government pays General Electric a negligible fixed fee to start and run a vast nuclear industry, is this private or public enterprise? Private, in that the workers are GE employees and not civil servants. But the government puts up all the money, and certainly audits all major decisions. So the whole development of the atomic and hydrogen bombs could by some be called "galloping socialism." (For peacetime atomic energy, the government is relinquishing some of its monopoly. But decisions about secrecy, about fusionable and fissile materials, about patents, will keep nuclear energy subject to public supervision.)

Finally, we should recognize that there has been a considerable rise of the federal payroll and in the number of government employees. Many of the latter are in the Washington executive offices, in regional laboratories, in the armed services, and so forth. Even if they are not producing private goods and services in competition with private industry, such resources are being directly used by the government, with government as employer.

Welfare expenditures Now we turn to an activity of government that has expanded tremendously since 1929 and that will continue to loom large in the decades ahead, namely, *government welfare expenditure,* which transfers purchasing power to the needy or worthy without regard to their providing a service in return. Payments are made to

---

[3]It is noteworthy that the war plants built by the government were, almost without exception, sold to private industry or shut down. Government research organizations and contracts do finance much of our research and development (R&D) efforts.

veterans, old people, the handicapped, pensioned workers and their families, and unemployed people. This category of "transfer expenditure" deserves further discussion. Because of it the modern mixed economy system is sometimes called the "welfare state."

TRANSFERS AND TAXES IN THE WELFARE STATE

A government check received by a veteran or needy family head differs economically from that received by a postal clerk or by a man who produces typewriters. It is important to understand why, because our later discussion of national income will involve this same distinction between items that are "transfers" and items that are directly parts of national production or of national income.

We shall see later that governmental payments to a postal clerk and stenographer or to a missile and typewriter producer are counted as parts of national income and output. Why? Because they do cover services rendered, they do use up resources and production, and they do provide collective direct or indirect consumption to the citizens of the United States. Whether they are financed by taxes, by the sale of postage stamps, or by any other means, the government uses its dollars to provide services for citizens' use. Such dollars are as much part of national income as the dollars used by a railroad company to provide transportation services for its customers.

A blind widow's pension is something else again. Socially, it may be one of our most desirable expenditures, but nevertheless it is not part of national output or national income. Why? Because the widow does not render any concurrent services to the government or its citizens in exchange for the pension. She does not provide any labor, land, or capital. The pension does increase her purchasing power, does permit her to live more adequately and to buy goods and services from other individuals. These goods and services *that she buys* are part of the national income and output; but they are *attributable* to the people and private factories that have produced them, not to her.

Minimum standards   Transfer expenditures have grown greatly in recent years. They grew partly as a result of the Depression, which made relief expenditures necessary, but they grew mostly because new minimum standards of health, nutrition, and security have been set up by the collective conscience of the American people. Society now rules that children shall not have rickets because of the bad luck or weakness of their parents, that poor people shall not die young because of insufficient money for operations and needed care, that the old shall be able to live out their years with some minimum of income. President Nixon's proposal for automatic payments to all families with low enough income (a version of the so-called "negative income tax") reflects this new view.

Are welfare expenditures anticapitalistic? We shall later see that, "on the first round," these expenditures do not directly consume goods and services; but by swelling the purchasing power of their recipients, they do create orders and jobs for free private enterprise "on the second round." The thing to note is that *the production induced by this process is both privately produced and privately consumed.*

Unless these expenditures are financed by new money creation or by bond borrowing, larger taxes will have to be levied on the public, and it is for this reason that they are usually called "transfer expenditures." Often the more fortunate citizens are paying for consumption of the less fortunate; and doubtless within reasonable limits, most people feel that this is proper.

In connection with welfare programs of the government, mention should be made of the fact that various *redistributions* of income among citizens are accomplished *by the form in which the government allocates the burden of the taxes it levies* on different groups and classes. The next chapter shows that there is a tendency in modern states for the well-to-do to be taxed absolutely and relatively more heavily than those below the median income level.

Thus, suppose there were no program of direct governmental transfers. But suppose the government made the very rich pay all the taxes for national defense and most of the taxes for civilian programs. Is it not evident, then, that it would be altering the inequality in the distribution of the after-tax disposable incomes that different classes have to spend on bread, cars, and anything else?

Along with transfer programs, one must include in the activities of the modern welfare state any *redistributions of income* it brings about by the way it differentiates in its tax system between the various income classes.

For the rest of this chapter, we can try to use some of the tools of economic analysis to understand the nature of the various governmental programs already surveyed.

GRAPHICAL ANALYSIS OF GOVERNMENT ACTIVITY

The production-possibility concept of Chapter 2, particularly Fig. 2-4 on page 22, gives insight into the nature of government activity. Figure 8-3(a) indicates on the next page how society can choose between (1) *private* goods (bread, shoes, gum, dictionaries), which families buy voluntarily out of their after-tax incomes at prices set by markets, and (2) *public* goods (battleships, roads and bridges, services of policemen and civil servants, defense, weather forecasts), which we consume collectively and which involve government expenditure (financed by taxes, deficit borrowing, printing of money).

What determines the actual E_1 position, which shows about a fourth of the total product being devoted to *public* goods and the rest to *private*? It is *legislative decision* that puts E_1 where it is and also determines the exact composition of the social expenditure as divided between the three levels of government.

What about the composition of the private sector at the point E_1? On reflection, one realizes that it does indeed depend on governmental decision making, but only in the following respects: (1) Welfare transfers by government help to determine the distribution of spendable incomes of people in the private community, money which they can spend voluntarily for different goods purchasable in the market. (2) Tax legislation by our representatives decides how to allocate the tax burden among different individuals and classes; such decisions impinge in a similar way on the allocation, in the background, of income distribution and E_1's private goods among persons.

Aside from these transfer and tax influences, the private consumption of goods is determined primarily by *voluntary market decisions of individuals*—as they decide to buy white rather than rye bread, beef rather than pork, boats rather than autos, and Scotties rather than Kleenex.

Cutting out waste is not the same as cutting scope of government:

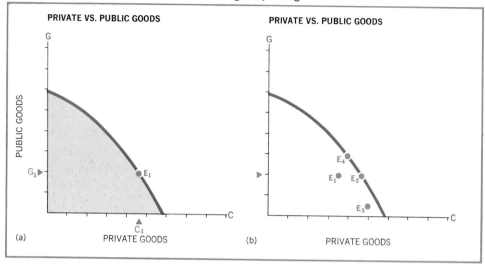

FIG. 8-3(a).   Along society's production-possibility frontier giving choices between private and public expenditure on goods and services, democratic voting decides on a point like E_1.

FIG. 8-3(b).   Cutting out waste and increasing governmental efficiency take society from E_1, inside the *p-p frontier*, out to it. This permits the previous level of government to be reached at E_2 with less sacrifice of private goods. (Cutting down on scope without change in efficiency would mean, however, moving inside the frontier down to E_3.) At E_4 the populace has decided to allocate the new affluence that efficiency has brought among new extra goods of both private and governmental type.

Suppose international tension ended, thereby permitting us to cut down greatly on defense expenditure and on taxes so as to leave people with more money to spend individually. Provided the economic system were made to run smoothly without significant unemployment, you should be able to show that the point E_1 would then move down the *p-p frontier* in Fig. 8-3(a), toward more private and less social spending.

Suppose the electorate agrees with Galbraith's *The Affluent Society,* and decides it would prefer to enjoy less private consumption of cars and such and enjoy more social consumption of roads, parks, schools, and hospitals. You should be able to show the upward and leftward movement of E_1 as it climbs the production-possibility frontier.

WASTE IN GOVERNMENT AND SCOPE

Our diagram helps to disentangle a common confusion. Government expenditure can be reduced in two quite different ways: First, the people can succeed in making their public activities more *efficient.* They can abolish graft and waste and insist on better planning of programs and on more efficient administration. This is sometimes called "cutting out fat without cutting muscle."

Second, they can change the *scope* of government, reducing public expenditure by having the government drop many of the functions it performs. The government can build fewer roads, provide less weather information, cease to do research, or abandon conservation activities.

Figure 8-3(b) helps keep the problem of efficiency in government distinct from the problem of scope of government. Its move from E_1 out to E_2 on the *p-p frontier* shows the result of a successful program of increasing the *efficiency* of government activity: we can now get the same quantity of government goods and services for less sacrifice of resources from the private economy. If the electorate wants to leave the scope of government unchanged, the new E_2 point will be due right of old point E_1, with same G_1 level of social consumption but with private goods now increased as shown. (This came about in the background in something like the following way: the savings in efficiency resulted in tax reduction large enough to give people the extra income sufficient to use up all the resources released by government.)

As an alternative to the above case, suppose people succeed in reducing government expenditure solely by cutting down on the *scope* of government activity. Then there will have been no change in efficiency. Inside the frontier, the nation moves down and to the right to E_3.

Consider still another alternative. Suppose everyone favors efficiency and we do succeed in getting out to the *p-p frontier*. But now suppose the electorate decides it will use its greater affluence for *both* private and additional social wants. If it decides to spend its extra real income on something from both categories, then it will move up and to the right to the point marked E_4.[4]

SOCIAL AND PRIVATE WANTS: EXTREME LAISSEZ FAIRE

Let us return from graphs to the basic issues. *Why is governmental use of goods and services ever required at all?* What light can economic analysis throw on this?

In the first place, suppose all goods could be produced efficiently by perfectly competitive enterprise at any scale of operations. And suppose that all goods were like loaves of bread, the total of which can be definitely divided up into separate consumptions of different individuals, so that the more I consume out of the total, the less you consume. And suppose that there were neither altruism toward other people nor envy of them. And suppose that each person had equal initial access to human and natural resources, had equal opportunity in every sense, and could carry on his activities independently of others, much as in frontier days.

If *all* these idealized conditions were met, would there be any need whatsoever for

---

[4]Recall Colin Clark's alleged law that no government can tax and spend more than 25 per cent of the national income without creating disaster. If there were an absolute real limit, the transformation curves would have a corner at the limit, moving off horizontally to the left of it. There appears to be no evidence of any such discontinuity. The possibility that inflation might be the consequence of going northwest of some critical E point is a quite different argument; after study of Part Two, one can appraise such an allegation. (Figure 39-2 will discuss the fact that as society taxes to transfer from private to social consumption, some distortions of incentives and efficiency are likely to result; in *changing the division* of the pie, you may *alter its size*. This constitutes one of the genuine costs of government, and sensible electorates will want to give it due weight in deciding whether this should lower or should expand government's proper scope.)

a mixed economy? Why should there be any government functions at all? Indeed, why speak of "a society" at all, since the world could then be regarded as an array of independent atoms with absolutely no organic connections among them? Clearly, such a case of zero government is at one extreme pole.

Yet even in this case, if there were to be a division of labor between people and regions, and if a pricing system such as that described in Chapters 3 and 4 and in Part Three were to work, the need would soon grow for government courts and policemen to ensure honesty, fulfillment of contract, nonfraudulent and nonviolent behavior, freedom from theft and external aggression, and guarantee of the legislated rights of property. This would be laissez faire with minimal government—and a good system it might be if the ideal conditions presupposed for it were truly present.

SOCIAL WANTS IN REAL LIFE

Each and every one of the idealized conditions enumerated above is lacking in some degree in real life as mankind has always known it. Abilities, opportunities, and ownership of property exhibit disparities, depending on biological and social history. It is a fact that many kinds of production can take place most efficiently only in units too large for "perfect competition" as defined exactly by the economist; and many other imperfections mar the simplicity of the scenario. All this forms the subject of analysis throughout this book—analysis designed to provide perspective for the important compromises that a free society must make. But here, in a chapter on public expenditure, we shall concentrate on the factors that call for governmental activity.

Let us consider national defense. Nothing is more vital to a threatened society than its security. But national defense, regarded as a commodity, differs completely from the case of a private commodity like bread. Ten loaves of bread can be divided up in many ways among individuals in a group; but national defense has to be provided *more or less automatically for all.* Many individuals will appreciate it, much as they appreciate quantities of bread; but even among them, some would be more willing, if necessary, to give up more bread for a given level of defense than others would. Some, who are pacifists, may profess that defense expenditure does not interest them particularly; while still others may actually experience pain from this social good and would require much bread to bribe them into voluntarily voting for national defense.

Could market laissez faire, with no political voting and coercion, give the group the national defense desired by the majority? Evidently not. If I knew that I was going to benefit anyway from the defense you had paid for, why should I come into the market place and exercise a dollar demand for it? Patriotism would of course motivate me; but it would show itself in the way that I and my neighbors *vote on election day* and in the way we acquiesce to the coercive fiats legislated by our responsive government, rather than *in our day-to-day private purchasing.*

To be sure, the example of national defense is a dramatic and extreme case. But when you think of the night policeman, the presiding judge, the appropriation for a park concert, or the damming of a river upstream to prevent floods downstream—indeed, when you think of government activities in general—you find the same common element:

The benefits from a social good, unlike those from a purely private good, are seen to involve *external consumption effects* on more than one individual. If a good can be subdivided so that each part can be *competitively* sold separately to a different individual with no external effects on others in the group, it is not a likely candidate for governmental activity.

In Part Three more will be said about external effects: so-called "external diseconomies," such as the smoke from my factory chimney which contaminates the air for all; and "external economies," such as the advantage your fruit trees get from the straying bees I raise to help pollinate my own fruit trees. It is enough here to give examples of government activities justifiable because of external effects.

Take our earlier case of a lighthouse to warn against rocks.[5] Its beam helps everyone in sight. A businessman could not build it for a profit, since he cannot claim a price from each user. This certainly is the kind of activity that government would naturally undertake. It would meet Abraham Lincoln's test: "The legitimate object of government is 'to do for the people what needs to be done, but which they can not, by individual effort, do at all, or do so well, for themselves.'"

Or take the case of government provision of research on corn farming. No one competitive farmer is large enough to do it; and he also knows he cannot retain the monetary advantage of the research financed by him. Nevertheless, there is great benefit to the group and to society from learning about and adopting any improvements that might be uncovered by research on farming. As a result of these considerations, because of a clear *externality* in the use of knowledge, no prudent private firm can be expected to invest its scarce dollars up to the point of best advantage to the group as a whole.

Therefore governmental activity in this area of research, whether in its own laboratories or by commissioning of private or university research, may well be a desirable act of representative democracy. (Where a government project, like an atomic pile, involves external *dis*economies, policy makers will have to take them into account.)

This concludes our brief economic analysis of the nature of government activity. In Part Three the discussion will go beyond the question of government finance and will develop the economic principles that determine when a government might prudently intervene in laissez faire to restrain monopoly, regulate it where it is inevitable, and use tax or subsidies to offset distorting external diseconomies and economies. The next chapter will discuss public finance as it relates to the tax systems of the federal, state, and local governments and will discuss expenditures of the states and localities and their coordination with the federal government.

---

[5] The analysis of this section owes much to the nineteenth-century analysis of Knut Wicksell and other economists and to the important recent treatise by Richard A. Musgrave, *The Theory of Public Finance* (McGraw-Hill, New York, 1959). In the lighthouse example, one thing should be noticed: The fact that the lighthouse operators cannot appropriate in the form of a purchase price a fee from those it benefits certainly helps to make it a suitable social or public good. But even if the operators were able—say, by radar reconnaissance—to claim a toll from every nearby user, that fact would not necessarily make it socially optimal for this service to be provided like a private good at a market-determined individual price. Why not? Because it costs society *zero extra cost* to let one extra ship use the service; hence any ships discouraged from those waters by the requirement to pay a positive price will represent a social economic loss—even if the price charged to all is no more than enough to pay the long-run expenses of the lighthouse. If the lighthouse is socially worth building and operating—and it need not be—a more advanced treatise can show how this social good is worth being made optimally available to all. Parts Three and Four go deeper into all this.

SUMMARY

1   The economic role of government has been a generally expanding one. More and more activities in our complex, interdependent society have been coming under direct regulation and control.

2   A larger fraction of the total output here and abroad has been going to collective consumption of *public* rather than *private* goods.

3   An increasing part of the national income is being "transferred" by taxation and government *welfare* expenditure from the relatively rich to the relatively poor. There has been in America, however, no trend toward state ownership of industry and of society's means of production and as yet little detailed government planning.

4   Since World War I, federal expenditure has far outstripped local and state expenditure. During the Depression of the 1930s, expenditures on relief, public works, and similar matters expanded the federal budget. But the post-World War II budget remains many times prewar levels because of increased defense and space outlays, interest on the public debt, and aid to veterans.

5   The production-possibility frontier of Chapter 2 can help distinguish between democratic voting to determine the level of *public goods* and day-to-day family spending decisions to determine the level of *private goods*. The *p-p frontier* can also distinguish between reducing government expenditure (*a*) by reducing governmental waste or (*b*) by reducing governmental scope of activity.

6   Economic analysis of private goods consumable solely by individuals points up the contrast with *social public* goods which involve "external consumption effects" on more than one individual in the group. National defense, research, law enforcement, conservation, lighthouse operation, and similar activities must pass the test of involving such "external effects" if they are to be easily justifiable as government activities.

QUESTIONS FOR DISCUSSION

1   Name things which government does now that it did not do in the past.

2   Between now and 1980, how would you expect the government's share in the national income to develop? Why? What factors affect your answer?

3   How much does the increasing economic cost of government reflect decreasing efficiency? How would you go about making a scientific study of this?

4   "The radical doctrines of three decades ago are the conservative doctrines of today." Is this ever true? Always true? Give favorable cases and exceptions.

5   "Government expenditure on goods and services represents public goods that in considerable degree are *produced* by market-operated private enterprise." Appraise.

6   "To bring back the federal budget to earlier levels, defense and veterans' programs will have to be the main items cut." Discuss.

7   Define transfer payments and redistributive taxes. Describe some welfare programs.

8   Evaluate critically the statement on the proper role of government attributed to Abraham Lincoln on the middle of page 151. Could believers in big government as well as believers in small government both appeal to it? See a Swarthmore College debate on this subject between Stigler and Samuelson in P. A. Samuelson, *Readings in Economics* (McGraw-Hill, New York, 1970, 6th ed.)

Review your understanding of the following concepts:

government spending
public debt and budget
laissez faire versus controls
fiscal policy

welfare state, socialism
transfer expenditures
private versus public goods
efficiency and scope

Economic Role of Government: Federal Taxation and Local Finance

9

Discussion of public finance continues in this chapter with an analysis of taxation. Then follows a survey of the federal tax system, of expenditure and taxation at the state and local levels, and of the interrelations among the different branches of government. Finally comes the problem of tax incidence—upon whom does the burden of each tax ultimately fall? How does the tax burden on rich and poor compare with their benefits from public expenditures?

ECONOMIC NATURE OF TAXATION

Financing real expenditures   The state needs money to pay its bills. It gets the dollars to pay for its expenditures primarily from taxes. However, what the state really needs to build a battleship or run a lighthouse is not so much money as *real economic resources:* steel and watchmen—in short, the use of society's scarce supplies of labor, land, and capital goods.

In deciding how to tax themselves, therefore, the people are really deciding how resources needed for social wants shall be taken from all the various families and from the enterprises they own and be made available for governmental goods and services.

Altering distribution of incomes   The state also spends on *welfare transfers*, which go to particular individuals in the community for them to spend on *their* private needs and wants. Again, money is a veil that cloaks the *redistribution* of command over real goods and services which results from action by the state to tax some and give to others.

Recall also that, even if there were no direct welfare transfers, the tax system is altering the distribution of incomes that results from laissez faire. In deciding who shall be made to pay for the resources spent on social goods and services, the electorate can vote taxes that will fall heavily on the rich rather than on the poor; on the energetic rather than on the lethargic; on the owners of tangible resources such as land and property, rather than on the owners of labor power.

Thus taxation and transfers help determine the distribution of private incomes.

In the distant past, taxes were levied by those in power against those out of power purely in terms of expediency. A nobleman at Louis XIV's court might go scot-free, while a merchant in Lyons or a peasant in Normandy was sorely burdened. When scholars tried to form more rational guides to taxation, what principles finally emerged?

Benefit versus sacrifice principles   Of the many principles concerning optimal taxation, two major groups can be distinguished:

1. There is the general notion that different people should be taxed in proportion to the "benefit" they can be expected to receive from public activity.

2. There is the general principle that people should be taxed in such a way as to lead to a desirable pattern of "sacrifice"; or what is really the same thing, that taxation should be arranged to accomplish whatever the good society regards as the proper and equitable *redistribution* of market-determined incomes.[1]

Such general principles are important; but they do not avoid difficult decisions with respect to just what is the desirable structure of taxes.

For instance, consider benefit taxation. If you and I were *exactly* alike, then the benefit we receive from the armed services, the public roads, and general governmental services would be the same; so we ought to pay equal taxes. Similarly, take redistributional taxation. If we were exactly alike, then the amount of sacrifice we each ought to make would again be equal. No one then will quarrel with the *dictum:*

Those who are essentially equals should be taxed equally.

This notion of equal treatment of equals was important in the past and still is. If Man A and Man B are alike in every respect except that A has red hair, that is presumably not a legitimate reason for taxing them differently—any more than, in a rule of law, the fact that A is a friend of the Prime Minister or President should relieve him from taxation. As we shall see, the existence of loopholes in tax laws shows how necessary it is not to forget the above dictum.

However, a corollary to this dictum *once again raises* all the hard problems:

If equals are to be taxed equally, then there is a presumption that *unequals are to be taxed unequally.*

On the basis of neither the general-benefit criteria nor the optimal-sacrifice criteria does this corollary by itself resolve society's policy issues.

---

[1]Economists who think the utilities of different persons can be added together to form a total social utility speak of taxing to produce maximum total utility, or to produce some specified pattern of utility sacrifice. Thus, if each extra dollar brings less and less satisfaction to a man, and if the rich and poor are alike in their capacity to enjoy satisfaction, a dollar taxed away from a millionaire and given to a median-income person is supposed to add more to total utility than it subtracts. See Chapter 22 and also Fig. 21-7 for more on this so-called "law of diminishing utility."

Imagine that Man A and Man B are alike in every respect except that B has ten times the property and income of A. Does that mean that B should pay the same *absolute* tax dollars for police protection as A? Or that he should pay the same *percentage* of his income as tax to defray police expense? Or that opulent B, inasmuch as the police have greater need to spend their time in protecting the property of the well-to-do, will not have paid his fair share of police expense unless he pays a *larger fraction of his income* in taxes?

The general philosophy of benefit or sacrifice taxation similarly leaves unanswered the question of the best tax formula. It is one thing to say that the rich have greater "ability" to pay taxes than the poor, that their "sacrifice" is less when they pay a dollar of taxes than when the poor pay a dollar. This still leaves open the question: *How much* differently should unequals in income be taxed? What do we mean by "equity?"

PRAGMATIC COMPROMISES IN TAXATION

How have modern mixed societies tended to resolve these difficult philosophical questions? Democracies have generally adopted pragmatic solutions that will please neither the enthusiasts in favor of benefit notions nor the enthusiasts in favor of thoroughgoing redistributional-sacrifice notions. Modern tax systems are a compromise.

Where various public services at the local and national levels are peculiarly for the benefit of recognizable groups, and where those groups have no special claim for favorable or unfavorable treatment by virtue of their average incomes or other characteristics, modern governments generally rely on taxes of the benefit type. Thus, local roads are usually paid for by local residents; taxes collected on gasoline may on the whole be devoted more specifically to roads than to schools or libraries; etc.

Progressive and regressive taxation   On the other hand, considerable reliance has been placed on *graduated income taxes*. A man with $20,000 of income is taxed more than a man with $10,000 of income. Not only does the higher-income man pay larger income tax, but he in fact pays a progressively *higher fraction* of his income. This "progressive graduation" of the rate of tax is in contrast to a strictly "proportional tax" that makes each man always pay exactly the *same proportion* of his income, and in even greater contrast to a so-called "regressive" tax, which takes a larger fraction from low incomes than it does from high.

Definition: **A tax is called** *proportional,* *progressive,* **or** *regressive* **depending upon whether it takes from high-income people the** *same* **fraction of income, a** *larger* **fraction of income, or a** *smaller* **fraction of income than it takes from low-income people.**

The words "progressive" and "regressive" can be misleading. They are technical terms relating to proportions that taxes bear to different incomes. They have to be appraised on their merits, and it would be wrong to read into the word "progressive" emotional overtones of being up-to-date or particularly right-minded.

A personal income tax that is graduated to take more and more out of each extra dollar of income is progressive. While many taxes on sales of goods will be seen to be regressive, the reader should realize that a tax on fine wine, which only the rich can afford, might well be progressive. Even a tax that is strictly proportional to size of estate left at death could be progressive, since the man with twice the income tends on the average to have and bequeath more than twice the wealth.

Direct and indirect taxes   Aside from their degree of progressivity, taxes can also be classified under the headings *direct* or *indirect.*

"Indirect taxes" are usually defined as taxes that are levied *against goods and services* and thus only indirectly on people. Examples are: excises or sales taxes; cigarette stamp taxes; tariff duties on imports; turnover taxes, which are levied every time a farmer sells wheat to a miller and a miller sells flour to a baker and on all transactions at any stage of production; value-added taxes, which tax only the costs added at each stage.

"Direct taxes" are levied directly on people (e.g., income, inheritance, poll tax).

When certain minimum income is exempt from tax, that is an element of progressivity. When there is a negative income tax at very low levels—as in the Nixon 1969 family-allowance plan, which automatically pays out money to very poor families—that is even more redistributively progressive.

There are, of course, many borderline cases that do not fall neatly into one category or the other. We generally associate direct and progressive taxes together; indirect and regressive (or proportional) taxes together. But there are many exceptions to such a rule: a poll tax of $2 per head is a direct tax, but a highly regressive tax in that it takes a larger fraction of income from the poor than from the rich; as mentioned, an indirect tax on yacht gasoline or rare brandy might well be progressive.

Modern tax systems are, to repeat, a compromise. They give some weight to benefit notions; some weight to sacrifice and redistribution notions; and, one may add, some weight to expediency and politics—and to the economic fact of life that increasing certain taxes, however favorable it looks to an ardent redistributionist, would at the same time be expected to do some harm to people's incentives and to the efficiency of society's use of resources.

FEDERAL TAXATION

The great variety of present federal taxes is indicated by Table 9-1. Of these, the first two, personal income taxes and death (estate) and gift taxes, bear down "progressively" more on people with higher incomes.

Payroll and sales taxes are relatively "regressive" in that they take a larger fraction of the poor man's income than they do of the rich man's.

The corporation tax is intermediate in its effects. In one way, it is progressive, since most dollars available for dividends accrue to people of more than median income. (Although it is true that many poor widows and orphans own some shares of stock, still the total that they own is not a large fraction of all stock shares.) But to the extent that corporations can pass the tax on to the consumer in higher prices, a tax on business profits may end up being regressive or proportional.

A brief glance at the various taxes will be helpful.

Personal income taxes and corporate income taxes are main federal revenue sources:

FEDERAL TAX RECEIPTS FISCAL 1970		
KIND OF TAX		RECEIPTS (in billions of dollars)
Progressive Personal income taxes		$ 90.4
Death and gift taxes		3.4
Intermediate Corporation income taxes		37.9
Regressive Employment or payroll taxes		39.9
Excise taxes		18.0
Tobacco and liquor	$6.7	
Manufacturing and retail excises	1.8	
Customs duties	2.3	
Highway trust fund .	5.0	
Miscellaneous	2.1	
Other taxes and receipts		9.1
Total tax collections		$198.7

TABLE 9-1. Three-fifths of federal tax revenues now come from personal and corporate income taxes. These respond quickly to changes in national income. Note that inheritance or death taxes do little these days to redistribute wealth and income. (Source: U.S. Bureau of the Budget.)

Sales and excise taxes In order of regressiveness, these would probably come first, and there has long been controversy over them. As far as *federal* finance is concerned, no *general* sales tax has been passed, but there are excise taxes on cigarettes, liquors, cosmetics, travel, and certain other items.

Social security, payroll, and employment taxes Most industries now come under the Social Security Act. Employees are eligible to receive old-age retirement benefits of so much per month, depending upon their previous earnings and not upon any humiliating demonstration of poverty. To help pay for these benefits and those of Medicare, the employee and employer in 1970 each contribute 4.8 per cent of all wage income below $7,800 per year; the self-employed pay 6.9 per cent.

Taken by itself, a payroll tax is regressive in its impact upon the poor and middle classes; but when combined with social security benefit payments, the degree of regressiveness is materially less.

Corporation income taxes After a corporation has paid all its expenses and reckoned its annual income, it must pay part of its income to the federal government. In 1971 a small corporation is scheduled to pay 22 cents of each dollar of its net income in taxes; but when its earnings get to be above $25,000 per year, it must pay 48 cents of each extra dollar of earnings.[2]

Some experts oppose taxing corporations on the ground that they are only fictitious legal persons. Besides, they say, the corporate tax becomes a cost that is passed on regressively in the price consumers pay. To the extent that it cannot be passed on, they think it is unfair "double taxation" for the government to tax corporate earnings and also to make the stockholders pay personal income taxes on the dividends received from corporations. They advise: Cut corporate tax rates; or alternatively, give the dividend receiver a more generous tax credit for the taxes his corporation has paid.

[2] In wars, this and other countries have had an "excess-profits tax" on corporations in addition to the above ordinary income tax. Thus, in the 1951–1953 Korean emergency period, some corporations were taxed 82 cents of extra dollars earned, keeping but 18 cents. Critics of direct progressive taxes have urged adoption of "value-added" taxes: these differ from "turnover" taxes that put a tax on every sale by business, in that value added is calculated after purchases of materials from other firms have been subtracted, as will be discussed in the next chapter. Aside from not pyramiding the tax burden through production stages, countries use value-added taxes to increase their foreign-trade advantages.

In opposition some experts argue that corporations should be taxed heavily, with the bigger corporations taxed at progressively heavier rates. They believe that, if government must collect large sums of money and if further increases in the personal income tax are not feasible, then a tax on corporations is better than a sales tax. Also, they point out that corporations do not distribute all their earnings to stockholders but retain some to be plowed back into the business. The stockholder may avoid personal income tax on these corporate savings by capital-gains loopholes, as we shall see. According to such critics, a corporation tax will at least partially remedy the situation.

THE PROGRESSIVE PERSONAL INCOME TAX

Spring used to be an unhappy season, as people had to make a lump-sum payment for taxes on the previous year's income, which had often already been spent. Now things are better. All through the year employers automatically *withhold* from each paycheck most of what we shall have to pay to the government. This puts us on a pay-as-you-go basis: by the end of the year our taxes are more or less all paid up.

For some 20 million families, with incomes below $10,000 and no appreciable property income, that is all there is to it. They simply turn in their withholding-tax receipts at the year's end; file a simple form; and the Treasury refunds them any excess paid. For still other millions of families, with moderate incomes and not incurring any extraordinary deductible expenses, there is merely a similar short form to fill out.

Those with sizable incomes must fill out a complex form.

How much does a typical person have to pay at each income level? Table 9-2 on page 160 gives the tax schedule as of 1973. (Rates are always changing, of course.) Column (2) shows about how much is the tax that people would have to pay on each of the incomes listed in Column (1). Note that the tax starts at zero for poor people (actually negatively when family-allowance schemes become law), and then rises rapidly in relation to income. Indeed, when property income climbs to $10 million, 69.7 per cent will go to the government. Never does the total tax quite reach 70 per cent. (On income from wages and personal effort alone, under President Nixon's tax proposals, the highest rate will only reach 50 per cent—much below the 70 per cent rate of the late 1960s or the highest 91 per cent rate of the early 1950s.)

Column (3) shows just how progressive the personal income tax really is. A $10,000-a-year man is made to bear a relatively heavier burden than a $3,000-a-year man—14.9 rather than 7.2 per cent; and a millionaire is made to bear a still heavier relative burden. Column (4) records an interesting fact; namely, the fraction of an *extra* dollar that taxes will take. Note that this begins at 14 per cent and then rises. This so-called "marginal (or extra) tax rate" finally reaches 70 per cent on nonearned income above $200,000.

Column (5) shows the amount of disposable income left after taxes. Note that it always pays to get more income: even when an heiress moves into a higher tax bracket, the move gives her more income to keep. As Column (4) shows, the government never takes more than 70 cents out of each *extra* dollar. At incomes around $50,000 it begins to take more than half of each *extra* dollar from a couple; a bachelor finds this happens at $32,000. Earned income dollars (wage, professional, etc.) pay a maximum 50 per cent.

The income-tax schedule climbs progressively as income grows:

FEDERAL INCOME TAX FOR A CHILDLESS COUPLE, 1973

(1) NET INCOME BEFORE EXEMPTIONS (but after deductions)	(2) PERSONAL INCOME TAX	(3) AVERAGE TAX RATE, PER CENT [= (2) ÷ (1)]	(4) MARGINAL TAX RATE (= tax on extra dollar)	(5) DISPOSABLE INCOME AFTER TAXES [= (1) − (2)]
Below $ 1,500	$ 0	0	0	$ 1,500
2,000	70	3.5	14	1,930
3,000	215	7.2	15	2,785
4,000	370	9.2	16	3,630
5,000	535	10.7	17	4,465
10,000	1,490	14.9	22	8,510
20,000	3,960	19.8	28	16,040
50,000	16,310	32.6	50	33,690
100,000	44,280	44.3	60	55,720
200,000	109,945	55.0	69	90,055
400,000	249,930	62.5	70	150,070
1,000,000	669,930	67.0	70	330,070
10,000,000	6,969,930	69.7	70	3,030,070

TABLE 9-2.   A bachelor would pay more; a large family less. (Taking the standard deduction, the couple would begin to pay tax at $2,500. On "earned income" a 50 per cent ceiling applies to dollars above $30,000.)

Taxation and inequality   The income tax tends somewhat to reduce the inequality of disposable income. Thus, in Fig. 9-1, the hypothetical effect of progressive taxes on the inequality of income is indicated in exaggerated form. Note how the area of inequality on the Lorenz diagram has been reduced; progressive taxation has shifted the curve somewhat nearer to the 45° line of equality.

Loopholes and erosion of tax base   The United States collects a larger fraction of its taxes from incomes than almost any other country. This is not because our professional and well-to-do people pay higher rates of tax; they pay generally less than do people at comparable real income levels in Sweden, Britain, and other welfare states. It is because our average citizen, who is so much better off, falls in a higher income bracket that our lower income-tax rates actually are able to produce relatively more revenues.

On paper our tax rates look progressive. But many items in the total income base escape taxation. First, there are exemptions of $750 per person and various minimum standard deductions as well. Second, real income in the form of owner-occupied homes avoids taxation. Third, there is also some illegal tax evasion—cheating by farmers, doctors, waiters, salesmen with fake expense accounts. The amount of such evasion can be estimated, and in advanced nations like Great Britain, the United States, and Scandinavia, it turns out to be surprisingly small. Fourth, more important than evasion is legal tax *avoidance*, which is possible because Congress has legislated so many tax "loopholes" permitting large amounts of income to go untaxed or to be taxed at lower levels.

If loopholes were closed and the erosion of the tax base corrected, rates on all income levels could be cut without revenue loss.

Here are a few facts. Before the 1969 tax reforms, less than half of all true income was included in the tax base. Those with incomes of over $1 million did not in fact pay an over-all rate of 70 or even 50 per cent: a sample showed they paid an effective rate of 48.2 per cent, which itself was an overstatement if one takes account of many true income items that could be treated as low-taxed capital gains. Eighty-five per cent of all income taxes came from the low-bracket rates of 20 per cent or less: It is not the rich who pay for the bulk of government; they are too few. It is the median-income group, who, by their numbers, predominate. Critics often say, "Uncle Sam digs deep into high incomes, but digs with a sieve."

By 1969, when voters learned that 155 persons with tax-sheltered incomes of over $200,000 paid not a cent of tax, a taxpayers' revolt threatened. Therefore, Congress lowered percentage depletion allowances for oil slightly, cracked down on excessive capital gains and tax losses claimed by gentlemen farmers, and ruled that some forms of tax-sheltered income had to be included in the tax base at trifling rates. In the end the revolt fizzled out.

Progressive taxes tend to reduce inequality of income distribution:

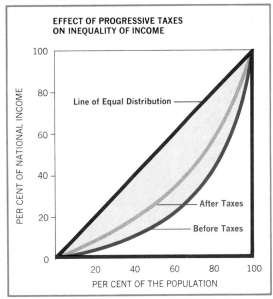

FIG. 9-1. The heavy curve represents the unequal distribution of income before taxes. The lighter curve shows how progressive (or "graduated") taxes create a more equal distribution of "disposable" income after taxes. The effect is exaggerated for emphasis.

PROGRESSIVE TAXES, INVESTMENT, AND SPENDING

Often, doubts are raised as to whether high income taxes do not discourage effort and risk taking. So far as effort is concerned, this is not an easy question to answer. For we shall later see that taxation will cause some people to work *harder* in order to make their million. Many doctors, scientists, artists, and businessmen, who enjoy their jobs and the sense of power or accomplishment that they bring, will work as hard for $30,000 as for $100,000; still others may prefer more leisure to more work as a result of progressive taxes. The net result is hard to evaluate. We shall return to this problem in Part Four.

The effects of progressive tax rates on *risky* investment could be quite adverse. In part, the government says to the taxpayer, "Heads I win, tails you lose." But recent reforms have improved the taxpayer's ability to "carry forward" or "carry backward" his losses, and also to spread out an extraordinarily high income by averaging it with the previous 4 years' income, thereby moderating greatly the penalty for erratic earnings from venturesome investment.

Careful studies at the Harvard Business School, cited elsewhere, confirm what has

Schools are the No. 1 state and local expense:

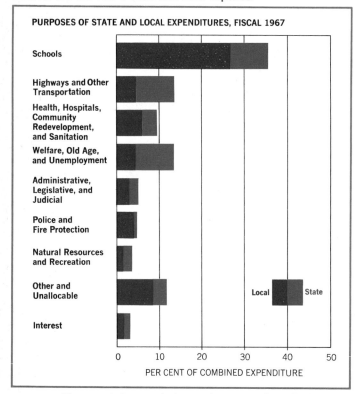

PURPOSES OF STATE AND LOCAL EXPENDITURES, FISCAL 1967

Schools

Highways and Other
Transportation

Health, Hospitals,
Community
Redevelopment,
and Sanitation

Welfare, Old Age,
and Unemployment

Administrative,
Legislative, and
Judicial

Police and
Fire Protection

Natural Resources
and Recreation

Other and
Unallocable

Interest

Local   State

0   10   20   30   40   50
PER CENT OF COMBINED EXPENDITURE

FIG. 9-2. The population explosion and move to the suburbs have put a strain on local and state finance, necessitating increased state and local debt issue. (Source: U.S. Bureau of the Census.)

just been said—that there are in fact sufficient perfectly respectable "loopholes" open to wealthy people so that they may typically pay but 50 per cent tax rates, not the higher rates shown in the table. They take risks and try for lightly taxed capital gains;[3] they invest in tax-exempt municipal bonds; they drill for oil, grow trees, or feed beef cattle—all more lightly taxed.

Opposing any unfavorable effect of progressive taxes on investments, jobs, and national growth, there is an offsetting effect. To the extent that dollars are taken from frugal wealthy people who spend small fractions of their extra dollars and are not taken from poor ready spenders, progressive taxes may tend to keep spending power at a high level—at too high a level if inflation is threatening. But statistics on how people spend extra dollars, as we shall later see, suggest that this effect on total spending may not be very great.

Economic science can point out but not itself resolve these various crosscurrents of progressive taxation. In the end, therefore, a voter must try to judge the costs and decide on ethical grounds whether he favors a more or less egalitarian society, greater or smaller rewards and incentives to initiative.

STATE AND LOCAL EXPENDITURES

Turn now to public finance other than federal. Although quantitatively the federal government's multi-billion-dollar expenditures exceed those of the states and localities, still these are important in their own right.

To see what the states and localities spend their money on, look at Fig. 9-2. All these items are more or less self-explanatory. Expenditure on schools—mostly by localities—is the biggest single item by far.[4]

---

[3] When we remember the loopholes discussed in this study, which show how the well-to-do can hope to convert heavily taxed income into lightly taxed capital gains from risky ventures, we find that *high tax rates may encourage risk taking by those who seek capital gains* and who know that Uncle Sam finances up to 65 per cent of their deductible costs.

[4] These figures represent net direct expenditure by the state and local governments. Funds transferred by the state to the local governments and spent by them are counted only once, as local expenditure.

STATE AND LOCAL TAXES

To see the main sources of funds to finance such expenditure, turn to Fig. 9-3 and Table 9-3. In terms of the previous discussion of kinds of taxes, the principal taxes of the states and localities are "regressive taxes."

Property tax   Note that the property tax still accounts for almost half the total revenues of state and local finance. Figure 9-3 and Table 9-3 show it is mainly the localities that levy property taxes.

The property tax is levied primarily on real estate—land and buildings. Each locality sets an annual tax rate. In a large city $55 on each $1,000 of assessed valuation (5.5 per cent, or 55 mils) might be the rate. If my house has been assessed at $10,000, my tax is $550. However, in many places assessed valuations tend to be but a fraction of true market value. Houses like mine may have a market value of $20,000, but be assessed at half that. My true tax rate is then less than 5.5 per cent.

The property tax is rather inflexible. Assessments and rates change slowly. In bad times, when real-estate values fall, the property tax is burdensome, giving rise to bankruptcy, mortgage foreclosures, and forced sales. In the zooming postwar economy, valuations and rates have been edging up.

In colonial days, a man's total income and wealth may have been connected with real estate; if so, the effect of a tax on such property would have been about the same as a proportional tax on income. Today, when so much of wealth and income is divorced from real estate, the property tax may be regressive relative to income—especially since small properties tend to be assessed relatively higher than large.

Highway-user taxes   As the name suggests, these revenues come from two primary sources: from a tax on gasoline and from license fees on autos, trucks, and drivers. In many states, more is collected in this way than is spent

The real-estate property tax still dominates local and state finance:

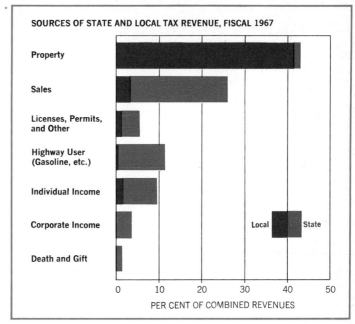

FIG. 9-3.   Most local and state taxes are of the regressive type, not easy to expand with needs. (Source: U.S. Bureau of the Census.)

Localities feel tax pinch and seek aid from federal government and hard-pressed states:

TAXES AND OTHER REVENUES OF STATE AND LOCAL GOVERNMENT, FISCAL 1967 (in billions of dollars)		
SOURCE	STATE	LOCAL
Taxes	$31.9	$29.3
Property	$ .9	$25.4
Other	31.0	3.9
Aid from federal government	13.6	1.9
Aid from state government		18.5
Fees and miscellaneous	15.6	15.7
Net total	$61.1	$65.4

TABLE 9-3.   While state and local taxes are almost equal, note that the latter are made up mostly of property taxes; and note that the federal government now gives as grants to the states two-thirds as much as the states give in grants to the localities. (Source: U.S. Bureau of the Census.)

on roads. The extra revenues are used for schools or old-age pensions or general government purposes, just as some colleges use profits from football games to buy fencing foils or even Greek manuscripts.

Highway and airplane taxes are usually justified on the ground that the taxpayer is simply paying for his *benefit* from using the roads and airports in much the same way that he pays for a railroad ticket or for his use of water and electricity.

Sales taxes   States are getting more and more revenue from general retail sales taxes. Each purchase at the department, drug, and grocery store pays a percentage tax. (Sometimes food and medicines are exempt.) Also, states usually add their own liquor and tobacco excises to the federal excises. (Some cities get into this act.) Most people—including many cigarette smokers and moderate drinkers—feel vaguely that there is something immoral about tobacco and alcohol. They somehow think two birds are being killed with one stone when these are taxed; the state gets revenue, and vice is made more expensive. (Note the element of self-contradiction here.)

The same moral attitude would hardly apply to a 5 per cent tax on everything a consumer buys: shoes, soap, a church candle. Rich and poor are taxed alike on each dollar spent: since the poor are forced to spend a larger fraction of their total dollars, one sees that a sales tax on nonluxuries is a regressive tax, taking a larger fraction of low than of high incomes.

Payroll and business taxes   States and localities often charge organizations license fees for their privilege of acting as a corporation, running a tavern, and so forth. Some states tax the net income of a corporation as well, and collect miscellaneous other fees from business enterprises.

In addition, all states have been bribed by the offer of federal aid into collecting a wage tax up to 3 per cent of payrolls in occupations covered by social security. The proceeds are used to provide "unemployment compensation benefits or insurance" when workers become unemployed.

Personal income and inheritance taxes   More than half the states imitate the federal government, but on a much smaller scale, by taxing individuals according to the size of their incomes. Such a method of taxation has already been discussed in connection with federal finance. A few important states, such as Ohio, do not rely at all on this relatively progressive tax.

Inheritance taxes on individuals who inherit bequests of property upon the death of a relative or friend are self-explanatory. They differ only in minor detail from estate taxes that are levied on the dead giver's estate. Gifts too are taxed, since wealthy people have every incentive to distribute their wealth before death to escape taxation.

Both the federal and the state governments share in estate and inheritance taxes. The federal government tries to act to prevent states such as Florida from advertising to old folks, "Come here to die and avoid all inheritance taxes." The federal government gives up part of its revenues to any state that passes such a tax law and accepts a state tax receipt as part payment of a citizen's taxes. State laws vary widely, however.

The inheritance and estate tax is called a progressive tax. The poor widow's inheritance usually pays no tax at all because of liberal exemptions, while the rich man's estate pays at a progressive rate. Social reformers attach great importance to death taxes for the purpose of preventing the development of a permanent moneyed caste, living not on its effort and intelligence, but on its property inherited from one generation to the next. Yet, in the 1970s the right to "split income," to make gifts, to set up complex "trusts" to escape capital-gains tax by death, and to bequeath tax-free insurance policies—all these have reduced death-tax collections to a low level. (This is also happening in Great Britain.)

There are other miscellaneous revenues. Some localities sell natural gas and electricity. Some, especially in Nevada, tax slot machines and racetrack betting. All collect some revenue from assessments on property owners who benefit from specific sewage and road improvements.

INTERGOVERNMENTAL GRANTS-IN-AID

An important revenue source is the financial aid that states receive from the federal government and that localities receive from the states.

Having access to more revenue sources, the federal government has increasingly been making grants to the states, and in lesser degrees to the localities. These are primarily for highways, public welfare assistance, and education. They help in part to offset the great regional differences in real incomes, as between North and South.

The Heller–Nixon plan   Because local and state needs burgeon and federal tax systems are most expansible, many authorities—such as Professor Walter Heller of Minnesota, former adviser to Kennedy and Johnson—have advocated massive (and unconditional!) grants to the states and localities by the federal government. Such revenue sharing has been much followed in Canada and Australia, and has been advocated by both Republicans and Democrats. President Nixon has proposed a revenue-sharing program of federalism for the 1970s.

Similarly, within the states there have been grants-in-aid to the localities—primarily for schools, highways, and public assistance (relief, old-age pensions, and so forth). Only in this way can the poorer parts of each state maintain certain minimum standards of schooling, roads, and living. In this way well-to-do suburbanites who have fled the city are made to share the burden.

Despite these grants-in-aid, there remain sizable differentials in minimum standards. It still matters where one is born.

CONCLUSION: THE THORNY PROBLEM OF TAX INCIDENCE

In ending this survey of taxes and other revenues, let us note a few warnings. Even if the electorate has made up its mind about how the tax burden shall be borne by individuals, the following difficult problems remain:

Who ultimately pays a particular tax? Does its burden stay on the person on whom

Experts try to answer the question, Who pays the taxes and gets the benefits?

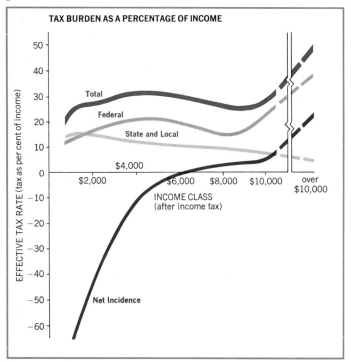

FIG. 9-4.   The blue curves show taxes as percentages of income broadly defined. Because the federal government levies payroll and excise taxes on the poor, even its tax structure is not progressive until one gets to the most prosperous quarter of the populace. However, as the brown curve of "net incidence" shows, after we take account of the favorable impact on the poor of government expenditure, the pattern is "progressive" and the brown curve rises with income. This means government has a balancing or equalizing effect upon the dispersion of real income. (Source: *Tax Burdens and Benefits of Government Expenditures by Income Class, 1961 and 1965*, Tax Foundation, Inc., New York, 1967.)

it is first levied? One cannot assume that the person Congress *says* a tax is levied on will end up paying that tax. He may be able to *shift* the tax: shift it "forward" on his customers, by raising his price as much as the tax; or shift it "backward" on his suppliers, who end up charging him less than they would have done had there been no tax.

Economists therefore say: We must study the final *incidence* of the tax—the way its burden ultimately gets borne, the totality of its effects on commodity prices, factor-prices, resource allocations, efforts, and composition of production and consumption. Tax incidence, thus, is no easy problem and requires all the advanced tools of economics to help toward its solution.

EXAMPLE: Does a tax on wheat raise the price to the consumer by as much as itself, so that the incidence is on the consumer? Or does the tax raise the price by half itself or not at all, so that the incidence is partially or wholly on the producers? Does it change oat prices? And does the tax kill off much of wheat production, so that it is having incidence effects beyond those which show up in money prices and wages and even beyond the burdens that you can allocate among the different citizens?

Parts Three and Four will develop some of the important tools that one needs to begin to tackle this thorny problem. Economists are not yet in agreement on final results. Some think the corporate income tax falls mostly on the consumer; some argue it falls mostly on stockholders or capitalists.

Figure 9-4 reports on a valiant statistical attempt to determine how progressive or regressive our over-all tax and expenditure system is. Experts agree that the results of such a study can be only approximate, since no one knows just how a corporate or other tax gets shifted. Even an expert is not a magician capable of making a controlled experiment in which he (1) measures things without taxes, then (2) measures things with taxes, and finally (3) determines tax incidence as the difference between these situations.

Note the sag in progression of tax around the median income level. The affluent do get taxed to help the poor, but the man in the middle is something of a forgotten man when it comes to tax burden. But, as the brown curve in Fig. 9-4 shows, when we consider which income classes *benefit* from government expenditure, the needy do show a more favorable "net incidence" than the affluent. With a negative income tax and federal revenue sharing, net incidence would be even more progressive.

SUMMARY

1   Taxes give the government the resources it needs for its *public goods.* Taxes also finance *welfare transfer* expenditures that change the distribution of income; and the over-all way taxes are levied affects the final distribution of incomes among people.

2   Notions of "benefit" and "proper sacrifice or redistribution" are two principal theories of taxation. Justice implies taxing equals equally, unequals unequally. Direct and progressively graduated taxes on incomes are in contrast to indirect and regressive excises.

3   About three-fifths of federal revenue comes from personal and corporation income taxes. The rest comes from "regressive taxes" on payrolls and excises. The personal income tax, except for loopholes and erosion of the tax base, is progressive, tending to redistribute income from rich to poor.

4   State and local expenditures have been rising in the postwar period: the principal items are education, highways, public welfare, and the ordinary police and safety functions of government.

5   The property tax is the most important source of local revenue. Sales taxes and excises are important for the state. In the postwar period, states and localities have been spending more than they tax, thereby increasing their debts.

6   The federal government gives large grants to the states, primarily for highways, matching grants-in-aid for social welfare, and education. Many (e.g., Heller and Nixon) advocate revenue sharing. The states help the localities—primarily in education, highways, and public assistance.

7   The incidence of a tax is its ultimate division of burden, its total effect on prices and other economic magnitudes. Those upon whom a tax is first levied may succeed in shifting part of its burden forward or backward. The economists' tools of Parts Three and Four will help in tackling this difficult problem. Progression in benefits seems to offset the regressive sag of our tax structure at middle income levels.

QUESTIONS FOR DISCUSSION

1   Make a list of different taxes in order of their progressiveness. What is the importance of each at the federal, state, and local level?

2   List different state and local expenditure categories in order of quantitative importance. Compare with federal expenditure categories of Chapter 8.

3   How do you think different government functions should be allocated among the three levels of government? How about revenues and grants-in-aid?

4   Should a citizen in Massachusetts be taxed to help a citizen in Arkansas? To help a citizen in Vermont? In Massachusetts? In Mexico or India?

5   "Since people don't change their smoking habits as a result of taxation, and since the poor smoke, a tax on cigarettes is really no different from a tax on bread." Do you agree? If so, what ought to be done?

6   From Table 9-2, calculate the personal income tax paid by a typical doctor, lawyer, teacher, stenographer, mechanic, and carpenter.

7   In the next decade there will be a political move to get the federal government to introduce a sales or value-added tax. Evaluate the pros and cons.

8   "More kids and cars mean local expenditure and debt." Evaluate.

9   Should marijuana be made legal and taxed to raise revenue? Should gambling be made legal everywhere, as it is in Nevada, to provide a cheerful source of tax revenues? Should bingo be legalized and taxed? Many foreign countries operate lotteries (like the New Hampshire and New York State sweepstakes). The Russians, instead of paying high interest on government bonds, give prizes to those who draw lucky numbers. Do you approve of such revenue sources? Might they lead to corruption in politics and gangsterism?

Review your understanding of the following concepts:

benefit and sacrifice notions	grants-in-aid, unconditional revenue sharing
direct and indirect taxes	budget surpluses and deficits
progressive and regressive	tax incidence and shifting

National Income and Product   10

The time has come, the Walrus
said, to talk of many things.
Of shoes, and ships, and
sealing wax, of cabbages—
and kings.
LEWIS CARROLL

One of the most important concepts in all economics is the national income—or, technically, the gross national product (GNP). This measures the economic performance of the whole economy. Of course, man does not live by bread alone. Nor does society live by GNP alone. But on our way to the state of affluence where material well-being will fall to the second level of significance, we do need a summary measure of aggregate economic performance.

This chapter's discussion of national income can serve as the unifying summary of Part One's introduction to the *basic economic processes and institutions* of modern mixed societies. Alternately, this analysis of national income, its anatomy and accounting structure, can be regarded as the introduction to the treatment of macroeconomics of Part Two—the study of the physiological forces that determine total employment, production, real income, and the price level. The concept of national income is indispensable preparation for tackling the great issues of unemployment, inflation, and growth.

THE YARDSTICK OF AN ECONOMY'S PERFORMANCE

What is national income? It is the loose name we give to the money measure of the over-all annual flow of goods and services in an economy. Often, instead of it, we use the almost equivalent precise term "national product" or "net national product" (NNP);[1] or the slightly different concept of "gross national product" (GNP).

If you asked an economic historian just what the Great Depression really meant, his best brief answer would be: "From a 1929 NNP of $95.8 billion there was a drop to a 1933 NNP of $48.8 billion. This halving of the money value of the flow of goods and services in the American economy caused hardship, bank failures, riots, and political turmoil."

[1] We shall notice later the special and narrow use of the term "national income" by the U.S. Department of Commerce.

Net national product is measured as flow of output or as equal flow of costs:

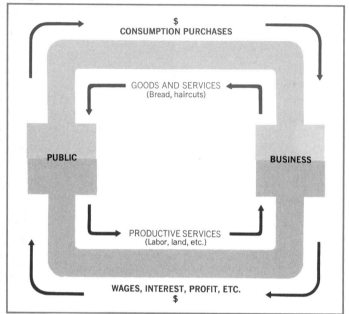

FIG. 10-1.   In the upper loop, people spend their money on final goods: the total dollar flow of these per year is one measure of net national product, NNP.

The lower loop measures the annual flow of costs of output: the earnings that business pays out in wages, rent, interest, dividends, and accrued profits. With profit properly reckoned as a residual, the two measures of NNP must always be identical.

In brief, national income or product is the final figure you arrive at when you apply the measuring rod of money to the diverse apples, oranges, and machines that any society produces with its land, labor, and capital resources.

TWO MEASURES OF NATIONAL PRODUCT: AS GOODS-FLOW OR EARNINGS-FLOW

How do we measure the net national product, NNP? The general idea is simple. Figure 10-1 shows the circular flow of dollar spending in an economy with no government and no accumulation of capital or net saving going on.

Flow-of-product approach Each year the public consumes goods and services: goods such as apples, oranges, and bread; services such as health care or haircuts. The public spends dollars for these consumer goods, as in the upper loop of Fig. 10-1. We add together all the consumption dollars spent for these final goods to arrive at the total of NNP.

Thus, in our simple economy, one can easily calculate national income or product as the sum of the annual flow of final goods and services: (price of oranges × number of oranges) + (price of apples × number of apples) + ...

Why use market prices as weights in evaluating and summing diverse physical commodities and services? Because, as we shall see in Part Three, market prices are reflectors of the relative desirability of diverse goods and services.

The *net national product*, or "national income evaluated at market prices," as it is technically named, is definable as the total money value of the flow of *final* products of the community.[2]

Earnings or income approach   There is a second, equivalent way to calculate NNP in so simple an economy. Go to the lower loop in Fig. 10-1: What is the total cost of output which business is paying out to the public? It is paying out wages, interest, rents, and profit. Why? Because these factor earnings of land, labor, and capital are the *costs* of production of the flow of product. (NOTE: Here the economist, unlike the accountant, does count profit as a cost or earning item.)

---

[2] In our first, simplest model, the only final product is private consumption expenditures. But in a moment we shall see that government expenditures on goods and services and private net investment are also to be included.

The statistician can measure the annual flow of such factor earnings or income in the lower loop.[3] In this way, he will *again* arrive at the NNP.

Net national product is also definable, from a second viewpoint, as the total of factor earnings (wages, interest, rents, and accruing profits) that are the costs of production of society's final goods.

Now we have calculated NNP by the upper-loop flow-of-product approach and by the lower-loop earnings-flow approach. Which is greater? Answer: They will be *exactly the same.*

Here is the reason for this identity. Recall that we have included "profit" in the lower loop—along with wages, interest, and rents. What exactly is profit? Profit is what you have left over from the sale of product (your oranges, apples, bread, and haircuts) *after* you have paid the other factor-costs—wages, interest, rents. *So profit automatically is the residual that takes on the size needed to make the lower-loop approach via earnings* exactly *match the upper-loop approach via flow of goods.*

This all reflects the useful device of double-entry which accountants use to keep the two sides of their books in perfect balance.

To sum up: NNP, or net national product, is measurable as the flow of product; but it is also convenient for the statistician to measure it via the earnings approach in the lower loop. With the proper definition of profit and its inclusion as an economic earning and cost, each approach will yield exactly the same NNP.

An example will show how to go from business accounts to national accounts in the simplest case, without government and investment, and where all final products are produced from land, labor, and capital in 10 million identical one-stage firms or farms.

INCOME STATEMENT OF TYPICAL FARM			
OUTPUT ATTRIBUTABLE TO FARMING		EARNINGS	
Sales of goods (wheat, apples, etc.)	$1,000	Costs of production	
		Wages	$ 800
		Rents	100
		Interest	25
		Profit (residual)	75
Total	$1,000	Total	$1,000

Adding all the 10 million farms gives the NNP account easily in this trivial case.

NATIONAL PRODUCT ACCOUNT (in millions!)			
UPPER-LOOP FLOW OF PRODUCT		LOWER-LOOP EARNINGS OR INCOMES	
Final output (10 × 1,000)	$10,000	Wages (10 × 800)	$ 8,000
		Rents (10 × 100)	1,000
		Interest (10 × 25)	250
		Profit (10 × 75)	750
NNP total	$10,000	NNP total	$10,000

Note that the definition of profit makes the firm's two sides balance; hence the two NNP approaches must still match after summation.

[3] When we leave our simple model, taxes (and government transfer items) will have to be introduced.

We deflate by a price index to correct for our rubber money yardstick:

	(1)	(2)	(3)
SAMPLE CALCULATION OF REAL NNP			
DATE	MONEY NNP (billions of current dollars)	INDEX NUMBER OF PRICES	REAL NNP (in billions of 1929 dollars) $(3) = \frac{(1)}{(2)} \times 100$
1929	96	100	$\frac{96}{100} \times 100 = 96$
1933	48	75	$\frac{48}{75} \times 100 = 64$

TABLE 10-1. Using price index of Column (2), we deflate Column (1) to get real NNP, Column (3). (RIDDLE: Can you show that 1929's real NNP was $72 billion in terms of 1933 prices? HINT: With 1933 as a base, 1929's price index is $133\frac{1}{3}$.)

REAL VERSUS MONEY NATIONAL PRODUCT: USING A PRICE INDEX TO "DEFLATE"

We saw that NNP uses the measuring rod of money prices in the market to combine diverse apples, oranges, and other goods to a single total figure. But one would hardly choose to measure things with a rubber rather than a wooden yardstick—one that stretched in your hands from day to day.

This is one of the problems economists have to solve when they use money as their measuring rod. Everyone knows that inflations and deflations can send most prices up or down. Or, as the economist puts it, "The value of money does change between years like 1929 and 1933, or 1939 and 1970, or 1970 and 1971."

What can be done about this? Economists can repair most of the damage due to the changeability of our measuring rod by using an *index number of prices.*[4] A 1929–1933 comparison will illustrate the process by which one uses a price index number to "deflate" a "current *money* NNP," converting it into a "*real* NNP in terms of dollars of unchanged 1929 purchasing power."

Table 10-1 gives the actual 1929 and 1933 NNP figures to the close approximations of $96 and $48 billion. It shows a halving of money NNP. But the government estimates that prices of goods and services dropped on the average about 25 per cent in the Depression. Using 1929 as a base of 100, this means the 1933 price index was about 75. So our $48-billion 1933 NNP was really worth somewhat more than half the $96-billion NNP of 1929.

How much more? Table 10-1 divides through by the price index number to "deflate" and shows that "*real NNP*" *fell only to two-thirds the 1929 level:* thus in terms of dollars of 1929 purchasing power, real NNP fell down to $64 billion. Hence, part of the halving shown by the *money* NNP was due to the optical illusion of the changing price yardstick.

Figure 10-2 shows in brown the history of money NNP (expressed in the actual dollars and prices that were current in each historical year). Then, for comparison, the real NNP (expressed in 1958 dollars) is shown in blue. Note that part of the increase in money NNP is really spurious, being due merely to inflation in the last 40 years of our money yardstick's price units.

---

[4]Computing a price index would be easy if all prices were to change by the same percentage. When all *P*s triple, the index rises from 100 to 300; when all halve, it drops to 50. If *P*s increase in different degrees, but all end up between double and triple their base, the index is certainly between 200 and 300. Just where? Evidently we need some kind of *average* of the price changes, each being *weighted* in accordance with its approximate economic *importance*. The official indexes are good approximations, but some basic problems remain: getting an accurate sample of prices; allowing for quality improvements; deciding which average to use (arithmetic or geometric mean, median, etc.); defining relative-economic-importance weights, in a statical and in a changing world.

AVOIDING "DOUBLE COUNTING" OF INTERMEDIATE GOODS

Returning to current money figures, we can now show how to handle "intermediate" goods (which are not truly *final* goods) and thus avoid counting anything two, three, or more times.

Ignoring intermediate goods   We do want to count bread in NNP, but we must *avoid also counting in the dough that goes to make the bread.* That would indeed be double counting, since the only reason we want the dough is for the final bread. Turn back to the two-loop Fig. 10-1. You could find bread (and haircuts) there; but you won't find any dough, flour, or wheat. Where are they? These are so-called "intermediate products" that are produced during all the stages leading up to the final bread product, and they are hidden in the block marked "business." That is as it should be. We don't want intermediate products to be double-counted along with final product.

Using "value added" to avoid double counting   A new statistician who is being trained to make NNP measurements might well be puzzled, saying:

I can see that, if you are careful, your upper-loop approach to NNP will avoid including intermediate products. But I'm a little uncertain whether or not you might find yourself in some trouble when you use the lower-loop approach. After all, don't we at the Commerce Department gather income statements from the accounts of firms? Won't we then be picking up what millers pay to farmers, what bakers pay to millers, and what grocers pay to bakers? Won't this result in double counting or even triple and quadruple counting of some items that go through several productive stages?

This is a legitimate question. Fortunately, we can give it a satisfactory answer. The statistician making lower-loop earnings or factor-cost measurements should always be very careful to use what he calls the "value-added" approach.

The value-added approach refuses to include *all* the expenses shown on each firm's business income statement in the lower-loop factor earnings. Which expenses are excluded? All purchases of materials and services from *other* firms are excluded, because those dollars will get properly counted in NNP from the reports of *other* firms.

EXAMPLE: Pepto-Glitter Co. buys electric power from the Edison Co. This expense on the Pepto income statement is *not* in-

How rising prices spuriously inflated our net national product:

MONEY NNP AND REAL NNP

NET NATIONAL PRODUCT (billions of dollars)

1,000

400

Real NNP (1958 prices)

Money NNP (current prices)

100

1930   1940   1950   1960   1970

FIG. 10-2. The rise in money NNP since the Depression and World War II exaggerates the rise in real NNP: because the price index has generally been rising since then, we must use it to deflate the money NNP in order to arrive at the real NNP trends.

NNP is the sum of value added of all the separate stages:

BREAD RECEIPTS, COSTS, AND VALUE ADDED (in cents per loaf)

STAGE OF PRODUCTION	(1) SALES RECEIPTS		(2) COST OF INTER- MEDIATE MATE- RIALS OR GOODS		(3) VALUE ADDED (wages, profit, etc.) (3) = (1) − (2)
Wheat	8	−	0	=	8
Flour	11	−	8	=	3
Baked dough	20	−	11	=	9
Delivered bread	30	−	20	=	10
	69	−	39	=	30
					(sum of value added)

TABLE 10-2.   To avoid double counting, we carefully calculate value added at each stage, subtracting all the costs of materials and intermediate products not produced in that stage but bought from other business firms. Note that every black intermediate-product item appears both in Column (1) and with opposite sign in Column (2); hence it is canceled out.

cluded in value added. Why should it be? It is not a wage, interest, rent, or profit payment. In fact, it is not a payment to any Pepto-Glitter productive factor; hence it never shows up at all in Pepto's own contribution to the lower loop. It stays inside the business block, where it and all other such expenditures by a firm on intermediate goods are carefully subtracted from Pepto's receipts. What is left? Pepto's true value added—which is exactly the sum of *its* wage, interest, rent, and profit costs.

Mind you, the electric power was produced by the Edison workers—and by the Edison interest, rent, and profit receivers. So do not fear that this electrical activity will get overlooked by the NNP statistician. It will not. He will pick it up in the lower loop as the value added of the Edison Co. This is as it should be: we want to count each thing once, not twice or three times.

Table 10-2 illustrates by means of the several stages of a loaf of bread how careful adherence to the value-added approach will enable us to subtract the intermediate expenses that show up in the income statements of farmers, millers, bakers, and grocers —ending up with the desired equality between (1) net value of final bread and (2) the lower-loop factor-costs embodying the sum of the value-added data of all stages. All this can be summarized as follows:

Value-added approach. **To avoid double counting, we take care to include in net national product only final goods, and not the intermediate goods that go to make the final goods. By resolutely sticking to the *value added* at each stage, taking care to subtract expenditures on the intermediate goods bought from other firms, the lower-loop earnings approach properly avoids all double counting and records wages, interest, rent, and profit exactly one time.**

Our earlier example with 10 million farmers can now have added to it 10 million second-stage manufacturers, who buy wheat and farm goods and add value to them by processing them into bread and other final products by the use of labor, land, and capital. Alongside the farmer's income statement we have the manufacturer's income statement.

INCOME STATEMENT OF TYPICAL MANUFACTURER

OUTPUT ATTRIBUTABLE TO MANUFACTURING		EARNINGS	
Sales of goods	$5,000	Costs or "value added"	
Minus goods bought from other		Wages	$3,500
firms	−1,000	Rent	100
		Interest	100
		Profit (residual)	300
Total	$4,000	Total	$4,000

To get total NNP for society, we can add the bottom items of the left-hand sides of the 10 million farmers *and* 10 million bakers; or to get lower-loop rather than upper-loop NNP, we add all the right-hand items for *all* these 20 million firms.

NATIONAL PRODUCT ACCOUNT (in millions)			
UPPER-LOOP FLOW OF PRODUCT		LOWER-LOOP EARNINGS OR INCOMES	
Final output (finished bread, etc.)		Wages (8,000 + 35,000)	$43,000
[50,000 = 10,000 (on farms)		Rent (1,000 + 1,000)	2,000
+ (50,000 − 10,000)	$50,000	Interest (250 + 1,000)	1,250
(in manufacturing)]		Profit (750 + 3,000)	3,750
NNP total	$50,000	NNP total	$50,000

NET INVESTMENT, CAPITAL FORMATION

So far we have banished all capital growth from our discussion. We talked of people as wanting currently to consume bread, apples, oranges, and haircuts.[5] In real life, however, people often want to devote part of their income to saving and investment. Instead of eating more bread *now*, they will want to build new machines to make it possible to produce more bread for *future* consumption; and they may want to add to the inventory of bread, dough, flour, and wheat. In short, we must recognize that the final goals of people do include net investment or capital formation, not simply current consumption.

If people are using part of society's production possibilities for capital formation rather than consumption, the economic statistician recognizes that he must include such outputs in his upper-loop flow of NNP. So really, we must modify our original definition to read:

Net national product is the sum of *all* final products, such as consumption goods and services, and including also *net* investment.

This net investment (or net capital formation) will include the net additions to our stock of (1) buildings, (2) equipment, and (3) inventories.

WARNING: To economists, investment always means real capital formation—production of added goods in inventories, or production of new plants, houses, and tools. To the layman, investment means merely using money to buy an outstanding share of General Motors stock, to buy a corner lot, to open a savings account. It is important not to confuse these meanings: If I take $1,000 from my safe and now put it in the bank or buy a common stock from a broker, the economist says that neither investment nor saving has gone up from this act alone. Only if some physical capital formation takes place is there investment; only if society consumes less than its income, devoting resources to capital formation, is there saving.

NET INVESTMENT EQUALS GROSS INVESTMENT MINUS DEPRECIATION

How does the economist get accurate figures on net investment?

First he has to make estimates of inventories and of their changes. Harder still is his task of estimating net investment in buildings and equipment.

[5]Indeed, the economic statistician counts in the NNP all consumption items that people want to spend *their* incomes on. He draws the line only at illegal expenditures, e.g., opium consumption or prostitution. During World War II when black-market operations were important, he found it necessary in some countries to supplement his statistics with estimates of black-market money transactions.

To get net investment, subtract depreciation from gross investment:

GROSS AND NET INVESTMENT (in billions of dollars)

INVESTMENT COMPONENTS	1929	1932	1946	1968
New construction	$ 8.9	$7.0	$14.0	$ 59.5
Producers' durable equipment	5.6	3.8	10.2	59.5
Change in business inventories	1.7	−6.2	6.4	7.3
Gross private domestic investment	$16.2	$4.6	$30.6	$126.3
Allowances for depreciation or capital consumption (also = difference between GNP and NNP)	−7.9	−7.4	−9.9	−73.3
Net private domestic investment	$ 8.3	$−2.8	$20.7	$ 53.0

TABLE 10-3. After subtracting capital depreciation from *gross* private domestic investment, we get *net* private domestic investment. (Source: U.S. Department of Commerce, which separately calculates data on foreign investment.)

Why can't he just jot down *all* the buildings built and *all* the machines produced, add them in with his calculated net inventory change, and let it go at that? He does indeed make such a calculation. But the resulting figure is too large—too gross. Recognizing this, he gives a new name to the result, namely, "gross investment" rather than "net investment."

Why the word "gross"? The statistician uses this word to emphasize that he has not yet made any *allowances for the using up of capital*, i.e., no allowance for capital *depreciation*. (Recall the accounting appendix of Chapter 5.)

One would not think much of a statistician who estimated the change in human population by ignoring deaths. If he just added up gross births without subtracting a good estimate for deaths, he would get an exaggerated notion of the net change in population. The same holds for economic equipment and buildings: net change is always gross births (of capital) minus deaths (or capital depreciation). This can be summed up:

Definition: **Net investment always equals gross investment minus depreciation.**

Table 10-3 gives typical figures relating net and gross investment. They differ only by depreciation; and fortunately, this is a sluggish item that changes only slowly over a period of a few years. That is why many forecasters, who really are interested in net investment, are satisfied to work with the gross investment figures, which are easier to find in the newspapers and official statistics.

GROSS NATIONAL PRODUCT VERSUS NET NATIONAL PRODUCT

Gross investment can be estimated fairly accurately, involving no difficult depreciation estimate. For this reason governments and the United Nations sensibly decided to calculate a gross national product figure *first* rather than a net national product figure.

Gross national product (GNP) is defined as the sum of final products such as consumption goods and gross investment (which is the increase in inventories plus gross births or production of buildings and equipment).

Table 10-3 suggests it will be easy enough to get NNP from GNP after we know what is the total depreciation figure that is to be subtracted from GNP.[6]

[6]Here is a convenient rule of thumb: NNP is usually about eleven-twelfths of GNP, depreciation nowadays being about one-twelfth of GNP. Figure 10-4 will soon bear this out.

The official statistics do present NNP data at stated intervals. Generally, though, they concentrate on GNP, for the good reason that depreciation cannot be quickly and accurately measured each quarter. Even if the economist—as in later chapters—likes to talk about NNP, he is content to work with GNP data, knowing that the two concepts do move together closely during any period that is not too long. For most general purposes, GNP and NNP can be used interchangeably.

GOVERNMENT EXPENDITURE ON GOODS AND SERVICES

Until now we have ignored government. We have talked about consumers but ignored the biggest consumer of all, namely, the federal, state, and local governments. Somehow NNP and GNP must take into account the billions of dollars of product that a nation collectively consumes. How?

After some debate, the income statisticians of the United States and United Nations decided on using the simplest method of all. To the flow of (1) consumption product and (2) investment product, they simply add (3) *all* government expenditure on goods and services. (Repeatedly in the next few chapters, you will see $C + I + G$, which stands for these three components.)

Here are examples. Along with bread consumption and net investment in NNP, we include in it government expenditures on roads (i.e., cement and road-builders) and jet bombers. We include government expenditure on the services of jet pilots, judges, policemen, national-income statisticians, firemen, and agricultural chemists.

In short, all the government payroll expenditures on its employees plus the goods (typewriters, roads, and airplanes) it buys from private industry are included in this third great category of flow of product, labeled G and called "government expenditure on goods and services."

Figure 10-3 pictures NNP and its three major components.

Exclusion of transfer payments   Does this mean that every dollar the government pays out is included in NNP? Definitely not. If you get an old-age pension from the government, we call that a "transfer payment" and do not treat it as part of NNP. Why

NNP is sum of consumption, investment, and government expenditures on goods and services:

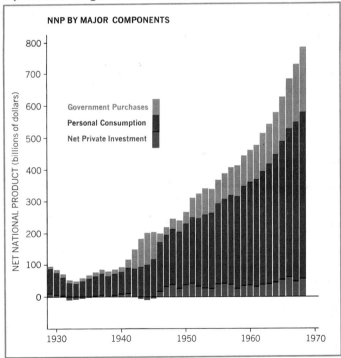

FIG. 10-3.   Though consumption dominates NNP, note the World War II and postwar growth in government expenditure and in investment. Note that in the Great Depression and the war, gross private investment fell short of replacement needs, and net private investment was negative. (Source: U.S. Department of Commerce.)

not? Because it is not a government expenditure on goods and services of this year. Or if your aunt gets a widow's assistance payment, and your cousin receives welfare aid, those welfare payments are also deemed to be transfer items. The same goes for pensions to the blind, veterans, and other welfare recipients. These transfers are not payments for *current* productive services.

Many other government transfer items[7] could be mentioned, but we can conclude with one large item: interest on the public debt. The interest paid on federal bonds was included years ago in NNP, but the fairly universal custom now is for countries to treat this as a transfer item. This is not now included in G, on the argument that it is not a payment for current goods and services.[8]

Do not think that the Treasury's budget fails to take account of all these government transfer payments. The budget back on page 143 did include these: the government surplus does equal taxes minus the sum of G *and* transfers. But do not confuse the usual budget with national-income accounts, which are related but distinct.

Treatment of taxes   In using the flow-of-product approach to compute NNP as $C + I + G$, we would not have to worry about taxes or how government finances itself. Whether the government taxes, issues interest-bearing IOUs, or prints new noninterest IOU green-backs, the statistician would compute G as the value of government expenditure on goods and services (evaluating items at their actual cost to the government, wherever the money came from) and then add in private $C + I$ at actual market prices.

It is all very well to ignore taxes in the upper-loop flow-of-product approach. But what about in the lower-loop earnings or cost approach to NNP? We do indeed have to take account of all taxes down there.

Consider wages, for example. Part of what my employer pays me in wages I have to give to the government in the form of personal income taxes. So these direct taxes do definitely get included in the wage component of the lower loop, and the same holds for direct taxes (personal or corporate) on interest, rent, and profit.

Or take the sales and other indirect taxes that manufacturers and retailers have to pay on a loaf of bread (or on the wheat, flour, and dough stages). Suppose these indirect taxes total 5 cents; and suppose wages, profit, and other value-added items add up to 30 cents in cost to the bread industry. (We do not care how much of this 30 cents goes to direct taxes.) What will the bread sell for in the upper loop? For 30 cents? Of course not. The bread will sell for 35 cents, equal to 30 cents of factor-costs plus 5 cents of indirect taxes.[9]

---

[7]The name "transfer payment," as used in Chapter 8 and here, is a little misleading. If the government taxes me to give a relief dole to my unemployed neighbor, that does sound like a "transfer." But suppose it prints a new green 20-dollar bill to give him, or borrows by selling bonds to make relief payments. He gets money that is not transferred from anybody else. Economists still call the relief payments transfers, regardless of how they are financed.

[8]How to treat government items in NNP is still somewhat controversial. (1) Some experts argue that G should be broken down into government current *consumption* and into government *net investment* (increase in its buildings, equipment, and inventories), just as private product is so broken up. And some nations do this. (2) Some experts say, too, that part of G is really "intermediate" rather than "final" product—much like dough rather than bread—in that it merely contributes to final private product already counted in (e.g., weather information for farmers who help give us our daily bread). But few nations make estimates of how much such double counting may be involved in the G figures.

[9]This is plainly so by definition of our residual profit and from the fact that residual profit is treated

Hence we definitely do always take account of taxes in the lower-loop cost approach to NNP and GNP.

Now that the government has been brought into the picture, a final comprehensive definition can be given.

GNP and NNP are definable as the sum of three major components: personal *consumption* expenditure on goods and services, plus *government* expenditure on goods and services, plus *investment* expenditure—where it is understood that in GNP gross investment expenditure on all new machines and construction is included, whereas in NNP only the net investment expenditure is included, there having been subtracted from the gross births of capital goods an appropriate depreciation allowance to take account of deaths, or using up of capital goods.

GNP and NNP are each definable, not only as an upper-loop flow of product, but also as a lower-loop total of costs: to factor-costs such as wages, interest, rents, and profit (always carefully excluding double counting of intermediate goods bought from other firms by the value-added technique), there will have to be added all the indirect business taxes that do show up as an expense of producing the flow of products; and in the case of gross national product there will also be included depreciation expense, whereas the net national product will be less by the amount of this estimated expense.

The two loops yield identical magnitudes by definition (i.e., by careful adherence to the procedures of "double-entry" bookkeeping).[10]

AMERICA'S NNP AND GNP

Armed with an understanding of the concepts involved, we can turn to the actual data in the important Table 10-4 on the next page, a table which merits lengthy study.

Flow-of-product approach   Look first at Table 10-4's left side. This gives the upper-loop *flow-of-product* approach to NNP. Distinguishing between domestic and foreign investment, we have four components. Of these, C and G and their obvious subclassifications require little comment.

Net private domestic investment does require one comment. Its net figure of $53.0 billion was arrived at in the way already described: from estimated gross private domestic investment of $126.3 billion was subtracted the estimated value of depreciation of $73.3 billion, just as in Table 10-3 of this chapter.

The final international item will be discussed further in the Appendix to this chapter and later in Chapter 33. If it were not for complications that arise from government

---

as a cost; but this result definitely says *nothing at all* about whether the tax is passed forward to the consumer or backward to the factors, whose wages and other returns might have been higher had there been no taxes. Chapter 20 analyzes such a "tax incidence" problem of the sort described in Chapter 9.
[10]Statisticians must always work with incomplete reports and must fill in some gaps by estimation. As will be seen in a moment, approximate guesses of the two definitions can differ somewhat by what is officially reported as the "statistical discrepancy." Along with the civil servants who are each heads of units called wages, interest, and so forth, there is actually a man with the title "head of the statistical discrepancy." If data were perfect, he would be out of a job; but as real life is never so ideal, his task of reconciliation is one of the hardest of all. (In the presentation of the balance of international payments given in Chapter 33 a similar "errors and omissions" item will appear.)

Here are the two ways of looking at NNP and GNP in actual numbers:

NET NATIONAL PRODUCT, 1968 (in billions of current dollars)					
FLOW-OF-PRODUCT APPROACH			EARNINGS AND COST APPROACH		
1. Personal consumption expenditure		$536.6	Wages and other employee supplements		$513.6
Durable goods	$ 83.3		Net interest		28.0
Nondurable goods	230.6		Rent income of persons		21.2
Services	222.7		Indirect business taxes and adjustments*		77.9
2. *Government* purchases of goods and services		200.3	Income of unincorporated enterprises (adjusted)		63.8
3. Net private *domestic investment* (126.3 − 73.3)		53.0	Corporate profits before taxes (adjusted)		87.9
4. *Net export* of goods and services (50.6 exports			Dividends	$23.1	
−48.1 imports)		2.5	Undistributed profits	26.7	
			Corporate profits taxes	41.3	
			Reported profits (unadj.)	$91.1	
			Inventory valuation adjustment	−3.2	
Net National Product		**$792.4**	**Net National Product**		**$792.4**
Depreciation (or capital consumption allowance)		73.3	Depreciation (or capital consumption allowance)		73.3
Gross National Product		**$865.7**	**Gross National Product**		**$865.7**

TABLE 10-4.   The left side measures flow of product (at market prices). The right side measures flow of costs (factor earnings plus indirect taxes). GNP, which includes Depreciation, is also shown. Be sure you understand the main items. (Source: U.S. Department of Commerce. The starred item includes the "statistical discrepancy" and arises from imperfect measurement of upper- and lower-loop data.)

transfer expenditures abroad, the $2.5 billion net export of goods and services could be interpreted as our net foreign investment, which has to be added to net domestic investment to arrive at the total of investment. In any case, along with C, G, and domestic I, net exports do represent a fourth component of the flow of product.[11]

Adding up the four components on the left gives the important total NNP of $792.4 billion. This is the harvest we have been working for: the money measure of the American economy's over-all performance for 1968.

Finally, note that if we add depreciation back into the figures, we have the GNP of $865.7 billion—which is larger because it contains gross rather than net investment in its measure of product and hence is swelled by the inclusion of depreciation.

Lower-loop flow-of-cost approach   Now turn to the right-hand side of the table. Here we have all the *value-added* items plus *taxes*.

[11]EXAMPLE: Of 100 chocolates of NNP, suppose 80 go to C, 10 to G, 6 to domestic I in the form of added inventory, and 4 are exported abroad with nothing being imported from abroad.

A few explanations are in order. *Wages*[12] and other employee supplements include all take-home pay and fringe benefits, and they also have in them the withheld and other income or payroll taxes that wage earners have to pay.

Net interest is a similar item. (Note again, interest on government bonds is not included as part of *G* or NNP, being treated as a transfer.)

Rent income of persons requires only one explanation. It, of course, includes rents received by landlords. In addition, if you own your own home, you are treated as *paying rent to yourself.* This is a so-called "imputed" item and makes sense if we really want to measure the housing services the American people are enjoying and do not want the estimate to be changed every time a tenant buys the house he has been renting. This imputed item has to be estimated, since no one reports rental receipts on his own home.

Indirect business taxes, as we earlier saw, do have to be included in the lower loop if we are to match the upper loop. Any direct taxes on wages, interest, or rents were already included in those items themselves.

Lastly, turn to profit. This should come last because it is the residual determined as what is left over after all other items have been taken into account. There are two kinds of profits: profit of corporations and profit of unincorporated enterprises, i.e., proprietorships and partnerships. "Income of unincorporated enterprises (adjusted[13])" refers to earnings of partnerships and single-ownership businesses. This includes much farmer and professional income. As we shall see in Parts Three and Four, really a good deal of this is a return to farmers and self-employed people for the labor, capital, and land they provide for their *own* businesses; but the statisticians count it all as profit.

Finally, "corporate profits before taxes (adjusted)" is shown. Its $87.9 billion includes corporate profits *taxes* of $41.3 billion. The remainder then goes to dividends or to undistributed corporate profits, the latter being what you leave or "plow back" into the business and called "net corporate saving."

Again, on the right side, the flow-of-cost approach gives us the same $792.4 billion of NNP and the same GNP figure of $865.7 billion, which was arrived at by adding back in the gross item of depreciation. The right and left sides do agree.

THREE RELATED CONCEPTS: DISPOSABLE, PERSONAL, AND NATIONAL INCOMES

Table 10-4 summarized the fundamentals of national-income accounting. For purposes of broad economic understanding, our task is over. But a businessman, citizen, or statesman

---

[12] The late Sir Arthur Bowley of the London School of Economics noted how remarkably constant over almost a century is wages' percentage share of national income. No one is sure why this should be so. (The wages' share does rise at the expense of profit during recession; in recent decades the wages' share has perhaps shown a slight upward creep, as seen in Chapter 37.)

[13] The term "adjusted" refers to an inventory valuation adjustment of the following type: If money prices change *within* the year, our yardstick for measuring profits is faulty. Part of the reported profit is simply a markup (or markdown, if the price level is falling within the year) of inventory. The statistician uses within-the-year price changes to estimate the amount of such overreporting of profits. Actually in 1968 wholesale prices were rising; so there has to be an inventory valuation adjustment of −$3.2 billion that gets subtracted from reported corporate profits of $91.1 billion to give a more meaningful adjusted figure of $87.9 billion. (In 1962, when prices fell, the adjustment was positive and *added* to reported corporate incomes.)

who wants to follow carefully what is happening from month to month and quarter to quarter in the American economy or abroad will benefit from a brief discussion of three other concepts that are measured and reported on by the U.S. Department of Commerce and similar official units elsewhere.

Disposable income, *personal* income, and (narrowly defined) *national* income are useful rearrangements of the above data.

Disposable income. How many dollars per year do private individuals and families have available *to them* to spend? The concept of disposable income tries to answer this question. Broadly speaking, to get disposable income, one subtracts all taxes direct or indirect from NNP, subtracts all corporate earnings that were not paid out in dividends but retained as net corporate savings, and adds in transfer payments of welfare or interest-on-federal-debt type. The result is, so to speak, what actually gets into the public's hands, to dispose of as we please.

Disposable income is an important series of data because, as will be seen in Part Two, it is this sum (suitably adjusted to take account of interest on loans that the consumer must pay) that people divide between (1) consumption spending and (2) net personal saving. Thus, in recent years people have been spending about 94 per cent of disposable income on consumption and interest, with about 6 per cent on net personal saving. It is this *DI* series that will be watched eagerly by a department-store head and a policy maker apprehensive over inflationary pressure or too little consumption spending.

Personal income. Unfortunately, *DI* data are available only every 3 months. For those who want up-to-date *monthly* information, the government publishes the series called "personal income." Like *DI*, *PI* removes corporate saving from NNP and adds back all transfers and consumer interest. If it excluded *all* taxes, *PI* would be identical with *DI*. Some taxes, however, are hard to estimate in a hurry, on a month-to-month basis. *PI* does eliminate some taxes that can be estimated fairly accurately in the short run: corporate income taxes and certain other payroll taxes; but it does *not* try to estimate the income taxes of people, and thus it does differ slightly from disposable income. However, if we did have a monthly estimate of *DI*, there is every reason to think that it would change in about the same percentage as *PI* most of the time. Therein lies the principal importance of personal income: it is a quickly available monthly figure that is

The different national-income aggregates tend to move together:

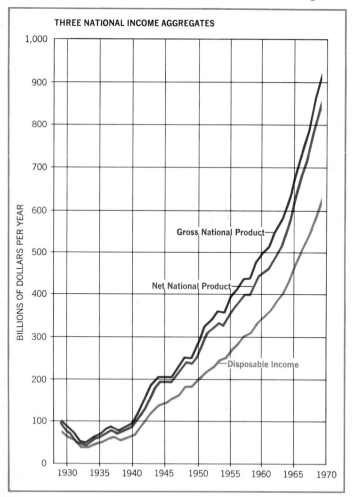

THREE NATIONAL INCOME AGGREGATES

BILLIONS OF DOLLARS PER YEAR

Gross National Product

Net National Product

Disposable Income

FIG. 10-4. NNP averages about eleven-twelfths of GNP. Because of taxes and corporate saving, the disposable income of people is smaller still. (Source: U.S. Department of Commerce.)

an excellent substitute for disposable income and is thus an indicator of what is happening to family well-being and spending.

National income, narrowly defined. We have followed the common practice and used the term "national income" to refer generally to *all* the concepts of this chapter—NNP, GNP, and so forth. Mention should be made of a narrower sense in which the U.S. Department of Commerce defines the term. In the narrow sense, national income, or *NI,* is simply NNP with all indirect business taxes (excises, cigarette stamps, gasoline taxes, and all sales taxes of any kind) taken out. But note that all direct taxes have been left in, as well as corporate income taxes.[14] (Figure 10-5 in the Appendix presents visually the relation among the different concepts.)

Figure 10-4 plots three of the important national-income concepts, GNP, NNP, and *DI,* and shows how much alike are their movements and how predictably slow are their drifts apart. That is why most people are content to watch GNP alone, occasionally supplementing it with data on disposable income.

This chapter has now given us the tools to chart the progress and health of an economy. It is a culmination of the introductory survey that is the task of Part One. It is a prelude to the subject of Part Two, the analysis of the *macro*economic forces that determine the level, trend, and cyclical fluctuations of the GNP and of the general level of prices.

SUMMARY

1   Net national product, NNP, is definable as a dollar flow of total product for a nation: the sum of consumption plus net investment (domestic and foreign) plus government expenditure on goods and services. NNP $= C + I + G$.

2   By use of price index, we can "deflate" money NNP (in current dollars) to arrive at a more accurate measure of "real NNP, expressed in dollars of one base-year's purchasing power." Use of such an average price index (of consumer-goods, investment-goods, and government-goods prices) is an approximate way of allowing for the rubber yardstick implied by changing levels of prices.

3   Because of the way we define residual profit, we can match the flow-of-product measurement of NNP by the lower-loop flow-of-cost measurement. This uses factor earnings, carefully computing *values added* to eliminate double counting of intermediate products. And after summing up all (before-tax) wage, interest, rent, and profit income, it adds to this total all *indirect* tax costs to business. (NNP definitely does *not* include *transfer* items such as receipt of interest on government bonds or receipt of welfare pensions.)

4   Net investment is positive when people are devoting part of society's resources to creating more inventory and more buildings and equipment than are currently being used up in

[14]If NNP can be called "net national product evaluated at market prices," then this version of national income can be called "net national product evaluated, not at market prices, but at the factor-costs (exclusive of indirect taxes) of that output."

the form of depreciation. Net investment equals gross investment minus depreciation. As depreciation is hard to estimate accurately, the statisticians have more confidence in their measures of gross than of net investment.

5   For the foregoing reason, the official statistics put greatest stress on gross national product rather than net. GNP = NNP + depreciation, always. Since depreciation is sluggish and rarely varies much from one-twelfth of GNP (or one-eleventh of NNP), we can generally use GNP and NNP interchangeably.

6   Disposable, personal, and (narrowly defined) national income are three additional official measurements. *NI* is simply NNP with indirect business taxes (gasoline, sales, and other nonincome taxes) removed. *PI* is simply a convenient monthly approximation to movements in *DI* and the other data that are available only on a quarterly basis. Disposable income is what people actually have left—after all tax payments, corporate saving of undistributed profits, and transfer adjustments have been made—to spend on consumption (and interest on loans) or to save.

  More information about national-income accounting is given in the Appendix to this chapter. Also given are some selected figures on the nation's recent economic history: the Federal Reserve Board's production index, which comes out monthly; and data on employment and unemployment. These vital aggregates chart a nation's economic health.

QUESTIONS FOR DISCUSSION

1   Compare the two-loop flow of money of Fig. 10-1 with Fig. 3-1 on page 42 which shows the way a pricing system solves society's WHAT, How, and FOR WHOM.

2   "You can't add apples and oranges." Show that money lets us do this.

3   Convince a skeptic that *services* do count as well as material goods—that we actually want most goods only for the consumption services they provide us (e.g. cars and rides).

4   Making a guess how prices have risen since 1968, e.g., 5 per cent in 1969 alone, test your knowledge of the deflating process by penciling in, on Fig. 10-2, recent money NNP and recent real NNP. How might you deflate for population change? If the United Kingdom has 1970 NNP of £40 billion, and if £1 buys what $3 will buy, how would you express U.K. NNP in U.S. 1970 dollars?

5   R. Crusoe produces upper-loop product of $1,000. He pays $750 in wages, $125 in interest, and $75 in rent. What *must* his profit be? Calculate NNP in the upper-loop and lower-loop way and show they must agree exactly.

6   From a recent *Federal Reserve Bulletin* or *Survey of Current Business* (Commerce Department), recalculate Table 10-4 for a later year than 1968. Explain the various items.

7   Distinguish between government transfer expenditure and the *G* that goes into NNP = *C* + *I* + *G*. To get disposable income, why remove all taxes from NNP and add in transfers? What about undistributed corporate profit?

Review your understanding of the following concepts:

NNP in two equivalent views
1975 money NNP in current dollars, and 1975 real NNP in 1958 dollars
intermediate goods, double counting, value added
gross investment − depreciation = net investment
GNP − depreciation = NNP

$NNP = C + I + G$
government transfers; indirect and direct taxes
net exports of goods and services
dividends, undistributed profits
income of unincorporated enterprise
valuation adjustment
NI, *PI*, and *DI*

APPENDIX: The Official National-income Data

The main text of this chapter has expounded the basic principles of national income. Here some special problems are elaborated.

A FEW BRAIN TEASERS

Readers often like to worry about fine points. Here are a few sample cases.

1. *Services of a housewife* do not get counted in the NNP. So if a man marries his housekeeper, the NNP may go down! Or if a wife arranges with her neighbor for each to clean the other's house in return for $5,000 a year, then the NNP would go up by $10,000.

This item is not omitted for logical reasons, but rather because it would be hard to get accurate estimates of the money value of a wife's services. So long as the number of women working at home does not change much in relative importance, the ups and downs of NNP will be about the same whether or not we count in this item or similar items such as home-grown vegetables and other do-it-yourself activities.

All this illustrates an important rule of approximate measurement in economics. *Often it does not matter which definition of measurement you use, so long as you stick to one definition consistently.*

2. For many items it is hard to know whether to put them in the *intermediate* or *final* class. EXAMPLES: A painter's ladder is certainly not to be charged as a final consumption item. Like bread dough, it is an intermediate expense item that has already been counted in as part of the fine homes he helps to create.

What about his overalls? His carfare from one job to another? His carfare from home to work? The coffee he buys a prospective customer? The coffee he himself drinks? The ball game he takes a prospective customer to, in his campaign for more business? Would you treat the last differently if he himself likes baseball?

Each of these items can raise an argument. Each has an element of intermediate business expense in it, and each an element of final consumption. The tax collector and the national-income statistician do not always agree on the treatment of these, and we can raise questions about each one's decisions. (EXAMPLE: The tax collector will not let anyone deduct his commuting costs to work *in town*; but out of town he may be able to deduct travel expenses from his taxable income. The ladder is clearly deductible from taxable income and from NNP; but the overalls are not if it can be shown that wearing them saved an ordinary suit's wearing out. So it goes. Close decisions and arbitrary ones.)

3. *Gifts* that are not disguised payments for work done or for goods and services are not included in NNP. They are like government transfers that we have already discussed. The same goes for the allowance a father gives his son. But what about the fee he pays the son for mowing the lawn? In logic it should be in NNP, but it rarely is.

4. If I buy an old painting, a corner lot, or a used car from someone else, that transaction is not a final transaction to be put into NNP. He and I have just *exchanged assets*: money for picture. Nothing has been produced.[1] So this is more in the nature of a special kind of transfer.[2] It illustrates an important fact: the total dollar volume of all intermediate transactions greatly exceeds the volume of the final trans-

---

[1]If a broker earns a fee for arranging the deal, that fee is counted as part of NNP. Just as some men produce satisfactions in the form of bread, brokers and salesmen produce satisfactions in the form of bringing transactors together.
[2]Do not confuse this kind of transfer with the government transfers we have talked about.

How the official statistics of national income are interrelated:

GROSS AND NET NATIONAL PRODUCT, NATIONAL INCOME, PERSONAL INCOME, AND DISPOSABLE INCOME (in billions of dollars)									
ITEM	1929	1933	1939	1945	1950	1955	1960	1967	1968
Gross national product	103.1	55.6	90.5	212.0	284.8	398.0	503.8	793.5	865.7
Less: Capital consumption (Depreciation)	7.9	7.0	7.3	11.3	18.3	31.5	43.4	68.5	73.3
Equals: **Net national product**	95.2	48.6	83.2	200.7	266.5	366.5	460.4	725.0	792.4
Less: Indirect business taxes	7.0	7.1	9.4	15.5	23.3	32.1	45.2	70.1	77.9
Business transfer payments	0.6	0.7	0.5	0.5	0.8	1.2	1.9	3.2	3.4
Statistical discrepancy	0.7	0.6	1.3	4.0	1.5	2.1	−1.0	−1.0	−2.5
Plus: Subsidies less current surplus of government enterprises	−0.1	0.0	0.5	0.8	0.2	−0.1	0.2	1.4	.8
Equals: **National income**	86.8	40.3	72.6	181.5	241.1	331.0	414.5	654.0	714.4
Less: Corporate profits and inventory valuation adjustment	10.5	−1.2	6.3	19.2	37.7	46.9	49.9	79.2	87.9
Contributions for social insurance	0.2	0.3	2.1	6.1	6.9	11.1	20.7	42.4	47.0
Excess of wage accruals over disbursements	0.0	0.0	0.0	0.0	0.0	0.0	0.0	0.0	0.0
Plus: Government transfer payments	0.9	1.5	2.5	5.6	14.3	16.1	26.6	48.8	55.8
Net interest paid by government and consumers	2.5	1.6	1.9	4.2	7.2	10.1	15.1	23.6	26.1
Dividends	5.8	2.0	3.8	4.6	8.8	10.5	13.4	21.5	23.1
Business transfer payments	0.6	0.7	0.5	0.5	0.8	1.2	1.9	3.2	3.4
Equals: **Personal income**	85.9	47.0	72.8	171.1	227.6	311.0	401.0	629.4	687.9
Less: Personal taxes	2.6	1.5	2.4	20.9	20.7	35.7	51.0	82.9	97.9
(Federal)	1.3	0.5	1.2	19.4	16.5	29.7	42.5	67.5	79.5
(State and local)	1.4	1.0	1.2	1.5	4.2	6.0	8.5	15.4	18.4
Equals: Disposable personal income	83.3	45.5	70.3	150.2	206.9	275.3	350.0	546.5	590.0
Less: Consumer interest payments plus transfers to foreigners	1.9	0.6	0.9	0.9	2.8	5.1	7.8	13.9	15.0
Less: Consumption expenditures	77.2	45.8	66.8	119.7	191.0	254.4	325.2	492.3	536.7
Equals: Personal saving	4.2	−.9	2.6	29.6	13.1	15.8	17.0	40.4	38.4

TABLE 10-5.   Read this together with Fig. 10-5 to understand the official data most easily. (Sources: U.S. Department of Commerce; *Economic Report of the President;* note that detail may not add to totals because of rounding.)

actions that we call national income or product. The loops of Fig. 10-1 include only a minority of the transactions that are taking place within the business and public blocks of that diagram.

Note, too, that we try not to let *capital gains due to mere price changes* enter into NNP. If Wall Street bids up my Ford stock, I may feel rich and spend more of my *DI*. But that windfall gain is not attributable to current economic activity, and the statistician tries to keep it out. For similar reasons he makes the inventory valuation adjustment in corporate profits.

5. In measuring NNP we are not interested in consumption and investment goods merely for their money value: *money is the measuring rod used to give some approximate figure to the underlying "satisfactions" or "benefits" or "psychic income" that comes from goods.* Strictly speaking, then, each time I play a phonograph record, shouldn't that act get into the NNP at its fair market value? In principle, Yes. And if I have put a dime in a juke box, it may in fact get directly into the NNP; but playing it at home will not get it directly into the NNP.

Indirectly, this enjoyment of a psychic pleasure does tend to get in the NNP to the extent that I wear out the record by playing it. Hence, as I replace my records, my consumption purchases at the store give a rough money measure of my enjoyments—but only a rough measure.

The statistician admits this, defending his practice by saying that a man's house is his castle and no accountant can enter his abode to measure his actual current consumptions; instead, he settles for treating a thing as consumed when it enters his abode. This all works well enough, except in one case.

More and more these days we spend our consumption dollar on durable consumers' goods. (This was seen in the breakdown of consumption into services, durable goods, and nondurable goods in Table 10-4.) Actually, then, in the years that we are building up our home inventories of such durable goods, our true psychic consumption is being overstated by our retail purchases; and vice versa in the years when we run home inventories down.

Some purists say, "In NNP, let's try to estimate

How to picture relations among official national-income data:

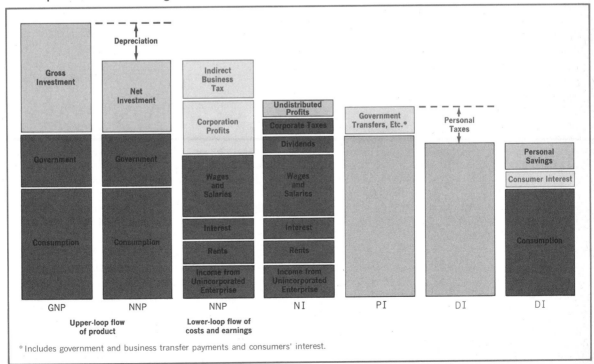

FIG. 10-5. This shows the operations in going from one concept to another, and is color-keyed to Table 10-5.

actual home consumption of services of durables and put that in C, not the mere retail purchases of the year." The Commerce Department thinks this too hard a job to do, but for special purposes economists have tried to make (from gas and mileage records, for example) more accurate estimates of auto consumption than are provided by new car sales.[3]

Fortunately, in the long run, the two methods tend to come to much the same thing, particularly if society is not growing too fast.

6. Should interest paid by consumers be included in disposable income, DI, in consumption expenditure, C, and in NNP? Before 1965 the official statistics did include consumer interest in C and NNP. But after 1965 the Commerce Department, with the approval of the United Nations Statistical Office, decided that this was not an item reflecting *current* (as against *past*) production. Hence, by a close but reasonable decision, net consumer interest payments (along with personal transfer payments to foreigners, a smaller item) are no longer in C and NNP.

But consumer interest is still in the official Department of Commerce disposable income, DI, figures. So, if we want to work with the money *income actually available* to be spent on C or on personal saving, we must first subtract from disposable income "consumer interest (and personal transfer payments to foreigners)." For 1970 this interest item came to about $17 billion. Thus,

$$DI = C + \text{NPS} + \text{consumer interest}$$

where C is consumption expenditure in current production and NPS is net personal saving. To get an idea of the size of these elements of DI, carefully read the bottom four lines of Table 10-5.

THE OFFICIAL STATISTICS

Figure 10-5 summarizes the relations of the different United States government statistics on national income or product. Many find careful study of this summary, together with Table 10-5, a great aid to understanding.

Table 10-6, along with national-income data, gives the other principal aggregates which business and public officials watch closely.

---

[3] It is interesting that in the case of a house, the most durable consumers' good of all, the officials do actually follow this principle: they do not take expenditures on a house as its C, but estimate the house use separately and count it as C.

INTERNATIONAL ASPECTS OF INCOME

Here is the place to give a few details on how net exports was arrived at.

From the beginning we agree to mean by United States NNP the income or product accruing to all "permanent residents" of the United States. This includes American citizens temporarily abroad and also unnaturalized immigrants who live permanently in the United States.

Note that, if an Englishman owns an acre of land in this country, his income therefrom is to be included in the United Kingdom NNP and not in ours. Similarly, if Americans receive dividends from British companies, this is part of the American income and not the British, being treated as payment for a property service that we have exported.

The previous paragraph shows that it is a considerable task to allow for international aspects of income. We must take account of exports, imports, dividends paid in and out of a country, and much more. As we shall see in the discussion of international finance in Part Five, a balance of international payments between the United States and the rest of the world can be drawn up of all such items. There is no need at this point of our national-income discussion to anticipate all the details of this subsequent discussion. We are interested only in the bare logic of the task of finding out the magnitude of net export of goods and services, which is the final component of NNP.

To get net export of goods and services we must calculate the surplus of all the goods and services we provide to foreigners over what they provide to us. Thus calculate (*a*), the total of our exports to them (wheat, shipping, . . .), plus our earnings from factors of production we own abroad (dividends and interest payable to us). Also calculate (*b*), the total of what we import from them and must pay them for their ownership of productive factors located in this country. The surplus of (*a*) over (*b*) represents our net export figures. We shall see that, just as net domestic investment can provide jobs, and expand the economy, so can net exports as well. Thus, when we write $C + I + G$, in I we add on top of domestic investment net exports (or foreign investments, to speak loosely) as well.

THE IDENTITY OF MEASURED SAVING AND INVESTMENT

To pave the way for the discussion of intersecting saving and investment schedules in Chapter 12, we can here show that the *national-income statistician*

These aggregates chart the nation's economic health:

YEAR	GROSS NATIONAL PRODUCT (current prices)	NET NATIONAL PRODUCT	GROSS NATIONAL PRODUCT (1958 prices)	DISPOSABLE INCOME	NET PERSONAL SAVING AS PERCENTAGE OF DISPOSABLE INCOME	GOVERNMENT EXPENDITURE ON GOODS AND SERVICES AS PERCENTAGE OF GNP	FEDERAL RESERVE BOARD INDEX OF INDUSTRIAL PRODUCTION (1957–1959 = 100)	CIVILIAN LABOR FORCE (thousands)	UNEMPLOYMENT AS PERCENTAGE OF CIVILIAN LABOR FORCE
1929	103.1	95.2	203.6	83.3	5.0	8.2	38	49,180	3.2
1931	75.8	68.0	169.3	64.0	4.1	12.2	26	50,420	15.9
1933	55.6	48.6	141.5	45.5	−2.0	14.5	24	51,590	24.9
1935	72.7	65.4	169.5	58.5	3.7	13.9	31	52,870	20.1
1937	90.4	83.3	203.2	71.2	5.3	13.1	40	54,000	14.3
1938	84.7	77.4	192.9	65.5	1.1	15.3	31	54,610	19.0
1939	90.5	83.2	209.4	70.3	3.7	14.7	38	55,230	17.2
1940	99.7	92.2	227.2	75.7	5.1	14.1	44	55,640	14.6
1941	124.5	116.3	263.7	92.7	11.8	19.8	56	55,910	9.9
1942	157.9	148.1	297.8	116.9	23.6	37.8	70	56,410	4.7
1944	210.1	199.1	361.3	146.3	25.5	45.8	83	54,630	1.2
1945	212.0	200.7	355.2	150.2	19.7	38.5	70	53,860	1.9
1946	208.5	198.6	312.6	160.0	9.5	12.9	59	57,520	3.9
1948	257.6	243.0	323.7	189.1	7.1	12.2	68	60,621*	3.8
1949	256.5	239.9	324.1	188.6	5.0	14.7	65	61,286	5.9
1950	284.8	266.4	355.3	206.9	6.3	13.3	75	62,208	5.3
1951	328.4	307.2	383.4	226.6	7.6	17.9	81	62,017	3.3
1952	345.5	322.3	395.1	238.3	7.6	21.6	84	62,138	3.0
1953	364.6	338.9	412.8	252.6	7.2	22.4	91	63,015	2.9
1954	364.8	336.8	407.0	257.4	6.4	20.4	86	63,643	5.5
1955	398.0	366.5	438.0	275.3	5.7	18.7	97	65,023	4.4
1956	419.2	385.2	446.1	293.2	7.0	18.7	100	66,552	4.1
1957	441.1	404.0	452.5	308.5	6.7	19.5	101	66,929	4.3
1958	447.3	408.4	447.3	318.8	7.0	21.1	94	67,639	6.8
1959	483.7	442.3	475.9	337.3	5.6	22.1	106	68,639	5.5
1960	503.8	460.3	487.7	350.0	4.9	19.8	109	69,628	5.5
1961	520.1	474.9	497.2	364.4	5.8	20.7	110	70,459	6.7
1962	560.3	510.4	529.8	385.3	5.6	20.9	118	70,614	5.5
1963	590.5	537.9	551.0	404.6	4.9	20.7	124	71,833	5.7
1964	632.4	576.3	581.1	438.1	6.0	20.4	132	73,091	5.2
1965	684.9	625.1	617.8	473.2	6.0	20.0	143	74,455	4.5
1966	749.9	685.9	658.1	511.9	6.3	20.9	156	75,770	3.8
1967	793.5	725.0	674.6	546.5	7.4	22.7	158	77,347	3.8
1968	865.7	792.4	707.6	590.0	6.5	23.1	165	78,737	3.6

TABLE 10-6. Forecasters like to use the production index because it moves more sensitively than income data. Statesmen worry about unemployment. (Sources: U.S. Department of Commerce; Federal Reserve Board; *Economic Report of the President*.) *From 1948 on 14- to 16-year-olds are not included in the civilian labor force.

defines the saving he measures as exactly the same thing as the investment he measures. This equality of measured saving and measured investment is an identity of double-entry bookkeeping and holds by definition.

What is the measure of investment? Forgetting government, we know I is the output in the upper loop that is not C. What is the measure of saving S? Again forgetting government and corporate saving, we know that S is that part of the lower-loop disposable income, or NNP, that is not spent on C. To summarize:

$$I = \text{upper-loop NNP minus } C$$
$$S = \text{lower-loop NNP minus } C$$

But the two loops must give the same measure of NNP. So $I \equiv S$: the identity between measured saving and investment.

Our task will be done once we bring the corporation and the government into the picture. Investment is just as before. But now saving S must be split into three different terms: (1) net personal saving, which people do out of their disposable incomes; (2) net corporate saving, that part of corporate incomes which they fail to distribute as dividends; finally, (3) net government surplus (or "saving"), which represents the algebraic excess of its tax revenues over its expenditure on goods and services *and* on transfers.

Our identity of measured S and I now has to be written in terms of the three components of total S.[4]

$$I \equiv \text{NPS} + \text{NCS} + \text{NGS}$$

[4]The eager reader can test his grasp of this fundamental identity (which must hold at all times whether or not an economy is in equilibrium or is galloping to or from an equilibrium) by going back to the discussion (page 188 and Table 10-6) of how disposable income is defined in terms of NNP − taxes − NCS + transfers + cons. interest, and how NPS $= DI − C −$ cons. interest. These relations combined with the $C + I + G$ breakdown of NNP can be used to give an algebraic demonstration of our identity.

Thus, from the definition of DI,

$$\text{NNP} \equiv (DI - \text{cons. interest}) + \text{NCS} + Tx - Tr$$

Adding and subtracting G and splitting up $(DI − \text{cons. interest})$ gives

$$\text{NNP} \equiv C + [\text{NPS} + \text{NCS} + (Tx - Tr - G)] + G$$
$$\equiv C + [\text{NPS} + \text{NCS} + (\text{NGS})] + G$$

But recall the upper-loop definition

$$\text{NNP} \equiv C + [I] + G$$

So we do indeed verify the saving-investment identity

$$[I] \equiv [\text{NPS} + \text{NCS} + \text{NGS}]$$

Determination of National Income and Its Fluctuations 2

Saving, Consumption, and Investment

11

We are all Keynesians now.
MILTON FRIEDMAN

In Part One the groundwork was laid for an understanding of the concept of national income. Now we can go beyond the anatomy of the problem to its physiology. What causes national income to rise? To fall? Why is NNP what it is at any time, rather than something larger or smaller? What causes too little total spending—recession and depression? What causes too much total spending—inflationary rises in the index of prices? Part Two analyzes these basic problems of "macroeconomics" (which is the study of the aggregate performance of the whole GNP and of the general price level).

This chapter provides an introduction to what is called the "modern theory of income analysis." The principal stress is upon the *level of total spending as determined by the interplay of the monetary forces of saving and investment.*

Although much of this analysis is due to an English economist, John Maynard Keynes (later made Lord Keynes, before his death in 1946), today the broad fundamentals of "the new economics" are increasingly accepted by most economists including, it is important to notice, many who do not share Keynes' particular policy views and who differ on technical details of analysis.[1]

The income analysis here described is itself neutral: it can be used as well to defend private enterprise as to limit it; as well to attack as to defend government fiscal intervention. When business organizations like the United States Chamber of Commerce, the Committee for Economic Development, or the Chase Manhattan Bank use

[1] Keynes himself was a many-sided genius who won eminence in the fields of mathematics, philosophy, and literature. In addition, he found time to run a large insurance company, to advise the British Treasury, to help govern the Bank of England, to edit a world-famous economic journal, to collect modern art and rare books, and to sponsor ballet and drama. He was also an economist who knew how to make money, both for himself and for King's College, Cambridge. His 1936 book, *The General Theory of Employment, Interest and Money,* created the greatest stir in economic thinking of the century and will live as a classic.

the apparatus of saving and investment, it is absurd to think this implies that they are "Keynesian," in the sense of belonging to that narrow band of enthusiasts associated with some of the policy programs that J. M. Keynes himself espoused during the Great Depression. Even Marxian economists, who at first resented Keynesian economics literally as a "mere palliative" to the ills of capitalism, have come to recognize its explanatory powers.

In recent years 90 per cent of American economists have stopped being "Keynesian economists" or "anti-Keynesian economists." Modern economists are "post-Keynesians," keen to render obsolete any theories that cannot meet the test of experience. Thus, in 1970, post-Keynesians accord an importance to the role of money in the process of income determination that would have surprised the first disciples of Keynes (but which would not at all have surprised that brilliant virtuoso of finance).

THE CLEAVAGE BETWEEN SAVING AND INVESTMENT MOTIVATIONS

The most important single fact about saving and investment activities is that in our industrial society they are generally done *by different people* and *for different reasons.*

This was not always so; even today, when a farmer devotes his time to draining a field instead of to planting and harvesting a crop, he is saving and at the same time investing. He is "saving" because he is abstaining from *present* consumption in order to provide for larger consumption in the *future*—the amount of his saving being measured by the difference between his net real income and his consumption. But he is also "investing"; i.e., he is undertaking net capital formation, improving the productive capacity of his farm. Not only are saving and investment the same things for a primitive farmer, but his reasons for undertaking them are the same. He abstains from present consumption (saves) only because he wants to drain the field (to invest). If there were no investment opportunity whatsoever, it would never occur to him to save; nor would there be any way to save for the future, should he be so foolish as to wish to.

In our modern economy, net capital formation or investment is carried on by business enterprises, especially corporations. When a corporation or a small business has great investment opportunities, its owners will be tempted to plow back much of its earnings into the business. To an important degree, therefore, some business saving does get motivated directly by business investment.

Nevertheless, saving is primarily done by an entirely different group: by individuals, by families, by households. An individual may wish to save for a great variety of reasons: to provide for his old age or for a future expenditure (a vacation or an automobile). Or he may feel insecure and wish to guard against a rainy day. Or he may wish to leave an estate to his children or to his children's children. Or he may be an eighty-year-old miser with no heirs who enjoys the act of accumulating for its own sake. Or he may already have signed himself up to a savings program because an insurance salesman was persuasive. Or he may desire the power that greater wealth brings. Or thrift may simply be a habit, almost a conditioned reflex, whose origin he does not himself know.

Whatever the individual's motivation to save, it often has little to do with the investment opportunities of society and business.

This truth is obscured by the fact that in everyday language "investment" does not always have the same meaning as in economics. We have defined "net investment," or capital formation, to be the net increase in the community's real capital (equipment, buildings, inventories). But the plain man speaks of "investing" when he buys a piece of land, an old security, or any title to property. For economists these are clearly *transfer* items. What one man is buying, someone else is selling. There is net investment only when *additional real capital* is created.

In short, even if there are no *real* investment opportunities that seem profitable, an individual may still *wish* to nonconsume—to save. He can always buy an existing security asset; he can accumulate, or *try* to accumulate, cash.

THE VARIABILITY OF INVESTMENT

Thus, we are left with our proposition: Saving and investing are often desired by different individuals and for independent reasons. While it is families who primarily decide to save, net capital formation takes place largely in business enterprise.

The amount of investment itself is *highly variable* from year to year and decade to decade. This capricious, volatile behavior is understandable when we come to realize that profitable investment opportunities depend on *new* discoveries, *new* products, *new* territories and frontiers, *new* resources, *new* population, *higher* production and income. Note the emphasis on "new" and on "higher." Investment depends largely on the *dynamic* and relatively unpredictable elements of *growth* in the system and on elements outside the economic system itself: technology, politics, optimistic and pessimistic expectations, "confidence," governmental tax and expenditure, legislative policies, and much else.

The extreme variability of investment is the next important fact to be emphasized.

The independence of forces operating upon saving and investment is like the independence of forces operating on Chapter 4's supply and demand schedules. While recognizing this independence, we should also recognize two qualifications: (1) often at the corporate level, decisions to invest are closely related to the funds that corporations are able to save out of their earnings and that need not be paid out in dividends; (2) at all times, but particularly in times of tight money and high interest rates, how much entrepreneurs can indulge their desire to invest in new profitable opportunities will depend on how much finance is made available to them by people's saving. Just as the independent forces operating on supply and demand are resolved by what happens to market prices, so we shall see that saving and investment decisions are resolved by what happens to the level of income and employment and to interest rates.

We shall see that an industrial system such as our own can do many wonderful things. It can mobilize men, tools, and know-how to respond to any given demand for goods. Over time it can improve upon its own response.

But there is one thing it cannot always do.

Unless proper macroeconomic policies are pursued, a laissez faire economy cannot guarantee that there will be exactly the required amount of investment to ensure full employment: not too little so as to cause unemployment, nor too much so as to cause inflation. As far as total investment or money-spending power is concerned, the laissez faire system is without a good thermostat.

For decades there might tend to be too little investment, leading to deflation, losses, excess capacity, unemployment, and destitution. For other years or decades, there might tend to be too much investment, leading to periods of chronic inflation—unless prudent and proper public policies in the fiscal (i.e., tax and expenditure) and monetary (i.e., Federal Reserve central bank) fields are followed.

Nor is there an Invisible Hand guaranteeing that the good years will by themselves equal the bad; or guaranteeing that scientists will discover just in the nick of time precisely enough new products and processes to keep the system on an even keel. From 1855 to 1875 railroads were built all over the world. In the next two decades nothing quite took the place of this activity. The automobile and public utilities produced a similar revolution in the 1920s. In the 1930s plastics and radio had no comparable effect on total net investment. In the years immediately following World War II, much of the time we were plagued by too much investment spending relative to the resources released by those acts of renouncing consumption which economists call "saving." Then in the Eisenhower years of the 1950s, America experienced sluggish growth, with increasing unemployment. By the Vietnam era of the late 1960s, inflation problems were back.

Thus we see that the instabilities are not all on the downward side. Economic history is, alas, a history of inflations. Anyone who comes of age today has seen prices almost double in his own brief lifetime. Unless proper policies are followed, he can look forward to gyrating prices for the rest of his life.

While a realist must recognize that an economy like ours of 1929 or of the 1970s will not *by itself* maintain stability of prices and full employment, critics should still recognize that there are certain elements in a pricing economy that can work toward stability if given a chance to operate and if helped by vigorous public stabilizing actions. As we shall see later, *the structure of interest rates*—which determines how costly and hard it is to get credit for investing activities—can be helped by Federal Reserve monetary policy to play a *stabilizing* role in moderating investment fluctuations. Also, to a considerable extent the frictions that keep various prices inflexible and sticky in a modern mixed economy can be offset by public fiscal actions.

This, then, is one of our most important economic lessons.

Where the stimulus to investment is concerned, the system is somewhat in the lap of the gods. We may be lucky or unlucky; and one of the few things you can say about luck is, "It's going to change." Fortunately, things need not be left to luck. We shall see that perfectly sensible public and private policies can be followed that have greatly enhanced the stability and productive growth of the mixed economy.

The next chapters will show how investment and saving determine the equilibrium level of national income. First, we must understand the important budgetary patterns, reflecting how people consume and save at different income levels.

BUDGETARY EXPENDITURE PATTERNS

No two families spend their money in exactly the same way. Yet statistics do show that there is a predictable regularity—on the average—in the way people allocate their

Family expenditures show regular income patterns:

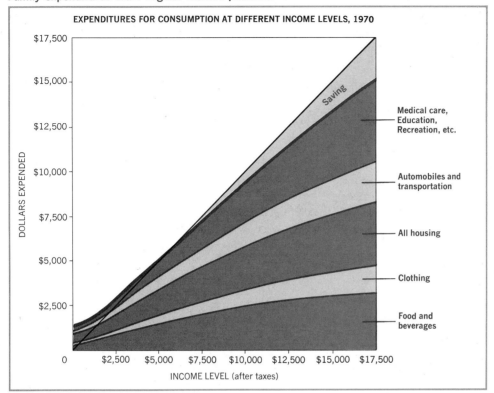

EXPENDITURES FOR CONSUMPTION AT DIFFERENT INCOME LEVELS, 1970

FIG. 11-1. Careful sampling of urban families verifies the importance of income as a determinant of consumption expenditure. Notice the drop in food as a percentage of higher incomes. Note also the rise in saving, from below zero at low incomes to substantial positive levels. (Source: Bureau of Labor Statistics and Department of Agriculture updated.)

expenditures on food, clothing, and other major items. Literally thousands of budgetary investigations have been made of the ways that people at different levels of income spend their money; and there is remarkable agreement on the general, qualitative patterns of behavior.[2] What are they? Figure 11-1 tells the story.

Poor families must, of course, spend their incomes largely on the necessities of life: food, shelter, and, in lesser degree, clothing. As income increases, expenditure on many food items goes up. People eat more and eat better. They shift away from cheap, bulky carbohydrates to more expensive meats and proteins—and to milk, fruit, vegetables, and labor-saving processed foods.

There are, however, limits to the amount of extra money that people will spend on food when their incomes rise. Consequently, the *percentage* importance of food expenditure declines as income increases. (Actually, there are a few cheap, but filling, items such

[2] Figure 11-1's behavior patterns are called "Engel's Laws," after the nineteenth-century Prussian statistician Ernst Engel (not to be confused with Karl Marx's friend Friedrich Engels). The average behavior of consumption expenditure does change fairly regularly with income; but averages do not tell the whole story. Within each income class, there is spread around the average.

as potatoes or sausage whose consumption decreases absolutely with income increase. These are called "inferior goods" in Part Three.)

After you get out of the very poorest income class, your proportion of income spent on shelter is pretty constant for a wide range. This is expressed in a familiar rule of thumb: One week's salary should cover one month's expenditure on rent and house utilities. The other rule of thumb—that you should pay about 2 years' income for a house—has a hollow ring these days.

Expenditure on clothing, recreation, and automobiles increases more than proportionately to after-tax income, until high incomes are reached. Of course, luxury items, by definition, increase in greater proportion than income; and in many ways, as we shall soon see, saving is the greatest luxury of all, especially at very high incomes.

THE PROPENSITY TO SAVE AND PROPENSITY TO CONSUME

An important use of after-tax income is saving for the future rather than consuming now. This saving facet is what interests us most. It is a matter of common observation that rich men save more than poor men, not only in absolute amounts but also in percentage amounts. The very poor are unable to save at all. Instead they "dissave," i.e., spend more every year than they earn, the difference being covered by going into debt or using up previously accumulated savings. Thus, income is a prime determinant of saving, as shown in Table 11-1.[3]

This table gives data on saving and consumption indicative of family patterns in the 1960s, the so-called "propensity to consume" and "propensity to save." Column (2) shows the net saving that accompanies each level of disposable income. The "break-even point," where the family neither saves nor dissaves, instead consuming all its income, falls at $6,000. Below this, as at $5,000 or $4,000, it actually consumes more than its income; it dissaves (see the −$110 and −$170 data). Above $6,000 it begins to do positive saving (see the +$150 data).

Column (3) shows the consumption pattern of each income level—the so-called "propensity to consume." Since each dollar of income is divided between the part consumed and the remaining part saved, Columns (3) and (2) are not independent: they must always exactly add up to Column (1). (Check that they do.)

Most saving is done by families with incomes above the average:

PROPENSITY OF FAMILIES TO SAVE AND CONSUME

(1) DISPOSABLE INCOME AFTER TAXES	(2) NET SAVING (+) OR DISSAVING (−)	(3) CONSUMPTION
$ 4,000	$ −170	$4,170
5,000	−110	5,110
6,000	0	6,000
7,000	+150	6,850
8,000	+400	7,600
9,000	+760	8,240
10,000	+1,170	8,830
11,000	+1,640	9,360
12,000	+2,150	9,850

TABLE 11-1. The break-even point at which people cease to dissave and begin to do positive saving is here shown at $6,000. How much of each extra dollar do people around this income level devote to extra consumption? How much to extra saving? (Answer: About 85 cents and 15 cents, respectively.)

[3] These data do not depict long-run behavior of each family when its income moves from a *permanent* low level to a *permanent* high level. Transitorily, saving rises much; but as people get accustomed to higher "permanent income," consumption rises and saving becomes more moderate. Surprising as it may seem, statistics show that people with $12,000 of *permanent* income save about the same fraction of their income as do people with $6,000 of *permanent* income. (NOTE. In this and later chapters, consumer interest, mentioned in Chapter 10's Appendix, is ignored.)

Economic analysis is interested not simply in the total figures of saving and consumption, but in the *extra* saving and consumption that each *extra* dollar of income brings. Thus, as income goes from $6,000 to $7,000, the extra $1,000 of income is divided between $850 of extra consumption and $150 of extra saving—split up 85 and 15 per cent, so to speak. (Where did these numbers come from? You get them from $6,850 minus $6,000 and from $150 minus $0. And verify that the division between consumption and saving of extra dollars beyond $7,000 is, respectively, 75 and 25 per cent, then 64 and 36 per cent. . . . Does it seem reasonable to you that richer people will consume a little less of each extra income dollar than will poorer?[4])

Family propensity-to-save and propensity-to-consume patterns have been rather stable. (Workers, however, have generally seemed to save less than the self-employed.)

To understand how saving and investment determine the level of national income and employment, we must continue to study in detail (1) the propensity-to-save schedule, relating saving and income, and its twin brother (2) the propensity-to-consume schedule, relating consumption and income.

THE PROPENSITY-TO-CONSUME SCHEDULE IN DETAIL

Table 11-2 on the next page rearranges these same data in more convenient form. First, verify its similarity to Table 11-1. Then disregard its Columns (3) to (5), and notice how consumption expenditure goes up at each higher level of income.

This same consumption-income relation can be shown even more vividly in diagrammatic form. In Fig. 11-2 on page 201 the total of consumption expenditure in Column (2) is plotted against family disposable income of Column (1); through the resulting circles *A*, *B*, *C*, *D*, *E*, *F*, *G*, and *H*, a smooth curve has been drawn.

This relation between consumption and income is called the *consumption schedule,* or *propensity-to-consume schedule,* or often simply the *propensity to consume.* It is a basic, important concept whose general properties we must study.

It will help you to understand its properties if, first, you look at the 45° line also shown in Fig. 11-2. Inasmuch as the vertical axis of consumption has been drawn to the same scale as the horizontal axis of income, any point lying on the 45° helping line has the following simple property: Its indicated consumption expenditure—measured by the vertical distance of the point from the horizontal axis—is exactly equal to 100 per cent of its indicated level of disposable income—measured by the horizontal distance of the point from the vertical axis. (Use your eye to verify that any point *not* on the 45° line cannot possibly be equidistant from the two axes. Reread the description of the 45° line.)

The "break-even" point The 45° line will tell us right away, therefore, whether consumption spending is equal to, greater than, or less than the level of income. The point

[4]Students at first find it hard to understand that, even when family income is below the break-even point and saving is negative, nonetheless each *extra* income dollar goes partly into positive extra saving and partly into positive extra consumption. To convince yourself, compare row 2 of Table 11-1 with row 1. Adding $1,000 to $4,000 of income gives $5,000. This extra income makes consumption go from $4,170 to $5,110, a gain of $940, with $60 of extra saving.

How we depict important consumption-income and saving-income patterns:

1st, A table presents the propensity-to-consume schedule:

	(1) DISPOSABLE INCOME (after taxes)	(2) CONSUMPTION EXPENDITURE	(3) MARGINAL PROPENSITY TO CONSUME (MPC)	(4) NET SAVING (4) = (1) − (2)	(5) MARGINAL PROPENSITY TO SAVE (MPS)
PROPENSITY TO CONSUME AND TO SAVE					
A	$ 5,000	$5,110		$−110	
			$\frac{890}{1,000} = 0.89$		$\frac{110}{1,000} = 0.11$
B	6,000	6,000		0	
			$\frac{850}{1,000} = 0.85$		$\frac{150}{1,000} = 0.15$
C	7,000	6,850		+150	
			$\frac{750}{1,000} = 0.75$		$\frac{250}{1,000} = 0.25$
D	8,000	7,600		+400	
			$\frac{640}{1,000} = 0.64$		$\frac{360}{1,000} = 0.36$
E	9,000	8,240		+760	
			$\frac{590}{1,000} = 0.59$		$\frac{410}{1,000} = 0.41$
F	10,000	8,830		+1,170	
			$\frac{530}{1,000} = 0.53$		$\frac{470}{1,000} = 0.47$
G	11,000	9,360		+1,640	
			$\frac{490}{1,000} = 0.49$		$\frac{510}{1,000} = 0.51$
H	12,000	9,850		+2,150	

TABLE 11-2.   Each dollar of income not consumed is saved. And each extra dollar of income goes into extra consumption or extra saving—giving us important concepts we need: MPC and MPS. (NOTE: $890 = 6,000 − 5,110. How about $850?)

on the consumption schedule where it intersects the 45° line shows us the level of disposable income at which families just break even. This break-even point is at *B*; here, consumption expenditure is exactly equal to disposable income; the family is borrowing nothing and on balance saving nothing.

Similarly, *anywhere else* on the propensity-to-consume curve, the family cannot be just breaking even. To the right of point *B*, the curve lies below the 45° line; the long brown arrow in Fig. 11-2 shows that the vertical distance (consumption expenditure) is less than the horizontal distance (disposable income). If the family is not spending all its income, then it must be saving the remainder. The 45° line tells us more than that, it enables us to find *how much* the family is saving. Net saving is measured by the distance from the propensity-to-consume curve up to the 45° line, as shown by the appropriate saving arrow in blue.

Similarly, to the left of point *B*, our 45° helping line tells us that the family is for the moment somehow spending more than the income it receives. The excess of consumption over income is its "net dissaving" and is measured by the vertical distance between the two curves. To review:

When the propensity-to-consume schedule lies above the 45° line, the family is dissaving. Where the two curves meet, the family is just breaking even. Where the propensity to consume lies below the 45° line, the family is performing net positive saving. And the amount of dissaving or saving is always measured by the distance between the two curves.

The "propensity-to-save schedule" This means that we can easily derive from the consumption schedule in Fig. 11-2 a new schedule: the propensity to save, or as it is sometimes called, the "saving schedule."

Graphically, this is shown in Fig. 11-3. Again we show disposable income on the horizontal axis; vertically we now show what the family *does not* spend; i.e., we show its net saving, whether negative or positive in amount.

This propensity-to-save curve comes directly from Fig. 11-2. It is simply the distance between the 45° line and the propensity-to-consume schedule. At a point such as A in Fig. 11-2, the fact that the family's savings were negative was indicated by the propensity-to-consume schedule lying above the helping line. Figure 11-3 shows this fact of negative saving directly, and similarly for the positive saving that begins when family income pushes past point B.

THE MARGINAL PROPENSITY TO CONSUME

In the next chapter, we shall be attaching much importance to the *extra* amount that people will want to spend on consumption if given an *extra* dollar of income. Economists are so interested in this concept that

2d, A schedule graphs the propensity to consume:

FIG. 11-2.   The curve through A, B, . . . , H is the consumption schedule, or the propensity to consume. Its slope at any point, measured by forming a little triangle and relating altitude to base, is the MPC, the marginal propensity to consume. The 45° line helps locate the break-even point and helps our eye measure net saving. Can you see how? (Source: Table 11-2.)

3d, The saving schedule is the exact twin of the consumption schedule:

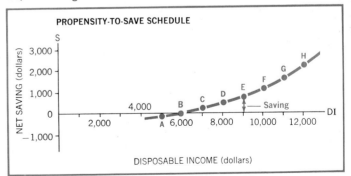

FIG. 11-3.   This saving schedule comes from subtracting consumption from income. (Graphically, we vertically subtracted the consumption schedule from the 45° helping line.) Note that the break-even point B is at the same $6,000 level as in Fig. 11-2. Measure MPS by the curve's slope at any point. Does MPS + MPC = 1 everywhere? (It had better!)

they have given it a special name, the "marginal propensity to consume," or MPC. (The word "marginal" is used by the economist to mean "extra"; thus, marginal cost will later be defined as extra cost of producing an extra unit of product; marginal utility as extra utility; marginal revenue as extra revenue; and so forth.)

Column (3) back in Table 11-2 shows how we compute the marginal propensity to consume. From B to C, income rises by $1,000, going from $6,000 to $7,000. By how much does consumption rise? Consumption grows from $6,000 to $6,850, or by $850. The extra consumption is therefore .85 of the extra income. Out of each extra dollar of income, 85 cents goes to consumption and 15 cents goes to saving. We therefore can say that the marginal propensity to consume, or MPC, is .85 between B and C, which agrees with Column (3) of Table 11-2.

You can easily compute MPC between other income levels. In Table 11-2, MPC begins at .89 for poor people and finally falls to .49 at higher incomes.

Now we know how to compute MPC numerically. What is its geometric meaning? It is a numerical measure of the steepness of slope of the consumption schedule.[5] Look again at Fig. 11-2. Near points B and C a little triangle is drawn. As we move to the right from B by $1,000, in order to stay on the schedule, we must go up by $850; this gives a numerical slope $850/$1,000, or .85. NOTE: If higher incomes have a lower MPC, the family consumption schedule will look slightly bowed (convex from above, concave from below).

THE MARGINAL PROPENSITY TO SAVE

Along with the marginal propensity to consume goes a Siamese-twin concept, the "marginal propensity to save," or MPS. This is defined as *the fraction of each extra dollar that goes to saving instead of to consumption.*

Why are MPC and MPS related like Siamese twins? Since each extra dollar of income must be divided between extra consumption and extra saving, it is obvious that, if MPC is .85, then MPS must be .15. (What would MPS be if MPC were .6? Or .99?) A comparison of Columns (3) and (5) of Table 11-2 confirms our common-sense feeling that at any income level, MPC and MPS must always add up to exactly 1, no more and no less.[6]

[5] By the numerical slope of the line XY, we always mean the numerical ratio of the length ZY to the length XZ. See the accompanying drawing. If XY were a curve, we could find the slope at any point on it (1) by placing a ruler tangent to it, and (2) by applying the procedure of this triangle to that tangential line.

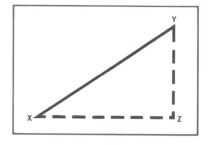

[6] You can also verify from Fig. 11-3 that the numerical steepness of slope of the propensity-to-save schedule is the geometric expression of MPS. This shows: The saving schedule will always have the opposite curvature to that of the consumption schedule; as MPC falls, MPS must rise. And since every extra dollar divides up between positive extra consumption and extra saving, it follows that neither the consumption nor the saving schedule *anywhere* has a slope as steep as the 45° line, which by definition has a slope of 1. Remember, we are here discussing *marginal* propensities. Thus, at point A, the family is spending more than its income; but that does not alter the fact that, at A, its *marginal* propensity to consume out of *extra* income is less than 1. (These family data show more exaggerated curvature than would seem realistic in the 1970s for *permanent* income levels.)

BRIEF REVIEW OF DEFINITIONS

For the record, let us jot down the main definitions now learned:

1. **The propensity-to-consume schedule (or consumption schedule)** relates in a table or a curve the level of consumption to the level of income.

2. **The propensity-to-save schedule (or saving schedule)** relates saving to income. Since what is saved is the same thing as what is nonconsumed, saving and consumption schedules are Siamese twins in the sense that

$$\text{Saving} + \text{consumption} = \text{disposable income}$$

3. **The "break-even point"** is the income level where net saving is zero. Below it, there is dissaving, or negative saving; above it, positive net saving. Graphically, the break-even point is where the 45° helping line intersects the consumption schedule, or where the saving schedule intersects the horizontal axis.

4. **The marginal propensity to consume (MPC)** is the amount of *extra* consumption generated by an *extra* dollar of income. Graphically, it is given by the slope of the consumption schedule—a steep slope meaning a high MPC and a flat one meaning a low MPC.

5. **The marginal propensity to save (MPS)** is the *extra* saving generated by an *extra* dollar of income, or the slope of the saving schedule. Because the part of each dollar that is not consumed is necessarily saved, MPS = 1 − MPC always. Hence, higher income that lowers MPC must raise MPS, implying a concave (from below) consumption schedule and a convex saving schedule.

THE COMMUNITY'S OVER-ALL CONSUMPTION SCHEDULE

So far we have been talking about the consumption patterns shown by families of different incomes. To study what determines a nation's income, we are interested in a propensity-to-consume schedule slightly different from the family-budget schedule. We want the "community propensity-to-consume schedule," relating total consumption to total "disposable (after-tax) income." This is because we are interested in how the total of *all* consumption spending in the United States changes as the total of our spendable income rises.

While aggregate income is not the only factor determining aggregate consumption, common sense and statistical experience tell us that it is one of the most important factors. Turn over to Fig. 11-4 to see how closely consumption seems to follow yearly disposable income; the only exceptional period is that of World War II, when goods were scarce and rationed and people were urged to save.

Figure 11-5 shows this relationship between consumption and disposable income in the form of a "scatter diagram" for the years 1929 up until 1970. Each dot marks the magnitude for each year. The resulting scatter of points shows no particular curvature; so a straight-line consumption schedule was drawn in. The actual data fall near, but not exactly on, the "fitted" consumption schedule,[7] reminding us that economics is not, like physics,

[7] So that no reader may think there is great accuracy in this line, let it be mentioned that it was fitted by stretching a black thread from the lower corner through all the data (excepting those for World War II) at what appeared a reasonable position. As in the case of supply and demand curves in Chapter 4 and Part Three, it will be convenient to go back and forth between drawing propensity-to-consume schedules as curved lines or more simply as straight lines when that does no gross violence to the actual facts. (Using full-year 1970 data, does the 1970 point fall near C?)

4th, Community consumption did move with national income:

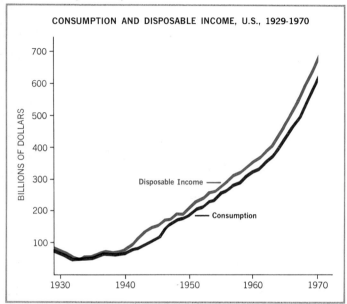

CONSUMPTION AND DISPOSABLE INCOME, U.S., 1929-1970

FIG. 11-4. Good forecasts of consumption come from income data. Can you see how great saving became during World War II's goods shortage and rationing? (Source: U.S. Department of Commerce.)

an exact science. A good rule of thumb is this: Out of each dollar of disposable income about 6 cents goes for saving, S, and 92 cents for consumption, C (the remaining 2 cents going for consumer interest).

QUALIFICATIONS

We are now prepared for the theory of income determination. We have introduced the crucially important concepts of consumption and saving schedules that will be used in the next chapter. But warnings are in order.

The community consumption schedule must be in some sense an aggregation of the family schedules. Yet even if we knew that the family schedules were perfectly reliable, we should still have to know something about the *distribution of incomes* before we could get the new points of total consumption of the national schedule. Thus, when a national-income rise is associated with the distribution of extra income that is *typical* for such a rise, we shall be moving upward on our unshifted community consumption schedule CC.

Aside from the distribution of income, there is a second factor that must be taken into account in any attempt to relate the family and national patterns. Suppose my income were to go from $9,000 to $40,000 a year. Would I spend and save my money in the same way that the budget studies showed $40,000-a-year people spend their money? Not necessarily. Especially at the beginning, I would be *nouveau riche* and have different patterns of behavior.[8]

A third reason why it is difficult to go from the family to the national consumption schedule is suggested by the expression "keeping up with the Joneses." Fifty years ago, if your family had $2,000 worth of purchasing power, you would have been quite well off and above the break-even point of zero saving. But today many people have incomes above that level. Because man is a social animal, what he regards as necessary comforts of life depends on what he sees others consuming. So today, with $2,000 of income, you would be desperately poor and unable to make ends meet. This fact that one man's consumption depends upon the incomes and consumption of others means that we cannot

[8]Modern theoretical and statistical researches by Professors James S. Duesenberry, Milton Friedman, and Franco Modigliani suggest strongly that if people were generally to get a prescribed percentage increase in their incomes that was permanent, they would probably add more to their long-run consumption expenditure than would be indicated by budget studies recorded for a single year such as 1950 or 1970. This warning, which appeared earlier in footnote 3, is worth repeating.

expect the final community pattern to be the simple sum of the separate family patterns. It also means that we must expect the consumption schedule to be shifting upward each decade as living standards rise. Hence, in Fig. 11-5, one would be foolish to push the line back to the income of 1900 or forward to 1999. It is a succinct description of history, rather than necessarily the best guess of the consumption schedule a bank or government economist would use in estimating next year's consumption.

A number of other important qualifications will occur to the reader. The community consumption schedule will shift as prices change and total population grows. Statisticians sometimes try to allow for this by working with per capita consumption and per capita income, expressed in real terms by means of a deflating price index of the sort discussed in the last chapter.[9]

We can think of still other reasons why the propensity-to-consume schedule might shift around. Thus, at the end of World

5th, The community consumption schedule in statistical form:

FIG. 11-5. The curve *CC* approximately fits the statistical points for all years except the World War II period. Can you verify its MPC slope of .91 and predict the 1970 point? (Source: Fig. 11-4.)

War II, many economists made a famous wrong prediction of deflation. They neglected the fact that people came out of the war hungry for goods and with greatly increased amounts of liquid assets (such as government bonds and bank deposits); for this and other reasons, the consumption schedule turned out to be at a higher level than many pessimistic predictions had indicated.

Again we are reminded that no social science can have great exactitude. We shall have to use tools such as the propensity-to-consume curve—or curves of supply and demand—which we know are subject to error and which tend to shift over time rather than remain stable.

The last chapter showed that the national-income accounts *always measure* an identity between saving and investment. This chapter showed that the *motives* and *desires* behind saving and investment are generally quite distinct—which certainly raises the suspicion that the total flow of dollar spending is not guaranteed to proceed at exactly the same

---

[9] Thus, instead of working with simple, total dollar *C*, statisticians may correct it for Price and Population, by working with doubly deflated $C/(\text{Price} \times \text{Population})$; likewise, they may replace *DI* by its doubly deflated $DI/(Pr \times Po)$, to get *per capita real* income.

rate year in and year out. The hard facts of history confirm this suspicion: at times the economy experienced overexuberant demand and inflation; at times—and they used to be of considerable duration—it experienced considerable unemployment and excess capacity; in the absence of determined public programs of fiscal and monetary controls, only at rare times have economies enjoyed full employment and steady price levels.

The next two chapters investigate how the forces of saving and investment interact to produce an equilibrium level of national income, which can be at high or low employment and which can be conducive to price stability or to price inflation.

SUMMARY

1 Motivations making people want to engage in saving and to engage in investing are different. History shows there is no automatic tendency for the same number of dollars to get spent always at the same rate. Hence, our modern mixed economy would be subject to inflationary and depression swings if proper public fiscal and monetary policies did not act to help stabilize the economy and reinforce its spontaneous internal mechanisms that strive to achieve stability.

2 Income is one of the most important determinants of consumption (food, clothing, total) and of saving. The propensity to consume is the schedule relating total consumption to total income. Because any dollar of income is either saved or consumed, the propensity-to-save schedule is the other side of the propensity-to-consume picture.

3 The characteristics of family or community propensity-to-consume and propensity-to-save schedules are summarized in the brief review of definitions on page 203 and must be thoroughly understood prior to the analysis of income determination in the next chapter.

4 We could aggregate the family consumption schedules to get the community propensity-to-consume schedule, (a) if we knew the distribution of income for each level of disposable income, (b) if families always stuck to the same consumption-income patterns in the short run and the long, (c) if we could forget the fact that one man's consumption is influenced by the income levels of his neighbors, and (d) if price levels, population, corporate saving, and taxes could be neglected.

The statistical data suggest that total consumption expenditure follows rather closely the changes in total disposable income. But in using the propensity-to-consume concept for the discussion of income determination in the next chapter, we must beware of forming an exaggerated notion of the accuracy and empirical stability of such a theoretical concept.

QUESTIONS FOR DISCUSSION

1 Summarize familiar budget patterns: food, clothing, luxuries, saving.

2 What are some of the reasons why people save? What are some of the forms in which they keep their assets?

3   Exactly how were the MPC and MPS in Table 11-2 computed? Illustrate between *A* and *B*. Explain why it must always be true that MPC + MPS = 1.

4   I consume *all* my income. Draw my consumption and saving schedules.

5   Do you think the break-even point is the same in New York as in Mississippi? What do you think is the current break-even point in your community? List a number of ways a person can incur negative net saving for a while.

6   "Along the consumption schedule, income changes more (absolutely) than consumption does." Why? Show that this is even more true on the saving schedule.

7   What factors must be taken into consideration if we want to aggregate family budgetary propensity-to-consume schedules to arrive at a community propensity-to-consume schedule? What would happen to the amount consumed out of $900 billion of income if the degree of inequality of income were increased? To the amount saved? What if total taxes out of the $900 billion were to increase? If people were to have more government bonds and bank deposits, how would that affect saving out of the $900 billion?

8   Contrast the meaning of this chapter's beginning quotation with the following 1966 letter to the editor of *Time Magazine* by Professor Milton Friedman of the University of Chicago.

   Sir: You quote me [Dec. 31] as saying: "We are all Keynesians now." The quotation is correct, but taken out of context. As best I can recall it, the context was: "In one sense, we are all Keynesians now; in another, nobody is any longer a Keynesian."

9   *Extra-credit problem:* Suppose the following equation for *CC* holds: $C = 200 + \frac{2}{3} DI$. Calculate the MPC as $dC/d(DI) = \frac{2}{3}$. From the identity $S + C \equiv DI$, verify the formula for the *SS* schedule: $S = -200 + \frac{1}{3} DI$. From this calculate MPS as $dS/d(DI)$ and verify that it does equal $1 - $ MPC.

   Review your understanding of the following concepts:

family motives for saving	break-even point and 45° line
business motives for investing	after-tax, or disposable, income
volatile investment decisions	permanent versus transitory income
consumption and saving schedules	community consumption schedule
propensity to consume or to save	versus family schedule
MPC and MPS	shifts of *CC* with price, time, and
MPC + MPS = 1	other changes

Income Determination: The Simple Multiplier Theory

12

Given the propensity to consume and the rate of new investment, there will be only one level of employment consistent with equilibrium.

J. M. KEYNES (1936)

Economists are agreed that an important factor in causing income and employment to fluctuate is fluctuation in investment. Whether we are to face a situation of inflationary bidding up of prices or are to live in a frigid state of mass unemployment can depend, as will be seen, upon the level of investment.

This chapter and the next one outline the modern theory of income determination. Because the problems are so important and because the analysis is so useful, the present chapter stresses the fundamentals—how saving and investment, or what is the same thing, how consumption and investment interact to determine the equilibrium level of national income at full employment, below full employment, or over–full-employment inflationary conditions; and how each dollar change in investment leads to more than a dollar—i.e., to a "multiplier"—change in NNP.

Once the tools of this chapter are mastered, we are ready to understand the next chapter's analysis of inflation and deflation, of how government expenditure and government tax policy can alter the income equilibrium, and of the paradox that sometimes when a nation *tries* to save more, it ends up only undermining actual investment.

USING THE CONSUMPTION AND SAVING SCHEDULES

The last chapter gave a simplified picture of the propensity-to-consume and the propensity-to save schedules for the community. As discussed, they are drawn up on the basis of our knowledge of the thriftiness of different families, the distribution of incomes between families, and so forth. (At the beginning, we shall make the further simplifying assumptions that there are no taxes, undistributed corporate profits, transfers, or government expenditure of any kind to worry about; hence, we do not have to concern ourselves for the moment with any distinction between net national product and disposable income, and we can use the word "income" to refer to either. Also, we shall initially neglect any changes in the price level.)

Figure 12-1 shows the community propensities to consume and to save. Each point on its consumption schedule shows how much the community will *want to continue to consume* at that level of disposable income. Each point on the saving schedule shows how much it will want to continue to save at that income level. Recall that the two schedules are clearly related: since $C + S =$ income always, the CC and SS curves are Siamese twins that will add up always to the 45° line.

HOW INCOME IS DETERMINED AT THE LEVEL WHERE SAVING AND INVESTMENT SCHEDULES INTERSECT

We have seen that saving and investment are dependent on quite different factors: Saving tends to depend in a "passive" way upon income, while volatile investment often depends upon "autonomous" factors of dynamic growth.

For simplicity, first suppose investment opportunities are such that net investment would be exactly $60 billion per year regardless of the level of NNP. This means that, if we now draw a schedule of investment against NNP, it will have to be a *horizontal* line—always the same distance above the horizontal axis. Observe Fig. 12-2 on the next page, where this investment schedule is labeled *II* to distinguish it from the *SS* saving schedule. (Note that *II* does *not* mean Roman numeral two.)

The saving and investment schedules intersect at E, which corresponds to a level of NNP equal to the distance from 0 to M as shown by the gold indicator.

This intersection of the *saving and investment schedules* is the equilibrium toward which national income will gravitate. Under our assumed conditions, no other level of income can perpetuate itself.

The remaining pages of this chapter are devoted to the single task of explaining and interpreting this important truth.

Let us see why the equilibrium income must eventually be at E, the point of intersection between the investment and saving schedules. We consider three cases.

Society's national income determines its consumption and saving:

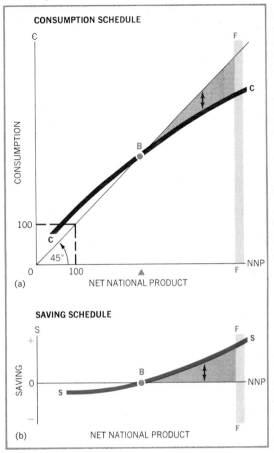

FIG. 12-1. *CC* is the propensity-to-consume and *SS* is the propensity-to-save schedule for the community.

Recall that these are closely related: the break-even point *B* is shown on the upper diagram where *CC* intersects the 45° line and on the lower diagram where *SS* intersects the horizontal axis. Can you explain why the vertically aligned arrows *must* be equal? (The curvature is slightly exaggerated here to help identify the two schedules. The two points marked 100 should help emphasize the important property of the 45° line: it depicts a vertical distance equal to exactly 100 per cent of the horizontal distance.)

The shaded area *FF* depicts the full-employment NNP. Above this critical level we know real product cannot increase, and beyond it we could no longer adhere to our simplifying assumption of ignoring price-level changes. (Source: Table 11-2, Fig. 10-2, and Fig. 10-3.)

The first case is that in which the system is *at E* itself, where the *II* schedule of what business firms *want* to invest and keep investing just intersects the *SS* schedule of what families *want* to save. Consequently, everyone will be content to go on doing just what he has been doing. Firms will not find inventories piling up on their shelves, nor will they find sales so brisk as to force them to produce more goods. So production, employment, and income spending will remain the same. NNP in this first case does truly stay at the point *E*; and we can rightly call that "equilibrium."

The second case is where the system is *first* at an NNP *higher* than at *E*, so that it begins east of *E*, at an income level where the *SS* schedule is higher than the *II* schedule. Why can't the system stay there indefinitely? Because at such an income level, families are saving—are refraining from spending on consumption—*more* than business firms will be *willing to go on investing*. Firms will thus find they have too few customers and that their inventories are piling up against their wishes, and they will not want to go on being forced into such undesired inventory investment. What can they do about it? They can certainly cut back production and lay off workers. This moves NNP gradually downward, which means westward in Fig. 12-2. Where does the system stop being in such disequilibrium? Only when it gets back to *E*, the equilibrium intersection point. There the longer-run tendency to change has disappeared.

The third case should be mastered by the reader. Show that if NNP were *below* its equilibrium level, strong forces would be set up to move it eastward back to *E*. (HINT: At any NNP level where families' *intended* saving falls short of business firms' *intended* investment, the result is consumption of more goods than are being currently produced. What does this mean? It means that business will find itself having to sell inventory off its shelves faster than its production line is producing such goods. Once businessmen notice that they are being forced into less investment, i.e., into more *in*voluntary inventory *disinvestment*, than the *II* curve shows they want, what will they do? They will then expand production and hire new men. This will complete the demonstration that the system does move back eastward until it gets to *E*.)

All three cases then lead to the same summary:

The only equilibrium of national income is at *E*, where the saving and investment schedules intersect. At any other point, the *desired* saving of families will not match the *desired* investment of business, and this discrepancy will cause businessmen to change their production and employment levels in such a way as to return the system to the equilibrium intersection.

Before we go on, a warning is in order. An equilibrium level like *E* is a point where the system tends to stay. But there is nothing necessarily *optimal* about every equilibrium point. Note the vertical shading at *FF* in Fig. 12-2 that depicts full-employment income. Note the fact that the *E* equilibrium shown is at a level of NNP *lower* than that corresponding to *FF*'s full employment.

We can show equilibrium determination of national income in the following equivalent ways:

1st, By intersection of saving and investment schedules:

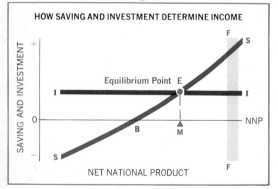

FIG. 12-2. *E* marks the spot where investment and saving curves intersect. Equilibrium is at intersection of *SS* and *II* curves because at no other level of NNP could the desired saving of families continually match the desired investment of business.

During a great depression, a capitalistic system may be firmly stuck at a point of very great unemployment. It is then at the E given by its low II schedule. No one would make the mistake of thinking that such a deep-unemployment equilibrium point is in any sense a good thing. Instead, the government would intervene in the economic system to try to shift the curves until a new equilibrium point E' was attained at a desirable level, as the next chapter explains.

INCOME DETERMINATION BY CONSUMPTION AND INVESTMENT

There is a second way of showing how income is determined, other than by the intersection of the saving and investment schedules. The final result is exactly the same, but our understanding and confidence in the theory of income determination will be increased if we work through this second approach.

This second approach is called the consumption-plus-investment rather than the saving-investment approach. The $C + I$ approach[1] takes advantage of the Siamese-twins property of the saving and consumption schedules. Thus it must always lead to exactly the same equilibrium income as does the saving-and-investment approach. This is shown by the fact that when you line up Fig. 12-3 vertically under Fig. 12-2, you always find that in both charts E marks exactly the same NNP equilibrium.

The $C + I$ approach has the advantage of concentrating on *total spending:* spending for consumption goods plus spending for investment goods. The $C + I$ approach vertically adds the II schedule of business' *desired* investment to the CC consumption schedule of families' *desired* consumption spending.

Only where these two *desired* amounts of spending add up to equality with the value of NNP being produced will there be equilibrium.

With what must the combined $C + I$ schedule intersect to depict this equilibrium? Figure 12-3 introduces a 45° line to provide our looked-for intersection point. The 45° line, we have seen, has the useful property that it lays out in the vertical direction a distance always exactly equal to the income shown on the horizontal axis. So the 45° line is admirably desired to depict the total expense that firms are incurring for the productive factors required to produce national output, and which they must be getting back if they are to feel safe to continue hiring the same number of men and producing the same level of NNP.[2]

2d, By intersection of $C + I$ schedule with 45° line:

FIG. 12-3. Adding II to CC gives the $C + I$ curve of total spending. At E, where it intersects the 45° line, we get the same equilibrium as in the saving-and-investment diagram. (Note the similarities between this figure and Fig. 12-2: the investment added to CC is the same as II of Fig. 12-2; B and F each come at the same place on the two diagrams, *and so must the E intersection.*)

---

[1] When government is brought into the picture, $C + I$ will become $C + I + G$.
[2] As the intermediate texts put it: If the system is not at this intersection, there will be *unintended* inventory investment or disinvestment and/or *unforeseen windfall* profits or losses. As a result, there

We can summarize the $C + I$ method of income determination thus:

The equilibrium level of national income is at the intersection of the $C + I$ schedule of desired total spending with the 45° line depicting value of total output.[3] This equilibrium E corresponds exactly to the saving-and-investment equilibrium because of the Siamese-twins relation between the consumption and the saving schedules.

We shall see in the next chapter that the $C + I$ approach has great advantages in helping to analyze government expenditure and fiscal policy. It easily turns itself into an exactly similar $C + I + G$ approach.

ARITHMETIC DEMONSTRATION OF INCOME DETERMINATION: A DIGRESSION FOR A THIRD RESTATEMENT

A thoughtful reader may still want to know more about *why* the equilibrium level of income will have to be at the intersection of the saving and investment schedules. What forces will push income to that level and no other?

An arithmetic example may help verify this important matter. Table 12-1 shows an especially simple pattern of the propensity to save against income. The break-even level of income where the nation is too poor to do any net saving on balance is assumed to be $820 billion. Each change of income of $90 billion is assumed to lead to a $30-billion change in saving and a 60-billion change in consumption; in other words, MPC is for simplicity here assumed to be constant and exactly equal to $\frac{2}{3}$ with MPS $= \frac{1}{3}$. For this reason, the saving propensity schedule SS in Fig. 12-4 takes on the especially simple form of a perfectly straight line.

What shall we assume about investment? For simplicity, let us suppose again that the only level of investment that can be voluntarily maintained indefinitely is exactly $60 billion, as shown in Column (4) of Table 12-1.

Now, Columns (5) and (6) are the crucial ones. Column (5) shows how much total expense business firms undergo at each level of national production for wages, interest, rent, *and* profit. This is the NNP of Column (1) copied once again into Column (5), because our repeated discussions in Chapter 10 showed that upper- and lower-loop measurements must be the same.

Column (6), on the other hand, shows what business firms would in fact be *getting back* in the long run in the form of scheduled or voluntary consumption spending plus scheduled or voluntary investment. (It's really the blue $C + I$ schedule of Fig. 12-3.)

When business firms as a whole are temporarily producing a high total product, higher

---

cannot be equilibrium; but rather a chain of new decisions will be set up to expand or contract output, and possibly to raise or lower prices. So the system will move in disequilibrium until it ends up at the intersection point of equilibrium. Those same intermediate texts point out that *measured* S and *measured I* stay *identical* even during the worst disequilibrium, by virtue of some people's experiencing unintended losses or gains and/or experiencing unintended investment or saving. (Remember that economists include profit in expense and recall Chapter 10's final Appendix remarks on $S \equiv I$.)

[3] Some writers like to call the $C + I$ curve an aggregate *demand* curve, and the 45°-line curve an aggregate *supply* curve. Then, using Chapter 4's language, they say: The equilibrium level of income is where the aggregate demand and supply curves intersect.

3d, The tendency toward equilibrium is shown by arithmetic table:

INCOME DETERMINATION BY SAVING AND INVESTMENT (in billions of dollars)						
(1)	(2)	(3)	(4)	(5)	(6)	(7)
		SCHEDULED OR PLANNED OR MAIN-	SCHEDULED OR PLANNED OR MAIN-	EXPENSE INCURRABLE BY BUSINESS	SCHEDULED SPENDING THAT WOULD PERMANENTLY	RESULTING
LEVELS OF NNP AND *DI*	SCHEDULED CON- SUMPTION	TAINABLE SAVING (3) = (1) − (2)	TAINABLE INVEST- MENT	TO PRODUCE NNP (5) = (1)	COME BACK TO BUSINESSES (6) = (2) + (4)	TENDENCY OF INCOME
$1,180	$1,060	$120	$60	$1,180 >	$1,120	Contraction
1,090	1,000	90	60	1,090 >	1,060	Contraction
1,000	940	60	60	1,000 =	1,000	Equilibrium
910	880	30	60	910 <	940	Expansion
820	820	0	60	820 <	880	Expansion
730	760	−30	60	730 <	820	Expansion

TABLE 12-1. The gold row depicts the equilibrium NNP, where the $60 billion that business-men will be willing to continue to invest is just matched by families' intended saving. (In higher rows, firms will be forced into unintended inventory investment and will respond by cutting production and NNP back to equilibrium. Interpret the lower rows' tendency toward expansion.)

than the sum of what consumers will buy and what business as a whole wants to be investing in equipment and inventory accumulation, businesses will find themselves forced involuntarily to pile up inventory of unsalable goods. At the same time their total sales revenue will be so low as to be putting disagreeable downward pressure on their profit position. With scheduled SS above *II*, therefore, they will want to contract their operations, and NNP will tend to fall. (Contrariwise, when *II* > SS and inventories are being involuntarily depleted and profit margins improving, they will increase their employment, and production and NNP will rise.)

When business firms as a whole are temporarily producing at an expense greater than what they can recover, they will want to contract their operations, and NNP tends to fall. When they are getting back more than their current expense for production, they increase their production and NNP rises.

Only when level of scheduled saving in Column (3) exactly equals scheduled investment in Column (4) will business firms stay continually in aggregative equilibrium. Their sales will there be just enough to justify continuing their current level of aggregate output. NNP will neither expand nor contract.

This same story is shown in Fig. 12-4. NNP can be read in either of two ways: on the horizontal axis or (from the nature of a 45° line) as the equivalent vertical distance from that axis up to the helping 45° line. The line SS represents the saving schedule; the line *II* represents the scheduled level of investment that can be maintained over time. Consumption can also be seen in the figure. Since income not saved is consumed, consumption is always the vertical distance from the saving schedule to the 45° line.

Now we can use Fig. 12-4 to confirm what has just been shown by the arithmetic

4th, A graph reinforces table's story of restoring equilibrium:

FIG. 12-4.   Only at E is there no gap between scheduled saving and investment. A gap like that shown at JK will soon cause firms to cut their production, which explains the westward gold arrow pushing NNP back to E's equilibrium level.

Show that the opposite gap at $J'K'$ will mean that firms find their sales so great as to deplete their inventories; interpret the eastward gold arrow showing that firms expand production to push NNP back to E.

of Table 12-1. No level of income can *long persist* if it is higher than the equilibrium level given by the *scheduled* saving and investment intersection at $1,000 billion. To the right of the intersection point E, the expense incurred by businesses would exceed the *amount received back* by businesses in the form of maintainable consumption plus maintainable investment.

Graphically, this is shown by the following: The amount continuously paid out by business is the whole distance up to the 45° line, i.e., from Q to R; but the amount that would continuously be received back by business would be only the sum of voluntary investment QK and consumption JR. There is a gap of JK.

Businesses face a real dilemma. For a while they could keep their prices high and let unsold goods pile up on their shelves, but that would not represent an equilibrium situation and could not persist. Or for a while they could lower prices on their goods and sell below needed cost with less profits; but that, too, could not last.

Thus, it is completely clear that income cannot *permanently* be maintained higher than the equilibrium level—*the level where the amount of saving that people want to do is matched by the amount of investment businessmen are willing to maintain.* A persistent gap of the JK type must, through attempts to cut down losses and excessive inventories, result in a contraction of employment and net national product back toward the equilibrium point, where there is no gap. Therefore the gold arrow near Q points leftward back toward the equilibrium level.

A similar argument shows why income will tend to rise from any place to the left of the equilibrium-intersection level. Indicate on the diagram the relation between business expense and what business can permanently receive back. Show that there will be a favorable gap (as at $J'K'$): Businesses either will be selling so much as to be depleting inventories on their shelves or will be temporarily raising their prices and earning extra profits. In either case, they will be tempted to expand their employment and production. And when they do, the result will be a rise in income back toward the equilibrium-intersection level.[4] Thus ends our digression.

---

[4]The recorded income statistics never show the gap depicted by JK and by Column (6) minus Column (5). Why not? Because these are gaps in people's *scheduled* quantities. They show levels that cannot

THE "MULTIPLIER"

Now that we have seen how the intersection of saving and investment determines the level of national income, we realize that an increase in investment will increase the level of income and employment. Thus, an investment boom may bring a nation out of a deep or mild depression—by having a higher *II* schedule cut the SS schedule at a higher equilibrium level for NNP.

An increase in private investment will cause income to expand; a decrease in investment will cause it to contract.

This is not a very surprising result. After all, we have learned that investment is one part of net national product; when one of the parts increases in value, we should naturally expect the whole to increase in value. That is only part of the story. Our theory of income determination gives us a much more striking result.

Modern income analysis shows that an increase in net investment will increase national income by a *multiplied* amount—by an amount greater than itself! Investment spending— like any independent shifts in governmental, foreign, or family spending—is high-powered, double-duty spending, so to speak.

This amplified effect of investment[5] on income is called the "multiplier" doctrine; the word multiplier itself is used for *the numerical coefficient showing how much of the above unity is the increase in income resulting from each increase in investment.*

Some examples will make this terminology clear. Let there be an increase of investment of $10 billion. If this causes an increase of income of $30 billion, then the multiplier is 3. If instead the resulting increase in income were $40 billion, then the multiplier would be 4.

Definition: **The multiplier is the number by which the change in investment must be multiplied in order to present us with the resulting change in income.**

No proof has yet been presented to show that the multiplier will be greater than 1. But by using ordinary common sense one can see why, when I hire unemployed resources to build a $1,000 garage, there will be a *secondary* expansion of national income and production, over and above my *primary* investment. Here is why.

---

continue to persist. On the other hand, the *measurable* statistics of saving and investment are definitionally equal no matter what income is doing: thus, when inventory is *involuntarily* piling up, the Commerce Department statistician cares not that its identity of investment and saving is the result of *unintended* investment. Why should it? It need never go beyond the anatomy of the problem. But we—interested in dynamic physiology of income determination—are vitally interested in schedules. (NOTE: In the last few pages, words such as "voluntary," "scheduled," and "maintainable" were repeated and stressed. This was done to call attention to the difference between a magnitude permanently persisting as a schedule, and the actual amounts measured after the fact in any disturbed short run. In the supply and demand schedules of Part Three, the same problem will recur; Chapter 4 showed that the wheat bought is *always* numerically identical with the wheat sold, but only at *equilibrium* market price do the *scheduled* amounts intersect.)

[5] Our later analysis will show that the multiplier can apply to government and other shifts in spending; but in this chapter we stick to the simplifying assumption of shifts up and down of a horizontal investment schedule only, leaving the government out of the picture and not letting the CC schedule shift and thereby itself initiate amplified multiplier effects.

My carpenters and lumber producers will get an extra $1,000 of income. But that is not the end of the story. If they all have a marginal propensity to consume of $\frac{2}{3}$, they will now spend $666.67 on new consumption goods. The producers of these goods will now have an extra income of $666.67. If their MPC is also $\frac{2}{3}$, they in turn will spend $444.44, or $\frac{2}{3}$ of $666.67 (or $\frac{2}{3}$ of $\frac{2}{3}$ of $1,000). So the process will go on, with each new round of spending being $\frac{2}{3}$ of the previous round.

Thus a whole endless chain of secondary consumption respending is set up by my primary $1,000 of investment spending. But, although an endless chain, it is a dwindling chain. And in toto it adds up to a finite amount. By either grade school arithmetic, in which we add the successive numbers until the decimals become insignificant, or by high school geometric progression,[6] we get

$$
\left.\begin{array}{c}
\$1,000.00 \\
+ \\
666.67 \\
+ \\
444.44 \\
+ \\
296.30 \\
+ \\
197.53 \\
+ \\
\vdots
\end{array}\right\} = \left\{\begin{array}{c}
1 \times \$1,000 \\
+ \\
\frac{2}{3} \times \$1,000 \\
+ \\
\left(\frac{2}{3}\right)^2 \times \$1,000 \\
+ \\
\left(\frac{2}{3}\right)^3 \times \$1,000 \\
+ \\
\left(\frac{2}{3}\right)^4 \times \$1,000 \\
+ \\
\vdots
\end{array}\right.
$$

$$
\begin{array}{cc}
\underline{\$2,999.9999} & \quad \underline{\dfrac{1}{1 - \frac{2}{3}}} \times \$1,000, \text{ or } 3 \times \$1,000 \\
\text{or} & \\
\$3,000 &
\end{array}
$$

This shows that, with an MPC of $\frac{2}{3}$, the multiplier is 3, consisting of the 1 of primary investment plus 2 extra of secondary consumption respending.

The same arithmetic would give a multiplier of 4 if the MPC were $\frac{3}{4}$, for the reason that $1 + \frac{3}{4} + (\frac{3}{4})^2 + (\frac{3}{4})^3 + \cdots$ finally adds up to 4. If the MPC were $\frac{1}{2}$, the multiplier would be 2. The size of the multiplier thus depends upon how large the MPC is; or it can be expressed in terms of the twin concept, the MPS. If the MPS were $\frac{1}{4}$, the MPC would be $\frac{3}{4}$, and the multiplier would be 4. If the MPS were $\frac{1}{3}$, the multiplier would be 3. If the MPS were $1/X$, the multiplier would be X.

---

[6] High school algebra says the formula for an infinite geometric progression is

$$
1 + r + r^2 + r^3 + \cdots + r^n + \cdots = \frac{1}{1 - r}
$$

as long as the MPC, r, is less than 1 in absolute value. If the MPC were changing along a curved schedule, in the multiplier formula we should have to use an MPC at an income level somewhere between the old and new levels. Footnote 7 in the next chapter handles a nonhorizontal II case.

By this time it is plain that the simple multiplier is always the upside-down, or "reciprocal," of the marginal propensity to save. Our simple multiplier formula is

$$\text{Change in income} = \frac{1}{\text{MPS}} \times \text{change in investment}$$

$$= \frac{1}{1 - \text{MPC}} \times \text{change in investment}$$

In other words, the greater the extra consumption respending, the greater the multiplier. The greater the MPS "leakage" into extra saving at each round of spending, the smaller the final multiplier.

GRAPHICAL PICTURE OF THE MULTIPLIER

Up to this point, we have discussed the multiplier in terms of common sense and arithmetic. Will our saving-investment analysis of income give us the same result? The answer must of course be, Yes.

Suppose, as back in Table 12-1 (page 213), the MPS is ⅓ and a new series of inventions comes along and gives rise to an extra $30 billion of continuing investment opportunities, over and above our previous $60 billion. Then the increase in investment should raise equilibrium NNP from 1,000 billion to what? To $1,090 billion if the multiplier is indeed correctly given as 3 by our previous analysis.

A look at Fig. 12-5 can confirm this. Our old investment schedule *II* is shifted upward by $30 billion to the new level *I'I'*. The new intersection point is *E'*. And lo, the increase in income is exactly 3 times as much as the increase in investment. This is because an MPS of only ⅓ means a relatively flat *SS* saving schedule. As the gold arrows show, the horizontal income distance is 3 times as great as the "primary" vertical saving-investment distance, the discrepancy being equal to the secondary "consumption respending."

In short, income must rise enough to bring out a volume of voluntary saving equal to the new investment. With an MPS of ⅓, income has to rise by how much in order to bring out $30 billion of new saving to match exactly the new investment? Only one answer is possible. By exactly $90 billion,[7] verifying our multiplier arithmetic.

Each dollar of investment can be "multiplied" into 3 dollars of income:

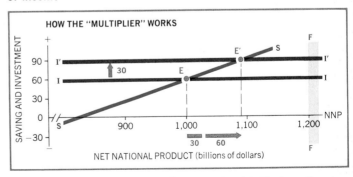

[7] Alter Table 12-1 on page 213 to verify this answer. In Column (4), we now put in $90 billion instead of $60 billion of investment. The new equilibrium level of income now shifts one row up from the gold equilibrium row. The multiplier can also work downward; thus a decline of $1 billion in investment spending will induce an endless chain of negative items, leading ultimately to a $3-billion *reduction* in equilibrium income. (Check by cutting *I* from 60 to 30 in Table 12-1.)

FIG. 12-5. New investment shifts *II* up to *I'I'*. *E'* gives the new equilibrium income, with income increasing 3 for each 1 increase in investment. (Note that the broken horizontal gold arrow is 3 times the length of the vertical gold arrow that shows the shift in investment, and is broken to show 2 of secondary consumption respending for each 1 of primary investment.)

THE SIMPLIFIED THEORY OF INCOME DETERMINATION RESTATED

Figure 12-6 pulls together in a simplified way the main elements of income determination. Without saving and investment, there would be a circular flow of income between business and the public: above, business pays out wages, interest, rents, and profits to the public in return for the services of labor and property; and below, the public pays consumption dollars to business in return for goods and services.

Realistically, we must recognize that the public will wish to save some of its income, as shown at the spigot Z. Hence, businesses cannot expect their consumption sales to be as large as the total of wages, interest, rents, and profits. Why not? Because dollars saved do not come back *as consumption sales.*

Some monetary cranks think this saving necessarily entails unemployment and depression. Such a view is simply incorrect. If there happen to be sufficiently profitable investment opportunities, business firms will be paying out wages, interest, and other costs *in part for new investment goods* rather than 100 per cent for consumption goods. Hence, to continue to be happy, business needs to receive back in consumption sales only *part* of the total income paid out to the public—only that part which involves the cost of current consumption goods. The *saving* that the public wants to make will do no harm to national income so long as it is not greater than what business can profitably continue to be *investing.*

In Fig. 12-6, investment is shown being pumped into the income stream at *A*. The handle of the pump is being moved by (1) technological invention, (2) population growth, and (3) other dynamic factors that affect the profitability of investment.

When the investment pump is going at a rapid, steady pace, NNP is high and is at its maintainable equilibrium rate where scheduled saving at Z just balances scheduled investment at *A*.

This demonstrates that the pessimistic monetary cranks who think that saving is always disastrous are plain wrong. But there is also a second misconception: some go to the opposite extreme and insist that saving and investment can never, in our modern mixed economy with all its frictions and rigidities, cause income to be too high or too low. They make the fatal error of automatically, and without regard to monetary policy and fiscal policy, connecting the pipe at Z with the pipe at *A*.

Many books have been written on this subject of equilibrium income determination, and it is only in the last few decades that economists have learned how to sepa-

Dynamic investment pumps national income up and down:

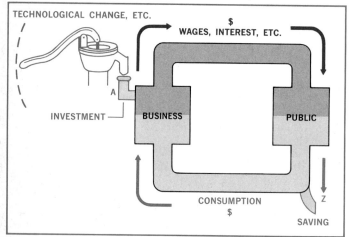

FIG. 12-6. Technological change, population growth, and other dynamic factors keep the investment pump handle going. Income rises and falls with changes in investment, its maintainable equilibrium level being realized only when intended saving at Z continues to match intended investment at *A*.

rate the truth and falsity of both extremes. The next 100 pages will deal with this important question, in its relation to income, banking, and business-cycle policy. More specifically, the next chapter will discuss fiscal policy's effect on "inflationary or deflationary gaps" and the effects of changes in the propensity to save.

SUMMARY

1 The motives that make people want to save are often different from those that make businesses want to invest. Net investment tends to depend on such autonomous elements as *new* population, *new* territory, *new* inventions, *new* tastes, and other *growth* elements. Consumption and saving tend to behave in accordance with passive schedules plotted against national income.

2 People's wishes to save and the willingness of business to invest are brought into line with each other by means of changes in income. The equilibrium level of national income must be at the *intersection* of the saving and investment schedules SS and *II,* or what is exactly the same thing, at the *intersection* of the consumption-plus-investment schedule C + I with the 45° line.

3 If incomes were temporarily above the equilibrium level, business would find itself unable to sell all it was producing at prices that fully covered required costs of production. For a short time inventories might pile up involuntarily and sales at a loss or untenable profit margin might take place, but eventually employment and production would be cut back toward the equilibrium level. The only equilibrium path of income that can be maintained is at the income level where families will voluntarily continue to save exactly as much as business will voluntarily continue to invest.

4 To sum up for the simplified case of this chapter: Investment calls the tune; investment causes income to rise or fall until voluntary, scheduled saving has adjusted itself to the level of maintainable investment.

Investment (and any autonomous schedule shift) has a multiplier effect on income. When investment changes, there is an equal *primary* change in national income. But as these primary income receivers in the capital-goods industries get more earned income, they set into motion a whole chain of additional *secondary* consumption spending and employment.

If people always spend about $\frac{2}{3}$ of each extra dollar of income upon consumption, the total of the multiplier chain will be

$$1 + \tfrac{2}{3} + (\tfrac{2}{3})^2 + \cdots = \frac{1}{1 - \tfrac{2}{3}} = 3$$

The multiplier works forward *or backward,* amplifying either increases or decreases in investment. The simplest multiplier is numerically equal to the reciprocal of the MPS; this is because it always takes *more* than a dollar's change in income to bring forth a dollar's change in saving.

QUESTIONS FOR DISCUSSION

1 Can you recall from the last chapter how the CC and SS schedules are in a Siamese-twins relationship, with MPC + MPS = 1 always? Why does the break-even point come at the same level of income (which will be on the horizontal axis in the lower part of Fig. 12-1 and on the 45° line in the upper part)?

2 If net investment were always zero, show that equilibrium would take place at the break-even point. (HINT: Income must fall to the low permanent level at which the amount that people would want to go on saving was zero—namely the break-even point.)

3 The saving-and-investment and the 45° line (or $C + I$) diagram are two different ways of showing how national income is determined. Describe each. Show their equivalence.

4 Reconstruct Table 12-1 assuming that net investment is equal to (a) $90 billion (b) $120 billion. What is the resulting difference in national income? Is this greater or smaller than the change in I? Why? When I drops 30 (or 1) below 60, how much must NNP drop?

5 Describe in a few paragraphs (a) the common sense, (b) arithmetic, (c) geometry of the multiplier. What are the multipliers when MPC = .9? .8? .5? When MPS = .1? .8?

6 Work out the explosive chain of spending and respending when MPC = 2. Explain the economics of the arithmetic of the divergent infinite geometric series.

7 If $C = a + bY = 200 + \frac{2}{3}Y$ and $I = \bar{I} = 100$, solve $Y = C + I = 200 + \frac{2}{3}Y + 100$ to get $Y^* = 900$. Increase $\bar{I}$ by 10 and verify that Y^* goes up by 30. What is the multiplier? Why? (NOTE: Y is NNP in billions of $.)

Review your understanding of the following concepts:

consumption schedule CC
saving schedule SS
45° helping line
break-even point
$C + I$ schedule
equivalent intersection of SS and II;
   or $C + I$ and 45° line
equilibrium intersection and forces
   moving NNP when not in equilibrium

intended maintainable saving and
   investment versus measurable
   identity of saving and investment
multiplier impact of primary I
   through secondary C spending

$$\frac{1}{1 - \text{MPC}} = \frac{1}{\text{MPS}}$$

$$= 1 + (\text{MPC}) + (\text{MPC})^2 + \cdots$$

Income Determination: Fiscal Policy, Inflation, and Thriftiness

13

The only good budget is a balanced budget.
ADAM SMITH
OF GLASGOW (1776)

The only good rule is that the budget should never be balanced—except for an instant when a surplus to curb inflation is being altered to a deficit to fight deflation.
WARREN SMITH
OF ANN ARBOR (1965)

The last chapter set forth the essentials of the modern theory of income determination. Here we must go on to discuss a number of important applications and qualifications.

How do changes in thriftiness—rises in the propensity to save and falls in the propensity to consume—affect the level of national income? What paradoxes lurk there?

How does the theory of income determination analyze inflation and deflation—the so-called "inflationary gap" or the "deflationary gap."

Finally, and most important for human welfare, what are the effects on national output, employment, and price stability of government fiscal policy—of public expenditure, of public taxation, of budget deficits and surpluses?

THE WASTEFUL "PRODUCTION GAP"

There is little need to emphasize the importance of the problem of income determination. In World War II and the Vietnam years, our economy was plagued by problems connected with *too high* a general money demand, with price increases, and with shortages.

From 1953 until the early 1960s, the American economy suffered from a growth in unemployment and an insufficiency of total money demand. Figure 13-1 on the next page shows how the economy, spurred on by the tax cut proposed by President Kennedy and passed in 1964, finally moved back toward the full-employment growth path in the middle 1960s.

Memories are short, and there is danger that we shall forget the tremendous costs that were associated with the mass unemployment of the prewar Great Depression. It is scarcely an exaggeration to say that the economic costs of that depression were of the same general magnitude as the *costs of all the economic resources which had to be used up in World War II itself.*

Cost of sluggish growth rivals that of war:

FIG. 13-1. The light blue area shows the gap between what we actually produced in recent years and what our economic system was capable of producing at reasonably high employment and capacity utilization. Public policy aims to reduce this "gap."

Figure 13-1 reminds us that the American economy, because of failure to maintain full-employment growth, has lost hundreds of billions of dollars worth of goods and services in recent decades. It reminds us that nations are subject to three kinds of poverty:

(1) ancient poverty due to famine and inadequate production potential

(2) unnecessary poverty in the midst of plenty, poverty due only to bad purchasing-power behavior of the system

(3) poverty due to uneven and bad distribution of an affluent total NNP

Long ago, for the advanced Western world, overt poverty was conquered by the triumphs of technology. But only with the development of modern income analysis has "poverty midst plenty"—like that of 1929–1939—been rendered obsolete. Here in Part Two, we learn how and why. Then in Part Six we can grapple with the third kind of poverty, which does still remain as a challenge.

HOW THRIFTINESS OR SHIFTS IN THE CONSUMPTION SCHEDULE AFFECT INCOME

We have seen that investment affects incomes. Let us now consider changes in thriftiness. By an increase in thriftiness we mean a shift in the SS saving schedule upward. Won't the new S'S' schedule intersect an unchanged II schedule in a *new* equilibrium E'? And with a new lower NNP?

The answers to these questions are, Yes and yes. Figure 13-2 shows that an upward shift in the saving schedule—and, what is the same thing, an equivalent downward shift in the consumption schedule—will tend in the absence of any change in the investment schedule to *lower equilibrium* NNP.

Common sense tells us why. If people consume less out of their incomes and if business will not willingly invest more, sales will fall and production must soon be cut. Cut how far? Until so much national income has been destroyed as to make people feel poor enough that they will finally end up not trying to save more than business will go on investing.

Perhaps this point seems obvious. But Fig. 13-2 tells us something more surprising. It shows that a $1 upward shift in the saving schedule will kill off $3 of income. Contrariwise, a $1 downward shift in the saving schedule, which means a $1 upward shift in the consumption schedule, will produce a similar multiplier $3 increase in income. (Note in Fig. 13-2 that the horizontal gold arrow is 3 times the vertical gold arrow.)

In short, just as investment spending is "high-powered spending" with multiplier effects on income, consumption spending that represents a genuine *shift* in the propensity to consume and save will also be "high-powered"!

We shall meet many examples of this. Thus, the last part of the chapter will show how reducing taxes can increase consumption and thereby expand income by more than that consumption shift. Or, for a second example, take the case of a famous Harvard economics professor of a past generation, Frank W. Taussig. During the Great Depression he went on the radio to urge everyone to save less, to spend more on consumption. What did he have in mind? That was before the modern theory of income de-

The saving-and-investment diagram has many applications. It shows how:

1st, Changes in thriftiness, or a shift in *CC*, will change income in a multiplied way:

FIG. 13-2. A desire to consume less at every income level will shift the saving schedule upward. With *II* unchanged, equilibrium drops to the *E′* intersection. Why? Because income has to fall until people feel poor enough to again want to save what the system can invest.

termination was known, but he presumably meant that such spending would on the first round give jobs and incomes to people; that their respending on consumption would create second-round jobs and income; and that it would continue thus in a multiplier chain.

A last example will arise in connection with the next section's so-called "paradox of thrift." The following summary paves the way for it.

If scheduled investment holds constant, an upward shift in the saving schedule—which means an equal downward shift in the consumption schedule—will kill off national income in a multiplier way until income falls low enough to bring people's new desired saving again into equality with investment opportunities. Thus an *attempt* to save may not lead to more saving, but instead may then simply reduce national income.

INDUCED INVESTMENT

Until now we have always treated net investment as an autonomous element, absolutely independent of national income. All our investment schedules have been drawn as horizontal lines, their level being always the same regardless of NNP. This simplification can now be relaxed.

Any practical businessman will tell you that he is more likely to add to his plant or equipment if his sales are high relative to his plant capacity. In the short run (before businessmen have had time to adjust their capital stock to a changed plateau of income), it is reasonable for us to redraw the *II* schedule in Fig. 13-3 on the next page as a rising curve. *An increase in employment and national product may* induce *a higher level of net investment.*

As before, the equilibrium level of (maintainable) national income is given by the intersection of the investment and saving schedules, or by *E* in Fig. 13-3. So long as the *SS* curve always cuts the *II* curve from below, businessmen's action must finally bring

2d, Higher income will induce businessmen to want higher investment:

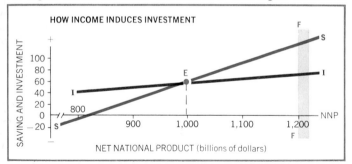

FIG. 13-3. Now we drop the assumption of a horizontal *II* sched- ule. Now *II* slopes upward, showing intended investment less than $60 billion at low NNP and more than $60 billion at high NNP. Equilibrium is still at *E*, where *SS* intersects *II* from below.

the economy back to the equilibrium level shown here at *E*.[1]

Induced investment means that anything which increases national income is likely to be good for the capital-goods industries; anything hurting national income is likely to be bad for them.[2]

THE PARADOX OF THRIFT

Induced investment throws new light on the age-old question of thrift versus con- sumption. It shows this:

An increased desire to consume—which is another way of looking at a decreased desire to save—is likely to boost business sales and increase investment. On the other hand, a decreased desire to consume—i.e., an increase in thriftiness—is likely to reduce inflationary pressure in times of booming incomes; but in time of depression, it could make the depression worse and reduce the amount of actual net capital formation in the community. *High consumption and high investment are then hand in hand rather than opposed to each other.*

This surprising result is sometimes called the "paradox of thrift." It is a paradox because most of us used to be taught that thrift is *always* a good thing. Ben Franklin's *Poor Richard's Almanac* never tired of preaching the doctrine of saving. And now along comes a new generation of financial experts who seem to say that the old virtues may be modern sins in depressed times.

Let us for the moment leave our cherished beliefs aside and try to disentangle the paradox in a dispassionate, scientific manner. Two considerations will help to clarify the whole matter.

The first is this. In economics, we must always be on guard against the logical fallacy of composition. That is to say, what is good for each person separately need not thereby always be good for all; under some circumstances, private prudence may be social folly. Specifically this means that the *attempt* of each and every person to increase his saving may—under the conditions to be described—result in a reduction in *actual* saving by all the people in the community. Note the italicized words "attempt" and "actual"; between them, in our imperfect mixed economy, there may be a world of difference when people find themselves thrown out of jobs and with lowered incomes.

The second clue to the paradox of thrift lies in the question of whether or not national income is at a depressed level. If we were at full employment, then obviously the more

---

[1]If the two curves crossed in the opposite way with *II* steeper than *SS*, the little arrows back in Fig. 12-4, page 214, would point out instead of in and we should have unstable equilibrium; then the economy would rush away—in either direction—from the intersection neighborhood. A physical analogy may help: An egg on its side is in "stable equilibrium"; given a slight disturbance, it returns to equilibrium. An egg on its tip is in "unstable equilibrium"; a light touch topples it.

[2]Note that induced investment makes the multiplier bigger; in addition to a secondary chain of induced *consumption* spending, there will be a reinforcing chain of secondary *induced investment* spending. See the final formula in footnote 7 of this chapter.

of our national product we devoted to current consumption, the less would be available for capital formation. If output could be assumed to be always at its maximum, then the old-fashioned doctrine of thrift would be absolutely correct—correct, be it noted, from both the individual and the social standpoints. In primitive agricultural communities, such as the American colonies of Franklin's day, there was truth in Franklin's prescription. The same was true during World War I and II, and during periods of boom and inflation: if people then become more thrifty, less consumption means more investment.

But according to statistical records, full employment and inflationary demand conditions have occurred only at intervals in our nation's history. Much of the time under laissez faire there were some wasting of resources, some unemployment, and some insufficiency of demand, investment, and purchasing power. When such is the case, everything can go into reverse. What once was a social virtue may then become a social vice. What is true for the individual—that extra thriftiness means increased saving and wealth—may then become completely untrue for the community as a whole.

Under conditions of unemployment, the *attempt to save* may result in *less*, not more, saving. The individual who saves cuts down on his consumption. He passes on less purchasing power than before; therefore someone else's income is reduced, for one man's outgo is another man's income. If one man succeeds in saving more, maybe it is because someone else is forced to dissave. If one man succeeds in hoarding more money, someone else must do without.

High C inducing high I   Thus, when there is stubborn unemployment, consumption and investment can be complementary, not competitive. What helps one helps the other. The attempt to cut down on consumption (to save) then only results in a reduction of income until everyone feels poor enough no longer to try to save more than can be invested. Moreover, at lower levels of income, less, and not more, capital goods will be needed. Therefore *investment will actually be less.* (As will be seen again and again, with prudent macroeconomic policies, our system will be restored to proper operation, so that the paradox of thrift can be robbed of its applicability.)

Let us clinch our common-sense understanding of this paradox by combining Figs. 13-2 and 13-3 into Fig. 13-4. An increase in thriftiness or the desire to save will shift the SS curve upward to S'S'. Note that the new intersection E' is now at a lower level of income. Because of induced *disinvestment,* the drop in income does also mean lower investment. Thus both income and investment have actually decreased! The attempt to save more in depression times has resulted in less actual saving.

If true, this is an important lesson. It will never again be a satisfactory measure to urge men in time of depression to tighten their belts, to save more in order to restore

3d, An attempt to save more could result in less actual saving and investment:

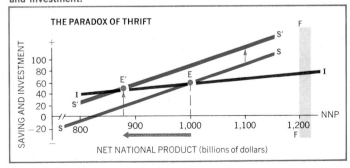

FIG. 13-4.   The shift of SS upward to S'S' depresses income; and the drop of income kills off some investment, moving us southwest along the sloping II schedule. (If the system were straining at the full-employment level of F, the effect of increased thriftiness might be different.)

prosperity. The result will all too likely be the reverse—a worsening of the vicious deflationary spiral. At such a time, many of the usual arguments go into reverse. An economic lobbyist of the capital-goods industries would, if he has their selfish interests at heart, advocate less thriftiness in depressed times, so that the consumption schedule will be pushed upward, and so that attempts to save—which then really lead only to decreases in income—will be discouraged. For only then will investment and sales of heavy capital goods flourish.[3]

Later, we shall see how fiscal and monetary policies can rid the paradox of thrift of its terrors.

THE DEFLATIONARY GAP

The multiplier is a two-edged sword. It will cut for you or against you. It will amplify new investment, as we have seen. But it will also amplify negatively any *decrease* in investment. Thus, if investment opportunities drop by $30 billion in our earlier examples, then national income will have to fall by 3 times as much—by $90 billion. If net investment drops away to zero, income will have to fall to the break-even point where the community is made poor enough to stop all net saving.

When $C + I$ spending that would be generated at full employment differs from the full-employment NNP, we call:

1st, Any spending deficiency a "deflationary" gap:

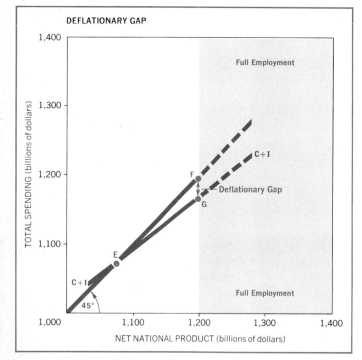

This reminds us once again that there may be nothing particularly good about what we have called the equilibrium level of national income. If investment is low, the equilibrium level of income will involve much unemployment and waste of national resources. The only level of national income that we are entitled to regard as a desirable goal is that near to full employment; but we shall end up at such a level of high employment only if investment opportunities happen to match full-employment saving.

Unless this full-employment saving is "offset" by private investment (or by public

[3] We have seen that this line of argument does not apply in conditions of full employment. It also requires some slight modifications to allow for the fact that thriftiness, by lowering income, may also lower interest rates and (as we shall see) thereby promote investment, or it may depress wages and prices and thereby increase the real purchasing power of people's money holdings enough to destroy their initial thriftiness. These qualifications are discussed later; in a mixed economy, with wage and price levels sticky and inflexible, they seem rather unimportant considerations during deep depression.

FIG. 13-5. The deflationary gap is always measured at the full-employment NNP level. It is the vertical distance there between the 45° line and the $C + I$ schedule, that is, FG. Such a deflationary gap will depress income in a multiplied way. (Later, after government is introduced, we'll relabel $C + I$ as $C + I + G$.)

policies), the nation cannot continue to enjoy full employment. There is then said to be a "deflationary gap," its size being measured by the deficiency of investment compared with full-employment saving.

We can picture the deflationary gap on a consumption-plus-investment graph, Fig. 13-5. Suppose that $1,200 billion represents the full-employment income. Suppose that, at this income level F, the scheduled total of $C + I$ adds up to only $1,160 billion, as shown at G. *This leaves a $40-billion deflationary gap between G and F.* Since obviously we cannot then remain at full employment, what will happen? Will income drop by only $40 billion? Clearly not. It must drop by some greater multiple of the original deflationary gap. If each dollar of reduced income results in a cut of $$\frac{2}{3}$ in consumption spending, income will have to fall until it has dropped 3 times as much as the original deflationary gap (see point E in Fig. 13-5).[4]

THE PROCESS OF PRICE INFLATION

2d, Any spending excess an "inflationary" gap:

FIG. 13-6. *FG'* measures the inflationary gap. People are trying to buy more than can be produced, and thereby they are inflating the price level. (With all prices changing and no longer ignorable, the *EE* point and spending schedules are likely to shift upward; so it would be a mistake to regard *E'* as an actually attainable equilibrium level of *real* income.)

Instead of a deflationary gap, we may have an *inflationary gap*. If scheduled investment tends to be greater than full-employment saving, then more goods will be demanded of business than it can produce, and prices will begin to rise. Figure 13-6 shows how we measure the inflationary gap as a vertical distance: The new $C' + I'$ curve lies *above* the 45° line at the full-employment level by the distance FG', giving us an inflationary gap of $30 billion.

If full-employment saving falls short of scheduled investment at full-employment, there is said to be an "inflationary gap," its size being measured by the excess of the $C + I$ schedule above the 45° line's full-employment level (which is the same thing as the excess of full-employment scheduled II over SS).

Now what will result from the $30-billion gap? Can production rise by $90 billion to give a new equilibrium at E'? Plainly not. Everyone is already fully employed, and

[4]What can be done about this? If we continue to leave the government out of the picture, we must have either an increase in investment or an increase in consumption. By how much must the level of investment or of the consumption schedule shift upward if full employment is to be restored? By the full $120 billion of lost income? No. Because of the multiplier, to wipe out a deflationary gap, the $C + I$ schedule need shift upward only by the amount of the gap itself, not by any multiple of the gap. (In a saving-investment diagram like Fig. 13-3 you measure the deflationary gap by the vertical distance between the SS and II schedules at the full-employment income FF.)

factories are producing at their practical capacity points. The region to the right of the vertical full-employment line through F is a never-never land. It shows us what we should like to be able to produce, but not what we are actually able to produce. Although an inflationary gap is the opposite of a deflationary gap, its effects upon employment and production are of a slightly different qualitative nature. A deflationary gap can move production leftward, down to 90 or even 70 per cent of a full-employment level; but an inflationary gap cannot possibly move employment rightward to 150 per cent of full or maximum employment. The economic system cannot move in *real terms* very far to the right in the full-employment shaded area.

The excess in purchasing power can result only in *price increases*—an inflationary spiral; *money* national income will rise because of "paper" price-tag changes, but *real* national product cannot go above its maximum full-employment level. Unfortunately, the upward movement of prices will continue for as long as there is an inflationary gap,[5] i.e., until we are lucky enough for investment or consumption demand to diminish, or smart enough as a nation to adopt corrective fiscal and monetary policies that will wipe out the inflationary gap.

Far from being "depression economics," modern income analysis has many of its most important applications in connection with the process of inflation and what can be done about it. During and after World War II, the concept of the inflationary gap was indispensable in indicating the quantitative magnitude of taxation needed to keep decontrolled prices from rising; and without understanding the rudiments of income analysis, one cannot follow the important economic issues discussed in Congress and the public press concerning the continued need for a Vietnam tax surcharge.[6]

FISCAL POLICY IN INCOME DETERMINATION: EXPENDITURE

When there is a large inflationary or deflationary gap, the government is called upon to do something about the price rise or the widespread unemployment. Tax and government expenditure policies—the general name for which is "fiscal policy"—will change the equilibrium level of income. So we must now for the first time explicitly introduce government fiscal policy into the picture to see exactly how income determination is affected. As you might guess, we now consider a $C + I + G$ spending schedule to show the equilibrium that results when government is in the picture.

It will simplify our task if in the beginning we analyze the effects of government expenditure with taxes held constant. When taxes come into the picture, we can no longer ignore the distinction between disposable income and net national product. But with the tax revenue first held constant, they will differ always by the same amount; and taking

---

[5] The process does not end with higher prices. The new higher price level will not equilibrate total supply and demand once and for all. On the contrary, since the higher prices received by businesses become in turn somebody's income—that of worker or property owner—demand again tends to shift upward and prices will continue to rise until taxes sop up the excess spending or until the money supply puts limits on demand. Attempts of labor to secure higher wages as compensation for the soaring cost of living may only cause the inflationary spiral to zoom at a dizzier speed. (Lord Keynes formulated this theory of inflation in 1939.)

[6] See Chapter 41, which includes along with the present kind of "excess-demand," or "demand-pull," inflation the possibility of "creeping cost-push inflationary tendencies."

account of such taxes, we can still plot the *CC* consumption schedule against NNP rather than against *DI*.

In Chapter 10 we learned that net national product consists of three rather than two parts; namely,

NNP = Consumption expenditure + private net Investment
+ Government expenditure on goods and services

$$= C + I + G$$

Therefore, on our 45°-line diagram in Fig. 13-7, we must now superimpose upon the consumption schedule not only private investment but also government expenditure G. This is because public road building is economically no different from private railroad building, and collective consumption expenditure involved in maintaining a free public library has the same effect upon jobs as private consumption expenditure for movies or rental libraries.

We end up with the three-layered *C + I + G* schedule showing the amount of total spending forthcoming at each level of NNP. We now must go to the intersection with the 45° line to read off the equilibrium level of national product. At this equilibrium NNP level, the total the nation wants to spend on all goods is just equal in value to the full costs of production of these goods.

Figure 13-7 shows that government expenditure, taken by itself and disregarding taxes, has a multiplier effect upon income just like that of private investment. The reason is, of course, that a chain of *respending* is set in motion by the road-builders, librarians, and other people who receive primary income from the government.[7]

To show the effects of an extra $20 billion of *G*, shift *C + I + G* in Fig. 13-7

[7]Our saving-investment diagram will give the same answer as the 45°-line diagram. The increase in government expenditure means an equivalent increase in the government deficit if taxes do not increase. Net saving must always equal private investment + government deficit. Therefore we add the deficit on top of the *II* curve and get our new greater equilibrium level of national income at the intersection with the *SS* curve. In more advanced discussions, we could employ Fig. 13-7 to show how induced investment or government expenditure (i.e., induced by a changed level of income) will enter into the multiplier. The final change in income resulting from a unit upward shift in the *C + I + G* schedule will always turn out to be $\frac{1}{1 - K}$, where *K* is the slope of the *C + I + G* schedule, and might be called the "marginal propensity to spend (inclusive of induced *C, I,* and *G* effects)."

Government expenditures act like consumption and investment in determining national income:

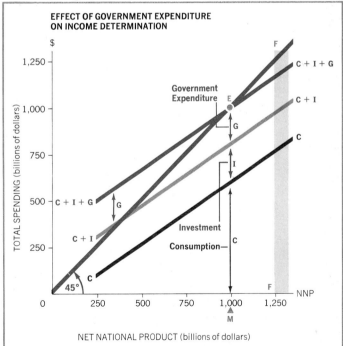

FIG. 13-7. On top of consumption spending and investment spending, we now add government spending on goods and services. This gives us the *C + I + G* schedule. At *E*, where this intersects the 45° line, we find equilibrium. (What if *G* increases or decreases? Can you show the multiplied changes in income?)

up to a new drawn-in $C + I + G'$ and show that the new E' will record a multiplier response of NNP to the new government spending.

TAXATION AND SHIFTS OF CONSUMPTION SCHEDULE

Now let us turn to the depressing effects of taxes on the equilibrium NNP level. Without graphs, our common sense tells us what must happen when the government (1) takes away more from us in taxes while (2) at the same time holding its expenditure constant. Extra taxes will mean we have lower real disposable incomes, and lower disposable incomes mean we shall cut down on our consumption spending. Obviously, if investment and government expenditure remain the same, a reduction in consumption spending will then reduce net national product and employment; or if we already are having an inflationary gap, the new taxes will help close the gap and wipe out excessive inflationary price increases.

Our graphs can confirm this reasoning: $I + G$ is unchanged, but now the increase in taxes will lower disposable income, thereby lowering consumption and shifting the consumption schedule downward; so in all, the $C + I + G$ schedule will shift downward. Pencil a new $C' + I + G$ schedule into Fig. 13-7 to confirm that its new intersection with the crucial 45° line must definitely be at a *lower* equilibrium level of NNP.

Figure 13-8 shows and explains how tax receipts shift the CC schedule downward. With CC down, $C + I + G$ in Fig. 13-7 will be down, and equilibrium NNP must drop.

REMARK: Now we know something that common sense did not immediately tell us. To offset a $20-billion upward shift in $I + G$, we must increase tax collections by *more* than $20 billion. Figure 13-8 shows needed taxes as $30 billion when MPC $= \frac{2}{3}$, if CC is to be lowered by $20 billion. This means that (1) when increased government spending on a Vietnam war is added to a full-employment economy with a balanced budget, then (2) taxes will probably have to be increased by *more than enough to balance the budget* if we are determined to avoid an inflationary gap.[8]

In connection with the massive Kennedy-Johnson tax cut of 1964, a reduction in tax rates served to *raise* the equilibrium level of national income. We can easily see this by reversing Fig. 13-8's analysis to explain why tax reductions help to fight a below-capacity economy. Each dollar of tax reduction leads, through an upward and leftward shift in CC, to an increase in people's disposable income by a dollar and to almost a dollar increase in initial consumption spending.

Hence, dollars of tax reduction are almost as powerful a weapon against mass unemployment as are increases in dollars of government expenditure.

Because tax potency is slightly less than expenditure potency, such a program may involve a larger budget deficit than an expenditure program would; but it also means that there is expansion of the private rather than government sector of the economic system. Both the United States and Japan used this tax-cut mechanism in the mid-sixties

---

[8]Advanced treatises call this phenomenon the "balanced-budget multiplier theorem." This very useful, but highly simplified, doctrine says: A *balanced* rise in G and T will raise NNP by just that amount; a balanced cut of $1 in G and T will cut NNP by $1. So it is not merely the budget deficit, $G - T$, that has NNP effects. The absolute size of the budget matters too.

to increase their employment and income levels, a remarkable example of modern fiscal policy at work. And the 10 per cent tax surcharge of 1969 was an attempt to close an inflationary gap by raising tax rates.

QUALIFICATIONS TO SAVING AND INVESTMENT ANALYSIS

The theory of income determination sketched in the last two chapters is a powerful tool.[9] It helps us to understand the ups and downs of the business cycle. It helps us to understand how foreign lending (which is one part of total net investment) affects domestic employment and income. It helps us to understand how governmental fiscal policy can be used to fight inflation and unemployment. All these topics are developed in later chapters.

But it would be a mistake to think that an economist can be made out of a parrot, simply by teaching him the magic words "saving" and "investment." Behind the scenes of these schedules a great deal is taking place.

It should be noted that an increase in the public's holding of government bonds and other wealth may shift the consumption schedule upward. Or rising living standards

Higher taxes will cut disposable income and consumption:

FIG. 13-8. Each dollar of tax lowers the *CC* schedule. Why? Because *CC* is shifted to the right by the amount of the tax. (EXAMPLE: First NNP = 960 at *U* with zero tax; *DI* = 960 also. *CC* shows consumption at *U* of 940. Now add tax of 30; NNP at *V* must equal 960 + 30 if *DI* is to remain 960 and consumption 940 there. So *UV* arrow shows *C'C'* is shifted rightward by exact amount of the tax.) A rightward *CC* shift means a downward *CC* shift. But the downward shift is only two-thirds of the rightward shift if *CC*'s slope of MPC = $\frac{2}{3}$. (Verify $WV = \frac{2}{3}UV$.)

With *CC* lowered, so will *C + I + G* in Fig. 13-7 be lowered. Show the drop in income there caused by such a tax increase.

(resulting from advertising and the invention of new products) may shift the consumption schedule up, just as it has in the past.

In short, it is an oversimplification to regard investment as always an autonomous factor, and consumption as always a passive factor depending upon income. True, this is a fruitful oversimplification. But as we have already seen, some of net investment may be "induced" by income changes in the short run; and, as we shall see, changes in interest costs, availability of credit, and stock of money can alter the swings in investment and total spending. Furthermore, consumption also will sometimes shift autonomously even though income has remained constant. And the reader can verify by experimenting with the saving-investment and the 45°-line diagrams the truth of our earlier assertion that such shifts in the *CC* or *SS* schedules do have multiplier effects upon national income—*exactly* like the multiplier effects of changes in *I* and *G*.

After the survey of our business-cycle history in the next chapter, the following chapters

[9] Advanced discussions show that corporate saving can be handled graphically much like taxes.

will discuss money and banking, to show how changes in credit, interest rates, and the supply of money may cause the spending schedules and their intersections to shift.

SUMMARY

1 Unlike ancient poverty due to famine in a preindustrial society or modern poverty due to uneven income distribution, the laissez faire economy used to suffer from "poverty midst plenty"—characterized by the "production gaps" between what full-employment operations could produce and what actual saving-investment intersections were causing to be produced. Now we study how fiscal policy can do something about improving macroeconomic equilibrium.

2 The *attempt* to save more is quite different from the achievement of increased saving for society as a whole. The "paradox of thrift" shows that an increase in thriftiness may reduce already depressed income and, *through induced effects on investment,* may actually result in *less* net investment. Only when employment remains full or unchanged are consumption and investment necessarily competing; only then are private virtues always social virtues.

   The moral is not for each individual to squander his money during a depression, trying to be patriotic. Instead, through proper national policies, we must re-create a high-employment environment in which private virtues are no longer social follies.

3 In short, we must avoid both *inflationary and deflationary gaps,* so that full-employment saving and investment just match without inflation. We measure the size of the deflationary or inflationary gap as (*a*) the vertical discrepancy at full-employment income between the saving and investment schedules, or what is exactly the same thing, as (*b*) the vertical distance between the $C + I$ (or $C + I + G$ when government is in the picture) schedule and the 45° line.

4 An increase in government expenditure—taken by itself with taxes and investment unchanged—has expansionary effects on national product much like those of net investment. The schedule of $C + I + G$ shifts upward to a higher equilibrium intersection with the 45° line.

5 An increase in taxes—taken by itself with investment and government expenditure unchanged—depresses the equilibrium level of national product. The schedule of consumption plotted against NNP is shifted downward and rightward by taxes; but since extra dollars go partly into saving, the dollar drop in consumption will not be quite so great as the dollars of new taxes. Therefore, to combat a given inflationary or deflationary gap, we may require an even larger change in taxation.

6 The art of economics consists in recognizing both the core of truth in the simple theory of income determination and also its needed qualifications. In later chapters we shall

see how the money supply and interest rates may also cause shifts in the schedules that determine levels of national income.

We leave to the final chapters of Part Two the analysis of government monetary and fiscal policy. In the intervening chapters we turn to an analysis of the wild dance of the business cycle, to the analysis of money, banking, and interest policy.

QUESTIONS FOR DISCUSSION

1   Just what is meant by "poverty midst plenty"? Illustrate by the United States, 1932 or 1958. Contrast with India, 1970. (Back on page 173, connect 1930 and 1942 on the real NNP curve by a straight line and shade in the depression production gap.)

2   "Even if the government spends billions on 'wasteful' armaments, during a depression that may help create jobs and several billions of new useful production." Discuss.

3   Give arguments for and against thriftiness. Contrast carefully (a) the individual and the community viewpoint and (b) boom and depression.

4   Describe effects upon income of (a) government expenditure, (b) taxes, (c) our sale of more goods and services to foreigners than they sell us (i.e., of net foreign investment).

5   "The purpose of fiscal policy is to help wipe out inflationary or deflationary gaps. Thus, if $C + I + G$ is too high, we have an inflationary gap; and we raise taxes to shift the new $C' + I' + G'$ schedule downward, thereby wiping out the inflationary gap." Explain. Show what you would do to taxes to fight a deflationary gap. To government expenditure.

6   Analyze the economics of the 1968–1970 debates on a 10 per cent surtax.

7   If cold-war military expenditure could be ended, how might we restore full employment? Explain your alternative programs in terms of shifts of the $C + I + G$ schedule.

8   Let $NNP = Y, DI = Y_d = Y - T$. Let $\bar{I} = 100$, and $C = 100 + \frac{2}{3} Y_d$. When $G = 0$ and $I = 100$, we use formula $Y = 200 + \frac{2}{3} (Y - T) + \bar{I} + \bar{G}$ to solve for $Y^* = 900$. Likewise, verify the values in the following quadruplets of values for $(\bar{I}, \bar{G}, \bar{T}, Y^*)$:(101,0,0,903), (100,1,0,903), (100,0,1,898), (100,1,1,901).

Review your understanding of the following concepts:

"production gap"	cumulative inflation
poverty midst plenty	underemployment equilibrium
multiplier effects on income of consumption or saving shifts	$C + I + G$ schedule
induced investment	fiscal policy (expenditure and taxes)
paradox of thrift	G effect on equilibrium
inflationary, deflationary gaps	tax effect on CC and equilibrium
	qualifications to the analysis

Business Cycles and Forecasting

14

The fault, dear Brutus,
is not in our stars—
but in ourselves. . . .
WILLIAM SHAKESPEARE

We have examined the economic forces operating to determine the level of national income—the balance of saving and investment. We now turn to the problem of how the level of national income has fluctuated, and how economists try to forecast the future. Any serious science should try to test bold theoretical formulation against a careful description of the empirical facts of life.

PROSPERITY AND DEPRESSION

Business conditions rarely stand still. Prosperity may be followed by a panic or a crash. National income, employment, and production fall. Prices and profits decline, and men are thrown out of work. Eventually the bottom is reached, and revival begins. The recovery may be slow or fast. It may be incomplete, or it may be so strong as to lead to a new boom. The new prosperity may represent a long, sustained plateau of brisk demand, plentiful jobs,

Are business cycles calming down?

buoyant prices, and increased living standards. Or it may represent a quick, inflationary flaring up of prices and speculation, to be followed by another disastrous slump.

Such, in brief, was the so-called "business cycle" that used to characterize the industrialized nations of the world for the last century and a half at least—ever since an elaborate, interdependent *money economy* began to replace a relatively self-sufficient precommercial society. Is the business cycle a thing of the past, a museum piece? This we must study.

No two business cycles are quite the same. Yet they have much in common. Though not identical twins, they are recognizable as belonging to the same family. No exact formula, such as might apply to the motions of the moon or of a simple pendulum, can be used to predict the timing of future (or past) business cycles. Rather, in their rough appearance and irregularities, business cycles more closely resemble the fluctuations of disease epidemics, of the weather, or of a child's temperature.

From these introductory remarks, it will be clear that business fluctuations are simply one further aspect of the economic problem of achieving and maintaining high levels of jobs, production, and progressive growth.

MEASURING THE BUSINESS CYCLE

Figure 14-1 shows how the economic system was plagued with the uncertainties of the business cycle throughout our history as a nation, although fortunately rarely with so sustained and costly a slump as the post-1929 Great Depression. With surprisingly few variations, the same pattern of cyclical fluctuations was long repeated in England, Germany, and other foreign nations. But it is a strange fact that the United States, supposedly one of the youngest and most vigorous of nations, always tended to have greater average

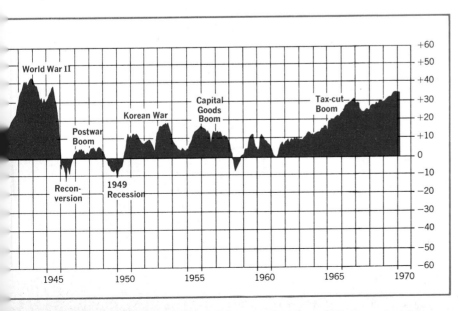

FIG. 14-1. For 30 years now we have had no significant depressions. But it was not always so in our history. (Source: Cleveland Trust Co.)

amounts of unemployment and greater variation in unemployment than most other countries. Not only was this true in 1933, when our percentage of unemployment rivaled even that of Germany, but it appears to have been the case for almost as far back as we have any records or indications. Only in the last 30 years have we avoided deep unemployment, but still our rates exceed those abroad.

Figure 14-2 shows a number of post-World War II economic "time series," presented together for comparison. Note the all-pervasive common pulse of the business cycle: the recessions of 1948–1949, 1953–1954, 1957–1958, and 1960–1961 are shown as shaded areas. These fluctuations show up in production, unemployment, incomes, and even such particular series as stock-market prices and building. Moreover, if data had been included on such noneconomic matters as marriages, births, suicides, and malnutrition, we could have seen the heavy hand of the business cycle in them too. Even political elections follow the business cycle: in slumps, the ins go out. Thus the 1960 Eisenhower recession helped elect President Kennedy, just as the Hoover depression of the 1930s helped elect Franklin Roosevelt.

Let us first stick to the facts and statistics. Later we can attempt to devise hypotheses and explanatory theories to account for the facts.

STATISTICAL CORRECTION FOR SEASONAL VARIATION AND FOR TRENDS

First, of course, we must remove from our statistical data irrelevant, disturbing factors such as *seasonal* patterns, and also certain so-called *long-term* "trends." If Sears' sales go up from November to December, 1960, we cannot conclude from this that the 1960 recession shown in Fig. 14-2 does not exist. Retail trade goes up every Christmas, just as Cape Cod hotels tend to be crowded in summer. The statistician attempts to remove the "seasonal influence" by carefully studying previous yearly patterns. If he finds that every December tends to involve about 150 per cent as much business as the average month of the year, and every January only 90 per cent, then he will take the actual raw monthly data and divide all the December figures by 1.5, all the January figures by 0.9, and so forth for each month. After this has been done, the statistician will end up with a time series of monthly department-store sales which have been "seasonally adjusted." These will show what we expected all along, that business was really still declining throughout all the best months of 1960, because December's improvement was less than the seasonal norm.

Another kind of problem arises when we examine the fluctuations through time of such a rapidly growing time series as electric-power production or personal income. (This last can be seen at the bottom of Fig. 14-2.) Such a growing series did not decline in any recent recession. But the recession is evident there, nevertheless. It rears its ugly head in the form of a *slowing down of the rate of growth* of the time series as compared with its normal or long-term "secular trend."

If we draw a smooth trend line or curve, either by eye or by some statistical formula, through the strongly growing components of NNP, we discover the business cycle in the twistings of the data above and below the trend line. If we measure the vertical

Most economic activities move up and down together:

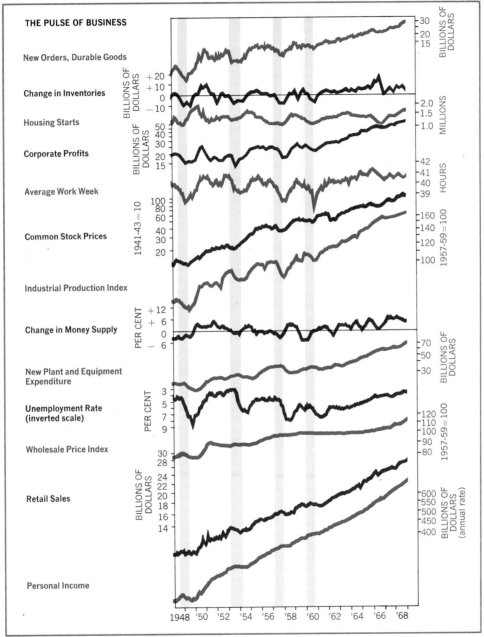

FIG. 14-2. The gold-shaded stretches show years of recession, in contrast to the unshaded periods of expansion. The top curves tend to represent investment items, which seem to be "early movers" and originators of causal movements. The bottom curves show less volatile elements that are more like consumption. Note how rare and short recessions have become in the post-World War II era. Similar charts for mixed economies abroad—Germany, Japan, and France—would show same tameness of mid-century cycles. (Source: Census Bureau.)

The business cycle, like the year, has its seasons:

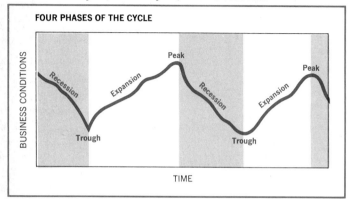

FOUR PHASES OF THE CYCLE

FIG. 14-3. Cyclical expansions follow recessions, with turning points in between. The National Bureau of Economic Research has dated these phases for America's history and for many other countries. Not every peak reaches "prosperity" in the sense of low unemployment. Nor does every threatened recession materialize.

deviations from the trend line and plot them on a separate diagram, we get a reasonably clear picture of the business cycle.[1] Let us take a look at it.

THE FOUR PHASES OF THE TRADITIONAL CYCLE

Early writers on the business cycle, possessing little quantitative information, tended to attach disproportionate attention to *panics* and *crises* such as the collapse of the South Sea Bubble in 1720, the panic of 1837, the Jay Cooke panic of 1873, the Cleveland panic of 1893, the "rich man's panic" of 1904, and, of course, the cataclysmic stock-market crash of "black Tuesday," October 29, 1929. Later writers began to speak of two phases of business: prosperity and depression, or boom and slump, with "peaks" and "troughs" marking the turning points in between. Today, it is recognized that not every period of improving business need take us all the way to full employment and true prosperity.

The cycle used to be broken up by many economists into four phases, the two most important ones being called the periods of "expansion" and "contraction or recession." The expansion phase comes to an end and goes into the recession phase at the upper turning point, or so-called "peak." Similarly, the recession phase gives way to that of expansion at the lower turning point, or so-called "trough." Thus, the four phases are supposed to keep repeating themselves as in the oversimplified picture shown in Fig. 14-3. Note that the emphasis here is not so much on *high* or *low* business activity as on the dynamic aspects of *rising* or *falling* business activity. (But do not forget the unemployment gap and the importance of growth trends.)

Each phase of the cycle passes into the next. Each is characterized by different economic conditions: for example, during expansion we find that employment, production, prices, money, wages, interest rates, and profits are usually rising, with the reverse true in recession. Each phase requires special explanatory principles. But let us continue with more facts before attempting analysis and theorizing.

Length of cycle How long have the traditional economic cycles been? This depends upon how many minor cycles you wish to count. Most observers have no trouble in agreeing on the major cycles, which were about eight to ten years in length. Everyone agrees that the late 1920s represent a period of prosperity and the early 1930s one of depression,

[1] The reader may be referred to any standard textbook on statistics for these technical procedures. However, cautious judgment must be exercised in using the mechanical tools of statistics. A beginner, carelessly "eliminating a trend," if not careful may throw out the baby along with the bath water.

and similarly with other past major business cycles. Not all economists, however, attach importance to the shorter minor cycles that are to be seen in economic charts. In 1924 and 1927, there were small dips in business activity. Shall we call the 1920s, therefore, three different (minor) cycles or one major prosperity period? In 1948–1949, 1953–1954, 1957–1958, and again in 1960–1961, we suffered mild recessions. Should these count as cycles? And if so, why not the "pauses" in 1951, 1962, and 1967?

In an elementary introduction of this type, it is perhaps best to stick primarily to major business cycles. For our purposes we may accept the summary that Harvard's illustrious Alvin Hansen gave to pre–World War II economic history:[2]

The American experience indicates that the major business cycle has had an average duration of a little over eight years. Thus, from 1795 to 1937 there were seventeen cycles of an average duration of 8.35 years. . . .

Since one to two minor peaks regularly occur between the major peaks, it is clear that the minor cycle is something less than half the duration of the major cycle. In the one hundred and thirty-year period 1807 to 1937 there were thirty-seven minor cycles with an average duration of 3.51 years.

. . . It appears that the building cycle averages somewhere between seventeen and eighteen years in length, or almost twice the length of the major business cycle. . . .

. . . American experience indicates that with a high degree of regularity every other major business boom coincides roughly with a boom in building construction, while the succeeding major cycle recovery is forced to buck up against a building slump . . . the depressions which have fallen in the interval of the construction downswing are typically deep and long. And the succeeding recovery is held back and retarded by the unfavorable depressional influence from the slump in the building industry.

The long swings in building construction and other series, which average anywhere between 15 and 25 years in length, are often called Kuznets cycles, being named for the scholar who first noticed them in 1930.[3] Work by A. F. Burns, S. Kuznets, M. Abramovitz, and other National Bureau scholars suggests that these pervasive swings have been associated with fluctuations in immigration and natural rates of population growth, in railroad building and capital imports, and in the rate of growth of the money supply. Scholars have noted them abroad too. Kuznets cycles are of interest because they seem to involve three factors: variations in the supply trends of labor and other resources available to the economy; variations in productivity trends relating to the efficiency with which those supplies can be used; and, what is still provisional but important, variations in the average intensity with which resources get used—in other words, variations in rates of unemployment.

[2] Alvin H. Hansen, *Fiscal Policy and Business Cycles* (Norton, New York, 1941), pp. 18–24.

[3] Kuznets cycles should not be confused with alleged *very long waves*, whose complete cycle length is about half a century. Thus, from the end of the Napoleonic Wars in 1815 to the middle of the nineteenth century, prices tended to fall and times tended to be unusually hard, on the average. After the Californian and Australian gold discoveries of around 1850, and as a partial result of the Civil and Crimean Wars, prices tended to rise. A new long cycle of falling prices followed the 1873 depression and lasted until the 1890s, when there was a great increase in gold production following the African and Alaskan gold discoveries. Whether these long waves are simply historical accidents due to chance gold discoveries, inventions, and political wars, it is still too soon to say. The interested reader may be referred to J. A. Schumpeter, *Business Cycles* (McGraw-Hill, New York, 1939), Chaps. 6 and 7, where long cycles are called "Kondratieffs" after the Russian discoverer.

Was the notable sluggishness of the American economy in the last part of the 1950s a reflection of our passing through a less favorable phase of the Kuznets cycle? Or, as some then thought, was it a forerunner of some more ominous trend? Or merely the natural relaxation after a postwar sprint?

Poring over the record book can take us only so far. Thus, the length of the Kennedy expansion after February, 1961, surprised those who tried to apply mechanical formulas from the past. "Since American expansions tend to average only 29 months," they reasoned, "by 1964 the expansion is living on borrowed time." But actually that expansion proved to be a veritable Methuselah—in tribute to the activism of the so-called "New Economics." For, as we shall see, fiscal and monetary policies can compensate for adverse phases of the Kuznets cycle—which modern man does not regard as one of those disasters, like earthquakes and volcanoes, which science can no longer do anything about.

A FIRST CLUE TO BUSINESS FLUCTUATIONS: CAPITAL FORMATION

Hansen's emphasis on *construction* gives us our first clue to the causation of the business cycle. Certain economic variables always show greater fluctuations than others in the business cycle. Thus, if we plot pig-iron production and cigarette consumption side by side, we hardly notice the business cycle in the latter. But in the pig-iron series there is little else to see but the business cycle. Why? Because cigarettes are nondurable consumers' goods, and in both good and bad times people are going to smoke the same amount. Pig iron, on the other hand, is one of the principal ingredients of capital and durable goods of all kinds: of plant equipment and durable machinery, of industrial and residential construction, and of automobiles, washing machines, and other durable consumers' goods.

Check this by reexamining Fig. 14-2. Note how volatile are the top three investment series, in contrast to the last two series of retail sales and personal income. Note that production and profit fluctuations coincide with investment fluctuations.

By their nature, durable goods are subject to violently erratic patterns of demand. In bad times their new purchase can be indefinitely postponed; in a good year, everyone may suddenly decide to stock up on a 10-year supply of the services of durable goods at the same time.

Our first clue to the nature of the business cycle lies, then, in the fact that it is the durable- or capital-goods sector of the economy which shows by far the greatest cyclical fluctuations.

Their swings are wide compared with those of the economic time series which represent primarily consumption of services, of nondurables, and the *services of* durable goods. Except for a few short, choppy surface disturbances in such series, the latter tend to follow the general flow of income in a rather passive fashion. Ordinarily, consumption movements seem the effect rather than cause of the business cycle; in contrast, there is good reason to believe that the movements of *durable* goods represent key causes in a more fundamental sense.

HOW SAVING AND INVESTMENT SCHEDULES APPLY

It is comforting to find that statistical analysis supports the emphasis in previous chapters on the crucial importance of the capital investment process. The income-determination theories of the last chapter do indeed help in understanding economic history. Here are but a few reminders:

1. *Wars* have always been great disrupters of an economy. How do they transmit their economic effects? Plainly, they lead to great swings in the G component of the $C + I + G$ schedule, and this causes even greater swings in the over-all level of production and incomes. Inflationary gaps appear at full-employment NNP, leading to wartime price inflation. The post-1965 Vietnam inflation is a case in point.

2. In minor cycles of the postwar type, it is common for considerable fluctuations in the rate of *inventory investment* to occur. In the years of expansion, inventory accumulation is at a positive rate as merchants seek to rebuild their stocks and accommodate them to the growing level of sales. When merchants veer from a positive rate of inventory accumulation to a negative rate, the I component in the $C + I + G$ schedule goes down: then the production line is cut back, men are put on fewer average hours per week or are laid off, wages and profits fall, and all this gets registered in a multiplier drop in NNP or in its failure to grow along a normal trend.

3. When there are longer waves in construction and equipment, the I component in the $C + I + G$ schedule causes the whole schedule and its equilibrium to go through slow swings of considerable amplitude.

4. While it is an oversimplification to say that the consumption schedule never shifts over time, S. Kuznets, M. Friedman, and R. Goldsmith have made National Bureau of Economic Research studies indicating the over-all stability of saving behavior relative to income over a long period. Their general finding is that, aside from short-term cycles, the percentage saved out of income has been remarkably the same over the last century.

The one situation in which we cannot regard consumption purely as a passive and predictable force comes in those times when consumer demand for autos and other durable goods fluctuates. (E.g., the record auto sales of 1962–1965 helped much to accelerate the long Kennedy-Johnson expansion of the 1960s.) Such *shifts* in the CC schedule also contribute to movements in the $C + I + G$ intersections, which, like any other shifts in autonomous factors, involve double-duty multiplier reactions.

A FEW THEORIES OF THE BUSINESS CYCLE

When it comes to explanations of why the income schedules shift, an industrious student could easily compile a list of separate theories of the business cycle that would run into the dozens.[4] Each theory seems to be quite different; but when we examine them closely

[4]We may mention just a few of the better-known theories: (1) the *monetary* theory—attributes the cycle to the expansion and contraction of bank money and credit (Hawtrey, Friedman, et al.); (2) the *innovation* theory—attributes the cycle to the clustering of important inventions such as the railroad (Schumpeter, Hansen, et al.); (3) the *psychological* theory—treats the cycle as a case of people's infecting each other with pessimistic and optimistic expectations (Pigou, Bagehot, et al.); (4) the *underconsumption* theory—claims too much income goes to wealthy or thrifty people compared with what can be invested

and throw out those which obviously contradict the facts or the rules of logic, or which just appear to be conveying an explanation when really they are not saying anything at all—when we do all this, we are left with relatively few different explanations. Most of them differ from each other only in emphasis.

One man believes the cycle to be primarily the result of fluctuations in total net investment, while another prefers to attribute the cycle to fluctuations in the rate of technological inventions and innovations, which act on business *through* net investment. These sound like two different theories, and in most advanced textbooks they might be given the names of two different writers, but from our standpoint they are but two different aspects of the same saving-investment process. As we shall see, this does not mean there is perfect agreement among all theories of the cycle or that there are not some important differences in emphasis among different writers.

EXTERNAL AND INTERNAL FACTORS

To classify the different theories, we may first divide them into the two categories of primarily *external* and primarily *internal* theories.

The external theories find the root of the business cycle in the fluctuations of something *outside* **the economic system—in sunspot cycles, in wars, revolutions, and political events, in gold discoveries, rates of growth of population and migrations, discoveries of new lands and resources, and scientific and technological discoveries and innovations.**

The internal theories look for mechanisms *within* **the economic system itself which will give rise to self-generating business cycles, so that every expansion will breed recession and contraction, and every contraction will in turn breed revival and expansion, in a quasi-regular, repeating, never-ending chain.**

If you believe in the sunspot theory of the business cycle—and no respectable economists today do—then the distinction between external and internal is rather easy to draw; although even here, when you come to explain how and why disturbances on the surface of the sun give rise to the business cycle, you begin to get involved in the internal nature of the economic system. But at least no one can seriously argue that the direction of causation is in doubt, or that the economic system causes the sunspots to fluctuate, instead of vice versa. However, when it comes to such other external factors as wars and politics, or even births and gold discoveries, there is always some doubt as to whether the economic system does not at least react back on the so-called "external" factors, thereby making the distinction between external and internal not such a hard-and-fast one. Still, no one will deny that any such "feedback" effects take us outside the traditional boundaries of economics, and this is our justification for distinguishing between external and internal theories.

(Hobson, Sweezy, Foster and Catchings, et al.); (5) the *overinvestment* theory—claims too much rather than too little investment causes recessions (Hayek, Mises, et al.); (6) the *sunspot-weather-crop theories* (Jevons, H. L. Moore). The interested reader should consult G. Haberler, *Prosperity and Depression* (Harvard University Press, Cambridge, Mass. 1958, 4th ed.), or other business-cycle texts for further information. We can add the newer "political" theory of Poland's Kalecki, which traces recessions to periodic political clamping down on creeping inflation.

PURELY INTERNAL THEORIES

As against the crude external sunspot theory, we may describe some simple examples of possible, crude internal theories.

"Echo" waves of replacement   If machinery and other durable goods all had the same length of life (say, 8 or 10 years), then we might (with radical Marx and conservative Taussig) try to explain a business cycle of the same length by this fact. If a boom got started—never mind how—then there would be a bunching of new capital goods all of the same age. A few years later, before these goods had worn out, there would be little need for replacement. This would cause a depression. But after 8 or 10 years all the capital equipment would suddenly wear out and would all have to be replaced, giving rise to an inflationary boom. This in turn would give rise to another complete cycle, with new echoing cycles of depression and boom every decade. Thus, self-generating "replacement waves" provide a purely internal business-cycle theory.

Actually, not all equipment has the same length of life; and identical automobiles produced on the same day will certainly not all be replaced at the same time. Consequently, any bunching of equipment expenditures will tend over time to spread itself out, at most giving rise to weaker and weaker replacement peaks. Twenty-five years after the Civil War one might have noted a deficit of births because of that conflict; but another generation later and the dip would be hardly noticeable; and today it is just as if there had never been that particular violent disturbance of population. Replacement waves, therefore, are like the vibrations of a plucked violin string: they tend to dampen down and die away, unless there is a new disturbance.

Psychological self-generating cycles   The laws of physics guarantee that friction will lessen any purely autonomous physical fluctuations. In social science, there is no law like the conservation of energy to prevent the creation of purchasing power. Therefore another example of a self-generating cycle would be the case where people became alternately optimistic and pessimistic, each stage leading as inevitably to the next as the manic stage of disturbed people leads to the depressive stage.

We cannot rule out such an internal theory. Nor can we be satisfied with it as it stands, for it says and explains little.

COMBINING EXTERNAL AND INTERNAL ELEMENTS

Everyone has observed how a window or a tuning fork may be activated into pronounced vibration when a certain note is sounded. Is this vibration externally or internally caused? The answer is, Both. The sounded note is certainly an external cause; but the window or tuning fork responds according to its own internal nature, coming into strong resonance, not with *any* sounded note, but only with one of a certain *definite* pitch. It takes the right kind of trumpets to bring down the walls of Jericho.

Similarly, we may look upon business cycles as not unlike a toy rocking horse that is subjected to occasional outside pushes. The pushes need not be regular; great technical innovations never are. But just as the wooden horse rocks with frequency and amplitude that depend partly on its internal nature (size and weight), so too will the economic system respond to fluctuations in external factors according to its *internal* nature. Both external and internal factors are important in explaining cycles.

Synthesis   Most economists today believe in a combination of external and internal theories. In explaining the major cycles, they place crucial emphasis on fluctuations in *investment* or *capital* goods. Primary causes of these capricious and volatile investment fluctuations are found in such external factors as (1) technological innovation and (2) dynamic growth of population and of territory. With these external factors, we must combine the internal factors that cause any initial change in investment to be *amplified* in a cumulative, multiplied fashion—as people who are given work in the capital-goods industries respend part of their new income on consumption goods and as an air of optimism begins to pervade the business community, causing firms to go to the banks and the securities market for new credit accommodation.[5]

Also, it is necessary to point out that the general business situation definitely reacts in turn on investment. If high consumption sales make businessmen optimistic, they are more likely to embark upon venturesome investment programs. Inventions or scientific discoveries may occur independently of the business cycle, but their appreciable economic introduction will most certainly depend on business conditions. When NNP moved up in the 1960s year after year, it was reasonable to expect that a considerable volume of capital formation (new machines, added inventories, construction) would be induced. Therefore, especially in the short run, investment is in part an *effect* as well as a cause of income movements.

In the longer run, no matter how high a plateau of income is maintained, the stock of capital goods will become adjusted at a higher level and new net investment will drop off to zero unless there is (1) a growth of income, (2) a continuing improvement of technology, or (3) a never-ending reduction in interest rates.

The first of these processes, showing how investment demand may be induced by *growth* of sales and income, has been given a rather high-sounding name—the "acceleration principle." Almost all writers bring it in as one strand in their final business-cycle theories. Let us examine how this internal cyclical mechanism works itself out and interacts with other factors.

THE ACCELERATION PRINCIPLE

According to this law, society's needed stock of capital, whether inventory or equipment, depends primarily upon the level of income or production. Additions to the stock of capital, or what we customarily call *net* investment, will take place only when income

---

[5] With two dice you can manufacture something that looks a little like a business cycle. Record the results of successive tosses—as in the random number sequence 7, 4, 10, 3, 7, 11, 7, 2, . . . Then take five-period moving averages—such as the successive numbers $(7 + 4 + 10 + 3 + 7)/5 = 6\frac{1}{5}$, $(4 + 10 + 3 + 7 + 11)/5 = 7, . . .$, etc. A plot of these will look not too different from NNP or price fluctuations! Explanation: The random numbers are like exogenous investment shocks; the moving average is like the economic system's (or the wooden horse's) internal smoothing reactions of $C + I + G$ type.

The acceleration principle shows how variations in a system's growth rate will induce variations in its level of investment:

TIME	YEARLY SALES	STOCK OF CAPITAL	NET INVESTMENT NI	GROSS INVESTMENT GI (NI + depreciation)
THE ACCELERATION PRINCIPLE (in millions of dollars)				
First phase				
First year	$ 6	$ 60	$ 0	1 machine at $3 = $3
Second year	6	60	0	1 machine at $3 = $3
Third year	6	60	0	1 machine at $3 = $3
Second phase				
Fourth year	$ 9	$ 90	$30	(1 + 10) machines at $3 = $33
Fifth year	12	120	30	(1 + 10) machines at $3 = $33
Sixth year	15	150	30	(1 + 10) machines at $3 = $33
Third phase				
Seventh year	$15	$150	$ 0	1 machine at $3 = $3
Fourth phase (to be filled in by reader)				
Eighth year	$14.7	$____	−$ 3	____machines at $3 = $____

TABLE 14-1. Investment fluctuates more than sales: to keep it from falling, sales must not even falter in their rate of growth.

is growing. As a result, a prosperity period may come to an end, not simply because consumption sales have gone down, but merely because sales have *leveled off* at a high level (or have continued to grow, but at a lower rate than previously).

A simplified arithmetical example will make this clear. Imagine a typical textile-manufacturing firm whose stock of capital equipment is always kept equal to about ten times the value of its yearly sales of cloth.[6] Thus, when its sales have remained at $6 million per year for some time, its balance sheet will show $60 million of capital equipment, consisting of perhaps 20 machines of different ages, with 1 wearing out each year and being replaced. Because replacement just balances depreciation, there is no *net* investment or saving being done by the corporation. *Gross* investment takes place at the rate of $3 million per year, representing the yearly replacement of 1 machine. (The other $3 million of sales may be assumed to be wages and dividends.) The first phase of Table 14-1 shows this.

Now let us suppose that, in the fourth year, sales rise 50 per cent—from $6 to $9 million. Then the number of machines must also rise 50 per cent, or from 20 to 30 machines. In that fourth year, 11 machines must be bought—10 new ones in addition to the replacement of the worn-out one.

Sales rose 50 per cent. How much has machine production gone up? From 1 machine to 11; or by 1,000 per cent! This *accelerated* effect of a change in consumption or other final items on investment levels gives the acceleration principle its name.

[6] To keep the discussion simple, we use the exaggerated ratio 10/1 and ignore changes in interest rates or degree of utilization of capacity. The reader can include inventory change and plant change along with equipment change in the analysis.

If sales continue to rise in both the fifth and the sixth years by $3 million, then we shall continue to have 11 new machines ordered every year.

So far, the acceleration principle has given us no trouble. On the contrary, it has given us a tremendous increase in investment spending as a result of a moderate increase in consumption sales. But now we are riding a tiger.

According to the acceleration principle, consumption has to continue to keep increasing in order for investment to stand still!

If consumption should stop growing at so rapid a rate—if it should level off in the seventh year even at the high level of $15 million per year—then net investment will fall away to zero, and gross investment will, for many years, fall back to 1 machine (see Table 14-1). In other words, a drop of zero per cent in sales has resulted in a 90 per cent drop in gross investment and a 100 per cent drop in net investment. (See the third phase of Table 14-1, and fill in the fourth phase with 0s and $147 at appropriate spots—i.e., zeros to signify that *nothing* is now being replaced.)

The acceleration principle can work in both directions. Should sales now drop below $15 million, gross investment would drop away to nothing for a long time; in fact, the firm would want to disinvest by selling some of its used machinery.

It is clear that a recession can set in just because sales have stopped growing so rapidly, even if not dropping off absolutely but only leveling off at a high rate.

INTERACTIONS OF ACCELERATOR AND MULTIPLIER

Needless to say, the curtailment of production in the machine-producing industries will curtail income and spending on food and clothing and will lead to still further "multiplier" changes in spending. This itself might ultimately cause textile sales to stop growing altogether, or even to decline. This in turn will cause a further accelerated drop in net investment.

Thus, we may be in a vicious circle where the acceleration principle and the multiplier interact to produce a cumulative deflationary (or inflationary) spiral.

Our example used machines. Does that mean the acceleration principle is not involved in the inventory "recessions" (such as 1920–1921, 1937–1938, 1948–1949, 1953–1954, 1957–1958, 1960–1961)? Not at all. The same principle—that stocks of capital goods tend to be held in some proportion to sales per unit time—is valuable to help explain short inventory cycles.

This analysis can also explain how a downturn can result from the previous expansion itself. Suppose, in a situation of unemployment, we get income growing again. The rising income induces, via the accelerator, new investment. The new investment induces, via the multiplier, further rises in income. Hence, the rate of growth of output may be "self-warranting."

But how can a system grow forever at 6 or 7 per cent if its labor force grows only at 1 or 2 per cent and workers' productivity grows only at 2 or 3 per cent? It can't. The self-warranting expansion, even if we are lucky enough to get and keep it, must ultimately bump into the full-employment ceiling. Like a tennis ball (and unlike a wad of gum), it is likely to bounce back from the full-employment ceiling into a recession. Why? Because the minute the system stops its fast growth, the accelerator dictates the end of the high investment supporting the boom. Like an airplane that falls once it loses its motion, the economic system plummets downward.

Similar accelerator-multiplier analysis may explain the ultimate end of a recession and the onset of an upturn. When output plummets downward rapidly, the acceleration principle calls for negative investment (or disinvestment) greater than the rate at which machines can wear out. This wear-out rate puts a floor on how fast disinvestment can take place, and hence a floor on how far it (the SS—II intersection) can push the economy below its break-even point.

Bumping along such a basement floor means that eventually firms will work down their capital stock to the level called for by that low level of income; and now the acceleration principle calls for a termination of disinvestment! Our image must shift from gum, ball, and airplane to that of an Olympic diver: once he stops moving downward under the water, he is buoyed back up again. A new cycle can begin and repeat itself.

It is easy to see that, in the acceleration principle, we have a powerful factor making for economic instability. If business sales go up and down, the acceleration principle can intensify their fluctuation. It induces net investment on the upswing, but causes about the same amount of net *disinvestment* on the downswing.

In the long run, if the system is growing because of population increase and technical progress, then the acceleration principle works primarily as a stimulating factor: growing national income causes extensive growth of capital, which in turn means brisk investment demand and relatively low unemployment.[7]

FORECASTING THE FUTURE OF BUSINESS ACTIVITY

Businessmen have to form guesses about the future in making their investment and production decisions. If they thought next year would bring a depression, they might want to reduce inventory now. If, on the contrary, they expected prices to rise greatly several months from now, they might hasten today to buy goods in advance and to add to equipment and plant. Similarly, speculators would like to know the future in order to be able to buy or sell common stocks and make a profit. And more important, policy makers in Washington would like to have a peek at next year's national-income accounts to be able to take remedial fiscal and monetary actions *now*.

Statisticians and economists cannot yet make accurate forecasts. Their guesses occasionally turn out to be quite wrong. Nonetheless, people insist that they do their best. Why? Because lack of any forecast usually itself involves an *implicit* forecast, and non-economists have an even worse long-run average score at making forecasts than do trained statistical economists.

Forecasting the economic future What methods do the best forecasters use? No simple description can be given, but here are a few of the most common practices.

[7] The Appendix of Chapter 37 discusses warranted growth further, in connection with so-called "Harrod-Domar models of growth."

1. They follow the national-income accounts very closely: GNP every quarter; personal income every month; new construction; equipment spending; the important short-run behavior of inventory change; estimates of coming government expenditures and taxes. They also watch monthly data: price indexes, the Federal Reserve Board index of production, changes in the rate of growth of the money supply, and reports on unemployment and job totals. In addition, they watch many diverse statistics as they become available: department-store sales each week; chain-stores sales (Woolworth, J. C. Penney); mail-order sales (Sears, Montgomery Ward) each month; new orders and inventory changes of manufacturing and trade each month.

2. In recent years, the forecaster can study various *surveys* of future events: the McGraw-Hill questionnaire of business intentions to invest, the SEC-Commerce official questionnaires on the same subject, and the Newsweek–National Industrial Conference Board surveys provide clues to fixed investment (plant or equipment) intentions. The attitudes reported by purchasing agents are important for inventories. For consumers, random sampling by the University of Michigan Group Survey Center and the U.S. Bureau of the Census gives information on whether or not the consumer is in a buying mood and what his spending intentions are. For businessmen generally, Dun & Bradstreet and *Fortune* take frequent polls of opinions about future and present intentions. In Europe this technique of polling heads of business has also made great progress.

3. Many forecasters, such as the President's Council of Economic Advisers, then try to draw up "$C + I + G$–type models" to make *approximate guesses* about future changes. They try to come out with *a range of probable answers*, not with a single answer accurate to two decimals.

4. Some reinforce these guesses by considering whether most diverse time series—such as those in Fig. 14-2—are going up or down. Are certain so-called "leading-indicator series," such as average hours worked per week, stock prices, construction awards, and new orders, predominantly signaling a turn now?

Men long looked for a statistical series (or group of series) that would manifest a turn a *fixed* number of months *before* business turned generally. Such a "leading indicator" would be invaluable for forecasting purposes; however, no such perfect guide has been discovered. Geoffrey Moore and Arthur F. Burns at the National Bureau of Economic Research, and Julius Shiskin at the Census Bureau, have found that certain series, such as have already been mentioned, can give some help in identifying turning points in advance and in confirming that they have just occurred. Forecasters cannot yet rely on indicators alone, for the reason that (as in 1951, 1962, and 1967) they may give misleading signals; in expansions, the indicators often turn down too many months before the true peak; in recessions, they turn up only a month or two before the upturn—by the time the data become available for smoothing, their main (important!) purpose is to tell us we have indeed already turned the corner. Economists look forward with interest to further improvements in these techniques, and practical forecasters do supplement their GNP estimates with this kind of information. See Fig. 14-4 for some improved efforts in this direction.[8]

[8] Dr. J. Shiskin has recently reversed the usual procedure of trend removal: he puts a trend *into* the leading indicators (1) to reduce the lead time at peaks, (2) to lengthen the lead time at troughs, and (3) generally to reduce the variability of leads and lags. Found among the useful leaders are new orders for durables, capital appropriations, housing permits, and inventory changes; rate of growth of the money supply; stock prices, corporate profits, and industrial materials prices; average workweek hours, unemployment-insurance initial claims, and new incorporations; etc.

Leading indicators call the business-cycle turns (usually!):

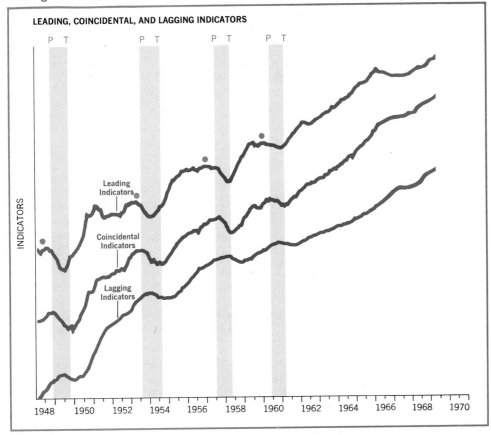

LEADING, COINCIDENTAL, AND LAGGING INDICATORS

FIG. 14-4. The coincidental indicators in the middle turn up and down in agreement with the peak-trough datings shown in gold shading. Note that the leading indicators above turn down about five months before the peaks. (Examine the gold dots that mark the peaks of the leading indicators and compare with the timing of onset of gold-shaded recessions.) Note that the leaders turn up scarcely two months before the troughs. (Can you pencil in with black dots the upper curve's troughs and compare with the shading?)

Experience shows that economic forecasts are indispensable for public and business decisions. Economists' forecasts, although not infallible, average out to be more accurate than those of readers of tea leaves, senatorial hunch players, computer robots, or simple extrapolaters of present levels and trends. Although not perfect, economists' forecasts are the best science can produce.

REQUIEM FOR THE BUSINESS CYCLE?

Is the business cycle dead? Has the New Economics ended once and for all this curse of historic capitalism, in the same way that modern medicine has ended such scourges as polio and smallpox?

Many people do believe that the business cycle has finally been tamed. And indeed, study of Figs. 14-2 and 14-4 shows that the American mixed economy has reduced recessions in the post-World War II period to brief and infrequent punctuations in the progress of sustained growth. It used to be the case, under historic capitalism, that the charts showed the shadings of recession half the time.

Yet, to paraphrase Mark Twain's comment on the report of his demise, "It is *premature* to speak of the death of the business cycle." Back in 1929, just before the great stock-market crash, experts spoke of the country as being in a "new era" of perpetual prosperity. The gods take their revenge on those who are too proud.

What can be said scientifically about the outlook for business fluctuations? Most economists would pretty much agree with the following formulation:

Although nothing is impossible in an inexact science like economics, the probability of a great depression—a prolonged, cumulative, and chronic slump like that of the 1930s, the 1890s, or the 1870s—has been reduced to a negligible figure. No one should pay any appreciable insurance premium to be protected against the risk of a total breakdown in our banking system and of massive unemployment in which 25 per cent of the workers can find no jobs.

The reason for virtual disappearance of great depressions is the new attitude of the electorate. By the $C + I + G$ analysis of earlier chapters, and the monetary analysis of chapters yet to come, economic science *knows how* to use monetary and fiscal policy to keep any recessions that break out from snowballing into *lasting* chronic slumps. If Marxians wait for capitalism to collapse in a final crisis, they wait in vain. We have eaten of the Fruit of the Tree of Knowledge and, for better or worse, there is no returning to laissez faire capitalism. The electorate in a mixed economy insists that any political party which is in power—whether it be the Republican or the Democratic, the Tory or the Labor party—take the expansionary actions that can prevent depressions.

Suppose we grant that great depressions are virtually a thing of the past. Does this mean that we must have perpetual prosperity—that recessions will never happen again, being replaced by what are euphemistically called "rolling readjustments" or mere "pauses"? Most scientists take a more cautious attitude, summarizing thus:

A mixed economy may still be subject to occasional *recessions:* inventory fluctuations can still occur; changes in cold-war spending can have initially destabilizing effects upon general business activity; attempts to bring inflation under control may sometimes result in downturns.

Nevertheless, now that the tools of income analysis are understood and their use is politically mandatory, the probability of recession in any one year is less in the mixed economy than it used to be. Expansion periods tend to be frequent and longer.

Lest we close on too optimistic a note, let us take warning that the forces of democracy are not so strongly balanced in the direction of controlling creeping inflation—as we shall see in Chapter 41. And future scientists may have to redefine the phases of the business cycle, so that in economies like Germany or the United States we count as unsatisfactory those years in which the economy actually *grows less than its potential grows,* thereby wasting its true productivity in mounting "gaps."

SUMMARY

1   The business cycle is a pulse common to most sectors of economic life and to various countries. Movements in national income, unemployment, production, prices, and profits are not so regular and predictable as the orbits of the planets or the oscillations of a pendulum, and there is no magical method of forecasting the turns of business activity.

2   The four phases of expansion, peak, recession, and trough can be separated for analysis and can be distinguished from seasonal and long-term trends. The resulting pattern of 8- to 10-year major cycles, shorter minor cycles, and longer Kuznets construction cycles has been carefully described by statisticians and historians.

3   To explain the cycle, our first clue is to be found in the greater amplitude of fluctuations of investment or durable-capital-goods formation. Although most economists agree on this fact, they differ in their emphasis upon *external* or *internal* factors. Increasingly, however, the experts are tending toward a *synthesis* of external and internal factors. On the one hand, importance is attached to fluctuations in inventions, in population and territorial growth, and in gold discoveries and political warfare. On the other hand, economists stress too the way that these external changes in investment opportunities are modified by the reactions of the economic system; the credit practices of banks and the monetary policies of the Federal Reserve; waves of optimism and pessimism; re-placement cycles; *the multiplier and the acceleration principle*, which bring in dynamic rates of change as well as levels; and other feedback effects of growth on investment.

4   Forecasting is still inexact. Those with the best long-run batting averages follow national-income and related statistics very closely. They rely heavily on surveys of government, consumer, and business intentions. They reinforce their $C + I + G$ and money-supply guesses with the study of leading, coincidental, and lagging indicators.

5   The business cycle has been tamed, even if not completely made a thing of the past. Although democratic mixed economies are unlikely to experience old-fashioned prolonged depressions ever again, recessions will no doubt still occur even though fiscal and monetary policies can moderate their frequency, intensity, and duration.

    Later chapters will provide the tools for understanding what public and private policy can do to modify the severity of business cycles and promote growth.

QUESTIONS FOR DISCUSSION

1   Describe the history of various business cycles in this country—pre- and post-1939.

2   Describe the different phases of the cycle. In what one are you now? How do you know?

3   Which theory or theories of the cycle do you like best? Why?

4   "The ups and downs of the traditional business cycle are less important objects of study today than 'unemployment gaps' and the trends in real growth and in prices." Appraise.

5   Write an explanation of the acceleration principle. Combine it with the multiplier.

6   Why is it important to be able to forecast the future of business activity? Give business and government examples. How would *you* forecast?

7   In the light of recent years' experience, reappraise the outlook for the business cycle.

8   The concept of the business cycle needs to be redefined in modern times as follows: "Expansion should be defined as years when GNP grows faster than *trend;* recession defined as years when GNP grows slower than *trend.* Then we will again have recession half the time on the average." Support the merits of this view.

Review your understanding of the following concepts:

business cycle, phases, crisis
peak, trough, expansion, recession
seasonal and trend corrections
internal and external theories
replacement waves, sunspots

acceleration principle, multiplier
forecasting methods
leading, coincidental, and lagging
   indicators
mixed economy improvements

Prices and Money   **15**

Earlier chapters showed how the modern economist finds it convenient to analyze the forces making for expanding or contracting money income in terms of saving and investment schedules—or what is the same thing, in terms of the components of consumption, investment, and government spending. For the most part, except in the inflationary-gap section, it was assumed that price levels would not change much until an approach to high employment was reached. Or alternatively, it was tacitly assumed earlier that all the schedules were expressed in terms of dollars which had been corrected for changes in the measuring rod of the price level. Accordingly, until now, a shift in the schedule of consumption-plus-investment-plus-government spending could be thought of as expanding employment and production.

Now we want to focus on changes in the *price levels*. Why do prices rise swiftly in major wars? Why do prices increase millionfolds in galloping inflation when a disorganized nation is printing new green currency by the bale? Why do prices begin to creep upward even before an expansion of $C + I + G$ spending restores the system to full or high employment? Why in a modern mixed economy might prices and wages rise even at a time of apparent excess plant capacity and slack labor markets?

These vital, and difficult, questions can be fruitfully approached by the following program. Section A first gives the facts about price-level changes and some of their effects. Then it discusses the concept of the money supply M. Then Section B analyzes the way M has generally moved in relation to long-term prices. In particular, the important "Quantity Theory of Money," in its crude and sophisticated forms, will provide an initial glimpse into the importance of banking and Federal Reserve monetary policies, as discussed in subsequent chapters.

We shall discover that changes in the money supply have an important role in causing the $C + I + G$ spending schedule to shift upward and downward.

A. PRICES AND THE MONEY SUPPLY

Wars bring sharpest price rises:

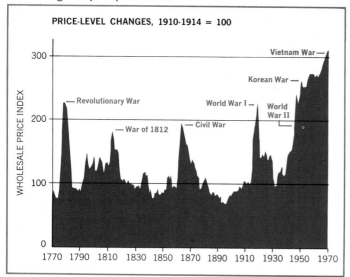

PRICE-LEVEL CHANGES, 1910-1914 = 100

FIG. 15-1. After each major war in the country's history there has been slightly less of a price drop. Indeed, after World War II there was no significant drop. For 75 years the price trend has seemed definitely upward. (Source: U.S. Census Bureau.)

Figure 15-1 shows the historical ups and downs of wholesale prices. Each war is clearly marked by a peak. At first glance there seem to be no general upward or downward trends. But the chart of consumer prices in Fig. 15-2 (page 263) pinpoints the general *upward* trend of prices in this century. The value of the dollar—as measured by what it can buy—has been about cut in half since today's college student was born.

As an omen for the future, note one terribly significant fact: After World War II there was no decline in prices at all comparable with what followed previous wars. Wages and prices seem to have become *sticky as far as downward movements are concerned;* also, government has become quick to act to stem any depression that begins to get under way. When the Vietnam war accelerated the rate of creeping inflation, the target for government policy was not price stability, for that was considered beyond the realm of feasibility. Instead, the target was to halve the rate of price increase, to bring it from 4 to 6 per cent per year down to 2 to 4 per cent. If prices rise in good times and scarcely fall at all in bad times, what is the indicated long-term direction for prices?

INFLATION, DEFLATION, AND REDISTRIBUTION OF INCOME AMONG GROUPS

First, some definitions will be useful.

By *inflation* we mean *a time of generally rising prices* for goods and factors of production—rising prices for bread, cars, haircuts; rising wages, rents, etc. By *deflation* we mean a time when most prices and costs are falling.[1]

Neither in inflation nor in deflation do prices all move in the same direction or in exactly the same proportion. As a result of changes in *relative* prices and in total spending, the two processes of inflation and deflation cause definite and characteristic changes in (1) the distribution of income among economic classes, and (2) total output.

---

[1] "Deflation" sometimes has a secondary meaning too, namely, a *drop in real output and an increase in unemployment* regardless of price behavior. And even our simple definition of inflation as rising prices will occasionally need modifying: thus in 1947 when wartime price controls were removed, prices shot upward. Did stability of prices mean no inflation before then? Hardly. As scarcities of goods increased from 1942 to 1947, we were having "suppressed inflation." The 1947 price rise was primarily a "symptom" of the disease we were *already* experiencing.

Unforeseen inflation tends to favor debtors and profit receivers at the expense of creditors and fixed-income receivers. Deflation has the opposite effect.

Suppose you lend $1,000 today and are paid back one year from now. If in the meantime prices have doubled, then your debtor will be paying back only one-half as much real purchasing power as you gave him. If prices were to increase a trillionfold, as they did in the German inflation of 1920–1923, then the wealth of creditors would be completely wiped out. This actually happened to German university endowments and life-insurance assets.

After 1939 an American who earned 6 per cent yearly on a mortgage found that, as a result of World War II, he was not even holding his own as far as the *real purchasing power* of the dollar was concerned. United States government savings bonds bought for $75 in 1969 pay off about $100 in 1975. But will one hundred 1975 dollars have as much purchasing power as seventy-five 1969 dollars did then?

On the other hand, one who invests his money in real estate, in common stocks, or in sacks of flour makes a great money profit during unforeseen inflation. The volume of business sales shoots up. Prices rise between the time that businessmen buy and sell their merchandise. Fixed or overhead costs remain the same; other costs rise, but not so rapidly as prices. For all these reasons profits increase—often faster than the cost of living. In periods of great inflation, every reckless fool can be a great financier.

In time of deflation, the shoe is on the other foot. Creditors and fixed-income receivers tend to gain at the expense of debtors and profit receivers. If prices fall between the time that a creditor lends money and is repaid, then he gets back more purchasing power than he lent. Between the time that a merchant buys and sells goods, he will have to take a loss.

The schoolteacher who keeps her job and whose pay is not cut too sizably finds that her real income has increased. The widow who withstood the temptation to buy common stock during the boom and instead put all her money into gilt-edge government bonds finds herself better off. At the same time the government finds the real burden of its public debt goes up relative to tax collections and national income. A hoarder who earns no money interest on his mattress cache finds the real value of his wealth increasing every day as prices fall. If prices fall at the rate of 10 per cent per year, he is being rewarded for his antisocial act of hoarding at a 10 per cent rate of interest in real terms, while the businessman who is foolish enough to give someone a job may find that he cannot even get back his original outlay, much less earn a profit.

Modern research suggests that the greatest redistribution of income resulting from inflation is from older people to younger people. The dollars one puts aside at 25 for retirement at 70 often shrink in purchasing power: if prices rise at an average rate of about 3 per cent per year, the real purchasing power of a dollar held for 45 years will halve and halve again in that period.[2]

---

[2] If an inflation goes on for a long time and is no longer "unforeseen," an allowance for a price rise may get itself built into the market interest rate. Thus, if we all expect prices to rise at 4 per cent per year, my pension funds invested in bonds and mortgages may pay me 8 per cent rather than 4 per cent. This adjustment of interest rates to strong inflation has been observed in Brazil and Chile, and even in the United States of the late 1960s and early 1970s.

EFFECTS OF CHANGING PRICES ON OUTPUT AND EMPLOYMENT

Aside from redistributing incomes, inflation may affect the total real income and production of the community.

An increase in prices is usually associated with high employment. In mild inflation the wheels of industry are well lubricated, and output is near capacity. Private investment is brisk, jobs plentiful. Such has been the historical pattern.

Thus, many businessmen and union spokesmen, in appraising a little deflation and a little inflation, speak of the latter as the lesser of the two evils. The losses to fixed-income groups are usually less than the gains to the rest of the community. Even workers with relatively fixed wages are often better off because of improved employment opportunities and greater take-home pay; a rise in interest rates on new securities may partly make up any losses to creditors; and increases in social security benefits may partly make up losses to the retired.

In deflation, on the other hand, the growing unemployment of labor and capital causes the community's total well-being to be less; so, in a sense, the gainers get less than the losers lose. As a matter of fact, in deep depression, almost everyone—including the creditor who is left with uncollectible debts—suffers.

The above remarks show why an increase in consumption or investment spending is thought a good thing in times of unemployment, even if there is some upward pressure on prices. When the economic system is suffering from acute depression, few will criticize private or public spending on the ground that this might be inflationary. Actually, most of the increased spending will then go to increase production and create jobs.

But the same reasoning shows that once full employment and full plant capacity have been reached, any further increases in spending are likely to be completely wasted in price-tag increases. (Recall Chapter 13's discussion of "inflationary gaps.")

GALLOPING INFLATION

Slow price increases are one thing. But when each increase in prices becomes the signal for an increase in wages and costs, which again sends prices up still further, we may be in the midst of a malignant, galloping hyperinflation. Nothing good can be said for a rapid rise of prices such as took place in Germany in 1920–1923 and more recently in China and Hungary. Production and even the social order are then disorganized. The total wealth of large groups of the population is wiped out as money becomes worthless. Debtors ruthlessly pursue creditors in order to pay off their obligations in valueless money. Speculators profiteer. Housewives rush to spend their husbands' paychecks before prices rise still further, but in doing so they only bid prices up even faster. As a Southerner said during the Confederate inflation:

We used to go to the stores with money in our pockets and come back with food in our baskets. Now we go with money in baskets and return with food in our pockets. Everything is scarce except money! Prices are chaotic and production disorganized. A meal that used to cost the same amount as an opera ticket now costs twenty times as much. Business is often at a standstill because no one knows how much to charge. (We'll settle after the war, some say.) As a result, everybody tends to hoard "things" and to try to get rid of the "bad" paper money, which drives the "good" metal money out of circulation. A partial return to barter inconvenience is the result.

Aside from hyperinflations of the German 1920–1923 type, we do see in countries like Chile and Brazil a state of chronic inflation—say, at the rate of 20 to 50 per cent per year—that goes on decade after decade. Somehow the people learn to live on such a merry-go-round. They hoard goods; buy houses; never, never lend money at ordinary interest rates; etc. Sometimes, as in Brazil, the economy manages to show real growth; too often, as in Chile, growth suffers.

Fortunately, there are few cases of hyperinflation except during war or in the backwash of war and revolution. The primary fear today for a mixed economy like America's is of a steady upward *creep* in prices. Will such a creep inevitably become a trot? A trot become a canter? A canter become a gallop? Few economic experts would regard such a development as inevitable or even likely. But they would still be concerned with too fast and steady a creep of prices.

In the first years after World War II, the rapid rise in prices drove some economists to the gloomy view: "We can never get near full employment without having rising wages and prices; only a price-fixing board can make full employment and price stability compatible." The 1936–1937, 1945–1948, 1956–1958, and 1965–1970 experiences did give this view some plausibility. On the other hand, 1951–1953 were mostly years of low unemployment and also years of falling wholesale prices and steady living costs. Wholesale prices were level from 1958 to 1964. Still, as we shall see repeatedly in later chapters, every mixed economy must face the problem of a tendency for full employment to result in creeping inflation. Chapter 41 discusses the fact that each has yet to find a so-called "incomes (or wage-price guidepost) policy" to help better this performance.

GOALS OF LONG-TERM PRICE BEHAVIOR

Ideally, we all want a progressive full-employment economy in which the excesses of the business cycle are moderated. We want to control the "mad dance of the dollar" as the business cycle passes from boom to crisis and slump. But as far as the *long-run trend* of prices is concerned, there are three possible programs that different economists sponsor as the soundest modern compromise:

1. *Prices—on the average—are to be stable.* As output increases over time because of population increase, capital formation, and technological progress, the total of dollar spending rises. Money wages and real wages also rise as a result of the increase in productivity over time.

2. *Prices are to be gently rising.* As high-employment output increases with productivity and growth, total dollar spending rises even faster than prices. Money wages also rise steadily; but the increase in real wages is not quite so great, because of the upward trend in the cost of living.

3. *Prices are to be falling steadily.* The total of money wages and property income remains almost constant. But the increase in output resulting from improved technological productivity is passed on to *all* consumers in lower prices. Real wages rise even though

money wages may remain constant. Such a fall in prices need not depress business activity unduly, provided that it results from previous reductions in cost.

All three solutions are tolerable if unemployment is kept at a low figure. And in some ideal frictionless system, it would not matter much which pattern were followed, as long as the trend in prices was foreseeable and all adjustments were made to it. However, economic history and analysis suggest that we do not live in an ideal frictionless system. In a modern mixed economy, high employment is least likely to be maintained under the third possibility of falling price levels.

Most vigorous periods of healthy capitalist development without political unrest came during periods of stable or gently rising prices. Capitalism itself developed during the centuries when Spanish New World silver and gold were raising prices—not because anyone planned it that way, but simply because monetary systems used to consist of precious metals, and Columbus accidentally discovered the ore-rich New World.

THE THREE KINDS OF MONEY: COINS, CURRENCY, AND BANK DEPOSITS

We saw in Chapter 3 that a specialized economy uses money rather than barter:

Money is the modern medium of exchange and the standard unit in which prices and debts are expressed. By controlling the behavior of money and credit, the government through its Federal Reserve System can hope to affect the balance of saving and investment expenditure.

By quickening or moderating the growth in the money supply, the Federal Reserve can hope to raise or lower the $C + I + G$ intersections of earlier chapters. Here lies the vital importance of monetary theory.

Let us list the main kinds of money in daily use: small coins, paper currency, and checking-account bank-deposit money.

Coins First, there are the *coins* we use for small change: copper pennies, nickel five-cent pieces, and silver-looking dimes, quarters, half dollars, and (in the Far West) dollars. These constitute our so-called "fractional currency." Children think them important; but in total they do not add up to very much—in fact, to less than one-thirteenth of the community's cash. Because the metal in all these coins is worth far *less* than their face value, they are termed "token money."[3] These coins are valued far beyond their metallic worth only because they can be readily converted into other money—20 nickels to the dollar, and so forth. Coins with negligible metallic value are not forced upon us; their quantity is limited by our demand for them to buy gum and newspapers.

Currency Far more significant is the second kind of money: *paper currency*. Most of us

---

[3]If a dictator insisted on supplementing the paper currency with coins whose metallic value equaled or came near their face values, he would show what an amateur he was at finance. Thus, as soon as platinum or silver rose enough in price on the auction markets of the world, the dictator would find his coins were being melted down for their metallic content. It is because coins and currency are made of cheap materials that they avoid this fate. Do facts bear out this theory? They do, as the next footnote will show: When the price of silver rose, the government had to stop using silver in dimes and quarters; to keep new coins from being melted down and hoarded, it substituted cheaper cupronickel materials.

know little more about a one- or five-dollar bill than that it is inscribed with the picture of an American statesman, that it bears the signature of one or another government official, and—most important of all—that each has a numeral showing its face value.

Examine a ten-dollar bill or some other paper bill. You probably find it says "Federal Reserve Note."[4] Also, it announces itself as "legal tender for all debts, public and private." Until recently it contained the further, and nonsensical, statement that it "is redeemable in *lawful money* at the United States Treasury or at any Federal Reserve Bank." Why italicize "lawful money"? Because for 30 years there was no such thing other than the "legal tender" bills under discussion, namely, Federal Reserve notes and so forth. In short, your old wrinkled ten-dollar bill was redeemable into a crisp new bill, into 2 fives, or into 10 ones if you prefer! But that was all.[5]

Today, all American currency and coin is essentially "fiat" money. It is money because the government decrees it is money, and because we all accept it. Metallic backing has no real meaning anymore (except, as will be seen later, when it serves to limit the total supply of fiat money).

Before 1933, it was common for good little boys and girls to be presented on their birthdays with five- or ten-dollar gold pieces; and gold certificates were often seen in circulation. These certificates were warehouse receipts promising the bearer redemption in gold upon application to the United States Treasury. But in 1933, when Congress raised the buying price of gold from about $21 to $35 an ounce, all gold—except that tied up in wedding rings, dental fillings, and rare coins—was called in. This was done so that holders or hoarders of gold could not make a 67 per cent profit as a result of the devaluation of the dollar. At the same time, all gold certificates were called in. Congress ruled that these certificates were not to be exchanged for gold upon being called in, but simply for ordinary paper dollars. A few absent-minded people still have not turned in their gold certificates, but once these are brought to a bank, they will be retired from circulation forever and replaced by other bills.[6]

---

[4] Some one-dollar bills used to bear the words "Silver Certificate." One who knows American politics and history realizes that these existed only because a few Western senators from mining states could persuade Congress to give silver mining a continuing subsidy by buying up quantities of silver for monetary use. Otherwise, silver has absolutely no *monetary* significance; many countries are abandoning it even for small coins, and it is finally losing its hold on the Orient. By 1963 silver for teeth, electronics, and photography rose in price to approach the point where melting dollars and turning in bills for metal became profitable. So Congress dropped the farce of requiring part of our money to take the form of silver certificates. No longer can you demand silver from the government.

Two-dollar bills, long considered to be bad luck, were so-called "United States Notes"—remnants of the greenbacks used to finance the Civil War. After 1966 they ceased to be issued. Some five-dollar bills are also United States Notes. Occasionally you may run into a bill that says "Federal Reserve *Bank* Note" or even a "National Bank Note" containing the name of some nearby national bank; these too are being gradually retired from circulation.

[5] A Cleveland businessman wrote to the Treasury asking for some "lawful money" in return for a ten-dollar bill. He received two polite letters, but no satisfaction. Actually, since 1934 the old distinction between "legal tender" and other money has ceased to have meaning. Since then, if you bring a thousand dollars' worth of pennies to settle a tax bill or contract, they are as legally acceptable in the federal courts as anything else; earlier a creditor could have insisted on certain specified "legal tender."

[6] The courts also upheld a statute that invalidated contracts calling for payment in gold; only payment in terms of dollars was permitted. Otherwise, creditors would have made a 67 per cent profit on the revaluation and debtors would have lost 67 per cent. In 1960 President Eisenhower prohibited the holding

From the standpoint of understanding the nature of money, it is perhaps simpler that gold certificates and coins no longer exist. The modern student need not be misled, as were earlier generations of students, by some mystical belief that "gold backing" is what gives money its value. Certainly gold, as such, has little to do with the problem. Every expert knows that the popular conception "money has more value if it is exchangeable into gold" exactly reverses the true relation. If it were not that gold has some monetary uses, gold's value *as a metal* would be much less than it is today. We should have cheaper inlays and wedding rings, and South African and Russian miners would be poorer.[7]

The sensible reason why a staunch conservative today wants to go back to gold-coin money is not that he thinks gold is needed to give money its value. Rather, he knows that governmental actions can today strongly affect the value of money, and he is convinced that *governments cannot be trusted to refrain from abusing this power;* so he favors taking away from the Congress, the Executive, and the Federal Reserve System their power in these matters and prefers to put his trust in the vicissitudes of mine discoveries rather than in fallible or allegedly corrupt representative governments.

As we shall see in subsequent chapters and in the international discussions of Part Five, gold still does have a limited role to play in financing international transactions and in determining the worldwide trends of international reserves. Therein lies its true role in twentieth-century economics.

Limitation in the supply of money is the necessary condition if it is to have value. If currency is so unlimited in amount as to become practically a free good, people would have so much of it to spend as to bid up all prices, wages, and income sky-high. That is why constitutional powers over money and banking are never given to private groups but are always vested in government.

WHY CHECKABLE DEMAND DEPOSITS ARE CONSIDERED TO BE MONEY

Demand deposits   There is also a third category of what economists call money. This involves *bank deposits subject to checking on demand.*

If I have $1,000 in my checking account at the Cambridge Trust Company, that deposit can be regarded as money. Why? Because I can pay for purchases with checks drawn on it. The deposit is like any other medium of exchange, and, being payable on demand, it serves as a "standard of value," or "unit of account," in the same sense that $1,000 worth of quarters do; i.e., both the deposit and the quarters are convertible into standard money or cash at fixed terms, dollar for dollar and penny for penny.

Possessing the essential properties of money, bank demand deposits might just as well be counted as money. And they are.[8]

---

of gold by American citizens even abroad. As we shall see in Chapter 17, the 12 Federal Reserve Banks still hold gold certificates of a special type, but this is a mere bookkeeping operation.

[7] That gold affects prices only through its ability to *limit or to expand the volume of paper money and total spending* was overlooked by foolish European chancellors of the exchequer who, after World War I, tried to stop inflation by *accumulating* new gold reserves through the purchase of gold on the open market with newly *printed* money! Of course, the effect was just the opposite. Only after they had reversed the process and used their gold to buy up and burn outstanding paper money did they enjoy any success.

[8] My balance on deposit in the bank is usually called money—not the checks I write.

Bank deposits form three-fourths of our total money supply:

MONEY SUPPLY OF THE UNITED STATES (in billions of dollars)				
KINDS OF MONEY	MARCH, 1939	MARCH, 1946	MARCH, 1960	MARCH, 1969
Coin	$ 0.6	$ 1.3	$ 2.3	$ 5.0
Paper currency (outside of banks):				
Federal Reserve notes	4.3	23.9	26.8	38.8
Silver certificates and				
U.S. notes	1.6	2.3	2.4	0.2
Other currency (largely in				
process of being retired)	0.3	0.6	0.2	0.2
	6.2	26.8	29.4	39.2
Bank money:				
Demand deposits of all banks				
(adjusted to exclude government				
deposits, etc.)	26.1	76.2	108.8	149.8
Total M_1	$32.9	$104.3	$140.5	$194.0
Time and saving deposits (includes				
mutual savings banks, postal				
savings, savings and loan agencies,				
certificates of deposit)	30.0	59.1	158.2	419.4
Total M_2	$62.9	$163.4	$298.7	$613.4
U.S. government bonds held by				
individuals and business				
(excluding banks, insurance				
companies, etc.)	12.0	83.2	84.3	94.2
Total "near-money" and money	$74.9	$246.6	$383.0	$707.6

TABLE 15-1. If to coin, currency, and demand deposits, we also add time and saving deposits, we get a broader and more rapidly growing concept of money—often called M_2 in contrast to M_1. (Source: *Federal Reserve Bulletin.*)

Actually, as was noted in the discussion of money in Chapter 3, bank money is quantitatively more important than currency because most transactions are made by check. The convenience of checks for mailing, for paying the exact sum of money due, for providing a receipt in the form of the canceled check voucher, for protecting against loss when stolen or misplaced (while unendorsed or, for that matter, endorsed)—all these advantages are obvious and explain the widespread use of bank money.

Table 15-1 illustrates the quantitative importance of the three components of money: coin, currency, and demand deposits. The total of these is called M_1, money as narrowly-defined.

TIME DEPOSITS, LIQUID ASSETS, AND OTHER NEAR-MONEY

Along with the total of money narrowly-defined, M_1, Table 15-1 also shows the total of money broadly-defined, M_2. Included in this broader definition of money are all kinds of saving and time deposits, whether in commercial banks, mutual savings banks, savings and loan associations, credit unions, etc. Although you cannot write checks on such time deposits, you can usually cash them in on short notice.

Suppose you have $10,000 on demand deposit and your brother has $5,000 on time deposit and $5,000 on demand deposit. Will your saving and consumption schedules be very different ones? At equal incomes, is he likely to save a much larger percentage than you? Probably not; and that is why M_2 is important. Time or savings deposits—in commercial banks, mutual savings banks, and federal savings and loan associations—have gained mightily on demand deposits in recent decades.

Because it is difficult to draw a hard-and-fast line at any point in the chain of things that do have a direct bearing on spending, the exact definition of M, the money supply, is partly a matter of taste rather than scientific necessity.

A century ago, demand deposits would not have been included in M. Today economists would include demand deposits, since even the most stubborn adherent of the old narrow concept has to admit that the existence of checking accounts does *economize* on the use of currency and thus acts much like an increase in the effective amount of currency. And a growing number of economists would argue along the same lines for inclusion of interest-bearing time deposits in the measurements of the money supply.[9]

Economists are not all agreed on nomenclature in this field. Many would go so far as to append to M_1 and M_2 a further category of liquid-wealth items called "near-money."[10] At the least, they would include in near-money the total of government bonds which anyone could present for redemption or sell for cash in the open market (albeit not at a stable price predictable long in advance). These near-money items have many of the properties of money. True, you do not pay your monthly expenses directly with government bonds, and so we hesitate to call such an item "money." Still, the fact that you have such an easily cashable asset means that your current spending habits are probably affected in much the same way as they would be if you owned a larger bank deposit instead of the government bonds.

Table 15-1 shows that all the different kinds of money are now many times greater than before World War II. For the most part, this book will follow the most common practice and define the total money supply thus:

M is the sum of coin and currency in circulation outside the banks, plus checkable demand deposits (after various routine adjustments have been made in this magnitude). Along with this narrow definition of M (which we may call M_1), it is sometimes useful to work with a broader definition (called M_2), which includes time and saving deposits in addition to coin, currency, and demand deposits.

See Fig. 15-2 for the more rapid growth of the broad measure M_2 in recent years.

---

[9] Some scholars have even attempted to include government bonds in money, rather than give them zero weight and exclude them; such writers prefer to give them some fractional weight and add them into a total called "effective" money supply, M_3. Because data on time deposits in commercial banks are easier to collect than those in S&Ls and mutual savings banks, we shall follow the custom of many scholars and often include only commercial-bank time deposits in our charts of M_2.

[10] It would not be illogical to subtract out from people's liquid assets their current liabilities (charge accounts, installment loans, etc.). Along with income, perhaps their resulting "net worth" would be the single most important determinant of their spending.

Both consumer prices and money supply show similar long-term upward trends:

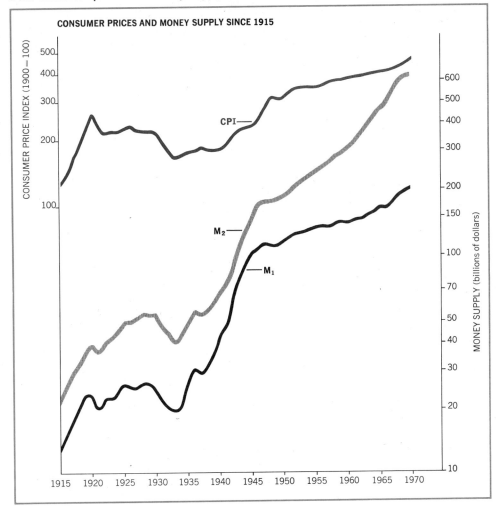

CONSUMER PRICES AND MONEY SUPPLY SINCE 1915

FIG. 15-2. Both prices and the money supply show generally similar movements. But money supply has grown faster than prices in this era of rising real output. (Sources: U.S. Department of Commerce, *Federal Reserve Bulletin;* Milton Friedman and Anna J. Schwartz, *A Monetary History of the United States, 1867–1960,* Princeton University Press, Princeton, N.J., 1963.)

B. THE DEMAND FOR MONEY AND THE QUANTITY THEORY

What are the functions of money? Here are some old ones from Chapter 3 and some new ones:

1. Money is a *medium of exchange* enabling us to transact our national income and product without recourse to hopelessly inefficient barter.

2. Money is the *unit of account* in which we express prices for current transactions, and also for future or deferred transactions (such as when I borrow $1,000 today and agree to pay back $1,200 three years from now).

3. Money is a safe *way of holding* at least part of one's *wealth*—safe against the ups and downs inherent in stocks, land, homes, and bonds. When all these are going down in price, the canny hoarder of money is the most successful speculator in the community. (When prices rise, however, many money holders suffer.)

4. Money holding is a necessary *precaution* against having a sudden expense occur or an unexpected delay in a receipt due from someone else. Similarly, it enables one to take advantage of a bargain in goods or in securities that might suddenly come up.

All these functions are worth paying for. And we each do incur a cost in holding a coin, a bill, or a demand deposit—namely, the *sacrificed interest and profit yield* that might be obtained from purchase of earning assets.

General Electric works just as hard to keep down its unnecessary cash as it does to keep down its unnecessary steel inventory and wastage. The business manager of a famous cartoonist was aghast to find that he had kept $120,000 idle in a demand deposit, earning no interest for years, and all merely because he never read his mail!

It is clear from the above that there are two main motives for holding money: (1) for the convenience of ordinary *transactions* needed at each level of income, and (2) to fill a prudent *precautionary* need arising from the uncertainties of safety and return from other forms of wealth, and the uncertainties of timing of expense outpayments and receipt inpayments.

At the turn of the century Alfred Marshall in Cambridge, England, and Irving Fisher in Yale summarized the factors involved in the demand for money thus:

Demand for money: The higher their annual incomes, the more dollars of business people will want to transact: with various allowances for economies of scale, men hold M at any time about in proportion to their *income* rate per year or month. This *transaction demand* for money will be shifted downward a little when the interest rates offered on good bonds, savings deposits, and other close money substitutes rise. At higher interest you will economize on your cash balance, making each dollar turn over more rapidly.

Men also hold M as a precautionary store of wealth, not wanting to put all their eggs in the basket of risky assets and wanting to be prepared for bargains or sudden expenses. This *precautionary* (or "asset") *demand* for money will be much affected by factors other than income: total wealth; level of sacrificed interest and profit yields; optimism, pessimism, and plain uncertainty about the future; expected changes in prices of goods and assets and expected changes in interest rates—all the speculative elements that any investments depend on.

The elements in the second paragraph of this summary are in Marshall and Fisher, but were not much emphasized until the 1930s, when Keynes and practical bankers noted that transaction demand could not account for massive changes in cash holdings. The pre-1930 discussions emphasized the M-and-income link by using the concept of "velocity of circulation of money," and to this we now turn.

VELOCITY OF CIRCULATION OF MONEY

It is historical fact that as dollar NNP has grown, so has M. With M now six times as large as before World War II, dollar NNP is even more than six times as large as its earlier figure. Nor is this merely history. If NNP grows from its present level of a trillion dollars to reach 2 trillion dollars a decade from now, the betting odds are that M will be nearly double its present amount then—a fair bet even before we know whether changes in M will be "cause" of changes in NNP or "effect."

Why should there be any connection? M is a stock magnitude, something you can measure at an instant of time like any other balance-sheet asset. NNP is a flow of dollar income *per year*, something that you can measure only from income statements that refer to the passage of time between two dates.

A new concept can be introduced to describe the Fisher-Marshall ratios between two such different magnitudes: it is called the "velocity of circulation of money" per year and is written as V.

Definition of velocity: **The rate at which the stock of money is turning over per year to consummate income transactions is called the velocity of circulation of money (or more exactly, the *income* velocity).**

If the stock of money is turning over very slowly, so that its rate of dollar income spending per year is low, V will be low. If people hold less money at each instant of time relative to the rate of NNP flow (price of apples × apples + price of oranges × oranges + . . .), then V will be high.

The size of V will tend to rise with interest rates. Also, V can change over time with changes in financial institutions, habits, attitudes, expectations, and relative distributions of M among different kinds of institutions and income classes; but these changes in V need not be abrupt, volatile, or completely unpredictable.

In every case, this formal definition of the velocity of circulation of money holds:

$$V \equiv \frac{\text{NNP}}{M} \equiv \frac{p_1 q_1 + p_2 q_2 + \cdots}{M} \equiv \frac{\text{sum } pq}{M} \equiv \frac{PQ}{M}$$

Here P stands for the average price level and goes up and down with an index of the price level, while Q stands for real (as distinct from current dollar) national product and has to be computed statistically by the mentioned process of "deflating" NNP with a price index.

Here is a helpful example. Table 15-1 indicates an M by 1970 of about $200 billion. NNP and GNP are indicated by then at annual rates of about $920 and $1,000 billion. So 920 per year divided by 200 gives us an income velocity of about 4.6 per year. This expression means that each unit of money was used for NNP transactions between four and five times a year; or putting this in an equivalent way, at any one time during the year people in the economy were holding money that amounted to a bit less than 3 months' average income.[11] (How do we similarly calculate GNP velocity? The ratio $1,000 per year/$200 calculates it at about 5 per year.)

---

[11]Economists sometimes calculate V for *all* transactions including transfers, intermediate goods, and everything. From recent statistics of bank checking transactions (or debits), one finds that urban bank deposits outside of New York City turn over some 47 times a year, and New York City deposits turn over some 140 times a year. Plainly, such overall velocity figures are much greater than income velocity.

THE QUANTITY EQUATION OF EXCHANGE: AN IDENTITY

After economists have invented the concept of velocity of circulation of money, they can rearrange its formal definition to get a new identity called the "quantity equation of exchange":

$$MV \equiv PQ$$

This comes merely from shifting M from the denominator of our last definition's right-hand side over to the numerator of the other side. By definition of V, the left-hand side in this new equation is equal to NNP, the rate of current national income or product per year. But the right-hand side, by virtue of what we have already defined P and Q to be, also is definitionally the same thing as NNP.

EXAMPLE: If there were only a single good in the NNP, a billion baskets of bread selling at a price of $5 each, then NNP $\equiv PQ = $5 billion per year; when there is more than one commodity, we sum all such $p \times q$ products; and if all their q's stayed unchanged and all their p's doubled, then the average price level as denoted by P would double, naturally giving us a $10- rather than $5-billion NNP.[12]

All the definitional equations have been written with the three-bar identity symbol rather than with the more common two-bar equality symbol. This is to drive home the fact that they are what logicians call a "tautology"—statements which by themselves tell us nothing about reality but which *would hold true by definition* even if the United States reverted to barter, or if its M halved while its NNP grew tenfold. (Although it is important to remember that the equation of exchange is such a tautology, it is not legitimate to infer from this fact that it must therefore be useless. It may, or may not, be a useful way of separating out for individual analysis the factors apt to lead to empirical relations which do best describe actual economic life. Subsequent chapters will show that careful description of income determination by $C + I + G$ schedules and how they are interrelated by changes in banking policy can *also* be expressed in terms of the magnitudes in the equation of exchange, and vice versa.)

THE QUANTITY THEORY OF MONEY AND PRICES: A HYPOTHESIS

The crude Quantity Theory   If 1970 M is six times 1939 M, then an adherent of what can be called the "crude Quantity Theory of Money and Prices" would have to predict that the 1970 price level P should be almost exactly six times 1939 P. The fact that prices have less than tripled in that period would be a refutation of this crude notion that the price level moves in direct proportion to the money supply.

Arithmetically, the crude Quantity Theory might be written as $P = kM$, where k is a positive proportionality constant that depends on units used; thus, if P and M are measured by index

---

[12] Some find the following "explanation" of this necessary equality helpful. Every income transaction involves sale receipts equal to $p \times q$, which leads to the PQ totals on the right. But it is M that is involved in such transactions. How much in a year? The stock M times its average velocity per year. Thus, value of money (that passes hands) equals value (*both* of what has been sold *and* bought), and the two sides must therefore be the same.

numbers which were 100 in the same base year, k could be replaced by 1.0 or omitted. Note that this relation is not intended to be an irrefutable definitional identity, but rather a useful empirical relationship about k's constancy.

The idea behind the crude Quantity Theory is simple. If the government effects a thousandfold increase in M, then one can predict that there will be a galloping inflation in which P rises a thousandfold—or, more cautiously, at least somewhere between 500-fold and 2,000-fold. Crude as this notion is, there is some usefulness to it. Thus when the head of the German central bank denied that its printing carloads of currency had anything to do with the 1920–1923 trillionfold increase in prices, his statement was nonsensical. If he had said, "I am just a civil servant, forced, by the clamor of the populace in a defeated nation with grave external and internal disorganization, to take part in an upward race between P and M"—if he had said this, we could feel sorry for him. But who can seriously deny the elementary fact that a vastly larger bidding of German marks for a limited supply of goods had to send prices expressed in marks skyward?

Money differs basically from ordinary goods like wheat or steel. We want wheaten bread for its own sake. We want money only for the work it does in buying us wheat or steel. If, in 1923, all German prices are a trillion times what they were in 1920, it is natural to want about a trillion times as much M as in 1920. Therein lies the valid core of the crude Quantity Theory. But we must be wary of extrapolating it to real-life cases where all Ps have not changed in the same balanced proportions.

Rudimentary as it is, then, the crude Quantity Theory linking P directly to M is useful to describe periods of hyperinflation and various long-term trends in prices, such as those in Spain and Europe after New World treasure was discovered.

Since galloping inflation can put an intolerable strain on a democratic society, it is well to preach the crude Quantity Theory in season and out of season—not because in its crudest form it is in season very often, but because it is so urgently needed in those disorganized times when its message is in season.

A sophisticated Quantity Theory   Few people still subscribe to the crude Quantity Theory. But we should not use its inadequacies to damn the valuable truth that money can have important effects on macroeconomic magnitudes such as investment, employment, production, and prices.

The next few chapters will show how *monetary policy* does have an important influence on the *total of spending*—on the $C + I + G$ intersections of GNP. This analysis can be translated quite easily into the language of V and M, even though it was not fashionable to do so a couple of decades back. Since there has been a revival of interest in the quantity theory by a number of competent American economists in recent years, it is worth taking an eclectic approach here and reviewing the fundaments of a sophisticated quantity-theory approach, leaving until later a more extensive reconciliation of the various approaches.

The proof of the pudding is in the eating, and the test of all theories is their correspondence with the facts. Figure 15-2 showed back on page 263 that consumer prices and the supply of money have both generally grown, but by no means in perfect concordance.

Economists such as Chicago's Milton Friedman are not surprised to find M growing sixfold while P scarcely triples; for they believe that only in time periods when real output remains roughly the same—say, at a high-employment level—can one expect M and P to be directly related. They expect M and GNP (or PQ) to be related. This belief is based upon the hypothesis that the velocity of circulation V can be predicted to be reasonably constant, or if not constant, is at least subject to predictable changes.

While it is a fact that NNP has climbed much faster than M since 1939, this rise in velocity has been a gradual one and perhaps one that might have been expected from the fact that 1939 was still a depressed year and still a time of very low interest rates and abnormally low V.

Historically, one observes that V exhibited a downward trend in the pre-1945 long run, moving down somewhat as real income has grown. The short-run cyclical swings in V are quite the opposite: when production and interest rates have gone up, V has tended also to have a short-run rise; when output has fallen in the short run, V has fallen too.

A sophisticated quantity theorist cannot be accused of believing that V is a fundamental constant of nature. What he does believe is that controlling the behavior of M *will help much* to control NNP, for the reason that the resulting changes in V will either be so small or so predictable as to make one confident that dollar NNP will still move *in the same direction* as M. Qualitatively, this is in agreement with almost any modern theory of income determination, and the only possible argument concerns the confidence with which one can predict the quantitative potency of effects on NNP of changes in M in comparison with other stimuli, such as fiscal policy and external investment swings.[13]

So, from every point of view, the discussions in the ensuing chapters—how the Federal Reserve pumps reserves into the banking system to cause the commercial banks to create new demand-deposit M, how a central bank such as the Federal Reserve itself operates, how monetary policy fits with income determination and with stabilizing fiscal policies—are of tremendous importance.

[13]There is general agreement, too, that whenever the dollar GNP gets pushed too high, there will be a strong tendency for P to rise. Also there is some agreement that inflexibilities in our mixed economy can keep wages and prices up in slack times; if so, *employment* and *production* will drop with the total of dollar GNP rather than having the drop in dollar PQ simply transmit its effects to lower P. There is still some controversy concerning the importance of a *cost-push* mechanism making for a price creep, as against inflationary effects of *excess dollar demand* alone. Later we shall attempt to appraise the measure of truth in both views. [It may be mentioned here that the *crude* Quantity Theory would be correct, if in the following rearrangement of the tautological equation of exchange $P \equiv (V/Q)M$, the expression in parentheses were a strict constant. Thus, if both V and Q changed little, or if their changes were always largely self-canceling, the crude theory would be correct. But once scholars agree that V may change appreciably when the economy goes from a 1929 high-interest prosperity to a 1939 low-interest depression, and that Q may fall from a full-employment 1929 level to a level that is far below full employment in some later year, they realize that a more sophisticated theory of money, production, interest rates and prices must be studied. A rather crude form of rejection of the significance of M was provided by the Radcliffe Committee Report published in 1959 by the British government. After arguing (correctly) that PQ is affected by over-all "liquidity" and bears no *simple* proportionality to M, it incorrectly inferred that induced changes in V are as likely as not to offset fully any contrived changes in M. The presumption in *all* modern theories is that a continued rise in M *will* definitely tend to expand PQ. Note the logical fallacy in Radcliffe's argument: "'Money alone matters' is false; *ergo*, 'money doesn't matter.'"]

SUMMARY

A. PRICES AND THE MONEY SUPPLY

1   It is unrealistic to expect that expansions in investment and other spending will have effects solely on employment and output. Changes in price levels must be expected as well. The effects and causes of a general rise in prices and wages (i.e., inflation) and a general fall in prices (i.e., deflation) are vital.

2   Historically, prices have shown their greatest swings in times of war. But in this century the trend in prices seems to have been more of a one-way climb: the absence of a drop in prices following World War II and in recent recessions is perhaps a sign that modern mixed economies are no longer likely to tolerate lengthy periods of unemployment, soft business conditions, and falling prices.

3   Inflations and deflations are never of the balanced type in which all prices and wages move in the same percentage relation, with no one helped and no one hurt by the process. Inflations typically favor debtors, profit seekers, and risk-taking speculators. Unforeseen inflation hurts creditors, fixed-income classes, pensioners, and conservative and timid investors. The old rather than the young are its prime victims.

4   Aside from redistributional effects of inflation out of a fixed level of production, mild inflations like those found throughout most of capitalism's history have been regarded as being a little more *likely* to keep employment high and business brisk than mild deflations do. But the cause of the inflation and the degree to which it is anticipated may make a difference. And the threat that a mild creep of prices could break into a trot or gallop shows that complacency about price rises could be harmful.

    If the processes were *foreseen* and steady, there would not be much difference between three possible long-term patterns that various economists favor: (1) steady prices, with money and real wages rising with productivity; (2) gently rising prices, with money wages rising even faster than real wages and productivity; (3) slowly falling prices, with money wages constant and real wages rising as every consumer's dollar buys more and more goods—a pattern perhaps not feasible in rigid mixed economies.

5   In addition to coin, currency, and demand deposits—whose sum is the money supply M—there are also very important other liquid-asset items: time or savings deposits (which pay interest and are de facto withdrawable at short notice, and which many economists include in a broad definition of money, M_2), "near-money" such as government bonds (which anyone can quickly liquidate into cash, at a price that depends on market forces at the time). However defined, M has increased mightily over the decades.

B. THE DEMAND FOR MONEY AND THE QUANTITY THEORY

6   The demand for money consists of a *transactions* demand importantly related to income, and a *precautionary* (or asset) demand much dependent on interest and profit rates, and

on wealth, volatile expectations, risk aversion, and speculative price expectations. (Chapter 18 will relate the demand for M to so-called "liquidity preference.")

7 The (income) velocity of circulation of money is defined as the ratio of dollar NNP flow to the stock of M. While V is definitely not a constant, its movements are subject to some regularity and predictability; and from its

$$V \equiv \frac{\text{NNP}}{M} \equiv \frac{PQ}{M}$$

definition comes the quantity-theory-of-exchange *identity*

$$MV \equiv PQ$$

8 The crude Quantity Theory of Money and Prices regarded P as almost strictly proportional to M. Useful as this view is in hyperinflation and for certain long-term trends, few would today uphold it in this crude form. It is generally agreed that action by the government and banks to affect the supply of money, its availability to investor borrowers, and the interest cost of such borrowings can have important effects on the total of *consumption + investment + government* spending, and thus on prices and wage levels. Both subscribers to a sophisticated quantity theory and national-income theorists will attach importance to the next chapters on banking and fiscal policy.

QUESTIONS FOR DISCUSSION

1 If sure of inflation ahead, what might you do to protect yourself? List some of the happenings that accompany galloping and mild inflation.

2 Explain what is meant by "near-money" and how it got its name.

3 If we printed and spent $100 billion in new greenbacks, what do you think would happen to prices? Is there some truth, then, to the crude Quantity Theory? Differentiate between the crude and sophisticated quantity theorists in terms of $MV \equiv PQ$.

4 Show that the Marshall-Fisher-Keynes summary implies nonconstant V.

5 In the last 25 years V has risen in almost every year. Could the fact that a bond pays 8 per cent in 1970 as against $3\frac{1}{2}$ per cent in 1945 help explain this rise in V? Why?

Review your understanding of the following concepts:

inflation, hyperinflation
redistribution and employment effects
  of price-level trends
real versus money wage
deflation and technological cost-price
  reduction

fractional coins, token money
demand versus time deposits
M_1, M_2, near-money
velocity definition
equation of exchange, $MV \equiv PQ$
crude Quantity Theory, $P \equiv kM$

The Banking System and Deposit Creation

. . . One rule which woe betides the banker who fails to heed it, . . . Never lend any money to anybody unless they don't need it.
OGDEN NASH

The importance of bank deposits as part of the community's money supply has been established. This chapter continues with two distinct topics. First, we examine briefly the important facts and functionings of the modern banking system, showing how the present-day commercial bank gradually began to keep only "fractional cash reserves" against its deposits. Second, we see just how the banking system "manufactures" bank deposits—the most important component of our money supply.

A. NATURE AND FUNCTIONING OF THE MODERN BANKING SYSTEM

Today there are over 13,000 banks in the United States that accept checking deposits. Only about a third of these are national banks, the rest being under state supervision. All national banks are automatically members of the Federal Reserve System, and in addition most of the larger state institutions are also members. Although this still leaves more than half of all the banks not members of the Federal Reserve System, they are sufficiently small in size so that their deposits are only about one-sixth of the total.[1] Moreover, since 1933, almost all commercial banks, state or national, have had their deposits insured by the FDIC (Federal Deposit Insurance Corporation). In 1970, the FDIC insured each deposit up to the sum of $20,000.

Unlike England or Canada, where a few large banks with hundreds of branches are dominant, the United States has tended to rely upon many independent, relatively small, localized units.[2] Until fairly recently, almost anyone

---

[1] Many state banks that are not full-fledged members nevertheless do belong to the Federal Reserve clearinghouse system and can use this service in handling checks of other banks.

[2] In California, the Bank of America has numerous branches all over the state, just as the Chase Manhattan Bank has branches all over New York City, and just as a few holding companies control many banks in Minnesota and Wisconsin. But by and large, the old American distrust of "big finance" has caused us to

could open a bank with relatively limited capital. It is not surprising, therefore, that the American history of bank failures and losses to depositors used to be a grievous one. Indeed, only about one-half the banks in existence in 1915 are still solvent; even in prosperous 1929, long before the Great Depression, no less than 659 banks with estimated total deposits of $200 million failed. Since establishment of the FDIC, a bank failure has become a rare—but not impossible!—event.

The primary economic function of commercial banks is *to hold demand deposits and to honor checks drawn upon them*—**in short to provide us, the economy, with the most important component of the money supply.**

A second important function of commercial banks is to lend money to merchants, homeowners, farmers, and industrialists; and to hold government and municipal bonds.

Banks also perform a variety of other functions in competition with other financial institutions. They usually hold savings or time deposits. Unlike demand deposits, these pay interest; although theoretically withdrawable only after 30 days' notice or more, they are in fact usually withdrawn (by their owners) on demand. (Recall that some economists include saving and time deposits in a broad M_2 definition of the money supply.) In this function, the commercial banks are, in parts of the country, competing with the so-called "mutual savings banks," which accept only time deposits; almost anywhere in the country the commercial banks are competing with cooperative building and loan societies and savings and loan associations. In selling money orders or travelers' checks, the banks are competing with the post office, Western Union, and American Express. In handling "trusts" and estates, they overlap with investment counselors and other fiduciaries. Even in lending money to individuals and businessmen, the banks are competing with finance companies and with so-called "factors" who provide corporations with working capital. In buying bonds, mortgages, and securities, they compete with insurance companies and other investors.[3] Large banks even do computing and counseling for corporations.

In summary, the commercial banks are by no means our only financial institutions. By definition, however, they are the only organizations able to provide "bank money," i.e., *checkable demand deposits* that can be conveniently used as a medium of exchange. Therein lies their primary economic importance. Their second, related function is that of credit: they help manufacture and transfer short-term credit for businesses and families; they make long-term mortgage loans; and despite the older view that banks should lend only seasonally, they increasingly provide intermediate-term credit through "term loans" of over a year's duration.

CREATION OF THE FEDERAL RESERVE SYSTEM

In 1913, the Federal Reserve Act was passed by Congress and signed by President Wilson. It sprang from the panic of 1907, with its alarming epidemic of bank failures: the country was fed up once and for all with the anarchy of unstable private banking. After half

---

hamper multiple-branch banking regardless of cost-saving efficiencies, to discourage bank mergers, and to limit nonbanking activities of one-bank holding companies.
[3] Massachusetts, Connecticut, and New York savings banks even sell life insurance.

a dozen years' agitation and discussion by both parties, the Federal Reserve System was formed—in face of strong banker opposition.

The country was cut into 12 Federal Reserve districts, each with its own Federal Reserve Bank (headquartered in New York, Chicago, San Francisco, Philadelphia, Boston, Cleveland, St. Louis, Kansas City, Atlanta, Richmond, Dallas, and Minneapolis). Their initial capital was subscribed by the commercial bank members of the Federal Reserve System, and so *nominally* each Federal Reserve Bank is a corporation owned by the "member banks." All are coordinated by the seven-member Board of Governors of the Federal Reserve System in Washington—popularly called the "Federal Reserve Board."

There is also a 12-man Federal Open Market Committee, with five representatives of the 12 districts as well as the seven-man Board of Governors. This has, with pardonable exaggeration, been called "the most powerful group of private citizens in America," for as we shall see, the Open Market Committee administers the single most powerful weapon of modern monetary policy.

The present-day realities of the Federal Reserve System can be summarized as follows.

The Federal Reserve Board in Washington, together with the 12 regional Federal Reserve Banks, constitutes our American "central bank." Every modern country has such a central bank, as, for example, the Bank of England, the Bank of France, and the Deutsche Bundesbank of Germany.

A central bank is a bank that the government sets up to help handle its transactions, to coordinate and control the commercial banks, and, most important, to help *control the nation's money supply* and credit conditions.

Although nominally a corporation owned by the commercial banks that are members of the Federal Reserve System, in fact the Federal Reserve (or the "Fed" as it is universally called by the financial press, with no disrespect intended) is a *public* agency. It is directly responsible to Congress; and whenever any conflict arises between its making a profit and the public interest, it acts according to the public interest without question. Its member banks receive fixed and nominal dividends from it; but so profitable is the Fed by virtue of its legal privilege that its dollars of profit above a certain level go *entirely* to the United States government. The Reserve authorities, meaning by this the regional and Washington officials, never think of its stockholders, the member commercial banks, as dictators of their actions, but instead act as a public body. (So the men on the Federal Open Market Committee are *not* private citizens even though their paychecks do not come from the government.)

Although the President appoints Federal Reserve Governors for 14-year terms and appoints their Chairman, the Board considers that its allegiance is primarily to Congress and not to the executive branch. Here is a case where the American practice is different from that of most countries. E.g., in Britain, the Bank of England has not only been nationalized, but well understands that it must in the last analysis be subservient to the will of the Cabinet, with a right to protest publicly but a duty to coordinate its policies with those of the Cabinet.

Prior to an "accord" signed in 1951 by the Treasury Department and the Fed, there

Demand deposits are important bank liabilities:

CONSOLIDATED BALANCE SHEET OF ALL MEMBER BANKS, JANUARY 1, 1969 (in billions of dollars)			
ASSETS		**LIABILITIES**	
Reserves	$ 27.2	Capital accounts	$ 30.1
Loans and discounts	220.3	Demand deposits	191.7
U.S. government		Time deposits	163.7
securities	47.9	Other liabilities	27.0
Other securities	56.9		
Other assets	60.2		
Total	$412.5	Total	$412.5

TABLE 16-1.   Reserves and demand deposits are the two key items of interest to our later economic analysis. Reserves are this large primarily because of legal requirements and not to provide against expected withdrawals. (Source: *Federal Reserve Bulletin*.)

was considerable pressure by the President and the Treasury on the actions of the Fed. In recent years the Fed has generally (but not always!) cooperated with the President; ultimately it feels its primary responsibility is to Congress.

BANKING AS A BUSINESS

Banking is a business much like any other business. The commercial bank is a relatively simple business concern. A bank provides certain services for its customers (depositors and borrowers) and in return receives payments from them in one form or another. It tries to earn a profit for its stock owners.

A member bank's balance sheet shows certain assets, certain liabilities, and certain capital ownership. Except for minor rearrangements, the bank's published balance sheet looks, on the whole, much like the balance sheet of any other business, and rather simpler than most. The only peculiar feature about the consolidated bank balance sheet shown in Table 16-1 is the fact that such a large portion of its liabilities are payable *on demand*; i.e., they are deposits subject to checking. And the vital reserves upon which its deposits depend are, as we shall see, created and controlled by the central bank.

This fact is intriguing to economists because we choose to call such demand liabilities money; but to the banker it is a familiar condition which has long since been taken for granted. He knows well that, although it would be possible for every depositor suddenly to decide to withdraw all his money from the bank on the same day, the probability of this is quite remote. Each day, as some people withdraw their money, others normally make deposits tending to cancel the withdrawals. In a growing community new deposits more than offset the withdrawals from an average bank.

This, however, need not be strictly true at any one moment, in any one day, or in any one week. By chance alone the amount of withdrawals might exceed deposits for some period of time—just as a coin may land with heads turned up rather than tails for a consecutive number of tosses. For this reason, the banker would voluntarily keep a little cash—but only a little—handy in his vaults and perhaps as a "reserve deposit" at the nearby Federal Reserve Bank.

HOW BANKS DEVELOPED OUT OF GOLDSMITH ESTABLISHMENTS

All these facts are so much taken for granted by every modern banker that he is hardly aware of them. But it was not always so. According to superficial but useful history, commercial banking began with the ancient goldsmiths, who developed the practice of storing people's gold and valuables for safekeeping. At first such establishments were simply like parcel checkrooms or warehouses. The depositor left his gold for safekeeping, was given a receipt, later presented that receipt, paid a small fee for safekeeping and got back his gold.

Quite obviously, however, money is wanted only for what it will buy, not for its own sake. Money has an anonymous quality, so that one dollar is just as good as another, and one piece of pure gold as good as another. The goldsmiths soon found it more convenient *not* to have to tag the gold belonging to any one individual so as to be able to give to him upon request exactly the same piece of gold that he had left. Instead, the customer was quite willing to accept a receipt for an amount of gold or money *of a given value*, even though it was not the identical particle of matter that he actually left. This "anonymity" is important. Therein lies a significant difference between today's bank and a checkroom or warehouse. If I check my bag at Kennedy Airport and later see someone walking down the street with that same suitcase, I call my lawyer and sue the airline. If I mark my initials on a ten-dollar bill, deposit it in my bank account, and later notice it in the hands of a stranger, I have no grievance against the bank management. They have only agreed to pay me on demand any old $10.

But let us return to the goldsmith establishments, which are supposed to typify the first embryonic commercial banks. What would balance sheets of a typical establishment look like? Perhaps like Table 16-2.

We assume the company has long since dropped its activities as a smith and is principally occupied with storing people's money for safekeeping. Over past time, $1 million has been deposited in its vaults, and this whole sum it holds as a cash asset. To balance this asset, there is a current deposit liability of the same amount. Actually, such a business need have no other assets (except the negligible value of its office space and vaults). But its owners could have—on the side, so to speak—subscribed $50,000 of capital to be lent out at interest or buy securities like stocks or bonds. On the asset side this is shown under the heading Loans and Investments; it is balanced on the right-hand side by a like sum in the Capital and Surplus account.

At this primitive stage, the bank would be of no particular interest to the economist. These investment and capital items have nothing to do with the bank's deposits; if all the bank's loans and investments should go sour and become worthless, the loss would fall completely on the stockholders, who have agreed to take that risk in the hope of making a profit. Every depositor could still be paid off in full *out of the 100 per cent cash reserves* held by the bank. The bank would still cover its overhead and clerical expenses by making its customers pay storage charges. These would presumably vary with the length of time the customer left his money for safekeeping, the average amount of his money requiring safekeeping, and the num-

The first goldsmith bank held 100 per cent cash against its demand deposits:

BALANCE SHEET OF EARLY BANK			
ASSETS		LIABILITIES AND NET WORTH	
Cash reserves	$1,000,000	Capital and surplus	$ 50,000
Loans and investments	50,000	Demand-deposit liability	1,000,000
Total	$1,050,000	Total	$1,050,000

TABLE 16-2.

ber of times the turnover of his account made a clerk wait on him and keep various records.

Economists could ignore such a bank's operations. The bank money[4]—the demand deposits created jointly by the bank's willingness to accept a demand obligation and the customer's willingness to hold a deposit—would *just offset* the amount of ordinary money (currency or coin) placed in the bank's safe and withdrawn from active circulation. The process would be of no more interest than if the public decided to convert some dollar bills into an equivalent amount of dimes. One says that the banking system has a *neutral* effect on spending and prices—not adding or subtracting from *total M* or its velocity.

MODERN FRACTIONAL-RESERVE BANKING

Let us return to our early goldsmith-banker to see how modern banks gradually evolved. If he were an alert fellow, he would soon notice that, although his deposits are payable on demand, they are not all withdrawn together. He would soon learn that, although 100 per cent reserves are necessary if the bank is to be liquidated and all depositors are to be paid off in full, such reserves are not at all necessary if his bank is a "going concern." As already seen, new deposits tend to balance withdrawals. Only a little till money, perhaps less than 2 per cent, normally seems needed in the form of cash.[5]

At first he probably thought this discovery too good to be true. Then perhaps he recalled the story of a rival bank whose dishonest clerk ran off with 95 per cent of its cash reserve—which was never discovered for a dozen years. No one ever had occasion to go to the back rooms of the vault because all withdrawals were financed by recently deposited money held in the front vaults.

We can imagine our intelligent banker—at first cautiously—beginning to acquire bonds and other earning assets with some of the cash entrusted to his care. Everything works out all right: depositors are still paid off on demand, and the bank has made some extra earnings. Gradually, the banker no longer feels it is necessary to conceal from his depositors what he is doing. If a depositor complains, the banker retorts, "Your money is safe. If you don't like my way of doing business, you are at liberty to withdraw your funds. Besides, haven't you noticed that the new method of fractional cash reserves has enabled me to *lower my service charges to you?* Also, it has enabled me to give a helping hand to our local businessmen who need more capital to buy new tools, buildings, and inventories. Such capital formation benefits consumers because they get better goods for lower prices. It also creates jobs for workers."

Little wonder, therefore, that banks should want to maximize their profits by putting

[4]The economist would consider the demand deposit as money as soon as the custom grew up for depositors to pay for the goods they bought by giving the storekeeper a little note to the bank saying, "Mr. Goldsmith, pay to the order of Sears, Roebuck $2.99, (signed) John Q. Doe." In other words, as soon as the use and acceptability of checks became customary.

[5]If the bank could pay off its depositors with one of its own checks (or as in former times with one of its paper bank notes), it might not have to keep any till money at all. By judiciously limiting the rate at which it was making loans and investments, the bank could ensure that the checks it received from other banks plus cash deposited were just matched by its outpayments. An occasional temporary outward drain of funds could be met by permitting the bank to pay by check what it owed to other banks for the few hours or days until some part of its asset portfolio could be liquidated or until it contracted its operations so as to get a surplus of inpayments over outpayments.

most of the money deposited with them in *earning assets* and keeping only *fractional* cash reserves against deposits.

Indeed, as long as business confidence remains high and bank managers are judicious in their loans and investments, there is no reason why the bank should keep much more than 2 per cent cash reserves against deposits.

But what if the banker makes a mistake in his investments? Since nobody's judgment is perfect and all investments involve some element of speculative risk, this is certainly a possibility to reckon with. To lessen the chance of extreme losses, the banker can try to diversify his investments, not putting all his eggs in one basket. Besides, a conservative bank will have a considerable amount of capital put up by the stockholders. For example, capital stock may have been issued equal to 10 per cent of demand deposits. Then, even if all the bank's assets are in earning investments rather than in nonearning cash, depositors are protected against all capital losses that do not exceed 10 per cent of the bank's investment portfolio. Ordinarily, this will be sufficient, as long as it keeps to high-grade bonds, mortgages, and conservative business loans.

There is one last requirement the bank must meet if we are to give it an A+. The management must watch the general trend in the size of its deposits to make sure that its locality is not becoming a "ghost town" and that it is not losing deposits steadily over time. Were that the case, the bank's investment portfolio would have to be arranged to hold securities and loans that could be gradually liquidated and converted into cash to meet depositors' withdrawals.

Even if the bank is not a declining business, prudent managers must still protect themselves against a *temporary* surge of withdrawals. To hold cash against such a contingency would be costly, since cash earns no yield. They will usually decide, therefore, to hold in their portfolios as "secondary reserves" some securities that always have a ready market and can be liquidated at short notice.

Short-term government bonds serve this purpose admirably. Called "bills," "notes," or "certificates," they vary little in value and can be liquidated simply by not buying new ones as the old ones come due every 90 days or 12 months. Even long-term government bonds, with 30 years of life before they mature, provide liquidity in the sense that in normal times they can always be transferred[6] to some other buyer at some quoted market price—albeit a varying price. In recent decades, a Federal Funds market has grown up, in which banks with surplus funds can lend on a daily basis to other banks at an interest rate comparable to yields on short-term Treasury bills.

LEGAL RESERVE REQUIREMENTS

When we compare a "going and growing" bank with any corporation, the surprising thing is not how little cash reserves the banks keep, but that they keep any at all (in

---

[6]There is a saying "You can sell government bonds even on Sunday." The important thing is not the *date of maturity* of the bond or loan, but rather how "shiftable" it is to some other investment institution. A 90-day loan to a local merchant, which is nonshiftable, is in this sense less liquid than a 90-year gilt-edge bond traded on a securities exchange.

Reserve requirements vary, depending on the location of the bank:

LEGAL RESERVE RATIOS FOR FEDERAL RESERVE MEMBER BANKS, JANUARY, 1970	RESERVE RATIOS REQUIRED, PER CENT	
KIND OF BANK	AGAINST DEMAND DEPOSITS	AGAINST TIME DEPOSITS
Reserve city banks (large and medium cities, Chicago, New York City)	17½	6
Other member banks (small-town or country)	13	6

TABLE 16-3.   These required reserve ratios have the purpose of controlling the volume of demand deposits and money supply. Congress gives the FRB the right to vary these rates within broad limits. (New York City and Chicago now are treated like other Reserve cities.)

excess of minimal till-money requirements). As long as financial skies are sunny, *we have seen that the same profit-maximizing logic which compels the abandonment of a system of 100 per cent reserves argues in favor of negligible reserves!*

Yet, if we turn to the facts, we find that a prudent modern bank is expected—and required by law!—to keep a substantial portion of its assets in nonearning cash. About a sixth or seventh of all demand deposits must be kept by banks immobilized in such nonearning reserve form. For the most part, a member bank holds these reserves on deposit with its regional Federal Reserve Bank; but in recent years the Fed has given each member bank the right to count as part of its reserves any cash it finds convenient to hold in its own vaults.

Table 16-3 indicates the level of required reserve ratios. Although they are changed at intervals by the Fed, they are roughly about one-sixth against demand deposits, depending on the category of the bank. Because one-fifth gives rounder numbers to work our numerical examples with, for the most part we shall refer to 20 per cent reserve ratios, it being understood that such a figure is only for expositional convenience and would have to be lowered a little to correspond with practice in the 1970s (as contrasted to some earlier decades when one-fifth was truly a better approximation than one-sixth and to the 1920s when one-tenth was more nearly the case).

The many, but unimportant, banks that are not members of the Federal Reserve System do not voluntarily keep such large amounts of nonearning cash reserves. Many experts think *all* banks should be subject to these same legal requirements, and if nonmember banks ever became important in total deposits, Congress might so legislate.

These legal reserve requirements need to be explained since they are so important a mechanism by which the FRB controls bank money.

Archaic geographical requirements   Why should the size of a town affect the legal reserve requirement? Before the Federal Reserve was created, the city banks held the precautionary reserves of smaller town banks. When a crisis came, the smaller banks tried to withdraw cash from the city banks. Therefore in the early days of the Federal Reserve System it seemed logical to make city banks, especially in the central reserve cities, New York and Chicago, hold higher reserve requirements.

Those days are past. Now it is the Federal Reserve Banks, not the big city banks, that hold the reserves of member banks. A new law finally removed all extra reserve requirements for New York and Chicago. Logically, all member banks—or nonmember banks, for that matter—might some day be given the same required reserve ratio.

Legal reserve requirements too high?   Many bankers think wistfully about how much they could earn on loans or bonds if they were free to use part of the money they are forced to keep as legal reserves against their own deposits. They argue thus:

Money we are required to keep as legal reserves doesn't earn us one red cent. So why do we have to keep such high legal reserves? One-sixth of our deposits is more than is really needed for safety. After all, our withdrawals never bunch up much; the laws of statistics take care of that. Besides, if we ever needed more, we could sell off some government bills or could turn to the Fed for help or could borrow temporarily from some other bank in the Federal Funds market. We bankers think that legal reserves of as little as 10 per cent—some of us would say 5 per cent!—are all that prudence requires in this age of insured deposits.

In part these bankers are right. Years ago the legal reserve requirements for the city and country banks were lower: they ranged between 7 and 13 per cent against demand deposits and 3 per cent against time deposits. After the mid-thirties Congress gave the Reserve Board the right to double these ratios, and the Board used its discretion to do this in a number of gradual steps.

But why did the Board raise the legal requirements? And why did it later ask Congress for authority to raise them still further? Because of the belief that such high legal ratios are needed to assure depositors of being able to withdraw their money when they want to? No.

The main function of legal reserve requirements is *not* that of making deposits safe and liquid, payable on demand. What, then, is it? Their vital function is to enable the Federal Reserve authorities to *control* the amount of demand deposits—or bank money—that the member banks can create. By imposing fixed legal reserve requirements, the Fed can limit the growth of bank deposits.

We shall soon learn just how this all works.

THE GOVERNMENT STANDS BEHIND THE BANKS

Banks are much safer than they used to be before the Depression. If this has little to do with legal reserve requirements, to what is it due?

Banks are safe today because everyone realizes that it is a vital function of government to stand behind them (and its Federal Deposit Insurance Corporation set up to protect depositors) should a depression and panicky "run" on the banking system ever recur.

No banking system with fractional reserves—i.e., none which keeps less than 100 per cent of its deposits in cash—can ever turn all its deposits into cash on a moment's notice. So every fractional-reserve system would be a "fair-weather system" if government did not stand ready to back it up. If panic ever came again, Congress, the President, and the Federal Reserve Board would all act, even using their constitutional powers over money to print the money needed to meet a national emergency!

Had this been said and done back in the black days of the early 1930s, history might have been different. Our country might have been spared the epidemic of bank failures[7]

---

[7] Some 8,000 banks with $5 billion of deposits became insolvent in 1930–1933. To keep all banks from collapse, Franklin Roosevelt's first act was to close them by declaring a "bank holiday" until they could be officially reopened with confidence restored.

that destroyed the money supply, creating fear and crisis for the whole capitalistic system. With the American people of both political parties realizing that the government stands behind the banking system, it is highly improbable that a panic could ever get started. Here is a case where being prepared to act heroically probably makes it unnecessary to do so.

KEEPING EACH BANK SAFE: A FINAL CHECK LIST

Just because the peril of a nationwide bank run has been overcome does not mean that each banker can stop worrying about *his* bank's safety. Numerous reforms have been introduced by government to alleviate the instability of laissez faire banking:

1. *Regulation of bank formation and activity.* For decades, either state or federal authorities have set down conditions under which banks could be formed—the minimum amount of capital they must have, etc. Bank examiners periodically scrutinize bank assets and pass on the bank's solvency, always keeping in mind that an ounce of prevention is worth a pound of cure.

2. *Formation of Federal Reserve System.* The next great step forward was the establishment of a central bank, whose emergency function is to stand as a Rock of Gibraltar in time of panic, to be ready to use the full monetary powers of the government to stem collapse of the banking system. The normal vital function of a central bank is to control money supply and credit conditions.

3. *Government insurance of bank deposits.* Following the bank crisis of 1933, the FDIC was belatedly set up to insure the safety of all bank deposits.[8]

The importance of this measure can hardly be exaggerated. From now on most banks will be closed by bank examiners and government authorities, not by the panicky behavior of depositors whose fears bring on the very contingency they are most afraid of. A single bank need no longer fear that its reputation, like that of a good woman, is compromised simply by being brought into question.

B. THE CREATION OF BANK DEPOSITS

CAN BANKS REALLY CREATE MONEY?

We now turn to one of the most interesting aspects of money and credit, the process called "multiple expansion of bank deposits." Most people have heard that in some mysterious manner banks can create money out of thin air, but few really understand how the process works. Few understand that all our money arises out of debt and IOU operations. Actually, there is nothing magical or incomprehensible about the creation of bank deposits. At every step of the way, one can follow what is happening to the banks' accounts. The true explanation of deposit creation is simple. What is hard to grasp are the false explanations that still circulate.

According to these false explanations, the managers of an ordinary bank are able, by

---

[8] In 1970, there were more than 100 million depositors in FDIC banks; the $20,000 limit insured about 97 per cent of all depositors, of whom 98 per cent were *fully* insured.

some use of their fountain pens, to lend several dollars for each dollar deposited with them. No wonder practical bankers see red when such power is attributed to them. They only wish they could do so. As every banker knows, he cannot invest money that he does not have; and money that he invests in buying a security or making a loan soon leaves his bank.

Bankers, therefore, often go to the opposite extreme, and sometimes argue that the banking system cannot (and does not) create money. "After all," they say, "we can invest only what is left with us. We don't create anything. We only put the community's savings to work." Bankers who argue in this way are wrong. They have become enmeshed in our old friend the fallacy of composition: what is true for each is not thereby true for all.

The banking system as a whole can do what each small bank cannot do: it *can* expand its loans and investments many times the new reserves of cash created for it, even though each small bank is lending out only a fraction of its deposits.

Our answer, then, to the basic question is in the affirmative: Yes, the banking system and the public do, between them, create about $5 of bank deposits for each new dollar of reserves that is created for the banks.

Figure 16-1 gives a preview of the process. The black box represents the banking system as a whole: Bank 1, which receives the initial new deposit, is at top; Bank 2, 3, . . . , and all other banks (not shown) are listed below. We shall study how $1 of new reserves, deposited at the left as input into the box, produces $5 of total deposit money, shown at the right. But Bank 1 cannot do this in one single step; as the blue arrows between the banks show, all the banks get involved in the lengthy secondary chain of money creation. Though the chain has many links, each is a dwindling fraction and the whole effect does add up to the 5 : 1 total.

Most of the remaining chapter explains this process of money creation.

HOW DEPOSITS ARE CREATED: THE FIRST-BANK STAGE

We begin with a brand-new deposit of $1,000 brought to a bank. Where it came from is not important. It could have been from a widow's hoard, from abroad, or more realistically, from someone's having just sold a bond to the regional Federal Reserve Bank (which may have paid for it by printing off 20 fifty-dollar bills). To avoid ambiguity, let us suppose

All banks together do what one can't do alone!

FIG. 16-1. For each dollar of new reserves deposited at left into a bank, the system as a whole creates at right about $5 of check money. The blue arrows in the box show that Bank 1 cannot do it alone. As we'll see, second, third, and other banks will get their share of the expansion.

Multiple-bank deposit creation is a story with many successive stages:

1st, A new deposit is added to the original bank's balance sheet:

ORIGINAL BANK IN INITIAL POSITION

ASSETS		LIABILITIES	
Reserves	+$1,000	Deposits	+$1,000
Total	+$1,000	Total	+$1,000

TABLE 16-4(a).

it arose from the government's giving a veteran $1,000 of newly printed money, which he deposited in his local bank. We shall see that *in the end* the banking system is going to manufacture $5,000 of new demand deposits out of this, thus taking in $1,000 of one kind of M (currency) and converting it into $5,000 of another kind of M (checkable demand deposits)—for a net gain of $4,000!

First-bank stage   Now, if banks were to keep 100 per cent cash-reserve balances, like the old goldsmiths, they could not create any extra money out of a new deposit of $1,000 left with them. The depositor would simply be giving up $1,000 of currency for a $1,000 checking deposit.

The change in the bank's balance sheet, as far as the new demand deposit is concerned, would be merely as shown in Table 16-4(a).[9]

The bank has not created this deposit *alone*. The customer had to be willing to make the deposit. Once he took the initiative, the bank was also willing to accept his checking account. Together the bank and the public "created" $1,000 of bank money, or deposit. But there is no multiple expansion yet, no 5 for 1 or anything else. So long as the banks keep 100 per cent reserves, the growth of bank M is just offset by the decline of currency-in-circulation M.

Suppose now that the bank does not have to keep 100 per cent reserves. Suppose that the law requires it to keep only 20 per cent legal reserves. (It can always keep larger reserves if it wishes to; but if there are many outstanding, relatively safe, interest-yielding government bonds or numerous profitable lending opportunities, the bank will not find it profitable to keep much more reserves than the law requires.)

What can Bank 1 now do? Can *it* expand *its* loans and investments by $4,000 so that the change in *its* balance sheet looks as shown in Table 16-4(b)? The answer is definitely, No. Why not? Total assets equal total liabilities. Cash reserves meet the legal requirement of being 20 per cent of total deposits.

True enough. But how did Bank 1 pay for the investments or earning assets that it bought? Like everyone else, it had to write out checks to those who sold the bond or signed the promissory note. If all such would promise not to cash the bank's check—or what is the same thing, to hold all such money frozen on deposit in Bank 1—then, of course, it could buy all it wanted to without losing any cash.

---

[9] For simplicity, all our tables will show only the *changes* in balance-sheet items. To simplify the arithmetic, we use reserve ratios of 20 per cent, which are a little larger than the legal rates of Table 16-3. Hence, wherever an expansion of 5:1 is mentioned, the meticulous reader can choose to think of a 6:1 or 7:1 expansion. If M_2 inclusive of saving deposits were studied, the expansion ratio would of course exceed 7:1. (Important reminder: When bankers refer to their loans and investments, by "investments" they mean their holdings of securities. They do not mean what we mean by I in $C + I + G$, namely, net capital formation for the community.)

But, in fact, no one will borrow money at 6 or 9 per cent just to hold it all in the bank. The borrower spends the money on labor, on materials, or perhaps on an automobile. The money will *very* soon,[10] therefore, have to be paid out of Bank 1. And if—as is likely—the bank is but one of many banks serving that city, county, state, and country, only a fraction of the sums withdrawn will ever come back to the original bank in another customer's deposit.

This loss of cash by a bank expanding its investments is even more clearly seen if Bank 1 buys a bond rather than making a local loan. When my Boston bank buys a government bond, what are the chances that the man who sells the bond will happen to have an account with it? The likelihood is negligible. Probably he lives in New York City; or Ames, Iowa. So my bank knows it will soon have to pay out *all* the money it places in bonds. A

2d, Of course the bank cannot then loan out four times the amount of the deposit:

IMPOSSIBLE SITUATION FOR SINGLE SMALL BANK			
ASSETS		**LIABILITIES**	
Reserves	+$1,000	Deposits	+$5,000
Loans and investments	+ 4,000		
Total	+$5,000	Total	+$5,000

TABLE 16-4(b).

3d, But what it can do is loan out four-fifths of the deposit:

ORIGINAL BANK IN FINAL POSITION			
ASSETS		**LIABILITIES**	
Reserves	+$ 200	Deposits	+$1,000
Loans and investments	+ 800		
Total	+$1,000	Total	+$1,000

TABLE 16-4(c).

bank cannot "eat its cake and have it, too." The New England bank cannot buy a bond and keep its cash at the same time. Table 16-4(b) gives, therefore, a completely false picture of what an individual bank can do.

Does this mean that Table 16-4(a) tells the end of the story? Must the bank, therefore, behave like the 100 per cent reserve goldsmith-bankers?

Of course not. Although the bank cannot jack its deposits up to five times its cash reserve, it certainly can *reduce its cash* down to one-fifth of its deposits. Nothing is easier. For, as just seen, all it has to do is acquire $800 worth of earning assets—bonds, loans, or mortgages. In a day or so it will lose practically all this cash as its checks come back for payment. Now its balance sheet will be as shown in Table 16-4(c).

As far as this first bank is concerned, we are through. Bank 1's legal reserves are just enough to match its deposits. There is nothing more it can do until the public decides to bring in some more money for deposit.

Before leaving the single first bank, note this important fact: It has created money! How? Clearly *it* retains from the initial $1,000 of original new reserves only $200 of cash M; and it has added $1,000 of bank-deposit M to the public's total. Thus, Bank 1's activity has created a net increase of $800 in money supply.

---

[10] If the bank made loans of $800 to its own customers, and they kept them on deposit, then for a brief period it would have deposits of $1,800. But as its borrowers spent their money, and unless the people who got that money were local customers who put the money back on deposit in this original bank, it would soon find itself forced toward the position of Table 16-4(c).

4th, The money loaned out by the original bank is soon deposited in other banks:

SECOND-GENERATION BANKS IN INITIAL POSITION			
ASSETS		LIABILITIES	
Reserves	+ $800	Deposits	+ $800
Total	+ $800	Total	+ $800

TABLE 16-4(d).

5th, Four-fifths of this new deposit will be loaned out by the second-generation bank:

FINAL POSITION OF SECOND-GENERATION BANKS			
ASSETS		LIABILITIES	
Reserves	+ $160	Deposits	+ $800
Loans and investments	+ 640		
Total	+ $800	Total	+ $800

TABLE 16-4(e).

6th, And similarly the four-fifths ratio applies to third-generation banks:

INITIAL POSITION OF THIRD-GENERATION BANKS			
ASSETS		LIABILITIES	
Reserves	+ ____	Deposits	+ ____
Loans and investments	____		
Total	+ ____	Total	+ $640

TABLE 16-4(f).

7th, Until finally the infinite, but dwindling chain of money creation takes place in all the generations of banks:

FINAL EQUILIBRIUM OF THIRD-GENERATION BANKS			
ASSETS		LIABILITIES	
Reserves	+ $128	Deposits	+ $640
Loans and investments	+ 512		
Total	+ $640	Total	+ $640

TABLE 16-4(g).   The final equilibrium is reached when every dollar of original new reserves, wherever it is written in the banking system, supports five dollars of demand deposits.

CHAIN REPERCUSSIONS ON THE OTHER BANKS

But the banking system as a whole cannot settle down yet. The people who sold the bonds or borrowed from the bank will presumably deposit the proceeds in some other bank or pay them to someone else who will make such a deposit. Our original bank has thus lost $800 *to some other banks* in the system.

Second-generation banks   If we lump these other banks all together and call them "second-generation banks" (or Bank 2), their balance sheets now appear as shown in Table 16-4(d). Of course, these banks are scattered all over the country. (Our original bank might even constitute a small part of the second generation as a few of its checks fell into the hands of its own depositors.) To these banks, the dollars deposited are just like any other dollars— *just like our original deposit;* these banks do not know, and do not care, that they are second in a chain of deposits. They do know, and they do care, that they are now holding *too much* nonearning cash. Only one-fifth of $800, or $160, is legally needed against $800 deposits. Therefore they can, and will, use the other four-fifths to buy $640 worth of loans and investments. Hence, in a few days, their balance sheets will have reached equilibrium as shown in Table 16-4(e).

So much for the second-generation banks. As shown back in Fig. 16-1 by the blue arrows connecting Bank 2 to Bank 1, part of the original reserves end up in these second banks, and they too have created money.

Thus far, the original $1,000 taken out of hand-to-hand circulation and put into the banking system has given rise to

$1,000 (first-generation deposits) plus $800 (second-generation deposits). The total of money has increased, and the end is not yet in sight. Let us continue the story through the infinite, but dwindling chain of other banks.

Later-generation banks The $640 spent by the second-generation banks in acquiring loans and investments will go to a new set of banks called the "third-generation banks." (Again, follow the blue arrow in Fig. 16-1 below Bank 2.) The reader should by now be able to fill in their balance sheets as they look initially [see Table 16-4(f)]. Evidently, the third-generation banks will at first have *excess reserves* of an amount equal to four-fifths of $640, or $512. After this has been spent on loans and investments—and only then—the third-generation banks will reach the equilibrium of Table 16-4(g).

The total of bank-deposit M is now $1,000 plus $800 plus $640, or $2,440. This is already almost $2\frac{1}{2}:1$ expansion of the original cash deposit. But a fourth generation of banks will clearly end up with four-fifths of $640 in deposits, or $512; the fifth generation will get four-fifths of $512, or $409.60; and so on, until finally, by the twenty-fifth round, we shall have all but a penny of the sum of the infinitely many generations.

8th, Through this chain process the banking system eventually creates total deposits equal to five times the original new reserves:

MULTIPLE EXPANSION OF BANK DEPOSITS THROUGH THE BANKING SYSTEM

POSITION OF BANK	NEW DEPOSITS	NEW LOANS AND INVESTMENTS	RESERVES
Original banks	$1,000.00	$ 800.00	$ 200.00
2d-generation banks	800.00	640.00	160.00
3d-generation banks	640.00	512.00	128.00
4th-generation banks	512.00	409.60	102.40
5th-generation banks	409.60	327.68	81.92
6th-generation banks	327.68	262.14	65.54
7th-generation banks	262.14	209.72	52.42
8th-generation banks	209.72	167.77	41.95
9th-generation banks	167.77	134.22	33.55
10-th generation banks	134.22	107.37	26.85
Sum of first 10 generation banks	$4,463.13	$3,570.50	$ 892.63
Sum of remaining generation banks	536.87	429.50	107.37
Total for banking system as a whole	$5,000.00	$4,000.00	$1,000.00

TABLE 16-4(h). (From the 7th generation on, all data have been rounded off to two decimal places.) Note that in every generation each *small* bank has "created" new money in the following sense: It ends up with final bank deposit five times *the reserves it finally retains*.

Final equilibrium What will be the final sum: $1,000 + $800 + $640 + $512 + $409.60 + · · ·? If we patiently work out the sum by arithmetic, we shall find that it leads to $4,999.999 · · · and "finally" to $5,000. Table 16-4(h) shows the complete effect of the chain of deposit creation; and we can also get the same answer in two other ways, by common sense and by elementary algebra.[11]

[11]This can be proved by algebra as follows:

$$\$1,000 + \$800 + \$640 + \cdots = \$1,000[1 + \tfrac{4}{5} + (\tfrac{4}{5})^2 + (\tfrac{4}{5})^3 + \cdots]$$
$$= \$1,000\left(\frac{1}{1 - \tfrac{4}{5}}\right) = \$1,000 \times 5 = \$5,000$$

Just as Chapter 12's multiplier made income rise threefold to generate the one-third of itself equal to the new dollar of I, here deposit M must rise fivefold so that 20 per cent of it will match the new dollars of reserves that started the chain. (NOTE: The arithmetic of M expansion is like that of the "Keynes multiplier" of Chapter 12. But don't confuse the two: the amplification here is from the stock of money reserves to the stock of total M_1; it does not refer to the extra income induced by investment.)

9th, Now we can see that all banks together can do what is impossible for one alone:

CONSOLIDATED BALANCE SHEET SHOWING FINAL POSITION OF ALL BANKS TOGETHER

ASSETS		LIABILITIES	
Reserves	+ $1,000	Deposits	+ $5,000
Loans and investments	+ 4,000		
Total	+ $5,000	Total	+ $5,000

TABLE 16-4(i).

Common sense tells us the process of deposit creation must come to an end only when no bank *anywhere in the system* has reserves in excess of the 20 per cent reserve ratio to deposits. In all our previous examples no cash reserves have ever leaked out of the banking system, but have simply gone from one set of banks to another set of banks. Everyone will be at equilibrium only when a consolidated balance sheet for all the banks together— for the first, second, and hundredth generation—looks as shown in Table 16-4(i). For if total new deposits were less than $5,000, the 20 per cent ratio would not yet be reached and equilibrium would not yet have been everywhere attained.

If the reader will compare Table 16-4(i) with Table 16-4(b), previously judged "impossible," he will see this:

The whole banking system *can* do what no one bank can do by itself. It can expand its deposits to five times the *initial* new deposit. *Bank money has been created 5 out of 1—and all the while each bank has invested and lent only a fraction of what it has received as deposits!*

Figure 16-1 on page 281 can be reviewed now with deeper understanding.

Who creates the multiple expansion[12] of deposits? Three parties do so jointly: the *public* by always keeping its money in the bank on deposit; the *banks* by keeping only a fraction of their deposits in the form of cash; the *public and private borrowers* who make it possible for the banks to find loans and attractive earning assets to buy with their excess cash. There is also a fourth party, *the central bank* (namely, the Fed), which by its activities determines how much will be the new reserves to come to the banking system. It will be the task of the next chapters to survey and explain this process.

Before leaving this section, test your knowledge of credit creation by tracing in detail what happens when the regional Federal Reserve Bank permanently kills off $1,000 of reserves by selling a government bond to a widow who withdraws cash from her demand deposit account to pay for it: (1) Her local bank loses $1,000 of reserves and $1,000 of deposits. But it previously held only 20 per cent cash reserves or $200 against her deposit. Clearly, it must have given up

---

[12] There is nothing paradoxical in the fact that total bank deposits are several times greater than the amount of paper cash in existence anywhere; the same is true of the total of government bonds and real-estate values. Deposits are something that banks *owe* their customers; cash is *left* in a bank, but it does not *remain* in that bank. Throughout its lifetime a dollar may have been *left* in many banks, just as it may be used over a long period of time to buy hundreds of dollars of merchandise. The one thing to keep firmly in mind is that bank deposits are one of the three forms of modern money and, quantitatively, the most important.

In effect, each small bank creates $1M$ out of $\frac{1}{5}M$, but not $5M$ out of $1M$. (NOTE: Whenever $1 of new reserves produces $5 of new demand-deposit money, the *net* creation of M is only $5 - 1 = 4$. So when one writes a $5:1$ expansion expression, it means that there is associated with this a $4:1$ *net-creation-of-M* expansion.)

to her some of its legally necessary cash reserves held against its other demand deposits. Show that its total reserves are now below the legal minimum. (2) Therefore it must sell $800 worth of investments or call in that many loans. The first-generation bank will be in equilibrium only when its balance sheet finally looks as shown in a newly constructed Table 16-5(a).

But in selling its securities, our original bank has drained $800 from a second generation of banks; and they in turn, by liquidating securities and loans, drain reserves from a third. And so it goes—until the widow and Fed's withdrawal of $1,000 of reserves from the banking system have produced a chain "killing off" $5,000 worth of deposits throughout the whole system and $4,000 of bank-earning assets. The reader should follow through each stage: hypothetical Table 16-5(b), Table 16-5(c), . . . ; and, in Fig. 16-1, reverse the arrow-flows and introduce minus signs.

10th, When a deposit is drawn out, a multiple contraction begins to take place:

EQUILIBRIUM POSITION OF ORIGINAL BANK LOSING A DEPOSIT			
ASSETS		LIABILITIES	
Reserves	−$ 200	Deposits	−$1,000
Loans and investments	− 800		
Total	−$1,000	Total	−$1,000

TABLE 16-5(a).

You should also be able to show how an initial deposit of $1,000 can result in $10,000 of bank deposits if banks keep only 10 per cent reserve ratios, as they did in the 1920s. And since the reserve ratios of Table 16-3 average below 20 per cent, you might show that 6:1 is a more accurate figure than 5:1.

A "MONOPOLY BANK"

In all the above processes, it was assumed that no cash leaked out of the banking system into someone's mattress or into permanent hand-to-hand circulation. The banking system was then in the enviable position of finding that its checks were always deposited somewhere within itself.

This condition being so, it is easy to see that a single "monopoly bank" with many branches, which served the whole nation and represented the consolidated banking system, would be able to do *at once* what we have said each small bank cannot do. Its balance sheet could quickly go to the condition shown in Table 16-4(b) or (i). It could write checks freely to pay for securities or loans, knowing that those who get them would always redeposit their proceeds in the one and only monopoly bank.[13]

SIMULTANEOUS EXPANSION OR CONTRACTION BY ALL BANKS

In the previous section we saw how the banking system can reach the limits of its expansion through many successive rounds or generations. If we allow half a week for checks to clear at each stage and for decisions to be made, then 5 to 8 weeks might be needed for the process to work itself out through more than a dozen rounds.

[13]In countries like England, where there is a "Big Five" group of branch banks, or like Canada, where there are a few large banks, or in states like California, where there are a few great multiple-branch banks—in such cases a bank may be able to lend out more than its legal excess reserves, knowing that part of the money will come back *to itself* in later "generations." However, these so-called "derivative," or "self-returning," deposits are not important for the United States and calling attention to them can confuse beginning students, as it did economists of half a century ago, when this process was still novel.

As a practical matter, it is not necessary to follow the chain of each dollar deposited through its successive rounds. Here is why. A rise in *initial* reserves will usually affect *almost all the banks at the same time.* They all receive some new deposits at about the same time. They *all* have excess reserves in the first instance, and *all* together make loans or buy securities. When a single small bank, alone by itself, writes checks to acquire securities, these checks go to other banks and it loses cash. But when *all* write checks simultaneously and in balance, there will tend to be a *cancellation* of new checks deposited and paid out in each bank. No one bank need lose cash reserves.

Hence, without going through the successive generations of the previous section, all banks together can simply and blithely expand their loans and investments—so long as each does not jeopardize its reserve position—until deposits are finally brought into a 5:1 relation to reserves. Then the banking system has reached the limit of its ability to create money.

One could follow through the similar process by which all banks *simultaneously* contract money 5:1 for each dollar of reserve withdrawn from the banking system, and one could also show how a monopoly bank would contract.[14]

TWO QUALIFICATIONS

Finally, two qualifications to the ideal condition must be made. We have shown that $1,000 of new reserves put into a bank can ultimately result in an increase of $5,000 of bank deposits. This assumed that all the new money remained somewhere *in* the banking system, in one bank or another at every stage, and that all banks could keep "loaned up" with no "excess reserves."

1. *Leakage into hand-to-hand circulation.* It is quite possible, however, and even likely, that somewhere along the chain of deposit expansion some individual who receives a check will not leave the proceeds in a bank but will withdraw it into circulation or into hoarding outside the banking system. As a matter of fact, in boom times when bank

[14]Here in Fig. 16-2 is the story of Fig. 16-1 retold for a monopoly bank or for simultaneous expansion.

FIG. 16-2.

In (a), there is no need for arrows within the box, since there is only one big bank. In (b), the arrows between the banks run in both directions and can be ignored.

deposits are expanding, there is usually at the same time an increased need for pennies, dimes, and paper currency.

The effects of such withdrawals on our analysis are simple. When $1,000 stayed in the banking system, $5,000 of new deposits were created. If $100 were to leak into circulation outside the banks and only $900 of new reserves were to remain in the banking system, then the new demand deposits created would be $4,500 ($900 × 5). *The banking system can always amplify in a 5:1 ratio whatever amount of new reserves is permanently left with it.*[15]

We have been concentrating here on checkable demand deposits. But remember that economists include time deposits in the broad M_2 definition of the money supply! Recall too that time deposits have legal reserve requirements, albeit (as Table 16-3 shows) lower ratios than do demand deposits. Hence, just as some of our original $1,000 of reserves will leak out of the banks as currency held by the public, so too will some leak into the time deposit division of the member bank as needed legal reserves for new time deposits. Obviously, the 5:1 amplification of demand deposits applies only to that part of the original reserves which does *not* leak out of the demand-deposit division in any shape, form, or manner.

2. *Possible excess reserves.* Our description of multiple deposit creation has proceeded on the assumption that the commercial banks stick fairly close to their legal reserve ratios. But there is no reason why a bank cannot choose to keep an *excess* over the legally required amount of reserves. Thus, suppose the original bank receiving a new $1,000 deposit had been satisfied to hold $800 of it in excess reserves. Then the whole process would have ended right there, with no multiple expansion of deposits. Or if, less absurdly, banks were always to keep 5 per cent excess reserves, on top of the 20 per cent legal requirement, we'd have an expansion chain of deposits $[1 + .75 + (.75)^2 + \cdots]$ rather than $[1 + .8 + (.8)^2 + \cdots]$, with only 4:1 instead of 5:1 expansion of deposits.

Back in the 1930s excess reserves—i.e., reserves over and above legally required reserves—were substantial, because bankers were then leery of loan opportunities and even of relatively safe government bills that were paying only $\frac{1}{8}$ of 1 per cent interest. Had the Fed then given the banking system $1,000 of new reserves, perhaps half might have gone into excess reserves. Today excess reserves are less important, as most banks find attractive uses in the Federal Funds market even for one-day funds.

In depressed times, the level of excess reserves depends more on the attitudes of banks toward the interest rates they can earn than on their fears that withdrawals will catch them unawares. When short-term interest rates become very low, and a banker finds that keeping an extra million dollars in idle reserves would not much change his earning position, he is not very anxious to get rid of all excess reserves. But as profit opportunities improve and become less uncertain, he becomes more aggressive in putting his idle reserves to work earning him a return.

The possibility that the excess reserves of banks can change over time is an important reminder that there is nothing mechanical and completely accurate about using a 5:1 or any other *fixed* ratio for money creation.

Accordingly, there is nothing automatic about deposit creation. Four factors are neces-

[15]In Figs. 16-1 and 16-2, pencil in holes at the bottom of the big box black, with arrows showing that part of the original blue $1 input leaks into currency held by the public.

sary: the banks must somehow receive new reserves; they must be willing to make loans or buy securities rather than hold new excess reserves; someone must be willing to borrow or to sell securities; and the public must choose to leave its money on deposit with the banks, not depleting them of reserves.

SUMMARY

A. NATURE AND FUNCTIONING OF THE MODERN BANKING SYSTEM

1   The American banking system consists primarily of relatively small-scale unit banks, chartered by the national government or by the states. Although less than half are members of the Federal Reserve System, member demand deposits include six-sevenths of the total of all deposits.

2   The functions of commercial banks are numerous and overlap with those of such other financial institutions as mutual savings banks, federal savings and loan associations, finance companies, and insurance companies. But in their function of providing demand deposit M, the commercial banks perform a unique and important economic role. Their checkable deposits constitute the single most important component of our money supply or medium of exchange. Also the banks are important sources for credit.

3   The Federal Reserve System (or Fed) consists primarily of (a) member banks, (b) the 12 regional Federal Reserve Banks, and (c) the Board of Governors (or Federal Reserve Board) in Washington. Although nominally corporations owned by the member banks, the Federal Reserve Banks are, in fact, almost branches of the federal government, possessing wide powers and being concerned with the public interest rather than profits. Responsible to Congress, in practice they do not act independently of Treasury and executive-branch policy. It is the primary responsibility of the Reserve authorities to control the money supply in order to help achieve full employment with stable prices (and backstop the banking system in time of crisis).

4   Modern banks gradually evolved from the old goldsmith establishments in which money and valuables were stored. It finally became general practice to hold far less than 100 per cent reserves against deposits, the rest being put into securities and loans for an interest yield. Fractional-reserve banking had evolved.

5   If the government did not stand ready to use its emergency powers to protect the banking system, an attempt by all depositors at the same time to withdraw their money would ruin any fractional-reserve banking system; but knowing the government is ready to act, people will never put it to the test.

   The member banks are required to keep legal reserves (on deposit with their regional Reserve Bank or in vault cash) in proportion to their deposits. (The geographical differences in required ratios are archaic and are diminishing.) These legal reserve requirements are *not* primarily to protect deposits but to permit the Federal Reserve to control the total supply of M and keep credit conditions conducive to proper over-all spending.

B. THE CREATION OF BANK DEPOSITS

6   If banks kept 100 per cent cash reserves against all deposits, there would be no net creation of money when currency was taken out of circulation and deposited in the banking system. There would be only a 1:1 exchange of one kind of money for another kind of money.

7   Modern banks are required to keep legal reserves of only about one-sixth or less of their demand deposits, depending on size of city. Consequently, the banking system as a whole— together with public or private borrowers and the depositing public—does create demand-deposit money almost 6:1 for each new dollar of reserves created by the Fed and left on deposit somewhere in the system (5:1 in our simplified examples).

8   Each small bank is limited in its ability to expand its loans and investments. It cannot lend or invest more than it has received from depositors; it can lend only about four-fifths as much. The system as a whole can expand at once, as each small bank cannot. This can be seen if we examine a monopoly bank in a closed community. The checks written by such a bank always come back to it; therefore the only restriction upon its ability to expand its investments and deposits (its assets *and* its liabilities in double-entry book-keeping) is the requirement that it keep one-fifth cash-reserve ratios against deposits. When deposits have expanded until they are five times the new reserves, the monopoly bank is "loaned up" and can create no further deposits until given more reserves.

9   In present-day America, there is no monopoly bank. Nevertheless, the same 5:1 expansion of bank deposits takes place. The first individual bank receiving a new $1,000 of deposits spends four-fifths of its newly acquired cash on loans and investments. This gives a second group of banks four-fifths of $1,000 in new deposits. They, in turn, keep one-fifth in cash and spend the other four-fifths for new earning assets; this causes them to lose cash to a third set of banks, whose deposits have gone up by four-fifths of four-fifths of $1,000. Obviously, if we follow through the successive groups of banks in the dwindling, never-ending chain, we find for the system as a whole new deposits of

$$\$1,000 + \$800 + \$640 + \$512 + \cdots$$
$$= \$1,000 \times \left[1 + \frac{4}{5} + \left(\frac{4}{5}\right)^2 + \left(\frac{4}{5}\right)^3 + \cdots \right]$$
$$= \$1,000 \left(\frac{1}{1 - \frac{4}{5}} \right) = \left(\$1,000 \quad \frac{1}{\frac{1}{5}} \right) = \$5,000$$

Only when each $1 of the new reserves retained in the banking system ends up supporting $5 of deposits somewhere in the system will the limits to deposit expansion be reached. Then the system is loaned up; it can create no further deposits until it is given more reserves.

10   In practice, it is not necessary to wait for the successive rounds in the chain of $1,000, $800, $640, . . . , to work themselves out. Usually, many banks tend to get new reserves at about the same time. If all simultaneously expand their loans and investments approxi-

mately in balance, their outpayments will tend to cancel each other. Thus, each loses cash; and *all together* can rather quickly expand their assets and deposits to the 5:1 limit.

11   As a minor qualification to the above discussion, we must note that there will be some leakage of the new cash reserves of the banking system into circulation *outside* the banks (and, indeed, some will go abroad) and into the time-deposit division of the banks for their legally needed reserves. Therefore, instead of $5,000 of new demand deposits created, as in the previous examples, we may have something less than that—the difference being due to what is withdrawn from the system. A second qualification results from the fact that a bank may keep *excess reserves* above legally required reserves. While large banks do not hold much excess reserves in prosperous times, others may hold varying amounts of excess reserves, depending upon interest rates and precautionary expectations. So there is nothing automatic about a 5:1 or other fixed-gear ratio.

In this chapter we have seen how bank deposits are kept at about five times the legal reserves of the banking system. In Chapter 17 we shall learn how the Federal Reserve Banks make bank reserves go up when an expansion of the total money supply is desired. When a contraction of the total supply of money is in order, the Federal Reserve authorities pull the brakes. Instead of pumping new reserves into the banking system, they draw off some of the reserves, and they are then able to reduce the quantity of money, not 1 for 1, but (as just shown) 5 for 1. Thus, within close limits, the Fed can control the rate of growth of the money supply along the pattern it thinks best.

QUESTIONS FOR DISCUSSION

1   Suppose that all banks kept 100 per cent reserves. How different would they be? What function do legal reserves perform? What are "excess reserves"?

2   Assume a 10 per cent reserve ratio. Trace the process of multiple bank expansion, duplicating Tables 16-4(a) to (i). Reverse the process.

3   Do bankers create deposits? Who does? If a banker receives a new deposit and new reserves, is he always able to find borrowers? Can he always expand his holdings of government securities?

4   "Banks borrow from their depositors at zero or low interest rates and invest most of the proceeds in higher-yielding loans and investments. They use the difference to pay their expenses, to provide us with low-cost mediums for monetary transactions, and to reward their stockholders for taking on the risks of declines in earning-asset values. They constitute an efficient method of allocating the saving and newly created M of the community to worthy local enterprises. One can scarcely imagine a better system than this, particularly with the recent reforms that insure depositors from loss and make psychological bank runs improbable." Appraise.

5   "My bank's books always balance. I merely *pass on* to investors the savings my depositors bring me. Who dares say a banker can create M or demand deposits?" Do you dare?

6 "The Fed should create new reserves indefinitely as long as we bankers can find good productive loans to make, because then each new M will be balanced by new product Q and prices won't rise and the community will get a higher real NNP indefinitely." This view was widely supported by the founders of the Fed in 1913. Can you see where the implied *elasticity* of M could be *harmful* in a world of fluctuating $C + I + G$ schedules? (HINT: Banks would expand M in booms and contract M in recessions: inflationary gaps and deflationary gaps might get worse.)

7 *Extra-credit problem:* Verify the following formulas for money expansion. Suppose M has several components, as, e.g., currency held by public; demand deposits of city member banks, of country member banks, of nonmember banks; time deposits; etc. And let the ith component of M follow the relation $M_i = m_i M$, where m_i is a positive fraction. And suppose the *reserves*, R_i, needed against M_i follow the rule: $R_i = r_i M_i$, where the r's are positive fractions, except for $r_1 = 1$ in case of the public's currency. Then, we have

$$M = M_1 + M_2 + \cdots = m_1 M + m_2 M + \cdots$$

and

$$R = R_1 + R_2 + \cdots = r_1 M_1 + r_2 M_2 + \cdots = (r_1 m_1 + r_2 m_2 + \cdots)M.$$

Hence, for each \$1 of new R the Fed creates, we have M expansion given by

$$M = \frac{1}{r_1 m_1 + r_2 m_2 + \cdots} R, \; M_i = \frac{m_i}{r_1 m_1 + r_2 m_2 + \cdots} R$$

EXAMPLE: $r_1 = 1$, $r_2 = .2$, $m_1 = 0$ gives $M = (1/.2)R = 5R$ of the text; $r_1 = 1$, $r_2 = .2$, $m_1 = 1/21$ gives $M = 4.2R$, $M_2 =$ demand deposits $= 4R$. Increasing any r_i alone will lower every M_i/R. Increasing any m_i share at the expense of any m_j with $r_j < r_i$ will also lower M/R, raise M_i, and lower all other M_j, but with M_i growing less than the other components together *all* shrink. E.g., a shift to time deposits raises M broadly-defined, because time deposits require less reserves than demand deposits do.

Review your understanding of the following concepts:

national, state banks; member banks, FDIC-insured banks

Board of Governors, 12 Federal Reserve Banks, Fed

bank balance sheet

goldsmiths and 100 per cent reserves, fractional-reserve banking

legal reserve ratio requirements

chain of generations

deposit creation for a monopoly bank versus a system of many small banks

simultaneous expansion by all banks

excess reserves, leakage of reserves into public's currency or time deposit reserves

Federal Reserve and Central Bank Monetary Policy

The Federal Reserve is a central bank, a bank for bankers and for the government. Every central bank has one prime function:

It operates to control the economy's supply of money and credit. **If business is getting worse and jobs are getting scarce, the Federal Reserve Board will try to expand money and credit. But if spending threatens to become excessive, so that prices are rising and there are many job vacancies, then the Federal Reserve authorities (the Fed) will do all that is possible to step on the brakes and contract money and credit. Monetary policy "leans against the wind" of prevailing deficient or excessive aggregate demand spending, to promote optimal real growth and price-level stability.**

In a nutshell that is the function of central banking. And all mixed economies rely on such a central bank. In this chapter we shall survey the weapons that the Federal Reserve uses to expand or contract money and credit.

HOW MONETARY POLICY WORKS TO CONTROL SPENDING

What is the exact process by which the Reserve authorities affect general spending? Here are five steps:

As shown in the last chapter, commercial or member banks must have *reserves* to support their assets and deposits. (So important are these "reserves" that we shall capitalize the word for the rest of this chapter.)

1. *The first step of the Fed, therefore, when it wants to put on the monetary brakes, is to act to cut down on the Reserves available to the banks.*

2. *Each dollar contraction in bank Reserves forces about a $5 contraction in total bank money, i.e., in total demand deposits.* (Recall the last chapter's analysis of multiple deposit creation in a fractional-reserve banking system.)

3. *The contraction in total money immediately makes credit generally "tight," that is, both dearer and less*

available. We shall see that less *M* will immediately raise interest rates. Just as important, less *M* will make credit less available to people.

Interest rates will rise for mortgage borrowers; for local governments that want to build schools and roads; and for businessmen anxious to build plants, buy new equipment, or add to inventory. Reinforcing higher interest cost will be credit's decreased availability. Thus, if you want to build a house, it matters to you that the interest rate has risen from 6 to $7\frac{1}{2}$ per cent. If you are like most families, it matters even more that you may now find it hard to get a mortgage with a low down payment. You may find your banker's manner a shade cooler; and he may discourage you from buying the $35,000 house that you really prefer to the $25,000 one you have been considering. When *M* is scarce, turndowns on loans become common. (During the Vietnam boom, all this happened. Housing starts plummeted for lack of credit both in 1966 and 1969.)

4. *With credit expensive and hard to get, private and public investment will tend to fall.* Why this downward shift in the *I* and *G* schedules?[1] Because people's decisions as to whether it is profitable to build a new house or plant, order a new machine, and hold more inventory usually depend upon how they can finance such investment spending. If they have to pay a high interest rate or find it very hard to get loans, they often scale down their investment plans. The same holds for state and local governments. The old road gets patched up and that new road postponed when the town finds it cannot float its bonds at any reasonable interest rate. The gymnasium and library are cut out of the new school plans when the citizens learn their tax rate is going up because it now costs 6 per cent to borrow, instead of 5 or $4\frac{1}{2}$ per cent.

5. *Finally, the pressure on credit and on investment spending will, through the downward shift in the I + G schedule, have downward effects on income spending, prices, and jobs.* The multiplier analysis of Chapter 12 showed how such a drop in investment will depress income spending sharply.

If the Fed has been right in its diagnosis of inflationary conditions, the drop in money income will be just what the doctor ordered to help the situation. *M* contraction will have succeeded in reducing the inflationary gap.

Indeed as a sixth, longer-run effect, the curb on *M* may *eventually lower* rather than raise interest rates. For suppose that raising interest rates from 6 to 8 per cent does succeed in reducing price inflation from a 5 per cent to a 2 per cent annual rate. Then at that time the swollen demand for credit will have been made to subside, and market interest rates will drop from the high 8 per cent level. No longer will lenders require so great a premium in the money interest rate to compensate for inflation, and what began as a 6 per cent interest rate could now go below 5 per cent without representing any reduction in the *real* (i.e., corrected-for-inflation) interest rate.

RECAPITULATION

This five-step sequence—from the Fed's changing the commercial banks' Reserves, to 5:1 changes in total *M*, to changes in credit's interest cost and availability, to changes

[1]Later chapters (particularly Chapter 30) show that higher interest rates tend to depress the market value of wealth items: land, bonds, buildings, equipment. With their total wealth now less and installment credit hard to get, people's *CC* schedule may also be shifted down along with their *II* schedules.

in private and public investment spending, and finally to multiplied changes in money income—is vital. By rereading the italicized parts of the previous section, you can consolidate your understanding of it. Better still, psychologists tell us one learns fastest by participating. The previous section was explained in terms of a time—like 1969—when the Fed wants to *contract* business activity. Tackle the problem of how things proceed when, as in 1960 or 1962, the Fed wants to *expand* business activity.

Suppose you are Chairman Burns of the Fed's Board of Governors at a time when the economy is mildly depressed. Suppose you are called to testify before a congressional committee—as Burns so often is—to explain to an interrogating senator just how your *expansionary* acts would operate. Retrace these detailed steps:

The Fed expands Reserves; member banks then engineer something like a 5:1 expansion in demand deposits; increase in society's *M* is associated with "easier money conditions," i.e., lower interest rates on loans, bonds, and mortgages and, equally important, more easily available credit to would-be investors and government spenders. There results an increase in *I*, *G*, and perhaps even in durable-goods *C* installment spending. And finally, there follow multiplier effects of the shift in the *C* + *I* + *G* schedule on income, employment, and possibly price levels.

BALANCE SHEET OF THE FEDERAL RESERVE BANKS

Now that we have surveyed the process of monetary policy with a telescope, let us study the mechanism in some detail. We shall not attempt to look at Federal Reserve policy under a microscope, since that is the job of an intermediate course in money and banking; but we do want to get a general idea of *exactly what weapons* the Fed can use to affect bank Reserves.

Look at Table 17-1. This lists the combined balance sheet of the 12 Reserve Banks. The first asset consists mostly of gold certificates, i.e., warehouse receipts from the Treasury to the Fed for so much gold. United States government securities make up most of the rest of the assets—the significance of this item will be explained soon. The smaller

Federal Reserve notes and deposits underlie our money supply:

COMBINED BALANCE SHEET OF 12 FEDERAL RESERVE BANKS, JANUARY 1, 1969 (in billions of dollars)			
ASSETS		LIABILITIES AND NET WORTH	
Gold certificates and other cash	$10.2	Capital accounts	$ 1.3
U.S. government securities	52.9	Federal Reserve notes	44.7
Discounts, loans, and acceptances	0.4	Deposits:	
Miscellaneous other assets	12.4	Member bank Reserves	21.8
(primarily "uncollected		U.S. Treasury	0.7
items")		Foreign and other	0.9
		Miscellaneous liabilities	6.5
Total	$75.9	Total	$75.9

TABLE 17-1. By (*a*) controlling its earning assets (government securities and discounts), the Fed (*b*) controls its liabilities (deposits and Federal Reserve notes), thereby (*c*) controlling the economy's money supply (currency and demand deposits) and affecting NNP.

Discounts, loans, and acceptances item is primarily loans or advances to member banks. (The interest rate the Fed charges banks for such loans, or "discounts," is called the "discount rate," which is usually about the same in all 12 Reserve Districts.)

The right-hand side lists the usual capital accounts: original capital subscribed by the member banks plus accumulated surplus. This would be much greater for so profitable a business were it not for the already-mentioned fact that the Federal Reserve gives *all* its excess profits back to the Treasury. (The Fed's profits come from the privilege the government gives it to issue Federal Reserve notes and bank deposits for the member banks at no interest cost; in return it acquires interest-yielding government bonds and loans. Hence, it is only fair that the government take back these privileged profits.)

Federal Reserve notes are the Fed's principal liabilities. These are the various dollar, five-dollar, and other bills we all carry in our wallets. The Fed is highly privileged to have been granted by Congress this power to issue currency (its "right to counterfeit"!).

Little comment is needed on several of its deposit liabilities: United States government deposits, foreign central bank deposits, and miscellaneous.

Of vital importance, though, are the member banks' Reserve balances kept on deposit with the Federal Reserve Banks and shown as FRB liabilities. Along with small amounts of vault cash, these are the Reserves we have been talking about. They provide the basis for multiple deposit creation by the member banks.

We shall see that the Fed, by altering its holding of government securities and discount assets, can create changes in the Reserves of the commercial banks—thereby starting off our earlier-mentioned five-step sequence. Later, Fig. 17-2 will show how these important balance-sheet and other items have changed in recent years. In summary, by varying its government-bond and other assets, the Fed can control the Reserves of the banks, (which, together with the currency held by the public, constitute the important so-called "monetary base") and thereby can control the rate of growth of the total money supply, M.

DISCRETIONARY MONETARY POLICIES BY THE FEDERAL RESERVE: OPEN-MARKET OPERATIONS

To initiate the five-step stabilization sequence, the Federal Reserve has three main weapons, which are, in order of their present importance, (1) open-market operations, (2) discount-rate policy, (3) changes in the *legal reserve ratio requirements* of the member banks. (We shall review its five minor weapons later in this chapter.)

By selling or buying government bonds in the open market (mostly in New York City), the Fed authorities can tighten member bank Reserves or loosen them. These so-called "open-market operations" are a central bank's most important stabilizing weapon.

At frequent intervals, even as you read this book, the Open Market Committee is meeting to decide whether to pump more Reserves into the banking system by buying Treasury bills (i.e., short-term bonds) or longer bonds; or whether to tighten things up a little by selling government securities. It is a never-ending job.

To see how an open-market operation changes Reserves, let us suppose that the Fed

Open-market sale cuts Reserves and cuts deposits 5 : 1:

(a) First, producing this change in the Federal Reserve Banks' balance sheet (billions of dollars)

FEDERAL RESERVE ASSETS		FEDERAL RESERVE LIABILITIES	
U.S. securities	−$1.0	Member bank Reserves	−$1.0
Total	−$1.0	Total	−$1.0

(b) Finally, producing this change in the member banks' balance sheet (billions of dollars)

MEMBER BANK ASSETS		MEMBER BANK LIABILITIES	
Reserves	−$1.0	Demand deposits	−$5.0
Loans and investments	− 4.0		
Total	−$5.0	Total	−$5.0

TABLE 17-2(a) and (b).   When an open-market sale kills off $1 billion of Reserves, it induces a $5 billion drop in total demand deposits. The member banks must call in loans and sell off their "investments" (i.e., their securities) up to $4 billion.

thinks the economic winds are blowing up a little inflation. Its Open Market Committee holds the usual secret meeting. They say: "Let's sell $1 billion of government bonds from our portfolio to contract Reserves and over-all money and credit." The motion is unanimously carried by vote of the seven Washington Governors and five Regional Bank Presidents.

To whom are the bonds sold? No one knows: to the open market. The dealers in government bonds—there are about half-a-dozen big ones—will not reveal the names of the buyers. But you can guess that they are primarily insurance companies, commercial banks, big business firms, and the dealers themselves.

The buyer will most likely pay for the bonds by a check to the Fed drawn on his bank account. The Fed will present this check for payment to his member bank. That member bank will *lose* an equivalent amount of its Reserve balances with the Federal Reserve. Table 17-2(a) shows the final effect on the Federal Reserve balance sheet. The open-market sale has cut down on the Fed's assets and liabilities. (It has also initially cut down on member bank Reserves and their demand deposits owed to the bond buyer.)

Actually, this shows only the *initial* potency of open-market sales. In all likelihood the $1 billion sale of government bonds will result in a $5 billion cut in the community's money supply. We've seen why before.

Reserves go down by $1 billion, and that tends to set off a $5 billion contraction of deposits. Table 17-2(b) shows the member banks' position after Reserves have been extinguished by the open-market operation. In the end, the Fed's open-market sale has put 5:1 downward pressure on bank-deposit M.

To test your understanding of open-market operations, consider the reverse process. Suppose incomes and jobs are at too low a level. What will the Open Market Committee want to do? Buy government bonds on the open market and thereby create new Reserves for the member banks? Produce thereby a 5:1 expansion in M, thus making credit cheaper and more easily available to investors, and consequently encouraging an upward shift in $C + I + G$ and a multiplier increase in NNP? Confirm all this.

DISCOUNT-RATE POLICY: A SECOND WEAPON

The Federal Reserve Banks also make loans to the member banks. These we call "discounts." When its discounts are growing, the banks are borrowing from the Fed, which is thereby helping bank Reserves to grow. When the Fed's discounts are dropping, it is helping bank Reserves to contract.[2]

Unfortunately, the Fed is not free to pursue a discount policy exactly the way it wants to. It cannot send salesmen out to drum up more discounts whenever it wants to expand them. All it can do is wait for banks to come to it. All it can do is name the "discount rate," which sets its interest charge in each of the 12 Federal Reserve Districts for such discounts or advances.

True, it can expect to get more business by lowering the discount rate or can discourage the volume of its discounts by raising the discount rate. But as far as discount policy is concerned, the Fed must play the passive role. It can sit and wait. It can veto. It can make its rate attractive. But it certainly cannot set its amount of *discounts* at precisely the figure it wants. Only in its open-market operations can it take the active role. But do not overlook the power of a veto. A bank knows it must not abuse the privilege of being able to discount; it must not *continually* use this source of funds. By being able to say No, the Fed has some power to put contractionary pressure on its discounts.

Changing the discount rate On New York's Wall Street, Chicago's LaSalle Street, and Boston's State Street, everyone keeps careful watch on the discount rate that the Fed charges for its discounts. Thus, on the Thursday when the discount rate is raised, stocks and bonds will usually fall in price. Even London and Paris find their interest rates and investment spending influenced by announced changes in our discount rate.

The discount rate is usually set to *follow* the market. After open-market sales have been forcing interest rates up, banks will more and more try to borrow from the Fed at the not-yet-raised discount rate. To discourage such a growth in its discounts and advances, the Fed will eventually have to raise the discount rate to bring it back into normal alignment with the market or else—as in 1968–1969—step up its distasteful need to ration and discourage use by banks of the discount privilege.

And when the Fed does raise the discount rate, very many in the market will say: "Aha, the Board still thinks the wind is blowing in the inflationary direction." Changes in the discount rate, as well as being *reflections* that follow the tightness of credit, can also have important reinforcing *causal* effects upon the credit market. The effective

[2] When the Federal Reserve System was started, it was thought that discount policy would be most important of all. The idea was to have member banks "rediscount" their customers' promissory notes, sending them over to the Reserve Banks in return for new cash. That way the neighborhood banks would never run out of money to accommodate worthy farm and business borrowers. It did not work out that way, for two reasons. First and most important, today experts realize that the last thing a healthy economy wants is an *elastic* money supply that will *automatically* expand when business is good and contract when it is bad. That way lies disastrous *reinforcement* of business cycles and inflation. Second, banks find that they prefer to borrow from the Fed on the basis of their numerous government securities rather than on their customers' promissory notes. Since 1935, most borrowing is on government securities, and that is why we now speak of the "discount rate" rather than of the old-fashioned "rediscount rate." (In England, they speak always of "bank rate.")

interest rate banks charge customers—such as the "prime rate" charged biggest corporate borrowers—may soon get forced up to maintain their differential above the discount rate.

These patterns are reversed when the Fed wants easier credit. The discount rate is lowered to reflect the ease *already* apparent in the market, and the announcement of its being lowered usually serves to ease the market *further*. Thus, in August, 1960, when the discount rate was cut from $3\frac{1}{2}$ to 3 per cent, stocks and bonds soared in price. By contrast, the April, 1969, announcement of a discount-rate rise caused bonds and stocks to plummet downward; now people realized the Fed would keep money tight to fight the Vietnam demand-pull inflation.

Discount-rate reform Few economists like the way discounting now works. When open-market operations tighten the reserve base by $1 billion, often this induces the banks to *offset* this by going to the discount window for some fraction of $1 billion of new borrowed Reserves. Why countenance such waste motion, which merely makes the needed initial open-market operation bigger?

Banks never quite know how free they really are to use the discount privilege. In 1969 some banks paid more than 13 per cent for funds from the Euro-dollar market and as much as 11 in the Federal Funds market when ostensibly they could still borrow from the Fed at the 6 per cent discount rate. They feared to do so. They feared rebuff or frowns. But most of all, they feared to use up the last-resort avenue which they might need more at some later date.

A massive study by the Federal Reserve in the late 1960s led to a proposal to make the right of the member banks to discount (part of the time, but never for *permanent* borrowing) *more automatic*. Of course, to keep banks from making a sure buck by borrowing at a low discount rate and lending at a high market rate, the proposal also contemplated having the discount rate follow market rates more closely than in the past. However, the Vietnam inflation of 1965–1970 put off the actual introduction of this proposed reform.

CHANGING RESERVE REQUIREMENTS: A DRASTIC AND INFREQUENTLY USED WEAPON

The Federal Reserve Board is given by Congress the limited power to raise or lower the required legal reserve ratio that the member banks must keep against their deposits. If the Fed wants to make credit tight very quickly, it can raise the required reserve ratios for the city and country banks to the 22 and 14 per cent statutory limits. (If it wanted credit still tighter, it would have to ask Congress to raise these limits, just as it would have to if it wished to raise the 10 per cent maximum time-deposit requirement.)

If the Fed wants to ease credit conditions, it can do the reverse. It can cut legal reserve ratios, doing this again and again until the banks are down to 10 and 7 per cent. (To go lower than that would require a new act of Congress.) And, as in 1969, the Fed can raise the required reserve ratios behind time deposits.

Changing reserve requirements is a powerful tool: it is used sparingly—a change comes only every few years, not every day as in the case of open-market operations. It could be used more often; but open-market operations can produce about the same effects.

Exactly how does an increase in required reserve ratios operate to tighten credit? Suppose the banks had built up deposits in a 5:1 fashion as a result of the required ratio having been 20 per cent, with excess reserves being negligible. Now suppose the Fed wants to tighten credit and Congress lets it raise the required ratio to 25 per cent. Even if the Fed does nothing by way of open-market operations or discount policy to change bank Reserves, the member banks now have to contract their loans and investments greatly—and their deposits as well.

Why? Because (as the last chapter showed) the bank deposits can now only be in a 4:1, not a 5:1, ratio. So there will have to be a drop by one-fifth in all deposits.

This painful cut will start to take place quickly. As soon as the Board signs the new fiat raising requirements to 25 per cent, banks find themselves deficient with

Raising Reserve requirements forces member banks to contract:

Before: when 1:5 prevails (billions of dollars)

MEMBER BANK ASSETS		MEMBER BANK LIABILITIES	
Reserves	$20	Demand deposits	$100
Loans and investments	80		
Total	$100	Total	$100

After: when 1:4 prevails (billions of dollars)

MEMBER BANK ASSETS		MEMBER BANK LIABILITIES	
Reserves	$20	Demand deposits	$80
Loans and investments	60		
Total	$80	Total	$80

TABLE 17-3. The same base of Reserves now supports only 4:1, not 5:1, of deposits. What will be happening on Main Street in the transition?

respect to Reserves. They will have to sell some bonds and call in some loans. The bond buyers will use up their demand deposits, and the borrowers whose loans are called will use up their demand deposits to pay back such loans. The process ends only after banks have brought down their deposits to 4 rather than 5 times their Reserves.

Table 17-3 shows how their combined balance sheets might look before and after the change. You may be sure that so great a change in so short a time would result in very high interest rates, in unavailable credit, in great cuts in I (and possibly in local G), and in great reductions in national income and employment. Hence, this powerful weapon of changing reserve requirements is sparingly used.[3]

MINOR WEAPONS: QUALITATIVE VERSUS QUANTITATIVE CONTROLS

The Fed also has used five further minor weapons: (1) "moral suasion," (2) selective controls over "margin requirements" for loans to buy stocks, (3) control over maximum interest rates banks can pay on time deposits, (4) selective credit controls over installment contracts and consumer credit, (5) selective controls over the terms of housing mortgage contracts. (The last two powers Congress let lapse in the early 1950s.)

[3] In 1936–1937 reserve requirements were sharply raised. But at that time banks found loans and bonds so unattractive that they were already holding heavy "excess reserves," i.e., holding more idle cash than the law required. So raising legal requirements did not have the great effects in lowering M or raising interest rates that it would have today. It should also be pointed out that such a sudden squeeze on banks' reserve positions would undoubtedly today cause them to borrow at the "discount window" even at a higher discount rate for some temporary period at least. And today, when reserve requirements are raised, their impact at first is cushioned by offsetting open-market operations.

Late in 1969 the Fed imposed a new 10 per cent reserve requirement against certain Euro-dollar borrowing by the member banks.

Moral suasion This refers to "jawbone control": the Reserve officials express their displeasure if banks are not doing what is wanted of them. Bankers are called in for heart-to-heart talks. An appeal to community spirit is made. Vague threats concerning future availability of credit may be made, and bank examiners may become especially zealous in going over the books.

Many economists doubt that slaps on the wrist will keep competitive bankers from doing what they want to do. Nevertheless, it is a tenable belief that moral suasion does have some significant effects, especially in the short run and especially when banks are heavily reliant on the privilege to "discount" at the Fed. After all, bankers are sensitive to public opinion just like anyone else. And bankers find it only prudent not to get in the bad books of the Federal Reserve (as their extraordinary compliance with the post-1966 voluntary program of control over foreign loans by banks did demonstrate).

Selective controls: margin requirements A selective or qualitative credit control is contrasted with an over-all quantitative credit control that operates merely by affecting over-all bank Reserves and over-all credit tightness. Selective credit controls can be very important in countries that have considerable central planning and supervision by the government of the detailed actions of business. To build a house there, you may need a permit; similarly, to float a new stock or bond issue.

The banks, particularly if, as in England, there are a few great ones, may be called in by the Chancellor of the Exchequer. He may say: "Look here. We want you to favor export industries in making your loans. And favor necessities. And cut back your total loans by 10 per cent before Christmas."

Such selective credit controls can be very powerful indeed. However, in normal peacetime it is the American custom not to rely on these detailed interferences with the pricing process—with one exception. The Federal Reserve is given power to set "margin requirements" that limit how much people can borrow in order to buy and carry listed common and preferred stocks. Thus, I could in 1970 borrow 20 per cent from my broker but had to put up the other 80 per cent myself. In 1958 I could borrow only 10 per cent, and in 1962, I could borrow as much as 50 per cent.[4]

Interest-rate ceilings When any bank can earn 6 per cent or more on safe short-term government bonds (or even more on riskier loans), it stands to gain when it can owe people demand deposits at a zero interest rate. Under competition, free banking would result in banks then bidding up the interest rate paid on demand deposits to a positive level. (That is what used to happen in the 1920s: Our grandfathers often got paid 5 per cent on their checking deposits! Or they could often draw checks on their saving or time deposits.)

[4]Back in the boom market of 1929, there were no rules at all: one could borrow 70, 80, or even 90 per cent of the value of any stock he bought. Little wonder that, once the crash came, brokers began to phone their clients for them to put up more "margin to cover the declining value of their stocks." Since many clients were already operating on a shoestring, they could not pony up the extra margin. Result: The broker had to sell their stocks; so just when stocks were already weak, the forced selling by low-margin holders added to the avalanche.

But during the Great Depression Congress made it illegal for banks to explicitly pay interest on checking accounts. This was for two reasons: Banks could earn practically nothing then on safe government bonds, and the industry felt that its earnings would be better if rivals were kept by law from bidding positive interest on demand deposits; aside from this cartel reason, many experts jumped to the conclusion that it was *over-competition* among banks that had given rise to unsound lending practices and which had led to the mass bank runs and failures.

This depression-born stricture against interest on demand deposits still stands. It explains why people and corporations have been putting less and less of their idle funds into demand deposits, keeping their check balances to a minimum and merely replenishing them from their savings accounts when they get too low. (And it explains the 1960s' rapid rise in the broadly defined M_2 money supply compared with the narrower M_1 definition including only deposits payable on demand. See Fig. 15-2, page 263.)

From the mid-thirties to the late fifties, the Fed also put low ceilings on the interest rates member banks could pay on *time* deposits. As long as competitive rates to be earned on government bonds remained low, this did not matter much. But when federal savings and loan associations could afford to pay 4, 5, and more per cent, people stopped leaving their money in commercial-bank savings accounts. They switched to nonmember banks and to S&Ls; in the case of firms, they switched to the Treasury-bill market. The big New York banks were especially hard hit when their foreign depositors began to withdraw deposits and to buy securities directly themselves.

In recent years, therefore, spurred on by the fear that foreign governments and firms would withdraw their money, the Fed, under so-called "Regulation Q," has raised the rates banks can pay on time deposits (to as much as $5\frac{1}{2}$-to-$7\frac{1}{2}$ per cent, depending on length of notice and account size). Critics feared that raising such ceilings would make money tighter. Actually, the reverse happened in 1962–1965, as competitive economic theory predicted it would: the member banks retained more funds than they otherwise would have, and the shift toward more time deposits at first had the good effect of keeping down the long-term interest rates so important for construction and investment loans, while permitting the Fed to tighten short-term rates so important to dissuade money from going abroad and worsening our gold problem.

In the tight-money years of 1966 and 1969 a new problem began to arise. During the 1960s the large New York banks pioneered a new kind of time deposit—the so-called "certificate of deposit." This was a negotiable instrument that would enable a corporation to deposit $100,000 or $1 million for 180 days (in 1969, say, at $6\frac{1}{4}$ per cent per annum); however, if at the end of a few days the firm should change its mind, it could sell the "C-D" to some other corporation and yet lose little or no interest. What was the result when credit became very tight in order to help calm down the Vietnam-induced inflationary gap? Investors started to withdraw their funds from West Coast savings and loan associations to put them into Eastern C-Ds. A few S&Ls were on the verge of bankruptcy after they began to lose funds in 1966; they now had to pay $5\frac{3}{4}$ per cent or more on time deposits, whereas they had obligated themselves to lend money on long-term mortgages that brought in a net yield of less than that!

To Congress it appeared that the competitive scramble for funds led to unwise and risky loans by banks and S&Ls desperate to hold onto their deposits. Therefore, Congress has led the Federal Reserve to use Regulation Q to limit interest rates that banks can pay on *low-denomination* C-Ds. (The poor get soaked!) Inasmuch as the government insures deposits in banks and in S&Ls, it has a burning interest in how competition works out in this area. But diddling maximum rates to protect S&Ls may not work long. Even if commercial banks are kept by fiat from offering competitive interest rates, depositors can withdraw funds from S&Ls and invest directly in higher-yielding Treasury bills, giving rise to what is called "disintermediation."

Ceilings on deposit interest interfere with the free flow of funds, in and out of housing particularly. Thus many economists urge the abolition of ceilings. Others argue, "While we have Regulation Q, let's recognize that it gives us an extra selective weapon to help achieve the goal of keeping housing from being the prime victim of tight-money programs. Let the S&Ls, which invest primarily in housing, have more generous interest ceilings than the ordinary banks to attract funds for housing. Later, when Fed policy eases generally, reverse this."[5]

Control over installment terms   Besides moral suasion and direct controls over margin borrowing and deposit terms, the Federal Reserve for many years had the power to set limits on installment contracts. Thus, in the years of the Korean conflict, the Fed made you put down a minimum amount when you bought cars, furniture, and other goods; and this same so-called "Regulation W" also required you to pay up on your charge accounts before buying more goods on credit. Regulation W seems to have been very effective, and the same has been true of similar regulations in Britain and elsewhere. But it became unpopular, and after the Korean crisis this important emergency power was allowed to lapse.

Control over mortgage terms   Congress had long empowered the Federal Reserve to set terms for mortgage down payments and the number of years for amortization of principal. This so-called "Regulation X" gave the Board powerful leverage over the pace of house-construction expenditure. By raising down payments and shortening the span of mortgages, homeowners would face discouragingly-high monthly payments, and thus the Board could choke off housing. By doing the reverse, it could stimulate construction.

This strong weapon of mortgage control was allowed by Congress to lapse in 1953. The Fed, with its philosophy of over-all quantitative controls rather than selective fiats, was perhaps not too sorry to see this power go; but it soon learned that Nature abhors a vacuum. If the central bank will not wield these powers, somebody else will. Financial intermediaries and governmental housing agencies competitive to the central bank have burgeoned.

Thus, much housing is subsidized by the government: the Veterans Administration (VA) guarantees mortgage loans, and so does the Federal Housing Authority (FHA). Also, there is the Federal National Mortgage Association ("Fannie Mae"), which buys mortgages to make credit for housing more available. The federal savings associations can borrow from the Federal Home Loan Bank, a government agency which threatens to become practically a second central bank, not always coordinated with the Federal Reserve.[6]

---

[5]See P. A. Samuelson, *Readings in Economics* (McGraw-Hill, New York, 1970, 6th ed.), for a Chase Manhattan Bank account of how Regulation Q caused more than a $10 billion run-off of C-Ds in the Vietnam inflation.

[6]These government agencies, which have no connection with the Federal Reserve, have often done what you might expect—they have worked at cross-purposes to the Board. Nowadays, public policy takes special interest in certain sectors of the credit market. It does not seem content to let interest rates find their own level in each market; it seeks to encourage activities such as housing and small business and to discourage others such as stock speculation. (Earlier we saw that finance and insurance companies perform many functions similar to the banks. But they are not under the tight reserve requirement and other controls exercised over the member banks. Some experts think that monetary policy would gain in potency and fairness if some *controls over financial intermediaries* were introduced. Others say, "After all, they don't directly create *M*, and in any case putting pressure on the banks does

INTERNATIONAL GOLD MOVEMENTS AND RESERVES

Until now we have been speaking as if all the movements in total M originate in actions of the Federal Reserve aimed to change bank Reserves in the direction desired by the authorities. There is, however, an *external* force that affects our M, namely, official gold movements and movements in and out of dollars that foreigners hold as international reserves.[7] These are primarily gold exports to or from abroad. Such movements tend to induce changes in M even when the Fed has done nothing. But it should be realized that the three already-discussed weapons of Fed monetary policy can enable the authorities to *offset* any such changes in M that are thought to be against the national interest.

Part Five will deal with international trade in detail; here we need only touch upon the banking aspects of gold flows. When American exporters are selling more goods abroad than importers are importing, and consequently foreigners are paying us by shipping gold here (or repatriating dollar currency held abroad), we shall see that the deposit of such gold in our banking system will give rise to the familiar 5:1 expansion process—just as in our earlier examples where a widow, or a seller of bonds to the Fed, or anyone else brought new Reserves to deposit in a member bank.

When, as has been more the custom in recent years, America is losing gold to pay for the excess of her total imports (including government spending abroad on military and foreign aid) over her total exports, there will then be a loss of gold and of Reserves by our banking system. Unless the Federal Reserve Board chooses to offset this loss of Reserves by some action, what must then happen to M? The money supply will be contracted in a 5:1 fashion.

GOLD AND INTERNATIONAL RESERVES AS A CONSTRAINT ON MONETARY POLICY

This completes the discussion of how international gold and dollar-reserve movements can themselves affect our money supply. As explained, such international influences on our M *can be offset* by planned Federal Reserve open-market operations acting in the opposite direction. All over the world, central banks have often chosen to offset the influences of international gold movements. In particular, for 25 years after 1933 the United States was in the position of having so much gold that she could determine domestic policy, completely ignoring her international balance of payments and blithely offsetting any gold movements she wanted to.

As we shall see in Part Five, dealing with international trade, this freedom no longer holds. When the Federal Reserve wants to lower interest rates in order to pursue a domestic stabilization policy of expansion, it must now take into account the following fact: If short-term interest rates are lowered here relative to those abroad, many foreigners will want to move their funds to higher-interest-rate markets abroad. There will be a resulting drain of "cool money" and gold from our shores; and, although we still have

---

put pressure on the intermediaries at one stage removed.") Government-guaranteed mortgages—under the Veterans or Federal Housing Administrations—often carry a maximum interest rate. When the free-market interest rates rise, money for them dries up—inadvertently increasing the potency of monetary policy.

[7] After 1970 official gold is to be supplemented by "paper gold" in the form of Special Drawing Rights in the International Monetary Fund, as Chapter 36 will discuss.

much gold, we can no longer afford to ignore such a drain. In an era when fear of losses of gold and international reserves dominates, there must be greater reliance on stabilizing *fiscal* policies rather than *monetary* policies.

FINANCE IN THE POST-WORLD WAR II PERIOD

The pyramid of credit   Figure 17-1 summarizes the relation between the commercial or member banks and the public; between these banks and the Federal Reserve Banks; and

The Federal Reserve provides our currency and bank Reserves—the monetary base for total *M*:

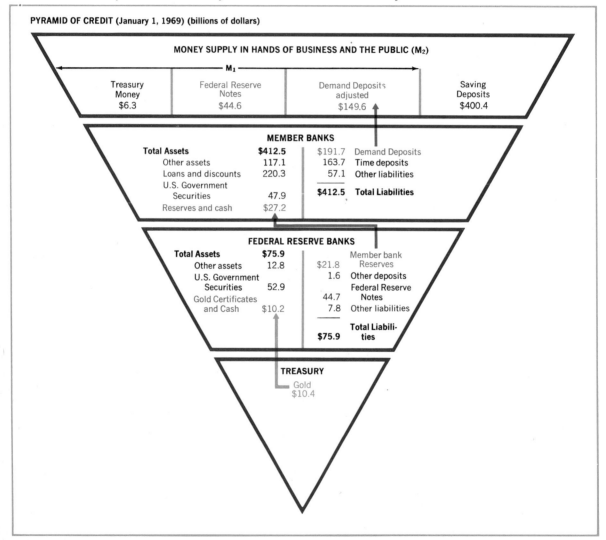

FIG. 17-1.   The small amount of gold at the bottom of this pyramid no longer puts limits on the money supply since Congress passed a law repealing all gold-reserve requirements on the Federal Reserve. The blue items summarize Fed control of bank Reserves and hence the money supply. Notice that the liabilities of one stage correspond to the assets of the next-highest stage. Total saving deposits include those of savings and loan and other noncommercial banks. (Sources: Tables 15-1, 16-1, and 17-1; 1969 *Federal Reserve Bulletin*.)

The Fed controls the monetary base—bank Reserves and currency—and hence shapes total *M*:

FIG. 17-2.   Money in circulation and Reserves underlying bank *M* have grown with the economy. The Fed has not let gold flows call the tune. Note that the drop in gold during the 1960s was not accompanied by a drop in Reserves! (Source: *Federal Reserve Bulletin.*)

between the Reserve Banks and the Treasury. At the bottom of the pyramid is a relatively small amount of gold held by the United States Treasury, about \$10½ billion worth in 1970. With minor exceptions not worth noting, this gold is matched by gold certificates in the coffers of the Federal Reserve Banks.

Moving up the pyramid from the Treasury to the Federal Reserve Banks, we find their total liabilities and total assets to be \$75.9 billion. Besides gold certificates, the Federal Reserve Banks hold about 12.8 + 52.9 billion dollars of loans and investments, primarily in short-term government bills. Matching their total assets, the Reserve Banks' biggest single liability consists of Federal Reserve note currency. This is held largely by the public.

The other principal liability of the Reserve Banks is Reserves of the member banks. Pyramided upon \$21.8 billion of Reserves is the volume of bank-deposit money held by the public. To show all the saving deposits held by the public, to the top layer we have added deposits in S&Ls, mutual savings banks, etc.

The pyramid of credit gives us a still picture. To see changes that have been taking place in recent years, refer to Fig. 17-2, which depicts the important economic variables published each month in the *Federal Reserve Bulletin.*

At the top is currency in circulation. It grew mightily in World War II and has since shown persistent growth. Demand deposits would be too large to show on the same chart, but they would show a pattern of somewhat slower growth.

The Fed seeks to control banks' Reserve positions:

FIG. 17-3. When discounts exceed excess reserves, net free reserves turn negative (becoming net borrowed reserves). Usually, this means credit is tight and interest rates are high.

When business slackens and the Fed pursues easy-money policies, its open-market purchases give banks new Reserves in order to encourage expansion of M and $C + I + G$. By lowering or raising the discount rate relative to short-term market interest rates (such as Treasury-bill rates), the Fed can encourage or discourage discounts.

Member bank Reserve balances, which together with vault cash constitute Reserves, show a similar but less dramatic pattern. Our major interest is to see how these Reserves change. Their trend has not been affected by the behavior of the gold stock and dollars held by foreigners. The Fed has not let undulations and declines in our gold holdings show up as changes in Reserves. It has been using open-market purchases to offset our loss of gold, thus keeping member bank Reserves from falling after 1958.

See Figs. 17-2 and 17-3 for the volume of *discounts*. Their total looks small, but their change in some years is significant in comparison with that year's net open-market purchases or sales. In the short run, these discounts operate at cross-purposes to open-market operations. Thus, note how discounts grew in 1966 and 1969, just when the Fed was trying to tighten credit. As mentioned, some economists, therefore, are critical of discount policy. But defenders say, "If it weren't for the safety valve of the discount privilege, the Fed wouldn't dare to have so tight a policy of open-market sales. Just as car brakes enable cars to go *faster*, the existence of discounting enables the Fed to pursue a sterner open-market policy."

Excess reserves, as shown in the top chart of Fig. 17-3, have been pretty small in recent years.[8] When discounts get above excess reserves—so that so-called "net free reserves" are negative—you can be pretty sure money is tight.

The middle of Fig. 17-3 plots the important concept *net free reserves*. It tends to be negative when "money is tight" and interest rates are high and to be positive when the Fed eases credit. Thus, as Vietnam inflation raged after 1967, the Fed, by engineering declining net reserves, made the money market tighten.

[8] In the mid-thirties you would have seen a tremendous bulge in excess reserves. Gold flowed here in great amounts; but with banks wary of loans and of further government securities, the result was no multiple expansion—merely a piling up of excess reserves. The Board, nervous always about inflation (even during the slump itself!), feared that these excess reserves might suddenly become the base of deposit expansion. So, as we have seen, they doubled reserve requirements, to bring excess reserves

REPORT CARD FOR THE FEDERAL RESERVE:
MONETARISM VERSUS THE MAJORITY

How has the Fed been doing? Expert opinion is divided. In the 1920s some thought the Federal Reserve had learned how to tame the business cycle forever. The Great Crash of 1929 and the following depression deflated that view, and ever since the majority of the experts think that monetary policy must be *reinforced* by stabilizing fiscal policies.

But there is one important minority dissent to this view. A school called the "monetarists," originating at the University of Chicago and led by the able economist Professor Milton Friedman, believe that essentially everything that can be done to control macroeconomic aggregates—inflationary gaps and epochs of depression and slow growth —has to be done by control of the money supply *alone*. Fiscal policy, Professor Friedman insists, is important in helping to shape how much of the macroeconomic total is in the public sector as against the private sector and in shaping the trend of interest rates and of the consumption share of GNP. But on the basis of his studies of the history of money in the United States and in many other countries, Professor Friedman is convinced that fiscal policy per se has essentially no predictable effect on the prospects for inflation or deflation, for high employment or mass unemployment.

Monetarism represents an extreme view.[9] But since it is proposed by economists with serious scientific interests, it should not be rejected just because it does not involve a mid-ground position. After all, scientific truth *could* turn out to be on one extreme rather than in the middle.

Monetarism versus the eclectic majority   The present author, having studied and weighed the evidence in favor of monetarism, has formed the opinion that where it differs from the majority eclectic view—which holds (1) that *both* fiscal and monetary policies matter much, (2) that the velocity of circulation of money is induced to increase systematically when interest rates rise and make it economical for people to turn over their cash balances more rapidly, and (3) that open-market purchases which create new M for the community have their stimulating effects on GNP spending somewhat offset by the reduction in the liquid interest-bearing government bonds now held by the community—where monetarism differs from this so-called "post-Keynesian neoclassical synthesis," it is essentially wrong and indeed an extreme.

Thus, I think that the tax cut of 1964 had a stimulating effect on the economy beyond that associated with the Fed's creation of new M to help finance that move. Professor Friedman disagrees. Professor Friedman believes that the tax surcharge of 1968–1969 had no effects on the current rate of inflation that are not attributable to the money-supply behavior of that period. Indeed to a monetarist, the unprecedentedly long post-Kennedy

---

under control. In brisk times, when banks can find attractive earning assets, excess reserves do not become substantial. As the Federal Funds market has developed, even the small country banks have cut down on their level of excess reserves.

[9] Reference can be made to M. Friedman and A. Schwartz, *A Monetary History of the United States* (Princeton University Press for the National Bureau of Economic Research, Princeton, N.J., 1963), and to articles pro and con monetarism by Friedman, Samuelson, and Walter Heller in P. A. Samuelson, *Readings in Economics* (McGraw-Hill, New York, 1970, 6th ed.).

expansion of the 1960s would have taken place even if the budget had been always in balance at a low level—provided the Fed had made M grow as it actually did during the decade. The majority of the experts do not believe this, arguing that interest rates early in the decade would have been much lower and GNP lower because of the difference in the velocity of circulation that would have been induced by increasing money alone.

Economics is not an exact science. We cannot repeat the 1960s under controlled conditions to settle the debate. Therefore, an author should present in his textbook a framework of analysis that can be shaded in favor of either of these two scientifically proposed models. And this edition, particularly, has been written to make this possible.

For even if, in the end, monetarism should be deemed by the jury of science to have been one-sided, (1) it is based on evidence; (2) an increasing minority of economists embrace it, both in the universities (e.g., Karl Brunner of Ohio State and Allan Meltzer of Carnegie-Mellon) and in business (e.g., Beryl Sprinkel, vice-president of the Harris Trust Company in Chicago, and Thomas Meigs, vice-president of the First National City Bank of New York); (3) it has an increasing following in Washington (among Nixon economists), in the Joint Economic Committee, and on the editorial pages of the *Washington Post* and *New York Times;* and (4) within the Federal Reserve System it is given increasing weight (even though it is only the Federal Reserve Bank of St. Louis that subscribes to its basic differences with the majority view).

Most important, Friedman's researches have *reinforced* the researches of post-Keynesians such as Yale's James Tobin and MIT's Franco Modigliani, to insist that *money does matter much,* to work out the channels by which it works, and to deny the view that some Keynesian followers took after 1939 (and which still prevailed in Britain's famous Radcliffe Report of 1959) that money does not matter much or at all.

Leaning against the wind   These disputes are not academic. They shape policy. You might think that a monetarist like Professor Friedman, convinced that money matters exclusively or most, would want to use control over the money supply to fight against the ups and downs of business activity. But you would be wrong. Dr. Friedman insists that *no* "fine tuning" will work. Money matters more than anything else, but even *its* effects are not perfectly predictable, there being always uncertain lags between cause and effect. Reinforcing his skepticism concerning fine tuning is Dr. Friedman's philosophical position that "rules" and not "discretionary authority by men or committees" should prevail. Hence, his sole recommendation for monetary policy is elegantly simple.

Monetarists tell the Fed to stabilize the growth of the money supply—every year and every month—at some agreed-upon constant rate—say, 4½ per cent per year, or at the least within the range of 4 to 5 per cent. Then, forgetting active fiscal policy and all fine tuning, let the free market take care of the rest—of interest rates, of unemployment, of the price level.

To illustrate this important difference in philosophy, consider 1966 and 1969.

In 1966 when Congress refused to raise taxes to prevent Vietnam inflation, the Fed slowed down the growth of M to a halt. There followed in early 1967 a pause or period of retardation but not a recession. Most experts think the Fed did pretty well in this period. But not the monetarists. They blame the Fed for not having made money grow at $4\frac{1}{2}$ per cent in 1966. Then in 1967 when it made money grow faster than $4\frac{1}{2}$ per cent to ensure that there would not be a recession (which the monetarists had said was "inevitable"), the Fed again gets a flunk from the monetarists. To the monetarists it is as if you compound the crime of running over a pedestrian, backing up your truck and running over him again; they get the Fed coming and going, for creating too much M at a time of inflation and too little at a time of battling inflation—rather than always creating a fixed amount.

To those who favor use of man's best intelligence to lean against the wind, one deviation tends to cancel out rather than aggravate the other. The helmsman tacks to the northeast and to the northwest to get north; he deserves a good mark for both decisions. Similarly in 1969, the monetarists espoused a gradual return toward their long-run growth number rather than the Fed's deliberate overshoot to below that number in order to make progress against the inflation. And in power, the Nixon economists sided with the majority, against the monetarists in this matter.

The future   Economics is an exciting subject because there is always much to learn. Unquestionably the Federal Reserve in the future will give less weight than it did in the past to stabilizing interest rates even when that meant destabilizing the economy and the rate of growth of the money supply. Undoubtedly the Open Market Committee will listen more carefully to the monetarists of the St. Louis region and less to those who tended in the past to overemphasize the target of "net free reserves" (recall Fig. 17-3's middle panel). That, in the author's opinion, will be the important contribution of monetarism to economic knowledge. But turning over the steering of monetary policy to an autogyro-robot formula would represent, I believe, an inefficient retreat to coarse tuning that would jeopardize real growth, full employment, and reasonable price stability.

SUMMARY

1   The Federal Reserve is a central bank, a bank for bankers. Its duty is to control the monetary base (currency plus bank Reserves) and through control of this "high-powered money" to control the community's supply of money. Its five-step mode of action goes thus: (1) it contracts bank Reserves, which (2) causes multiple contractions in total M deposits, which (3) makes credit expensive (high interest rates) and hard to get, which (4) depresses private and public investment spending, which (5) puts a multiplied damper on money income and prices.

2   The powerful weapons the Fed uses are (*a*) open-market operations, (*b*) discount-rate policy, and (*c*) changes in legal reserve requirements. Minor weapons used at times by central banks are moral suasion and selective controls over time-deposit interest ceilings, margin borrowing, installment sales, and mortgage credit terms.

3   Sales by the Fed of government securities to the open market represent a positive act which reduces its assets and liabilities and which reduces the Reserves of the member banks, and hence their base for deposits. People end up with less M and more government bonds. Open-market purchases do the opposite, ultimately expanding M at the expense of outstanding bonds. Powerful day-to-day open-market operations should be understood by every student of monetary policy.

4   Outflows of official gold and dollars will reduce Reserves and M unless offset by FRB open-market purchases of bonds (as was done in recent years). Inflows have opposite effects.

5   The main facts of finance, as shown by the still picture of the credit pyramid or by the charts of changing Reserves and money supply, are to be understood in terms of this chapter's analysis. The view of monetarists—that the money supply dominates aggregate demand and that it should be set always at a fixed growth rate—clashes with the view of the majority's post-Keynesian synthesis—that, while M matters much, so also do tax, expenditure, and investment shifts in $C + I + G$, and that "leaning against the wind" will improve on automatic M rules.

QUESTIONS FOR DISCUSSION

1   In what Federal Reserve District are you? Where is the nearest branch?

2   Trace the effects of a $1 billion open-market purchase. An open-market sale.

3   Trace the effects of a doubling of reserve requirements; a halving. Which alters bank earnings more: open-market or reserve-requirement action?

4   List the weapons of monetary control of the Reserve authorities. How powerful are they to control (*a*) M, (*b*) interest rates, (*c*) prices, and (*d*) employment and unemployment?

5   What are the effects of ceilings on time deposits on monetary controls and housing?

6   "Gold movements affected prices only because we used them as a barometer, signaling us to expand or contract total M supply. Of course, the gold standard was a stupid system; but it was wiser to tie ourselves to such an imperfect system than to trust corrupt legislatures whose tendency is always to print inflationary paper money." Discuss.

7   Discuss the following 1939 FRB statement: "The Federal Reserve System can see to it that banks have enough reserves to make money available to commerce, industry, and agriculture at low rates; but it cannot make the people borrow, and it cannot make the public spend the deposits that result when the banks do make loans and investments."

8   Give both sides of the debates between monetarists and the post-Keynesian majority. How have post-1970 events tilted the scientific issues?

Review your understanding of the following concepts:

the five-step sequence
high-powered monetary base:
   currency plus bank Reserves
availability and cost of credit
Federal Reserve balance sheet
open-market purchases and sales
discount rate, discounts
legal reserve ratio requirements

selective controls
moral suasion, interest ceilings
margin requirements
pyramid of credit
net free reserves (+ or −)
net borrowed reserves (− or +)
offsets to gold movements
monetarism, leaning against the wind

Synthesis of Monetary Analysis and Income Analysis

18

About this time there was a cry . . . for more paper-money. . . . I was on the side of an addition, being persuaded that the first small sum struck in 1723 had done much good, by increasing the trade, employment, and number of inhabitants in the province, since I now saw all the old houses inhabited, and many new ones building. . . . The utility of this currency became by time and experience so evident, as never afterwards to be much disputed. . . . Tho' . . . there are limits beyond which the quantity may be hurtful.

BENJAMIN FRANKLIN

Chapters 12 and 13 showed how saving and investment schedules intersect to determine the level of national income. And the last chapters have shown how changes in Federal Reserve policy affect the community's stock of money.

This chapter relates these two analyses. Monetary analysis is seen to fit in well with modern theory of income determination. And the stage is set for combined stabilization policy: (1) central bank monetary policies and (2) government fiscal policies (public expenditure and taxation, with the implied budget deficit or surplus). Monetary and fiscal policies have to be coordinated to achieve the goal of a progressive economy that enjoys reasonable price stability and lives up to its production potentialities.

This chapter shows how stabilization policies work and interact. We leave more detailed study of fiscal-policy issues for the final chapter of Part Two.

MONEY, LIQUIDITY PREFERENCE, MARGINAL EFFICIENCY, MULTIPLIER

The last chapters showed that M expansion by the central and commercial banks can shift upward the $C + I + G$ intersection point of Chapter 12. What is the same thing, an increase in M shifts upward the SS-II intersection point of Chapter 12, as follows:

When the Fed increases the money supply, M, this primarily affects investment, shifting II upward. Its expansion of M bids up bond prices and thus bids down interest rates and makes credit loans more easily available to investors. Therefore, it has become more profitable to undertake new investment projects. In the simplest case, the sequence is this:

$$M \text{ up} \rightarrow i \text{ down} \rightarrow I \text{ up} \rightarrow NNP \text{ up, up}$$

New graphs can illuminate this and also the process by which a shift in $C + I + G$ schedules—as, e.g., due to a technical investment boom or to a budget deficit—can, in the $MV = PQ$ relation of Chapter 15, shift upward the velocity of circulation (V) and thereby increase GNP beyond any change originating in M itself.

Chapter 15 (page 264) showed that the demand for money, along with depending positively on the level of income transactions, also depends inversely on the interest and profit yields sacrificed in order to have the safety and convenience of holding M. To get more M held by the community, the Fed must therefore bid down interest rates enough to make people find it advantageous to economize less on their cash balances and hold more M. The so-called "liquidity-preference schedule" of Fig. 18-1(a) summarizes how an increase in M resulting from monetary policy (open-market purchases, etc.) leads initially to a reduced interest rate—from A's 6 per cent to B's 4 per cent.

Figure 18-1(b) picks up the story to show how reduced interest rates (and what does not show on the graph but is lurking in the background, namely, greater *availability*

Central bank affects money, interest, investment, and output:

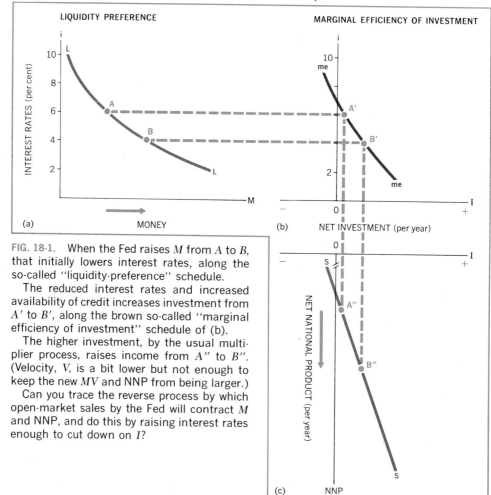

FIG. 18-1.   When the Fed raises M from A to B, that initially lowers interest rates, along the so-called "liquidity-preference" schedule.

The reduced interest rates and increased availability of credit increases investment from A' to B', along the brown so-called "marginal efficiency of investment" schedule of (b).

The higher investment, by the usual multiplier process, raises income from A'' to B''. (Velocity, V, is a bit lower but not enough to keep the new MV and NNP from being larger.)

Can you trace the reverse process by which open-market sales by the Fed will contract M and NNP, and do this by raising interest rates enough to cut down on I?

of credit) make more investment profitable. On Fig. 18-1(b)'s brown so-called "marginal efficiency of investment schedule," the drop in interest rate induces the rise in investment from A' to B'.

Figure 18-1(c) is merely Chapter 12's saving-investment diagram, page 210, turned on its side to line it up with Fig. 18-1(b)'s investment axis. Note that the interest-rate drop from A to B led to the investment rise from A' to B', and this (through the multiplier) has led to the NNP rise from A'' to B''.

To clinch understanding of this vital sequence, consider the following reverse case where monetary policy is contracting to wipe out an inflationary gap:

Monetary contraction (open-market sales, increased legal reserve ratios, etc.) bids up interest rates[1] and decreases credit availability. This depresses investment spending, and via the multiplier depresses income by even more. The basic sequence is now

$$M \text{ down} \rightarrow i \text{ up} \rightarrow I \text{ down} \rightarrow \text{NNP down, down}$$

Retrace the reverse BA, $B'A'$, and $B''A''$ sequence in Fig. 18-1 to see how money and income determination interact.

Depression model. This reconciliation of the theories of money and of income determination is, of course, oversimplified and needs some qualifications. For example, it does not emphasize what can happen in *severe depression* when the liquidity-preference curve is practically *horizontal* because interest rates are already so low that people are quite indifferent whether they hold M or the near-M government Treasury bills that the Fed wants to swap for M. In such a rare, but possible, case, the potency of monetary policy is at least temporarily very low. This is summarized in the aphorism "The central bank can pull on a string (to curb booms), but it can't *push on a string* (to reverse deep slumps)." Indeed, in such depressed times the profit expectations of businessmen are likely to be so low that they would not employ men and machines on new investment projects even if you let them borrow temporarily at a zero interest rate. In this case, the brown marginal-schedule of Fig. 18-1(b) is practically vertical; and again the chain of monetary action loses potency. (It is these "depression models" which are often, but wrongly, associated with the name of Keynes; and if they were his sole cases, his ideas would only rarely be of great interest in modern times.)

Classical case. The opposite "classical" or "monetarist" case, equally extreme, occurs when the liquidity schedule is practically vertical, so that each unit of M is under a strong compulsion to circulate at a constant velocity (with V a hard constant).[2] As most economists interpret the history of the last few centuries, this extreme case is not deemed realistic. They cannot agree with the extreme classical view known as "Say's Law of Conservation of Purchasing Power." The Appendix to this chapter discusses this matter further. It is enough here to characterize Say's Law as alleging:

"There cannot be any such thing as a saving-and-investment problem. What is not consumed is surely destined to be spent on investment goods, without the possibility of any snag."

Qualifications Eschewing polar cases, we must notice a point raised by experts in corporate finance. They point out that many firms, particularly large ones, finance their investments *out of retained earnings* and the cash flow generated by their own operations. Many

[1]Of course, if this monetary constriction is successful in ending rapid price inflation, interest rates in the longer run will not have to include a premium to cover depreciation of the dollar's real purchasing power. So the *initial* rise in interest rates from M restriction may well be reversed *in the end*.
[2]Or where the marginal-efficiency schedule is so horizontal that the slightest reduction in interest rate is enough to wipe out any deflationary gap and the slightest rise in interest is enough to wipe out any inflationary gap. Appendix readers will find more on these polar cases there.

avoid going to the banks or outside markets for borrowings or stock flotations. (EXAMPLE: The giant Du Pont Company has not borrowed a cent for more than 40 years, and yet it has been an important source of progress in the chemical field.)

To the degree that investment depends upon internal funds that are insulated from market fluctuations in interest-rate and credit availability, the potency of monetary policy is just that much less: it then takes greater action by the Fed on M to offset fluctuations in V. (One could go on to give other bits of evidence used to play down the importance of monetary policy, as for example the fact that when investors are uncertain about the future, small changes in safe-asset interest rates may have little effect upon the high profit rates investors require as inducement to undertake investment; and hence I may be insensitive to Fed policy. Both in 1966 and 1969, the only obvious impact of hard-money policies was on construction—not on business-equipment or inventory spending.)

Qualifications are not all in the direction of playing down the importance of M. We have noted in passing that credit policy does have some influence on G and C in $C + I + G$. Higher market evaluations of land, plant, and equipment, and of securities generally, may shift CC up. In the long run, if the increase in M comes, let us say, from Fed financing of a new government deficit (and not merely from a swap by the Fed's Open Market Committee of M for near-M), the new M *adds directly to people's net worth*, and this does lead them, other things equal, to spend more on C, on I, and on G.[3]

FISCAL POLICY AND INCOME DETERMINATION

Let us now resurvey fiscal-policy powers of government. Aside from the central bank, the government has another major way of affecting current spending, as we have seen in Chapter 13. As part of its *fiscal policy* the government can expand its *expenditures:* build useful public roads and schools, hire more civil servants, increase defense expenditure, do a hundred and one useful (or foolish) things to expand total spending. This could all be shown in a saving-investment diagram like Fig. 18-1(c).

But better still, we can show it as an *upward shift in the G component* of the $C + I + G$ schedule that was used as an alternative way to show income equilibrium. Figure 18-2(a) recapitulates the demonstration on page 229 of how an expansion of public expenditure G leads to an expansion of income.

The same type of chart[4] can show, in Fig. 18-2(b), the other side of fiscal policy—changes in tax collections. To raise NNP the fiscal authorities cut taxes: this gives people

---

[3] Some economists used to hope that higher interest rates would stimulate saving and kill consumption; i.e., they hoped an interest rise would shift up the SS schedule in Fig. 18-1(c), thereby reinforcing the effect of a downward shift in II. Experience, and the analysis of Chapter 31, suggest that outside the area of installment-financed consumer durables, these effects are probably weak and cannot be much counted on. (WARNING: The B points in Fig. 18-1 are final equilibria only if the Fed now creates just enough further M to satisfy enhanced *income* needs for new transaction balances; otherwise, we repeat the cycle with LL shifted up by the raised NNP level, finding final equilibria somewhere generally north of the midpoint between A and B. See the Hicks-Hansen diagrams in the Appendix for a rigorous handling of this transactions-need feedback problem.)

[4] The treatment here recapitulates the treatment on page 231 of Chapter 13 and best handles the effects of personal income taxes. For more complicated analysis of indirect and other taxes, also taking account of tax effects on investment, see intermediate texts.

higher disposable income, and since they have a propensity to consume out of extra income, this means they will consume more.

How can we show the increased consumption on Fig. 18-2(b)? We can show the effect of reduced taxes as an upward shift of the CC schedule, which is plotted against NNP and is a major component of the pictured $C + I + G$ schedule. With taxes lower, we subtract less from each level of NNP to get the corresponding level of disposable income. So, with higher disposable income corresponding to each NNP, we must show higher consumption—hence the higher CC curve.

Fiscal policy means government expenditure and tax policy:

FIG. 18-2(a). An increase in government expenditures on goods and services will shift $C + I + G$ up to $C + I + G'$, raising income to E'. Moreover, there is involved the usual multiplier effect of induced consumption spending (and, for that matter, induced private investment spending).

FIG. 18-2(b). Lowering taxes has similar expansionary effects on income, as was seen after the 1964 Kennedy-Johnson tax cut. Lower tax collection gives you more disposable income out of NNP, and hence shifts the consumption schedule upward. We go from E to E' as a result of the new $C' + I + G$ schedule. (Dollar for dollar, tax reduction is a little weaker than G increase. Why? Because some tax rebate is saved rather than used to shift CC up. A cut in taxes of 10 shifts CC *leftward* that much, but *upward* only by $\frac{2}{3} \times 10 = 6\frac{2}{3}$ when the MPC is $\frac{2}{3}$. Recall Fig. 13-8.) Show that the 1968 Vietnam tax surcharge shifts $C + I + G$ rightward and lowers E.

We may summarize the effects of fiscal policy:

Increased G raises income by raising the GG component of $C + I + G$. Reduced taxes raise the CC component of the $C + I + G$ schedule. Both together—which also means deficit financing or a reduction in the budgetary surplus—result in an even greater upward shift of the $C + I + G$ schedule and of equilibrium income. In the reverse case of contractionary fiscal policy, the final $C + I + G$ schedule shifts downward.

Here is a good test of one's understanding of the mechanics of fiscal policy:

Show the effect on NNP of the massive 1964 tax cut; and then see what the effect would have been if there had been a matching cut in G, as some people then recommended. For such matching changes, expenditure change slightly outweighs tax change.

THE SYNTHESIS AT WORK: TECHNOLOGICAL UNEMPLOYMENT?

To appreciate how modern tools of income and monetary analysis really work, let us here apply them as a case study to one of the great problems of our day.

A notable feature of our time is the development of "automation." Will this "new industrial revolution," in which machinery plays a new role, be a curse or a blessing to mankind? In particular, does it not confront the modern economy with the threat of mass unemployment?

Our tools enable us to give an optimistic answer; but our optimistic answer is quite different from the old-fashioned one, which simply *asserted* that inventions would *necessarily* create new jobs *just as fast* as they killed off old ones. Such a view was based upon an uninformed faith, and it was not persuasive. Sometimes experience accorded with it; sometimes experience went against it. In short, it made the outcome depend merely on *luck*. Our contemporary optimistic answer is truly more optimistic.

What automation is   The word "automation" was coined in 1947 by Del Harder, vice-president of Ford Motor Company, to apply to "automatic handling of parts between progressive production processes." At about the same time John Diebold, a management engineer, shortened the word "automatization" into automation. Diebold stressed the use of control devices that operate by means of "feedback."

Automation has still other meanings. Giant electronic calculators, which are a million-fold faster than hand machines, have simplified data processing and record keeping. One pretty machine does the work of a hundred pretty girls. Numbers recorded on magnetic tape can make a milling machine or lathe turn out intricate copies of a master pattern. Some modern digital computers can beat a good player at checkers, but none can yet beat a champion. None can yet play a really fine game of chess; at simple games such as ticktacktoe, the machine plays a perfect game.

Displacement of labor?   Whether one thinks automation is something absolutely new or represents a great postwar quickening of developments already known in principle, everyone admits it is a force to reckon with. Automation will presumably increase productivity; otherwise it would not be installed. Does this mean it will reduce the total need for labor and create mass unemployment? Back in the depression of the 1930s, long before we knew the term "automation," there was much fear of "technological unemployment." Should we again worry that modern man will become obsolete?

The late Norbert Wiener, MIT mathematician and one-time prodigy, who coined the name "cybernetics" (from the Greek word for "helmsman"), has pronounced on this subject in the following dramatic way:[5]

The industrial revolution has . . . displaced man and the beast as a source of power. . . . The factory of the future . . . will be controlled by something like a modern high-speed computing machine. . . . We can expect an abrupt and final cessation of the demand for the type of factory labor performing repetitive tasks . . . an intermediate transitional period of disastrous confusion. . . . Industry will be flooded with the new tools to the extent that they appear to yield immediate profits, irrespective of what long-time damage they can do. . . . It is perfectly clear that this will produce an unemployment situation, in comparison with which the present recession and even the depression of the thirties will seem a pleasant joke.

The forward look Any increase in productivity will indeed, *if output does not increase,* throw men out of work. In the Great Depression men readily believed total product would remain the same, that desired output would fail to grow with the growth of productivity. This view makes you look at unemployment in the following way: "Why did those unemployed workers over there lose their jobs? Which machines displaced them?" And so forth.

Modern students of income determination urge a more fruitful tack. They say:

Regardless of why those men lost their jobs, why aren't there enough *new* jobs for them? What fiscal and monetary policies are needed to create the new dollar purchasing power necessary for them to be hired anew?

"Satchel" Paige, a great baseball player, once said: "Never look backward; someone may be gaining on you." This is good advice in economics, too. Do not look back to find what caused past layoffs; look forward to see what you have to do to restore high employment. This is more efficient—and more helpful.

Better still, this approach means you do not have to decide whether the pessimists are right who argue that inventions will kill off more jobs than they create. Why care? *In every case we know that high employment without inflation will require monetary and fiscal policies of the correct magnitudes and mixed economies know what needs doing.*

Graphical restoration of high-employment equilibrium To apply this fruitful approach, we can use our consumption + investment + government spending schedule and look for income equilibrium where the $C + I + G$ schedule just intersects the 45° helping line. Figure 18-3 on the next page illustrates this.

Suppose that automation makes labor 30 per cent more productive. This means that the same full-employment labor force could produce 30 per cent more real national product; hence, the FF full-employment line of Fig. 18-3(a) is now shifted rightward 30 per cent to $F'F'$. Let us make quite unfavorable assumptions: (1) that government leaves its expenditure G as it was; and that the new machines are so cheap and short-lived that they can be introduced just by using up the depreciation allowances of the wearing-out

[5] N. Wiener, *The Human Use of Human Beings* (Houghton Mifflin, Boston, 1950), pp. 180–189.

The income-determination diagrams before and after automation:

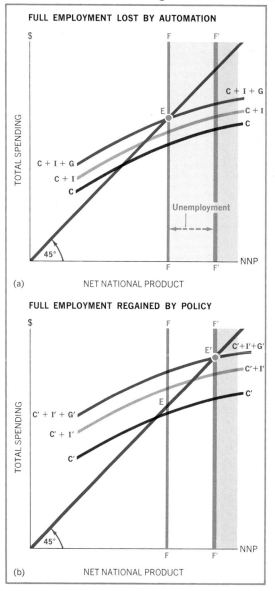

FULL EMPLOYMENT LOST BY AUTOMATION

(a) NET NATIONAL PRODUCT

FULL EMPLOYMENT REGAINED BY POLICY

(b) NET NATIONAL PRODUCT

FIG. 18-3(a). If inventions raise productivity 30 per cent, FF of producible full employment shifts 30 per cent rightward to $F'F'$. If C, I, and G schedules were not to change, the intersection would still be at E, but now alas with mass unemployment. (Under laissez faire no one can predict what the net final effect of such inventions on the total of $C + I + G$ would be. They *might* tempt consumers to less thrift, and investors to more capital formation. But they might instead undermine $C + I + G$.)

FIG. 18-3(b). Regardless of inventions' effect on old spending schedules, expansionary monetary policy can raise I by the needed amount. Expansionary fiscal policy can raise G to G'; and can lower taxes, raise disposable incomes, and shift up the consumption schedule to $C'C'$. Full-employment equilibrium will be restored at E', where $C' + I' + G'$ has been shifted upward the needed amount by macroeconomic policy.

machines, so that (2) net investment I is no greater than before; finally, that automation gives people the same things for less but does not whet their appetites for new gadgets, which means that (3) the propensity-to-consume schedule (and propensity to save) will be exactly the same as before in terms of disposable income.

In short, we assume the $C + I + G$ schedule has none of its components shifted as a result of automation. Then the schedule must continue to intersect at the same E point as before. Whereas this E point was previously a full-employment equilibrium, with automation it now represents a point of mass unemployment. A large fraction of the populace is now out of work, and many are working only part time. Were this the case, who can doubt that unions and government would agitate to cut the length of the working week and sabotage new methods and machines? And who could blame them?

New Economics to the rescue   Even this pessimistic case can be cured by proper therapy. Here is how. Let the Federal Reserve fight this slump by increasing M and making credit much cheaper and much more freely available. (Recall open-market purchases, lowering of reserve requirements, and lowering of discount rates.) What will this do to the I schedule? Push it up. At the same time, let the government cut down on the heavy taxing it was doing in the previous full-employment situation. This will increase people's disposable incomes, will increase their consumption spending, and thus shift upward the C part of the $C + I + G$ schedule. (Maybe I will get further shifted, too.) Without increasing government expenditure directly, we could thus shift the $C + I + G$ schedule far enough upward until the new $C' + I' + G'$ schedule intersects the 45° line at the new full-employment level E'. Alternatively, since there are always pressing program needs in the public sector that merit doing when society gets new economic resources, an expansion of G could be used to help shift $C + I + G$ up to the target level.

Figure 18-3(b) shows how these upward shifts have restored the full-employment equilibrium. By proper policy we have converted the machine from a curse to a blessing. People now enjoy 30 per cent more output. They are not forced into bread lines. They are not made to work short hours and do not have to take Mondays off because the limited work has to be shared. They do not have to throw their cigarette cases into the works of the new machinery to protect their jobs and take-home pay.

You should be sure you know how to use the same diagram to handle the case where automation or new inventions spontaneously increase investment a great deal and tempt people onto an upward-shifted consumption schedule. You can then show how the desired E' equilibrium could come about spontaneously. Indeed, to test your powers, you should analyze the possible case where automation causes *too great* a burst of investment and consumption spending. You should then show which contractionary monetary and fiscal policy would be needed to wipe out the resulting inflationary gap and to bring the new $C + I + G$ schedule successfully back to the proper intersection.

Of course, the higher dollar demand engineered by fiscal and monetary policy cannot be expected to provide the same kind of jobs using exactly the same skills and paying exactly the same wage rates. Inevitably there will still be important transitional problems for *particular* workers, firms, and regions. Programs of retraining and of increasing labor mobility and flexibility are vital (as Chapter 41 discusses), along with policies to ensure proper aggregate dollar demand.

THE NEW MIXED ECONOMY

Critics used to regard the classical principles of economics as out of date. Looking at the long bread lines and the men selling apples on street corners, they said:

Why speak of scarcity? Or efficiency? Or growth? Or fairness? Throw away your tools of supply and demand, your finespun theories of market pricing. Tear up the rule book. We live in a new era in which everything is upside down: attempts to save kill off investment; a hurricane or war is a blessing in that it creates jobs and gives food to the starving unemployed. Capitalism is doomed to collapse in a crisis of underconsumption and overproduction.

What is the modern economist's answer to all this? He says:

You are right to question the classical principles. All principles should be subjected to the closest examination with respect to both their logic and their factual relevance. The classical arguments were oversimple, and they admittedly did not allow for the facts of nineteenth- and twentieth-century life. Experience since 1932, and careful logical reasoning, suggest that money and aggregate $C + I + G$ spending *will not manage themselves*. A laissez faire system is doomed to wasteful ups and downs of the business cycle and perhaps to long fits of stagnation.

But even among the economists of Eastern Europe there has developed a recognition of the new scientific knowledge about macroeconomic policy.

Simple capitalism has been replaced virtually everywhere by the mixed economy ("the managed economy"). Everywhere in the Western world,[6] governments and central banks have shown they can win the battle of the slump if people want them to. They have the weapons of fiscal policy (expenditure and taxes) and of monetary policy (open-market operations, discount-rate policy, legal reserve ratio policy) to shift the various schedules that determine national income and employment. Just as we no longer meekly accept disease, we no longer need accept mass unemployment.

Under the managed macroeconomics of the mixed economy, many of the old classical principles of microeconomics will again apply; but now they apply because our macroeconomics has validated their premise of adequate demand—not because the world is lucky enough to have them apply automatically and at all times.

This is a brave answer, and essentially—most careful economists would today say—an accurate answer. But let us not be too boastful of our modern conquest of instability. There is no warrant for smugness. Let us quietly add the following qualifications:

The worst consequences of the business cycle, which Chapter 14 showed plagued capitalism from its beginning, are probably a thing of the past; but that does not mean that the cycle is gone. "Fine tuning" is not yet here. We still shall have minor inventory fluctuations, still shall have transitions from war to peace and from one kind of boom to another. The difference will be this: the age-old tendencies for the system to fluctuate will still be there, but no longer will the world let them snowball into vast depressions or into galloping inflations—no longer will we let our banking system fail and our nation go through the most painful debt deflation and bankruptcy.

We should recognize that all the political pressures in a democracy do work to make a drastic slump unlikely. But can we be so sure that the same pressures will operate to prevent mild inflation? Even if fiscal and monetary policies could prevent such chronic mild inflation of a couple of per cent per year, can we be sure that they will be used to do so? Chapter 41 will return to these vital problems.

The Appendix explores deeper the analytics of money and of income determination.

---

[6] This, of course, includes Australia and New Zealand; Japan, India, and other Asian nations; Latin America; and the new African states.

SUMMARY

1 Monetary policy by the central bank is an important way of shifting the saving and investment schedules, or the total schedule of consumption-plus-investment-plus-government-spending.

2 Along the downward-sloping "liquidity-preference schedule," higher M induces a lower interest rate—enough lower to persuade people to hold all the new M. Along the downward-sloping "marginal efficiency of investment schedule," lower interest rate and more available credit make it profitable for new investment projects to get done. Along the familiar saving-investment multiplier-type diagram, the induced increase in I leads to higher production and incomes.[7]

3 Fiscal policy means governmental tax and expenditure policy. It, too, affects income determination by shifting the spending schedules. Higher public expenditure directly raises the G component of the $C + I + G$ schedule and thus raises its equilibrium intersection. Taxes work in reverse: *reduced* tax rates, by shifting the CC schedule leftward and upward, push *up* the $C + I + G$ schedule; increased tax rates have the opposite, contractionary effect; and in either case, tax changes are, dollar for dollar, a little less potent than changes in government expenditure on goods and services.

4 The important case of technological invention shows how, by combination of fiscal and monetary policies, a modern economy can ensure the restoration of high-employment equilibrium even in the worst case where automation is reducing the need for men to do any given amount of work and is not bringing in its train any spontaneous expansion of dollar demand elsewhere.

5 Modern mixed economies have the fiscal and monetary tools, and the political will to use them, to end chronic slumps and galloping inflations. This makes obsolete the fear of overproduction and underconsumption, and obviates the need to bolster purchasing power by military or imperialistic programs. But it does not solve problems of income inequality or of monopolistic and other imperfections at the microeconomic level. Part Two's successful handling of macroeconomics merely sets the stage for the again-relevant microeconomic problems of Parts Three and Four.

QUESTIONS FOR DISCUSSION

1 Redo Fig. 18-1(a), (b), and (c) to show tight monetary policies. Trace out the steps.

2 Wipe out a 1975 automation-created deflationary gap by (*a*) fiscal policy alone, (*b*)

---

[7] If there is a deep-depression inelasticity of investment response to interest and/or a deep-depression horizontality of LL representing indifference to money holding, the effect of M will fall to nil. In quantity-theory language, then and *only* then will the contrived rise in M be completely negated by a compensating fall in V, leaving $NNP = P \times Q$ quite unchanged. Usually the induced drop in interest rates will cause V to decrease, but by not enough to offset the new M in the now-higher MV. Only in the other extreme case of monetarism will V be a hard constant, responding in no systematic way to i, CC, II, and GG changes. The great neoclassical writers—Marshall, Walras, Wicksell, Pigou, Irving Fisher—never believed in this monetarism.

monetary policy alone, and (c) any blend of them. Which path leads to full employment with slowest growth (i.e., least capital formation for the future)?

3   "Fiscal and monetary authority should be in one agency, or at least be coordinated. Otherwise the authorities may conflict, one undoing what the other does." Discuss.

4   Use Fig. 18-2 to show that increasing G and taxes at the same time will tend to have canceling effects on income. Difficult question: Can you follow the intricate reasoning which has argued that, dollar for dollar, changes in G are a little more potent than changes in taxes—so that a balanced-budget decrease in G is likely to be somewhat deflationary?

5   The tools that handle automation problems can handle any threat of unemployment that might come from sudden peace and disarmament. Explain, anticipating Chapter 41.

6   Explain critically the new look in macroeconomics.

Review your understanding of the following concepts:

M down $\rightarrow i$ up $\rightarrow I$ down $\rightarrow$ NNP down $= MV$ down	liquidity-preference schedule
shift of $C + I + G$: through monetary policy and through tax and expenditure changes	marginal-efficiency schedule
	tax versus expenditure potency
	automation and unemployment
leftward CC shift from tax cut	mixed economy
	"new look" macroeconomics

APPENDIX: Mechanisms of Monetarism and Income Determination

This is a brief discussion of how money, interest, investment, income, prices, and velocity of circulation are interrelated. Classical views that there can never be unemployment, and depression versions of the Keynesian system, will turn out to be alternative poles of such an analysis. And what most economists would consider to be the most realistic description of how our economy works and what are the potencies of policy weapons will fall somewhere on the continuum between these extreme poles.

The topics will be covered in this order: velocity interrelations; classical and monetarist models; liquidity preference and income determination.

BEHAVIOR OF VELOCITY

Instead of the chain $M \rightarrow i \rightarrow I \rightarrow$ NNP (or its even further elaboration to take account of wealth-capitalization effects and effects on G and C schedules), some proponents of monetarism prefer to short-circuit the process and use the concept of velocity. They write

$$M \rightarrow MV \equiv \text{NNP}$$

This asserts that an increase in M, unless *offset fully* by an induced shift in V of the type that neither they nor the believers in the four-link chain consider likely, will serve to increase dollar NNP with all the implied effects on the product $P \times Q$.[1]

These different modes of language can formally represent the same facts, just as an account in English or an account in French can be given of any sequence of events. In a sense, therefore, reasonable men will not argue about terminology and semantics.

At a deeper level, however, those who prefer one terminology usually think that certain hypotheses about the real world are more fruitful than others.

[1]Some proponents would think V will stay constant after a sizable change in open-market operations; others would not think this a necessary assumption. Some, impressed by the empirical fact that in past short-term upswings, rises in M and V have tended to coincide, might choose to extrapolate this *post hoc* experience. Others would set up more complicated hypotheses, depending on the environment upon which the open-market operation impinged. Many will agree with our later liquidity-preference theory, whose Hicks-Hansen diagrams can be thought of as a theory of velocity—i.e., a theory in which V is an increasing function of the interest rate i.

Thus, those who like to use MV usually have more definite views about the probable behavior of V, and its invariance under a wide range of alternative conditions, than do those who like to use the $C + I + G$ and liquidity-preference approach explicitly. While the bulk of economists today incline toward the latter view, there is no need to be dogmatic about the matter. If the day ever arrives when the proponents of the velocity approach can prove by their researches that theirs is the more convenient tool, pragmatic scholars will welcome all its help. In any case, post-Keynesians and monetarists both agree that "money matters much."

CLASSICAL PRICE FLEXIBILITY

More basic than the question of whether to use or not use the terminology of either school is the contrast between a *frictionless* system in which all market prices are *flexible* and the *realistic* world of a mixed economic system that exists here and elsewhere in the West. Many classical economists thought unemployment to be quite impossible because in their frictionless models whatever is not spent in one direction gets automatically spent in another.

Say's Law This view, named for the 1803 French writer J. B. Say, has been much debated because of the ambiguous form in which it was expressed. Thus, Say and other classical writers felt that overproduction was impossible by its very nature, since all value relations were relative—shoes being comparable with spoons at some proper relative price; they felt that what a worker saves gets spent as truly on employing men in the machinery trades as what the worker spends on giving work in the food or other consumers' industries; they had at least a vague supposition that the interest rate in a flexible capital market would always find a level at which (full-employment) saving and investment schedules would intersect; they, or their more sophisticated followers, had the notion that, if only the money wage would fall flexibly far enough, it would always bring out job offers for every willing worker. So went the rather vague arguments.

In the years since 1800, there were often short periods of considerable unemployment, and on a few occasions there were longer periods of considerable unemployment or of *under*employment. So economists wanted to go beyond the simpler formulations of Say's Law: to deny some of its implicit presumptions about flexible prices and wages, or to abandon it and work from alternative hypotheses.

Today it is clear that the alternative approaches are fully capable of being reconciled, so that there is only a difference of degree and realism between them, not a difference of kind. A. C. Pigou of Cambridge University showed in 1943 how his older cherished beliefs could be related to what he had first thought were Keynesian heresies; his reconciliation goes thus.

Pigou effects Let there be a certain M in the system that consists of coins or of imperishable paper currency. Suppose that initially there is unemployment because the SS and II schedules intersect to the left of the full-employment level. Suppose interest rates are in equilibrium on every bond and security market, with auctioneers finding matching supply and demand bids. And just to complete the simplified discussion, suppose there is no central banker or fiscal authority to do anything about the situation.

A sophisticated follower of Say would now assert: "There is just one flaw in this equilibrium. Men who want to work at going wages are not employed. To be fair, whether or not this is realistic, you should also imagine an auctioneer for the labor market. He makes the wage rate expressed in money fall whenever there is excessive labor supply."

Pigou agrees. He lets the wage rate fall. Money wages being an important cost of production, for all the reasons discussed in Parts Three and Four, this drop will result in considerable lowering of all prices. When prices and wages are low enough, what will happen to the SS and II intersection? Suppose I am a typical man who previously owned an acre of land, a machine, and $100 in cash. (I also may have owed on a mortgage or may have held someone's IOU stated in terms of money; but for the community as a whole, such interpersonal money liabilities and assets have to *cancel* out. Recall also that there are no government bonds in the picture to worry about.)

For dramatic effect, suppose that wages fall to one-thousandth (.001) of their previous level; suppose, although it is unnecessary except for simplicity to stick to exactly the same number, that prices of all things also fall to .001 of their previous levels. This means that my acre of land and machine will fall to .001 of their previous value. Everything falls in value—except one item. My $100 bill is still a $100 bill. But now, in terms of its real purchasing power, I own the equivalent of what was $100,000 before. I am rich!

Will I spend the same amount on consumption and on saving out of *income* levels that are the same as before either in money or in real terms? I will not. I am rich and can consume more before I die.

At some point, because of the enhanced *real wealth effect* of the incre₌sed purchasing power of the hard

money in the economic system (induced by a large enough wage and price fall), *CC* schedules will shift up in real (not money) terms, and *SS* schedules shift equivalently downward. The new *SS* and *II* intersection can thus be moved up to the full-employment level. So, even if there were no favorable effects of the price-level or of interest change on the *II* curves, *by getting money wages and prices far enough down, the condition of "full employment" could theoretically be achieved.* **QED.**

Pigou thus vindicated abstract classical principles by recourse to this "hard-money effect," which economists today call the "Pigou effect" in his honor.[2] But being a realistic observer of the difficulties of getting wages to move flexibly downward in a mixed capitalistic society, and having lived through eras in which the dynamic process of debt deflation led to bankruptcy, riots, slump, and even revolution, Pigou hastened to point out that he did not recommend such hyperdeflation to cure capitalism's unemployment. He much preferred to accomplish the same thing by increasing dollar *M*; and actually, he adhered to the general notions of Part Two of this book. The fact that he often liked to use the word "velocity" in his Keynes-like theory shows that mere semantic matters are indeed of limited importance.

Crude Quantity Theory in the classical model   Recall now the crude Quantity Theory, which held that prices must always be proportional to the amount of money —so that doubling *M* must exactly double *P*. For many situations in the real world—with its sticky prices, booms, recessions, and thousands of changes always going on to confound the experiment—we saw that the crude Quantity Theory was not a good predicting device. But if we confine our attention to the *perfectly frictionless model* of the classical type used by Pigou and others in the above discussion, we can find an important *nucleus* of truth in the crude Quantity Theory; and we can understand better the reasons why it has a degree of predictive value during galloping inflations and over certain long time intervals.

Recall Pigou's fantastic but happy equilibrium which has made the representative man feel rich enough to save as little as society can invest at full employment. Now suppose his $100 bill had been a $10 bill. Do you

see that merely by having all prices go down still another nine-tenths, the equilibrium could be *exactly restored,* with every relative price and wage just the same as before and every physical commodity and input the same as before? *Cutting M to one-tenth has cut P to exactly one-tenth* in this classical model.

In this abstract model the crude Quantity Theory has come into its own. In the tautological equation of exchange $MV \equiv PQ$, there has been no slightest reason for the *Q*, *i*, or *V* to have changed (waiving all dynamic questions of how the system gets into the new equilibrium and "forgets" past price levels). So *P* does equal kM, where *k* is the ratio V/Q, whose numerator and denominator will have been constant in the abstract example, however much they may vary in reality.

This long-period full-employment frictionless classical model does have the property that *no* change in interest rates can come from the *balanced* change in *M*. As David Ricardo argued, if all prices and wages change in exactly the same proportion, so that what used to be called 4 pence is now 2 pence, then any asset that used to pay 5 per cent per annum in the form of 50 pence on 1,000 pence will now be paying 5 per cent in the form of 25 pence on 500 pence.

It should not be necessary to stress that the real world as we know it is a far cry from the abstract model. This is true especially in the short run; in the longer run, to the degree that all price adjustments get made and other disturbances are ruled out, the abstract model fits somewhat better. The art of economics is to know how to blend the elements of absurdity and of relevance of such a model in interpreting living events and policy.

Permanent public debt   Even in the extreme classical model, all *P*s would not be proportional to *M* alone! Interest-bearing public bonds, which correspond to no government capital formation and which no taxpayer rationally expects to have to help retire *in his lifetime,* have effects similar to those of the noninterest *IOU*s we call *M*. Thus, the Pigou effect from hyperdeflation involves an increase in the real value of such bonds *along with* an increase in the real value of hard-money *M*. Since a rational taxpayer will reckon that he *will* have to help pay taxes to keep up the interest payments (during his lifetime) on the public debt, $1 of such debt will not have the potency to produce as much spending as will $1 of *M*. Even so, believers in a crude quantity theory for an extreme classical model *should* reformulate their theory to say:

Doubling *M and* permanent public debt will, other things equal, double all *P*s and leave all relative *P*s, physical quantities, and interest rates unchanged in the new long-run equilibrium. *Doubling M alone represents a nonneutral change* whose substantive effects are the greater the shorter is taxpayer life expectancy and the higher is the interest rate.[3]

LIQUIDITY PREFERENCE AND INCOME

We have seen that the amount of money people will hold depends upon the interest rate and is a declining function of it in the sense that you must contrive lower yields on securities to coax people to be willing to hold more money. Figure 18-1(a) showed this liquidity-preference link between money and interest.

But as already noted, there is a *transactions* motive for holding money along with the *store-of-wealth* or asset reason for holding money. So part of the money held can be said to depend upon the level of income: this so-called "active" component of the money supply is a function of the level of NNP, rising as NNP rises. Indeed, if velocity were a strict constant for *all* money and not just for this idealized active-money component, there would be no room at all for a nonvertical liquidity-preference curve *LL* in Fig. 18-1(a).

This dependence of money on income as well as on interest was not depicted in the important sequence of Fig. 18-1(a), (b), and (c). The chapter's first footnote warned us that the diagram did not take into account the full feedback effect of the transactions demand for money induced by a successful expansion of NNP contrived by an increase in *M*. We can here make good this deficiency, and verify that the chapter's story is essentially correct, even if oversimplified in the telling; now we consider what is known as a Hicks-Hansen diagram, named originally for Sir John Hicks of Oxford and for Alvin Hansen of Harvard who popularized it.

The brown curve labeled *IS* in Fig. 18-4 recapitulates in a single income–interest-rate diagram the story told by Fig. 18-1(b) and (c), quite independently of (a). We saw back on page 314 that when we change the interest rate we do end up changing the NNP level, as shown here on the brown curve. In Fig. 18-1, this took place in two steps: (1) the marginal-efficiency step of 18-1(b) in which changing interest rate changed investment in the opposite direction; and (2) the old multiplier relation of 18-1(c), inherited from our saving-investment analysis of Chapter 12, in which the change in investment resulted in an amplified change in income in its same direction, owing to primary spending and secondary respending. We call this result of the two steps the *IS* relation, because it shows the resulting

[3]WARNING: Doubling *M* and *PD* does not mean you can add *M + PD* and treat that magnitude as if *P*s were proportional to it. Rather it is the case that (2*M*, 2*PD*) implies 2*P*.

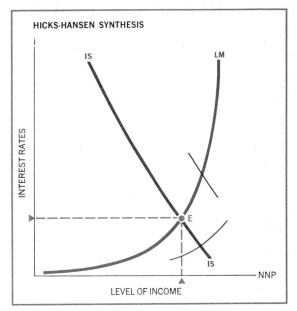

FIG. 18-4.

correspondence between interest rate and income when scheduled saving and scheduled investment have been kept equal. (Recall this is the definition of maintainable NNP equilibrium.)

The new element in Fig. 18-4 is the blue *LM* schedule. This relationship between the interest rate and the level of income is labeled *LM* because it is the complete liquidity-preference relationship between money and income after we have taken into account *both* the dependence of money holding on interest *and* on income. I.e., we have recognized the *transaction* motive for "active money," which depends primarily on income; and also what page 264 called the *precautionary* (or "asset") store-of-wealth motive for holding money, which depends upon the interest rates that investors speculate could be earned on alternative stores of wealth (bonds, stocks, land, real capital goods—earning assets in general). Figure 18-1(a) reflected this.

It is important to emphasize that the *LM* schedule is drawn up on the proviso that the total amount of *M* is fixed. Why then does *LM* slope upward? Because an eastward increase in NNP will require more active *M* for transactions, leaving less *M* for people to hold as a wealth asset. The smaller amount of *M* for wealth holding can only be rationed out at a higher (or northward-moving) interest rate, which is needed to coax people more into securities and more *out* of money.

Now we must combine the marginal-efficiency-multiplier brown curve *IS* with the blue liquidity-

preference curve *LM*, to show that their interaction does determine the equilibrium level of income and of interest rate for each given total of *M*. *E* shows the equilibrium intersection. There and only there has the existing amount of money produced just low enough interest rate and just high enough investment to lead to a maintainable level of income: at this indicated NNP and *i* rate, the existing *M* supply just covers the transactions and holding demand for money. QED.

What if the Fed engineers an *increase* in *M*? What will that do to the *LM* curve? Now with more money to be held at each level of income, the interest rate will have to be bid down. Hence, the *LM* curve clearly shifts downward (and thus *rightward*, as shown by the new thin blue curve in Fig. 18-4). What about the *IS* curve? In this simplified version, *IS* does not have the money supply in it anywhere; *IS* stays unshifted by an *M* change. The downward shift of *LM* moves the equilibrium NNP upward and the equilibrium interest rate downward (just as, in Chapter 4, page 62, an increase in supply *ss* intersected an unchanged demand curve *dd* in a higher *Q* and lower *P*). Pencil *E′* in.

By contrast to monetary policy, which shifts the *LM* curve, fiscal policy shifts the *IS* curve. How? An increase in government expenditure *G* (just like an increase in any component of a *C* + *I* + *G* schedule) will shift the *IS* schedule *rightward* (as in the new thin brown curve). Why? Because it leads to a higher NNP level at the same interest rate. Thus, you can show that expansionary fiscal policy leads to a new *E* higher on the unshifted *LM* curve, with equilibrium NNP and *i* higher. (The reader should test himself by penciling in on Fig. 18-4 the new higher *E″* intersection.)

Figure 18-5 shows at the ends of the *LM* curve the extreme "classical" pole and the extreme "depression" (or so-called "liquidity-trap") pole. Where *LM* turns almost vertical, no shift in the *IS* curve can increase NNP: that is because money's velocity has reached its limit. (Note the near-constancy of NNP at E_1 and E_2.) At this classical pole, then, fiscal policy would accomplish little unless accompanied by central banking change in the money supply. Few modern economists think present-day mixed economies operate in such an extreme classical region.

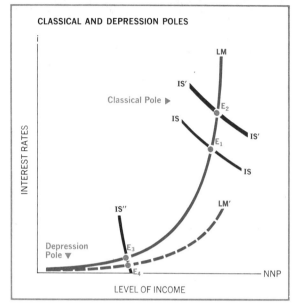

FIG. 18-5.

At the other extreme, at vanishingly low interest rates such as prevailed in the late 1930s, the *LM* curve might turn horizontal. If the Fed engineered an increase in *M* by open-market purchases which involved swapping a close-money substitute Treasury bill for *M* itself, the Fed would merely succeed in shifting the *LM* curve rightward, leaving its horizontal part virtually unchanged. At such a pole, and particularly where extreme inelasticity of the depression marginal-efficiency curve makes *IS* almost vertical, monetary policy is practically impotent to affect NNP.[4] (Note the virtual identity of the E_3 and E_4 intersections.)

The Hicks-Hansen diagram not only succeeds in synthesizing fiscal and monetary policy, the theory of income determination and the theory of money; in addition it helps synthesize the monetarist and Keynesian theories of macroeconomics by providing a definite and general theory of the velocity of money.

[4] Sometimes the "depression model" is called the "Keynesian model," but most authorities agree that this is bad terminology, since Keynes' *General Theory* covered *all* cases from the beginning and not merely that of the Great Depression.

SUMMARY TO APPENDIX

1   The causal interrelations between *M*, *i*, *I*, and NNP could also be expressed in *MV* language. So long as one expects any induced changes in *V* to be such as not *fully* to offset the original

change in M, then changing M can in one step be described as changing NNP. Semantics alone would be involved, were it not true that special hypotheses about constancy of V may seem tenable to monetarists who use this concept.

2   In a perfect classical world without frictions and with an inflexible hard-money public-debt base, Pigou proved in the 1940s that a sophisticated version of Say's Law could be asserted. For policy and realistic description, he preferred not to rely on hyperdeflation to produce such "Pigou effects." Pushing such a full-employment model to its logical limits, however, does enable one to reaffirm the crudest Quantity Theory in which P is strictly proportionate to M and public debt (the degree of the proportion varying only when extraneous *real* changes take place). Hicks-Hansen diagrams synthesize classical and depression poles.

QUESTIONS FOR DISCUSSION

1   Is it reasonable for you to hold relatively less M and have a faster V when i is 9 rather than 1 per cent? When inflation is galloping? Use your answer to criticize simple monetarism.

2   Explain the Pigou-effect mechanism for restoring full employment when wages and prices are perfectly flexible. What is the public debt's role?

3   *Extra-credit problem:* Intermediate texts can use mathematical symbols to summarize a simple version of this Appendix. Let real saving, S, depend on real income, $Q = \text{NNP}/P$, namely: $S = S(Q) = .1Q$, say, much as in Fig. 18-1(c). Let real investment, I, depend inversely on the interest rate, as in Fig. 18-1(b)'s marginal-efficiency schedule, namely: $I = I(i) = 1/i$, say. In the equation of exchange $MV = PQ$, let velocity, V, be an increasing function of the interest rate, namely: $V = V(i) = 4.4i/(1+i)$, say. Pick units so that full-employment output is $Q_F = 1$ (trillion dollars, perhaps); and suppose that, prior to full employment, prices are constant (as determined by sticky wage-cost levels, etc.), so that by choice of units $P = 1$ until an inflationary gap lifts the price level. Finally, let the money supply, M, be set by the Fed at the level $\overline{M}$. Then to determine our two unknowns, Q and i, in Fig. 18-4 we have the two equations for the IS and LM schedules

$$S(Q) = I(i) \qquad \text{or} \quad .1Q = 1/i, \qquad\qquad \text{marginal efficiency and multiplier}$$
$$\overline{M} = PQ/V(i) \qquad \text{or} \quad \overline{M} = Q/[4.4i/(1+i)], \qquad \text{liquidity-preference theory of } V$$

Solving (by simple substitution or otherwise), we get Q as an increasing function of $\overline{M}$, and i as a decreasing function. After $\overline{M}$ has become so large that full-employment Q_F has been reached, along with its corresponding i_F and V_F, we put Q_F in both equations and solve for the price level P, with P now simply proportional to $\overline{M}$ (in accordance with the classical Quantity Theory of Money), namely: $P = (V_F/Q_F) \, \overline{M}$. NOTE: for the suggested special formulas above, substitution gives $i = 10/Q$, $V = 44/(Q+10)$, $\overline{M} = Q(Q+10)/44$, a quadratic equation for Q in terms of $\overline{M}$. To get full-employment $Q_F = 1$, evidently, $\overline{M} = 11/44 = 1/4$ (i.e., a quarter of a trillion dollars, with $V_F = 4$ per year, or once every 3 months on the average); and $i_F = 10/Q_F = 10$ per cent per year. For underemployment equilibrium, the quadratic's relevant root is given by $Q = -5 + \sqrt{25 + 44\overline{M}}$. Verify that $\overline{M} = 1/4$ does yield $Q = 1$.

Review your understanding of the following concepts:

Say's Law and classical models	liquidity preference:
Pigou effects	M dependence on both NNP and i
crude Quantity Theory	V dependence on i
induced changes in V	Hicks-Hansen LM and IS intersection
public-debt effects	depression and classical poles

Fiscal Policy and Full Employment without Inflation

19

The Congress declares that it is the continuing responsibility of the federal government to . . . promote maximum employment, production, and purchasing power.
EMPLOYMENT ACT OF 1946

We have seen in earlier chapters that the behavior of saving and investment determines the level of national income and employment. We have seen that investment and other spending often fluctuate widely from year to year. History shows how painful and wasteful the business cycle has been in the past. Today everyone is in agreement that we must continue to succeed in laying to rest the ghost of instability, chronic slump, and snowballing inflation. The historic Employment Act of 1946 brought the United States up to the other mixed economies in this respect. It set up a Council of Economic Advisers and a Joint Economic Committee to help ensure full employment and healthy growth.

What prescription follows from our economic diagnosis? Earlier chapters have shown that the Federal Reserve System can do much, by way of monetary policy and interest, to moderate instability. Reinforcing central bank actions, powerful help is still needed from the weapon of public *fiscal policy* (i.e., governmental tax and expenditure policies).

OLD-FASHIONED FINANCE

Forty years ago the chapter in an economic textbook dealing with public finance read just as it had in Adam Smith's time. From 1776 to 1929 there was little discernible progress. Moreover, the Democratic President Grover Cleveland differed not a bit in his ideology of finance from Republican William McKinley, or for that matter from Calvin Coolidge and Herbert Hoover.

What were the clichés of oldfangled shirt-sleeve economics, the doctrines our grandfathers were taught and preached? Here are a few:

1. The budget should be balanced in every year (and at a low level, with expenditure prudent and purposes strictly limited).

2. The public debt is a burden on the backs of our

children and grandchildren (just as though each of us has to carry on our shoulders heavy boulders). All debt is evil; public debt, absolutely evil.

3. Everything that is true of an individual or family is also true of the government. If a husband and wife spend more than their monthly income, they go bankrupt and misery follows. The same is true for Uncle Sam (or John Bull or Kaiser Wilhelm).

4. In agreement with one of Adam Smith's four fundamental "canons of taxation," a good tax is one that produces *the same revenues in good times as well as bad.*

You can extend the list in any club locker room or bar. What is interesting about it is that today no experts agree with it or the reasonings on which it relies. And no nations, even in the heyday of Victorian capitalism, came anywhere near to living up to it; for, fortunately, they could not do so. During each depression and recession, *automatically* budget deficits developed at the same time that the conventional wisdom was deploring the phenomenon. For centuries, in times of distress, local and national governments have resorted to work on the roads and other public works to relieve the distress. For centuries, poorhouse relief and other transfer expenditures have ebbed and risen with the dance of the business cycle.

As will be seen in this chapter, experienced researchers into the facts and the analytical principles of public finance have today, all over the world, quite different answers to these questions from those of our forefathers. The problem for an introductory text is to explain the logic and experience underlying modern doctrines, not indoctrinate the student into any one view. Objective analysis of the issues—both pros and cons—should be helpful in giving each person the materials from which he can form his own understanding of the fiscal practices followed by mixed economies all over the world.

A. SHORT-RUN AND LONG-RUN FISCAL POLICY

By a positive fiscal policy, we mean the process of shaping *taxation* and *public expenditure* in order (1) to help dampen down the swings of the business cycle and (2) to contribute toward the maintenance of a growing, high-employment economy free from excessive inflation or deflation.

Suppose the economic system in a particular year is threatened with a deflationary gap. Suppose private consumption and investment spending are too weak to provide adequate employment. What action would then be called for?

The Federal Reserve will use expansionary monetary policy to try to stimulate private investment. To the degree[1] that its efforts are not fully adequate, the fiscal authorities would still be faced by a deflationary gap. This would be the signal for Congress and the President to introduce tax and public-expenditure policies designed to help reachieve stable full employment.

Similar action would be called for in the case where private investment and consumption decisions were threatening the economy with an inflationary gap. With prices rising and employers vying desperately for nonexistent workers, the Fed would initiate contrac-

[1]How much of the stabilizing load is carried by monetary and how much by fiscal policy depends, as Chapter 41 will discuss, on public-growth targets and international-payments constraints. Also, the financing of deficits and surpluses can itself help shape the course of money-supply growth.

tionary credit programs aimed to reduce the inflationary gap. But if the saving-investment or $C + I + G$ intersections still threatened the economy with a sustained inflationary gap, it would then be the duty of Congress and the President to initiate higher tax rates and/or lower-public-expenditure programs in the attempt to restore a high-employment equilibrium without inflation.

In summary, fiscal policies dealing with taxes and public expenditure, in cooperation with stabilizing monetary policies, have for their goal a high-employment and growing economy—but one without price inflation. The fiscal and monetary authorities "lean against the prevailing economic winds," thereby helping provide a favorable economic environment within which the dynamic forces of private initiative can have the widest opportunity for achievement.

OUR IMPORTANT "BUILT-IN STABILIZERS"

One might get the impression from the above remarks that fiscal policy helps stabilize the economy only so long as government officials are carefully watching trends, are successfully anticipating future developments, and are meeting promptly to take decisive action. Such "discretionary fiscal policies," involving the making and changing of explicit decisions, are important; fortunately, they are but part of the story.

The modern fiscal system has great inherent *automatic stabilizing* properties. All through the day and night, whether or not the President is in the White House, the fiscal system is helping to keep our economy stable. If in 1975 a recession got under way while Congress was out of session, powerful automatic forces would go instantly into action to counteract it before there were any committee meetings or the exercise of special intelligence of any form.

What are these mysterious stabilizers? They are primarily the following:

1. *Automatic changes in tax receipts.* We saw in Chapters 8 and 9 that our federal tax system depends progressively on personal and corporate incomes. What does this mean for stability? It means that as soon as income begins to fall off, and even before Congress makes any changes in tax rates, the tax receipts of the government also fall off. (Today, for each 10-billion-dollar drop in NNP, total tax receipts drop by about $3\frac{1}{2}$ billion. After President Nixon's variant of the negative income tax becomes law, this fraction may become considerably larger.)

Now, reductions in tax receipts are just what the doctor prescribes in case of a dip in income. So our present tax system is a mighty and rapid built-in stabilizer.

NOTE: Taxes stabilize *against upward* as well as downward movements. In times of inflation, this is a good thing; but when built-in rises in taxes stand in the way of healthy real growth, we call it "fiscal drag"—a subject discussed on page 339.

A century ago, writers thought that *stability* of tax revenue was a good thing, and they would have looked with disapproval on the present-day tendency for tax receipts to rise and fall with national income. (Recall Adam Smith's canon of prudent taxation!) Today, most economists believe that just the reverse is the truth. Thus, to dampen a boom, a budgetary surplus is desirable. There are two ways to produce such a surplus: by a reduction in government expenditure, yes; but also by an increase in tax receipts. To fight a recession, there are likewise two ways open: raising expenditures, or cutting tax rates. How lucky we are, therefore, that our present tax system has to some degree "automatic flexibility," with its receipts tending to rise in inflationary times and to fall in times of depression. This is a powerful factor stabilizing the economy and moderating the business cycle.

2. *Unemployment compensation and other welfare transfers.* In the last 40 years we have built up an elaborate system of unemployment compensation. Soon after men are laid off, they begin to receive payments from the unemployment compensation funds. When they go back to work, the payments cease; and the taxes collected to finance unemployment compensation rise when employment is high. During boom years, therefore, the unemployment reserve funds grow and exert stabilizing pressure against too great spending; conversely, during years of slack employment, the reserve funds are used to pay out income to sustain consumption and moderate the decline.

Other welfare programs—such as family relief payments outside the Social Security system—also show an anticyclical automatic behavior of a stabilizing type.

3. *Farm aid programs.* The various parity programs to aid agriculture, which we shall discuss later in Part Three, act like built-in stabilizers. When dollar spending drops off and farm prices fall, the federal government pays out dollars to farmers and absorbs surpluses. When inflation brews and prices soar, the government warehouses put forth farm goods and absorb dollars, thus cushioning any movement.[2]

4. *Corporate savings and family savings.* Not all the applause goes to the government. Our private institutions also have built-in stabilizers. Thus, the custom of corporations' maintaining their dividends, even though their incomes change in the short run, does cause their retained savings to act like a shock absorber or built-in stabilizer.[3] And to the extent that families try to maintain previous living standards and are slow to adjust their living standards upward—to this extent, they too help stabilize. (To the extent that they rush out to spend extra income on down payments or hysterically cut down on consumption when economic clouds arise, they hinder stability.)

Still other stabilizers could be mentioned, but these are the main ones.[4]

LIMITATIONS OF AUTOMATIC STABILIZERS

Before leaving the subject of automatic stabilizers, we should stress two things. First, the built-in stabilizers are our first line of defense, but are not by themselves sufficient to maintain full stability. Second, reliance on them in preference to discretionary programs raises some philosophical and ethical questions. Let us examine these points.

[2] By pushing up the prices of raw materials, parity formulas can also have an "escalating," or destabilizing, effect; and to the extent that they simply limit supply at all times, they redistribute and lower rather than stabilize income. Defense stockpiling of metals is at times stabilizing, at times not.

[3] To the extent that corporate investment is itself linked to corporate saving, this stabilizing influence is negated. A rise in the wages-profits ratio is a stabilizer on dips, as Cambridge's Nicholas Kaldor insists (but which is only partial in the view of most of his critics).

[4] Many experts advocate increasing the stabilizers by having Congress pass a law making tax *rates* vary *automatically* with changes in various aggregative price and income indices. But Congress so far has not been willing even to vote discretionary power over tax rates to the President, as the Commission on Money and Credit had recommended.

The automatic tendency for taxes to take away a fraction of each extra dollar of NNP means that the size of the "multiplier" is cut down. Each dollar swing in investment—whether caused by sunspots, inventions, or anything else—will now have its destabilizing effect on the system reduced *but not wiped out completely.* Instead of such disturbances having their effects on NNP multiplied 3 or more times, there will now—because of the automatic stabilizing effect of taxes—be a multiplier effect of only 1.5 or 2 times.[5]

In short, a built-in stabilizer acts to *reduce part* of any fluctuation in the economy, but does not wipe out 100 per cent of the disturbance. It leaves the rest of the disturbance as a task for fiscal and monetary discretionary action.

Philosophically, some reformers dislike the need to have human beings decide policy. They speak of a "government of laws and not of men." They advocate setting up automatic rules and mechanisms that would go into action without ever depending on human decisions. At the present time an automatic gyropilot can keep an airplane pretty stable while the pilot catches a nap; but when something unusual comes up, the human pilot must still take over. No one has yet found a gadget with all the flexibility of man. Similarly in the social field: we have not yet arrived at a stage where any nation is likely to create for itself a set of constitutional procedures displacing the need for discretionary policy formation and responsible human intelligence.

DISCRETIONARY FISCAL POLICY

The principal weapons of discretionary fiscal policy—programs which involve explicit public decision making—are (1) varying public works and other expenditure programs, (2) varying transfer-expenditure programs, and (3) varying tax rates cyclically.

Public works   When governments first began to do something active about depressions, they tended to initiate work on public investment projects for the unemployed. Often these were hastily devised, and in that they aimed primarily to make work for people, they often were rather inefficient; e.g., road building using as little machinery as possible to make the work stretch, leaf raking during the Depression by the WPA relief workers, trumped-up pork-barrel projects of low utility and lacking careful planning. The extreme case is the mythical program where men dig holes and then refill them.

The day is long past when a modern nation will let its economy collapse to the point where its only rescue must come from hastily contrived and wasteful public-works spending. The modern emphasis has, rightly, shifted away from such "make work" projects. Indeed, where a recession is expected to be a short one, economists today would wish

---

[5] Intermediate texts show that in the simple multiplier formula $1/(1 - MPC)$, we have to cut MPC down to .65 MPC now that .35 of each NNP dollar goes to taxes and only .65 to disposable income. What effect on the multiplier does this attenuation of MPC have? In the case of a multiplier of $3.0 = 1/(1 - \frac{2}{3})$, it cuts the $\frac{2}{3}$ down to .433 and the final multiplier down to only 1.8. (The propensity of corporations to distribute only a fraction of their earnings has similar attenuating effects on the multiplier; but their tendency to let a rise in income induce I and their tendency to increase their I merely because they have some retained profits will work to increase the multiplier.) Transfer expenditures on welfare, which tend to fall when NNP rises, act like taxes to reduce the multiplier.

to rely much more on a temporary reduction in tax rates than on an increase in public works.

Why this shift away from public works as a recession cure? Men now realize that it takes a long time to get a post office started or to put into effect a road-building and slum-clearance program. Plans must be made; blueprints drawn; land acquired by purchase and court condemnation; existing buildings razed; and then new structures and roads constructed. All this may take five or more years; and, at the least, half of this time may elapse before any sizable amount of money will get spent on labor and materials. Suppose the recession turns out to last a year at most, followed by two years of steady advance. Then, just in the third year, when the economy may have gone all the way from too little demand to too much demand, there will suddenly come onto the market the government spending that was intended to help a recession. Such timing would of course make fiscal policy an aggravator of instability, not a reducer.

The above remarks should not be construed as an argument against public works. Slum clearance, urban rehabilitation, road building, and public construction are deemed by the American people to represent urgent use of their social resources. Therefore, such programs should be pushed hard; but—and this is the point—they should not be pushed hard under the guise of a program designed *merely* to achieve short-run stabilization. They should be carried out for their own sake and over that long period of time which is necessary if they are to be done well and efficiently.

Of course, the case will often arise where the economy is in a recession or pause and where it may be possible to move ahead the date of carrying out a long-term public-expenditure program that the people had already agreed ought to get done anyway. An intelligently planned shelf of blueprints for desirable public-works projects, even though some costs would be involved in arranging them ahead of time and keeping them up to date, could much improve fiscal timing. As Secretary of Commerce and President, Herbert Hoover long advocated this, and since 1931 we have had such laws. Likewise, it was logical for President Nixon, during the 1969 Vietnam inflation, to freeze most of new federal construction programs.

Welfare expenditures We saw that existing welfare programs, such as unemployment compensation and old-age retirement payments, do act as automatic stabilizers, rising automatically when incomes fall and needs increase.

In addition to such built-in stabilizers, it is possible for the government to institute various discretionary programs of transfer expenditures that will stabilize further. Thus, the government could refrain from giving some pending veterans' bonus in inflationary times and push forward such disbursements in depressed times. If it intends to lower parity farm payments, Congress might hope to time the change to coincide with a boom period. Most important, in times of prolonged unemployment, the federal government has moderated the decline by aiding the states in prolonging the period for which the jobless can get paid unemployment compensation. It is precisely in times of *sustained* unemployment that the present system is most deficient, and it is in such times that there will be minimal harmful effects on job mobility and incentives from increasing unemployment disbursements.

Variation of tax rates   If there is good reason to think that a recession will be brief, a temporary cut in income-tax rates can be a very good way of keeping disposable incomes from falling and of preventing a decline from snowballing. Under our withholding system, the moment Congress or the executive branch decides the economy needs stimulus through tax reduction, employers can begin to withhold less from salary paychecks. Varying tax rates can be used also to help control an inflationary gap and long-run sluggishness. Thus, belatedly, Congress and both Presidents Johnson and Nixon relied on a 10 per cent tax surcharge to help moderate the Vietnam-induced inflation, and the investment tax credit was suspended to help curb the 1966 and 1969 investment booms.

Aside from the obvious political difficulty that it takes Congress a long time to debate and act to make tax changes, there is a minor weakness in the case for heavy reliance on discretionary varying of tax rates for stability purposes. An objection to "temporary" suspension of tax rates to counter a recession comes from the political fact of life that in a democracy it may be hard to get tax rates *back up* after the emergency decline is over. Political sentiment to fight unemployment is often easier to mobilize than sentiment to fight inflationary gaps and more-than-full employment. (In long slumps this may be good.) Furthermore, if people know tax changes are to be temporary and will not be altering their permanent incomes much, they may not vary their consumption spending very much.

SURPLUS AND DEFICIT FINANCING: STAGNATION, EXHILARATION, AND CONTRIVED GROWTH

So far we have been talking only about ironing out the business cycle. If the business cycle were around some "normal" level, most people would not worry too much so long as the boom-time budgetary surplus were always matched by the depression budgetary deficit. With such regularity, *the budget would be balanced over the business cycle* even though not balanced in every single year or month. There would be no secular trend upward in the public debt, nor downward.

But how can one be sure that the cycle will be so regular? What if America is in for what in 1938 Harvard's Alvin Hansen called "secular stagnation"—which means a long period in which (1) slowing population increase, (2) passing of the frontier's free land, (3) high corporate saving, (4) the vast piling up of capital goods, and (5) a bias toward capital-saving inventions—all of which will imply depressed investment schedules relative to saving schedules? Will not an active fiscal policy designed to wipe out such deflationary gaps then result in running a deficit *most of the time*, leading to chronic growth in the public debt? The modern answer is, "Under these conditions, yes; and over the decades the budget should not necessarily be balanced."

Contrariwise, suppose population is proliferating, new inventions are zooming, and investment is generally excessive relative to full-employment saving. If this threatens to go on most of the time, will not active fiscal policy require a budgetary surplus most of the time? Hence, will not such a condition of "secular exhilaration" lead to a long-term *decline* in the public debt? The modern answer is, "Under these conditions, yes,—and a good thing."

In the longer run, deficits may cancel out or public debt may trend upward or downward:

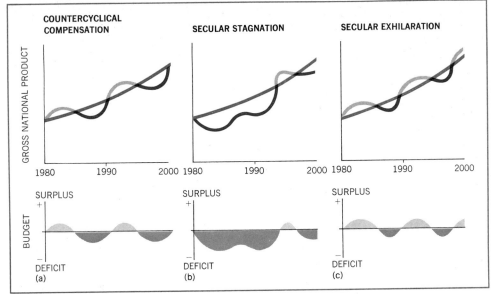

FIG. 19-1. In every case the trend line of policy-achieved full-employment output is shown in gold. How the GNP would grow in absence of active fiscal policy is shown in brown. The indicated budget policy, of successful "leaning against the wind," is shown in blue below. In (a), the light areas of surplus cancel out the dark areas of deficit over the business cycle. In (b)'s case of secular stagnation, the dark deficits prevail over the surpluses and the debt trends upward. In (c), surpluses predominate on the average and debt declines.

A new, third possibility will be discussed in Chapter 41. Suppose a democracy is concerned to accelerate its own rate of growth. Suppose its representative government wishes to increase the fraction of its full-employment income that gets devoted to capital formation rather than to consumption. If public policy succeeds in stepping up net investment by militant easy credit or other policies, how can consumption spending be cut down to prevent excessive dollar demands from precipitating inflation? Primarily by having the government pursue an austere fiscal policy; raising tax rates and cutting down on marginal expenditures, thereby contriving a *chronic* budget surplus to offset easy money.

In brief, one cannot set in advance the optimal trend of surplus or deficit. A diagram can summarize long-term budget alternatives. Figure 19-1 illustrates three variants of modern fiscal policy, all in contrast to a budget balanced in every single year.

In 19-1(a), we see *simple compensatory finance* to iron out the business cycle, with boom surpluses canceling out depression deficits.

In 19-1(b), under secular stagnation, surplus periods are rarer and do not suffice to keep the public debt from having a tendency to grow chronically. (In the last half of the chapter, we study the consequences and true burdens of public-debt growth.)

In 19-1(c), with private $C + I$ spending either spontaneously strong or made strong by expansive Federal Reserve policy, the tendency for the system to run inflationary gaps much of the time is countered by budget surpluses most of the time, with the public debt tending to decline in the long run.

THE NEW ECONOMICS AT WORK

For 10 years after World War II, total demand was exuberant, real economic growth was unusually rapid, and by 1953 unemployment was down to what seems in retrospect a glorious minimal amount. During the 1950s unemployment became higher at each successive peak: $2\frac{1}{2}$ per cent in 1953, 4 per cent in 1957, 5 per cent in 1960. Real growth was sluggish in the Eisenhower years: businessmen complained of a "profit squeeze"; and critics of the mixed economy began to wonder whether it was not subject to the debilitating disease of "structural unemployment" that could not be cured by macro-economic measures. Long-term stagnation had again reared its ugly head.

At this point President Kennedy introduced the "New Economics" into American public policy. Elected in 1961 on the pledge to "get the country moving again," he realized that this would require fiscal actions and not just words. In the first years of the 1960s, the United States government for the first time in its history *explicitly tried to add to a recession deficit in the interests of higher employment and better growth.*

At first, the New Frontier fiscal actions took the form primarily of an increase in government expenditure. But by the end of 1962 President Kennedy had become convinced that the country needed a massive tax cut. To cut taxes when there was already a budget deficit was indeed "new" economics. Only after a long campaign of education did businessmen, laborers, and the man in the street generally become persuaded of the following precepts:

1. To the extent that a tax cut succeeds in stimulating business, our progressive tax system will collect extra revenues out of the higher income levels. Hence, a tax cut *may* in the long run imply little (or even no) loss in federal revenues, and hence no substantial increase in the long-run public debt.

2. There is no need to balance the budget, or try to balance it, in every year. In a growing economy prudent policy does not even require that the budget be balanced over a decade, or over a business cycle. So long as continuous deficits do *not result in the public debt growing faster than GNP grows,* good economic health can prevail. For the economy, "balance" means full employment and healthy growth with no wasteful gap between our potential and our actual real output, and also no inflationary gap.

At first the nonexpert public remained skeptical about these new doctrines. But when President Johnson, after Kennedy's assassination, persuaded Congress to introduce a massive tax cut early in 1964, it worked well enough to impress even the most skeptical. What were the effects of the more than $10-billion tax cut? Scientists have studied this experiment more carefully than almost any other in our economic history, and here are their main conclusions.

The cut in taxes did not prove impotent to change consumption and investment spending, as extremists had argued. Nor did it succeed miraculously in producing full employment overnight, as other extremists had argued.

Instead, the tax cut resulted in just about the gradual rise in consumer spending that the propensity-to-consume concept had predicted. It also had the expected direct stimulus on investment spending. And then the multiplier doctrine worked very much as modern economic textbooks had suggested it would. Moreover, Federal Reserve actions reinforced the fiscal actions with the appropriate monetary policies needed for a steady return toward full employment.

In economics, of course, controlled experiments are not possible. Other things will not remain constant, and by 1966 the unplanned upswing in Vietnam military expenditures caused the economy to overshoot the goal of full employment and enter into a period of demand-pull inflationary gap. Despite advice of most economists to raise taxes, Congress procrastinated from mid-1965 to mid-1968 before introducing the 10 per cent tax surcharge, and by that time prices had been rising for so long that stubborn inflationary expectations were aroused. The resulting rise in $C + I$ spending and in prices proved hard to quell by monetary and fiscal policy.

FISCAL DRAG OR DIVIDEND[6]

In concluding this discussion of deficits and surpluses, and before taking up the issue of the public debt, we should notice some new principles which were developed in the 1960s. First, there is the important concept of "fiscal drag or dividend." Second, there is the related concept of the "full-employment budgetary surplus (or deficit)" as contrasted with the actual surplus or deficit experienced at whatever NNP actually happens to be.

We have seen that a progressive income-tax structure results in vast increases in tax revenues when incomes grow. Thus, every year that the American economy shows 6 or 7 per cent growth in money NNP, the government collects about $15 billion extra of revenue. Every year! Since existing government expenditures do not automatically grow by this amount, we are provided in effect with a "fiscal dividend" that can be used for public purposes.

If inflation is taking place, this built-in stabilizer is a great thing—just what the doctor ordered. But suppose the economy is in a normal healthy state of full employment without inflationary or deflationary gap? Then a collection of billions of new dollars of tax revenue can prove a *deflating* influence that may kill off full employment. And in this case we call it "fiscal drag," and know that we must get rid[7] of it either by cutting taxes, raising federal expenditures, or giving financial aid to the states and localities, with their burgeoning social needs and inflexible tax systems.

Definition: **"Fiscal drag or dividend" is the name for the automatic growth in tax revenues in an economy with a progressive tax structure and steady over-all growth. Unless needed to fight an inflationary gap, fiscal drag has to be offset by (1) federal-expenditure increase on public goods deemed vital, (2) tax-rate cuts that increase people's disposable incomes and expenditures in the private sector, (3) revenue sharing with the states and the localities, or (4) combinations of all of these.**

THE FULL-EMPLOYMENT BUDGET SURPLUS

As a way of dramatizing this ever-recurring problem of fiscal drag, economists have learned not to look at the actual budget deficit. When, as in 1961, we had 7 per cent

---

[6]The next two sections may be skipped in brief courses.

[7]As will be seen in Chapter 41, if there is no international constraint on expansionary monetary policy, fiscal drag can be offset by inducing higher private investment to accelerate national growth.

The New Economics introduces new concepts: full-employment budget and fiscal drag:

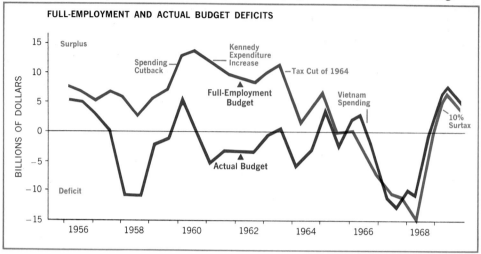

FIG. 19-2. Even though the brown curve shows that the actual budget was in deficit most of the time from 1958 to 1968, the blue curve shows that there was a surplus in the full-employment budget (which measures what the story would be if output and tax receipts were at the full-employment level). Growth of the economy would have enlarged the full-employment surplus every year and produced "fiscal drag," if the Kennedy-Johnson administrations had not deliberately raised expenditures at the beginning of the 1960s and deliberately cut taxes in the mid-1960s. To fight a post-1965 demand-pull inflation, can you show that you want to reinforce fiscal drag by raising the full-employment surplus through judicious tax-rate increases? (Source: Federal Reserve Bank of St. Louis; Council of Economic Advisers.)

unemployment and a large gap between our actual output and our full-employment potential, we were of course running a budget deficit.

But modern economists make a new calculation, asking: "Suppose we were now at high or full employment, say, with only 3½-to-4 per cent of the labor force unemployed and with firms at their desired 95 per cent of capacity. With all the higher tax revenues that such an increase in GNP would bring, what then would our budget deficit be?"

Figure 19-2 shows by the blue curve that in the early 1960s there was really a "full-employment surplus," even though the brown line indicates an actual budget deficit at that time.

To summarize, the "full-employment budget surplus or deficit" measures what *would* be the budget position *if* the economy were at full employment and the legislated tax and spending structures were in effect. Unless tax rates are cut or expenditures increased, there would be in every healthily growing economy an increase in the full-employment surplus and a resulting fiscal drag.

By now we have come a long way from the old-fashioned views of the man in the street. Economic emphasis has been put on the economy's healthy growth without inflation and not on the balancing of the budget. But is this sound economics? Can the economic system *prudently bear the implied burden of the public debt?* To that vital question we turn for the remaining section of this chapter.

B. THE PUBLIC DEBT AND MODERN FISCAL POLICY

As a result primarily of World War II, the public debt of the federal government is about $360 billion—more than a third of a trillion dollars. What are the various economic problems created by such a debt? Are there any false problems associated with it? What are the important noneconomic factors that must be reckoned with in any discussion of this vital political issue?

In appraising the burdens involved in a public debt, we must carefully avoid the unscientific practice of making up our minds in advance that whatever is true of one small merchant's debt is also necessarily true of the government's debt. Prejudging the problem in this way comes perilously close to the logical fallacy of composition; and instead of permitting us to isolate the true—all too real—burdens of the public debt, it may only confuse the issue.

No introduction can go into all the intricacies involved in correct appraisal of the public debt. But modern economists give attention to the debt's true burden and diagnose its problems in a way significantly different from the approach the layman used to take.

BURDENS AND BENEFITS OF THE PUBLIC DEBT

The man in the street, if asked to make a list of important economic problems, will usually put the size of the public debt near the top of his list. A panel of economic experts, in this country or anywhere in the Western world, will usually put the debt toward the bottom of any such list, and indeed some will actually include it on the credit side as a positive blessing.

Why this difference of opinion? And why is it that in countries like Germany, Britain, Japan, and Holland, statesmen, editors, and the citizenry never even know what their current budgetary deficits (as *we* measure the concept) are? These are interesting *psychological* questions that do not belong primarily in a course on economics. It is our task here to make sure we understand in an objective and dispassionate way the *economic* effects of debts, deficits, and surpluses. The facts agreed on by economic scholars can be briefly summarized in the main body of this chapter. The Appendix will present a survey of the deeper analysis that underlies the economics of public debt.

As the Appendix shows,

The main way that one generation can put a burden on a later generation is by using up currently the nation's stock of capital goods, or by failing to add the usual investment increment to the stock of capital.

Thus, the bulk of our $360 billion of federal debt came from World War II. The primary burden of that war came from the need *then* to eat up capital goods without replacing them in order to maximize our effectiveness against the enemy and shorten the conflict. (Hence, it was the prohibition against car manufacture or building construction and repair that produced this real burden, and not the happenstance that Congress decided to finance part of the war effort on a loan-deficit basis rather than on a full tax-as-you-go basis.)

Looking to the future, we can say that (1) *increases in public debt which are incurred in time of full employment* and involve no government capital formation, but *which* (2) *do require that private investment be held down* (by Federal Reserve policy or by inflation itself), do in fact represent a "burden." On the other hand, incurring debt when there is no other feasible way to move the $C + I + G$ equilibrium intersection up toward full employment actually represents a *negative* burden on the immediate future to the degree that it induces more current capital formation than would otherwise take place!

There is a second aspect of the American public debt needing stress. An *external* debt (owed to foreigners), as the Appendix shows in detail, does involve a net subtraction from the goods and services available to the American people, to the degree that we have to send goods abroad to pay interest on that debt. An *internal* debt (owed by the government to its own citizens) is quite a different matter. Certainly one cannot blithely ignore an internal debt on the ground that "we all owe it to ourselves." There definitely are problems involved in an internal debt, but they do differ from those of an external debt.

Two internal-debt problems   First, there are the *transfer* payments of interest that must be made to some people and the taxes that are levied upon all people for this purpose. To the degree that the people involved are different and that the interest receivers are wealthier, more thrifty, or deemed less in need of income, there will be some (admittedly minor) *redistributional* effects to reckon with. But even if the same people are taxed to pay on the average the same amounts they receive in interest, there will still be the *distorting effects on incentives* that are inescapably present in the case of any tax. (The Appendix shows that taxing Peter to pay Peter interest may make Peter work less hard or harder—and either of these may be a distortion of efficiency and well-being.[8]) Second, because we do not live forever, we tend as individuals to treat the public debt as something of an addition to our net worths (added onto the value of the land, structures, and machinery we own). This feeling of greater wealth may well cause us to consume a bit more and save a bit less. Thus the existence of a large outstanding public debt may have some long-run influence on interest-rate levels. Some writers fear that channeling investment funds into the purchase of government bonds will raise the rate of interest to private borrowers. Thus, if people want to hold a certain total of assets to provide for their old-age retirement, the existence of government bonds may substitute for ownership of deeds to machinery and buildings.

Alexander Hamilton, the spokesman of the conservative Federalist party, argued that the debt could lower interest rates. He felt that, rightly managed and in the right amounts, a public debt would be "a national blessing" because it would provide a secure gilt-edge asset that would give businessmen an income and enable them to trade for smaller profits. Notice, too, the beneficial effects of interest payments to banks, colleges, widows, and other *rentiers*. If there were no public debt, or if interest rates were to fall substantially, (1) charitable institutions would have to be supported by public and private current contributions more than by interest on endowments, (2) social security and annuities would have to take the place of *rentier* interest, and (3) service charges by banks would have to be relied upon instead of public bond interest.

[8]But recall that back on page 143, debt interest is listed as only one-twelfth of the total tax level.

Still other effects are analyzed in the Appendix. But in general, when economists evaluate the magnitude and trend of the public debt, with rare exceptions, they agree that its present level does not merit the psychological excitement that used to be accorded it and that often still is. They also agree, however, that *recklessness* concerning deficit spending and debt formation could become an important social evil if it emasculates all public self-discipline, and they point to historical instances of ruinous inflations.

EFFECTS ON PRIVATE EMOTIONS AND INVESTMENT

Never forget that there is a tremendous amount of emotion involved in people's attitudes toward the debt, and this we must not dismiss lightly. Like sex or religion, the public debt is a subject we all love to discuss. Many people used to predict the end of the world when the debt reached one-hundredth, one-tenth, and one-fifth of its present level; each year when the dire disaster had not appeared, they renewed their predictions for subsequent years.

Such attitudes may affect private investment. What if private investment is frightened off by government expenditure or by the deficit? This is certainly possible. Businessmen may say, "With that man in the White House spending recklessly, we're going to abandon even the little private investment we had planned." Or a private utility company may curtail investment because it fears the threat of public dam projects. Or when government spending gives people money to buy in retail stores, the effect in time of deep depression may simply be to permit merchants to work off inventory of surplus merchandise; if they don't reorder production goods, the public expenditure has been just neutralized by induced private *disinvestment* (in inventory), and the multiplier chain is stopped dead in its tracks.

On the other hand, there are expansive effects on private investment that are just the opposite of these unfavorable repercussions of government finance. When current production is at a low ebb and there is excess plant capacity, no prudent businessman feels like undertaking new capital formation. If the government is able to boost retail sales and the production of consumption goods, then businessmen will have the financial ability and at least some motive to renew equipment and build new plants.[9] Sometimes purely psychological fears about the public debt and deficit could *accentuate* an inflation situation, even one with its origin outside the fiscal sphere.

Where there are two such opposing tendencies—expansive and contractionary effects upon private investment—facts rather than arguments must be our guide. Although economics does not permit us to make controlled experiments to settle the point conclusively, the bulk of the statistical data seems to suggest that private investment tends on the whole to move sympathetically with the level of national income. The cash register calls the tune.

Proof of the pudding   Some Congressmen have said, "Deficit financing was tried in the Great Depression and proved to be a failure." MIT's E. Cary Brown studied the fiscal

[9] An example of this was provided by the discussion in Chapter 14 of the acceleration principle relating induced investment to the upward change in sales.

facts of the 1930s to see whether this was true. His careful measurement of the actual statistics of NNP, G, and deficits showed that the historical facts agreed remarkably well with multiplier theory: despite the hysterical criticisms of the New Deal deficits as being gigantic, they in fact were what we would consider small today in relationship to the existent deflationary gap—much too small for any scientist to predict that they would restore full employment; but the fiscal actions of the 1930s did, *per dollar*, produce the expansionary effects predicted by multiplier theory.

THE QUANTITATIVE PROBLEM OF THE DEBT

To assess the importance of the present public debt, we must turn to the facts. Do interest payments on it swallow up most of the national income? How does the total of all interest payments, public and private, compare with past years and with the experience of other countries? What about the future?

To see how the present debt compares with the past and with Britain's debt, look at Table 19-1. It shows for selected times and places the size of national debts and their relationship to size of national income and interest payments. Thus, in 1970 our national debt of about $360 billion represented little more than one-third year of our trillion-dollar GNP (or about 5 months of 1970 national income), and the debt's interest payments represented only about 2 per cent of national income. Note that England in

Growing debt holds little peril for a dynamically growing economy:

PUBLIC DEBT AND INTEREST CHARGES RELATIVE TO NATIONAL INCOME					
(1)	(2)	(3)	(4)	(5)	(6)
				SIZE OF DEBT IN YEARS OF NATIONAL INCOME	INTEREST CHARGES AS A PERCENTAGE OF NATIONAL INCOME
		INTEREST CHARGES ON			
	NATIONAL	NATIONAL	NATIONAL		
YEAR	DEBT	DEBT	INCOME	(5) = (2) ÷ (4)	(6) ÷ 100 = (3) ÷ (4)
United States (billions):					
1970	$360	$16½	$815	$5/12$	2.0
1945	278.7	3.66	181.5	1.5	2.0
1939	47.6	0.95	72.6	0.7	1.3
1929	16.3	0.66	86.8	0.2	0.7
1920	24.3	1.02	79.1	0.3	1.3
1916	1.2	0.02	38.7	0.0+	0.0+
1868	2.6	0.13	6.8	0.4	1.9
Britain (millions):					
1967	£31,986	£1,198	£31,148	1.0	3.8
1946	24,000	500	8,100	3.0	6.2
1923	7,700	325	3,950	1.9	8.2
1913	625	20	2,400	0.3	0.8
1818	840	31	400	2.1	7.7

TABLE 19-1. The $40-billion debt that so worried people in the 1930s looks small against the subsequent rise in our income. (Sources: *Economic Almanac*, U.S. Department of Commerce; U.S. Treasury; United Nations; *Statistical Abstract of United Kingdom*.)

1818, 1923, and 1946 had an internal debt estimated at two or three times national income, and interest on the debt as a percentage of national income far exceeded anything that we need look forward to; yet the century before World War I was England's greatest century—greatest in power and material progress. Furthermore, as the table shows, her national debt was not substantially reduced; but with the steady growth of her national income, the debt and its charges shrank to almost nothing in relative magnitude!

In the light of these statistics and by careful qualitative analysis, the reader must form his own judgment as to whether the national debt can be rationally regarded as a problem of the first magnitude in comparison with the problems of national defense, the nuclear bomb, urban blight, racial tension, unemployment, and inflation. Whether productivity will continue to rise in the future, whether labor and management can learn to bargain collectively without strikes and inflation—to many observers these seem much more important than the debt itself.

Growth in the economy In dispassionately analyzing the growth of the debt, there is one error we must avoid: *We must not forget that the real national product of the United States is an ever-growing thing.*

Our population grows lustily. As to productivity, there is no indication that man-hour efficiency and new techniques have begun to slacken off. Upon this, "stagnationists" and "exhilarationists" both agree. What seemed like a big debt in 1790 would be nothing today. What our children will come to regard as a big debt, our great-grandchildren will deem relatively unimportant.

This explains why England and France, in the crucially formative years of the capitalistic system and the Industrial Revolution, were able to go on—not only decade after decade, but century after century—with their budgets in balance less than half the time. The historian Thomas Macaulay, more than a century ago, said the last word on the debt and growth:

At every stage in the growth of that debt the nation has set up the same cry of anguish and despair. At every stage in the growth of that debt it has been seriously asserted by wise men that bankruptcy and ruin were at hand. Yet still the debt went on growing; and still bankruptcy and ruin were as remote as ever. . . .
The prophets of evil were under a double delusion. They erroneously imagined that there was an exact analogy between the case of an individual who is in debt to another individual and the case of a society which is in debt to a part of itself. . . . They made no allowance for the effect produced by the incessant progress of every experimental science, and by the incessant efforts of every man to get on in life. They saw that the debt grew; and they forgot that other things grew as well. . . .

Figure 19-3 on the next page shows that the growth of our economy since 1945 has drastically reduced the ratio of United States public debt to gross national product. (This, properly, excludes FRB and Treasury holdings; but the point would be the same if these exclusions had not been made.) This fact of growth explains why, in the United States, where money GNP doubles in less than 15 years, the public debt might increase by another $360 billion in that time without its relative percentage burden growing at all.

This would give the wildest believer in government spending an average deficit of tens of billions of dollars per year before he would have to turn to such even more

While private debt outstripped NNP growth, public-debt ratio fell steadily after World War II:

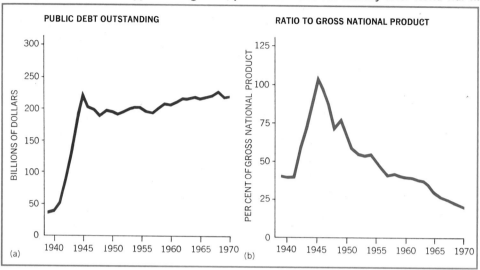

FIG. 19-3. Most of the federal debt held by the public came from wars. In the last 25 years, its ratio to the growing GNP or NNP has declined steadily. (Source: U.S. Treasury. FRB and government holdings of bonds are excluded from the total of federal debt.)

unorthodox financial expedients as printing money or selling interest-free bonds to the Federal Reserve Banks.

Could a nation fanatically addicted to deficit spending pursue such a policy for the rest of our lives and beyond? Study of the mechanics of banking and income determination suggests that the barrier to this would not be financial. The barrier would have to be political; and the effects of such a policy depend crucially upon whether it impinges on an economy that is already inflationary or deflationary. And if the electorate and Congress learn the half-truth that expenditure is expansionary, while forgetting the fact that unpleasant taxes may be necessary to curb undue expansion, then the long-term outlook may indeed be in the direction of rising prices.

PRIVATE AND PUBLIC ANALOGIES[10]

Undoubtedly the major reason for concern about the public debt does not involve sophisticated questions of whether or not it affects the stock of real capital goods. The major concern has to do with the fact that people are uncomfortable at the prospect of anything that may go on growing forever. We all are made uncomfortable by infinity; we are all frightened of the way things grow at compound interest. Some psychologists attribute this to the fact that every child is frightened of the prospect of dying, of *not* living forever. The following case study of the public debt in comparison with the debt of the American Telephone and Telegraph Company adds little to sophisticated analysis of the economics of the matter; but it does bring psychological comfort where it is needed most, to those fearful of ultimate national bankruptcy.

[10] This section may be skipped by brief courses.

"How can the government go on running up debt? If I or my wife lived beyond our means and ran a debt, we'd soon learn what trouble is." The person speaking has overlooked the fallacy of composition: What is true for each unit may be false for the whole of society.

"Why do conservatives complain about the size of the public debt? Private debt has grown tremendously faster in the postwar period than public debt, and you don't hear complaints about that. All credit involves debt. The pyramid of credit could be called the pyramid of debt. If people are to have liquid assets, other people or institutions must have liabilities—d--t to the squeamish." The speaker here is also trying to use analogies with private finance, but this time to the advantage of a program for large deficits.

Both analogies are in principle suspect. Each contains some element of truth, but every strand of such arguments needs critical testing. Thus, it is true that private debt is more than twice the public debt, and that it more than doubled in the last 20 years, while federal debt grew little in absolute amount and has actually dropped from being 62 per cent of all debt in 1945 to being only 20 per cent in the late 1960s. But it is also true that the private assets to back up that private debt have gone up too. And it is true that one could imagine an economy—not ours!—where everything was financed by *equity* issues without fixed debt.

With the warning that no analogy is conclusive, here is an analogy between a private corporation like the American Telephone and Telegraph Company and the United States government.

AT&T has grown all this century. It has floated new debt throughout this century, with never an end to it. If our economy remains healthy, AT&T will undoubtedly have a rising bond debt for the rest of this century. This is prudent finance, not unsound finance. It is prudent to buy that bond debt, but not for the reason that the company has plants and equipment bought from that debt financing and which it could liquidate in a pinch. There is no one to whom AT&T could sell such specialized items in an emergency, since they are good only for the telephone business in which AT&T has complete local monopolies.

Why is never-ending growth in AT&T debt prudent? It is prudent because *the dollar receipts the company can earn from its telephone services are sure to grow along with the population and GNP.* The interest on the debt, and the occasional refunding (but not retirement) of the debt, can be paid for out of the revenues from the telephone company's customers. If they all became impoverished, say, by atomic war, AT&T would have to go bankrupt and not repay its debt. But in a growing economy, no going concern proceeds on the assumption that all the people will go bankrupt.

What does the federal government use to pay its debt interest and refundings? Obviously, *it is the taxable capacity of the country's national product that any government can rely on.*

So long as the money NNP (or GNP) grows at 5 or 6 per cent from now until kingdom come, the public debt of the federal government can grow at those rates, ultimately passing one, two, or any number of trillion dollars. No inflation need result if the process takes place in balance. And no bankruptcy or increase in relative tax burden. And no embarrassment to the Secretary of the Treasury. Like life itself, there is no end to the process.

The above analogy is given only for those who feel a psychological need for reassuring analogies and as an antidote to misleading pessimistic analogies. It says nothing about the great harm governments can do if they spend their taxed or borrowed funds rashly and feed fuel to inflationary gaps when such exist. It says nothing about the proper scope and efficiency of government, because those issues were already clarified in Chapter 8. It says nothing about the proper rate of capital formation and rate of current consumption.

Now we have looked carefully at the facts about the public debt here and abroad and have given the economic principles that underlie the burdens of a public debt. We have seen that there are certain definite problems involved, but that laymen often have mixed-up notions as to what are and are not genuine burdens.

There are many major problems ahead for our economy: inflation, slump, conservation and congestion, adequate growth, international balance of payments, and scores of others. Prudent fiscal and monetary policies impinge on them all; but in a sober man's list of grave problems, the present magnitude of the public debt does not come near the top.

CONCLUSION: MACROECONOMICS OF THE MIXED ECONOMY

The Employment Act of 1946 stated that the government had a responsibility to act to keep employment high and to moderate cyclical instability (and many have suggested that it be amended to mention explicitly a similar government concern for "reasonable stability" of the price level). Even if there were no such legislative proclamations, it is a fact all over the world that the populace of modern mixed economies require their representative governments to pursue economic policies that attempt to keep employment high, growth strong, and prices stable.

Part Two has presented the economic *tools of macroeconomics:* how the various schedules determine levels and movements in incomes and prices; and how monetary and fiscal policies can shift those schedules so as to avoid deflationary and inflationary gaps and promote growth. In Part Six certain special problems connected with the modern era—growth, demand-pull and cost-push inflation, and so forth—will be discussed in greater detail. The millennium has not yet arrived.

The finding of our macroeconomic analysis rejects both the classical faith that laissez faire must by itself lead to utopian stability and the pre–World War II pessimism that classical microeconomic principles have become inapplicable to the modern world. Instead we end with the reasoned prospect that appropriate monetary and fiscal policies can ensure an economic environment which will *validate* the verities of microeconomics—that society has to choose among its alternative high-employment production possibilities, that paradoxes of thrift and the fallacies of composition will not be permitted to create cleavages between private and social virtues or private and public vices.

By means of appropriately reinforcing monetary and fiscal policies, a mixed economy can avoid the excesses of boom and slump and can look forward to healthy progressive growth. This being understood, the paradoxes that robbed the older classical principles dealing with small-scale "microeconomics" of much of their relevance and validity will now lose their sting. The broad cleavage between microeconomics and macroeconomics has been closed by active public use of fiscal and monetary policy.

With good conscience we can turn to the analysis in Part Three of how the great social aggregates of national income and employment *get determined in their detailed parts* and to Part Four's analysis of *income distribution.*

SUMMARY

A. SHORT-RUN AND LONG-RUN FISCAL POLICY

1   When private investment and consumption spending create an inflationary (or deflationary) gap, it is the task of fiscal and monetary policy to offset the gap in the attempt to preserve price stability, high employment, and growth.

2   Fiscal weapons refer to taxation and expenditure policies. In this connection, the modern economy is blessed with important "built-in stabilizers." Requiring no discretionary action, tax receipts change *automatically* when income changes, thereby reducing the size of the multiplier and serving to wipe out part of any disturbance. (The same stabilizing effect is created by unemployment compensation and other welfare transfers that automatically grow as income falls, as well as by farm aid programs and the propensity of corporations to pay out in dividends only part of their current earnings.)

3   Because the automatic stabilizers never *fully* offset the instabilities of an economy, scope is left for *discretionary* programs. Public works and other expenditure on goods and services can involve such time lags in getting under way as to make their use to combat short recessions undesirable. Discretionary variations in transfer expenditures and in tax rates—politics aside—have greater short-run flexibility.

4   When men began to drop the notion that the government's budget had to be balanced in every year or month, they first thought that it would be in balance over the business cycle—with the boom-time surpluses just matching the depression deficits. It is today realized that only by coincidence would the prosperity years just balance in their intensity the recession years and with the desired mix of consumption and capital formation.

   If, as a few believe, we are faced by "secular stagnation," with private saving and investment schedules tending much of the time to produce deflationary gaps, fiscal policy will probably succeed in maintaining stable high employment only by having a *long-term* increase in the public debt. If, as others believe, we are in for "chronic exhilaration," with demand so brisk as to lead much of the time to inflationary gaps, then active fiscal policy will probably mean a bias toward surplus financing and a secular downward trend in the public debt. Perhaps the majority of economists feel there is no need to try to predict what the distant future has in store, being prepared to advocate programs that the developing situation calls for.

5   To get a better measure of changes in discretionary fiscal policy, economists supplement knowledge of the *actual* budget surplus or deficit with the hypothetical "full-employment budget surplus of deficit," which measures what the existing tax and spending structure *would* entail if GNP were at the full-employment level. In a growing economy, there would automatically be a steady growth in the size of the full-employment surplus and resulting "fiscal dividend" or "fiscal drag"—unless offset by expenditure increases, tax cuts, or sharing of tax revenues with states and localities. In time of inflation, automatic fiscal drag is a good thing; and at all times a dividend from genuine growth provides resources for new public or private activities.

B. THE PUBLIC DEBT AND MODERN FISCAL POLICY

6   The public debt does not burden the shoulders of a nation as if each citizen were made to carry rocks on his back. To the degree that we now follow policies of reduced capital formation which will pass on to posterity less capital goods, we can directly affect the production possibilities open to them. To the degree that we borrow from abroad for

some transitory consumption purposes and pledge posterity to pay back the interest and principal on such external debt, we do place upon that posterity a net burden, which will be a subtraction from what they can later produce. To the degree that we bequeath to posterity an internal debt but no change in capital stock beyond what would anyway have been given them, there may be various *internal transfer effects* as one group in the community receives a larger share of the goods then produced at the expense of another group. At any one time there is no "net burden" of such internal transfers quite like the net subtraction involved in the external debt payment, but at most important *transfer effects* between people of different ages then alive and certain effects within each generation's lifetime on how much they will receive of consumption and at what ages. And the process of taxing Peter to pay Paul, or taxing Peter to pay Peter, can have definite costs: these can involve various distortions of production and efficiency, but should not be confused with actually sending goods abroad.

Aside from the above "real" effects, there may also be psychological effects upon the minds of men, and men's resulting actions must of course be regarded as real. Moreover, the fact that there are more rather than less bonds being owned by people in the community can be expected to have quite real effects on their propensity to save and consume out of income. Each person regards his government bond as an asset, but the future taxes to service these bonds he does not count in fully as a current personal liability, even though all society will have to pay taxes equal to such debt service. (This is not irrational from his viewpoint, since the tax rates he will be subject to have little to do with his personal holding of the debt, as the Appendix discusses.)

This summary point has been written at some length to indicate the complexity of the problem. We see that a debt does have important impacts on the economy, even if they are not primarily those that orators and editors preach about.

It is important, also, to know roughly what the size of the post–World War II federal debt is in relation to national income and interest charges, in order to assess the present, both in terms of the past and in terms of the future. The growth of the debt must be appraised in terms of the growth of the economy as a whole. Since 1945 the ratio of public debt to private debt and national product has been substantially declining.

7   A full- (or high-) employment program has as its goal a level of total spending that is neither too little nor too great—so that the saving and investment schedules intersect in the region of full employment. The Employment Act of 1946 represents an important innovation, affirming responsibility of the government for employment opportunities and setting up executive and congressional machinery for policy action.

QUESTIONS FOR DISCUSSION

1   "No nation can avoid having a fiscal policy. With the government such an important part of the present-day economy, it is almost impossible even to define a 'neutral fiscal policy.' It is even harder to give rational reasons for preferring such a policy to an active fiscal program aimed at preventing inflation and deflation." Examine critically.

2   List various "built-in stabilizers." Show how they work in the 1970s.

3 What phase of the business cycle (if any) are you now in? What tax and expenditure policies would seem appropriate? Qualitatively, how would you vary the relative mix of taxes (income-tax rates and exemptions, sales taxes, property taxes) to fight unemployment or inflation?

4 From the early 1870s to the middle 1890s, depressions were deep and prolonged, booms were short-lived and relatively anemic, the price level was declining. What long-run fiscal policy should have been followed in that quarter of a century? Would your answer be the same for the following 20 years leading up to World War I, a period of rising prices?

5 "In the AT&T–debt versus public-debt analogy, it should be noted that along with the private debt went new capital goods—machines, buildings, etc.—which *themselves* enabled growth of real GNP. The same is not true of public-debt growth to finance current public-consumption programs." Verify the element of truth in this.

6 Show briefly why "burden of the debt" is a complicated economic issue.

7 Formulate and evaluate the "New Economics."

Review your understanding of the following concepts:

inflationary and deflationary gap
tax receipts and tax rates
government expenditure on goods
   and transfer expenditures
built-in stabilizers and the reduced
   multiplier
discretionary fiscal programs
fiscal drag and fiscal dividend
the full-employment budget surplus

internal versus external debt
present versus future generations and
   bequeathal of real capital
debt-income ratios here and abroad,
   today, yesterday, and tomorrow
AT&T versus U.S.A.
chronic stagnation, exhilaration, and
   trends in the public debt
Employment Act of 1946

APPENDIX: False and Genuine Burdens of the Public Debt

We have seen that the public debt, prorated over the population, is sometimes regarded to be a load on each man's back. According to this same image, when Congress adds a dollar to the debt by running a current deficit of a dollar, that is like just one more rock added to the load our children or grandchildren will already have to carry on their backs.

This image is misleading in two ways. First, it exaggerates the burdens that are truly involved. Second, by giving a mistaken view of the debt burden, it lays itself open to refutation and thereby to the mistaken conclusion that there are, after all, *no* burdens connected with the public debt. In other words, superficial and wrong analysis offers genuine comfort neither to the conservatives, liberals, or radicals.

As a preview to a judicious appraisal, see how vulnerable the foregoing image is.

A DIALOGUE

Suppose all debt came from World War II. This war is over. Suppose all America's families (1) share equally in ideal nondistorting taxes, (2) hold equal shares of public-debt bonds, (3) all live forever (as individuals or as a cohesive family). With no debt held abroad, (4) "we all owe it to ourselves."

"Then such bonds are not rocks on our shoulders, or even paperweights. If we unanimously voted to abolish the bonds, there would be no real difference. If an enemy bombed our homes and factories, that would be a genuine personal and national burden. But if an enemy bombed our bond lockboxes out of existence, that would merely save us the red tape of taxing ourselves to pay each of us back in bond interest just what the extra tax took away."

So goes the argument. Notice how simple the above refutation is. And how clever in taking the wind out of the sails of those who use the oversimplified rock-burden image. Moreover, the refutation is—granted its assumptions—logically rigorous.

Has the refutation proved that the war involved no grievous burden? It has been cunningly silent on that matter. The Devil's Advocate who produced the refutation would, if pressed by a Tireless Truthseeker, have to concede much.

Devil's Advocate: Yes, the war did involve a grievous economic burden at the time. We had to work hard and long hours. We had to cut wartime consumption to the bone: do with little meat, no cars, no travel, no urban development—make do with few of the things that make life enjoyable rather than merely tolerable.

Tireless Truthseeker: With severe rationing controls, the contemporaneous wartime burden of sacrificed consumption would, according to your view, be much the same even if the war had been financed by pay-as-you-go wartime taxes instead of deficit?

D.A.: Precisely. Postwar canceled tax receipts, instead of bonds, would make no difference.

T.T.: But surely, we used up capital goods during the war by not replacing them. The enemy had to be fought with current 1941-1945 goods and not with 1970 goods. By using up capital goods *then*, we could throw more resources into the war effort. And that did put a real burden *on us in the postwar period* since we inherited less capital goods at war's end. In the postwar period we've had to consume less in order to rebuild those capital goods; and we've had to consume less than we could have if 1941-1945 had given us the normal peacetime increase in capital goods.

D.A.: True. But wartime rationing produced that result. If no wartime deficits and bond indebtedness had been created, that *genuine burden* on the postwar group due to the war would still have had to take place.

T.T.: I feel there must be a catch somewhere. Your argument sounds too facile.

1. I can't help feeling that the existence of the public debt leads (*a*) to tax distortions as we collect taxes to pay its interest, and (*b*) to a lower consumption schedule when poor people with higher MPC pay taxes for bond interest to wealthier people with a lower MPC.

2. Moreover, people don't live forever, and it is not irrational of them to feel wealthier because of the public debt (since they need count on paying taxes for debt interest *only through their remaining lifetime*). This increase in the CC propensity to consume could be at the expense of net capital formation in a full-employment postwar year, requiring contractionary M policy that hurts investment.

3. Besides, a small part of our public debt (about 1 in 20) is external and held abroad: sending foreigners goods to cover the interest payments does constitute a definite subtraction from our GNP available for domestic consumption and investment.

4. While it may be true that transfers of purchasing power—between individuals living at one time, between individuals at different ages of their life-spans, and between individuals alive today and yet unborn—can be engineered by the government without using the device of the public debt at all, yet I can't help believing that society is led by the presence of the debt to make some transfer decisions that it probably wouldn't otherwise have made.

5. If the decision to have a deficit in depression times (or in times when the international balance of payments makes expansionary monetary policy infeasible) merely prevents unemployment, then I admit the implied deficit adds to, rather than subtracts from, the capital stock bequeathed to the postdepression times. (Maybe $50 billion of the depression deficit and some of the 1958-1964 deficit was such a blessing.) But when a decision to have a deficit leads to a compensating cut in private capital formation through inducing more restrictive FRB monetary policy than would otherwise be the case, I say that such a way of increasing the public debt does *itself* put a real burden on the backs of later citizens.

6. Of course, I admit that floating a public debt to add to useful government capital is as legitimate as floating private debt to build useful private capital—because in each case the new paper assets are matched by real income-creating assets.

7. But in a well-run full-employment system, I have to regard loan finance for *current* public consumption as putting a kind of burden on the future through its effective cutting down on net capital formation at the time, and subsequently through its wealth stimulus on consumption that may be competitive with investment.

D.A.: I've never denied anything you are saying. I merely assumed away most of your genuine burdens. If I may say so, you are now shifting over to the side of the angels and are beginning to analyze the true and false burdens rather than using analogies that obscure rather than illuminate the truth.

SUMMARY OF DEBT BURDENS AND BENEFITS

1. Capital-bequeathed burden   The principal way one generation puts a burden on itself later or on a later generation is by bequeathing it less real capital than would otherwise have been the case. Any growth of public debt that has this effect—as in the case of full-employment borrowing for current public consumption that has to be offset by contractionary monetary policy which will lower investment—most definitely does involve a genuine "burden."

2. External-debt burden   Any public debt that is externally held does involve a current burden on the citizens at home, since in the end they have to send goods abroad corresponding to the interest payments and debt service. (Of course, if the original borrowing from abroad resulted in equivalent fruitful capital goods here, their fruits will cover the external-debt service; so the net effect of such external borrowing, taken as a complete package, would be favorable to our economy.)

3. Transfer effects   Taxing Peter to pay Paul bond interest, even if they are the same person, is certain to cause some harmful distortions of personal and business decisions. (EXAMPLE: Peter is taxed 10 per cent of his income to pay himself $1,000 of bond interest. He is under the illusion, and rightly so as an individual, that he can work less and cut down on his tax; but if all do so, we simply have to increase the tax rate. Result: We all end working less because taxes on each individual matched by exactly equal interest payments to him do not economically cancel out!)

Correlated with public-debt operations, but not always in an intrinsic way, are certain transfers that take place between different individuals living at the same time, between the same individual at different periods of life, and between successive generations.[1]

---

[1] EXAMPLES: Twin Jane Day worked hard in World War II; twin Rose did not. Because our government used deficit financing, Jane ended up in 1945 with bonds rather than tax receipts. (Jane may have been motivated to work harder by the bribe of postwar command over goods.) Since 1945 Jane has been receiving a larger share of consumption than Rose; Rose is being taxed more than would otherwise have been the case in order to help pay interest and principal to Jane. Moral: A public debt can definitely involve *internal transfer effects* between individuals of the same or different ages.

4. Wealth stimulus to consumption   The existence of public debt, for reasons already seen, makes the average man feel wealthier. For good or evil, it raises his propensity-to-consume schedule: this may, in a poorly functioning system, be a great thing to reduce unemployment and increase both consumption and investment. But in a system where employment can be counted on to remain full by virtue of price flexibility, luck, or monetary management, the increase in C may be at the expense of I and reinforce the less-capital-bequeathed burden.

5. Effects on interest and money policy   A large debt gives the Fed great leverage for massive open-market operations to achieve stabilization—unless, as in 1946–1951, the central bank is pressured by the government to sacrifice the goal of stabilization to the dubious goal of keeping down the interest charges on the public debt. Many experts believe that the existence of a broad market in government securities makes possible extensive open-market operations of a stabilizing type and tends to enhance the effectiveness of monetary policy. Debt management by the Treasury and Fed by a proper policy of open-market operations in bonds of all maturities that was properly carried out could enhance the stability of a modern system.

6. Effects on discipline and ideology   It would be a tragedy if people, in giving up their irrational fears of deficit spending, were thereby led to call the sky the limit. Unlimited spending can produce inflation, chaos, and waste.

It is to be hoped that the discipline of rationality can replace the discipline of superstition and misunderstanding. After the shibboleth of a balanced budget has lost its power to limit public spending, the good society will have to replace it by a calculus of cost-and-benefit.

Even if Jane Day had died in 1965, she could have consumed more in 1945–1965 by selling off her bonds. The burden of *this* extra consumption could be imposed on those born after 1965 (1) by causing a reduced capital stock after 1965 due to lowered investment in 1945–1965, but also (2) by having an intermediate generation of young postwar workers (employed in 1945–1965 and who have bought Jane's bonds out of their personal saving) supported in *their* old age by the 1980 workers who will then pay taxes on the public debt.

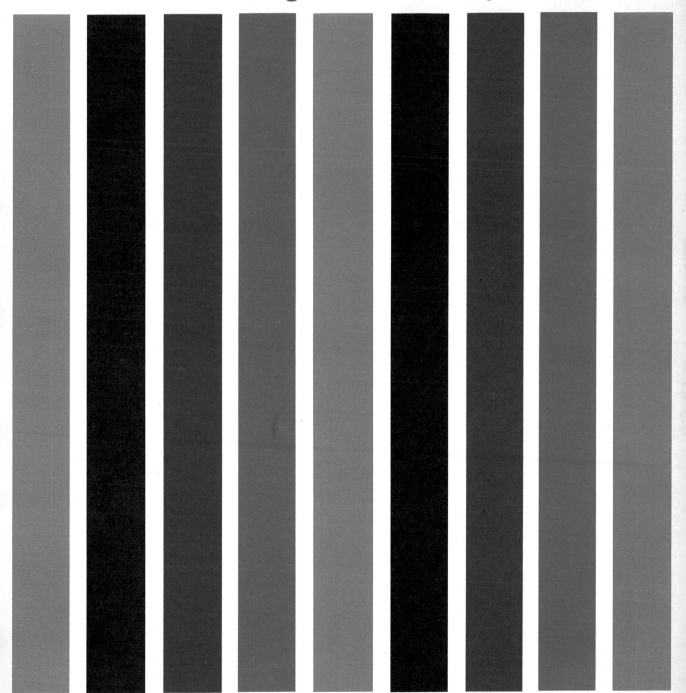

The Composition and Pricing of National Output 3

Determination of Price by Supply and Demand

20

The end is easily foretold,
When every blessed thing you hold
Is made of silver, or of gold,
You long for simple pewter.

When you have nothing else to wear
But cloth of gold and satins rare,
For cloth of gold you cease to care
Up goes the price of shoddy.
GILBERT AND SULLIVAN
The Gondoliers

Part One of this book described the modern economic system and discussed the nature of national income. Part Two gave the modern theory of income determination: it showed why and how incomes, job opportunities, and levels of price fluctuate; it showed how money and banking fit in with income analysis; and most significantly, it showed how fiscal and monetary policy can keep the aggregate system working tolerably well. Today such analysis is called *macro*economics.

PREVIEW

Now Parts Three and Four analyze *micro*economics dealing with the following important questions: What determines the relative prices of *particular* goods? What determines the quantitative breakdown of the national-income aggregates into various goods and services?

In order to understand the *system* of market prices which strikes an equilibrium among people's tastes for different goods and the scarcities of total resources that can produce them, Part Three studies in detail the tools of supply and demand that Chapter 4 introduced briefly.

Part Four follows with a closely related supply-and-demand analysis of what determines the prices of factors of production. Why are wages growing? Why does the share of land rent in the economy move in this way or that? What determines interest? Why have unskilled wages been falling relative to white-collar wages? Are workers being increasingly "exploited" in the sense of receiving an ever-lower share of GNP? Such problems constitute the subject of "distribution of income" in Part Four.

We shall see that the concepts of supply and demand as they are developed further in this chapter are vital tools for mastering the analysis of varied branches of microeconomics. (As a matter of fact, the supply-and-demand tools are indispensable in explaining the international trade problems of Part Five and the current economic issues of Part Six.)

MICROECONOMICS VERSUS MACROECONOMICS?

Macroeconomics deals with the big picture—with the macroaggregates of income, employment, and price levels. But it is not true that microeconomics deals with unimportant details. After all, the big picture is made up of its parts. Mere billions of dollars would be meaningless if they did not correspond to the thousand and one useful goods and services that people really need and want. And who would be impressed by a vast national income if its distribution among human beings was a matter of caprice and pointless inequality?

There is really no opposition between micro- and macroeconomics. Both are vital. You are less than half-educated if you understand one while being ignorant of the other. We cannot even say which comes first: some books begin with one; some with the other. And surveys show that even books like this one, which begin with macroeconomics, are used by about 40 per cent of the courses to teach microeconomics first.

Thirty years ago our society had such poor mastery over its macroeconomics as to make people naturally give less emphasis to microeconomics. With millions starving because of a slump, who could get excited about whether mutton or pork was in a proper relative-price configuration? Or who thought much about white-collar wage trends relative to unskilled wages, when the unemployed tramped the street in every kind of shirt?

Today we can hope all that is changed. Man has gained considerable mastery over his macroeconomic problems, and hence it is natural for the classical problems of microeconomics to move again to the forefront of his attention.

REVIEW OF FUNDAMENTALS OF SUPPLY AND DEMAND

Chapter 3 discussed how a system of pricing and of markets performs the task in any mixed economic system of determining WHAT shall be produced, How goods shall be produced, and FOR WHOM they are to be produced. Then Chapter 4 introduced the basic concepts of supply and demand: their description in terms of schedules of numbers and in terms of intersecting curves. It will be assumed that each reader has this material fresh in his mind, or has gone back to review what was learned earlier, or will stop and take time to master it now.

Our task here is to put the tools of supply and demand to work: to show how they help explain changes in price, in the short run and in the long run; to help predict what effect a tax will have on competitive price; to evaluate various policies that interfere with the laws of supply and demand.

We shall make repeated efforts to see what it is that market pricing is accomplishing in terms of the *efficiency* with which the economy fulfills its basic functions.

All through Part Three new tools of economic analysis will be introduced and the old tools will be gradually developed. But it would be a mistake for any reader to become enamored of tools for their own sake. It is the application of the tools to the richness of modern economic life that makes them exciting. Experience shows that one cannot understand the economic world of the present and the future without having at his command a systematic method of analyzing it. And the testimony of generations of students is that, however far away they later move from formal schooling and examinations, their understanding of the basic economic processes is forever keener, once they have mastered the elementary tools of economic analysis.

Review   Glancing back at the supply-and-demand diagram in Fig. 4-3 (page 61), we see how equilibrium P comes at the intersection of competitive dd and ss curves. We note that any departure of P above equilibrium creates an "oversupply" condition leading back to equilibrium, and that any fall in P below equilibrium creates an "excess demand" that bids P back up to restore the equilibrium.

The succeeding diagram, Fig. 4-4(a) on page 62, shows how a shift in supply, such as might be brought about by a bad harvest, will be likely to increase the equilibrium price P and decrease the equilibrium quantity Q. The new E' intersection point is found to be higher on the unshifted demand curve—just far enough up to cut consumption down to the depressed harvest level.

This illustrates well that important principle, the law of downward-sloping demand—the fact that the demand curve slopes down toward the southeast, in reflection of the observation that people will buy more at lower prices and buy less at higher ones. Likewise, Fig. 4-4(b) showed how an upward shift of the demand curve leads to a higher equilibrium price. So much for review.

A. ELASTICITY OF DEMAND AND SUPPLY

Second-graders, it is found, know that an increase in supply, whether because of an abundant harvest or for whatever reason, is likely to depress price. So it is no surprise that Gregory King, the English writer of the seventeenth century mentioned on page 62, should have remarked on this fact. But that same writer observed a fact perhaps less obvious: King's statistical studies convinced him that farmers as a whole received *less* total revenue when the harvest was good than when it was bad!

This fact, that high agricultural Q tends to be associated with low $P \times Q$, is one that every President of the United States has had to reckon with in facing the farm problem. To understand it and to lay the groundwork for the discussion of farm problems in Chapter 21, we must in this chapter consider and master a new and important economic concept, "elasticity of demand." Henry Ford, and any businessman tempted to *cut* his price in order to sell more goods and make more profit, is also interested in the concept of elasticity. And when the ICC lets a railroad *raise* its prices in order to cut down on passenger-service losses, the elasticity concept is crucially involved.

ELASTICITY OF DEMAND

Various goods differ in the *degree* to which the Q bought will respond to changes in each respective P. Wheat Q may go up much less than 1 per cent for each 1 per cent cut in wheat P; Henry Ford's Q may rise far more than 1 per cent for each 1 per cent reduction in its P; in between is the borderline case of a good whose Q would just halve whenever its P doubled—where the percentage changes are just in balance.

Elasticity of demand is a concept devised to distinguish these three cases. Thus, the first case of weak percentage response of wheat Q is put into the category of "inelastic demand." The second case of great percentage response is put in the category of "elastic demand." The borderline case is called "unitary elasticity of demand."

Here is how the economist goes about defining the three cases:

The crucial thing to concentrate on is the *total dollar revenue* that buyers pay to sellers. If consumers buy 5 units at $3 each, what is total revenue? Total revenue is always, by definition, price times quantity, or the $15 product $P \times Q$. By arithmetic multiplication, total revenue can always be calculated for each point in a demand schedule or diagram.

Elasticity of demand is important primarily as *an indicator of how total revenue changes* when a fall in P induces a rise in Q along the demand curve.

Definition of elasticity of demand: **This is a concept devised to indicate the degree of responsiveness of Q demanded to changes in market P. It depends primarily upon** *percentage* **changes and is independent of the units used to measure Q and P. Elasticity ends up qualitatively in one of three alternative categories:**

1. When a cut in P raises Q so much as to *increase* **total revenue $P \times Q$, we speak of** *elastic* **demand—or of elasticity of demand** *greater than unity.* **The percentage change in Q exceeds the percentage change in P.**

2. When a percentage cut in P results in an exactly compensating percentage rise in Q so as to leave total revenue $P \times Q$ exactly *unchanged,* **we speak of** *unitary elasticity of demand*—**or of elasticity of demand that is numerically** *exactly equal to unity.*

3. When a percentage cut in P evokes so small a percentage increase in Q as to make total revenue $P \times Q$ fall, we speak of *inelastic* **demand—or of elasticity of demand that is** *less than unity* **(but not less than zero).**

Figure 20-1 gives a graphic example of the three cases. In each case, P is halved from A to B, but it would be just as much in order to have used a very small percentage change in P. Perhaps at a first glance, it will be easiest to begin with the borderline case of unitary elasticity of demand.

In Fig. 20-1(b), the doubling of Q exactly matches the halving of P, with the result that the total revenue collected remains unchanged at $1,000. This can be shown graphically by comparing certain rectangular areas. How? Price and quantity can be easily read off the curve at any point; but how do we read off total revenue, which is their arithmetic product $P \times Q$? When we recall that the area of a rectangle is always equal to the product of its base times its altitude, the answer is easy:

Total revenue at any point is always as shown by the area of the rectangle which that point makes with the two axes. (Check that the shaded rectangle at A does have a base equal to Q and an altitude equal to P.) Hence, if our eye watches how the area of each point's rectangle changes as we cut price and move down the demand curve, we can know in which of the three categories of elasticity such a movement happens to fall.

Clearly, in the middle diagram, the areas are remaining exactly the same because of offsetting changes in their Q bases and P altitudes; consequently, this is the case neither of elastic nor of inelastic demand, but rather is the borderline case of unitary elasticity of demand.

The reader can now verify that Fig. 20-1(a) does correspond to *elastic* demand, with total revenue going up when P is cut and elasticity hence greater than unity. And Fig.

Elasticity of demand comes in three cases, depending on how total revenue moves:

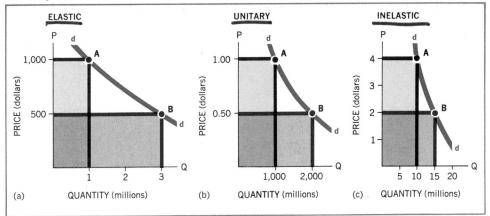

FIG. 20-1. In cutting P from A to B, we raise, leave unchanged, or lower the rectangle of total revenue, depending on whether demand is elastic, unitary elastic, or inelastic. That is, elasticity depends on percentage response of Q to each percentage change in P.

20-1(c) corresponds to the opposite case of *inelastic* demand, with total revenue falling off when P is cut and elasticity less than unity. [Which diagram represents the Gregory King finding that smaller harvests meant higher total revenues for farmers? Which represents the early belief of Henry Ford that if only he could reduce his cars' P, he would meet a great increase in cars sold? Surely, 20-1(c) and 20-1(a), respectively.]

NUMERICAL MEASUREMENT OF ELASTICITY: A DIGRESSION[1]

The general notion of elastic, inelastic, and unitary elasticity as an indicator of the percentage responsiveness of quantity to price and as an indicator of how total revenue behaves is now clear. But some readers will be curious to know how these qualitative cases can be given exact numerical measurement by economists. What does it mean to say that the elasticity of demand is 1.0? 2.3? .5? To answer this question, we give the following definition for a coefficient of elasticity E between two different price points on a demand curve:

$$\text{Elasticity coefficient } E = \frac{\text{per cent that } Q \text{ has risen}}{\text{per cent cut in } P}$$

Note that the movements along P and Q are in opposite directions because of the law of downward-sloping demand. Note, too, the use of *percentages*, which brings in the nice property that the units of a good or of money—bushels or pecks of wheat, dollars or pennies—do not affect elasticity.[2]

---

[1] In a short course the next two sections may be skipped.
[2] Units will affect the *slope* of the demand diagram, just as the draftsman can make a curve look steep or flat in slope by changing the scale of one of his axes. So the purpose of the next section is to help you avoid confusing *slope* and *elasticity*. As Fig. 20-1(b)'s curve with $E = 1$ shows, it is not a straight line with constant slope that corresponds to a curve of constant elasticity, but rather one whose slope varies in order to keep the percentage changes in the same ratio. (Mathematicians call the unitary-elastic curve a ["rectangular"] hyperbola.)

Dividing percentage price cut into percentage quantity rise gives numerical elasticity:

NUMERICAL CALCULATION OF ELASTICITY COEFFICIENT						
P	$-\Delta P$	Q	ΔQ	$\dfrac{P_1 + P_2}{2}$	$\dfrac{Q_1 + Q_2}{2}$	$E = -\dfrac{\Delta Q}{(Q_1 + Q_2)/2} \div \dfrac{\Delta P}{(P_1 + P_2)/2}$
6		0				
	2		10	5	5	$^{10}/_5 \div {}^2/_5 = 5 > 1$
4		10				
	2		10	3	15	$^{10}/_{15} \div {}^2/_3 = 1$
2		20				
	2		10	1	25	$^{10}/_{25} \div {}^2/_1 = .2 < 1$
0		30				

TABLE 20-1.   Each P cut, $-\Delta P$, is related to the average P, $(P_1 + P_2)/2$; each Q rise, ΔQ, to the average Q, $(Q_1 + Q_2)/2$; the resulting ratio gives numerical E, a measure expressed in percentage (dimensionless) units, not in absolute slope units.

Do not get bogged down in numerical details of E calculation. Now that you have mastered the general idea of elastic, inelastic, and unitary demand, you can proceed to the following numerical examples.

Always there is a slight ambiguity about percentage changes. Suppose a grocer buys bread for 15 cents and sells for 25. Is that the $66\frac{2}{3}$ per cent markup that comes from relating the change of 10 to the lower base 15? Or is it the 40 per cent change that comes from relating 10 to the higher base 25? No one answer can be said to be right, and no one definitely wrong. Fortunately, when it comes to very small percentage changes, as from 100 to 99 or from 100 to 101, the difference between $\frac{1}{100}$ and $\frac{1}{99}$ becomes hardly worth talking about. For small changes, it does not matter much how you calculate the percentage changes; but for larger ones it may make quite a difference, and no single answer can be declared to be the right one.

What is a good rule to use? Long experience suggests this: As good a rule as any is to relate the price change to neither the higher nor the lower of the two Ps, but to their average. Thus, is a cut from 101 to 99 a change of $\frac{2}{99}$ or $\frac{2}{101}$? By our convention, it is neither: we call it a change of $\frac{2}{100}$, because the average of 99 and 101 is $(99 + 101)/2 = {}^{200}/_2 = 100$.

Table 20-1 is self-explanatory: it shows how to calculate E for three movements along a dd curve. We shall be seeing that most dd curves start out elastic at high P and end up inelastic at low P, passing through unitary elasticity at an intermediate position where total revenue $P \times Q$ is at its maximum. Table 20-1 illustrates this.

GRAPHICAL MEASUREMENT OF ELASTICITY: A DIGRESSION

Students tend to make a simple mistake: They often confuse the slope of a curve with its elasticity; they think a steep slope on dd must mean inelastic demand, and a flat slope must mean elastic demand. This is not quite true. Why not? Because slope of dd depends upon *absolute* change in P and Q, whereas elasticity was seen to depend upon *percentage* changes.

The straight line dd in Fig. 20-2(a) illustrates the fallacy of confusing slope and elasticity. Everywhere it has the same absolute slope. But toward the top of the line, where

Absolute slope and percentage elasticity are not the same:

ELASTICITY AT A POINT

PERFECT INELASTICITY

INFINITE ELASTICITY

FIG. 20-2. All points on *dd*'s straight-line demand in (a) have same absolute slope: but above the midpoint price, demand is elastic; below it, demand is inelastic; at it, demand is unitary. Only in the case of perfectly vertical or horizontal curves, as in (b) and (c), can you infer inelasticity and elasticity from slope alone.

(1) P is high and its percentage change low and (2) Q is very low and its percentage change therefore almost infinitely great, our numerical formula for E results in a very high elasticity.

Thus, above the midpoint M of any straight line, demand is elastic, with $E > 1$; at the midpoint, demand is of unitary elasticity, with $E = 1$; below the midpoint, demand is inelastic, with $E < 1$.[3]

[3] Intermediate books tell how to calculate E at any one point on a straight line: E equals the length of the line segment below the point divided by the length of line segment above it. Since M is halfway, the formula there gives $E = 1$, unitary elasticity. At B, it gives $3/1 = 3.0$; at R, $E = 1/3 = .33$.

Knowing how to calculate E for a straight line enables you to calculate it for any point along a curved *dd*. (1) Draw with a ruler the straight line tangent to the curve at your point (e.g., at B in Fig. 20-3); (2) calculate the E for the straight line at that point (e.g., E at $B = 3/1$); (3) identify your resulting E as the correct elasticity for the *dd* curve at your chosen point. Question 7, page 378, proves the truth of the geometrical rule for calculating E.

NOTE: E at a point can be shown to be mathematically equivalent to the following limit:

$$\frac{-\Delta Q}{Q} \div \frac{\Delta P}{P} = -\frac{P}{Q}\frac{\Delta Q}{\Delta P} \rightarrow -\frac{P}{Q}\frac{dQ}{dP}$$

as ΔP goes to zero, taking ΔQ with it and making it immaterial which of the Ps and Qs or their averages we use to compute percentage changes. Intermediate texts show that, when you plot *dd* on double-log paper, it becomes correct to identify slope with elasticity—because double-log paper does measure percentage changes. (See footnote 12, p. 378, for more on this.)

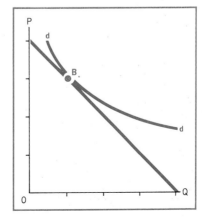

FIG. 20-3.

When many people make the same mistake, there is usually a reason. The limiting cases of *completely vertical* and *completely horizontal* demand curves, shown in Fig. 20-2(b) and (c), do validly portray the limiting cases of *completely inelastic* and *infinitely elastic* demands. But do not think that the in-between cases, where most of reality falls, can have their elasticities depicted by slope alone.

Now, we go back to the mainstream of demand and supply.

ELASTICITY OF SUPPLY

What we did for demand, we can do also for supply. Economists introduce the concept of "elasticity of supply" to give an indication of the percentage increase in the amount of Q supplied in response to a given percentage rise in competitive P. (Note that in the case of a *rising* supply curve, we now speak of an *increase* in P, rather than of a *decrease* in P as was done in the case of a downward-sloping demand curve.)

If the amount supplied is perfectly fixed, as in the case of perishable fish brought to today's market for sale at whatever price they will fetch, we face the limiting case of perfectly *inelastic*, or vertical, supply. If we have a horizontal supply curve (the "constant-cost case"), so that the slightest cut in P will cause Q to become zero and the slightest rise in P will coax out an indefinitely large supply, we are at the other extreme of *infinitely elastic* supply. Between such extremes, we call supply elastic or inelastic depending upon whether the percentage rise in Q is respectively greater than or less than the percentage rise in P bringing it about.[4]

Supply elasticity is a useful concept but not quite so useful a concept as demand elasticity, for the reason that elasticity of demand has the major additional function of telling us what is happening to total revenue.

There is, however, an important fact that supply elasticity can help describe. A given change in price will tend to have greater and greater effects on amount supplied as we move from the momentary situation to a short-run period of time and on to the long-run period. This means:

Elasticity of supply tends to be greater in the long run, when all adjustments to the higher price have been made, than in shorter periods of time.

Let us see why.

[4]A numerical coefficient of supply elasticity E_s is defined thus: $E_s =$ (percentage change in Q)/(percentage change in P). Figure 20-4 shows three straight-line supply curves: at A the line going through the origin has elasticity of exactly 1.0; the steeper curve with intercept on the Q axis is inelastic, with elasticity coefficient less than 1; and the flatter curve is elastic, with elasticity coefficient greater than 1. (If—as we shall see can happen—the supply curve actually bends up backward, elasticity of supply as here defined could actually become negative.) Also, for a supply curve with curvature, one can reckon its elasticity at a point A' by drawing a straight line with a tangential ruler and seeing which curve of Fig. 20-4 it resembles; or plot it on double-log paper and study its slope at A'.

FIG. 20-4.

MOMENTARY, SHORT-RUN, AND LONG-RUN EQUILIBRIUM

Alfred Marshall, Cambridge's great economist at the turn of the century, helped forge these tools of supply and demand. We can review our understanding of equilibrium and at the same time advance our knowledge if we survey Marshall's important emphasis on the *time element* of the problem.

He distinguishes at least three time periods: (1) *momentary* equilibrium, when the supply is fixed; (2) *short-run* equilibrium, when firms can produce more within given plants; and finally (3) *long-run* equilibrium (or "normal price"), when firms can abandon old plants or build new ones and when new firms can enter the industry or old ones leave it.

Let us imagine that the demand for a perishable good, such as fish that cannot be preserved, increases from *dd* to *d'd'*. With the amount of fish supplied unchanged, the stronger demand will sharply bid up the momentary price of fish. This is shown in Fig. 20-5(a), where the fixed supply curve $s_m s_m$ runs up to the new demand curve *d'd'* to determine the new sharply higher momentary equilibrium price shown at *E'*. The price has had to rise so much in order to *ration* the limited supply of fish among the now eager demanders.

But with so high a price prevailing in the market, skippers of the fishing boats will be motivated to hire more men and to use more nets. Even if they do not have the time to get new boats built, they will in the short run begin to bring to the market a greater supply of fish than they did at the old momentary equilibrium. Figure 20-5(b) shows the

Effect of demand increase on price varies in the three time periods:

1st, The new momentary equilibrium raises P to ration out the unchanged supply:	2d, Short-run equilibrium coaxes out increased supply from existing plants:	3d, Normal long-run equilibrium comes when new plant, all resources, and costs get adjusted:

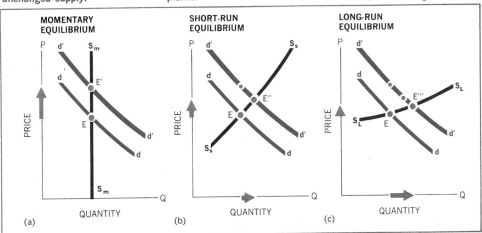

FIG. 20-5. Marshall distinguishes three different time periods, depending upon whether supply elements have time to make (a) no adjustments, (b) some adjustments of labor and variable factors, (c) full adjustment of all factors and costs to price. (The upward slope of $s_L s_L$ puts this case in the "increasing cost" category. What would $s_L s_L$ be like in the "constant-cost" case? Why might a very small industry have constant costs?)

new $s_s s_s$ short-run supply schedule, and shows that it intersects the new demand curve at E'', the point of short-run equilibrium. Note that this equilibrium price is a little lower than the momentary E' price. Why? Because of the extra supply of fish induced in the short run by more intensive use of the same number of boats.

Figure 20-5(c) shows the final long-run equilibrium, or "normal," price. The higher prices that long prevailed have coaxed out more shipbuilding and attracted more trained sailors into the industry. Where the long-run supply curve $s_L s_L$ intersects the demand curve $d'd'$ at E''' is the final equilibrium reached after *all* economic conditions (including number of ships and shipyards) have adjusted to the new level of demand.

Note that the long-run equilibrium price is not as high as the short-run equilibrium price, and not nearly as high as the momentary equilibrium price. Yet it is a little bit higher than the price that prevailed previously when demand was lower. Marshall would call this a case of "increasing cost" and would regard it as the normal one to be met in most sizable competitive industries. Why normal? Because when a large industry (which has already achieved the economies of large-scale production) expands, it must coax men, ships, nets, and other productive factors away from other industries by bidding up their prices and thus its own cost. So the long-run supply curve $s_L s_L$ will usually be sloping gently upward as in Fig. 20-5(c). Only if the industry is small compared with the total of all other users of its factors will Marshall's $s_L s_L$ curve in Fig. 20-5(c) be horizontal—which is called the case of "constant cost."[5]

The reader can test his understanding of all the foregoing discussion by now assuming a downward shift in the demand curve back to *dd*. Show what happens in the new momentary run; in the short run; and in the long run. The Appendix to this chapter presents various cases of supply and demand. Chapters 23 and 24 will give in greater detail the factors and processes underlying the various supply curves.

B. APPLICATIONS AND QUALIFICATIONS OF SUPPLY AND DEMAND

Other things being equal, as economists are fond of saying, there is a unique schedule of supply or demand in any period of time. But other things will not remain equal. The demand for cotton is declining over the years because of reductions in the price of synthetics. The supply schedule of gasoline is shifting because technological progress permits more to be produced at the same cost. As costs and tastes change, as incomes vary, as the prices of rival products (coffee in relation to tea) or of cooperating products (sugar in relation to tea) change, our schedules will shift. What will be the effects on consumption, production, and price? That we must now study.

All beginners in the field of economics must beware of a common error. They must take care not to confuse an increase in *demand*—by which is meant a *shift* of the whole curve to the right and upward, as more is now bought at each same price—with an increase in the *quantity demanded* as a result of moving to a lower price *on the same demand curve*. By "demand" is meant the whole demand curve; by "supply" is meant the whole supply curve; by an "increase" in demand or supply is meant a *shift* of the

---

[5] See the cases in the Appendix.

whole curve in question to the right. To indicate a single point on a demand curve, we speak of the "quantity bought" or the "quantity demanded" *at a particular price.* A movement *along* the same curve is "a change in the quantity demanded as a result of a price change." It does not represent any change in the demand schedule. The need for this warning will appear in a moment.

INCIDENCE OF A TAX

We can illustrate the case of a shift in the entire curve by referring to supply and demand schedules for a good like wheat. Figure 20-6 shows an equilibrium price at *C* of $3 per bushel before a tax is imposed.

Let us now introduce a new factor, which will disturb this equilibrium. In particular, assume that the government imposes a sales tax on wheat. On each and every sale, the producer is required to pay a tax of $1 per bushel of wheat.

What is the final effect, or what economists call the "incidence," of the tax? Is its burden shifted back completely onto the producer, who must pay it legally in the first instance? Or may it be shifted forward in part to consumers? The answer can be derived only from our supply and demand curves.

There is no reason for the demand curve of the consumers to have changed at all. At $3, consumers will still be willing to buy only 12 (million) bushels; they neither know nor care that the producers must pay a tax.

But the whole supply curve is shifted upward and leftward: leftward because at each market price the producers will now supply less as a result of the tax; upward because, to get the producers to bring any given quantity to market, say, 12 (million) units, we must give them a higher market price than before—$4 rather than $3, which is higher by the exact amount of the $1 tax the producer must pay.

The student should be able to fill in a new supply column, resembling Column (3) in Table 4-3, page 61, but with each price raised by $1. Here in Fig. 20-6, the demand curve *dd* is unchanged, but the supply curve *ss* has been shifted up everywhere by $1 to a new vertically *parallel* supply curve *s's'*.

Where will the new equilibrium price be? The answer is found at the intersection of the new demand and supply curves, or at *C'*, where *s's'* and *dd* meet. Because supply has decreased, the price is higher. Also, the amount bought and the amount sold are less. If we read the graph carefully, we find that the new equilibrium price has risen from $3 to about $3⅔. The new equilibrium output, at which purchases and sales are in equilibrium, has fallen from 12 (million) per month to about 10.6 (million) bushels.

Wheat tax falls both on consumer and producer:

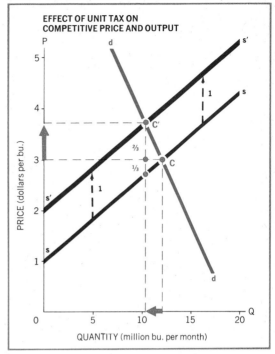

FIG. 20-6. A $1 tax shifts *ss* up $1 everywhere to give parallel *s's'*. This intersects *dd* in new equilibrium at *C'*, where price to consumer has risen $⅔ above old *C* equilibrium and where price to producer has fallen by $⅓. The gold arrows and dots show change in *P* and *Q*. (Had *dd* been very elastic and flat relative to *ss*, most of the $1 tax would have fallen on the producer. Had *ss* been completely horizontal, the whole $1 tax would have been shifted forward onto the consumer.)

Who pays the tax? Well, the wheat farmers do in part, because now they receive only $2\frac{2}{3}$, ($3\frac{2}{3}$ − $1), rather than $3. But the consumer also shares in the burden, because the price received by the producer has *not* fallen by as much as the tax. To the consumer, the wheat now costs $2\frac{2}{3}$ plus the $1 tax, or $3\frac{2}{3}$ in all. Because consumers want wheat so badly, they pay $\frac{2}{3}$ of the tax, and producers pay $\frac{1}{3}$ of the tax.[6]

To check his understanding of the above reasoning, the student should consider the case of an opposite shift in supply. Let the government pay producers a subsidy of $1 per bushel of wheat instead of taxing them this amount. Shift *ss* down to the new curve *s″s″*. Where is *C″*, its intersection with *dd*? What is the new price? The new quantity? How much of the benefit goes to the producer? How much to the consumer?

Summary: **A sales tax on a good will raise its price most and reduce its quantity least when supply and demand curves are most *inelastic*. (When they are elastic, *Q* changes much and *P* changes little.)**

The tax is shifted forward onto the consumer when *dd* is very inelastic. The tax is shifted backward onto the producer when *ss* is relatively the more inelastic. Only with the apparatus of supply and demand can one analyze the incidence of various different taxes—import tariffs, cigarette and liquor excises, payroll and corporation taxes, etc.

A COMMON FALLACY

By now the student has mastered supply and demand. Or has he? He knows that a tax will have the effect of raising the price that the consumer will have to pay. Or does he know this? What about the following argument of a kind often seen in the press and heard from the platform:

The effect of a tax on a commodity might seem at first sight to be an advance in price to the consumer. But an advance in price will diminish the demand. And a reduced demand will send the price down again. Therefore it is not certain, after all, that the tax will really raise the price.

What about it? Will the tax raise the price or not? According to the editor's written word and the senator's oratory, the answer is, No. Evidently, we have here an example of the treachery of words. One of the four sentences in the quotation is false because the word "demand" is being used in the wrong sense. The student has already been warned against confusing a movement *along* an unchanged curve with a shift in the curve. Actually, the correct answer[7] would be more or less as follows:

A tax will raise the price to the consumer and lower the price received by the producer, the difference going to the government. At the higher price a smaller quantity will be bought by consumers. This is as it should be, because producers are also supplying a smaller quantity at the lower price which they receive. Thus the amounts willingly bought and sold out balance where the new supply and demand schedules intersect, and there will be no further change in price.

[6]There is another and equivalent way to handle this tax problem. If the consumer were thought of as paying the tax in the first instance, you could subtract $1 everywhere from his *dd* curve. This new *d′d′* will intersect *ss* at the same new *Q*, and the same $2\frac{2}{3}$ and $3\frac{2}{3}$ prices will prevail. It goes without saying that all these figures are hypothetical.
[7]H. D. Henderson, *Supply and Demand* (Cambridge, London, 1922), p. 27, explains this.

IS THE LAW OF SUPPLY AND DEMAND IMMUTABLE?

Competitive price and quantity are determined by supply and demand. But does not price depend on other factors, such as the amount of gold production or whether there is a war going on? Actually, price does depend on many such factors. However, they are not *in addition* to supply and demand, but are included in the numerous forces which determine or *act through* supply and demand. Thus, if new gold production gives everyone higher incomes, it will shift demand curves and raise prices. But it is still true that competitive price is determined by supply and demand.

At this point a thoughtful reader should be moved to voice protest. Little has been said about price as being determined by cost of production. Should not this be listed as a third factor in addition to supply and demand? Our answer is stubbornly, No.

Competitive price is affected by cost of production only to the extent that such cost affects supply.

If God sends nutritious manna from heaven without cost but in limited supply, then its price will not be zero but will be given by the intersection of the demand and supply curves. On the other hand, if it would cost $50,000 to print the national anthem on the head of a pin, but there is no demand for such a commodity, it simply will not be produced and would not command $50,000 if it were produced. (What the market price of something nonexistent should be called is left to the reader's pleasure.)

This does not mean that cost of production is unimportant for price determination. Under competition it is especially important. But its importance shows itself *through its effects upon supply*. Businessmen produce for profit. If they cannot get a price high enough to cover their past costs, then they will not like it. Nevertheless, once the crop is in, so to speak, there is not much they can do about it under competition. They have no choice but to minimize their short-term losses. But they will not continue *in the future* to supply goods at prices that fail to cover the *extra* costs incurred to produce these goods. Thus supply depends intimately on cost, especially on what Chapter 23 and later chapters will call "extra" or "marginal" cost; and so too must price.

Moreover, to say that price equals cost does not in itself tell us which is the cause of which. In many cases where an industry uses a productive factor highly specialized to itself (e.g., baseball players, opera singers, vineyard land), *price determines cost rather than vice versa*. Grain land is dear because the price of grain is high. Apartment buildings sell for much because rents are high. This type of relationship was overlooked by the Massachusetts dairy farmers who petitioned during World War II for a higher milk price "because the price of cows is high." If their request had been granted, they would soon have observed the price of cows chasing the milk price upward.[8]

Useful categories Thus, supply and demand are not ultimate explanations of price. They are simply useful catchall categories for analyzing and describing the multitude of forces,

[8] Where a factor of production is inelastic in supply, as in all these cases mentioned here, its cost is "price-determined" rather than "price-determining" and its return is called an "economic rent." For more on this, see Case 3 in the Appendix and Chapter 28.

causes, and factors impinging on price. Rather than final answers, supply and demand simply represent initial questions. Our work is not over but just begun.

This should help to debunk the tendency of neophytes to utter sagely, "You can't repeal the law of supply and demand. King Canute knew he could not command the ocean tide to retreat from his throne on the seashore. No more can government get around, or interfere with, the workings of supply and demand."

It would be better not to have learned any economics than be left with this opinion. Of course the government can affect price. It can do so by affecting supply or demand, or both. In Chapter 21 we shall examine how government programs for restricting farm production can raise price and income by cutting down on supply. Similar programs by government cartels have been pursued all over the world: Brazil has burned coffee to raise its price; Britain during the 1920s tried artificially controlling the price of rubber; sugar and cocoa are still under international control.

These governments have not violated the law of supply and demand. They have worked (not always to good purpose) through the law of supply and demand. The state has no secret economic weapons or tricks. What is true for the state is also true for individuals. Anyone can affect the price of wheat as long as he has money to throw on the market or wheat to hold off it.

Trade-unions often influence wages, or try to, by directly or indirectly affecting the supply of labor. Anyone with a somewhat distinctive commodity may try by advertising to increase the demand for his product and, by restricting supply, to raise price above his extra costs of production. It should be emphasized, however, that as soon as individual producers grow in size and become important enough to affect the price of the things they sell, they then cease to be perfect competitors in the strict sense, and their behavior has to be analyzed in terms of a blend of monopoly and competition, i.e., in terms of imperfect competition as described in Chapters 25 and 26.

PRICES FIXED BY LAW

There is one genuine interference with supply and demand whose effects we must analyze. The government sometimes sets by law a maximum price or a minimum wage. During World War II, ceilings were placed on items in the cost of living. In 1970, a floor of $1.60, in the form of a minimum hourly wage, applies to most workers. These interferences by law are quite different from government actions, previously described, which work *through* supply and demand.

Price ceilings and rationing Consider, say, the market for sugar, which has ordinary curves of supply and demand such as we have repeatedly met in this chapter. Suppose that the government through an Office of Price Stabilization (OPS) establishes an order prohibiting sugar from rising above 7 cents a pound (retail). Now, because of prosperity or bad crops, let demand be so high and supply so small that the equilibrium price would have been 20 cents a pound if the government had not intervened. This high price would have contributed to "profiteering" in that industry, it would have represented a rather heavy "tax" on the poor who could ill afford it, and it would only have added fuel to an inflationary spiral in the cost of living, with all sorts of inflationary reactions on workers' wage demands. So go the arguments of price fixers.

Therefore the government, through Congress and the OPS, decides to hold the line on prices. It passes a law putting a maximum price on sugar at the old level of 7 cents a pound. The ceiling-price line *CJK* in Fig. 20-7 represents the legal price ceiling. Now what will happen?

At the legal ceiling price, supply and demand do not match. Consumers want thousands of pounds of sugar in excess of what producers are willing to supply. This is shown by the gold gap between *J* and *K*. This gap is so large that there will not long be enough sugar on grocers' shelves or in the warehouse to make up the difference. Somebody will have to drink bitter coffee. If it were not for the maximum-price law, this somebody would gladly bid the price up to 8 or 18 cents or more, rather than do without sugar. As in our earlier discussion (Fig. 4-3, page 61), we could have shown this by putting an upward-pointing arrow perpendicular to *JK*. Such an arrow would not stop pointing upward until price had been bid up to the equilibrium level of 20 cents.

But it is against the law for the consumer to bid a higher price. Even if the consumer should be so unpatri-otic, the seller could not legally take the higher price. There follows a period of frustration and shortage—a game of musical chairs in which somebody is left without a seat when the music stops playing. The inadequate supply of sugar must somehow be rationed. At first, this may be done by "first come, first served," with or without limited sales to each customer. Lines form, and women have to spend much of their time foraging for food. But this is no solution, since somebody must be left at the end of the line when the sugar is gone.

The price mechanism is stymied and blocked. Nonmonetary considerations must deter-mine who is the lucky buyer and who the unlucky one: the warmth of the smile that the customer flashes on the grocer, her previous standing at the store in question, the amount of other things the customer is willing to buy, or the accident of being in the store when the sugar is put on the shelves.

Nobody is happy, least of all the harassed grocer. Were it not for the community's elementary sense of fair play, the situation would soon become intolerable. Patriotism is more effective in motivating people to brief acts of intense heroism than to putting up day after day with an uncomfortable situation. It is no wonder that black markets occasionally develop; the really surprising thing is that they do not occur sooner.

If for political or social reasons market price is not to be permitted to rise high enough to bring quantity demanded down to the level of quantity supplied, the ultimate solution may require outright allocation of *ration* tickets.

A legal maximum price, without rationing, leaves a gap between demand and supply:

FIG. 20-7.   Without a legal price ceiling, price would rise to *E*. At the artificial ceiling price, supply and demand do not balance and some method of rationing, formal or informal, is needed to allocate the short supply and bring the effective demand down to *d'd'*.

Once rationing is adopted, most people heave a sigh of relief, because now sellers need not turn people away and now buyers can count upon getting their fair quota of the limited supplies. Of course, there are always some cranky customers, longer on intuition than brains, who blame their troubles on the mechanism of rationing itself rather than on the shortage. "If only the government could print more ration tickets," they sigh. Such people are like the ignorant ancient kings who used to slay the messengers bringing them bad news. Their complaints need not be taken seriously; they only serve to add spice to the human comedy.

Just how do ration coupons work out in terms of supply and demand? Clearly, the OPS tries to issue just enough of them to lower the demand curve *to d'd', where supply and the new demand balance at the ceiling price.* If too many coupons are issued, demand is still too far to the right and we encounter the old difficulties, but in lesser degree. If too few coupons are issued, stocks of sugar will pile up and P will fall below the ceiling price. This is the signal for liberalizing the sugar ration.

One goes to an insane asylum to learn to appreciate normal human behavior. So, too, the breakdown of the price mechanism during war gives us a new understanding of its remarkable efficiency in normal times.

Goods are always scarce, in the sense that there is never enough to give everyone all he wishes. Price itself is always rationing scarce supplies: rising to choke off excessive consumption and in order to expand production; falling to encourage consumption, discourage production, and work off excessive inventories.

Minimum floors and maximum ceilings   Even in peacetime, when there arises any kind of emergency or state of general shortage and inflation, political pressures for wage and price freezes develop. Experience has taught most economists, whether they be liberals or conservatives, that such emergency measures work very well in short emergencies but do create more and more distortions the longer they are in effect. Economists therefore tend to recommend that such direct fiats be reserved for emergency periods and not squandered on minor peacetime situations.

Nevertheless, as Adam Smith well knew when he protested against the devices of the mercantilist advisers to the earlier kings, most economic systems are plagued by inefficiencies stemming from well-intentioned inexpert interferences with the mechanisms of supply and demand. Here is a brief list of such interferences (shown in Fig. 20-8).

1. *Minimum wage rates.* These often hurt those they are designed to help. What good does it do a black youth to know that an employer must pay him $1.60 per hour if the fact that he must be paid that amount is what keeps him from getting a job?[9]

2. *Rent ceilings.* Everyone hates a landlord and loves a farmer. To protect the poor from being gouged by landlords, maximum rentals are often fixed by law. These fiats may do short-run good; but they may also do long-run harm. Thus, France had practically no residential construction from 1914 to 1948 because of rent controls. If new construction had been subjected to such controls after World War II, the vigorous boom in French residential building since 1950 would never have taken place. New York City rent controls

[9] See P. A. Samuelson, *Readings in Economics* (McGraw-Hill, New York, 1970, 6th ed.), for arguments pro and con minimum-wage legislation. See also Chapter 22's Appendix for graphical analysis of economic inefficiency of controls and rationing.

When government by fiat sets maximum or minimum prices, troublesome discrepancies between supply and demand may emerge:

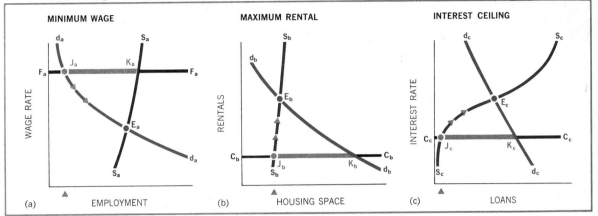

FIG. 20-8(a). Setting minimum-wage floor at F_aF_a, high above free-market equilibrium rate E_a, results in forced equilibrium at J_a. The too-high floor freezes workers into unemployment from J_a to K_a. Lowering the minimum wage will move us down along dd, as shown by gold arrows, increasing employment. (If dd is elastic, total wage payrolls rise though hourly rate falls!)

FIG. 20-8(b). Setting maximum rental ceiling at C_bC_b, far below free-market equilibrium at E_b, causes fringe of unsatisfied renters between forced equilibrium at J_b and K_b. Raising the ceiling rate moves the system up s_bs_b, as shown by gold arrows: new construction provides more living space, and old quarters are used more efficiently.

FIG. 20-8(c). Setting maximum interest rates at C_cC_c, far below free-market equilibrium rate E_c, results in drying up of available funds. Desperate borrowers at J_cK_c turn to loan sharks. Raising interest ceiling moves system toward more loans, as shown by gold arrows on s_cs_c.

do favor those lucky enough to find a cheap apartment; but they inhibit new private building of low-cost housing, and they discourage economies of space utilization that high rents tend to induce.

3. *Usury laws.* Interest rates have always been an object of suspicion. No longer is lending at interest a crime, but in most places a maximum rate is set by law. Unfortunately, the ceiling is often far below what would be set by the competitive supply-and-demand market, after account is taken of riskiness and administrative expense connected with small loans. The result? Funds dry up completely.

The cheap money you can't get does you little good. Veterans who tried to get mortgages learned this in the 1950s; college students trying to get tuition loans from the banks learned this in the 1960s. Federal Reserve ceilings on bank-deposit interest (so-called "Regulation Q") periodically causes massive withdrawals (the so-called "disintermediation" of Chapter 17).

EFFICIENCY OF SUPPLY-DEMAND PRICING AND "EQUITY"

We do not study competitive pricing for the beauty of the subject. Nor for its realism alone, since often monopoly elements spoil the competitive picture. We study it for the light it throws on *efficient* organization of an economy's resources. The pathology of interference with supply and demand helps to bring out the remarkable efficiencies produced by perfect competition.

Why then do politicians and the populace keep interfering with the mechanism?

Primarily, because man does not live by efficiency alone. He is interested in the question: Efficiency for what? And for whom? Most of these floors and ceilings are set in the name of "equity"—to help some group deemed deserving at the expense of some other group deemed already affluent and amply well-off. Just as Robin Hood "robbed the rich to help the poor," these devices try to create or restore a distribution of real income considered more equitable. Their advocates are willing to pay some price in the form of lower efficiency and higher waste to bring about a "fairer" distribution of income. Economic science cannot pronounce that they are necessarily wrong if they face the cost.

MONOPOLY INTERFERENCES WITH SUPPLY AND DEMAND

Aside from governmental interferences, there are serious monopolistic interferences with supply and demand. Competitive supply and demand is one way of organizing an economy. It is one way of getting the job done, but of course it is not the only way relied on in actual modern society. Certainly, when one or a few producers can get monopoly control of an industry, they can move the final outcome away from the competitive equilibrium point. As we shall see later, a monopolist can reduce output and make the consumers travel up their demand curves to higher prices.

Is such an interference with supply and demand a "good thing"? If the monopolist were a more worthy soul than the rest of us, or if he were much poorer and had greater need for money than the rest of us, some might rise to defend his act of raising price. Or if he took our money and devoted it to better causes (charity, scientific research) than we should do, some might still defend him as a modern-day Robin Hood.

Chances are, however, that anyone in a position to contrive a monopoly will be at least as well off as his customers, and there is not much reason to think he would be of finer clay than anyone else. And though Robin Hood may have been all right in his day, in our day we tend to think it is the government that ought to do any subsidizing of worthy causes, not self-appointed monopolists; and we hope government can be more efficient in financing its good causes out of tax revenues than any monopolist could ever be. So what probably needs emphasis is this:

Any *haphazard* interference with competitive supply and demand is likely—save in some exceptional circumstances—to be a bad rather than a good thing.

Thus, a monopolistic interference in Industry A reduces output there needlessly relative to Industry B. The fact that it produces such scarcity is reflected in the higher P_A/P_B ratio it creates, relative to the citizenry's desires for the goods and to their true relative costs as measured along the production-possibility frontier or by undistorted competitive costs. The monopoly may also lead to a bad distribution of income in that it may give extra income to one who already has as much income as he deserves.

At this point monopoly's *restriction in output* relative to that of competitive industries perhaps needs more stressing than its distortion of the income distribution. For what if we taxed away the monopolist's ill-gotten gains?[10] We should then have rectified the

---

[10]Or what if many monopolists entered the industry, with all keeping their price too high but with total business so divided up among them that none ends up making any exorbitant monopoly profit? Then the evil effect on the income distribution would not exist, but the resulting wasteful pattern of

income-distribution distortion of monopoly. But the community would still be left enjoying less of the (monopolized) consumption goods that it really does want in terms of what it really can produce.

Like sin, monopoly is one of those things most people are against. Therefore one need not labor the point that monopoly interferences with supply and demand are probably a bad thing. Still, it is better to know analytically why.

GOVERNMENT INTERFERENCES WITH SUPPLY AND DEMAND EVALUATED

In conclusion let us appraise government interferences. Surely the government means well and its interferences are not to be as harshly judged as those of a monopolist?

Well, that all depends. If the government happens to know better than people what is really good and evil, its interferences may improve matters. An example might be opium. We do not treat the consumer as a sovereign who can decide how much opium he will spend his money votes on. Where opium is concerned we adopt a paternalistic attitude, treating the consumer a little the way we treat the insane, minors, and other "incompetents." Society is similarly beginning to move against cigarettes.

But where eight-cylinder cars or bubble gum is concerned, we usually are content to let the consumer spend his own dollars in his own way. We recognize that advertising has given us one set of tastes, which may not be intrinsically better than some other set, but in the interests of freedom we do treat the consumer as sovereign.

As we have seen, the matter becomes more complicated if the sellers or the buyers in a market happen to be especially rich, or especially poor, or especially "deserving," or especially "undeserving." For example, imagine an artificial case where 1 million very rich producers sell milk in competitive markets to 50 million very poor people. Some people would then be tempted to approve of any interference that lowered milk price. "That leads to what we call a fairer income distribution," they might say.

Without foisting his ethical judgments on others, the economist can remind us:

Interfering with the competitive supply-and-demand mechanism is an inefficient[11] way of correcting the income distribution. Whatever distribution you want to end up with

FIG. 20-9.

---

overcapacity in the industry and too high price could persist until doomsday. More on all this when Chapter 26 treats imperfect competition along the lines of Harvard's late E. H. Chamberlin.

[11] The fact that buyers and sellers are different people who may have different incomes or wealth hides the truth that the competitive equilibrium point has certain allocative efficiency properties in solving the WHAT and How economic problems. So consider a simplified case where I trade only with myself. I have 10 hours of leisure worth exactly $2.50 per hour to me. I can produce 1 Q unit with each hour of work or sacrificed leisure. Suppose the first Q unit is worth exactly $4 to me, and successive Q units are worth $3, $2, $1, and $0. Figure 20-9 shows *my* supply and demand for Q. Equilibrium is at E, where I consume exactly 2 of Q. I get $4 + $3 of "satisfaction" from them (as shown by light shading) and 8 times $2.50 from my 8 hours left of leisure (as shown by heavy shading), or $27 of satisfaction

can often be more efficiently attained by using the tax system to redistribute income rather than using ad hoc Robin Hood interferences in a single market.

Indeed, if taxation always could be counted on to keep society's FOR WHOM problem optimally solved, then perfect competition (were it to prevail!) could be counted on to solve most WHAT and How problems efficiently.

Naturally, all this is a controversial area. There is no one answer, and any observer of the modern world can see that nations everywhere do interfere with the price system at many points. EXAMPLES: Blood for transfusions is not primarily obtained by commercial bidding, but rather through much voluntary effort. (Why?) Doctors often charge rich patients more than poor ones, in part subsidizing the latter from revenues of the former. (Why this private system of taxation?) Milk and other basic foods are often subsidized. And to the degree that our demands reflect merely manipulated fads, engineered by profit-seeking advertisers, the merits of "consumer sovereignty" fade away.

The next chapter will deal with the extensive agricultural aid programs which the government has been following. And later chapters will discuss the effects of monopolistic imperfections of competition once competitive demand has been related to utility and competitive supply has been related to cost.

SUMMARY

A. ELASTICITY OF DEMAND AND SUPPLY

1   A basic problem of microeconomics is the mechanism of market pricing: how it grapples with the economy's problems WHAT, How, FOR WHOM. The supply and demand curves in Chapter 4 explain what goes on in each particular competitive market.

2   Elasticity of demand depends on what happens to total revenue as price is cut. Demand is elastic, inelastic, or unitary, according to whether a reduction in price increases, decreases, or does not change total revenue. The numerical coefficient of elasticity of demand is defined as "the percentage increase in quantity divided by the percentage cut in price." Depending upon whether the percentage rise in Q exceeds or falls short of the percentage fall in P, we have $E > 1$ or $E < 1$, with $E = 1$ in between. (Elasticity is dimensionless, involving percentages; it is not to be confused with absolute slope, as numerical tables and graphical measurements make clear.)

3   Elasticity of supply measures percentage responsiveness of amount Q supplied by producers when market P is raised by a given percentage.

---

in all, as shown by the sum of the areas. You can show that any disturbance which makes me work 1 hour too much, or too little, kills off 50 cents of my satisfaction. Distortion of a second hour kills off $1.50 of satisfaction; each further distortion takes a heavier and heavier toll, as shown by the growing discrepancy between *dd* and *ss*. (See Figs. 22-4, 26-4, and 32-2 for more on "consumer's surplus," which can be used to demonstrate monopoly harm or price-control inefficiency. Also see Chapter 22 Appendix.)

4   Marshall stressed the time element: (a) *momentary* equilibrium of fixed supply; (b) *short-run* equilibrium with output varying within fixed plants and firms; (c) *long-run* equilibrium of normal price, when numbers of firms and plants, and all conditions, adjust to the new level of demand.

B. APPLICATIONS AND QUALIFICATIONS OF SUPPLY AND DEMAND

5   The apparatus of supply and demand enables us to analyze the effects of shifts in either curve, or in both simultaneously. Beginners must avoid the pitfall of confusing the expression "an increase in demand" (i.e., an outward *shift* of the whole demand curve) with "an increase in quantity demanded" as a result of a reduction in price (i.e., a movement *down* an unchanged demand curve).

6   A tax of so many dollars per unit of a good will lead to a new equilibrium intersection and will be borne more largely by consumers rather than producers to the degree that the demand is inelastic relative to the supply. The more elastic *dd* and *ss* are, the smaller the *P* changes and the greater the *Q* change.

7   A thousand forces affect price; but in a free competitive market they do so only by acting *through* supply and demand. For example, cost of production affects competitive price only through affecting supply, not otherwise.

8   Although the government usually affects price by *operating* on either supply or demand, occasionally it sets maximum ceilings or minimum floors that *interfere* with the workings of competitive markets. Under such circumstances, supply and demand need not be equal; some producer or consumer may *wish* to sell or buy more than he is able to do at the legal price. Distortions and inefficiencies result. Unless the discrepancies are parceled out by legislation (rationing, etc.), disorder and black markets may result.

9   Haphazard, arbitrary interferences with supply and demand will often be harmful. Monopoly interference provides an obvious case, and here the evil is not so much that the distribution of income is distorted as that society has to put up unnecessarily with reduced relative output of a good that it really wants and really can afford.

   Even in cases where government is interfering with supply and demand for the purpose of achieving some desired distribution of income or some other social goal, there may be hidden costs in the use of so *inefficient* a device—and often the same goal would be accomplished better by use of the tax system and preservation of the efficiency of market pricing.

QUESTIONS FOR DISCUSSION

1   What factors might increase the demand for wheat? The supply?

2   Which do you think has the most inelastic demand: perfume, salt, penicillin, cigarettes, ice cream, chocolate ice cream, Sealtest chocolate ice cream? Why?

3   When demand is elastic (inelastic, or unitary), what will a rise in P do to total revenue? What will higher Q do in the three cases?

4   "Elastic demand means elastic supply, since the curves meet." Refute.

5   Explain Marshall's three time periods, their equilibria, the slope of $s_L s_L$.

6   Examine the diagram below, which shows demand and supply curves for wheat for different years. Identify gold historical intersection points. Fill in the columns at the right showing the price and quantity of wheat for each of the four years. (Note how hard it would be to estimate demand or supply curves from a plot of gold intersections.)

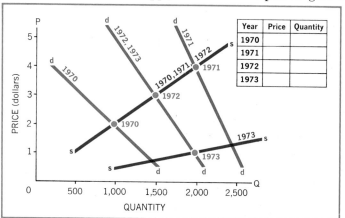

Year	Price	Quantity
1970		
1971		
1972		
1973		

7   As an extra-credit problem for those who like simple geometry and algebra,[12] try to justify the E rule given in footnote 3 (page 363) for a straight line. In the triangle below, the dd has the equation $Q = b - (b/a)P$, where b is the Q intercept and a the P intercept, and the absolute inverted slope of dd is $-(dQ/dP) = -\Delta Q/\Delta P = b/a$. Now apply the formula $E = -(dQ/dP)(P/Q)$ to get $E = (b/a)\{P/[b - (b/a)P]\} = P/(a - P)$—the ratio of the lower vertical bracket to the upper. Can you show, by the property of similar triangles, that $E = P/(a - P) = bC/aC$, equals "the length of the straight line below the point divided by its length above the point," as stated in footnote 3?

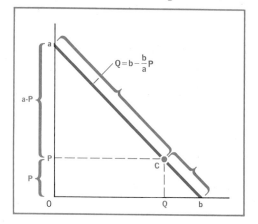

$$Q = b - \frac{b}{a}P$$

---

[12] Those who tackled the mathematical question 10 of Chapter 4, page 71, can calculate E from the demand function $Q = f(P)$. Define

$$E = \lim_{\Delta P \to 0} \frac{-\Delta Q}{\Delta P} \frac{(P_1 + P_2)/2}{(Q_1 + Q_2)/2} = \frac{-dQ}{dP} \frac{P}{Q} = \frac{-P\{df(P)/dP\}}{f(P)}$$

For $f(P) = b - (b/a)P$, calculate $E = P/(a - P)$. Show E to be respectively 1, 2, 1/3, k for $f(P)$ successively c/P, c/P^2, $c/P^{1/3}$, c/P^k. Taking logarithms (to any base) of the last expression, verify $\log Q = \log c - k \log P$ does give $E \equiv k$. [HINT: $(dQ/Q) \div (dP/P) = d \log Q/d \log P \equiv -k$.]

Review your understanding of the following concepts:

microeconomics, macroeconomics
total revenue, $P \times Q$
elastic, inelastic, unitary elastic
$E = \% Q$ rise $\div \% P$ cut
elasticity of supply
Marshall's three time periods
demand versus amount demanded
shift vs. movement along a curve
incidence of a tax
government actions to influence
    supply and demand curves

cost of production, supply, and price
rationing and price fixing
    maximum-price ceilings
    maximum-interest ceilings
    minimum-wage floors
monopoly reduction of relative outputs
    versus monopoly distortion of income
    distribution
possible efficiencies sacrificed when govern-
    ment interferes with supply and demand
    to achieve a worthy goal

APPENDIX: Cases on Supply and Demand[1]

PROPOSITION 1: (*a*) As a general rule an increase in demand—supply being constant—will raise price.

(*b*) Probably also, but less certainly, increased demand will increase the quantity bought and sold. A decrease in demand has opposite effects.

PROPOSITION 2: An increase in supply, demand being constant, will almost certainly lower price and increase the quantity bought and sold. A decrease in supply has opposite effects.

These two important propositions summarize the *qualitative* effects of shifts in supply and demand. But the exact *quantitative* degree of change in price and quantity depends upon the specific shapes of the curves in each instance. Here, then, are a number of possible cost and supply situations.

Case 1. Constant cost   Imagine a manufactured item, like pencils, whose production can be easily expanded by merely duplicating factories, machinery, and labor. To produce 100,000 pencils per day simply requires us to do the same thing as when we were manufacturing 1,000 per day, but on a hundredfold scale. In this case the supply curve *ss* in Fig. 20-10 is a horizontal line at the constant level of unit costs. A rise in demand will shift the new intersection point E' to the right, raising Q but leaving P the same.

What will be the effects of a sales tax of, say, 5 cents

FIG. 20-10.

per pencil, on output and price paid by the consumer? Fill in the diagram in the Fig. 20-6 manner.

Case 2. Increasing costs and diminishing returns Suppose an industry like wine-grape growing requires a certain kind of soil and location (sunny hillsides, etc.). Such sites are limited in number. The annual output of wine can be increased to some extent by

---

[1] Many courses may prefer to study this Appendix after Chapter 23 or 24.

INCREASING-COST CASE

FIG. 20-11.

Thus there is only one *Mona Lisa* by Leonardo. Nature's original endowment of the "natural and indestructible" qualities of land can also often be taken as fixed in amount. Raising the price offered for land cannot create more than four corners at State and Madison in Chicago. High-paid artists and businessmen who love their work would continue to work at their jobs even at low pay. Once a bridge is built, it must earn "what the traffic will bear" regardless of past sunk costs.

In all such cases the supply curve goes *vertically* up and down, at least in the relevant region. Look at Fig. 20-12. A higher price cannot elicit an increase in Q; nor is the higher price necessary to bring out the existing Q, for even at lower prices the same amount will still be forthcoming. Because it is price-*determined* rather than price-*determining*, the return to such a factor of production is called a "pure economic rent," or "surplus," which need not be paid to call out the required supply.

If demand now shifts upward, the whole effect is to raise price. Quantity is unchanged. And the rise in price exactly equals the upward shift in demand. (More on this in Chapter 28.)

Likewise, if a tax is placed upon the commodity, its whole effect is to reduce the price received by the supplier by exactly the amount of the tax. The tax is shifted back completely to the supplier, who absorbs it all out of his economic rent or surplus. The consumer buys exactly as much of the good or service as before and at no extra cost.

adding more labor and fertilizer to each acre of land and by bidding away more hill sites from other uses. But as we saw in Chapter 2, the law of diminishing returns will begin to operate if variable factors of production, like labor and fertilizer, are added to fixed amounts of a factor like land. Why is that? Because each new *variable addition* of labor and fertilizer has a *smaller proportion* of land to work with. By the same token, each fixed unit of land has more labor and fertilizer cooperating with it. Therefore land's productivity and earnings are higher. The result: Getting extra amounts of wine sends total costs up more than proportionately. Therefore the cost per unit of wine is rising. The supply curve travels upward from southwest to northeast because at lower market prices, less will be supplied. At higher prices, more will be supplied.

Figure 20-11 shows the rising supply curve *ss*. What will be the effect on price of an increase in demand? Effect on quantity?

[Show by a diagram that a tax of so much per ounce of wine will raise price to the consumer by less than a similar tax on pencils did. Why? What will be the effect on the price received by the producer? If the original demand curves for wine and pencils are similar, show that the fall in output will be *greater* for pencils than for wine. Why?]

Case 3. Completely fixed or inelastic supply and economic rent Some goods or productive factors are completely fixed in amount, regardless of price.

PURE-RENT CASE

FIG. 20-12.

FIG. 20-13.

Case 4. A backward-rising supply curve Early explorers into new lands often noted that, when you raised the wages of natives, you received *less* rather than more labor. If wages were doubled, instead of working 6 days a week for their minimum of subsistence, the natives might go fishing for 3 days. The same has been observed among so-called "civilized" people. As improved technology raises real wages, people feel that they ought to take part of their higher earnings in the form of more leisure, less work. (In Chapter 22, the discussion of the marginal utility theory, or of "income- and substitution-effects," will explain why a supply curve might bend backward.)

Figure 20-13 shows such a supply curve of labor. At first it rises as higher wages coax out more labor, but beyond the point T, higher wages induce *more leisure* and *less work*. An increase in demand does increase the price of labor in agreement with Proposition 1(a). But note how lucky we were to have added the words "but less certainly" in 1(b)! For the increase in demand has *decreased* the quantity of labor.

A partial verification of such a possibility is found in the fact that a decrease in demand for farm products during a depression often causes farmers to work harder in order to restore their incomes. The result:

More rather than less is produced in response to a decrease in demand.

Case 5. A possible exception: decreasing cost Heretofore our examples have agreed with Proposition 1(a), that an increase in demand raises price. But what about the often-observed case where an increase in demand is followed by economies of mass production and decreasing costs?

A good theory must make room for all the facts. So we must frankly admit that our first proposition may break down and have exceptions. Of course, we can save some face by pointing out that many of the important reductions in cost following an increase in demand really represent *permanent downward shifts* in the supply curve rather than downward movements *along* a falling supply curve.

Illustrate this by the case where the government increases its demand for radar. The first few sets built must be constructed in the laboratory by experimental methods. They are tailor-made and very expensive per unit. But the know-how gained in the process makes possible the production of further sets for much less per unit. Even if demand went back again to its previous level, price would not return up to its previous level. In traveling along the arrow EE' marked with a question mark in Fig. 20-14, we are not moving reversibly along the supply curve. Instead, the supply curve has shifted *irreversibly* downward from ss to $s's'$, so that even when demand is back again at dd, the price is now lower at E'' than it was originally.

FIG. 20-14.

The case discussed here really does not come under the heading of Proposition 1, but under Proposition 2 dealing with shifts in supply. The final result agrees with the latter's conclusion that an increase in supply will lower price and increase quantity. (Compare E and E'' in Fig. 20-14.) But the present case is still an unusual one because the shift of supply has been *induced* by a shift in demand.

In economic history, there have been important cases of reduced cost over time as a result of technological progress that was partly induced by the expansion of a mass market. Goods are constantly being improved in quality and cheapened in price.

What about the case of genuine *reversible* economies of large-scale production—cases where going back to small-scale production does send costs up again? The alert modern economist will not deny its importance; but he will suspect that some monopolistic imperfection of competition is present. He will point out that in a competitive industry each firm would have *already* expanded its output to where the *extra* cost of producing a unit of output has begun to turn up. This would be because each competitive producer has no fear of spoiling his own market and has every incentive to expand his production through and beyond the decreasing-cost stage.[2] (Later chapters analyze the imperfect competition that results when a few firms have decreasing cost and hence expand to capture much of the market.)

Case 6. Shifts in supply   All the above discussion, with the exception of part of Case 5, dealt with a shift in demand and no shift in supply. To analyze Proposition 2, we must now shift supply, keeping demand constant. This is done in Fig. 20-15.

If the law of downward-sloping demand is valid,[3]

CASE OF SHIFTING SUPPLY

FIG. 20-15.

[2] There remains the possibility mentioned in Chapter 24: the case of an $s_L s_L$ curve that is downward-sloping because of Marshallian *external* economies.

[3] In Chapter 22 we shall meet the legitimate exception to the law of downward-sloping demand in the case of the Irish peasants who might be forced by higher potato P to consume *more* of such necessities. Another exception is provided by items such as diamonds or chic hats, which are valuable, not for their intrinsic qualities so much as for their "snob appeal" and expensiveness, and which may therefore fall off in demand if their price is cut. What appears to be another exception is the case in which a short-run rise in P may make people expect future P to be still higher, thus causing them to buy more rather than less now and thereby leading to unstabilizing speculation; but this is more properly to be interpreted as a case where the whole demand curve is dynamically shifting, rather than as a northeast move along dd.

then increased supply must send us *down* the demand curve, decreasing price and increasing quantity. The student may verify, by drawing diagrams or by comparing automobiles and wheat, the following quantitative corollaries of Proposition 2:

(*a*) **An increased supply will decrease price most when demand is inelastic, decrease it least when demand is relatively elastic.**

(*b*) **An increased supply will increase quantity least when demand is inelastic, most when demand is elastic.**

What are common-sense reasons for these? Illustrate with elastic autos and inelastic wheat.

Case 7. Dynamic cobweb   There is a famous economic case which can be used to show that the tools of supply and demand are not restricted to handling static and unchanging situations, but can also be used fruitfully to analyze dynamic situations of change. (The time-pressed reader may skip the next sections.)

Suppose that a competitive crop—let us take the conventional example of hogs for pork production—is auctioned off in the market in the usual way so as to fetch the P given by running vertically up from any given Q to the dd demand curve.

But now we want to make the supply side dynamic. Suppose farmers look at today's P and use it to determine the Q they will bring to market in the *next* period: specifically, if today's P is high, they begin to breed many new pigs, to feed and fatten them, and finally to bring them to market some months from now. The farmers do indeed have an *ss* supply curve, but it acts *with a time lag* and connects next period's Q with this period's P. (It is understood that we define a period as the time involved in producing hogs.)

If the market price were at the intersection of *ss* and *dd* in Fig. 20-16, this would represent an unchanging equilibrium in exactly the same way that it did in the nondynamic cases. Today, tomorrow, and in the period after that, the farmers would be on their *ss* curve producing the amount shown by E; and the amount consumers would gladly demand at that P would just match what farmers will gladly supply. As yet, then, no difference.

But suppose that, for some reason, such as hog cholera, the crop initially drops to Q_1, which is below the equilibrium amount $Q*$. We run up to the demand curve to E_1 and see that we get the higher P_1 corresponding to the reduced crop. But that is not the end of the story. We are not at long-run equilibrium; because how much will the farmers produce tomorrow at this higher P_1? They will run over rightward to their supply curve and produce in the second period at the point marked F_2. We can see that this amount of Q is above the equilibrium $Q*$. What will it sell for in the

competitive market? We run down to the demand curve and see that P_2 will have to fall to the level shown at E_2. But we are not yet in final equilibrium. At this low price, farmers will plan to cut down tomorrow's production by going leftward to their *ss* curve, ending up at F_3. From there we move upward to the *dd* curve, to find the P_3 given at the E_3 point.

And thus it goes on and on. First Q is low and P is high. But high P makes next period's Q high and next period's P low. So—like a man on a tightrope who goes too far on one side, then corrects himself by going too far on the other—market price oscillates in successive periods above and below equilibrium, tracing out a spiderlike cobweb.

What is the final outcome? Figure 20-16 was drawn with the supply curve's slope at E *steeper* than the demand curve's falling slope. So, as can be seen from the diagram, the oscillations finally do dampen and die out: the cobweb winds inward to E. We are then back at equilibrium, where we can stay forever. Forever? Well, at least until the next outside disturbance comes to set off still another dying-out oscillation.

Not all equilibrium points are so dynamically stable. On the next page, Fig. 20-17 puts a microscope on the region around E in a number of other possible situations. Thus, in its first diagram, *ss* has been made *flatter* than *dd*, and the cobweb diverges outward in an explosive oscillation.

In the middle diagram, the straight lines are of the *same slope* and we get a perfect cobweb: depending upon how severely it is disturbed, the market will oscillate endlessly around equilibrium, getting neither more nor less violent in its swings. (This is like the case of an ideal frictionless pendulum which would repeat its swings forever.)

The last diagram is designed to show that there is no need to stick with straight lines. Because its *ss* is flatter (more "elastic") than *dd* at the equilibrium point, any small disturbance will *at first* send the system into increasing oscillations. But no explosion can go on forever in real life; and the curvature of the schedules finally brings the system to the stable "box," indicated by the letters $ABCD$. Ultimately, then, the system oscillates repeatedly in an every-other-period box and the amplitude or degree of the oscillation will be determined by the curvatures of *dd* and *ss*. After any new disturbance, the system tends to come back to this box from within or without; and even if stationary equilibrium were restored at E by accident, the slightest new shock would send the market away from such an unstable equilibrium point. (The thoughtful student may ask at this point: Could prices swing forever in this every-other-period fashion without

DYNAMIC COBWEB

FIG. 20-16.

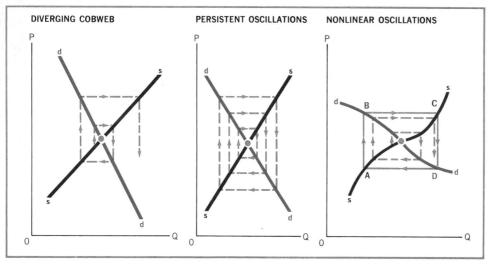

FIG. 20-17.

shrewd speculators beginning to notice the pattern? Would they not then tend to buy at low P, store, and resell at high P, thus tending to wipe out the price differentials? The Appendix to the next chapter deals with dynamic speculation and suggests that just this might indeed happen.)

There was space here for only the briefest account of this cobweb model.[4] Statistics show that a corn-hog

cycle like this has been part of modern history. And our simplified model throws some light on the business-cycle phenomena dealt with in Part Two, where a free enterprise system would tend to fluctuate if not moderated by public policy and equilibrating market mechanisms. Corporations, like pig farmers, can swing from one extreme to the other, thus causing instability.

---

[4] This cobweb model enabled Columbia's pioneering econometrician of half a century ago, H. L. Moore, to crack the problem of how to "identify" either the supply or the demand curve from historical data depicting gold (P, Q) intersections. Recall question 6, page 378, which illustrated the difficulty. Moore assumed that the blue points (E_1, E_3, E_2 in Fig. 20-16 and B, D in Fig. 20-17), which depict *unlagged* (P_t, Q_t) values, defined the *dd* curve for him. Moore assumed that the brown points (F_3, F_2, and A, C), which depict *lagged* variables (P_t, Q_{t+1}) defined his *ss* curve. Biological scientists, trying to "identify" the relation between cigarettes and longevity, can sympathize with the economist's difficulty in making controlled experiments. Here, briefly, are other methods econo-

metricians use to "identify" *dd* and *ss* elasticities quantitatively: (1) If *ss* is very shifting (say, because of weather) and *dd* very stable, the resulting (P_t, Q_t) scatter traces out the blue points along the stable *dd* schedule. (Reverse the roles to get brown *ss* points.) (2) Or suppose Q_t of *dd* depends on another variable, say, GNP_t, as well as on P_t; and suppose Q_t of *ss* depends on a quite different other variable, say, fertilizer cost, F_t. Then by generalized multiple correlation techniques, separate blue and brown relations between P and Q can be "identified." (DRAMATIC EXAMPLE: Suppose GNP_t changed only in odd years and F_t changed only in even years. Then odd-year (demand) changes would trace out brown *ss* points; and even-year (supply) changes would trace out blue *dd* points.)

Supply and Demand as Applied to Agriculture

21

American farm leaders are correct in arguing that our agriculture still must look forward to a definite "surplus" problem. What they tend to overlook, however, is of what our "surplus" consists. Fundamentally America's long-term agricultural problem is not one of "surplus" cotton, wheat or grapefruit. Rather it is one of "surplus" farmers.
WILLIAM H. NICHOLLS

The economist's model of perfect competition, in which a homogeneous product is produced by many different people and auctioned off in a well-organized market, does not fit most of American life at all closely. Therefore, in later chapters we shall have to supplement it by the new tools of imperfect, or monopolistic, competition.

There is, however, one great area that does provide a valuable application of the basic tools of supply and demand. Agriculture is an important problem area. It makes the news. It shifts votes. Moreover, our rich food potential is a vital resource in connection with foreign aid to hungry peoples abroad. No one can possibly understand the major policy issues in the field of agriculture without first understanding the basic economic concepts of supply and demand. This chapter puts these tools to work.

RELATIVE DECLINE OF AGRICULTURE

Farming is still our largest single industry. But the percentage of people engaged in it has been declining steadily for the last two centuries. We used to be a nation of farmers. That is no longer true. Though farmers still swing much political weight, only 1 in 20 Americans today works in agriculture!

Figure 21-1 shows that farm prices have been generally losing ground to other prices. The trends of parity shown there reveal that only in the two major wars have farm prices risen relative to nonfarm.

Why this relative shift away from farming? People seek the higher incomes of the city, shorter hours, and what many seem to regard as the better social life in town; they flee from ancient discriminations. (But, as Chapter 40's analysis of urban and race problems will show, the migrants to the city encounter new problems there.)

Differential birth rates   In a way, this out-migration from the country is lucky. For, as we saw in Chapter 2, birth

Parity is ratio of prices farmer gets to prices he pays:

FIG. 21-1.   If the change since 1909–1914 in prices farmers receive for their products just matched the change in the prices they pay for goods, the parity-price ratio curve would be at 100. Its being recently around 75 shows that prices received by farmers have not risen as much as have prices they have to pay. (Source: U.S. Department of Agriculture)

rates are higher in rural areas than in cities. If it were not for this migration, cities might grow smaller and smaller; the rural share of total population would grow larger and larger. What does the law of diminishing returns tell us such an eventuality would mean? It would mean a great reduction in the productivity of each man-hour spent on the farm. The land would become crowded with many people, each producing little and each unable to buy many of the comforts of life with his produce.

Does this sound far-fetched? It is a true picture of about two-thirds of the globe. In Asia especially, standards of living are pitifully poor. With three out of every four persons engaged in producing the food necessary for life, only one out of four can be producing the bare comforts of life. Contrast this with the United States, where each producer is efficient enough today to feed 50 other people and feed them well.

Technological change and patterns of taste   Besides the differential in birth rates, there are two other reasons why agriculture is a problem area:

Technological progress has been greatly reducing the number of people needed to produce any given total of food and fiber. Use of the tractor, the combine, the cotton picker, irrigation, fertilizer, selective breeding of hybrid corn and livestock, and numerous other examples come to mind.

Coupled with the improvement in labor-saving technique is the unshakable fact that, _as we get richer, we do not want to expand our food consumption by as much as we_ *want to expand our consumption of city products.* This has been shown by almost every statistical investigation of income elasticities here and abroad. Hence,

<u>Birth rates, tastes, and technology dictate that agriculture must go on exporting people to industry.</u>

AGRICULTURE'S LONG-RUN DECLINE: GRAPHICAL ANALYSIS

One single diagram is more useful in explaining the sagging trend of farm prices than libraries of orations and editorials.

In Fig. 21-2 let the point E represent the initial equilibrium of supply and demand at some earlier period. Now see what happens to these curves as the years go by. We know that dd' will shift rightward as population grows and as higher real incomes make people want to consume more food at the same price; but we've seen that basic foods are the kinds of necessities which do not grow in the family budget at all proportionately to increases in real income, and we realize that United States population no longer grows at the prodigious percentage rates of the nineteenth century. So the rightward demand shift to $d'd'$ is of modest amount.

What about supply? Though many make the mistake of thinking of farming as a backward business, statistical records show that productivity in American agriculture has increased at a pace even faster than productivity in industry. So each new improvement helps to shift the ss curve a great deal to the right.

What, then, must be happening to the new equilibrium E' that would prevail in the market if the government did not intervene? Certainly a shift in supply that outstrips the shift in demand must lead to a *downward trend of market prices* (relative, of course, to the general price level, so that effects of over-all inflation are disregarded). Naturally, this declining price trend means financial pressure and hardship on those farmers and rural workers whose efficiency has not undergone tremendous increase; and it means that there will be considerable pressure for people to leave the countryside for jobs in industry. It also means that consumers are paying lower prices for the raw-material component of their foods[1] and that the economy is reallocating its resources toward the things that are *now* most demanded in our growing society.

And, as we know, it means strong political pressures for government aid to agriculture.

One diagram goes far to explain the farm problem:

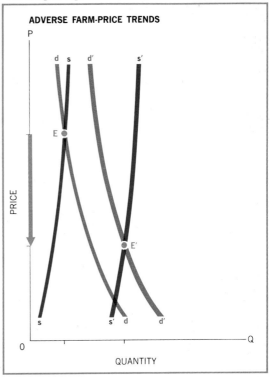

ADVERSE FARM-PRICE TRENDS

FIG. 21-2. As the years go by, the increase in demand for farm products generated by population and income growth tends to be less than the vast increase in supply generated by technological productivity improvements. Thus free prices fall. With both schedules highly inelastic, prices fall hard; farm incomes deteriorate. And small shifts in inelastic curves generate large price fluctuations.

[1] Even though the price the farmer gets for the food he sells will fall, the retail price need not fall so much—or may even rise. Why? Agricultural experts claim this is not so much because railroads, packers, and supermarkets extort an undue share of the food dollar as that we consumers today want our food more and more fabricated (e.g., frozen, cut, cleaned, cooked, minutely packaged, premixed

INSTABILITY IN AGRICULTURE

Farming is an up-and-down industry. Corn, wheat, beef, pork, and other farm products are sold in highly competitive markets whose prices change yearly, daily, hourly, and by the minute. The farmer swings at the very end of our seesawing economy. Good times bring him great percentage increases in income. Depressions cause his cash income to drop away to very little. The farmer particularly benefits from wartime demand conditions. But for a quarter century farm income has been sliding downward relative to other incomes, both in total and in per capita terms.

If we look closely at farm statistics, we note a surprising fact:

Farm *incomes* fluctuate between boom and bust to a greater degree than nonfarm incomes, but farm *production* is remarkably more stable than industrial production. Stability of farm output contrasts with instability of farm prices!

Even the weather, which is a great threat to stability of income in *any one* farm region, does not cause sizable fluctuations in *total* farm crops over the whole nation. During the last quarter century, industrial production had an average year-to-year variation of about 8 per cent, while agricultural production had less than 3 per cent.

No wonder the farmer feels he is at the mercy of a fluctuating market. His supply curves are relatively inelastic for many reasons: (1) When *P* is low, his own effort to increase output may increase, as he desperately tries to maintain family income; (2) many of his costs go on anyway, whether he produces much or little, and he can save but little extra cost by cutting his *Q*.

Figure 21-1 showed that fluctuations in the prices received by farmers are greater than the fluctuations in the prices of the things they must buy. In the Great Depression days of the 1930s, prices received by farmers dropped about twice as far as did prices elsewhere. Even in the prosperous 1920s the farmer did badly; and, to make things worse, he then carried a heavy burden of mortgage debt left over from the war boom.

GOVERNMENT AID TO AGRICULTURE

Agriculture may be the unlucky stepchild of nature, but it is often the favored foster child of government. From the beginning of time, the public seems always to have hated a landlord and loved a farmer. So there is fairly widespread support among the electorate at large for aid to the farmer even though the voting strength of the farm bloc itself has shrunk considerably.

Prior to 1929, the principal government aid to agriculture came through our *public land policy* aimed at getting acreage into the hands of settlers, and through the elaborate *practical and scientific* aids to improved agricultural methods and conservation. The work done in agricultural experiment stations, at the so-called "state land-grant colleges" (Michigan State, Iowa State, etc.), is well known; and in every farm district, the gov-

---

for baking, and so forth) and that greater technological progress may be taking place in producing raw food than in processing and marketing it. In the 1970s the farmer gets but one-third of the retail food dollar, as compared with about one-half in earlier years of high farm prices.

ernment-paid county agent provides an important source of help toward efficient farming.

But in 1929, under the Hoover administration, the Federal Farm Board was set up. A new era of direct aid to farmers began. Subsequently, under various alphabet agencies (the AAA, the CCC, etc.), the government stepped in to "interfere with the natural laws of supply and demand" to try to increase the stability and level of farm incomes.[2] Both political parties have pledged themselves to a continuation of such activities; the powerful Farm Bureau Federation, the Grange, and the Farmers' Union maintain close contact with Washington to make sure Congress knows farmers' wishes.

The parity concept The years 1909 to 1914 are often looked back upon as the golden age of agriculture. So, over the years, there has been increasing political pressure to have the government somehow guarantee to the farmer prices as relatively favorable as then prevailed. This is the root notion of "parity"—the simple feeling that if a bushel of wheat or farm goods sold for enough in 1909–1914 to buy a certain market basket of city goods and services, then in the 1970s it should still be able to buy the equivalent of that same market basket.

Parity, as shown back in Fig. 21-1, perhaps sounds simple; and perhaps rather fair— especially since we all like farmers and their votes. Why, then, the fight over it?

Deeper analysis shows that, as demand and supply change over a long period of time, the attempt to peg price at an arbitrary high level results in an avalanche of surplus farm goods. (Show the gap between the $s's'$ and $d'd'$ of Fig. 21-2 at prices kept higher than E'; and show how that gap will grow over time.) The dollar costs of aid become astronomical. The distortions of production become cumulatively greater and greater. Thus, the government storage bins are often bursting, and even the mothball fleet of abandoned warships has had to be used for storage; grain has even had to be stored on the ground itself.

The reason for this farm surplus, we have already seen. More rapid technical progress in the farm than in town means that an hour of rural labor now produces many more bushels of food than it did in 1909–1914; and if an hour of city labor does not now produce relatively as many more market baskets of industrial goods, why should these city and farm items still swap at the same "parity" terms?[3] In short, the real costs of production have gone down immensely since then; so pegging prices at the old levels calls forth a supply much larger than will be bought in the market at the parity prices. For the efficient farmers, parity maintenance may mean incomes running into six figures. For the marginal farmer, it may mean a pittance. And it keeps some inefficient farmers from going to higher-productivity occupations.

Farmers boast of their independence; and when they come to the government for

---

[2] Also, the Farm Credit Administration and the Rural Electrification Administration are government agencies set up to help the farmer borrow at low interest rates and enjoy electricity.

[3] Even if productivity were to grow at about the same rate in the two areas from now on, it would still be necessary to have some differential in earnings on and off the farm in order to coax the socially desirable shift of labor to production of those goods and services which expand in people's demand more rapidly than do food and fiber.

help—as they most certainly do—they claim they do not want a handout, but rather that they want to "earn" their subsidies. But actually, in some of the years following World War II, more than half of what the farmers collected in the market place for certain crops—such as peanuts, sorghum grain, and others—resulted from government aid programs!

Then along came a food shortage in the mid-1960s: soybean crop failure in China; poor wheat harvests in Russia; hungry mouths in India and elsewhere. After our government had forced and bribed farmers to limit acreage and production, the world suddenly faced a temporary scarcity of food. This illustrates the need to understand the shiftings of demand and supply once the State steps in to interfere with market mechanisms.

FORMS OF GOVERNMENT AID

What are the economic mechanisms by which government can help, or seem to help, the farmer? They are principally five in number:

1. Outright *gift* or relief payments, given to needy farmers who have established their need and misery (e.g., the negative income tax)

2. Programs by the government that aim to *increase the demand* for farm products or *cut their real* cost of production

3. *Crop-limitation* programs (such as acreage allotments or crop quotas to each farm) that aim to cut down on supply and raise price

4. *Purchase-loan storage* programs to guarantee farm prices, or at least give them some support

5. Finally, *purchase-and-resale differential subsidy* plans connected with the names of Eisenhower's Secretary of Agriculture Benson and Truman's Secretary Brannan

Gifts and relief There is nothing complicated about outright gifts or transfer payments, which might well be adjoined to our Social Security system or be part of Chapter 39's negative income tax. The organized farm pressure groups do not particularly want such aids, even though in strictest economic logic they may be the most defensible of all: If our Republic wants to alleviate the burden on farmers (or the poor anyplace!) and provide minimum standards, outright gifts will clarify exactly what is involved and what it costs, thereby enabling the electorate to decide rationally what it wants to accomplish.

Less than a fifth of our farms correspond to the public image of a "family farm" earning a decent living. Most farms by number are poverty enterprises. Only one out of three farms produces over $10,000 of sales per year; and they produce five times as much as the 2 million poorest farms! As it is now, billions of dollars of farm subsidies per year trickle down only in small fractions to those in greatest need: the Southern sharecropper who lives in credit peonage, the less fortunate tenant farmers, owners of small marginal farms, and paid farm laborers.

Demand promotion and research Little need be said about attempts by the Department of Agriculture to find new chemical uses of farm products or to send out circulars telling people to improve their diets. (The Department may also get Congress to provide funds to finance cheap school lunches, food stamps for the hungry, and other demand-raising programs.) Such activity goes a long way back in our history, as does government aid to land-grant colleges' experimental work to increase farm productivity. Not only will the Agriculture Department send a farmer a pamphlet on baking an angel-food cake or running a Halloween party; it will also send a county agent to teach the farmer good conservation methods, how to keep records, and how best to till his soil. Some observers think it odd that while one branch of the government is trying to get the farmer to produce less, another branch is trying to improve his productivity.

Probably the most important promotion of demand for farm products has come from Public Law 480 (the Agriculture and Trade Redevelopment and Assistance Act, 1954). This permits underdeveloped countries like India, Pakistan, and Egypt to buy our wheat and other grains. But they do not have to pay dollars for these goods; at worst they can pay the United States government in their own currencies (rupees, pounds, etc.). These "counterpart funds" are of limited usefulness to our government, although some of this local currency may be used for American propaganda purposes, cultural activities, or exchange fellowships.

Of course, our farmers get paid for their grain in American dollars that come from the budget and, indirectly, from the general taxpayer. In effect, the government is subsidizing agriculture by shifting the *dd* curve for food upward and to the right; then it proceeds to "dump" these goods abroad where they are much needed, as part of our foreign-aid program. All this is to the good; but we should ponder the warnings of Hendrik Houthakker, professor at Harvard and Economic Adviser to President Nixon:

The program has been popular with American farmers, who regard it as a legalized form of dumping. One danger which has appeared recently is that some countries (especially India) have become so dependent on food imports from the United States. . . . This may be good for farmers, but it does not help in maintaining stable domestic prices or in improving the balance of payments. An unintended result of Public Law 480 has been that the United States now exports much of its farm products to nations that cannot pay, while its competitors (especially Canada) sell for cash to the more solvent customers.

Often farmers have warred among themselves. The very large commercial farmers want freedom to produce; the middle-size farmers want protection; the poor farmers are largely politically invisible.

Yet in the 1970s, the basic outlook for American agriculture is perhaps improving. Chronically bad crops in Russia and China, plus the flowing of resources all over the world into more prosperous industry, have created recognition of the important role that efficient American and Canadian commercial farms have in helping feed the world. As we shall see in Part Five's discussion of international trade, America does enjoy what is called a "comparative advantage" in the production of food and fiber on highly mechanized large-scale farms.

ECONOMICS OF THREE MAIN AID PROGRAMS

To understand the final three programs listed on page 390, our economic tools of supply and demand are absolutely necessary. Let us see how each case works.

(Case 1.) **Crop restriction** If farmers produce a smaller total Q, they will each receive a higher P. Because the demand for farm products is generally *in*elastic, limiting total Q will actually *raise* the total revenues received by farmers—as the last chapter showed.

Of course, the consumers will be hurt by scarcity of goods and by higher prices, just as they would be if flood or drought created a scarcity of foodstuffs. In deliberately restricting farm Q, society is deliberately shifting economic resources away from places that produce the extra goods which people's dollar votes in the market place show they really want. Either those resources go into idleness, as occurs with land no longer cultivated, or they may go into secondary uses for which they are ill-fitted and which involve producing items that people do not much want.

A silver lining is provided by the fact that *soil conservation and flood control* may be achieved if land gets a rest or is put into forests and pasture. And to the degree that some of the benefits from the monopolistically contrived higher prices accrue to poverty-stricken farm families, there may be certain Robin-Hood-like social gains to offset the social costs: current suffering may be alleviated; and some of the benefit may be used to get the young people out of low-productivity agriculture.

On the other hand, some of the desirable long-run shifts and economic adjustments may be *slowed down* by the farm aid programs. And it can be shown that many of the methods used to cut down on Q—such as holding wheat acres down to a quota, but leaving farmers free to use tremendous doses of fertilizer to expand production on the quota land—will lead to inefficient use of resources in producing the reduced Q. (In terms of the production-possibility frontier of Fig. 2-4, not only are people pushed farther west than their true food and nonfood tastes would dictate, but in addition, society is pushed *inside* the producible frontier by the inefficient methods of Q restriction.)

Does the situation described above mean that farm aid is bad? Not necessarily, since noneconomic ethical and political issues are also involved. But it does suggest that each bit of benefit to some farmers is being bought at a greater sacrifice to the rest of the community than is economically and technically necessary. It does suggest that society look around for *more efficient* methods.

Regardless of sermons or partisan debate, advocates of any view will want to understand the mechanics of how

A cut in farm supply raises price and total revenue:

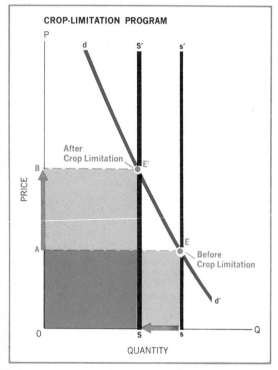

CROP-LIMITATION PROGRAM

FIG. 21-3. Before government intervenes, the *ss'* supply curve intersects the inelastic *dd'* curve at the low price shown at E. As an individual competitor, each farmer has no motive to do anything to improve the situation. But if all together can get government to put monopolistic limits on their total Q, they can benefit.

When production controls cut supply from *ss'* to *SS'*, P rises to E'. Because demand is inelastic, total gross farm income is thereby increased. (Recall that $P \times Q$ revenues at E and E' are measured, respectively, by the *OsEA* and *OSE'B* rectangular areas. Let your eye confirm that the gain in E' height over E outweighs the rectangle's loss in width; with elastic demand, the reverse would have been true.)

Q output restriction works. Figure 21-3 on page 392 tells its own story, which can be summarized as follows:

If the demand for farm products is inelastic rather than elastic, then a program of crop reduction will result in higher total receipts to the farmer. And since he also saves a little on total costs when he produces less, his net revenue goes up by even more than his total receipts do.

Case 2. Parity price through loan support or government purchase   This case is a little harder. Now government guarantees the farmer a price higher than would have prevailed in the market. This "price floor" is shown by the gold line BB' in Fig. 21-4. At so high a price, consumers will not buy all the crop supplied. Consumers will be on the demand curve at C. But farmers are supplying the full amount shown by F. If government does nothing, price must fall to E, which is below the parity price.

So what does the government have to do? By outright purchase or through some kind of loan red tape, it must acquire the unsold portion between C and F, marked with an arrow. This will go into storage, or be dumped abroad (as part of foreign aid, perhaps), or be left to rot. What, then, has the final result been?

The government has increased the price received by the farmer from E to F. But unlike the setup in the previous case, the farmers can now sell as much as they want to; so the increased price is gravy to them, representing a clear increase in their incomes. The consumers are now paying a higher price and buying less; to them Case 2 is just as bad as Case 1.[4] Who, then, is footing the bill for the extra income now received by the farmers? Obviously, the government: The public Treasury is having to shell out an amount of dollars equal to the part of the crop it must buy times the full market price. In terms of area, the Treasury's expense is shown by the shaded area $MCFs$. Can you explain why?

Of course, if the demand curve dd' were in later years to shift upward so that it intersected the supply curve at F or above, then the Treasury would not have to do anything to ensure parity. Indeed, it might in such a prosperous year exactly reverse the above procedure; instead of buying part of the crop to add to storage, it might take food out of storage and sell it. The interested reader can draw a new dd', to see how such an "ever-normal granary" program of stabilization purports to work.

Government loans or purchases support price by acquiring unsold surplus:

FIG. 21-4. The government keeps price at indicated floor or support price BB' (near or at parity) by acquiring for storage unsellable surplus shown by CF. The shaded area shows the total cost to the government of raising market price from E to F. Note that domestic consumers pay the higher price and get no current benefit from the CF part of the crop.

[4] Such Q as is being produced is presumably being produced *efficiently*. In this case, unlike Case 1, society is not *inside* its production-possibility frontier. It is merely too far southeast on Fig. 2-4's *p-p frontier*, producing more food than spontaneous dollar votes call for. Case 1 led to the opposite.

Benson-Brannan plan pays farmers gap between actual consumer's price and producer's supported price:

SIMPLIFIED RESALE PLAN

FIG. 21-5. The government lets price to consumer fall to *E*. It then makes up, by direct payments to farmers of *EF* per bushel, the difference between the low market price and the desired support price. Farmers end up with total price return shown at *F*. The shaded area shows the cost to government of the direct payments involved in such a two-price system.

Case 3 Subsidized producer-consumer price differential This is the hardest case of all. It involves paying an artificially high price to farmers, but reselling food to consumers at whatever low price the market will set. Although originally proposed by Truman's Secretary of Agriculture Brannan for perishable goods, this resale proposal was also advocated by Eisenhower's Secretary Benson with respect to butter and was passed by the Republican Congress with respect to wool.

Here the farmer is again guaranteed the *BB′* parity price, just as in Case 2. But Fig. 21-5 shows the new fact that food, instead of being left to rot in storage, is to be resold to the public for current consumption at whatever market price it will bring.

How is the farmer to receive the parity price if market price proves to be below that figure? The Department of Agriculture *simply writes him a check for the difference.* In effect, then, it is much as though the government had bought the crop at the parity price—as in the loan support of Case 2—but had then sold it on the open market for whatever price it would bring.

Every bit produced, as shown by the *ss′* supply curve, will now go to the consumer. Consumption will end up at the original point *E*. Why? Because the "law of supply and demand" tells us that, for consumers to buy the full crop, price must fall to the point where the demand curve intersects the market supply. But producers are promised the parity price for their entire crop. So the price they are to receive is indicated by *F* (just as in Case 2). Who pays the difference? The government—by sending each primary producer a check, whose amount per bushel is shown in Fig. 21-5 by the vertical arrow *EF*.

How much does it cost the government? The answer is clear, once we realize that the government must pay the difference between the producer's and consumer's price *on each and every unit produced!* (In terms of area, the expense to the government is the shaded rectangular area *AEFB*. Here the shaded rectangle goes all the way leftward to the price axis, whereas back in Case 2 the shaded rectangle of government expense went all the way downward to the quantity axis.)

An important but tricky question is the following: Will the Benson-Brannan plan of Case 3 cost the Treasury more or less than the plan of having the government withhold from the consumers part of the crop as outlined in Case 2? The answer turns out to depend upon our old friend the elasticity of demand and upon nothing else.

Look at the problem this way: Under either plan the *producers* are equally well off, being at *F* in both cases and receiving the same total income. Remember, too, that under either plan the producer's revenue can come from only two sources: the total revenue paid by the consumers plus the government's contribution. Hence, to answer the question, "Which plan costs the government more dollars?" we need only answer the much simpler question, "Which plan collects (for the government, so to speak) the greater total revenue from consumers: the plan where the consumers pay a high price and buy little, or the plan where consumers pay a low price and buy much?"

But note: this is nothing but the question we have met repeatedly in connection with the definition of elasticity. A point high up on the demand curve, such as *C*, will collect more total revenue than a point low down, such as *E*, provided the demand is *inelastic* in that interval. If demand were *elastic*, then the reverse would be true.

So now we can answer the question of relative cost as follows:

The Benson-Brannan plan of making more food available to consumers will currently cost the Treasury more money than will a purchase-for-storage-or-destruction program provided the demand curve is *inelastic*. If it had been *elastic*, the reverse would have been true. (Of course, wasteful storage costs militate against Case 2.)

From the standpoint of political economy, a plan which brings price to the consumer more nearly down to the social cost of producing food would have much to be said for it even if it should happen to result in costing the Treasury more money. If farmers are to get the same income in one way or the other, the important thing to us consumers is not so much how we divide our payments between market purchases and taxes as that food be produced and consumed up to the point where marginal utilities and costs are more nearly in balance[5]—as the next chapters will demonstrate.

ISSUES IN FARM AID

In the early New Deal days, the emphasis was on crop reduction. Acreage was cut, but technical progress and intensive cultivation often kept Q from declining. Later, the emphasis shifted from Case 1 to price supports through purchase or loan. These Case 2 programs became colossally expensive as rightward shifts of the supply curves made the free-equilibrium price fall further and further below 100 per cent or 80 per cent of parity. Government warehouses bulged (except during war and cold-war periods, when the surplus turned out to be a godsend). As we've seen, grain rotted;[6] the mere cost of holding and storing became great.

Government, with the backing of the associations of larger commercial farmers, has in recent decades favored lowering price supports below parity and closer toward free-market levels. But to avoid too precipitous a fall in farm prices, government has relied on a mixture of crop reduction, loan support, and direct subsidies: in return for generous price supports, farmers are to vote to limit their production quotas severely—a reversion to the Case 1 methods of the 1930s. The resulting rise in their income is thus to be financed in effect primarily by a hidden excise tax on food (in the form of higher prices for scarcer food supplies) rather than by glaring expenditure items in the federal budget.

[5] If *ss'* were drawn more realistically so as to be somewhat upward-sloping, we should have the evil of slightly too much Q being coaxed out by the too high government subsidy; consumers would be getting too much farm Q at a price to them below true social costs of resources used.
[6] Admittedly, we gave some of the surplus to our poor, through school lunch, stamp, and other programs. And, as already seen, we shipped food and fiber abroad under Public Law 480. So all was not waste.

WHAT ECONOMIC ANALYSIS CAN SUGGEST

As other chapters in Part Three demonstrate, there is often a strong case for sticking to the competitive market's outcome. The main exception is (1) when the people helped by government interference are for some reason strongly preferable ethically to those who are hurt and (2) when it can be shown that there is no better way of helping them out of general taxes. How does this apply to the farm problem?

Many tough-minded economists would argue that much of our government aid now goes to very prosperous commercial farmers, with too little filtering down to the really poor farmers, whose poverty makes them most deserving. (In 1970, 95 per cent of economists sampled would be found to be critical of our farm programs!) They favor new programs which give whatever aid it is decided to give to farmers in a more efficient way—so as to leave the rest of us with more than we now get. Such programs would involve more pinpointing of the aid given to those who actually merit it from the standpoint of need—as through a negative income tax.

Such a turnabout would involve more reliance on market forces in determining food and fiber prices. As prices fell, consumers generally would be able to afford more food, and especially more of the expensive protein foods such as milk and meat. The United States would be better able to export the food and fiber she is well suited to produce. Commercial farmers would feel pressure on them to become more efficient, and many of the remaining family farmers would find their incomes so low in agriculture as to be speeded into industry or into part-time jobs off the farm. The really poor farmers would receive welfare aids under such a program—not so much because they are farmers, but for the same reason that government aid is given to any who are poverty-stricken and need rehabilitation.

The economists who argue along this line say:

In terms of resource allocation, the American people so little value an extra unit of food relative to other things, and our technology so easily permits us to produce an extra unit of food, that it is most worth while for us to equate supply and demand for food at low prices—low enough to coax resources out of agriculture and into industry, where they will produce things for which there is a demand in the form of consumers' money votes unbuttressed by artificial government aids.[7] Resources should both be forced out, and attracted out, of agriculture. The transitional distress should be alleviated by outright subsidies which will not involve inefficient distortion of production and which should be made to taper off after a set number of years. Human suffering merits the same aid anywhere.

THE LONG-RUN SOLUTION?

Does all this sound cruel and heartless—hard-boiled? It is perhaps a bit extreme in giving too little weight to the argument that a civilization is happier when it seeks to protect any group in it from *sudden and drastic* changes in status.

Nonetheless, this economic analysis succeeds in pointing out the only ultimate solution.

[7] Footnote readers can refer to page 375 for a graph of the argument that uninterfered-with pricing has a property of being "efficient," even if not necessarily "equitable."

That solution, as suggested in the quotation from Vanderbilt's expert agricultural economist W. H. Nicholls, is *to reduce our surplus of farmers*. No doubt this has to be done gradually. And it is actually happening all the time: each year there are fewer and fewer people in agriculture.

Before mourning this century-old trend, consider the following parable:

Back in Andrew Jackson's day, the American people discovered that cheap Western land was depressing farm prices. So they introduced an AAA program. Later the Whigs stepped up this program, and in the Grant administration, following the Civil War, the program was stepped up still further.

To restore the golden age of 1820, the government bought and burned crops. This became so expensive that the government also had to set acreage quotas. By 1860 each farmer had to leave an acre fallow for each acre he cultivated. By 1900 he could cultivate only 1 acre in 10. By 1984, so rapid was technological innovation that he could cultivate only 1 acre in 40. And even then, the government found itself taxing one-third the Net National Product for purchases of crops to burn. Yet America's 50 million people—her population could not grow much under such a regime!—were so dedicated to helping agriculture that they cheerfully voted the burden. And why not? More than half of the working force had to farm on the 1 acre in 40 in order to support the other half. The average income per head was, in 1984, below that prevailing in Japan, a country not lucky enough to have a wonderful farm aid program.

Everybody was happy. Except for one thing. Americans feared that with so low an income they would be unable to equip a strong army against the Enemy, who each year foolishly encouraged his own farm and city productivity and who looked with longing eyes on all 40 out of each 40 lush North American acres.

Of course, this is a rather silly parable. It overstates the case, and that is not fair. And yet . . . and yet . . . for all its overstatement, are there not some important economic insights to be gleaned from it?[8]

RURAL POVERTY

Looked at properly, America's real farm problem is that of rural poverty. Real incomes on the farm and in small towns average below those elsewhere. Twelve million people fall below the rural poverty line in 1970. Although only three-tenths of the populace is rural, four-tenths of the impoverished live in the country. Many are black; some are Indians; some are of Mexican descent; most, by absolute (but not relative!) number, are white. Silently, invisibly, they lead miserable lives in Appalachia, along the Mexican border, in the Deep South, in the Ozarks, in the upper Great Lakes regions (and, in Canada, in the Maritime Provinces and Quebec).

Solutions for them will not come from the mechanisms of supply and demand. The solutions must come—as Chapter 39 shows—from transfer-payment programs, from education subsidies, from relocation and retraining, and from family-planning clinics. The mixed economy, and not laissez faire, must provide the solutions.

[8] All this will remain for a long time a political issue. No one will begrudge the farmer his desire to be free from wildly fluctuating prices. In the Appendix we shall see how private speculators on an organized exchange are supposed in traditional economic theory to be able to iron out any *foreseeable* fluctuations. The question remains whether, gifts aside, we can expect the government to make better forecasts of the uncertain future than private speculative markets can, and whether we can expect the government, through its storage program, to be better than private markets in stabilizing prices.

SUMMARY

1   Although the rural birth rate is higher than the urban, a persistent cityward migration means that the percentage of the population engaged in agriculture is declining. Improvements in agricultural techniques mean that supply increases greatly and that the same total of food can be produced with fewer workers; also, as incomes increase, the increase in demand for food is less than proportionate.

   So free-equilibrium prices for agriculture tend to fall. Farm income tends to be both low and unstable; as a result, government has adopted a variety of programs to support farm-product prices and maintain farm incomes.

2   Pegging prices at any ancient parity formula, despite its superficial plausibility and fairness, utterly disregards basic changes in demand and real costs of production. As time passes, such a parity will produce prices differing sharply from "natural competitive" levels here and abroad. The result: huge surpluses, with the wrong goods being produced and with growing distortions of efficiency.

3   Aid programs involving direct gifts or promotion of demand and of cost research require no deep economic analysis. But the tools of supply and demand are needed to understand the three aid programs: (1) crop limitation by acreage or other allotments, (2) government price support by purchase-loan storage programs, (3) resale to consumers at competitive market prices of food bought at a pegged price, with the government footing the bill for the differential. Hybrids of all three are frequently legislated. The resulting programs are colossally expensive, economically inefficient, and satisfactory to no groups.

4   The long-run solution must involve maintenance of prosperity outside agriculture, so that people can continue to move to the lines of highest productivity and so that demand for agriculture will be optimally high. But mere prosperity in industry is not enough. The 1920s and 1960s show that the city and town can prosper while the country's economic position deteriorates.

   In the long run, resources have to be helped to move out of low-efficiency rural uses and into more productive uses. That means a continuation of the trend toward fewer but more efficient farmers, and a need for short-run aids to speed the reconversion and to ease its human burdens. It also means flexible pricing practices that permit efficient American farms to help feed the world. And, as Chapter 40 shows, the rural exodus creates urban problems elsewhere.

5   The real problem of agriculture is seen to be that of poverty. All the creative energies of the mixed economy are needed to cope with this basic challenge.

QUESTIONS FOR DISCUSSION

1   Contrast long-term and cyclical patterns of agriculture and industry.

2   Describe government indirect and direct farm aids. Explain "parity."

3   Why might limiting a farm's acreage in one crop not reduce the total of it much? How would it affect noncontrolled crops? Fertilizer demand?

4   Debate the merit of taking a dollar from the 19 in 20 people employed outside farming and giving it to the 1 in farming. Distinguish ways of giving him the dollar.

5   What does Professor Dudley Johnson of the University of Washington mean here? "Major premise: Society should help poor people. Minor premise (of doubtful validity as stated): Farmers are poor people. (Dubious) Conclusion: Therefore society should help farmers. Actually, if society is to subsidize individuals, it should not be done on the basis of their occupations, but because they are *poor*—i.e., aid on an *income* basis."

6   Why might a welfare program like the negative income tax help the farm problem?

Review your understanding of the following concepts:

inelastic farm demand and supply
farm technology and declining percentage
   of income spent on food
free-farm-price trends
parity, 1909–1914 golden age
Public Law 480

Q limitation; P support; direct
   payments with consumer and
   producer Ps different
pros and cons of free farm prices
long- and short-run solutions
rural poverty

APPENDIX: Economics of Speculation, Risk, and Insurance

Here we apply the tools of supply and demand to analyze price relations across space and time and the important problems involved in risk, speculation, and gambling. We deal not only with the purchase and sale of actual commodities such as corn or cocoa, but also with the purchase and sale of something more mysterious—of bits of paper.

These bits of paper are called "commodity futures": they are contracts that brokers deal with on organized commodity exchanges like the Chicago Board of Trade or the New York Cocoa Exchange. You and I may buy or sell such commodity futures even though we have never seen any *real* corn or cocoa. As speculators in such futures, the last thing in the world we should want to happen would be for a truck to roll up to our door seeking to deliver honest-to-goodness corn or cocoa.

Yet, as we shall see, even though speculators never touch the real thing, they may under certain conditions be helping to even out the consumption of the crop between harvest times and to carry over the proper amount of food and fiber between seasons.

In his autobiography, the elder statesman Bernard Baruch said that 10 years after he heard Professor George B. Newcomb lecture on supply and demand at CCNY, he had made more than a million dollars from speculation—implying that those lectures might have had something to do with it. Certainly, this Appendix is not designed to make you rich, and if you skip it, your knowledge of the rest of the book will not suffer. But speculation is a fascinating topic and can serve as an example of important applications of supply and demand. Inevitably, it is a complicated subject which no introduction can pretend to treat completely.

GEOGRAPHICAL PRICE PATTERNS

In a well-organized competitive market, there tends to be at any one time and place a single prevailing price. This is due to the action of professional speculators or "arbitragers" who keep their ear to the market and, as soon as they learn of any price differences, buy at the cheaper price and sell at the dearer price, thereby making a profit for themselves—at the same time tending to equalize the price.[1]

[1] On the floor of the Chicago Board of Trade, the important market for grain, some hundred important "pit scalpers," or dealers, are said to make all their profits on price changes within each day, closing out all their transactions every night and sleeping peacefully until the next day. Specialists on the floor of the Stock Exchange act similarly.

Two markets at a considerable distance from each other may have different prices. Wheat in Chicago may sell for a few cents more per bushel than identical wheat in Kansas City, because of shipping, insurance, and interest charges involved in transportation. If ever the price in Chicago should rise by more than the few cents of shipping costs, speculators will buy in Kansas City and ship to Chicago, thereby bringing the price up in Kansas City and down in Chicago to the normal maximum differential.

Nobody legislates these patterns. They follow from supply and demand.

SPECULATION AND PRICE BEHAVIOR OVER TIME

In an ideal competitive market there tends to be a definite pattern of prices *over time* just as there is over space. But the difficulties of predicting the future make this pattern a less perfect one: we have an equilibrium that is constantly being disturbed but is always in the process of re-forming itself—rather like the ocean's surface under the play of the winds.

Stabilizing seasonal patterns Consider the simplest case of a grain, like corn, that is harvested at one period of the year. This crop must be made to last all the year if privation is to be avoided. Since no one passes a law regulating the storage of grain, how is this desirable state of affairs brought about? Through the attempts of speculators to make a profit.

A well-informed speculator who is a specialist in this grain realizes that, if all the grain is thrown on the market in the autumn, it will fetch a very low price because of the glutting of the market. On the other hand, months later, with almost no grain coming on the market, price will tend to skyrocket.

The above description tells what would tend to happen were it *not* for the action of speculators. Speculators realize that by (1) purchasing some of the autumn crop while it is cheap, (2) withholding it in storage, and (3) selling it later when the price has risen, they can make a profit. This they do. But in doing so, they increase the autumn demand for grain and raise its autumn price; and they increase the spring supply of grain and lower its spring price. At the same time that they are equalizing the price over the year, they are also equalizing the supply coming on the market in each month—which is as it should be.

Moreover, if there is brisk competition among speculators, none will make an excessive profit over the costs that he incurs (including, of course, the wages

For a good to be stored, expected price rise must match storing cost:

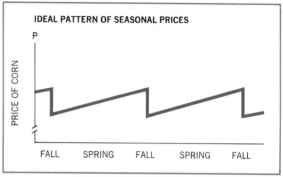

FIG. 21-6. Ideally, P is lowest at harvest time, rising gently with accumulated storage costs until the next harvest. This flexible pattern tends to even out consumption over the seasons—as compared with a harvest glut's causing very low autumn price and summer scarcity's causing sky-high price.

necessary to keep him in this line of activity). The speculator himself may never touch a kernel of corn or a bag of cocoa, nor need he know anything about storage, warehouses, or delivery. He merely buys and sells bits of paper. But the effect is exactly as described.

Now there is one and only one monthly price pattern that will result in neither profits nor losses. A little thought will show that it will not be a pattern of constant prices. Rather, the ideal price pattern will involve lowest prices in the autumn glut and then gradually rising prices until the peak is reached just before the new corn comes in. The price must rise from month to month to compensate for the storage and interest costs of carrying the crop in storage—in exactly the same way that the price must rise over space from one mile to the next to compensate for the cost of transportation.[2] Figure 21-6 shows the behavior of prices over an idealized yearly cycle.

Stabilizing foreseeable fluctuations Not all fluctuations in activity can be so accurately forecast as the seasonal harvesting of a crop. No one can predict with confidence next year's weather or the likelihood of a

[2] Do I, as a warehouse storer, need a crystal ball to tell me price will rise enough to pay me to store corn today? No. The market today will quote me a future price—for delivery of corn some months hence—and when this future price sufficiently exceeds the current spot price for physical corn, I get the signal to store corn.

recession in the near future. But to the extent that speculators can form any accurate guesses today about the future *scarcity* of a commodity, they will tend to buy it now for *future* delivery, thereby causing (1) a withdrawal of present supply, (2) an increase of present price, (3) an increase in amount stored, (4) an increase in future supply, (5) a reduction in future price—or in all a relative stabilization of price and consumption over time.

The reader should try to visualize the opposite process by which speculators stabilize prices when they correctly foresee an exceptionally large future crop and a low future price: how they then "sell short"[3] for future delivery, tending to depress current prices, raise present consumption, and reduce carry-over of stocks.

Spreading of risks Aside from their influence toward stabilizing prices, speculators have another important function. By being willing to take risks on their own shoulders, they enable others to avoid risk.

For example, a warehouse owner must carry large inventories of grain in the course of his business. If the price of grain goes up, he makes a windfall capital gain; if down, he incurs a windfall loss. But let us suppose that he is content to earn his living by storing grain and wishes to forgo all risk taking. This he can do by a process called "hedging." This complicated procedure is rather like a man who bets on Army to win the Army-Navy game and then washes out this transaction, or covers it, by placing an equal bet on the Navy. Whichever side wins, he comes out the same, his left hand winning what his right hand loses.

To get a notion of how the complicated process of hedging works out, here is a highly simplified example. Suppose I am buying and storing corn in the late fall.

[3] There is nothing mysterious about selling short. I simply put in an order to my broker in which I agree, in return for a certain price *now*, to deliver *at some later date* an amount of grain. Usually, at the time of putting in the order, I do not have the grain on hand. But I can legally fulfill my contract by later "covering," i.e., buying the grain and making delivery. If I later have to pay a higher price in covering than I now receive when selling short, then I take a loss. But if I have guessed right and prices do fall in the intervening period, then I "buy in" for less than I have sold and make a profit.

Selling short in the stock market works out similarly, except that I am free to cover and make future delivery of the stock at any time I please. Meanwhile, the man who has bought the stock receives his stock shares. How? As a result of the fact that my broker, obligingly, lends me the stock certificates to make delivery. Later, when I cover, I buy in some stock and turn over the certificates to my obliging broker.

I am a specialist in running a warehouse and wish to stick to my last rather than become involved in the risky business of taking speculative bets as to whether the price of corn will change between now and next spring, when I expect to stop storing corn and to sell it. In effect, I should really like to sell it now for an agreed-upon price that will compensate me for my 9-cent-per-bushel storage expenses between now and later delivery time. If a speculative market exists, that is precisely what I can do by the device of hedging.

How do I hedge? For each 5,000 bushels of corn I buy in November to put into storage until next May, let us suppose I have to pay $1 a bushel to local Illinois farmers. I look up the price quoted today, November 30, on the Chicago Board of Trade for next May corn futures and see that this quotation is $1.09. I realize that this 9-cent excess over today's price will give me a fair return for my expenses of storage and that is why I am glad to store. I now hedge by *selling* a 5,000-bushel May corn-future contract. (The brokerage commission on this "short-sale" transaction will be less than $\frac{1}{2}$ cent per bushel; my broker will require that I put up less than 10 cents per bushel as "margin" to ensure that I fulfill my contractual obligation, and he neither knows nor cares whether I actually have some physical corn with which to make later delivery.)

Now I am hedged. I happen to own 5,000 bushels of physical corn in storage. I also have sold 5,000 bushels of May corn futures.

What will happen if slack corn demand and a tremendous winter wheat and oats crop cause the price of corn to fall to 90 cents by next May?

My brother, who owns a warehouse and bought corn in the fall as I did *but did not hedge*, will now lose 10 cents per bushel. Indeed, he is worse off than that, because he is also out the 9 cents that it costs him to keep his warehouse going (watchmen's pay, and so forth). So he has really lost 19 cents per bushel in toto.

What about me, the cagy hedger? I do lose 10 cents a bushel *on my physical corn* because of the unforeseen change in price. But when, as May arrives, I look in the paper for the Board of Trade quotation on my May future, I am relieved to see that it has fallen from $1.09 all the way down to 90 cents—at which price I buy in, or "cover," my futures. Thus, *on short sale of my futures* I have gained 19 cents, or exactly as much as I (and my brother) have lost in toto on the sale of physical corn. *The hedge has protected me from all price fluctuations:* my left futures pocket has gained what my right physical-corn pocket lost. I am left with my 9-cent costs well covered. The speculator who made my hedge possible took the price risks off my shoulders.[4]

To the extent that speculators forecast accurately, they provide a definite social service. To the extent that they forecast badly, they tend to aggravate the variability of prices. Were it not for the detailed statistical information provided by the Department of Agriculture and private agencies, the traders of the Chicago Board of Trade would find themselves at the mercy of every idle rumor, hope, and fear. For speculation is often a mass contagion, like the inexplicable dancing crazes that swept medieval villages, the Dutch tulip mania that sent the price of a single bulb higher than that of a house, the South Sea Bubble in which companies sold stock at fabulous prices for enterprises which would "later be revealed."

GAMBLING AND DIMINISHING MARGINAL UTILITY[5]

The defenders of speculation resent the charge that it represents simply another form of gambling, like betting on the horse races or buying a lottery ticket. They emphasize that an uncertain world necessarily involves risk and that someone must bear risks. They claim that the knowledge and the venturesomeness of the speculator are chained to a *socially useful purpose*, thereby reducing fluctuations and risks to others. (We have just seen that this is not always the case and that speculation may indeed be destabilizing; but certainly, no one can deny all validity to the above claims.)

Why is gambling considered such a bad thing? Part of the reason, perhaps the most important part, lies in the field of morals, ethics, and religion; upon these

[4]To check your understanding, work through the case where a war scare sends up the price of physical corn in the May market to, say, $1.19. Now my unhedged brother, in addition to his 9-cent return as a warehouseman, makes an additional windfall risk profit of 10 cents per bushel. What about me? On my physical corn which I bought at $1 and sell for $1.19, I gain; but I lose 10 cents on having to buy in my May futures at 10 cents more than I sold it for. So I end up making my 9-cent warehouse return and no more—regardless of what can happen to corn price fluctuations.

Actual hedging of millers, farmers, and storers can become more complicated. Also, it could happen that, in order to coax out speculators, the quotation in November of the May future would on the average have to sell for a little less than the $1.09 such physical corn can be expected to sell for in May; this means that the risk-bearing speculators require a premium for the insurancelike risk taking they are providing—a premium (called "normal backwardation") that, like any cost, must be borne by producers and ultimate consumers.

[5]Some of this material leans on (and illustrates!) the later discussion of marginal utility, beginning on page 410.

the economist as such is not qualified to pass final judgment. There is, however, a substantial economic case to be made against gambling.

First, it involves simply *sterile transfers of money or goods* between individuals, creating no new money or goods.[6] Although it creates no output, gambling does nevertheless absorb time and resources. When pursued beyond the limits of recreation, where the main purpose after all is to "kill" time, gambling subtracts from the national income.

The second economic disadvantage of gambling is the fact that it tends to promote *inequality* and *instability of incomes*. People who sit down to the gaming table with the same amount of money go away with widely different amounts. A gambler (and his family) must expect to be on the top of the world one day, and when luck changes—which is the only predictable thing about it—he may almost starve.

Law of diminishing marginal utility and chance   But why is inequality of income over time and between persons considered such a bad thing? One answer is to be found in the widely held belief that the gain in utility achieved by an *extra* $1,000 of income is not as great as the loss in utility of forgoing $1,000 of income. Where that is the case, a bet at fair odds involves an economic loss: the *money* you stand to win balances the money you may lose; but the *satisfaction* you stand to win is *less* than the satisfaction you stand to lose.

Similarly, if it could be assumed that individuals are all "roughly the same" and are ethically comparable, so that their utilities can be added, then the dollars gained by the rich do not create as much "social welfare" or total utility as the dollars lost by the poor. This has been used not only as a criticism of gambling, but as a positive argument in favor of "progressive" or steeply graduated taxation aimed at lowering the inequality of the distribution of income. (The issue of

[6]Actually, in all professional gambling arrangements, the participants lose out on balance. The leakage comes from the fact that the odds are always rigged in favor of the "house," so that even an "honest" house will win in the long run. Moderate gambling among friends may be considered a form of consumption or recreation activity whose cost to the group as a whole is zero. Oddly, some people who do not trust their ability to save do use steady purchase of lottery tickets as a way to cut down on current consumption and put themselves in the position of occasionally accumulating larger sums of money. In some past and present societies, the enhancement of inequality of income distribution by gambling may have made a roundabout contribution to social thrift and capital formation.

incentives must also enter into forming any decision on policy, since discussions elsewhere show that redistributing the national pie may lessen its total.)

Just as Malthus saw the law of diminishing returns as underlying his theory of population, so is the "law of diminishing marginal utility" used by many economists to condemn professional gambling. According to this theory (discussed in next chapter) as money income increases, each new dollar adds something to utility, but less and less. Similarly, each extra unit of any good that can be bought with money contributes less and less satisfaction or utility. When we get as much of a good as we wish (e.g., air), it becomes a "free good" because still further units add nothing new to our utility.

WHY IDEAL STABILIZATION BY SPECULATORS IS OPTIMAL

We can now use the tools of marginal utility to show how ideal speculation would maximize total utility over time. Suppose every consumer has a utility schedule that holds for each year independently of any other year. Now suppose that in the first of two years there was a big crop—say, 3 units per person—and in the second a small crop of only 1 unit per person. If this crop deficiency could be foreseen, how should the consumption of the two-year 4-unit total be spread over the two years?

If we agree, for simplicity, to neglect all storage, interest, and insurance charges and all questions of utility commensurability over time, we can prove this:

Total utility for the two years together will be maximized only if consumption is equal in each year.

Why is uniform consumption better than any other division of the available total? Because of the law of diminishing marginal utility. Here is the reasoning: "Suppose I consume more in the first year than in the second. My last unit's marginal utility in the first year will be low, and then it will be high in the second. So if I carry some crop from the first to the second year, I shall be switching from low to high marginal utilities —and that will maximize my total utility."

But is not that exactly what the following ideal speculation pattern would accomplish? Yes, it is.

If speculators can neglect interest, storage, and insurance charges and happen to forecast accurately next year's low crop, what will they do? They will figure it pays to carry goods over from this year's low price resulting from the high crop, hoping instead to sell at next year's scarcity price. But as each speculator subtracts from this year's supply and adds to next year's, what must finally happen? Equilibrium can be reached only when the two prices have been equalized! Then there will be no further incentive to carry over more crop.[7] (Of course, a small payment for the speculator's

---

[7]A graph can illuminate this argument. If utility could be measured in dollars, with each dollar always denoting the same marginal utility, the demand curves would look just like the marginal utility schedule on page 411. The two curves of Fig. 21-7 show what would happen if there were no carryover—with price first determined at A_1, where s_1s_1 intersects dd, and second at A_2, where the lower supply s_2s_2 intersects dd. Total utility of the blue shaded areas would add up only to $(4 + 3 + 2) + 4$, or \$13 per head. But with optimal carryover to the second year of 1 unit by speculators, Ps and Qs will be equalized at E_1 and E_2, and now the total utility of the blue areas will add up to $(4 + 3) + (4 + 3)$, or \$14 per head. (Show that the gain in utility of \$1 is measured by the dark block, which represents the excess of the second unit's marginal utility over the third unit's marginal utility; one can show that equality of marginal utilities is optimal.)

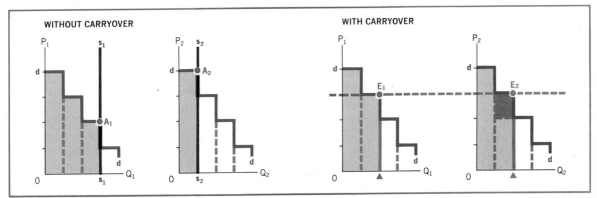

WITHOUT CARRYOVER   WITH CARRYOVER

FIG. 21-7. The blue areas measure total utility enjoyed each year. Carrying one unit to the second year equalizes Q and also P, and increases total utility by amount of dark block. (Footnote 9 suggests other applications.)

effort might have to be included—but we have agreed to waive all costs just to keep the example simple.)

Do not for a moment get the impression that real flesh-and-blood speculators can guess the future correctly. They often make mistakes and often are prey to rumors and mass enthusiasms. So the process is not as ideal as here pictured. Still, to the degree that speculators can intelligently foresee the future—and those who have a terrible batting average may get eliminated fast as their capital is lost—they (and for that matter, *farsighted* government agencies, too) may help to provide a useful stabilizing function.

ECONOMICS OF INSURANCE

We are now in a position to see why insurance, which appears to be just another form of gambling, actually has exactly opposite effects. For the same reasons that gambling is bad, insurance is economically advantageous.[8] Whereas gambling creates risks, insurance helps to lessen and spread risks.

In buying fire insurance on his house, the owner seems to be betting with the insurance company that his house will burn down. If it does not—and the odds are heavily in favor of its not burning—the owner forfeits the small premium charge. If it does burn down, the company must reimburse the owner to the tune of the agreed-upon loss. (For the obvious reason of removing temptation from hard-up home owners who like fire engines and excitement, the face value of the policy tends to be something less than the money value of the property insured.)

What is true of fire insurance is equally true of life, accident, automobile, or any other kind of insurance. Actually, at the famous Lloyd's of London, which is a place for insurance brokers to come together, you

---

[8]The astute reader will note (1) that economics proves that those subject to diminishing marginal utility should not gamble and should insure, but that a man with *increasing* marginal utility will maximize his expected utility by gambling and by noninsuring; and (2) that any economist who uses observations on a person's reaction to situations involving probabilities as his test of how marginal utility varies for that person may end up with the following circular reasoning: those who gamble should gamble; those who insure should insure. So the case for prohibiting gambling must rest on extraneous ethical or religious grounds; or must be withdrawn; or must be based on the notion that society knows better than individuals what is truly good for them; or must be based on the notion that we are all imperfect beings who wish in the long run that we were not free to yield to short-run temptations. Some political economists feel that moderate gambling might be converted into socially useful channels.

can arrange to insure a ball team or vacationer against rain, dancers against infantile paralysis, *and* a hotel keeper against a damage suit from the widow of a man killed in a fight with another man who bought a drink in the hotel's cocktail lounge; and you can get numerous other bizarre policies. But by the common law, Lloyd's may refuse to bet $10,000 with me that it will not snow on Christmas, since I do not have an "insurable interest" of that amount and the bet would be unenforceable in the courts. However, a ski-resort owner, who stands to lose that much if it does not snow, would have such an insurable interest and could certainly buy such a policy. Economic theory shows that the difference between these two cases is that insuring the resort owner *stabilizes* income while insuring me *destabilizes* it.

The insurance company is not gambling, because what is unpredictable and subject to chance *for the individual* is highly predictable and uniform *in the mass.* Whether John C. Smith, age twenty and in good health, will live for 30 more years is a matter of chance, but the famous *law of large numbers* guarantees that out of 100,000-odd twenty-year-olds in good health, only a definite proportion will still be alive at the end of such a period. The life-insurance company can easily set a premium at which it will not lose money. Hence, the company certainly is not gambling.

What about the buyer of insurance? Is he gambling? The reverse can be shown to be true: The man who does not insure his house is doing the gambling. He is risking the whole value of his house against the small premium saved. If his house does not burn down in any year, the noninsurer has won his bet; if it does, as occasionally must happen, he loses his bet and incurs a tremendous penalty.

At this point, a sporting man will say, "So what? Of course, a man gambles when he doesn't buy insurance. But the odds on such a bet are not unfavorable. In fact, they are favorable, because we know that the insurance company is not in business for its health. It must keep records, it must support insurance salesmen, and so forth. All this costs money and must be 'loaded' onto the insurance premium, detracting from the perfect mathematical odds of the buyer and making the odds for the nonbuyer a little better."

To which a rational man will reply: "When I am among friends, I don't mind a small game of chance for relaxation even at slightly unfavorable odds. But when a big bet is involved, even if the odds are favorable, then I pass. I insure my house because I hardly miss the premium each year; but if it burned down without being covered, I'd feel the loss an awful lot.

When I insure, my living standards over time and my income remain the same, come what may. When I don't insure, I may be up for a while, but I risk going way down."

Obviously, the law of diminishing marginal utility—which makes the satisfaction from wins less important than the privation from losses—is one way of justifying the above reasoning.[9] *This law of diminishing marginal utility tells us that a steady income, equitably divided among individuals instead of arbitrarily apportioned between the lucky and unlucky people whose house did or did not burn down, is economically advantageous.* (Also, when a family chooses to buy hospital and medical insurance, it may express the belief that this will be relatively-painless, forced "saving against a rainy day." This self-imposed "compulsory-saving" feature is another benefit of insurance.)

WHAT CAN BE INSURED

Undoubtedly, insurance is a highly important way of spreading risks. Why, then, can we not insure ourselves against *all* the risks of life? The answer lies in the indisputable fact that certain definite mathematical conditions are necessary before sufficiently exact actuarial probabilities can be determined.

[9] Figure 21-7 of this Appendix can show all this. Change the titles "Without Carryover" and "With Carryover" to "Without Insurance" and "With Insurance" to see the gain in utility from insuring. To prove the loss from gambling, relabel once again the left-hand figure "After Gambling" and the right-hand one "Before Gambling." To illustrate that equal incomes maximize the sum of ("social") utility of two ethically commensurable persons, relabel Fig. 21-7 still once again to read "Before Redistribution" and "After Redistribution."

First, we must have a *large number of events.* Only then will a pooling of risks and a "cancellation" and "averaging of extremes" be possible. The bank at Monte Carlo knows there is safety in numbers. The lucky streak of an Arabian prince one night will be canceled by his next night's losings or by the losings of a fake Balkan countess. Once in a blue moon someone may "break the bank"; but in a few more lunar cycles the "house" will more than break even.

But large numbers are not enough. No prudent fire-insurance company would confine itself to the island of Manhattan even though there are thousands of buildings there. *The uncertain events must be relatively independent.* Each throw of the dice, each chance of loss by fire, should stand relatively by itself. Obviously, a great fire like that of Chicago in 1871 or of the San Francisco earthquake would subject all the buildings in the same locality to the same risk. The company would be making a bet on *one* event, not on thousands of independent events. Instead, it must diversify its risks. Private companies cannot, without government aid, bear the risks of nuclear-war insurance. Nor is it possible to buy unemployment insurance from a private company. Depressions are great plagues which hit all sections and all classes at one and the same time, with a probability that cannot be computed in advance with any precision. Therefore only the government, whose business it is to take losses, can assume the responsibility of providing unemployment compensation.

There still remain, and probably always will, numerous risks of personal and business life. No one can insure the success of a new beauty shop, a new mousetrap, or a hopeful opera singer. Without error there cannot be trial; and without trial there cannot be progress.

SUMMARY TO APPENDIX

1 The intelligent profit-seeking action of speculators and arbitragers tends to create certain definite *equilibrium patterns of price over space and time.* To the extent that speculators moderate price and consumption instability, they perform a socially useful purpose. To the extent that they provide a market and permit others to hedge against risk, they perform a further useful function.

But to the extent that speculators pile onto price changes and cause great fluctuations in stock and commodity prices, and in foreign-exchange rates, they do social damage.

2 The economic principle of diminishing marginal utility is one way of showing why consumption and price stability is good, and why gambling is economically unsound and insurance is sound. There are fundamental differences among what can be insured by private rather than social agencies and what can scarcely be insured at all.

QUESTIONS FOR DISCUSSION

1   How does ideal speculation work to stabilize seasonal prices? To spread risks?

2   "Insurance reduces total risk; gambling increases the total. Therefore the former is good and the latter is bad." Explain.

3   "I love the thrill of gambling, or risking all on the turn of a card. What do I care for odds or economic principles?" Can economic science pass judgment on such a person?

4   Can you reverse the reasoning on the desirability of gambling and insurance so that it will apply to two individuals with increasing rather than decreasing marginal utility of income?

5   If $1 of gain is worth less than $1 of loss, show that people will prefer to hold a portfolio of *diversified* securities.

6   List some important differences between private and social insurance.

7   *Extra-credit problem* (for students of statistics): Suppose each of four cab companies faces accidents "normally distributed," with a standard deviation, $\sigma_i = \$3,000$, around a mean loss of $50,000. Let them now pool risks through mutual reinsurance. Show that this gives a total mean loss of $200,000 (or still $50,000 for each one's fair share; but now total variance is only $4 \times (\$3,000)^2$, or $\sigma^2 = 4\sigma_i^2 = \$36,000,000 = (6,000)^2$). So each ends up with a standard deviation of only $1,500 = \$6,000/4$—halving the risk through quadrupling the size! (Suppose at the beginning of Fig. 21-6, the harvest were many times the average crop. Then it would be rational to spread it over two crop years, not one. Can you show how P would drop so low in the first Fall as to lead to a *steady* rise thereafter for two years, and with *no* drop in P at the time of the next intermediate autumn harvest?)

Review your understanding of the following concepts:

spatial P equality but for transport costs
ideal seasonal price pattern
hedging, speculation, and short-sale
law of diminishing marginal utility

consumption stability versus instability
gambling versus insurance
insurable and uninsurable risks
social versus private insurance

The Theory of Demand and Utility

22

What is a cynic? A man who knows the price of everything, and the value of nothing.
OSCAR WILDE

In a competitive market, price is determined by the schedules of supply and demand. But what principles of economics lie behind the demand schedules? What principles behind the supply schedules?

In this chapter we shall investigate briefly the economic principles of *total utility* and *marginal utility* which underlie the market demand schedule. The later chapters will survey the cost concepts which underlie the competitive supply schedule and the behavior of monopolists.

SUMMING INDIVIDUAL DEMANDS TO GET MARKET DEMAND

The demand curve for a good such as tea is arrived at for the whole market by summing up the amounts of tea that will be demanded by each consumer. Each consumer has a demand curve along which the quantity demanded can be plotted against the price of tea. It generally *slopes downward* and to the right, declining from northwest to southeast. If all consumers were exactly alike in their demands and there were 1 million consumers, then we could think of the market demand curve as a millionfold enlargement of each consumer's demand curve.

But people are not all exactly alike. Some have high incomes; some low. Some greatly desire tea; others prefer coffee or concerts. What must we do to the demand schedules or curves of each consumer to arrive at the total market *dd* curve?

All we have to do is calculate the sum total of what *all* the different consumers will consume at any given price; we then plot that total amount as a point on the market demand curve. Or if we like, we may set the total down in a demand table like that first seen in Chapter 4.

Summary: We sum individual demands at each price to end up finally with the market demand curve. (Figure 22-1 adds demand curves "horizontally.")

To get market demand, we add all consumers' demand curves:

FIG. 22-1. At each price, such as $5, we *horizontally* add quantities demanded by each man to get market quantity demanded.

DEMAND SHIFTS FROM INCOME AND OTHER CHANGES

Factors other than changes in the price of tea can change the quantity demanded of tea. We know from budget studies, from historical experience, and from thinking about our own behavior that an increase in money income is a factor that will normally tend to increase the amount we are willing to buy of any good. Goods that are necessities tend to be less responsive to income changes, and goods that are luxuries tend to be more responsive; a very few abnormal goods, called "inferior" goods, may actually go down in quantity bought when we get enough income to be able to afford to replace them in the budget by other goods. (Potatoes, rye bread, bologna, soup bones and offal, lard, and oleomargarine might be examples of inferior goods, but the species is so rare that we can usually neglect it in our discussions.)

Let us now show what all this means in terms of the demand curve. This curve is, of course, simply the graphical picture of the response of quantity bought of a good to the change in its *own* price. But quantity bought may change also as a result of changes in the *prices of other goods* or as a result of a change in the consumer's *income*. The demand curve is drawn on the assumption that these other things do not change. But what if they do? Then the whole demand curve will *shift* to the right or to the left.

Figure 22-2 illustrates such changes. Given a certain income and established prices for all other goods, we can draw the consumer's demand for tea, *dd*. First, assume price and quantity are at the point A. Suppose now that his income rises. Even though the price of tea is unchanged, he will in all probability buy more tea than before; hence the demand curve will have shifted to the right, say, to *d′d′*, with A′ indicating his new total purchase of tea. If his income should fall, then we may expect a reduction in quantity bought—there *must* be a reduction if income falls far enough. This downward shift we illustrate by *d″d″* and by *A″*.

Income is only one of many factors that the position of the demand curve depends on. An increased taste or fashion for tea would also shift the demand to the right, and a decreased taste would have the opposite effect. Advertisers seek to shift the *dd* curve. Even if each person consumed the same amount of a good, a growth in population would have the effect of increasing the total market demand for a product. If people think that a boom is about to get under way, they may increase their purchases now in order to beat the gun.[1] Still other factors operate all the time to shift demand.

CROSS RELATIONS OF DEMAND

Everyone knows that raising the price of tea will decrease the amount demanded of tea. We have seen that it will also affect the amounts demanded of other commodities. For example, a higher price for tea will lower the demand for a commodity such as lemon; i.e., it will shift the whole demand schedule of lemon downward. But it will also increase the amount demanded of coffee. Probably it will have little or no effect on the demand curve for salt.

Demand curve shifts with change in income or in another good's price:

SHIFTS IN THE DEMAND CURVE

FIG. 22-2. Higher income will shift *dd* to *d′d′*. (Explain why; and why lowering income will shift *dd* to *d″d″*.) Similarly, a rise in price of coffee, which is a substitute for tea, might shift tea's *dd* out to *d′d′*. (What would a cut in coffee price do? Can you explain why a great rise in price of lemon, a complementary good used with tea, might shift *dd* leftward to *d″d″*?)

We say, therefore, that tea and coffee are rival, or competing, products, or *substitutes*. Tea and lemon, on the other hand, are cooperating, or complementary, commodities—so-called *complements*. In-between pairs such as tea and salt are said to represent *independent* commodities. The reader should classify such pairs as beef and pork, turkey and cranberry sauce, automobiles and gasoline, truck and railroad freight, oil and coal.

Besides showing effects of income changes, Fig. 22-2 also illustrates the effect of these changed prices of other goods. A fall in the price of coffee may well cause our consumer to buy less tea; the demand curve shifts to, say, *d″d″*. But what if the price of lemon were to fall? The resulting change on this *dd* may not be very large. But if there is any change, it will be in the direction of *increased* tea purchases—a rightward shift of *dd*. Why this difference in response? Because coffee is a rival, a *substitute* product for tea; lemon is a *complementary* commodity to tea.

---

[1]In fact, when I see in today's paper that the price of tea is going up, I may rush out to buy more: this may seem superficially to be an exception to the law of downward-sloping demand, but (as discussed on page 382, footnote 3) it can be reconciled with that law when we realize that I am buying more because of the *rising* price of tea and because I want to be able to buy less of it tomorrow when its price will have stabilized at a high level. Despite this *dynamic* effect of *changing* prices, it remains true that at a steady high price for tea, I shall consume less than at a steady low price.

THE LAW OF DIMINISHING MARGINAL UTILITY

Return to the law of downward-sloping demand, which is so basic a law that we have to investigate the economic principles operating in the background to justify and explain it. A century ago economists hit upon the fundamental notion of "marginal utility," and it was from this analysis that they felt able for the first time to derive the demand curve and explain its properties. There is space here only to sketch the basic notions underlying such theories, leaving refinements and developments to specialized treatises on advanced economic theory.

As a customer you will buy a good because you feel it gives you satisfaction or "utility." A first unit of a good gives you a certain amount of psychological utility. Now imagine consuming a second unit. Your total utility goes up because the second unit of the good gives you some additional utility. What about adding a third and fourth unit of the same good?

A century ago economists proclaimed an important law that sounds like the law of diminishing returns; but instead of referring to the extra output added by successive doses of an input (as in Table 2-2 on p. 24), this is a law about the behavior of psychological utility as you add more and more of a good. It can be described by words, by a table of numbers, and by two curves.

The law of diminishing marginal utility. **As you consume more of the same good, your** *total* **(psychological) utility increases. However, let us use the term marginal utility to refer to "the extra utility added by one extra last unit of a good." Then, with successive new units of the good, your total utility will grow at a slower and slower rate because of a fundamental tendency for your psychological ability to appreciate more of the good to become less keen. This fact, that the increments in total utility fall off, economists describe as follows:**

As the amount consumed of a good increases, the *marginal utility* of the good (or the extra utility added by its last unit) tends to decrease.

Column (2) of Table 22-1 shows that *total utility* enjoyed increases as Q grows, but at a decreasing rate. Column (3) measures *marginal utility* as the increment of total utility resulting when one last unit of the good is added; the fact that marginal utilities in the table are declining exemplifies the law of diminishing marginal utility.

Figure 22-3(a) pictures how total utility increases, but at a decreasing rate. Figure 22-3(b) depicts marginal utilities—increments of utility (not the total of utility itself). Whether we work with sizable units of the good and measure utilities by blocks and steps, or whether we smooth the drawings by use of the brown and blue curves to reflect continuously divisible units, the law of diminishing marginal utility means that the relations in Fig. 22-3(b) must slope downward and—what is exactly the same thing—that the total utility relations in Fig. 22-3(a) must look concave (from below), reflecting total utility's growth becoming less and less.

The validity of the law of diminishing marginal utility seemed probable to economists of an earlier generation as they looked into their own minds for their own psychological reactions to extra consumption. These findings of *introspection* seemed strengthened when they learned about numerous laboratory experiments by psychologists of the 1850s.

The law of decreasing marginal utility can be shown by numbers or curves:

(1) QUANTITY OF A GOOD CONSUMED	(2) TOTAL UTILITY	(3) MARGINAL UTILITY
0	0	
		4
1	4	
		3
2	7	
		2
3	9	
		1
4	10	
		0
5	10	

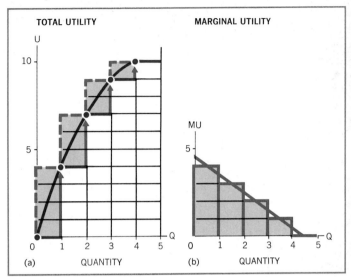

TABLE 22-1. Although *total utility* rises with consumption, it does so at a decreasing rate. This means that marginal utility—the extra utility added by each last extra unit of the good—will be decreasing. From this psychological fact, older economists prepared their demonstration of the law of downward-sloping demand. (Note similarity to Chapter 2's law of diminishing returns.)

FIG. 22-3. The blue blocks show the extra utility added by each new unit. The fact that total utility increases at a decreasing rate is shown on the right by the declining steps of marginal utility. If we make our units smaller and smaller, the steps in total utility are smoothed out and total utility becomes the smooth brown curve. Now *smoothed marginal utility is shown in (b) by the blue downward-falling smooth curve, and* marginal utility becomes indistinguishable from the *slope* of the smooth curve of (a).[2]

Suppose you blindfold a man and ask him to hold out his hand, palm up. Now place a weight on his palm; he certainly will notice it. As you add more units of weight, he notices their addition too. But after his palm is carrying a good deal of weight, you can add just as big a weight as you did in the beginning, and yet this time he will reply that he is not conscious of any addition. In other words, the greater the *total* weight he is already carrying, the *less* will be the effect of an extra or *marginal* unit of weight.

When older economists learned that perception of sound, light, and other sensations seemed to show a similar *Weber-Fechner* law of decreasing marginal effect, this—rightly or wrongly— gave them even greater confidence in the economic law of diminishing marginal utility.[3]

---

[2]NOTE: It will be found that the sum of all the marginal utilities in Table 22-1's Column (3), if reckoned above some point, must equal the amount of total utility in Column (2) at that point. [Thus, 4 + 3 + 2 does give us the 9 shown in Column (2). What does 4 + 3 give?] In terms of Fig. 22-3(b), the area under the marginal utility curve, as measured by blocks or by the area under the smooth curve, must add up to equality with the numerical height of the total utility curve shown in (a)—it being understood that we make our comparison at a specified quantity level. All this portrays the fact that total utility is the sum of all the marginal (or extra) utilities added from the beginning.

[3]The modern generation, however, has found that the exact way in which one measures utility is not particularly important to explain the price-quantity demand curve. Some economists would still use introspection. Others would want to observe whether you had to give a man 2/1 odds to get him to wager on the toss of a fair coin the loss of a new hat against the winning of a second new hat; and

THE PROCESS OF RATIONAL CHOICE

What is the fundamental equilibrium condition that has to be satisfied if a consumer is spending his income on the variously priced goods so as to make himself truly best off in terms of utility or well-being? Certainly he would not expect that the last egg he is buying brings him exactly the same marginal utility as the last lamb chop he is buying. For lamb chops cost much more apiece than eggs. On reflection, it would seem more reasonable that he should keep buying a good which costs twice as much per unit as another until it ends up in his equilibrium bringing him just twice as much in marginal utility. .

In short, if he has arranged his consumption so that every single good is bringing him marginal utility just exactly *proportional* to its price, then it would seem that he could not better himself by departing from such an equilibrium. This fundamental condition can be stated as follows:

"Marginal utility proportional to respective price" means that there must be exact equality among the *ratios* of each good's marginal utility divided by its price. These *MU/P* ratios for each good are called the marginal utility *per dollar* that the consumer gets from spending his money on that good.

So final equilibrium of maximized well-being will require that there be *equality* of each and every good's *marginal utility per dollar.*

For those who like numerical examples, the next section digresses to work out a food and clothing case (and can be skipped at a first reading).

NUMERICAL EXAMPLE OF OPTIMAL CHOICE

Let's apply this MU/P reasoning to an actual two-good choice. Table 22-2 considers the case of clothing and food. Clothing price, P_1, is assumed to be $1. Column (2) of Table 22-2 lists clothing's marginal utility per dollar, MU_1/P_1: thus, the first dollar spent on clothing brings you 1 clothing unit and $MU/P_1 = 4$. A second dollar spent on it brings in a marginal utility of only 3 utils. Why? Because of the law of diminishing marginal utility. Total utility has gone up from 4 to 7 (but not to 8!). What would a third and fourth dollar spent on clothing alone bring? Evidently they bring marginal utilities per dollar of 2 and 1, with total utility from 4 clothing units ending up at 10 utils.

To have a problem of choice, you must be confronted with at least two goods. So Column (3) brings into the picture a new good, food. It also is assumed to cost $1; that is, $P_2 = \$1$. Being a necessity, food starts out with a very high MU_2 per dollar, namely 10. And at first its MU_2/P_2 drops very little, being 9 for the second unit. But once you

---

they would conclude from this that the marginal utility of the second hat decreases to half the marginal utility of the first hat. Such economists thus hope to measure his marginal utility "behavioristically" rather than introspectively. Probably the majority of economists in advanced graduate theory today would feel that what counts for consumer demand theory is whether certain situations have *more* total utility than others. These economists would not care to look for any numerical measure of utility beyond such "greater or less than" comparison; they would use the "indifference curves" of the Appendix to this chapter. By any of these methods, the general properties of the market demand curve can be securely established. (NOTE: Demand theory never has any need to make *interpersonal* comparisons of utility that involve adding or comparing utilities of *different* minds.)

You maximize utility by choosing items with greatest marginal utility per dollar, until equality is reached:

MARGINAL UTILITIES PER DOLLAR WHEN EACH GOOD HAS $P = \$1$		
(1)	(2) GOOD 1 CLOTHING MU_1/P_1	(3) GOOD 2 FOOD MU_2/P_2
UNIT OF GOOD		

TABLE 22-2. Food, being a necessity, has its MU_2 falling faster than MU_1 of clothing falls. In choosing how to spend each last dollar, the rule that gives you most total utility is this: Select any item whose MU/P is largest; if $MU_1/P_1 = MU_2/P_2$, you can be indifferent. (Hence, successive dollars of income go for food first, food second, clothing third, clothing fourth, . . . —because $10 > 9 > 4 > 3. \ldots$)

INCOME BUDGETARY PATTERN OF DEMAND								
INCOME (per day)	$1	$2	$3	$4	$5	$6	$7	$8
Clothing (demanded)	0	0	1	2	3	3	——	4
Food (demanded)	1	2	2	2	2	3	——	4

TABLE 22-3. By choosing items in Table 22-2 with highest MU/P (i.e., marginal utility *per dollar*), you find your optimal equilibrium pattern of demand. Thus, second dollar of income goes all to double food, and third dollar finally brings in clothing.

are fed, your MU_2 and MU_2/P_2 drop very rapidly—to $1\frac{3}{4}$ for the third unit of food and to $\frac{3}{4}$ for the fourth unit.[4]

Now to choose. Start out with daily income of only $1. Your best buy is food: 1 unit. Why? Because 10 utils from a dollar spent on food is better than 4 utils from a dollar spent on clothing.

Now consider $2 of income. Again, all goes for food. The second food unit brings you 9 utils, which still beats the 4 utils that could come from the first clothing unit.

But now get $3 of income. At last you have enough to buy a luxury: 1 unit of clothing along with your 2 of food. (Why a first unit of clothing rather than a third of food? Because $MU_1/P_1 = 4 > MU_2/P_2 = 1\frac{3}{4}$. QED.)

Table 22-3 shows your budget pattern of food-clothing purchases at different income levels. How was it derived? Verify that you did maximize your total utility from all sources only if you always followed the rule of picking that unit of a good which gives you the larger MU/P. (Can you fill in the $7 blanks as 3 food and 4 clothing? Why?)

So much for the important budgetary patterns of expenditure at different incomes with prices fixed. Can we derive the usual *demand curves with respect to price* from the utility data of Table 22-2? Yes, we can. Imagine that the price of food has halved, to $P_2 = 50$ cents. We want to show that, at unchanged income levels and with P_1 held at $1, the cut in P_2 will indeed increase the quantity demanded of Q_2.

Clearly Table 22-2's clothing column of MU_1/P_1 remains unchanged at 4, 3, 2, 1. But food's column now is $MU_2/\$\frac{1}{2}$ instead of $MU_2/\$1$; this means that the numbers 10, 9, $1\frac{3}{4}$, . . . , to be comparable, would have to be *doubled* to read 20, 18, $3\frac{1}{2}$, ...

---

[4]WARNING: Goods 1 and 2 in Table 22-2 are assumed to have *independently* addable utilities. If they had been rival goods, like tea and coffee, the MU of the third tea unit would go down when you got one more coffee unit. If they had been complementary goods, like tea and lemon, the MU of the third tea unit would go up when you got one more lemon unit. The $MU_1/P_1 = MU_2/P_2$ rule would still hold in maximizing equilibrium; but you couldn't get these from *separate* columns. You would need the Appendix indifference contours to handle such a case, or more complicated analysis.

Now let us make our controlled experiment. Hold income constant at $1 per day and P_1 at $1, but cut P_2 to 50 cents. Now for each dollar we can buy 1 clothing unit, as before, or 2 food units. Because the new numbers 20 and 18 are both greater than 4, our first two half-dollars will both be spent on food. Consequently, comparing this 2-of-food result with the first entry in Table 22-3, which had shown only 1 of food bought, we see that the price reduction of food has definitely caused its quantity bought to increase—even though it is a necessity. (Actually, its price elasticity, as calculated by any of the formulas for Chapter 20, happens by accident to turn out to be unity here, since the same total receipts are spent on it at both prices.)

We shall omit the calculations to show how any other level of income would be spent in the new situation,[5] and how any other cuts in the price of P_2 do tend to increase Q_2 bought.

EQUILIBRIUM CONDITION: EQUAL MARGINAL UTILITIES PER DOLLAR FOR EVERY GOOD

After our digression for a numerical example, we restate the basic principle.

A consumer with a fixed income and facing given market prices of different goods can come into his equilibrium of maximum satisfaction or utility only when he acts thus:
Law of equal marginal utilities per dollar. **Each good—such as sugar—is demanded up to the point where the marginal utility per dollar (or penny) spent on it is exactly the same as the marginal utility of a dollar (or penny) spent on any other good—such as salt. If any one good gave more marginal utility per dollar, the consumer would gain by taking money away from other goods and spending more on that good—up to the point where the law of diminishing marginal utility brought its marginal utility per dollar down to equality. If any good gave less marginal utility per dollar than the common level, the consumer would buy less of it until the marginal utility of the last dollar spent on it had risen back to the common level.[6]**

This fundamental condition of consumer equilibrium can be written in terms of the marginal utilities and prices of the different goods as follows:

$$\frac{MU \text{ Good } 1}{P_1} = \frac{MU \text{ Good } 2}{P_2} = \frac{MU \text{ Good } 3}{P_3} = \cdots = \text{common } MU \text{ per dollar of income}$$

The logical meaning of this condition rather than the rote memorizing of a formula is, of course, what matters.

Nor need all this apply just to spending money. Suppose you have only a certain number of hours to spend on study for examinations. If you are so uncreative as to seek merely to maximize your grade average, how should you allocate your time? By spending equal hours on each course? Not necessarily. You have to shift from history to chemistry, from

[5] See Figs. 22-9 and 22-10 in the Appendix for a rigorous derivation of demand responses to income and price changes. The next footnote discusses some problems due to lumpiness of units.
[6] At a few places in economics the indivisibility of units is important and cannot be glossed over. Thus, Cadillacs do not come like peas, and their indivisibility may matter. Suppose I buy one but definitely not two Cadillacs. Then the marginal utility of the first car is enough larger than the marginal utility of the same number of dollars spent elsewhere to induce me to buy this first unit. The marginal utility that the second Cadillac would bring is enough less to ensure I do *not* buy it. When indivisibility matters, our equality rule for equilibrium can be restated as an inequality rule. NOTE: As mentioned, the validity of the equilibrium condition can be made quite independent of how, or whether, we measure utility *numerically*. Only relative marginal utilities matter.

German to economics, until you are getting *the same marginal grade advantage from the last minute spent in each alternative use.*[7] The same marginal rule can show you how to allocate your time on a pleasant weekend. Our marginal equilibrium condition is not merely a law of economics; it is a law of logic itself.

A final remark may be in order at this point. A consumer is not expected to be a wizard at numbers or graphs, nor need he be, to approximate the demand behavior of this chapter. He can even make most of his decisions unconsciously or out of habit. As long as he is fairly consistent in his tastes and actions, all he has to do to make the present analysis relevant is to avoid repeating those mistakes which he found in the past did not give him the goods and services he most wanted and to avoid making wild and unpredictable changes in his buying behavior. If enough people act in this way, our scientific theory will provide a good measure of approximation to the facts.

SUBSTITUTION- AND INCOME-EFFECTS: A DIGRESSION

The concept of marginal utility has lent credence to the fundamental law of downward-sloping demand. A different way of looking at the demand's downward sloping makes no mention of marginal utility explicitly; but it does lead rigorously to the desired result, and does provide an interesting insight into the factors that tend to make the elasticity of response of quantity to price very great or very little.

Substitution-effect   The first factor explaining diminishing consumption when price rises is an obvious one. If the price of tea goes up while other prices do not, then tea has become relatively dearer. It pays, therefore, to *substitute* other goods for tea in order to maintain one's standard of living most cheaply. Thus tea becomes a relatively dearer source of stimulation than before, and less of it will be bought and more of coffee or cocoa. Similarly, a rise in price of movies relative to stage plays may cause the consumer to seek less of his amusement in the dearer direction. The consumer is doing here only what every businessman does when rises in the price of one productive factor cause him to adjust his production methods so as to substitute cheap inputs for the dear inputs. By this process of substitution, he is able to produce the same output at least total cost. Similarly do consumers buy satisfaction at least cost.

Income-effect   In the second place, when your money income is fixed, being forced to buy a good at a higher price is just like having a decrease in your *real* income or purchasing power, particularly if you have been buying a great deal of the raised commodity. With a lower real income you will now want to buy less tea. Thus, unless a good is an "inferior" good like bologna or margarine, the income-effect will *reinforce* the substitution-effect in making the demand curve downward-sloping.[8]

---

[7] This does not mean that you study to get the same 89 grade in all classes. Your average may be maximized with grades of 93, 92, 90, and 81, but with each marginal hour of study adding one-tenth of a grade point to any subject.

[8] Income- and substitution-effects not only explain the downward slope of demand but also explain a possible, albeit extremely rare, exception to that law. When the 1845 Irish famine greatly raised the

Of course, the quantitative importance of each of these effects varies with the good in question and with the consumer. Under some circumstances the resulting demand curve is very *elastic:* as where the consumer has been spending a good deal on the commodity and where ready substitutes are available—for example, a drunkard's demand for one brand of gin. But if a commodity, such as salt, involves only a small fraction of the consumer's budget, is not easily replaceable by other items, and is needed in small amounts to complement more important items, then demand will tend to be *inelastic.*

THE PARADOX OF VALUE

The preceding theories help to explain a famous question that troubled Adam Smith in *The Wealth of Nations.* He asked, How is it that water, which is so very useful that life is impossible without it, has such a low price—while diamonds, which are quite unnecessary, have such a high price?

Today even a beginning student can give a correct answer to this problem. "That's simply explained," he can write on an examination. "The supply and demand curves for water are such that they intersect at a very low price, while the supply and demand curves for diamonds are such that they intersect at a high price." (Today he could add that water is no longer all that cheap.)

This is not an incorrect answer. Adam Smith could not have given it because supply and demand curves as descriptive tools had not yet been invented, and were not to be for 75 years or more. But after he had mastered the new lingo, old Adam Smith would naturally ask the question, "But *why* do supply and demand for water intersect at such a low price?"

The answer is by now easy to phrase. It consists of two parts:

Diamonds are very *scarce,* the cost of getting *extra* ones is high; and water is relatively *abundant,* with its cost low in many areas of the world. This first part would have seemed reasonable to even the classical economists of more than a century ago, who would probably have let it go at that, and would not have known how to reconcile these facts about *cost* with the equally valid fact that the world's water is more *useful* than the world's supply of diamonds. In fact, Adam Smith never did quite resolve the paradox. He was content simply to point out that the "value in use" of a good—its total contribution to economic welfare—is not the same thing as its "value in exchange"—the total money value or revenue for which it will sell. Smith had not arrived at the point where he knew how to distinguish *marginal* utility from *total* utility!

Today, we should add to the above cost considerations a second truth:

---

price of potatoes, families who consumed a lot of potatoes merely because they were too poor to consume much meat might have ended up consuming *more* rather than less of the high-*P* potatoes. Why? Because now they had to spend so much on potatoes, the necessary of life, as to make it quite impossible to afford any meat at all and hence were forced to become even more dependent than before on potatoes. In brief, the substitution-effect was here overcome by the perverse income-effect applicable to a peculiar "inferior" good, such as the potato, which tends to *decrease* in the poor man's budget when incomes *rise.* This *curiosum* is attributed to Sir Robert Giffen, a Victorian economist. (NOTE: In the case of ordinary inferior goods on which we spend little money, the perverse income-effects will not outweigh the substitution-effects and produce the odd Giffen case.)

The *total* utility of water does not determine its price or demand. Only the relative marginal utility and cost of the *last* little bit of water determine its price. Why? Because people are free to buy or not buy that last little bit. If water is priced higher than its marginal utility, then that last unit cannot be sold. Therefore the price must fall until it reaches exactly the level of usefulness of the last little bit, no more and no less. Moreover, because every unit of water is exactly like any other unit and because there is only one price in a competitive market, *every unit must sell for what the last least useful unit sells for.* (As one student put the matter: The theory of economic value is easy to understand if you just remember that the tail wags the dog: concentrate on *marginal* and not on *total* utility.)

Paradox resolved: The more there is of a commodity, the less the relative desirability of its *last* little unit becomes, even though its *total* usefulness grows as we get more of the commodity. So, it is obvious why a large amount of water has a low price. Or why air is actually a free good despite its vast usefulness. The many *later* units pull down the market value of *all* units.

CONSUMER'S SURPLUS

The foregoing discussion emphasizes that the accounting system which records the "total economic value" or revenue of a good (price × quantity) differs from the measurement necessary to record "total welfare." The total economic value of air is zero; its contribution to welfare, very great.[9] Similarly, if we increase the quantity produced of a good, we increase the community's welfare; but if it is a good like wheat, whose demand is inelastic, we do at the same time destroy some economic value.

Thus, there is always a sort of gap between total utility and total market value. This gap is in the nature of a *surplus*, which the consumer gets because he "receives more than he pays for."
   Nor does he benefit at the expense of the seller. In a swap, one party does not lose what the other gains. Unlike energy, which cannot be created or destroyed, the well-being of all participants is increased by trade.

It is easy to see how this consumer's surplus arises. Each unit of a good that the consumer buys costs him only as much as the last unit is worth. But by our fundamental law of diminishing marginal utility, the *earlier* units are worth *more* to him than the last. Thus, he enjoys a surplus on each of these earlier units. When trade stops benefiting him and giving him a surplus, he stops buying.

As final clinching evidence that the consumer always receives a surplus, we may cite the fact that a ruthless seller could present the consumer with an ultimatum—what is called an "all-or-none" offer: "Either you pay me an extra amount of money for the whole block of the good that you are consuming, or you must go without all the units, from first to last. Take it or leave it!" The consumer would certainly be willing to pay extra rather than do altogether without the good of this discriminating monopolist.

[9] Or, as Adam Smith would say, its value in use is very great; its value in exchange, negligible.

How is the concept of consumer's surplus used? It is sometimes needed to help make correct social decisions. Suppose a new branch road would cost your town $100,000. Being free to all, it is expected to bring in no dollar revenues, and all the utility it gives to each user will represent his consumer's surplus. (To avoid extraneous interpersonal difficulties, let us assume there are 1,000 users all exactly alike in income and in their benefit from the road, and all equally worthy.) If each such similar man enjoys $100 (the road's *per capita* cost) or more of consumer's surplus from the road, they should all vote to build the road. If the consumer's surplus of each is less than $100, it is uneconomical for them to tax themselves for this public project.[10]

Many ingenious ways have been suggested for measuring consumer's surplus, but they are of no particular significance here.[11] The important thing is to see how lucky the citizens of modern efficient communities really are. The *privilege of being able to buy a vast array of goods at low prices cannot be overestimated.*

This is a humbling thought. If ever a person becomes arrogantly proud of *his* economic productivity and *his* level of real earnings, let him pause and reflect. If he were transported with all his skills and energies intact to a primitive desert island, how much would his money earnings buy? Indeed, without capital machinery, without rich resources, without other labor, and above all without the technological knowledge which each generation inherits from society's past, how much could *he* produce? It is only too clear that all of us reap the benefits of an economic world we never made. As L. T. Hobhouse said:

The organizer of industry who thinks that he has "made" himself and his business has found a whole social system ready to his hand in skilled workers, machinery, a market, peace and order—a vast apparatus and a pervasive atmosphere, the joint creation of millions of men and scores of generations. Take away the whole social factor and we have not Robinson Crusoe, with his salvage from the wreck and his acquired knowledge, but the naked savage living on roots, berries, and vermin.

SUMMARY

1   The market demand curve for all consumers is derived by adding *horizontally* the separate demand curves of each consumer. A demand curve can shift for many reasons, such as

[10] See page 615, footnote 4, for a diagram illustrating this all-or-nothing social decision.

[11] In the special case where money provides a firm measuring rod of utility, consumer's surplus is easily measured and depicted. In Fig. 22-4, when the consumer buys *OM* sugar at *ON* price for each, he pays the total revenue indicated by the blue rectangular area *OMEN;* but that much sugar gives him total utility (expressed in money) which is the whole area *OMER;* the light triangular area *NER* left over is his consumer's surplus, and it obviously will be greater the lower the price becomes.

This geometrical concept is useful in illustrating how taxes, farm quotas, and monopolistic interferences create social inefficiency and loss.

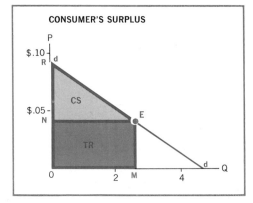

FIG. 22-4.

the following: Normally, a rise in income will shift *dd* rightward, thus increasing demand; a rise in the price of a *substitute good* (coffee for tea, and so forth) will also create such an upward shift in demand; a rise in the price of a *complementary good* (such as lemon in its relation to tea) will represent a cross effect that shifts the *dd* curve downward and leftward. Still other factors—such as changing tastes, population, or expectations—can increase or decrease demand.

2   The concepts of total and marginal utility were introduced to explain the law of downward-sloping demand. The fact that *total utility* rises with each new marginal addition of a good but at a decreasing rate of growth can be expressed in a technical way. With equal additions to a good's quantity, its *marginal utility* (which is the increment of utility coming from adding a last extra unit of quantity) tends to decrease.

3   To get the most utility, the consumer must achieve a fundamental marginal condition for demand equilibrium: A consumer has not maximized his well-being until he has succeeded in *making equal the respective marginal utilities per dollar spent on each and every good.* (BEWARE: The marginal utility of a $25-per-ounce bottle of perfume is not equal to the marginal utility of a 10-cent glass of cola; but their marginal utilities divided by price per unit—that is, their marginal utilities per last dollar, MU/P—are all to be equalized in optimizing equilibrium.)

This is a fundamental rule of logic that transcends demand theory: If you want to allocate any limited resource among competing uses, whenever the marginal advantage in one use happened to be greater than in another, you can benefit by transferring from the low-marginal-advantage use to the high—until a final equilibrium is reached at which all have become equal.

4   Without using the marginal utility concept explicitly, we can gain new insight into the factors making for downward-sloping demand by analyzing the effect of a price rise into (1) its *substitution-effect* component and (2) its *income-effect* component. When P for a good rises, you tend to maintain the same level of well-being by *substituting* other goods for the good that has just become dearer. Reinforcing this decrease in a good's Q that arises out of substitution is the income-effect: Since you ordinarily buy less of the good in question when your family income is lower, the rise in its price—which has produced a *drop in your real income* or purchasing power—thus induces a further cut in consumption as the result of your now having a lower real income.

5   Adam Smith's paradox of value—that a commodity important for welfare may sell for less in the market than one less important—is clarified by the distinction between the concept of marginal and total utility. The scarcity of a good, as determined by its cost (i.e., supply conditions), interacts with the market demand for the good as determined by the usefulness of its *marginal* unit (not the usefulness of the *total* stock of the good).

6   The fact that market price is determined by marginal rather than total utility is dramatized by the concept of *consumer's surplus.* Since we pay in the market the same

price for each unit that the marginal unit is worth to us, we reap a consumer's surplus on all the previous units. This consumer's surplus reflects the benefit we gain from being able to buy at low prices, rather than being confronted by a ruthless monopolist who insists we pay him for the whole of our consumption just what that total is worth to us. However difficult it may be to quantify consumer's surplus, advanced treatises show it is a concept relevant for many social decisions—such as deciding when the community should incur the heavy initial expenses of a road or bridge.

Without reading the Appendix, we can go from the utility background of demand to the next chapter's cost background of supply.

QUESTIONS FOR DISCUSSION

1   As you add horizontally the demands of more and more people, the aggregate market curve begins to look flatter and flatter on the same scale. Show that this merely reflects the fact that the same cut in price induces more new sales from many buyers than from few. (NOTE: Elasticity need not change. Guess why. HINT: E is dimensionless, unaffected by scale changes.)

2   List several goods in order of their responsiveness to higher income.

3   Which of the following goods do you think could be classified as *complementary, substitute,* and *independent* goods: beef, ketchup, lamb, mint sauce, cigarettes, gum, pork, butter, paperbacks, taxis, and oleomargarine? Illustrate the resulting shift in the demand curve for one good when price of another good goes up. How would a change in income affect the demand curve for butter? The demand curve for oleomargarine?

4   Explain the difference between marginal and total utility. State the law of diminishing marginal utility. Be sure you understand what it means in terms of numbers and diagrams.

5   Why is it nonsensical to say, "In equilibrium, the marginal utilities of all goods must be exactly equal"? Reword to give a correct statement and explain.

6   If you wanted to avoid using the marginal utility concept, show that you still can justify the law of downward-sloping demand by reasoning that involved (1) substitution-effect and (2) income-effect.

7   How much would you be willing to pay rather than give up *all* movies? How much do you spend on movies? Estimate roughly your consumer's surplus.

Review your understanding of the following concepts:

market versus individual demand

demand shifts from income and
   other changes

substitute, complementary, and
   independent goods

income-effect and substitution-effect

law of diminishing marginal utility

equating marginal utility of last dollar
   spent on each good, $MU_1/P_1 = MU_2/P_2$

value in use versus value in exchange

paradox of marginal versus total utility

consumer's surplus

APPENDIX: Geometrical Analysis of Consumer Equilibrium

It is instructive to show graphically, and without using the language of numerical utility, exactly what the consumer's equilibrium position looks like.

THE INDIFFERENCE CURVE

We start out by considering a consumer who buys only two commodities, say, food and clothing, at definite quoted prices. We suppose the consumer can tell us whether (1) he prefers a given combination or batch of the two goods, say, 3 units of food and 2 of clothing, to some second combination or batch, say, 2 units of food and 3 of clothing, or (2) he is "indifferent" as between the two combinations.

Let us suppose that, actually, these two batches are equally good in the eyes of our consumer—that he is indifferent as to which of the two he receives. Let us go on to list in Table 22-4 some of the other combinations of goods between which he is likewise indifferent.

Figure 22-5 shows these combinations diagrammatically. We measure units of clothing upon one axis and units of food upon the other. Each of our four combinations or batches, A, B, C, D, is represented by its point. But these four are by no means the only combinations that would leave our consumer just indifferent as between them. Another batch, such as $1\frac{1}{2}$ units of food

and 4 of clothing, might be ranked as equal to any of A, B, C, or D above, and there are many others not shown.

The curved line of Fig. 22-5, linking up the four points, is an "indifference curve." *Every* **point thereon represents a different combination of the two goods; and the indifference curve is so drawn that, if our consumer were given his choice of any point on it, he would not know which one to choose. All would be equally desirable to him, and he would be indifferent as to which batch he received.**

It should be noted that this indifference curve is of convex curvature viewed from below. As we move downward and to the right along the curve—a movement which implies increasing the quantity of food and reducing that of clothing—the slope of the curve becomes flatter. The curve is drawn so because this illustrates a property which seems most often to hold true in real life and which we may call the "law of substitution":

The scarcer a good, the greater its relative *substitution* **value; its marginal utility rises relative to the marginal utility of the good that has become plentiful.**

Food-clothing batches which give equal utility are "indifferent":

INDIFFERENCE COMBINATIONS		
	FOOD	CLOTHING
A	1	6
B	2	3
C	3	2
D	4	$1\frac{1}{2}$

TABLE 22-4.   Getting more of one good compensates for giving up something of the other. The consumer likes situation A exactly as well as B, C, or D.

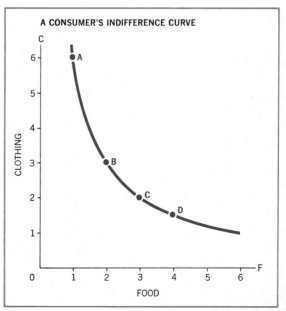

FIG. 22-5.   The food-clothing combinations that yield equal satisfaction can be plotted as a smooth "indifference curve" (or so-called "equal-utility contour"). This is convex (from below) in accord with the law of substitution, which says: As you get more of a good, its "substitution ratio," or "indifference slope," diminishes.

For example, the consumer who is at position A in Table 22-4 is willing to give up 3 units of clothing in order to get a second unit of food; thus, at A, he would swap 3 of his 6 clothing units in exchange for 1 extra food unit. But when he has moved to B, he would sacrifice only 1 of his remaining clothing supply in order to obtain a third food unit—a 1-for-1 swap. For a fourth unit of food, he would sacrifice only $\frac{1}{2}$ unit from his dwindling supply of clothing.

If we join the points A and B of Fig. 22-5, we find that the slope of the resulting line (neglecting its negative sign) has a value of 3. Join B and C, and the slope is 1; join C and D, and the slope is $\frac{1}{2}$. These figures—3, 1, $\frac{1}{2}$—are simply the "swapping terms" that we noted just above.

But to move from A to B is to move a considerable distance along the curve. What about the swapping terms for smaller movements? If the consumer is at A and we consider a movement to the intermediate position (not shown in Table 22-4) of $1\frac{1}{2}$ food and 4 clothing, the swapping ratio would be 4. And it is clear that, as the movement along the curve grows smaller, then the closer the swapping terms come to the actual slope of the indifference curve.[1]

So the slope of the indifference curve is the measure of the terms on which—for very small changes—the consumer would be willing to exchange a little of his supply of one good in return for a little more of the other.

And an indifference curve which is convex in the manner of Fig. 22-5 conforms to the law of substitution earlier noted. As the consumer's food goes up —and his clothing goes down—food must become relatively cheaper and cheaper in order for him to be persuaded to take a little extra food in exchange for a little sacrifice of clothing. The precise shape and slope of an indifference curve will, of course, vary from one consumer to the next; but for this introductory discussion, it seems reasonable to assume that the general convex shape as shown in Fig. 22-5 is typical.

---

[1] By the arithmetic slope of the indifference curve, we mean this: To find the slope of the curve at, say, point B, take a ruler and place it so that it is just tangent to the curve at B—it touches the curve, but does not cross it either above or below B. Mark the points at which the ruler's edge crosses the two axes. The slope is the ratio of the distance cut off on the vertical axis to the distance cut off on the horizontal axis; e.g., at B, the slope is 6/4, or $1\frac{1}{2}$. Intermediate texts refer to the slope of the indifference curve at any point as the "substitution ratio," or "the marginal rate of substitution," or the "*relative* marginal utility ratio" at that point.

THE INDIFFERENCE MAP

Table 22-4 is but one of an infinite number of possible tables. We could have started out with a still higher level of satisfaction or indifference and listed some of the different combinations that belonged to it in the mind of our consumer. One such table might have begun with 2 food and 7 clothing; another with 3 food and 7 clothing. Each table could be portrayed graphically; each has its corresponding curve. Figure 22-6 shows four such curves; the old curve of Fig. 22-5 is now labeled U_3. This figure is analogous to a geographical contour map. A person who walks along the path indicated by a particular height contour on such a map will find that he is neither climbing nor descending; similarly, the consumer who moves from one position to another along a single indifference curve enjoys neither increasing nor decreasing satisfaction from the change in the flow of goods he is getting. Of course, only a few of the possible indifference curves or equal-utility contours are shown in Fig. 22-6.

Note that, as we increase both goods and hence move in a northeasterly direction across this "map," we are crossing successive indifference curves; we are

Every point lies on one of the many indifference curves:

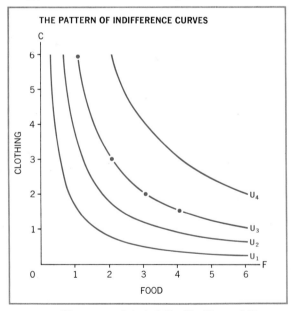

FIG. 22-6. The curves labeled U_1, U_2, U_3, and U_4 represent indifference curves, or equal-utility contours. (Why is it better to be on a farther-out indifference curve?) U_3 is the indifference contour of Fig. 22-5.

Fixed income and market Ps imply limited consumption possibilities:

ALTERNATIVE CONSUMPTION POSSIBILITIES		
	FOOD	CLOTHING
M	4	0
	3	1½
	2	3
	1	4½
N	0	6

TABLE 22-5. The costs of these budgets (reckoned as $1.50F + $1C) all add up to $6 income.

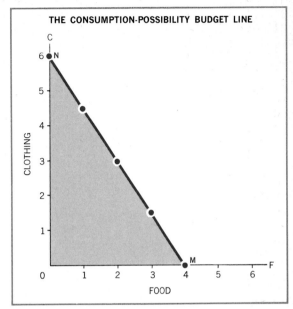

THE CONSUMPTION-POSSIBILITY BUDGET LINE

FIG. 22-7. *NM* is the consumer's consumption-possibility budget line. When he spends just $6 daily, with food and clothing prices $1.50 and $1, he can choose any point on this line. (Why is its slope $1.50/$1 = 3/2?)

reaching higher and higher levels of satisfaction. Unless the consumer is satiated, he would be enjoying increasing satisfaction from receiving increased quantities of *both* goods. Hence, curve U_3 stands for a higher level of satisfaction than U_2; U_4, for a higher level of satisfaction than U_3; etc.

THE CONSUMPTION-POSSIBILITY BUDGET LINE

Now let us set the consumer's indifference map aside for a moment and give him a fixed income. He has, say, $6 per day to spend, and he is confronted with fixed prices for each food and clothing unit—$1.50 for food, $1 for clothing. It is clear that he could spend his money on any one of a variety of alternative combinations of food and clothing. At one extreme, he could buy 4 food units and no clothing; at the other, 6 clothing units and no food. Table 22-5 illustrates some of the possible ways in which his $6 could be allocated.

Figure 22-7 shows these five possible positions on a diagram with axes similar to those of Figs. 22-5 and 22-6. Each position is indicated by a small dot, and it will be noted that they all lie on a straight line, which is labeled *NM*. Moreover, any other attainable point, such as $3\frac{1}{3}$ food units and 1 clothing unit, would lie upon *NM*. The straight line *NM* sums up all the possi-

ble positions that our consumer could occupy in spending his $6 of budget income.[2]

The slope of *NM* (neglecting its sign) is 3/2, which is necessarily the ratio of food price to clothing-price; and the common sense of line *NM* is clear enough. Given these prices, every time our consumer gives up $1\frac{1}{2}$ clothing units (thereby dropping down $1\frac{1}{2}$ vertical units on the diagram), he can gain 1 unit of food (i.e., move east 1 horizontal unit). Or what is the same thing, he can exchange 3 clothing units for 2 food units. We can call *NM* the consumer's "consumption-possibility" (or "budget") line.

THE EQUILIBRIUM POSITION OF TANGENCY

Now we are ready to put our two parts together. The axes of Fig. 22-7 were the same as those of Figs. 22-5 and 22-6. We can superimpose the consumption-

[2]This is so because, if we designate quantities of food and clothing bought as F and C, respectively, total expenditure on food must be $1\frac{1}{2}F$ and total expenditure on clothing, $1C$. If daily income and expenditure is $6, the following equation must hold: $6 = $1\frac{1}{2}F + $1C$. This is a simple linear equation, the equation of the budget line *NM*. NOTE:

Arithmetic slope of $NM = $1\frac{1}{2} \div 1
$$= \text{price of food} \div \text{price of clothing}$$

Equilibrium is where consumer has reached highest satisfaction level:

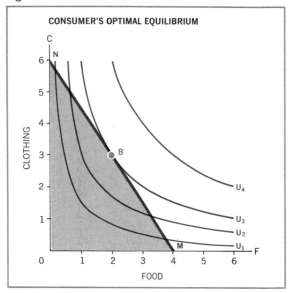

CONSUMER'S OPTIMAL EQUILIBRIUM

FIG. 22-8. At B the consumer reaches highest indifference curve attainable with his fixed income. B represents tangency of consumption-possibility budget line with highest indifference curve. (Why? If slopes were unequal, NM would *intersect* a U contour and he could cross over onto higher satisfaction levels.) At tangency point B, substitution ratio equals price ratio P_F/P_C. This means that all goods' marginal utilities are proportional to their prices, with marginal utility of the last dollar spent on every good being equalized—as demonstrated in the chapter's main text.

possibility budget line NM upon the consumer's indifference map, as in Fig. 22-8. He is free to move anywhere along NM. Positions to the right and above NM are barred to him unless he has more than $6 of income to spend; and positions to the left and below NM are unimportant, since we assume that he will want to spend the full $6.

Where will the consumer move? Obviously, to that point which yields the greatest satisfaction; or, in other words, to the highest available indifference curve, which in this case must be at point B. At B, the consumption-possibility line just touches—but does not cross[3]—the indifference curve U_3; at this point of tangency is found the highest utility contour he can reach.

[3] At any point on NM other than B, NM is crossing indifference curves. And as long as the consumer can keep crossing indifference curves, he can keep moving to higher ones.

Geometrically, the consumer is at equilibrium where the slope of his consumption-possibility budget line is exactly equal to the slope of his indifference curve. And as already noted, the slope of the consumption-possibility line is the price of food ratio to clothing

We may say, then, that optimal equilibrium is attained when the consumer's *substitution* ratio is just equal to the ratio of food price to clothing price.[4]

CHANGES IN INCOME AND PRICE

Our understanding of the process will be furthered by considering the effects of (1) a change in money income and (2) a change in the price of one of the two goods.

Income change   Assume, first, that the consumer's daily income is halved, the two prices remaining unchanged. We could prepare another table, similar to Table 22-4, showing the consumption possibilities that are now open to him. Plotting these points on a diagram such as Fig. 22-9, we should find that the new consumption-possibility budget line occupies the position $N'M'$ in Fig. 22-9. The line has made a *parallel* shift inward.[5] The consumer is now free to move only along this new budget line. Again he will move to the highest attainable indifference curve, or to the point B'. A similar tangency condition for optimal equilibrium again applies.[6]

Single-price change   Now return our consumer to his previous daily income of $6, but assume that the price of food rises from $1.50 to $3. Again we must examine the change in the consumption-possibility budget line. This time we find that it has pivoted on the point N and is now NM'',[7] as in Fig. 22-10.

The common sense of such a shift is clear. Since

[4] The substitution ratio, or slope of the indifference curve, can be shown to be nothing but the ratio of the marginal utility of food to the marginal utility of clothing. So our tangency condition is just another way of stating that a good's price and its marginal utility must be proportional in equilibrium—the consumer there getting the same marginal utility from his last penny spent on food as from his last penny spent on clothing (in agreement with page 414).

[5] The equation of the consumption-possibility line is now $3 = 1\frac{1}{2}F + 1C$.

[6] Join B' and B by a smooth gold curve to generate the important budgetary income-expenditure patterns of Fig. 11-1, page 197, or Table 22-3, page 413.

[7] The equation of the consumption-possibility line is now $6 = 3F + 1C$.

When income or a price changes, we find new equilibrium:

FIG. 22-9. An income change shifts the consumption-possibility budget line in a parallel way. Thus, halving income to $3 shifts NM to $N'M'$, moving equilibrium to B'. (Show what doubling income to $12 would do to equilibrium. Pencil in a new tangency point.)

FIG. 22-10. A rise in the price of food makes the consumption-possibility budget line rotate from NM to NM''. New tangency equilibrium is at B'', with less food and either more or less clothing. (Can you handle a change in P_C?)

the price of clothing is unchanged, the point N is just as available as it was before. But since the price of food has risen, point M, which meant 4 food units had been purchasable, is no longer attainable. With food costing $3 per unit, only 2 units can now be bought with a daily income of $6. So the new consumption-possibility line must still pass through N, but it must pivot around N and pass through M'', which is below M. (The new line has a slope of 3/1. Why?)

Equilibrium is now at B''; we have a new tangency situation in that equilibrium. Higher food price has definitely reduced food consumption; higher P_F may change clothing consumption in either direction. (The dd demand curves of this chapter were derivable by plotting the P_F, Q_F data you can read off from the gold curve passing through B and B''.)

To clinch understanding, the interested reader can work out the cases of an increase in income and a fall in the price of clothing or food. (He can connect all the tangency points generated by income changes to get the Engel's budgetary patterns of Chapter 11.)

Balanced-price changes Suppose *all* prices exactly *double*. Then it is easy to see that this is exactly like a *halving* of income. Hence Fig. 22-9's halving of NM to get $N'M'$ will handle this case. This illustrates an important property of consumer demand.

Changing all prices and income in exactly the same proportion leaves equilibrium quantities demanded quite unchanged.

This provides the germ of truth underlying the Quantity Theory of Money and Prices (of Chapter 15 and Chapter 18 Appendix).

SUMMARY TO APPENDIX

1   An "indifference curve" or "equal-utility contour" depicts the points of equally desirable consumption. The indifference contour is usually drawn convex from below, in accordance with the empirical law of diminishing relative marginal utilities (or of substitution ratios).

2   If a consumer has a fixed money income, all of which he spends, and is confronted with market prices of two goods, the consumption-possibility budget line upon which he is free to move is a straight line. The steepness of the line's slope depends on the ratio of the two market prices; how far out it lies depends on the size of his income.

3   The consumer will move along this consumption-possibility line until he reaches the highest indifference curve attainable. At this point, the consumption-possibility line will touch, but not cross, an indifference curve. Hence, equilibrium is at the point of *tangency*, where the *slope of the consumption-possibility line* (the ratio of the prices) exactly equals the *slope of the indifference curve* (the substitution ratio or relative-marginal-utility ratio of the two goods).

4   A fall in income will move the consumption-possibility line parallel inward, usually causing less of both goods to be bought. A change in the price of one good alone will, other things being equal, cause the consumption-possibility line to pivot so as to change its slope. In any case, whatever change has occurred, a new equilibrium point of highest satisfaction will be reached. It is a new point of tangency, where the marginal utility per dollar has become equal in every use. By comparing the new and old equilibrium points, we trace out the usual *dd* demand curve and income pattern.

QUESTIONS FOR DISCUSSION

1   Explain why one indifference curve will go through any point on an indifference map, and why two such curves never cross.

2   If the consumer is at a point on his consumption-possibility line where it *crosses* an indifference curve, explain why he cannot have reached equilibrium. How will he move?

3   Can *you* generate the ordinary *dd* food demand curve from Fig. 22-10? The *dd* for clothing?

4   Give Robinson Crusoe (or Utopia) a production-possibility curve between food and clothing like the curve of Chapter 2. Give him the indifference curves like those of this Appendix. Can you depict the basic equilibrium of any economy from the resulting tangency and interpret its price aspects?

5   *Extra-credit problem* (but only for the brave): Indifference maps can help solve the problem of calculating a "true cost-of-living index number." In Fig. 22-10, begin at B with original $1.50 and $1 prices for F and C. Now double F's price (as in moving from Los Angeles to New York, or from 1975 to 1980). By how much does ($3, $1) exceed ($1.50, $1)? Since clothing P has not gone up, it would be an exaggeration to say that the price level (i.e., the "average" price) has doubled to 200. Here is a better guess: Since we happen to be spending the same fraction of income on the two goods (by coincidence, both before and after in 22-10's example), we average a doubling with no change to get $\frac{1}{2}2 + \frac{1}{2}1 = 1.50$, or an index number of 150, representing a 50 per cent increase in the cost of living.

   This is a good approximation. But actually, Fig. 22-10 can show 150 is a bit too high, as can be seen from two considerations. (1) Suppose your boss, in order to compensate you for the 150 index, does raise your income from $6 to $9. Now you can buy the 2 of F and 3 of C again as at old B. (Verify by arithmetic.) Geometrically, if your boss shifts your NM'' outward by 50 per cent, your new steep budget line will go right through B. (That's really how our averaging computed the number 1.50!) But note that given your choice on this new *steep* line, you will no longer find B to be an equilibrium *tangency*. You can do a bit better by moving northwest of B to a new higher tangency *above* the U_3 contour. So 150 was a bit too high.

   (2) Now we have the hint on how to calculate the *exact* cost-of-living index. Define it as "the minimum ratio by which you must change money income so that the *same level of well-being* can be attained at the *new* prices as was obtained at the *old* prices." (Read and re-

read.) By geometric exploration in Fig. 22-10 you will find that a parallel increase in NM'' of 41 per cent (giving "true" $141 < 150$) will bring you to tangency with the U_3 contour at a point just northwest of B. (Mark it B''' at about $4\frac{1}{4}$ for C and about $1\frac{7}{17}$ for F.) See an advanced text like R. G. D. Allen, *Mathematical Analysis for Economists* (Macmillan, London, 1936) for a thorough treatment of this topic. On reflection you will realize that a rich man's index may differ from a poor man's, if the latter's U_1 contour is of a quite different shape from the former's U_4. Actually, New York City has a higher rich-man's than poor-man's index.

6   Geometry buffs can interpret the accompanying diagrams to show how the efficiency of rationing can be improved on. Before war, Man 2 at brown B_2 is richer than Man 1 at blue B_1. With food scarce in wartime, both men are rationed to R_1 and R_2 points of each's food consumption. Because men have unequal substitution slopes there, gold areas show how *both* can be made better off if the rich man can buy some of the poor man's food ration.

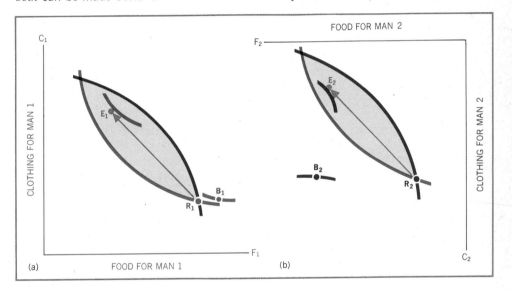

They trade on parallel gold arrows, ending at gold E points (of equal slopes!) where no further mutually beneficial moves are possible. (Can you show that pure competition equilibrium at B_1 and B_2 was "efficient" in the sense that *both* could *not* be made better off? HINT: Slope at B_1 equals slope at B_2 because of common tangency to common market-price ratio. NOTE: Final efficient E situation might also have been reached by a heavy money tax on the rich, with scarce goods being auctioned off to all men at common E_i price ratio. *Reference:* Question 4 of Chapter 27's Appendix uses a similar geometric technique of "box diagram" useful for more advanced "welfare economics" and you might reread the two together.)

Review your understanding of the following concepts:

indifference curves or contours
slope or substitution ratio
consumption-possibility budget line

optimal tangency equilibrium:
P_F/P_C = substitution ratio = MU_F/MU_C
parallel and pivoted shifts

Competitive Supply

23

Cost of production would
have no effect on
competitive price if it
could have none on supply.
JOHN STUART MILL

The last chapter looked behind the market demand curve for its base in terms of the marginal utilities of individuals. It showed how the demand curves of the different individuals in the marketplace can be summed to form the aggregate market demand schedule.

In this chapter we look behind the supply curve of the industry to find its base in the costs of the different competitive firms. A new concept—that of "marginal" or "extra" cost—is seen to be crucial.

We are interested in competitive supply not merely as a descriptive device. Here in this chapter, we are also interested in showing that the marginal cost concept has a crucially important role to play in allocating for any society its resources in the most efficient manner. (We leave to the following chapter a detailed view of the different kinds of costs that are important in economics.)

SUMMING ALL FIRM SUPPLY CURVES TO GET MARKET SUPPLY

Figure 22-1 showed how we add horizontally all individual demand curves to get the aggregate market demand curve. The same horizontal addition now applies to supply.

Suppose we are dealing with a competitive market for fish. How much of this commodity will be brought to market at each different level of market price? Firm A will bring so much to market at a particular price; Firm B will bring so much at this same price; Firm C will bring the amount shown on its supply curve; and so it goes. The total Q that will be brought to market at a given market P will be the sum of all the qs which firms will want to supply at that price. And similarly at any other price.

Summary: **To get the aggregate SS supply curve for a good, we must add horizontally the ss supply curves of the independent producers of that good.**

This is illustrated for two firms by Fig. 23-1. Recalling that the firms' momentary-run supply curves are defined

To get market supply curve, we add all firms' supply curves:

FIG. 23-1. At each price, such as $40, we add quantities supplied by each firm to get total market quantity supplied. This applies to any number of firms. In fact, if there were 1,000 identical firms, the market supply curve could be made to look just like the supply curve of each firm by a careful thousandfold change of horizontal scale in the third diagram; if no horizontal scale change is made, aggregate supply must look flatter than each firm's.

as the inelastic supplies in a time period so short that no variability in output is possible, we can say:

To get the *industry's* vertical momentary supply curve $S_m S_m$, add horizontally, at the same *P*, all firms' vertical momentary supply curves.

Now recall from Chapter 20 (page 365) that Marshall's "intermediate" or "short run" is defined as that period of time in which the firm is stuck with certain fixed commitments, but in which some variable factors of production can be altered so as to produce more output along the various firm's supply curves:

Again, to get the industry's *short-run* supply curve $S_s S_s$, add horizontally at the same *P* the *short-run* supply curves of the fixed number of firms which exist in that short run.

Our problem is to see how a firm's supply curve is determinable from its costs.

DEFINITION OF MARGINAL COST NUMERICALLY AND GRAPHICALLY

Basic to industry supply is Marginal (or extra) Cost. Table 23-1 on page 430 shows how we calculate Marginal Cost: By subtracting the $16,000 total cost of producing $q^* = 400$ units from the $16,040.05 total cost of producing $q = 401$, we find $MC = \$40.05$ for producing 1 more unit beyond q^*; to produce 1 less unit involves a difference, $MC = \$39.95$, or $\$16,000 - 15,960.05$. So at q^* itself we may, by disregarding or averaging over the trifling differences caused by the trifling lumpiness of units, estimate $MC = \$40$.

***Definition:* Marginal Cost at any production level q is the extra cost of producing one extra unit more (or less);[1] it comes from subtracting total dollar costs of adjacent outputs.**

---

[1]WARNING: *MC* is usually not the same as average cost per unit, which we get by dividing total cost by number of units produced: *MC* is extra cost, or incremental cost, or differential cost; or, as we have seen from the use of the word "marginal" in connection with *extra* utility, the appropriate name is indeed Marginal Cost.

Marginal or extra cost can be shown numerically by subtraction:

CALCULATION OF MARGINAL COST

(1) QUANTITY PRODUCED q	(2) TOTAL COST TC	(3) MARGINAL COST MC
399	$15,960.05	
		$39.95
400	16,000.00	40.00
		40.05
401	16,040.05	

TABLE 23-1. The difference in total dollar cost from producing an extra unit is found by subtracting adjacent items of total dollar cost in Column (2). At $q^* = 400$, $MC = \$40$ to a high degree of approximation (as shown by the light-brown average of MC data).

Just as we can calculate MC for $q^* = 400$, we can calculate it for any and every q. Table 23-1 had put a microscope on cost behavior around 400 and 401 units. To see the big picture,[2] let us stand off and see how the Marginal Cost curve behaves at *all* levels of output. Figure 23-2 and Table 23-2 show that Marginal Cost is related to Total Cost in the same way that Fig. 22-3, page 410, related Marginal Utility to Total Utility. From Fig. 23-2(b), you will see this:

MC tends to be U-shaped: ultimately it is rising, even though there may be an initial phase in which MC is falling.

Why can you expect Marginal Cost to be ultimately a rising curve? This takes us back to the law of diminishing returns of Chapter 2, pages 22 to 25. Behind the dollar costs of the firm lies the production relationship between the firm's output and the labor and other inputs it hires. This will be discussed in depth in Chapter 27, but here we can indicate the general logic of the situation.

Suppose some factor is held fixed in the short run we are considering: it could be fixed land, or, in manufacturing, it could be fixed plant capacity. Suppose that we get our varying amounts of q by hiring varying amounts of some input such as labor. If we can always buy labor at the same wage per unit, the only reason why our marginal or extra cost of getting more q should rise would be because the extra product added by each successive unit of labor is going down. Hence, if we do get diminishing returns to the varying labor factor, we shall certainly get increasing Marginal Cost.

Costs and productivity returns are merely opposite sides of the same relationship.

Why does MC often decline *at first*, as shown in Fig. 23-2(b)? Recall that the law of diminishing returns tends *ultimately* to hold: at the beginning, it might be negated by a strong tendency toward *increasing* returns, owing to the economies of large-scale production associated with indivisibility of the productive process and the chance to introduce more elaborate division of labor as scale expands. If at first we have strong *increasing* returns, we must at first have *declining* rather than increasing Marginal Cost.[3]

---

[2] Figure 23-2 and Table 23-2 measure q in units of hundreds; hence, $q = 300, 400, 401, 500$ in Table 23-1 would show here as $q = 3, 4, 4.01, 5$, etc.

[3] Later we shall examine the behavior of Marginal Cost in the long run. Suppose we consider so extended a period of time that nothing can be regarded as fixed. Old plants can wear out and be replaced. New plants can be designed and built. Old land obligations can expire. New land contracts can be made. And so forth. In the long run, as a small firm, we may be able to buy *all* the factors of production in balance at unchanged prices. Now what will happen to long-run costs, particularly long-run MC, if the firm has no fixed factors and can enjoy "constant returns to scale"? (This is defined as a state where there is no reason for diminishing returns to operate, since *all* factors grow in balance, and where all economies of large-scale production have already been realized.) *Answer:* If long-run constant returns to scale holds, then doubling all inputs will exactly double their total dollar costs and will at the same

Marginal Cost is to Total Cost as Marginal Utility is to Total Utility:

(1) OUTPUT (in hundreds) q	(2) TOTAL COST TC	(3) MARGINAL COST MC
0	$ 55	
		$30
1	85	
		25
2	110	
		20
3	130	
		30
4	160	
		50
5	210	

MARGINAL COST

TABLE 23-2. To find the *MC* of producing the fifth unit, we subtract $160 from $210 to get $50. This table can be compared with the Marginal Utility Table 22-3 on page 413. (Source: Table 23-1 but with *q* measured in hundredfold coarser units.)

FIG. 23-2. In (a) a smooth curve has been drawn through the points of *TC*. In (b) a smooth *MC* curve has been drawn through the steps of extra cost. Ultimately *MC* is rising (because of diminishing returns), but it may at first fall, giving the curve a U-shaped contour.

We can summarize the relationship between the productivity laws of returns and the laws of Marginal Cost:

A tendency for varying factors to show diminishing returns when applied to fixed factors implies a tendency for *MC* to be rising. If at first there is increasing returns, there is at first declining *MC*—ultimately followed by diminishing returns and increasing *MC*.

_____

time exactly double total output. Hence, there will be constant Marginal Cost, *MC* being *horizontal* rather than rising or falling. (See page 447 of Chapter 24 for the long-run envelope cost curves.)

HOW TO DETERMINE MAXIMUM-PROFIT COMPETITIVE SUPPLY BY *MC*

It is evident that costs are vital determinants of how much a firm will be willing to supply. It would supply nothing if market P were too low to cover its out-of-pocket expenses, and would supply much if P were very high. To decide how much to supply at each market P, the firm will want to know the *extra* or *marginal* cost to it of each extra unit of q. Thus, consider Firm A back in Fig. 23-1, which was shown supplying 4 (hundred) units at a market price of $40 per unit. Why does $q = 400$ and not 401 or 399?

At first you might be tempted to reply: "Firm A has no choice but $q = 400$ because that is all it can sell at $40—no more, no less." What is wrong with such an answer? It overlooks the fact that this is a model of *perfect competition.*

Definition: A perfect-competitor is too small and unimportant to affect the market price. Like a wheat farmer, he is a "price taker" who can sell *all* he wishes to at the ruling market price. In terms of elasticity of demand, a perfect-competitor faces a (virtually) horizontal *dd* demand curve for *his* product—his elasticity of demand being infinite.[4]

Granted that a perfect-competitor can sell *any q* he chooses at the going P, how does he pick his best q supply response? A perfect-competitor picks the quantity he will supply by referring to his marginal-cost curve, so that $P = MC$. Why? He will do this because he is interested in maximizing the total profit he can earn. Profit is the difference between the total revenue he receives from selling his output and the total cost incurred in producing that output. He increases his total profit so long as the *extra* revenue brought in from the last unit sold is greater than the *extra* cost which that last unit entailed. Total profit reaches its peak—is maximized—when there is no longer any extra profit to be earned by selling extra output. The last little unit he produces and sells is just in balance as far as extra revenue and extra cost are concerned. What is that extra revenue? It is price per unit. What is that extra cost? It is marginal cost.

Specifically, back in Fig. 23-1(a), why did you choose to produce quantity $q^* = 400$ at $P = 40$? Only one answer is correct: Because the 401th unit would involve you in extra (or so-called "marginal") cost of just over $40; and the 399th unit involved you in extra cost of just under $40; so best-profit $q^* = 400$ involves an *extra* or *marginal cost* just exactly equal to price P of $40. (Reread page 430's Table 23-1 for an example.)

DERIVING THE FIRM'S SUPPLY CURVE FROM ITS *MC* CURVE

We have now demonstrated that a competitive firm is at its Maximum-profit position when it is definitely producing all units that had MC less than P, and is definitely not

[4] Figure 23-3 shows the contrast between the industry demand curve *DD*, relating P to the sum of firm demands $Q = q_1 + q_2 + \cdots$, and the *dd* curve facing any one small competitor. If there are thousands of firms in the industry, the draftsman will have to rescale the horizontal axis and focus a microscope on point A of the industry *DD* curve to show how this sloped curve will reappear as the horizontal *dd* curve to the lilliputian eye of the firm.

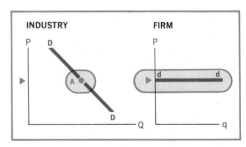

FIG. 23-3.

producing further units for which *MC* is definitely greater than *P*. Evidently, its Maximum-profit equilibrium comes when it follows the rule

$$\text{Price} = \text{Marginal Cost} \quad \text{or} \quad P = MC$$

This means that the firm's supply curve is given by its rising *MC* curve as shown in Fig. 23-4. Thus, at the indicated horizontal *d'd'* level of $50, the firm will find its Maximum-profit supply response at the intersection point *A*. (To check this, note that the loss of profit from producing a little less than at *A* is shown by the gold-shaded triangle, depicting the surplus of *P* over *MC* on the last little units.)

Alternatively, suppose the firm were faced by a horizontal *dd* at $40. Its Maximum-profit supply response is shown at the intersection point *B*. It happens, as our original cost Table 23-1 shows, that the firm just breaks even there, covering all its long-run costs at this point.

Or suppose the firm faced *d''d''*. At this price below $40, the firm cannot break even; but it does *minimize its short-term losses* (or maximize its "algebraic" profit) there at the *C* intersection on the *MC* curve (as you can show by penciling in a gold-shaded triangle like *A*'s).

Thus, the firm's rising *MC* curve does indeed constitute its competitive supply curve.

TOTAL COST AND SHORT-RUN SHUTDOWN CONDITIONS[5]

Recall that earlier the "short run" was defined as that period of time in which certain equipment, resources, and commitments of the firms are fixed; but it is a period long enough for the firm to vary its output by hiring more or fewer variable factors of production, such as labor, raw materials, and so forth. It is certainly not a precise period of time which will be the same for all industries. Even within an industry, we can be asking questions about "short-run" periods of different duration. At one ultrashort extreme, so many decisions have already been frozen as to make the resulting Marginal Cost curve practically a vertical and inelastic line. Or at the other extreme, we can permit so much time to pass as to let more and more of the equipment have a chance to wear away or be replaced, thereby making the resulting Marginal Cost curve almost as flat as it will be in the longest run, when *no* fixities are possible except those associated permanently with the management of the firm itself.

Now consider a firm making its short-run decisions. It has a certain "fixed cost": this is defined as the total of costs that will go on anyway because of its fixed commitments that are already frozen in the short run; examples would be bond interest, rentals, over-

Profit-maximizing competitor has supply curve determined by rising Marginal Cost:

FIG. 23-4. If you can sell all you wish at *P* given by horizontal *d'd'*, your Maximum-profit equilibrium comes at its intersection with the *MC* curve at *A*: your maximum profit is positive; and the gold-shaded triangle shows you would lose some profit if you produced less than at *A*, since your extra revenue of *P* would exceed your extra cost, *MC*.

If *P* dropped to *d''d''* level, you maximize profit at *C*: *P = MC* there minimizes your unavoidable short-run loss. If *P* falls below Shutdown point, your revenue fails to cover out-of-pocket expenses and you will shut down. If *P* is at Break-even point *B*, your maximized profit (inclusive of normal return to your labor and capital) is just zero: new firms will not enter, and old ones will not leave.

---

[5] This section may be skipped in a brief course.

head salaries, franchise taxes, and so forth. The rest of its "total cost" is called "variable cost": this is defined as the sum of all costs that vary with output; examples are cost of materials, wages for workers on the production line, and so forth. Chapter 24 will discuss all these in detail.

But now consider the firm facing lower and lower P. It has the option of producing nothing at all. How much will it then lose? With its revenue zero and all its fixed cost going on anyway, its shutdown loss will exactly equal its fixed cost. When P falls so low as to give it *less revenue than the variable cost it incurs* from producing positive q, it will prefer to shut down completely: why should it produce if that means it incurs loss greater than the fixed cost it incurs when shut down? So this rule holds:

Shutdown point. At the critically low market price, where the firm just recovers its variable cost by producing, it will be on the verge of shutting down. Below that point, it will produce nothing at all.

Above that P, it *will* produce along its short-run Marginal Cost curve. For, at such $MC = P$ points, the firm will be getting something toward covering its fixed cost; and either it will be getting maximized positive profits, or at least will be minimizing its losses (and in that sense maximizing its algebraic profit).

The location of the Shutdown point was shown in Fig. 23-4. The MC curve continues down below that blue point, but it no longer corresponds to an *ss* supply curve.

SYNTHESIS OF MARGINAL COST AND MARGINAL UTILITY

We can summarize what has now been established. Just as Marginal Utility lies behind the demand curve, Marginal Cost lies behind the supply curve. *The supply curve of an industry is seen to be the summed rising MC curves of the firms in that industry.*[6]

Having described market equilibrium, we are now in a position to understand *how important the MC concept is in helping society to organize its production efficiently and responsively.* We can now combine cost and utility, or more precisely Marginal Cost and Marginal Utility.

Robinson Crusoe Begin with the simplest case—that of Robinson Crusoe. A single man, so the story goes, works so many hours picking strawberries. (1) Each extra berry brings him *diminished* marginal utility. (2) Each extra hour of sweaty labor brings him *increasing marginal disutility.* (3) Working with fixed land, each extra minute of work, because of the law of *diminishing returns,* brings less and less extra berries.

It must follow from these assumptions that Crusoe will work up to the critical equilibrium intersection where a declining marginal-utility-of-berries curve (which looks like both an MU and a *dd* curve) intersects with a rising marginal curve of disutility involved in providing the effort needed for additional berries (which is like an MC and *ss* curve).

Figure 23-5 gives the Robinson Crusoe welfare equilibrium.[7] The brown curve now

---

[6] The next chapter will discuss the longest-run case in which new firms can come into the industry and old firms leave it.

[7] To keep matters at their simplest, suppose we can ignore the increasing marginal disutility of sweaty labor, measuring all our welfare in fixed "disutils" of labor time; or better, what is the same thing, we consider each hour of forgone-leisure as having a constant marginal utility so that we can arith-

rises because diminishing returns makes the *MC* of extra strawberries rising; the blue curve falls because of diminishing *MU*. Welfare is maximized at *E*, where *MU* of berries is in balance with *MC* (measured, remember, in utils of forgone-leisure). The "triangular" blue area *AEB* represents the consumer's (net) surplus, and it is larger at *E* than anywhere else. (The shaded gold "triangle" beyond *E* shows the loss of well-being from producing too many berries. You can pencil in a similar blue "triangle" to the left of *E* reflecting what you would lose of consumer's (net) surplus if you did *not* produce the last units.)

Communal state   Economics is a science of *society,* not of a single isolated individual. Still, we can keep our story simple if we now apply it to a communal state, where all families are treated exactly alike or where some single benevolent or malevolent dictator provides the utility and disutility magnitudes that are to be maximized.

Figure 23-5 still serves to show optimal welfare for a monistic, communal state, just as it did for the one-man Crusoe world. Now a Planner, using computers or market devices, would want to realize the same *MU* and *MC* equality shown there.

Indeed, both Crusoe and a planning board might achieve the *MU = MC* equilibrium by introducing a price of strawberries, *P*.[8] Then by equating *MU = P* and *MC = P*, they would succeed in achieving their welfare optimum.

Many goods   One last complication before considering the real world. Crusoe or a planning board would have to cope with many goods: strawberries versus tea versus cotton gloves, etc. Suppose labor is freely transferable among the different activities—tea, berries, etc. And, to keep the parable simple, suppose that *varying* labor is applied to different grades of *fixed* land, each land being completely specialized to its industry. Clearly, then, each good will have a rising *MC* curve in terms of labor (and hence leisure-utils) applied to it.

What about society's (or Crusoe's) marginal utility from berries, tea, gloves, etc.? For simplicity suppose each good *independently* has its own total utility and marginal-utility schedules like last chapter's Fig. 22-3. Now comes the vital question. How should Crusoe or the Planner most efficiently allocate labor among the different industries to effect the optimal-welfare pattern of berry production, tea production, etc.?

Supply-demand intersection can help solve the Planner's welfare optimum of Marginal Utility and Marginal Cost:

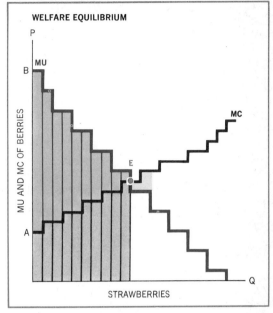

FIG. 23-5. Here Robinson Crusoe or a communal-state Planner utilizes apparatus of supply and demand to determine optimal well-being output. Blue *MU* curve intersects brown *MC* curve at *E*. Cost of picking strawberries is given by brown area, measuring "utils" of forgone-leisure. Vertical slabs of blue area under *MU* give excess strawberry utils over utils of cost. Hence blue-shaded area of consumer's net surplus is maximized by producing at *E* intersection (gold area to the right of *E* shows loss from producing too much).

metically reckon all utilities and costs in these leisure-labor utils. This important notion of "forgone-opportunity" cost" will be discussed again in the next chapter.
[8]This price could be in units-of-utility-of-forgone-leisure. Or, if we defined labor so that $1 equals the wage of 1 unit of work and 1 unit of forgone-leisure, then strawberry *P* could be expressed in dollars.

Obviously, to maximize welfare and allocation efficiency we must in each industry[9] get a balance of *MU* and of *MC*. If tea involves twice the *MC* of strawberries, its *P* must be twice as great. These $P_i = MC_i$ equivalences are vital in any society aiming to solve WHAT and How efficiently.

By now, the essential point should be obvious enough. But in leaving it, please notice that a simple "labor theory of value" will not properly solve the problem. Only if you reckon the *Marginal Cost* of a good can you get its proper price in terms of labor or of anything else! And setting prices merely proportional to labor used in an industry does not properly adjust for the scarcity of nonlabor inputs.

EFFICIENT MARKET ALLOCATION OF PRODUCTION

Now forget parables. Forget Robinson Crusoe. Forget a communal state. What about the anarchy of a million small competitors? Can a perfectly competitive market really achieve the same optimal *MC* equilibrium?

Qualifications   The answer is, "Yes." Better still, "Yes, maybe." First, you must rule out monopoly: no one expects that an unbridled profiteer will achieve the social optimum. Second, you must not be considering cases where people's demand curves *deviate* from true utility. I.e., don't try to apply the theory to heroin production. Or, if you believe that Madison Avenue advertisers have manipulated consumers into demanding worthless gadgets that don't deserve to have the word "utility" applied to them, don't try to apply the theory to that area. If there remains a group of goods and industries—say shoes, beef, housing, etc.—where there are many reasonably informed consumers and many mutually competing competitive producers, then you may hope to achieve efficiency[10] by market pricing along *MC* lines.

---

[9] For each new industry, we draw a new diagram like Fig. 23-5, and again maximize the blue area of "consumer's (net) surplus" where $P_i = MC_i$ and P_i reflects *MU* of the *i*th good as determined from consumer *dd* curves. (WARNING: if coffee is not *independent* of tea, you could not draw its diagram *independently* of that of tea. Also, if the transferable inputs in terms of which we measure the MC_i did not satisfy our simplifying axiom of strict constancy of forgone utils, the consumer's-surplus exposition here would have to be made more complicated; advanced economics handles the problem rigorously by the more complex tools of intermediate economic treatises. Fig. 23-6 here uses the methods of the Appendix to Chapter 22 to show the same welfare optimum as did Fig. 23-5. Robinson Crusoe maximizes welfare at *E*, where MC_{tea}/MC_{gloves} (as measured by the brown slope of his *p-p frontier*) and MU_{tea}/MU_{gloves} (as measured by the blue slope of his indifference curves) are each equal to the market P_{tea}/P_{gloves} (as measured

FIG. 23-6.

by the gold slope of the price-line through *E*). Verify that *E* does represent the highest well-being possible for this simplified society. The same holds if the blue curve depicts Planner's preference.

[10] If the dollar votes of different consumers represented an "equitable" allocation, so that each person's dollar represented as ethically deserving a pull on the market as any other's, there would be no need to make the following important qualification: Efficient production and pricing does not mean that the FOR WHOM problem of society is being properly solved; it only means that the WHAT and

Competitive-industry market integrates consumer demands and producer's minimized cost:

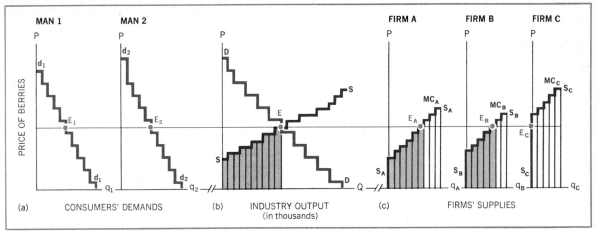

FIG. 23-7(a).   Individual demands (as derived from Chapter 22's marginal utility considerations) are shown on the left. If there were 1,000 consumers like Man 1 and 1,000 like Man 2, we would add (horizontally) all their dd curves to get industry DD curve in the middle.

FIG. 23-7(b).   The market brings together all consumer demands and firm supplies to reach equilibrium at E. The horizontal gold line shows where each consumer on left and each firm on right reaches equilibrium. [NOTE: Brown area under SS represents total cost (e.g., labor-leisure) of Q, and this area is at a minimum when all MCs are equal].

FIG. 23-7(c).   For each of these competitive firms, profits are maximized when supply curve is given by rising MC curve. Brown area represents firm's cost of producing. When $MC_A = P = MC_B$, we have Least-cost efficient allocation for industry!

Market synthesis   Now turn to Fig. 23-7 to see how a competitive system does bring out a balance between utility and cost. On the left, we add horizontally the demand curves for all consumers to get the market DD curve in the middle. (Recall Chapter 22, p. 408.) On the right, we add all the separate firm's MC curves to get industry SS curve in the middle. Note what the equilibrium price at the E intersection achieves: it gives people on the left what they are willing to pay for and buy of the good at the P reflecting efficient social MC. On the right, we see that the equilibrium market price does allocate production most efficiently. (I.e., the brown area under SS in the middle does represent the minimized sum of brown cost areas on the right![11])

Summary: **The ideal competitive market is a device for synthesizing (1) the willingness of people to pay for goods with (2) the actual (minimized) marginal costs of those goods. Without conscious planning, the competitive market does achieve the Robinson Crusoe or Planning most efficient allocation of resources.**

Although Fig. 23-7 shows only one good, say, wheat, it can be duplicated to show how shoe production gets organized. Remember that labor and other resources are trans-

---

How problems are being solved in the best way they can be solved consistent with the *existing distribution* of dollar-voting power and of sharing in national wealth and GNP. This qualification is vital.

[11]Because dollar-voting power may not have been distributed so as to reflect ruling ethical notions of proper welfare and equity, the area under the market DD curve has not been shaded blue: for that would involve "adding" incommensurable utilities of different persons' dollars and an illegitimate leap from consumer's surplus to consumers' surplus.

ferable not only between different wheat farms but also between the wheat and the shoe industries. Their respective MC_i reflect these social costs; and without the $P_i = MC_i$ conditions being satisfied, economic allocation would be "inefficient" in the following strong sense: "Unless *all* $P_i = MC_i$, one can reorganize production and make *everybody* better off—the poor, the rich,[12] wheat producers, shoe producers, etc!" Who pays for such an improvement? No one. It comes from cutting out deadweight waste and inefficiency in social allocation!

FINAL SUMMARY OF EFFICIENCY OF MARGINAL-COST PRICING

A coldly objective scientist, who wanted to know nothing beyond how to describe and analyze competitive supply behavior and who had not the slightest interest in society's welfare, would consider the Marginal Cost concept extremely important. But what about a person who was concerned also with human happiness and with the social efficiency of a pricing system? He would find the equating of price to Marginal Cost even more interesting. Our analysis has demonstrated the following remarkable truth:

Only when prices of goods are equal to Marginal Costs is the economy squeezing from its scarce resources and limited technical knowledge the *maximum* of outputs. Only when each source of industry output has had its rising *MC* equated to *any* other source's *MC*—as will be the case when each *MC* has been set equal to the common *P*—can the industry be producing its total *Q* at *minimum Total Cost*. Only then will society be out on its production-possibility frontier and not inefficiently inside the frontier.

This equal-marginal-cost dictum is as applicable to a communist, socialist, or fascist society as it is to a capitalistic society. Unless wheat cultivation has been pushed in different parts of the Soviet Union so as to equalize Marginal Costs (including transportation), the Planners there will be failing to achieve the abundance of wheat and other goods that could be theirs with more efficient allocation of resources. (Perhaps it is not surprising to learn from reading the recent debates in their own economic journals that they are gradually becoming aware of this basic fact of logic and economics.)

Because Marginal Cost has this optimality property, it can with some care be used as a yardstick to detect inefficiency in any institutional setup. Thus, if perfectly competitive industries did not exist at all, or if they were rarer even than they are today, one would still derive great benefit from defining and studying the concept of Marginal Cost.

NONOPTIMALITY OF COMPETITIVE LAISSEZ FAIRE PRICING

But we must not leave the subject of efficient pricing without a warning. We have not proved that laissez faire with perfect competition maximizes the greatest good of the greatest number. We have not proved that it produces a maximum of social utility. We have not proved that it results in the best attainable level of social welfare. For people are not equally endowed with purchasing power: some are very poor through no fault of their own. Some are very rich, and not necessarily because of any virtue or effort that

---

[12]Of course, the gains from getting rid of inefficiency *could* be used to help only those deemed *most* in need of help.

they or their ancestors have ever performed. So the weighting of dollar votes, which lie behind the individual demand curves on the left of Fig. 23-7, is not necessarily equitable or even tolerable as judged by many ethical systems (various forms of Christianity, Buddhism, "fair shares," etc.). In terms of many ethical systems the social welfare might be improved by redistributive taxation, rather than letting the end result depend upon laissez faire pricing of the property ownership that happens to prevail. All that marginal-cost pricing has been demonstrated to achieve in these discussions is the property of helping to lead to efficiency—efficiency in the sense that there is no "deadweight loss" in the system (i.e., *no possibility of making everybody better off*). When we depart from $P = MC$ pricing, along with any existing inequities of distribution we compound the inefficiency of deadweight loss. Marginal-cost pricing is part of the recipe for getting the good society; it is not alone a sufficient condition for having achieved it.

This completes our discussion of the relationship between Marginal Cost and industry supply, and of marginal-cost pricing in its relationship to efficient allocation of resources. The next chapter will go more deeply into the nature and variety of concepts of cost. And later chapters will examine the important cases that deviate from perfect competition—such as monopoly or oligopoly or external nuisances on other people.

SUMMARY

1   In a competitive market, aggregate supply of a group of independent firms comes from adding horizontally their separate supply curves.

2   The short run is defined as that period of time in which some of the firm's productive factors and costs are fixed and some are variable. For a firm we can define Marginal Cost as its *extra* or incremental cost of producing an *extra* unit of output, and can compute the instantaneous rate of Marginal Cost at each output from a smoothed schedule or graph of costs.

3   Trends of costs and of productivity returns are reverse sides of the same coin: when the law of diminishing returns ultimately holds, the MC curve ultimately rises; when there is an initial stage of increasing returns, MC initially falls; if *all* factors of production could be bought in balance at unchanged prices and output were to then show constant returns to scale, long-run Marginal Costs could be horizontal forever.

4   A perfectly-competitive firm is defined as one which is able to sell all it wants to at the posted market price. To maximize its (algebraic) profit, it will move along its (horizontal) demand curve until it reaches its rising Marginal Cost curve. At this intersection, $MC = P$, and the firm is maximizing its profits (or minimizing its short-run losses). So the industry supply curve from a given number of firms will come from adding horizontally their relevant Marginal Cost curves.

5   Out-of-pocket costs (or avoidable, variable costs) must be taken into consideration in determining a firm's short-run "Shutdown point." Below some critical P the firm will

not even be recovering in price revenues the variable cost that could be saved completely if it shut down; so rather than end up losing more than its fixed cost, it will shut down and produce nothing at lower Ps.

6 Beyond its importance for describing and explaining *competitive supply*, the concept of Marginal Cost has great importance for *welfare economics*. The problem of How goods are to be produced is being solved most efficiently only if every source of production for a good is being utilized up to the same MC level—an optimal result that is achievable when $P = MC$ everywhere. The problem of WHAT goods are best to be produced and in what amounts is solved in a Robinson Crusoe or Planning world by equating Marginal Utilities and Marginal Costs. Just as MU lies behind dd, so does MC lie behind ss; the competitive market, despite its surface appearance of anarchy and chaos, does provide one method for achieving economic efficiency. (WARNING: By itself, competitive pricing cannot ensure that the FOR WHOM distribution of dollar-voting power is ethically optimal; taxes and transfers might be needed for that, after which competitive pricing could do the rest of the job.)

QUESTIONS FOR DISCUSSION

1 Show that the differences between momentary, short-run, and long-run periods are a matter of degree and not of kind. In reality, there is a continuum of time periods in which there are fewer and fewer factors that are *fixed*.

2 "If a good can be stored, momentary supply will not be vertically inelastic. When P gets very low, producers will *reserve* some product, storing it for future sale at a higher P." Justify. Can you show that this would make $S_m S_m$ have a rising slope?

3 Give reasons why (positive) Marginal Cost might at first fall and later rise.

4 Why will you ever supply goods at a loss along a short-run MC curve?

5 "If I can get more than enough to cover my fixed costs, I will produce, forgetting my variable costs." Show that two words have been exactly reversed here.

6 Appraise this dialogue. A: "What does efficiency matter if the wrong people have all the money?" B: "Why risk making everybody worse off? Besides, use the tax system for redistribution rather than deviate from competitive pricing at $P = MC$ since the latter method of redistribution is an inefficient device." A. "But will the tax system be so used?"

Review your understanding of the following concepts:

summing ss curves to get SS
Marginal (or extra) Cost
$P = MC$, Maximum-profit condition
identity of firm ss supply curve and rising MC curve

diminishing returns and rising MC
Shutdown point
Robinson Crusoe or Planner welfare optimum at $MU = MC$
market efficiency of $P = MC$

Analysis of Costs and Long-run Supply

24

A class in economics would be a real success if the students gained from it a real understanding of the meaning of cost in all its many aspects.
J. M. CLARK

The last chapter introduced the definition of marginal cost, a fundamental concept that was seen to lie behind the supply curve of the competitive firm. Here in this chapter we shall go deeper into a variety of different cost concepts.

To understand the Maximum-profit equilibrium of any firm—whether it be the most perfect competitor, the most complete monopolist, or anywhere in the vast terrain of imperfect competition—we need to know how marginal and total costs are related to other cost concepts (such as average, or unit, costs) and to the breakdown between fixed costs and variable costs. Then we shall be ready in Chapter 25 to see how the marginal cost of *any* firm, whether competitive or not, has to be related to a similar concept on the demand side—namely, Chapter 25's *marginal* (or extra) *revenue*—in order to arrive at the Maximum-profit equilibrium of the firm.

TOTAL COST: FIXED AND VARIABLE

Consider a typical firm that produces the output q. At this stage, we do not care whether it is a perfect- or imperfect-competitor. At any one time, it has a certain state of technical knowledge, and it is confronted with the prices of the labor and other inputs it must buy. Now its accountants have been able to calculate what will be *its total dollar costs for producing each different level of q.*

Table 24-1 shows the simplified Total Cost[1] for each different level of output q. Columns (1) and (4) are the crucial ones, showing that TC goes up as q goes up. This

[1] These data depend upon engineering technology *and* upon the market prices of labor, land, fertilizer, and other factor inputs that the firm needs to produce each output of the good in question. Before its accountants and production men were able to write down the numbers in Table 24-1, they had to make efficiency decisions in *engineering*, ensuring that the physical inputs cannot be combined to give more physical output. And what is not so obvious until we have studied production theory in Part Four, the firm must also have made minimizing decisions of an *economic* kind in arriving at its lowest expense for each q produced.

From schedule of firm's Total Cost, all other costs can be computed in a table—

VARIOUS COST CONCEPTS

(1) QUANTITY q	(2) FIXED COST FC	(3) VARIABLE COST VC	(4) TOTAL COST $TC = FC + VC$	(5) MARGINAL COST PER UNIT MC	(6) AVERAGE COST PER UNIT $AC = \dfrac{TC}{q}$	(7) AVERAGE FIXED COST PER UNIT $AFC = \dfrac{FC}{q}$	(8) AVERAGE VARIABLE COST PER UNIT $AVC = \dfrac{VC}{q}$
0	55	0	55	34	Infinity	Infinity	
				30			
1	55	30	85	27	85	55	30
				25			
2	55	55	110	22	55	$27\frac{1}{2}$	$27\frac{1}{2}$
				20			
3	55	75	130	21	$43\frac{1}{2}$	$18\frac{1}{3}$	25
				30			
4*	55	105	160	40	40*	$13\frac{3}{4}$	$26\frac{1}{4}$
				50			
5	55	155	210	60	42	11	—
				70			
6	55	225	280	80	$46\frac{4}{6}$	$9\frac{1}{6}$	$37\frac{3}{6}$
				90			
7	55	—	370	100	$52\frac{6}{7}$	$7\frac{6}{7}$	45
				110			
8	55	—	480	120	60	$6\frac{7}{8}$	$53\frac{1}{8}$
				130			
9	55	555	610	140	$67\frac{7}{9}$	$6\frac{1}{9}$	$61\frac{6}{9}$
				150			
10	55	705	760		76	$5\frac{5}{10}$	$70\frac{5}{10}$

*Minimum level of Average Cost.

TABLE 24-1. All the costs can be calculated from Column (4)'s rising TC. Columns (5) and (6) are the important ones to concentrate on: incremental Marginal Cost, calculated by sub-traction of adjacent rows of TC and shown in blue; the light numbers of smoothed MC come from Fig. 24-1(b). In Column (6) note the point of minimum cost of $40 on the U-shaped AC curve. (Realize why the gold MC = gold AC at the minimum.)

is natural because it takes more labor and factor inputs to produce more of a good, and these extra factors involve an extra money cost. It costs $110 in all to produce 2 units, $130 to produce 3 units, and so forth. [Figure 24-1(a) verifies all this.]

Fixed Cost Columns (2) and (3) break down Total Cost into two components: total Fixed Cost, FC; and total Variable Cost, VC. Figure 24-1(a) shows the breakdown.

Even when the firm produces zero output, it must honor its short-run commitments (contractual rentals, watchmen's pay) and continue to incur its total Fixed Cost of $55. By definition, FC is the amount of cost that goes on independently of output; so it remains constant at $55 in Column (2). Another name for Fixed Cost is overhead cost.

Variable Cost Column (3) shows total Variable Cost. By definition, VC begins at zero when q is zero. It is the part of TC that grows with output; indeed, the jump in TC

and also in diagrams:

(a)

(b)

FIG. 24-1(a). The total Fixed Cost curve is horizontal by definition. Adding on top of it the rising total Variable Cost gives the rising Total Cost curve.

FIG. 24-1(b). The blue curve of Marginal Cost falls and ultimately rises, as in Chapter 23. *MC* is shown as a smooth curve after the steps of incremental cost are smoothed out; the numbers from the smooth *MC* curve are given in light blue in Column (5) of Table 24-1 [and also correspond to the slope of *TC* curve shown above].

By dividing *TC* by *q*, we can plot Average Cost: $AC = TC/q$. Similarly, *AFC* comes from FC/q, and *AVC* comes from VC/q. At any point, we can add these two brown curves and also get the *AC* curve at that point.

Note that *MC* intersects the U-shaped *AC* at *AC*'s minimum. This is no coincidence. To the left of *M*, *MC* is less than *AC* and hence is pulling *AC* down. To the right, $MC > AC$ and hence is pulling *AC* up. At the *M* minimum point, $MC^* = AC$; hence *AC* is horizontal there, being neither raised nor lowered by the equivalent *MC*. Also, *MC* cuts the *AVC* curve at its bottom.

between any two outputs is the same as the jump in *VC*. Why? Because *FC* stays constant at $55 throughout and cancels out in any such comparison. (Fill in by subtraction the missing *VC* data of the third column.)

Definitions: "Total Cost" represents lowest aggregate dollar expense needed to produce each level of output *q*. *TC* rises as *q* rises.

"Fixed Cost" represents the total dollar expense that goes on even when a zero output is produced. It is often called "overhead cost" and usually includes contractual commitments for rental, maintenance, depreciation, overhead salaries and wages, etc. It is a sunk cost that is quite unaffected by any variation in *q*; in the time period for which it is sunk, the only rule is this: Disregard Fixed Cost because *FC* cancels completely out of every decision.

"Variable Cost" represents all items of *TC* except for *FC*—as, for example, raw materials, wages, fuel, etc. Always, by definition,

$$TC = FC + VC$$

(Note that *TC* and *VC* always show exactly the same increments of *MC* as *q* changes, because *FC* is a strict constant.)

In Fig. 24-1(a) the rising *TC* curve is shown broken down into its constant *FC* and rising *VC* components.

MARGINAL COST REVIEW

We saw in Chapter 23 how Marginal Cost is defined as the increment of Total Cost that comes from producing an increment of one unit of *q*. (Recall that "marginal," whether applied to utility, cost, or anything else, always means "extra" in economics.)

The blue *MC* numbers in Column (5) of Table 24-1 come from subtracting the adjacent *TC* numbers in Column (4). Thus *MC* is $30 in going from 0 to 1 unit of *q* (i.e., $85 − $55 = $30). *MC* is seen to be $110 − $85 = $25 in going from *q* = 1 to *q* = 2. *MC* is $20 for the third unit of *q*, $30 for the fourth, and thereafter rising steadily until it is shown as $150 in going from *q* = 9 to *q* = 10. (What is it in going from *q* = 5 to *q* = 6? Pencil in your answer in blue.)

Instead of getting *MC* from the *TC* column, we could as easily get the *MC* number by subtracting each *VC* number of Column (4) from the row below it. Why? Because Variable Cost always *grows* exactly like Total Cost, the only difference being that it must—by definition—start out from 0 rather than from the constant *FC* level. (Check that 30 − 0 = 85 − 55, and 55 − 30 = 110 − 85, . . .)

Figure 24-1(a) and (b) shows the behavior of Total Cost (in brown) and Marginal Cost (in blue). Note that the *q* axes of the graphs on page 443 are just lined up so that the eye can see the correspondence between *TC* and *MC*.[2]

This example shows *MC* to be U-shaped—at first falling, but ultimately rising. We saw why on page 430: At first there may be great economies in using some or all of the productive factors on a larger scale; and so *MC* at first falls down to a minimum positive number before again rising. If we stick to the short run where some factors of production

---

[2] As on page 431, we have assumed that units can be made indefinitely small, so that the smoothed-instantaneous *MC* values can be plotted and read off to give the light numbers of Table 24-1, Column (5). To help understand the smoothed-instantaneous *MC* at a point *q*, see Fig. 24-2. It helps to clarify the distinction already mentioned between *MC* as an increment of cost for a finite step between two points of *q*, and *MC* as a smoothed-out instantaneous rate depicting the tangential slope at which *TC* is rising at one given *q* point. The distance from *a* to *b* represents one extra unit of output. The distance from *b* to *a′* represents the resulting increase in Total Cost, which is the first and simplest definition of incremental Marginal Cost. The second definition is given by the slope of the Total Cost curve at point *a*—and what mathematicians call $d(TC)/dq$—or what is the same thing numerically, by the distance from *b* to *c*. In the limit, as the size of the extra units becomes small and we reexamine the ratios in the new smaller triangle, the discrepancy between the two definitions becomes relatively negligible. (I.e., $ba′ \div bc$ approaches one as *a′* approaches *a*.)

FIG. 24-2.

are fixed, ultimately the old law of diminishing returns will operate to reduce the extra product that comes from adding equal physical and dollar increments of the varying factors onto the fixed factors. So the cost of getting extra product will ultimately become more expensive, and the short-run curve of Marginal Cost will ultimately be rising.

Marginal Cost has many uses. We saw in the last chapter that the rising MC curves of the firms provide us with the rising short-run ss supply curves which we sum horizontally to get the industry's short-run SS supply curve. In the next chapter we shall see that any firm—monopolistic or competitive—will find its Maximum-profit equilibrium by nicely balancing its extra cost against its extra revenue (i.e., by finding an intersection of its Marginal Cost curve and what will be defined as its "Marginal Revenue" curve).

AVERAGE OR UNIT COST

But first turn back to Column (6) of Table 24-1. This gives Average Cost (per unit), which is simply the Total Cost divided by the number of q units produced.

$$\text{Average Cost} = \frac{\text{Total Cost}}{\text{output}} = \frac{TC}{q} = AC$$

In Column (6), when only 1 unit is produced, Average Cost has to be the same as Total Cost, or $85/1 = 85$. But for $q = 2$, $AC = TC/2 = 110/2 = 55$, as shown. Note that Average Cost is, at first, falling lower and lower. (We shall see why in a moment.) But AC reaches a minimum of $40 at $q = 4$, and then slowly rises.

Figure 24-1(b) gives a careful plotting of U-shaped AC, nicely arranged below the TC it came from. We can now break down Average Cost into its two components, fixed and variable, just as earlier we had the breakdown of TC into FC and VC. By dividing each of the last two by q, we get Average Fixed Cost, $AFC = FC/q$ of Column (7); and Average Variable Cost, $AVC = VC/q$ of Column (8).

Average Fixed Cost Since total Fixed Cost is a constant, dividing it by q gives in Column (7) a steadily falling Average Fixed Cost curve. The brown-dashed AFC curve in Fig. 24-1(b) looks like a unitary demand curve, or hyperbola that approaches both axes: it drops lower and lower, approaching the horizontal axis as the constant FC gets spread over more and more units. If we allow fractional and zero units of q, AC starts infinitely high, as the finite FC is spread over tinier and tinier units of q.

Average Variable Cost AVC of Column (8) and Fig. 24-1(b) at first falls and then ultimately rises. We could have predicted this U-shaped behavior of AVC from the U-shaped behavior of MC. When MC at first falls, each new q is pulling down the Average Variable Cost calculated over all the items.

The points of Minimum Average Cost Figure 24-1(b) is an important economic diagram. Fix it on your eye's retina. Note particularly the typical U shape of the AC curve.

The AC curve is always pierced at its minimum point by the rising MC curve. This is no coincidence. And now we can explain why this has to be the case.

Competitors are in long-run equilibrium where Price equals Minimum Average Cost:

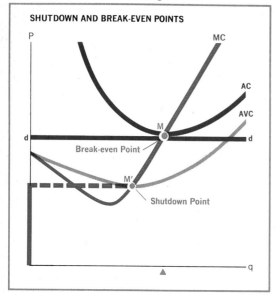

SHUTDOWN AND BREAK-EVEN POINTS

FIG. 24-3. The Break-even point is at M where dd is tangent to AC and AC is at its minimum. The short-run Shutdown point is similarly at the bottom of the AVC curve.

Any average curve is pulled downward when MC is less than AC: if the last increment of cost is less than the average of all previous ones, it must pull the average down! But when MC gets as big as AC, AC no longer is pulled down; it now turns sideward or level. Then, if MC rises above the AC, it must of course pull AC up. So at the point where rising $MC = AC$, and only at that point, shall we find the point of Minimum AC.[3]

Summary: So long as Marginal Cost is below Average Cost, it is pulling Average Cost down; when MC gets to be just equal to AC, AC is neither rising nor falling and is at Minimum AC; after MC is above AC, it is pulling AC up. Hence:

At bottom of U-shaped AC,
$MC = AC = $ Minimum AC

Likewise, the MC curve cuts the AVC curve at the bottom of its U, pulling it down before this point because $MC < AVC$ and pulling it up beyond that point because $MC > AVC$.

Now that we know how the MC curve intersects the AC and AVC curves where their U's bottom out, we can describe exactly how the firm's Shutdown and Break-even points of Fig. 23-4, page 433, had been determined. The Break-even point of long-run no-profit competitive equilibrium is seen here in Fig. 24-3 to be at the bottom of the U-shaped AC curve, in accordance with

$$P = MC = \text{Minimum } AC, \text{ in long-run equilibrium of zero excess-profits}$$

Likewise, the Shutdown point would come at M', once the horizontal dd of the firm had fallen to a level of P so low as to just cover minimum AVC. A price below this level would cause the firm to produce zero output.

LONG-RUN PLANNING ENVELOPE CURVE[4]

We now have all the technical apparatus of the various cost concepts needed to permit us to tackle the problem of how any firm will find its Maximum-profit equilibrium. But one last technicality is needed to explain how a firm may *in the longest run* be able to have lowest costs through adapting and varying the size of its plant.

Recall that, once the firm has a fixed plant, it has a short-run U-shaped AC curve (call

---

[3] Here is an explanation of the MC and AC relationship in terms of college grade averages. With MC below AC, Average Cost keeps being pulled down by the lowered cost of the final unit—just as one's cumulative grade average is pulled down when one's incremental average in the junior year is less than one's cumulative average up to that time. Only when one's "marginal or current" grade average crosses above or below one's cumulative grade average will the latter reverse its direction.

[4] This section may be skipped in brief courses.

In the long run, a firm can choose its best plant sizes:

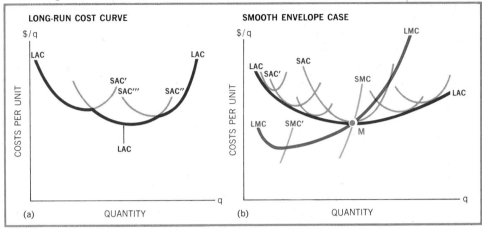

FIG. 24-4.   In the long run, the firm can alter its plant size and number of plants. In (a) its *LAC* is the brown "envelope" or lower frontier of the three possible choices of plant. In (b) there is an indefinite number of choices and we get *LAC* as a smooth brown envelope. In the usual manner we can derive from the brown *LAC* curve its blue marginal curve, *LMC*.

it *SAC* to emphasize its short-run nature). If the firm builds a larger plant, the new *SAC* curve must be drawn farther to the right. Now, suppose the firm is still in the planning stage, still quite uncommitted by any fixed obligations. It can write down *all possible* different U-shaped *SAC* curves, and then choose to select for each prescribed output the *SAC* that gives it the lowest costs. As *q* changes permanently, the firm hops to a new *SAC* curve.

Figure 24-4(a) shows how, in the longest run, the firm selects *SAC'* for low *q*; for intermediate *q*, it does better to plan to use *SAC''*; for still larger *q*, *SAC'''* leads to lowest costs. The heavy brown curve of Long-run Average Cost (*LAC*) is composed of the three *lowest* branches. Figure 24-4(b) shows the same lower limit in the case where the firm has choice of infinitely many smooth short-run *AC* curves (*SAC*, not *AVC*!): now *LAC* is the U-shaped smooth "lower-envelope" curve; and *its* well-behaved *LMC* provides the firm's long-run Marginal Cost curve, emerging from the *LAC* minimum point with a gentler slope than the short-run *SMC* curve there.

TASKS ACCOMPLISHED AND TASKS YET TO COME

The first half of this chapter is done. The important concepts of cost have been introduced: Total Cost, and its breakdown into total Fixed and total Variable Costs; Marginal Cost; all the different Average Costs (per unit), *AC*, *AFC*, and *AVC*; the interrelations between marginal and average concepts, including their intersection at the minimum point of the U-shaped average curve; finally, long-run envelope cost, *LAC*, when the number of plants and all elements can be adjusted to the level of production.

Since competitive firms must in the longest run realize a price equal to average cost—so that total dollar revenue equals total dollar cost, with no excess-profit—we are now equipped to carry on the analysis of longest-run competitive supply.

TOTAL COST AND LONG-RUN BREAK-EVEN CONDITIONS

Once I am stuck with certain fixed cost commitments, I will be willing to produce in the short run along my *MC* curve above the Shutdown point—even though I am not earning enough to cover *all* my costs—as the last chapter showed. But only at some higher point on my *MC* curve will I be earning enough to cover *all* the costs that have to be met if I am to stay in business after the short run is over and I have regained my long-run freedom (1) to renew my old commitments or (2) to move to another industry.

There is, then, a critical "Break-even point" below which *long-run P* cannot remain if I am to stay in this business. If every other firm were exactly like me, the long-run supply would dry up completely below this critical Break-even level which covers all costs of staying in business.

Now let us suppose further that entry into the industry is absolutely free in the long run, so that any number of firms can come into the industry and manage to produce in exactly the same way and at exactly the same costs as the firms already in my industry. Under such conditions of free "replication," it is obvious that long-run *P* cannot remain above this same critical Break-even point at which they all cover their long-run total costs—including in these (1) all labor, materials, equipment, taxes, and other expenses; (2) all wages payable to the identical managers at the level determined competitively by the bidding in all industries for people of such talents and industriousness; and (3) the interest yield that any of them could get on the amounts of capital that they tie up in this industry instead of investing it elsewhere.

Long-run Break-even condition: This comes at a critical *P* where the identical firms just cover their full competitive costs. At lower long-run *P*, firms would leave the industry until *P* had returned to the critical equilibrium level; at higher long-run *P*, new firms would enter the industry replicating what existing firms are doing and thereby forcing market price back down to the long-run equilibrium *P* where all competitive costs are just covered.[5] Thus, as shown back in page 446's Fig. 24-3,

$$P = MC = \text{minimum competitive costs, the long-run Break-even equilibrium}$$

IMPLICIT- AND OPPORTUNITY-COST ELEMENTS: A DIGRESSION

It is important to stress that the "full competitive minimum costs" which have to be just covered by normal price include more than accountants usually include in costs. Economists include a normal return to management services, as determined competitively in all industries; and a normal return to capital, as determined competitively everywhere by industries of equal riskiness. In the above sense we may say that "normal profits" are included in costs and that "excess-profits" are competed away by entry of new firms, and "abnormal losses" are eliminated by long-run exit of firms.

[5]If investors tend to be overoptimistic and repeatedly produce an oversupply in the industry so as to create permanent losses on the average, full competitive costs might be defined compatibly with such chronic losses resulting from repeated miscalculations.

Implicit-cost elements The return to a factor of production is economically important regardless of how it happens to be owned. To the economist, the returns that go to factors of production owned by the firm itself are so important as to deserve a new name: in contrast to wages that are *explicitly* paid to outside labor, we defined the concept of "implicit wages" as the return to the labor provided by the owner himself; and similarly, implicit rent and interest would be the returns to the land and capital provided by the owner himself rather than hired from outside owners.

Through miscalculation, a person may fail to receive his implicit wages in the short run; on the other hand, he may in the short run be getting more than the needed implicit return, the difference being a transient profit that has not yet been competed away. If he owns some special factors of production, like rich ore land, exceptional know-how, or fertile soil, his accounts may show a high return even in the long run; but we realize this is not so much profit as a return to that special factor of production he is lucky enough to own.[6]

Opportunity-cost elements Related to the above discussion is an even broader notion about cost. The man in the street can clearly recognize costs that are actual cash payments; the accountant must go well beyond that. But the economist goes even further. He realizes that some of the most important costs attributable to doing one thing rather than another stem from the *forgone opportunities* that have to be sacrificed in doing this one thing. Thus, Robinson Crusoe pays no money to anyone, but realizes that the cost of picking strawberries can be thought of as the sacrificed amount of raspberries he might otherwise have picked with the same time and effort or the sacrificed amount of forgone-leisure. This sacrifice of doing something else is called "opportunity cost." (Note that opportunity cost would still exist even if he loves to spend that hour in doing both kinds of picking and recognizes not the slightest disutility or sweat in performing that type of work.)

How does all this apply to industry supply and the firm's Break-even costs? In this way: The long-run Break-even level of costs includes, in addition to *explicit* cost outlays, those *implicit* costs that accrue to factors which might otherwise be used in alternative ways. If my labor in wheat could have been used in rye or even in some other man's wheat patch, then its value in those uses has to be met[7] or I shall not continue to supply it to my own wheat patch. For these reasons, full competitive cost intimately involves *opportunity cost*. The latter is an important concept, which covers much more territory than does the notion of implicit costs. The prices of labor and other factors that competi-

---

[6] If he happens to own very fertile land and persists in cultivating it by uneconomical methods, he will be paying for his folly or stubbornness by forgoing the high return such land is capable of yielding; in dollars, the land becomes worth more to others than to him, and if he refuses to rent or sell it, he is as surely spending his sustenance to please his own tastes as he would be doing if he sold the land and spent the proceeds on wine, song, or being a country squire. A young person with high IQ and versatile talents who stays in a dull dead-end job or dying industry is similarly squandering his economic potential.

[7] The *best* alternative use is of course the proper one to use in reckoning opportunity cost. If alternatives exist along an infinite and smooth continuum, such opportunity cost will set a tight limit on costs to this industry. If alternatives come in steps, then the next-best alternative may give us only a lower limit on factor-price, leaving a possible area in which it has to be determined by the "rent" analysis of Part Four.

tive farmers in an industry are forced to pay out explicitly depend importantly on the forgone opportunities for use in other industries or for leisure; and this means that all competitive costs involve opportunity costs in the background.

The terminology of economists is not uniform in this connection, but the concept of opportunity cost is important and we shall run into it again and again.

LONG-RUN INDUSTRY SUPPLY AND FIRMS' BREAK-EVEN POINTS

Now we can return to the behavior of industry supply as firms can enter or leave the industry. We resume the story begun way back in Fig. 23-1's short run and carried on up to Fig. 24-4.

Figure 24-5(b) pictures industry's long-run supply in relation to the supplies of firms— actual firms and *potential* firms.

Figure 24-5(b) shows the long-run horizontal supply curve $S_L S_L$ that would result if we can postulate conditions of replicability and absolutely free entry at precisely the level of the firm's Break-even point in Fig. 24-5(a), which is essentially a reproduction of Fig. 23-4, page 433. This horizontality also depends on a postulate that should now be made explicit: It assumes that this industry (1) is very small compared with the total of other industries, or (2) uses *all* the factors of production (land, skilled and unskilled labor, and so forth) in proportions very near to those of the rest of the economy that is contracting as this industry is expanding. Both of these assumptions assure that expansion of this industry (and contraction of other industries) does not significantly alter the prices

Short-run and long-run industry supply depends on firms' costs:

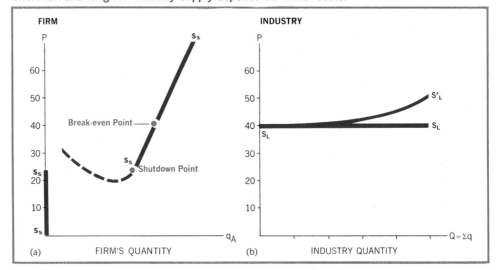

FIG. 24-5. With details omitted, Fig. 23-4 is shown again here in (a). In (b) the industry supply curve is shown. With entry and exit free and any number of firms able to produce on identical unchanged cost curves, the long-run SS curve will be horizontal at each firm's Break-even level. If industry cannot attract all the factors it uses at unchanged factor-prices, the $S_L S_L'$ supply curve will have to slope upward as each firm's cost curves are all shifted upward.

of any of the productive factors that the identical producers (and potential producers) are using in this industry—so that even a vast increase in demand for this industry will leave all our cost curves unchanged.

If this additional postulate were not made, the long-run expansion of this industry as more firms come into the market and as each firm expands its output would produce an increase in the market prices of those factors of production that are in peculiarly heavy use in this industry. (EXAMPLE: If wine production were much expanded, those special hillsides needed for vineyard production could not be drawn away from other uses at constant rental rates.) What would be the effect upon the S_LS_L supply curve when an increase in industry Q raises the prices of those factors of production peculiarly important in this industry? It would certainly be to *shift upward* the marginal and other cost curves of the new and old firms. And the final result would be that the long-run supply curve of the industry will slope upward from the horizontal.

The law of diminishing returns is likely to become involved in the increasing-cost case.[8] As discussed in Chapter 2 and on page 365, if the sizable industry needs a specific factor—say, able seamen—more intensively than do the rest of industries, expanding its Q will put special upward pressure on that factor's relative price. To be sure, the scarcity of this factor can be partially compensated for by adding other factors to it. But remember what happens when the industry has to add variable factors to a relatively fixed one. They experience diminishing returns. The industry gets less from them, and that sends its long-run costs up. That this industry's S_LS_L' curve is upward-sloping comes from the fact that expansion of its Q relative to other industries' outputs makes its factor-costs (and therefore its price) rise relative to theirs, fulfilling the expectation implied by the curvature of the production-possibility frontier of Chapter 2.

The relative rise in this industry's P and in its peculiar-factors' prices is a fact, but it also can be termed a desirable fact. Why? Not because the consumers who must pay more for this good are undeserving, nor because owners of the peculiarly scarce productive factors are especially deserving of higher incomes. Then why? Because any expansion of Q ought to be accomplished *efficiently* with least possible sacrifice of other Qs: the especially scarce factors have now to be severely rationed and be given more of other factors to work with; this will come about, not by a planning board's edict, but by a rise in the prices of this good and its peculiar factors, which will both signal the news of what must be done for efficiency and actually induce people to make the substitution needed if society is not to be inefficiently inside its *p-p frontier*.

If entry is really free, not only has perfect competition the nice property of ensuring that *each firm* ends up on an efficient curve and at the minimum point on it, but in addition the Invisible Hand ensures that *industry* gets its Q from the proper number of firms as some are squeezed out or attracted in.[9]

---

[8] The discussion here concerns the *industry* level and does not merely repeat the earlier analysis relating the firm's rising MC to its short-run experience of diminishing returns. Even if each small firm had horizontal long-run MC, when *all* firms expand, the factor-prices faced by each firm will rise and thereby *shift up* each MC curve, thereby causing *the industry* to travel up the S_LS_L' curve. (Chapter 27's Appendix extra-credit final question gives diagrams to show how the *p-p frontier* is attained.)

[9] If industry demand is large enough to permit numerous firms, then the optimal quantity each firm should produce is at the bottom of its U. It can be proved that the no-profit no-loss condition of ruthless competition will then achieve the most efficient number of firms to *minimize TC* for the industry's Q. For why force more expensive extra output from an existing number of firms if it can be got cheaper by replication of firms? And why not be sure that each of the identical firms produces neither too much nor too little, instead producing that Break-even q where $P = MC$ and where likewise P equals the lowest Average Cost per unit that will keep the firm in business in the long run? (If market demand is not large enough to keep numerous competitors viable, there will arise problems connected with the discreteness of firm sizes that will be discussed in Fig. 25-2.) See final question 10 for more on this.

It will be noted that in industries where $S_L S_L'$ slopes upward, owners of mines, land, know-how, and any other productive factors peculiar to this industry will earn a higher income (or what will be called "rent") from those factors as the industry expands.

If you do not like their earning such an extra return, you might take some of this away from them by taxes or other devices. But any special price ceilings placed on them in order to keep them from reaping such a return will definitely interfere with the equality-of-marginal-cost condition that is needed for maximal social efficiency—and such egalitarian legislation should be passed only if no better way of achieving this purpose can be found and the game is deemed worth the candle it will cost.

DECREASING COSTS AND THE BREAKDOWN OF PERFECT COMPETITION

Economic textbooks of years ago used to supplement the cases of horizontal supply and upward-sloping supply by a third case in which Marginal Costs of the firms were falling rather than rising and in which this was thought to create an industry long-run supply curve that sloped gently downward. Actually, if we review our argument of page 432 telling us why a maximizing firm will want to produce where $MC = P$, we see that the argument *fails completely* in the case where the firm's MC curve is a downward-sloping one. For if you move to the right of a point on a falling MC curve, you find that your additional P per unit is in excess of the now lower MC; and so in the case of decreasing Marginal Cost, the firm will expand its output more and more beyond the MC curve to gain extra profit.

Under decreasing Marginal Cost, the first firm to get a head start will find its advantage increasing the greater it grows. As it forces other firms to contract their qs, their disadvantage will become aggravated as they are forced to travel back up their falling MC curves.

The result must be obvious:

Under persisting decreasing costs for the firms, one or a few of them will so expand their qs as to become a significant part of the market for the industry's total Q. We shall then end up with one of the following three cases:

(1) a single monopolist who dominates the industry

(2) a few large sellers who together dominate the industry and who will later be called "oligopolists"

(3) some kind of imperfection of competition that, in either a stable way or in connection with a series of intermittent price wars, represents an important departure from the economist's model of "perfect" competition wherein no firm has any control over industry price

As the next section will show, when the firms in this industry all expand together, they could create what are called *external economies* (or *diseconomies*). Thus, a school for fishermen might become feasible only at high industry Q; and this training might cause a downward shift of every firm's cost curves as the industry total Q rises. The result could be an industry $S_L S_L$ curve that slopes *downward* owing to *external* economies. But this does not deny the fact that ("internally") decreasing cost for a firm destroys perfect competition, as Chapter 25 will discuss further.

EXTERNAL ECONOMIES AND DISECONOMIES[10]

Our discussion of decreasing costs has shown that it would be wrong to draw a curve of downward-sloping industry supply based upon costs falling *internally* within the firm. There is, however, a possible theoretical case in which the expansion of the industry's Q somehow causes each firm's cost curves as plotted against its q to *shift downward*. Alfred Marshall deemed this a case of downward-sloping industry supply based upon what he called *external* economies.

An "external economy" is defined as a favorable effect on one or more persons that emanates from the action of a different person or firm; it shifts the cost or utility curve of each person it helps, and such an *externally* caused shift should be distinguished from any *internal* movement along the affected individual's own cost curve.

An "external *dis*economy" is defined in the same way, except that it refers to external *harm* that is done to others. The case where expansion of fishing by others in limited waters serves to shift up each boat's cost curves would be an example of an external diseconomy; another case would be one where each man's haste to drill for oil near his neighbors' boundaries lowers the amount of oil ever recovered. Smoke nuisance and water pollution are two familiar other instances.

External economies have a considerable importance in connection with government activities that provide benefits to many individuals (so-called "public goods"). They are important too in connection with growth, where the building of a public road or some kind of "social overhead capital" like a hospital or dam has favorable external repercussions on many families, firms, and industries. The kinds of favorable external economies that are peculiarly associated with expansions along an industry supply curve—our main subject here—are not so easy to find. But here are a few examples.

As fishing Q expands, the number of trained fishermen that any firm might find to hire may go up. Or it may now pay the government, or some profit-seeking monopolist, to build a training school for fishermen, whereas previously such a school could not pay because of its high marginal cost at low scales of operation. A similar case would be one where specialized machinery for the fishing industry was producible by another industry only at decreasing marginal cost. Or if all of us in a neighborhood keep bees, I may find that I gain more wandering bees from your nearby acres when total Q of the honey industry rises; whereas when total honey Q is small, I find that some of my bees wander uselessly off to neighboring cornland and my neighboring corngrower has few bees that might in return wander back to me. Or one might conjure up the case where, when I drain my mine of water, I cannot help but make your neighboring mine somewhat drier and thereby confer an external economy on you.

It is easier to find examples of so-called "external diseconomies" resulting from higher industry Q. Recall that these are defined as harmful effects upon other people that result from one man's production. Thus, expanding along a supply curve for steel will cause great belching forth of smoke. This external effect is not only a nuisance, it may actually be harmful to good health and costly in terms of needed cleaning bills. Smog in many

[10]This section may be skipped at a first reading.

cities comes from the external diseconomies of each man's auto and factory. The greatest external diseconomy of all results from one country's setting off nuclear bombs.

One does not need the case of the nuclear bomb to know that wherever there are externalities a strong case can be made for supplanting complete individualism by some kind of group action: consumers should be made to pay for the smoke damage that their purchases make inevitable, as would be the case if we supplemented laissez faire by a tax or by coercive ordinances; a conservation subsidy to farmers, so that they will keep trees growing and thereby prevent disastrous floods hundreds of miles downstream, might represent rational social policy; regulations that prevent smallholders from digging oil wells frenziedly at the edge of their neighbors' property would be economically efficient. The reader can think of countless other externalities where sound economics would suggest some limitations on individual freedom in the interest of all.[11]

No more need be said at this point about externalities. They can shift firm cost curves and thereby alter the slope of industry supply curves upward and downward. But even more important is their general role in connection with causing free pricing to be non-optimal, thereby creating a prima facie case for zoning laws, government controls, and alert planning.

The main cost concepts, and their relation to supply in the short and long run, have now been introduced. In the next chapter we can pit cost against revenue to learn how any firm finds its Maximum-profit equilibrium.

SUMMARY

1 Total Cost can usefully be broken down into its Fixed and Variable Cost components. *FC* cancels out of all decisions relevant to the period for which it is truly fixed.

2 Marginal Cost is the increment of extra Total Cost resulting from one increment of extra *q*. (If our units are divisible, *MC* can be defined as the slope of the smooth *TC* curve at any *q* point, and this slope will give a close approximation to the extra cost of producing one more small *q* increment.)

3 Average (total) Cost, *AC*, is the sum of ever-declining Average Fixed Cost and of usually

---

[11]The late Professor A. C. Pigou, Marshall's prize pupil at Cambridge, was the economist who most emphasized the problem of externalities. There is a clear-cut economic case for a tax (or a subsidy) whenever an external diseconomy (or economy) creates a divergence between private pecuniary Marginal Cost as seen by a firm and true social Marginal Cost. But this truth is quite independent of the supply slope of the industry in question. And Marshall and Pigou erred in thinking that a tax should be put on an industry whose supply curve rises, in the fashion of Fig. 24-5(b), because some *pecuniary* factor-costs are raised to the firm externally by the expansion of industry *Q*—as Allyn Young pointed out half a century ago. We may add, they erred equally in thinking an industry should be subsidized if its *SS* curve slopes down because of pecuniary reductions in its input prices, reductions which shift firms' curves down externally: so long as government assures that such an input is sold at *its* declining *MC* price, the pecuniary external economy it creates for *our* industry can be safely ignored. Young correctly emphasized that external *technological* economies and diseconomies merit interference. He showed that rent collecting on private property in land succeeds in preventing it from becoming overcrowded by rugged individualists. Similarly, in the case of overcrowded fishing waters, subdividing the sea might somewhat reduce social inefficiencies; but certain government fees and rules of the road might well be devised which would do still better than would ordinary private ownership of the sea's acres.

U-shaped Average Variable Cost. AC is U-shaped, being intersected at its bottom by the rising MC curve. Similarly, AVC is cut by MC at its bottom.[12]

4   In the long run, when all fixed commitments expire and a firm is free to plan to operate any number of plants, the long-run cost curve LAC (and LTC) must be the lower-envelope frontier of best choice of plant for each level of output. This frontier will be a smooth envelope, containing at any point a tangential short-run cost curve, if potential plant sizes are smoothly continuous. Usually the long-run curve LAC, and its associated marginal curve, will be U-shaped: ultimately it will rise if not all factors of production (including management) are expandable at constant prices; and at very small outputs, indivisibilities in the inputs or the methods of combining them will cause costs initially to fall.

5   An industry's long-run supply curve, $S_L S_L$, must take into account the entry of new firms and exodus of old ones. In the long run all the commitments of any firm will expire, and it will decide to stay in business only if price at least covers all its long-run costs— whether they be "explicit" out-of-pocket payments to labor, lenders, material suppliers, or landlords; or whether they be "implicit" wages (defined as the "opportunity costs" of its owners' labor which could be employed elsewhere in producing or in leisure) or implicit interest and rent on the property assets owned by the firm (and whose opportunity costs are measured by what they will fetch in other equally risky uses).

6   Under conditions of free entry, where no one firm has any particular advantages of location, skill, or resources specialized to this industry, one can expect in the long run that free entry of would-be competitors will compete away any excess profits earned by existing firms in the industry. So, just as free exit means P cannot fall below the Break-even point, free entry means it cannot persist above that point in the long-run equilibrium. Where an industry can expand by replication without pushing up the prices of any factors peculiar to it or used in peculiarly large proportions by it, the resulting long-run supply curve will be horizontal. More likely, any but the smallest industry will generally use some factors of production in large enough amounts to force up their prices slightly. As a result, its long-run supply curve will be sloping upward, at least gently.[13]

7   It is not true that *downward*-sloping Marginal Cost curves of competitive firms can serve as their supply curves—for the very good reason that their profits will be at a minimum along such curves and they will rush away in either direction from such points. As a result, one or a few firms will tend to expand and the remaining firms will tend to contract. Thus lasting decreasing costs that are *internal* to firms implies the destruction of perfect competition. So it is wrong to talk of decreasing supply curves in such a case, or of competitive supply at all.

---

[12] See no. 9 in the Questions for Discussion section for useful rules about AC and MC curves.

[13] Or in extreme cases, where the labor it uses actually is supplied by families in reduced amounts when Q expansion bids up the wage, the industry $S_L S_L$ curve could even bend backward toward the northwest, as in Case 4 of the Appendix of Chapter 20.

8   There is, however, the possibility that *external economies* could prevail in an industry. In such cases expansion of *industry Q* could *shift* downward the cost curves of *single firms;* and in the complicated adding of the resulting supplies of all firms, the industry supply curve could end up as downward-sloping.

The concept of external economies or diseconomies is important beyond any such Marshallian application to industry supply. By definition, such externalities involve good and bad economic effects *upon others* resulting from one's own behavior. Since one person takes into account in the search for individual gain and well-being only private money benefits and costs as seen by him, there will then be a divergence between *social* costs and *pecuniary-private* costs. This means that there is a prima facie case in such instances for group action, by subsidy or public control, to expand situations fraught with external economies; and a similar case to contract, by tax or fiat, activities involving external diseconomies.

QUESTIONS FOR DISCUSSION

1   Make a list of cost elements: wages, salaries, fuel, rentals, etc. Divide them into the Fixed and Variable categories. (Your division will depend on your time periods.)

2   Explain the difference between Marginal Cost and Average Cost. Why should AVC always look much like MC? Why is MC the same when computed from VC as from TC?

3   To the \$55 of Fixed Cost of Table 24-1, add \$90 of additional FC. Now calculate a whole new table, with the same VC as before but new $FC = \$145$. What happens to MC, AVC? To TC, AC, AFC? Can you verify that minimum AC is now at $q^* = 5$ with $AC = \$60 = MC$? (You can check MC and TC of your table against Chapter 25's Table 25-3.)

4   Explain why MC cuts AC and AVC at the bottom of their U's. Recall, in connection with the last chapter, that minimum AVC can be shown to provide the short-run Shutdown point, and minimum AC to provide the long-run Break-even point.

5   Explain how the long-run envelope cost curve is defined as the lower frontier of all short-run curves. Illustrate with (a) the case of a few plant sizes, and (b) the case of infinitely-continuous plant sizes.

6   Relate the rising MC curve to the law of diminishing returns. Contrast the falling part of the curve with that law.

7   Interpret this dialogue. A: "How can competitive profits be zero in the long run? Who'll work for nothing?" B: "It is only *excess*-profits that are wiped out by competition. Managers get paid for their work; owners get a normal return on their capital in long-run equilibrium—no more and no less."

8   Give examples of external economies. External diseconomies. What public interferences might you possibly suggest? What rights to sue in court?

9   *Extra-credit problem:* With the help of the adjoining diagram, puzzle out the meaning of the following rules. *First rule:* If a Marginal Cost curve is below its associated Average Cost curve, it is pulling the AC curve down; if MC is above AC, it is pulling AC up; if $MC = AC$, AC must be horizontal. *Second rule:* If AC is a straight line, as in (a), (b), or (c), MC will be a straight line starting from the same vertical intercept point but with twice the slope of AC. (NOTE: This tells us how to find the MC point above or below

the *AC* point on *any* non-straight-line *AC* curve. At a chosen *q* in (d), merely draw the tangent straight line to *AC*; from that line's vertical intercept, draw an *MC* line with twice the slope; read off from this last line the *MC* value at your chosen *q* level. Of course, you must draw two new straight lines for every different *q* level.) Final query: Note fine black line in (b); label it *dd* for perfect-competitor's demand. Shade in triangle formed between *dd* and *MC* and note that you gain by increasing your *q* indefinitely!

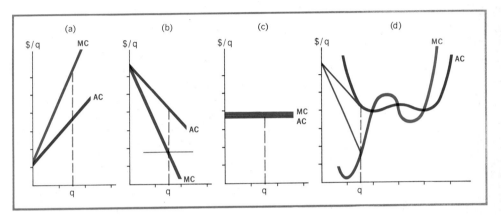

10 *Extra-credit problem:* Can you interpret the diagram below to show that society does get industry *Q* at lowest dollar and resource cost when each of many firms is at bottom of its U-shaped *AC*? First U on left comes with 1 firm. Second U comes with *Q* divided equally between 2 firms (so second U is merely the first with twice the horizontal scale; and similarly for the *n* = 3, 4, . . . U's). Beyond the // break, *n* is large—say, 100 firms. Naturally, industry *Q* is procured at least cost on *heavy lower curve*, with lower and lower gold switch points at which it just pays to add one new firm. Then to see how costs *for each typical firm* drop as *Q* and *n* grow, concentrate on the markings on the left side of the first U. With *n* = 1, the sky is the limit. For *n* = 2, the gold 2 shows highest that *AC* can ever be for any firm; for *n* = 3, gold 3 gives lower highest *AC*;

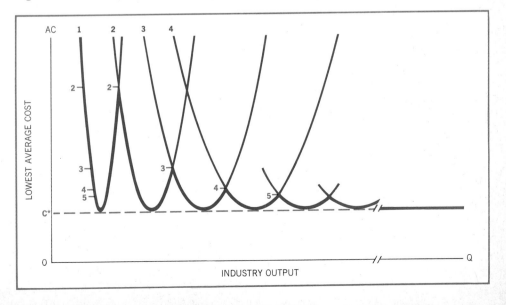

and gold numbers (which are drawn at exact level corresponding to respective switch points) drop to minimum *AC* when *DD* is big enough for numerous competitive firms to survive. So beyond the // break, with many firms, the heavy industry curve looks smoothly horizontal.

Review your understanding of the following concepts:

Total Costs: Fixed and Variable
$TC = FC + VC$
$AC = TC/q = AFC + AVC$
Marginal Cost (incremental and
   smoothed)
long-run envelope of cost, *LAC*
   and *LMC*

Break-even point at $P = MC = $ Min *AC*
Shut-down point at $P = MC = $ Min *AVC*
horizontal and rising $S_L S_L$
implicit costs and opportunity costs
decreasing costs and breakdown of
   competition
external economies and diseconomies

Maximum-Profit Equilibrium: Monopoly

25

Both monopolistic and competitive forces combine in the determination of most prices.
EDWARD H. CHAMBERLIN

In the last several chapters we have studied the workings of competitive supply and demand in considerable detail. For the most part, we have been studying the case called "perfect competition."

Perfect competition means something very definite to the economist. As we saw, the economist means by it something *much stronger* than the man in the street and the businessman do when they talk of "strong rivalry and keen competition among different business firms and industries."

The special case of perfect competition is very important. But it is only one case, and economists pay it so much attention because of the light it throws on the *efficiency* of resource use. Certainly, it cannot faithfully represent many of the facts about modern industries. The real world—as we know it in America, Europe, or Asia—contains significant *mixtures of monopoly imperfections* along with *elements of competition*. The real world, then, is for the most part to be classified in the realm of "imperfect competition": it is neither perfectly competitive nor perfectly "monopolistic."

The remaining chapters of Part Three, therefore, will give us the tools to analyze imperfect as well as perfect competition. They will show what modifications have to be made in any conclusions that were based on an analysis of perfect competition. We shall see that the way a pricing system succeeds in solving the basic problems of WHAT, HOW, and FOR WHOM is affected to an important degree by any elements of monopolistic imperfection that may be involved in numerous modern industries.

Part A of this chapter gives an overview of *patterns of imperfect competition and of real-world market structure*. It also presents a new important tool—the concept of Marginal Revenue. Part B portrays the equilibrium analysis of an idealized monopoly firm, to show how it *achieves maximization of profit by balancing its Marginal Cost and Marginal Revenue*. We then are ready to appraise at the end of this chapter the *inefficiency* inherent in imperfection of competition, and to develop in the Appendix some principles of public regulation.

A. OVERVIEW OF MARKET STRUCTURE AND THE CONCEPT OF MARGINAL REVENUE

PERFECT COMPETITION CONTRASTED WITH IMPERFECT COMPETITION

Figure 25-1(a) reminds us that, to an economist, a perfect-competitor is defined as a firm that has no control over price—in the sense that it faces an essentially *horizontal dd* curve along which it can sell as much or as little output as it likes.

Remember how strict this definition of perfect competition is. Think of any commodity that comes to mind: razor blades, toothpaste, steel, aluminum, potatoes, wheat, cigarettes, tobacco, nylon, cotton. Which will fit in with our strict definition? Certainly not razor blades or toothpaste or cigarettes. Who ever heard of an auction market for blades, toothpaste, or cigarettes?

Neither aluminum nor steel meets the definition of perfect competition. For a long time there was only one aluminum company, Alcoa (Aluminum Company of America); and even today there are only Alcoa, Reynolds, Kaiser, and one or two others. Contrast this with the case of thousands, if not millions, of cotton and wheat farmers.

What about steel? United States Steel and Bethlehem are the industry giants. Together with Republic Steel, Jones & Laughlin, and the few others that constitute Little Steel, they produce a large fraction of the total market. It is true that one plant's steel output may be much like another's, but it is not true that Bethlehem and Republic are so weak that each could never depress the price of steel by throwing on the market as much as it could comfortably produce.

When you go down the list, you will find that only potatoes, tobacco, wheat, and cotton come within our strict definition of perfect competition. Nylon must compete with cotton; that is very true. But in the economist's strict sense, nylon is not a product supplied under "perfect competition," nor is each of its few producers a "perfect-competitor" in the economist's sense of the term.[1]

The acid test for imperfect competition is slope of firm's demand:

FIRM DEMAND UNDER PERFECT COMPETITION

FIRM DEMAND UNDER IMPERFECT COMPETITION

FIG. 25-1. The perfect-competitor firm can sell all it wants to along its horizontal *dd* curve, never depressing market price. But the imperfect-competitor firm will find that its demand curve slopes downward as its increased *q* forces down the *P* it can get. And unless it is a sheltered monopolist, a cut in its rivals' *P*s will appreciably shift its own *dd* leftward to *d'd'*.

[1]Sometimes economists use various synonyms for perfect competition: they often call it "pure competition," in contrast to "impure, or imperfect, or monopolistic competition"; or they occasionally call it "atomistic competition," to convey the notion of numerous small firms which combine like a multitude of tiny atoms to make up the industry. Occasionally, too, an economist will say: "By perfect, I mean really perfect. The

IMPERFECT COMPETITION DEFINED

But suppose the single firm finds itself facing a demand curve which slopes appreciably downward as in Fig. 25-1(b)—which means that when it insists on throwing more on the market, it definitely does depress price along its *dd* curve—then the firm is classified by the economist as an "imperfect competitor."

Definition: "**Imperfect competition**" **prevails in an industry or group of industries wherever the individual sellers are imperfect competitors, facing their own** *nonhorizontal* *dd* **curves and thereby having some measure of control over price.**

This does not mean that a firm has absolute monopoly power over the price it can charge; as we shall see, there are varying degrees of monopolistic imperfection in different imperfectly competitive markets.[2]

Mind you, we are not saying that the owner of an imperfectly competitive firm is of poor character, that he beats his wife, or fails to pay his bills. Nor does the fact that a firm is an imperfect competitor mean that it is not keenly seeking to outsell and outadvertise its rivals. Intense commercial rivalry and "perfect competition" are not at all the same thing; indeed, Farmer Jones, perfect-competitor, will do no advertising at all. Why should he? He can sell all the wheat he can produce without depressing market price. But American Products Co., producer of Pall Mall cigarettes and an imperfect competitor, will spend much of its energies in trying to outsell Winston cigarettes, the snuff industry, and even the candy industry.

COST PATTERNS AND STRUCTURE OF MARKET IMPERFECTION

At the end of Chapter 24 we saw that continuing decreasing cost is incompatible with perfect competition. If every, or even *any*, firm in an industry could always bring down its Marginal and Average Cost in the long run merely by expanding its output q, it would soon expand to become an important fraction of the industry. In short, it would expand to become some kind of monopolist, ceasing to be a price taker and now having some measure of control over the price it gets. As soon as it has control over price, it will cease to follow the $P = MC$ rule for profit maximization. Presently we shall see why. And as soon as somebody in the system raises Price above Marginal Cost, a critic is able to find a flaw of inefficiency in the economic organization of society.

wheat market isn't 'perfect competition' unless everyone in it is perfectly *informed* about all the future, there being nowhere any *uncertainty.*" However, that is not the sense used here for perfect competition. The price of wheat will fluctuate in a way that no one can now foresee, but as long as *no seller can appreciably influence wheat price,* we shall agree to call the wheat market *perfect.* (Naturally, once you bring government control programs into the wheat picture, as in Chapter 21, you are bringing monopolistic imperfections into this perfect-competition setup.)
[2] The standard book on all this is E. H. Chamberlin, *Theory of Monopolistic Competition* (Harvard University Press, Cambridge, Mass., 1963, 8th ed.). Chamberlin prefers the term "monopolistic competition" for what is here called "imperfect competition," but that may give the impression to the layman that there is something especially nasty, or illegal, in not being a perfect-competitor, which is not Chamberlin's view. Also, confusion can result from the fact that "monopolistic competition" is sometimes used by Chamberlin as a name for Fig. 26-3's special large-group case of symmetric sellers of differentiated products, a nomenclature avoided in this book.

To avoid monopoly, costs must turn up soon:

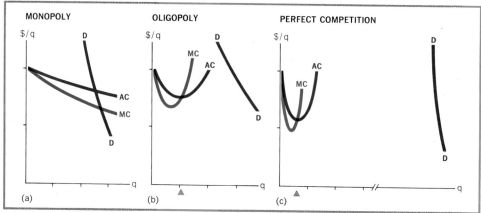

FIG. 25-2. When costs fall indefinitely, as in (a), any one firm can expand to monopolize the industry. In (b) costs eventually turn up, but not soon enough relative to total industry demand *DD*. Coexistence of numerous perfect-competitors is impossible; some kind of few-seller oligopoly is likely. In (c) total industry demand *DD* is so vast relative to efficient scale of any one seller as to permit viable coexistence of numerous *perfect-competitors*. (What if firms contrive to differentiate their product in (c), fragmenting the market and moving *DD* far to the left, ending up in some kind of Chamberlinian imperfect competition—like (b) or (a)?)

Figure 25-2 illustrates some patterns of costs which lead to a breakdown of perfect competition. In Fig. 25-2(a) the firm is shown to have Average and Marginal Costs that fall forever. It displays "increasing returns to scale": as *q* grows, the firm finds more elaborate ways of specializing its equipment; it organizes its work gangs in larger and more efficient units; it can afford ever-larger boilers and machines, which display greater net efficiency. All this without end. No matter how big is the demand for its product—no matter how far out the industry *DD* curve happens to lie, the most efficient operating size for this one firm will be greater, and peaceful competitive coexistence of thousands of price takers will be quite impossible.

Perhaps the pattern of unlimited decreasing cost is unrealistic. Perhaps *ultimately* the economies of scale will all have been achieved, and the cost curves will level out or turn up. Figure 25-2(b) illustrates such a case: the firm's long-run *MC* and *AC* curves do finally turn up. But, alas, they do not turn up soon enough to avoid the breakdown of perfect competition. For note where the industry total demand curve *DD* now lies: it does not provide a big enough market to enable *numerous* firms to coexist at the efficient level of operation called for by the indicated cost curve. We shall still end up in some kind of monopoly or few-seller "oligopoly" situation. (*Oligos* means "few" in Greek.)

In Fig. 25-2(c), the outlook is more favorable for perfect competition. Why? Because the industry *DD* (even in each local market) is so great compared with the optimum size of each firm, we can hope to replicate the large number of firms needed for truly perfect competition.

There is one encouraging feature of the modern industrial state. Large corporations find it pays them to produce many *different* products, not just the single *q* shown in these diagrams. Thus, Ford produces trucks, tractors, refrigerators, precision equipment, and not just automobiles. It is a big company—but it is really not big in the refrigerator or tractor or equipment markets. It must compete with General Electric, Litton Industries, Sears, IBM, and other giants in these markets. As far as producing more refrigerators is concerned, its costs will not continue to fall, as in Fig. 25-2(a) or (b), until it has a dominant position. Actually, because of the competition of numerous other conglomerate giants, Ford's costs relative to each diverse market's demand might look more like that of Fig. 25-2(c). The result is encouraging because it may lead to a tolerable approximation to the P and MC equivalences of efficient, perfect competition.

As Adam Smith said, "Specialization is limited by the extent of the market." He meant by this that you often cannot use the most efficient known methods when serving a *small* market. And this provided him with good ammunition for attacking the mercantilistic interferences by governments of his time that served to fragment the DD demands into many smaller DD demands—one for each country or county. He might have gone on to add this:

If you are *still* in the stage where efficient specialization is being limited by the extent of the market, then you are not yet in the state appropriate for perfect competition; instead, not-yet-exhausted economies of scale leave you in some area of imperfect or monopolistic competition. In such a case there is all the more reason for society to promote measures that will extend the market.

One more important point. Suppose we begin in the Fig. 25-2(c) situation where DD is large enough relative to the efficient size of firm operation to permit coexistence of numerous viable competitors. But suppose something arises to fragment the aggregate DD demand into much smaller separate demands for the different firms. Then perfect competition will be dethroned. Since the new DD curve confronting any firm or segment of the market will then be moved far to the left, we are really put back in Fig. 25-2(b) or even 25-2(a).

Such a case arises when restrictive tariffs are used to fragment markets and create a monopolistic situation. "The tariff is the Mother of trusts," is a slogan from American history showing that even the man in the street understands the point. And one of the purposes of the Marshall Plan for reconstructing Europe was to help create the Common Market, so that DD curves would become large enough relative to efficient production levels to promote vigorous and effective competition.

DIFFERENTIATION OF PRODUCTS

What is not so obvious is that the DD demand curves for an industry can be *deliberately fragmented* into smaller segments by the profit-seeking activities of firms. This is what the late Edward Chamberlin of Harvard called "differentiation of product."

Contrived product differentiation   Each seller tries to make his product a little different from that of any other sellers. He avoids the price competition of classical "perfect competition." Instead, he introduces brand quality competition, precisely because it is a profitable form of imperfect competition.

EXAMPLE: He makes penicillin a little different chemically. He seeks patent protection. He advertises, or sends so-called "detail men" to call on doctors, to make them think his penicillin is different, whether or not it significantly is; or more important, he advertises so that you will attach significance to such differences as are there.

What is the result when everybody successfully differentiates his product? The result is that the *DD* curves of Fig. 25-2(c)'s model of perfect competition are moved so far to the left as to become like those of the models of monopoly or oligopoly shown in Fig. 25-2(a) and (b). Fortunately, each firm is not able at will to differentiate its product successfully to any degree that it wishes, even though Galbraithian converts do exaggerate the unilateral power of advertisers.

Chamberlin would agree with much that has been said here. But he would resent the implication that all product differentiation is an artificial, contrived thing whose only purpose is to increase monopoly power and bilk the consumer. Rather, he would insist that people's tastes differ: different people want different degrees of sourness of cider; and even the same person may not want all his units of cider to be of the same sourness. Creating a great variety of differentiated products is often, Chamberlin insists, a genuine catering to basic human wants and needs. Chamberlin does not agree that we would be better off if we all agreed to wear a few basic styles of clothes, each of which is produced in long and efficient factory runs. He would stress that all tastes, including noble tastes for Bach and Rembrandt, are made by society rather than arising from the individual himself. The change of fashion, frivolous though it be, adds zest to life.

In effect, Chamberlin is *reemphasizing the importance of decreasing costs* in making perfect competition *unviable.* He is saying, "Once we replace a homogeneous output Q of the industry (or what is the same thing, the homogeneous output q of a typical firm) by a whole complex of somewhat different $Q_1, Q_2, \ldots$, then the demands will just not be big enough to permit you to have many different producers at the bottom of their efficient U-shaped cost curves." Chamberlin is arguing, "You think that as *DD* grows in Fig. 25-2(b), with population or for any other reason, society will move from the imperfect-competition model of (b) to the perfect-competition model of (c). But you are wrong. With the *bigger scale* of *DD* will come a bigger opportunity for making *more,* and more minute, *differentiations of product.*"

Natural product differentiation Even if we do not agree with Chamberlin's implication that the world is perpetually assigned to the realm of imperfect competition regardless of increases in scale, we must concede that he does have a valid and important point. His general *Weltanschauung*—that the economic world cannot be properly understood in terms of the simple models of perfect competition or complete monopoly, but must be interpreted in terms of a richer theory that involves phenomena not to be described as mere blends of these polar cases—is made more convincing by the following:

Products are often differentiated by natural as well as man-made causes. Space itself, and the transport costs associated with it, provides one important example.

Consider the steel industry. It involves very large-scale production. Yet this is a big country. So you might argue that we can tolerate numerous replications of the most efficient-sized plant. But what follows? The United States does not constitute one single market for steel. Because of transport costs, each region and each part of each region provide us with relevant *DD* curves to compare with the efficient large-scale U of cost. It would be ridiculous to think that even New York City could have the dozens or hundreds of independent integrated steel producers needed for the market model of perfect competition. And if the lobbyists of the steel industry got the import quotas they crave, the departure from competitive *MC* pricing would become even worse.

Similarly with electric-power production. In order to reach minimum Average Cost, one might today want to build a generating plant of more than 2 million kilowatts of capacity. But that efficient size is already much too big for perfect competition to prevail. Any *compact region* that had 10 such competing plants would be plagued with dreadful overcapacity.

We may conclude as follows:

Patterns of returns in which costs still decline relative to the effective size of the market imperil the realism of perfect competition and of $P = MC$ efficient social pricing. This problem is accentuated by man-made or natural differentiations of product which lower the effective *DD* levels of demands relative to the bottom of the U levels of efficient production, making competitive coexistence of numerous competing units simply non-viable. On the other hand, if larger firms produce many, many different kinds of products, each firm may be checked in its monopoly power in any one market by the fact that it meets the competition of *many* other large firms in each separate line.

Let us now survey the principal patterns of imperfections of competition.

IMPERFECT COMPETITION: MONOPOLY, OLIGOPOLY, AND DIFFERENTIATED PRODUCTS

Monopoly   How imperfect can imperfect competition get? The extreme case would be that of a *single* seller with practically complete monopoly power. (He is called a "monopolist," from the Greek word *mono* for "one" and *polist* for "seller.") He is the only one producing in his industry, and there is no industry producing a close substitute for his good. (Back in Fig. 25-1(b) on page 460, a change in another firm's price would shift his *dd* curve negligibly.)

Exclusive monopolies, like public utilities or telephones, are usually regulated by the government; and even they must usually take account of the potential competition of alternative products—oil for gas, or cables for telephones. This shows how relatively unimportant complete monopolies are.

Oligopoly   We have seen that this horrible-sounding word means "few sellers." Oligopolists are of two types.

First, an oligopolist may be one of a *few* sellers who produce an *identical* (or almost identical) product. Thus, if A's steel delivered in the New York area is much the same as B's, then the smallest price cut will drive the consumer from A to B. Neither A nor B can be called a monopolist. Yet, if the number of sellers is few, each can have a great effect on market price.

This first kind of oligopoly is thought to be common in a number of our basic industries where *product is fairly homogeneous* and size of enterprise is large—as in the aluminum and nylon industries. Another example would be that of moving freight between New York and Chicago by any of the three or four alternative rail routes. In the old days when rail rates were unregulated, there would be periodic price wars in which each railroad undercut the other in an attempt to gain more of the business: sometimes it would become cheaper to move freight from New York to Chicago than to move it from New York to Buffalo; and occasionally it might be cheaper to move freight from New York to Buffalo via Chicago, with all the implied wasteful cross-haulage.

The second kind of oligopoly is typified by the case where there are *few* sellers who sell *differentiated* (rather than identical) products. The Big Three in the auto industry are examples: three producers dominate the industry, but the Fords, Chevrolets, and Plymouths that they make are *somewhat differentiated* products. In the cigarette industry, a few large sellers own the numerous brands and types (filter, king-size, and regular) that compete for and get the bulk of the business. In heavy machinery, such companies as General Electric, Westinghouse, Allis-Chalmers, and others illustrate the case of an oligopoly that has few sellers and some differentiation of product.

Many differentiated sellers   This is the last in our list of imperfect competitors. Here there are many sellers, but now they do *not* produce *identical* products as in the case of many perfect-competitors. Instead, they produce "differentiated products," i.e., products which differ somewhat in real qualities or which the buyer thinks differ in real qualities. My toothpaste is a little different from yours; and if I raise my price above yours, I may still hope to sell a good deal to those consumers conditioned by my advertising or by past use of my product.

Advertising, brand names, trademarks, patents, and custom may explain why there is product differentiation. Or it may merely be that a given barber shop or grocery store is in a locality near to certain consumers: the fact of this nearness may give it a measure of monopoly power; and yet, if its price gets too high, it will find itself losing trade to more distant competitors. (This time back in Fig. 25-1(b), when your rivals cut their P, your *dd* curve shifts leftward and downward *appreciably*.)

All these four categories of market structure overlap. They range in degree from perfect competition to a large number of differentiated sellers, to the two kinds of oligopoly, and finally to the limiting case of monopoly.

BRIEF SUMMARY OF KINDS OF COMPETITION AND MARKET STRUCTURE

Table 25-1 gives a brief picture of the various possible categories of imperfect and perfect competition. It merits close study, for we shall later examine each of its cases.

The remainder of this chapter will analyze the principles of profit maximization, concentrating mostly on the limiting case of a complete monopoly. As has been mentioned, few firms in real life enjoy anything like a complete monopoly: usually some other products will be partially substitutable for the ones you sell. If for some unnatural reason you were in a position of practically unchecked monopoly, we can be sure that the modern

Most industries are imperfectly competitive—a blend of monopoly and competition:

KIND OF COMPETITION	NUMBER OF PRO-DUCERS AND DEGREE OF PRODUCT DIF-FERENTIATION	PART OF ECONOMY WHERE PREVALENT	DEGREE OF CONTROL OVER PRICE	METHODS OF MARKETING
TYPES OF COMPETITION				
Perfect competition	Many producers; identical products	A few agricultural industries	None	Market exchange or auction
Imperfect competition:				
Many differ-entiated sellers	Many producers; many real or fancied differences in product	Toothpaste, retail trade; conglom-erates		
Oligopoly	Few producers; little or no difference in product	Steel, aluminum	Some	Advertising and quality rivalry; administered prices
	Few producers; some differentiation of products	Autos, machinery		
Complete monopoly	Single producer; unique product without close substitutes	A few utilities	Considerable	Promotional and "institutional" public-relations advertising

TABLE 25-1.

mixed economy would make you subject to public regulation. The example of public regulation of such utilities as electricity, gas, and telephones comes immediately to mind; and by the end of the chapter we shall be in a position to understand the proper principle of monopoly regulation.

The tools useful to understand Maximum-profit equilibrium for the complete monopoly—namely, Marginal Cost and Marginal Revenue—turn out to be the tools needed to understand Maximum-profit equilibrium in the more realistic cases of oligopoly and various forms of imperfect competition. They lay the groundwork for Chapter 26's study of antitrust policies of government to prevent and control monopolies.

PRICE, QUANTITY, AND TOTAL REVENUE

What is the Maximum-profit output q that a monopolist will try to produce in any situation? What is the accompanying Maximum-profit price P that it should charge?

It turns out that old and new *marginal* concepts provide the key to the common-sense

Marginal Revenue numbers come from demand-schedule P and q data, and

TOTAL AND MARGINAL REVENUE

(1)	(2)	(3)	(4)
QUANTITY q	PRICE $P = AR = R/q$	TOTAL REVENUE $R = P \times q$	MARGINAL REVENUE MR
0	$200	$ 0	+ $200
			+ 180
1	180	180	+ 160
			+ 140
2	160	320	+ 120
			+ 100
3	140	420	+ 80
			+ 60
4	120	480	+ 40
			+ 20
5	100	500	0
			− 20
6	80	480	− 40
			− 60
7	60	420	− 80
			− 100
8	40	320	− 120
			− 140
9	10	180	− 160
			− 180
10	0	0	

TABLE 25-2.   Total Revenue is easily computed from demand curve data. To get blue Marginal Revenue, we increase q by a unit and calculate the difference in Total Revenue it brings. Note MR is at first positive, but after demand turns inelastic, MR becomes negative. Price never becomes negative, but MR lies below P because of loss owing to the necessity to lower price on previous units if the new unit of q is to get sold. (Light data of instantaneous Marginal Revenue come from smoothed MR curve of Fig. 25-3(a).)

trial-and-error procedure of maximizing profit. The final results will agree with common sense, after analysis discloses the good sense in common sense.

As far as costs are concerned, all the tools that we shall need have already been developed in Chapter 24's discussion of costs (MC, AC, TC, and so forth).

Here, therefore, we can begin with the sales revenue side of things. From the firm's demand curve dd, we know the relation between P and the q it can sell. Table 25-2 indicates this relationship, for a hypothetical firm, in Column (2). And Fig. 25-3(a) depicts, in brown, the dd demand curve for this monopolist (who is given, for simplicity, a straight-line demand curve). Column (3) of Table 25-2 shows how to get the firm's Total Revenue by multiplying $P \times q$: thus 0 units bring in $TR = 0$; 1 unit brings in $TR = \$180 \times 1$; 2 units bring in $\$160 \times 2 = \$320$. The general rule is this: $TR = P \times q$.

Total Revenue at first rises with q, since the reduction in P needed to sell the extra

also Marginal Revenue curve comes from demand curve:

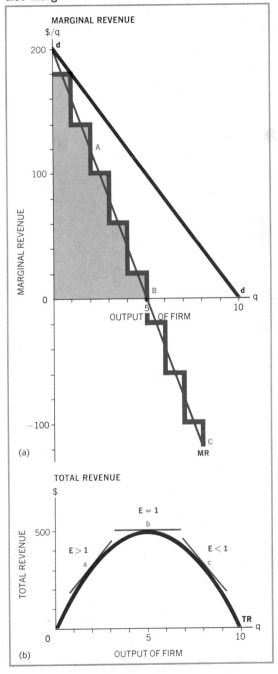

(a)

FIG. 25-3(a). The blue steps show the increments of Total Revenue from each new unit of output as calculated from Table 25-2 (or from the *TR* of Fig. 25-3(b) below). *MR* falls below *P* from the beginning, actually dropping twice as fast as the straight-line *dd* curve. *MR* becomes negative when *dd* turns inelastic. Smoothing the incremental steps of *MR* gives the blue *MR* curve, which in the case of straight-line *dd* will always have twice as steep a slope as *dd*. (NOTE: These values for smoothed *MR* are the same as the light numbers in column (4) of Table 25-2.)

FIG. 25-3(b). Total Revenue is dome-shaped, rising from zero (where $q =$ 0) to a maximum (where *dd* has unitary elasticity) and then falling back to zero (where $P = 0$). *TR*'s slope gives instantaneous smoothed *MR*, just as jumps in *TR* give steps of incremental *MR*.

q is moderate in this first *elastic* range of the demand curve. But when we get to some intermediate point on *dd*, *TR* reaches its maximum—at $q = 5, P = \$100$, and $TR = \$500$. Increasing q beyond this point brings you into *inelastic* demand regions, and now the percentage cut in P needed to sell 1 per cent more q is so much greater than 1 that it cuts down on TR. Figure 25-3(b) shows TR to be dome-shaped, rising from zero to a maximum of $500 and falling back to zero when P has become vanishingly small.

Already Table 25-2 illustrates an important fallacy: "A firm out to maximize its profits will always charge what the 'traffic will bear.' That means charging the highest possible price." This statement is wrong. A profit maximizer may not be an altruist; but that does not mean he is a fool. To charge the highest possible price is to sell *no q* at all and to get no TR at all! Even if we reinterpret this doctrine to mean charging the highest price at which anything at all can be sold, it is obvious that selling but one unit even at a high price is not the way to maximize your profit. Even if we neglect (for a moment) all costs, the correct interpretation of charging what the traffic will bear must mean that we find the best *compromise* between a high P and a high q if we are to get the best profit. In Table 25-2, it is at $q = 5$ that $P \times q = TR$ is at a maximum: this is the point where demand elasticity turns into demand inelasticity.

Before proceeding now to introduce the important concept of Marginal Revenue, we can note the fact that the *Price* at which each q is sold could be called *Average Revenue* to distinguish it from Total Revenue. Thus, we get $P \equiv AR$ by dividing TR by q (just as we earlier got AC by dividing TC by q). Verify that if Column (3) had been written down *before* Column (2), we could then have filled in Column (2) by division. To test understanding, fill in the blanks of Columns (2) and (3).

MARGINAL REVENUE AND PRICE

We need a test to determine by how much Total Revenue is gaining or losing as we increase q. Marginal Revenue is the convenient concept for this purpose.

Definition: "Marginal Revenue" is defined as the increment of Total Revenue (plus or minus) that comes when we increase q by an increment of one unit. **MR is plus when demand is still elastic, minus when demand is inelastic, and just crosses zero when demand turns from being elastic to being inelastic. (If units of q are divisible, the blue MR steps of Fig. 25-3(a) can be replaced by a smooth MR curve.)**

The blue numbers of Marginal Revenue are shown in Column (4) of Table 25-2; they are calculated by subtracting the TR we get by selling q units from the TR we get by selling $q + 1$ units, the difference being our extra revenue or MR. Thus, from $q = 0$ to $q = 1$, we get $MR = \$180 - 0$. From $q = 1$ to $q = 2$, MR is $\$320 - 180 = \$140$.

MR is positive until we arrive at $q = 5$, and negative from then on. That does not mean you are giving goods away at a negative price. Actually, Average Revenue, which is P, continues to be positive. It is merely that, in order to sell the sixth unit of q, you must reduce the price so much on *all* the units as to end up getting less TR—which is what the negative MR is telling you.

This warns us: Do *not* confuse Marginal Revenue with Average Revenue or Price. The table shows they are different. Review Fig. 25-3(a) and note that the plotted blue steps of MR definitely lie below the brown dd curve of AR. In fact, MR will have already turned negative when dd is only partway down toward zero.

Just why is *MR* definitely less than *P* (or *AR*) for the imperfect competitor? True, I sell my last unit of *q* for *P*. But what did I have to do to coax out that last unit of sale? Clearly, I had to lower my *P*, since I didn't face a perfect-competitor's horizontal *dd*. But in lowering my *P* for the last new buyer, I also had to *lower* P *for all the previous buyers.* So my extra revenue, my *MR*, is evidently less than *P* by this loss on previous units from the price drop. QED.

Summary: **With *dd* demand sloping,**
$$P > MR \ (= P - \text{Loss on previous } q)$$

In Column (4) of Table 25-2, the light numbers of smoothed *MR* are also seen to be less than Column (2)'s *P*s.

Only under perfect competition, where the sale of extra units will never depress price at all, is the loss-in-revenue term zero. Only then will Price and Marginal Revenue be identical. Graphically, a straight-line *MR* curve always has twice the steepness of the *dd* curve. But if *dd* is horizontal, as in perfect competition, so then must *MR* be: thus, a perfect-competitor's *dd* and *MR* coincide as the same horizontal line!

This completes our analysis of Marginal Revenue and equips us for the task of finding Maximum-profit equilibrium of the firm.

B. MAXIMUM-PROFIT MONOPOLY EQUILIBRIUM: DIVERGENCE OF PRICE AND MARGINAL COST

Now suppose the firm wants to maximize its Total Profit. To do this it must bring in, along with the Total Revenue information it gets from its demand side, the Total Cost information described in Chapter 24.

Definition: **Total Profit equals Total Revenue minus Total Cost:**
$$TP = TR - TC = P \times q - TC$$
To maximize its profit the firm must seek out the equilibrium price and quantity, *P**
and *q**, that gives it the largest difference, *TR − TC*.

Common sense tells us this Maximum-profit will occur only where the firm's Marginal (or extra) Revenue has just come into balance with its Marginal (or extra) Cost.

We may now bring all our relevant facts together in a supertable, Table 25-3 on the next page. Total Profit is, of course, the column of greatest interest in this table.

What quantity *q** will maximize Total Profit, and at what price? The easiest way to solve this problem is to compute Column (5), Total Profit, which is simply the difference between Total Revenue and Total Cost. Running our eyes down this column tells us:

The optimal quantity is 4 units, with a price of $120 per unit. After taking account of Total Cost, we see that no other situation will give us as much profit as the $230 at *q** = 4 and *P** = $120.

Another way of arriving at the same result is to compare Marginal Revenue, Column (6), and Marginal Cost, Column (7). (*MR* is computed from the *TR* column, as in Table 25-2. Recall from the last chapters that *MC* is similarly calculated from *TC*.)

As long as a step toward extra output gives us more Marginal Revenue than Marginal

Equating Marginal Cost to Marginal Revenue gives the firm its Maximum-profit q and P—

SUMMARY OF FIRM'S MAXIMUM PROFIT

(1) QUANTITY q	(2) PRICE P	(3) TOTAL REVENUE TR	(4) TOTAL COST TC	(5) TOTAL PROFIT TP	(6) MARGINAL REVENUE MR	(7) MARGINAL COST MC	
0	200	0	145	−145	+200	34	
					+180	30	MR > MC
1	180	180	175	+5	+160	27	
					+140	25	
2	160	320	200	+120	+120	22	
					+100	20	
3	140	420	220	+200	+80	21	
					+60	30	
4*	120	480	250	+230	+40	40	MR = MC
					+20	50	
5	100	500	300	+200	0	60	
					−20	70	
6	80	480	370	+110	−40	80	
					−60	90	
7	60	420	460	−40	−80	100	
					−100	110	MR < MC
8	40	320	570	−250			

* Maximum-profit equilibrium.

TABLE 25-3. Total and Marginal Cost of production are now brought together with Total and Marginal Revenue. The Maximum-profit decision is where $MR = MC$, with $q^* = 4$, $P^* — \$120$, and maximum profit $TP = \$230 = \$120 \times 4 − \$250$. (NOTE: For convenience, the light MR and MC numbers are put in to give the smoothed instantaneous values at each q point itself: disregarding these, we could get the same result.)

Cost, our profit is *increasing* and we continue to produce more output. But whenever Marginal Cost exceeds Marginal Revenue, we *contract* output. Where is equilibrium?

Maximum-profit equilibrium is where Marginal Revenue and Marginal Cost are equal. $MR = MC$, the Maximum-profit point

This second way of finding the optimum point by comparing Marginal Cost and Marginal Revenue is neither better nor worse than the first method of simply examining Total Profits. They are essentially exactly the same method.

GRAPHICAL DEPICTION OF FIRM'S MAXIMUM-PROFIT POSITION

The curves of Fig. 25-4 illustrate these procedures. In Fig. 25-4(a), MC intersects MR at E, the Maximum-profit point, where $q^* = 4$. We run up vertically from E to the dd curve to G, where $P = \$120$. The fact that G lies *above* F, the point on the AC curve at $q^* = 4$, guarantees a positive profit. (We cannot read directly the amount of Total Profit unless we calculate the area of the shaded rectangle.)

The same story is told in Fig. 25-4(b) with total curves. Total Revenue is dome-shaped.

and graphs of marginal and total curves can show this same Maximum-profit equilibrium:

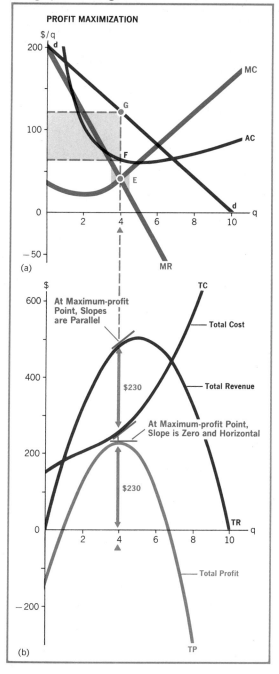

(a)

FIG. 25-4(a). At E, where MC intersects MR, equilibrium position of Maximum-profit is found. Any move from E will lose some profit. Price is at G above E; and since P is above AC, the maximized profit is a positive profit. (Can you understand why the shaded gold rectangle measures Total Profit? And why the blue triangle of shading on either side of E shows the reduction in Total Profit that would come from a departure from $MR = MC$—i.e., the greater loss of extra revenue in comparison with extra cost?)

(b)

FIG. 25-4(b). This tells the same story of maximizing profit as above, but uses total concepts rather than marginal concepts. Total Profit is given by vertical distance from TC up to TR. This is at a maximum where the two brown total curves have equal and parallel slopes, $MR = MC$. This is necessary if gold Total Profit curve is to be at a maximum, with its blue slope horizontal as MR cancels out MC.

Total Cost is ever rising. The vertical difference between them is Total Profit, which begins negative and ends negative. In between, TP is positive, reaching its maximum of $230 at $q^* = 4$, where the blue slopes of TR and TC are equal and parallel: if these

MR and *MC* slopes were pointing outward in a nonparallel fashion (as at $q = 2$), we should gain a little extra profit by expanding q. At $q^* = 4$ things are at their best balance. This is verified by the Total Profit curve, whose blue slope is horizontal at its peak: *TP*'s slope is clearly the difference $MR - MC$, and this slope should definitely have a zero value at the maximum.[3]

Excess of *P* above *MC*. For the firm with some monopoly power, maximizing profits by equating Marginal Revenue to Marginal Cost leads to a price that is *above* Marginal Cost. The canny seller *contrives an artificial scarcity of his product* so as not to spoil the price he can get on the earlier premarginal units.

PERFECT COMPETITION A SPECIAL CASE OF IMPERFECT COMPETITION

This completes our discussion of Marginal Revenue and Marginal Cost as tools to maximize profit. It will add to your confidence in the result if you find that the general $MR = MC$ rule is consistent, when applied to a *perfect-competitor*, with Chapter 23's $P = MC$ rule for a profit-maximizing perfect-competitor. Is it? Yes, indeed. Here is why:

For a small perfect-competitor, Marginal Revenue works out to be exactly the same thing as Price. With no need to cut your *P* to sell an extra unit of *q*, the incremental Marginal Revenue it brings you is precisely the *P* received for that last unit, with no loss on previous units being subtracted.[4] Hence, $MR = MC$ and $P \equiv MR$ do lead to the special rule for profit maximizing by a perfect-competitor:

$$P = MR = MC \text{ at a perfect-competitor's Maximum-profit point}$$

These tools to show how a rational firm will find its Maximum-profit equilibrium will later apply to firms under monopoly, oligopoly, or anything else.

BYGONES AND MARGINS

While economic theory does not aim to make you necessarily a successful businessman, it does introduce you to some new ways of thinking. Here is one instance.

The economist always stresses the "extra," or "marginal," costs and advantages of any decision. He says:

Let bygones be bygones. Don't look backward. Don't moan about your sunk costs. Look forward. Make a hard-headed calculation of the *extra* costs you'll incur by any decision and weigh these against its *extra* advantages. Cancel out all the good things and bad things *that will go on anyway*, whether you make an affirmative or negative decision on the point under consideration.

---

[3] Those who know elementary calculus need not use the finite-step definitions of *MR* and *MC* as ΔTR and ΔTC. Instead they can use the smoothed instantaneous slopes of the *TR* and *TC* functions of q; i.e., define $MR = d(TR)/dq$ and $MC = d(TC)/dq$, and note that maximizing $TR - TC$ of profit requires finding the q^* root of the equation: $d(\text{profit})/dq = 0 = d(TC)/dq - d(TR)/dq = MR - MC$. QED. (See Extra-credit problem, question 7, on page 478 for more on this.)

[4] If you redraw Fig. 25-4(a) for a perfect-competitor, make *dd* horizontal and coinciding with *MR*. Then proceed to find the *MR* and *MC* intersection as usual (which gives the old *MC* supply story of Chapter 23). In the new version of Fig. 25-4(b), *TR* merely becomes a straight line, rising from the origin, but the slopes of *TR* and *TC* must still match at the Maximum-profit equilibrium point.

This disregarding of bygones is extremely important, and most successful decision-makers practice it intuitively, even if they have not had a formal course in economics. Here is an application of this principle:

The King taxes a monopolist a flat sum for his match-monopoly franchise—say $100 per day, no matter what he does. How will this affect the new Maximum-profit P and q? If you have grasped the tools of this chapter, you will discover that a flat-sum tax will not shift either the MR or MC curve. If the monopolist successfully maximizes his profits before and after the tax and if nothing else changes and if he stays in business, the *flat-sum tax will have absolutely no effect on price or output*, but will be borne completely by the monopolist! (Can you verify that adding $100 to every TC number in Table 25-3 merely subtracts $100 from every profit in Column (5), leaving you with the same Maximum-profit $q^* = 4$ and $P^* = \$120$?[5])

HOW IMPERFECTION OF COMPETITION AFFECTS RESOURCE ALLOCATION

In the next chapter we shall study some of the important cases of imperfect competition—oligopoly and so forth. This will involve us in important public questions that lie in the field of "antitrust policy." As preparation, let us recall again how deviations from perfect competition affect the efficiency with which a free-price system solves the important problems of WHAT, HOW, and FOR WHOM.

Under free pricing, when firms face a sloping demand curve, their Marginal Revenue is below their Price. Then, to the degree that such imperfect competitors intelligently pursue their self-interest, they will *not* be led by Adam Smith's Invisible Hand to perform the acts needed to promote the general interest.

Let us recapitulate how this divergence between Price and Marginal Cost will affect the goodness or badness of the way the economy is organizing its production and distribution. We have already met this complex question, and will do so again.

Excess profit of monopoly First, the imperfect competitor may be earning more than he would if the government made him compete like a perfect-competitor. If so, is that excess-profit a good or a bad thing? Is he a more worthy man than most? Is he poorer than most, and more in need? (And will he use his gains to subsidize the arts, or to pay for vulgar display? Will he use any monopoly profits to sponsor new industrial research? Or to sponsor research in ways to convince consumers that his product is better than others'.)

[5]Suppose the King put a flat-sum tax of $230 on Fig. 25-4's monopolist to wipe out all his profit. The new Fig. 25-5 shows the story. MR, MC, and dd are exactly as before. (Why?) But now AC has been shifted up because of the added tax, Fixed Cost. Only at the price of G, where the dd curve is *tangent* to the new AC curve, can the firm break even: everywhere else it makes a loss; maximizing profit by finding $MR = MC$ now means avoiding loss. (But see the next section and the Appendix for a demonstration that taxing away monopoly profit does still leave society with a discrepancy between Price, or Marginal Utility, and Marginal Cost.)

FIG. 25-5.

When the man in the street thinks of the monopoly problem, he gives most weight to the above question—to the way it affects the FOR WHOM problem of distribution.[6] Yet, *even if it has no harmful effect on income distribution by creating excess-profits, monopolistic imperfection can still be shown to represent an important economic evil.*

Deficient output of monopoly   To see this, imagine that all money votes are distributed properly and A is the only imperfect competitor in the system. Everyone else is a perfect-competitor, who keeps his MC equal to his P. Price is the signal that consumers use to indicate how much they value various goods. Costs, and particularly Marginal Cost, are the indicators of how much of society's valuable resources each good's production utilizes: scarce land, sweaty labor, and other resources that could produce other goods. Everywhere else, competitive firms are giving people what they most want by producing right up to the point of $P = MC$, where goods are shown to be worth what they cost.

But take the imperfect competitor A—the one deviant. What is he doing? A is not forcing people to buy from him. But the fact that A faces a sloping demand curve shows he does have some control over P. How is he using that power? Does he produce goods up to the point where their social cost—as measured by his MC—is equal to what the last unit of the good is worth to society—as measured by market P resulting from consumer money votes? No.

The imperfect competitor is contriving to keep things a little scarce. He is contriving to keep P above MC because in that way he sets $MR = MC$ and thereby maximizes his profit. So society does not get quite as much of A's good as it really wants in terms of what that good really costs society of produce![7]

Do not think A is a villain. If he did not intelligently try to maximize his firm's long-run profits, he might be displaced by the stockholders or be sued. Even if A owned the company and chose to lower P to MC, he would be shunting money from his wife and kids to the public at large. While there is no law against his being such an altruist, such a Santa Claus, the betting odds are against this. And in any case such an optimal solution to the problem *by chivalry* has nothing to do with Adam Smith's Invisible Hand—which insisted that *self*-interest (not altruism) would perform, under ruthless competition, the miracle of providing for the general interest.

The clue to the Invisible Hand paradox is this: Adam Smith would have to rely on

---

[6] In Fig. 25-5 of the last footnote, the monopolist was stripped of his excess-profit by taxes, but the vertical arrow showing the discrepancy between P (at G) and MC (at E) shows that monopoly q is still too small and should be expanded as shown by the lower horizontal gold arrow.

As the next chapter shows, imperfect competition of many differentiated producers might result in no one's making a profit if there is "free entry" into the Chamberlinian industry in question. Yet P might still stay above MC, and so the result might still be tremendous wastage of resources because we have too many corners with too many gasoline stations, each with too many idle attendants (who in the end are not even well rewarded for being imperfect competitors). To be sure, more gas stations could mean shorter walks for people out of gas and more consumer convenience generally; but who is to say that the optimal amount of such differentiation-of-product convenience is being provided under any particular regime of imperfect competition?

[7] As Fig. 20-9, page 375, showed, it is a social inefficiency when monopolists' outputs are too small and competitors' outputs get expanded beyond their optimal amounts. Chapter 23's Fig. 23-7 clinched the point with its comparison of competitive MC pricing with a Crusoe-Planner optimum of welfare. (See this chapter's Appendix, pages 479–480, for more on this.)

strictly defined "perfect competition" to get his result. As soon as we have imperfect competition in the real world, we have left the Garden of Eden and there arises the problem of how to minimize the evil and wastes involved in such imperfections of competition. Chapter 26 analyzes the main forms of imperfect competition and surveys the antitrust policies of modern governments. And the brief Appendix to this chapter indicates the *economic* principles that should underlie public regulation of monopoly and imperfect competition and should underlie antitrust philosophy and law.

SUMMARY

A. OVERVIEW OF MARKET STRUCTURE AND THE CONCEPT OF MARGINAL REVENUE

1 Most market situations in the real world can be thought of as falling on a line between the limiting poles of perfect competition and complete monopoly. Imperfect competition involves some control by each of its firms over its own price, by virtue of the fact that there are not *a very large number of rivals* who sell *exactly the same product* as it does. (Note the italicized words.) Important cases are (1) *Oligopoly*—few sellers of similar or differentiated products—and (2) *many sellers of differentiated* products.

2 Decreasing-cost tendencies are destructive of perfect competition, since one or a few corporations then kill off the numerous sellers needed for the competitive model. (However, big conglomerates, which produce many products and invade each others' markets, may each find themselves constitutional rather than absolute monarchs, unable to dominate their separate markets.)

3 From the firm's demand curve, we can easily derive its Total Revenue curve. From the schedule or curve of Total Revenue, we can easily derive its Marginal Revenue—the extra revenue resulting from the sale of an extra unit of output. Ordinarily, Marginal Revenue will fall short of Price because of the *loss on all previous units* of output that will result when we are forced to drop our price in order to sell an extra unit of output.

B. MAXIMUM-PROFIT MONOPOLY EQUILIBRIUM: DIVERGENCE OF PRICE AND MARGINAL COST

4 A firm will find its Maximum-profit position where the last little unit it sells brings in extra revenue just equal to its extra cost. This same $MR = MC$ result can be shown graphically by intersecting $MR = MC$ curves, or by the equality of the slopes of the Total Revenue and Total Cost curves. In any case, *Marginal Revenue = Marginal Cost* must hold at the equilibrium position of Maximum-profit.

5 Economic reasoning leads to an emphasis upon *marginal* advantages and disadvantages—to a *cancellation of bygones* and factors that go on no matter how you make a decision.

6   Imperfection of competition, by putting P above MC for some goods, acts as one extra deterrent to Adam Smith's Invisible Hand, which tried to convert mankind's selfish interest to a best solution of society's WHAT, HOW, and FOR WHOM problems.

QUESTIONS FOR DISCUSSION

1   List distinguishing features of perfect and imperfect competition. How might you characterize U.S. Steel? Bethlehem Steel? AT&T? A & P? Sears? Farmer Jones?

2   "A corporation charges what the traffic will bear." Interpret.

3   What is the numerical value of MR when dd has unitary elasticity and TR is constant?

4   Relate MR to P, at $q = 4$ or 5 in Tables 25-2 and 25-3, showing loss on previous units.

5   Figure 25-4(a) and (b) describes the Maximum-profit equilibrium position. Explain in detail that it really shows two different ways of describing exactly the same fact, namely, that a firm will stop when the extra cost of a further move just balances its extra revenue.

6   Here is a hard question. "If a monopolist is big enough to affect the P for the good he sells, he may also be big enough to affect the price of materials and the labor he buys. (He becomes what is called a 'monopsonist'—or 'single buyer.') In computing MC as it *looks to him*, he will debit against the last unit of q the *rise* in wage forced on all the *previous* units of labor by his need to hire more labor. Private pecuniary MC, so computed, is higher than the true MC society wants P equated to for efficiency." Interpret this if you can (but if you cannot, don't worry as Chapter 29's footnote 4, page 562, will return to this.)

7   *Extra-credit problem:* Firm A has dd demand function, $P = 15 - .05q$, and hence $TR = qP = 15q - .05q^2$. Its $TC = q + .02q^2$. Verify: $MR = d(TR)/dq = 15 - .1q$, $MC = d(TC)/dq = 1 + .04q$. So $d(\text{profit})/dq = 0$ at $MR = MC$ or at $15 - .1q = 1 + .04q$ or at $q^* = 100$. Then $P^* = 15 - 5 = \$10 > MC^* = \$5$. Maximum-profit $= \$1,000 - (100 + 200) = \$700$. Can you show that a tax of \$1/unit will add $1q$ to TC, cutting q^* by $100/14$ units and raising P by $5/14$ units? Had the firm been competitive, with dd at the \$5 level, its Maximum-profit on $q^* = 100$ would have been $\$500 - \$300 = \$200$; and now a \$1/unit tax would cut competitor's q^* by much more than monopolist's— namely, by $100/4 = 25$ units. [HINT: Now maximize $\{5q - (q + .02q^2)\} - 1q$]

Review your understanding of the following concepts:

perfect versus imperfect competition
decreasing costs and monopolistic
   imperfection
monopoly, oligopoly, product differentiation
rivalry versus perfect competition
$MR = MC$ condition at Maximum-profit

MR in relation to P (loss on
   previous units)
$MR = P$, $P = MC$, for perfect-competitor
bygones versus relevant alternatives
inefficiency of $P > MC$
imperfection of competition and
   Smith's Invisible Hand

APPENDIX: Monopoly Regulation and Exploitation; Game Theory

Figure 25-6 repeats a monopoly equilibrium like that of Fig. 25-4(a). The monopolist is seen to be (1) making a profit, as shown by the gold-shaded rectangle near G; and (2) charging a P above MC, as shown by the EG discrepancy.

Suppose a public-utility commission is set up to regulate the monopolist. Or suppose the antitrust department of the government threatens to arrest him. If the regulators decide to make him charge a price that will wipe out his excess-profits, they will move him to H, the intersection of his dd and AC curves. Here $P = AC$, and price covers only normal costs.

How good is this solution? Economically speaking, it probably does represent something of an improvement. First, the owner of the monopoly is probably no more deserving, or poorer, than the consumers. So there is no reason to let him extort monopoly profits

from them to him. By wiping out monopolistic profit, we probably have a more "equitable distribution of income." (WARNING: Value judgments that go beyond technical economics are involved in such a conclusion.)

Second, the regulators have lowered the discrepancy between Price and Marginal Cost in making the monopolist cut his P from G to H. Why deem this an improvement? Because (equity considerations aside and assuming that dollars truly reflect social utilities and social costs) the expanded q units are worth more to people in Marginal Utility than their extra or Marginal Cost. (PROOF: Between G and H, dd lies above the MC curve.)

IDEALLY REGULATED PRICING

If $P = MC$ is such a good thing, why shouldn't the regulators go all the way and make the monopolist lower P until he is at the intersection point of the dd and MC curves (at J)?

Actually, requiring $P = MC$ *is* the ideal target for optimal efficiency. But with a decreasing-cost situation like this one—and we saw in Fig. 25-2, page 462, that much of monopoly, oligopoly, and other forms of imperfect competition come from decreasing-cost cases—setting $P = MC$ while AC is still falling will involve the firm in a *chronic loss*. (REMEMBER: Falling AC means $MC < AC$; or $P = MC < AC$.)

How can society achieve its ideal of $P = MC$, where the Marginal Utility of output just matches its Marginal Cost at the equilibrium amount? The answer involves a *permanent government subsidy* to the decreasing-cost producer. Where does the subsidy come from? From the general budget (and ideally from taxes collected on a "lump-sum" basis so that people's marginal decisions are not distorted by attempts to minimize taxes).[1]

Under unregulated monopoly, price is set too high:

FIG. 25-6. Maximum-profit equilibrium for the unregulated monopolist is at G, directly above the intersection of MR and long-run MC, with P above MC and with monopoly profit shown by the shaded rectangle.

Public-utility regulation of the monopoly would set its price down to the H intersection of demand with long-run average cost; this wipes out excess-profit; more important, it brings price down closer to the Marginal Cost level at J, where marginal social costs and benefits are appropriately balanced.

Ideally, P should be forced all the way down to MC at J, with the chronic loss being covered by permanent government (lump-sum) subsidy.

---

[1] Some qualifications are given in advanced treatises. (1) If lump-sum taxes are not politically feasible, the evil from $P = MC$ must be balanced against the distortion from taxation. (2) As Fig. 32-2 will show, a decision has to be made whether the money needed to subsidize the J point could not be used better elsewhere, with this q set equal to zero. (3) If the consumers of this good are especially "deserving"—or if this should be a good that society deems even more worthwhile than the valuations that consumers themselves act on—there may be a case for even greater subsidy. (Reverse the argument if the good is opium or is something bought only by those who already have too large a share of society's income.) (4) Recall Fig. 25-5 (and see Fig. 26-3), where it is

What if dd in Fig. 25-6 shifts to intersect MC at J', beyond the bottom of U-shaped AC? Then the regulators should insist on having P at the profitable J' point, not at the new H' Break-even point. But, as with profitable TV channels, the government should auction off licenses or tax away all their excess-profit.

Helping all　We can now demonstrate that if $P_1 > MC_1$ in one monopolized industry and $P_i = MC_i$ in *all* other perfectly competitive industries, then it is possible to expand the monopoly Q_1 and contract the competitive outputs in such a way as to make *any* (and hence, if we wish, *every*) consumer or worker better off.[2]

Suppose we define units of goods so that monopoly P_1 equals competitive P_2 (i.e., we could use a dollar's worth of monopolized berries and of competitive wheat as our amounts). Since only the monopolist's P exceeds MC, this means that the ratio of MC in monopoly to MC in the competitive industries is less than 1. But recall from Chapter 22 that for each consumer $MU_1/P_1 = MU_2/P_2$. Hence for any single consumer the ratio of Marginal Utilities is exactly one, and is thus greater than the ratios of Marginal Costs. This means that the monopoly good is being kept so scarce that it is still yielding more MU_1 than its true MC_1 cost.

Any one sovereign consumer could command: "Transfer a small amount of labor from competitive industry 2 to monopoly industry 1. This will give you *more* than 1 unit of new Q_1 for each lost unit of old Q_2, because $MC_1 < MC_2$, (that is, the resources in one extra unit of Q_1 are less than the resources in one extra unit of Q_2). Now freeze everyone in the United States except me at their old consumption levels. Then they are certainly *as well off as before.* But when you give me more than 1 new Q_1 for 1 sacrificed old Q_2, I am certainly *now better off* since previously each good has had the *same MU* to me. Hence, any one man like me can be made better off by removing monopoly imperfections without hurting anyone else! QED."

Monopoly exploitation of labor　This sagacious consumer might even add: "Actually, if you had divided up the benefits more evenly, you could have made *all* people who consume the two goods better off.

"And furthermore, any worker who now chooses to work an extra new minute picking berries in the monopolized industry will find that the true amount of new berries he picks is greater than what he could buy at the monopolist's P_1 with his last minute's wage— because the monopolist is marking up P_1 over true Marginal Cost. (NOTE: the same improvement is *not* possible under competition.)

"Hence, the monopoly imperfection is indeed inefficient in the sense that there is seen to exist a way to depart from it and improve any worker while at the same time not hurting *anyone* else (i.e., have the worker spend an extra minute picking berries and eating them)! QED again."

Summary: Monopolistic deviation from $P = MC$, means "exploitation" of labor (and other transferable resources), in the sense that society's labor is misapplied as between goods and leisure or as between too-scarce monopolized goods in relation to too-plentiful competitive goods.

We shall have more to say about exploitation in Parts Four and Six. But one warning is in order here. Often monopolies can afford to pay workers *even more* than competitive industries can, sharing so to speak a mite of the monopoly swag with the workers. So raising wages in monopoly industries by trade-union action is *not* the way to get rid of *this* kind of exploitation.[3] It is *all* society that is being exploited, and it is a task for antitrust policy to reform the situation.

ECONOMIC WARFARE: THE THEORY OF GAMES

Oligopoly sometimes breaks out into intermittent warfare. Vanderbilt and Drew used to cut and recut shipping rates on their parallel railroads. By undercutting competitors' prices, John D. Rockefeller used to drive them to the wall or into mergers. When Boeing and Douglas first brought jet planes to market, each had to wonder how high his rival would set his price, asking, "What do they think we think they will do?"

Such a situation, "where two (or more) *free wills* each choose strategies that will affect both *interdependently*," constitutes the essence of the philosophical problems involved in the theory of games. This

---

shown that a flat-sum tax could wipe out the monopolist's profit but leave you with the socially inefficient $P - MC$ discrepancy. (5) If in many other industries $P > MC$, it may not be optimal to bring P all the way down to MC in this industry alone.

[2] When it is impossible to make everyone better off, advanced books speak of "Pareto optimality," named after Vilfredo Pareto. This concept does not come to grips with "interpersonal equities," but it does throw light on "efficiency."

[3] See footnote 4, on page 562, for union actions that can offset "*monopsonistic* exploitation of labor" by employers who have monopoly-bargaining buying power in the labor, not the Q-good, market.

When irresistible force meets immovable object, something must give:

FIG. 25-7.

theory, which sounds frivolous in its terminology borrowed from chess, bridge, and war, is fraught with significance and was largely developed by John von Neumann(1903–1957), Hungarian-born mathematical genius and one of the three coinventors of the United States hydrogen bomb.

Here we can only sketch the general notions involved in game theory.[4] Figure 25-7 shows a case of perpetual price cutting. The New York department store Macy's used to advertise, "We sell for 10 per cent less." But its rival, Gimbel's, advertised, "We will not be undersold." The vertical blue arrows show Macy's (or Blue's) price cuts; the brown horizontal arrows show Gimbel's (or Brown's) responding strategies of matching them.

It is just as if Blue and Brown were playing a chess game: at Blue's turn, he moves north-south; at Brown's turn, he moves east-west. Here the game ends in mutual ruin, at zero price, where 90 per cent of nothing is compatible with equal (zero!) prices.

But finally Macy's gets wise and realizes that when it cuts its P_1, the other P_2 will not stay constant but

[4]Aside from the classic by von Neumann and Morgenstern cited in next chapter's footnote 2, the reader might study John McDonald, *Strategy in Poker, Business and War* (Norton, New York, 1950).

will follow it downward. Only if it is shortsighted does it think it can move south; actually as Brown reacts to match, both move southwestward together toward lower profits for both. If there were but two sellers and no antitrust laws to worry about, the two might collusively raise price to the monopoly level that maximized joint profits and represented $P > MC$.

Our joint-strategy diagram can be replaced by an equivalent two-way table (or "game-payoff matrix"). In Table 25-4, Blue picks his P_1 strategy by selecting a row. Brown's P_2 strategy involves his choosing a column. Then in each of the four cells A, B, C, D the blue number represents Blue's profit-payoff at those prices and the brown number gives Brown's profit-payoff. Thus, in Cell A joint profits of 6 + 6 (thousand dollars) are maximized at the common monopoly price, $2 = P_1 = P_2$. But A is not "stable," in that if Blue knew Brown would really stay in his first column, Blue would gain by cutting P_1 down to C, getting the lion's share of the business there with payoff 9 > 6. But, of course, Brown will now prefer to match Blue's $1 P_1, taking us from Cell C to D.

Here at D (whose excess-profits just happen to be minimal), the competitive solution is stable. (I.e., 0 is the largest blue number in the *column* Brown has picked, and 0 is the largest brown number in the *row* Blue has picked. Verify this gold-dot equilibrium.)

But we must be warned. The competitive solution is not stable as against a "collusive" move from D to

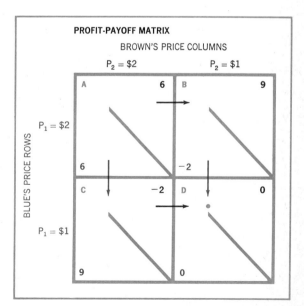

TABLE 25-4.

A. This might come about by overt agreement or by tacit agreement. (If Blue were reluctant to follow suit, Brown might in Hitler fashion blackmail him by threatening mutual ruin through cutting *P* far below any cost levels.) The only safe guarantee of competition is thus the potential pressure of really numerous sellers.

These game-theoretic considerations show the importance to oligopolists of finding some way to "agree." And they help explain, along with next chapter's "kinked" demand curve, why oligopoly prices tend to be administered in a "sticky" or rigid way. Were prices to change often, tacit agreements would be hard to identify and enforce.[5]

[5]Collusion is less worrisome in the simpler two-person games studied by von Neumann, the "constant-sum" games in which the brown and blue payoffs add up to the *same* constant in *every* cell, as in the accompanying Table 25-5(a) and (b).

In (a), cell D is a stable solution—representing what is called a "saddlepoint," i.e., a cell which gives maximum blue numbers in *its* column and *minimum* blue (and hence, maximum brown) numbers in its row.

But in (b), which can be given a penny-matching interpretation as Brown's "tails" matches Blue's in Cell A, you will find no such minimax or gold-dot stable saddlepoint. (Thus, from A, Blue moves to C; then Brown moves to D; then Blue to B; then Brown back to A; and so we oscillate counterclockwise forever!)

Von Neumann proves this remarkable theorem about (b); namely, each player should introduce *randomized* strategies: thus if each charges $1 or $2 with equal and independent probabilities, neither can then gain in *average* payoff by departing from this stable, minimax saddlepoint solution.

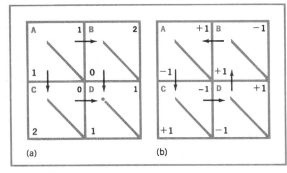

TABLE 25-5.

Using probabilities, every constant-sum matrix has a saddlepoint. (Von Neumann proves many other fascinating theorems. E.g., chess is as "trivial" as ticktacktoe. This means that when played "correctly," it must *always* end in the *same* one of the following: a draw, first man wins, second man wins—but what that outcome is for chess with its multiplicity of moves, no one knows, not even the electronic computer.)

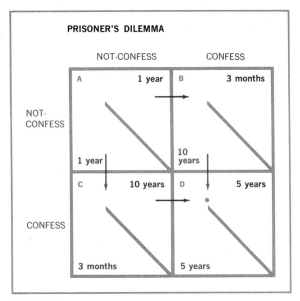

TABLE 25-6.

Prisoner's dilemma and love Game theory can throw light on one of the great needs of our age—the need for altruism. (In a more sentimental time, love might be the word.)

In the game matrix of Table 25-4, self-interest (in a word, selfishness) was channeled by the mechanism of economic competition to bring the system to cell D, which happens in this context to be the optimum state. Thus, by a happy accident so to speak, there does exist a facet of social life—the perfectly-competitive market, when that is strictly applicable and viable—where Adam Smith's Invisible Hand does contrive the maximum of well-being out of the motivation of selfishness.

But that is a lucky accident, unlikely to be realized in other social situations. The following model, or fable, called "prisoner's dilemma," illustrates this basic truth in game-theoretic language. Table 25-6 is like Table 25-4, but reinterpret it in terms of prisoner's dilemma so that Blue and Brown are two prisoners who have been caught in a joint crime. The district attorney interviews each separately, saying "I have enough on both of you to send you to jail for a year. But if you *alone* will confess to the 10-year crime, I'll make a deal with you: You'll get off with a 3-month sentence, while your partner will serve 10 years. But if you *both* confess, you'll both get 5 years."

What should Blue do? Confess and hope to get only a short sentence? That's better than the year from not confessing. But wait. There is an even better reason for confessing. For suppose Blue doesn't confess and unknown to him, Brown does confess. Blue stands to get 10 years! Better than *that* is to confess and get no worse than 5 years.

Brown is in the same dilemma: If only he knew what Blue is thinking (or what Blue thinks Brown thinks Blue is thinking . . .).

Note that selfishness leads inevitably to long prison terms—5 years—in cell D of Table 25-6. Only by altruism—or social agreement (in this case, collusion)—can the best *common* state of the world, cell A, be realized.

To see the need for altruism—or failing that, for collective decision making—apply Table 25-6 to the air pollution problem. (Replace not-confess by not-pollute, . . . , etc. And assume that when I pollute and you do not desist from polluting, I will be somewhat worse off if I alone decide to desist.) Then the same logic as in Table 25-6 proves that individualistic pursuit of self-interest leads to everyone breathing the same foul and polluted air that shortens life expectancies.

Thus, game theory does point up the need for brotherhood and common rules of the road.

FOR REVIEW

Review your understanding of the following concepts:

$P = MC < AC$ regulation
improving all when $P_1 > MC_1$
monopoly exploitation of labor
profit-payoff game matrix
row and column strategy
stable point

collusion
prisoner's dilemma
constant-sum game
randomized strategies and
    necessarily-existent stable
    saddlepoint or minimax

Imperfect Competition and Antitrust Policy

26

The last chapter gave us the tools for analyzing the actual markets of the real world. Now we focus on the real world of the modern mixed economy in the last third of the twentieth century. We seek answers to questions like the following: How do firms factually go about setting their prices? What is the role of the theoretical tools developed to analyze profit maximization? What are some of the important patterns of imperfect competition? How does Galbraith's "new industrial state" change the conventional wisdom of the past? Part A deals with these subjects.

Part B then takes up the basic problem of the relevance of economics to improving the workings of the system. What are the important issues for public antitrust policy that patterns of imperfect competition raise?

A. ANALYTICAL PATTERNS OF IMPERFECT COMPETITION

DO FIRMS MAXIMIZE PROFITS?

To what degree do businessmen actually try to maximize their profits? To what extent do they succeed if they do try to? It is not easy to give precise answers to these questions. Certainly, this much is true:

If a firm is absolutely reckless in calculating costs and revenues, then the Darwinian law of survival of the fittest will probably eliminate it from the economic scene. Therefore those firms which do manage to survive cannot be completely oblivious to the maximization of profits.

But this does not necessarily mean that every oligopolist or monopolist is seeking desperately to squeeze the last ounce of profit from every transaction. As soon as the firm becomes of any considerable size and begins to enjoy some control over price, *it can often afford to relax a little* in its maximizing activities.

Moreover, it is probably good business to take the long

view and not concentrate on purely immediate gains. Many acts of altruism and apparent generosity can be amply defended in terms of public relations and the maximization of *long-run* profits.

Consider a firm that is maximizing its profits in a fairly sensible manner. Does this mean that it is calculating elaborate geometrical curves of cost and revenue and from them deriving elaborate measures of marginal cost and revenue? Obviously not, as you will soon learn if you inquire about current business practices.

But even if the firm is not itself tackling the problem with conscious awareness of the particular marginal tools of the theoretical economists, *to the extent that it is truly making a pretty fair guess as to where its highest profits are realized,* it will be succeeding in making marginal revenue and marginal cost approximately equal. It does this without curves, just by feeling its way to the optimum by trial and error. And increasingly managerial economics is becoming a sophisticated art, utilizing giant computers and involving the statistical and mathematical techniques of operational research, linear programming, and probabilistic decision theory.

MARKUP PRICING

One reason why business is a challenge is the fact that best guesses must be made in terms of incomplete information. It is no small task for a business to make an estimate of the demand curve for its products. A railroad can only guess whether a cut in fares will bring many more customers. Because other things do not remain equal, a firm has no exact way to judge accurately the demand elasticity for its many products.

Many observers claim that modern business firms—even the largest—cannot in real life accurately determine marginal revenue and marginal cost. They cannot determine their optimum price and output with neat exactitude. Yet the day's work must somehow get done. Prices must be set on their products. Here is where average, or unit, cost is often thought to play an important role. The argument goes as follows:

Put yourself in the position of the president of a company producing many products. Prices are partly at your disposal. Your last year's sales are known to you, but your next period's sales can only be guessed even if you leave prices unchanged. Not knowing the extent or elasticity of demand for your products, you are unable to determine marginal revenue. What will you do?

Probably, you call in your accountants and sales managers and ask, "What is our likely volume if we stay on our toes and keep our share of the market?" In answering, the sales force has to guess at the probable level of business activity, consumers' needs and how your advertising can reshape them, results of market surveys, and much else.

After they have made their estimates, you turn to the cost experts and probably ask for the average cost of producing each product in question at those levels of output. There will be plenty of headaches in aiming at any sort of figure. For example, how should the administrative and plant overhead costs be allocated between different products? Or if a given process simultaneously creates joint products like meat and hides, how should the costs be allocated between them? Or if a building will last for many years, how much should be charged against current operations?

Headache or no headache, it is the practice of accountants to come out with some sort of answer as to average costs. Management must now decide by how much to mark up price over the cost figure. Depending upon its estimate of the consumers' reaction and the pricing policy of its competitors, the firm may perhaps decide on a 5, 10, 30, or 110 per cent markup.[1] Whether aware of it or not, the businessman is making some kind of implicit guess about his demand elasticity in setting his markup.

In bad times, when price competition is particularly keen, businessmen may even set prices at less than "full costs" because they realize that fixed expenses will go on whether or not production is at a low level. But price will never be set below average *variable* costs unless the item in question is being used as a "loss leader" to attract other business now and in the future, or unless the firm is willing to incur temporary losses in order to crush a rival and drive him out of business completely.

Investigators of actual business pricing policies have testified that corporations often do follow the above-described practice of quoting administered prices on a "cost and markup" basis, hoping thereby not only to recover their "full cost outlays," but also to make a return on their investments. This theory therefore seems realistic. But it is not very informative. It stops tantalizingly short of telling us *why* the average markup is 40 per cent in one industry and 5 per cent in another; it cannot tell why, before World War II, General Motors in the auto industry was able to earn 30 per cent on the book value of its invested capital while Ford, almost as large, could earn but $\frac{1}{2}$ of 1 per cent. Demand and cost just have to be regarded as lurking in the background of any business case.

Careful reading of the foregoing accounts suggests that it is compatible with the principles outlined in Chapter 25. So long as the percentage markup is subject to the pressures implicit in *MC* and *MR* analysis, markup pricing may hinge on the same conditions as in the simplified theory.

BREAK-EVEN POINTS AND "ADMINISTERED PRICES"

Businessmen often speak of their break-even points. You will hear them complain that union wage demands during the long expansion of the 1960s have raised the level of their break-even points to a dangerous degree, so that, if there is any slackening of the peak levels of sales, profits may soon turn into losses. What might I, a hypothetical business-man, mean by my "break-even point"?

Suppose that I have already fixed upon the price to be charged. Probably I used some sort of markup rule to do so, guessing at the most profitable price range, but it does not much matter how I made the decision.

If I am like most firms, I shall not be changing my *P* every day. Probably (as in the last section) I name a so-called "administered price" and—subject to varying discounts and other reflections of demand elasticity—I stick to it until further notice.

So long as my *P* is above *MC* and *AVC*, it is clear that my profits will grow with sales. As a matter of fact, at small outputs I shall not even be earning enough to cover fixed costs; but as sales increase, this loss will dwindle, and I shall reach a point where I just cover fixed and variable costs. My sales have now reached the break-even point.

Beyond this break-even point, my profits will begin to materialize. Anything I can do to increase sales will be all the more to the good. I am quite unlike a perfect-competitor on the farm: he can always sell *all he wants to produce* at the market price; but as an imperfect competitor, with $P > MC$, I would be glad to sell more q at the market price. That is why I advertise and hire salesmen. And that *willingness to sell more* marks me as no perfect-competitor.

GALBRAITH'S NEW INDUSTRIAL STATE

Prior to John Kenneth Galbraith's 1958 masterwork, *The Affluent Society*, this versatile giant emphasized in his 1954 *American Capitalism* the notion of "countervailing power." Thus a mammoth corporation like General Electric produces, among many other things, refrigerators. It is, of course, checked somewhat in its market power in selling them by the competition of Westinghouse, Philco, General Motors, and many other selling rivals (particularly in this post-Galbraithian era of proliferating "conglomerates," which merge into one large corporation unrelated activities that cut across scores of industries).

Competition by selling rivals is old-fashioned competition, which may or may not suffice to prevent monopoly. Galbraith's emphasis is on something different.

Countervailing power This is the check upon a giant corporation that comes from the organized competition among the units it buys from and among the units to which it sells. Countervailing power is the check on GE that comes from its being faced with a giant trade union in the market where it buys its labor; from its being faced with a government-led cartel of farmers and miners when it buys its raw materials; from its being faced by powerful chains of retail stores (Sears, Allied Stores, Korvette Discount Stores), consumer cooperatives, and Pentagon purchasing agents to which it must sell, and which use their mass purchasing power to bargain down price and keep profits in check.

Essentially then, *countervailing* power adds, along with the conventional competition of rival sellers, the checks and balances of competition between giant buyers and sellers at every stage in the productive and distributive process.

To the degree that it does prevail, countervailing power will improve the performance of a mixed economy in comparison with the unlimited oligarchy of the giant trusts of 1900. But it does take us a long way from the world of simple laissez faire, and inevitably it puts a great premium on lobbying and participation in politics to influence economic activity. (The whole concept of the "military-industrial complex" takes on a new potential in a world of countervailing power.)

The technostructure In his 1967 *New Industrial State*, Galbraith views the large corporation as the strategic economic unit of our time. Having much at stake, the corporation desires *stability*, not adventure or uncertainty. Desiring growth, growth, growth, it embraces rational *planning*. Needing *experts*, it increasingly uses, and *is increasingly taken over by*, a new breed of technicians. These bureaucrats are professional managers, who possess the esoteric skills of science, engineering, and social psychology. Members of this technostructure go back and forth between New York and Washington. This year the graduate of Groton (or Bronx Science High), Yale, and the Harvard Business School is merging seven companies; next year he is in Washington, helping negotiate an arms treaty with the Russians.

It is Galbraith's contention that all over the world—in Los Angeles or Leningrad, in Peking or Poona—there is a *convergence* toward the same kind of society. On the other side of that bargaining table, the expert faces someone who is essentially his twin—the graduate of the top Moscow Institute, or the Inspecteur de Finance who led his class at the Ecole Polytechnique or the Ecole Supérieure. In what may be Galbraith's own Walter Mitty dream of glory, the new establishments everywhere are converging to the same pattern—to a "meritocracy" based on expert skills, in short, to a "technostructure."

Pluses and minuses   Critically how are we to evaluate these new ideas? To say they are nonsense would itself be nonsense. To insist that they are not new—that Veblen had prophesied the triumph of the engineers 50 years ago, that James Burnham had stressed the role of the bureaucracy, that every tired radical of the 1930s took it for granted that consumer preferences were shaped by advertising efforts and did not well out of the spontaneous nature of man—is beside the point: those who live on in the history of thought and ideas are not those who first think of a notion, but rather those who synthesize its various meanings, who package it, and put it across.

Scholarly research is still going on to document quantitatively the merits and demerits of the Galbraithian vision. The results seem, all over the Western world, to be converging to a balance sheet something like the following.

1. Experts are increasingly in demand. But Galbraith exaggerates the unilateral power that they can exercise. Those who control the plurality of stockholders' votes—themselves usually a minority—still call the tune. The minute the company hits upon hard times and slow growth, the whiz-kid expert is reminded of the layman's definition of the expert—"a bastard from out of town."

2. Large corporations do certainly have the elbow room for unilateral action denied to a small farmer or conventional family enterprise. They can give money to slum clearance. They can relax in their pursuit of profit. They can pursue growth even when it is more that of cancerous than of healthy cells. They can tempt consumers to buy the goods that the corporation would like to sell.

But the large corporation is not an absolute monarch. Ford could not sell Edsels. Lever Brothers could not, with all the wizardry of Madison Avenue, sell Swan soap. Montgomery Ward was gradually dethroned by the stubborn stupidity of Sewell Avery. If one minority group of management lets profits languish so that the common-stock holders do not get capital gains, another ring of capitalists will stage a successful "take-over." The new crew may not be gentlemen from Harvard, but this is the mixed economy's way of cutting its losses.

3. Having said all this, the objective scholar must assert that economics will never quite be the same as in the days before the Galbraith trilogy.

OLIGOPOLY: COMPETITION AMONG THE FEW

Table 25-1, page 467, gave a classification of different forms of market structure. It is important enough to warrant reproducing again here as Table 26-1.

Most industries are imperfectly competitive—a blend of monopoly and competition:

TYPES OF COMPETITION AND MARKET STRUCTURE

KIND OF COMPETITION	NUMBER OF PRODUCERS AND DEGREE OF PRODUCT DIFFERENTIATION	PART OF ECONOMY WHERE PREVALENT	DEGREE OF CONTROL OVER PRICE	METHODS OF MARKETING
Perfect competition	Many producers; identical products	A few agricultural industries	None	Market exchange or auction
Imperfect competition:				
Many differentiated sellers	Many producers; many real or fancied differences in product	Toothpaste, retail trade; conglomerates	Some	Advertising and quality rivalry; administered prices
Oligopoly	Few producers; little or no difference in product	Steel, aluminum		
	Few producers; some differentiation of products	Autos, machinery		
Complete monopoly	Single producer; unique product without close substitutes	A few utilities	Considerable	Promotional and "institutional" public-relations advertising

TABLE 26-1. (Source: Table 25-1, page 467.)

Monopoly (one seller) is a rare case. Duopoly (two sellers) happens occasionally, particularly in geographically distinct markets where a couple of steel makers or a couple of railroads dominate the market. More common still is the case of oligopoly (few sellers). We saw in Chapter 5, page 93, that most large-scale industries are dominated by a few giant firms: In automobiles, the Big Three saturate most of the market; in aluminum, a few big firms dominate; and so it goes in the cigarette, steel, aircraft, meat-packing, soap, and communications industries.

An economic theory of oligopoly has been developed to try to account for the facts of *administered* prices which change infrequently, and to account for the prevalence of markup pricing. Let us consider the case of three or four dominant firms. Already we know that the pattern of costs and returns is likely to be such that the *optimal size of efficient production*—at the bottom of the U-shaped long-run *AC* curve (recall page 462 and elsewhere)—*will be very large relative to the total market demand.* That is why the three or four firms do not become thirty or forty, or three hundred, or three thousand.

Thus, it probably costs a billion dollars to produce an integrated steel plant. Kaiser

Oligopoly means few sellers of the same or differentiated products:

OLIGOPOLIST'S EQUILIBRIUM

FIG. 26-1. After experience with disastrous price wars, each of the few rivals who dominate a given market is almost sure to recognize that price cutting *begets* canceling-out price cutting. So the typical oligopolist will estimate his demand curve *DD* by assuming others will be charging similar prices (and by taking into account the potential entry of new oligopolists). Since he gains little from cutting *P*, he will settle for sizable markup of *P* over *MC*.

Steel is the only integrated producer on the West Coast. If steel could be produced at the scale that wheat is produced, there would be thousands of West Coast steel companies, and Kaiser would have to fear much more competition than it now gets from Japanese imports and shipments from the eastern United States.

Figure 26-1 shows the large-scale operation of a typical oligopolist. The most acute case threatening instability of oligopolistic competition is that in which the different firms produce virtually *identical* or *homogeneous* products. If Firm A's sulfuric acid undersells Firm B's by even $1 a cartank, A will get practically all the business. In this case, we oligopolists are practically sure to recognize our "mutual interdependence"[2]—namely, that we must end up charging about the same prices, and that any initial advantage I get in undercutting your price will be lost when you are induced to cut your price in return. That is why the *DD* demand curve shown for Corporation A in Fig. 26-1 is *not* drawn up on the assumption of "other things (including rivals' prices) being held constant"; instead A's *DD* is about as inelastic as the whole industry's *DD*, since it is A's prorated one-third or one-fourth of the shared market.

Where is the Maximum-profit equilibrium for the oligopolist? It is shown in Fig. 26-1 at *E*, the intersection of his *MC* and *MR* curves, with *P* at *G* on *DD* just above *E*.

If you turn back to page 473, you see that this oligopoly equilibrium looks much like the simple monopoly equilibrium of Fig. 25-4(a).

Inflexible, administered pricing But there is an important difference under oligopoly. A monopolist might be expected to change his price every time his *DD* or *MC* curve shifts, which could be every year, every quarter, every month. We need an economic theory to explain the more inflexible price quotations administered typically by oligopolists. We deduce the needed theory of *P* inflexibility from the fact that rivals may behave one way when you *cut* your price—namely, matching your cuts and thwarting your hope

---

[2] A century of theorizing by economists about what Mind A thinks Mind B will do if *he* thinks A will do such-and-such culminated in J. von Neumann and O. Morgenstern, *The Theory of Games and Economic Behavior* (Princeton University Press, Princeton, N.J., 1953, 3d ed.). This mathematical theory, while it cannot clear up all the philosophical problems of how two omniscient minds will act against each other in an interdependent world, does offer many incisive insights for political warfare as well as economics. (EXAMPLES: A teacher picks quiz questions *at random* from a book; a watchman makes his rounds at random, not in a discernible pattern. Facing you as a smart rival, I shall work hard to maximize my *most vulnerable* defense, knowing you will find out the weakest link in my chain. I bluff at poker, not simply, as some think, to win a pot with a *weak* hand, but rather to ensure that all players do *not* drop out when I bet high on a good hand.) The previous Appendix surveys game theory.

for new business; and they behave another way when you *raise* your *P* above the customary level—namely, holding their prices constant in order to pick up some of your customers. In consequence, you have little motive to change your price in either direction. Instead you "administer" your price in a rigid fashion, particularly since each oligopolist learns from game-theoretic experience that it is easier to agree—tacitly or explicitly—on a common *P* that is fixed rather than on one that is changing from month to month.[3]

Figure 26-2 illustrates the "kinked" or "cornered" demand curve that economists postulate to explain rigid price behavior. The equilibrium price *G* is shown in both diagrams at about that markup level over costs which the oligopolists think will be best for them in the long run.[4]

But at *G* there is a kink in the effective demand and marginal revenue curves of Oligopolist A. Why? Because if he cuts his *P* below *G*, his rivals will follow him, and he moves down the old steep *DD* curve. But what if he *alone* raises his *P* above the tacit customary price at *G*? No rival will follow him, because they all hope to pick up some business at his expense. Most, but not all, of his customers are likely to leave him: hence, for *increases* in *P*, he is on the more elastic *dd* curve that reflects what he would sell when he *alone* changes *P* while all rivals *hold their prices constant* at the customary *G* level.

Geometrically, the corner on the demand curve implies the vertical discontinuity in the *MR* curve marked *FC*.[5] And now we see that the *MC* level for the firm could shift considerably—anywhere between *F* and *C*—without changing the *q** intersection of *MC* and *MR* or the Maximum-profit *P** at *G*.

A "cornered" or "kinked" demand curve around an administered level of markup price—because *P* cuts are matched and *P* increases are not—can help explain rigidity of oligopoly price compared with both perfect-competition and complete-monopoly flexible price. Also, this rigidity makes tacit agreement more easily possible.

A kinked or cornered demand curve can explain rigidity of oligopolists' administered price:

KINKED OLIGOPOLY DEMAND

FIG. 26-2.   The *DD* curve through *G* is the demand curve when all sellers move prices *together* and share total market. However, *dd* is the more elastic demand curve when this firm *alone* changes its price and loses sales to its rivals. Below *G*, as others match your price cut, *DD* prevails. Above *G*, when rivals do not match your price increase, *dd* prevails. Geometrically, the different demand curves generate different *MR* curves, with the *FC* vertical discontinuity (or "kink") resulting from the corner at *G*. Considerably shifting *MC* curves will still lead to intersection on *FC*, and hence unchanged oligopoly price and quantity at *G*.

---

[3] The remainder of this section may be skipped if desired.
[4] Actually, it would be realistic for them to draw up their *DD* curves allowing for entry of *potential* rivals who might be tempted into the industry if they collude on so high a *P* as to make it profitable for new firms to come in. In consequence, each firm's *DD* might be somewhat more elastic than that for the whole industry, but still more inelastic than the *dd* that results from no change in rival's *P* induced by your change in *P*.
[5] The straight-line geometry of page 457's diagram can demonstrate this. The flat *dGd* straight line generates the flat *MR* line; the steeper *DGD* line generates the steeper *MR* line; between these *MR* lines comes the vertical "kink," *FC*.

Collusion, tacit or explicit   We see why the antitrust laws should be greatly concerned with the problem of oligopoly collusion. Even where there is some differentiation of products, if there are but two, three, or a few sellers, they may come to realize that their prices are closely *interrelated*. Each will guess, or may soon learn from experience, that when it cuts its price, its rivals tend to meet or to exceed such a price cut. Economic warfare may result, until the few sellers come to realize that they are in the same boat.

Back in the old days before the antitrust laws were important, such oligopolists might have formed a merger, or a tight little cartel or trust. Meeting at celebrated dinners, such as those that Judge Gary of the United States Steel Corporation held decades ago, the sellers would collusively set some kind of monopoly price. A full monopoly price? Sometimes, if they were sure they could keep newcomers out. But in the more realistic case where the oligopolists had to take account of the fact that setting a high price would tempt new rivals into their field, they would agree on a price higher than the purely competitive one but set with some moderation for fear of attracting new entry.

Today it would be illegal in the United States, and a few other countries, for cartels to set prices collusively and shamelessly in order to maximize their mutual profits. On the other hand, if a few large firms encounter the same problem, experience suggests that they may—without ever meeting, phoning, winking, or corresponding—arrive at a *tacit* mode of behavior that avoids fierce price competition. With or without a price leader, the sellers may be quoting rather similar prices[6]—prices which come nowhere near the level of *MC*, as would have been the case of the perfectly competitive industry discussed in Chapter 23.

The richness of possible outcomes would exhaust a specialized book on the subject. The final equilibrium may end up much or little above the firm's marginal-cost level. If fear of entry is great and if the number of existing sellers is considerable, then the *DD* curve might be quite near to horizontal and give results not too different from perfect competition. But if sellers are few, and if they are large relative to the total demand, not very fearful of new entrants, and keenly conscious of the mutuality of their interest, the tacit price pattern may become a very high one relative to long-run or short-run marginal cost.

Also, oligopolists love to shift rivalry and competition into dimensions other than price: into advertising, into changing the wrapping of their product and the size of its replacement parts, into providing quick and reliable service.

Some of this is undoubtedly valuable; some is definitely wasteful. What is the net balance of advantage over disadvantage? A priori reasoning alone cannot tell us; even study of the facts cannot lead to a conclusive answer completely independently of ethical value judgments. But what needs emphasizing by the economist is this:

Once the rules of perfect competition are left behind, there is no Invisible Hand principle which sets up a presumption that the working out of laissez faire is likely to be in the direction of satisfying wants most efficiently.

[6] In 1946 the Supreme Court held that cigarette oligopolists could be guilty of price fixing even when there was no overt collusion!

MANY DIFFERENTIATED SELLERS: WASTE UNDER FREE ENTRY

Let us leave few-seller oligopoly and turn to the case of many sellers, but not of a homogeneous single product. This important case is the brainchild of the late E. H. Chamberlin.

In Fig. 26-3 a typical firm is briefly in short-run equilibrium at G'. His $d'd'$ is sloped because his product is a little different from anyone else's.

However, we assume that *entry is free* for new firms to produce their own differentiated products on as favorable terms as our typical firm can produce his. Since he and all the other initial sellers are seen to be making good profits at the initial G', new firms are tempted into the market. These new entrants cut into his demand and shift his $d'd'$ curve leftward to dd until it just touches (and does not cross above) his AC curve.

Thus, final long-run equilibrium for the typical seller ends up at the *tangency* point G—the only point at which the firm can avoid losses. Note that downward-sloping dd means that tangential AC must be falling and that final output is smaller than the Q^* corresponding to the bottom of the U-shaped AC curve.[7]

Chronic excess capacity and waste. **Free entry into the large group of sellers of differentiated products merely divides up markets, leading to excessive prices at the tangency points of downward-sloping demand curves with still-falling long-run AC curves. Minimum-average-cost scale of production is not attained. The imperfect competitors make no monopoly profits, but price does not get lowered to the bottom-of-the-U level. The consumer has to pay for chronic excess-capacity operation of too many sellers, each producing too little.**

Free entry of many imperfect competitors can wipe out profit but leave waste:

FIG. 26-3.   The typical seller of one of many differentiated products can be forced by free entry into a long-run no-profit tangency at G. Such rivals split up the markets without depressing price to the marginal-cost level as in perfect competition. He and all his rivals end up with P above MC; and each producer is on the left-hand declining branch of his long-run AC curve with output less than the particular Q^* which is at the bottom of the U.

[7] The Chamberlin excess-capacity tangency of Fig. 26-3 should not be confused with the tangency under *perfect* competition shown here in Fig. 26-4. As discussed in earlier chapters, this typical perfect-competitor is one of so many producers of an identical good that he faces a practically horizontal ("infinitely elastic") dd curve, even though the industry's very much larger DD curve can be very much more inelastic. If there is free entry-and-exit of well-informed firms that can replicate the cost conditions of any other firm, long-run equilibrium at E will involve no excess of profit over competitive costs (including properly computed implicit- and opportunity-cost returns). Society is getting its total output most efficiently, in recognition of the $P = MC$ condition of Chapter 23; and it is not forcing out of existing firms any output that could be obtained more cheaply by adding new firms (as page 457's diagram showed).

FIG. 26-4.

These wastes are different from those of complete monopoly, and of course different from the efficiency of perfect competition.

If consumers were willing to sacrifice the differentiation of product, a lower equilibrium *P* would be possible as fewer firms were used more intensively to produce a more standardized output. But laissez faire has no way of deciding how much extra people *ought* to pay in return for the extra variety of products they enjoy in Fig. 26-3.[8]

B. MODERN ANTITRUST PROBLEMS

SOME WASTES OF IMPERFECT COMPETITION RECAPITULATED

Before going into the legal, historical, and institutional aspects of antitrust legislation, we ought to remind ourselves what the economic evils are that are associated with various monopolistic and other imperfections of competition.

Monopoly restrictions   Recall that it is not the profit a monopoly (or oligopoly, for that matter) makes that constitutes its greatest evil, but rather its setting too high a price in relation to social marginal-cost pricing.[9] To recall this, imagine our taxing away all the monopolist's profit by imposing on him a franchise tax of the right size.

Clearly, the monopolist would end up with no profit. The state would get that profit, but the monopoly would not lower its *P* or raise its *Q*. Why not? Because the intersection of *MR* and *MC* would be unchanged by a lump-sum franchise tax: since such a tax is a fixed cost that varies not at all with *Q*, it will not affect *MC*; and *MR* depends only on the demand curve, not on costs or franchise taxes.

So the consumer goes on getting too little of the product and paying too high a price. The state has now become the villainous recipient of monopoly profit and has failed to correct the misallocation of resources.

The moral: It is the contrived divergence between *P* and *MC* that constitutes the true additional burden of monopoly.[10]

[8] Even if, as Chamberlin insists, people may want some of the extra variety of differentiated products that the tangency solution of Fig. 26-3 makes possible, that pattern cannot be ideally efficient. For it can be shown that wherever *P* exceeds *MC* anywhere, there definitely exists a new configuration (possibly involving subsidies, as in Chapter 25's Appendix) in which *everyone* can be made better off. This point is alluded to again on page 496, note 11.
[9] Figure 20-9, Chapter 23's Robinson Crusoe parable, and Chapter 25's Appendix elaborate on this.
[10] Advanced treatises use the accompanying Fig. 26-5 to approximate the "deadweight loss" due to monopoly. At the competitive ideal *I*, each similar consumer enjoys Marshallian consumer's surplus given by the whole triangular area *NIR*. When monopoly raises *P* to the Maximum-profit point *G*, the consumer loses to the monopolist that part of his consumer's surplus represented by the profit rectangle *NEGN'* and is left with but *N'GR*. What happens to the little triangle *EIG*? It is lost to everybody and represents "deadweight loss." Thus consumers lose more than the monop-

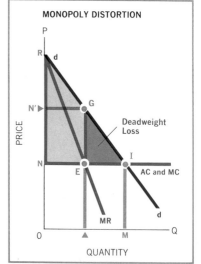

FIG. 26-5.

Overentry and "sick" industries   Many fields are characterized by an excessive number of firms. Most of these do a small volume of business and remain in the industry only until they have lost their capital. Grocery stores, taverns, undertakers, restaurants, nightclubs, and gasoline stations are typical examples taken from retail trade. But much the same thing is true of the textile trade, the dress trade, the shoe or plastic business, and many others that require little initial capital.

Why don't such unprofitable concerns leave the industry? The answer is, They do. But as fast as they leave, new firms enter the industry, leaving the total number unchanged and even growing. Why do new firms enter the industry in the face of the fact that most existing firms are incurring losses? Apparently, partly out of ignorance and partly out of misplaced hope.

Such chronically overcrowded industries need not be what the economist has called "perfectly competitive"—although in the case of agriculture or "cotton gray goods," they may happen to be approximately so. Having too many firms in a perfectly competitive industry is an undesirable condition, involving as it does wastes of resources and losses. But at least in such a *competitive* industry the consumer partly gains, through lower prices, what the overoptimistic producers are losing.

Unfortunately, in most chronically overcrowded sick industries, market competition is quite *imperfect*. Being inefficient producers, the small concerns do not sell very cheaply. Instead of competing on a price basis, they tend to charge fairly high prices and simply to *divide* the business.

The resulting economic situation under this form of free-entry numerous-seller imperfect competition may be worse even than under complete monopoly: not only is price excessive, but in addition valuable resources are wasted because each firm has too much idle plant and manpower. The situation is triply bad: producers incur losses, resources are wasted, and the prices charged the consumer are too high.

Our earlier diagram from Chamberlin, Fig. 26-3 on page 493, showed how imperfect competition may result in wastage of resources, too high price, and yet no long-run profits for the imperfect competitors. Figure 26-3 portrayed such a typical imperfect competitor, say, a local barbershop that can count on some customers' being unwilling to walk a long way to get a haircut. Its original demand $d'd'$ slopes downward; and hence it has been marking up P above MC. It is maximizing positive profit and charging more than full unit costs.

But now other barbers see this profit opportunity. They move in. There is now one barbershop for every three blocks rather than every four. What happens to the demand curve for our typical barber? Clearly, entry of new competitors divides up the existing business and causes demand to shift downward and leftward to dd, with each barber wasting more time in frustrating idleness. Now at the new maximum-profit point, each barber makes no profit, as can be seen from the fact that the new demand curve just touches the average cost curve tangentially. Marginal cost is equated to new marginal revenue—but that serves only to avoid losses, not to produce a positive profit.

---

olist's profit; and even if we took back the *NEGN'* profit by lump sum taxation, we would be losing to the devil of inefficiency the "deadweight triangle" which benefits *nobody*.

The long-run equilibrium at G, which Marshall might shudder to call "normal," very clearly shows that price is higher than the most efficient cost level which prevails at the bottom of the U-shaped average cost curve. The barbershop has excess capacity, with empty chairs much of the time. (Of course, customers have to walk only three blocks now, not four, and may have to wait less. And that is worth something. But note that they have never, in most cities, really been given the choice of a slightly longer walk and haircuts at the lower prices that efficient capacity utilization would make possible.[11])

(If there is lasting overentry of overoptimistic barbers, draw in a $d''d''$ curve still lower than dd and show wasteful social losses and turnover of disappointed entrepreneurs. You can do the same in the case of perfect competition illustrated in Fig. 26-4.)

Evils of oligopoly   Antitrust regulators must be even more aware of the economic effects of oligopoly. Recall the already-mentioned railroad price wars of the past century. Customers shipping goods from Chicago to New York always picked the route that offered even a few-pennies saving. Thus, each of the three or four trunk lines would intermittently undercut the existing rate schedules, until finally a disastrously low level of rates was reached. At the same time, for short hauls where shippers had no alternative, the railroads would jack up the rates, thus creating an anomalous, discriminatory pattern of charges.[12]

Even without government regulations, in industries characterized by heavy overheads, decreasing costs, and identical products, there is often a realization that competition is ruinous. Therefore, tacitly or explicitly, the firms try to agree on a price that maximizes the long-run profits of all. Trade associations, keeping one eye on the Justice Department lawyers who enforce the Sherman Antitrust Act, may impose penalties on any chiseler in the industry who makes secret price concessions. Occasionally, as new conditions or firms upset the status quo, another price war may break out—to last until everyone has again learned his lesson and the morale of the industry is restored.

In appraising oligopoly we must note that the desire of corporations to earn a fair return on their *past* investments can at times be at variance with the well-being of the consumer. Too much plant capacity may have been built in the industry in the past; but that is not justification for continuing high prices and scarce output. Competition, which the businessman regards as destructive, cutthroat, and ruinous, may actually be the only way to get the redundant plant capacity into operation or to discourage its maintenance. (Having made the mistake of building the plants, society ought not to add the further error of failing to use them to best advantage.) Losses or subnormal profits is the free enterprise way of discouraging excess capacity.

---

[11]Repeatedly, in our discussion of pricing "efficiency," we have seen what is proved rigorously in advanced texts: Price in excess of marginal cost leads to a state from which it would be possible theoretically to make *everybody* better off—barbers, bald people, long-haired people who hate long walks and waits, and everybody else. But do not leap from this to the invalid inference that variety does not matter or that enforcing $P = MC$ everywhere would (in decreasing-cost situations with differentiated products) lead spontaneously to the "ideal" amount of variety. Here is a case where defining an optimum is actually a difficult social task.

[12]We have seen that the Interstate Commerce Commission was established in 1887 to regulate railroad rates and earnings and prevent such unstable price conditions. (Alas in modern times the ICC too often *protects the railroads*, not the consumers!)

The steel and other metal industries are examples of this pattern of imperfect competition. How does all this work out these days in practice? In 1954, 1958, and 1960 we hit a lull. Steel production went down to half its capacity. Some feared this would initiate a wave of price cuts which would reduce steel companies' earnings to the break-even point or below. Did it work out that way? Not quite. The industry discovered it could still make money at levels far below capacity; price morale stayed high in the industry. Even massive competitive steel imports have not forced steel prices down to marginal-cost levels.

In a perfectly competitive industry, when demand shifts leftward, P will fall. Profits will decline greatly. Yet competitive Q may not fall much at all, being sold for whatever it will fetch. The consumer does benefit from what the producer loses, and in time output will adjust to the new state of demand.

By contrast, under oligopoly, price tends to stay firm with output taking up the great variation. Plants stand partially idle, and the product is not cheapened in the hope of coaxing out new quantity demanded.

This downward inflexibility of "administered" (or named) prices, many economists fear, adds to the danger of Chapter 41's creeping inflation. Why? Because if prices and costs rarely ever fall, there is but one way for the price index to go.

DYNAMIC RESEARCH AND MONOPOLY

All is not evil in any field. Some arguments concerning the *virtues* of imperfect competition can also be made. A common industrial pattern is that of a firm that has considerable control over price by virtue of its technological efficiency, its patents, its trademarks, and its slogans. Its "monopoly profits" are plowed back into further research and advertising, so that it is always able to keep abreast or ahead of its rivals. General Electric, RCA, and Du Pont are perhaps typical of such companies.

Because research and advertising are expensive and their results cumulative, success tends to breed success, and profits tend to breed more profits. Therefore small business claims that it cannot always effectively compete with such firms. In other words, industrial research may be subject to economies of large scale which small businesses cannot enjoy.[13] And yet, when John Jewkes traced the source of the more important inventions of this century, he found that less than half came from laboratories of large corporations.

Furthermore, instances of beer, cigarettes, and soap remind us that advertising and research are quite different things. Budweiser beer sales may stay large because a national audience has been persuaded of its merits. Much soap advertising is aimed more to solidify the sales of one brand than to expand total soap use and cleanliness. Yet in many cases it will not be easy to decide whether a certain bit of applied industrial research is for the purpose of technical improvement or merely for market improvement.

Reread Schumpeter's eulogy of the dynamic innovational contribution of monopolists

---

[13] Also, large firms are great "poolers of risks," being favored by the statistical fact that when you aggregate independent risks you cancel out much of the variation. (In fact, quadruple the size of the firm and its independent risks and you halve the average risk per dollar—as probability books show.)

(page 94). Weigh this with the claims that many of our best discoveries come from small business, government, lone-wolf inventors, and university researchers. A sensible student realizes this is indeed a controversial matter.

While admitting the efficiency and progress of some of the firms described, critics go on to argue that society would be *still* better off if the full advantages of efficiency were passed on to consumers or plowed back into research aimed at technological improvements and not simply at profits; and if fewer dollars were spent on "soap operas" and jingles and more went into fundamental science rather than into patentable gadgets.

Obviously, we are dealing here with moot issues, on which each citizen must form his own judgment. Obviously too, the giants of the new industrial state must be placed under ever-vigilant public scrutiny and surveillance.

WHAT TO DO ABOUT MONOPOLY IMPERFECTIONS

Is there no hope for limiting monopoly and oligopoly? Yes, there is.

For one thing, if we make sure that *barriers to entry are kept to a minimum*, the fear of potential competition and the actuality of that competition may help to keep the oligopoly prices down.

For a second thing, if government antitrust policy bears down hard on the slightest sign of collusion designed to keep prices firm and to control supply, the oligopolists may find it harder to equate their marginal revenue and cost at a level high above society's true marginal cost.

For a third thing, some economists—such as George J. Stigler—would argue that large firms should be broken up into many small pieces. He thinks the bottom of U-shaped cost curves comes early enough to make this a practical possibility and one will not sacrifice any appreciable economies of large-scale production. With sellers now numerous, he hopes that competition can become much more like perfect competition than like oligopoly. (Needless to say, Stigler is against any mergers that might reduce numbers still further; and he believes that many of today's giants grew from mergers which had as their goal not *productive efficiency*, but rather monopoly *control over market price*.)

Government regulation and government antitrust laws are the principal weapons a mixed economy uses to improve the workings of the price system. This is plainly a developing and dynamic area. Even the Supreme Court has been gradually changing its mind on the legalities of the issues, as we shall see.

PUBLIC-UTILITY REGULATION

To show what government can do about monopoly, let us consider in detail a monopoly licensed by the state and under government regulation. Such "public utilities" include gas and light companies, telephone and communication services, railroads and public carriers, and so forth. Since it seems uneconomical to have two local sets of telephone wires, an exclusive franchise is given to a single company. (Why not the same for milk delivery—which is no easy question.)

But having given the utility company a complete monopoly, the state steps in to protect the consumer by setting maximum rates. Usually this is done by public regulating commissions, which specify the *maximum prices* that can be charged for each kind of service.

In setting such prices it has long been customary to pick prices that will try to give the company "a fair return on its capital." Rates such as 6, 7, or 8 per cent are often selected as representing a fair return. (Of course, any "guarantee" of a rate of return raises the problem of *motivating* the utility to keep efficient and cost-conscious.)

It is a complex problem, that of determining the *capital-value* base of the company to which this "fair rate" is to be applied. Three measures of fair capital value have been suggested at times: (1) *original cost* (minus depreciation)—or the sum of all past prudent investments; (2) *current reproduction or replacement cost* (minus depreciation)—or the cost of replacing the company's equipment *at present prices,* corrected for age and condition of the property; and (3) *capitalized market value* of the public utility's securities or assets.

Advantages and disadvantages of different methods of regulation   Of these methods, the third is universally recognized to be nonsensical. As was shown in the earlier discussion of good will (Chapter 5), the market value of any income-earning property is given by capitalizing its annual return by the interest rate.[14] For a regulating authority to use capitalized market value as a base for measuring capital would be tantamount to recognizing *any level of earnings*, high or low, as fair. (E.g., let the earnings be high—excessively high. The stock market will then pay a lot for them.) Once having been capitalized into a new base, excessively high earnings will appear as only moderate interest returns, and the same is true of excessively low earnings. The method of capitalized earnings begs the question that the authorities must answer!

The American courts have therefore vacillated between *original* cost and *reproduction* cost. So long as the general price level does not change, the two are not very different. But over a period of decades, when prices may greatly increase, reproduction cost will involve higher earnings and rates than original cost. In periods of declining prices, the reverse discrepancy is to be observed. On the whole, reproduction cost leads to a more flexible price structure and gives less weight to the dead hand of past costs.[15]

---

[14] The capitalization process is more fully discussed in Chapter 30.

[15] From the standpoint of the advanced discussions of "welfare economics," neither method is ideal, as the last Appendix made clear. Some writers in this field have set up a perfectionist formula that would involve pricing of public-utility services at not more than the extra or marginal costs of services. (We have seen why $P = MC$ is "efficient" already many times.) However, marginal-cost pricing is a doctrine which, as a practical matter, few economists would endorse all the way. It could lead to excessive returns to the owners if demand was large in comparison with capacity. But with decreasing-cost situations so likely in the public-utility area, it would more likely give *inadequate* returns to original investors. Although the state could then, if it wished to, *by a subsidy* secure justice for investors without interfering with the desirable output or price, this would represent a considerable departure from present practice and seems unlikely to come about fully. The great regional power projects such as the TVA and Bonneville Dam are from one viewpoint partial approaches toward such a system of pricing. However, the fact that the government can raise capital in larger sums and at lower costs than private industry, and the fact that the same set of dams can simultaneously achieve the ends of national defense, navigation, flood control, and irrigation, make any simple yardstick comparison between private and public operations difficult, if not impossible.

OVERVIEW OF ANTITRUST POLICY

Around the turn of the century, America went through a period of widespread trust formation. Big and small companies combined collusively to limit supply and raise price (often putting voting stock of the different firms into a so-called "trust" agreement that provided for collective action and profit sharing). Small companies were flagrantly merged into big combines. Price cutters were punished brutally by competitive retaliation. Huge stock-market promotion schemes flourished.

The common law had long forbidden monopolistic conspiracies. And often these doctrines had been used against the youthful trade-union movement. But it was apparent toward the end of the last century that antitrust legislation would be needed if the game of effective competition was to be maintained.

Any history of antitrust policy must take into account (1) the history of *legislative acts*—e.g., the Sherman Act (1890), the Clayton Act (1914) and the Federal Trade Commission Act (1914), the Celler-Kefauver Antimerger Act (1950); (2) the history of attempted *enforcement of the laws by the Department of Justice*—e.g., inaction in the 1890s, Theodore Roosevelt's activism, the lull from 1911 when Standard Oil and American Tobacco were broken up until Franklin Roosevelt's late New Deal days when Thurman Arnold became so active in prosecuting cases that wags referred to the Sherman Act as the "Thurman Act," the increased activism of federal lawyers under Kennedy, Johnson, and Nixon; and (3) the history of *federal court decisions*—e.g., the post–1911 period when the Supreme Court followed its 1911 "rule of reason" doctrine and refused to break up U.S. Steel; the post–1945 period when the Court in effect reversed itself and held that the Aluminum Company of America was guilty just by virtue of controlling most of the market, even if it did not engage in particularly predatory practices; and the increasingly tough decisions of the courts since mid-century.

Moreover, any survey of the field must take note that some of the antitrust legislation has acted actually to *increase* monopolistic imperfection of markets rather than *decrease* it—to protect inefficient businesses from the competition of larger efficient firms, by means of the Robinson-Patman (1936) anti-chain-store legislation and the related Miller-Tydings Act (1937) designed to help enforcement of "retail price maintenance" agreements.

Legal technicalities rather than economic realities have often been dominant. The *act of monopolizing* has been the target rather than the condition of *existing* monopoly; two firms acting in concert have been hit harder than one giant firm which has continued the same excess of price over marginal cost! Punishment *after* the fact rather than *prevention* of bad market behavior and bad market structure has often been emphasized. And the distinction between bad *market structure* (per se) and bad or unreasonable *market conduct* has often been blunted by the legal mind.

Yet these criticisms should not blind us to the fact that the antitrust activity of government has been evolving into a stricter pattern. Nor blind us to the fact that without our antitrust acts the imperfection of competition in America would presumably be significantly heightened. When one looks at monopoly and cartel patterns of behavior abroad, in such countries as Germany and Japan, we understand why so many foreign nations have in recent years been imitating the American policies. Indeed, many experts feel that the whole of our antitrust programs adds up to more than the sum of the parts: the system seems to work better than anyone can account for.

BRIEF HISTORY OF ANTITRUST POLICY

Sherman Act (1890)   This made it illegal to "monopolize trade" and outlawed all "combination or conspiracy in restraint of trade." On paper, this act represented a major advance over the previous common-law restrictions on monopolistic conspiracies. But it was adopted with little discussion, indeed without attracting much attention of a favorable or unfavorable nature; and beyond an antipathy toward "monopolizing," there is no evidence that anyone had clear notions as to which actions were to be regarded as legal or illegal.

In the early 1900s, the Republican administrations of Theodore Roosevelt and William Howard Taft witnessed the first surge of activity under the Sherman Act. Thus, the Supreme Court prevented J. P. Morgan and E. H. Harriman from using a holding company to bring about a merger of their Northern Pacific Railroad with Hill's Great Northern. In 1911, the Supreme Court ordered the American Tobacco Company and Standard Oil each to be broken up into a number of separate companies.

In condemning these flagrant monopolies, the Supreme Court enunciated the "rule of reason": Only *unreasonable* restraints of trade (agreements, mergers, predation, and the like) were to come within the scope of the Sherman Act and to be considered illegal. Thus, although Eastman Kodak and International Harvester were clearly near-monopolies, the court used its rule of reason to acquit them of guilt, arguing that they had not engaged in *visible* coercion or attack on rivals to build up their monopoly position.

The "rule of reason" doctrine almost emasculated the antitrust program, as shown by the U.S. Steel Case (1920). Although J. P. Morgan had put together this giant by merger, and enjoying as it did in the beginning 60 per cent of the market, the court held that mere size per se was no offense. Only monopoli*zing* and not monopoly seemed to constitute an offense to the legal mind! Until the 1930s, the antitrust programs hibernated under the probusiness Coolidge and Hoover administrations.

Clayton Act (1914) and FTC (1914)   To spell out the vague intent of the Sherman Act and strengthen it, the Clayton Act was passed. It outlawed *price discrimination* to lessen competition and "tied" contracts (in which you forced a buyer or seller to deal exclusively with you). It banned *interlocking directorates* designed to lessen competition, and *mergers* for this purpose formed by acquiring common stocks of competitors. The Clayton Act emphasized prevention before the fact as well as punishment after the fact. In contrast to the early common law, which had been used particularly against organized labor, the Clayton Act specifically excluded labor as a commodity in the sense of antitrust. (Today many critics of the monopoly power of labor would like to subject unions to new antitrust legislation; however, many experts in the field argue that this would exacerbate rather than moderate intransigent union behavior.)

Also in 1914 the Federal Trade Commission (FTC) was established. It was to have powers to investigate, hold hearings, and issue cease-and-desist orders. But the courts construed away most of its powers. And it was not until a 1938 amendment (Wheeler-Lea) that it acquired its primary present-day function—that of banning false and deceptive advertising.

New Deal activism   Congress passes laws, the courts enforce them, but nothing happens unless the Department of Justice brings suit to execute them. Thus President Cleveland's Attorney General disapproved of the Sherman Act after it was passed and refused to prosecute under it. As we have seen, Theodore Roosevelt instituted a more activist phase after the turn of the century; but it was only in the late 1930s, when Franklin Roosevelt put Thurman Arnold in charge of antitrust, that a real burst of prosecutions got under way. Arnold tackled the notoriously backward building industries, glass, cigarettes, cement, and many others.

Today the Department of Justice has hundreds of lawyers in its Antitrust Division, as against the few of Teddy Roosevelt's time. And it needs them: 45 or more cases are prosecuted each year, in contrast to the 2 or 3 of earlier times. Certain classes of cases average $6\frac{1}{2}$ years in duration!

The Aluminum Company Case (1945) represents a culmination of this new activity. Reason and rules had changed since the disastrous U.S. Steel Case. Monopoly and not simply monopoliz*ing* was declared illegal. For Alcoa had gained its 90 per cent of the market by subtle and nonpredatory means: building ahead of market demand, keeping its price low enough to forestall competition, etc. For the first time the Court emphasized market *structure* rather than so-called market *conduct*. In the Cigarette Case (1946) the Supreme Court found the Big Three guilty of *tacit* collusion: recognizing that Camels and Luckies must sell at the same price per pack, Reynolds and American Tobacco did not need to hold secret meetings or telephone conversations; they had only to recognize mutual interdependence and engage in *parallel* action. (Though punishing them as oligopolists, the Court could not tell them how to avoid sin and turn over a new leaf: if one undercut the other's price, that would be predatory oligopoly; if they matched prices, that was tacit oligopoly. Apparently moderate exercise of monopoly power would be the prescription for a quiet life.)

THE FEW ANTITRUST LAWS WHICH WEAKEN COMPETITION

The Sherman and Clayton Acts and most of the antitrust laws, have contributed enormously toward improving the degree of competition in our system. All who value social reliance on decentralized markets and economic efficiency should applaud this kind of public intervention which helps to lessen the imperfections of competition.

But unfortunately, during the Great Depression a movement developed to pass laws that were called "antitrust laws" but which actually tended to make competition more *im*perfect. Thus, the NRA (National Recovery Act of 1933), under the guise of recovery from depression, blatantly promoted industry-wide codes and cartels with collusive price maintenance. (This act was later declared unconstitutional.)

Another example, already mentioned, is the Robinson-Patman Act (1936). This tries to keep one businessman from vigorously cutting his prices by selling the same product under a different brand name, and in various other ways serves to limit competition. Rather than concentrating on bringing *P* down for the consumer, it concentrates on keeping many firms in business, even though some may be inefficient.

Still other examples are provided by *resale price maintenance* laws of the Miller-Tydings (1937) type. These try to make it hard or impossible for one merchant to undersell another on given brand-name products. Recently these price-maintenance laws have more and more been under heavy attack by courts and the public; but Congress is still lobbied by their proponents.

Often legislators, lawyers, and judges have been against bigness *even when it promoted efficiency and lower consumer prices*. Thus, in the A & P Case, the worst crime, in many eyes, was that the size of the company made it possible for its chain of stores to sell groceries at a much smaller markup than its myriad of competitors could. Terrified by the quite unrealistic possibility that its price cutting would drive out all competitors and *then* permit it to raise its prices high, critics tried to use the antitrust laws against the A & P. (Actually, it is A & P that has been losing ground in recent years.)

From these perversions of the antitrust philosophy, one can see that the economists' preoccupation with how well the pricing system serves to determine WHAT, HOW, and FOR WHOM is not quite the same thing as the judge's preoccupation with who is a nasty man who has been doing nasty things and with whom.

MODERN ANTITRUST

In the decades since World War II the Justice Department and the courts have been increasingly vigorous in their prosecution of the antitrust laws. Thus the Cement Case (1948) abolished the "basing-point" system of quoting prices at any place in a region at a differential, reflecting transport costs, above the price at a given point—like the old "Pittsburgh-plus" pricing of the steel industry. In 1961, the electric equipment industry was found guilty of collusive price agreements. Executives of the largest companies— such as General Electric and Westinghouse—were held to have met in hotels secretly for that purpose. Although the top men in these companies apparently were unaware of what the vice-presidents just below them were doing, they had put much pressure on them for results. The companies agreed to pay extensive damages to their customers for overcharges; and some of the executives involved spent time in jail on criminal (as against civil) prosecutions initiated by the Eisenhower administration.

Celler-Kefauver Antimerger Act (1950)   Because the Clayton Act had only ruled out mergers resulting from acquisition of stock, there was a loophole in the law that permitted mergers via acquisition of assets. In 1950 this loophole was plugged up. Today *horizontal* mergers—as, for example, where one retail chain takes over another retail chain in the same area—are close to being ruled illegal per se. Former Chief Justice Warren actually stated in the Brown Shoe Case (1962) that a merger achieving 5 per cent control might further "the oligopoly Congress sought to avoid." Contrast this with an earlier view of the Supreme Court that a 60 to 64 per cent share of the market might be admissible. Indeed, in the Von Grocery Case (1965) a merger of two supermarkets leading to only a $7\frac{1}{2}$ per cent share of the Los Angeles market was disallowed. Vertical mergers—as, for example, when Reynolds Aluminum tried to expand its fabrication and sale of aluminum wrappings—tend to be frowned on too.

CONGLOMERATES AND BACKLASH

Conglomerate mergers, where a company in one industry takes on a company in another unrelated industry, present more difficult cases. In 1957 the Supreme Court ruled that Du Pont unduly dominated General Motors and made Du Pont get rid of its GM stock. In the Phillips-Tidewater Case (1966) the head of the Justice Department started prosecution on the ground that if Phillips Petroleum were refused the merger, it would start hundreds of new gas stations in that area and thereby increase the degree of competition. Similar reasoning was involved in the prosecution by the government of the proposed merger by Bethlehem Steel, which had no plant in the Chicago area, and Youngstown Steel, which did have such a plant. By forcing Bethlehem to build a new plant there, it was hoped that one extra competitor would be established. In the Pabst case (1966), mere fear of size as such—quite independently of considerations of dominant share of market—was used against mergers by Judge Warren Burger (later Chief Justice of the Supreme Court).

By the 1970s, antipathy against conglomerates had become almost a mania of the Nixon Justice Department. Litton Industries, International Telephone, and others had been the darlings of Wall Street during the 1960s, each taking over dozens and dozens of smaller firms in unrelated industries. A host of imitators sprang up, of course.

Thus, Ling-Temco-Vought began with an airplane company but soon acquired scores of companies by clever offers of new varieties of Ling securities- preferred stock, convertible preferred, second convertible preferred, convertible bonds, bonds with attached (but detachable) warrant options to buy the common. One had to be an Einstein of finance to calculate the amount of dilution of ownership that would occur if all convertible securities were ultimately to be converted into common stock. (Professor Warren Law of the Harvard Business School admitted the Ling prospectus was beyond him!) Often, little conglomerates would take over giant cash-rich companies many times their own size, using in the end the cash of the company taken over to pay for the acquisition. Thirty-year-old whiz kids pyramided thousands of dollars into tens of millions almost overnight.

Each new successful acquisition increased total sales and reported per share earnings, thereby enabling the conglomerates to acquire still more companies at lower and lower cash cost. (Often the reported gain in earnings was misleading, being merely the product of imaginative accounting, which ignored potential dilution by conversion, treated once-and-for-all paper gains on security sales as if they were recurring operating earnings, juggled the accounting treatment of good will, and reported as current income items for which payment would be received only in future installments. Franchise and land companies were some of the worst offenders.)

But what, after all, did the airplane business have in common with meat packing? Or typewriters with birth-control pills? Or computer leasing with passenger-bus operations? Good modern management, coupled with adequate finance, can of course help in any line of activity. And the history of the East India or Hudson Bay companies does remind us that in underdeveloped countries the only way to get the efficiencies associated with large-scale corporations may be through conglomerates. (Fancifully, if Harold Geneen has the genius to run scores of unrelated activities under the headship of International Telephone & Telegraph, could he be the prototype and forerunner of Galbraith's expert-planner under socialism or some equivalent form of organization of the future industrial state?)

By the late 1960s the bubble had burst on the conglomerates. It was a chain-letter form of growth which had to grow ever faster in order not to lead to disillusionment and collapse. When even the mighty Litton Industries had a pause in earnings growth, the jig was up for the Lings, Gulf & Westerns, and later imitators. Now "conglomerate" became a dirty word. Conglomerate stocks dropped. Acquisitions failed. Mergers were blocked by the Nixon Justice Department. A scapegoat was needed by Congress and the public: conglomerates provided a convenient target. Bigness as such was held against them, on the *simpliste* theory that the unit with the "deeper pocket" can outbargain and destroy its competitors. There were threats to tax them, or take away from them the usual privilege of having bond interest tax-deductible. Fear of "reciprocity"—the practice of one big business to buy products from its own branches or from those other companies who reciprocate with purchases from it, even at unfavorable market terms—became rampant in the Antitrust Division and in the courts. Nonetheless, Professor Stigler, in a task force investigation for President Nixon, concluded that reciprocity is quite trivial in economic importance and that much of the hostility to conglomerates is hysterically irrational. Often those seeking take-overs represented "outsiders," self-made newly arrived chaps who had not belonged to Yale's Skull and Bones or been vetted by the existing business establishment. Their crudities were thus specially to be resented. And yet, corporate oligarchies that had grown soft and arrogant under previous minority rule were often goaded into reform by fear of take-over or were even replaced by those better able to utilize the corporation's resources.

Take-overs, like bankruptcy, represent one of Nature's methods of eliminating deadwood in the struggle for survival. A more open—and more efficiently responsive—corporate society can result. But, without public surveillance and control, the opposite could also emerge. The Darwinian jungle is not guaranteed to produce a happy ending.

FUTURE OF ANTITRUST POLICY

In summary, both Republicans and Democrats are spending more and more money on lawyers and investigators to enforce the antitrust laws with ever-increasing vigor. Firms no longer dare to use group practices which used to be standard in American industry. Aside from civil and criminal suits initiated by government, they face the threat of suits for triple damages initiated by aggrieved rivals.

Judges are tougher in their judgments. More and more they weaken the powers that a business firm has to exploit its patents and its market advantages. Even after a case has been decided against a company, it is not off the hook. It may feel forced to enter into "consent decrees" which bind it to follow certain policies, and the judge may for years afterward keep his careful eye on the firm's performance. (The United Shoe case is a good example, where the company had to agree to sell its machines instead of only renting them. Like a truant schoolboy, it had to keep reporting to the federal judge.

In a similar way the FTC has kept the giant meat packers under surveillance literally for decades.)

As we have seen, the economist and the lawyer do not always see eye to eye. The economist often feels that lawyers and the courts have concentrated on the letter of the law, without defining its spirit with any precision. If a businessman should be caught with an indiscreet set of letters in his files, the court throws the book at him. But if another company has consistently done the same thing in less overt fashion, it is immune from prosecution.

To illustrate this, consider the striking fact that the most prosecutions under the antitrust laws have been in the food-processing industries, the building industries, and the service trades. Are these the most concentrated industries? Certainly not. They are characterized by rather large numbers of firms. Apparently, complaints arise from frictions between firms, while giant companies that dominate a field and exercise quiet monopoly power tend to be overlooked. Some cynics, decades ago, argued that the antitrust laws even encourage bigness, because in practice they are so much harsher on agreements *between* firms than on what the economist would consider the same price–marginal-cost discrepancies engineered by *intrafirm* practices that require no furtive meetings at midnight or incriminating letters.

Too often the law—as drawn up by Congress, enforced by the Department of Justice, and adjudicated by the courts—regards various vigorous forms of competition that tend to eliminate firms and reduce the discrepancy between price and marginal cost as crimes rather than benefits. The legal mind is not to much concerned with the distortion of prices, which it has no means of measuring, as it is with the methods by which prices are set. Yet the economic and legal minds do seem today to be coming closer together.

As to the future evolution of antitrust policy, there are two opposing philosophies. Carl Kaysen, formerly of Harvard and now director of the Institute for Advanced Study in Princeton, together with Donald F. Turner, professor at Harvard Law School and formerly President Johnson's head of the Antitrust Division, believe the test should be whether a firm has "market power per se," stemming from its monopolistic market *structure*. Independently of its *conduct*, Kaysen and Turner would say there is a prima facie case for breaking up such a company. At the opposite pole is the view that an updated "rule of reason" should be applied to every case. If even the biggest monopoly is found to display marvelous Schumpeterian innovation, it should be left undisturbed by antitrust litigation. Evidently there is an unresolved conflict here, and all that can be said at this point is that economists tend on the whole to lean toward the market-structure viewpoint.

FINALE

Our discussion of antitrust has concentrated on United States experience, for the very good reason that this country has been a pioneer in such legislation. For many years countries such as Britain, Germany, and Japan, as well as other European nations, appeared to us to take a very lax view of the legality of monopolistic arrangements. After World War II, American occupational authorities in Japan and Germany tried to introduce legislation in those countries to break up their old combines. For a while this seemed to succeed. Then, as those nations began to stand on their own feet, there was some backsliding. However, the Common Market countries have been strengthening their antitrust statutes, and it remains to be seen in what spirit the letter of the regulations will be interpreted. And Britain has belatedly begun to adopt antitrust practices. (Many nations, like the United States in the Webb-Pomerene Act, 1918, lighten their antitrust rules for their own exporters; many more exempt them completely.)

While no one would claim that American antitrust legislation and enforcement have been completely logical or have come anywhere near complete success, one has but to look abroad to realize how much worse off our economy might have been were it not for the omnipresent threat of legal prosecution. American enterprise is kept on the defensive and would never dream of adopting the flagrant devices that are all too common in most places.

Professor Richard Caves has compared American antitrust action to traffic laws. Most citizens do not consider breaking the traffic laws mortal sins. And the police tend to act only against the most flagrant offenders—the driver who goes 80 in a school zone. But the fact that the policeman may be there, *ready to make an arrest,* does keep drivers generally more in conformity with the laws of the road. "The guilty flee where no man pursueth." And so, often, do the innocent. To cynics, part of the efficacy of the antitrust laws may even result from their arbitrariness: like the emperor who would take out a general at random and shoot him—"in order to encourage the others"—the antitrust program hangs like the sword of Damocles over every businessman, limiting his temptation to exercise monopoly power.

By laissez faire one does not automatically get perfect competition. To reduce imperfections of competition, a nation must struggle perpetually and must ever maintain its vigilance.

Workable competition   Repeatedly, in Part Three, we have stressed the basic problem of how a pricing system solves society's questions WHAT, HOW, FOR WHOM. This frames the rational goal of antitrust policy.

We cannot expect competition to become everywhere "perfectly perfect," in the strict sense of the economist. But what we must strive for is what the late J. M. Clark of Columbia University years ago called "workable competition." By public and private policies we can hope to improve the efficiency with which market prices reflect underlying individual needs, desires, and wants against the background of true costs of goods—marginal costs in terms of alternative goods that could be produced and in terms of used-up scarce productive factors which involve sweat and disutility. Just as concentration in control of share of market was made to decrease from 1900 to mid-century, so by the century's end can monopoly imperfections be weakened further. But laissez faire cannot be counted on to do this. Public vigilance and support for antitrust will be required.

Part Four will be concerned with identical problems that arise in connection with the pricing of land, labor, and capital. Again, the function of such pricing in trying to solve society's problems is the focal point of interest.

SUMMARY

A. ANALYTICAL PATTERNS OF IMPERFECT COMPETITION

1   Few business firms are able to develop exact curves of cost and revenue. This does not mean that they are oblivious to profit maximization. Through trial and error, they may be doing a tolerably good job of keeping alive as a business entity and of achieving long-run optimum profits.

2   Under imperfect competition, a firm may have to make rough guesses in setting its price. Often it will use some kind of *markup* over an estimate of unit cost. Nonetheless, it is often market conditions that determine how much of a markup any firm can safely count on getting; so in a sense the problem is merely re-posed. Only factual investigations of each market situation can tell what the result is likely to be.

3   In Galbraith's vision of the new industrial state, bureaucrats of the technostructure exercise unilateral power to mold consumer tastes. They may be checked by the "countervailing power" of their large-scale suppliers or customers; and despite Galbraith's prose, even the largest corporations are subject to checks of numerous rival conglomerates, making collusion difficult and despotic rule shortsighted.

4   Various patterns of competition lend themselves to economic analysis: (1) monopoly, (2) oligopoly, in which few sellers compete with similar or differentiated products, (3) Chamberlinian models of many sellers of differentiated products, and finally (4) the case of perfect competition itself. The kinked demand curve of oligopoly helps to explain its rigid administered pricing around a level that can be agreed upon. The no-profit tangency equilibrium of Chamberlin's large group leaves society with the wastes of excess capacity and overdifferentiated products.

B. MODERN ANTITRUST PROBLEMS

5   The economic evils of such imperfections transcend the mere matter of monopolistic profits: entry may cut out excess-profits *without* bringing prices down to marginal costs; overentry of imperfect competitors may waste resources without giving the consumer the benefit of lower prices; monopolistic and oligopolistic pricing above true marginal costs brings distortion of resource allocation (inefficiency and nonresponsiveness) even if the firms involved have their excess-profits taxed or competed away.

6   Against the evils of monopoly and oligopoly must be weighed the possible Schumpeterian *dynamic* efficiencies which they may introduce. A large firm in a protected market may have the wherewithal to develop new inventions and also the assurance that it will not lose to competitors the advantages of its own research efforts. In strongly decreasing-cost industries, there is no hope for viable *perfect* competition, and substitute checks on the powers of few dominating firms have to come from public control.

7   By public regulation of utilities and by various formal and informal antitrust activities of the state, some of the checks and balances that are not automatically enforceable by perfect competition can be achieved by governmental action.

8   The history of American antitrust legislation and enforcement has been an irregular one. Inaction has been followed by vigorous action; and sometimes by various backward steps, including price-maintenance laws which seem to reduce rather than enhance effective price competition. Although the legal mind of judges and legislators has not always concentrated on what economists consider the key pricing issue—e.g., being excessively concerned with "reciprocity," conglomerates, and bigness as such—evolutionary progress toward "workable competition" has been made. And many nations abroad are beginning to imitate our methods. After economists realize that perfect competition is not spontaneously attained or enforceable, the problem of defining and approaching "workable competition" becomes paramount. Here is the frontier for economic policy.

QUESTIONS FOR DISCUSSION

1   Give examples of behavior by business firms suggesting that they do seek to maximize their profits. Give some apparent exceptions.

2   Suppose you ran an electric company. How could you go about maximizing profits? How would you estimate elasticity of demand? Would an economics textbook be the source for learning how to be successful in this respect?

3   What is meant by markup and administered pricing? Show how these might work.

4   Describe the pattern of imperfect competition in the auto industry, cigarette industry, aluminum industry, mousetrap industry, women's-dress trade, retail grocery trade, barbershop trade, undertaking industry.

5   "The tragedy of monopolistic competition often has nothing to do with excessive profits. Rather, there may be no profits at all, the high price being frittered away in small volume and inefficient production." Discuss.

6   Recapitulate highlights of antitrust activity here and abroad.

7   "It is utopian to try to break up monopolies into even a few effectively competing units, because the basic cause of monopoly is the law of decreasing cost with mass production, and, in any case, a few competitors are not enough to duplicate the pricing patterns of perfect competition." Discuss both parts of this statement.

8   "The A & P Company is not bad just because it is big." Discuss.

9   Show that companies may be tempted to merge in order to gain tax advantages. (HINT: Suppose the New York Central Railroad has sizable losses and the Pennsylvania Railroad has profits. Losses can be "carried forward" to offset later profits.)

10 Eisenhower's Justice Department permitted Hudson and Nash to merge as American Motors, permitted Studebaker and Packard to merge, but forbade the merger of the Bethlehem and Youngstown steel companies. All these decisions were made in the interest

of promoting competition. Do you think they are necessarily inconsistent? Give arguments pro and con.

11 "The modern corporation is a good pooler of risks. Other things being equal, the larger the firm, the more it can cancel off one risk against another, the more it can economize on inventory and excess peak capacity, and the more it can spread the indivisible costs of the best-grade research among its many units. Larger size tends to help, and if it emulates the example of General Motors and other efficient decentralizers of decision making, there are almost no penalties from larger size. I conclude that trying to prevent monopolies is a fight against nature." Comment critically.

12 *Extra-credit problem* to illustrate operations research and decision theory: Page 36 presented a least-cost-diet problem in linear programming. Here is a transportation version. Your Plants 1 and 2 each produce 13 and 9 (thousand) units. Your Markets 1, 2, and 3 each need 5, 11, and 6 (thousand) units. You know the cost of transporting each unit of your good from Plant i to Market j, as given by the coefficients C_{ij} of the amounts you ship from i to j, X_{ij}. Mathematically, you have to solve the linear programming problem

$$\text{Minimize } Z = \sum_{1}^{2}\sum_{1}^{3} C_{ij}X_{ij} = \begin{aligned}40X_{11} + 50X_{12} + 60X_{13} \\ + 20X_{21} + 30X_{22} + 80X_{23}\end{aligned}$$

subject to

$$X_{11} + X_{12} + X_{13} = 13, \; X_{21} + X_{22} + X_{23} = 9, \qquad X_{11} \geq 0, X_{12} \geq 0, X_{13} \geq 0$$
$$X_{11} + X_{21} = 5, \; X_{12} + X_{22} = 11, \; X_{13} + X_{23} = 6, \qquad X_{21} \geq 0, X_{22} \geq 0, X_{23} \geq 0$$

By trial and error can you verify that Plant 1 ships 6 to Market 3 and 7 to Market 2, while Plant 2 ships 5 to Market 1 and 4 to Market 2? This gives least $Z = 930 = 40(0) + 50(7) + 60(6) + 20(5) + 30(4) + 80(0)$. (HINT: a two-way table might help, with Plant totals placed at the right of its two rows, and Market totals placed below its three columns. Experiment with two of the Markets' each being satisfied from only one Plant.)

Review your understanding of the following concepts:

markup pricing, administered *P*

Galbraithian countervailing power
  and technostructure

oligopoly, with or without tacit
  collusion, kinked demand

free entry

no-profit equilibrium of producers
  of differentiated products

evils of imperfect competition

utility rate regulation

fair return on original or reproduction
  cost or on market valuation

Sherman, Clayton, Celler-Kefauver Acts

NRA, resale price maintenance

Robinson-Patman

conglomerates

Schumpeterian dynamic advantages

challenge of "workable competition"

Distribution of Income: The Pricing of the Productive Factors 4

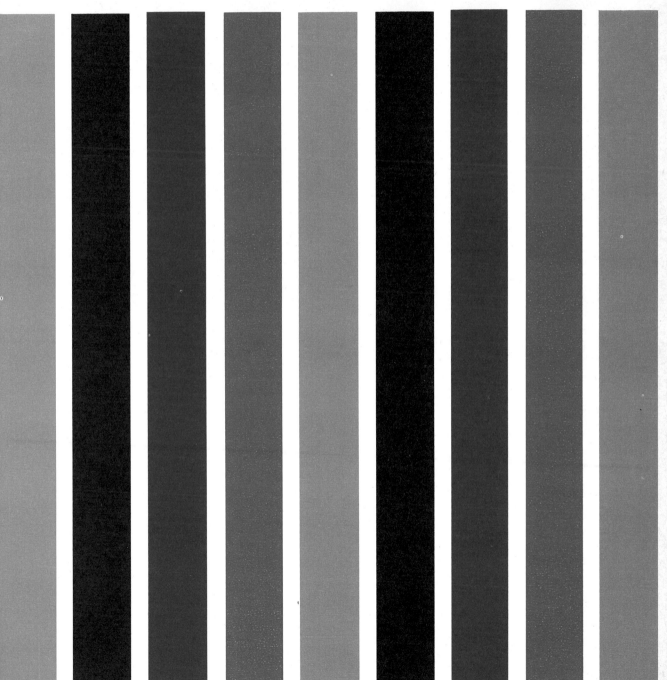

Theory of Production and Marginal-Products

27

Knowledge is the only instrument of production that is not subject to diminishing returns.

J. M. CLARK

In the next few chapters of Part Four we shall be primarily concerned with how factors of production get priced in the market place; that is, we shall analyze the determination of (1) *rents* of land and other resources (Chapter 28), (2) *wages* of various kinds of labor (Chapter 29), (3) *interest* rates on capital assets (Chapter 30), and (4) *profit* (Chapter 31), and grand summary (Chapter 32).

Economists call this the problem of "distribution." They do not mean by this term what the man in the street means when he refers to distribution as the marketing of goods and the carrying of goods to the final consumer. Instead Part Four distribution deals with the problem of FOR WHOM goods are to be produced. It is pricing of factors of production by supply and demand that is helping determine FOR WHOM. This same factor pricing also operates to solve the problem of How society is to produce.

Why are wages some three-quarters of the total national product? To understand this we must study the forces that determine market wage rates, market land rentals, market interest rates. Thus, if technological changes, reflecting automation in industry, lowered market wage rates relative to the returns to property, the wage share might fall. Because the number of owners of property is so much smaller than the number of owners of labor, the result would be to shift the Lorenz-curve measure of inequality toward greater income inequality. We can understand the economic question of distribution primarily by focusing on the markets where factors of production get priced. This will give us insight into optimality equilibria and into "exploitation."

The key to such factor pricing will turn out to be provided by the economic *theory of production.* So, as a prelude to our general discussion of distribution of income, this chapter will investigate the theory of production. It will define the important economic concept of "marginal-product" and relate this to the familiar law of diminishing returns. Finally, the chapter will show that the demand curves for the various factors of production—the demands for labor, land, and so forth—are to be expressed in terms of their marginal-products.

DEMAND FOR FACTORS A DERIVED DEMAND

Begin with some elementary observations about factor demand.

Why do consumers demand a finished output like a magazine or an overcoat? They do so because of the satisfaction they hope to enjoy from its use. But why does a business-man demand a factor input such as fertilizer or sulfur or unskilled labor? Surely not for the *direct* satisfaction he hopes to get. He wants the productive factors because of the production and revenue that he hopes to secure *indirectly* from them.

Satisfactions are in the picture, but at one stage removed. The satisfactions that consumers get from an overcoat help to determine how much a textile company can sell the coat for and how many coats it can sell. Therefore you would be right to insist that consumer demands do *ultimately* determine the firm's demand for inputs. The firm's demand for labor is *derived indirectly* from the consumer demand for its final product. So economists speak of the demand for productive factors as a "derived demand."

Definition: **Derived demand refers to the fact that, when profit-seeking firms demand a factor of production, they do so because that factor input permits them to produce a good which consumers are willing to pay for now or in the future. The demand for the factor of production is thus derived ultimately from consumers' desires and demands for final goods.**

In short, effort involved in making coats or sewing machines is of no interest to society for its own sake; we pay men and machines to sew because of the satisfaction believed to be gained from the finished product. Sometimes the derived demands go through many stages: Wool is wanted to spin yarn; yarn is wanted to weave cloth; cloth is wanted to make coats. All the previous demands are derived from the ultimate consumer demand for the satisfactions to be secured from the finished product.

DEMAND FOR FACTORS A JOINTLY INTERDEPENDENT DEMAND

Another peculiarity about the demand for inputs stems from this technological fact: Factors usually do not work alone. A shovel by itself is worthless to me if I wish a cellar; a man with his bare hands is equally worthless. Together the man and shovel can dig my cellar. In other words, the quantity of a good produced depends *jointly* upon all the available inputs.

Sir William Petty, an early economist, put the matter in this striking way: Labor is the father and land the mother of product. One cannot say which is more important in producing a baby—a mother or a father. So, too, one cannot in most cases hope to demonstrate how much of the physical product has been *caused* by any one of the different factors *taken by itself*. The different factors *interact* with each other. Usually they reinforce each other's effectiveness, but sometimes they are substitutes for one another and they compete with, rather than complement, each other.

There is an important consequence of this jointness, or interdependence among the productivities of the different factor inputs, namely: The amount of labor demanded will depend on its wage rate, but the labor demanded will also depend upon the price of machines. The same is true of the demand for machines. By raising miners' wages, John L. Lewis created good business for power tools.

Thus, the demand for each input will depend upon the prices of *all* inputs, not on its own price alone. *Cross elasticities* **between different factors are as important as regular** *"own"* **elasticities.**

It is this interdependence of productivities of land, labor, and capital goods that makes the problem of distribution complex. For suppose we had to distribute at one harvest time the whole aggregate of output constituting the NNP. If land by itself had produced so much, and labor by itself had produced so much, and some third factor had by itself produced the rest, distribution might seem easy indeed. Crude notions of fairness might suggest that each factor share be simply set at what each has alone produced. Ethics aside, under free supply and demand if the separate factors could produce goods by themselves, they could jolly well make sure that they got the fruits of their activity; so, ethics aside, this would be a good description of the facts.

But reread the above paragraph and underline such words as *"by itself* produced" and *"has alone* produced." They refer to an *independence* of productivities which we know is simply lacking in the real world. If land and labor *together* produce the corn harvest, just how do you unscramble the separate contributions that supply and demand will parcel out to each?[1] A proud American worker might reflect on what *he* would produce and get in India or in 1900 America.

How is the problem of distribution resolved? It gets resolved by the processes of supply and demand, operating in perfectly or imperfectly competitive markets and modified by government laws. A brief analysis of the economic theory of production provides the indispensable key.

TECHNICAL LAW RELATING OUTPUT TO INPUTS: THE "PRODUCTION FUNCTION"

The theory of production begins with specific engineering or technological information. If you have a certain amount of labor, a certain amount of land, and certain prescribed amounts of other inputs such as machines or raw materials, how much output of a particular good can you get? The answer depends upon the state of technology: if someone makes a new invention or discovers a new industrial process, the obtainable output you

---

[1] Labor leaders used to say, "Without labor there is zero product. So attribute to labor *all* the product." Spokesmen for capital used the same bad logic to produce the opposite result: "Take away all capital goods, and labor scratches a bare pittance from the earth; so practically all the product should go to capital." The trouble with such foolish proposals is that, taken together, they allocate 200 or 300 per cent of the total product to the two or three factors, whereas there is only 100 per cent of the harvest to be allocated. And it makes no sense to say, "There is some truth on both sides; so let us apply the Golden Mean and, by a rule of unreason, give each of the factors the largest equal shares that will use up the available 100 percent of product." A real-world economy is not a courtroom where nimble legal minds illogically split hairs in order to solve society's problem of FOR WHOM.

can get from given factor inputs will go up. *But at any time, there will be a maximum obtainable amount of product for any given amounts of factor inputs.*

This technical law relating inputs to output is so important that economists have given it a name. They call it the "production function."

Definition: **The production function is the technical relationship telling the maximum amount of output capable of being produced by each and every set of specified inputs (or factors of production). It is defined for a given state of technical knowledge.**

Here is an example. An agricultural engineer lists in a thick book the various combinations of land and labor that will produce various quantities of corn. On one page of the book he lists the alternative combinations of land and labor needed to produce 100 bushels of corn; on another page, the alternative input combinations that will produce 200 bushels of corn; and so forth. Another example of a production function would be the chemical engineer's listing of the various ways of producing gasoline of a given octane rating.

There are thousands of different production functions in the American economy: at least one for each of the innumerable firms or productive units. A purpose of this chapter is to show how the firm's production function lies behind its Total Cost curve (discussed in Chapter 24) and to show how this provides the basis for the firm's derived demand for land, labor, capital, fertilizer, and numerous other productive inputs that it goes out into the market to buy.

Thus, the firm is poised between two kinds of markets: (1) the commodity market in which it appears as a supplier, selling its wares along the demand curve *of its customers;* and (2) the markets for factors of production in which it itself appears as a demander, buying inputs so as to minimize its total costs of production and to produce its Maximum-profit output. It is these factor markets which put prices upon the various productive inputs of the community and thus determine the distribution of income (wages, rent, interest, and so forth).

THE AGGREGATE AMERICAN PRODUCTION FUNCTION

Suppose, first, we put away our microscope and train a telescope on the aggregate magnitudes for American manufacturing of total labor, total capital, and total product. Such magnitudes must be measured with care, involving innumerable index-number problems of correct weighting; yet they are useful in giving a broad description of society. Back in the late twenties, former Senator Paul H. Douglas, then a University of Chicago professor of economics, won an important prize for his pathbreaking statistical measurement of America's production function. Later MIT's Robert Solow carried these researches a significant step further by showing how technological progress has been improving the productivity of American labor and capital.[2]

[2] P. H. Douglas, *Theory of Wages* (Macmillan, New York, 1934); R. M. Solow, "Technical Change and the Aggregate Production Function," *Review of Economics and Statistics,* vol. 39, 1957, pp. 312–320. Neither study measures land's separate contribution and share. In the 1970s this would probably be only about 5 per cent for the whole economy, and much less for manufacturing alone; but early in the century it was perhaps double that. Further work by E. Denison will be cited in Chapter 37, where modern growth models are discussed.

What have Douglas and Solow shown? Their statistics suggest that labor is the single most important factor of production in a certain subtle sense. Both labor and capital are needed in production: take away all capital, or alternatively all labor, and you will be left with negligible total product. But they find that a 1 per cent increase in labor seems to increase output about three times as much as would a 1 per cent increase in capital.[3] This largely corresponds with the widely known fact that wages are about three-fourths of the national product, while one-fourth (which is one-third of wages) is about the share of property incomes. There are numerous other findings from such studies, many of which have received important corroboration from similar researches by the nonprofit National Bureau of Economic Research. Here are a few of the most important empirical findings:

1. The productivity of both labor and capital has been increasing throughout this century because of improved technology and skill. The average rate of improvement appears to be between 1 and 2 per cent per year.

2. The amount of capital has been growing at a faster rate than the labor supply because of successful thrift on the part of society as a whole and slower growth in man-hours worked. As a result, each laborer has more capital goods to work with, and hence his productivity wages have tended to rise even faster than the 1 to 2 per cent attributable to technological growth alone.

3. The return per unit of capital might have been expected to encounter diminishing returns because each capital unit now has less labor to cooperate with it. Yet capital's return per unit has in fact remained about the same. Why? Because of the offsetting effect of technological progress. Technical improvements by themselves would probably have raised profits on capital had not the diminishing returns to increasing capital per laborer been taking place as an offset. In consequence of these simultaneous offsets, the sharing of the growing social pie has remained not too far from the same three-fourths and one-fourth level—a remarkable fact in view of the growing union movement, the vast structural changes in our economy since 1900, and the widespread notion that "automation" has downgraded the value of human brain power and skills.

Similar statistical measurements all over the globe help to put flesh on the bare bones of the economic theory of production and distribution, and serve as factual tests of the validity of economic principles—principles that Chapter 37 will use for growth theory. But now let us put the production function under a microscope.

MARGINAL-PRODUCTS DEFINED

In Chapter 2, the law of diminishing returns was defined. Figure 27-1 reproduces the table (shown earlier on page 24) of diminishing *extra product* for varying extra labor units added to fixed land. Back there, we were using the production-function concept without yet knowing the name.

Now we can introduce the economist's name for extra product. Recall that in economic

---

[3]Consistent with the law of diminishing returns, discussed in Chapter 2 and in the next sections of this chapter, a 1 per cent increase in either factor *alone* increases product by *less* than 1 per cent: actually by $\frac{3}{4}$ per cent in the case of labor and by $\frac{1}{4}$ per cent in the case of capital.

Diminishing returns restated as law of diminishing marginal-physical-product:

(1) UNITS OF LABOR	(2) TOTAL PRODUCT	(3) MARGINAL-PHYSICAL-PRODUCT
0	0	
		2,000
1	2,000	
		1,000
2	3,000	
		500
3	3,500	
		300
4	3,800	
		100
5	3,900	

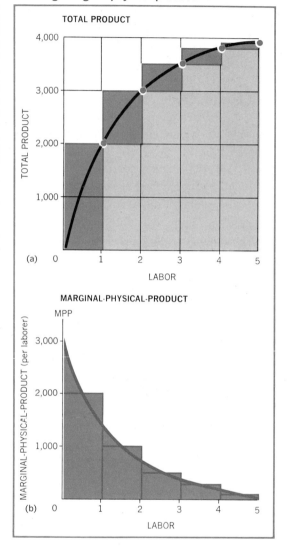

FIG. 27-1.   In the lower diagram the rectangles of marginal-physical-product have been smoothed by a curve. The area under the marginal-physical-product curve (or of the rectangles) adds up to the total product shown above. (E.g., 2,000 + 1,000 + 500 = total product of 3,500 for three men. What gives total product for four, or five, men?)

theory the word "extra" is typically replaced by the word "marginal." It is natural, then, to define terms as follows:

Definition: The "marginal-product" of a productive factor is the extra product or output added by one extra unit of that factor, while other factors are being held constant. Labor's marginal-product is the extra output you get when you add one unit of labor, holding all other inputs constant. Similarly, land's marginal-product is the change in total product resulting from one additional unit of land, with all other inputs held constant—and so forth, for any factor.[4]

[4] Chapter 30 will discuss some intricacies involved in defining "capital."

Note that the marginal-product of a factor is expressed in *physical* units of product per unit of extra input. So careful economists often speak of "marginal-physical-product" rather than plain marginal-product, particularly when they want to avoid any possible confusion with a later *dollar* concept called "marginal-revenue-product."

MARGINAL-PHYSICAL-PRODUCTS AND DIMINISHING RETURNS

Column (3) of the table in Fig. 27-1 can now be identified with the term "marginal-physical-product." Note the drop from 2,000 to 100, in accordance with diminishing returns. The same marginal-product is pictured in the lower diagram, which shows the steady drop of labor's marginal-physical-product. This reflects the fact that the upper chart shows total product rising in ever-smaller steps as we hold land constant and add equal extra units of labor. The law of diminishing returns, we see, could be renamed the "law of diminishing marginal-physical-product." (For brevity, one often skips the word "physical" when no misunderstanding is possible and writes MP for MPP.)

What is true for one input is also true for another. We can interchange land and labor, now holding labor constant and varying land. We can make up a new table, showing land's marginal (physical) product in its column. And this would also presumably obey the law of diminishing returns. Why? Because now each of the extra land units would have less and less of the fixed labor factor to work with.

DISTRIBUTION SOLVED BY MARGINAL-PRODUCTS

Now the riddle of the Sphinx—how to allocate among two (or more) cooperating factors the total product they *jointly* produce—can be solved by use of the marginal-product concept. John Bates Clark, a distinguished Columbia University economist, provided a simplified theory of distribution around 1890. It can be applied to competitive price-and-wage determination when there are any number of goods and factor inputs, but it is most easily grasped if we concentrate on one total harvest output—call it corn, or a basket of goods, or just Q. A production function tells how much Q is produced for each amount of man-hours, L, and number of acres of homogeneous land, A.

Although diminishing returns applies when one factor is added to the other fixed factor, perfect competition is best maintained when there are "constant returns to scale" when *all* factors are increased simultaneously in the same proportion. (Thus, when Clark doubles land *and* labor, he finds output has just doubled; when he increases L and A by any equal per cent, Q increases by that same per cent. For if Q were to grow by a greater per cent, there would be long-run decreasing costs for each firm, and the firm that grew largest first could reap so great an advantage as to create a monopoly.)

Now Clark reasons as follows. A first man produces great marginal-product because he has so much land to work with. Man 2 adds a large, but slightly smaller, vertical slab of marginal-product contrast. But the two men are alike: they must get exactly the same wage. Which wage? The MP of Man 1? The lower MP of Man 2? The average of these? Under free competition, where landowners are free to employ as few or many L as they like, the answer is plain. Landlords will never freely hire that second man

Marginal-product principles determine factor shares of income:

FIG. 27-2. ·Total wage is blue rectangle's area: the wage-rate altitude times labor-quantity base. Rent gets what is left over, as shown by the gold residual triangle. Total product, the sum of wage-rectangle plus rent-triangle areas, is area under demand curve of society's marginal-product (the sum of all the vertical slabs added by each new worker).

if the market wage they must pay him exceeds his marginal-product. So the *dd* demand curve for labor will ensure that *all* the men who get hired will receive *the lowest marginal-product of the last man.*

What happens to the excess of *MP* produced by the first man and all the earlier men up to the very last? That stays with the landlord. It is his rent. In free competitive markets, no one can take it away from him. Is he "profiteering"? Not in the usual sense of the word. Each landowner is but one of thousands: any acre of his is no better and no worse than the acres of the rest. Just as worker competes with worker for jobs, landowners compete with landowners for workers. There are no conspiracies, no employer associations, and no unions in Clark's competitive world.

Figure 27-2 shows that the marginal-product curve of labor gives the *dd* demand curve of all employers in terms of real wages (in corn, or market baskets of goods, or *Q* units). The population supply gives us *ss*, and the equilibrium wage comes at *E*. The total wage share of labor is given by $w \times L$ (for example, $w = 5$ and $L = 1$ million, total wages $= 5$ million); this is indicated by the blue area of the rectangle at *E*.

We have determined not only the distributive share of labor but also land rent. The indicated gold rent triangle simply measures all the "excesses over final marginal-product that the early workers brought and never got paid in wages." Whether fair or unfair, all the men are alike; all landlords are free competitors who can demand or not demand as they like; so it is inevitable that all workers get paid the *MP* of the last worker and, because of diminishing returns, that there be left the residual triangle of rent that goes to the landowners.

This completes the marginal-productivity theory of distribution. Note that labor wages exceed property rents in this example: the wage rectangle of *MP* is about three times as large as the residual rent triangle of property. That is realistic, but it depends on the facts of technology. If a new invention made the *dd* of labor marginal-product *MP* fall very fast, property's triangle might swallow up 60 to 80 per cent of the total NNP!

If mass immigration or seven children per family increased *L* so much as to move society down the *dd* curve to a low wage, the rectangle share of labor *might* fall relative to the rent triangle of land. It might, but might not. Here is the explanation:

An increase in *L* along the *dd* curve of *MP must* always raise the absolute total of land's rent triangle. (Try it.) What about the absolute total of labor's rectangle? The elasticity discussion of Chapter 20 reminds us that labor's total wage rectangle will most certainly increase if *dd* has more-than-unitary elasticity. But can labor's rectangle grow *as great* in percentage as land's triangle, or even greater? Although not obvious until you experiment with drawing in *dd* curves, the answer is definite: Yes, the relative share of wage's rectangle can increase and the relative share of land's triangle decrease if the marginal-product curve slopes downward slowly enough.

Senator Douglas' researches, corroborated for England and elsewhere by the late Sir Arthur Bowley, suggest that labor's relative share remains surprisingly constant over the decades, despite changing birth rates and technology!

Generalizations Before summarizing the marginal-productivity theory of wages, let us appreciate J. B. Clark's advance over such classical economists as David Ricardo, a follower of Adam Smith, and a leader of economic thought in the early 1800s. Ricardo would have soon grasped, and agreed with, Clark's Fig. 27-2; it fits in well with Ricardian rent theory. But Clark said more than that. He also proved these remarkable facts:

You can switch the roles of labor and land. Now hold labor constant. Add successive units of variable land to fixed labor. Calculate each successive acre's marginal-product. Draw a *d'd'* curve showing how many acres labor-owners will demand of land at each rent rate. In the new version of Fig. 27-2 that you draw, find a new *E'* point of equilibrium. Identify land's *rectangle* of rent as determined by *its MP*. Identify labor's *residual* wage triangle. Ricardo would recognize the complete symmetry of the factors: that *all* factors can be thought of as having their distributive shares determined simultaneously by their respective interdependent marginal-products.

That is not all. Instead of labor and land, suppose the only two factors were labor L and some versatile capital goods K. Suppose a smooth production function relates Q to L and K, with the same general properties as in Fig. 27-2. Then you can redraw Fig. 27-2 and get an identical picture of income distribution between L and K.[5]

Summary Marginal productivities provide the clue to competitive pricing of factor inputs—of labor or of skilled and unskilled labor, of each grade of land, of capital goods (i.e., rentals for their use), of fertilizer, and of other inputs.

Profit-maximizing employers in competitive factor markets will have their demand curves for inputs determined by what additions to their product successive units of a factor will bring, i.e., by marginal-products. In the simplified Clark case of a single Q output, firms' physical *MP*s are added horizontally—as *dd* and *ss* curves were added in Chapters 22 and 23—to get the market demand *dd* for labor or any other factor. At the level determined by intersection of each *dd* with its factor-supply *ss*, we get

Wage = Marginal-product of labor
Rent = Marginal-product of land
And so forth for any factor.

This distributes 100 per cent of Q, no more and no less, among all the factors of production.

---

[5] That is still not all. Suppose we have three (or more) factors of production: L, A, and K. Again assume that a well-behaved production function gives Q output in terms of all three inputs. Again vary L alone; calculate its *MP*s. Then vary K alone; calculate its *MP*s. Vary A alone; calculate land's diminishing *MP*s. Now set up *three* simultaneous, interdependent demand curves of marginal-products. Set up three supply curves for the factors. It will follow that all Q, and no more, will get distributed by competition among the three factors according to equality of each factor-price to its marginal-product: $P_L = MP_L$, $P_A = MP_A$, P_K = price charged for use of capital good $= MP_K$. All of any factor gets what its last unit produces of *MP*; the residual surplus, of early units' *MP*s over final *MP*, provides just enough Q to pay the other factors their final *MP*s. (Some qualifications of this simple Clark model will occur in the Appendix to this chapter. Note here that monopoly bidding by employers would require alterations in the Clark model, as shown in page 562's footnote.)

COMPETITIVE EQUILIBRIUM A GOOD THING?

We have now completed a sketch of how the marginal-product theory "distributes" total product between two factors—land and labor—in a simplified world.

We have simply been observing how hard-boiled competition would work itself out under simple conditions. Just as the jungle has its laws without regard to right and wrong, so does the competitive market have its brute facts.

But did you notice one efficient thing that happened? Without a planning board, *society got its food produced in the most efficient way.* How did that happen? Well, efficiency certainly requires that the homogeneous land and labor be everywhere combined for food in exactly the same proportions. (PROOF: Suppose society were using much labor on half its land and little labor on the other half. The law of diminishing returns tells us that the marginal-product of the workers will be less on the dense than on the sparse half. So we can get some extra Q by shifting men to the sparse acres with higher MP. Maximum output comes when marginal-products are equal on both halves, i.e., when labor and land are combined in the same proportions on both halves. QED.)

Ruthless competition with only the commercially fittest surviving did bring about the desirable equality everywhere of factor proportions and marginal-products. How did it do this? By landlords' seeking maximum rents; by workers' seeking maximum wages; by market prices' being forced to lowest costs of production. These were the vital processes. (WARNING: A tendency toward "increasing returns to scale" would have killed off perfect competition and have brought in monopoly to spoil the whole story. Note also that if different acres were of different qualities, we would no longer use the same proportion of labor on each; instead the desirable equality of marginal-products of transferable labor would be achieved by competition's making sure that relatively more laborers get used on the better lands—a sensible result!)

We shall see again, in Chapter 32, that competitive pricing can help solve efficiently the How problem of any society. We shall see that charging a rent for God-given land is necessary if such scarce land is to be rightly allocated. But notice that we have not proved that the competitive result is "fair" or "equitable": efficiency by itself does not necessarily imply justice. To this issue we now turn.

THE CONCEPT OF EXPLOITATION

For two centuries socialist critics of the present order have asserted that labor has the right to the full product of society. What price the efficiency of marginal-product distribution if it gives a sizable fraction of the total product to property owners? This, they asserted, represents "exploitation" of labor.

It is naïve to think that if a word exists, there must always then exist some obvious real phenomenon corresponding to it. Thus, if I can say the name of a unicorn, need there be in some jungle somewhere such an animal? Or, if I can think of a perfect God-Being, *ergo* must He exist? Or, if the dictionary contains the word "exploitation," must there surely be some simple meaning to the concept that anyone can understand even *before* he has studied economics? To the scholar who studies economics and does research in the field, a naïve approach must be replaced by an attempt to analyze and isolate the meaningful and true concept of the concept of exploitation.

The late Oskar Lange, after spending a sojourn in the United States from 1934 to 1944 as a distinguished professor of both Marxian and non-Marxian economics, returned to his native Poland to become Ambassador to the United Nations and subsequently to serve as Vice President of Poland and a professor of economics. In his view, all that Marx wished to convey by the concept of "exploitation of labor" could be achieved without the trappings of the "labor theory of value" (which seemed to deny that scarce land and tools also contributed to competitive costs and to true social costs). Said Lange in effect, "The fact that people, who don't deserve to own the tools of production which work with labor and which are given their positive marginal-products out of the total product that might otherwise go to labor, receive a substantial fraction of the GNP, is ethically bad. The cure is to see that labor owns the tools of production and nature's gifts of land and other natural resources. Then labor, either in the form of wages or in the form of *its* share of property income, will indeed get all of the national product. Anything else is exploitation even in a prosperous capitalistic system where wages are very high (and much higher than are total incomes in egalitarian socialist societies)."

When we come to discuss land reform and increased education for labor, we shall see how laborers may come themselves to get a larger part of the property income of society. But before leaving the subject of exploitation, notice that the Lange version of the concept does not depend upon monopoly or upon any imperfections of bargaining power between employer and employees.[6] What is involved here is a "value judgment" about the distribution of wealth ownership, not an alternative scientific finding.

MARGINAL-PRODUCT THEORY OF THE SINGLE FIRM [7]

Our main task is done. But there remains the need (1) to tie up these theories of production and distribution with Maximum-profit decisions of the firm; and (2) to show that the cost curves of Part Three were implicitly based on the marginal-productivity decisions of this chapter.

Marginal-revenue-product and maximizing profit   Exactly what does each last worker bring to my firm in cash dollar terms? He brings his marginal-physical-product—that we have seen. But he does not want his wage paid in toothpaste: the market wage is in *dollars*, not q units. And I, the employer, want to maximize dollars of profit.

---

[6] See Chapter 29, page 547, for a discussion of a quite different concept of exploitation based on employer monopoly power in the buying of labor (so-called "monopsony"). Still a third concept of exploitation of a factor like labor comes from what Cambridge's Joan Robinson calls "monopoly power of the firm in its product markets." As will be seen in the next sections, such a firm will be paying its factors less than the money value for which their marginal-products actually sell. Instead they get marginal revenue (which is less than price) times their marginal-products. Since the biggest and most monopolistic firms usually are the ones that actually pay the highest wages, such Robinsonian exploitation really means merely that monopolists are producing too little of their goods, that society at large is being exploited by this inefficiency, and that workers cannot from their wages buy for themselves the last extra product that an extra hour of work might actually produce.

[7] Brief courses may skip the rest of this chapter without discontinuity.

Under perfect competition, the answer is easy. The physical-marginal-product the worker brings me, MPP_L, can all be sold at the market price for my q output, P_q, which I as a perfect competitor cannot affect. If his MPP_L is 8 units of q and each sells for $P_q = \$5$, clearly, the dollar value of the last worker to me is $\$40 (= \$5 \times 8)$. Generally, then, under perfect competition, each laborer is worth $P_q \times MPP_L$ to the firm, namely, the dollar value of his marginal-products. (For acres of land, this would be $P_q \times MPP_A$.)

But perfect competition is merely one limiting case of imperfect competition. It is the case of a horizontal dd schedule for my q. In the more common case of imperfect competition, dd is somewhat downward-sloping: Chapter 25 taught that the actual marginal revenue I then get from each extra physical q is less than market P_q (because of loss on previous units). With $MR_q < P_q$, the laborer's marginal-physical-product of 8 units will *not* each be worth the market $P_q = \$5$ to me. How much, then? If $MR_q = \$3 < \$5 = P_q$, the answer is clear-cut: his final MPP_L is worth to me only $\$3 \times 8 = \$24$.

Generally, then, a firm's demand curve for a factor, such as labor, is given in dollar terms by "marginal revenue of q" times "marginal-physical-product of L." This important concept is given a name and defined as follows:

Definition: **"Marginal-revenue-product" is defined as marginal-physical-product multiplied by the marginal revenue the firm gets for its extra physical goods sold:**
Marginal-revenue-product of $L = MR_q \times$ marginal-physical-product of L
Marginal-revenue-product of $A = MR_q \times$ marginal-physical-product of A
And so forth.

Now we can put the new concept to work.

Rule: The firm's demand curve for any factor is given by its curve of marginal-revenue-product for that factor, a curve which declines because of (1) diminishing physical returns and (2) the downward slope of the MR_q curve that usually prevails under imperfect competition.

In Maximum-profit equilibrium, every firm faced with competitive factor-prices—the money wage, the money rent rate per acre of land, and so forth—will aim to achieve
Marginal-revenue-product of L = Price of L
Marginal-revenue-product of A = Price of A
And so forth.
Maximum-profit equilibrium is attained when every factor is hired until its marginal benefit and costs are equated.[8]

Marginal-products and Least-cost Chapter 24 presented Total Cost data for each firm q. How did such minimal TC estimates get made? Marginal-productivity theory can now give the answer. Engineers told the firm it could produce $q = 9$ units with much land and

[8] Repeatedly in Part Three, we saw that departures from the conditions of perfect competition led to inefficiencies and to nonoptimal responsiveness to people's dollar-vote desires. It is to be understood here, therefore, that such aberrations will be ruled out *only* in the special case where $P_q = MR_q$ and $P_L = P_q \times MPP_L$, etc. This is actually what happened in the Clark model, where perfect competitors produced a homogeneous Q and had no "spoiling of the market problem" to bring MR_q below P_q and distort resource use.

little labor or with little land and much labor. Which is a more efficient choice: $A = 10$ and $L = 2$, or $A = 4$ and $L = 5$? Evidently, that must depend on the wage and rent rates the firm faces. If $P_L = \$5$ per hour and $P_A = \$2$ per acre, 10 acres and 2 hours give lower TC than do 4 acres and 5 hours. [Why? Because $(\$2 \times 10) + (\$5 \times 2) = \$30 < (\$2 \times 4) + (\$5 \times 5) = \$33$.]

What is the rule to follow to get lowest TC? The Least-cost position for producing each q comes from studying the marginal-physical-products of land and of labor. If labor and land each cost $\$1 = P_L = P_A$ and if I stopped where $6 = MPP_L > MPP_A = 4$, I should be foolish. Another dollar spent on labor and taken away from land would bring me a gain in product of $MPP_L - MPP_A = 6 - 4 = 2$ units, *at no* extra cost! So I should hire more L and drop A. But more L means diminishing returns for MPP_L, perhaps bringing it down to $MPP_L = 5$. And what is less obvious, the law of diminishing returns requires that, with *less* land, its MPP_A must *rise*. Say, MPP_A rises to 5.

Now am I at Least-cost equilibrium? Yes. Each last dollar allocated to labor gives me the same marginal-physical-product as does each last dollar devoted to land. My marginal-physical-return-per-dollar is now given by $MPP_L/P_L = 5/\$1$ and $MPP_A/P_A = 5/\$1$. I have found the cheapest TC to produce $q = 9$. (The reader could repeat the exposition for $q = 8$ or 10 or 1 or anything—ending up in each case with the Least-cost condition of equal marginal-product-per-dollar.)

We are now in a position to state the Least-cost rule for every case, not just the case where the factor-prices were equal. If an acre of land cost $P_A = \$200$, which is 100 times larger than an hour of labor's factor-price $P_L = \$2$, no one in his right mind would expect Least-cost to come from achieving equal *physical*-marginal-products of land and labor. Since land costs 100 times as much, it should give us 100 times the MPP of labor. It is evident that what has to be equalized is the MPP per dollar spent on each factor. (Recall Chapter 22's similar equating of marginal-utilities-per-dollar.)

Least-cost rule: **To get the lowest Total Cost at each point on its TC curve, a rational firm will hire factors until it has equalized the marginal-physical-product-per-last-dollar spent on each factor of production.**

$$\frac{\textbf{Marginal-physical-product of } L}{\textbf{Price of } L} = \frac{\textbf{Marginal-physical-product of } A}{\textbf{Price of } A} = .., \textbf{ at Least-cost}$$

An obvious corollary of the above[9] can now be stated.

Substitution rule: If the price of one factor, like labor, rises while other factor-prices remain fixed, it will generally pay the firm to produce its same q outputs by substituting, for the factor now become dearer, more of the remaining factors. (A rise in P_L will thus reduce MPP_L/P_L and cause L to be fired and A hired until equality is restored, thus lowering the amount of needed L and increasing the demand for land acres; a fall in P_L will do the reverse. A rise in P_A alone will, by the same logic, cause labor to be substituted for now dearer land.)

*   *   *   *   *

---

[9]The Least-cost rule involves no mention of marginal revenue, because it applies for *all q* on the TC curve even before the firm's demand curve has been mentioned. The Appendix will relate it to the marginal-revenue-product rule of Maximum-profit where $MR_q = MC$.

Finale We have shown that the bird's-eye view of Clark's aggregate distribution is completely compatible with the realistic microeconomic pricing of any number of goods produced by any number of factor inputs. The triad of forces which determines competitive microeconomic distribution and value theory is seen to be (1) technology (the production function), (2) tastes and dollar-vote-power to demand various goods (the ultimate demand curves for goods, from which factor-price demands are derived), and (3) relative factor supplies (as determined by nature's abundance, inherited and acquired abilities, disutilities of different occupations).

The picture is oversimplified but important.

SUMMARY

1 Distribution is concerned with the determination of different people's incomes, or with the basic question of FOR WHOM economic goods are to be produced. To understand what determines labor's and property's share in national product, and to understand forces acting on the degree of equality of income, distribution theory must study the problem of how the different factors of production—land, labor, capital, entrepreneurship and risk taking—get priced in the market. Thus it must study how supply and demand interact to determine all kinds of wages, rents, interest yields, and profits.

2 To understand why the demand curves for the factors of production are what they are, we must investigate the theory of production and cost within each firm. This is because the demand for inputs is a *derived demand*—derived indirectly from the final demand by the consumer. The problem is complicated by the fact that the demand for factors is a *joint demand*—joint because the factors interact in producing final product.

3 The relationship between quantities of available inputs—land, labor, machines, fertilizer—and quantity of output is called the production function. By varying one factor in successive small increments, we define its marginal-physical-product. Diminishing returns implies falling *MPP* of any factor if other factors are held fixed. But when *all* inputs increase *in balanced proportion*, the J. B. Clark model of competition presupposes that there will be exactly *constant* returns (i.e., constant returns to scale).

4 Competition of numerous self-seeking landowners and labor-owners will ensure that total product gets allocated among the factors by each having its factor-price equal to its marginal-product. That will allocate *exactly* 100 per cent of the product. Any factor, not just labor alone, can be the varying factor: because each of it gets paid only the *MP* of the last hired, there is enough of a residual surplus left (from the triangle of excess-of-early-over-last-*MP*s) to pay the other factors their exact marginal-products. Hence, the Clark neoclassical theory of distribution, although simplified, is logically complete and a true picture of idealized competition.

5 Ambitious attempts to measure an aggregate production function for the whole of American manufacturing seem to provide rough corroboration for the theories of produc-

tion and marginal-products. In this century, technological progress has been shifting the productivities of both labor and capital upward. At the same time capital has been growing faster than the labor supply, with the following implications: (*a*) the increase of capital per worker has shifted his productivity wages up even faster than technological change would alone; (*b*) the tendency of each unit of capital to encounter diminishing returns has just about been canceled by technological innovations; (*c*) the relative shares of labor and property incomes have remained at about three-quarters and one-quarter despite the vast institutional changes in union organization and in automation of production. (Chapter 37's growth theory will return to this.)

6   When the marginal-products of a factor in different uses are all equal to their common market wage, society's resources are being most efficiently allocated. (Any deviation from this inequality, whether under centralized planning or under monopoly imperfections interfering with perfect competition, means that we are inside rather than out on Chapter 2's production-possibility frontier.) To socialists, like Poland's Oskar Lange, the efficiency of the marginal-product method of distribution in enlarging the size of the social pie was not an excuse for labor's not receiving all of the product. If owners of scarce land and scarce tools could withhold them from workers except when they command a fraction of the GNP through their competitive marginal-product prices, then to Lange that represented "exploitation" even if he had no particular use for Marx's labor theory of value (and even if other kinds of exploitation associated with monopoly power of firms in commodity or in labor markets were absent).

7   If he is given ruling market prices of all factors and is given engineering, technical information about the effects of factor changes on final product, the businessman can simultaneously solve the two problems (*a*) of substituting the different factors for each other so as to realize the Least-cost combination—at which he has *equalized the marginal-physical-product-per-dollar spent on every factor used*—and (*b*) of finally determining which of all possible outputs is his Maximum-profit position, where $MR = MC$.

8   An exactly equivalent condition of factor equilibrium is the following: *equality* of marginal-*revenue*-products to factor-prices. Why must this hold in the Maximum-profit equilibrium? Because any businessman with common sense will stop hiring any factor at the point where what its marginal-physical-product will bring in to his firm in actual dollars of marginal revenue begins to fall short of the market price he must pay to hire as much or little as he wants.

9   Our analysis has shown why, when a factor-price rises, the quantity of it that is demanded will tend to fall. Higher labor price will cause other factors to be substituted for it in producing each output; and higher labor cost probably means that the Maximum-profit output will be at a lower level where MR equals a now higher MC. What is the same, the marginal-revenue-product demand curve for the factor tilts downward because of technical diminishing returns, reinforced by spoiling of the monopolist's market. (This last fact reminds us that monopolists produce too little and hire too few factors.)

In the next few chapters we shall apply these principles to show how supply and demand operate in the factor markets to determine rents, wages, and other factor-prices. The Appendix to this chapter provides a review of the theory of production for those interested in a more geometrical approach.

QUESTIONS FOR DISCUSSION

1 Give examples of derived demand and joint demand.

2 Explain the "production-function concept" and various marginal-products.

3 Explain Clark's distribution theory, varying land in a new version of Fig. 27-2.

4 Define marginal-revenue-product, distinguishing it from marginal-physical-product. Give a common-sense explanation to show that Maximum-profit is not attained unless each factor-price exactly equals its marginal-revenue-product.

5 Convince a skeptic of the truth of the rule that to reach a Least-cost point you must equalize the marginal-productivity-per-dollar spent on every factor. Show this to be true even when we have not yet decided on the Maximum-profit output.

6 Suppose NNP grows in a mixed economy faster than labor supply in every decade. If, contrary to Karl Marx's predictions, wage share stays about the same fraction of NNP, show that real wage rates must rise.

Review your understanding of the following concepts:

For Whom, How, factor pricing, distribution theory
derived demand, joint demand
production function
diminishing returns
aggregate production function
symmetry of land and labor
marginal-product

MP rectangle, residual rent triangle
exploitation as low competitive returns and as monopoly victimization
marginal-physical-product, marginal-revenue-product, and factor-prices
marginal-physical-product-per-last-dollar spent on each factor equalized
monopoly output and misallocated factors

APPENDIX: Graphical Depiction of Production Theory

The production theory of this chapter can be graphically presented. Table 27-1 is a numerical example of a simple production function relating output to two inputs, labor and land. It is in the form of a two-way table, looking like a baseball or mileage schedule.

Along the left-hand side are listed the varying amounts of land, going from 1 unit to 6. Along the bottom are listed amounts of labor, also happening to go from 1 to 6. Output corresponding to each land row and labor column is listed inside the table.

If we are interested in knowing exactly what output there will be when 3 units of land and 2 units of labor are available, we count up 3 units of land and then go over 2 units of labor. The answer is seen to be 346 units of product. Similarly, we find that 3 units of land and 6 of labor will produce 600 units of output.

Thus, for any combination of labor and land, the production function tells us how much product we shall have (using, of course, the best engineering methods known).

THE LAW OF DIMINISHING
MARGINAL-PHYSICAL-PRODUCT

Table 27-1 can nicely illustrate the law of diminishing returns.

First recall that we have given the name "marginal-physical-product of labor" to the extra production resulting from *one* additional unit of labor, land being held constant. At any point in Table 27-1 the marginal-physical-product of labor can be derived by subtracting the given number (representing product at that point) from the number on its right lying in the same row. Thus, when there are 2 units of land and 4 units of labor, the marginal-physical-product of an additional laborer would be 48, or 448 minus 400 in the second row.

By the "marginal-physical-product of land" we mean, of course, the extra product resulting from one additional unit of land, labor being held constant. It involves a comparison of adjacent items in a given column. Thus, when there are 2 units of land and 4 units of labor, the marginal-physical-product of land is shown in the fourth column as 490 − 400, or 90. The reader should be able to compute the marginal-physical-product of labor or land at any point inside the table.

Having defined what we mean by the marginal-physical-product of an input, we are now in a position to restate the law of diminishing returns:

As we hold a fixed input constant and increase a variable input, the marginal-physical-product of the variable input will decline—at least after a point.

To illustrate this, hold land constant in Table 27-1 by sticking to a given row, say, that corresponding to land equal to 2 units. Now let labor increase from 1 to 2 units, from 2 to 3 units, and so forth. What happens to product at each step?

As labor goes from 1 to 2 units, product increases from 200 to 282 units, or by 82 units. But the next dose of labor adds only 64 units, or 346 − 282. Diminishing returns has set in. Still further additions of a single unit of labor give us, respectively, only 54 extra units of output, 48 units, and finally 42 units. The reader should check some other row to verify that the law of diminishing returns holds there too. He should also verify that the same law holds true when labor is held constant and land is added in a number of steps. (Examine the changes in product in any *column.*)

At this point, it is well to recall the explanation given for diminishing returns. In Chapter 2, it was attributed

The production function summarizes technology:

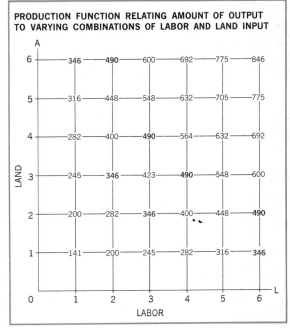

TABLE 27-1. When you have 3 land units and 2 labor units available, the engineer tells you your maximum obtainable output is 346 units. Note the different ways to produce 346, and to produce 490.

to the fact that the fixed factor decreases *relative* to the variable factor. Each unit of the variable factor has less and less of the fixed factor to work with. So it is natural that extra product should fall off.

If this explanation is to hold water, there should be no diminishing returns when both factors are increased in proportion. When labor increases from 1 to 2 and land *simultaneously* increases from 1 to 2, we should get the same increase in product as when both increase simultaneously from 2 to 3. This can be verified in Table 27-1.[1] In the first move we go from 141 to 282, and in the second move the product increases from 282 to 423, an equal jump of 141 units.

Also, this explanation of diminishing returns in terms of the *proportions* of the inputs would lead us to expect that increasing land will improve the marginal-physical-product of labor. Again this can be

---

[1] Not all production functions met within real economic life would have these special properties of so-called "constant returns to scale." Recall from Chapter 2 the discussion of increasing returns to scale, or economies of mass production.

How we graphically find Least-cost point:

1st, Factors can be substituted to produce the same output:

EQUAL-OUTPUT FACTOR COMBINATIONS

	LABOR L	LAND A	TOTAL COST WHEN $P_L = \$2$ $P_A = \$3$	TOTAL COST WHEN $P_L = \$2$ $P_A = \$1$
A	1	6	$20	—
B	2	3	13	$7
C	3	2	12	—
D	6	1	15	—

TABLE 27-2.   More labor can be substituted for less land to produce 346 units. When $P_L = \$2$ and $P_A = \$3$, calculate total of wage cost plus land cost to verify that their combination gives lowest cost $12 at C. Show that lowering P_A to $1 causes land to be substituted for labor as it pays to move from C to B.

verified from our table: The fifth unit of labor adds 48 units of product when there are only 2 units of land; but at 3 units of land, a fifth unit of labor adds 58 units of product.

LEAST-COST FACTOR COMBINATION FOR A GIVEN OUTPUT

The numerical production function shows that the engineer is not able to tell us definitely how any given output is to be produced. There is more than one way to skin a cat. And there is more than one way to produce any given output. Thus, the blue numbers in Table 27-1 show that the output $q = 346$ can be produced in any one of the ways shown in Table 27-2.[2]

As far as the engineer is concerned, each of these combinations is equally good at producing an output of 346 units. But the accountant, interested in keeping profits of the firm at a maximum and costs at a minimum, knows that only one of these four combinations will give Least-cost. Just which one will depend, of course, on the respective factor-prices.

Let us suppose that the price of labor is $2 and price of land $3. Then the sum of the labor and land costs in situation A will be $20 (= 1 × \$2 + 6 × \$3). And costs at B, C, and D will be, respectively, $13, $12, $15. At these stated input prices, there is no doubt that C is the best way to produce the given output.

If either of the input prices changes, the equilibrium

[2]You can make a similar table for $q = 490$.

proportion of the inputs will always change so as to use *less* of the input that proportionately has gone up most in price. This is just like the substitution-effect of Chapter 22. Thus, if labor stays at $2 per unit but land falls to $1 per unit, the new optimal combination will be B, where more land is substituted for reduced labor and where total cost is only $7. The reader should verify this by computing the new total expense of all other combinations and seeing that they are higher. (Pencil in missing costs in Table 27-2.)

Exactly the same sort of thing can be done for any other output; as soon as all input prices are known, we can experiment until we have found the Least-cost input combination. (To guarantee your understanding of the principles involved, work out the optimum production decision and cost for output equal to 490 units when price of labor is $4 and price of land is $3. See that 3 labor and 4 land units will turn out to produce Least-cost of $24 for $q = 490$.)

EQUAL-PRODUCT AND EQUAL-COST CONTOURS: GRAPH OF LEAST-COST POSITION

The common-sense numerical analysis of the way in which a firm will combine inputs to minimize costs can be made more vivid by the use of diagrams. From the production schedule we can draw a picture of the different input combinations that will produce a given output. Figure 27-3 is the exact counterpart of Table 27-2. In it the smooth curve indicates the different combinations of labor and land that yield an output of 346 units. This could be called a "production-

2d, Equal-output factor combinations can also be graphed:

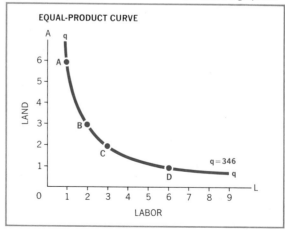

FIG. 27-3.   All the points on the curve represent the different combinations of land and labor that can be used to produce the same 346 units of output.

indifference curve" by analogy with the consumer's indifference curve of the Appendix to Chapter 22. But a more expressive name would be to call it an "equal-product" curve. (You should be able to draw in on Fig. 27-3, as a dotted curve, the corresponding equal-product curve for output equal to 490 by getting the data from Table 27-1. You should realize that an infinite number of such equal-product contour lines could be drawn in, just as a topographical or weather map could be covered with an indefinitely large number of equal-altitude or equal-pressure contour lines.)

Given the price of labor and land, the firm can evaluate the total cost for points A, B, C, and D or for any other point on the equal-product curve. Obviously, it will be maximizing its profits only when it has found that optimum point on the equal-product curve at which it reaches Least-cost.

Purely as a graphical trick, the firm might try to save itself much tedious arithmetical computation by evaluating once and for all the total cost of every possible factor combination of land and labor. This is done in Fig. 27-4, where the family of parallel straight lines represents all possible equal-cost curves when the price of labor is $2 and the price of land $3.

To find the total cost for any point we have simply to read off the number appended to the equal-cost line going through that point. The brown lines are all straight and parallel because the firm is assumed to be able to buy all it wishes of either input at constant prices. The lines are somewhat flatter than 45° be-

4th, We move on equal-product curve to Least-cost line:

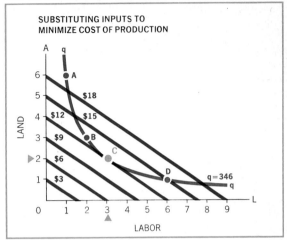

FIG. 27-5.   Where the equal-product curve touches (but does not cross) the lowest total-cost contour is the Least-cost optimum position. This tangency means that factor-prices and marginal-physical-products (or "substitution ratios") are proportional, with equalized marginal-physical-products-per-dollar.

cause the price of labor P_L is somewhat less than the price of land P_A. More precisely, we can always say that the arithmetic value of the slope of each equal-cost line must equal the ratio of the price of labor to that of land[3]—in this case $\frac{2}{3}$.

It is now easy to recognize the optimum equilibrium input position of the firm at which total costs are minimized for the given output. The single blue equal-product curve has superimposed upon it the family of brown equal-cost lines. This is shown in Fig. 27-5. The firm will always keep moving along the blue convex curve of Fig. 27-5 as long as it is able to cross over to lower cost lines. Its equilibrium will therefore not

3d, Equal-cost contours are parallel lines:

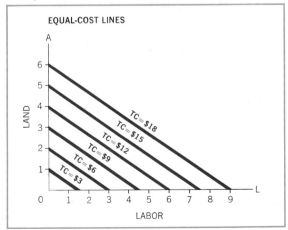

FIG. 27-4.   Every point on a given line represents the same total cost. The lines are straight because of constant factor-prices, and they all have a numerical slope equal to the ratio of labor price to land price, $2/$3, and hence are parallel.

[3] The careful reader will notice the parallel between the geometry of this section and that of the analysis of consumer equilibrium in the Appendix to Chapter 22. Each equal-cost line indicates all the possible different quantities of labor and of land that the firm might buy for any given outlay. Each line is straight since its equation is $TC = \$2L + \$3A$. In the Appendix to Chapter 22, the consumer is buying goods, not factor services; otherwise his "consumption-possibility line" exactly parallels the equal-cost lines we are now discussing. We can explain, similarly, why the slope of an equal-cost line equals the ratio of the two prices involved.

But note this difference: The consumer was assumed to have a fixed budget; hence, he had but one consumption-possibility line. The firm is not limited to any particular level of costs; so it must consider many equal-cost lines before discovering its Least-cost equilibrium.

be at A, B, or D. It will be at C, *where the equal-product curve touches (but does not cross) the lowest equal-cost line.* This is, of course, *a point of tangency,* where the slope of the equal-product curve just matches the slope of an equal-cost line and the curves are just kissing.

We already know that the slope of the equal-cost curves is P_L/P_A. But what is the slope of the equal-product curve? This slope is a kind of "substitution ratio" between the two factors, and it depends upon the *relative* marginal-physical-products of the two factors of production—just as the rate of substitution between two goods along a consumer's indifference curve was earlier shown to equal the ratio of the marginal, or extra, utilities of the two goods (Appendix to Chapter 22).

LEAST-COST CONDITIONS

Thus, our Least-cost equilibrium can be defined by any of the following equivalent relations:

1. The ratio of the marginal-physical-products of any two inputs must equal the ratio of their factor-prices.

Substitution ratio, or

$$\frac{\text{marginal-physical-product of labor}}{\text{marginal-physical-product of land}} = \frac{\text{price of labor}}{\text{price of land}}$$

2. The marginal-physical-product-per-dollar received from the (last) dollar of expenditure must be the same for every productive factor.

$$\frac{\text{Marginal-physical-product of } L}{\text{Price of } L}$$
$$= \frac{\text{Marginal-physical-product of } A}{\text{Price of } A} = \ldots$$

Relation 2 is discussed in detail in the main body of the chapter. (It could also be derived from relation 1 by transposing terms from one numerator to the other denominator, i.e., by "interchanging means," as is always algebraically permissible.)

But the student should not be satisfied with any such abstract explanation. He should always remember the common-sense economic explanation which shows how a firm will redistribute its expenditure among inputs if any one factor offers a greater return for each last dollar spent on it. Finally, we may state the above Least-cost relations in the following form:

3. Input prices and their marginal-physical-products must be proportional, the factor of proportionality being marginal cost.[4]

MC of output $\times$ marginal-physical-product of labor = Price of labor
MC of output $\times$ marginal-physical-product of land = Price of land
And so on for any number of inputs.

The Least-cost relationships 1, 2, and 3 are all equivalent. Each holds at every point along the Total Cost curve, *whatever the output.* They do *not* tell the firm where it should finally produce.

MARGINAL-REVENUE-PRODUCT CONDITION OF MAXIMUM-PROFIT

But now we add the Maximum-profit condition that $MR = MC$; and we recall the definition of "marginal-revenue-product" as equal to "marginal-physical-product times marginal revenue." Then we can combine the Least-cost relations of item 3 just above and the Maximum-profit relationship to reach our final equilibrium condition:

Marginal-revenue-product of labor = Price of labor
Marginal-revenue-product of land = Price of land
And so on for any number of factors.

Thus, our graphical analysis has arrived at the same final result as our common-sense reasoning of this chapter—which tells us that we shall stop hiring more of a factor only at the point where the marginal-revenue-product it brings just matches its market price. This is what lies behind the firm's demand curve for a productive factor.

FIXITY OF PROPORTIONS

An important qualification must sometimes be made. We have calculated the marginal-physical-product of any one input by (1) holding all the other inputs constant and then (2) increasing the input in question by 1 unit. The resulting increase in physical product was then measured, and that was identified as the factor's marginal-physical-product. But in some technological processes the factor inputs work very intimately together, so that, when you increase only one of them, holding the others constant, you get *zero extra product;* and when you decrease one factor alone, you lose the *whole product* produced by both together. Only when you change both factors *in combination* do you seem to get a nice smooth curve of marginal-physical-product.

---

[4]Why are these marginal-physical-products-per-dollar each equal to the reciprocal of marginal cost, or to $1/MC_q$? Because

extra output per dollar is nothing but the upside-down of extra dollars per unit of product, which is what we mean by MC.

Certainly, such discontinuities can sometimes happen, but perhaps they do not occur quite so often as some critics have claimed. Thus, critics often point out examples where one man is always using one shovel or where it seems to take a certain amount of gold to produce a watchband and no amount of labor can substitute for this gold. But actually, in any digging operation, extra shovels must usually be kept on hand; and if shovel prices were very high and wages were low, workers on different shifts might use the same implements so that the shovel requirements could be kept to a minimum; also, we might in time change the size of the shovels or introduce bulldozers, thereby changing the proportions of the factors. Or in the above case of the gold watchband, there will almost certainly be some waste of metal in the form of shavings and dust; and if wages were low enough relative to the price of gold, it would pay us to hire more men to produce the same number of watchbands out of less gold—the labor being, in effect, a substitute for the use of more gold.

Other arguments and examples could be given in reply to those who stress fixity of factor proportions and discontinuities in substitutability and marginal-products. Nonetheless, in some technical processes, there may not be continuous substitutability between the various inputs, and so the calculated marginal-physical-products may become erratic and lumpy.

It was once thought that lack of substitutability would spoil the economic theory of production; but that is fortunately not necessarily so.

To see the case of fixed-proportions, we would have to replace the smooth blue contour of Figs. 27-3 and 27-5 by a blue L-shaped equal-product contour. Regardless of how high or low the positive P_L/P_A ratio is, the Least-cost point of "tangency"—where the blue contour touches but does not cross the minimal brown line of TC—comes always at the corner of the L. Hence, the Least-cost condition is even more easily found in the fixed-proportions case. (There now will be *no* substitution when one factor becomes dear relative to another, for the reason that no technical substitutability is possible.)

The derived demand of firms for factors is still well determined, but with the difference that there may be inelastic stretches and some discontinuities in the factor-input demand curve. In Fig. 27-2, both *ss* and *dd* curves being vertical would spoil the simple Clark tale of determinate rectangle and residual triangle.

Fortunately, dropping the one-good assumption of Clark and replacing a single Q by many goods (Q_1, Q_2, . . .) can sometime restore determinacy of distribution. Let's see why.

INTERCOMMODITY SUBSTITUTION AND QUALIFICATIONS

It is not hard to show what happens when we drop the simplified case of a single product. As any factor, such as unskilled labor, becomes more plentiful, its marginal-revenue-product and rental will tend to fall. Not only will more of it tend to be substituted for other factors in each line of production, but in addition, those special goods which happen to use much of this factor in their production will fall in price more than will prices generally. This relative price drop will tend to cause consumers to use more of such cheapened goods, and in this way the derived demand for the factor will become even more elastic.

Thus, *in addition to intracommodity technical substitutability between factors, there is also intercommodity substitutability resulting from differential price effects.* This suggests how distribution will be determined even when the continuous-substitutability assumptions of the marginal-product theory of production break down. If factors must be used in fixed proportions, their derived demands are still perfectly well determined. These demands, together with supply relations, help determine all prices. Intercommodity substitutions now become extremely important, as do the supply conditions for the factors.[5]

[5] An example illustrates how intercommodity substitutions can determine factor-prices even in the worst case of fixed-proportions, e.g., where 1 unit of land *and* 1 unit of labor are needed to produce a unit of wine and where 1 unit of land *and* 2 units of labor are needed to produce a unit of bread. Assume that wine sells for $10 per unit and bread for $12. Bread differs from wine by $2 in price and cost; and in terms of inputs, it differs by what? By 1 extra unit of labor. Hence wages must be exactly $2 per unit (= $12 − $10), and land use must be priced at $8 per unit (= $10 − $2, or $12 − 2 × $2). So from commodity prices we can obtain factor-prices—even in this fixed-proportions case.

You will realize that the prices of wine and bread had also to be determined by supply and demand and will depend in part upon how much income goes to hungry laborers and thirsty machine owners and upon the initial supplies of the factors. For example, imagine that we started with a supply of 200 acres of land and 300 laborers, and let us summarize the resulting general equilibrium.

If we had started with factors in a 1/1 ratio—say, 200 of each—and *if* we required them to be fully employed, they would *all* have to go into wine production. We could not produce any bread and still keep all our factors employed. Similarly, if our factor totals had been in a 1/2 proportion—say, 200 acres of land, 400 laborers—we should have to produce nothing but bread to preserve full employment.

But we start with a halfway ratio—200/300. Common sense and simple algebra tell us that we must then split our

To understand the different aspects of the problem of distribution is to begin to understand much of the history of the classical and modern theories of distribution and of competitive pricing. But it does not tell us much about the cases of imperfect competition: (1) where there may be economies of scale that lead to a few firms' gaining semimonopoly power and (2) where consumers may develop a special preference for products that can be produced only by factors owned by a single firm. As Chapter 31 shows, in these cases the firms may earn "monopoly profits" or "monopoly rents" which the attempted competition of other firms may not take away from them. To "natural scarcity" is then being added artificial "contrived scarcity," brought about by someone's holding in his supply for fear of "spoiling the market."

---

land half and half between the two industries, thereby using up the total of both factors in producing 100 wine units and 100 bread units. The prices of these supplies of goods would then be determined by the interplay of competitive supply and demand for the two goods and for the two factors, and thus we end up at the above equilibrium prices for goods and

---

services. (NOTE: A factor-price can be made zero by some demand and supply patterns, but this "free factor" possibility is neglected for simplicity. If both goods used both factors in the same ratio that they are inelastically supplied, we would indeed be in a singular case where equilibrium would be indeterminate.)

SUMMARY TO APPENDIX

1   A production function lists, for each labor row and each land column, the output that is producible. Diminishing returns, to one variable factor applied to a fixed factor, can be shown by calculating the falloff of marginal-products in any row or column.

2   An equal-product contour, usually drawn to be convex (from below), depicts the alternative input combinations that produce the same level of output. The slope, or substitution ratio, along such an "isoquant" equals relative marginal-products (e.g., MPP_L/MPP_A). Contours of equal Total Cost are parallel lines with slopes equal to factor-price ratios (P_L/P_A). Least-cost equilibrium comes at tangency point, where equal-product contour touches but does not cross the lowest TC contour. There marginal-products are proportional to factor-prices, with *equalized* marginal-product-per-dollar spent on all factors (e.g., equalized MPP_i/P_i).

3   Of all points on TC curve, the Maximum-profit equilibrium comes where $MR = MC$; there each factor has marginal-revenue-product just equal to its price. (I.e., the Least-cost condition $P_i = MC \times MPP_i$ becomes at Maximum-profit $P_i = MR \times MPP_i$ as in main chapter.)

QUESTIONS FOR DISCUSSION

1   Show that raising labor wage while holding land rent constant will steepen the brown equal-cost lines and move tangency point C in Fig. 27-5 northwest toward B with now cheaper input substituted for now dearer one. Should union leaders take this into account?

2   (The remaining questions are not easy and can be skipped by those who have no interest or training in geometry and elementary calculus.) The famous statistical equation of Senator Douglas related Q output to L labor and C capital by the formula $Q = 1.01\ L^{.75}C^{.25}$. [Ignoring the 1.01 scale factor and identifying marginal-products with partial derivatives, show that labor's relative share is given by $WL/PQ = L(W/P)/Q = L(\partial Q/\partial L)/Q = L(.75L^{.75-1}C^{.25})/L^{.75}C^{.25} = .75$. Show also that capital's share is $C(\partial Q/\partial C)/Q = .25$.]

3   Let $P = P(q)$ be the declining demand curve for a monopolist firm, with $TR = qP(q) = R(q)$. Let its total costs be given by $TC = P_LL + P_AA$. Let its production function be written as $q = q(L,A)$, with marginal-products given by $MPP_L = \partial q/\partial L$, etc. Then Maximum profit requires the maximization of $R - C = R[q(L,A)] - P_LL - P_AA$. Such a maximum requires differentiating partially with respect to each input, giving us by the chain rule for the calculus the equality of marginal-revenue-products to factor prices. Verify

$$\partial\{R[q(L,A)] - P_LL - P_AA\}/\partial L = R'[q] \times \partial q/\partial L - P_L = 0$$

and likewise for the $MR \times MPP_A$ equivalence. In the case of perfect competition, set $P(q) \equiv P$, a constant; then $R[q] \equiv Pq$, $R'[q] \equiv P$, and you derive the equivalence of factor-price and value of its marginal-product. Do it.

4   As a test of creative free association, use the following geometry to understand an important theorem in modern welfare economics: "Planners or markets are socially efficient, being out on and not inside society's production-possibility frontier for butter and guns (or, better, for food and clothing) only if the ratio of labor's marginal-physical-product to land's marginal-physical-product has been equated in every industry—equated to a common wage-rent ratio."

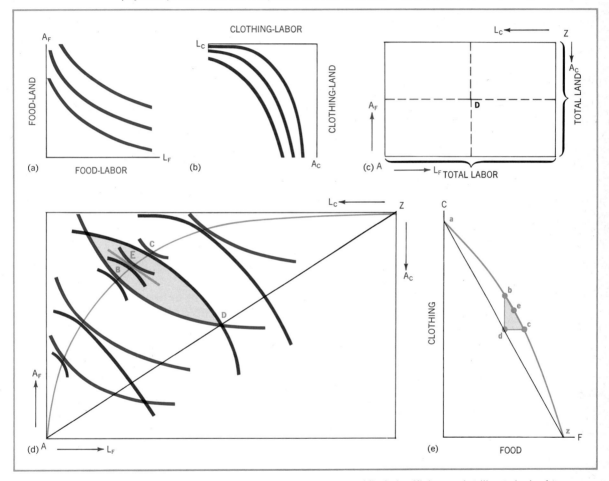

HINT: We superimpose (a) and (b) on (c) to get (d). At inefficient point like D, lack of tangency leads to gold area of waste. At typical efficient frontier point on gold AZ curve, blue and brown MPP ratios are equal to common wage-rent as shown by mutual tangency to gold line through E.

FOR REVIEW

Review your understanding of the following concepts:

convex equal-product contours
parallel equal-TC lines
substitution slope $= MPP_L/MPP_A$

Least-cost tangency, $MPP_L/MPP_A = P_L/P_A$
    or $MPP_L/P_L = MPP_A/P_A$
Maximum-profit condition, $MR \times MPP_L = P_L, \ldots$

Pricing of Factor Inputs: Rents of Land and Other Resources

28

The price of pig,
Is something big;
Because its corn, you'll understand,
Is high-priced, too;
Because it grew
Upon the high-priced farming land.

If you'd know why
That land is high,
Consider this: its price is big
Because it pays
Thereon to raise
The costly corn, the high-priced pig.
H. J. DAVENPORT

The last chapter showed how each firm decides on its demand curve for any factor of production that it wants as an input for its production function. This chapter will show in detail how the demand curves of all firms and industries are added together to form the aggregate market demand for any factor of production. Such a demand curve, together with the supply curve for the factor, will be found to determine its market price; in this way a market economy determines the distribution of income to owners of the different factors of production.

The interesting special case of the rents to lands and other resources serves to illustrate these general principles. The following chapters will provide still other important applications to wages, interest, and profit.

AGGREGATE MARKET DEMAND CURVES FOR OUTPUT AND FOR EACH INPUT

Figure 28-1 shows how the demand for a given input, such as fertile cornland, must be regarded as derived from the consumers' demand curve for corn. This assumes, of course, that we hold constant the prices of such cooperating inputs as fertilizer, labor, and farm machinery. The last chapter showed this: At each land-rent price prevailing in the market place, any small farmer must decide on the Least-cost combination of the various inputs, and he must also decide on the Maximum-profit scale of his output to throw onto the market. Therefore each farmer will want to hire more and more of cornland up to the point where its marginal-revenue-product is equal to its market rental. At that point, the last unit just brings in an amount equal to its extra cost. That is why it is the equilibrium point at which the farmer ceases to demand more or less.[1]

[1] We are dealing with a competitive industry in which the single farmer is too small to affect the market price of corn. In such a competitive industry, no one need worry about spoiling the

FACTOR-PRICE DETERMINATION BY SUPPLY AND DEMAND

Until now we have worked only with the demand curve for a factor, taking its market price as given to the demanding firms. But obviously it is *all the firms together* that determine the factor's market price which each small firm faces. Let us see how the total demand curve of all firms for the factor, together with its total supply curve, will interact to determine the equilibrium price tending to rule in the market place.

Figure 28-2 repeats the total derived demand curve for cornland *dd*. It was arrived at by adding together the demand curves of all the firms.

Now it is one of the peculiarities of land that, unlike most things, its total supply is relatively fixed by nature and in general cannot be augmented in response to a higher price for it or diminished in response to lower land rentals. (This is not strictly true. Land can sometimes be created by drainage, and the fertility of existing land can be depleted by overcropping.)

Nonetheless, we can accept the complete fixity of land's supply as its characteristic feature. By tradition, we may confine our discussion to the "original and inexhaustible gift of Nature" whose total supply is by

market for the previous units of corn being sold; consequently, marginal revenue and price are the same thing. It follows that marginal-revenue-product will be exactly the same thing as marginal-physical-product times corn price. For such a special perfectly-competitive case, as we have already seen, economists often use the special name "value of the marginal-product" instead of marginal-revenue-product.

Five principles governing elasticity of this factor demand will perhaps seem reasonable. Demand for a factor tends to be the more inelastic (1) the more inelastic is the demand for the product; (2) the less important is the fraction of total cost of this factor ("It is important to be unimportant"); (3) the less other factors can be technically substituted for this factor; (4) the more inelastic are the supplies of other factors; and (5) the more inflexible is the administered price at which the firm continues to sell its product. (Skilled electricians meet all the first four requirements: little is spent on them; they are indispensable; other labor, such as carpenters and masons, is inelastically supplied; and the demand for new structures is quite inelastic.)

Demand for factors is derived from demand for the goods they produce:

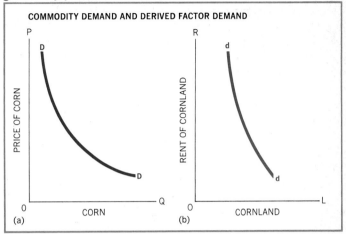

FIG. 28-1. The blue curve of derived demand for cornland comes from the brown curve of commodity demand for corn. Shift the brown curve up, and up goes the blue curve. (Make the brown commodity curve more inelastic and vertical, and in part the same tends to happen to the blue factor curve.)

Fixed land must work for what its demanders bid:

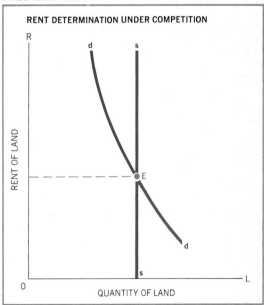

FIG. 28-2. Perfect inelasticity of supply characterizes the case of so-called "pure economic rent." We run up *ss* curve to factor demand curve to determine rent. (Aside from land, we can apply rent considerations to oil and mining properties and anything in inelastic supply.)

definition *completely inelastic*. **It was the price or return to such a factor that the classical economists of the last century called "rent."**

This differs from ordinary usage in which rent or rental is the money paid for the use over a period of time of anything—of a house, truck, and so forth. (For the rest of Part Four we shall use the word "rent" to refer to the return to a factor whose supply is completely inelastic and "rental" to refer to money paid for the services, over a period of time, of any factor.)

In Fig. 28-2, the supply curve for land *ss* is made to be completely inelastic because of the fixity of its supply. The demand and supply curves intersect at the equilibrium point *E*. It is toward this factor-price that the rent of land must tend. Why? Because if rent rose above the equilibrium price, the amount of land demanded by all firms would be less than the existing amount that would be supplied; some property owners would be unable to rent their land at all; therefore they would offer their land for less and thus bid down its rent. By similar reasoning, the rent could not long remain below the equilibrium intersection. If it did, you should be able to show how the bidding of unsatisfied firms would force the factor-price back up toward the equilibrium level. Only at a competitive price where total amount demanded of land exactly equals the total supply will there be equilibrium. It is in this sense that supply and demand determine any factor-price.

Note that the man who owns land does not have to be a particularly deserving citizen in order to receive this rent. A virtuous and poor landowner will be given exactly the same rent by competition as will a wealthy wastrel. It is the productivity of the acre of land that is being paid for, and not the personal merits of the landowner.

Even this productivity of the land is not something absolute. For example, what would happen if the price of corn were to fall greatly because people began to desire other goods? Then the derived demand for cornland would shift drastically downward and to the left. What would happen to the rents received by landowners? After a time, rents would have to sink down to a new equilibrium intersection. The land is not less productive in a technical sense than it was before, and the landlords are neither more nor less virtuous than they were before. But factor demand-and-supply intersection has changed.

A factor of production like cornland is said to earn a "pure economic rent" (1) when its total supply is regarded as perfectly inelastic; and (2) when we can assume that the land *has no other uses*, such as in the production of sugar or rye. Adam Smith's great follower in England, David Ricardo, noted in 1815 that the case of such an inelastically supplied factor could be described as follows:

It is not really true that the price of corn is high because the price of corn land is high. Actually the reverse is more nearly the truth; the price of corn land is high because the price of corn is high! Land's total supply being inelastic, it will always work for whatever is given to it by competition. Thus the value of the land is completely derived from the value of the product, and not vice versa.[2]

---

[2] Land is not the only factor whose return may be considered economic rent. For an example where most of a wage payment is a "pure rent," see page 555. And in the short run, the supply of a machine or plant may be entirely fixed; thus a hydroelectric plant takes a long time to build, still longer to

RENT AND COSTS[3]

Some economists went so far as to say: "Rent does not enter into the cost of production." As a digression let us see why.

The last section shows that there is a grain of truth in this. But still it is very dangerous terminology. If you were a farmer trying to go into the corn-raising business, you would certainly find that the landlord has to be paid like anybody else. You would certainly include rent in your costs of production; and if you could not pay your rent, you would go out of business.

Implicit versus explicit returns   Even if you were a farmer who owned your own land, it would be a mistake to think that rent does not enter into your costs of production. After you had paid all your other bills, including wages to yourself at least as great as what you could earn elsewhere in the market, there would have to be left an amount at least equal to the market rental value of your land. For what if there were not? Then you would soon find that it would be better for you *to rent out your farm on the open market* and hire out your own labor to somebody else.

Sometimes economists call rent paid by a man to himself "implicit" rather than "explicit" rent. Very clearly, implicit rent is as much a part of long-run competitive costs as are any other costs, and the same can be said of the implicit wages or implicit interest earned on any other factors that you could sell rather than use personally. The reader is urged to refer to the discussion of opportunity cost in Chapter 24 (page 449), which bears on this point.

Relativity of viewpoint   When some economists claim rent does not enter into society's cost of production, what are they driving at? As already noted, they are saying:

Since rent is the return to an inelastically supplied factor that would still be supplied to the community even at much lower prices, the direction of causation goes as follows: "The prices of goods really determine land rent—rather than having land rent determine the prices of goods."

But at this point we must avoid our old enemy "the fallacy of composition." What appears as a cost of production to each and every small firm using a particular kind of land may, as we have seen, be to the whole community merely a derived price-determined rent expense rather than a price-determining one. More than that, suppose the land is specialized and can be used only for the production of one industry. If a grade of land is inelastically supplied to one industry and, having no place else to go, will always work for whatever it can earn there, its return may appear to every small firm as a cost like any other. But as scientific observers of the whole industry, we still must recognize that the land return is a price-determined rent and not a price-determining cost.

---

wear out. The return to any factor in temporarily fixed supply is sometimes called a "quasi rent"— "quasi," because in the long run, its supply need not be fixed. Those farmers who petition for higher farm prices because of higher land and cow prices, without knowing it, illustrate rent and quasi-rent doctrines.

[3] This theoretical digression may be skipped by brief courses.

Now let us move on to an alternative case. Suppose this land can be used for a variety of industries: for corn growing, rye growing, buckwheat growing, cattle grazing, and so forth. Then to each small industry (such as buckwheat growing), land's return will definitely appear as a necessary expense that the consumers of buckwheat will have to pay as cost before they can get their buckwheat. One small industry is just like any one small firm in this case: although the total of land is *inelastic* in supply for *all* uses, to any *one* small firm or industry it is in completely *elastic* supply.

To conclude: Whether rent is or is not a price-determining cost depends upon the viewpoint: that of a small firm, small industry, large and even exclusive-user industry, or whole economy. What is a price-determined rent return to a factor which is inelastic in supply to the whole community or dominant industry may, to each firm and to any small industry that is only one of many potential users, appear as a price-determining cost.[4]

HENRY GEORGE'S SINGLE-TAX MOVEMENT: TAXATION OF LAND "SURPLUS"

In the last part of the nineteenth century, a western frontier still existed in this country. As more and more people came here from Europe, each acre of land had more and more people to work with. In a sense, therefore, the land became more productive. In any case its competitive rental value certainly tended to rise. This created handsome profits for some of those who were lucky or farsighted enough to get in on the ground floor and buy land early. As Will Rogers put it, "Land is a good investment. They ain't making no more."

Nor was this true only in agriculture. Men still alive in the Middle West can remember when towns first began. They will tell you how they might have been rich if their fathers had recognized 100 years ago that the corner of State and Madison would eventually become the center of town and grow tremendously in value as a result of the great increase in urban populations. *Urban sites with good locations earn rents in the same sense that fertile areas do.* Many people began to wonder why lucky landowners should be permitted to receive these so-called "unearned land increments."

Henry George, a printer who thought much about economics, crystallized these sentiments in the single-tax movement. This movement had a considerable following a century ago, and there are still some adherents to it; but it is not likely that anyone running on the single-tax ticket will again come so close to being elected mayor of New York City as George did in 1886. Nor is it likely that anyone will soon come along and write so persuasive a bible for the movement as Henry George did in his *Progress and Poverty,* a book which sold millions of copies.

[4] The Davenport verses opening this chapter hint at such a conclusion. To cover cases like this, economists invented the technical expression "opportunity cost." (Again see Chapter 24's discussion.) To each owner of land, using it in his own business is wise only if its marginal-product there will be sure to cover his "opportunity cost," or cost forgone in not selling it in the market for others to use. Similarly, a competitive industry can employ a factor only if its derived worth there at least measures up to the opportunity cost of using it elsewhere. In the terminology of Chapter 2's production-possibility frontier: The cost of guns is the forgone (or opportunity) cost of not producing butter with the same resources; gun cost can be measured in terms of sacrificed butter even if every factor were in inelastic supply, involving no disutility and involving price-determined or "residual" rents that are quite *unnecessary* to elicit the factors' supply and effort.

This is not the place to attempt any assessment of the merits and demerits of George's political movement. But one important principle of distribution and taxation can be illustrated by his valid central tenet:

Pure land rent is in the nature of a "surplus" which can be taxed heavily *without distorting production incentives or efficiency*.

Let us see why. Suppose that supply and demand create an equilibrium land rent, as in Fig. 28-3 at *E*. Now what would happen if we were to introduce a 50 per cent tax on all land rents? Mind you, we are not taxing buildings or improvements; for that certainly would affect the volume of construction activity. All we are supposed to be taxing is the yield of the *naturally fixed supply* of agricultural and urban land sites, assuming that this can somehow be identified.

There has been no shift in the total demand curve for land; firms are still willing to pay the same amount as before for the same amount of land. Hence, with land fixed in supply, the market price that they pay must still be at the old intersection *E*. Why? Because supply to users has not changed and neither has demand. Because at any higher price than before, some land would have to go without any demanders. Hence, competitive rents could not permanently be raised to land users.

Tax on fixed land is shifted back on landlords, skimming off pure rent:

EFFECT OF 50 PER CENT TAX ON LAND RENTS

FIG. 28-3.   A tax on fixed land leaves rentals paid by users unchanged at *E* but reduces rent retained by landowners to *E'*. (What can the landowners do but accept less return?)

Of course, what the farmer pays and what the landlord receives are now two quite different things. As far as the landlords are concerned, once the government steps in to take its cut of 50 per cent, the effect is just the same as if the *net* demand *to the owners* had shifted down from *dd* to *d'd'*. Landowners' equilibrium return *after taxes* is now only as high as *E'*, or only half as high as *E*. *The whole of the tax has been shifted backward onto the owners of the factor in inelastic supply!* The landowners will not like this. But under competition there is nothing they can do about it, since they cannot alter the total supply and the land must work for whatever it can get. Half a loaf is better than none, or even than one-fourth of a loaf.

Whether or not it is a fair thing to take away part of the return of those who own land is quite another question. Perhaps many voters will feel that such owners are not less deserving than are investors who have put their money into other things; perhaps many will feel that no one should have the right to benefit from nature's windfall gifts of oil, minerals, or soil fertility.[5] But these are political questions that must be brought out at the polls. What is relevant is to point out that a similar 50 per cent tax put upon a different factor of production whose total supply is *not* completely inelastic would

---

[5] In most countries, unlike America, the owner of land is not permitted to claim the full reward from lucky mineral discoveries on "his" terrain. Here, to encourage exploration, we introduce tax loopholes like so-called "depletion allowances."

certainly produce definite effects on the factor-prices charged in a competitive market. To some extent this tax would distort the pattern of production, and it would shift part of the burden *forward* onto the users of the factor and onto consumers. Thus, if the same acre of land were to be taxed differently when used for wheat rather than corn production, this would certainly have distorting effects on the price of wheat relative to that of corn.

Since statistics quoted in the last chapter show that pure land rent today is barely 5 per cent of the total GNP, if Henry George were alive today and facing the need of government for more than 25 per cent of GNP, he would undoubtedly change the name of his movement from "the single tax" to "the useful tax on unearned land surplus."

SUPPLY AND DEMAND FOR ANY FACTOR

The competitive determination of land rent by supply and demand is only one instance of the general analysis applicable to *any* factor of production. How is the rental value per week of a tractor to be determined in a competitive market?

We first sum up the derived demands of all business firms for tractors. (Of course, these derived demands have behind them marginal-revenue-product considerations of the last chapter; but this behind-the-scenes relation need not concern the observer of the aggregate market demand for this factor.) Along with the *dd* curve shown in Fig. 28-4, we must also have a supply curve such as *ss*. But there is now no reason why the supply curve should be perfectly vertical. It may now be positively elastic, rising upward toward the northeast. (EXAMPLE: The case of tractor supply, dependent on rising marginal costs of production.) Alternatively, if the factor of production were labor, it might be that people would feel they could afford to work *fewer* hours when wages rise, so that the *ss* curve might eventually bend backward and northwestward from the vertical, rather than rising forward.

In any case, whether the supply curve is vertically inelastic, positively elastic, or negatively elastic, there will be an *ss* curve as in Fig. 28-4.

Where the derived demand curve for a factor intersects its supply curve, the final equilibrium factor-price will be set. And if the demand curve for the factor shifts up, its market price will tend to rise; on the other hand, if the supply offered of a factor increases, so that the supply curve shifts rightward, then the factor-price will tend to fall.

In a competitive market economy, therefore, factor-prices and the distribution of income are not determined at random. There are definite forces of supply and

Factor supply and derived demand together determine income distribution:

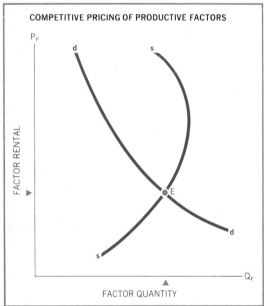

COMPETITIVE PRICING OF PRODUCTIVE FACTORS

FIG. 28-4. Land's share in national income rises when its rent is bid up. In the same way skilled and unskilled labor shares are determined, in competitive markets, by interplay of factor supply and demand. The same would hold for any factor of production.

demand operating to create high returns to scarce factors that are very useful in producing the things wanted by people with purchasing power. And, of course, any factor's
earnings tend to drop if more of it becomes available, or if other close substitutes for it
are found, or if people stop wanting the goods that this factor is best suited to make.
Competition gives, and competition takes.

FACTOR PRICING AND EFFICIENCY: RENT AND FACTOR-PRICES AS DEVICES TO RATION SCARCE RESOURCES

Competitive supply and demand helps determine the FOR WHOM problem of society.
Whether or not we like its answer to this distribution question—and in the case of rent,
Henry George certainly did not—we have to admit that it does contribute to an *efficient*
solution of the How problem for society.

Thus, as a result of supply and demand in markets for goods and for factors, in America
where land is plentiful and labor scarce, we find extensive agriculture. In Europe or Asia,
where people are plentiful relative to land, we find intensive agriculture.

Why? Because of government planning? No, not necessarily.

Rather it is the *signaling* of market pricing that results in efficient How. Land has
to be auctioned off at a low price here; labor, auctioned off at a high price here. So
every farmer, seeking his Least-cost combination lest he go bankrupt, substitutes land
for labor here. Contrariwise abroad, cheap labor gets substituted for land. (More than
that: with labor scarce here, we find that fussy vegetables, which require much care,
get priced relatively higher than those which lend themselves to extensive methods. So
the resulting high commodity prices tend to make us *substitute the cheaper land-intensive goods* in our diet for the more expensive labor-intensive ones. Abroad the opposite
commodity substitutions take place. Hence, the pricing system signals best commodity
substitutions as well as best factor substitutions!)

Thus, we see that charging rent has a function—even if you later tax part or all of
it away. And we can now appreciate examples showing how troubles in the real world
come from the fact that in some areas there is no way to charge the appropriate rents.

Item: The sea is free to all. So everyone fishes in it until the fish are all killed off or
decimated. If society could somehow charge rents for commercial fishing licenses, we
might in the long run all be better off—including fishermen! Refer to the discussion of
external diseconomies in Chapter 24, and show that letting workers overrun Iowa farmland at zero rents would lower society's efficiency in using those acres.

Item: Our roads get very crowded on weekends and during rush hours. We usually
cannot charge tolls or rents. If we could, we might coax shoppers and people who are
on the margin of indifference to do their driving at some less crowded time.

Item: Even if policemen can inspect and make collections from parking meters at a
negligible fraction of the cost of the revenue collected by parking meters, it may be
socially desirable to keep the tolls of such meters high enough to create a rational use
of limited curb space.

Other examples of how charging rent leads to efficient How could be given. But this
does not justify the status quo of taxation or of unequal land ownership. That must be

attacked or defended in terms of ethical value judgments concerning the proper FOR WHOM resolutions in society.

CONSERVATION AND LAND TENURE

Ricardo and Henry George emphasized the original, unaugmentable, and indestructible gift of Nature. Actually, much of the land we use *has* been augmented by man: it has been drained, filled, and fertilized by investment effort quite like that which builds machines and plants. Equally important, Nature's gifts *can* be destroyed. There are now deserts where green acres once flourished. There are used-up mines; deforested timberlands; eroded and depleted topsoils. Part of the rental element in the sale of Minnesota iron ore was a return of capital for this exhaustible resource. More and more we must go abroad for the raw materials to feed our machines.

Charging rents for use of resources may slow down their rate of depletion and serve to ration out such scarce, exhaustible resources. But in a freely competitive system, the self-interest of owners may well lead to the rapid using up of natural resources. The resulting depletion is not merely to the owner, who is left with nothing more to sell or rent. Unsightly and unhealthy slag piles may also be created. There may be short-term and long-term regional unemployment. There may be deforestation that causes floods and soil erosion downstream. All these "external diseconomies" create a presumption toward public concern and toward governmental regulation or coordination.

Land-use programs As Chapter 40 will discuss, civilization pollutes the atmosphere, rivers, lakes, and even seas. Urbanization and irrigation deplete water reservoirs and depress the level of the water table below ground. Fresh water becomes a vital scarcity, and regions fight over the disposition of scarce water: Colorado versus California; northern versus southern California; Illinois versus Michigan versus Canada. That is one reason why huge dam projects are undertaken publicly—TVA in Tennessee, Bonneville and other projects in the Northwest and Canada, the Aswan Dam on the Nile, the Volta in Ghana: for irrigation, conservation, electric power, and defense purposes.

As we shall see in Chapter 38's discussion of underdeveloped nations, at the village and farm level, inefficient systems of land tenancy may keep society inside its production-possibility frontier and even depress that frontier. Absentee landlords will not put money into the land; tenants on short and uncertain tenure have every incentive to mine the land and to refuse to make needed long-term improvements; credit is lacking for productive investment; and peasants who pay 40 per cent interest to moneylenders in order to tide them over until the new harvest alleviates starvation can hardly be expected to make capital investment in the land or even maintain it.

Thus, the choice is not between ideal perfect competition and public regimentation. It is between imperfect laissez faire and imperfect public coordination; between inefficient government fiats and rational democratic programming.

This is why most of the mixed economies put some limits on freedom to use land. They make zoning restrictions and draw up regional and urban plans. They employ the right of eminent domain, in which owners are made to sell their land at publicly determined prices. Parklands, owned by government, are used to create "external economies" and common consumption benefits. In Britain, Italy, France, Sweden, and elsewhere, limitations are put on the windfall capital gains that can be secured by those lucky enough to own farmland where a new city is to be located or those clever enough to speculate successfully on future developments.

CONCLUSIONS

The same general principles determining land rent also determine the prices of all inputs: capital goods, natural resources, or labor. Thus the rentals of threshing machines or of trucks are determined in essentially the same way. One can even say that wages are the rentals paid for the use of a man's personal services for a day or a week or a year. This may seem a strange use of terms, but on second thought, one recognizes that every agreement to hire labor is really for some limited period of time. By outright purchase, you might avoid ever renting any kind of land. But in our society, labor is one of the few productive factors that cannot legally be bought outright. Labor can only be rented, and the wage rate is really a rental.

The next chapter deals with the peculiar problems of wages and labor markets. Chapter 30 will analyze the problems of capital and interest, which will be seen to be important in determining the supply of durable goods available for rental and use.

SUMMARY

1   Factor demand curves are derived from commodity demand curves. An upward shift in the latter causes a similar upward shift in the former; and inelasticity in commodity demand makes for inelasticity of derived factor demand.

2   We add up for all the firms their derived demands for a factor in order to get the aggregate demand curve. This, together with the specified supply curve of the factor, can be expected to determine an equilibrium intersection. At the equilibrium market price for the factor of production, the amounts demanded and supplied will be exactly equal—only there will factor-price have no tendency to change. Anywhere above the equilibrium price, suppliers will tend to undercut the market and to cause price to fall; anywhere below the equilibrium price, shortages will cause demanders to bid the price upward, restoring the equilibrium.

3   The unchangeable quantity of natural land is an interesting special case where the supply curve happens to be perfectly vertical and *inelastic*. In such a so-called "*pure* rent" case, competition will still determine an equilibrium market rental. But in this case, we are faced with a cost element that is more price-*determined* than price-*determining*; the land rent is more the result of the market prices for the finished commodities than their cause. (Yet we must not forget that, to any small firm or to any industry too small to affect appreciably the total demand for land, rent will still seem to enter explicitly or implicitly into the cost of production just like any other expense. To such a small industry, rent

reflects the opportunity cost of using land elsewhere and appears to be as much price-determining as any other cost element.)

From the standpoint of the community as a whole, the rent of an inelastically supplied factor will be reckoned in the national income at its full dollar value, like anything else. But below the veil of money, it still remains true that this factor would be willing to work for less if it had to, and in that sense its return is in the nature of a "surplus" rather than in the nature of a reward necessary to coax out the factor supply. This provides the basis for Henry George's "single-tax" program, proposing to tax the unearned increment of land value—and without any shifting forward of the tax to the consumer or distorting effects on production.

4   Whatever some may feel about the ethical nicety of its answer to the FOR WHOM problem, proper factor pricing does under perfect competition contribute to efficient solution of society's How problem. Indeed, *not charging rents* may cause inefficient overcrowding and bad choice of use in many situations.

Because land utilization is fraught with "neighborhood and externality effects," zoning fiats and public controls on land use are common. Exhaustibility of natural resources, conservation, and distorting forms of land tenure raise special problems of economic analysis for land.

5   The general principles of supply and demand can also be used to explain the competitive price determination of all services other than those of land. The rental of all inputs—including the wages that have to be paid for the use of the services of human beings and the rentals of durable machines—is determined in a competitive system by supply and demand.

QUESTIONS FOR DISCUSSION

1   Define the "pure rent" case. Explain the sense in which price of such a factor is "price-*determined*" rather than "price-*determining*." Show that, nonetheless, an increase in supply of the rent-earning factor will depress its return and lower prices of goods that use it much.

2   What was the Henry George single-tax movement all about? Use a diagram to show the effect of taxing pure rent. Apply this to a ballplayer's inelastic supply.

3   Discuss why it might avoid confusion if you reserved the word "rent" for the strong case of inelastically supplied factors and used "rentals" for the more general case.

Review your understanding of the following concepts:

derived demand
inelastic supply of God-given land,
   pure rent
single tax, backward shifting of land
   tax, unearned increment
price-*determined* expense versus price-
   determining expense

supply-and-demand equilibrium
factor-price equilibrium
price signaling of efficient factor and
   commodity substitutions
How, FOR WHOM, and rents
resource exhaustibility and conservation
land zoning and public policies

Competitive Wages and Collective Bargaining

29

The labourer is worthy
of his hire.
NEW TESTAMENT

A man is much more than a commodity. Yet it is true that men do rent out their services for a price. This price is the wage rate, and of all prices it is by far the most important. For the vast majority of the population, the wage is the sole determinant of family income. And when we remember that much of the income of farmers, of professional people (such as doctors and lawyers), and of nonincorporated enterprises is in actuality a form of labor income, we realize that wages must constitute almost 80 per cent of the national income.

What is supposed to determine wage rates under competitive conditions? This is the first problem we shall tackle, in Section A below. Then in Section B, we shall investigate the effects of deviations from competitive conditions. Developing further the problems introduced in Chapter 7, we shall analyze the economics of collective bargaining between trade-unions and employers.

A. WAGE DETERMINATION UNDER PERFECT COMPETITION

Wage rates differ enormously. The average wage is as hard to define as the average man. An auto executive may earn $700,000 a year at the same time that a clerk earns $7,000 and a farmhand $3,500. In the same factory, a skilled machinist may earn $190 a week, while an unskilled man gets $100. Experienced women may be paid $90 a week at the same time their younger brothers are starting at $110. Part of any theory of wages must explain these differentials.

But important as these wage *differences* are, we must not overlook the general wage *level*. Wages of virtually every category of labor are higher than they used to be half a century ago. Wages are higher in the United States than for similar categories of labor in Europe; and they are higher in Europe than in Asia. Economic analysis must be applied to understanding of such basic facts.

Favorable resources, management, skills, and technology explain high American wages:

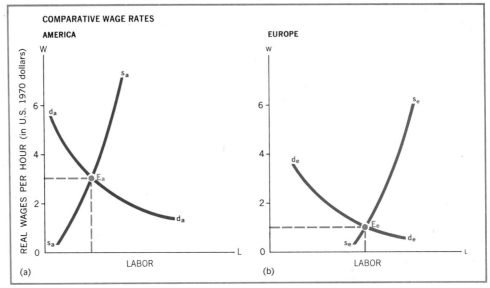

FIG. 29-1. Supply and demand determine a higher competitive wage in America than in Europe.

REAL WAGE DETERMINATION FOR A SINGLE GRADE

Let us begin by examining the simplified case of wages paid for similar jobs to laborers who are all exactly alike in skill, effort, and every other respect. Then competition will cause their wage rates per hour all to be exactly equal. No employer would pay more for the work of one man than he would pay for his identical twin, and no worker would be able to ask more for his services.

How is this single market wage determined? If we know the supply and demand curves for these laborers—as in Fig. 29-1(a)—then the competitive equilibrium wage must be at E, the intersection point. If the wage rate were lower than E, spirited bidding by frustrated employers would restore the equilibrium.

We are interested in *real wages*—in what the wage will buy—and not just in the money wage. Therefore, in our illustrations, we express wages in money units whose purchasing power over goods is held constant at the level of some particular year and place, e.g., in terms of American dollars of 1939 or 1970 purchasing power. By definition, an index of the real wage represents an index of actual money wages deflated (or divided) by an index of the price level. (EXAMPLE: Money wage rates doubled since 1955; however, since prices increased $33\frac{1}{3}$ per cent in that period, real wages increased by only one-half; i.e., $200/133\frac{1}{3} = 1\frac{1}{2}$.)

Imagine that Fig. 29-1(a) represents the state of affairs in America and Fig. 29-1(b) that in Europe. Why are wages so much higher in America than in Europe? Is it because we have unions and they do not? Or because we have passed higher minimum-wage laws than they? Experts doubt that these factors can explain the difference. In any case, such factors are ruled out in our simplified competitive case. A true answer would be:

Supply and demand are such in America, compared with Europe, as to lead to a higher real wage here.

But *why* are supply and demand such as to lead to high American wages? What lies behind these schedules? Why is labor's marginal-product so high here?

RESOURCES, CAPITAL, AND TECHNOLOGY

In the first place we recall that the derived demand schedules for labor slope downward. The law of diminishing returns suggests that adding more and more labor to the same American natural resources and land area will tend to diminish labor's marginal productivity and wages. Suppose you let American population increase so as to shift the supply curve *ss* far to the right in Fig. 29-1(a). Then the wage might fall to the European level or even lower.

One important explanation of high American wages, therefore, lies in the sphere of economic geography:

Compared with the size of our working population, we are generously supplied with land, with coal, with iron, with oil, and with water power.

The per capita supplies of these vital sinews of modern industrial production are less in Europe and still less in many other regions.

But economic geography does not tell the whole story. Two regions may be exactly alike in endowment of natural resources; but if one uses superior managerial and technological methods, its productivity and real wages may be much higher than the other's. In part, using superior technological methods involves better know-how, better applied science, better economic laws and customs, better management, more highly skilled and educated people, and better work methods; in part, it involves relative abundance of capital goods—of man-made machinery, materials, and plants.

Just why America developed a superiority in know-how and capital availability is not well understood by economic historians. Our lead seems to be narrowing slightly, as know-how spreads abroad. But the truth of this superiority is not in doubt.

IMMIGRATION AND RESTRICTIONS OF LABOR SUPPLY

This raises the question, Why don't Europeans move from their low-wage area to our higher-wage area? People *did* migrate to this country in great numbers during the three centuries prior to World War I. A few came to seek religious freedom, many because they liked our system of government, but by far the greatest number came to better their economic condition.

After World War I, laws were passed severely limiting immigration. Only a trickle of immigrants has been admitted since then. This is a first example of interference with

Incomes reach a peak where population is not too large or small:

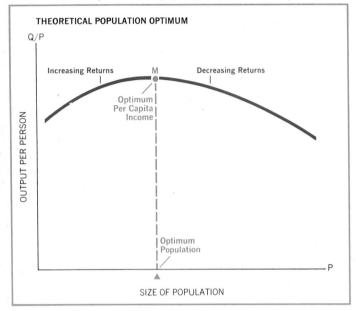

FIG. 29-2.   At the point where decreasing per capita returns begins, output per person is at its very highest. Unfortunately, economists are unable to estimate just where the optimum is for a modern nation. No doubt many nations in Asia have population density well beyond the optimum. But for the advanced nations, loss of privacy and of an unpolluted environment are probably more important than diminishing returns in terms of food.

the free play of competition in the wage market. By keeping labor supply down, immigration policy tends to keep wages high. Let us underline this basic principle:

Limitation of the supply of any grade of labor relative to all other productive factors can be expected to raise its wage rate; an increase in supply will, other things being equal, tend to depress wage rates.

The law of diminishing returns makes it easy to understand why the trade-unions have favored restrictions on immigration. The same analysis helps to explain why they have pressed for (1) a shorter and shorter working week and more days of vacation per year; (2) restrictions on child labor, encouragement of early old-age retirement, and exclusion of women from some areas of labor; and (3) restrictions on degree of effort and speed-ups. The old labor jingle

Whether you work by the week or the day,
The shorter the work the better the pay

expresses the hope that workers can travel upward on the demand curve for labor.[1]

THEORY OF THE OPTIMUM POPULATION

At this point we must be careful not to overstate the law of diminishing returns. Working against it, for a range at least, is a counterlaw: *the law of increasing returns to scale,* or of *economies of mass production.*

One of the reasons the United States is so prosperous is that ours is so *large* a free-trade area. Modern technology increasingly requires larger and larger plants: unless you can produce a thousand electric refrigerators per day, you will not realize the full economies of large-scale mass production. Before the Common Market brought down trade barriers in Europe, a small country with a limited domestic market found it difficult to have an efficient domestic industry.

This raises a question: Would the per capita living standard be higher for the United States in the 1970s if our population were cut by one-half? If you apply the law of

[1]Union policy today is by no means uniform in pressing for these restrictions upon supply. In recent years, some unions have revised their views on retirement age, now opposing compulsory retirement at sixty-five. The AFL-CIO helped pass the immigration reforms of the 1960s that lessened sociological and ethnic discrimination. Many unions still featherbed, but some encourage high productivity.

diminishing returns uncritically, the answer is, Yes. But in view of the counterlaw of increasing returns, the answer is in doubt.

This discussion suggests a rather interesting theory of population. Why not have the best of both situations? Why not take advantage of increasing returns per capita as well as of diminishing returns? Specifically, why not aim at letting population grow up to the exact point where increasing returns begin to be outweighed by decreasing returns? This point will give the highest level of real wages or real incomes and is called the "optimum population." Figure 29-2 illustrates how the optimum is defined at the very top of the productivity curve.

THE IRON LAW OF WAGES: MALTHUS AND MARX

In Chapter 2, we encountered the Malthusian theory of population, and we shall meet it again in Part Six. According to this theory, you should draw in on Fig. 29-1(a) a *horizontal* long-run supply curve of labor. This should be drawn in at the wage level corresponding to the subsistence standard of living at which people will just repro-duce their numbers. A century and a half ago, economics was called "the dismal science" because many classical economists believed wages tended toward the bare minimum of subsistence. Our survey of rising living standards and growing pop-ulations showed how unrealistic for the West is this notion of a bare-minimum long-run supply curve of labor.

A quite different version of the gloomy law of wages was provided by Karl Marx. He put great emphasis upon the "reserve army of the unemployed." In effect, employers were supposed to lead their workers to the factory windows and point to the unemployed workers out at the factory gates, eager to work for less. This, Marx thought (or is interpreted as having thought), would depress wages to the sub-sistence level.

Let us try to show this on our diagrams. Figure 29-1(a) is redrawn as Fig. 29-3. Sup-pose that the wage is at $5 per hour in 1970 prices. Employment is at the level indicated by the point A. At this high wage, there would indeed be unemploy-

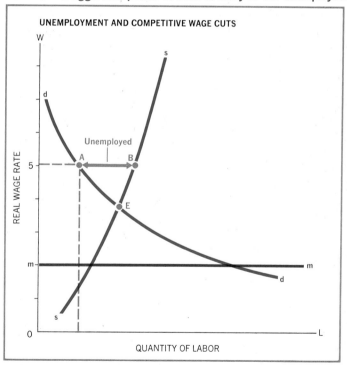

Karl Marx exaggerated power of reserve army of the unemployed:

FIG. 29-3. Contrary to Marx, the "reserve army of the unemployed" —as shown by *AB*—need not depress real wages to the *mm* "minimum-subsistence" level. It can only depress competitive wages from *A* to *E*. If labor supply became so abundant that *ss* intersected *dd* at *mm*, the wage would be at a minimum level, as in many underdeveloped regions; but institutional or legal changes can do little when marginal productivity remains abysmally low.

ment, as alleged. The amount of unemployment would be represented by the distance between the labor supplied and demanded *AB*. In our simple, idealized model of competition, such unemployment could certainly be expected to put downward pressure on wages.

But does the basic Marxian conclusion follow? Is there any tendency for real wage rates to fall to a *minimum-subsistence level* such as *mm* in Fig. 29-3? None at all. There is absolutely no reason why in our simple model real wage rates should ever fall below the equilibrium level at *E*. In a country well endowed with capital and natural resources, this competitively determined equilibrium wage might be a very comfortable one indeed. In a less fortunate country, we should expect it to be lower. Thus we reach an important principle:

If competition in the labor market were really perfect, there would be no necessary tendency in an advanced country for wages to fall to any minimum-subsistence level.

Employers might prefer to pay low wages. But that would not matter. In a competitive market they are unable to set wage rates as they would *like*. As long as employers are numerous and do not act in collusion, their demands for any grade of labor will bid its wage up to the equilibrium level at which the total forthcoming labor supply is absorbed. The workers may aspire to still higher wages, but under competition they do not get what they would *like* either; as long as they do not act collusively to limit the labor supply, their wishes will not serve to make wages rise above the competitive level.

LUMP-OF-LABOR FALLACY AND THE THIRTY-HOUR WEEK

It would be wrong to think that diminishing returns alone explains why unions pursue policies to restrict labor and effort. There is a related and still more powerful reason why workers fight for shorter hours. They fear unemployment; they tend to think the *total amount of work to be done is constant* in the short run. So what happens if a foreigner is put to work? Or a woman comes into the labor market? Or an old man refuses to retire? Or a fellow worker works too efficiently? Or a machine replaces a man? Or men work overtime? Each of these looms up as a threat to a worker's job and livelihood.

This attitude, that there is only a fixed amount of work to be done, is sometimes called by economists the "lump-of-labor fallacy." We must give this notion its due. To a particular group of workers, with special skills and status and stuck in one region, the introduction of technological change may represent a real threat. Viewed from their personal standpoint, the lump-of-labor notion may not be so fallacious.

True enough, in a great depression, when there is mass and chronic unemployment, one can understand how workers generally may yield to lump-of-labor philosophy. But the lump-of-labor argument implies that there is only so much useful remunerative work to be done in any economic system, *and that is indeed a fallacy.*

If proper monetary, fiscal, and pricing policies are being vigorously promulgated, no mixed economy need resign itself to mass unemployment. Although technological unemployment is not to be shrugged off lightly, its optimal solution lies in offsetting retraining policies that create adequate job opportunities and new skills, rather than in restrictions on production. Retraining is to be coupled at the macroeconomic level with expansionary fiscal and monetary policies.

There are, of course, still other arguments for or against cutting standard working hours from, say, 40 per week to 30. As our standards of living and productivity rise, it is only natural that we should feel we can afford more leisure. Historically, working hours have been progressively shortened, as we have already seen. Saturday work will no doubt become rarer and rarer in American industry. Probably there will be a trend toward increased vacations with pay—not so much because the vacation will improve workers' productivity as that people get enjoyment from summer and winter vacations. Taking more time off will probably be one of the ways in which we shall choose to enjoy the fruits of technological progress. No doubt, too, our grandchildren will choose to work a still shorter week; but that should reflect choice, not necessity.

Still, at this stage of history would American workers really wish to purchase 10 extra hours of leisure per week if this meant forgoing a sizable fraction of real and money income—say, 20 per cent of what potentially might be earned? The facts do not bear this out. As our economy approached full employment in the 1960s, agitation for the 30-hour week declined. This suggests that the unemployment rather than the leisure argument really carried most weight. Moreover, when a union leader favors a shorter week, he at the same time asks that there be no cut in take-home pay. What worker could be against a free present of more leisure? A few pages later we shall investigate the degree to which unions can squeeze higher wages out of employers. But there is no doubt that drastic shortening of hours would imply lower real earnings than a full-employment economy is capable of providing.

GENERAL SUPPLY CURVE OF LABOR

Return now to the case of perfect competition. What is the supply curve of labor like? How does the wage rate affect population? Affect people's desire for a longer or shorter average working day? Influence the number of people *not* in the labor force (via age of retirement, years of schooling, and women workers)? Will higher wages motivate people to work more effectively or make them feel they can afford to relax?

These questions show that the supply of labor involves at least four dimensions: (1) population, (2) proportion of the population actually in the labor force, (3) average number of hours worked per week or year by workers, and (4) quality and quantity of effort and skill that workers provide.

These four labor-supply dimensions all depend on sociological as well as economic forces.[2] The third, though, is of particular economic interest.

"Substitution-effect" versus "income-effect"   What effect will wage rates have on the number of hours worked per year? We have already touched on this earlier. A diagram may help to make the issues clear. Figure 29-4 shows the supply curve of total hours that a group of people will want to work at each different wage. Note how the supply

[2]The labor force sometimes tends to grow in recessions: when a husband is thrown out of work, his wife and children may seek jobs. Tending to cancel this is the fact that women and other workers are, under prosperous conditions, attracted into jobs by plentiful employment opportunities. The labor force grew less from 1957 to 1965 than demographers had expected: apparently the high level of unemployment discouraged new entrants. When full employment finally reappeared, new entrants were coaxed back into the labor force only to withdraw again in the 1969–1970 Nixon slowdown.

**At a high enough wage we can afford
to work less:**

BACKWARD-BENDING SUPPLY CURVE

WAGE RATE

QUANTITY OF LABOR

FIG. 29-4. Above the critical point *c*, raising the
wage rate reduces amount of labor supplied. (Income-effect overcomes substitution-effect: at
higher income, you feel you can afford more leisure even though each extra hour of leisure is
costing you more than before.)

curve rises at first in a northeasterly direction; then at the
critical point *c*, it begins to bend back in a northwesterly
direction. How can we explain why higher wages may
either *increase* or *decrease* the quantity of labor supplied?

Put yourself in the shoes of a worker who has just
been offered higher hourly rates and is free to choose
the number of hours worked. You are torn two different
ways: On the one hand, you are tempted to work some
extra hours because now *each hour of work is better
paid.* Each hour of leisure has become more expensive—
hence you are tempted to *substitute* extra work for
leisure. But working against this so-called "substitution-
effect" is an opposing "income-effect."[3] With the wage
rate higher, you are, in effect, *a richer man.* Being
richer, you will want to buy more clothes, more insurance, better food, and more of other consumer goods.
But most important for the present problem, *you will
tend also to buy more leisure!* Now you can afford to
take Saturday off, have a week's vacation in the winter
or an extra week in the summer.

Which will be more powerful, the substitution-effect
or the income-effect? Or will they just balance each
other and cancel each other out—so that the supply curve
neither rises forward nor bends backward, but rises
perfectly vertically and inelastically? There is no one answer. It depends upon the individual. In Fig. 29-4, from *s'* to *c* the substitution-effect outweighed the income-effect.
But from *c* to *s''*, the income-effect was the more important.

RENT ELEMENTS IN WAGES OF UNIQUE INDIVIDUALS

Generally, one could expect that, after people receive a comfortable margin over what
they consider to be conventionally necessary, further increases in wage will not bring
forth further hours of work. This was tested by a tax lawyer who studied his professional
and business friends in New York City to learn the effect on them of heavy graduated
taxes. Somewhat to his surprise, he discovered that taxes seemed to make them work
harder so as to maintain their previous standards of living. Apparently, the short-run
income-effect of reduced after-tax wages was more powerful than the substitution-effect.
But probably most powerful were their nonmoney drives—desire for achievement and

[3] See Chapter 22 for a discussion of "substitution-effect" and "income-effect" in connection with
consumption, and Case 4 of the Appendix to Chapter 20. The income-effect of a wage increase is defined
as its tendency to make you feel richer and able to afford more pleasurable leisure. Its substitution-effect
is its tendency to make you want to react to the higher price of leisure—higher because of the higher
hourly wage you now forgo to get each hour of leisure—by substituting for leisure the new goods your
higher pay will buy. The two effects of a wage change oppose each other; when the income-effect
wins out over the substitution-effect, labor's supply curve bends back.

liking for their work. A Harvard Business School study gathered similar evidence, as did a recent study of English accountants and solicitors.

As we shall see in Chapter 31 on profits, the most harmful effects on incentives of graduated tax rates seem to involve risk taking and venture capital rather than any connection with the supply of effort by gifted people. Most of the high earnings of outstanding individuals can probably be classified as "pure economic rent." Babe Ruth earned $100,000 a year playing baseball, something he liked to do anyway. Outside the field of sports it is doubtful if he could have counted on earning more than, say, $5,000 a year. Between these two limits his supply curve was almost completely *inelastic*, not affected by tax rates; and hence economists can term the excess of his income above the alternative wage he could have earned elsewhere *a pure rent*, logically like the rent to nature's fixed supply of land as discussed in the last chapter.

EQUALIZING DIFFERENCES IN WAGES

Turn now from the problem of supply of labor in general to investigate the vital problem of *differentials in competitive wages* among different categories of people and jobs. Supply conditions now become all-important in explaining the tremendous wage differentials observed in everyday life.

When you look more closely at the differences among jobs, some of the observed pay differentials are easily explained. Jobs may differ in their unpleasantness; hence wages may have to be raised to coax people into the less attractive jobs. Such wage differentials that simply serve to *compensate for the nonmoney differences among jobs* **are called "equalizing differences."**

Steeplejacks must be paid more than janitors because people do not like the risks of climbing flagpoles. Workers often receive 5 per cent extra pay on the 4 P.M. to 12 P.M. "swing shift" and 10 per cent extra pay for the 12 midnight to 8 A.M. "graveyard shift." For hours beyond 40 per week or for holiday and weekend work, $1\frac{1}{2}$ times the base hourly pay is customary. And when you observe a doctor who earns $40,000 a year, you must remember that at least a part of this is an equalizing difference needed to induce people to incur tuition costs and endure the lack of pay for years. (When you allow for the extra hours he puts in, the doctor is not all that much ahead of other professionals.)

Jobs that involve dirt, nerve strain, tiresome responsibility, tedium, low social prestige, irregular employment, seasonal layoff, short working life, and much dull training all tend to be less attractive to people. To recruit workers for such occupations you must raise the pay. On the other hand, jobs that are especially pleasant or attractive find many applicants, and remuneration is bid down. Many qualified people like white-collar jobs, and so clerical wages are often lower than blue-collar pay.

To test whether a given difference in pay is an equalizing one, ask people who are well qualified for both jobs: Would you take the higher-paying job in preference to the lower? If they are not eager to make such a choice, then it is fair to conclude that the higher-paid job is not really more attractive when due weight is given to all considerations, nonmonetary and monetary.

NONEQUALIZING DIFFERENTIALS: DIFFERENCES IN LABOR QUALITY

If all labor were homogeneous, we have seen that every observed competitive wage differential could be explained as an equalizing difference. But turn to the real world. True, some of the observed differentials can be regarded as equalizing. Yet everyone knows that the vast majority of higher-paid jobs are also *more pleasant*, rather than less pleasant. Most wage differentials cannot therefore be of the equalizing type.

Are they perhaps due to the fact that competition is imperfect? Undoubtedly, some observed differentials are of this type. Studies show that workers do not have anything like perfect knowledge of job opportunities. Trade-unions or minimum-wage laws or a monopoly by the workers in a particular occupation can also explain part of the existing nonequalizing differentials. If you removed these obstructions due to monopolistic or imperfect competition, enough people would flow into some of the higher-paid jobs to bring pay in these jobs into equality with that prevailing elsewhere. We shall analyze these interferences with competition in a moment.

But never forget that many of the observed differentials in wages have little to do with the imperfections of competition; they would still persist if there were no monopoly elements. Even in a hypothetically perfect auction market, where all the different categories of labor were priced by supply and demand, equilibrium would necessitate tremendous differentials in wages.

This is because of the tremendous *qualitative* differentials among people.

No one expects the competitive wage of a man to be the same as that of a horse. Then why expect one man to receive the same competitive wage as another man or woman? A zoologist may call us all members of the same *Homo sapiens* species, but any personnel officer who is trying to equalize the marginal-physical-product-per-dollar expended in every direction knows that people vary much in their abilities and contributions to a firm's dollar revenue.

There are more than 80 million people in our labor force. There is no single factor of production called labor; there are thousands of quite different kinds of labor. If you are hiring men to shovel railroad trains out of a blizzard, it will probably pay you to lump together as one indistinguishable factor of production all adult males of certain ages who appear to be reasonably healthy, muscular, and sober.

Thus, the labor market will always group people into certain general classifications for purposes of wage determination. But even after groupings are made, many distinguishable categories of labor remain, with wide dispersion of their wage rates.

"NONCOMPETING GROUPS IN THE LABOR MARKET"

A century ago, economists began to call these different categories of labor "noncompeting groups in the labor market." Instead of being a single factor of production, labor was recognized to be many different factors. Economists expected that as many different wage rates would result as there were noncompeting groups. Their instinct was sound, but there is some danger of misunderstanding their terminology.

In the first place, we must not think that in a perfectly competitive labor market the so-called "noncompeting groups" would disappear. We should still have different categories of labor—just as in the wheat market we have winter wheat, spring wheat, grade 2 red wheat, etc. Second, no one can doubt that these different groups are in some sense competing with each other. Just as I decide between hiring a horse and a tractor, so must I decide between hiring a very skilled, fast-working, high-paid worker and a lower-paid, less skilled one.

The essential point, then, is this: The different categories compete with each other; yet they are not 100 per cent identical. They are *partial rather than perfect substitutes* for each other.

Workers can to some degree cross over from one category into another. If welders' wages were to become $100,000 a year, I might study the art and quit being a teacher. Or if I did not, others would. Therefore, even when the wages of the different categories of labor are different, quantitative wage differences are still subject to the laws of supply and demand. "Cross elasticity" of supply becomes very important: The wage you must pay to recruit foundrymen depends on what the nearby auto plant is paying men on the assembly line.

Or take the case of skilled surgeons. They receive high pay in all countries compared with butchers. Why? Because their work is important? Only in part on this account. For suppose that (1) as many babies were born every year with the capacity necessary for a surgeon as with the capacity necessary for a butcher, (2) we knew how to train surgeons in no time at all, and (3) a surgeon's activities and responsibilities were not regarded as less pleasant or more taxing than those of a butcher. Then do you really think that surgeons would continue to receive higher earnings than butchers? And if you think the sanctity of human life is the key explanation, how do you account for the fact that the best plastic surgeons are higher paid than the best heart surgeons?

Chapter 40's analysis of the economics of racial and other discrimination will emphasize that some of the differences in "quality" are in the eye of the beholder. If employers think that skin color denotes lower efficiency, that can become a stereotype built into the demand and supply schedules. All categories are dynamic, not static, being changeable by training, custom, and legislation.

GENERAL EQUILIBRIUM OF LABOR MARKET

In real life as we know it, distinctions are not absolute. There is some mobility between different jobs; differences in wages will tend gradually over a long period of time to encourage greater and greater mobility; nor is it necessary for all workers to be mobile—a few movers are enough.

But there will still remain certain permanent barriers to mobility that depend upon the irreducible differences in biological and social inheritance. Hence, wage differentials will persist even in the long run.

How big will these differentials be? Suppose we made it easy for people to get the education they are fitted for and to travel from one region to another where their skills can be better used. And suppose we provided people with the best possible information about job opportunities and about their personal potentialities. Then differentials would

Market wage structure shows great variety of patterns under competition:

COMPETITIVE WAGE DETERMINATION

SITUATION	RESULT
1. People all alike—jobs all alike.	No differentials.
2. People all alike—some jobs differ in disutility.	Equalizing wage differentials.
3. People differ, but each type of labor is in unchangeable supply ("noncompeting groups").	Wage differentials that are "pure economic rents" or "surpluses."
4. People differ, but there is some mobility between groups ("partially competing groups"; "cross elasticity" important).	General equilibrium pattern of wage differentials as determined by general demand and supply (includes 1–3 as special cases).

TABLE 29-1.

be much reduced. But for such differentials as remain, how exactly are they determined? The answer is provided by supply and demand.

The market will tend toward that equilibrium pattern of wage differentials at which the total demand for each category of labor exactly matches its competitive supply. Then and only then will there be general equilibrium with no tendency for further widening or narrowing of wage differentials. Table 29-1 sums up our conclusions.

B. IMPERFECTIONS OF THE LABOR MARKET AND COLLECTIVE BARGAINING

Real-world labor markets are far removed from the ideal model of perfect competition. You can grade wheat into neat market categories, but you cannot do that with human beings. No auctioneer allocates workers to the highest bidders. Studies of areas such as New Haven, Connecticut, show that workers often have only the most imperfect knowledge of nearby wage rates.

Wage stickiness   Two tests indicate that the labor market is imperfect. When there is a considerable increase in unemployment—as in the sluggish 1950s—do wage rates drop as they would in a competitive market? History answers, No.

You may be every bit as capable as someone who has a job, and yet there is no way that you can take his job away by underbidding him. Just imagine going to General Motors or any large corporation when the next depression comes, brandishing your degrees and certificates of IQ and excellence, and offering to work for less than they are paying. Only the naïve think they could get a job that way.

Wage policy of firms   The fact that a firm of any size *must* have a wage policy is additional evidence of labor market imperfections. In a perfectly competitive market, a firm need not make decisions on its pay schedules; instead it would turn to the morning newspaper to learn what its wage policy would *have* to be. Any firm, by raising wages ever so little, could get all the extra help it wanted. If, on the other hand, it cut the wage ever so little, it would find no labor to hire at all in a perfectly competitive labor market.

But just because competition is not 100 per cent perfect does not mean that it must be zero. The world is a blend of (1) competition and (2) some degree of monopoly power over the wage to be paid. A firm that tries to set its wage too low will soon learn this. At first nothing much need happen; but eventually it will find its workers quitting a little more rapidly than would otherwise be the case. Recruitment of new people of the same quality will get harder and harder, and slackening off in the performance and productivity of those who remain on the job will become noticeable.

Availability of labor supply does, therefore, affect the wage you set under realistic conditions of imperfect competition. If you are a very small firm, you may even bargain and haggle with prospective workers so as not to pay more than you have to. But if you are any size at all, you will name a wage for each type of job, then decide how many of the applicants will be taken on; and in terms of the number of applicants who respond, you may alter your wage rate over time. Even in the absence of unions, you will find it a perplexing task to decide on an optimal wage policy.

Inequality of bargaining power   One of the reasons given in the past for starting trade-unions was the feeling that unorganized workers, facing financially strong employers, lacked "equality of bargaining power." By union organization it was hoped that a greater equality of bargaining power could be restored. But exactly how one goes about measuring equality or inequality of bargaining power remains a difficult research task for the economic theorist.

It is safe to say that prior to the formation of labor unions, the labor market was not a perfectly competitive one in the economist's sense of the term. And after the formation of unions it continues to differ from the perfectly competitive model. Moreover, a number of the features of labor markets usually associated with unions are also present even where there are no unions. Thus, large companies without unions will typically introduce a standard trend-rate of pay and be slow to change it, even though the number of workers locally unemployed might go up or down. In years of labor market slack these firms raise their wage rates as much as unionized trades do, despite the fact that competitive theory might expect them then to be cutting rates. [EXAMPLE: Du Pont raises wages about the same in (a) its nonunion plants as in (b) its few unionized plants and (c) its few plants with a "company union."]

FOUR WAYS UNIONS SEEK TO RAISE WAGES

Leaving the oversimplified picture of perfect competition behind, we can use economic theory to analyze how trade-unions operate. How might unions hope to raise wages in a particular industry?

There are four main methods by which a union might hope to raise wages: (1) Unions can reduce the supply of labor. (2) They can use their collective bargaining power to raise standard wage rates directly. (3) They can cause the derived demand curve for labor to shift upward. (4) Unions can resist exploitation of laborers facing an employer with

To raise pay, unions restrict supply and enforce standard wage rate:

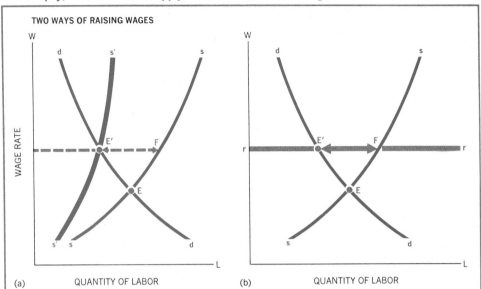

FIG. 29-5. Raising the standard wage to rr in (b) has exactly the same effect on wages as reducing the effective supply from ss to $s's'$ in (a); the workers from E' to F are excluded from employment in either case.

monopoly bargaining power. These four devices are much alike and often are reinforcing; but they also display significant differences.

1. Restriction of labor supply   We have already seen that a union may restrict the supply of labor in order to travel upward on the derived demand curve for labor. Immigration barriers, maximum-hour legislation, high initiation fees, long apprenticeships, refusal to admit new members into the union or to let nonunion members hold jobs—all these are obvious restrictive devices that have been used in the past.

In addition, there are other, more subtle restrictions on labor supply: explicit union limits on work loads (artificial limits put on number of bricks per day, width of paintbrush, stand-by orchestras, number of looms attended, and similar "featherbedding" labor practices) and implicit understandings forcing a slowdown of the working pace.

2. Raising standard wage rates   Direct limitations on the labor supply are today no longer so necessary to unions, except to reinforce the ability of the union to secure a high standard wage rate and to maintain it. Union leaders have learned this important economic fact:

If you can persuade or force employers always to pay a high standard wage—a wage rate that is publicly known and adhered to—then the supply of labor will take care of itself. At the standard rate, employers will hire the number of men they want, and any surplus job applicants will be *automatically excluded* from the labor market.

Figure 29-5(a) and (b) contrast *direct* restriction of labor supply and *indirect* restriction via a high standard wage. In Fig. 29-5(a) the union cuts down supply from *ss* to *s's'* by insisting on long apprenticeships and high training fees. The wage consequently rises from *E* to *E'*. (Test your understanding of this: Explain the effects on doctors' earnings of a policy that reduced the number of students going through medical schools relative to the total population.)

Alternatively, in Fig. 29-5(b), the union gets all employers to agree to pay wages no lower than the minimum standard rate, as shown by the horizontal line *rr*. Note that here, too, the equilibrium is at *E'*, where *rr* intersects the employer's demand curve. The workers from *E'* to *F* are as effectively excluded from jobs as if the union had directly limited entry. What now limits supply? It is the lack of job opportunities at the high standard wage rate.

This helps explain what used to puzzle many observers of modern unionism. At the same time that many unions were liberalizing restrictions on union membership, wage rates were often being pushed up by collective bargaining.

3. Shifting the derived demand curve upward   A union may hope to increase wages by any policy that improves the demand for labor. Thus, like the International Ladies' Garment Workers' Union, it may study ways of reducing garment prices by improving productivity of labor and management, or it may help the industry advertise its products. *Or* the union may agitate for a tariff to protect its industry, hoping thereby to raise the demand curve for domestic workers. *Or* it may persuade the government to pay higher rates on public contracts and to write make-work featherbedding restrictions into building codes. *Or* it may help the employers in an industry to maintain a high monopoly price, with some of the extra profits going into higher wages.

Moreover, if collective bargaining raises wages, and *if increased wages increase the marginal productivity of labor*, then labor will have shifted its own demand curve upward. Figure 29-6 depicts the case in which an increase in the wage from *rr* to *r'r'* itself results in an upward *shift* in the demand curve for labor—from *dd* to *d'd'*. Note that, at the new equilibrium *E'*, both wage and employment have increased.

In the old days, the standard example of this was the case where workers were being paid so little that they were malnourished and hence inefficient; higher wages might then have made them more efficient and thus resulted in lower rather than higher production costs. Today, in this country, few workers are so physiologically undernourished. But psychological elements can be as

Some union policies try to shift the labor demand curve upward:

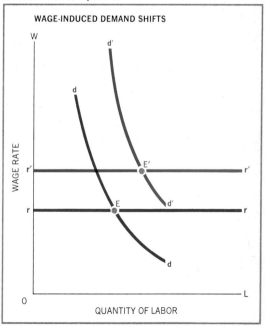

FIG. 29-6.   Raising wages (from *rr* to *r'r'*), by making ill-fed workers stronger or resentful ones more energetic, in this case shifts the curve of demand productivity upward (from *dd* to *d'd'*), with employment actually increasing (from *E* to *E'*).

important as physiological. Many an employer has found that too-low wages are bad business even from a hard-boiled dollars-and-cents standpoint.

It can be argued that high wages have a favorable "shock effect" on the employer's efficiency in using labor. One reason advanced for the high productivity of American industry, even back in the nineteenth century when unions were unimportant, was the fact that high farm earnings made it necessary for industry to develop good machine methods in order to be able to pay high wages and still stay in business. Adversity, in the form of a kick in the pants from unions or from fate in general, can at times galvanize businessmen into finding improved ways of doing things. How much there is to this shock-effect argument, nobody knows. It has therefore to be used with caution.

4. Removing exploitation by monopolist of labor (the "monopsonist")   Finally, there is the case where unions arise to offset monopoly power that employers may have in a labor market that has been far from competitive. Suppose there is a company town: unless you work for the dominant firm, you are unemployed; your alternatives are few or non-existent, and you must take what the employer offers. In this case the employer does not think of himself as too small to affect appreciably the wage he pays; he does not hire factors up to the point where their marginal-revenue-products (as defined in the chapters just preceding) are equal to the wage he pays. Instead, the employer realizes that hiring an extra worker will raise the wage he must pay to all, and hence he had better not hire that worker unless the worker's marginal-product is much *greater* than the wage.

In this situation (which many modern economists call "monopsony," after the Greek words for the situation in which there is a "single buyer," just as "monopoly" means the situation in which there is a "single seller"), organizing a union can result in higher wages and without any decline in employment! Once the employer realizes the union is going to see to it that he must pay the standard wage, he will again be a "wage taker" who will hire men up to where their marginal-product fully equals that standard wage.

The lessening of exploitation by union organization is more important in isolated places, like the tin mines of Bolivia or the lumber camps of American history, than it is in a modern economy where people are, in fact, mobile in moving to better job opportunities. There do still, however, remain areas of agriculture where employers hire workers below the market because of the workers' lack of other opportunities or their ignorance of such opportunities as do exist.[4]

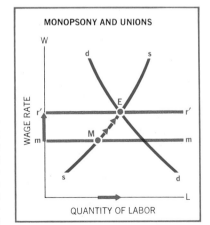

MONOPSONY AND UNIONS

[4] Intermediate economics texts show that, where an employer was previously possessed of monopoly-buying-power over labor, collective bargaining can—if not pushed to excess—right the balance, leading to both increased wages *and* increased employment. Before unionization, the employer monopsonist who is on his toes will set his equilibrium wage at *mm* in Fig. 29-7. This will be lower than the so-called "competitive wage" at *E*. Why will the monopsonist's equilibrium be at a point like *M*? The monopsonist will not want to travel upward from *M* to *E* because he

FIG. 29-7.

WAGE INCREASES AND REDUCTIONS IN EMPLOYMENT

If raising wages means simply that you climb up the existing demand curve for labor, then employment will decrease in consequence. This is because demand curves almost always slope downward and to the right.[5] The amount of unemployment created in a particular occupation by wage increases would depend upon the elasticity of the demand curve for that particular category of labor. We saw in earlier chapters that a factor demand is a "derived demand," and we discussed (page 537, footnote) some of the conditions that determine how elastic or inelastic the derived demand might be. Here are two cases to help review those principles:

Case of inelastic derived demand   Suppose that a particular building-trades union, such as the electricians', raises wages. This case emphasizes the factors making for inelastic demand and a small resulting drop in employment of electricians. (1) Note that, in the short run, employers *cannot substitute* other factors—such as machines or plasterers—for electricians. (2) Do not forget *the importance of being unimportant:* The total cost of a house will be little affected by a change in the wage rate of electricians alone. This fact will tend to cause only a mild reduction of employment as a result of an increase in their wages. (3) Suppose there is a great housing shortage so that people feel they need homes desperately. *In*elasticity of demand for the final product, housing, will lower the derived elasticity for electricians. (4) Suppose that all practicing electricians must be in the union, so that an increase in wages is not followed by a great increase in nonunion labor supplied. This inelasticity of supply of other factors will tend to make the demand for union electricians inelastic. (5) Suppose, finally, that administered pricing or public regulation will not permit the prices at which houses are available to change much. This will make for a little quantity of houses sold and hence inelastic demand for the factors that build houses.

Case of elastic demand   On the other hand, suppose you were a union leader in the glass-blowing industry. Suppose that labor costs are an important part of the total expense but that new mechanized processes exist which substitute machinery for men. Suppose, too, that a large part of the industry is not unionized, particularly those nonskilled workers who run the new machines. And finally, suppose that there are many commodity substitutes for glass, such as tin and paper. You can apply our principles to show qualitatively (1) that the demand for labor would then be quite elastic, and (2) how disastrous in terms of employment it would then be to raise wages.

---

realizes that any employment increase beyond M will raise the wages paid to *already hired workers* by more than the extra revenue resulting from hiring the new men. But now let the union raise the wages toward E by collective bargaining; the monopsonist employer now reluctantly travels up the *ss* curve, as shown by the gold arrows. Note we do not travel up the marginal-revenue-product curve *dd*. Wages and employment both rise together. (QUERY: Suppose collective bargaining raises the standard wage to a level $r''r''$ that lies *above E*. By drawing in the resulting arrows *above E* on *dd*, show that now unemployment will follow. What then will happen to employment? Draw in the resulting gold arrows on the demand curve.)

[5] Cases have been noted where short-run demand is virtually completely inelastic.

THEORETICAL INDETERMINACY OF COLLECTIVE BARGAINING

Just as unions sometimes realize it would not be to their interest to ask for higher wages, managements sometimes take the view that an increase in wages would improve their long-run corporate earnings. But both these views are exceptional. Usually, at any collective bargaining conference, the workers are pressing for higher wages and fringe benefits than management wishes to pay.

What will be the terms of the final agreement? Unfortunately, this is one important question that no economic theory can answer with precision. The game-theoretic result depends on psychology, politics, and countless intangible and unpredictable factors. As far as the economist is concerned, the final outcome of bilateral monopoly is in principle indeterminate—as indeterminate as the haggling between two millionaires over a fine painting.

Eight main arguments will be appealed to during the bargaining:

1. If the cost of living is rising, the union economist will talk a great deal about the workers' *standard of living;* but if prices are falling, the employer brings this up.

2. If the company and industry have been prosperous, the union will stress *ability to pay;* but if the industry has had low profits, the employer will emphasize this fact.

3. If *productivity* has risen or fallen recently, this will be brought into the negotiations by one of the interested parties.

4. If other firms in the same area are paying *going wages* higher or lower than the firm in question, this fact will be brought out.

5. Labor will extol the philosophy of high wages as a means of bolstering *purchasing power* and prosperity; management will emphasize higher-cost aspects of wages.

6. If a *national pattern* of "fourth- or nth-round" wage increases of so much per hour has already been set by a few "key bargains" in large industries such as coal, steel, or automobiles, that will have great weight in the deliberations.

7. American workers and employers have grown accustomed to steady money-wage increases. Almost as certainly as spring brings robins, it brings wage increases. So General Motors and many firms build into their wage agreements a steady upward trend—the so-called "improvement factor." This may mean an average 3 to 4 per cent wage boost each year in addition to any cost-of-living escalator wage clauses.

8. The government may set forth guideposts for wages and prices, and these may be appealed to or be ignored depending on the interests of the bargaining parties. Such guideposts broadly aim to have money wages increase with *national* productivity: then if prices are lowered in industries of above-average productivity growth and raised in those of below-average, the general price level can be stable and customary wage-property shares be preserved.

Most often labor and management will arrive at a new yearly contract after some days of negotiation. But sometimes when they get stalled, a government mediator may try to narrow down the few-cents disagreement. Or there may be an understanding that a disinterested "arbitrator" will render a decision, which both parties will accept. Unfortunately, economic theory cannot tell us how such an arbitrator will arrive at his final decision. All the previously mentioned factors will be weighed in his mind, plus the all-important question, What decision is likely to be *acceptable* to both sides?

Strikes and collective bargaining Both sides realize that failure to reach agreement will mean a costly strike. It may sometimes happen that management refuses to go above $4.50 an hour while labor refuses to take less than $4.55. A "work stoppage" will result. Should we call this an "employees' strike" or an "employer's lockout"? Popularly, it will certainly be referred to as a strike. But since each party knows it can end the work stoppage by agreeing to the other party's terms, we could call it either.

Newsmen ask why workers go out on strike just because of a 5-cent disagreement; they point out that it might take two or three years for the workers to recover—at 5 cents an hour—their loss of earnings during the strike. But the workers look at it differently. To them the employer caused the strike by his stubbornness. They point out that the employer will also lose more by the strike than refusing the extra 5 cents would save him in many years.

Actually, a strike is *not* over just the last 5 cents of wage disagreement! The workers believe that the employer would not have been forced from $4 up even to $4.50 except for the threat of a strike, which hangs over the negotiation like a time bomb. To keep the bomb from going off, both sides must agree.

Threats become hollow unless occasionally carried out. Both parties must show that they are truly prepared to incur at some point the costs of a strike. Thus, suppose the employer was deprived, voluntarily or by law, of the right to refuse any wage demand if it would bring on a strike. Would this cost him only 5 cents an hour? Obviously not. There would then be no reason why the union might not hold out for a 90- rather than a 50-cent wage increase. Similarly, if the union could never exercise the right to strike, why should not the employer offer $3 rather than $4 per hour if he can get labor at that rate?

QUALIFICATIONS

Has unionization raised wages? The advocates of organized labor claim unions have raised real wages; the critics blame unions for having done just that and for having thereby distorted the efficient use-pattern of resources. Despite this agreement that unions raise real wages, the true facts are not at all clear.

Since 1933, for example, low-paid, nonunionized occupations (such as domestic service and farm work) have shown greater percentage wage increases than unionized trades. In this same period of tremendous organization of labor, there has been a general tendency toward higher wages, but with wage differences remaining about the same in *absolute* terms. This means that *percentage* differentials are diminishing. (For example, suppose you are a unionist earning $4 an hour, and I earn $2 in a nonunion trade. Now we both get a $1 increase; this leaves the absolute differential unchanged; but you no longer get twice my wage; instead you receive $5 to my $3.)

Most other countries also show a lessening of percentage wage differentials in recent decades, a trend in part quite independent of union trends.

It is true that the average wage in unionized industries is about 18 per cent higher than the average wage in nonunionized industries. But that in itself does not prove that unions are responsible for the difference. The industries that are unionized tend also to be those dominated by large rather than small enterprise and by firms which use workers of higher-than-average skills. Even before they were unionized, these same industries paid higher-than-average wages.

Arthur Ross, formerly Commissioner of the Bureau of Labor Statistics, is one of many who have studied the change in wage rates since 1933 in union and nonunion industries.[6] He finds that the industries most recently unionized do seem to show a slightly greater wage increase since 1933 than do similar industries that have either never been unionized or that had already been unionized prior to 1933. (That is, if we examine Industries A, B, and C, all of which were paying about the same wages in 1933, then A, the recently unionized industry, seems to show a slightly greater wage increase than does B, the never-unionized industry, or than does C, the industry unionized before 1933.)

ONE WARNING: Such statistics on the differential movements of union and nonunion wages cannot give the whole answer to the question whether unions have raised wages. Labor spokesmen claim that unions also help raise wages for the unorganized workers. Thus, a nonunion industry's policy may be to follow any changes in the wage scale hammered out in unionized plants nearby. If an industry raises wages in order to keep the union out, the union will get no credit for its influence in the figures. On the other hand, suppose the targets for union organizers are profitable, expanding, high-productivity, concentrated industries; then the union may be riding aboard a moving demand curve and be given credit for wage increases that would have occurred even in its absence. Which is cause and which effect?[7]

Pitfalls in the concept of a general demand for labor   A second important warning must be given. It is legitimate to draw up a demand curve of the usual general shape for one *small* labor market: as long as *all other* prices and wages are more or less unaffected, it is indeed true that a higher money wage in one sector is the same as a higher real wage there; it is true also that employment there can be expected to fall off somewhat at the higher wage.

But remember the fallacy of composition. What is true for any *small* sector of the economy need not be true for *the whole aggregate*. If all wage rates rise, it is dangerous to suppose that commodity prices will remain constant. Thus, doubling all money wages *might* well result in a doubling of all prices. Were that the case, the real wage would not be changed at all. And hence, in a diagram such as Fig. 29-1, we should be moving neither upward nor downward on the demand curve. (Turn to Fig. 29-1 and note that the vertical axis represents real wages in dollars of *constant purchasing power*.)

Remember that wages are not simply costs: they also represent *incomes* of most of the population. Therefore the sales revenue of business enterprises is vastly affected by

---

[6] A. M. Ross, *Trade Union Wage Policy* (University of California Press, Berkeley, 1948). See L. G. Reynolds and C. H. Taft, *The Evolution of Wage Structure* (Yale University Press, New Haven, Conn., 1956), and H. G. Lewis, *Unionism and Relative Wages in the United States* (University of Chicago Press, Chicago, 1963), for references to confirming later studies by R. A. Lester, A. E. Rees, J. T. Dunlop, and others.

[7] Study of the 1960 census suggests that union power can keep wages higher than what they otherwise would have been for male production workers in monopolistically concentrated industries. Many studies also suggest that unions keep wage rates from falling, as they would competitively, in declining high-wage industries such as coal, railroads, etc.

a substantial change in wage levels. Since the demand for labor is a demand derived from the demand for business products, it is clear that any change in general wages must shift the general demand curve for labor. Hence, it is dangerous to argue in terms of an unchanged demand curve for labor.

To illustrate this pitfall, ask the following question: In 1932 or 1960, when there was widespread unemployment, would an all-round cut in money wages have *increased* employment? Or, as claimed by the trade-unionists, would such a decrease in general money wages have decreased "purchasing power" and *decreased* employment?

To the extent that a halving of wages would result in a halving of all prices, of all money incomes, and of all money spending, the answer must be obvious. Such a completely balanced deflation would neither help nor hurt the unemployment situation.[8] This serves as a warning against accepting the superficial claims of those critics of labor who argue in terms of simple *dd* curves, and of those friends of labor who argue in terms of "purchasing power."

Summing up We may cautiously conclude discussion of the economic effects of unions by quoting in turn from two leading students of labor economics, Princeton's Albert E. Rees and Yale's Lloyd G. Reynolds. According to Rees,[9]

We tend to overemphasize the role of the unions, both in . . . their own industries and . . . the economy as a whole. . . . The other two thirds may have their wages and salaries influenced by what the unions do, but I feel there are very strong independent forces on the demand side that govern their rates of pay. . . . Even in the . . . unionized [one-third] there are some very weak or almost impotent unions that have had very little to do with the wages of their members. . . .

In a series of rough guesses, I would say perhaps a third of the trade unions have raised the wages of their members by 15 per cent to 20 per cent above what they might be in a nonunion situation; another third by perhaps 5 per cent to 10 per cent, and the remaining third not at all. . . . The high figures tend to be found, not in periods of inflation, but in periods of prosperity combined with stable prices. . . . In [an inflationary] period like 1946–1948, for example, the

[8]Today most economic theorists believe that the favorable effects during recession of any over-all general wage cut will depend upon how it affects the balance of saving and investment, or total real demand. If (1) lower wages cause prices to drop and (2) people's cash and holdings of government bonds do not drop in proportion, then the increase in people's *real wealth* may have expansionary effects on the real propensity to consume and on employment. But falling prices may aggravate debts and bankruptcy and, by making people pessimistic, may harm investment; consequently, most advanced treatises in economics seem to advocate expanding people's real wealth and real consumption schedule by means of expansionary bank and financial policy rather than by deflation. (Chapter 18's Appendix discusses this so-called "Pigou effect" on page 325.)
[9]The Rees quotation is from *Wage Inflation* (National Industrial Conference Board, New York, 1957), pp. 27–28; the Reynolds quotation, from Reynolds and Taft, *op. cit.*, pp. 194–195. Cf. the following quote from Sumner Slichter, J. Healy, and E. R. Livernash, *The Impact of Collective Bargaining on Management* (Brookings Institution, Washington, 1960), p. 951: "Collective bargaining seems to have greatly encouraged the development of management. . . . companies that have been relatively successful in union-management relations gave evidence of following wise basic policies, of negotiating balanced general policies, of developing good implementing and procedural arrangements to make policy effective at the operating level, and of having considerable initiative in labor relations administration. The challenge that unions presented to management has, if viewed broadly, created superior and better-balanced management, even though some exceptions must be recognized."

union people may even lag behind simply because of the rigidities involved in the collective bargaining process.

And Reynolds states the following conclusions of his researches:

Summing up these diverse consequences of collective bargaining, one can make a strong case that unionism has at any rate not worsened the wage structure. We are inclined to be more venturesome than this, and to say that its net effect has been beneficial. This conclusion will doubtless strike many economists as surprising. . . .

  Fears that complete unionization will bring seismic disruption of the wage structure do not seem to be well founded. . . . The countries with the strongest union movements appear to have a wage structure which is more orderly and defensible than the wage structure of countries where unionism has been weak.

In Part Six's Chapter 41 we shall face the important problem, as yet unsolved, of finding an "incomes" or "guidepost" policy that will make full employment compatible with reasonably stable price levels.

SUMMARY

A. WAGE DETERMINATION UNDER PERFECT COMPETITION

1 In perfectly competitive equilibrium, if all men and jobs were exactly alike, there would be no wage differentials. The equilibrium wage rate would be determined by supply and demand. To the extent that Country A has (1) more natural resources per worker than Country B and (2) better productive methods (because of capital availability and technical knowledge), A's competitive wage is likely to be higher than B's.

2 The law of *diminishing returns* suggests that a reduction of labor relative to natural resources might be expected to raise real wages. While this principle lies back of labor's immigration policy and similar restrictions, historical examples of economies of mass production do point to the operation of a countertendency of *increasing returns*. In theory, the *"optimum* population" size is at the point where the two countertendencies have reached a balance of maximum per capita income.

3 Though Malthusian overpopulation threatens many an underdeveloped country such as India, there is no tendency for population growth in the United States and developed nations to push real wages down to a minimum-subsistence level. Pressure exerted on real wages by the "reserve army of the unemployed" tends to depress real wages only to the *equilibrium* level. In the Western world, this equilibrium wage is much above the physiological *subsistence* level and increases with every decade.

4 Fear of unemployment leads often to acceptance of the "lump-of-labor" fallacy. This belief, that there is only a fixed amount of useful work to be done, may result from experiencing technological unemployment or depression. It lies behind much of the agitation for a 30-hour week and featherbedding work rules. But unemployment calls for policies to furnish adequate job opportunities, not for defeatist restrictionism.

5   The supply of labor has four dimensions: population size, percentage of people gainfully employed, average number of hours worked, and quality of effort.

6   As wages rise, there are two opposite effects on the supply of labor: The "substitution-effect" tempts each worker to work longer because of the higher pay for each hour of work; the "income-effect" exerts influence in the opposite direction—in that higher wages mean that workers can now afford more leisure along with more commodities and other good things of life. At *some* critical wage, the supply curve may bend backward. The labor supply of very gifted, unique people is probably quite inelastic; their wages are likely to contain a large element of so-called "pure economic rent."

7   Once we drop the unrealistic assumptions concerning the uniformity of people and jobs, we find that substantial wage differentials will characterize even a perfectly competitive labor market. "Equalizing wage differences," which compensate for nonmonetary *differences in disutility* between jobs, explain some of the differentials.

8   But differences in the *quality* of various grades of labor are probably the most important cause of wage differences. Although it cannot be claimed that labor consists of wholly "noncompeting groups," it is nonetheless true that there are innumerable categories of partially competing groups. When the relative wage of one category rises, there are substantial cross-elasticity effects on labor supply as some people switch to the improved-pay occupation. The final pattern of wages would, in a perfectly competitive labor market, be determined by the general equilibrium of the interrelated schedules of supply and demand, as shown in Table 29-1's final category.

B. IMPERFECTIONS OF THE LABOR MARKET AND COLLECTIVE BARGAINING

9   Labor markets are not perfectly competitive in real life. With unions or without them, employers usually have some control over wages, but their wage policy must be conditioned by the available supply of labor.

10   Unions affect wages by (*a*) restricting labor supply, (*b*) bargaining for standard rates, (*c*) following policies designed to shift upward the derived demand schedule for labor, and (*d*) countering exploitation of labor by employers with monopoly bargaining power (i.e., by so-called "monopsonists").

11   Relative increases in wages will in most industries result in less employment there. This is based on the assumption of a movement *along* a given demand schedule (i.e., no demand shifts from higher productivity).

12   At the collective bargaining table the following are some of the determining factors around which argument is likely to center: (1) cost and standards of living, (2) ability to pay and profits, (3) productivity trends, (4) "going wages" paid elsewhere in the lo-

cality and in the industry, (5) the influence of higher wages on purchasing power and on the level of costs, (6) the "national pattern" as determined by "key bargains" in important industries, (7) continuous increases based upon improvement factors from long-term technical improvements, and (8) government guideposts designed to keep increases in money wages in line with *average* productivity increases of the economy, with prices coming down in industries of over-average productivity increase by enough to cancel out price increases in industries of below-average productivity increase. Economic theory cannot tell just what the final wage bargain will be, it being theoretically indeterminate.

13   Usually a compromise settlement will be possible, without government intervention, formal arbitration, or a strike. But the *threat* of strike is ever present and conditions the whole bargaining procedure. In vital industries, however, the interest of the public transcends the individual interests and rights of the disputing parties; consequently, voluntary collective bargaining is on trial in such strategic areas and is subject to government controls whenever damaging work stoppages occur.

14   Historically, the extent to which unions have succeeded in raising wages is in doubt. Since 1933 union membership has greatly increased, but in this same period wage differentials seem to have remained about the same in absolute terms. There seems to have been here and abroad a narrowing of percentage wage differentials. While it is true that *recently unionized* industries seem to show slightly greater wage increases since 1933, the quantitative difference is not great and it is not clear which is cause and which effect. Heavily concentrated and expanding industries may have been targets for unionization, and the high wages may have been the result of factors associated with or causing unionization rather than of unionization as such.

15   A final warning is in order: We must beware of the fallacy of composition in ascribing to the *demand curve for labor in general* the shape characteristic of the *demand curve for one small category of labor*. Wages are more than costs; they also constitute much of the income of consumers and react heavily back upon the demand for products of business. A general change in money wage rates can be expected to have important effects on prices. It is even possible that real wages will not change at all. To the extent that a general wage change is balanced by an equivalent percentage change in *all* prices, little substantive effect upon unemployment may result.

QUESTIONS FOR DISCUSSION

1   Explain narrowing of wage differentials from competition of like people.

2   What factors of technology, economic geography, and legislation help to determine the level of real wages? Show how diminishing returns and countertendencies are linked with the theory of optimum population.

3   Define and contrast "equalizing and nonequalizing differences in wages." Which concept is exemplified by high wages that contained much "pure economic rent"? What about noncompeting groups?

4   Give a list of imperfections in the labor market. Show that not all are related to monopoly power or to trade-union organization.

5   Give three ways unions try to influence wages, as described in this chapter. Contrast the first two, and gauge their importance. Do the same for the third method.

6   "Unions can raise real and money wages in a particular industry, but the result will be less employment." Evaluate, utilizing the elasticity of demand for labor.

7   What is the public interest in voluntary collective bargaining?

8   Explain dangers involved in treating the general demand for labor like a particular group's demand. Show that wages are costs *and* sources of demand.

9   "In his 1964 State of the Union message, President Johnson suggested that a penalty might be put on firms that chronically offer overtime work. This is defeatism, and could have been avoided with activist macroeconomic policies (fiscal and monetary)." Evaluate.

10 President Nixon tried in the 1970s to keep the government out of collective bargaining. Do you think this is possible; in a (a) rail strike, (b) steel strike, (c) longshoreman or teamster strike, (d) one-town-newspaper strike, (e) auto strike? Where draw the line?

Review your understanding of the following concepts:

general equilibrium
optimum population
subsistence wage level
backward-bending supply curve
income- versus substitution-effect
rent element in wages
equalizing and nonequalizing wage differences

noncompeting groups
standard rate
monopoly-employer exploitation
elastic, inelastic derived demand
collective bargaining
strike, lockout, work stoppage
percentage and absolute differentials
structural unemployment

Interest
and Capital

30

How to have your cake
and eat it too:
lend it out at interest.
ANONYMOUS

The last chapters have sketched the determination of the rents of resources and the wages of labor. Now in this chapter we turn to the third great category of productive factors, capital; and to the determination of its special price, which is called "interest."

Capital theory is one of the most difficult parts of economic theory. For this reason, an introductory treatment cannot hope to grapple with all the important issues. It seems best, therefore, to proceed as follows:

The main part of this chapter summarizes in an uncritical way the key notions involved in capital and interest. Then, at the end, are briefly given some of the key qualifications that ought to be made concerning the oversimplified traditional treatment. For the Appendix are reserved certain special topics of classical capital theory and modern doctrines of income determination.

LAND, LABOR, AND CAPITAL

Our traditional account of capital theory begins with a rather arbitrary division of all productive factors into three categories:

1. *Natural resources* provided by Nature in fixed supply, which cannot be augmented or used up. The return of this inelastic factor is called (pure economic) *rent*.

2. Human *labor* resources, not produced in response to economic conditions, but taken by the economist as determined by social and biological factors. The return of this human factor is called *wages* (which includes the salaries for brain and managerial workers as well as wages for manual workers).

In the oversimplified traditional account, factors (1) and (2) are called "primary factors of production"—primary in the sense that their supplies are determined largely outside the economic system itself. To them we must now add an "intermediate" factor.

3. Capital goods, *produced by the economic system itself*

to be used as productive inputs for further production of consumption and other goods and services. These capital goods can be long- or short-lived. They can be rented out in the competitive market just the way acres of land or hours of labor can be. Their rents—or perhaps we might use the term "rentals," to avoid confusion with pure economic rent to natural resources in fixed supply—these rentals of capital goods are determined by the same demand conditions of marginal productivity discussed previously.

However, in the traditional capital theory, the return or yield of capital is not taken to be the *rentals* of capital goods. What, then, is it? The yield of capital is the *interest rate per annum*, which is a pure percentage per unit time—independent of dollar or other value units. Of what is the interest rate 5 per cent per annum the yield? Obviously, it is the yield applied to the *dollar* value of capital goods.[1]

CAPITALIZATION OF ASSETS

Now we can take a brief look at the important economic process by which capital goods get priced in the market at their "capitalized value." The interest rate plays a key role, and when this rate drops from a high down to a low level, we shall see there must result a considerable rise in the capitalized value of machines, bonds, annuities, or any asset providing a stream of future property revenues.

To see how assets get capitalized, look at the simplest case of a piece of land or an annuity contract that is certain to pay you the *same* number of dollars each year from now until *eternity*. It turns out we can quite easily write down the formula for the present capitalized value V of any *permanent* income stream of \$1 per year or \$$N$ per year. We ask, "How many dollars put out every year at the market rate of interest i per annum will give us exactly the same return of \$1 per year or \$$N$ per year?" The answer is summarized in the rule

$$V = \frac{\$N}{i}$$

where V = present capitalized value (often called "present discounted value")

   $\$N$ = permanent annual receipts

   i = interest rate in decimal terms (e.g., .05, or $5/100$, corresponding to 5 per cent)

Thus, if the interest rate will always be 5 per cent, any permanent income will sell for exactly 20 (= $1 \div 5/100$) times its annual income.[2] (To check our formula, realize that

[1] In taking a census of total capital, we should not add to the 1-million-dollar value of a firm's plant, equipment, and inventory the 1-million-dollar value that its common-stock shares may sell for on Wall Street. It is double counting to add the left side of a balance sheet to its right side. The value of all assets, or society's left side, should equal the *net* value of all individuals' right-side ownership: thus, if we reckon Crusoe's net worth by taking care to subtract from his gross assets his liabilities to Friday, the sum of their two net worths should equal the value of the island's goats, land, huts, and tools. If they are blessed with a government which has issued paper money and a public debt which cannot be expected to be retired during the lifetimes of Crusoe and Friday, they may include money and government bonds in their personal net worths; if they do, the sum of goat-and-other-real-assets will fall short of the sum of personal net worth by the amount of the government debt liabilities and money.
[2] In the Middle Ages, they called this "20 years' purchase" and thus got around the taboo against interest. Show that 4 per cent interest means 25 years' purchase; 6 per cent, $16\frac{2}{3}$ years'. (See the Appendix

a principal of $20 at 5 per cent will yield $1 every year; so $20 must be the perpetuity's capitalized value.)

NET PRODUCTIVITY OF CAPITAL

Now we ask ourselves this question: Why do people ever bother to transform the primary factors of labor and land into intermediate capital goods or into capital? The answer is plain: It is a technological fact of life that you *can get more future consumption product by using indirect or roundabout methods.*

To see this, imagine two islands exactly alike. Each has exactly the same primary factors of labor and land. Island A uses these primary factors directly to produce consumption product; she uses no produced capital goods at all. Island B, on the other hand, for a preliminary period sacrifices current consumption; instead she uses some of her land and labor to produce intermediate capital goods such as plows, shovels, and synthesized chemicals. After this preliminary period of sacrificing current consumption pleasures in the interests of net capital formation, she ends up with a varied stock of capital goods, i.e., with a sizable amount of capital. Now let us measure the amount of consumption product she can go on permanently producing with her land, labor, and constantly replaced capital goods.

Careful measurement of Island B's "roundabout" product shows it to be greater than Island A's. Why is it greater? Why does B get *more* than 100 units of future consumption goods for her initial sacrifice of 100 units of present consumption? That is a technological engineering question. To sum up, the economist traditionally takes the following answer as a basic technical fact:

There exist roundabout processes, which take time to get started and completed, that are more productive than direct processes.

From this basic technological fact we can now draw an important economic conclusion:

After allowing for all depreciation requirements, capital has a *net productivity* (or real interest yield) that can be expressed in the form of a percentage per annum; and the only reason you do not take further advantage of this opportunity to get more product by roundabout methods is that you would have to cut down on present consumption if you are to speed up capital's rate of growth and future consumption.

DEFINITION OF NET PRODUCTIVITY OF A CAPITAL GOOD OR INVESTMENT PROJECT

We need an exact definition of the net productivity of any capital project. We first calculate the original dollar cost of the factors you bought to begin each roundabout

---

for discussion of capitalization of nonpermanent income streams.)

NOTE: After land has been capitalized, its rent may appear as *interest* earned on its market value. In principle, *all* the nonwage part of NNP could be reported as interest on the value of property: if selling ourselves into slavery were not illegal, even wages might be reported as interest on the capital value of men! As is also noted in Parts One and Six, investing in human capital by education and training is important: much of the wage of a high-income surgeon can be regarded as interest and return of principal on his father's or wife's investment in his training.

process. Then we calculate the total receipts that the roundabout methods give. We know very well that the receipts total must add up to more than the original cost total, or else there is no net productivity. Having satisfied ourselves that there is indeed a positive net productivity, we need a way of measuring it quantitatively so as to make diverse projects comparable—projects involving apples and oranges, projects involving 50-year bridges and 5-month beer. Our final solution is to look for a measure that is a *percentage per annum*.

We end up defining the net productivity of a capital project thus:

A capital or investment project's net productivity is that annual percentage yield which you could earn by tying up your money in it. What is the same thing, the project's net productivity is that market rate of interest at which it would just pay to undertake it.

EXAMPLE: I buy grape juice for $10, and a year later sell it as wine for $11. If there are no other expenses and no risk or effort to me, my interest yield (or "net productivity") is 10 per cent per annum—equal to $1/$10.[3]

As a community transfers part of its resources away from current consumption and toward capital accumulation, projects with lower and lower net productivity will be undertaken. Thus, this 50-year bridge with a net productivity of, say, 10 per cent will not be worth building if the market rate of interest is 11 per cent. But when the market interest drops to 10 per cent or below, you will build the bridge.

The law of diminishing returns is invoked as more and more capital goods of all types become available to work with the limited supply of natural resources and land, and with the more slowly growing number of workers. This law implies that society and the private investors will run out of new projects with net productivities as high as the previous ones. And unless offset by technological innovations, this law of diminishing returns would result in interest rates and investment yields falling through time. For without such a fall, the low-yielding long-lived projects would not get undertaken.

A BIRD'S-EYE VIEW OF INTEREST DETERMINATION

We can now define the rate of interest and summarize the forces determining its competitive level.

Definition: The market rate of interest is that percentage return per year which has to be paid on any safe loan of money, which has to be yielded by any safe bond or other type of security, and which has to be earned on the value of any capital asset (such as a machine, a hotel building, a patent right) in any competitive market where there are no risks or where all risk factors have already been taken care of by special premium payments to protect against risk.

Thus, in an ideal capital market, the riskless rate of interest might be set by supply and demand

---

[3] Here are two more examples. I plant a pine tree at labor cost of $50 plus 25 years' land rental cost—paid in advance—of $50, or $100 in all. At the end of 25 years the grown tree sells for $430. The net productivity of this capital project is then 330 per cent per quarter-century, which, interest tables tell us, is equivalent to a net productivity of 6 per cent per year. Or I buy a $10,000 truck. For 10 years it earns annual rentals of $5,000, but I pay $3,000 annually for fuel, driver, and maintenance. Its scrap value is zero. What is its net productivity or yield? The same as the annual percentage yield of an annuity of $2,000 per year payable for 10 years and bought for $10,000. Compound interest tables for annuities show this truck's yield to be 15 per cent per year and that its value depreciates with age.

at 6 per cent, just as the rent of fertile land is set at $20 an acre per year and the wage of skilled labor is set at $150 per 40-hour week.

That does not mean that I shall make a small loan at this low a rate to an applicant whom I do not know and who has lost three jobs in 6 months' time: I may have to charge him as much as 20 per cent per annum to compensate me for having to investigate him, dun him for collection, and cover the risk premium from default and costly litigation. Nor shall I buy risky mining stock that yields only 6 per cent. At any time there is a whole spread of interest rates for ventures of different riskiness, and this whole spread will move up or down when the pure, riskless rate of interest changes.

What are the changes in supply or demand that could move the pure interest rate up or down? Certainly, if scientists and engineers create new projects for capital investment, which have their *net productivities increased greatly* from the previous equilibrium, this will tend to bid up the market rate of interest. Contrariwise, if people become *less impatient* to consume now rather than in the future, their successful attempt to save—to shift resources from consumption-goods production to formation of capital goods—will bid down the interest rate, as more and more capital accumulation leads to diminishing returns and creates the need to take up capital projects with lower and lower net productivities.

As Yale's great expert Irving Fisher put the matter a half-century ago:

Supply-and-demand determination of the interest rate means that its level is determined by interaction between (1) people's *impatience* to consume now rather than accumulate more capital goods for future consumption, and (2) *investment opportunities* that exist to procure higher or lower net productivities from such capital accumulated.

The market rate of interest has two functions: it *rations out*, into the uses with highest net productivities, society's *existing scarce supply of capital goods;* and in the long run, it may (or may not[4]) induce people to *sacrifice current consumption and add to the stock of capital.*

GRAPHICAL DETERMINATION OF INTEREST

Supply-and-demand diagrams can amplify this survey of interest determination. But in the field of capital theory, they become rather complicated. At this point we can greatly simplify the exposition of the traditional theory if we agree to concentrate on the case where all physical capital goods are exactly alike. (Of course, in the real world, they

[4] There is evidence that some people save *less* rather than more at higher interest rates; and that many people save about the *same* amount regardless of the level of the interest rate; and that some people are induced to consume less only by the promise of higher interest returns. As we saw in the discussion of substitution- versus income-effects, in Chapters 22 and 29, economic principles alone cannot give us a decisive prediction. The bulk of the evidence suggests that the level of interest tends to cancel out of consumption and saving decisions, even though a rise in the rate paid by one savings bank may bring *it* increased business because people will tend to transfer their assets from commercial banks or mutual funds (without their having altered consumption one bit). Some classical economists sought to justify interest as the reward for the pain of abstinence and waiting, just as they justified wages as the reward for sweat and psychic disutility. This gave rise to jests among Continental socialists concerning Baron Rothschild's painful sacrifices!

are not all alike; and therefore advanced treatises have to go through a rather lengthy discussion to show how the diversity of capital goods is to be handled.[5])

Figure 30-1 illustrates how the interest rate is determined in traditional capital theory. Curve *dd* shows the demand curve for the stock of capital. Remember how the demand for labor was formed from the marginal productivity curve for labor. Similarly, the demand for capital is a "derived demand"—derived ultimately from the value of the extra consumption goods that extra capital makes possible. The demand for capital is made up of its *net productivity curve* (reckoned as a per cent per annum, as we have seen).

Diminishing returns We see the law of diminishing returns applying to capital as well as to other factors. This is shown by the *dd* curve's sloping downward; e.g., at levels where capital is very scarce, there are some very profitable roundabout projects that yield 12 or more per cent per annum. Gradually, through thrift, capital

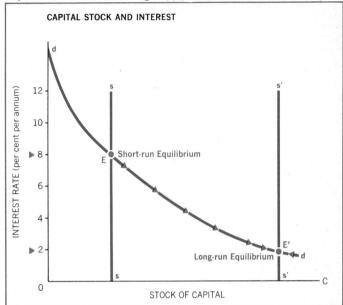

Capital demand intersecting supply determines interest rate:

FIG. 30-1. Existing supply of capital intersects net productivity schedule to determine a moving equilibrium rate. Continued capital formation shifts *ss* sideward and leads to the indicated fall in interest rate along *dd*. Long-run equilibrium interest rate is at *E'*, where net saving ceases.

formation takes place and the community finds it has exploited all the 12 per cent projects; with total labor and land fixed, diminishing returns to the varying capital have set in. The community must then invest in 11 and 10 per cent projects as it moves down *dd*.

In Fig. 30-1, capital formation has taken place in the past until the existing supply of the stock of capital is given by the vertical supply curve *ss*. The equilibrium rate of interest must in the short run take place at the intersection of the *dd* demand curve and the *ss* short-run supply curve. Why? Because below the equilibrium interest rate, there would exist too many investment projects; and the community's stock of capital is only big enough to take care of the projects yielding the shown equilibrium interest rate of 8 per cent.

Short-run equilibrium Why is the equilibrium at *E* only a short-run, moving equilibrium? Because 8 per cent is a rather high rate; and even though capital is currently scarce enough to keep us at *E*, people would probably want to go on saving part of their income there. This means the community will have capital formation continuously taking place;

[5] See the Appendix's Fig. 30-3, page 587, for some further discussion of this problem and of the Irving Fisher analysis.

so as time passes, the community will be moving southeast on the *dd* curve as shown by the gold arrows.

Specifically, (1) we move east because the accumulating amount of positive investment and capital formation means that the capital stock, and therefore the short-run supply curve, is being pushed more and more rightward. (In each new short run, the curve will again be vertical but farther to the right.) Now why does the interest rate move downward? (2) It moves downward because the law of diminishing returns tells us—other things such as labor, land, and knowledge of technology remaining unchanged!—that the net productivity of the increased stock of capital goods falls to ever lower percentages.[6]

Long-term steady-state equilibrium   The equilibrium at *E* is in the nature of a short-run equilibrium; short-run, in the sense that people are still saving at the interest rate shown there. Capital is still growing, as is indicated by the gold arrows; we are still moving down the *dd* curve. The interest rate at *E* was just big enough to keep us growing at the rate we were growing. But the interest rate at *E* was not yet low enough to choke off all desire to save, not yet low enough to make the community's average propensity to consume equal to 100 per cent of income.

It is at *E'* that *long-run equilibrium* is finally achieved. Again, the existing stock of capital is being auctioned off in the market for the highest short-run interest rate it can fetch. (You run vertically up the *s's'* supply curve and read off the *E'* interest rate.) But now interest is so low that the net saving is zero; now capital stops growing, and the supply curve no longer shifts rightward. The arrows converge on *E'*: at higher interest, capital would grow through positive saving and investment; at lower interest, it would decline through positive disinvestment and dissaving. So *E'* represents the stable long-run equilibrium that could prevail in the absence of technical change.

ANCIENT MISCONCEPTIONS ABOUT INTEREST

Before proceeding to criticize and qualify its oversimplifications, we can use the traditional theory of capital and interest to clear up some ancient debates.

Fairness and inevitability of interest   Pointing out that money is "barren," Aristotle said it was unfair to charge positive interest for loans. Many sophisticated medieval Schoolmen followed him in this view that interest represents unjustified usury. Indeed interest was forbidden by canon law throughout the Middle Ages, and many were the dodges to get around these restrictions.

How do we answer this view? First, we could point out what has been shown in earlier chapters—that holding a cash balance often does serve a useful function for which people will gladly pay up to a point. But let us meet the issue head on. Let us make the realistic assumption that when I borrow money from you, my purpose is not to hold onto the

---

[6]The process of accumulating capital goods faster than labor grows is important, and will be called "deepening of capital" in Chapter 37 (in contrast to mere duplication of capital goods to match a growing labor force, called "widening of capital"). The steady-state equilibrium shown at *E'* could, if population were growing at, say, 2 per cent per year, be a moving equilibrium in which capital is being accumulated *in balance* with labor, with no "deepening" but only "widening." See page 588, footnote 2.

cash: instead I use the borrowed cash to buy capital goods; and, as we have seen, these intermediate capital goods are so scarce as to create a net product over and above their replacement cost. Therefore, if I did not pay you interest, I should really be cheating you out of the return that you could get by putting your own money directly into such productive investment projects!

Consumption loans   The Biblical utterances against interest and usury clearly refer to loans made for consumption rather than investment purposes. Suppose I, a poor man, borrow from you, a rich man, so that I can eat more today or pay a hospital bill. (1) Is it fair that I should have to pay you interest? (2) How do such consumption loans affect the short-run and long-run equilibrium interest rates?

The answer to the second question will help answer the first. Consumption lending is today less important than productive-investment lending; therefore productive investment primarily determines the behavior of interest rates.[7]

Now we can treat the fairness question. Are we assuming that there is effective competition in the money market for consumption loans so that no one—rich or poor—can take unfair *monopoly* advantage of anyone else by preventing him from borrowing at the cheapest available terms? If we explicitly assume effective competition *and* that people will not rashly sacrifice their future well-being just to consume more now, then it is hard to see why there is anything more unfair about *loan* transactions between rich and poor than there would be in *other* competitive transactions between rich and poor, e.g., when a rich butcher sells a poor consumer a pound of meat. Of course, the poor man would rather pay nothing for the meat than have to pay a positive price. But being a scarce good, the meat commands a positive price and one that changes with supply and demand. The same holds for interest. If the existing distribution of income seems unfair to the populace, the field of taxation would seem to offer the best remedies—not random interference with competitive loan or other market transactions.

Is a zero interest rate possible?   In a world of perfect certainty, it is hard to see how people could ever save enough to bring the net productivity of capital all the way down to a zero interest rate. As long as there is a single hilly railroad track left, it would pay at a zero rate of interest to make it level. Why? Because in enough years, the savings in fuel would pay for the cost. As long as any increase in time-consuming processes could be counted on to produce any extra product and dollars of revenue, the yield of capital could not be zero. Also, as long as any land or other asset exists with a *sure perpetual net income*—and as long as people are willing to give only a *finite* amount of money today in exchange for a perpetual flow of income spread over the whole future—then we can hardly conceive of the rate of interest as falling to zero.[8]

[7]Nonetheless, to the extent that there is a desire to borrow now for present consumption purposes, we can take this into account in Fig. 30-1. If some people want to dissave, their consumption borrowing will make the community less thrifty as a whole than it would otherwise be. So we find the *ss* curve of the stock of capital shifting *more slowly* rightward; and we thereby progress more slowly downward on the *dd* curve from E toward E', with interest not falling so fast or far as otherwise.

[8]Under realistic conditions of uncertainty, we must qualify the above. Before you have recovered the costs of leveling the roadbed of the railway, airplanes might make railways obsolete—or earthquakes might undo your work. In 1932 people expected and experienced zero or negative returns from most

A zero rate of interest is a little like an "absolute zero of temperature" in physics. We can imagine getting closer and closer to it, but we can hardly imagine actually reaching the limiting state of a zero equilibrium rate of interest. Thus, interest is a basic phenomenon that would not disappear even in the most ideal economic world.

Interest under socialism? Our economic analysis suggests that thinking is superficial if it concludes that interest is solely a monetary phenomenon of predatory capitalism. Students of planning in a centralized socialistic society have discovered that even such a society must introduce a concept like the interest rate into its plans. Every known society has, since Eden, had some limits on its supply of capital goods. Every society, therefore, has the important task of screening out investment projects, giving first priority to those that are most immediately productive of the things that society wants. Even in Utopia, you simply cannot do everything at once.

How, then, does the screening out among possible projects take place, so that definite priorities can be given? Clearly, there is no alternative but to choose (1) how much of present resources are to be used, and (2) how much of future useful products will be created. To reduce all the alternative patterns into a final single figure is not easy; but something like our earlier calculation of net productivities must be made. Unless you are satisfied to toss a coin or proceed by guess in your collectivist's society, *you have to introduce first those investment projects with the higher net productivity.* After much investment has gone into these in the past and diminishing returns has brought down the yield, you can go on to lower-net-productivity projects.

At some point, therefore, something like the interest rate necessarily comes into being. Recent studies show that the social engineers of the Soviet Union are anxious not to be denounced as capitalistic apologists; yet they need some form of interest rate (or "discount factor," or "payoff period") for making efficient investment calculations. As a result, about a dozen different accounting methods are in vogue there for introducing a thinly disguised interest-rate concept into Soviet planning procedures. But, of course, no one necessarily receives interest income from them.

SUMMARY OF INTEREST DETERMINATION

We have now seen what determines interest rates over time. If Robinson Crusoe (or a Communist dictator or the average citizen in a free economy) cuts down on current consumption, then capital formation can be high and capital goods can grow in number. The more capital goods there are, the lower their net productivities will tend to be. Why? Because of the good old law of diminishing returns: with population and natural resources unchanged, when you add more and more physical capital goods—or, what is closely related, when you make production more and more roundabout and time-consuming—you will add to total product, but generally at a decreasing rate.

capital projects. That is why investment ceased. Even today, if the profit rate (pure interest rate plus premium to cover risk) got forced down to 10 or 12 per cent before taxes, business as a whole might be unwilling to undertake an investment level equal to desired full-employment saving. See Appendix, page 588, for more on this.

When you have built the bridges, dams, factories, and production lines that yield a net productivity of 20 per cent, you have then to go on to investment projects with 19 per cent and still lower net productivities. The market rate of interest that can be earned on investments will thus fall, and this will be the signal for investors to undertake projects which were previously unprofitable at the earlier higher rates of interest.[9]

Two kinds of thrift are involved. First, people must resist the temptation to eat up some of the capital that was amassed in the past; they must "abstain" from consuming more than their current incomes, that is, continue to replace capital and abstain from making net saving become negative. Second, if there is to be positive net capital formation, the community must usually be willing to undergo "waiting"—waiting in the sense of giving up consumption goods now in return for more such goods in the future.

All in all, consumption-saving decisions plus the technical net productivity of capital goods are needed to explain behavior of interest rates over time.[10]

SOME MAJOR QUALIFICATIONS

Now the main task of this chapter is done. But any traditional account of capital theory is in need of some important qualifications. This chapter concludes with only brief mention of the more important ones. The Appendix provides further discussion.

Technological disturbance   In real life we cannot hold other things constant while the system proceeds to accumulate capital and travel down the road of diminishing returns. In particular, new inventions and discoveries are constantly being made. Such technological changes will often raise the net productivity and the interest rates to be earned on the community's stock of capital and on its extensions. So, instead of there being a movement down an unchanged schedule, inventions may cause an upward shift of the net-productivity-of-capital schedule.[11] All this is not a fanciful possibility. Historical studies suggest that, for America and the West generally, the tendency toward falling interest rates via diminishing returns has been just about canceled out by technological progress: though real wage rates have been rising, the real interest return on capital has not been generally falling in this century, as would have been expected from a primitive classical analysis of capital accumulation.

If technical change came to an end, the rate of interest might again march down toward zero or to the point where no saving took place. But, actually, new inventions are constantly coming along to give interest rates an upward lift. Some economists (such

---

[9] What is the same thing, a lowering of the interest rate at which we calculate present discounted values (as indicated on page 589) will raise more and more investment projects above their initial cost—and they will be undertaken to society's advantage.

[10] As we shall see, the government—through its monetary and fiscal policies that favor or retard the rate of capital formation and ensure against the paradox of aborted thrift—is also an important determinant of investment and interest rates. So two economies in which *private* individuals and corporations show the same thrift propensities may develop very differently over a decade or century, depending upon the policies being followed by government.

[11] Some inventions may be "capital-saving" and twist the net productivity relationship downward, often tending to lower interest. (See Chapter 37.) Note that inventions may also destroy some capital by making it obsolete; and changes in consumer tastes can have similar disturbing effects.

as Schumpeter) have likened the process to a plucked violin string: other things being equal, the string will gradually come to rest as competitive capital formation undermines net yield; but before this can happen, some outside event or invention comes along to pluck it once more and to set it again into motion. (See Chapter 37 and its Appendix for more on this.)

Uncertainty and expectations Our exposition of the traditional capital theory has assumed perfect foresight. This is a serious oversimplification. In real life no one has a crystal ball to read the future: all evaluations of capital and all investment decisions, resting as they do on estimates of future earnings, must necessarily be guesses—accurate guesses based on much thought and information in some cases, wild guesses in other cases, but in every case uncertain guesses. Each day we wake up to learn that our expectations were not quite accurate and have to be revalued; each night we go to bed realizing that the next morning will have some surprises for us.

The next chapter will show how significant uncertainty is for profit theory. Here, in connection with interest theory, we must note an important effect of uncertainty:

Investors' optimism about future yields and risks can change markedly in a very short time; hence all relations are very *shiftable*. They shift with changes in opinion and rumor; with changes in population trends; with changes in technology and innovation; etc.[12]

Shifts in schedules with income Even without disturbing outside factors, there is a serious drawback to traditional schedules. Changes in the level of *real income* profoundly *shift* classical saving and investment schedules at each rate of interest. (Only recall our long statistical and theoretical discussions of Part Two dealing with the propensity to consume and to save at different levels of income. Also recall discussions of investment induced by increases in the level of income relative to fixed capacities of capital—or what is closely related, the "acceleration principle" of our business-cycle discussions in Chapter 14.)

Shifts of the basic schedules—as, e.g., of *dd* in Fig. 30-1—represent serious weaknesses in the traditional theory. Many classical economists of a century ago were unaware of this problem because they had the comfortable view that chronic unemployment was impossible and income would not fluctuate. They did not always know why they believed full employment was inevitable. But they did believe that "supply always creates its own demand and general overproduction is an impossibility."[13]

Real versus money interest rate In Brazil interest rates often exceed 40 per cent a year. During the 1923 German inflation, they were often 1 million per cent per month! Americans who bought government savings bonds almost a decade ago, with a nominal yield

---

[12] To illustrate this subjective volatility, Keynes once characterized the 1929 crash as "a sudden collapse in the [net productivity or] marginal efficiency of capital"—a true, but surface, explanation.

[13] E.g., some believed in a miraculous law of conservation of market purchasing power: what was not spent in one direction they said *had* to be spent in another. A more defensible version of the theory claims that, if only wages and prices were never sticky, then flexible decreases in all prices and wages would ultimately so increase the real purchasing power of the coin and currency in each man's pocket as to reduce his thriftiness enough to restore full employment. The modern version of this hyper-deflation theory we have associated with A. C. Pigou, who did not recommend it for policy purposes. (See Appendix to Chapter 18 on Say's Law and Pigou effects.)

of $4\frac{1}{4}$ per cent, can actually buy less today with $100 than with the $75 the bonds cost—entailing a "real interest return" of less than zero per cent.

These examples stress the need to define the "real interest rate" as the "money interest rate" minus "the percentage price rise." Thus, if the money rate is 8 per cent for Americans and the annual price rise is 5 per cent, then the true real rate of interest is $8 - 5 = 3$ per cent. So to speak, 100 market baskets of goods lent today gives you next year only 103 (not 108!) market baskets in return.

As people come to anticipate a steady rate of inflation, they build into their interest-rate supply and demand schedules an allowance for the inflation. They begin to prefer common stocks, shunning low-interest bonds. Thus, in the post-1965 Vietnam years, interest rates of 8 and 10 or more per cent became common. High rates? Yes, in money terms. But the calculated real interest rate held steady for 1965 to 1970 at the rather moderate level of 3 per cent.

PUBLIC AND PRIVATE POLICY IN DETERMINING CAPITAL FORMATION

Concretely, how does modern macroanalysis fit in with the valid elements of the traditional microeconomic theory? Here is its basic contribution:

Fiscal and monetary policies interact with private thrift to determine how fast society builds up its capital.

E.g., consider a successful pattern of full-employment equilibrium without inflation. Recall that this requires the saving and investment curves of the theory of income determination in Chapters 12 and 13 to be intersecting at full employment, with no inflationary gap and no deflationary gap. Two instances are shown here in Fig. 30-2.

Mix of monetary and fiscal policy determines rate of capital growth:

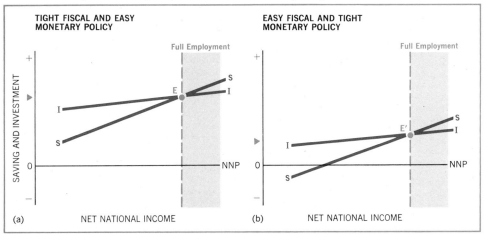

FIG. 30-2.   (a) By tight fiscal and easy monetary policies, the first economy is causing full-employment saving and investment to reach equilibrium at E, with rapid rate of capital formation. (b) The second economy uses easy fiscal policy (low taxes and deficits) matched by tight monetary policy to create a low-saving-and-investment (high-consumption) full-employment equilibrium. Note that E' is much lower than E in investment.

The community's propensity-to-save-out-of-income curve will crucially depend upon budgetary fiscal policy. To see this, suppose tax rates are very high, so that revenues collected at full employment are very high relative to expenditure, the budget being overbalanced. Suppose, too, that the taxes fall most heavily on the relatively thriftless lower-income groups. Then the community's propensity-to-consume schedule will be a low one at every level of national income, including the full-employment level. The amount not consumed (equal to net personal saving plus the government surplus) will then be very great at every level and—what interests us here—SS will be great at the full-employment level of income shown in Fig. 30-2(a).

Will such a depressed consumption level cause unemployment? Not if macroeconomic management[14] is working. Aggressive easing of monetary policy (open-market purchases, lowered reserve requirements, lowered discount rate, and possibly aggressive selective credit programs) will push the community's investment schedule upward. Result: Tight fiscal policy plus very expansionary monetary policy have given us a full-employment income characterized by very high capital formation and relatively low consumption. (See *E* in Fig. 30-2(a).)

We can work out the opposite mix of tight monetary and easy fiscal policies appropriate for a community that seeks a high-consumption low-investment full-employment income, as in Fig. 30-2(b). Looked at together, the two diagrams (a) and (b) show the alternative rates of capital formation in two societies, each characterized by the same degree of private thrift (as measured by family budget studies at each level of disposable income), but with alternative public policies. Note the resulting differences in capital formation, and remember that diminishing returns would be operating to bring down interest more rapidly in the high-investment society unless offset by special technological progress there.

A sobering public responsibility We conclude, then, with two reminders. Macroeconomic management can banish the paradoxical possibility of thrift becoming abortive and can in this sense validate the classical notions concerning capital formation and productivity. On the other hand, modern societies necessarily are engaging in monetary and fiscal policies—and it is these public policies that to an important degree do shape the resulting pattern of high-employment consumption and investment.

This power over the community's rate of capital formation constitutes an exhilarating—and sobering—responsibility for the voters in any modern democracy.

SUMMARY

1   We can apply *primary* factors of production, land and labor, in indirect ways by introducing *intermediate* productive factors called *capital goods*. It is taken as a technological fact that this "roundaboutness" yields a *net productivity* over and above all replacement costs, expressible as an annual interest percentage and subject to the usual law of diminishing returns. (Read again the exact definition of net productivity.)

[14]See pages 321–322 and page 591.

2   To get the capitalized value of an asset, the interest rate is needed. It is also the device society uses to select investment projects that are most urgent and economical. When interest is high, only projects with highest net productivities can qualify. Gradually, after much past capital formation has invoked the law of diminishing returns, the interest rates will be falling. This provides the signal for introducing capital projects with lower net productivities.

3   Thrift, in the sense of *abstaining* from consuming past capital accumulations and *waiting* for future consumption goods rather than consuming now, interacts with the technical net productivity of capital goods to determine the developing pattern of interest rates and capital formation. Even outside a collectivist world, government monetary and fiscal policies play an important role in this process.

4   Even a planned state which is not run for private profit or gain would have to use some device like an interest rate as a sieve to determine which of the many possible investment projects represent the best use of the resources available today after present consumption needs have been determined. "Come the revolution"—come laissez faire—Nature's law of diminishing returns is likely still to be in business.

5   Consumption loans, while they are of minor importance today, do have some influence on the rate at which the community accumulates capital rather than consumes. Like the subjective factors of thrift, abstinence, waiting, foresight, impatience, and so forth, (1) personal borrowings do interact with (2) the technological fact of opportunity to invest in long-lived projects that yield a net productivity.

    Critics of interest had in mind the occurrence of consumption loan transactions in highly imperfectly competitive markets where the poor are at the mercy of the rich lender's bargaining power. Today no one would be in favor of usurious overcharges that take advantage of the poor man's inadequate access to competitive loan markets or his desperate neglect of his own future; but economists and philosophers recognize that the net productivity of capital is the technological fact most basic to modern-day interest: when you lend me money, you are giving up the opportunity to invest in land, machines, bonds, and stocks—forgone opportunities of which interest is the rough measure.

6   Important qualifications of the oversimplified traditional capital theory include the following: Lack of perfect foresight means that the capital net productivity is very *shiftable* as expectations, technology, and income levels change. Also, a classical theory that ignores deviations from full-employment income does need modification. Finally, to get the real rate of interest, one must subtract from the money rate the anticipated percentage rate of price inflation.

7   A great variety of compensating monetary and fiscal policies can succeed in maintaining reasonably full employment. Stable employment being assumed, Fig. 30-2 gives the needed qualification to the traditional theory; and it reveals that public policy has great responsibility for determining whether the composition of the full-employment national

income will be heavily weighted toward investment or toward consumption; this means that the central bank and the legislature between them shape the environment within which private thriftiness provides one part of total social thriftiness.

QUESTIONS FOR DISCUSSION

1   Give some examples of efficient roundabout processes. Of "produced" or "intermediate" inputs.

2   Contrast three "prices" of capital: (*a*) rental of a capital good, (*b*) market price of the capital good, and (*c*) interest yield on the value of the good.

3   Irving Fisher wrote a book with the title *The Theory of Interest*. He gave it the subtitle *As Determined by Impatience to Spend and Opportunities to Invest*. Explain what these mean. Defend the following: "Fisher should have added 'and as affected by government monetary and fiscal policies.'"

4   "The interest rate was simply a bourgeois device for exploitation." Discuss.

5   Protestant, Catholic, and Jewish organizations today issue mortgages to build local places of worship, and they invest any surplus funds in bonds, or possibly, as in the case of the Church of England, in equity stocks. How might they ethically distinguish this from "taking usury"?

6   How do innovations and expectations affect traditional interest theory?

7   Interpret macroeconomic management in a modern mixed economy. Contrast full employment involving "tight money" and "easy fiscal policy" with an opposite full employment.

8   Explain the rule for calculating present discounted value of a perpetual income stream. At 5 per cent, what is the worth of a perpetuity paying $100 per year? Paying $200 per year? Paying $N per year? At 6 or 8 per cent, what is the worth of a perpetuity paying $96 per year? What does doubling of the interest rate do to the capitalized value of a perpetuity—say a perpetual bond?

Review your understanding of the following concepts:

net productivity of capital	abstinence and waiting
indirect, roundabout methods and diminishing returns	uncertainty and technological change
interest rate per annum	real versus money interest rate
capitalization by $V = \$N/i$	austere fiscal policy and easy monetary policy, or opposite
choosing among investment projects	public responsibility for rate of capital formation
zero interest under any ism	

APPENDIX: Theoretical Aspects of Interest, Money, and Policy

Here, very briefly, can be mentioned some elaborations and qualifications of this chapter's discussion.

PRODUCTIVITY OR IMPATIENCE?

Some people like to find a single cause for everything, and such people ask: "Is interest caused by the productivity of capital? Or by the fact that savers must be paid for the unpleasant task of 'abstinence' or 'waiting'? Which is more important: opportunity to invest or impatience to spend?"

Our previous argument shows this is a false antithesis. *Both* factors operate to determine the time path of interest: the impatience to spend, or the tendency to prefer the present to the future, limits the growth rate and attained size of capital; and the productivity factor tells us what is the interest or net productivity that can be earned as we have various amounts of diverse capital goods. Just as both blades of a scissors are needed to cut—so that you cannot say that one blade rather than the other is doing the actual work—similarly, both factors, impatience *and* productivity, interact to determine the behavior of interest rates.[1]

DETERMINATION OF THE INTEREST RATE

Can our account of interest determination avoid the use of Fig. 30-1's simplifying concept of a stock of homogeneous capital? Yes, in a number of ways, some too complex to discuss in an introductory work. Thus, we may work with a variety of different physical capital goods and processes, being careful never to add their heterogeneous units together, noting that the sum of their capitalized market values does depend (in a virtuously, and not viciously, circular way) on the market interest rate, and never forgetting that it is machines and not hunks of dollars which enter into physical production functions. If the realistic problem of uncertainty about the future and the risks thereby implied could be ignored, advanced treatises can show rigorously how an equilibrium interest-rate pattern can be defined in such a heterogeneous model.

This is clearly not the place for such refinements. But it is desirable to mention that a theory of equilibrium interest rates can be given which avoids the homogeneous-capital assumptions of Fig. 30-1.

The key to a simple approach comes from Fisher's

[1] Those who have mastered the indifference-curve graphs of the Appendix to Chapter 22 can use Fig. 30-3 to see that

diagram, Fig. 30-3, in the preceding footnote, which states the following fundamental fact about the whole theory of interest:

Society can exchange present consumption goods for future consumption goods at a trade-off rate depicted by the rate of interest.

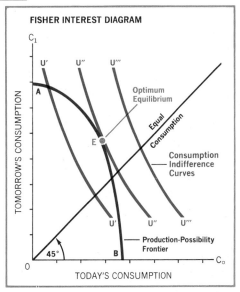

FISHER INTEREST DIAGRAM

FIG. 30-3.

positive interest is caused by two factors: (1) a vertical bias of the *AB* production-possibility frontier between present and future consumption goods, and (2) a general vertical bias of the typical consumer's indifference contours between present and future consumption goods. Hence, the tangency-equilibrium at *E* has a slope steeper than 1.0, corresponding to positive interest. The experienced reader will recognize that these can be related to Böhm-Bawerk's three famous causes for interest. His third cause, technological superiority of roundabout processes, and his first cause, the expectation by the typical consumer that his future dollars will have lower marginal utility because his income will be higher in the future (as a result of technological progress or of the productivity of roundaboutness), relate to factor (1). Böhm's second cause—systematic time preference by consumers for present rather than future goods, for rational reasons of life's uncertainties and brevity or for irrational reasons—relates to (2). [Suppose we were to rule out factor (1) by making *AB* "symmetrical around the 45° line" and rule out factor (2) by making the indifference curves "symmetrical around the 45° line." Having thus ruled out net productivity and time preference, we should find that the equilibrium interest rate must then be zero. Leaving one in leaves interest positive.]

Long-run equilibrium How long could this accumulation process of sacrificing current consumption go on? Just as Fig. 30-1 suggested, it can go on until the interest rate is zero, or until people want to do no net saving. At the zero rate of interest, if we could ever quite reach this point on the horizon, the plateau of consumption would be as high as is technically possible with the given labor, land, and primary resources. It would be a kind of "golden age."[2]

In real life three or more things keep us from reaching the golden age:

1. People may be so impatient and conscious of death that at some interest rate like 3 per cent, society won't want to do net saving.

2. Inventions may come along and offset diminishing returns by shifting upward all curves *like dd* in Fig. 30-1.

3. There is always riskiness in a dynamic society: long before the pure interest rate reaches zero, the profit-rate-inclusive-of-premium-for-risk may have hit a floor below which investment lags. We must examine this important matter.

AN UNCERTAINTY FLOOR TO RISKY RETURNS AND INVESTMENT?

It may be that under conditions of perfect certainty, persistent thrift can lead to no floor for interest except that of zero. But what about the real world where a measure of uncertainty must always be feared for any actual investment project? Can it not be the case that investors will dislike the task of taking risks on their shoulders? That they will insist on a rate of return on such investments which includes a certain definite positive percentage premium? Thus, even if the rate of interest to be earned on perfectly safe holdings were forced down to zero, might not people still insist on a 5 per cent after-tax return on a risky investment

in a machine or in the purchase of land that produces an uncertain yearly rental?

This floor at 5 per cent, or at some positive level above zero, might be a realistic problem to contend with. And if it were to materialize, some serious problems for full-employment policy might one day arrive. Here is why: Suppose that Federal Reserve expansionary policies lowered the rate of interest on very safe short-term government bonds toward zero; this could be expected to bring the rates of return on risky enterprises down from, say, 12 per cent to 8 per cent. And since at the lower rate many new investment projects would now pay, an upswing in investment spending might result that, through the mechanism of the familiar multiplier process, would lift output, income, and employment.

But suppose all this were not enough to reestablish full employment. Then the Federal Reserve could do more of the same. *But by no amount of expansionary moves could it reduce the safe interest rate below the floor of zero.* And it might well be the case that a zero floor on safe holdings could pull the rates on risky investment down only to their floor of 5 per cent—and no further. Then it would be quite conceivable that the sticky 5 per cent floor would bar further reduction in rates needed to coax out a pace of current job-giving investment big enough to restore full employment.

Therefore it is conceivable that an impasse, a kind of Day of Judgment for our mixed system with its inflexible wage and price levels, might arrive when conventional measures to stimulate investment could not restore full employment and let our optimistic "managed money" work itself out smoothly and fully.[3]

---

[2] Advanced books show that this golden rule must be modified if primary resources such as labor are *all* growing at 3 or 5 per cent per year. Then the golden age of maximal per capita consumption comes when the interest rate has been brought down also to 3 or 5 per cent: then the young earners in society, who are saving for their old age, are just enough more numerous than the retired earners, who are eating up what they had earlier saved; and then there is just enough net saving and investing to keep all capital goods growing in full proportion to the growth in primary labor. Then we have an equilibrium, a nice moving equilibrium with balanced growth. (If land will not grow at all, Malthus reminds us that this Eden must, in the absence of inventions, come to an end with ultimate stationary population.)

[3] Without risk the problem of placing my assets is easy. I put all my wealth in Bank A if it offers me $5\frac{3}{4}$ per cent while Bank B offers only 5 per cent. I put all my wealth in building stores or tools if these projects offer more than Bank A's $5\frac{3}{4}$ per cent. So long as I know I can get any safe positive interest return, I hoard no money, keeping only minimal balances for transaction purposes. Without any risks, so long as interest yields remain positive, we'd never run out of investment opportunities and into unemployment problems on this account.

With risk, if I obey the law of diminishing marginal utility of Chapter 22, the Appendix of Chapter 21 showed that I shall avoid gambling and want insurance (since a gain in my wealth will be worth less to me than an equivalent *dollar* loss). Now I refuse to put all my eggs in one basket: I put some money in both banks in case one should fail; I prefer $5,000 in General Motors and $5,000 in General Electric to $10,000 in either one alone; I buy many independent stocks for my

While this pessimistic possibility may not now be at hand, a prudent society has to keep it in mind. And if that unhappy day should ever approach, more extensive remedial programs (such as insurance of loan risks or new institutions to provide venture capital) would have to be imaginatively explored.

MARKET CAPITALIZATION OF ASSETS EQUALS THEIR PRESENT DISCOUNTED VALUE

Here we can go beyond page 573's simple case of perpetual annuities to the general case. Under conditions of absolute certainty, anyone can borrow or lend as much as he wishes at the single competitive market rate of interest. Every asset must be yielding that same market rate of interest. This equality of yield results from the way competitors bid up or bid down the market price of any asset—whether it be a bond, stock, patent, going business, corner lot, or any earning stream of net rentals whatsoever.

What exactly is the formula for the capitalized market value of *any* asset?

Under absolute certainty, every asset will be capitalized *by the price bids of buyers and sellers* in the market place at the *present discounted value* of all its future net receipts. These dollar receipts cannot simply be added up regardless of the date when they are received. The farther off in the future a given dollar receipt is, the less it is worth today. Why?

Because the positive market rate of interest means that all future payments must be *discounted*. A building far off looks tiny because of spatial perspective. The interest rate produces a similar shrinking of time perspective. Even if I knew you would pay $1 to my heirs 999 years from now, I should be foolish to advance you more than a cent today. To see why, let us review the arithmetic of this discounting process.

At 6 per cent interest I can set aside about 94 cents today, and it will grow to $1 within the year. Hence, the *present discounted value* of $1 payable a year from

Future dollar receipts are discounted to get their present value:

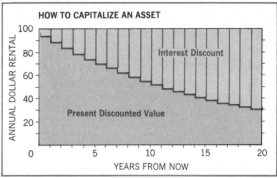

FIG. 30-4. The present value of a machine giving net annual rentals of $100 for 20 years (with interest rate prescribed at 6 per cent) is shown by the lower area. The upper area has been discounted away. (Show that raising the interest rate depresses the market price of an asset such as a machine or bond. It does so by enlarging the gold discount area subtracted.)

now is today only 94 cents (or to be exact, $100/1.06 = 94\frac{36}{106}$ cents). The present discounted value of $1 payable in 2 years' time is only about 89 cents, or $\$1/(1.06)^2$. Similarly, any tables of compound interest will show how to compute present discounted values.[4]

The way to arrive at any asset's present discounted value is straightforward. Let each dollar stand on its own feet; evaluate the present worth of each part of the stream of future receipts, giving due allowance for the discounting required by its payment date. Then simply *add together* all these separate present discounted values. Thus we have arrived at the asset's capitalized market value, or what is called its "present discounted value."

Figure 30-4 shows this graphically for a machine that earns steady net annual rentals of $100 over a 20-year period and has no scrap value at the end. Its present value is not $2,000, but only $1,147. Note how

---

portfolio; I particularly buy both war and peace stocks so as to be hedged against the worst that can happen. For safety's sake I always hold some idle cash even though it pays no interest. When the pure interest rate is below 2 per cent, I might just as soon hoard cash equal to a large fraction of my wealth or just as soon hold less. This is why Part Two's problem of great unemployment can persist—When a low investment schedule intersects the saving schedule at a point of low-employment NNP, and with profit and interest rates already at their bottom, there is relatively little that conventional banking policy can do in such unlucky times. Then we thank Providence for fiscal policy!

---

[4] The general rule for present discounted values is the following: To figure out the value today of $1 payable t years from now, ask yourself how much must be invested today at compound interest to grow into $1 at the end of t years. Now we know that at 6 per cent compound interest any principal grows in t years proportionally to $(1 + 0.06)^t$. Hence, we need only invert this expression to arrive at the final answer. Therefore the *present discounted value* of $1 payable t years from now is only $\$1/(1 + 0.06)^t$. What if the interest rate were 8 per cent per annum?

much the later dollar earnings are scaled down or discounted because of the time perspective we have been talking about. The total area remaining *after* discounting (the blue-shaded area) represents the total of the machine's *present discounted value*—its capitalized market value.[5]

Acting to maximize present discounted value Our formula tells us how to write down on our balance sheets the value of any asset once we know how that asset will be used. But note that an asset's future receipts usually depend on our business decisions: Shall we use a truck 8 or 9 years? Shall we overhaul it once a month or once a year? Shall we replace it with a cheap nondurable truck or an expensive durable one?

[5]Can you now verify our V = N/i perpetuity formula? In high school algebra we learn to sum a convergent geometric progression

$$1 + K + K^2 + \cdots = \frac{1}{1 - K}$$

for K any fraction less than 1. If you set $K = \dfrac{1}{1 + i}$, you can with a little work verify our capitalization formula for a permanent income stream: write out *all* the discounted terms

$$\frac{\$N}{1 + i} + \frac{\$N}{(1 + i)^2} + \cdots$$

$$= -\$N + \$N \left\{ 1 + \frac{1}{1 + i} + \left(\frac{1}{1 + i}\right)^2 + \cdots \right\}$$

$$= -\$N + \$N \frac{1}{1 - \dfrac{1}{1 + i}} = \frac{\$N}{i} \quad \text{[QED]}$$

But note that common-sense economics gives us an equally convincing proof: At interest i, N/i is the only sum *whose earnings will exactly match the $N per year of income.*

(A FINE POINT: Sometimes you cannot be sure just which of two machines is the more "durable" one that will be brought into use at a lower interest rate. Suppose Machine A yields $100 of output one period from now and $132 of output three periods from now. Let Machine B yield $230 units of output two periods from now, and let it cost the same as A. Which is more durable? More capital-intensive? We can't say. At low rates of interest, present discounted value or *PDV* of A exceeds *PDV* of B, since 100 + 132 > 230. At very high rates of interest, *PDV* of A exceeds *PDV* of B, since the second and third periods' outputs are discounted away to almost nothing. But at intermediate interest rates, between 10 and 20 per cent per period, calculation shows *PDV* of B exceeds *PDV* of A, and B will be chosen. This "reswitching" phenomenon spoils any simple diminishing-returns story, as advanced treatises show.)

There is one golden rule for giving correct answers to all investment decisions:

Calculate the present discounted value resulting from each possible decision. Then always act so as to achieve the maximum present discounted value. That way you will have more wealth, to spend whenever and however you like.[6]

MONEY, INTEREST, AND PUBLIC POLICY

Our final brief task is to suggest how the classical theory of interest fits in with the modern macroeconomic theory of effective demand and money.

Do changes in the amount of money affect the interest rate?

If you believed that employment was always full and that changes in money always resulted via a strict "Quantity Theory" in proportional changes in *all* prices then interest rates would indeed be independent of monetary policy. This extreme classical version of neutral money is today believed by nobody to be applicable to short-run events. (Some economists would, as we saw earlier, grant it a measure of long-run validity even today: refer back to Chapter 15's discussion of the "crude quantity theory.")

In Part Two we saw that an alternative to holding earning assets is holding money as an asset. Suppose people make no change in their current propensities to save and consume out of a given income when faced by a given interest-rate structure. But suppose they do decrease their desire to hold cash. Then they bid for existing stocks, bonds, and titles to earning assets. This raises capital values and immediately *lowers interest rates;* it also may set capital to growing at a more rapid rate; but only after a time period of higher investment can the volume of real capital goods be appreciably increased. Unless offset by contractionary fiscal policy, all this will raise employment and/or expand wages and prices.

Note that the central bank can create exactly the same chain of events by engaging in expansionary monetary policies. (Recall from Chapter 17 the open-market operations, reserve-rate and discount-rate changes, ...)

[6]This rule shows that business decisions in an ideal capital market would be independent of the decider's *personal* consumption-saving time preference. Why? Because it is always better to be able to sell out now for a larger money sum than for a smaller sum, no matter in what time pattern *you* decide to spend on consumption. In imperfect markets, personal time preference may matter.

How do we reconcile this increase in investment that results from no change in personal thriftiness with classical notions? We do so by recognizing that moving interest downward and relaxing credit generally may raise employment and income and thereby increase achieved capital formation—thus sending us down capital's schedule of net productivity at a faster rate.

SYNTHESIS OF CLASSICAL THEORY OF INTEREST WITH THEORY OF INCOME DETERMINATION: REVIEW

The successful macroeconomic management referred to earlier shows how private and public thrift patterns interact. It shows that private thrift need no longer be feared lest it cause a depression and paradoxically abort itself. It deals with a well-running system that is kept near inflationless full employment by matching central bank and fiscal policies.

Thus, if we desire a high-investment full-employment condition, the central bank uses its "bag of tricks" to increase investment. Of course, given the community's private thrift patterns and technological-expectational investment patterns of the moment, we can stay at the full-employment level aimed at by the central bank only if Congress adopts a compensating fiscal policy.

What are the requirements of this compensating fiscal policy? Taxes and expenditure must be just contractionary enough to affect disposable incomes enough to cut the consumption propensity down to equality with full-employment product minus investment. (Describe what central bank and fiscal authorities must do to create full employment with high consumption, reversing all of the above steps.[7])

[7]See the Hicks-Hansen diagrams in Chapter 18's Appendix. We can be, and stay, at full employment by having contractionary fiscal policy shift the *IS* curve rightward while expansionary central bank policy shifts the *LM* curve rightward. (Can you show how to get a high-consumption low-investment full employment by reversing this prescription?)

SUMMARY TO APPENDIX

1   Technical opportunities to invest (to swap present consumption for future consumption goods) interact with people's subjective time preferences (about how much to consume or to add to the accumulated stocks of past capital formation) to determine the interest rate. As in all markets, *both* supply and demand factors interact.

2   Avoiding the highly useful device of homogeneous stock of physical capital, we can still have a complete interest theory along Fisher lines. The interest rate equals terms of trade at which we can get next year's consumption goods for today's—106 chocolates next year for 100 today means a real 6 per cent interest rate per annum.

3   The formula for capitalizing the asset value of a perpetual constant income can be extended when receipts are neither constant nor perpetual. Each dollar payable t years from now is worth only its "present discounted value" of $\$1/(1 + i)^t$. So for *any* net receipt stream (N_1, N_2, . . . , N_t, . . .),

$$PDV = \frac{N_1}{(1 + i)} + \frac{N_2}{(1 + i)^2} + \ldots + \frac{N_t}{(1 + i)^t} + \ldots$$

4   Under conditions involving no uncertainty and no technical innovations, if the community insisted on accumulating more and more capital, diminishing returns might finally force capital's net productivity and the interest rate indefinitely down toward zero. Under real-life conditions of great uncertainty, there is the possibility that the floor on risky returns would be considerably higher than the floor of zero return on risk-free loans. So we cannot rule out the pessimistic possibility of a future Day of Judgment, where the authorities would have to supplement the orthodox methods by which the central bank eases interest rates if they are to succeed in coaxing out the volume of job-creating investment needed to keep employment high or full. But that day seems remote for mixed economies of the 1970s.

5   The classical assumption that changes in the amount of money merely change the nominal price level and leave all relative prices, interest rates, and production and employment levels

unchanged is in need of drastic modification in today's world, where wages and other prices are sticky in the short run, where wages may be hard to get down even in the long run, *and where the degree of unemployment may vary considerably.*

Increases in money (or decreases in people's desire to hold idle money) will often bid up security prices, lower interest rates, raise investment, and expand money and/or real incomes.

6   But the classical analysis can be usefully applied if we make the New-Economics assumption that central bank and fiscal policies will be so meshed as to preserve stable high-employment levels without undue inflation. (The central bank, so to speak, sets interest to achieve the desired investment level, and the fiscal authorities regulate taxes and expenditures to validate the needed thrift. Recall Fig. 30-2. Of course, both policies are to be *simultaneously* applied.)

QUESTIONS FOR DISCUSSION

1   After the H-bomb was discovered, my time preference for present over future consumption increased. After having learned that my uncle will bequeath me a fortune a decade from now, the same happened. Was this rational? Thinking of a lobster dinner tonight, I offer you $6 on Saturday for $5 now. Is this irrational?

2   Two communities have the same technological production functions. Why might they show different interest-rate patterns in history?

3   Give reasons why lower interest rates might increase investment demand.

4   What might higher M do to interest? Why? What does higher income do? Explain why *independent* monetary and fiscal policies need not lead to full employment. Show that there is more than one investment rate compatible with full employment because of changing mix of policies.

5   *Extra credit problem:* If a doubling of i halves the *PDV* of a perpetuity, can you show that the truck in Fig. 30-4 will *less* than halve in capitalized value? (HINT: The perpetuity has a rectangle that goes on forever, with its blue area getting less and less. The truck lacks this infinite tail off to the right. Now the early year receipts get hardly changed in value at all, since (say) .96 is not much changed when it becomes .92. So the average change in all the truck's blue area is less than that for the perpetuity. By similar reasoning establish the rule: Interest changes have their biggest effects on *long-term* bonds; their least effects on *short-term* bonds—whose principal will be repaid soon and is therefore hardly affected by any discounting.

Review your understanding of the following concepts:

abstinence, impatience, waiting	interest rate and planning
opportunity to invest	uncertainty
present discounted value	technical progress
trade-off between today's c and tomorrow's	public policy and capital growth

Profits and Incentives

In addition to wages, interest, and rent, economists often talk about a fourth category of income: profit. Wages are the return to labor; interest the return to capital; rent the return to land. What is profit the return to?

The answer that economists give is a complex one. This chapter will show that the word "profits" has many different meanings in everyday usage. From these different possible meanings, the economist, after careful analysis, ends up relating the concept of profit to dynamic innovation and uncertainty-bearing, and to the problems of monopoly and incentives.

We shall first discuss the main notions of profit. The usual profit figures bandied about will not check with any of these, as we shall see. Then, after analyzing the main notions, we shall conclude the chapter with a summary of the role profit and loss play in the market pricing solution to society's problems WHAT, How, and FOR WHOM.

REPORTED PROFIT STATISTICS

When a United Nations or U.S. Department of Commerce statistician gives newspaper reporters a figure involving profits, what does he usually include?

Certainly he includes *corporation earnings*—whether they are paid out as dividends or retained as undistributed profits. (In some reports he includes and in some he excludes corporate profit taxes, and sometimes he "adjusts" corporate profits for changes in evaluation of inventories due to price-level changes. So you must be careful in using published statistics.) He may also give another figure that has the flavor of profits about it, namely, *income of unincorporated enterprises* (farmers, self-employed, doctors, partnerships, and so forth).

We understand how he arrived at such a statistical figure of profits for a corporation or unincorporated enterprise. From the sales revenue of the firm, he subtracted its costs:

cost of materials, wage payments to employees, bond interest, depreciation, land rents, and the rest. What is left goes into the figures as profit.

FIRST VIEW: PROFIT AS "IMPLICIT" FACTOR RETURNS

To the economist, such statistical profits are a hodgepodge of different elements. Obviously, part at least of reported profits is merely the return to the owners of the firm for the factors supplied *by them*. Thus, part may be the return to the personal work provided by the owners of the firm—by the farmer and his family, by the doctor, by the partners, or by corporate executives who also happen to be principal stockholders. Part may be the rent return on self-owned natural resource. Part may be the equivalent of interest on the owner's capital. (Recall Chapter 24's discussion, page 449.)

This shows us the first fact about profit:

Much of what is ordinarily called profit is really nothing but interest, rents, and wages under a different name. *Implicit* interest, *implicit* rent, and *implicit* wages are the names economists give to this part of profit, i.e., to the earnings of *self-used* factors.

SECOND VIEW: PROFIT AS THE REWARD TO ENTERPRISE AND INNOVATION

Suppose we lived in a dreamworld of perfect competition, where we could read the future perfectly from the palms of our hands and where no innovations were permitted to disturb the settled routine of things. Then the economist says there would really be no profits at all! Here is what he means.

The statistician might still be reporting some profit figures to the press; but we know that, under these ideal equilibrium conditions, the *implicit returns* to the labor and property supplied by owners *would exactly swallow up all the profits reported*. Why? Because owners would hire out their factors on the market if they did not get equal rewards from using them in their own businesses. And because people who previously were hiring out their labor and property services would soon go into business for themselves if they knew they could earn more in that way.

Perfectly free entry of numerous competitors would, in a static world of perfect knowledge, bring price down to cost and squeeze out all profits above and beyond competitive wages, interest, and rent.[1]

We do not live in such a dreamworld. We never shall. In real life somebody must act as boss to decide how a business shall be run. Competition is never "perfectly perfect." Somebody must peer into the future to guess the demand for shoelaces or what will be the price of wheat. And in the world as we know it, there is a chance for a man with a brand-new idea to invent a revolutionary machine or a softer soft drink—to promote a new product or find a way to lower costs on an old one.

Let us call the man who does any of these things an *entrepreneur*, or *innovator*. Although it is hard to draw the line, let us distinguish him from the bureaucratic executive or

---

[1]If people like running their own business, they may gladly take lower implicit wages. If, by contrast, people dislike having to boss other people and if it is tiring to take responsibility for management decisions, then management wages may have to be higher.

manager who simply keeps an established business running. Many economists—such as the late Joseph Schumpeter, Austrian-born economist who taught at Harvard—do not think of the wages of management as profit: they think of the wages of management as wages—implicit or explicit, and high as they may be in the competitive market for gifted managers. But they think of *profit as the return to innovators, or entrepreneurs.*

Today it is easier for us to understand this distinction than it used to be half a century ago. We are all acquainted with huge corporations run by managers who own less than 1 per cent of the common stock. Although these executives run the business, they are paid wages much like anybody else. Management of this type is a skill not different in kind from other skills, such as being able to keep books or supervise production. People who possess this skill are bid for in the market place, and like any other factor, they move into those jobs where they will receive the highest wages.

The innovator is different. Though he may not always succeed, he is trying to carry out new activities. He is the man with vision, originality, and daring. He may not be the scientist who invents the new process, but he is the one who successfully introduces it. Maxwell developed the scientific theory of radio waves, Hertz discovered them experimentally, but Marconi and Sarnoff made them commercially profitable. On the other hand, De Forest, who discovered the triode tube, also sought to put his inventions to commercial use; yet he went broke a number of times and on each occasion disappointed the hopes of investors who had put money into his enterprises. Many try; a few succeed.[2]

The dollars earned by the successful innovators are defined by some economists—like Schumpeter—as profit. Usually, these profit earnings are temporary and are finally competed out of existence by rivals and imitators. But as one source of innovational profits is disappearing, another is being born. So altogether, these innovational profits will continue to exist.

THIRD VIEW: RISK, UNCERTAINTY, AND PROFIT

If the future were perfectly certain, there would be no opportunity for a bright young man to come along with a revolutionary innovation; everything would already be known. This shows that innovators' profits are closely tied up with risk and uncertainty. Frank Knight, a famous University of Chicago economist of the last 50 years, has an important theory that *all true profit is linked with uncertainty.* Innovators' profits, discussed in the preceding section, represent one important category of uncertainty-induced profit.

A factual examination of the great fortunes of the past shows a strong luck element in many of them. Oil discoveries, fortunate patents, marketing and speculative successes are examples of the chance elements in a profit-and-loss system.

In examining any profit figures, we must always keep uncertainty and risk in mind. We saw in earlier chapters that some low-grade risky bonds may appear to be yielding 9 per cent at the same time that high-grade safe bonds yield only 5 per cent. But if

---

[2] Incidentally, the problem of innovation provides a partial defense of patents. Society deliberately gives a man a monopoly; this contrivance permits him artificially to keep something *partially* scarce. But society hopes the offered bribe of temporary monopoly will encourage the invention of things that would otherwise be 100 per cent scarce.

the chances are that 1 out of 20 low-grade issues will default on their principal in the coming year, then you are fooling yourself if you think that these bonds are a better buy. Actually, the extra 4 per cent may be no more than enough to cover the risk of default.

While people who buy lottery tickets face uncertainty, the promoter of the lottery faces no risk. He knows *he* will come out ahead. Similarly, a large insurance company may rely on mathematical laws of probability to reduce its relative riskiness. Why? Because the different risks tend to be canceled by each other if the numbers are large enough. To the extent that we can eliminate uncertainty by pooling and spreading risks, the problem of profits fails to arise. It arises only for the irreducible minimum of riskiness that remains.

In some years, the total losses may be greater than the total profits. Then risk bearers as a whole have paid out to labor, to capitalists, and to landowners more than those factors would have earned if the future had been certain. In another year, the algebraic total of Knight-defined profits may turn out to be positive—so that the factors of production have then received less than they would have if the future were certain. An important question is this:

Are risk bearers on the whole overly optimistic? As a class do they lose money and subsidize the other factors of production? Or are risk bearers as a class overly "pessimistic"—as claimed in most economics textbooks—so that profits represent a net positive payment for the service of risk bearing? Many economists think that businessmen on the whole act as if they dislike mere riskiness, and hence they must on the average be paid a positive premium or profit for shouldering risks.

Risk-premia as costs   All this means that for risky industries long-run costs of production must be high enough to include, along with wage and interest costs, *a positive profit premium* to compensate for aversion to risk and coax out the supply of risk bearing.

EXAMPLE: Wheat involves harvest risks due to weather. Production of synthetic rubber does not. Suppose both involve the same wage costs per unit; suppose both involve the same capital outlay per unit. Suppose capital in rubber pays a sure return of 10 per cent, but that in wheat there are even odds that on each dollar invested you double your money or lose half of it. Your average return is then $\frac{1}{2}(2.00) + \frac{1}{2}(.50) = 1.25$, or 25 per cent per year. The 15 per cent premium, over and above the safe 10 per cent interest return, is competitively needed profit; and at the intersection of the long-run dd and ss schedules of the wheat industry, such profit will be included as a cost that must be covered.

We summarize the notion of profit as the reward of risk bearing thus:

If people generally act like risk averters, feeling that the marginal utility of the dollars they gain is less than that of the dollars they lose, they will prefer smaller steady incomes to erratic incomes even when those average out to a higher figure. Therefore *economic activities that involve much uncertainty and risk*, which will fall on the people who engage in them, *will be forced by competitive entry and exit of risk takers to pay*, over the long run, a *positive profit premium to compensate for aversion to risk*. The yield on capital invested in such industries will involve, in addition to pure interest corresponding to safe investments, an extra element corresponding to positive profit.

FOURTH VIEW: PROFIT AS A "MONOPOLY RETURN"

We have noted three aspects of profit: (1) profit as *implicit* rents, wages, and interests; (2) profit as the temporary return to daring but unforeseen *innovations;* and (3) profit as the divergence—thrown up by the fact of *uncertainty*—between what people had *expected* to happen and what actually happened, tending to average out positive if people dislike risk and must be paid a positive cost premium to shoulder it.

If you point out the above to a person who feels vaguely critical toward profit, you may confuse him and make him uncertain as to what it is that he is against. His hazy notion of a capitalist as a fat man with a penchant for arithmetic, who somehow exploits the rest of the community, calls attention to a fourth possible meaning of profit, namely, *profit as the earnings of monopoly.* Like most people, he may have an exaggerated notion of how much of each dollar spent on an automobile or a pork chop goes to profit receivers—according to any of our definitions. Most likely, he thinks that about 50 per cent of each dollar goes to wealthy monopolists; the prosaic truth is that, even in terms of the catchall statistical definition, corporate profits after taxes are less than *one-fifth* of corporations' wage payrolls (even after personal taxes).

Perfect competition redefined   Still, to be objective we must not close our eyes to this fact: In the world as we know it, competition is not "perfect" as rigorously defined by the economist. Some elements of monopolistic imperfections do certainly exist. Perfect competition means that each seller has *absolutely no control* over price; it means that his demand curve is perfectly horizontal and *infinitely* elastic; it means that no person is able to control any significant fraction of the total of any category of productive resource.

We have seen in Chapter 25 and elsewhere that perfect competition is a far cry from the real world. Most firms, outside farming, can raise or lower their prices without losing or gaining *all* the customers in the market. Instead, their demand curves are somewhat sloped, and there is a discrepancy between price and marginal revenue. Most markets are imperfectly competitive—a blend of competition and monopoly. (So common a condition is by no means necessarily illegal or immoral, but, as already seen, competitive imperfections have distorting effects on What, How, and For Whom.)

Now let us return to the fourth view of profits. When we examine the ownership of productive factors, we see that no two factors are quite alike. Your abilities as a worker and those of your neighbor are somewhat different. If we define your precise pattern of abilities as a separate factor of production, then we must admit that you do own and control an appreciable fraction of the total of that unique factor of production—100 per cent, in fact. Or you may be the sole owner of the patent to a particular process, or own the only site where the river narrows down to its most suitable place for a bridge. Or there may be no acre of Iowa land quite like yours.

Let us see how this ties in with imperfect competition. Your neighbors are a little different from you, certainly. But probably they are enough like you that the hourly wage rate for your services would not be appreciably higher even if you *withheld* some from the market. You really do not possess any appreciable monopoly power because the demand for the factor you own is for practical purposes infinitely elastic.

The same is true of your acre of good Iowa cornland. If you let half of it stand idle, the price of corn would not be affected; and the derived price for each acre of your land would be unchanged, even though you and your family know that there is really no other farmstead quite like it.

And note this: If the land is sufficiently fertile, you will, of course, be making a fine living off your farm. Perhaps you may even be in the top 2 per cent of the income distribution. Even though competition is perfect, this rent return to the land you own *cannot* be competed away by rival farmers. As long as the Good Lord made only a limited amount of fertile Iowa farmland, it will earn a rent for its owner—regardless of how he originally acquired title to the land. *Competitively determined rents are the results of a natural scarcity.* They yield a "surplus" but not a pure profit.[3]

"CONTRIVED SCARCITIES" VERSUS "NATURAL SCARCITIES"

It is quite a different matter if the demand for one of your factors of production is negatively inclined rather than infinitely elastic. (Let us review what this means: It means that, when you raise your price, you still can sell *some* of your factor; this is the sense in which you have some monopoly control over price.) If you are the sole owner of an important patent, it will pay you to charge a price so as to limit its use. If audiences swoon to your singing as to nobody else's, then you will have to remember that the more you sing, the lower will be the price the customers will pay for your singing. If you own the best site for a bridge, then you must be careful not to sell anyone else the lot next to it; otherwise he will be able to offer the bridge builders a site nearly as good as yours, and this will limit the dollars you can derive from yours. Thus, part of the rent you earn on Nature's bridge site has a monopoly element in it by virtue of your withholding its use for fear of spoiling your dollar market.

What does all this add up to? It means that, *as soon as there is an appreciable deviation from perfect competition, it will pay you to take account of the fact that you will spoil the market the more you offer of your factor.*

Any prudent firm takes account of the loss on all previous units resulting when it sells an extra unit of product, and it is its marginal revenue—lower than price because of the loss on previous units—which a prudent firm concentrates on. Again with you as the owner of a factor: you are interested in the *marginal,* or *extra, revenue* that the factor brings you. You will not withhold all the factor from the market—that would bring you in *no* revenue at all. Nor will you provide so much of the factor that it becomes a free good and brings in no revenue. As a quasi-monopolist, or imperfect competitor, what should you do? You will withhold just as much of that service as will bring its marginal revenue down to zero.[4]

[3] If there is great inequality in the distribution of ownership of factors of production, then even under the most perfect competition (where pure profit is zero) there can still result a very rich, possibly idle, minority of plutocrats surrounded by masses of lower-income people. Recall Chapter 27's discussion of exploitation, pages 522–523.
[4] Of course, there may be some discomfort to you in rendering the service, or you may have the opportunity of selling the service in some other market—as in the case where you could use your bridge

Our principle is this: *Under imperfect competition, it pays people to limit the supply of their factors somewhat.* By definition, natural scarcities are such that nothing can be done about them. But under imperfect competition, we encounter in addition so-called "contrived scarcities."

MONOPOLY EARNINGS AS THE RETURN TO "CONTRIVED SCARCITIES"

Hence, the fourth view of profits as a monopoly return is often reformulated in the economics textbooks to read as follows:

Part of what is called profit is the return to a contrived or artificial scarcity. **This return takes the form of rent, wages, or interest, depending on the nature of the factor in question and on the contractual relations set up to handle the particular situation. (For example, an investor may buy the bridge-site land at the full capitalized value of its monopoly earning power. To him, the return will seem to be interest.) So monopoly profits are inextricably tied up with wages, interest, and rent.**

Wherever contrived scarcities exist, they distort the optimum pattern of resource use. They may also create high earnings for the people involved. But high earnings do not always follow. Thus, under imperfect or monopolistic competition, there may be many taxicabs or grocery stores. Each owner may have a sloping demand curve and may be setting a price in excess of marginal cost. Yet there may be so many imperfect competitors that none of them is earning more than he could get in a perfectly competitive industry. Wiping out the imperfections and illegally contrived scarcities might improve the pattern of production, but it still might or might not have much effect on relative distribution of income (see the Chamberlinian Fig. 26-3, page 493).

ETHICAL ATTITUDES TOWARD PROFITS

Any sampling of public opinion shows some hostility toward profit. A statistician recently asked a random sample of businessmen if they "tried to maximize their profit." To a man, they all denied this firmly, perhaps because they pictured a profit maximizer as some kind of chiseling extortionist or miser. But then the investigator asked the same businessmen whether they thought any change in their present price policies could be counted on to make them better off in the long run. To a man, they all replied that they were already doing as well as they could hope to do.

It is misleading to talk about "a profit system." Ours is a *profit-and-loss* system. Profits are the carrots held out as an incentive to efficiency, and losses are the kicks that penalize using inefficient methods or devoting resources to uses not desired by spending consumers. This metaphor of carrots and kicks is ancient, but apt.

Within the framework of law and custom—where it is both illegal and uncustomary to put sand in sugar—what does the pursuit of profit mean? It means that the businessman,

---

site to grow corn. In these cases, you will obviously equate marginal revenue to some defined positive marginal *cost* rather than to zero.

like anybody else, is trying to get as much as he can for the resources at his disposal. (This is not different from what a worker is doing when he changes occupations or joins a union.) If competition is perfect, the businessman will end up with no *excess profits*. If competition worked perfectly, the attempt by all to reap excess profits would result in none succeeding. Competitors would have to run hard in order to stay in the same place! This is a paradox, but it is true nonetheless.

Would the competitive disappearance of profits mean that the businessman's land, acumen, sweat, and financing would go without reward? No, certainly not. Even under perfect competition, his factors would earn wages, interest, and rent. *Much of the hostility toward profit is really hostility toward the extremes of inequality in the distribution of money income that comes from unequal factor ownership;* this should be kept distinct from hostility toward profit created by imperfections of competition.

THE IMMEASURABILITY OF "PROFIT": TAX EFFECTS

How large are these four different categories of profit? We have no way of knowing. It would be nice if we could say that so many billion dollars of the reported total of profit is implicit wages, so many billions implicit interest, and so many billions implicit rents and, of the remainder, so much is innovator's profit and so much is the algebraic total due to uncertainty generally. It would be nice, too, if we could divide the total of all factor incomes into two separate parts: (1) the return to so-called "contrived scarcities" and (2) the competitive rent return to so-called "natural scarcities."

But probably we shall never be able to do this with precision. And what good would it do us if we could? Well, for one thing, some reformers believe that, if only Congress could easily identify every situation of an illegally contrived scarcity, it might act to bring about a more efficient use of resources. Or some citizens may think that, if Congress could identify the temporary profits due to innovation, it might try to tax them more heavily. And some may agitate for reversal of the present light treatment of capital gains[5] and propose that Congress tax the profits arising from luck and uncertainty more heavily than it taxes ordinary income.

Taxing profits   Since many people think of profits as an unnecessary surplus not really needed as an incentive for production or as a deserving reward, governments often seek to tax profits particularly heavily. Thus, during war emergencies an excess-profits tax is

---

[5] Thus, a movie star borrows from a bank to drill for oil; he knows his interest will be paid 70 cents on the dollar by the government through his tax savings; he knows he can deduct his intangible drilling expenses on the same 30-to-70 cent basis; he knows too that when he finds oil, he can sell it and pay only 25 per cent long-term capital-gains tax—or, holding on to the successful oil well, he can collect tax-free 20+ per cent oil-depletion allowance. (WARNING: Tax loopholes change constantly.) A 1953 Harvard Business School study suggests that the rich men it examined were able to keep their tax rates down to 50 per cent on the average, and that taxes pushed some toward venturesome investment. "Appreciation-minded investors . . . may have been so stimulated by the tax structure to seek out investments offering unusually large capital gains potentialities, such as promising new ventures, as actually to increase the flow of capital to such situations." J. K. Butters, L. E. Thompson, L. L. Bollinger, *Effects of Taxation: Investment by Individuals.*

often passed. (In World War II, and again during the Korean war of the 1950s, corporate earnings were taxed at rates much, much, much higher than 50 per cent.)

Chapter 28 showed that in some cases of inelastically supplied productive factors, such as Henry George's unearned Ricardian land rent, all the return is indeed a surplus. But in most cases of a trillion-dollar GNP, we are quite unable to identify, say, $200 billion as a taxable surplus and $800 billion as needed incentive payments. Only occasionally, as with mines and oil wells or with lucrative franchises to own TV stations or filling stations on toll roads, can the government appropriate by taxes a "monopoly" return.

As always, when seeking greater equality of income by redistributive taxation, some costs in the form of distortions must be borne.

A SERMON ON PROFIT AND WHAT, HOW, AND FOR WHOM

Back in Chapter 3 we surveyed how a price system helps solve society's basic problem of WHAT, HOW, and FOR WHOM. In Part Three we studied the tools of supply and demand that determine competitive market price. And we examined important effects of monopolistic imperfections of competition. The case for and against profit should be ruthlessly examined prior to the next chapter's complete review, in order to summarize the role of profit and loss in the over-all pricing process.

1. Each person seeks his own advantage. Workers seek highest wages; landlords, highest rents; capitalists, highest interest returns. Some of these factor returns will be implicit returns. Still other returns may arise from innovation and/or uncertainty, and for those reasons they may be called profit.

2. In the most general sense, profit seeking is simply seeking of self-advantage. Does this all lead to a jungle—"red in tooth and claw," and chaotic? Not if there are complete checks and balances. These checks and balances are most complete if competition is perfect; incomplete, if it is imperfect. Adam Smith's Invisible Hand cannot be counted on under monopolistically imperfect competition.

3. Where competition is perfect, or nearly so, there results a pattern of order, of efficiency. But not, mind you, any proven condition of utopia, with the poor become prosperous and the rich brought down near the mean.

Of course, shirkers get low incomes. And earnest people, born stupid and with weak muscles, also get low incomes for all their earnestness. Smart go-getters get high incomes. Highly intelligent altruists, who seek the well-being of other people, themselves get low incomes. Smart girls, born of smart and lucky fathers, get high incomes. Stupid girls, born of smart and lucky fathers, get high incomes. Those who get a good education from five to twenty, or four to twelve, stand to gain at the expense of those who do not. Without deliberate legislative interferences, the Lorenz curves of income distribution will record persistent patterns of inequality subject only to slow (and unpredictable) drift.

4. Profits and losses signal the advantages of activities. When a man is doing what some buyers in society want, he finds his wage or profit return rising. So he keeps on doing this. If he overdoes it, he gets penalized. Or, through no fault of his own, he gets penalized when someone better comes along. He may then get kicked into the next best thing for him to do.

Profit as a coordinating device   Where knowledge is imperfect, a man may make money by correctly guessing the future. If he thinks wheat will be scarce in Kansas, he ships wheat there; or grows more wheat there; or makes a bet about wheat's scarcity on the board of trade, and by making this bet may activate someone else to grow more wheat, eat less, or ship more—or he may just gain from another bettor.

In a free pricing system, each man may use his initiative to create a new product or process. If his guess about the future is wrong, he stands to lose. And so do all the people who guessed that he was right—his workers who gave up other jobs, his capitalist backers, and so forth. If he turns out right, he strikes it rich; and his rival may go to the poorhouse. Any entrenched way of doing things can, under the freest competition, be bested and changed.

Profits and high factor returns are the bait, the carrots dangled before us enterprising donkeys. Losses are our penalty kicks. Profits go to those who have been efficient in the past—efficient in making things, in selling things, in foreseeing things. Through profits, society is giving the command over new ventures to those who have piled up a record of success.

To understand this last point, imagine a bureaucratic board that awards money to people who apply to it for new projects. If a man was very successful in his last five projects, the board is likely to act favorably on his new application. Well, profits that a man with high innovating abilities has piled up from the past automatically give him the go-ahead signal in his future enterprises. (But in life, and in the case of the bureaucratic board, how do you get your first start?) The apologist for profits sums up his case:

Profits are the report card of the past, the incentive gold star for the future, and also the grubstake for new ventures.

5. Under perfect competition a man could get ahead only by doing things of value to himself or someone else. With knowledge perfect, he could not spread lies about fake uranium mines and make money that way or from false advertising claims. A perfect competitor would not cut down on his output in equating marginal revenue to marginal cost ($MR = MC$). Instead he would have no control over market price and would be doing what the utopian Invisible Hand says everyone has to do if the pricing system is to be 100 per cent efficient; namely, he would be equating price to marginal cost ($P = MC$). And he could not be making monopoly profits from contrived scarcity, because under perfect competition there are no monopoly positions.

And if a pricing system were really utopianly perfect in its working, no activity would be pouring smoke into the air without being made to share the cost that such smoke imposes on the rest of the community. No one would refuse to do basic research for fear that he could never tap its full advantage to society and thereby recover his own private research costs. All "external" benefits or costs connected with every activity would be correctly counted in. So when each maximized his own advantage, the checks and balances of perfect pricing would ensure that the benefit of all with money votes was being efficiently achieved.

6. The above remarks show that you would be wrong to say: The trouble with perfect competition is that it has never been tried. For could it ever be tried? Can we institute perfection? Monopoly aside, can we banish "external effects"? Obviously, no one can

institute perfection. And obviously, no one can identify the existing world with perfect competition, or identify a government-do-nothing world of laissez faire with perfect competition.

To the degree that public action can (1) lessen monopolistic imperfections, (2) increase imperfect knowledge and (3) bring total social benefits and costs into closer alignment with private benefits and costs—to this degree will there be a creative economic role for the state worth the costs involved.

7. Where a democracy does not like the For Whom pattern that results from laissez faire, it puts in tax changes, school and other expenditures, fiats, and subsidies to change the pattern. This helps some incomes, hurts others.

These redistributions are acquired at a cost. What cost? The cost of distortions of incentives, distortions which somewhat lessen the efficiency of the most efficient market system. There are costs, too, in tax collection and transfer. If the citizenry believes in notions of equity and greater equality of opportunity and incomes, it will knowingly incur such costs up to a margin.

Our sermon on pricing is over. Taking into account the real world as we know it, students of the modern economy realize why, revolutions aside, it has to be—from its very nature—a mixed economy. Market pricing must carry most of the burden of solving society's What, How, and For Whom. But constructive public policies are needed to keep the system competitive and provide the favorable environment in which private initiative can achieve the common good.

SUMMARY

1 Profit is a highly miscellaneous category. In national-income statistics, it is the total of lumped-together corporate earnings and the income of unincorporated enterprises. But economically we must distinguish four profit concepts.

2 Much of what is called profit is really *implicit* interest, rent, and wages payable for the productive factors provided by the owners of the business.

3 The special category of *high temporary earnings resulting from innovation* is often termed profit by many economists. Routine management earns wages, they say, but profit may accrue to genuine entrepreneurship.

4 *Uncertainty* is the all-pervading fact of life. It makes innovation possible and also creates positive and negative divergences between what factors expect to earn and what they actually end up earning. Pure luck determines much of the dispersion of incomes under free private enterprise. Knight and other economists define profit and loss as the *unforeseeable discrepancies created by uncertainty.* If people are generally averse to risk and erratic returns and resist being overoptimistic, a positive premium of profit will be required to coax out their limited supply of risk bearing. Goods involving risks in their production will have to be priced to cover sweat costs of labor, abstinence costs of capital, and risk-premium costs of uncertainty (i.e., will cover wages, interest, and "profits").

5   Still another definition of profit is the return accruing as the result of some kind of monopoly position. This concept is sometimes varied to describe profit as part of the return resulting from a "contrived or artificial scarcity."

6   The taxation of any of these categories of profit can be expected to have definite repercussions, some undesirable from any viewpoint. A fifth notion of profit as *an identifiable and taxable surplus rather than incentive payment* is oversimple. If the public wishes, it can use the tax system to modify the distribution of opportunity and living standards, facing up to the costs involved and deeming them worth the improvement gained.

7   Profit or advantage seeking does, under perfectly-competitive pricing conditions, lead to efficient How. If the distribution of initial wealth, abilities, and opportunities were made ethically optimal (and were continually adjusted to changing relative prices), and if there were no externalities or monopolistic imperfections of technology and markets, then the checks and balances of perfect competition could lead to a "best" solution of WHAT, HOW, and FOR WHOM.

   In a mixed economy, public policies try to provide needed correctives and checks and balances and try to help align social and private benefits—in short, try to promote the best environment within which private initiative can function.

QUESTIONS FOR DISCUSSION

1   Define "implicit" factor earnings. Contrast with other profit concepts.

2   Give cases of innovation; of risk taking. How will taxes affect them?

3   What is meant by perfect competition? By imperfect competition? Can you specify a monopoly profit that all will think bad? Can you identify natural and contrived scarcities?

4   Cornflakes factories face riskless and steady demand, so that unemployment insurance rates are low for them; machine-tool demand is unpredictably volatile, so that unemployment compensation rates are high for them in many states. Compare this pair of goods with the wheat and rubber example of the chapter. How will long-run competitive prices adjust to these risk patterns?

5   Discuss ethical and incentive aspects of taxing so-called "profits" or higher incomes generally. (E.g., corporate income tax favors bond finance. So?)

   Review your understanding of the following concepts:

reported statistics of profits	imperfections of competition, monopoly
implicit versus explicit factor returns	contrived versus natural scarcity
wages of management	rent and surplus, incentive payments
reward for risk taking	initial and after-tax distribution of wealth
innovation, uncertainty	external effects, and divergence of private
probability, large-number of risks	and social benefit and cost
profit as premium for risk bearing	ethical questions and value judgments

Epilogue to Microeconomic Pricing

32

Truth can never be told
so as to be understood
and not be believed.
WILLIAM BLAKE

Parts Three and Four are now completed. We can now give a bird's-eye review of the broad principles of *value* and *distribution*.

SURVEY OF THE INTERDEPENDENT PRICING PROCESS

We have seen:

1. How competitive supply and demand operate in a *single* market, in both the short and long run.

2. How the relative marginal utility (or indifference) preferences of men lie behind their respective demand curves.

3. How marginal costs lie behind the competitive supply curves.

4. How the technical production function relating output to factor inputs lies behind the total and average cost curves, which have been minimized by the firm's demanding inputs until their marginal-physical-products are proportional to factor-prices.

5. How these marginal-physical-products and marginal-revenue-products, summed for all firms, provide the "derived demands for the factors."

6. How these derived demands for land, labor, or capital goods interact with their market supplies to determine factor-prices such as rent, wages, rentals, and so forth.

7. How primary resources like labor and land are used to make produced capital goods, which are in turn used in roundabout ways to increase society's final output; how this "net productivity of capital" is reflected in the rate of interest, which, in the absence of technical change, is generally subject to diminishing returns much as labor and land are subject to that law; and how competitive markets evaluate all assets at their "present discounted values," using interest yields to screen out best investments.

8. Finally, how pursuit of profit and avoidance of loss furnish the motive force behind the whole competitive process; how, paradoxically, under static conditions free

of uncertainty and innovational change, competitive profits (other than implicit factor returns and wages of management) would tend to zero; but how uncertainty brings income dispersion depending on luck, and how the persistence of risk coupled with a general aversion to risk taking, on the ground that dollar gains have less marginal utility than dollar losses, would lead to profit return as a systematic positive premium for risk bearing.

SIMULTANEOUS MUTUAL DETERMINATION

Notice how, in the listing of the eight steps above, each follows from the preceding one—from step 1 to step 2 and then step 3, until finally we come to step 8. In the textbook chapters they follow in about the same order.

But in real life, which comes first? Is there any order and sequence, with prices being determined in single markets on Monday, consumers evaluating preferences on Tuesday, businessmen reckoning costs on Wednesday and marginal-products on Thursday? Obviously not. All these processes are going on at one and the same time.

That is not all. These different processes do not go on independently side by side, each in its own little groove, careful not to get in the way of the other. All the processes of supply and demand, of cost and preference, of factor productivity and demand—all these are really different aspects of one vast simultaneous *interdependent* process.

Thus, the supply curve for wheat given in the first chapter of Part Three is itself the resultant of the cost calculations given at the end of Part Three, of the production considerations given early in Part Four, and of the wage and rent and interest determinations given late in Part Four. Actually, you can take any one of the eight steps in the outline and draw arrows connecting it causally *with every other step.*

Figure 32-1 gives a summary picture of the interdependent system which economists call "general equilibrium." Recall the circular-flow diagram on national income (Fig. 10-1, page 170), showing plumbing pipes carrying dollars clockwise from business to families and from families to business. That gave what economists call the "aggregative," or "macroeconomic," picture of the nation's grand economic totals.

Now turn to Fig. 32-1. It also gives the circular flow of dollars. But this time we take a microscopic approach—what economists call the "microeconomic" picture. Now we do not talk about the grand total of factor incomes; instead we show derived demand by business for skilled labor, unskilled labor, good vineyard land, and every other factor of production. Nor do we speak of total consumption: we specify; we show the consumer's demand for coffee, tea, shoes, and each and every commodity or service.

Note that in the lower loop we have for each factor *both* a supply and a demand. (QUERY: Which of these schedules comes from business? Which from the public? Match blue and brown colors.) And in the upper loop, you see *both* a business supply and consuming-public demand for each good. (Match colors there.)

Thus, we can give an optimistic answer to the logical purist who poses the embarrassing question: "Your economic system isn't determinate until you have found conditions to determine a price *and* a quantity for each output and for each input. Do you have enough simultaneous conditions (or equations) to make your interdependent equilibrium system determinate?"

WHAT, HOW, and FOR WHOM is determined by general equilibrium pricing:

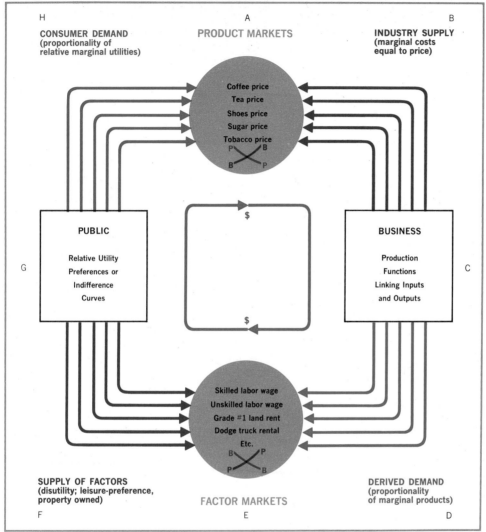

FIG. 32-1.   The clockwise money flow is broken up to show consumer demand meeting industry supply at *A* to determine equilibrium price and quantity of each good. Similarly, derived factor demands of business meet public's supply of factors at *E* to determine equilibrium factor-prices and amounts. (Interpret what is going on behind *B*, *D*, *F*, and *H*—and inside *C* and *G*—and compare this with the WHAT, HOW, and FOR WHOM of Fig. 3-1, on page 42.)

Fortunately, we can answer: "We do have for each output or input *both a supply and a demand condition*. So we can hope that the system will, by trial and error in the market place, finally settle down—if left undisturbed!—to a determinate competitive equilibrium."[1] And we can add: "The final competitive equilibrium is an 'efficient' one. Because

[1] Léon Walras, a French economist three-quarters of a century ago, is usually credited with the discovery of general equilibrium. But W. S. Jevons of England, C. Menger of Austria, Alfred Marshall of England, J. B. Clark of America, Vilfredo Pareto of Italy, and Knut Wicksell of Sweden all made significant contributions; and even in Adam Smith you can hunt out the germ of the idea of general equilibrium.

prices equal marginal costs, output is being maximized, inputs minimized; because prices reflect relative marginal utilities for each consumer, people who like apples are not being given oranges, etc. From so efficient a final point, you can no longer make everyone better off. You can help Joe only by hurting Tom."

Figure 32-1 is the final development of the figure on page 42 of Chapter 3, where we first asked how a price system goes about solving WHAT, How, and FOR WHOM. Only after mastering the tools of Parts Three and Four are we able to present this culmination of our original inquiry.

IMPERFECTIONS OF COMPETITION

This survey proceeded on the basis of some heroically abstract assumptions: no monopolies, no imperfections, no dynamic innovations or unforeseen disturbances, no governmental distortions, and so forth. Figure 32-1, therefore, is like the no-friction model of the physicist; it is not a picture of the real world as we know it when we step outside the library and rub elbows with real live breathing people on the street.

Yet, even though every engineer knows he must meet friction, he does find the frictionless model a valuable tool in throwing light on complicated reality. So it is with our ideal competitive model. In the long run, many imperfections turn out to be transient. *The competitive model, therefore, may suggest in its oversimple way some interesting hypotheses that turn out to have a measure of long-run validity!*

EXAMPLE: An invention cuts cost of aluminum; the competitive model says price will fall and pressure will be put on use and price of steel. The sophisticated student of imperfect competition says the real world is not perfectly competitive, so no hard-and-fast conclusion can be drawn. Still, bet with him that the prices will fall *in the long run*—and probably you will win his money. A sure thing? No, but often a good bet.

Even if we agree that the perfect-competition model does give some approximate descriptions of reality, we cannot be satisfied with such crude approximations. Forty years ago an economics textbook would have had to confine itself to the case of perfect competition, and let it go at that. Thanks to the pioneering work in the theory of imperfect and monopolistic competition over the last generation, economists now have the tools (marginal revenue, etc.) to analyze oligopoly, monopoly, differentiation of products of numerous sellers, collective bargaining, and various intermediate cases. (Recall Chapters 25 and 26.)

We have seen that prices are often inflexibly administered, changing rarely and subject only to minor hidden discounts, which is in contrast with the minute-to-minute volatility and year-to-year gyrations of competitive prices. We have seen that two workingmen may work in the same city at different wage rates for comparable work; that interference by a union with wage setting may correct a previous monopsony condition of unequal bargaining, or may increase the departure from the model of perfect competition. We have seen Chamberlinian cases where free entry may squeeze out profits while still leaving price above minimum average costs. We have seen that prejudice under laissez faire may lead to unequal employment opportunity and both social inefficiency and inequity.

There is no need, therefore, to warn against overemphasis on the elegant model of perfect competition as a close description of economic reality.

A WORD ON WELFARE ECONOMICS

Even if perfect competition were a poorer descriptive tool than it is, students of economics would still want to study it intensively and master its principles. This is so for a reason unconnected with mere description. The competitive model is extremely important in providing a bench mark for appraising the *efficiency* of an economic system. The Russians, the Chinese, the Indians, as well as the Swiss need to study its analytical principles.

For the most part in any science, scholars discuss what *is* and what will be under this or that situation. The task of positive description should be kept as free as is humanly possible from the taint of wishful thinking and ethical concern about what ought to be. Why? Because scientists are cold-blooded robots? No, rather because experience shows again and again that a more accurate job of positive description will be achieved if one tries to be objective. (Experience also shows that, try as we may, we humans never succeed in separating completely the objective and subjective aspects of a discipline. Indeed, the very choice of what scientists choose to measure, and the perspective from which they observe and measure it, and the reactions the observer produces in that which is observed —all these make the distinction between *is* and *ought*, between objective and subjective issues, at bottom a matter of degree rather than kind. Recall, for example, Chapter 1's bird-antelope paradox.)

The citizenry, unlike the specialist, is in the end most interested in problems of "norms," of what *ought* to be done, of policy rather than mere description. That citizenry is best served by the scientist who can give it the most accurate description of what is relevant, and of what the consequences of different policy actions will be.

Very briefly then, in this epilogue, let us again devote a few lines to implications for economic welfare that have been developed in Parts Three and Four.

Efficiency optimality   First, we have seen repeatedly that a regime of perfectly competitive pricing would have certain efficiency properties if conditions were really present for the maintenance of perfect competition. Therefore Adam Smith, in his talk about an Invisible Hand, which led the selfish actions of individuals toward so harmonious a final result, did have some point. Smith never could state or prove exactly what that point was, but modern economics can state this property of ideal competitive pricing:

Under perfectly perfect competition, where all prices end up equal to all marginal costs, where all factor-prices end up equal to values of marginal-products and all total costs are minimized, where the genuine desires and well-being of individuals are all represented by their marginal utilities as expressed in their dollar voting—*then* the resulting equilibrium has the efficiency property that "you can't make any one man better off without hurting some other man."

What does this mean exactly? It means that a planner could not come along with a slide rule and find a solution, different from the laissez faire one, which could improve the welfare of everyone.[2]

---

[2] If *A* is the competitive equilibrium, there is no point *B* the planner could devise which could be approved over *A* by a *unanimous* vote. Some would be hurt in going to *B*, some might gain; but the gainers could never find it worthwhile to give big enough bribes to win the losers over to approving the move to *B*. Graduate treatises call this a case of "Pareto optimality," named after Pareto's work at the turn of the century as elucidated in our time by Abram Bergson of Harvard University.

Arbitrary distribution of dollar votes What does it not mean? It does not mean that actual laissez faire, with the imperfections of competition that will go with it, leads to efficiency or necessarily even to a close approximation to efficiency. And inefficiency aside, it does not mean that the people who are deemed by various religious or ethical observers to be most worthy, most deserving, or most needy will necessarily get their ethically best share of goods and services.

Laissez faire perfect competition *could* lead to starving cripples; to malnourished children who grow up to produce malnourished children; to perpetuation of Lorenz curves of great inequality of incomes and wealth for generations or forever. Or, if the initial distribution of dollar-wealth votes, genetic abilities, conditioned motivations, and training happened to be appropriate, perfect competition might lead to a rather egalitarian society characterized by uniformity greater than might please many an aristocratic ethical tradition.

In short, Adam Smith, in the famous passage quoted on page 37, had no right to assert that an Invisible Hand channels individuals selfishly seeking their own interest into promoting the "public interest"—as these last two words might be defined by a variety of prominent ethical and religious notions of what constitutes the welfare of a nation. Smith has proved nothing of this kind, nor has any economist since 1776.

Redefining the Invisible Hand doctrine If Smith were alive today, he would agree with all this; and one ventures the guess, from his biography, that he would probably reword his doctrine pretty much along the following lines.

1. Only if abilities and *dollar-wealth votes were originally distributed in "an ethically optimal" manner*—and kept so distributed by nondistorting, nonmarket interventions—could even perfectly competitive pricing be counted on (*a*) to produce an efficient configuration of production out on society's production-possibility frontier (and not inside it), and (*b*) to give people what they really deem is best for them, in accordance with their dollar votes that now reflect equally significant social utility. If laissez faire were abandoned in favor of an ethically proper distribution of wealth and opportunity, then perfect-competition equilibrium could be used to attain optimally efficient and equitable organization of society.

2. Admittedly, *the demands of people in the market place sometimes do not reflect their true well-beings* as these would be interpreted by even the most tolerant and individualistic of ethical observers. (EXAMPLES: A dope addict's craving for opium even at the expense of his food or his children's food; a child's desire for a seventh lollipop; a diabetic's craving for sweets; a spendthrift's mortgaging his house for an advertised sports car.) As a pragmatist, were Smith alive today, he would say, "People are entitled to make their own mistakes in many matters, but it is arrogant to think that anyone who is not a minor or a lunatic is in every respect a sovereign will; as men conscious that we were born not perfect and as inhabitants of a post-Freudian world, we shall sparingly and for good cause want (with due process) democratically to place restrictions on our own behavior. So again, laissez faire perfect competition would not inevitably be the ideal."

Then, after emphasizing the need for tolerance and the virtues of freedom, Smith might strike a more technical note.

3. Where there are monopolistic imperfections that produce deviations from ideal competitive marginal-cost pricing—and in situations of strong increasing returns and decreasing costs, such deviations are practically inevitable—of course there is a prima facie case that laissez faire pricing is not efficient. Public scrutiny, to see whether democratic controls would make the situation better or worse, has to be presumed in such quasi-monopoly situations.

4. Finally, Smith would add that wherever there are "external economies and diseconomies" (such as were analyzed at the end of Chapter 24 and in the discussion of public versus private goods in Chapter 8), there is a prima facie case for study to see whether zoning laws, taxes or subsidies, and government expenditure and regulation should be initiated in some degree. Where the checks and balances of perfect competition are not operative, the Darwinian struggle for existence is not led by an Invisible Hand to any kind of an optimum. The creative role of government in economic life is vast in an interdependent crowded world.

CONCLUSION

The reader is warned that all the above issues of welfare economics can be given varying interpretations and can lead to controversial debate which cannot be presumed to be settleable within positive science. Conservatives may legitimately interpret the above principles in terms of their version of the good society. Middle-of-the-roaders may do the same for theirs. And radicals may call for small or large reforms of the present structure of a mixed economy by giving their interpretation of these principles. That means the reader may do so, too. Economic science arms one for the great debate.

The following Appendix gives in greater depth a view of the efficiency aspect of the system of interdependent economic pricing under capitalism or socialism.

APPENDIX: Review of Commodity and Factor Pricing: General Equilibrium and the Parable of Ideal Welfare Pricing

PARABLE OF UTOPIAN PRICING

Economists used to be twitted that their books always harp on Robinson Crusoe. True enough: we do find that the economic decisions of a single man furnish a dramatic way of simplifying our basic principles. But these days we have an even more dramatic device for illustrating the fundamental facts of economic life: we use the example of a fully collectivized society. This retains the same simplicity of ultimate decision making, but at the same time it involves the social interactions between people that the Crusoe model lacks. The con-

trast between such a model and our realistic everyday world is, of course, enormous. And therein lies its value. By examining the logic of such a model, we get new insight into the nature of our own pricing system.

Let us, therefore, examine how our economic analysis of pricing can be applied to a completely artificial planned society of the kind never seen in Russia or anywhere else. Call it Utopia or call it Hades. In analyzing the problem of pricing in a planned socialist state, we kill two birds with one stone:

1. We get one of the best possible reviews of the over-all working of a perfect *capitalistic* price system.

2. We get an introduction to "welfare economics," the study of what is considered right and wrong about any economic system. This depends, of course, upon ethical points of view, themselves necessarily a-scientific. But the economist, as a disinterested observer, may help to throw light on how successfully an economic system realizes any suggested ethical *goals*.

A DILEMMA FOR CENTRALIZED PLANNING

The earlier chapters of this book have shown how a system of market prices operates to solve the basic economic problems of WHAT, HOW, and FOR WHOM. To drive home what all this really means, try a mental experiment. Suppose you were given the job of making the blueprints for a completely planned economic system. How might you begin?

First, let us suppose you are interested in giving people what they want, not in telling them what they ought to want. Obviously, you cannot give them everything they want: land, labor, capital goods, and technological knowledge are limited in amount. So you must make compromises and choices.

You may say: This is merely a complicated mathematical problem, calling for the use of lots of high-powered electronic high-speed calculating machines. But remember that we shall have to deal with the millions of items that are to be found in department stores, with thousands of grades of productive factors, and with numerous individuals and families. The number of unknowns of the mathematical problem will be in the millions, and the number of steps to its solution in the billions of billions. No known set of computing machines can even begin to tackle such a problem.

You are stumped. And discouraged. Perhaps you will lower your sights and stop being a perfectionist. Instead of giving people exactly what they think they want, you may decide that there will be only a few types of, say, shoe styles and sizes, so that the calculation problem will be simplified. Or you may abandon individual freedom of choice and start to give people goods that *you* find it convenient to give them.

One thing is clear: If centralized planning means that one centralized person or committee must have in mind all the myriad intricacies of detail, then it is an impossible job to do with any efficiency. So you will naturally begin to experiment with various devices to *decentralize* the job. And quite probably you will end up by introducing a *pricing* system in many ways like that of capitalism.

How might such a system work?

PRICING IN A UTOPIAN STATE: CONSUMPTION GOODS PRICES

In your new society, the consumer will still have *freedom of choice* and will not have dictated to him the relative amounts of different commodities which he is to "enjoy." As in the capitalist system, each person will receive a sum of money or abstract purchasing power to spend among different commodities as he wishes. Thus, vegetarians will not have to eat meat, and those who most prefer meat will be able to do so.

How will relative prices between salmon and ham or any other consumers' goods be set by the socialist state? Generally speaking, prices will be set with the same double purpose as in a capitalist society: (1) just high enough to ration out the existing supplies of consumers' goods, so none are left over and none are short; and also (2) just high enough to cover the socially necessary extra costs of producing the goods in question—or, in technical terms, relative prices are to be set equal to relative "marginal utilities" and "marginal costs."

THE DISTRIBUTION OF INCOME

So far the process has worked much like the capitalistic system. Almost by definition, however, socialism means a society in which most land and capital goods or nonhuman resources of all kinds are owned collectively by society and not individually by people. In our society, an Astor who owns 500 parcels of New York City land, each of which produces $60,000 of net rents per year, will receive an income of $30 million per year—which may be 10,000 times what a night watchman is able to earn, and 2,000 times what the average skilled engineer can earn. In a society where most property is owned collectively rather than distributed with great inequality among different individuals, an important source of inequality of income would be absent.

Many people profess to hold the ethical and philosophical belief that different individuals' wants and needs are very much alike, and that the present market mechanism works inadequately because the rich are given so many more votes in the control of production than the poor—which makes the market demand for goods a faulty indicator of their true social worth. Such people with a relatively egalitarian philosophy will welcome a great reduction in the spread of incomes between the lowest 90 per cent of all families and the highest 10 per cent. They may argue that taking away $1,000 from a man with an income of $100,000 and giving it to a man with an income of

$2,000 will add to social well-being (by taking dollars from a place deemed low in marginal social utility to a place deemed higher). After the distribution of income between families has been determined correctly, according to society's fundamental (a-scientific) value judgments, then and only then will it be true that the dollars coming on the market will be valid indicators of the value of goods and services; and only then will they be serving to direct production into the proper channels and goods into the right hands. Hence, *lump-sum taxes and transfers will be used in Utopia to give ethically proper income distribution.* So goes the argument.

How is what is considered the proper ethical distribution of income to be achieved aside from the negative act of wiping out unduly high property owning and the appropriate lump-sum taxing of individuals?

Perfectionists have two answers: (1) in part by letting people get some of their income in the form of wages; but (2) in part by having these wages supplemented by receipt of a lump-sum *social dividend payment* or negative income tax. This cash payment in an egalitarian society might involve differences to compensate for numbers of children, age, health, and abilities acquired or inherited.

It is an ethical rather than a scientific question as to just how large, relatively, each person's final income ought to be. As a pure science, economics can concern itself only with the best means of attaining given ends; it cannot prescribe the ends themselves.

Indeed, if someone decided that he preferred a feudal-fascistic kind of society, in which all people with little black mustaches were to be given especially high incomes, a pathological economist could set up the pricing rules for him to follow to achieve his strange design best. He would be told to determine his social dividend payments to achieve the required optimal distribution of income, after which each dollar coming on the market could be regarded as correctly representing (that eccentric philosopher's) true social values.

The social dividend differs from a wage because it is to be given to every individual *regardless of his own efforts.* That is why it is called a "lump-sum" dividend or transfer.[1] (Any bonus based upon productivity or effort is to be treated as a wage.)

We have not yet seen how wages are to be determined, but before doing so, let us first turn to another important problem.

PRICING OF NONHUMAN PRODUCTIVE RESOURCES AND INTERMEDIATE GOODS

What should be the role of land and other nonhuman productive resources as an element of cost in such a utopia? Some people would say that such nonhuman resources should not enter into cost at all; that only human sweat and skill are the true source of all value; and that any extra charges based upon the cost of land or machinery represent a capitalistic surplus which the owners of property are able to squeeze out of the exploited laboring masses by virtue of the private monopoly of ownership of the means of production. We have seen that this view is the traditional "labor theory of value," of Karl Marx and John Locke. Learned scholars dispute over just what Marx meant by the "labor theory of value" and whether he meant it to apply to a socialist economy in the short or long run.

We need not enter into this dispute. However, it is important to note that, in its simple form, *the labor theory of value will lead to incorrect and inefficient use of both labor and nonlabor resources in even the most perfect socialist society.*

So long as any economic resource is limited in quantity—i.e., *scarce* rather than free—the socialist planners must give it a price and charge a rent for its use. This price need not, as in the case of the Astor millionaire under the capitalistic system, determine any individual's income. It can be a purely bookkeeping or accounting price (or so-called "shadow price") set up by the planners, rather than a market price. But there must be a price put upon the use of every such resource.

Why? First, we must price nonhuman resources to ensure that society is deciding How goods shall be produced in the best way, so that we really end up on the true production-possibility frontier of society and not somewhere inside it.[2] It would be absurd to get rid of the capitalistic system with its alleged wastes due to unemployment, and then, by stupid planning, end up far inside society's true production potentialities.

Related to the above point is the second need for all resources to be given a value if correct prices are to be charged for those final goods *that use up a great deal of scarce resources.* In other words, for society to

[1] If the state is providing public goods for the people which require greater use of resources than the state owns, most of the social dividends may have to be negative—lump-sum taxes rather than transfers.

[2] See Exercise 4 of Chapter 27's Appendix for geometric proof.

find itself in the best choice among all possible positions on the production-possibility frontier, we must price such consumption goods as food and clothing to reflect their true relative (extra or marginal) costs of using up *all* scarce resources. Otherwise, even with incomes equitably distributed, the free choice exerted by consumers on their dollar spending will not truly maximize their own and society's preferences, with utilities and costs properly balanced at the margin.

THE EXAMPLE OF LAND RENT

The foregoing two reasons may be hard to grasp. However, let us try to make the necessity for nonlabor pricing clear by considering a single land example. Suppose there are twins in a farming utopia. What if one were to produce wheat on an acre of good land, and the other were to produce less wheat by the same year's work on an acre of bad land. If they are identical twins, working equally hard, we would certainly have to agree that their wages ought to be the same.

Now, if wages were to be treated as the only cost, in accord with the simple labor theory of value, then the same price could not be charged for the two different outputs of wheat, even though the kernels of wheat were identical. The good-land wheat would have involved lower labor costs and will have to sell for less than the poor-land wheat.

This, of course, is absurd. A well-wishing social planner might try to get around the dilemma by charging the same price for both, losing money on the poor-land wheat and gaining on the other. Or what is almost the same thing, he might say, "To keep the costs of the two wheats the same, let us pay the twin on bad land lower wages; but then let us make the richer brother share his wages with the poorer."

Such a solution is not absurd, but it falls short of achieving the desired best results: maximum production and equal pay for equal human effort. In particular, *it fails to shift more labor onto the more productive land.*

The only correct procedure is to put an accounting price or rent tag on each land, with the good land having the higher tag. The prices of both kinds of wheat will be equal, because the land cost ("Ricardian rent") of the good-land wheat will be just enough higher than that of the poor-land wheat to make up the difference.

Most important of all, the socialist production manager must try to minimize the combined labor and land cost of producing each kind of wheat. If he does so according to the marginal-product principles dis-

cussed in Part Four, he will accomplish something undreamed of by the simple believer in the labor theory of value.

He will find it pays to work the good land more intensively, perhaps with the time of $1\frac{1}{2}$ men until the extra product there has been lowered by the law of diminishing returns so as to be just equal to the extra product of the $\frac{1}{2}$ man's time on the poor land. Only by putting a price upon inert sweatless land are we using it, and sweating breathing labor, most productively! The price or rent of land rises in order to ration its limited supply among the *best* uses.

Note, too, that the most finicky humanitarian will have nothing to complain of in our solution. By transferring labor from one acre to the other until labor's marginal productivity has been made equal, we get the largest possible total production of wheat.[3]

The two brothers are paid the same wages because they have worked equally hard. But their wages are not high enough to buy all the wheat, since part of the cost of the wheat has come from (bookkeeping) land-rent charges. However, the people through their government own the land equally. The land's return does not go to any property owner but is available to be distributed as a lump-sum social dividend to both brothers and to others according to their ethical deserts.

By putting a proper accounting price or rent on land, society has more consumption than was otherwise possible!

If we turn now to the production of more than one consumer good, it will be obvious that their cost prices must be made to reflect the amount of socially limited land and machinery which they each use up. Field crops like wheat require little labor and much land compared with garden crops like tomatoes. If we price each good on the basis of labor costs alone, wheat will sell for too little, and too much land will be forced out of tomato production. All will be worse off.

MARGINAL-COST PRICING

One last point concerning the final determination of a product's cost and price. After the costs of all neces-

[3] As earlier discussions of marginal productivity have shown, *total product will be at a maximum only when labor has been transferred from the land where its marginal-product is low to the good land where its marginal-product is high. Every such transfer must necessarily yield us extra product, until finally no further increases in output can result when the marginal-products have been equalized in the two uses.*

sary factors of production have been added together to arrive at total cost, the planning authorities must set their prices at the marginal cost of production. Or more accurately, the socialist managers of a plant must behave like a perfect competitor: they must disregard any influence that their own production might have on market price and must continue to produce extra units up to the point where the last little unit costs just as much as its selling price.

For many industries, such as railroads, where unit costs are constantly falling, setting marginal costs equal to price will imply that *full* average costs are not covered. In a noncapitalistic society the difference would be made up by an (accounting) lump-sum grant from the state; for if a railroad system is worth building, it is worth being utilized well.[4]

---

[4] The long-run question as to whether to build a railroad in the first place may involve an "all-or-none decision," which cannot be made step by step. In such a case, there must still be a balancing of the extra (or marginal) advantage and extra cost to society of the enterprise. But for such a big step, price is no longer a good indicator of total welfare, since—as we saw in Chapter 22—there is always an element of consumer's surplus in the total amount of goods a person consumes over what he has paid for them.

Figure 32-2 pictures a case where *dd*, which we assume reflects true marginal utilities to society, everywhere lies below

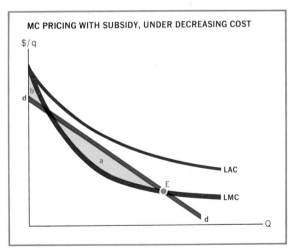

MC PRICING WITH SUBSIDY, UNDER DECREASING COST

FIG. 32-2.

decreasing long-run *AC*. So pricing at long-run *MC* can never recover full long-run social costs. Yet, with the *a* area a little larger than the *b* area, the total-utility area under *dd* is greater than the total-cost area under *LMC*. So society should produce at *E*, giving a lump-sum subsidy to cover the inevitable loss

SUMMARY OF RESOURCE PRICING

Correct social planning requires that all scarce resources, whether human labor or not, be given accounting prices at least. The final costs of consumer goods should include the sum total of *all* extra costs necessary to produce each good, or in short, should equal *marginal cost*. The demand for consumer goods is really an indirect demand for all productive resources, a demand which can be kept in proper check only by putting appropriate valuations on productive resources.

Otherwise, society's valuable nonhuman—and human!—resources will be incorrectly allocated and the market pricing of finished goods will not lead to maximum consumers' satisfaction. It is to be emphasized that the accounting prices of land and other nonhuman resources need not, in a socialist state, be part of the incomes of anyone. In the language of the visionary critic of private enterprise: no one is "exploited" by having a property owner skim off part of the final product. Instead, the contribution of capital and land to production is given to deserving people in the form of government goods and the algebraic *social dividend.*

THE ROLE OF THE INTEREST RATE IN UTOPIA

We have seen that the interest rate has an important function in a capitalistic, socialistic, or any other kind of economic system. Capital goods have a "net productivity." As long as resources can be invested for the present or the future, it will be necessary to make important decisions with respect to capital. Shall we apply present land and labor to the production of a corn crop this year or to apples 15 years from now? Shall we have grape juice today or wine 10 years hence? Shall we replace a worn-out loom with a new expensive one which yields its services over a period

---

or somehow getting people to pay more for their earlier units that yielded great consumer surplus. (EXAMPLES: A railroad line to a country region; a monorail for urban commuters.) If *dd* shifted down enough to make *a* < *b*, the whole project should be abandoned. Even if *dd* shifted up a bit, so that part of it lay above *LAC* and price could cover all costs, *P* still should be kept down to *LMC* for efficient pricing. (All this needs qualifications if dollars do not represent true and constant marginal utility and true social costs, as in a world of many monopolies and in making big decisions.) Also, taxing to finance the subsidy may involve some distortions: so we may have to settle for a second-best solution with *P* between *LMC* and *LAC*.

of 20 years or buy a cheap one that will last only 14 years? Every one of these questions can be answered only by using an interest rate to relate future and present economic values. Without such an interest rate, the existing stock of fixed and circulating capital cannot be devoted to its best uses; and whatever amount of national income society has decided to invest in capital formation cannot be embodied in the best form without such an interest rate.

The interest rate acts as a sieve or rationing device: all projects that can yield 10 per cent are undertaken before any projects that yield only 8 per cent.

It should be added that many economic writers on socialism do not think that the rate of interest should also determine—as it does in our economy, to some degree—the rate at which capital growth is to take place at the expense of current consumption. The decision as to how much should be saved would be determined by the state "in the light of national and social needs," and not by the "haphazard" notions of individuals with respect to the future. But the level of social saving and capital growth once having been determined, the interest rate must be used to allocate scarce "capital supplies" optimally and to determine the priority of alternative projects.[5]

WAGE RATES AND INCENTIVE PRICING

We must now return to the problem of how the utopian planners would set wage rates, and then we are done. If the amounts of labor of all kinds and of all skills were perfectly fixed, there would be no reason why labor should not be given accounting prices just like any other productive factor. Workers would receive no wages at all. They would then receive all the national income in the form of an enlarged *social dividend.*

However, if heterogeneous people are to be free to choose their own occupations and given the choice of working a little harder and longer in return for extra consumption goods, then it will be necessary to set up a system of *actual market wages* at which people can sell their services. These wage rates will be set just high enough to equate demand and supply.

Wages may differ depending upon how the irksomeness of the job affects voluntary labor supplied; and unlike now, the pleasanter jobs may then be lower paid, and the ditchdiggers or garbage collectors may

have to be higher paid to attract people into these jobs. Occupations that require much training and skill will receive high pay, but much of that pay may be spent by the state in providing the education necessary to acquire those skills. Piece rates might be used, and a worker with a 20 per cent higher productivity will be receiving higher (pretax and pre-social-dividend) wages. Workers will in every case be offered wages equal to their marginal, or extra, productivity.

Therefore, it is not necessarily true that all incomes will be at a dead level in the utopian society. They will differ somewhat as a result of two distinct factors: (1) society's appraisal of the "needs and worth" of different individuals and families—as reflected primarily in the size of the individuals' lump-sum *social dividends* —and (2) the need for wages to differ to provide incentives and to compensate people for extra disutility and effort. Incomes need not differ, however, because of inequality in the ownership and inheritance of property and genetic talents. Wage rents (like Babe Ruth's) could be heavily lump-sum–taxed, exactly like Henry George's surplus land rents.

SUMMARY OF UTOPIAN PRICING

1. A utopian system could make use of four different kinds of pricing: (a) consumer-goods prices, (b) wage and incentive rates, (c) accounting prices of intermediate goods or produced inputs, and (d) final lump-sum dividends (when positive, transfers; when negative, taxes). The first three prices would be determined by supply and demand.

2. To give people free choice among consumer goods, market prices would be set for such goods. Similarly, to provide freedom of choice of occupation, to give people incentives, and to provide compensation for differences between occupations, wage rates would get set to correspond to (marginal) productivities and disutilities.

3. Accounting prices would have to be set on all nonhuman productive resources to ration them in their best uses where their (relative) marginal productivities are equal and highest. Similarly, there would have to be a rate of interest to ration the existing and growing stock of capital among its best uses. Any consumption good would be produced up to the point where the full marginal cost of production (necessary to keep all resources from other uses and from leisure) is just equal to the price.[6]

[5]There is no logical reason why individuals who are willing to forgo present for future consumption should not be permitted to do such voluntary extra saving and receive an interest return equal to the net productivity of capital.

[6]The decentralized managers of industries could generally achieve this by seeking to maximize their net algebraic profits, measured in accounting points or actual dollars, but with *all* Ps taken as given parameters. (NOTE: Under cost

4. Lastly, the final distribution of income would be made to correspond to what society regards as the ideal distribution pattern by means of payment of a lump-sum social supplement or dividend to people, depending upon "need, wants, and deservingness," but not—like a wage—on effort or performance. In Utopia, it might be felt that a much more nearly equal distribution of income will be necessary before the dollar votes of consumers can be expected to reflect true social preferences. However, this is an a-scientific, ethical question; and a misanthrope could use the same economic principles to make blueprints for an *in*egalitarian utopia.

5. None of these processes except the last requires detailed *comprehensive planning by a central agency.* Mathematicians would not have to be called in to solve thousands and thousands of simultaneous equations. Instead, the *decentralized planners* would proceed by successive approximation, by trial and error—setting provisional market and accounting prices and cutting them or raising them, depending upon whether available supplies are piling up or running short.

It would be naïve to think that any actual society would succeed in reaching the ideal equilibrium positions described above. Errors of foresight would inevitably be made. Existing vested interests, anxious to preserve their security in a dynamic world of change, would resist and sabotage such change in the same qualitative fashion as they have done in historical societies. Even where politicians and the electorate do not pay much attention to the incentive mechanisms outlined in the preceding pages, the importance of this discussion is that it teaches us how to appraise the mechanical efficiency of pricing in a *non*socialist society.[7]

WELFARE ECONOMICS IN A FREE ECONOMY

On the basis of the above principles of pricing, we are in a position to see what friendly and unfriendly critics think is wrong in our system, or not necessarily right from various ethical viewpoints. Critics list the following possible deviations from the social optimum:

1. The existing distribution of property, income, education, and economic opportunity is the result of past history and does not necessarily represent an optimum condition according to the ethical philosophies of Christianity, Buddhism, paganism, the American creed, or other ideologies. Defenders of the capitalist system point out that such deviations from the optimum distribution can be corrected by appropriate tax policies, if that is desired. There are, however, some costs to be incurred in our capitalistic system from such policies because of taxation effects upon incentives, risk taking, effort, and productivity.

2. The widespread presence of monopoly elements in our system and the limited appearance of perfect competition mean that production is rarely being pushed to the optimum point of equality of marginal cost to price; because the elasticity of demand is not infinite to imperfect competitors, production is pushed only to the point of equality of marginal cost to marginal revenue. Because of the fear of "spoiling the market," monopoly price is then too high and its output is too low relative to competitive outputs.

This is related to a further Chamberlinian evil under imperfect competition when entry of new firms into an industry is very easy. There may then tend to be an inefficient division of production among too many firms; the P charged is too high, but through wasteful use of resources, no one need be making any profits.[8]

---

conditions suitable for viable laissez faire, such behavior is actually policed by competition, but where bureaucrats "play the game of competition," there may be a hard administrative problem to make sure they do act in the prescribed price-taker manner.)

[7] A brief history of welfare pricing doctrines may be of interest. From Smith's time at least, men saw beauty in the laissez faire mechanism and inferred that it must have teleological significance in giving efficiency. But they were often uncritical, and often they overlooked the assumption that dollar votes were to be distributed in the ethically desired way; and they could not prove what they believed. Around 1900 Pareto showed that an ideal socialism would have to solve the same equations as competitive capitalism. Around 1920, Ludwig von Mises, perhaps unaware of Pareto's proof, set forth the challenging view that rational economic organization was *logically* impossible in the absence of free markets. Fred Taylor of Michigan, A. P. Lerner of England and California,

and Oskar Lange of Poland answered Mises with the view that socialism could conceptually solve the problems of economic organization by a decentralized process of bureaucratic trial and error—"playing the game of competition" and "deliberately planning not to plan." F. A. Hayek has argued that this answer overlooks the problem of giving *each man the initiative* to better the existing order and that only with actual free enterprise do you efficiently utilize the dispersed information which each of us may possess. See Chapter 42 for the movement in Soviet Russia to rely more on prices and profitability.

[8] Another evil, discussed in Chapter 24, is the fact that individual firms, in making their decisions, do not take into account some possible effects of their production decisions on *other* firms or industries. In digging his oil well, Pat does not mind that he may be robbing Mike's oil pool; and the same with Mike—with the result that less oil is obtained in the end, and with more cost. Because of such so-called

3. Finally, of course, as shown in Part Two, under a laissez faire system, there may be great wastes due to unemployment and the business cycle. Consumers, labor, farmers, and business, together with public fiscal and monetary policy, must be mobilized in a never-ending war against this social scourge—poverty which has no real cause but stems only from an intricately misbehaving monetary society.

"external diseconomies or economies" apparent "private marginal costs" do not reflect true "social marginal costs"; and certain lines of activity deserve to be contracted and others to be expanded. Compare A. C. Pigou, *Economics of Welfare* (Macmillan, New York, 1932).

The paradox that really perfect competition would discourage people from inventing (since they would know their profits would disappear) can be understood in terms of external economies: my pecuniary reward from an invention may be much less than its social value after it has been widely imitated. Governmental activities are needed when "public goods" involve external benefits to more than one person at the same time, as shown in Chapter 8. See, too, Chapter 24's discussion.

SUMMARY TO APPENDIX

1   In a pure unmixed competitive society, the economic problems of WHAT shall be produced, HOW, and FOR WHOM are solved in an interdependent manner by the impersonal workings of profit-and-loss markets. Each variable depends upon every other, but all tend to be simultaneously determined at their general equilibrium values by a process of successive approximations and readjustments.

2   Unless a utopian economy were uninterested in efficiency and economizing, or in freedom of choice of goods and jobs, it would have to institute a system of pricing. However, some prices would be purely accounting or bookkeeping figures; in addition, the final determination of the distribution of income would involve an outright social dividend or tax, in various lump-sum amounts to people as determined by explicit a-scientific ethical decision of government and society designed to make dollar votes properly reflective of society's value judgments.

3   From the standpoint of welfare economics, it is seen that any capitalistic system may depart from what is considered a social optimum in three main ways: through improper distribution of income, monopoly and externalities, and unemployment.

   Each one of these evils can, in various degrees, be ameliorated by appropriate policies, within the framework and logic of the mixed economy.

QUESTIONS FOR DISCUSSION

1   Summarize how a pricing system works to solve the three fundamental economic problems. Illustrate their interdependence.

2   Discuss the four kinds of prices in a utopian state.

3   What do you deem to be imperfections in our economic order? Virtues? What defects would plague a collectivist society?

Review your understanding of the following concepts:

interdependence, general equilibrium
determinate final equilibrium
efficient final equilibrium
labor theory of value versus proper pricing of
   nonhuman resources
interest rate in capitalism and socialism
social dividend: lump-sum tax or transfer

wage rents, incentive wages
accounting prices versus actual prices
monopoly restrictions
"external" divergences between social
   and private benefits and costs
welfare economics, ethical distribution
   questions, value judgments

International Trade and Finance **5**

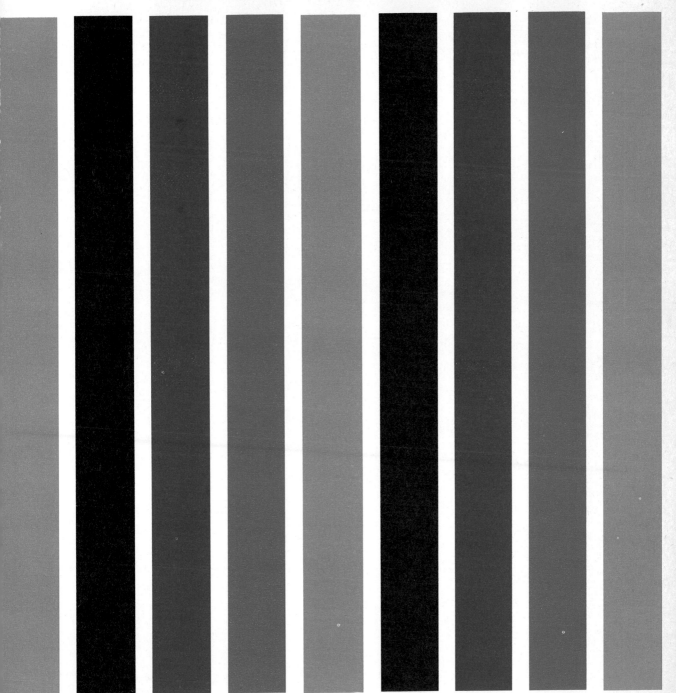

The Balance of International Payments

33

MISS PRISM: Cecily, you will read your political economy in my absence. The chapter on the fall of the rupee you may omit. It is somewhat too sensational. Even these metallic problems have their melodramatic side.
OSCAR WILDE,
The Importance of Being Earnest

In the earlier chapters of this book we took international trade more or less for granted. Here in Part Five we wish to analyze explicitly the interesting economic problems arising as soon as an economy engages in foreign trade.

This chapter and its Appendix deal with the monetary mechanisms involved in international trade. Then the next two chapters concentrate on the basic real factors which underlie international trade and which are often obscured by the monetary veil that covers all international transactions. These basic real factors are involved in any rational appraisal of the problems raised by tariffs and other barriers to the international division of labor. In the final chapter all the principles are put to work to help understand the contemporary international economic scene.

International trade is important for the following basic reason:

Foreign trade offers a "consumption-possibility frontier" that can give us more of all goods than can our own domestic production-possibility frontier!

EXAMPLE: Men in Malaya give us rubber; we give Englishmen wheat; Englishmen give Malayans cotton shirts. *Each of us ends up consuming more than he could produce alone.* The world is out on—and not inside—its true production-possibility frontier. That is the essence of foreign trade. So simple. And yet apparently so hard for congressmen and voters to grasp and remember.

Our task in Part Five is to study the mechanics of international trade and finance: foreign exchange rates; balance of international payments; foreign lending and giving; tariff duties on imports, and import quotas; the so-called "principle of comparative advantage," which tells what kinds of trade will take place and why; and finally, the international economic problems of the 1970s —the United States balance-of-payments deficit, gold drains and hoardings, rigid versus flexible exchange rates, the European Common Market, foreign aid, the International Bank, the International Monetary Fund, long-term

621

international liquidity problems, and new ("paper-gold") Special Drawing Rights. These are anything but abstract economic problems. They make the difference between fruitful international exchange and chaos.

A. MECHANISMS OF FOREIGN EXCHANGE AND TRADE

FOREIGN EXCHANGE RATES

First, how does trade take place? If I buy oranges from Florida or ammonia from Chicago, I naturally want to pay in dollars. Also, the grower and ammonia producer expect to be paid in dollars, for the reason that their expenses and their living costs are all settled in dollars. Within a country, economic transactions seem simple.

If, however, I wish to buy an English racing car directly, matters are more complicated. I must ultimately pay in British money, or what is called "pounds sterling," rather than in dollars. Similarly, an Englishman must somehow get dollars to an American producer if he wants our merchandise. Most Americans have never seen a British pound note. Certainly they would accept pounds only if they could be sure of converting them into American dollars.

Clearly, therefore, exports and imports of goods between nations with different units of money introduce a new economic factor: the foreign exchange rate, giving the price of the foreigner's unit of money in terms of our own.

Thus, the price of a British pound was about $2.40 in 1970. There is also a foreign exchange rate between American money and the currencies of each and every country: 27 cents to the German mark; 18 cents for the French franc;[1] less than $\frac{1}{6}$ cent for an Italian lira; etc.

Given the foreign exchange rate, it is now simple for me to buy my English car. Suppose its quoted price is £2,000 (i.e., 2,000 British pounds). All I have to do is look in the newspaper for the foreign exchange rate for pounds. If this is $2.40 per pound, I simply go to a bank or post office with $4,800 and ask that the money be used to pay the English car exporter. Pay him what? Pounds, of course, the only kind of money he needs.

Whether I use the post office or a bank or a broker is of no particular importance. In fact, it is all the same if the English exporter sends me a bill requesting payment in dollars or if he deals with me through an American garage. In any case, he ultimately wants pounds, not dollars, and will soon trade the $4,800 for £2,000. (Needless to say, we are neglecting all commission charges and the cost of money orders.)

You should be able to show what a British importer of American grains has to do if he wants to buy, say, a $24,000 shipment from an American exporter. Here pounds must be converted into dollars. Why, when the foreign exchange rate is $2.40 per pound, will this cost him £10,000?

---

[1] There are also foreign exchange rates between the pound and the German mark. But these rates between other countries need not interest us much, particularly since, in a free competitive market, the pound-mark rate can be simply calculated from the pound dollar and mark-dollar rate, because sharp-eyed international arbitragers see to it that relative "cross rates" do not get out of line: thus a pound must sell for a little less than 9 (= $2.40/$.273) marks. Of course, these 1970 examples have to be modified when official exchange rates are altered.

The businessman or tourist does not, as an individual, have to know anything more than this to get his imports or exports transacted. But the true economics of the problem cannot be grasped until we find out *why* the foreign exchange rate is at the level it is. What economic principles determine foreign exchange rates?

STABLE EXCHANGE RATE UNDER THE CLASSICAL GOLD STANDARD

There are three important cases to study:

1. The working of some kind of pure or modified *gold standard.*

2. The case of *free foreign exchange rates,* available to every person in either country, but fluctuating from day to day according to *market demand and supply* (quite like the case of wheat, which is available to all at a price that fluctuates from day to day, depending upon competitive supply and demand).

3. The case of *controlled* international trade, where each transaction requires a government license and where the foreign exchange rate may be different for different kinds of transactions, being set according to the will of the state.

The gold-standard case has been historically most important; in severely modified form, it prevails today; and some vestige of it may be with us in the years ahead. It is also one of the easiest cases to master.

Gold bars   Suppose people everywhere insisted on being paid in bits of pure gold metal: weight alone would count, and its shape—whether round like a ball or a coin, or irregular like a sliver, or cylindrical like a broom handle—would not matter so long as there were a guarantee of its purity and weight. Then buying grain in Chicago would merely require payment in gold at a price expressed in ounces of gold; and buying a car in Britain would involve the same kind of payment. By definition, there would be no foreign-exchange-rate problem.

Gold coins   Since slivers and blobs of gold are inconvenient to carry and to assay for purity and for weight, it became customary for the state—in those days, the prince—to stamp out in coin form a specified number of ounces of gold carrying the seal of the state to guarantee purity and weight. (The edges were milled, so that removal of the edges would reveal light weight and fraud. Even so, since gold is soft and rubs off, merchants and banks weighed the coins.)

With gold coins as the exchange medium, would not foreign trade still be like domestic trade? Yes, essentially. But with some minor differences: If we used ounces and France used grams to measure weight, you would merely have to have a table of units' conversion. And the same problem would arise if Queen Victoria chose to make her coins about $\frac{1}{4}$ ounce of gold (the "sovereign") and President McKinley chose to make his $\frac{1}{20}$ ounce of gold (the dollar). In that case, the pound sovereign, being five times as heavy as the dollar, would naturally have an exchange rate of $5 to £1.

Now that is essentially how the pre-1914 gold standard actually worked. Of course, local pride tended to keep us using our coins and the English using their coins. But anyone was free to melt down our coins and get them converted into English coins (at very nominal costs). So except for the trifling costs of melting down, shipping across the ocean, and recoining, *all countries on the gold standard had essentially stable exchange rates whose par values, or parities, were determined by the gold content of their local money unit.*

Minor qualifications. Gold being quite inconvenient to carry around for spending purposes, inevitably governments issued paper certificates that were pledged to be redeemable in gold metal. People had the right to turn in gold for certificates and certificates for gold, and they often exercised that right. Also, in those days ocean transport was slow and costly: so there were "gold points" around the true mint parities within which the pound and dollar exchange rates could fluctuate. Thus, if it cost 2 cents to ship $\frac{1}{4}$ ounce of gold either way across the Atlantic Ocean (inclusive of insurance and interest costs), could the exchange rate depart a little from $5? Yes. In New York, the quoted price of a pound could rise to as much as $5.02 before it would pay to get gold bars and ship them to London to be exchanged for pounds; a price higher than $5.02 could not prevail because enough gold would be flowing to keep the price no higher than the upper gold point. It should be evident that the pound could fall below the mint parity of $5 by 2 cents to $4.98. When the exchange rate got down to this lower gold point, it would be cheaper for gold to be shipped from Europe to America. All this actually happened (except that $5 is substituted here for the correct pre-1914 parity of $4.87 to simplify the arithmetic, and the shipping costs are given only approximately). Before 1914, the foreign exchange rate of the pound and dollar stayed essentially constant, varying but a trifle from these weight-determined mint parities until the gold points were touched and gold had to flow in the indicated direction.

The Hume gold-flow equilibrating mechanism   Now that the mechanics of the problem are understood, we probe deeper to answer this question:

Under the gold standard, what kept America from buying more goods from England than England bought from us—which, after all, would have required us to keep shipping gold in final payment? Why wouldn't we be drained of all our gold?

This is a good question, and the mercantilist writers, who preceded Adam Smith and his friend the noted philosopher David Hume, gave a plausible but superficial answer. The mercantilists said:

"A country will lose its gold unless the Prince introduces tariffs and quotas to cut down on imports of goods; and unless he gives subsidies to encourage exports; and unless he forbids skilled workmen to take their knowledge abroad and makes sure that all shipping takes place in our own boats, however dear they may be." As an afterthought, almost too obvious to require mention, they said: "Of course, losing gold is a terrible thing for a nation. Don't ask why. Everyone knows it to be one of the worst tragedies that can happen to a nation."

David Hume in 1752, and economists ever since, have given the refutation to this line of reasoning. First Hume noted that it could not be true that everyone would all the time be losing gold under free trade. Where would it go—into the sea? And he demonstrated that it is no tragedy at all if a country goes permanently from having 10 million ounces of gold to having 5 million, or even 1 million. *If* halving half the amount of gold means merely that *all* prices are exactly halved, no one in the country is the least bit better or worse off. So, losing half or nine-tenths of a nation's gold is nothing, Hume pointed out, to worry about if the nation merely ends up with an equivalently reduced price level.

Here it is well to recall the crude Quantity Theory of Money and Prices discussed in Chapter 15. David Hume, along with John Locke and earlier writers, was one of the first to enunciate and hold to this theory concerning the proportionality of all prices to the stock of money (in this case M being gold).[2]

Now comes the second and important part of Hume's classical refutation of mercantilism and defense of free trade. He went on to assert that there is a four-pronged mechanism that tends to keep in equilibrium the international balance of payments of countries on the gold standard. Briefly, the Hume mechanism is this:

Whenever one country imports too much and begins to lose gold, its loss of gold *reduces its price and cost level*, thereby (1) *decreasing its imports* of foreign goods that have become relatively dear, and (2) *increasing exports* of its home-produced goods that have become relatively cheap.

The other country, which had been having a so-called "favorable balance of trade," in which it was sending more goods abroad than it was importing and merely receiving barren gold in exchange, now has (via the Quantity Theory) its price and cost levels of goods *raised*. This is a further reason (3) for its now-expensive *exports to go down* in physical amount and (4) for its citizens to import *more* of the now-cheap goods of the first country.

The result of this four-pronged gold-flow price-level mechanism is to improve the balance of payments of the country which was losing gold and worsen that of the country with the favorable balance of trade—until equilibrium in international trade is established at relative prices that keep imports and exports in balance with no net gold flow. The equilibrium is stable and self-correcting, requiring no tariffs and other state interference.

FLEXIBLE EXCHANGE RATES

Having seen how an idealized gold standard works, we turn now to the case where supply and demand are left free to determine the foreign exchange rate. In the absence of any tie to gold, the pound in the 1940s might have had an average price of $4 or $5, and in this decade, an average price of $2.40. Who knows, perhaps next decade it could be at $4.50, or $3 or $1.50, once floating exchange rates become the rule.

The forces of supply and demand will determine the answer. If Americans want to buy so many English goods at the existing $2.40 level and Europeans want so few American goods, then we might be demanding more pounds as our needed foreign exchange than they will be wanting to supply us with. What then will happen? If there is no longer a gold standard, one cannot get gold and ship it over so as to keep the foreign exchange rate within narrow gold points around the $2.40 parity. Instead, our urgent demand will bid up the foreign exchange rate. How far? Just far enough so that, at the new higher price of, say, $3 for the pound, our total demand for foreign exchange will be brought again down into equality with their enhanced supply of foreign exchange.

[2] He admitted that the equilibrium predicted by the Quantity Theory would not take place instantaneously; indeed, he was one of the first to recognize that a period of rising M and rising prices, when it was first happening and was not foreseen, would give profits to businessmen by causing their prices to rise more than their costs; he thought this would be good for full employment and capital formation in the short run.

Demand bids up, supply bids down a free foreign exchange rate:

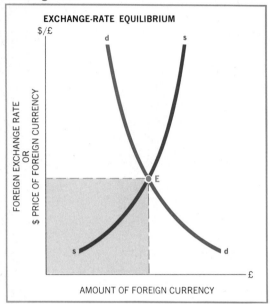

FIG. 33-1   Behind our *dd* is our desire to import British goods, buy British securities, visit the Bard's grave, and so forth. Behind their *ss* supply of pounds to be traded for dollars is their desire for our export goods and other items. If the rate were above *E*, there would be an excess of foreign currency that they would want to supply us over what we should want to demand. Such an excess of supply would bid the rate back down to *E*, where the market of foreign currency for dollars is just cleared. (Test yourself by replacing £s by 27-cent German marks.)

Two main steps are involved: (1) With the pound rate more expensive, it will cost more to import British bikes and our physical demand for them will fall off in the usual fashion. (2) With the dollar now cheaper, our goods will cost less to Europeans and they will want to demand more of our export goods. (If we look at these two effects, from both their viewpoint and our own, we have something like the four-pronged action of Hume. But with certain important differences. Our whole *domestic* price level need not change, and neither need theirs. The change in foreign exchange rate can *itself* bring about directly enhanced relative dearness and cheapness *of export and import* price levels.)

The familiar curves of supply and demand developed in Chapter 4 and Part Three are used in Fig. 33-1 to show equilibrium determination of flexible exchange rates.

America's *dd* curve comes from our desire for foreign exchange rate to buy import goods, to make tourist visits, to hire shipping and insurance services, to finance our troops abroad and our foreign-aid grants, to pay the dividends and interest we owe to foreign owners of our securities and property; and also to finance long-term investment abroad by American firms or stock buyers, and short-term investment in foreign near-term bonds or savings accounts.

What is behind their demand for dollars—which shows up as the *ss* supply curve of the pound-foreign-exchange they offer us? The exactly similar items in their balance of payments: desire to import our export goods, need to pay us dividends, etc.

At the *dd* and *ss* intersection, the flexible foreign exchange rate will get set, having then no tendency to rise or fall from this equilibrium level.

What will happen if tomorrow we send more troops abroad, travel abroad more, find new bargains in their catalogues and expand our dollar demand for their goods, and are forced by domestic inflation to raise our export-goods prices? Such changes will obviously shift our *dd* upward and rightward and also their *ss* leftward and upward. With what resulting intersection? With a new higher equilibrium level of the exchange rate; as described above, just enough higher to coax out more American exports and choke off imports from Europe. The exchange rate at which we buy foreign currencies has risen; the dollar's relative value has fallen.

A classical economist like Hume would understand all this very well. In fact, he (and Ricardo around 1817 and Sweden's Gustav Cassel around 1917) would offer this clue to the equilibrium level of a flexible exchange rate:

Purchasing-power parity. Let America and Europe be at equilibrium, say, at $2.40 per £1. Now let America double *all* her prices by domestically inflating her *M*; and let Europe keep her *M* limited enough to produce a steady price level. Then, other things being equal (such as employment remaining full and there being no inventions, crop failures, tariffs, or change in tastes), the new *dd* and *ss* intersection will come at twice the old $2.40 rate, namely, at $4.80 per £1.

Hume's reasoning would be classically simple. With all wages and prices here *exactly doubled* (and *M* doubled here to finance them), we can *buy exactly the same* physical imports and *sell exactly the same* physical exports at the new exchange rate that has doubled like everything else. (It is just as if every American old dollar is now called two American dollars, period.)[3]

Depreciation, appreciation, and devaluation   A doubling of the pound is a halving of the dollar. By definition, the fall in the price of one currency in terms of one or all others is called a "depreciation." A relative rise in the price of a currency in terms of another currency is called an "appreciation." Evidently, the pound has appreciated in our example, and the dollar has undergone a large depreciation.

The term "devaluation" is often confused with the term "depreciation." Devaluation usually is defined to mean a rise in the price of gold: thus, in 1933, Roosevelt devalued the dollar, raising the price of gold from about $21 an ounce eventually to its present price of $35 an ounce. When the Swiss or French stayed on the gold standard at their previous parities, the devaluation of the dollar meant depreciation of the dollar relative to the undevalued French franc and Swiss franc; but relative to the Canadian dollar and Philippine peso, which devalued equally with us, there was neither depreciation nor appreciation. (Check that the French franc then underwent appreciation.)

Devaluation defined. When gold officially goes up in price relative to a currency—as from $21 an ounce to $35—we say the currency has been devalued.

Depreciation defined. When the price of a foreign currency rises relative to a given currency—e.g., when the price of the German mark rose about 9 per cent in 1969, from $0.250 to $0.27⅓ per mark—we say the (domestic) currency has *depreciated*, and that the foreign currency has had a relative *appreciation*.

If *all* countries *simultaneously* raised the price of gold by 100 per cent, there would be no depreciation or appreciation, but there would be a devaluation.

If prices and wages lack the flexibility to make the needed trade adjustments under the gold standard, the deficit country may find itself forced into a devaluation; this rise in the price at which it will buy and sell gold will imply a depreciation of its currency relative to any currency that remains at the old gold parities.[4] If all countries devalue

---

[3] Cassel and other writers developed the doctrine of purchasing-power parity to predict how much World War I currencies would depreciate when internal inflation sent their price levels up by 100 or more per cent. His long-run predictions worked out better than his short-run predictions, but neither had perfect accuracy. In the real world, unlike the classical model, other things did not stay equal.

[4] At the end of this chapter's Appendix, there is discussed a compromise proposal that has some of the stability advantages of the gold standard's fixed exchange rates, and some of the flexibility advantages of floating exchange rates set by market forces of supply and demand. It is called the "crawling peg," and it permits limited changes in the exchange rate each year; over several years an orderly change in parity can then be achieved.

together and in balance—to restore international liquidity or for any other reason—no appreciation or depreciation of currencies relative to each other takes place.

Generally, a depreciation of the currency that has been running an international deficit can be expected[5] to help restore the equilibrium. Although this alternative happens less frequently, equilibrium could also be restored by having the surplus country *appreciate* its currency—an example would be the 5 per cent appreciation of the mark and guilder engineered by the Germans and Dutch in 1961 and the further 1969 appreciation of the mark, or the World War I appreciation of the Swedish krona.

EXAMPLES: Britain was forced by her international deficit into depreciating the pound from $2.80 to $2.40 in 1967. Slowly, this did improve her export competitiveness; but, if she had let wages and costs rise within the country by as much as the depreciation, she would have frittered away all its benefit. Again, in August, 1969, France devalued the franc by 11 to 12 per cent; 1968 unrest had sent up French costs, and De Gaulle's stubborn refusal to depreciate had encouraged a speculative run on the franc.

MODIFIED GOLD AND DOLLAR STANDARDS

Now that we have surveyed the idealized cases of a pure gold standard and a completely flexible exchange-rate system, we can describe the international system as it has in fact operated in recent decades, paving the way for Chapter 36's discussion of future modifications that are on the way.

Evolution of the gold standard There is nothing sacred about gold. Silver, platinum, lead, or for that matter paper napkins would do, provided they had convenience for exchange, could not be falsified, and were enough limited in supply to keep the price level from soaring. Actually, the old gold standard was in its heyday only for a brief half-century prior to 1914. Before the nineteenth century, England had been more on a silver than on a gold standard, and had stumbled onto the gold standard as a result of market revaluations of the two precious metals without anyone's realizing it. Her great prestige caused France, the United States, and the rising empires of Germany and Japan to adopt the gold standard later.

Even in its brief heyday, several crises caused the gold standard to break down periodically (as, for example, when our Civil War forced us off gold for more than a decade). Moreover, the price level was at the mercy of the happenstance of gold discoveries. If world physical production was increasing in the years 1875 to 1895 at the rate of 5 per cent per year, the gold supply would—according to the quantity theory

---

[5] There is a theoretical possibility that the relative price changes brought about by depreciation of the dollar could make the deficit worse rather than better if international demands turn out to be very inelastic rather than elastic. In such cases, lowering the £ prices of American export goods will not expand our physical sales much; therefore Englishmen will actually offer fewer pounds for dollars rather than more pounds. And this could outweigh the reduction of pounds we pay England for our reduced physical imports. Thus, the price reaction to a depreciation of the dollar may be a perverse rather than an equilibrating one: The dollar would have to depreciate still further until demands ceased to be so inelastic; paradoxically, currency *appreciation* might in this perverse case wipe out a country's import deficit.

of Money—have to increase by 5 per cent per year to keep prices stable. But mines, because of the ending of the Californian and Australian gold rushes, were not producing this much gold then; and as a result price levels were sagging all over the world in the last third of the nineteenth century.

This gave rise to much social unrest. In an ideal world of perfect price and wage flexibility, where the Quantity Theory worked smoothly both down and up, falling prices should not have mattered much. But as Hume himself insisted, prices and wages tend to be sticky downward; and falling price levels tend to lead to labor unrest, strikes, unemployment, and radical movements generally. Precisely that happened in the United States and other countries during the 1875-1895 era of populism. (Recall Chapter 7's account of the rise of the Knights of Labor.) Since gold seemed to be squeezing prices downward, there was a clamor on the part of farmers and workers for use of silver to supplement gold. This culminated in the historic speech by William Jennings Bryan in favor of "bimetallism" at the 1896 Democratic Convention, where the "Boy Orator of the Platte" warned against crucifying mankind on a cross of gold.[6]

Fractional-reserve banking and the gold-exchange standard   With Germany and Japan going on the gold standard, the deflationary pressure on prices would have been even worse had it not been for growing methods of economizing on gold. Modern banks, which hold only fractional reserves, began to develop: the demand-deposit M they created meant that not quite so much gold was needed to keep up with growing total output. Moreover, most of the countries on the gold standard did *not* keep 100 per cent gold reserves to back up the token coins and paper currency they issued. Thus, if the typical country held only one-fourth gold against its paper money, only a quarter as much gold would have to be mined to support the same world price level.

This process of domestic banking evolution to economize on the use of gold is important. For, as we shall see, it foreshadows the modern international development of economizing on and displacing gold by creating so-called "paper gold" (i.e., SDRs, or Special Drawing Rights).

Another development helped economize on gold. Many countries, particularly small ones (like the Philippines), kept their money exchangeable at fixed rates with respect to gold. But they held little or no gold. Instead, they would hold the money of some

---

[6] Bimetallism would mean that the Treasury would exchange dollars for *either* gold or silver, at some agreed-upon ounce ratio, such as 16 ounces of silver to each ounce of gold. Unless all countries agreed on the same 16/1 ratio, there would be a one-way movement of each metal to the place where it was most valued; and the place where gold was most valued would be on the gold standard; while the place where silver was most valued would be on the silver standard. As a result, with every change in the relative supplies and demands for the two metals, there would be an ensuing fluctuation in the foreign exchange rates between the two countries. (The percentage size of the fluctuation could be only two-sixteenths if their respective bimetallic parities were 16/1 and 18/1. Even if all countries went on the same 16/1 ratio, any tendency for mines to pour out the two metals at substantially different rates would lead to the free market's bidding their price ratios to some figure other than 16/1; and in this case, by a form of what is known as Gresham's Law—"Cheap money drives out good"—the result would be that the cheapest metal in the market place would all be given to the treasuries of the different countries, and in effect the world would be on a single standard again—that of the cheapest metal. Today no one, not even a Kansas farmer, favors bimetallism.)

big country (like the United States) which was on the gold standard. So long as the small country could stay on such a "gold-exchange standard," the effect would be much like the pure gold standard, but with great economizing on gold.

Fortunately for those who favored the gold standard, the deflationary pressures eased some when gold was discovered in the Klondike and South Africa in the mid-nineties and when the cyanide process greatly increased the output of gold mines. Together with the increasing leverage attained by having smaller and smaller fractional-reserve ratios and more and more gold-exchange standards, the increase in mining enabled the world to keep on the gold standard and stave off deflation up until the 1929 crash. But this did involve a strain on international liquidity, and some experts actually attribute that slump to an increasing shortage of world liquidity.

The dollar standard   During the Great Depression of the 1930s, political unrest and fear of Hitler's aggression caused an avalanche of gold to flow into the United States. After World War II *the world was in fact on a dollar standard.* The pound sterling and the American dollar were the "key currencies" in terms of which international trade and finance were carried on. Private and governmental reserves were kept largely in the form of dollar and sterling balances (i.e., in cash, bank deposits, and liquid short-term securities). Whereas before 1914 the pound had been king, by 1945 the dollar was established as *the* key currency.

EXAMPLE: As Chapter 36 will show, the Bretton Woods Conference of 1944, which set up the International Monetary Fund and the World Bank, defined in its Charter the parities of currencies not simply in terms of gold, but in terms of dollars (the equivalent of $\frac{1}{35}$ ounce of gold).

The fact that the dollar served as a key currency gave America, in effect, something of the same privilege of creating money out of thin air that the commercial banks enjoy domestically (as Chapter 16 discussed). To a degree, this key position gave America the right to get a certain amount of goods at no real cost. But it also put a special responsibility on America to keep its balance of payments in order.

In the 1970s the international standard is still undergoing evolution with the role of gold as a metal becoming less and less pivotal.[7]

EXCHANGE-RATE MECHANICS CONCLUDED

We have now surveyed the fundamentals of foreign exchange rates. Although money prices are quoted in international trade, in the longest run there must really be an international *barter* of goods and services against goods and services. Under a stable exchange-rate system like that of the modified gold standard, gold flows are supposed to lead to price-level adjustments big enough to restore equilibrium on the export and import side. Under flexible exchange rates, it is fluctuation in the foreign exchange rate that alters the relative costs and prices of foreign and home goods enough to restore an equilibrium balance in international trade.

---

[7]Chapter 36 will discuss the post-1968 creation of a "two-tier" gold system: within the official tier, a fixed total of gold exchanges at stable parities; but then in the unofficial tier, gold is bought and sold in the London, Zurich, and Paris markets at whatever price is determined by the shifting supply of mined gold and the shifting demand by jewelers, dentists, the Mafia, industrial users, and hoarders.

The remaining section of this chapter will go behind the demand and supply curves of international trade to examine each item involving foreign exchange payments and see how they all combine.

B. BALANCE OF INTERNATIONAL TRADE AND CAPITAL MOVEMENTS

THE BALANCE OF INTERNATIONAL PAYMENTS

The time has come to explain exactly what we mean when we speak of a country's "balance of international payments." We mean the statement that takes into account the values of all goods, all gifts and foreign aid, all capital loans (or "IOUs"), all gold and key-currency reserves coming in and going out, and the interconnections among all these items that lie behind Fig. 33-1's curves.

The balance of international payments summarizes these important relations. If you understand it, you have a fairly good grasp of foreign trade.

The U.S. Department of Commerce keeps records and makes official estimates of all international transactions during a year: merchandise exported and imported, money lent abroad or borrowed, gold movements, tourist expenditures, interest and dividends received or paid abroad, shipping services, and so forth. They all go to make up the "balance of international payments"—which is simply a double-entry listing of all items, drawn up in such a way that it must always show a balance.[8]

The balance of international payments is listed in three sections:

I. Current account
    Private:
        Merchandise (or "trade balance")
        Invisibles:
            Transportation (shipping services, etc.)
            Travel expenditure (tourists, etc.)
            Income on investments (interest, royalties, dividends, etc.)
            Private gifts (immigrants' remittances, etc.)
            Miscellaneous services
    Governmental:
        Government export of military goods to allies
        Unilateral grants of United States government (aid programs, military aid)
II. Capital movements
    Long-term:
        Private
        Government
    Short-term:
        Private
        Government
III. Gold-and-reserve-assets movements (out and in)

---

[8]Smuggling and some innocent items elude the record keepers; so it is necessary to introduce a miscellaneous category of omitted items, as in NNP's "statistical discrepancy."

Balance on current account   The totality of items under section I is usually referred to as the "balance on current account." This important magnitude summarizes the difference between our total export of goods and services and our total import of goods and services.

In a moment, we shall see how any surplus or deficit balance on current account is "financed"—or, more precisely, is offset—by gold and reserve assets or by capital movements under sections III and II. But before doing this, we shall describe briefly I's major current items under the headings Private and Governmental.

Centuries ago, when *merchandise* items predominated, writers concentrated on them alone. If merchandise exports were greater in value than merchandise imports they spoke of a "favorable balance of trade"; if imports exceeded exports, of an "unfavorable balance of trade." This is not a good choice of terms, for we shall see that a so-called "unfavorable" balance of trade may be a fine thing for a country.

In addition to such so-called "visible" merchandise items, we must not forget the important role played these days by the "invisibles." These consist of such items as shipping and insurance services which we provide for foreigners or which they provide for us, American tourist expenditures abroad, our earnings from abroad, and the gifts that immigrants send back home. On reflection, one realizes that an invisible item such as an American's expenditure for a drink in Paris has the same effect on the final balance of payments as does his import of French wine to be drunk here at home in America. And when we provide shipping insurance service, that acts like an export.

Debits and credits   A good way to decide how any item should be treated is to ask the following question: Is the item like one of our merchandise exports, providing us with more foreign currencies? Such an export-type item is called a "credit item" and gives us a supply of foreign money. Or is the item like one of our merchandise imports, causing us to use up our stock of foreign currencies and making it necessary to get more foreign currency? Such an import-type item is called a "debit item" and gives us a demand for foreign money.

To show how this rule works, ask the following question: How shall we treat interest, royalty, and dividend income on investments received by Americans from abroad? Clearly, they are credit items like exports, in that they provide us with foreign currencies. The reader can reverse the argument to show that such items which foreigners receive from us must be treated like debit items—like imports, they use up our foreign currencies.

At this point a close look at Table 33-1 will be helpful. It presents official data on the balance of international payments of the United States for 1968. Note its three main divisions into current, capital, and gold-and-reserve items; in addition, it has an item (line 25) to account for statistical errors and omissions. Each row is numbered to make reference easy. Then, after each item has been listed by name in Column (*a*), we list in Column (*b*) the credits, i.e., the amounts of those items that are like exports in earning us foreign currencies. Next, in Column (*c*), we list the debits, i.e., the amounts of the items that use up foreign currencies because of our need to pay for imports, etc.

Thus, in 1968 our merchandise exports gave us credits of $33,598 million, but our merchandise imports gave us debits of only $32,972 million. The net difference between credits and debits is in this case +$626 million. It is shown listed in the last column,

These figures summarize international transactions:

U.S. BALANCE OF INTERNATIONAL PAYMENTS, 1968 (in millions of dollars)

NO.	(a) ITEMS	(b) CREDITS	(c) DEBITS	(d) NET CREDITS (+) OR DEBITS (−)	
	I Current				
	Private:				
1	Merchandise (adjusted)	$33,598	$32,972	+$626	
	Invisibles:				
2	Transportation	2,924	3,248	−324	
3	Travel expenditures	1,770	3,022	−1,252	
4	Income on investments (interest, royalties, dividends, etc.)	8,213	2,231	+5,982	
5	Private remittances		753	−753	
6	Miscellaneous services	1,546	625	+921	
7	Current private balance				+$5,200
	U.S. governmental:				
8	Exports of military goods and services (+)	1,427			
	Military aid payments (−) to allies		1,427	0	
9	Other military transactions	838	3,103	−2,265	
10	Other grants and payments		2,950	−2,950	
11	Miscellaneous government transactions	1,117	1,451	−334	
12	Current government transactions				−$5,549
13	Net balance on current account				−$349
	II Capital account, net exports of our IOUs (+) or net imports (−)				
	Long-term loans (−) or borrowing (+)				
14	Private			−1,259	
15	Government			−449	
16	Net long-term foreign investment				−1,708
17	**Net balance on current account + long-term investments (the "basic deficit in U.S. balance of payments")**				−$2,057
	Short-term loans (−) or borrowing (+)				
18	Private			+988	
19	Net foreign purchase of U.S. equities			+3,094	
20	Government			−428	
21	Net investment in short-term debt				+3,654
	III Net gold and reserve assets, exports (+) or imports (−)				
22	Gold			+1,173	
23	Reserve assets			−2,053	
24	Net change in gold and reserves				−880
25	Errors and omissions				−717
26	Offset to basic U.S. "deficit"				+$2,057
27	Over-all net balance of international payments				0

TABLE 33-1. Although our current balance on private account exceeded $5 billion (more exactly being $5.2 billion), that was not large enough to cover our $6 billion of government aid and long-term investments and our over $1 billion of long-term private investment. (Source: Adapted from U.S. Department of Commerce data.)

Column (d), of the first row. (Be sure you know why the algebraic sign is shown $+$ rather than $-$.) Even today one hears this export merchandise surplus called by the misleading title "favorable balance of trade."

The reader can interpret each line of the invisible items. He will know why the American tendency to travel abroad results in a negative—or net debit—entry under travel expenditures. He will also know why gifts by private Americans to relatives or charities abroad serve to use up foreign currencies and are listed as debits in line 5. (Of course, in their balance of payments, foreign countries would think of *our* debit as *their* credit, and of these last two items as "making more *dollars* available.")

Table 33-1 shows that as far as the private current items are concerned, the final effect of invisible items was to reinforce greatly our small trade surplus of credits over debits —primarily because of our interest and dividends from abroad.

The whole net credit balance of the first seven private rows cannot quite offset the governmental items of the next five rows. Government military transactions and various foreign-aid grants and payments[9] resulted in the balance of $-\$5,549$ million in line 12, more than enough to wipe out much of the positive private balance and make the final "net balance on current account" (line 13) equal to $-\$349$ million, a deficit.

In computing the net balance on current account, we have completed the first great block of Table 33-1. How must a nation offset its net balance on current account? Either by gold- and reserve-assets payments (e.g., we could export gold and, on a dollar standard, export dollar assets), as in section III of the table, or by net borrowing as in section II. *For it is a tautology that what you get you must either pay for or owe for.* And this fact of double-entry bookkeeping means that the whole table of the balance of international payments must show a final definitional balance. (Statistical errors and omissions, as in the case of the GNP statistical discrepancy discussed in Chapter 10, must of course be reckoned with if the double-entry bookkeeper is not given all the accurate facts; but this should not affect the *logic* of the perfect balance.)

Capital movements   We can now turn to capital movements: the long-term and short-term loans *private* citizens make or receive from foreign private citizens (e.g., when General Motors builds an automobile plant abroad or when I buy a French bond or deposit funds in a Swiss bank; or when Belgians buy New York real estate or treasury short-term bills here); and long-term and short-term *government* loans and credits through various direct or intermediate channels.

It is easy to decide which are credit and which debit items in the capital accounts if you use the following rule: Always think of America as exporting and importing *capital securities*—or, for short, exporting and importing IOUs. Then you can treat these exports and imports like any other exports and imports. When we lend abroad, is it a credit or debit? Obviously, we are importing IOUs—and imports always give rise to debits. Therefore it is a debit.

[9]It will be seen that direct government gifts of equipment to, say, the German Army would appear in line 8 as a self-canceling item in that it was produced here at home and simply left with the Germans as a gift; if counted as an export credit, it also is matched by the debit act of giving. Other military transactions, such as pay to the Germans for petrol for our troops there or their maintenance, and other United States government foreign programs would show up in lines 9 through 11.

Similarly, when we are borrowing from abroad on balance, this export of IOUs creates a net credit. If you do not follow this rule, you will find yourself getting confused: when we lend abroad you will be tempted to think of us as exporting capital abroad and thereby earning a credit. This is wrong: we are then importing IOUs, and these imports are debit *offsets* enabling us to be paid for a surplus of credit exports on current account.

Line 16 shows that in 1968 America was a net long-term foreign lender: we were doing more long-term lending or investing abroad than foreigners were lending or investing here. We were the net importers of long-term IOUs by −$1,708 million. (During 1968, there was a rush by foreigners to profit from the Wall Street boom by buying our stocks in billions of dollars. Being volatile and easily reversed, these portfolio investments are not here included in long-term investment, but are shown in line 19. By mid-1969 foreigners had already begun to pull out money from Wall Street, confirming how volatile and unreliable portfolio investment can be.)

Basic deficit   Now let us depart from a simple consideration of current, capital, and gold items. Let us investigate the important concept of America's "basic deficit." Certain short-term capital movements take place to make up for, and offset, our inability to generate enough credit items. (Examples are holdings of treasury bills and bank deposits, or volatile portfolio purchases of our common stocks.) So we exclude such short-term items in order to discover where we really stand on a sustainable longer-term basis.

Line 17 totes up the score of *all* our current transactions and long-term capital movements. So great were current government debits and long-term private investment debits as to give America a so-called net "basic deficit"—for 1968, a basic deficit of −$2.1 billion.

It is somewhat dangerous to speak of a "deficit in the balance of payments," for, as we have just seen, the whole balance of payments must always be in tautologically perfect balance because of the identities and conventions of double-entry bookkeeping. What, then, do newspapers and congressmen mean when they refer to the American deficit in the balance of payments for the years 1958–1969? They probably[10] have reference to something like line 17, which is the sum of the current account deficit and the long-term (nonportfolio) investment deficit. It is this basic deficit that must definitely be paid for either by gold or by having foreigners choose to acquire liquid American assets on short-term capital account, knowing they can always change their mind and ask for gold if they decide that other financial markets offer them a higher interest rate or better capital-gain opportunity on short-term funds than does New York City.

Gold and reserve movements   The $2 billion basic deficit was covered up in largest part by the shorter-term capital movements in lines 18 and 19. Attracted by high United

---

[10]This "basic deficit" should not be confused with two other international deficits to be encountered later in Chapter 36, and which appear more commonly in official government statistics. The "basic deficit" used here was developed in President Kennedy's first official 1961 message (except for the author's debatable decision to exclude portfolio investment from the long-term category). For 1968 the Official Settlements balance was +$1.6 billion, as opposed to the −$2.1 billion basic deficit of Table 33-1. When, as in 1969, our banks pay 10, 11, and even 12 per cent to borrow in the so-called "Euro-dollar" market, these borrowings add to the Liquidity Deficit (even though the dollar is thus enabled to be strong rather than weak; and even though the Official Settlements Deficit may be quite unaffected, with no government transactions being involved).

States interest rates, +$988 million of short-term funds moved here. Attracted by the boom in Wall Street, portfolio purchases of our equities brought in another +$3,094 million. However, line 25's Errors and omissions probably represented hidden capital outflows that had to be offset against these inflows.

Line 22 shows we exported gold (most of it before March, 1968, when the two-tier system of gold was set up, after which we no longer fed gold to the free-market hoarders). The +$1,173 million gold export, taken together with our net imports of volatile IOUs, resulted in our accumulating back from foreigners the $2,053 debit item of Reserve assets [dollars of currency held by them, dollar deposits, or short-term liquid (dollar) securities].

Thus we finally achieve the formal balance shown in line 27. The balance of international payments taken as a whole is built out of double-entry debit and credit items, so that it will always show this formal balance. This was true even of the period from 1946 to 1949 when we were gaining gold and liquid assets from abroad (during the so-called "dollar shortage" when European factories were noncompetitive with ours). This formal balance holds true even in recent times—when there has seemed to be the opposite of a dollar shortage, namely, a "chronic deficit" in the American current and long-term capital balance which is being matched by an outflow of gold and the short-term dollar obligations that foreigners have been piling up instead of taking all in gold.

STAGES OF A COUNTRY'S BALANCE OF PAYMENTS

Historically, the United States has gone through the four stages typical of the growth of a young agricultural nation into a well-developed industrialized one. A review of this history may be useful to consolidate understanding.

1. *Young and growing debtor nation.* From the Revolutionary War until after the Civil War, we imported on current account more than we exported. England and Europe lent us the difference in order to build up our capital structure. We were a typical young and growing debtor nation.

2. *Mature debtor nation.* From about 1873 to 1914, our balance of trade appears to have become favorable. But growth of the dividends and interest that we had to pay abroad on our past borrowing kept our balance on current account more or less in balance. Capital movements were also nearly in balance, our new lending just about canceling our borrowing.

3. *New creditor nation.* In World War I, we expanded our exports tremendously. At first, private American citizens made loans to the warring Allied Powers. After we got into the war, our government lent money to England and France for war equipment and postwar relief needs. We emerged from the war a creditor nation. But our psychological frame of mind had not adjusted itself to our new creditor position. We passed high tariff laws in the 1920s and in 1930. Because we refused to import, foreigners found it difficult to get the dollars to pay us interest and dividends, much less repay principal.

So long as we remained in this third stage of being a new creditor country—so long, that is, as we kept making *new* private foreign loans all through the 1920s—everything momentarily appeared all right on the surface. We could continue to sell more than we were buying, by putting most of it "on the cuff." The rest of the world met our export surplus by sending us gold and by sending us IOUs. As long as Wall Street bankers could interest Main Street investors in foreign bonds, everything seemed rosy. But by 1929 and later, when Americans would no longer lend abroad, the crash finally came. International trade broke down. Debts were defaulted. America, as much as the rest of the world, was to blame.

West Germany in 1970 seems to be repeating many of the phases—and errors!—of the United States in the 1920s.

4. *Mature creditor nation.* England reached this stage some years ago, and as in all such cases, her imports exceeded her exports. Before we feel sorry for her because of her so-called "unfavorable" balance of trade, let us note what this really means.

Her citizens were living better because they were able to import much cheap food and in return did not have to part with much in the way of valuable export goods. The English were paying for their import surplus by the interest and dividend receipts they were receiving from past foreign lending.

Fine for the English. But what about the rest of the world? Were they not worse off for having to send exports to England in excess of imports? Not necessarily. Normally, the capital goods that England had previously lent them permitted them to add to their domestic production—to add *more* than had to be paid out to England in interest and dividends. Both parties were better off. Nineteenth-century foreign lending was twice blessed: it blessed him who gave and him who received. Of course, international trade and finance did not always operate quite so smoothly. Some investments proved unwise. Political problems of colonies and nationalism complicated the situation. And the whole process went awry and broke down after World War I.

By virtue of our cold-war foreign-aid and defense commitments, America finds herself needing the income from investments to meet her current requirements from abroad. We need huge current surpluses to cover aid and investment programs.

BASIC SIGNIFICANCE OF INTERNATIONAL CAPITAL MOVEMENTS

Return now to the problem of capital movements. If political problems of nationalism and domestic problems of unemployment did not enter the picture, the fundamentals of international lending would be easy to understand. We could cut through the fog of money and finance to concentrate on the real aspects in terms of goods and resources.

How does capital grow within a country? By our diverting labor, land, machinery, and other resources away from the production of current consumption goods. Instead, we plant trees, drain rivers, or build new machinery and buildings. All these add to our future income and consumption.

We are postponing present consumption for future consumption; in fact, for an even *greater* amount of future consumption. Where does the increase in future consumption come from? As Chapter 30 showed, *capital goods have a "net" productivity.* This constitutes the real aspect of the interest rate.

Different parts of the world have different amounts of resources: labor, minerals, climate, know-how. Were it not for ignorance or political boundaries, no one would push investment in North America down to the point of 5 per cent returns *if elsewhere there still existed 10 per cent opportunities.* Some capital would certainly be invested abroad. This would give foreign labor higher wages, because now the foreign worker has more and better tools to work with. It would increase foreign production. By how much? Not only by enough to pay for the constant replacement of used-up capital goods but, in addition, by enough to pay us an interest or dividend return on our investment. This interest return would take the form of goods and services which we receive from abroad and which add to our standard of living. An all-wise scientist would probably approve of the process. It would make sense to him because capital is going into the regions where its productivity is highest.

When would we be repaid our principal? So long as we are earning a good return, there is no reason why we should ever wish to have it repaid. However, the once-backward country may finally become rather prosperous. It may wish to pull in its belt as far as consumption is concerned and to use its savings to buy out our ownership in its factories, farms, and mines. But suppose that we are rich, with plenty of savings and with so much capital at home that our rate of interest is low. We might not particularly wish to sell out or be repaid. We might raise the selling price of our farm and factory holdings abroad. In other words, we might be content with a smaller percentage interest return. Thus, there is no necessary reason why a country should ever be paid off for its past lending, unless it has become relatively poorer.

When nationalism rears its head, matters change. Within the United States, interest and dividends may stream from South to North and West to East until doomsday. A few people may grumble about absentee ownership; but the courts and police are there to see that property rights are respected. Not so between nations. When a country is poor, it may be anxious to borrow. After it has become richer, it becomes unhappy to have to pay dividends and interest abroad. It chooses not to remember that its prosperity stemmed in part from its past borrowing. More than an economic burden is involved; politically, countries do not like the principle of absentee ownership by foreigners. They are prone to insist upon getting rid of their international liabilities—paying them off at a fair or unfair price, or often by outright default.

Economics and politics mix in ways too complicated to resolve. Some say "trade follows the flag." Others say the flag follows trade. Some say the pursuit of economic gain is the primary motive behind the imperialistic search for colonies. Others claim that national power (offensive and defensive) is an end in itself; that economic well-being is sacrificed to this end; and that economic resources are sought for their contribution to military strength (offensive and defensive) rather than for their contribution to economic well-being. According to this view, without wars and nationalism, anyone could invest and trade anywhere, and sensible people should prefer to live in small countries unhindered by costly military establishments and colonial administration. At the opposite extreme is the view that victory in battle, rather than comfortable living, is the only worthy end in life; that the foreigner is of no importance compared with the fatherland; that he can be stripped of his goods and land, and be made to work for the conquerors. The world of the last few centuries lies somewhere between these extreme cases.

FINANCIAL VERSUS REAL ASPECTS OF FOREIGN LENDING

Let us turn from politics back to economics to see how foreign investment takes place in financial terms. Money throws a veil over the real aspects of capital movements. Usually, a foreigner borrows *money* from us rather than capital goods directly. He gives us an IOU in the form of a bond, note, or stock certificate. We give him dollars. If he simply holds the dollars or puts them in an American bank or invests them in an American security, there has not yet been a net capital movement. We have some form of his IOU; he has some form of ours. In the capital-movements section of the balance of payments, the difference cancels out. Only when the foreign borrower uses the receipts of the loan to import goods (or gold) in excess of his exports to us does a real and a financial capital movement take place.

When the time comes for interest payment, the foreigners must sell us more goods than they buy in order to get the extra dollars to remit to us. Our balance of international payments then will show an import trade surplus, balanced by the invisible credit item, interest, royalties, and dividends.

Should a nation feel glad or sorry when it is exporting more than it is importing? If we never had to worry about unemployment, we would certainly regret having to give away goods that might better serve our own well-being. Only the consolation of later receiving goods in return could serve to compensate us for this present loss. Altruism aside, if we could look into a crystal ball and see that the investment was sure to go sour later and never be repaid either in principal or interest, then we should certainly conclude that the capital movement was a bad and not a good thing.

A century ago, John Stuart Mill properly stressed that *it is imports and not exports that add to a nation's well-being*. Before World War II, countries were handling the problem of maintaining full employment so badly that they began to revert back to mercantilism, putting the cart before the horse and treating exports as if they were an end for their own sake. Fortunately, nations are learning how proper monetary and fiscal policies can restore to validity the fundamental principles of classical economics. And to this degree Mill's sensible stress on imports comes back into its own.

SUMMARY

A. MECHANISMS OF FOREIGN EXCHANGE AND TRADE

1 Buying or selling abroad presupposes a foreign exchange rate between home and foreign currencies. Two countries on a gold standard have a stable foreign exchange rate set by the stable parity prices at which they each buy and sell gold—whether gold bars, coins, or fractional-reserve banking and gold-exchange standards are used.

2 Classical economists (such as David Hume) relied on gold movements to alter relative price levels, (a) raising exports and (b) curbing imports of the deficit country, and (c) cutting exports and (d) raising imports of the surplus country.

3 Once stable exchange rates under a gold standard are abandoned, flexible foreign rates get set by interaction of supply and demand schedules for foreign exchange. The adjustment now involves changes in export and import prices and not necessarily absolute domestic price levels.

4 Gold coin and bullion evolved into gold-exchange standards internationally and fractional-reserve banking domestically. Gradually the dollar as a key currency gained over the pound, and since World War II the world has been de facto on a dollar standard—which, as Chapter 36 will show, is badly in need of basic structural reform.

B. BALANCE OF INTERNATIONAL TRADE AND CAPITAL MOVEMENTS

5 The balance of international payments refers to all the transactions that use up foreign exchange or make foreign exchange available to us. It relates the total of our exports of goods and services to our imports. Our exports of goods, services, gold, or IOUs are

credit items, making foreign currencies available to us. Our imports of those items are debits, using up foreign currencies.

6 Our net balance on current account comes from adjusting our merchandise trade balance for "invisible" service items and taking into account our unilateral government aid programs. It and net long-term capital movements constitute the "basic deficit" which must be offset by short-term capital movements and shipments of gold and reserve assets.

7 As a nation passes from the "young debtor" to the "mature creditor" stage, its payments go through a characteristic sequence of stages.

8 No problem in international finance is more important than that of understanding the real and the monetary aspects of capital movements in their effect upon the industrial development of nations.

QUESTIONS FOR DISCUSSION

1 Contrast free and stable foreign exchange rates. Explain each.

2 What are the gold points exactly? Suppose transport costs diminish.

3 Draw up a list of items that belong on the credit side of the balance of international payments and another list of items that belong on the debit side. What is meant by a "favorable balance of trade"? By the balance on current account? By the "basic deficit"? Why the term "invisible items"? What is the difference between short- and long-term capital movements?

4 Construct hypothetical balance sheets for a young debtor country, a mature debtor country, a new creditor country, and a mature creditor country.

5 "Foreign lending causes war. Foreign giving postpones war. Free foreign trading prevents war." Comment.

Review your understanding of the following concepts:

gold standard versus free exchange rate
currency depreciation and devaluation
gold-exchange and dollar standard
debits and credits
balance of international payments,
   trade balance, invisibles, current
   account, government aid items

"favorable balance"
America's "basic deficit"
gold movements
IOUs, capital movements
net foreign investment
historical capital movements, financial
   and real, in politics and economics

APPENDIX: Income and Unemployment Aspects of International Trade

FOREIGN-TRADE MULTIPLIER

The classical mechanism of Hume depended primarily on relative prices. It seems to have assumed, essentially, that employment is always full: that in the long run, trade simply moved a society from one point on its domestic production-possibility frontier to another; that foreign trade never moved society inside its *p-p frontier* or pushed it outward toward that frontier from an initial underemployment equilibrium.

Yet we saw in Part Two that a laissez faire system is not automatically always at full employment. That cannot be guaranteed unless stabilizing monetary and fiscal policy is brought to bear on it (or unless there is more ideal flexibility of wage and price levels than modern mixed economies have.)

What, then, will be the effects of international forces on the $C + I + G$ equilibrium of Part Two? One can guess that additional exports and foreign investment will have the same expansionary effects on domestic production and employment as will additional domestic investment.

That guess is correct: similar multiplier effects are involved. New exports do have exactly the same multiplier effects on output and prices. They raise incomes directly, but in addition they set up a chain of further spending and respending.

Thus, $1 billion worth of new export orders to New England machine-tool factories will create $1 billion of primary jobs and income. Then workers and owners may respend perhaps two-thirds of their new income on the consumption products of Indiana and California; two-thirds of this extra income is in turn respent. The process finally comes to a halt only when the total adds up to

$$3 = 1 + \tfrac{2}{3} + (\tfrac{2}{3})^2 + \cdots = 1/(1 - \tfrac{2}{3})$$

—i.e., to $1 billion of initial expenditure plus $2 billion of extra secondary consumption expenditure.

Besides introducing a multiplier effect of exports, international trade has a second important effect. Our higher American GNP will increase our imports, let us say, by one-twelfth out of every extra dollar. This means that our chain of induced domestic purchasing power will peter out faster than in the above example. At each step, these imports act as "leakages," just like the marginal propensity to save.[1]

Therefore, out of the original $1 billion of income in the export industries, perhaps only $\tfrac{7}{12} (= \tfrac{2}{3} - \tfrac{1}{12})$ rather than $\tfrac{8}{12}$ will be respent on *American* consumption goods (in Indiana, California, and so forth). And so it will go at each stage. The whole multiplier will now add up to only

$$1 + \tfrac{7}{12} + (\tfrac{7}{12})^2 + \cdots$$

or only to

$$1 \div (1 - \tfrac{7}{12}) = 1 \div \tfrac{5}{12} = 2\tfrac{2}{5}$$

[1]Applying the foreign-trade multiplier analysis to a small city or country, you will find that secondary multiplier effects upon the workers of that region are almost negligible, since most extra income leaks out to other regions.

instead of to 3. Note that $\tfrac{1}{12}$ of our extra $2\tfrac{2}{5}$ billion of generated income—or $\tfrac{1}{5}$ billion in this case—tends to go abroad for extra imports. A general rule can be stated:

Exports raise domestic income, but with a multiplier reduced by our induced imports. So long as some fraction of income at every stage is leaking into domestic saving, a new dollar of exports will raise income, but can never lift it by enough to call forth a full dollar of new imports.[2]

In conclusion, we may say that variations in income generated by international trade will often go partway to effecting the needed adjustments; but they do not obviate the need for some price or exchange-rate reductions, since a spontaneous increase in demand for our exports can never create a large enough induced expansion of our imports to cancel out all final effects on the balance of payments between us and abroad.

OVERVALUATION OF A CURRENCY AND UNEMPLOYMENT

Consider two countries. Call them A and E for America and Europe. Although Germany is not identical with Europe, let the respective currencies be called dollars and marks. Let A and E begin in long-run foreign exchange equilibrium with 4 marks to the dollar or $.25 per mark.

Now let productivity in Europe, even though it begins far below that in America, grow faster than in America. If all money wages and profits grew in E as quickly as productivity, there need be no lasting disturbance to the equilibrium: thus, doubling productivity and money wages and factor payments in E will leave her prices just as they were in relation to A's unchanged prices. The real income level in E has grown relative to that of A, perhaps closing some of the gap between them. But so long as Engel's laws imply that A's goods are as much in demand at higher income levels at E's, there need be no disturbance of the equilibrium. A is not yet hurt or helped by E's improved real income.

[2]Suppose that each extra dollar of income is always split up into the three fractions: c for American consumption goods; b for America's propensity to import goods from abroad; a for the remaining amount going into saving. Then let exports go up by 1 unit. The multiplier tells us that our income will go up by $1/(1 - c) = 1/(b + a)$. Multiplying this extra income by the fraction b, we get induced imports of $b/(b + a)$, which is certainly less than our original 1 of new exports—to the extent that the marginal propensity to save a is positive.

If there is any induced domestic investment, it can be thrown in with c, and our result will still hold for any "stable" system with positive "leakage" a.

However, it is more realistic to assume that money wage and other factor-costs do not *at once* grow abroad as fast as productivity does, even though they grow much faster than in relatively stagnant A. Now E's goods are bargains. Even if A has not had domestic wage or other inflation, A's goods are now relatively dear. What is the effect? E's exports expand physically and (probably) in value; A's exports dwindle physically and (probably) in value. If payments were in balance before, now A runs a chronic international deficit.

We can say: Before at 1 dollar to 4 marks, the dollar was neither undervalued nor overvalued; now at 1 to 4, the dollar is definitely an "overvalued currency," running a chronic deficit and having too high a cost level. This results from the more rapid technical change abroad, which partially closed the gap between their technology and ours and lowered their relative costs.

The deficit disequilibrium in A's balance on current account will probably be aggravated by a tendency for A's investors to want to invest in E, where profitability is likely to be very high as a result of (1) rapid growth in E; (2) rapid technical change in E; (3) great opportunity for A firms to profit from applying their "know-how" in E.

Effects of overvaluation 1. If in A we previously had full employment, our loss of export production (and perhaps of domestic production displaced by cheap imports) implies a multiplier drop in employment and real GNP.

2. We cannot use Federal Reserve easy money to stimulate domestic I, for fear that low interest yields will drive cool money to seek higher yields in E.

3. If, like Kennedy and Johnson in the 1960s, we use militant fiscal policy, expanding G expenditure and cutting tax rates to expand C and I, we can overcome our unemployment; but the resulting increase in GNP will wipe out the drop in our imports from E that had resulted from our income drop (and which has *partially* relieved our international deficit).

4. If E previously had full employment, she now is threatened with overemployment, with demand-pull and cost-push inflation. If E previously had some slack, she would be delighted with her good fortune to have become an *undervalued*-currency nation, with the extra NNP and employment thereby implied. If previously at full employment, E will now complain bitterly that she is "importing inflation" from profligate A.

5. Actually, now that E is quoting prices low relative to those A is quoting, the disturbed-equilibrium terms of trade—the ratio of our export to import prices—

have moved in favor of A. E is, so to speak, throwing away goods to A. Not only is A getting cheap goods—the goal of rational nonmercantilistic nations—but we in A are, for the moment, getting some goods in return simply for our shipping out barren gold or mere IOUs.

Correcting overvaluation What can correct the situation? We in A can wait for inflation in E to raise E's prices and end the undervaluation of E's currency. If E's productivity continues to show miracles of growth, the wait may be a long and grueling one.

Or, in premodern times, A could try to deflate her own wage and cost level by 10 or 20 per cent. This seems not very practical in a mixed economy of rather rigid administered prices and wages: blood has often run in the streets of nations trying to adjust to an overvalued currency by internal cost deflation.

Or A might pray for a miracle that would increase her productivity. Exhortations to have us all work harder and more skillfully will no doubt be forthcoming in abundance.

Or E might *ap*preciate the mark.[3] When the mark has risen from \$.25 to \$.27, German exports will be dear and imports from America cheap. Thus, there may again be equilibrium, with neither currency overvalued.[4] However, let us suppose that for the years in question appreciation is simply not politically feasible.

If A's gold is large enough to meet the chronic drain and E's willingness to take A's IOUs is sufficiently great, the disequilibrium situation may go on for a long time. Perhaps in that time luck will shift the winds of demand in A's favor; or A's productivity might grow; or A may become a more profitable place for investors in either country to want to place their long-term funds; or the government in A may, reluctantly, cut down on its troop and its aid expenditures abroad.

A country with an overvalued currency will be under

[3] Or A might *de*preciate the dollar.
[4] If E's improved productivity has occurred across the board in all industries, she will be better off in the new equilibrium and we need not be hurt or helped. (E.g., a relative 10 per cent improvement in her productivity and costs relative to ours could be just offset by a 10 per cent appreciation. We import the same German goods at the same dollar costs as before; they now can buy 10 per cent more of their domestic goods from an hour's work at home and 10 per cent more of imports from us at the 10-per-cent-cheapened dollar.) But suppose, as is more likely, that Germany's productivity is biased to rise more in goods that she had been on the borderline of importing from America. Then there is a presumption that in the new equilibrium our export prices will fall relative to what we now pay for imports. Europe's progress has hurt us a bit, as we now lose "consumer's surplus" from no longer being able to trade at so "favorable terms of trade."

great internal pressure to interfere with free trade. Employers and workers will clamor for protective tariffs and quotas. Congress will consider preventing costly tours abroad, curbing free flow of capital abroad, introducing comprehensive exchange controls, initiating export subsidies, tying up foreign aid, and requiring purchase of military equipment at home even at prices twice as high. The President will exhort business to moderate profitable investments abroad by a "voluntary" and mandatory capital investment program, and will introduce so-called "interest equalization taxes" which place perhaps a 10 to 20 per cent tax on long-term foreign loans.

Most chronically overvalued currencies in history have resulted in suspension of freely convertible currencies and in controlled international trade. Moreover, once the overvaluation of the currency has been handled in this way, there is no possibility of removing the controls: when controls are ended, the international payments deficit reappears. History is replete with cases of premature dashes toward convertibility, which ended in fiascoes and return to controls.

The Achilles' heel of classicism What needs emphasis here is the economics of overvaluation. We shall discover that all the discredited notions of the mercantilists—fear of gold drain, insistence on import curbs and export subsidies, wish to export unemployment abroad, desire to give goods away cheaply rather than dearly, etc.—make some sense in the case of an overvalued currency. The skilled classical and neoclassical arguments of Hume, Smith, and Samuelson no longer carry the day because their major premise of equilibrium currency valuation is explicitly denied.

The next two chapters will elucidate the pro-and-con arguments for tariffs and will demonstrate the basic theory of comparative advantage that justifies mutually advantageous geographical division of labor and trade. If prices and wages were everywhere perfectly flexible and/or exchange rates could be counted on to be neither overvalued nor undervalued, the arguments of these chapters would be unanswerable. Here is an example:

Chapter 34 points out that the veil of money and foreign exchange merely covers the true barter nature of trade. It says, "One country cannot undersell the other in *all* goods, but only in those in which it has a comparative advantage, being undersold by the other country in those goods in which that country has a comparative advantage." That is absolutely true in a Ricardian model where the wage ratio between the two countries moves flexibly so that the resulting foreign exchange rate is neither overvalued nor undervalued.

But it is still quite obvious that if one country insists on pricing its goods sky-high in money terms (because of sky-high wage rates *or* profit markups), it can certainly price itself out of the market, bringing upon itself an overvalued currency, unemployment, and international deficits. After all, any one of us can do that by insisting on $100,000 per hour; and any region, such as New England, could be undersold by the South in everything if it insisted on prices that cleared no markets. So this can certainly happen internationally as well as intranationally.

A CRAWLING (OR SLIDING) PEG

We have seen that stable exchange rates promote fruitful trade. We have also seen that a flexible, freely floating exchange rate, determined by momentary supply and demand as in Fig. 33-1, prevents long-term balance-of-payments disequilibrium of the kind that will be discussed in Chapter 36. A number of economists[5] have therefore suggested as a new reform measure an interesting compromise between exchange-rate stability and flexibility.

1. The "gold points," which surround the parity exchange rate, are to be widened (and freed from any dependence on a fixed price of gold or the cost of shipping gold).

Thus instead of holding fluctuations of the £-$ rate within the range $2.40 ± .02, let it now freely move with supply and demand within the range of, say, $2.40 ± .20. I.e., in any year the pound rate might fall from $2.60 to $2.20 if Europe's import debits were threatening to exceed her export credits.

Within the widened range, equilibrium would take place as a result of permitted, orderly rate adjustments (appreciation or depreciation).

2. Over a period of years, the midrange parity, around which the widened limits are drawn, would be permitted to rise or fall by, say, 1 or 1½ per cent per year.

Why? So that if Europe's cost structure were showing a long-term tendency to rise more than ours, the threatened fundamental disequilibrium could be averted. (Merely widening the upper and lower points would give only limited relief: for, if Europe's costs and prices rise chronically, the exchange rate would always be at the $2.20 floor; only by gradually lowering

[5] J. M. Keynes proposed widening of the gold points in the 1920s. In the 1960s, A. W. Phillips, J. E. Meade, and J. Black of the United Kingdom proposed a crawling peg; and a large number of American experts endorsed the combined scheme in a 1965 petition. Chapter 36 will return to this subject.

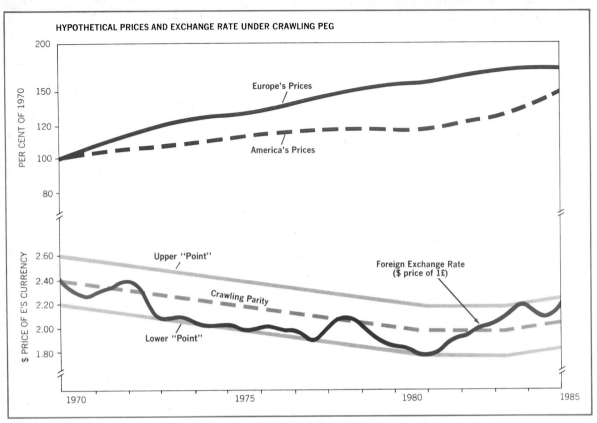

FIG. 33-2.

that floor could the growing dearness of Europe's exports be offset by long-term, orderly depreciation of the pound.)

The slowness of the long-term slide in the exchange-rate peg should go far to discourage speculators from "piling on" to a one-way movement, thereby aggravating it and making it even more disorderly.

Figure 33-2 shows how the scheme might work in a hypothetical future period.

Note that in the early years, European prices (costs, wages, etc.) are rising faster than American prices (these are shown in brown above). By the "purchasing-power parity" doctrine of this chapter, that should

depress the pound rate toward its floor. (Of course, momentary ups and downs of supply and demand change the blue exchange rate within the widened limits.)

Since Europe's relative price rise is chronic and not temporary, the blue tracks all move in one direction, at 1½ per cent per year. In a decade, an orderly 15 per cent exchange-rate adjustment has been made!

Best of all, the process can be a two-way street. If, much later, American prices outsoar European, it can be the dollar's turn to depreciate: now the pound appreciates toward the ceiling limit, and the tracks gradually rise.

FOR REVIEW

Review your understanding of the following concepts:

foreign-trade multiplier
"leakage" into imports
overvaluation, undervaluation

unemployment and overvaluation
crawling peg of parity
widened "gold points"

International Trade and the Theory of Comparative Advantage

34

The benefit of international trade—a more efficient employment of the productive forces of the world.
J. S. MILL

Again and again we have seen how specialization increases productivity and standards of living. Now we must show exactly how this works out in the field of international trade, going behind the facade of international finance.

Why did the United States specialize a century ago in the production of agricultural goods and exchange these for the manufacturing output of Europe? Why is she today able to export highly complex mass-produced goods to the far corners of the globe? Why is the agriculture of Australia so different from that of Austria? How great would the costs of complete self-sufficiency be to a modern country? How do all countries benefit from trade?

The key to such questions, and many more, is provided by the theory of comparative advantage, or comparative cost. Developed more than a century ago by David Ricardo, John Stuart Mill, and other followers of Adam Smith, the theory of comparative advantage is a closely reasoned doctrine which, when properly stated, is unassailable. With it we can identify gross fallacies in the political propaganda for protective tariffs aimed at limiting imports. With it we can identify the germs of truth that sometimes appear in the heated claims for tariff protection.

DIVERSITY OF CONDITIONS BETWEEN REGIONS OR COUNTRIES

For simplicity, begin by imagining two countries or continents, each endowed with certain quantities of natural resources, capital goods, kinds of labor, and technical knowledge or know-how. The first link in the comparative-cost chain of reasoning is the *diversity in conditions of production between different countries.*

Specifically, this means that the production possibilities of the different countries are very different. Although people could try to produce something of every commodity in any region, it is obvious that they would not succeed; or if they did succeed, it would only be at a terrific cost. Smith pointed out that, with hothouse procedures and forcing methods, wine grapes could perhaps be grown in Scotland; but the cost in terms of economic resources would be exorbitant, and the resulting product would be scarce fit to drink.

Even if by chance two countries can both produce the same commodities, they generally find that it pays for each to concentrate its production especially on some goods and trade for other goods.

If we consider trade between, say, the northern temperate zones and the southern tropics, the foregoing proposition will seem true and trite. Of course, resources near the equator are more productive in the growing of bananas, and northern resources are better designed for wheat growing. Everyone can readily see that in this case specialization and trade will increase the amount of world production of both goods, and also each country's ability to consume both goods.

It is not so immediately obvious, but it is no less true, that

International trade is mutually profitable even when one of the countries can produce *every commodity* more cheaply (in terms of labor or all resources) than the other country. Can America with $5-an-hour wages benefit from trade with Japan at $1 an hour? Yes, asserts the theory of comparative advantage.

One country may be *absolutely more efficient* in the production of *every* good than is the other country; and this means the other country has an absolute disadvantage in the production of every good. But so long as there are differences in the *relative* efficiencies of producing the different goods in the two countries, we can always be sure that even the poor country has a *comparative advantage* in the production of those commodities in which it is relatively most efficient; this same poor country will have a *comparative disadvantage* in those other commodities in which its inefficiency is more than average. Similarly, the rich, efficient country will find that it should specialize in those fields of production where it has a comparative advantage, planning to import those commodities in which it has a comparative disadvantage.

A traditional example used to illustrate this paradox of comparative advantage is the case of the best lawyer in town who is also the best typist in town. Will he not specialize in law and leave typing to a secretary? How can he afford to give up precious time from the legal field, where his comparative advantage is very great, to perform typing activities in which he is efficient but in which he lacks *comparative* advantage? Or look at it from the secretary's point of view. She is less efficient than he in both activities; but her relative disadvantage compared with him is least in typing. Relatively speaking, she has a comparative advantage in typing.

So with countries. Suppose America produces food with one-third the labor that Europe does, and clothing with one-half the labor. Then we shall see that America has comparative advantage in food and comparative disadvantage in clothing—this, despite the fact that America is absolutely most efficient in everything. By the same token, Europe has comparative advantage in clothing.

A SIMPLE CASE: EUROPE AND AMERICA

Let us illustrate these fundamental principles of international trade by a simplified example. Consider America and Europe of a century ago, and concentrate on only two commodities, food and clothing. In America land and natural resources were then very plentiful relative to labor and capital; but in Europe, people and capital were plentiful relative to land.

This contrast is best seen if we look at the *intensive* agriculture of a country such as Belgium. There, in order to get the greatest possible output, small plots of land have to be cultivated assiduously by many people using much fertilizer. Compare this with the extensive agriculture of early America: here one family cultivated many acres, and national product was maximized by each man's "spreading himself thin" over the virtually free land. A Belgian would have thought this wasteful. But in view of the relatively high cost of our labor or capital and the low cost of land, it was prudent.

Of course, if surplus population could have all migrated from Belgium to the United States, the law of diminishing returns implies that real wages here would fall toward equality with rising wages there; and high land rents there would fall toward equality with rising rents here.[1]

But suppose that immigrants from abroad are to be kept out of the United States in order to keep labor scarce here and wages high. From this same selfish point of view, should the United States also impose a protective tariff designed to keep out imports from abroad? Or should it not? To answer this important social question we must measure carefully the amounts of food and clothing that will be produced and consumed in each country (1) if there is no international trade and (2) if trade, according to comparative advantage, is permitted to follow its own course.

THE LAW OF COMPARATIVE ADVANTAGE

David Ricardo, stockbroker and self-made millionaire, expert on the theory of land rent and of currency, came up in 1817 with the beautiful proof that international specialization pays for a nation. This is the famous theory of comparative advantage, or, as it is sometimes called, the "theory of comparative cost."

For simplicity Ricardo worked with only two countries; we shall call them America and Europe, and assume they are both about the same size. For simplicity he worked with only two goods; we shall call them food and clothing. For simplicity Ricardo chose to measure all costs in terms of hours of labor; we shall do the same, recognizing that more advanced treatises and the Appendix to this chapter can give some of the needed qualifications when our simple assumptions are relaxed. The germ of truth in the principle of comparative advantage will still remain.

Uncommon sense   Using common sense, people will probably agree that trade between America and Europe is likely to be mutually profitable in a first simple case where European labor has greater productivity in one good and American labor has greater productivity in another.

---

[1] Actually, this would have tended at the same time to increase *total world production*. Why? Because the transfer of workers from their poor Belgian farms to rich American farms would increase their productivity and total world product. Factor mobility shifts the world *p-p frontier* outward.

Comparative advantage depends only on productivity ratios:

AMERICAN AND EUROPEAN LABOR REQUIREMENTS FOR PRODUCTION		
PRODUCT	IN AMERICA	IN EUROPE
1 unit of food	**1** day's labor	3 days' labor
1 unit of clothing	2 days' labor	4 days' labor

TABLE 34-1. Even though America's 1 and 2 are, respectively, less than Europe's 3 and 4, we have *comparative* advantage in food and Europe has it in clothing. Why? Because our 1 ÷ her 3 is less than our 2 ÷ her 4 (or equivalently, because our 1/2 is less than her 3/4).

In this case, to produce a unit of food in America requires a smaller number of labor days than is needed in Europe to produce it, while to produce a unit of clothing takes a smaller number of labor days in Europe than in America. The man in the street needs no Ricardo to tell him that in such a case America will probably specialize in food production, exporting some food for Europe's clothing exports.

But Ricardo showed much more than this. He showed that even if American labor (or resources generally) were more productive than Europe's *in both* food *and* clothing, trade is still likely to be mutually advantageous.

Table 34-1 illustrates this principle of comparative advantage. In America a unit of food costs 1 day's labor and a unit of clothing costs 2 days' labor. In Europe the cost is 3 days' labor for food and 4 days' labor for clothing. By forming the proper two ratios of these four crucial numbers, Ricardo is able to prove conclusively that America and Europe will *both* benefit if America specializes in food and exports it for the clothing exports that Europe specializes in.

Before examining this, listen to the European in the street as he says:

Mon Dieu! Trade could never be profitable for us with that American colossus. Her efficiency will enable her to undersell us in every line—food and clothing. We need import tariffs to protect the honest European worker.

Now listen to what is being said here in America by the man in the street and the congressmen who have not grasped the law of comparative advantage:

The European wage level most assuredly will be far below that of this most prosperous (and productive) nation on earth. If we subject the American workers to the unbridled competition of the European pauper laborers, who subsist on less per day than we do, the real wage of the American worker must drastically fall. A protective tariff against cheap imports is desperately needed to maintain the American standard of living.

What Ricardo shows is that both arguments are wrong. The European and American workers *both* can get higher real wages by international trade. Prohibitive tariffs on either or both sides will reduce real wages in both places. (And we may add in our day that there are better tools than protective tariffs to make sure that there are plenty of job opportunities and stable price levels in both places; namely, proper fiscal and central-bank monetary policies.)

Before trade If we start with a prohibitive tariff that has prevented all international trade, Table 34-1 shows that the real wage of the American worker for a day's work will be 1 unit of food or $\frac{1}{2}$ unit of clothing. The European worker is even less well off and gets for a day's labor before trade only $\frac{1}{3}$ unit of food or $\frac{1}{4}$ unit of clothing.

Evidently, under domestic competition in each isolated continent, the price ratios of food and clothing will be different in the two places because of the difference in relative labor cost ratios. In America clothing will be 2 times as dear as food because it takes twice as much labor. In Europe clothing will be only $\frac{4}{3}$ times as dear as food.

After trade   Now we repeal the protective tariff and make trade free. The relative prices of clothing and food must now come to a common level, just as the water in two connecting pipes must come to a common intermediate level once you remove the barrier between them. Why?

Competitive merchants buy where things are cheap and sell where they are dear. With clothing relatively more expensive in America, merchants will soon ship clothing from Europe to America and ship food from America to the European markets, where it has been relatively dear. Our clothing industry will feel the keen price competition of imports, and if the figures in Table 34-1 do not change, it may lose *all* its workers to the American food industry. The opposite will happen in Europe: workers will leave the food industry for the clothing industry, in which it has a comparative advantage.

America as a whole has benefited. Like any merchant who will buy electric power from another firm if he cannot produce it as cheaply himself, America has taken advantage of the fact that clothing does cost us less by barter than by domestic production. The same goes for Europe's benefit from specializing in clothing and getting her food more cheaply by barter.

Example of benefit: Each unit of American labor still gets the 1 unit of food it produces here. But now 1 American food trades for *more* than $\frac{1}{2}$ unit of clothing. How much more? Certainly not more than the 3/4 ratio set by Europe's costs. The common ratio after trade will be *somewhere between 1/2 and 3/4*. American labor gains in clothing by any degree that it exceeds 1/2. Similarly, European labor gains in bartering clothing for food by any degree that the ratio falls short of 3/4. (See the Appendix for elaborations.)

Granted that Ricardo has proved that both countries have benefited from trade in accordance with comparative advantage, what about the workingman in each place? Table 34-1 can show that his real wages have improved in both places. Now the American worker's day of labor will buy him the same food as before, but he gets *more* imported clothing for a day of labor and can now afford to consume more of *both* goods. Likewise, the European worker can get more of the cheapened imported food for a day of his labor, and inasmuch as he gets the same real wage in clothing, his budget is also better off. It is the expanded *world* production of both goods, which specialization and trade created, that makes it possible for *everyone* to be better off.

1. *The principle of comparative advantage restated:* **Whether or not one of two regions is absolutely more efficient in the production of every good than is the other, if each specializes in the products in which it has a *comparative advantage* (greatest *relative* efficiency), trade will be mutually profitable to both regions. Real wages of productive factors will rise in both places.**
2. **An ill-designed prohibitive tariff, far from helping the protected factor of production,**

will instead reduce its real wage by making imports expensive and by making the whole world less productive through eliminating the efficiency inherent in the best pattern of specialization and division of labor.

This simple principle provides the unshakable basis for international trade.[2]

OTHER CAUSES OF INTERNATIONAL TRADE

Decreasing costs   If economies of mass production are overwhelmingly important, costs may decrease as output expands. This would strengthen the case for international exchange of goods. In fact, decreasing costs are a second great factor—in addition to differences in comparative costs—explaining why specialization and trade are profitable. For, as was discussed in Chapters 3 and 25, large-scale specialization is most fruitful when there is a widely expanded market.

In fact, even if there were no differences in comparative costs between two countries, it might pay for them to toss a coin to decide who was to produce each of two goods subject to increasing returns or decreasing costs. Complete specialization would increase world production of both goods. This may be illustrated by our example in Chapter 3

---

[2] To see this graphically, look at Fig. 34-1(a), which shows America's blue domestic production-possibility frontier, with its slope depicting a 1/2 food-to-clothing price ratio.

Europe's brown domestic production-possibility frontier has its 3/4 slope. (Since Europe's population happens to be about equal that of America, why is the brown curve this much "smaller" than the blue? Because America has double or more the productivity of Europe.) Ricardo says, "It is the difference in slopes that makes profitable trade possible." How profitable? The limits (as explained in the Appendix) are shown by the gold areas between (a) each country's domestic curve and (b) a line drawn parallel

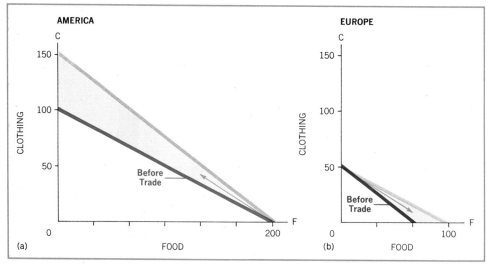

FIG. 34-1.

to the other country's curve passed through each point of specialization. Thus the intermediate gold arrows, with slopes intermediate between A's 1/2 and B's 3/4, are one possible outcome: at posttrade equilibrium with food selling for two-thirds clothing (i.e., at 2/3), A gains by producing food alone and exporting it for clothing: E gains by producing clothing and exporting it in exchange for food.

of the identical Indian twins who, despite their similarity, still find it advantageous to specialize to reap the efficiencies of "mass" production. The European Common Market (France, West Germany, Italy, Belgium, the Netherlands, Luxembourg) hopes to reap the advantages of such an extended division of labor.

Moreover, there is one very practical aspect of international trade to be observed under decreasing cost. Peculiarly under such conditions, perfect competition is likely to break down and be succeeded by monopoly, or imperfect competition. By excluding foreign competition, protective tariffs only serve to consolidate the position of the monopolist. This is recognized in the old slogan, "The tariff is the mother of trusts." Freer international trade is often an efficient way of breaking up monopoly positions.[3]

Differences in tastes or demand   Here is a third possible cause for trade. Even if costs were identical in the two countries and were increasing, trade might take place as the result of differences in *tastes*.

Thus, it might pay both Norway and Sweden to produce fish from the sea and meat from the land in about the same amounts. But if the Swedes have a relatively great fondness for meat and the Norwegians for fish, then a mutually profitable export of meat from Norway and fish from Sweden would take place. Both parties gain from this trade. The sum total of human happiness is increased, just as it is when Jack Spratt trades fat meat for his wife's lean. Both get some "consumer's surplus" from the swap.[4]

We have now gone beyond the financial facade of international trade to the real fundamentals. Now we can handle the remaining two chapters of Part Five.

FOREIGN-TRADE SUPPLY-AND-DEMAND CHARTS[5]

The foregoing theory of comparative advantage stripped international trade down to its barter essentials. It said nothing about dollars, pounds, or foreign exchange rates. How does the matter appear to the perfect competitors in one small food or clothing industry in America? Why does competitive P settle down so that America exports this item of wheat but not that item of cloth? How do the supply and demand curves look in the competitive market for a small clothing item exported by Europe—say, linen cloth?

Figure 34-2 first takes up the case of an American export good, wheat, in the simplest case where every European unit of money—call it a pound—is always worth exactly \$3. Figure 34-2(a) shows the American demand and supply curves $d_a d_a$ and $s_a s_a$ for wheat expressed in dollars (which, by a 1/3 scale change, can also be read in pounds). Figure

---

[3] Still, one must concede that decreasing-cost situations might under free trade lead to bigger monopolies, and that decreasing-cost situations may have in them some of the valid elements of the "infant-industry" argument to be met in the next chapter.

[4] Even two individuals with identical amounts of two goods and the same tastes may in rare instances trade. Two sailors, each with a fifth of rye and a fifth of gin, might toss a coin to decide which is to have two fifths of gin and which two fifths of rye. You can reason out why the same might be true of herring and chocolate, but not of corned beef and cabbage. Such cases of trade are oddities (and can be shown in more advanced treatises to result from a reversal of curvature of the convex indifference contours of Chapter 22's Appendix).

[5] The next two sections are quite independent of the rest of this chapter, except for points 5 and 6 in the Summary. The next chapters do not require them or this chapter's Appendix.

Supply and demand here and abroad determine export Ps:

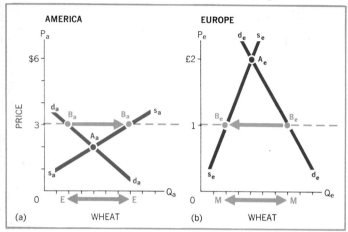

FIG. 34-2.   With zero trade, American wheat price is at A_a, below European price at A_e. With free trade, goods flow from low- to high-price place, finally equalizing Ps at that golden level where the export arrow just matches the import arrow.

34-2(b) shows the European supply and demand for wheat as $d_e d_e$ and $s_e s_e$ (in pounds, with vertical scales nicely aligned so as to be read in dollars or pounds).

Suppose trade in wheat were prohibited by quotas, tariffs, or sky-high transport costs. Where would *autarky* equilibrium be in each country? Under such an assumption of no trade, equilibrium would be at the separate intersection points A_a and A_e: Wheat's price (per bushel) in America would be $6, or £2. Both markets are cleared; being forbidden, exports and imports are, of course, zero.

Now open up trade in wheat. If there are zero transport costs, quotas, and tariffs, both markets must have the same price. Why? Because sharp-eyed arbitragers could buy where wheat was cheap and send it for sale where it was dear. With what result? Evidently, P_e would fall and P_a rise until equality was achieved. How much would the price changes be? That would depend on the slopes of each country's *dd* and *ss* curves.

The condition for the free-trade equilibrium is that the new common price should coax out an import demand abroad just equal to our export supply.

Free-trade equilibrium is at the $3 and £1 level, where America's export arrow *EE* or $B_a B_a$ just matches (and opposes in direction) Europe's import arrow *MM* or $B_e B_e$. No other equilibrium can persist.

Figure 34-3 shows exactly the same phenomenon for the case of Europe's clothing export, linen. Who decides that linen will be Europe's export and wheat will be America's? The levels of the no-trade equilibria intersections decide: goods flow uphill toward higher prices under free competition! (Because A_e is below A_a, Europe exports linen.)

The reader could draw a new figure for the case where the no-trade Ps happen to start out equal and where free trade leads to zero trade. This is a rare razor's-edge case of coincidental levels. However, in real life, there are always transport costs that impede trade. Thus, although bricks may seem to be cheaper in America, if the difference between the no-trade equilibrium intersections is less than the substantial *costs of shipping* heavy and bulky bricks, each country will produce its own bricks and there will be neither exports nor imports. Goods try to flow uphill toward higher prices, but transport-cost or tariff impediments can inhibit their flow.

This supply-and-demand analysis is a simple extension of that given in Chapter 4 (or Part Three). It is useful. But note that we should have to go to Ricardo's deeper analysis of comparative advantage to explain *why* both countries' *dd* and *ss* schedules will be such as to give America a money-cost advantage in exporting this food item. That same analysis of basic comparative advantage is needed to explain why the clothing item, linen, will have *dd* and *ss* intersections causing Europe to export it.[6]

EFFECTS OF TARIFFS AND QUOTAS

Prohibitive tariff   Figure 34-3 can be used to illustrate the effect of an American tariff (or "customs tax") on the import of linen. If we tax linen imports by more than the difference in prices ($9 \equiv £3 = \$12 - \$3$) shown between the no-trade A_a and A_e intersections, how much linen will get sent here? Absolutely none: the tariff of more

Supply and demand here and abroad determine import Ps:

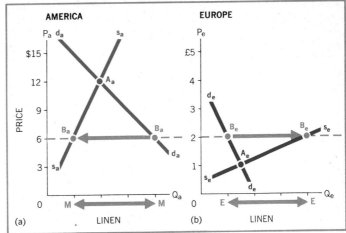

FIG. 34-3.   Lower European *P* at zero or *autarky* trade means linen will be imported from Europe when trade is permitted. Common *P* is where imports and exports match. (Quotas, tariffs, or transport costs will make *P*s unequal.)

than $9 will be a *prohibitive* one, shutting out all imports. Why? Because any importer who tries to buy linen at the European A_e price of $3 (or £1) can sell it here for at most $12 (or £4). But the tariff the importer has to pay would come to *more* than that difference! Hence, such a tariff kills off *all* the advantage of specialization and trade.

A smaller tariff will kill off some linen imports, in that sense partially "protecting" our domestic industry.

Social cost of tariffs   What happens to our domestic linen industry? The tariff gives it a higher price than under free trade. The effect of a tariff that "protects" against imports is to raise the price to the domestic consumer.[7]

But does not the government collect in tariff revenue about what the consumers now pay in extra prices? Our special example of a prohibitive tariff points up the negative answer that can be generally given. Here consumers pay more but the government collects nothing! This needs emphasis, and shows how foolish it is to try to measure a tariff's height and capacity for doing harm by the tax revenue it brings in. Also, any tariff that limits imports will make consumers pay a higher *P* for all the *domestically supplied* output, and *none* of this shows up in government revenue.

The higher *P* lowers the satisfaction and well-being of consumers. Whom does it benefit? The suppliers of this particular industry do benefit. If linen were a monopoly industry

---

[6]As economists put this matter: Marshall's supply and demand curves depict only "partial equilibrium." They must be anchored on "general equilibrium" analysis, of which Ricardo's is a special case.

[7]The price rise need not be as great as the tariff itself; it will be that great only if the industry abroad is so large compared with our use of the product that one or both of their *ss* and *dd* schedules can be regarded as practically horizontal, our imports being too small to affect their prices appreciably.

here, the monopolist would benefit and could afford to lobby for tariffs. Some of the benefit would trickle down to his employees and to owners of resources especially fitted for linen production. Even if, as in Fig. 34-3(a), there is perfect competition, the productive factors specialized for the protected industry do stand to get some benefit (higher P for linen, more jobs, higher wage rates, higher economic rents on factors inelastically supplied to that industry).[8] When the wife of one of these specialized employees complained about the high cost of linen and of living generally, resulting from a high-tariff program, her husband could reprimand her: "Stop complaining. *We* get more than *we* give as a result of the tariff. It's *the rest of the community* that experiences the net harm from the cessation of linen imports."

In wheat and other nonprotected industries, wives and husbands can both legitimately complain about this linen tariff. Indeed, let us consider (1) the harm done to consumers, (2) the revenue collected by government, and (3) the benefit received by suppliers. What is the net effect, on the supposition that rich and poor, worthy and unworthy, are equally involved on all sides of the argument? It is shown in the Appendix to this chapter that the harm of a prohibitive tariff outweighs its gain, in this sense:

A system of prohibitive tariffs puts a society inefficiently *inside* the consumption-possibility frontier that would be available if the efficiencies of international exchange and division of labor were utilized. This is absolutely true of the world as a whole, and particularly true for a country that cuts off all imports and becomes self-sufficient.[9]

Quotas The effect of a prohibitive tariff could be achieved by imposing a zero quota on all imports. The prices would find their A_a and A_e levels in both markets as in the no-trade cases already discussed. Consumers here will be hurt; and in the sense described above, they will be hurt more than producers are helped.

Suppose the quota is set, not at zero, but, say, at half the level of free-trade imports. The reader can verify that, in the special case of Fig. 34-3's straight-line curves, the

[8] Indeed, if $s_a s_a$ were completely vertical, all the money newly extorted from the consumer would be transferred to the producers in extra rent: this would presumably be a switch from not particularly unworthy consumers to not particularly worthy producers. More commonly though, with $s_a s_a$ having some positive elasticity, the higher P will coax out extra domestic Q; this will represent a definite social inefficiency, to the degree that resources are drawn from fields where America has a comparative advantage into protected industries where she has a comparative disadvantage. In the extreme case of a horizontal $s_a s_a$, where factors are indifferent between this and other industries, *all* the tariff's benefits to producers are frittered away in inefficient resource allocation, and not even those in the industry derive a selfish benefit at the expense of the hard-hit consumers.

[9] It is also true with rare (and unimportant) exceptions for a country that levies prohibitive tariffs on a subset of its goods. The exceptions apply to a country large enough to affect appreciably the relative prices of the goods it imports. By levying sufficiently-small shrewdly-gauged tariffs, it might exploit its monopoly power to "make the foreigner pay" for its tariff. [This is an esoteric point, which could be illustrated by means of utility-disutility areas under the schedules in Fig. 34-3(a). But readers of Chapter 25's discussion of marginal revenue (and the loss taken on all earlier units when an extra unit of q is sold by a monopolist) can understand the point thus: The last little unit of import under free trade brings us zero marginal benefit; that is why it is the last unit. If we impose a tiny tariff to keep it out, we do force a reduction in the P we pay on *all* previous units imported. So we could benefit a little from such a move (unless the $s_e s_e$ and/or $d_e d_e$ curves were horizontal). However, Europe could do the same to our wheat, and when all play this game, there is some presumption that world inefficiencies will make all (or most) worse off.]

American P will rise half the distance between the free-trade B_a price and the no-trade A_a price. (In Europe P will fall halfway.) Only at these new respective Ps of $9 and £1$\frac{1}{2}$ will the arrow of Europe's linen export match our import arrow. (Verify.)

The quota has produced a price difference between here and abroad. As just said, that equilibrium difference is defined as just large enough to make exports and imports match. (NOTE: A tariff on each unit import of linen, which was exactly equal to this price difference, could have achieved the same equilibrium.[10])

There is thus no essential difference between tariffs and quotas. Except this: A non-prohibitive tariff at least gives revenue to the government, in part offsetting the net harm done to the importing country by the restriction on imports. A quota, on the other hand, puts the profit from the contrived price difference into the pocket of the importer lucky enough to get a quota license. He can afford to wine and dine the officials who give out import licenses; or if they are not already his kinfolk or political cronies, he can afford to bribe them.

This is why economists generally regard tariffs as a lesser evil than quotas. "At the least," they advise, "if you must introduce inefficient restrictive quotas, be sure that the government auctions off the scarce import-quota licenses so that the Treasury gains the swag and so that bureaucracy is not put under the strain of corruption and exercise of arbitrary power and caprice."

The harmful effects of a nonprohibitive tariff or quota are of the same type as, but lesser in degree than, those of prohibitive tariffs or quotas. Generally, there is net harm done to the citizenry as it is forced to curb its consumption of the goods it desires most and to channel resources from lines of true comparative advantage to economically inefficient uses. Generally, real wages and average living standards are hurt by tariffs and quotas.

Transportation costs The economic costs of moving bulky and perishable goods also lessen the extent of profitable regional specialization.

The effects are like those produced by the passage of artificially restrictive tariff legislation. In the case of transportation costs, the evil is unavoidable, whereas protective tariffs or artificial barriers to interregional trade within a nation are squarely the responsibility of man.

This ends two sections of digression on particular markets' price equilibria under trade and tariffs. We now return to our discussion of basic comparative advantage.

QUALIFICATIONS AND CONCLUSIONS

Of course, comparative advantage holds for *any* two countries and goods, not just for America and Europe and food and clothing. (Ricardo used England and Portugal and

---

[10]This gives the clue to how to compute the new equilibrium prices for any tariff rate between the prohibitive and zero levels. In Fig. 34-3, shift the exporting country's whole diagram *upward* by the amount of the tariff (so that its vertical-scale prices now differ from the importing country's vertical scale by the amount of the duty). Then move a horizontal ruler up and down until you have located exactly equal export and import gaps (gold arrows) between the respective schedules.

cloth and wine in his examples.) The following Appendix shows how the principle of comparative advantage can be generalized to handle any number of goods; and more advanced books show how it can handle any number of countries or regions. Instead of using simple labor cost examples, we could easily measure costs in terms of "doses" of labor, land, and capital goods of fixed-proportions. We can also allow for changing factor proportions and diminishing returns. For this and more, see the Appendix.

Perhaps a more serious defect of comparative advantage is its static assumptions. The theory is stated in terms of barter and relative price ratios. It disregards all stickiness of prices and wages, all transitional inflationary and overvaluation gaps, and all balance-of-payments problems. It supposes that when workers go out of one industry, they always go into another more efficient industry—never into chronic unemployment. No wonder this abstract theory sold at a discount during the Great Depression. Recently its prestige has been coming back. To the extent that we can in the future count on the successful macroeconomic management, which mobilizes modern theories of monetary and fiscal policy to banish chronic slumps and inflations—to that extent will the old classical theory of comparative advantage retain its vital social relevance.

If theories, like girls, could win beauty contests, comparative advantage would certainly rate high in that it is an elegantly logical structure. Indeed, one must admit that it is a simplified theory. Yet, for all its oversimplification, the theory of comparative advantage provides a most important glimpse of truth. Political economy has found few more pregnant principles. A nation that neglects comparative advantage may pay a heavy price in terms of living standards and potential growth.

SUMMARY

1   As soon as there are diversities of productivities within a country, specialization and exchange become profitable. The same holds for nations: international exchange is an efficient way for us to transform one good into another, more efficient than having to rely solely on domestic production.

2   Without much study of economics, people see that trade is mutually beneficial between the tropics and the temperate zones—or between two countries where one is more efficient in producing one good and the other is more efficient in producing the other good. But it takes the important Ricardian principle of *comparative* advantage to see that trade is no less mutually beneficial between two countries (or as in the case cited of the lawyer and stenographer, between any two units) even when one of the countries happens to be absolutely more efficient in every industry than is the other.

As long as there is a difference in *relative* efficiency, there will be powerful benefits derived from *specializing* in those goods in which there is a comparative advantage, *trading* them for goods in which the other nation has a comparative advantage.

3   The law of comparative advantage not only predicts the geographical pattern of specialization and direction of trade; it also demonstrates that *both* countries are made better off and that the real wages (or, more precisely, returns to the factors of production taken

as a whole) are improved by trade and the resulting *enlarged* totals of world production. Prohibitive tariffs that re-create *autarky* (i.e., national economic self-sufficiency) will hurt real wage and total factor returns—not help them.

4   Decreasing costs (economies of scale) are an important cause of specialization and regional trade. Differences in tastes can also cause trade.

5   In supply-demand markets for one small good, completely free trade will equalize prices, causing the good to be exported from the place with lowest zero-trade price. The equilibrium common P is at the level equating physical exports to physical imports.

6   A tariff or quota, by lowering imports, will cause a rise in domestic P and a fall in foreign P. (So long as some imports continue, the Ps will differ by the amount of the tariff.) The harm done to the domestic economy, from higher P and decreased home consumption and from wastage of resources on goods lacking comparative advantage, will generally exceed the benefit to producers. Transport costs also cut down on trade and well-being.

7   The important law of comparative advantage must be qualified to take into account certain interferences with it. Thus, if money wage rates are rigid in both countries or if fiscal and monetary policies are poorly run in both countries, then the blessing of cheap imports that international specialization gives might be turned into the curse of unemployment.[11] With proper public policies, modern nations can achieve a managed macroeconomics which need not sacrifice the great benefits from trade, but rather can re-create the environment in which the principle of comparative advantage will apply.

QUESTIONS FOR DISCUSSION

1   "Buying a good cheaper abroad than we can produce it at home is to our advantage." Is this consistent with comparative advantage? Show that it indeed is.

2   Are real wage levels, like water in connecting pipes, brought to the same level by completely free international trade? Why not? Are international prices? Why?

3   What happens if two countries are exactly alike in productivity and efficiency? Explain. Justify the slogan *"Vive la différence!"*

4   What if (1,2; 3,4) in Table 34-1 became (1,2; $1\frac{1}{2}$,3)? Can you show that all trade is killed off? And that this certainly would be a worse position for America? (Footnote readers: redraw Fig. 34-1 with equal *p-p* slopes.) Show that if it now becomes (1,2; $1\frac{1}{2}$,4), Europe will export food.

5   Can a country once have a comparative advantage, say, in steel, and then lose it? What then *will* happen? Should it?

6   Why might a new continent have a comparative advantage in food?

[11] See the Appendix to the previous chapter for a demonstration that overvaluation of a country's currency can undercut these basic classical principles.

7 "If some goods continue to be imported after a new tariff, the sum of the rise in domestic *P* and the fall in foreign *P* must equal the new tariff." Can you show why?

Review your understanding of the following concepts:

personal and regional diversity and
  specialization
absolute efficiencies versus comparative
  advantage

barter versus home production
international price equilibrium
quota and tariff equilibrium
prohibitive tariffs and real wages

APPENDIX: Comparative Advantage Amplified and Qualified

Our discussion of comparative advantage has until now followed Ricardo and measured all costs in terms of labor. Modern economists know that the theory is still valid even if you do not want to assume a labor theory of value.

The production-possibility, or transformation, frontier that we used in Chapter 2 to discuss guns and butter is the tool that enables us to dispense with labor units: users of the production-possibility frontier choose to measure the cost of clothing in terms of the food we must sacrifice to get more clothing. (This is sometimes so-called "opportunity cost.")

The first part of this Appendix follows through in detail an America-Europe food-clothing case, showing the irrelevance of absolute labor costs.

AMERICA WITHOUT TRADE

In Chapter 2, we saw that every economy has a production-possibility (or transformation) schedule indicating how much of one commodity, food, can be produced if all resources are diverted to it; also how much of the other commodity, clothing, can be produced if all resources are diverted to its production; and how either good can be transformed into the other.

For simplicity, let us suppose food can always be transformed into units of clothing in America at the *constant ratio* of 10/3. For each 10 units of food sacrificed, we can always get 3 units of clothing. We further assume that, when all resources are diverted to food production, America will have altogether 100 (million) units of food.[1]

We may put all this in the form of a schedule, as shown in Table 34-2. Or it may be plotted in Fig. 34-4, just as was done in Chapter 2, Fig. 2-3 (page 21). The solid *AK* is America's production-possibility frontier. This new production-possibility frontier is a straight line, whereas the earlier one was rounded, being concave when looked at from below. The straight-line production-possibility schedule has been introduced in order to keep the argument simple—to relieve the student from having to remember many different cost ratios. As will be seen later, this will not seriously affect the validity of the argument. The few qualifications needed are made later.

So far we have been talking only about production. However, if the United States is isolated from all trade, what she produces is also what she consumes. Let us suppose, therefore, that the gold quantities for *H* in Table 34-2 and Fig. 34-4 represent the amounts produced and consumed by America in the absence of trade; or in numbers, America then produces and consumes 30 units of food and 21 units of clothing.

Why was this particular combination decided upon rather than one of the other possibilities? We know from earlier chapters that in a competitive system nobody "decides" upon this, but that the price mechanism, operating through supply and demand for goods and services, determines WHAT shall be produced, How, and FOR WHOM. Well, the indicated quantities are the WHAT. Very little need be said here about the How, except for the obvious remark that agricultural food production will require more land relative to labor than will more highly fabricated clothing output. As to the

---

[1]Note that labor is never mentioned in the following discussion. But if you wanted to relate this discussion to Ricardo's labor treatment, you could merely change the numbers in

Table 34-1 from (1,2; 3,4) to (3,10; 8,10), or more generally to (3*a*, 10*a*; 8*b*, 10*b*), where *a* and *b* are arbitrary positive numbers depending only on units and absolute efficiencies.

America can produce food or clothing, consuming before trade what she produces:

PRODUCTION-POSSIBILITY SCHEDULE OF AMERICA (10/3 CONSTANT-COST RATIO)		
AMERICA		
POSSIBILITIES	FOOD (millions of units)	CLOTHING (millions of units)
A	100	0
B	90	3
C	80	6
D	70	9
E	60	12
F	50	15
G	40	18
H	30	21
I	20	24
J	10	27
K	0	30

TABLE 34-2.

AMERICA'S PRODUCTION-POSSIBILITY FRONTIER

FIG. 34-4.   The constant-cost line AK shows America's domestic production possibilities. The new line AK' indicates an increased ability to produce clothing and means that America can move northeast from AK, enjoying more of both goods.

FOR WHOM, we need only remark parenthetically that scarcity of labor in the United States will mean rather high wages for workers, while superabundance of land here will mean low rents (per acre) for landlords.

Technical progress   Let us proceed to introduce Europe into the picture. Before we do so, it will pave the way for the later argument to interject a question. What would happen if some American (like Eli Whitney, inventor of the cotton gin, for example) should make a clever invention, allowing each 10 units of food to be transformed into 6 rather than 3 units of clothing? Would America be potentially better off?

The answer is, obviously, Yes. The production-possibility frontier has shifted outward and upward and is now shown by the broken line AK' in Fig. 34-4. (Show that America could now go from H northeast to a new point H' and have *more of both* food and clothing.)

EUROPE WITHOUT TRADE

We can now do for Europe exactly what was done above for America, but with an important difference. Europe's plentiful endowment of labor relative to land would give her a different cost or transformation ratio between food and clothing. She might have a

comparative advantage in clothing rather than in food. For her, each 10 units of food may be transformable into, say, 8 units of clothing. She gets 5 more than was true of the United States because of her comparative advantage in clothing. However, in terms of food, America gets 10/3, or 3.33 units, for each unit of clothing sacrificed, while Europe's comparative disadvantage in food production gives her only 10/8, or 1.25 units of food, for each sacrificed unit of clothing. *The important thing to concentrate upon is the difference in the two cost ratios: 10/3 for America and 10/8 for Europe.*

We shall still keep the two continents isolated. What is Europe's exact production-possibility schedule? Let us suppose that Europe's population is so large and her land area such that before trade she was at C, producing and consuming 50 units of food and 80 of clothing. This fact, plus the constant-cost ratio 10/8, tells us all we have to know to draw up Europe's complete production-possibility schedule as in Table 34-3 (page 660). Check this against Fig. 34-5's production-possibility frontier.

THE OPENING UP OF TRADE

Now, for the first time, let us admit the possibility of trade between the two regions. Food can be bartered

Europe's production possibilities favor clothing, in which she has comparative advantage:

PRODUCTION-POSSIBILITY SCHEDULE OF EUROPE (10/8 CONSTANT-COST RATIO)		
EUROPE		
POSSIBILITIES	FOOD (millions of units)	CLOTHING (millions of units)
A	150	0
B	100	40
C	50	80
D	0	120

TABLE 34-3.

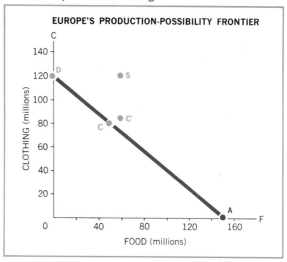

FIG. 34-5. Before international trade, Europe is on her domestic production-possibility frontier at *C*, consuming just what she produces. (Disregard the points *C'* and *S* until later in the chapter.)

for clothing at some *terms of trade*, i.e., at some *price ratio*.[2] To dramatize the process, let us suppose that in mid-ocean there stands an impersonal auctioneer whose business it is to balance supply and demand —offers of clothing and offers of food. He does this by calling out to both countries an exchange rate or price ratio between food and clothing. Until supplies and demands are balanced, he keeps the bidding going. When he finally hits on the equilibrium price level *at which supply and demand balance*, he raps his gavel three times and says, "Going, going, *gone!*"

Probably, he will suspect in advance that Europe is going to specialize in clothing production, in which she has a comparative advantage, and that she will wish to export part of her clothing production in exchange for food imports. But he has no idea what the final exchange ratio, or terms of trade, between food and clothing will be—whether it will be 10/3, 10/8, 10/5, 10/6, or anything else. For that matter, if the auctioneer is very new at the game or very stupid, he may think that the final equilibrium exchange level, or terms of trade, will be 10/1 or 10/12.

Actually, neither of these last two can be the final exchange ratio. He would soon learn this from bitter experience. For let him tell America and Europe that they can get all the clothing they want in exchange for food at the rate of only 1 unit of clothing for every 10 units of food. What will America do? By producing at home, she can get 3 units of clothing for each 10

of food. Clearly, she will not be persuaded into trading food for clothing on those terms; she would rather remain self-sufficient.

That is only half the story. Why should not America go to the other extreme and export clothing in exchange for food imports? Each 1 unit of clothing gets her 10 units of food from the auctioneer. What will 1 unit of clothing get at home in domestic food production? Obviously, from Table 34-2 and Fig. 34-4, only 10/3, or 3.33, units of food. At 10/1, therefore, we should certainly shift all our resources to clothing production; we should export some surplus clothing for food imports.

Now, what about Europe? At home she gets only 10/8, or 1.25, units of food for each unit of clothing. At 10/1, she too will want to trade clothing for food. We see, therefore, what a green hand the auctioneer was. By calling out 10/1, he brings a flood supply of clothing on his head and only demands for food. Since he has no supplies of either good up his sleeve, he must now change his tactics. He must raise the price of food relative to the price of clothing. He had better try the ratio 10/2, or perhaps even 10/9. You are now in a position to reason why neither of them will do: why 10/2 will still induce a tidal wave of clothing and, on the other hand, why 10/9 represents the opposite error, in which there is a tornado of food.

Clearly, *the final exchange ratio cannot be outside*

[2] Terms of trade (or an exchange ratio) of, say, 10 food for 6 clothing means that clothing is more expensive than food, with the price ratio, (clothing price)/(food price) = $1\frac{2}{3}$ = 10/6.

the original two-country limits of 10/3 *and* 10/8! Anywhere between is a possibility—with America following her comparative advantage and specializing in food, and Europe following her comparative advantage and specializing in clothing.

EXACT DETERMINATION OF THE FINAL PRICE RATIO

Just where between the domestic cost ratios will the terms of trade settle down? Some of Ricardo's immediate followers were foolish enough to say, "Split the difference between the two countries' cost ratios, and pick the "halfway" point 10/5½ as the equilibrium ratio."[3]

Actually, as John Stuart Mill, the third great classical economist (after Smith and Ricardo), showed a little later, *the exact final level of the terms of trade between the two cost ratios will depend upon the strength of world supply and demand for each of the two commodities.* If people have an intense desire for food relative to available supplies of food and clothing, the price ratio will settle near the upper limit of 10/8; if clothing is much demanded by both countries, the final price ratio will settle nearer to 10/3.[4]

Mill did what our auctioneer would have to do. He drew up a schedule showing supply and demand at *each possible price ratio:*[5] how much food America would wish to export and how much food Europe would want to import; and at the same time, how much clothing Europe would be willing to export at each price ratio in comparison with the amount of clothing America expected to import. At one, and (usually) only one, intermediate price ratio, exports and imports will

balance. At this equilibrium price, exports and imports will "mesh" (or match), quantitatively as well as qualitatively; the auctioneer and Mill will heave a sigh of relief, and trade will continue indefinitely until tastes or technology have changed.

For our numerical problem it has been assumed that the equilibrium terms-of-trade ratio is 10/6, a little "nearer" to Europe's pretrade ratio than to America's.

America concentrates her production completely on food. In Fig. 34-7 on page 662, America is production-wise at A. But since she can now trade freely at 10/6, America is no longer limited to her old production-possibility frontier. By trading, she can now move on the solid line AK' *just exactly as if a fruitful invention had been made.* Is America made potentially better off by trade? Indeed she is. Just where she will stop on this solid line, which we may call her new *consumption-possibility curve,* depends upon the workings of her internal price system. We assume that this causes her to stop at the point H', where 40 units of food and 36 units of clothing are consumed. The gold arrows show America's exports ($+$) and imports ($-$).

All this is summarized in America's rows in Table 34-4 on page 662. This table should be studied carefully. To understand it thoroughly is to understand the doctrine of comparative costs.

As a result of specialization and trade, America has become better off; she has more food and more clothing to consume. The same is true of Europe. What is the black magic by which something seems to have been got for nothing? In Table 34-4 the rows marked

---

[3] Or would they have said "halfway" between 10/3 and 10/8, at 110/48, which corresponds to 10/4⁴⁄₁₁? Both are silly.

[4] Also, if America were very small relative to Europe, so that its supplies made hardly a "dent" on the market, then the price ratio might even stay at Europe's 10/8. America would then be specializing in food and importing clothing, but all America's food exports would amount to so little that Europe would still have to produce some food for herself. This is possible only at a price of 10/8. America would in this case get *all* the gains from international trade. It pays to have a large (different!) neighbor.

[5] Chapter 22's indifference curves can be used to summarize each country's tastes for food and clothing. Together with the p-p curves, these could derive the reciprocal demand curves of Mill, shown in Fig. 34-6. Unlike ordinary dd and ss curves, C is trading against F, not against money; hence, relative prices P_C/P_F, rather than money P_C, are plotted. (If tastes and incomes vary within each country, aggregate indifference curves would be replaced by more elaborate analysis.)

FIG. 34-6.

America specializes in food and imports clothing:

FIG. 34-7. The line AK represents America's domestic production-possibility curve; the line AK', her new consumption-possibility curve when she is able to trade freely at the price ratio 10/6 and in consequence has decided to specialize completely in the production of food (at A). The gold arrows from S to H' and A to S show the amounts exported (+) and imported (−) by America. As a result of free trade, she finally ends up at H' with more of both goods than before at H.

World, which represent the sum of the American and European rows, show this: *World production of both goods has been stepped up by specialization and trade.*

Actually, the sixth row gives the data the auctioneer would be most interested in. He is assured that equilibrium has been reached by two facts shown there: (1) World consumption of each product is identical with world production—no more, no less; and (2) the

International trade makes larger world production possible:

SUMMARY SHOWING SPECIALIZATION AND GAIN FROM TRADE ACCORDING TO COMPARATIVE ADVANTAGE

AREA COMPARED	EXCHANGE RATIO OF FOOD FOR CLOTHING P_C/P_F	FOOD PRODUC- TION	FOOD CON- SUMP- TION	FOOD EXPORTS (+) OR IMPORTS (−)	CLOTHING PRODUC- TION	CLOTHING CON- SUMP- TION	CLOTHING EXPORTS (+) OR IMPORTS (−)
Situation before trade							
America	10/3	30	30	0	21	21	0
Europe	10/8	50	50	0	80	80	0
World	none	80	80	0	101	101	0
Situation after trade							
America	10/6	100	40	+60	0	36	−36
Europe	10/6	0	60	−60	120	84	+36
World	10/6	100	100	0	120	120	0
Gains from trade							
America	———	———	+10	———	———	+15	———
Europe	———	———	+10	———	———	+4	———
World	———	+20	+20	———	+19	+19	———

TABLE 34-4.

amounts that each country exports are just balanced by the amounts that the other country wishes to import. Thus the price ratio 10/6 is the right one.[6]

This completes our explanation of comparative advantage. You might test your full understanding by filling in on Fig. 34-5 for Europe everything that has already been filled in for America on Fig. 34-7. Europe's new consumption-possibility line, made possible by trade, pivots around the point D on the vertical axis and goes to C'. Draw in the arrows from D to S representing the amounts exported ($+$) and imported ($-$) as was done in Fig. 34-7. Note that Europe's arrows match America's but are opposite in sign. Why is this quantitative meshing of exports and imports necessary at equilibrium?

The eager reader could add labor measurements and wage data to the example. But the thing to note is that comparative advantage, not absolute labor advantage, is the all-important condition.

MANY COMMODITIES

Very briefly, we now show what happens when we remove some of the oversimplifications in the foregoing discussion. The conclusions are not essentially changed, and even the changes in details are minor.

First note that until now we have simplified the discussion by considering only two commodities, food and clothing. Obviously, food stands for many different items (beef, milk, etc.), and likewise clothing. Moreover, the advantages of exchange are equally great when we consider the thousand and one commodities that can and do enter into international trade.

As is shown in advanced treatises,[7] when there are many commodities producible in two countries at constant costs, they can be arranged in order according to their comparative advantage or cost. For example, the commodities automobiles, flax, perfumes, watches, wheat, and woolens might be arranged in the comparative-advantage sequence shown in Fig. 34-8. This means that wheat costs are lowest relative to all other commodities in America; Europe has its greatest comparative advantage in perfumes; its advantage in watches is not quite so great; and so forth.[8]

From the beginning we can be almost sure of one thing. The introduction of trade will cause America to produce wheat, and Europe perfume. But where will the dividing line fall? Between automobiles and flax? Or will America produce flax and Europe confine herself to watches, woolens, and perfumes? Or will the dividing line fall on one of the commodities rather than between them, so that, say, flax might be produced in both places at once?

You will not be surprised to find that the answer depends upon the comparative strength of international demand for the different goods. If we think of the commodities as beads arranged on a string according to their comparative advantage, the total demand-and-supply situation will determine where the dividing line between American and European production will fall. And an increased demand for automobiles and wheat, for example, may tend to turn the terms of trade in the direction of America and make us so prosperous that it will no longer pay us to continue to produce our own flax. Also, there is the

FIG. 34-8.   (Source for this example of ordering: Table 34-5, page 664.)

[6] To find this equilibrium the auctioneer could have made up a whole book of such tables, each page corresponding to a different price ratio. Generally, only one page is the right one, however, because at all other prices the algebraic total of exports and imports would not cancel out. Thus, at 10/7, America's desire for clothing imports would surpass Europe's willingness to export clothing. The world as a whole would be trying to consume more clothing than had been produced. Since the auctioneer has no inventories to draw upon, he would have to turn the pages toward a higher price for clothing and a lower price for food. On the right page the price ratio would be an equilibrium one: exports would balance imports, at the E intersection of Fig. 34-6.

[7] For example, G. Haberler, *Theory of International Trade* (Macmillan, New York, 1937). Haberler also pioneered the use of *p-p frontiers* in trade theory.
[8] This ordered array of goods might have arisen from the numerical data of Table 34-5 on page 664, which are presented only for the curiosity of the more advanced reader and are not essential for the above discussion. As before, it is not necessary to measure costs in terms of money or labor, but only in terms of the relative commodities into which any good can be "transformed." Suppose that we choose to measure the costs of every good in both countries in terms of woolens— selected arbitrarily because it comes last alphabetically. Then our data might be arranged alphabetically as in Table 34-5.

possibility that a new scientific discovery permitting America to grow flax on the desert might rearrange the order of the comparative advantages of the different commodities and alter the pattern of specialization and trade.

MANY COUNTRIES

So much for the complications introduced by many commodities. What about many countries? Europe and America are not the whole world, and even they include many separate so-called "sovereign nations."

Introducing many countries need not change our analysis. As far as any one country is concerned, all the other nations with whom she trades can be lumped together into one group as "the rest of the world." The advantages of trade have no special relationship to state boundaries. The principles already developed apply between groups of countries and, indeed, between regions within the same country. In fact, but for historical accident, they would be more applicable to trade between our Northern and Southern states than to trade between the United States and Canada.

From the standpoint of pure economic welfare, the slogan "Buy American" is as foolish as "Buy Wisconsin" would be, or "Buy Oshkosh, Wisconsin," or "Buy South Oshkosh, Wisconsin." Part of our great prosperity comes from the fortunate fact that there are no restrictive customs duties within our 50 states, which form one great free-trade area.

This means that in America one must give up the production of 1,000 units of woolens to get 1 automobile, while in Europe the cost of 1 automobile is the sacrifice of 3,000 units of wool production. Therefore the comparative cost of automobiles relative to woolens is in Europe three times that in America, and so forth for the other goods.

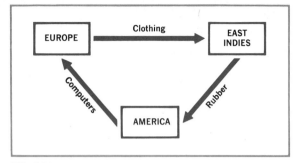

FIG. 34-9.

There is, however, one new aspect introduced by the existence of many countries. America may find it very profitable to trade *indirectly* with Europe. America sells Europe much, including finished commodities such as computers. It buys little from Europe; but it does buy rubber and raw materials from the East Indies. They in turn do not usually buy goods from America; however, they do buy clothing and other goods from Europe. Thus, we have a very advantageous *triangular* trade, as shown in Fig. 34-9. The arrows indicate the direction of exports.

What would happen if all countries tried to sign bilateral trade agreements, so that America could not and would not buy from the Indies unless they bought an equal amount from us? And suppose the same bilateralism held for every two nations? Clearly, trade would be cut down severely. Imports would balance

---

Obviously, Europe's relative cost advantage is greatest in perfumes and least in wheat; in between, the commodities are arranged as was shown in Fig. 34-8. The fact that the figures in the last column are predominantly greater than 1 in no way reflects on the efficiency of Europe; it merely comes from the accidental fact that we chose woolens as our common denominator in which to express costs. Had we selected wheat or watches, the opposite would have been the case, and yet none of our results would be any different—except for a "scale factor" (such as converts inches to feet or yards).

TECHNICAL NOTE: Anyone who feels he must bring in labor productivities can write the respective American requirements in labor days as $A, B, C, \ldots$, and Europe's as $a, b, c, \ldots$. The whole analysis can then be worked out in terms of comparative ratios of the form $A/B, C/B, \ldots$, and $a/b, c/b, \ldots$; to explain trade patterns it is never necessary to compare absolute advantages between countries $A/a, B/b, \ldots$. Of course, if he wants to compare money and real wages, these absolute advantages are necessary: by extending the analysis of Table 34-1, it can be shown that the ratio of European to American real wage must lie between the least and greatest of $A/a, B/b, \ldots$; just *where* between depends on the working out of reciprocal demands.

(1)	(2)	(3)	(4)
	AMERICAN COST RATIO, IN TERMS	EUROPEAN COST RATIO, IN TERMS	COMPARATIVE EUROPEAN COSTS, IN TERMS OF AMERICAN COSTS
GOODS	OF WOOLENS	OF WOOLENS	(4) = (3) ÷ (2)
Automobiles	1,000	3,000	3.0
Flax	0.8	1.6	2.0
Perfumes	5.0	3.0	0.6
Watches	50	75	1.5
Wheat	0.2	0.8	4.0
Woolens	1.0	1.0	1.0

TABLE 34-5.

exports, but at the level of which is the lower. Each region would end worse off.

INCREASING COSTS

Returning again to two countries and two commodities, we must now drop the assumption that costs are constant. The production-possibility frontiers of Figs. 34-4, 34-5, and 34-7 should have been concave, as they generally were in Chapter 2. It is no longer possible to specify a single cost figure for each country.

On the whole, America is better endowed for food production than Europe; still, after a great amount of American food is produced, the cost of *extra* food will begin to exceed that in Europe. Even after American competition has drastically lowered the price of food relative to clothing, a little of the best land in Europe will be able to hold its own in food production. Similarly, that first little bit of American clothing production which can be achieved at low costs will continue even after international trade has reached an equilibrium level. However, any attempt to expand American clothing production further would entail higher extra costs and competitive losses.

We may summarize the modifications in international trade made necessary by increasing costs:[9]

As a result of international trade, each country will tend to specialize, as before, in the commodity in which it has the greatest comparative advantage; and it will export some of that commodity in exchange for the other country's surplus exports. But because of increasing relative costs, specialization need not be complete: something of both commodities may still be produced in either country, because even the less favored commodity may have low enough costs to compete when its production is small.

INTERNATIONAL GOODS MOVEMENTS AS A SUBSTITUTE FOR FACTOR MOVEMENTS

Having acknowledged the law of increasing costs described in Chapter 2 and elsewhere, we now examine implications of the related law of diminishing returns within each country.

After international trade takes place, resources in Europe flow from food to clothing production. Because clothing requires relatively much labor and little land, the pressure of population on the limited land of Europe is relieved. Land is no longer relatively so dear; rents fall compared with wages. In America the reverse happens after trade: concentration upon food production, in which labor is economized and land heavily utilized, tends to raise rents relative to wages.

In each case the free international movement of goods has effects which are partly like those following from the free international movement of factors of

---

[9] For the geometrically minded, Fig. 34-10 may be helpful. It shows America's condition before and after trade when increasing costs prevail. The production-possibility frontier is now bowed out. Before international trade, America is consuming and producing at H. The domestic price ratio is

10/3, just equal to the ratio of extra costs of getting (at H) a little more clothing for a little sacrificed food. This is shown by the slope of the AK curve at H.

After trade, when the common price ratio is 10/6, American production shifts to B, toward less clothing but not away from clothing altogether. The new production point B will be reached as a result of competition, because the slope of the curve there—i.e., the ratio of costs of extra clothing for extra food—is 10/6, or just equal to the common international price ratio. At B, and only there, will the value of America's national product (evaluated at the 10/6 price ratio) be at a maximum.

The straight line represents the new consumption-possibility curve America can achieve as a result of trade. It is straight and not bent because the auctioneer offers to trade freely, giving America at the 10/6 ratio as much or little clothing for food as she wishes. The final levels of consumption, determined by supply and demand, are given by the point H'. As before, arrows indicate exports and imports.

There are still gains from trade; but because of diminishing returns and increasing costs, there is not so much specialization as before, and not quite such large gains. Note that at the equilibrium point, where no further trade is possible, relative (extra, or "marginal") production costs in the two countries are equal, each to the common price ratio 10/6.

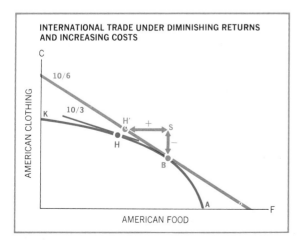

INTERNATIONAL TRADE UNDER DIMINISHING RETURNS AND INCREASING COSTS

FIG. 34-10.

production. Just as the movement of labor from Europe to America would relieve the scarcity of labor in America and of land in Europe, so the movement of clothing from Europe to America and of food from America to Europe tends to make the superabundant factor in each country less abundant and the scarce factor less scarce.

The person who has most clearly emphasized how commodity trade partially relieves the scarcity in all countries of the less abundant factors of production is the Swedish economist and statesman Ohlin (pronounced O'Lean).[10] He has made this important addition to the classical doctrine of comparative cost:

[10] Bertil Ohlin, *Interregional and International Trade* (Harvard University Press, Cambridge, Mass., 1933).

Free movements of labor and capital between countries will tend to equalize wages and factor-prices. *However, even without any movements of productive factors across national boundaries, a tendency toward equalization of factor-prices will often result from the free movement of goods in international trade.*

It is clear, therefore, that although international trade increases national product in Europe, it may at the same time so reduce the share of particular groups that *they* are made worse off. Thus, the large British landowners who a century ago constituted the backbone of the Conservative party may have been selfish in opposing the famous repeal of the English corn-law tariffs in 1846, but they were not necessarily unintelligent in making their unsuccessful last-ditch fight to retain protective tariffs on imported grains.

SUMMARY TO APPENDIX

1   If nature endows two regions unequally with factors of production, the *relative* cost of transforming one commodity into another domestically will probably be different for the two areas. (E.g., a land-rich area will have a comparative advantage in food and other land-intensive goods. A labor-rich area's comparative advantage will be in labor-intensive goods.)

2   Under free trade, goods will exchange for each other at a price ratio somewhere *intermediate* between the original domestic cost ratios of the two countries (depending on reciprocal supply and demand).

3   Each country will specialize in the commodity in which it has a comparative advantage and export its surplus of that product for imports from abroad.

4   Each country is made better off by trade and specialization: America can get by trade more units of clothing than when she domestically transforms food into clothing; Europe does better when she trades clothing for food, doing better than when she domestically transforms clothing into food.

5   Trade is *indirect* production. It is efficient production. Efficient production is always better than inefficient production. (Note that advantages of trade have nothing to do with *relative wage rates.* Under free trade, a country's wage tends to be pulled up to the higher levels of productivity of its export industry, not down to the low-efficiency level of its import industry.)

6   Free movements of productive factors, can, without trade, equalize factor-prices. But even without migration of any factors, free movement of goods in trade can work to reduce or sometimes eliminate the differences in factor-prices that result from different geographical factor proportions.

QUESTIONS FOR DISCUSSION

1   Suppose two countries have the same-sloped *p-p frontiers* that are straight lines. Will self-sufficiency be different if one greatly exceeds the other in labor productivity all around?

2   Show that I benefit if your *p-p frontier* is as different from mine as possible.

3   Why would you expect land-rich Canada to export wheat to labor-rich China?

4   *Extra-credit problem:* Even where there are many goods and many countries, verify the correctness of the simple rule: For any two goods, say wheat and water, and any two countries, say France and Japan, we can calculate (from labor productivity data) which country has the comparative advantage in which good; and no country *can ever* export to the other country that good in which it has a comparative advantage. (WARNING: It may be that neither Japan nor France will produce any of either good; but that does not violate the stated rule!)

5   *Extra-credit problem:* Add to Table 34-5 the information that woolens happen to cost 1 day's labor in each country. Begin with $3 to £1. With wages here $6 an hour and £1 there, show that the cost-price of flax will be the same in both countries. Which goods will A produce cheapest? Which goods will B? Now let our wage rise relative to theirs, or let the $ depreciate relative to the £. Show that our exports will suffer and our imports will rise.

FOR REVIEW

Review your understanding of the following concepts:

straight-line *p-p frontier*
specialization point
pre- and post-trade
  equilibria

matching trade arrows
many-good ordered array
triangular and multilateral trade
concave frontiers and tangencies

The Economics of Tariff Protection and Free Trade

35

To the Chamber of Deputies: We are subjected to the intolerable competition of a foreign rival, who enjoys such superior facilities for the production of light that he can *inundate* our *national market* at reduced price. This rival is no other than the sun. Our petition is to pass a law shutting up all windows, openings and fissures through which the light of the sun is used to penetrate our dwellings, to the prejudice of the profitable manufacture we have been enabled to bestow on the country.
Signed: Candle Makers.
F. BASTIAT

It would be absurd to try to decide whether God exists or not by counting on one hand all the arguments in the affirmative and on the other hand all the arguments in the negative, and then to award the decision to the side with the greater *number* of points. It is as absurd to evaluate the case for tariff protection by a mere count of unequally important pros and cons.

Indeed, as was shown in the previous chapter, there is essentially only one argument for free or freer trade, but it is an exceedingly powerful one, namely:

Unhampered trade promotes a mutually profitable international division of labor, greatly enhances the potential real national product of all countries, and makes possible higher standards of living all over the globe.

Recall that putting on a tariff duty (i.e., tax) discourages imports and raises prices to the domestic consumer. By killing off the fruitful international division of labor, it "protects" the relatively inefficient domestic producer. Import quotas do the same.

The arguments for high tariff protection against the competition of foreign imports take many different forms. They may be divided into three categories:

1. Those that are definitely economically false: some so obviously and palpably as hardly to merit serious discussion; but some whose falsity can be detected only by subtle economic reasoning.

2. A few that are without validity in a perfectly competitive "classical" static full-employment world, but that do contain some kernels of truth for a sizable nation which monopolizes some crop, or for a nation undergoing economic development and subject to underemployment and an overvalued currency.

3. Certain noneconomic arguments that may make it desirable national policy to sacrifice economic welfare in order to subsidize certain activities admittedly not economically efficient.

NONECONOMIC GOALS

Let us begin with the last category of arguments, for they are most simply disposed of. If you ever are on a debating team and are given the assignment to defend free trade, you will strengthen your case at the beginning by conceding that economic welfare is not the sole goal of life. Political considerations are also important. Thus, it may be necessary to become partially self-sufficient in certain lines of activity, even at great cost, because of fear of future wars.

An example is the production of oil. If oil reserves and capacity are considered necessary for national defense and if the needed amount of capacity is not able to survive under free trade, the economist cannot assert that national policy should be against protection of this industry. But he can suggest that a *subsidy* to domestic production might be preferable to a tariff. This would bring the domestic price down to the international price instead of raising the price to the consumer up to the domestic cost; also, the subsidy would show clearly what the total costs of national defense are and would better enable the public to decide whether the flame is worth the candle. Moreover, a policy of encouraging imports of oil plus a subsidy to exploration would leave us with more oil in the ground at a time of future emergency than would the present policy of keeping out cheap oil imports.

The question of a national policy to foster the American merchant marine is a similar one. Doubtless the United States does *not* possess a comparative advantage in building or operating a merchant fleet. As soon as American seamen, through trade-unions or on their own, insist upon living conditions and wages remotely resembling those in Detroit factories, then we cannot compete with Dutch, Greek, Japanese, and Norwegian ships. If we give no weight to America's "glorious seafaring tradition"—a long way back!—and consider purely economic welfare, the correct policy is obvious. If America has a comparative advantage in factory production, let men go to factories where their real productivity is high. American international trade need not suffer by being carried in other countries' bottoms.

However, if national defense makes a large merchant marine necessary, that is another matter. Mail subsidies and subsidies for building ships with the extra speed to escape submarines may then be justified. Likewise subsidizing for defense reasons domestic steel capacity at a limited level of, say, one-fifth present capacity might be preferable to protecting domestic producers whose costs exceed those in Japan and Europe.

The problem of deciding how much to spend in peacetime on national defense is a perplexing one, especially since armament races are both *cause* and effect of international disunity. The economist can claim no special competence to advise on this problem. He can point out that selfish economic interests often wrap themselves in the flag and try to justify uneconomic projects in terms of national defense. He can ask suspiciously, "Would an increase in tariffs on Swiss watches be really justified by our defense needs for precision workers? Or is this merely a case of political pressure?" Finally, the economist can also point out that mutually profitable international trade may help to promote international understanding and unity, and that political interferences with trade have in the past provided some of the frictions that led to war.

In conclusion, it is well to point out other noneconomic goals that may deserve consideration. Society may feel that there is some special sanctity about farm life, something worth preserving in the way of life of the "stout agricultural yeoman or happy peasant." (It is to be doubted that people who rhapsodize in this fashion typically come from farms.) Or some may agree with the Soviet Union that rural living is worth fostering because the country has a higher birth rate than the cities.

In such cases, subsidies rather than tariffs seem called for. A tariff is simply a rather indirect and clumsy form of subsidy that draws attention away from the problem.

Do not be left with the impression that the political noneconomic arguments are generally favorable to tariffs. They are not. Every congressman knows that America has a tremendous diplomatic interest these days in winning friends and allies. And nothing is so disruptive to our popularity abroad as our reputation for being a high-tariff country. Foreigners are convinced that as soon as they carve a piece of the American market, we will clamp down with quotas or tariffs. We do not deserve that reputation as much as we used to. So it is all the more to our political interest to resist many of the pressures that make for restrictions on international trade.

GROSSLY FALLACIOUS ARGUMENTS FOR TARIFFS

Keeping money in the country   To Abraham Lincoln has been attributed the remark, "I don't know much about the tariff. But I do know that when I buy a coat from England, I have the coat and England has the money. But when I buy a coat in America, I have the coat and America has the money."

There is no evidence that he ever actually said this; but it does represent an age-old fallacy typical of the so-called "mercantilistic" writers of the seventeenth and eighteenth centuries who preceded Adam Smith. They considered a country lucky which *gave away* more goods than it received, because such a "favorable" (!) balance of trade meant that gold would flow into the country to pay for its export surplus.

In this day and age it should be unnecessary to labor the point that, while an increased amount of money in the hands of one person will make *him* better off, doubling the money in the hands of everybody in a full-employment economy will only serve to raise prices. Unless the single individual is a demented miser like King Midas, the money makes him better off, not for its own sake, but for what it will buy or bid away from other individuals. For society as a whole, once full employment is reached, new money cannot hope to buy any new goods.[1]

A tariff for higher money wages   Today it is agreed that extreme protection can raise prices and attract gold into one country, if all other countries do not retaliate with tariffs. The tariff may even increase *money* wages; but it will tend to increase the cost of living by more than the increase in money wages, so that *real* wages will fall as labor becomes less productive. It is simply not the case that our general living standards can be raised by protecting every domestic industry threatened by cheaper imports.[2]

---

[1] Of course, our gold might be spent abroad. But this perfectly sensible way of improving welfare by importing was precisely what the mercantilist "bullionists" were arguing against.
[2] See Chapter 34's discussion of comparative advantage and effects of a tariff.

One could go on endlessly giving examples of protectionist fallacies that every thoughtful person can explode in a minute by subjecting them to analysis. This does not mean that such crude fallacies can be dismissed as unimportant. Actually, they are most important of all in shaping legislation, the other fancier arguments simply being used as window dressing.

Tariffs for special-interest groups The single most important motivation for protective tariff is obvious to anyone who has watched the "logrolling" in Congress when such legislation is on the floor. Powerful pressure groups and vested interests—both business and labor—know very well that a tariff on their products will help *them*, whatever its effect on total production and consumption. Outright bribery was used in the old days to get the necessary votes; today powerful lobbies exist in Washington to drum up enthusiasm for the good old crockery, watch, or buttonhook industry.

Economically the case for freer trade may be strong, but politically the case for protection tends to exert undue pressure. Why? Because *freer trade helps everybody a little*, while *protection helps a few people a lot*. Does it matter politically that the bad points of protection outweigh the good? Not if those few who benefit from protection (or who are kept by protection from suffering harm) are politically active in pressing for this cause. It is much harder to organize the masses of consumers and producers to agitate for the even larger gains that they get from an efficient pattern of national specialization and trade. If political votes were in exact proportion to *total* economic benefit, every country would selfishly legislate most of its tariffs out of existence.

SOME LESS OBVIOUS FALLACIES

A tariff for revenue First, there is the claim that the tariff should be used to raise government tax revenue. Actually, a customs duty on imports is only one form of regressive sales tax, and a rather bad one. A customs duty or tariff is especially bad because it draws economic resources away from their best uses. If the people who advance the revenue argument were sincere, they would advocate a sales tax which would *also* fall on domestic production. But this would provide no protection. (In some of the underdeveloped countries about the only tax source that can be administratively handled is that on imports or exports. So, admittedly, a case for revenue tariffs can be made in their cases.)

To clinch the case in advanced countries against the revenue argument, only remember that a prohibitively high tariff, which perfectly "protected" us from imports, would collect no revenue at all! Back in 1890, the so-called "billion-dollar Congress" found itself with a surplus of tax revenue over expenditure. Since there was no suitable debt to retire, Congress found the situation embarrassing. It finally met the problem of excessive tariff revenues, not by lowering tariff rates, but by *raising them high* enough to reduce the total of revenue collected.

Tariffs and the home market A second argument, which by itself is on the whole false but whose fallacy is rather difficult to spot, goes as follows: "Farmers should support a tariff for industry because that will gain them a large home market for their products."

Henry Clay, the perennial candidate who turned out to be neither "right" nor "President," used this argument.

Its falsity can be seen from different points of view. First, by cutting down industrial imports we are really at the same time indirectly tending to cut down our farm exports. Thus the farmer is hurt directly. "But," Clay might remonstrate, "what about the extra home market for farm produce?"

Well, what about it? Our detailed example of comparative cost showed that isolation from foreign trade *decreases the total of national product or real income.* The total domestic demand for farm products will certainly be less at a low level of real income than at a high level. So unless it can be buttressed by one of the quite different arguments for protection coming later, the slogan about "creating a home market" is seen once again to be fallacious.

Competition from cheap foreign labor   A third argument for protection has been the most popular of all in American history, because it appealed to the large number of labor votes. According to its usual version, "If we let in goods produced by cheap pauper foreign labor—by Chinese coolies who live on a few cents' worth of rice per day or by low-paid Japanese textile workers—then the higher standard of living of American workers cannot be maintained." So stated, the argument cannot stand up.

We have seen that trade is mutually profitable even if one country can produce every good more cheaply in terms of resources than the other. The important thing is comparative advantage, not absolute advantage. In the last analysis, trade boils down to two-sided barter. At the current exchange rate one country cannot indefinitely undersell the other in every line of merchandise.

Earlier we showed that full employment at home need not depend in the long run on foreign trade. If, then, everyone in this country remains fully employed at his most suitable occupation, is it not to *our selfish advantage* for the workers of other countries to be willing to work for very little? To put the matter another way:

The comparative-cost doctrine shows that we benefit most by trading with countries of the Far East or the tropics which have economies *very different* from ours, rather than with countries such as England or Germany which have an industrial economy like our own.[3] Against the pauper-labor argument, there is the clinching fact that the analysis of comparative advantage showed that absolute wage levels had nothing to do with the long-run increase in national income that resulted from trade.

So much from a theoretical point of view. If we turn to the real world, we find the arguments to be even more incorrect. In Europe and in Asia the workers beg for tariffs, saying, "Protect us from the 'unfair competition' of high-paid, efficient American workers who have skill and machinery far better than our own." The rest of the world lives in fear of competition from American mass-production industries. The English protectionist

---

[3] This argument must be qualified and amplified. Backward countries, so poor that they have little real purchasing power with which to import, at best can export little to us. Most trade today is between industrialized countries. As a backward country advances industrially, it buys more from industrial countries, not less; but perhaps not proportionally more, and perhaps there is *less consumer's surplus from trade* accruing to both parties.

claims that the American worker in Bridgeport, Connecticut, who is paid $4.50 per hour is more than three times as efficient as the English worker who gets paid $1.50 an hour. This is perhaps an overstatement, but it is close to the important truth.

High American real wages come from high efficiency, not from tariff protection. Such high wages do not handicap us in competing with foreign workers.

A tariff to raise wage share   Thus far we have had nothing but adverse criticism for the "cheap pauper foreign labor" tariff argument. To be objective—and without objectivity there can be no science—we must admit that it may have the following iota of possible truth. The Ohlin proposition in the Appendix to the preceding chapter suggested that free trade in goods may serve as a partial substitute for immigration of labor into the United States. This implies that labor scarcity in the United States could be alleviated by our international specialization in labor-economizing products and that real wages might actually fall under conditions of free trade. Real national product would go up, but the relative and absolute share of labor might go down.[4]

Although admitting this as a possibility, most economists believe its grain of truth for a typical country is outweighed by more realistic considerations. No doubt immobile laborers such as textile workers might be hurt by removing a tariff. But since labor is such an important and flexible factor of production, it seems likely that other laborers would gain from expanded trade more than those hurt would lose. Labor as a whole would presumably share in the increased national product from trade.

A tariff for retaliation   Some people admit that a world of free trade would be preferable to a world of tariffs. But they say that as long as other countries are so foolish or so wicked as to pass restrictive tariff legislation, there is nothing that we can do but follow suit in self-defense.

Actually, however, a tariff is much like an increase in transportation costs. If other countries were foolish enough to let their roads go to ruin, would it pay us to chop holes in ours? The answer is, No. Analogously, if other countries hurt us and themselves by passing tariffs, we should not add to our own hurt by passing a tariff.

To make sure that you grasp the point that our tariff harms *us* as well as the foreigner, you should realize that there are four gains when a trade-agreement program succeeds in getting another country and ourselves to lower tariffs reciprocally. The other country's tariff reduction bestows gains (1) on us and (2) on them. Our tariff reduction adds two more gains: (3) for ourselves and (4) for them.

Therefore the only possible sense in the argument that we should retaliate when a foreign country raises tariffs is that our threat of retaliation may deter them from raising tariffs, and our promise to reduce tariffs may persuade them to reduce theirs. This would justify our passing an occasional tariff as a bluff, but if our bluffs do not work, we should give them up.

[4] A study by W. Leontief of Harvard suggests that in America capital rather than labor is the relatively scarce factor! If correct, this would be an argument for raising real wage share of GNP by *lowering* tariffs. (The presumed explanation for this Leontief Paradox of alleged capital scarcity is that each United States worker is technically like three foreign workers, but we lack triple the capital per head.)

Most realistic students of political science infer from historical studies that retaliatory tariffs usually lead other nations to raise theirs still higher and are rarely an effective bargaining weapon for multilateral tariff reduction.

The "scientific" tariff   This is one of the most insidious arguments for a tariff; insidious because it often sounds plausible and moderate but, if taken literally, would mean the end to all trade! According to its usual form, tariffs should be passed to "equalize the cost of production at home and abroad." The last chapter showed all the advantage from trade to rest on *differences* in cost or advantage. If tariffs were passed raising the costs of imports to that of the highest home producer, no goods would come in at all.[5]

There is nothing scientific about such a tariff. It is a grave reflection on the economic literacy of the American people that this least defensible of all protectionist arguments had tremendous political importance in our history, and was even written into law upon occasion.

Peril-point tariff argument   According to this congressional argument, America is to keep tariff duties low on an industry. However, if this results in so many imports that the very existence of that domestic industry is threatened, we have reached the so-called "peril point." When that point is reached, we are to increase duties or tighten quotas to keep our domestic industry from disappearing or becoming perilously small.

What about this argument? While it may sound moderate, note that its basic philosophy runs completely counter to the economic theory of comparative advantage. Our nation gains from trade by *specializing*, i.e., *by giving up* certain activities and moving their resources into other industries in which we have a greater comparative advantage. The industries in which we have strong comparative disadvantage should never have come into existence. And suppose an industry (like, say, steel) formerly had a comparative advantage but has lost it—because other industries have had greater technological improvements, because the domestic factors it uses have become more expensive through becoming more valuable elsewhere, because factors for that industry have become relatively cheaper abroad, or for any other reason. Then this industry *ought* to be imperiled. It ought to be killed off by the competition of our more productive industries. It ought to reach and pass the peril point.[6]

This sounds ruthless indeed. No industry willingly dies; no region gladly undergoes conversion to new factor uses. In truth, any field that is imperiled is probably already a sick industry with a past history of suffering. So the already weak industry and region feel they are being singled out to carry the burden of getting the country into a more productive configuration.

Perhaps the best policy, then, is to introduce tariff reductions gradually, so that vested factors will have time to move; and, as in the 1962 Trade Act, to give financial aid to retrain and relocate factors of production. This tends to speed the transition, share the

---

[5] With nonconstant costs the scientific-tariff formula is indeterminate. A zero tariff may equalize foreign costs with those of our few most efficient producers; an almost prohibitive tariff equalize with our high-cost producers. Where can one scientifically draw the line?

[6] Of course, national-defense and other valid arguments for tariffs might apply; but if they do, it is *those* arguments, and not the peril-point argument, that have to be respected.

burden among strong and weak, and perhaps lessen effective opposition to the needed reorganization of national production. Bicycles, glass, watch manufacture (as distinct from domestic assembly of Swiss movements), oil, basic chemicals, wool growing, china, textiles, generating equipment, and steel are some of the weak sisters that feel imperiled. Politics has forced protective concessions to some of these.

Fortunately, in a growing economy the ineffective industries gradually dwindle in importance relative to the dynamic effective ones. Fortunately, too, the strength of our export industries and the effective use of fiscal and monetary policies can keep over-all employment opportunities high, so that with good conscience the nation can strive for the increase in real income made possible by specialization according to the principles of comparative advantage.

THE "FOREIGNER WILL PAY" OR TERMS-OF-TRADE ARGUMENT[7]

After dealing with fallacious tariff arguments, we find it refreshing to come now to a possibly valid one—which hopes tariffs will shift the terms of trade against the foreigner. Indeed, it is about the only argument that would be valid even under static competitive conditions, and it goes back 150 years to John Stuart Mill. Paradoxically, valid arguments for protection seem mostly to have come from free traders, not protectionists!

If we put a tariff on rubber, Mill would argue, that will raise the price here over its price abroad. But with our demand now curtailed, and as we are an important demander of rubber, the price abroad will be bid down. So part of the tariff really falls on the foreigner. (Show that a very small country could not use this argument, since a tiny country cannot budge world prices.)

In summary, a judicious tariff might improve an important country's terms of trade (defined as the ratio of her export to her import prices).

But here is a warning. *Prohibitive* tariffs, which suit the protectionist who really is against all trade, could never be justified by this terms-of-trade argument. Why? Because killing off *all* trade would kill off *all* the advantage you get from shifting the terms of trade in your favor. Mill and modern economists therefore insist that the "optimal tariff" is one just large enough to improve your terms of trade and just small enough to keep your physical exchange of imports and exports at the level most favorable to your own country.

Most economists think that all this would imply rather small tariff rates for most countries. And they hasten to point out that when all nations pursue such terms-of-trade tariff policies, the world pattern of production and exchange becomes less efficient: most (if not all) tend to end worse off under such beggar-my-neighbor policies.

ARGUMENTS FOR PROTECTION UNDER DYNAMIC CONDITIONS

At last we are arriving at a point in the protection versus free-trade debate where those in favor of tariffs can begin to score some weighty points. Three important arguments

---

[7] The argument is exactly like that of a domestic monopolist who raises his price above marginal cost but does not raise it sky-high, instead stopping where $MR = MC$.

fall in this category: (1) a tariff may help reduce unemployment; (2) tariffs may create diversified industries more immune to risk; and (3) temporary tariff protection for an "infant industry" with growth potentialities may be desirable.

Tariffs and unemployment   Historically, one of the strongest arguments for protection has been the desire to make or preserve jobs. Earlier we discussed the favorable multiplier effects of exports and foreign investment on jobs and domestic spending, and also the unfavorable "leakage" effects of imports. So beggar-my-neighbor high-tariff policy might increase employment in the short run before other nations retaliated.

But can we accept such measures as a valid part of our national full-employment program? Is not freer trade much like a scientific discovery of new machinery and methods? Both represent increases in our *potentially producible* level of real national output; but either *might* in the short run tend to lower our actual *attained* level of output and employment. And yet, there is no need, in either the short or the long run, to tolerate a gap between actual and potentially producible product, for that represents an unnecessary frittering away of the gains from progress.

How, then, do we meet the arguments relating unemployment to too low tariffs? We refute these arguments just as we refute arguments concerning "technological unemployment." We point out the existence of domestic monetary, foreign-exchange-rate, and fiscal policies that can successfully *and efficiently* solve the problem of economic slump. (Recall our hundreds of pages on macroeconomics.[8]) If workers displaced by imports can find other jobs in a strong labor market, this protection plea falls down.

Once again, we realize how vitally important it is to insist on rational macroeconomic management that employs the tools of monetary and fiscal analysis to create the favorable environment for stability and growth which is vitally necessary if the classical principles of economics are to be relevant and valid.

A further point needs emphasis. Today we include in a rational program the requirement that the foreign exchange rate not be a disequilibrium one. If the dollar parity represents "overvaluation," unemployment may result (as was shown in Chapter 33's Appendix). Of course, a tariff might work a little to offset such an overvaluation. But it is much more efficient—and equitable too—to lower the exchange rate rather than rely on quotas, tariffs, and exchange controls.

Diversification to reduce terms-of-trade risk   Comparative advantage might tell a country to specialize completely on one good or a few goods. So she is to put all her eggs in one basket. But then what will happen if the prices of those goods drop? Or if her export prices oscillate? She will find such variations in her terms of trade very destabilizing to her real income; and she may be left with an industry become permanently unprofitable.

To avoid the perils of "monoculture," Latin American economists advise the introduction of tariffs. Just as an investor in securities will diversify to reduce risk rather than keep all his eggs in one basket, so they tell a country to use tariffs to induce diversification.

This argument certainly deserves careful examination. Note that it assumes private

---

[8] If money wage rates are generally too high, the dollar may be "overvalued" (as defined in Chapter 33's Appendix). Chapter 36 shows this could call for a new exchange-rate parity.

citizens are neglecting to take account of the riskiness in future prices of the industries they put their money and labor skills into. This argument has to assume that the government is better informed than private investors, or at least that the government is more farseeing than private investors in taking account of the future perils of price drops and price gyrations. If the future risks are genuine and are foreseen by private investors, those investors will not be misled by temporarily high profits into investing in these few industries; in truth, such industries will not then have a genuine long-run comparative advantage, and there will be no effective tendency to specialize in them.[9]

At this point a related Latin American argument for tariffs should be mentioned. Dr. Raúl Prebisch, long chief economic adviser to the United Nations Economic Commission for Latin America, argued that *the long-run terms of trade are always shifting against agricultural products.* So nations that specialize in them are betting on the wrong horse. He argued their governments should instead impose tariffs aimed at building up manufacturing industries whose future terms of trade will be more favorable. (Against this argument is the following: If past and future reductions in food prices are matched by even greater drops in food's real costs, as agriculture undergoes great technological progress, then long-run comparative advantage might still validly tell a nation to specialize in food to improve its real income or at least to minimize its losses.)

This argument is really an argument about what the *future* comparative advantage of the countries in question will be. To the degree that governments are smarter than private investors in discerning trends threatening to the terms of trade, a valid case can be made for their interfering with free-market forces. But if government is wrong in its comparative-advantage forecasts, the loss in real income to the nation can become very considerable, and the nation may find its rate of development slowed down rather than speeded up.

Tariffs for "infant industries"   Alexander Hamilton, in his famous "Report on Manufactures," raised this argument. It is also associated with the name of a nineteenth-century German economist, Friedrich List, and it has received the cautious blessing of John Stuart Mill, Alfred Marshall, Frank Taussig, and other orthodox economists.

According to this doctrine, there are activities in which a country would really have a comparative advantage, *if only it could get them started.* If confronted with foreign competition, such infant industries are not able to weather the initial period of experimentation and financial stress; but given a breathing space, they can be expected to develop economies of mass production and the technological efficiency typical of many modern processes. Although protection will at first raise prices to the consumer, once the industry grows up it will be so efficient that cost and price will actually have fallen. If the benefit to consumers at that later date would be enough to more than make up for the higher prices during the period of protection, a tariff is justified.

---

[9]Suppose private employers do foresee the risk, but think they can fire workers when export prices drop, thereby throwing the burden of the unemployed workers on the state. Then we face a genuine so-called "external diseconomy," which might justify government intervention in the form of tariffs, quotas, or other programs. Also, recall the limited conditions under which the "foreigner will pay" argument has terms-of-trade validity. Followers of Prebisch might also claim that fostering industry will improve labor's share of the social pie more than it reduces the size of that total pie.

There is certainly something to this, at least as a possibility. Historical studies have turned up some genuine cases of infant industries that grew up to stand on their own feet; but history reveals even more cases of the contrary—of perpetual infants! Unfortunately for the practical importance of this argument, even promising infant industries cannot swing many votes. It is not they who get protection from Congress, but rather the old vested interests who have never shed their diapers for lo these many years.

The "young-economy" argument   Probably the infant-industry argument had more validity for America a century ago than it does today, and it has more validity for present-day undeveloped nations than for those which have already experienced the transition from an agricultural to an industrial way of life. In a sense, such nations are still asleep; they cannot be said to be truly in equilibrium. All over the world, farmers seem to earn less than industrial workers. Consequently, there is everywhere a relative growth of industry and a decline of agriculture. Populations migrate cityward, but this movement is not rapid enough to achieve an equilibrium of earnings and productivity. A strong case can be made for using moderate protection to accelerate these economically desirable long-run trends. Such a defense of protection might better be called a "young-economy" rather than an infant-industry argument.

One final word: Please note that the infant-industry or young-economy arguments are not contradictory to the principle of comparative advantage. On the contrary, their validity rests upon the presumption of an induced, dynamic shift of the production-possibility frontier outward and in the direction of a *new* comparative advantage in the lines needing temporary protection.

CONCLUSION

While this chapter has usually spoken of tariffs, almost everything it has said would apply equally well to any other impediments to trade. Thus, quotas have all the bad effects of tariffs, and often quotas are even more restrictive. An insidious modern development is to use political pressure to get exporters abroad "voluntarily" to place quota limits on their exports to us. Textile quotas by the Japanese and by Hong Kong and "voluntary" steel quotas by Europe and Japan are notorious cases.

Finally, we should mention the so-called "invisible tariff." In many countries—and the United States is no exception—the complicated administration of the customs can be as bad as the monetary duty that has to be paid. If an importer's shipments are unduly delayed or if a foreigner's exports to us are refused admittance for complicated reasons of health or of failure to comply with arbitrary regulations, then such red tape can be as harmful to trade as outright tariffs or quotas. Work toward simplification of customs administration still has a long way to go.

This completes our discussion of the tariff controversy. No fair-minded reader who takes the trouble to think the matter through can fail to see how shallow are most of the economic arguments for tariff protection. The only serious exception is the infant-industry or young-economy argument.

Tariffs were long a political football:

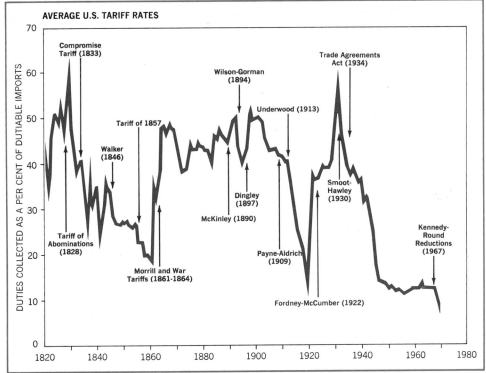

FIG. 35-1. America is no longer a high-tariff nation. Tariff rates have gone up and down in our history. Note how low they have become in the post-World War II era. If comparable figures were compiled for other countries, it would be seen that America no longer deserves her reputation as one of the most protectionist of all nations. Study of comparative quotas and exchange controls would confirm this vital change. (Source: U.S. Department of Commerce, *Statistical Abstract of the United States*, selected editions and author's estimates.)

It is not surprising, therefore, that economists—who are supposed to agree on almost nothing—have been overwhelmingly in favor of the Hull Reciprocal Trade Agreements and GATT (General Agreement on Tariffs and Trade), aimed at lowering trade barriers. The Kennedy Trade Act (1962) gives hope for further multilateral progress, as does the "Kennedy Round" of international negotiations to reduce tariffs multilaterally as the 1970s come into view. President Nixon, too, has asked Congress to lower tariffs.

See Fig. 35-1 for a dramatic illustration of the fact, too little appreciated at home and abroad, that America has at long last ceased to be a high-tariff nation.

SUMMARY

1   The case for freer trade rests upon the increased productivity that international specialization, according to the law of comparative advantage, makes possible. Higher world production is made possible, and all countries can have higher standards of living. Trade between countries with different standards of living is especially profitable.

2 Most arguments for tariff protection are simply rationalizations for special benefits to particular pressure groups and do not stand up under analysis.

3 An exception to the law of comparative advantage is provided by the need to favor certain uneconomical lines of activity for reasons of national defense. Perhaps outright government subsidies would be better in such cases.

4 The only other exception of any practical importance in a full-employment economy[10] is provided by the case of infant industries or young economies that need temporary protection in order to realize their true long-run comparative advantages. To the degree that public planning for development can discern long-term trends better than the free market can, trade interventions to spur industrialization might turn out to be beneficial.

QUESTIONS FOR DISCUSSION

1 What do you think is the single most favorable argument for a tariff or quota?

2 Make a list of fallacious tariff arguments. Weigh pros and cons. (Apply, say, to steel.)

3 Comment critically on the infant-industry and young-economy arguments. What is their relation to comparative advantage?

4 Mention some noneconomic considerations relevant to tariffs.

5 Relate the peril-point and "scientific-tariff" arguments to comparative-advantage theory.

6 Suppose labor productivity grows mightily abroad, and American goods start to be undersold in every line. Suppose that a mixed economy like ours has sticky wage rates. Suppose devaluation of the dollar is not feasible. Show that new tariffs might then be a stopgap measure.

7 *Extra-credit problem:* To understand the fact that the foreigner can be made to pay part of a tariff, go back to linen imports in Fig. 34-3(b). Suppose a new tariff lowers the gold arrows of imports shown there. Can you see that the new equilibrium position must involve lower price of linen there? So America is helped by the tariff to buy a bit more cheaply.

Review your understanding of the following concepts:

tariff protection, quota
scientific tariff and peril point
national-defense arguments

terms of trade
specialization and risk
infant industry and young economy

---

[10]The "foreigner will pay" argument, for all its theoretical attractiveness, is probably of limited actual importance for most countries. Chapter 33's Appendix shows how overvaluation of a currency gives comfort to the enemies of fruitful international trade. And the next chapter will discuss, in the context of America's gold problem, what might be done about such an overvaluation of the dollar.

Current International Economic Problems

36

We must now turn to the main international economic problems facing the United States and the rest of the world in the years ahead. How can we understand the important facts? Which economic policies must we avoid? Which policies must we follow?

Economists have achieved more unanimous agreement about the principles of international trade than about any other aspect of their subject. Yet the gulf between the plain man's beliefs about international finance and those of the experts is almost as wide as elsewhere in economics. Fortunately, that gulf has seemed to be narrowing in recent decades. Section A provides a survey of the main historical and contemporary trends in foreign trade. Section B analyzes the threatened breakdown in the international system—America's chronic gold drain, shortage of international liquidity, and other trade problems. Against this background, Section C surveys the basic reforms in international finance now under way.

A. MODERN TRENDS AND INSTITUTIONS OF INTERNATIONAL FINANCE

TRENDS, 1914–1950

Exports and jobs   When the war broke out in 1914, the belligerent nations—England, France, and Russia—increased their imports from the United States. The effect of this could not be analyzed by the tools known at that time to the highest experts; but the multiplier analysis of Part Two can, as the Appendix of Chapter 33 and common sense show, explain what actually happened—a multiplied expansion of GNP.[1]

---

[1] Suppose (as on page 641) we each spend $8/12$ of each extra dollar on goods, but that $1/12$ represents expenditures on imports from abroad and only $7/12$ represents domestic respending. Then a $1 billion increase in exports will give rise to an ultimate multiplier chain of $[1 + 7/12 + (7/12)^2 + \cdots] = 1/(1 - 7/12) = 12/5 = \$2\frac{2}{5}$ billion increase in NNP.

When the warring countries suddenly became avid customers for our exports, we sent them goods in return for barren gold and fancy gilt-edge certificates. The result was a shift from a prewar recession to great prosperity in America. In the period after we entered World War I, when our shipments of shot and shell increased, again there resulted all the trappings of prosperity booms—high prices and jobs aplenty.

During the 1920s, when we were making many foolish private loans to the rest of the world and whooping it up for tariffs, allegedly to "protect the American workers' standard of living," a contributing factor to our prosperity was heavy foreign lending. Like domestic investment or government deficit expenditure, the foreign-trade balance was adding to total money spending and jobs.

The hard-boiled businessmen summed it up: "Of course, many of our foreign loans later turned sour, and investors lost their money, but while we were shipping goods abroad, jobs were created. It didn't matter, as far as *current* jobs and prices in the twenties were concerned, whether 10 years later the loans turned out good or bad or whether they represented public or private gifts." Or, as Leon Fraser, who used to be president of J. P. Morgan's First National Bank of New York, put it: "It is better to have lent and lost than never to have lent at all."

The Great Depression   After the 1929 stock-market crash, foreign loans became worthless, new foreign lending ceased, and in every country there was much unemployment and unrest. With jobs scarce at home, the political forces of protectionism became rampant. Tariffs were raised, quotas imposed, and in many countries exchange controls were also imposed. Against the advice of almost 100 per cent of the economics profession (who signed a petition to Congress), the Hawley-Smoot (1930) high tariff was passed. Cynics were delighted at the spectacle of a country *trying to collect debts from abroad and at the same time shutting out the import goods that could alone have provided the payment for those debts.* H. L. Mencken, who never failed to call attention to the comedy of American life, rubbed his hands to see farmers—who were net exporters and not importers of goods—being given import tariffs on their export(!) products in exchange for their voting for tariffs on manufactured imports.

The fallacy of composition was at work. Each country believed that, if *it* could develop a favorable balance of trade, *its* employment would increase at the expense of its neighbors; in effect, it would be succeeding in exporting some of its joblessness. But for everybody to run a favorable trade balance simultaneously is a self-contradiction—as impossible as for everybody to be taller than anybody else.

Of course, the attempt to be taller—that is, to generate a favorable surplus of exports over imports—could be predicted to cut down on the fruitful division of labor. And precisely that happened. As much as domestic and total world production declined, the volume of international trade declined still more. The situation reached its height of absurdity when countries would trade with each other only on a *bilateral* basis: A would buy from B only as much as B would buy from A; under Hitler's economic adviser Schacht, Latin American countries were sending staples to Germany in return for aspirin, which was piling up in warehouses.

It was a non-Euclidean world, with triangles whose angles added up to anything or nothing and with intersecting parallel lines. Inefficiency was putting the world and each nation well inside its production-possibility frontier. But since contractionary monetary and fiscal policies were being urged as the only penance for the sinful practices followed during the prosperity, destruction of goods seemed the order of the day. Farmers were pouring milk into gutters, wheat was being burned to keep sharecroppers warm, the government was paying people to plow under the unripened corn, and the windows of empty factories were the targets for bored men who had been on relief for years. Eliminating the efficiency of international trade was not out of line with the idiocy of the day.

Today, even schoolboys ask why the people did not insist on deliberate programs of fiscal and monetary expansion. It is only too easy to remake history *after* the fact. But —and this is what concerns us here—one reason a single nation could not introduce expansion at home was the genuine fear that if she increased her GNP while others kept their GNP depressed, her imports would grow in the face of languishing exports. Thus, she would lose gold and, under the gold standard, she would either have to contract again or be forced into devaluation or bankruptcy.

As it happened, by 1931 England was forced off the gold standard along with Scandinavia and the Commonwealth. With the pound depreciated, these countries could afford to push their *internal* expansion; and if you look at the records, you see that Sweden and Britain were already recovering nicely from the Depression when the United States, Germany, and France were experiencing the worst of it. Doubtless, some of the gains to the depreciating countries were at the expense of those who stayed orthodoxly on gold. But most authoritative studies suggest that the gain to the expanding countries came *primarily from the freedom it gave them to expand domestically.*

Was old-fashioned virtue rewarded? Not in the 1930s. Belgium clung precariously to the old gold mint parities, even after Roosevelt deliberately devalued the dollar. Political unrest and depression were Belgium's reward—until 1936, when she gave up the struggle and, instead of being smitten by thunderbolts for her apostasy, she immediately registered relief in her production and unemployment statistics. France, having been the wayward inflationist in the 1920s, practically tore herself apart politically by clinging to the old gold parity into the late 1930s. Only Switzerland seemed to be able to afford Euclidean geometry in a world gone non-Euclidean.

War   The Depression, which hit Germany and the United States especially hard, contributed to Hitler's rise to power. His preparations for war "solved" Germany's mass-unemployment problem and proved—in a tragically unnecessary way—the potency of Keynes-like fiscal and monetary policies. When World War II came, deficits in every country, financed with a new supply of money, engineered vast increases in the G of $C + I + G$. This had the predictable effect of, first, expanding production enough to get rid of unemployment, and second, swelling total demand so much as to create inflationary gaps and outright inflation. As in World War I, shipments of exports for the warring nations again brought full employment and enhanced real product to the United States.

War meant scarcity, not superabundance. So again the world turned Euclidean. Mercantilistic notions, that it is good *to give away goods* abroad in return for as few imports as possible, went into discard. The emphasis again was on extending production-possibility frontiers outward and on making sure to be on those frontiers, and not inside. The classical theory of comparative advantage came into its own as the Allied Powers allocated to each nation the tasks it could perform *relatively* most efficiently.

The period of "dollar shortage"   When the war was over, the scarcity of resources remained. Only the United States had not been physically devastated by the war. Elsewhere there was a great need to rebuild, to develop, and to make up for wartime scarcities. At the prevailing exchange rates, the American dollar was vastly "undervalued."

Undervalued dollar and dollar shortage defined: **The total demand abroad for American dollars to finance needed imports from us was much greater than the total of dollars our private citizens would want to supply (to pay for trips, imports, direct investments, etc.). If we had not introduced a governmental policy of providing relief and reconstruction aid, of making loans and gifts, no country would have had the needed amount of gold or credit worthiness to finance its international deficit with us. In a free-trade, flexible-exchange world, the price of the dollar would have been bid sky-high.**

Under the conditions of 1945–1950, in the absence of vast American aid programs and tight regulation abroad of imports and capital movements, the *dd* and *ss* schedules of Chapter 33, Fig. 33-1, page 626 would have shown a tremendous "dollar gap" at existing foreign exchange rates; this could have been met only by dropping to an equilibrium intersection where the dollar was much, much dearer in terms of foreign currencies— perhaps at $2 per £1 rather than $4, which was then prevailing, and likewise for the needed appreciation of the dollar relative to the mark, franc, and yen.

That is the technical meaning of the term that used to be heard so widely then, namely, the "dollar shortage," or "dollar gap." (Reread the above brown paragraph.)

How was the gap handled? Not by immediate postwar depreciations abroad (although later in 1949 Britain and most nations did have to depreciate, the pound dropping from $4 to $2.80). Instead, the so-called "dollar gap" was handled primarily by comprehensive exchange and import controls on the part of the nations with "overvalued currencies" and, as we shall see, by vast American aid and loan programs.

MARSHALL PLAN, MILITARY AID, AND OTHER PROGRAMS

Table 36-1 shows how enormous the American aid programs have been. After the United Nations Relief and Rehabilitation Administration (UNRRA) had helped meet the immediate postwar emergency needs, we introduced our dramatic Marshall Plan for European recovery. Subsequently, our aid shifted toward grants to the North Atlantic Treaty Organization (NATO) and other military alliances. (Thus, the "Truman Doctrine" brought financial aid to Greece when that country was threatened by communism. Even Yugoslavia has received aid along with the Chinese Nationalists, the South Koreans, and the South Vietnamese.) Our aid to the neutral countries of Asia, Africa, and Latin America, for economic development, has been on a scale without precedent in all history.

Undoubtedly, the motive for many of these programs was our fear of the spread of communism. Full stomachs may not save a democracy, it was argued, but empty ones

For relief, recovery, development, and military security, we gave:

UNITED STATES GOVERNMENT POST-WORLD WAR II FOREIGN AID (billions of dollars, fiscal years)					
TYPE OF AID	1945–1950	1951–1956	1957–1962	1963–1967	TOTAL POSTWAR PERIOD
Net nonmilitary grants	17.1	11.0	11.2	7.6	46.9
Western Europe	10.9	5.4	1.0	0.0	17.3
Asia, Africa, and Near East	4.6	5.0	8.3	6.3	24.2
Rest of world	1.6	0.6	1.9	1.3	5.4
Net government loans	9.4	1.5	2.5	8.0	21.4
Western Europe	8.1	0.2	−2.1	−0.1	6.1
Asia, Africa, and Near East	0.7	0.8	2.8	6.4	10.7
Rest of world	0.6	0.5	1.8	1.7	4.6
Net military grants	1.8	16.7	12.1	7.2	37.8
Western Europe	0.3	11.0	4.2	1.0	16.5
Asia, Africa, and Near East	1.4	5.1	7.3	6.1	19.9
Rest of world	0.1	0.5	0.6	0.2	1.4
Net total, grants and loans	28.3	29.2	25.8	22.8	106.1

TABLE 36-1.   Excludes International Bank and Fund operations. (Source: U.S. Department of Commerce.)

can seal its doom. Putting modern guns into the hands of our friends was intended both to help their defense and save American soldiers' lives. Since other advanced nations—such as Britain, Germany, and the Soviet Union—have also given foreign aid, an element of emulation and competition also entered our motivations.

However, a close study of the events leading up to the Marshall Plan and other foreign-aid plans will show that America in the postwar period has also had intermittent "do-good" motivations. Call this altruism if you wish, or call it long-run expediency. The fact that the globe holds 15 non-Americans to every American makes our very future depend upon a stable international order not overly hostile to Western society. Close study of the facts does not well bear out the hypothesis that we embraced aid programs because that was the only way to prevent a great depression at home. On the contrary, we gave most *at times when domestic inflation problems were most pressing;* and one of the gravest costs of aid was aggravation of our concurrent internal scarcities.

The Point Four program   Aside from providing substantial material aid, there is one important thing we do for foreign countries that costs us very little, namely, *help them acquire the technical know-how to enable them to increase their levels of productivity and living standards.* This is known as the "Point Four" program because it was first enunciated as the fourth point in the 1949 inaugural address of President Truman.

Fourth, we must embark on a bold new program for making the benefits of our scientific advances and industrial progress available for the improvement and growth of undeveloped areas. . . . I believe that we should make available to peace-loving peoples the benefits of our store of technical knowledge in order to help them realize their aspirations for a better life. . . . We invite other countries to pool their technological resources in this . . . world-wide effort for the achievement of peace, plenty, and freedom.

Besides these government plans, we have been privately exporting our "know-how." Many of our largest companies are establishing branch factories abroad; often the capital is largely raised there, with Americans supplying the technical knowledge.

Some people throw up their hands in horror at the thought of our helping foreign nations to become our industrial competitors. Despite the statistical fact that international trade is largest between developed industrial nations and not between highly developed and backward countries, in terms of selfish long-run economic interest there is some factual basis for this gloomy view—as the post-Marshall Plan economic revival of Europe and Japan well illustrates. However, in terms of both long-run political interests and altruism, helping others to develop is deemed definitely good policy for the United States, albeit embraced by the electorate in less enthusiastic degree as the 1970s progress.

THE INTERNATIONAL BANK AND FOREIGN LENDING

Since the United States is more developed industrially than the rest of the world, there is no doubt that South America, the Orient, Europe, and Africa could profitably use our capital for their industrial development. Such capital could be expected to increase their production by more than enough to pay generous interest and repay the principal.

But private American citizens were long loath to lend. Though American corporations will build branch plants abroad and will invest in oil or mineral resources, substantial private lending through Americans' buying risky foreign bonds or stocks disappeared sometime in 1929, seemingly forever. Yet American citizens do have savings which they would be glad to lend if such capital transactions could be made safe; and the American nation would benefit by a higher future standard of living from such sound foreign lending.

Therefore the leading nations of the world (except Soviet Russia by her choice) came together in 1944 to form the International Bank for Reconstruction and Development and its sister institution, the International Monetary Fund. As its name implies, the International Bank is formed to provide sound long-term loans for reconstruction and development. (The International Monetary Fund is concerned, as we shall see shortly, with short-term credit and the cooperative stabilization of foreign exchange rates.)

The International Bank is easy to understand. The lending nations subscribe toward its capital stock in proportion to their economic importance. (The United States quota is about one-third.) The bank can use its capital to make sound international loans, to people or countries whose projects seem economically sound but who cannot get private loans at reasonably low interest rates.

The International Bank's true importance arises from something greater than the loans that it can make out of its own capital. More important is the fact that it can float bonds and use the proceeds to make loans. (It has successfully floated bonds in the United States, in Switzerland, and elsewhere.) The bonds are safe because they are backed by the credit of all the nations (up to their 100 per cent of quotas). Also, the International Bank can *insure* loans in return for a ½ or 1 per cent premium; private parties can then put up the money, knowing that the Bank's credit is behind the loan.

As a result of extending long-term credits, we can expect to see goods and services in the years ahead flowing out of the advanced nations aimed at international development. If sound, these loans will be repaid in full. If some go sour, the loss will be paid out of the Bank's interest or premium earnings. If still more go sour, the loss will be spread over all the member nations. While the loans are being made, the advanced world is getting jobs and, if spending is already too great, some increase in their inflation problems. When the loans are being "serviced" or repaid, the advanced nations should have an import surplus of useful goods. Production in the borrowing lands should have risen by more than enough to pay interest on the loans; wages and living standards generally should then be *greater*, not less, because of what foreign capital has added to the GNP of the borrowing country.

Has the Bank been a financial success? Decidedly. If anything, until Robert McNamara (formerly of Ford and the Pentagon) became its activist head in the late 1960s, the Bank may have long been too conservative in its practice of lending to self-liquidating projects. By 1970 an embarrassing volume of profits had accumulated. An increasing proportion of this now goes to the International Development Agency, set up by the Bank to make "soft loans" to nations for education, roads, hospitals, etc.; and to its International Finance Corporation, set up to make loans to foreign development banks for financing private investment projects.[2]

THE INTERNATIONAL MONETARY FUND

The International Monetary Fund, like the International Bank, grew out of the 1944 international conferences held in Bretton Woods, New Hampshire. The IMF hopes to secure the advantages of the gold standard without its disadvantages; e.g., exchange rates were in the beginning envisaged to be relatively stable, but with international cooperation to replace the previous automatic mechanism. Also, countries are to be spared the need for making adjustments that involve *deflating themselves into drastic unemployment.* And the IMF hopes to lessen need for import controls.

Ordinarily, a country pays for its imports by means of its exports or long-term borrowing. Suppose a country, say, England, is in need of short-term credit from the Fund. How does the Fund enable such a debtor country to get hold of dollars, for instance? It does this by extending "purchasing rights." It simply permits the British to buy with British currency some of the Fund's own holdings of dollars. After the British balance of payments has improved, Britain is expected to buy back with gold (or with dollars or, as we'll see, with the new SDRs of "paper gold") the pounds it has sold to the Fund.

The Fund tries to set up rules and procedures to keep a country from going too deeply into debt, year after year. After a country has been piling up debts for a considerable period, certain financial penalties are applied. More important, the Fund's directors

---

[2]Our own Export-Import Bank also makes foreign loans, e.g., enabling an American exporter to sell machine tools to Brazil on credit.

consult with the country and make recommendations for remedying the disequilibrium. However, they do not advise a country to create a depression in order to cut its national income down to such a low level that its imports will finally fall within its means. Instead, the country itself is permitted first to depreciate (or appreciate in opposite situations) its currency by 10 per cent. This tends to restore equilibrium in its trade by expanding its exports and contracting imports.

If this is still not enough to correct the so-called "overvaluation" of the debtor country's currency, the Fund authorities may, after proper consultation, permit still further depreciation of the debtor country's exchange rate. But note this: All changes in rates are to take place in an orderly way. Most of the time, there is to be international stability. There is also provision for flexibility when needed, which is better by far than waiting for a great smash.

By the 1960s the IMF realized that it must also shift onto the surplus countries an obligation to help restore basic equilibrium. Thus, Germany may be encouraged to *appreciate* the mark (as she did in 1961 and finally in 1969). She may be encouraged to lower import barriers and export subsidies; to lend abroad and enlarge her foreign aid; to reflate her economy if she is stagnating.

At first the Fund was rather a disappointment. The postwar strains turned out to be much larger than people realized in 1944; and the Fund's resources were inadequate to cope with those disequilibria. Since 1955 and the end of the dollar gap, the IMF has become increasingly important. For example, the United States has reinforced its own international resources by drawing on the Fund.

As an example of the renewed importance of the IMF, consider the sterling crisis faced by the British Labor Government in the years before the 1967 devaluation of the pound from $2.80 to $2.40 per pound. Britain borrowed several billion dollars from the IMF to support the pound, making the United Kingdom the greatest user of the Fund since its formation. In addition, the IMF helped coordinate the billions of dollars of support for the pound from the United States and continental European countries (the other members of the "Club of Ten").

In any future major reforms of international liquidity or any future dollar problems, the International Monetary Fund will undoubtedly play a pivotal role, as we shall see.

THE EUROPEAN COMMON MARKET AND THE FREE-TRADE AREA

The last few chapters analyzed the economic gains from freer trade. One way of getting trade impediments down is for several countries to form a customs union. Within such a union, tariffs and quotas might be reduced or banished; but they might still persist with respect to external trade. History provides us with many examples. The 50 states of the United States can be thought of as a large customs union. A century ago the many independent German states formed a *Zollverein,* or customs union.

One of the most exciting international developments of the century has been the formation of the six-nation European Common Market. In 1957 Belgium, France, Italy, Luxembourg, the Netherlands, and West Germany signed treaties to create a Common Market. Subject to exceptions, by 1973 each nation is to eliminate tariffs and import quotas on nonfarm goods produced *within* the area; to set up a common tariff against goods from countries outside the Common Market; and to allow free movement of capital and labor. It looks to become the second-largest free-trade area in the world. If Great Britain were to get in, the Common Market might become the largest area of all.

Anxious over the progress of the Common Market, seven other European nations formed the "Outer Seven" free-trade area: this consists of Austria, Denmark, Norway, Portugal, Sweden, Switzerland, and the United Kingdom. This loose federation (EFTA) aims eventually at free trade, but its development does not compare in importance with that of the Six and ultimately it may merge with the Common Market.

Some economists have worried whether the lowering of tariffs between countries of a bloc is truly a movement toward a more efficient world pattern: "Won't there be a danger that the lower-than-average tariffs between the countries in the union will distort the 'normal' pattern of trade even more than it is already being distorted by separate nations' tariffs? Won't the difference between the ins and the outs be magnified and represent as serious a distortion as the previous situation?"

Others have replied: "Two wrongs don't make a right. If you can't get rid of trade impediments everywhere, at least get rid of them where you can. Then maybe a few great customs unions can ultimately merge into a worldwide free-trade area."

No definitive answer will cover every case. Perhaps most economists would venture the guess that lowering of tariffs in Europe could have such good effects there on the division of labor as to lead to net benefit for these countries, and ultimately for others.

FREER MULTILATERAL TRADE: GATT

The Cordell Hull reciprocal-trade program for reducing American and other tariffs has now been with us for more than a third of a century. Contrary to common opinion, our high 1930 tariffs have been cut substantially (in some cases they have been halved and then halved again, as you can see by referring back to Fig. 35-1, p. 679). As a result, careful measurement of the degree to which all the nations of the world restrict trade will show that in 1970 the United States is near the top of the list of "relatively free traders." To be sure, we ought (in our interest as well as in the interest of others) to go even further; and admittedly, foreigners never know when Congress will raise tariffs. Still, those who talk about American trade policy should study the true situation, and not become guilty of the informational lag that was already pointed out at the end of the preceding chapter.

All stand to gain if fruitful multilateral trade can be restored. As mentioned before, GATT (the General Agreement on Tariffs and Trade) is a most important development toward international cooperation. The Kennedy Trade Act (1962) aimed at a new round of reciprocal tariff cuts, a fitting memorial to the man.

This so-called "Kennedy Round" for multilateral tariff reductions is a good example of the gradual progress being made toward trade liberalization. Actually the late-1960s effort was the sixth round of tariff reduction under the auspices of GATT, earlier efforts having taken place in 1947, 1949, 1951, 1956, and 1961. Agreement was made difficult by the wish of certain members of the Common Market, most notably France, to increase protective tariffs on agriculture. Thus, although most geographers and economists are impressed by America's comparative advantage in farm products, the French have always insisted that their higher-cost producers be protected, even if this would entail higher prices to German and other consumers. Indeed, the repeated difficulties placed in the way of Britain's entrance into the Common Market have been related to the strong French stand on this and other matters.

B. THREATENED BREAKDOWN OF THE INTERNATIONAL SYSTEM

Now that we have surveyed the post-World War II institutions of international finance, we can face up to the burning issues that confront America and the world.

FROM DOLLAR SHORTAGE TO DOLLAR GLUT

The Marshall Plan and other aid programs soon began to have spectacularly favorable effects on the less-than-most-affluent countries—Japan, Germany, Holland, France, and Italy. Primarily on their own, by a process no one had predicted, they began a miraculous sprint of productivity growth in the 1950s. This miracle persists into the 1970s.

This growth in the *competitiveness* of foreign economies, plus the expensiveness of America's *cold-war programs* (the Korean conflict, the Vietnam war, the NATO alliance, etc.), plus our *civilian foreign-aid programs* (in Asia, Latin America, and elsewhere), plus the burgeoning outflow of *direct foreign investments by American corporations* facing juicy profitability opportunities abroad—all these factors led to a gradual cessation of the dollar shortage and an actual swing toward a shortage of foreign currencies.

The "dollar shortage" of the 1950s turned into the "dollar glut" (i.e., draining of gold from America, with chronic balance-of-payments deficits) of the 1960s and early 1970s. Relatively high costs here meant "overvaluation of the dollar."

At first the drain on our gold supply went unnoticed. But after 1958, everybody could see that a new trend was in the making.

Figure 36-1(a) shows how America has turned into a deficit nation in her balance of payments.[3] How was this international deficit financed? As Fig. 36-1(b) shows, in part it was financed by our shipping gold abroad. By 1970 our gold stock had dropped from its peak of $24 billion in 1949 down to around $10 billion. But in larger part the international deficit was financed by foreigners accepting our short-term IOUs. Figure 36-1(b) shows how liquid claims on us have grown to exceed our gold holdings.

Since America probably had a disproportionate share of the world's gold supply in 1950, American experts rather welcomed the first part of the gold drain. Even now, American economists would not be displeased with our present gold stock if they thought that an equilibrium was in clear sight. But Fig. 36-1 gives no assurance of this.

For the 25 years from 1933 to 1958, thanks in part to Hitler and the political uncertainties that sent gold to our shores for safekeeping, American economic policy was

---

[3] The deficit shown here is not the "basic deficit" described in Chapter 33. It is the Official Settlements Balance of Payments that is now commonly used. Thus, for 1968 the United States "basic balance" was shown on page 633 to be $-\$2,057$ million ($= -\$349$ million deficit on current account plus $-\$1,708$ million long-term investment outflow). The Official Settlements balance is shown in Fig. 36-1 to be about $+\$1$ billion, the difference coming from short-term capital movements. The government also reports a "liquidity" deficit, which differs from the Official Settlements balance because some private foreign capital *inflows* into the United States (such as our private borrowings from the Euro-dollar market) are included in it.

Chronic foreign deficits weaken the dollar, cause hemorrhage of gold:

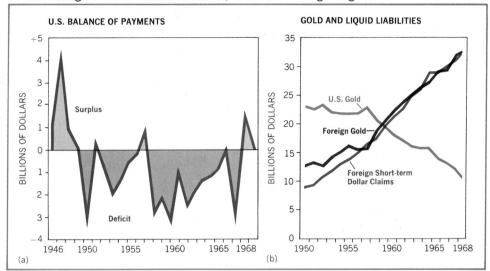

FIG. 36-1.   The continued international deficit shows the swing from dollar shortage to over-valuation of the dollar. Although America is still the owner of the largest amount of gold, its gold stock has dropped steadily. The rest of the world has increased its amount and share of total gold and has been accumulating short-term liquid claims on us. (Source: U.S. Department of Commerce. This deficit, on an official reserve transactions basis, differs from *basic* deficit of Chapter 33 in that it is affected by changes in short-term investments.)

emancipated completely from any concern for our international balance of payments. Now the honeymoon is long since over. America has rejoined the human race: we too have a balance-of-payments problem. We had to take it into account when, as in 1960–1965, we wished to lower interest rates in order to help achieve full-employment levels of investment and stimulate the capital formation that leads to faster growth rate of our producible NNP.

Every decision made about defense and civilian aid to underdeveloped countries has in the 1960s been limited by the constraint: What will it do to our balance of payments?

REASONS FOR CHRONIC INTERNATIONAL DEFICIT, 1955–1970

Many reasons are given for America's chronic international deficit. Most have an element of truth in them, but we shall see that the crucial cause for the 1955–1970 period is probably to be found in the vast improvement of technical productivity abroad in recent years. Below are the causes commonly named for the deficit:

1. Too much inflation here at home   If a country has more rapid wage increases than its neighbor, and if these are not matched by compensating differentials in worker productivity gains, then it is indeed likely to find itself running into a deficit in the balance of international payments.[4]

---

[4] For further analysis, see Chapter 33's Appendix discussion on overvaluation of a currency.

If we turn from conjecture to fact, an examination of any of the usual over-all index numbers of money prices and wages will show that up to 1965, there had not been more inflation here than abroad. On the contrary, a list of the 20 principal countries of the world shows that the United States came almost at the bottom in terms of price-level increase in the last decade. The same is true of index numbers of money wage rates. Only after 1965 did our price indices begin to soar.

There is this grain of truth, however, in the overpricing allegation. If one leaves over-all indices and turns to certain important sectoral price indices, it will indeed be found that American steel prices long rose relative to those abroad. No wonder that Japanese steel invades the Pacific Coast; that foreign steel products such as *barbed wire* (and what could be more American that *that?*) have taken over many of our traditional home markets; that steel from England and Belgium, helped by lengthy domestic strikes and fears of strikes, has got a foothold in our markets. Similar occurrences are found in several of our machinery industries. There the great burst of demand in the equipment boom of 1956–1957 sent our prices soaring, whereas the price rise in steel was thought by the Joint Economic Committee of Congress to be more the result of "cost-push" by wages and maintained profit margins.

We shall see that full employment, incident to the post-1965 Vietnam escalation, has created a price-level escalation that has caused deterioration of our private current balance of exports over imports. Hence, from 1965 to 1970, America's basic deficit problems worsened.[5]

2. Overgenerosity in our aid and military programs   It is natural when aiming to reduce our trade deficit by a billion dollars to think of simply cutting out that much foreign aid and military spending. However, it is somewhat misleading to think that such a cut will reduce the deficit by that same billion, since many of our export credit items are present in the balance of payments *only because our government programs have given foreigners the "tied" funds to pay for them.* Hence, cutting such programs by $1 billion will thereby cut into our private exports and in turn reduce our deficit by something less than $1 billion, how much less being hard to estimate.

Until Vietnam, our governmental foreign-aid and military programs had not grown much in relative size; rather, it was more the case that, with the growth in private long-term investment, our surplus on current *private* account was no longer large enough to let our aid programs be as generous as they had been previously.[6] After 1965, Vietnam did become an important aggravator of our payments deficit.

---

[5]If you plot (1) our declining share of world exports against (2) the post-World War II rise in the ratio of our export prices to those abroad, the result does look a little like a downward-sloping *dd* curve, with the rise in our relative P explaining the loss in our relative Q.

[6]Even some experts do not realize how high America's surplus on current private account must be if we are to stay in healthy equilibrium with free long-term investment and are to carry on desired government operations abroad. Equilibrium might then require us to expand our exports of goods and services, in comparison with our imports, by enough to create a current private surplus of as much as $8 to $10 billion! It is quite wrong to think that developing such a sizable surplus would do harm to our trading partners. On the contrary, financial equilibrium and equilibrium of comparative advantage require that this be achieved; inasmuch as we are already supplying the rest of the world with the means to finance our enlarged surplus, they are in no genuine sense harmed. The private surplus must` be large enough, however large that is, to fit in with over-all international equilibrium.

3. Lack of trust in the dollar   From 1933 to 1955, the dollar was considered everywhere to be a holding even better than gold. It was *the* key international reserve currency. But what happens when people and governments begin to believe that America is in international disequilibrium? And when they become apprehensive that the dollar *might* be devalued relative to marks, francs, or gold? It is natural enough, under these circumstances, that some governments and private persons should, before the 1968 two-tier gold system made our gold unavailable to private persons, want to take out gold from the United States rather than continue to hold dollar currency or dollar IOUs. This so-called "shift in international liquidity preference" can help explain some of the chronic 1955–1968 gold drain from our shores.[7]

4. Discriminations abroad against American goods   While the dollar was in short supply abroad, it was understandable why barriers against our exports would have been common in other countries. With the dollar weak not strong, there is good reason to argue that remaining discriminations against American goods be removed or reduced, and some progress has taken place.

5. The rapid growth of productivity abroad   From a long-run viewpoint, the fundamental cause of the change in America's international position would seem to be the remarkable speeding up of productivity increase in Western Europe and Japan.

Their production technology is still largely behind ours, but the gap, particularly in the goods which we customarily export and specialize in, has been narrowing.

Even with real wages rising abroad more rapidly than here, productivity improvements abroad enable foreigners to produce for themselves more cheaply than we have been producing for them. Hence they can outsell us increasingly in third markets, and can even begin to outsell us in our home markets.

6. High investment abroad by American firms   The miraculous productivity spurt abroad created tremendous profit opportunities for American corporations. In the last decade, instead of wishing to invest in the underdeveloped world, they hastened to build branch factories in Europe and Japan: when a market is growing by 10 per cent a year, how can you help but make high profits?

By 1965 the outflow of direct investments by American firms had become so large that the government introduced a *voluntary* capital control program. The Federal Reserve administered the program as applied to commercial bank loans; the Department of Commerce administered it as applied to corporations. In 1968, the voluntary program

---

[7]On the other hand, some experts—such as MIT's C. P. Kindleberger, Stanford's Emile Despres, and Princeton's Fritz Machlup—think the distrust of the dollar is a foolish state of mind that could be easily changed by a bold policy in which America makes the following kind of announcement: "Come exchange your dollars for gold right now at $35 per ounce—if you are foolish enough to want to do so. But don't think you can count on America to buy back that gold from you at a guaranteed price of $35 once again. Instead America may, at *its* pleasure, reduce its buying price of gold—perhaps abandoning gold altogether!" Given such an ultimatum, gold hoarders will realize the error of their ways and, so the argument goes, will swing over in liquidity preference to the dollar. Under the two-tier system, the Kindleberger-Despres doctrine takes a slightly modified form, as we shall see.

became mandatory, and quotas were tightened. Despite the 1970 easing of quotas by the Nixon administration, the control program, like all such programs, tends to decrease in effectiveness with the passage of time—as greater inequities develop and strains are put on public spirit and altruism.

EQUILIBRIUM IN THE 1970s?

Is the world moving toward international equilibrium in the 1970s? Here are the salient facts to show fundamental structural reform cannot long be delayed.

1. Certainly the decade of the 1960s began with the dollar and pound in fairly serious *disequilibrium* relative to the surplus countries of the Common Market.

Our patterns of comparative advantage were changing, and that is rarely a comfortable transition period. Moreover, it was not simply a question of our shifting factors from one industry to another. So long as our dollar costs tended to be high *all around*, the American currency could be called an "overvalued currency." A country with an overvalued currency tends to incur international deficits, to be undersold in most goods, to have capital outflow, and to be threatened with high unemployment and excess capacity. What may be needed is for her money prices and wages to fall relative to those in other countries, either falling absolutely or rising less rapidly than theirs. Even if no *real wage* change were needed, we know that it is very far from easy in a modern democratic mixed society to have a deflation in money wage and other costs and in prices.[8]

2. For the first half of the decade there were definite signs of improvement for the dollar. Perhaps the principal reason for this was the over–full employment on the Continent, which sent its wage and other money costs rising faster than costs in the more sluggish American economy.

3. After 1965, America too reached the goal of full employment. This, combined with the Vietnam conflict, tended to increase our imports relative to our exports. No longer did our costs grow more slowly than those in many of the surplus countries. By 1970 the experts were no longer certain that the dollar disequilibrium was about to cure itself and enable dismantling of the ad hoc measures used to defend the dollar ("tying" of aid, interest-rate equalization tax, voluntary and mandatory capital control program, etc.).

THERAPY FOR A CHRONIC DEFICIT

Economists know what are the programs generally needed to reverse a chronic international deficit. These are easy to preach but not so easy to follow.

1. American workers and industry can be urged to *increase domestic technical productivity.* Urging does not accomplish much. More important in the long run are supports for scientific research and investment.

2. American exporters can be urged to *improve selling practices* abroad. Since foreign salesmen are also similarly urged, mere exhortation accomplishes little.

---

[8] A rise in productivity abroad can often increase real wage here by cheapening imports. But (1) if it takes the form of improvement in productivity there in goods we have been specializing in and (2) if it reflects the discovery by American corporations that their know-how can be applied to non-American workers, then the whole process could actually slow up the rate of real wage growth here and could result in a *loss* of American consumer's surplus from international trade. Cf. Chapter 33's Appendix.

3. America can press for further *reductions in discriminations against the dollar.* There are still trade impediments, and the Common Market threatens more.

4. We can ask that the prospering nations of the free world take up a *larger share of the aid, development, and defense burdens.*

5. We could *keep our economy depressed* at home, eschewing low interest rates needed for expansion and growth, diminishing our demand for imports, and putting pressure on profit margins in export industries and making them hungry to drum up export business.[9] During the 1960s, the Kennedy-Johnson administration rejected a policy of deliberate creation of unemployment and sluggish growth in order to lessen international deficits. But in 1966–1970, the British Labor Government had to introduce a deliberate slowdown in order to strengthen the balance of payments, and so did President Nixon in 1969–1970.

6. There could be a *depreciation of the dollar* relative to other currencies, with or without a unilateral *devaluation* relative to gold (in the official tier), or by some other move.

Second-best measures   Any or all of the above measures are designed to get rid of any overvaluation of the dollar relative to other currencies. But suppose that they are not feasible in the needed amount, and that America will have to live with an overvalued dollar for some time. A host of new, and somewhat distasteful, measures can combat overvaluation.

7. We can *"tie" foreign-aid grants and loans further,* requiring that their proceeds be spent directly in the United States even if our goods cost more. Also we have tied our own military expenditures in the sense that an item must be bought at home even if it costs 50 per cent more than abroad. This is but one of many piecemeal devaluations or depreciations of the dollar that take place when outright devaluation is not feasible.

8. We can *limit tourism,* by cutting down on the amount of goods that travelers can bring home free of duty. If matters got worse, free tourism could be interfered with, as is the case in so many other nations. Thus, Wilson's Labor Government in the late 1960s had to cut down travel allowances for the British to a derisory sum per year.

9. *Restrictions or tax penalties can be put on foreign investment.* Attracted by the high profits that growth and productivity improvements abroad make possible, as we have seen, there has been a vast outpouring of investment abroad by firms and individuals. Except for the obvious special case of oil discoveries in the Near East and Latin America, the bulk of this investment has not gone to the underdeveloped countries so much as to the developed nations. If one wanted to be simple-minded, one could blame this upsurge of long-term investment for most of the basic deficit.[10]

Reluctantly, Congress imposed a so-called "interest equalization tax" of $11\frac{1}{2}$ per cent or more on any purchase by an American from a non-American of a foreign stock or long-term bond. This is intended as a curb on foreign portfolio investments by Americans, a reinforcement of the already-mentioned compulsory program of foreign capital investment control that was introduced in 1965 on commercial bank lending abroad and direct corporate foreign investment. Tax rebates on exports could also help our deficit.

[9] To the degree that unemployment at home means low profit opportunities, it might worsen our balance by encouraging more foreign investment (i.e., more debits)!
[10] In the long run, earnings from these investments would begin to help our deficit.

10. We could revert to *protectionism* generally. Tariffs and quotas will not raise *real* wages, for the reasons seen in the previous chapters, but they can compensate a little for sticky money wages and an overvalued currency. Such a solution will be deplored by all who value the advantages that come from specialization according to comparative advantage and by all who think America's political advantage lies in our living down our old reputation as a bad neighbor.

11. Finally, to bring the list to a close, we could hope that *the surplus countries of Europe and Japan would again experience an acceleration of inflation in their cost and price-levels.* Money wages on the Continent did in 1959–1965 grow faster than productivity there, and this fact probably did more to promote an ultimate solution of America's basic balance than anything else. Alternatively, if surplus nations would undertake the politically unpopular task of *appreciating* their currencies (as West Germany and Holland did in 1961 and Germany belatedly did in 1969), the overvalued dollar could be cured without any depreciation on our part or inflation on theirs.

C. STRUCTURAL REFORM OF INTERNATIONAL FINANCE

Is the gold drain from the United States merely symptomatic of a more widespread malaise? Growing world production requires growing money supplies; but can gold mining keep up with this need? Growing international trade, and freer trade in a world more susceptible to political and economic irregularities, require larger liquid reserves for countries to hold as protection against swings in their balance of payments—particularly in mixed economies that will not let the rules of the gold standard dictate internal inflation or depression to achieve Hume's classical equilibration. Will world gold supplies be adequate for this need, particularly in an environment where key currencies like the pound and dollar no longer command the respect that enabled them once to serve as a substitute for gold reserves?

Many economists, remembering the sobering experience of 1929, strongly believe that the whole world is in need of some basic structural reforms to provide needed elasticity in international reserves.

THREE MAJOR PROBLEMS OF STRUCTURAL REFORM

By 1970 what was already evident to experts became unmistakably clear to government officials and financial men generally—namely, that the international dollar-and-gold standard was in serious trouble, and was probably not viable without fundamental reform. Three basic defects characterized the system and were in need of repair.

Inflexible exchange rates   A quarter of a century after Bretton Woods, experience showed the system set up there to be flawed at the core by its reliance on exchange-rate parities that were to be *constant*. Economic theorists know that modern mixed economies are prone to drift apart through the years in their trends of price levels, wage costs, and productivities.

Hence, suppose the dollar and mark have exchange rates in equilibrium in 1949. Why should those rates still be suitable 20 years later? German productivity might outstrip American in an unpredictable way—and that is what happened. America might get involved in military programs necessitating vast offshore expenditures—and that too happened. Inventions may affect different regions differently in terms of their international competitiveness. Consumer tastes may change, causing what was an equilibrium parity to become a currency overvaluation or undervaluation. In a world where *everything changes*, where no price remains constant, why try to build an international edifice on a foundation of *inflexible* exchange rates?[11]

Dollar disequilibrium   Compounding this basic flaw of inflexibility of exchange rates has been the fact that the dollar itself—the linchpin of the system—became progressively out of equilibrium in the 15 years following 1955.

"The dollar is even better than gold." Such a statement involved a genuine truth for the two decades following 1933, decades when there had been the dollar shortage and when our currency was an undervalued one. But by the 1960s, after a decade of chronic American balance-of-payments deficits, the attractiveness of dollars as a key international asset began to evaporate. Central bankers in Europe began to offer bets of champagne with former Federal Reserve Chairman Martin that the dollar would be depreciated, devalued, or both.

Increasingly in the 1960s central banks and foreign governments began to insist upon America's meeting its deficit with gold; only a part of the deficit would they accept in the form of dollar assets. (And undoubtedly if large official holders of dollars, such as Germany, Japan, and Italy, had not known very well that an attempt on their part to cash in those dollars for gold would be met by our suspending gold payments, they would have asked for still more gold. In other words, a good deal of the dollar holding was *involuntary* and not voluntary, and the decade loss of gold by America would have been even greater if it had reflected the spontaneous laws of supply and demand.)

Private individuals and corporations, in France and other Continental countries where legal taboos on the holding of gold were not operative, felt free to hoard gold and did so increasingly. Speculators, scenting that the existing gold parities could only move upward and were not likely to do so, piled onto the bandwagon. And so private gold hoards mounted, depleting central banks and official authorities of their gold reserves.[12]

Long-run gold and liquidity shortage   This brings us to the third basic flaw in the international system. The long-run supply of gold cannot possibly keep up with the liquidity needs of growing international trade.

[11]The architects of Bretton Woods did provide for *occasional* discontinuous exchange-rate adjustments by international agreement with the IMF. But what they did not sufficiently realize was the fact that such adjustments would be made only *after* the disequilibrium state had become apparent to all, and that this recognition would provide a field day for speculators who could sell the weak currency short, knowing that there was no risk of its moving against them and a great chance that it would move in their favor. Moreover, the speculators acting in concert could hope to precipitate the crisis which would make them their profit.

[12]Continental hoarders could not *directly* get gold from the U.S. Treasury. But when they got gold from their central banks, those institutions acted as a conduit and exercised their right to get gold from the U.S. Treasury.

Year in, year out, the volume of international trade increases annually at a 7 or 8 per cent rate. But world gold production from the dwindling mines of South Africa and Russia can increase at barely a 2 per cent annual rate. And much of this new gold, hoarding quite aside, is preempted for normal *industrial* use. Hence any international system *dependent inflexibly* on gold for its reserve base is doomed to ultimate liquidity shortage and chronic emphysema.

As mentioned earlier, the replacement of gold coin by paper currency and the development of fractional-reserve banking systems served to economize domestically on gold in the last 75 years. Even then the system was being afflicted with sagging price levels until luck in the form of Alaskan and African gold rushes intervened. By 1929 luck had given out, and again by 1968 the gold-exchange and dollar-standard economizing and international devices for stretching out the use of gold had reached dangerous limits.

As long ago as 1955 Yale's Robert Triffin correctly prophesied the need for fundamental institutional reform to increase international liquidity.[13] Although the long-run liquidity-shortage problem would have been inevitable quite independently of the dollar disequilibrium, the fact of America's chronic payments deficit in the years after 1950 led to our hemorrhaging gold. Since our gold hemorrhage provided a gold infusion to the Common Market countries and the rest of the world generally, the problem of dollar disequilibrium served inadvertently to cover up and divert attention for a time from the long-run inadequacy of gold. (Refer back to Fig. 36-1, page 691.)

THE TWO-TIER GOLD SYSTEM

By 1968 time had run out on the precarious gold-and-dollar standard. When the rush for gold by hoarders became a stampede which would have stripped Fort Knox of all our gold within a matter of weeks, the 10 leading nations of the world met during March, 1968, in Washington and Stockholm. They suspended all gold payments from official central banks to the free market. Henceforth there was to be a two-tier system.

The official tier   In the official tier, gold payments are made only between governments, and always at the official IMF parities. Thus, within the Club of Ten, if Germany has an export surplus with the United States that is to be partially paid for in gold, each $35 million payment will involve our sending Germany (or, more likely, merely earmarking in the vaults of the New York Federal Reserve Bank) a million ounces of gold. Since the mid-1969 IMF parity of the mark is 27+ cents, or about 3.6 marks to the dollar, the million ounces of gold represent 126 (or 3.6 × 35) million marks to the Germans.

Essentially, all the gold in the official reserves as of March, 1968, was frozen in forever. None can ever go outside the Club of Ten and the hundred other nations that belong to the IMF.[14] With the exception of South Africa, no government in the Club is to buy gold from any government that ever deals with the free market in gold.

[13] Indeed Lord Keynes at Bretton Woods in 1945 had already proposed a gold substitute—a new currency unit for international reserves called "Bancor." In addition to the Triffin Plan there have been a Bernstein Plan, a Stamp Plan, a Posthuma Plan, and a number of similar proposals for creating new reserve units, credits, or versions of "paper gold."

[14] At first General de Gaulle had tried to block the new system. But the 1968 French student riots

The free-market tier   Outside the IMF Club, gold has finally been completely demonetized. Its price is freely set by supply and demand, just like the price of copper, wheat, silver, or salt. Thus in 1970 the few American gold mines sell their output at a price near that set by auction in London or Zurich.[15] When you buy a wedding ring, your jeweler pays the $40 an ounce, or $42 or $36, that happens to be quoted at the time in question.

Hoarders in the Near East and India can hoard to their heart's content. French merchants and international Mafia operators, out to evade taxes, can hide gold in their wine cellars and Swiss bank vaults. Speculators, in countries where citizens are allowed to deal in gold, can hope to make capital gains if they are able to sell gold at a higher price than they have bought it at. But note this: With the price floating above any official floors, speculation and hoarding are now *two*-way streets. You can make a bundle if you buy at $40 and sell at $45, but you can lose your shirt if you buy at $43 and have to sell at $36—or even at $33 if an avalanche of dishoarding should take place.

Evaluation   How has the two-tier system worked? Up until 1970 it has been working very well indeed. The fear that some small central bank would buy gold at the $35 official price and surreptitiously feed it to the free market, making a neat profit of, say, $41 − $35 an ounce, has proved to be exaggerated. For the first time in 15 years the international financial structure has been able to be completely indifferent to the vagaries of hoarders and the ups and downs in free-market gold prices.

The two-tier system works well, but it is only a halfway house, a stopgap arrangement. The frozen and limited total of official gold would soon put a throttle on the expansion of total world trade were it not for the new plan adopted by the IMF to create "paper gold" in the form of Special Drawing Rights—as we shall see.

ALTERNATIVE PROPOSALS FOR REFORM

Before looking into the new plan for creation of paper gold, we should explore the main reforms currently being debated. The most important are (1) "massively increasing the official price of gold"; (2) complete demonetization of gold, ejecting it even from the official tier and replacing the Hume gold-flow adjustment mechanism with its stable exchange rates by a new system of "freely floating, completely flexible exchange rates"; (3) a system of a "sliding or crawling peg," in which stable exchange rates are abandoned but in which within any year the change in parity is limited to, say, 1 or 2 per cent.

Increasing the price of gold   This position was associated with De Gaulle and his economic adviser Jacques Rueff and with Sir Roy Harrod of Oxford.

---

and general strike so depleted France's gold reserves as to make him and his successor Pompidou hasten to return to the fold.

[15] Newly mined gold from South Africa provides an exception. South Africa would like to be able to sell part of her output in the free market at prices *above* $35 an ounce, and to sell the remainder to the Club at that official price—getting the best of both possible worlds. In 1970 a compromise was reached. In return for South Africa's agreement not to manipulate the free-price of gold, the IMF agreed to buy her residual new-mined gold at the official $35 an ounce—thus providing something of a floor under the free market.

2
3
4
5

Increase the price of gold from \$35 to \$70 or \$100 per ounce. Similarly increase gold's price in terms of *all* other currencies. This massive "devaluation" of all currencies, being in balance, will result in no "depreciation" or "appreciation" of any currency relative to another. But at the stroke of a pen, the shortage of international liquidity will have disappeared.

What are we to think of this plan? Naturally the South Africans love it. So does the Soviet Union, the other principal gold-mining nation. So do the gold hoarders. So do those nations that were least cooperative in the 1960s in resisting the temptation to hoard gold officially. So do the speculators, lusting after a quick capital gain.

Self-interest aside, what are the plan's merits and demerits? For Rueff, an archconservative, the price of gold is to be raised once and for all, *and then mankind is to go back onto a rigid gold standard.* Gold is to serve as a *discipline* for governments. The moment a nation inflates, it will lose gold and be forced back into deflation. If capitalists disapprove of their government, they can hoard gold coins and take their money abroad, creating a run on the currency and bringing down the ruling government. (This happened repeatedly in the history of France and other countries during the capitalist era.)

For Sir Roy Harrod, a Keynesian expansionist, doubling or tripling the price of gold is favored for reasons diametrically *opposed* to those of Rueff. With one stroke of the pen, governments everywhere will be given their freedom to pursue *expansionary* policies for another quarter of a century. After that time, another stroke of the pen. . . .

Most experts regard gold as an anachronism. How absurd to waste resources digging gold out of the bowels of the earth, only to inter it back again in the vaults of Fort Knox, Kentucky! And why adopt a plan that gives a windfall profit to South Africa, Russia, speculators, and private or official hoarders? But the even more important objection to reliance on a rise in the price of gold is this:

Modern mixed economies will not go through the agony of deflating themselves, running the risk of mass unemployment and stagnation, merely to obey the rules of the automatic gold-standard game. And if the gold-standard game is *not* played according to its rules, small disequilibria will not be prevented from accumulating into major disequilibria with ultimate crisis and breakdown.

Even though the world will not revert to the automatic gold standard, it is a fact that official gold does exist and is an important part of official international reserves. Hence the new IMF reforms are able, as we shall see, to *build around* gold and *supplement* it by new reserve assets.

Freely flexible exchange rates   This reform is at the other extreme from that of restoring the automatic gold standard. In effect, it proposes:

1. Turn all exchange rates completely over to the free market, avoiding all official interventions.

2. Forget about the balance of payments. *Let supply and demand intersect to produce whatever pattern of exchange rates will clear the market.*

3. Rely on the development of a speculative market in foreign exchange which will offer importers and exporters the opportunity—at a price, of course, but under vigorous

competition not necessarily a very high price—to "hedge" their international merchandise and capital transactions.[16]

For the mechanics of how freely floating exchange rates work, the reader can refer back to Chapter 33's pages 625–628. The main point to emphasize is that now a country can be free to do anything it wishes domestically, letting the exchange rate move to adjust in consequence. Thus, if the United States wilfully inflates its domestic prices to double or quadruple previous levels, there is nothing to stop it. (But, of course, as Chapter 33's discussion of purchasing-power parity shows on page 627, the foreign exchange rate for the dollar—in terms of the mark or the currency of any other country which has kept its prices stable—will automatically *depreciate* to about a half or a quarter of its previous level, going from, say, 4 marks to a dollar down to 2 marks, or even 1.

It is precisely this *autonomy* of domestic policy under floating exchange rates which opponents criticize in flexible exchange rates. They claim that healthy hedging possibilities and fruitful international trade will be possible only if exchange rates *do not move chronically in one direction*—i.e., only if a nation does not chronically induce or countenance inflation. "But," these critics point out, "if, after all, the country is going to have to *desist* from chronic inflation, there has been no true escape from the disciplines of the gold standard in the end; and one might as well have the advantages from the beginning that come with the traditional *fixed* exchange rates."

Pros and cons They go on to argue, "Within the 50 states, we do not have floating exchange rates. That would hurt the intranational volume of trade and division of labor. So why give up stability of exchange rates internationally?"

How do the advocates of flexible exchange rates reply? First, they stress that within a country like the United States there is one central government, one Federal Reserve and money system, and one labor market in the sense that workers can migrate to a low unemployment region. All these features are lacking internationally.

Second, advocates say that flexible exchange rates were never intended as a panacea. What they can do is make the effects of unavoidable creeping inflation and price rigidities

---

[16]To ensure against the risk that the foreign exchange rate for marks will rise 10 per cent between now and the time my import of German dyestuffs arrives, I turn today to the forward market and buy marks 90 days ahead. Who sells them to me? Possibly an American exporter who wants to play safe and know exactly how many dollars he's going to get for the computer he is shipping today to Germany, and for which he will be paid marks in 90 days. But even if export and import transactions in both directions don't balance out, some speculators with sporting blood will sell marks forward hoping to be able to buy them cheaper later. If speculators are overoptimistic, they may end up providing this hedging service even at a loss to themselves; or if risk taking is so irksome as to require a positive premium for hedging, that cost will be added onto the price of international goods and, to a degree, will lessen the volume of and gains from trade. (The analysis of hedging and speculation in a market for corn, as described in the Appendix of Chapter 21, cannot be confidently applied to foreign exchange markets. Speculation in foreign exchange is more in danger of being destabilizing, since there is no natural par of supply and demand set by crop conditions and basic human demands for wheat. Instead, when the dollar is weak, all the speculators will pounce on it and make it weaker; they will force America into depreciation and into internal inflation, and thereby the new proper level for the dollar will be permanently lower, rewarding the speculators for their bear raid. If the authorities resist such raids by keeping a tight rein on the domestic money supply, price level, and GNP level, they are as much restrained by the balance of payments as under a stable exchange standard: so why give up advantages of stable exchange rates if you are going to have, in any case, their disadvantages?)

Crawling peg provides compromise between floating and rigid exchange rates:

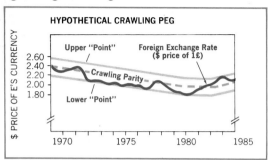

FIG. 36-2. Instead of fixed parity at $2.40, under this plan the parity can crawl downward or upward by 1 or 1½ per cent per year, achieving in a decade's time the 10 or 15 per cent needed to adjust for drifting apart of cost levels. Also at any one time the band between upper and lower "points," within which supply and demand can freely operate, are considerably widened. (Source: Figure 33-2, page 644.)

in the mixed economy *a little more tolerable*. Advocates of flexible exchange rates still insist that the economy will function best only if chronic inflationary and deflationary gaps are avoided by proper macroeconomic policy.

THE CRAWLING OR SLIDING PEG WITH WIDENED "GOLD POINTS"

This provides a compromise between the inflexible exchange rates of the gold standard and Bretton Woods setup and a system of indefinitely floating exchange rates.

1. Within any one year the exchange-rate parity is to be permitted to move some maximum stipulated amount, say, 1 or 1½ per cent.
2. This slowly crawling parity level is to be surrounded by a *widened band*, within which limits supply and demand is free to set the actual exchange rate.

Even if foreseen, such a crawl in parity is not great enough to tempt out an avalanche of speculation. But it produces enough flexibility to permit a 10 or 15 per cent adjustment of exchange rates over a decade! And that should be sufficient to compensate for the normal drifting apart of wage and price levels due to technological change, changing tastes, and differential degrees of wage-push inflation in the various mixed economies.

For the economics of the crawling peg, the reader can be referred to Chapter 33's Appendix, particularly to Fig. 33-2, page 644. Part of that figure is reproduced here as Fig. 36-2. In this example, the dollar-pound parity begins at $2.40 in 1970. But now the exchange rate is no longer held within the $2.38-to-$2.42 band formerly set by the "gold points." Now the exchange rate can vary between $2.20 and $2.60 per pound. And next year, with parity moved[17] to, say, $2.35 by Britain's deficit, the range would be $2.15 to $2.55.

It is evident that academic opinion of the 1970s is virtually unanimous in favoring a move toward some measure of exchange-rate flexibility. And the practical men in government and the banks, impressed finally by the bitter experience with periodic international crises, have come privately to agree with this academic view.

Thus the crawling peg seems to provide the most likely compromise that could be practically agreed upon for reform in the adjustment mechanisms of international trade.

However, "How to get from here (the old inflexible system) to there (a system with some flexibility)" is a conundrum no one has yet been able to solve.

---

[17]There are a variety of details proposed for the crawling peg. Thus, some would have the change be gradual within the year; some would permit the change to be determined by the governments involved; some would make the movement of the crawling peg to be determined by an automatic formula in terms of certain averages of previous months' deficits or surpluses in the balance of payments.

SDRS AND PAPER GOLD

We conclude this discussion of current international problems with a description of the long-awaited plan for (1) augmenting official gold as international reserves by (2) the creation of a new reserve asset—the Special Drawing Rights, or SDRs, created by the International Monetary Fund. Because these SDRs will serve all the purposes of gold, they are usually called "paper gold."

The SDRs are set up by vote of the IMF members, subject to a veto by 15 per cent of the voting quotas. The exact amount newly created per year is determined by the Director General of the IMF, in consultation with the voting members. But the allocation of the new SDRs among the members is determined strictly in proportion to their quotas in the IMF. Thus, in the year 1970 $3.4 billion of new SDRs were created, the United States getting $867 million, Canada $124 million, Britain $410 million, West Germany $202 million, France $165 million, India $126 million, Japan $122 million, etc. Similar sums are set for 1971 and 1972, and after that a new schedule will be adopted.

Thus, at long last the straitjacket of the happenstance of gold mining can be replaced by a rational international system whereby nations, through multilateral agreement, create the optimal amount of new international reserves—not too little so as to cause deflation, or too much so as to cause inflation.

Success of the system is not yet assured, but if it does evolve at all according to plan, the system of paper gold will represent a significant step forward.

It would be even more hopeful if the new SDR system could be combined with some degree of exchange-rate flexibility—e.g., the crawling peg. And, since the SDRs will not solve the problem of existing exchange-rate overvaluations and undervaluations, the new system should ideally be accompanied by an *initial realignment of major currency parities*—with the mark, the yen, and other *surplus* currencies *appreciating* relative to the *depreciation* of the dollar and other *overvalued currencies* subject to chronic balance-of-payments *deficits*. When all this is done, we can forget unofficial gold, letting it become the concern of dentists, jewelers, the Mafia, and smugglers.

SUMMARY

A. MODERN TRENDS AND INSTITUTIONS OF INTERNATIONAL FINANCE

1   Expanded exports—as in World Wars I and II—will have multiplier expansionary effects on a country. If previously it had unemployment and excess capacity, the result will be more jobs and output. If previously it had inflationary pressures, the result will be an intensification of them. The beggar-my-neighbor policies of the depressed thirties, by which each nation vainly tries to export its unemployment abroad, are self-defeating.

2   The International Bank, the International Monetary Fund, Marshall Plan and military-aid programs, Point Four, the reciprocal-trade program for tariff reduction, the European Common Market—all these are important factors in the postwar bid for more rational world trade.

3   The first decade after World War II was the period of "dollar shortage." The dollar was "undervalued" in the sense that the other countries of the world, disrupted by war and with high cost structures, were avid to buy from us more than we wanted to buy from them. The sizable devaluations abroad in 1949—plus our Marshall Plan and other aid programs, America's cold-war spending, and finally, the miraculous spurt of productivity in the Common Market and Japan—all brought dollar shortage to an end.

B. THREATENED BREAKDOWN OF THE INTERNATIONAL SYSTEM

4   In the last decade, *basic disequilibrium* in America's balance of payments became evident: our surplus on private current account simply was not large enough to offset (*a*) our substantial government defense and aid programs, and (*b*) the large volume of long-term foreign investment by American firms seeking the high profits offered in the miracle-growth countries abroad. The testimony of this "basic international deficit" was reinforced by the testimony of the more conventionally reported international deficit, shown in Fig. 36-1, which reveals growing distrust of the dollar.

5   No single factor can account for the reversal of dollar shortage. Certainly a basic cause seems to be the more rapid rate of growth in productivity in Western Europe and Japan than in America rather than any upswing in our generosity or—until Vietnam!—domestic inflation. This "basic imbalance" in the annual international flows places important constraints on domestic growth and stabilization policies.

No single remedy for a chronic payment disequilibrium can be prescribed. Steps to improve the situation would include sharing by others of the aid and military burdens, lessening of discriminations, programs designed to improve our productivity and selling efficiency, better control over the cost-push pressures at home, and various other measures. Resort to protectionism and controls on foreign investment and trade would involve a sacrifice of economic and political advantage, and be inferior to a devaluation of our seemingly overvalued currency which would be a last desperate act of emergency. The recent increase in well-being abroad should be noted even if it means adjustments here (and even possibly a slight retardation in our growth in real wages and consumer's surplus from international trade).

C. STRUCTURAL REFORM OF INTERNATIONAL FINANCE

6   America's gold drain long covered up (*a*) the basic weakness in a world of change (and in which mixed economies will not submit to deflation and inflation) of a dollar-and-gold standard system based on *fixed* exchange rates; (*b*) the growing disequilibrium of the (overvalued) dollar over 15 years, a fact of especial importance in view of the dollar's role as key currency; and (*c*) long-run liquidity shortage of reserves in a world where foreign trade grows at 7 or 8 per cent per year while gold from mines grows at barely 2 per cent (and part of which goes into nonmonetary uses).

7   The major proposed reforms involve (*a*) a massive increase in gold price; (*b*) freely

floating, flexible exchange rates set completely by supply and demand; and (c) some version of a "crawling peg," providing limited flexibility of parity in any year, but needed long-run flexibility. (Usually widened "gold points" are proposed as part of the crawling peg.)

8   The two-tier system of gold, plus the introduction of paper gold in the form of Special Drawing Rights by the IMF, provides transition reforms. Coupled with initial parity realignments and perhaps with some crawling peg, they would provide the world with a more rational—and viable—system.

QUESTIONS FOR DISCUSSION

1   Describe analytically post-World War II changes in the position of the dollar.

2   Contrast and compare the International Bank and Monetary Fund.

3   Draw up a list of what you consider our most important postwar economic problems. If you were in Congress, what would you do about them?

4   What effects can one expect from the European Common Market?

5   "Not a single American industry should be sacrificed in the name of the GATT program for realizing freer multilateral trade." Do you agree?

6   Describe the extent of our postwar aid to the rest of the world. Was this merely "generosity"? Did generosity play any important role?

7   Contrast "dollar shortage and glut." Diagnose and prescribe.

8   Apply to an overvalued pound the reasonings used earlier for the dollar.

9   Why would you expect an interest-rate equalization tax on all foreign long-term securities to help our capital accounts and international deficit? As control programs on bank and corporate investing abroad begin to spring leaks, how might explicit taxing of foreign investment help us buy the time needed to reattain equilibrium?

10   Give pros and cons of flexible exchange rates, changing gold price, two-tier system.

11   What do you understand the term "paper gold" to mean?

Review your understanding of the following concepts:

exports, foreign investment
   foreign-trade multiplier
International Bank and Fund
Marshall Plan and other aid programs
Point Four
common market, customs union
dollar shortage and glut, chronic deficit

floating versus stable exchange rates
financial discipline
overvaluation, undervaluation
devaluation and gold's price
international liquidity plans
crawling or sliding peg
paper gold: SDRs

Current Economic Problems 6

The Theory of Growth

37

. . . When you can measure what you are speaking about, and express it in numbers, you know something about it; when you cannot measure it, when you cannot express it in numbers, your knowledge is of a meager and unsatisfactory kind; it may be the beginning of knowledge, but you have scarcely, in your thoughts, advanced to the stage of science. . . .
LORD KELVIN

In the final section of this book, we can mobilize the tools of economic analysis to show their relevance to the burning issues of our age. To theories of economic growth (Chapter 37). To the processes by which the less-developed countries can better their economic well-being (Chapter 38). To the problems of growth and price stability in the advanced economies (Chapter 41).

As old problems get partially solved, new problems are forced onto the social agenda. Chapter 39 deals with the stubborn problems of poverty and economic inequality, with the quality of economic life as against its mere quantity. Chapter 40 faces up to the ancient plague of racial discrimination, a phenomenon of first importance at home as well as abroad; it is part and parcel of the urban blight that mars the face of both the rich and the poor nations. Finally, in Chapter 42, comes economic analysis of alternative economic systems: pure capitalism, the mixed economy, fascism, socialism, and communism.

All the tools of economic analysis developed in this book are needed to throw light on such difficult and important social problems. This chapter will apply the *principles* of economic theory to the process of growth and development, in preparation for the next chapters' applications.[1]

STAGES OF HISTORY

Napoleon agreed with Voltaire that history is but "a fable agreed upon." It was long the fashion to regard economic development as proceeding according to a timetable. Dr. Spock can guess that a baby at so many weeks will begin to see things, and he can make predictions about when it will walk and talk. Often he may err, but *it is remarkable how predictable the stages of biological growth prove to be.* Scholars used to think economic history could be treated in the same way.

[1]For a short course, this chapter may be skipped, particularly the theoretical discussion of pp. 712–721.

Friedrich List, in his 1841 *National System of Political Economy*, was one of the first to divide economic history into stages. Especially in Germany, this became a popular notion a century ago. A new group of scholars, called the Historical School, came near to saying: "Throw away fancy theories. Grub in the facts. Collect them. Sort and sift them. Let them tell their own story."

The first step for any scientist is indeed to maintain a respect for the facts. But alas, it is not the last step. *The facts never tell their own story.* Truth, like beauty, is oft in the eye of the beholder. No two writers ever seem to be told the same fables of development by the accumulated almanac of facts. Some, and they included Karl Marx (1818–1883), saw in history a one-way evolution:

Primitive culture   First, there were marauding hunters and self-sufficient tribal families cultivating crops. (Supposedly they still survive in some isolated jungles.)

Feudalism   Gradually, as elbow room began to be scarce, the primitive economy was succeeded by feudalism. In the Middle Ages, a settled chain of command and exploitation, from nobility down to serf, governed all economic and social life.

Capitalism   Whether or not one thought the Middle Ages idyllic, feudalism in its turn was brought to an end when the periods of the Renaissance and Reformation ushered in the commercial and industrial revolutions. Peasants were alienated from the soil and forced into the cities as a proletariat. Rivers were dammed to harness water, and the invention of the steam engine enabled the energy of wood and coal to replace the energy of beast and man. The Calvinist ethic helped to create business-minded entrepreneurs. As if in a play, the curtain came down on feudalism and mankind was supposedly ushered onto the stage of bourgeois, middle-class capitalism. (Of course, isolated countries like Russia and Japan were not expected to move from feudalism to capitalism in exactly the same time periods; but when their time came, the process could be expected to be qualitatively similar even if more compressed in duration.)

Self-satisfied historians of the Victorian age, such as Macaulay or Herbert Spencer, looked upon the evolution of society as an ascent of man toward higher forms. But now that the more or less perfect state of Victorian capitalism had been reached, they thought evolution could have its final rest. All that remained was further progress toward removing tariffs and the few other governmental fiats still interfering with the laissez faire market place. Spencer could contemplate with mathematical certainty the withering away of the state and the supremacy of free markets. Invention by science, better education of the masses, and individual initiative could be expected to produce steady gains in living standards in this best of all possible worlds. (In our time, Friedrich Hayek in Freiburg and Milton Friedman in Chicago look back to the Victorian Whig society as a golden age, to be reattained by democratic dismantling of the welfare state.)

Socialism and communism   Having eaten of the fruit of the tree of evolution, why should men think that the play of history has to be written in only three acts? In a country like Germany, which had never been imbued with the tradition of individual and business

freedom, philosophers thought that capitalism, too, was but a passing stage, to be succeeded in its turn by state socialism or communism, just as capitalism had succeeded
dying feudalism. Marx and Engels wrote in *The Communist Manifesto:* "The modern
bourgeois society has sprouted from the ruins of feudal society. . . . The modern laborer
. . . becomes a pauper. . . . What the bourgeoisie therefore produces . . . are its own
grave diggers. Its fall and the victory of the proletariat are equally inevitable."

FACT AND FICTION

Events rarely agree with fable.[2] Thus, the revolutions in France and Germany that Engels
and Marx predicted to each other in their letters failed to materialize in the weeks,
months, and years as they had confidently projected. And real wages, instead of falling
or remaining constant in the decades since Marx's 1867 *Das Kapital,*[3] turn out on statistical
examination to have been rising dramatically under industrial capitalism. Even the rate
of profit stubbornly refused to follow the law of decline predicted for it and instead
oscillates and wanders without any strong trend.

It is true that *around the turn of the century there seemed to be a burgeoning of
monopolies in advanced economies.* But it turned out that even the most capitalistic
democracy, the United States, could and did produce antitrust legislation to limit this
development; and study of the statistics of concentration of market shares among a few
big oligopolists suggests that monopolistic concentration is less at mid-century than it
was at the beginning. It is true that the Great Depression of the 1930s was one of the
worst the capitalistic system has ever known; but it is also true that a mixed economic
system subsequently replaced rugged individualism and laissez faire. The mixed economy
introduced fiscal and monetary policies to moderate business cycles and control chronic
slumps. We live in a world no prophet ever predicted!

Mid-century miracle?   What has been the single most surprising economic development
of the mid-twentieth century?

Rapid progress under communism? No, in that few experts in 1950 expected the Soviet
Union, China, and the Eastern European planned economies to do much better or
worse than they have since performed.

Reversion to beneficent laissez faire and free private enterprise? Certainly not that,
since except for the usual ebb and flow of political elections, there has been no trend
back to the Victorian condition. When a Conservative party, in Britain, Norway, or
Australia, ousts a so-called "socialist" regime, most of the apparatus of a mixed economy
is retained. When a Nixon succeeds a Johnson or an Eisenhower succeeds a Truman, only
marginal changes in the American *Zeitgeist* emerge.

---

[2]M. I. Rostovtzeff, *Social and Economic History of the Roman Empire* (Oxford University Press, New
York, 1926), showed that an elaborate system of international markets and trade in nonluxury goods
existed long before the Middle Ages. Compound interest appears on Babylonian cuneiform tablets, and
some nations are repeating in the 1970s the worst errors of historic mercantilism. Neither progress nor
perpetual oscillation correctly portrays the richness of economic history.
[3]Translated as *Capital,* and ultimately including posthumous Volume II (1885) and Volume III (1894).

The single most surprising development of our age has been the unpredicted vigor of the modern mixed economy. The miracles of sustained growth in production and living standards have taken place in the second-level countries—Japan, Germany, Italy, France, Scandinavia, Western Europe generally—rather than in the most advanced countries like the United States and Canada or in the less-developed countries of Latin America and Asia.

Social prophets of our day, such as Schumpeter and Toynbee, to say nothing of the earlier Veblen or Spengler, thought of the mixed economy as "capitalism in an oxygen tent." But the growth experience of the years 1950–1970 revealed that a market economy enriched by government planning and macroeconomic control could perform favorably in comparison to past epochs of both capitalist and communist development.

We are thus warned to place limited confidence in the allegedly scientific proofs that one stage in history must inevitably be succeeded by a particular next stage. When Nikita Khrushchev said to an American audience, "We will bury you . . . your grandchildren will be communists," he was repeating what is taught in elementary Russian economics textbooks. (WARNING: Critics of Russia should not make a similar mistake about immutable timetables of development. It may involve wishful thinking to argue, as some scholars have done: "True, the U.S.S.R. is now showing a faster percentage rate of growth than the U.S. But wait until she becomes as mature as we; then she'll *have* to slow down!" Right-wing determinism is as poorly founded as left-wing.)

This sketch of the development of the mixed economy is all too brief, but it represents a fair summary of the views of historians on this side of the Iron Curtain. Since this view of the mixed economy is completely rejected by communist scholars, Voltaire and Napoleon were wrong: apparently, "history is a fable *not* agreed upon." Let us turn now to various economic models which can help us to understand history rather than to compress it into neat explanations that pretend to predict the future with certainty. Our task is to understand the actual development of wages and profits, of labor and capital, and of national product.

THE "MAGNIFICENT DYNAMICS" OF SMITH AND MALTHUS

In *The Wealth of Nations* (1776), Adam Smith wrote a handbook of economic development. Achievement-oriented, Smith preached the great efficiency that comes from specialization, division of labor, and exchange. He stressed the need to remove the blundering hand of mercantilistic governments; to cultivate attitudes of honesty, zeal, and thriftiness; to unleash the competitive profit motive, which would—as if led by an Invisible Hand—achieve the maximum well-being of all.

Labor theory of value in a golden age   Smith had also a theory of dynamic development. He and Malthus began with a hypothetical golden age—"that original state of things, which precedes both the appropriation of land and the accumulation of stock"—when labor alone counted, when land was freely available to all, and before the use of capital had begun. What determined pricing and distribution in this simple and timeless state? Answer: The labor theory of value.

To see this, consider Smith's famous case of deer and beaver. Suppose 2 hours of hunting yields 1 deer; or 4 hours yields 1 beaver. Then the price ratio between deer and beaver will be set by comparative labor time alone: the price of 1 beaver will equal 2 deer. Why 2 deer per beaver? Because the price ratio can be computed in necessary labor time as 4 hours (of sweaty work)/2 hours (of sweaty work). This determination of price by labor cost alone would apply no matter how many goods there were; and it would be enforced in any primitive market by having hunters shift from one good to the other if ever that other good's price got out of line and offered a profit advantage. It is still true that supply and demand is operating in this golden age; but the situation is so simple that we do not need elaborate *dd* and *ss* curves. The long-run *ss* curves for the different goods are simple horizontal lines at the stated labor costs; so long as there is enough demand to have the goods produced at all, labor costs will be determining. (NOTE: Demand is still there in the background; thus, if it would cost 10 hours to hunt a skunk, and yet nobody received any utility from skunks, skunks would not be hunted and would not be bought and sold at a price of 10 hours, or of 5 deer.)

Population growth   Now consider Smith-Malthus dynamics. Life is pleasant in the golden age. Babies are born, and the population doubles about every 25 years. Since there is plenty of land, people move west and spill over onto more acres. National output exactly doubles as population doubles. Price ratios of deer and beaver remain exactly as before. What about real wages? Real wages still get *all* the national income, there being as yet no subtractions for land rent or interest on capital. What is the real wage per hour? So long as land can expand proportionally to the expansion of labor, the law of diminishing returns cannot come into operation. The wage rate per hour remains at one-half deer or at one-fourth beaver, as determined by labor productivity.

That would be the end of the story, until, say, some clever inventor found a new way of doing in 1 hour what used to take 2 hours. This would raise the national product per capita. Such a balanced improvement would leave the price ratio of beaver to deer unchanged; but it would double the real wage rate.[4]

---

[4]The graphical production-possibility frontier of Chapter 2 can show all this. For a society with 100 hours of labor, the *p-p frontier* must now be drawn as a straight line going from the intercept on the vertical axis of the 50 deer producible with that much labor to the intercept on the horizontal axis of 25 beaver. The absolute slope of this *p-p frontier* would give the 2/1 price ratio prevailing at any point where both goods were being produced and consumed. (The marginal-utility and indifference-curve analysis of Chapter 22 would still be needed to tell *where* society ends up on the *p-p frontier*.)

A doubling of labor productivity in all industries would move the *p-p frontier* out in a parallel position so as to depict an exact doubling of national product. The interested reader can show that an invention which tripled the productivity of beaver hunting, while only doubling that of deer hunting, would flatten the shifted-out curve, changing the price ratio from 2/1 (equals 4 hours per beaver ÷ 2 hours per deer) to 4/3 (equals 4/3 hours per beaver ÷ 1 hour per deer). Now the real wage rate has risen, but unequally when computed in terms of the different goods: the real wage has tripled in terms of beaver, but only doubled in terms of deer; lovers of fur coats have gained more than lovers of venison. (NOTE: Suppose laborers are not homogeneous. If men are *everywhere* twice as productive as women, Marx and Ricardo would redefine socially necessary labor units, treating 1 man as 2 *basic* labor units, etc. But if men are *unequally* superior to women in different jobs—being twice as productive in beaver, thrice as productive in deer, and half as productive in potatoes—the labor theory of value breaks down: now we must know the demand condition of non-Marxian economics to determine equilibrium prices.)

Scarce land and diminishing returns Even had golden ages ever existed, they could not have lasted once all land became fully populated. As we saw in Chapter 2, Malthus pointed to a fatal flaw in the happily expanding economy. Once the frontier of virgin land disappears, new laborers begin to crowd onto existing cultivated soils. For the first time, private property in land springs up; now land is scarce, and a rent is charged to ration it.

Growth does take place in this classical world of Smith-Malthus following on the golden age. Population grows, and so does national product. But product can no longer grow proportionally to labor. Why? *Because with new laborers added to fixed land, each worker now has less land to work with.* Naturally, therefore, the law of diminishing returns (of Chapters 2 and 27) comes into operation. The increasing labor-land and decreasing output-land ratios mean a declining contribution of each last (or marginal) worker to product, and hence declining real wage rates.

As David Ricardo, a later classical economist, pointed out:

A conflict of interests arises between classes. More babies mean lower per capita incomes and wage rates; lower wage rates mean higher rent rates per acre of land. Landlords gain as labor loses. This is why Carlyle criticized economics as the "dismal science."

To understand the brute fact of economic inequality, we have to jettison the simple labor theory of value and study the effects of scarcity in the productive factors that labor needs access to.

Paradise lost and regained How bad can things get? Gloomy Malthus thought, at least in his first edition of 1798, that the end of economic development could be only an equilibrium down at *the minimum level of subsistence.* Above this subsistence wage, population would continue to grow; below it, population would die off; only at this level could there be lasting equilibrium (as we saw in earlier discussion of Malthus).

Biological fecundity was a fact of nature; diminishing returns was a fact of nature. Only sentimentalists could refuse to face the sad facts of life prevailing once man had left the golden Garden of Eden. It is for precisely these reasons that Adam Smith had earlier said: Lucky is a nation that is growing rapidly, for it has not yet made its sad rendezvous with its destined equilibrium at the minimum of subsistence. Sad is that nation which has reached the stationary equilibrium of the subsistence level, where deaths just cancel out births.

What did Malthus forget, or at least underestimate? He failed to realize how technical innovation could intervene—not to *repeal* the law of diminishing returns, but to *more than offset* it. He stood at the brink of a new century and failed to anticipate that the succeeding two centuries would show the greatest scientific gains in history.

DETAILED ECONOMIC ANALYSIS OF SMITH-MALTHUS

To understand the world's population problem for the next centuries—and the problems of India, Indonesia, and China in the next two decades—we must master the above classical model, which may have more *future* relevance than it has had for the West

Diminishing returns from population growth ends classical golden-age of development:

RELATION OF OUTPUT TO LABOR AND LAND

	(1) ACRES OF LAND	(2) MAN-DAYS OF LABOR	(3) OUTPUT OF FOOD	(4) WAGE IN FOOD PER DAY	(5) LABOR'S SHARE OF GNP (%)	(6) RENT IN FOOD PER ACRE
A	1,000	500	4,000	8	100	0
		501	4,008			
A'	1,000	1,000	8,000	8	100	0
		1,001	8,008			
B	1,000	3,000	20,000	5	75	5
		3,001	20,005			
E	1,000	6,000	33,600	4.2	75	8.4
		6,001	33,604.2			
Z	1,000	8,000	39,000	0	0	39
		8,001	39,000			

TABLE 37-1. Higher labor-land density reduces output per man, lowers the marginal-product wage, and hence raises rent per acre.

since Malthus' time. As a bonus, the same graphical tools will apply when we investigate the role of capital formation as a factor of growth for Germany, Japan, the United States, and the less-developed countries of the world.

Table 37-1 and Fig. 37-1 show succinctly how the tendency of population to grow when the wage is above the level of minimum of subsistence will (1) end the golden age of abundant and free land, and (2) lead to an economic growth path that approaches a stationary equilibrium at the minimum of subsistence.

Table 37-1 shows the decline in wage rate when the fixity of land keeps output from growing as fast as labor. Column (1) shows unchanged land. Column (2) shows growing labor. Column (3) shows the resulting growth in output, which, because of the fixity of land, is *less* than proportional to labor growth. All the remaining information can be computed from these production-function data alone.

To get the declining wage rate of Column (4), we have to repeat Chapter 27's calculation of what the *last* worker *adds* to total product. (Recall that this is termed the marginal-physical-product of each of the identical workers.) Let us add one worker to 1,000 existing workers at A'. Note that output rises from $Q = 8,000$ to $Q = 8,008$ units. This gives extra product per extra worker of 8; so the marginal-product and real wage rate must then be 8 units of output per worker. Check that the extra product and wage later falls to 5.0 at B; to 4.2 at E; and finally to zero at Z, where land is so overcrowded as to be unable to produce any extra output regardless of added labor.

To get the relative share of labor in the net national product, we multiply the wage rate of each worker by the number of workers. Then we divide this total wage bill, wL, by total GNP, Q. Note that labor's share in Column (5) soon falls from 100 per cent of GNP to 75 per cent, and ultimately down to 0 per cent. Who gets the remaining

Population grows until Malthus subsistence state is reached:

FIG. 37-1. Population growth moves us from the golden age of A, A', and a down the diminishing-returns marginal-product curve dd to the Malthusian equilibrium at intersection with ss supply curve of subsistence wage. The fall in real wage rate from a to b to e implies rising rent rates along the "factor-price frontier" ff. Because inventions shift dd and ff upward and rightward, historically the real wage rose from B to B' to B'' levels, with rent also rising from b to b' to b''.

share? By our assumption that there is no capital to clutter up the labor-and-land model, all other returns must go for land rent. With total acres unchanged, we simply divide up land's calculated share of total output by the fixed number of acres. Obviously, the rent per acre must therefore *rise* in Column (6) as the wage rate *falls* in Column (4), just as David Ricardo warned.

GRAPH OF MALTHUSIAN DEVELOPMENT

Figure 37-1 depicts all this. In Fig. 37-1(a), we see the wage rate declining as the law of diminishing returns pushes labor's marginal productivity downward along dd (which goes through d, A', B, E, and Z). What keeps the wage from falling down to zero on this dd demand curve for labor? Actually, the wage stops falling where dd intersects the ss horizontal supply curve set by the minimum wage at which people can subsist and just barely reproduce their numbers. The Malthusian equilibrium at E is a gloomy one, anything but golden.

Gloomy or not, it does represent a *stable* equilibrium. Test it. Let a plague temporarily reduce numbers, moving us to the left of E. Real wages then become high (as they actually did after the Great Plague of 1665), standing at a point on the dd curve above E. But the system cannot stay there. With wages high enough to cause population to grow, we again move gradually back toward the equilibrium at E, as indicated by the converging blue arrows. (Show that a temporary growth of population beyond E, as used to result from an unusual run of good harvests, will mean a wage rate so much below subsistence as to kill people off until the arrow moves us up dd back to E.)

Figure 37-1(b) shows that the rent rate per acre rises as the wage rate per hour falls. On what may be called "the factor-price frontier" (shown as ff), landlords are seen to be better off at the high-rent Malthusian subsistence equilibrium e than they were in the earlier golden age at a. No wonder some landlords greeted with joy the introduction of the white potato, which enabled people to live on cheaper calories, and hence in effect lowered the old ss subsistence curve and raised equilibrium rents. And no wonder some few landlords regarded the spreading of birth-control information as a threat to their own standards of living. One man's slavery is another man's comfort.

The Ricardians actually exaggerated the conflict of class interest. While population growth might imply higher rent per acre, they were wrong to think it *had to* imply a larger *percentage share* of NNP going to land. Note in Column (5) of Table 37-1 that labor happens to continue to get 75 per cent of the total, even when the wage rate drops from B to E and the rent rises from b to e.[5]

END OF THE LABOR THEORY OF VALUE

The simple labor theory of value, which said that the price ratios of goods can be predicted from labor costs alone independently of the utilities which bring out a demand for the goods, has thus had to be dropped to account for the facts of land scarcity. Costs of production now include rent as well as wage payments. Two goods, like food and clothing, may now have equal labor costs per unit, but if food requires more land cost per unit than clothing does, they will no longer sell on a one-to-one basis.

Worse than that from the standpoint of an advocate hankering for a labor theory of value, suppose that people in a capitalistic or socialistic state shift their demand toward producing more food and less clothing. This must make the price of food *rise* relative to that of clothing. Why? Because food requires more land per worker than clothing does. Hence, the fixed land becomes more scarce when people want more of the product that is "land-intensive," thus bidding up rent at the expense of the wage.

Under neither socialism nor capitalism can we succeed in predicting commodity prices from labor requirements alone, taking no account of the pattern of tastes and demand and its effects on scarcity of nonlabor factors.[6]

What about labor's right to *all* the product? Labor is the only input that is human and can sweat, laugh, cry, and pray. True. Yet, even though dirt cannot sweat or cry, it does contribute toward the growing of potatoes and needs to be economized in the good society.

One who wants to make a logical case for labor's being "exploited" should not handicap himself by a simple labor theory of value. He may challenge the *title* to land of those who call themselves landlords and their *right* to rents. He may claim that only the peasants

---

[5]Historically, pure land rent has become a declining fraction of NNP. Edward Denison, in his study of American growth, estimates that land accounts for barely 3 per cent of product today as against 9 per cent before World War I. Colin Clark's estimates for various countries of the world also suggest that industrialized nations are able to substitute capital and labor for scarce land. E. Denison, *The Sources of Economic Growth in the United States* (Committee for Economic Development, New York, 1962); C. Clark, *Conditions of Economic Progress* (Macmillan, London, 1957, 3d ed.). Although modern science enables us to make nitrates and nylon out of air and of plentiful products like coal and oil rather than having to pay high rents to scarce natural nitrate resources in Chile or to silkworm-cultivation facilities in Japan, natural resources still command high scarcity rents; they represent a generalization of the simpler classical concept of nature's gift of fixed land. Land is not included in the later capital statistics.

[6]Footnote 4 has pointed out that, in the golden age of free land, society's production-possibility schedule was a straight line with slope determined by labor productivities alone. Now with land scarce and more important in food than in clothing production, the production-possibility schedule is bowed out for the reasons explained in Chapter 2's discussion of the law of increasing (relative) cost. (Cf. also Appendix to Chapter 27, final question.) The slope of the *p-p frontier* which determines the competitive price ratio now depends on where people's demand leaves us. (It can be shown that Ricardians erred in thinking they could "get rid of land as a complicating factor" by going out to "the external margin" of poor, no-rent land upon which output was so low that all its costs have to go to labor alone.)

have a valid title to the land and to rent, or that only the state does. Who receives rents is an ethical or legal problem. But whatever its solution, rational use of land does require that a rent cost be charged the consumers who buy its products and the factors that are best fitted to work with it. (Recall Chapter 27's earlier discussion of exploitation and the Appendix to Chapter 32 on efficient socialist pricing.)

Chapter 40 will return to problems of exploitation and racial discrimination.

TECHNICAL ADVANCE AND CLASSICAL GROWTH THEORY

As mentioned, real wages have risen historically, not fallen. Population has not stabilized. Land rents per acre have risen surprisingly little and, relative to other factor-prices, have actually declined. It is evident that life has not consisted of a movement down an unchanged factor-price frontier or marginal-product curve. Inventions of science, of engineering, and of managerial practice have *shifted* the curves of Fig. 37-1 rightward and upward. The black lines of progress—*BB'B''* and *bb'b''*—show the actual course of history; the reader is invited to draw on his copy of Fig. 37-1 the shifted *dd* and factor-price frontiers that run through *B'* or *B''* and through *b'* or *b''*. Such shifts have more than won the race with diminishing returns, making the Malthusian equilibrium point of subsistence unrealistic in Western economies.

Not all inventions are *equally* favorable to labor and land. Thus, inventions which help to drain swamps or to grow more food on the same acres of land might help wages more than they help rents. Some economists would call these "land-saving inventions." In contrast, any inventions that tended to raise rents more than wages, thereby tending to increase landlords' share of GNP, might be called "labor-saving inventions." In between would be the case of inventions that raised both factor returns by the same percentage, leaving relative shares of GNP unchanged: these might be called "neutral inventions." In the history of the West, inventions have appeared to be land-saving on balance; but few inventions have been so land-saving as actually to lower rents *absolutely* along with lowering them relative to wages.

The ghost of Carlyle should be relieved to know that economics, after all, has not been a dismal science. It has been the impatient science of growth.

RICARDO-MARX-SOLOW MODELS OF CAPITAL ACCUMULATION

So far we have stressed the classical preoccupation with scarce land. In the remainder of this chapter, we shall survey the more important model of capital and labor, pushing land to the side as being less important for the developed part of the world. We can now use exactly the same tools.

Basic assumption of capital-labor model: One production factor grows relative to the other. Now population will be regarded primarily as a noneconomic variable, being stationary (or growing slowly for sociological reasons). Accumulation will make capital the varying factor. In an oversimplified model where output is produced by a relatively fixed and a relatively varying factor, the law of diminishing returns sets in. The return of the augmented factor falls; the return of the relatively scarce labor factor rises. In the absence of technical change, a stationary state of equilibrium will be approached.

Notions of capital   It is now capital,[7] written as K, that is the factor growing relative to labor, L. Capital goods consist of a great variety of things: machines of various kinds, plants and houses, tools, raw materials and goods in process (seed grain, growing wheat plants, harvested wheat, flour, dough, warm loaves, wrapped and delivered bread), and canned and frozen edibles. Society can sum the market values of these physical goods to get total wealth or total capital value; but it cannot command a million dollars of electric generators to transmute themselves into a million dollars of oil-refining equipment.

It is true, however, that as generators wear out, the resources which could have gone to replacing them can be shifted to turn out extra refining equipment; the financial counterpart of this physical alchemy is to have investors in the generator industry take the money funds accruing on account of depreciation there and transfer them over to finance extra investment in the equipment industry. Result: although the total balance sheet of money capital may show a practically unchanged total and although the national-income statistician shows only a cancellation of one kind of disinvestment against another kind of investment, still society has managed to change the physical composition of its capital stock without undergoing any change in current consumption of goods.

Effects of capital deepening   What happens to per capita output when capital grows relative to labor? Recall what happened to output per acre when labor grew relative to land. Output there grew less than proportionally to the growth in the varying factor (labor), and its factor-price (the wage) had to *fall*. A similar law of diminishing returns comes into operation in our oversimplified model whenever one factor (such as capital) grows faster than the other factor (such as labor) with all technical change absent:

1. Output will not grow in proportion to the growth in the capital stock.

2. The return to capital, the interest rate per annum—or what is the same thing if we rule out risk and technical change, the profit rate—will fall as capital deepens.

3. What happens to the wage rate now that each man works with more capital goods and with the more intricate capital goods that the economy can now afford in the environment of a lower interest and profit rate? Just as the rent earned by relatively scarce land rose in Fig. 37-1, here the competitive wage return to relatively scarce labor will rise, as men become worth more to capitalists and meet with spirited bidding up of their market wage rates. (NOTE: Competition, not altruism, is at work.)

4. Higher wage rates and lower interest rates do *not* necessarily imply a higher percentage *share* for labor at the expense of the percentage share of capitalists. Why not? Because the increase in capital relative to labor might offset (or even more than offset) the decline in the interest rate and the rise in the real wage.[8]

5. Finally, since output (per capita or total) grew less than in proportion to the increase in capital (per capita or total), the capital-output ratio would rise in the absence of technical change (e.g., from capital value being 3 times annual NNP up to $3\frac{1}{2}$ times).

---

[7] Chapter 30 and Appendix discussed capital theory and problems of measuring it.

[8] EXAMPLE: Let capital double from 1 million dollars to 2 million dollars, while labor stays at 30 men; let interest drop from 5 to 4 per cent, and the wage rise from $5,000 per year to $8,000. Total wage share then continues to be 3 times that of capital's, each having risen by 60 per cent from their initial respective shares of $150,000 and $50,000 per year.

Here is a final summary:

Deepening of capital (unchanged technology)

Capital/labor up; interest or profit rate down; wage rate up; capital/output up

DEEPENING OF CAPITAL IN DIAGRAM FORM

Figure 37-2(a) and (b) are like Fig. 37-1(a) and (b); but now capital is the relatively growing factor. Capital's amount per capita is given on the horizontal axis of (a), and its interest or profit return goes on the vertical axes. And now labor is the relatively fixed factor, and its wage goes on the horizontal axis of (b) just the way land rent did in Fig. 37-1(b).

In the absence of technical change, capital accumulation takes us down the dd curve from A to B and perhaps ultimately to the Ricardian equilibrium point E at which people feel it no longer pays them to save any per cent of their incomes for enhanced future consumption. On the factor-price frontier ff in Fig. 37-2(b), society can successively be at a; or at b with the higher wage rate and lower interest rate that are implied by an augmented capital stock (more machines available of every kind per man); or at e with a still higher capital-output and capital-labor ratio. The earlier literary summary of the effects of capital deepening is verified by these graphs.

TECHNICAL PROGRESS AND WAGES

Now let us reintroduce improving technology. This will shift the dd and ff curves outward, for example, to $d'd'$ and $f'f'$. Instead of moving from B down to E, society may find that diminishing returns are offset; and the economy might in actual historical fact move from B to B', negating or concealing the Ricardo-Marx law of the declining rate of profit from capital deepening. Note in Fig. 37-2(b) that the real wage rate must definitely rise, with or without technical improvements, so long as the profit rate stays the same or falls.[9]

An alternative theory would ascribe the rise of wages under capitalism to (1) trade-union pressure, (2) government regulation of monopoly, and (3) interventions of a welfare and regulatory kind by democratic governments reacting to militant political pressures from the masses. This cannot be rejected as without substance, for we have seen throughout this book that government actions do have consequences for both good and evil. But the magnitude and pattern of the rise in real wages in this last century have been such as to cast doubt on union or political action as an important element in its explanation. Thus, America in the 1920s was run on the basis of limited government intervention: trade-unions were weak; monopoly was certainly not shrinking in that decade; yet real

---

[9]Indeed, we shall see later in the chapter that, unless a competitive industry's invention is so "labor-saving" as to raise the profit rate enormously, the invention must definitely boost the real wage rate. In real life, a monopolist's invention might not be so beneficent.

wages rose strongly. Similarly, Japan and West Germany have shown sharp growth in real wages linked with sharp growth in labor productivity, and this at times when government seemed probusiness rather than prolabor.

With the advance of technology and the piling up of a larger stock of capital goods, it would take a veritable miracle of the devil to keep real wages of men from being bid ever higher with each passing decade. Who fails to see that, fails to understand economic history as it actually happened. Economic theories that do not fit these facts have to be junked and replaced by others that do.

THE APPROXIMATE FACTS OF MODERN DEVELOPMENT

Let us summarize our theoretical researches.

First we studied the crucial role of limited land and growing labor in economic progress. Then we passed from the Smith-Malthus world to one that studied the role in economic growth of capital accumulation relative to labor. Last, but far from least, we stressed the factor of technological change and innovation. A look at the facts will now show why present-day economists think that scientific and engineering progress has been quantitatively the single most important factor for growth in the advanced countries.

Accumulation of capital raises output and wage, tends to depress interest rate:

FIG. 37-2.   Adding more and a greater variety of capital goods to fixed labor will, in the absence of technical change, add less and less to total product, causing interest rate earned to fall along *dd* from B to E, which is the Ricardian equilibrium point at which saving will cease. Along *ff*, fall in interest rate from *b* to *e* must raise the real wage earnable from labor's higher productivity.

Historically, technical innovation has shifted *dd* and *ff* rightward just about fast enough to offset diminishing returns and to keep the interest and profit rate almost unchanged, as shown by horizontal arrows from B to B' and *b* to *b'*.

Thanks to Professor Simon Kuznets and his co-workers at the National Bureau of Economic Research,[10] to Professor Robert Solow of MIT, and to Dr. Edward Denison of Brookings Institution (earlier, of the Committee for Economic Development), we can formulate certain general uniformities of economic development in the United States and the advanced nations of the world. On the next page, the ratio chart of Fig. 37-3 shows the great trends of economic development for America in this century. Similar findings apply to the leading nations abroad. Figure 37-3 is crucially important. Linger over it.

The top chart shows the growth since 1900 of labor, capital, and hence of real output.

[10] S. Kuznets, *Capital in the American Economy* (Princeton University Press, Princeton, N.J., 1961), gives reference to pioneering National Bureau researchers, such as A. F. Burns, D. Creamer, S. Fabricant, R. W. Goldsmith, and J. Schmookler. See also J. W. Kendrick, *Productivity Trends in the United States* (Princeton University Press, Princeton, N.J., 1961), a pioneering National Bureau study.

Economic growth has displayed long-run regularities:

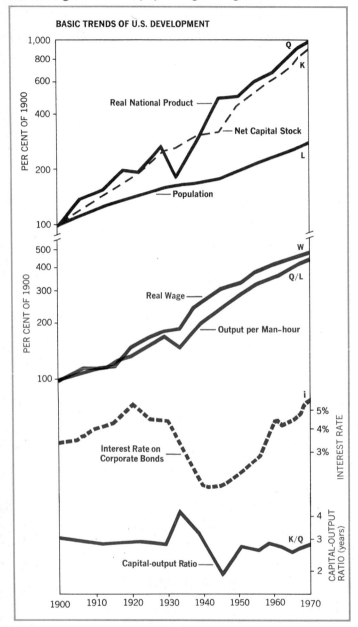

BASIC TRENDS OF U.S. DEVELOPMENT

FIG. 37-3. The upper black curves show capital and output growth steadily outpacing labor growth. The middle curves show that the real wage and output per man-hour have risen together, leaving the relative shares of labor and capital about the same. The interest (or profit) rate displays no diminishing returns, and the capital-output ratio displays no steady rise. Hence, the statical curves of Fig. 37-2 must have been shifted by technological advance.

Population has more than doubled in 70 years of steady growth. (Taking into account shortening of the working week and changes in age distribution and in labor-force participation, the growth in total number of man-hours has been even more modest.) While labor has about doubled, the stock of physical capital has increased about eight-fold! Thus the substantial increase in capital per worker, the K/L ratio, does represent a significant amount of "capital deepening."

What about the growth in output? Has output grown less than in proportion to capital, as in the model that ignored technical change? No. The fact that the Q curve is not *in between* the two factor curves, but actually lies *up near* the capital curve itself, shows that there must have been technical change in actual history. The close proximity of the output and capital curves shows that the capital-output ratio has not risen as in the simple deepening model; instead, as the lowest curve in the bottom chart shows, the capital-output ratio has remained remarkably close to 3 years (i.e., a balance-sheet calculation of current value of all capital goods would show it to be approximately equal to 3 years of total product).[11]

Rising wages and trendless profit The real wage has indeed risen steadily, in accordance with what one would expect from the growth in capital tools cooperating with labor and from favorable technolog-

[11] Many charts show a stronger tendency for the capital-output ratio to decline in the last part of the period. Much of such a decline in K/Q results from measuring the numerator to deflate out of it the relative rise that has taken place in capital-goods prices compared with other prices. In Fig. 37-3, the components of K/Q are each measured in current dollars deflated by a *common* price index.

ical trends. The interest rate—or, if we could get complete statistics, the rate of profit actually earned on more risky investments—does *not* show the decline that would be predicted from simple deepening of capital and diminishing returns. Interest rates and profit rates fluctuate much in business cycle and war, but display no strong trend upward or downward for the whole period. Either by coincidence, or as the result of some economic mechanism that needs study, technological change has just about offset diminishing returns.[12]

Output per man-hour is the blue curve shown in the middle chart. As could be expected from the deepening of capital and from technological advance, Q/L has risen steadily. Moreover—and this too represents a remarkable coincidence or the result of some economic mechanism needing study—the percentage growth in wage rates per hour has almost exactly matched the percentage growth in product per man-hour. This does not mean, as some Wall Street arithmetic has implied, that labor has captured *all* the fruits of productivity advance. It means, rather, that labor has kept about the *same share* of total product, with property also earning about the same relative share throughout the period. (A closer look at the middle chart suggests that there *might* have been a slow upward creep in the share of labor in NNP, with property's share dropping gently; but part of this might be the return to capital invested in education.)

SIX BASIC TRENDS OF ECONOMIC DEVELOPMENT

These basic facts of economic history in the advanced nations can be summarized approximately by the following trends:

Trend 1. Population has grown, but at a much more modest rate than the capital stock, resulting in a "deepening of capital."

Trend 2. There has been a strong upward trend in real wage rates.

Trend 3. According to what is often called Bowley's Law, the share of wages and salaries relative to the total return to property has shown considerable constancy in the long run (but perhaps with slight signs of an edging upward of labor's share).

Trend 4. Instead of observing a fall in the rate of interest or profit, we actually observe their oscillation in the business cycle but no steady upward or downward trend in this century (particularly if we deflate interest and profit rates of their price-change component, and deal with *real* rates).

Trend 5. Instead of observing a steady rise in the capital-output ratio as the deepening of capital invokes the law of diminishing returns, we find that the capital-output ratio has been approximately constant in this century.

Trend 6. The ratio of saving to output has oscillated in the business cycle—reaching about the same level at various high-employment phases of the cycle. Or taking into account the approximate constancy of the capital-output ratio, we can convert this

---

[12]Resist the temptation to think diminishing returns is not operating: if, instead of being merely hidden, it were actually not operating at all, the interest rate would have had to *rise* strongly as a result of technical change alone. (If we corrected interest rates for price changes—e.g., subtracting 1969's high percentage price rise from 1969's bond yields, as was done in earlier chapters—we would find the "real rate of interest or profit" to have been even more steady.)

approximate constancy of the ratio of investment to income into the following: national product has generally been growing at a roughly constant percentage rate per year.[13]

ANALYZING THE LAWS OF MOTION OF THE MIXED ECONOMY

While these are only approximate truths and not like the unrepealable laws of physics, they portray fundamental facts about economic growth. How can we explain them?

Trends 2 and 1—higher wage rates when capital deepens—fit nicely together with classical and neoclassical theories of production and distribution. Trend 3—Bowley's Law that the wage share is approximately constant—is an interesting coincidence that would be consistent with a *statical* neoclassical model only if it possessed a special kind of production function relating Q to L and K (what in advanced treatises is called the "Cobb-Douglas function," for which relative factor shares are constant).

Trends 4 and 5, however, warn us that neoclassical theory cannot hold in *static* form! A steady profit rate and a steady capital-output ratio are incompatible with the more basic law of diminishing returns under deepening of capital. We are forced, therefore, to introduce *technical innovations* into our statical neoclassical analysis to explain these dynamic facts. And a good thing it is that we are told to introduce technical change, since we have much independent evidence of the importance of science and engineering in the modern era.

In terms of the analysis back in Fig. 37-2, we are forced to introduce an outward shift in the dd and ff curves there to account for all the trends. Thus, the eastward move in Fig. 37-2(a) from B on dd to B' on $d'd'$, which corresponds to the eastward move in Fig. 37-2(b) from b to b', will be consistent with trends 1 to 6. The tendency toward diminishing returns has just been offset by the technical shift, with interest remaining at the same horizontal level and the wage rate rising just as much as output per head. The capital-output ratio, which cannot easily be read in Fig. 37-2, must stay constant if the interest return on capital is to constitute the same relative share as before.[14]

Professor Solow, utilizing his own methods of analysis and corroborating the independent findings of numerous scholars at the National Bureau of Economic Research and elsewhere, has come up with the following remarkable conclusion:

Less than half of the increase in America's productivity per capita and in real wages can be accounted for by the increase in capital itself. Considerably more than half of the increase in productivity seems to be attributable to technical change—to scientific and engineering advance, to industrial improvements, and to "know-how" of management methods and educational training of labor.

This important finding needs careful interpretation.

First, although it is customary to measure and speak of the enhanced productivity of

---

[13] EXAMPLE: Figure 37-3 shows K/Q about 3 and the percentage growth of capital per annum almost $3\frac{1}{3}$ per cent per year. Only if net capital formation is about 10 per cent (equals $3\frac{1}{3} \times 3$) of output is this possible, as footnote 14 and the Appendix make clear.

[14] As shown in the Appendix, trends 3, 4, and 5 cannot be independent, since arithmetically the constancy of any two of the three magnitudes (iK/Q, i, K/Q) implies the constancy of the third. (These basic trends can be rationalized by the hypothesis that invention has increased labor's efficiency by just enough to keep the ratio capital/labor-measured-in-efficiency-units constant. Hence, the static model predicts constant i and K/Q.)

labor, there is no necessary implication that all of it (or most of it, or little of it) came from greater effort on the part of workers, or from more intensive conditions of sweat and strain; from more effort and education, or from more initiative and incentives of the human labor force. The facts do not point to any simple interpretation.

Second, it is artificial to separate capital formation and technology completely. New techniques do tend to be *embodied* in new kinds of equipment. It is possible to imagine a stationary state—like the optimistic one of John Stuart Mill—in which there is no net saving and investment, but in which there is considerable technical progress as the depreciation charges of worn-out equipment finance their replacement by technically better equipment. Still, no one will deny that innovations can be introduced faster in a society which is performing *net* investment in addition to the gross investment corresponding to replacement. We all do learn from actually doing, and the society which gets to try out more new things will run that much ahead of the one which does little or no net saving.

ARE INVENTIONS LABOR-SAVING OR CAPITAL-SAVING?

Any invention that wins its way under competition must raise the real wage rate or the interest rate or both.[15]

However, some inventions will by their nature have a tendency to increase the relative share of labor; others to increase the relative share of capital and property generally; and others to affect both factors in about the same degree. This suggests the convenience of the following definition:

Definition: **An invention is called "labor-saving," "capital-saving," or "neutral," depending upon whether it tends to lower the relative share of labor, lower the relative share of property, or leave relative shares unchanged.**

An extreme example of a labor-saving invention would be one that enabled unmanned machines to turn out robots that could do any of the manual and intellectual tasks of human labor. This would no doubt reduce the competitive wage drastically and could conceivably drop labor's share of NNP from its present level of about 75 to 80 per cent to below 50 per cent. An example of a capital-saving invention would be the case of a cheap computer that enabled firms to get along with much less inventory; or the invention of Kleenex tissue to replace durable handkerchiefs; or the invention of easily launched wave-reflecting satellites that made ocean cables unnecessary.[16] It is easy to

---

[15] In terms of Fig. 37-2(b)'s factor-price frontier, *ff* must be shifted outward and upward or the invention will not succeed in the competitive market. Karl Marx erred in overlooking this. He promulgated the "law of the declining rate of profit [or interest rate]" alongside the "law of the immiserization of the working class [falling real wage rate]." Unless one invokes diminishing returns to land in the Malthus fashion—and Marx, who hated Malthus as an apologist for the rich and as a "plagiarist," paid insufficient attention to such phenomena—one has to give up one or both of the Marxian "laws."

[16] A capital-saving invention tends to twist Fig. 37-2(a)'s productivity curve of capital down toward the vertical and toward greater inelasticity, thereby tending to reduce the fruits of sacrificing current consumption and accumulating capital. A neutral technical change would be one that shifts Fig. 37-2's curves generally outward and upward. Advanced treatises deal with various distinct definitions of what is meant by labor-saving; the discussion here is left general so as not to be inconsistent with either the definition associated with J. R. Hicks or that different one associated with R. F. Harrod.

specify innumerable examples of capital-saving or labor-saving innovations and of neutral innovations in between.

The steady rise in wage rates is thought by many economists to *induce* employers to come up with labor-saving inventions. This tendency is often offered to help explain the failure of the profit-and-interest rate to fall as capital is accumulated. Marx a century ago had used such an explanation to account for the success of capitalists in resisting a rise in wages and in creating an industrial reserve army of the unemployed. Sir John Hicks of Oxford has in our day advanced similar arguments of an inherent bias toward labor-saving innovation.

Whatever the ultimate merits of such arguments, we must recognize that *any* invention which lowers cost of production can benefit the first competitor who introduces it. Furthermore, since the relative share of wages in total costs has been approximately constant for a century, any employer who is planning his research expenditures over the coming years will reasonably take this into account and will do well to spend now the same number of pennies on experimentation designed to save a dollar of future cost, whatever its source.[17]

We have seen that economic analysis can throw much light on the laws of motion of the mixed economy.

Growth theory is still at the frontier of economics, and the experts are not all agreed on the mechanisms of past and future paths of economic development. Some alternative theories are presented in the Appendix to this chapter. However, we are now armed to tackle in the next chapters the problems of growth in less-developed economies, advanced economies, and collectivist economies like the Soviet Union.

SUMMARY

1 Many writers have tried to read into economic history a linear progression through inevitable stages, such as primitive economy, feudalism, capitalism, and some form of communism. The actual facts have not agreeably stuck to such timetables; in particular, the mixed economies that dominate the Western world came into being without the permission of social prophets.

---

[17] A theory of induced technical change can explain and unify all the six basic trends of economic development as follows: (1) Suppose any increase in capital relative to labor will raise labor's relative share. (2) Suppose that effort devoted to making each laborer the new equivalent of more than one laborer will go up when labor cost increases as the share of total costs (and like efforts to "augment" capital go down). (3) Finally, assume that a constant fraction of income is always saved and invested and that labor population grows at a constant slow rate. Then it will follow that the system will ultimately grow in "golden-age balance": (*a*) Capital and output will grow at the same high rate with a constant K/Q ratio; (*b*) labor population will grow at a slower rate, but because of induced technological invention, "labor in effective or efficiency units" will grow at precisely the same rate as capital and output; (*c*) now with Q, K, and effective L growing in balance, there will be no diminishing returns to capital and hence there will be a constant interest rate and constant relative labor share; (*d*) finally, the real wage will grow because each worker is having his effectiveness raised by the induced technical change. QED: Rigorous proof of this was presented by several authors in the mid-1960s.

2   The classical models of Smith and Malthus describe economic development in terms of fixed land and growing population. A simple labor theory of value prevails so long as land is superabundant; and output develops steadily with population in this golden age where labor gets all the national product.

3   In the absence of technical change, increasing population ultimately exhausts the supply of free land. The resulting increase in population density invokes the law of diminishing returns: Fixity of land keeps output from growing proportionally to increased labor; with less and less of land to work with, each new man adds less and less extra product; the decline in labor's marginal-product means a decline in the competitively earned real wage. As each acre of land gets more and more labor to work with, its marginal-product and competitively earned rent go up. A fundamental factor-price frontier depicts how the rent rate must rise as the wage rate falls; but no one can predict what will happen to the *relative* shares of land and labor in national product.

4   The Malthusian equilibrium comes when the wage has fallen to the subsistence level, below which the supply of labor will not reproduce itself. However, in realistic fact, technical change has kept economic development going in the West by continually shifting the productivity curve of labor upward. How fast wages will rise must depend upon whether the technical changes are labor-saving or land-saving or neutral.

5   The Ricardo-Marx-Solow model stresses the deepening of capital, i.e., the process of accumulating capital goods of varied types faster than the growth in population and labor hours. In the absence of technical change, an increase in capital per capita will not be matched by a proportional increase in output per capita because of diminishing returns. Hence, capital deepening lowers the interest rate (which is the same as the "profit rate" if risk is ignored), raises the real wage along the factor-price frontier, and raises the capital-output ratio.

6   Historically, trends 1 and 2 on page 723—a rise in K/L and in w—are consistent with the *statical* model. Trend 3's approximate constancy of relative shares of labor and property—as measured by wL/Q and iK/Q, where $Q = wL + iK$—is not mandatory in the statical model, but is consistent with a special technical case of it (Cobb-Douglas). However, trends 4 and 5—the failure of the interest and profit rate to fall and of the capital-output ratio to rise—show clearly that technical change must be brought into the analysis. Trend 6—approximate constancy of the investment-income ratio—taken together with the constancy of the capital-output ratio, arithmetically implies a constant percentage growth of output per decade.

7   The facts suggest the hypothesis that capital accumulation is second to technical change in explaining rising productivity. But innovation and investment interact, as new techniques get embodied in new equipment and people learn by trying new investments. Increasing productivity can be expressed conveniently in terms of labor productivity—i.e., Q/L—but this does not necessarily imply anything about the reasons for the rise.

8 Inventions are defined as labor-saving, capital-saving, or neutral, depending upon whether they reduce labor's relative share of national product, reduce property's relative share, or leave shares unchanged. Experience with rising wage rates makes firms expect the trend to continue; whether or not they try for, and succeed in making, labor-saving inventions, firms will want to cut down on any cost items (labor, natural resources, capital costs).

Either by coincidence or by cancellation of offsetting trends or as the result of economic mechanisms needing study,[18] the pace of invention has turned out to be just about enough to offset the effect of diminishing returns to capital on the interest and profit rate; and innovations have not turned out to be so labor-saving or capital-saving as to cause much change in the relative shares of labor and property.

QUESTIONS FOR DISCUSSION

1 Does the mixed economy fit any of the timetables of history? Was it so hard to foresee?

2 "If the democratic state subsidizes science and invention, controls the business cycle, augments full-employment thrift by a budget surplus, and introduces sensible planning, we can expect growth that would astound the classical economists." Evaluate critically.

3 Draw the parallels between the models of Figs. 37-1 and 37-2: rising labor-output ratio and rising capital-output ratio; falling wage and falling interest rate; the two factor-price frontiers; technical shifts of dd and ff in both cases; land-saving or labor-saving and neutral innovations in both cases; relative factor shares; and other parallelisms.

4 "Saving helps capitalists today, workers tomorrow." Assess this filter-down view.

5 "Without technical change and unemployment, persistent capital accumulation would ultimately mean euthanasia (death) of the capitalists." Use Fig. 37-2 to explain this.

6 Since labor's share shows a slight uptrend and the capital-output ratio a slight downtrend, since the interest and profit rate fluctuates considerably, since the ratio of private net investment to NNP shows fluctuation and in recent years signs of an uptrend—in view of these facts, would you be much surprised if basic trends were to show future changes?

7 Give examples of labor-saving and capital-saving inventions.

8 "Had America saved less but spent more on experimentation, we'd be richer." Comment.

Review your understanding of the following concepts:

stages of history	capital deepening, K/L rise
Smithian golden age	capital-output ratio, K/Q
labor theory of value	interest rate and profit rate
Malthusian subsistence wage	technical progress
factor-price frontier ff	labor-saving
marginal-product dd	neutral
diminishing returns	capital-saving
relative factor shares	Q growth from inventions, from more K

[18] Such as that described in footnote 17.

APPENDIX: Modern Discussions of Development Theory

Economics, not being a settled subject, is itself still undergoing development. While the broad facts of historical development discussed in the chapter are not in dispute, different interpretations of them are given by different authors. Some of the ideas associated with the names of the late Joseph A. Schumpeter, Sir Roy Harrod of Oxford, W. W. Leontief of Harvard, Professors Joan Robinson and Nicholas Kaldor of Cambridge University, and various current American economists will be sketched briefly in this Appendix.

While an elementary textbook cannot pretend to resolve advanced topics, today one would consider an introduction to physics old-fashioned if it did not somewhere give the reader a glance at fundamental issues on the frontiers of knowledge: atomic theory, elementary particles, generalized relativity, and so forth.

Similarly many beginning students of economics will want to have a glimpse of the issues at the frontier of current economic analysis. Without mastering every intricacy of this Appendix, the interested reader can capture the flavor of developing economic thought from it. In particular, many readers who are not concerned with the rest of the theories discussed in this Appendix may still want to turn to its final discussion (pages 736–738) of the fascinating and useful subject of Leontief input-output analysis of interindustry flows.

SCHUMPETERIAN INNOVATION

Joseph Schumpeter (1883–1950) of Vienna and Harvard was author of two economic classics:[1] *The Theory of Economic Development* (English ed., Harvard University Press, Cambridge, Mass., 1934) and the posthumous *History of Economic Analysis* (Oxford University Press, Fair Lawn, N.J., 1954).

Schumpeter emphasized the role of the innovator —i.e., the inventor, the developer, the promoter, the man who initiates and recognizes technical improvements and who succeeds in getting them introduced. Like Carlyle's faith in the role of the great man in history, Schumpeter's theory regards the innovator as the dynamic actor of capitalism, who rules profitably for a day, only to have his profits nibbled away by imitating competitors.

Figure 37-2(a) back on page 721 well represents Schumpeter's notion of what would happen if all innovations ceased. Competition and capital accumulation would quickly push society down the diminishing-returns curve dd; indeed, Schumpeter thought that the long-run ss horizontal line at which the supply of new saving will disappear would be at a zero rate of interest and profit, being properly drawn in Fig. 37-2(a) down on the horizontal axis itself. (His theory of a zero rate of interest in the innovationless stationary state can be replaced by a positive-interest-rate floor without appreciably altering his theory of cycles or development.)

But now Schumpeter plays his trump card. Innovation is periodically shifting the dd curve upward and outward. The violin string is plucked by innovation; without innovation it dies down to stationariness, but then along comes a new innovation to pluck it back into dynamic motion again. So it is with the profit rate in economic life.

The profits due to innovation, we have seen, will be competed away by imitators, with labor and consumers benefiting from price reductions. The innovation-induced rise in interest rates will soon coax out saving and capital formation, until the accumulation of the augmented capital stock leads to diminishing returns, a "profit squeeze," and minimal interest. But then along comes a new burst of innovations—railroads, electricity, automation, semiconductors—to pluck the system back into dynamic motion, and we are off on a new repetition of the process of development.

Ignoring Schumpeter's specific theories of the business cycle, we see that his theory of development is completely consistent with the first two trends of economic history: rising real wage rates, and capital increase outstripping population increase. Although his general theory does not specifically call for constant relative shares, a trendless profit rate, a constant capital-output ratio, or a trendless average pro-

---

[1] As can be seen by readers of his stimulating *Capitalism, Socialism and Democracy* (Harper, New York, 1942), Schumpeter was more than an economist. Believing the economic system to be itself essentially stable, Schumpeter advanced sociological and political reasons for his predicted decay of capitalism: he held that the very efficiency of capitalism will be its ruin, as intellectuals and the masses come to despise the market ideology and contrive to introduce hampering government interferences in the name of welfare. Unlike Marx, who thought capitalism would die of its own cancers, Schumpeter thought it would eventually commit suicide for psychosomatic reasons. The tremendous resurgence of *mixed* economies in the 25 years since Schumpeter cheerfully gave his gloomy prediction is, apparently, a deviation from *his* timetable of history, but the disaffection of affluent college activists may be testimonial to his prophetic insight.

pensity-to-consume-and-save, still all or any of these could be quite consistent with his general schema.

UNEMPLOYMENT IN THE STATIONARY STATE?

Ricardo, Alfred Marshall, and Schumpeter had one thing in common with Lord Keynes of *The General Theory of Employment, Interest and Money*. They all thought that profit rates would be pushed to minimal levels in the absence of technical change. But Ricardo and company all thought that when this day of judgment came, the economy would be voluntarily consuming 100 per cent of its full-employment income; although positive investment would cease, people would then be spending enough on consumption to maintain full employment. (In terms of the diagrams of Part Two, in the Ricardian stationary state the $C + I + G$ curve would be intersecting the 45° line at the full-employment level, with $C + I + G$ actually equal there to $C + zero + G$, because net investment ceases in the stationary state.)

Keynes, on the other hand, feared that such minimal rates of interest and of profit on risky ventures might create a stationary state of stagnation with chronic unemployment:

People might still *want to save* at full employment, but no *matching real investment* would be forthcoming when the promised profit rate is too low to coax out risk taking; and when the interest to be earned on short-term gilt-edge government bonds has become so low as to make people indifferent between hoarding much or little safe, idle money,[2] central bank policy cannot do much to prevent stagnation.

This notion of a troublesome stationary state did not die with the 1930s. Prominent followers of Keynes at Cambridge University, such as Professors Joan Robinson, Lord Kahn, and Nicholas Kaldor, have grave doubts concerning the possibility of a successful deepening of capital accompanied by full employment in a mixed economy. At the least they would stress that it will never happen by itself in a country that confines itself to orthodox fiscal and monetary policies. At the most they would harbor grave doubts that "managed capitalism" could, or would, pursue the

unorthodox policies of monetary and fiscal expansion implied by a successful synthesis of neoclassical and post-Keynesian analysis.

Readers who go on to advanced economics can be referred to writings of these and other authors.[3] Here, briefly, will be presented some of the points that need to be considered in doing justice to both sides of the argument as it bears on long-term economic development: no attempt will be made to identify ideas and writers meticulously.

UNCHANGEABLE CAPITAL-OUTPUT RATIO?

The land-output and labor-output ratios were not constants in the first Smith-Malthus model of development. And the capital-output ratio in the Ricardo-Marx-Solow model of Fig. 37-2 was likewise not supposed to be a technical constant. In the absence of technical change, successful capital formation by society would enable output to grow; and the resulting phenomenon of diminishing returns would imply a *smoothly growing* capital-output ratio as capital deepening was taking place. On this view, dynamic technical change has seemed historically to provide about the extra productivity needed to offset statical diminishing returns, keeping the measured capital-output ratio constant.

Many modern economists—Professors Robert Eisner of Northwestern, Alvin Hansen of Harvard, and others—are of the view that the capital-output ratio is very nearly a technical *constant,* and that any attempt to accumulate capital beyond the rate required by the annual growth in output will soon be unsuccessful. Profits or rents from equipment will fall off badly after any surge of capital investment like those of 1955–1957 and 1964–1970. Excess capacity will follow, and the resulting profit squeeze will kill off private investment, as it did in the sluggish years following 1957. Therefore, they argue, any long-term theory must utilize an *invariable* capital-output ratio like that shown in the historical data of Fig. 37-3.

HARROD-DOMAR GROWTH MODELS

These concepts can be illuminated by some interesting models of balanced compound-interest (or "exponential") growth developed by Sir Roy Harrod in England

[2]This floor on the profit-and-interest rate could help account for the historical constancy of the profit rate named in trend 4 (page 723), particularly if someone could supply reasons for a profit ceiling. With the profit rate allegedly running between two channels, its constancy would be removed from the realm of coincidence. (Recall also earlier discussion; page 328's "liquidity trap" or "depression pole," when elevated by riskiness, might provide such a profit floor.)

[3]J. Robinson, *Economic Philosophy* (Aldine, London, 1962), Chap. 5; *Accumulation of Capital* (Macmillan, London, 1956); N. Kaldor, *Essays on Value and Distribution; On Economic Stability and Growth; On Economic Policy* (Duckworth, London, 1960).

and Professor E. Domar in America.[4] This theory has two aspects: the long-term "natural rate of growth" and the so-called "warranted rate of growth."

The natural rate of growth The historical data of Fig. 37-3 can help explain Harrod's arithmetic; and, in turn, a simple Harrod-Domar model can give an oversimplified "explanation" of those historical trends.

Suppose hours of labor L grow steadily at about 1 per cent per year.[5] And for extreme simplicity, assume that technical change is in effect making every man's efficiency as a laborer grow at another 2 per cent per year. Either because of more scientific methods of production or better education, it is as if 98 men can this year do what it took 100 to do last year; and this is repeated indefinitely. To coin a phrase, while *actual* L in its human man-hour units is growing at but 1 per cent per year, the number of "efficiency units of labor" L^* is growing at 3 per cent per year because of the annual 2 per cent efficiency improvement. This leads to the concept of the natural rate of growth.

Definition: **The *natural rate of growth* of a simplified Harrod system is the percentage growth per year of its labor supply expressed in "efficiency units" (which means natural labor units as augmented by the presumed increase in technical effectiveness of each man-hour); as a condition of *balanced* growth, output and capital must also be growing at this same natural rate per year.**

With NNP (or Q) and with L^* growing steadily at this natural rate of 3 per cent per year, the stock of capital K must also grow at the same natural rate of 3 per cent per year so as to keep in balanced pace. How much investment is required each year to keep K growing at this natural rate of 3 per cent? Or, in other words, how much must people be steadily saving and

investing out of their annual full-employment product to keep growth nicely balanced?

Evidently the needed saving-income ratio must depend on the numerical value of the capital-output ratio K/Q times the natural growth rate.[6]

We are now in a position to write down the arithmetic formula relating three historical things: the Harrod natural rate of growth of .03 per year, or in the general case g per year; the historical capital-output ratio of, say, $3\frac{1}{3}$, or in the general case K/Q; the required saving-income ratio of .10, or in the general case s. We get

$$s = g \times \frac{K}{Q} \text{ or } .10 = .03 \times 3\frac{1}{3}$$

This relationship determines the amount of voluntary saving *and* investment that is needed if the Harrod natural rate of growth is to be an *equilibrium* situation.[7]

Explaining the trends Can this simplified Harrod-Domar model of balanced natural rate of growth account for all six of the basic trends listed on page 723? Yes. Let us check them off.

The model certainly gives a deepening of capital relative to man-hours of actual L, since K grows at 3 per cent and L only at 1 per cent. (In this simplified model, an observer who concentrates only on L^*, labor in efficiency units, will see a constant K/L^* with no "deepening" going on but merely an apparent "widening of capital" to keep K and L^* balanced.)

Trend 2 is verified also. The wage rate rises—actually at 2 per cent per year. Why? Because each actual man (L, not L^*) collects the marginal product of the increasing efficiency units *in him*, and these units work with their full quota of capital goods.

Trend 3 is verified and is no longer a coincidence. Because technical change was so nicely neutral as to

---

[4]R. F. Harrod, *Towards a Dynamic Economics* (Macmillan, London, 1948); E. D. Domar, *Essays in the Theory of Economic Growth* (Oxford University Press, Fair Lawn, N.J., 1957). The discussion of interacting accelerator-multiplier models in Chapter 14 is here applied to the trend of economic development rather than to the business-cycle deviations from that trend.

[5]Expansion of an industrial sector through the utilization of an unlimited supply of rural labor is associated with the name of Sir Arthur Lewis, an eminent economist now at Princeton but originally from Jamaica. Such diverse economists as the conservative Gustav Cassel of Sweden and the nonconservative Karl Marx had put forth similar Ricardian notions.

[6]Thus, suppose Q is 1,000 billion dollars per year, and that the capital stock is about $3\frac{1}{3}$ times as great, being 3,333 billion dollars. Then to add 3 per cent to K this year we must have net investment of 100 billion dollars (equals $.03 \times 3.333$ billion dollars), which means that people must be saving and investing exactly 10 per cent (equals $3\% \times 3\frac{1}{3}$) of their incomes. [Check your understanding by showing that a 4 per cent natural growth rate would in this case require a $13\frac{1}{3}$ per cent (equals $4\% \times 3\frac{1}{3}$) saving ratio out of income; and that a 3 per cent natural growth rate with a K/Q ratio of only 2 would require only a 6 per cent saving-income ratio.]

[7]This is really the $I = S$ schedule equality of Part Two. For in the case of the natural growth rate, $g = I/K$ or $I = gk$; hence, $I/Q = S/Q = s = g(K/Q)$, the Harrod condition.

make each man take on "the strength of ten," the balanced growth in K and L^* means we are *dividing shares between the factors in precisely the same way as before*. (Recall that an observer of L^* alone merely sees balanced *widening* of capital, not deepening.)

Trend 4's constancy of the interest rate is now precisely verified, being neither an approximation nor a coincidence. Each unit of K, being matched exactly by the same amount of L^* as before, experiences no diminishing returns and has imputed to it the same competitive interest rate. (If degree of risk is the same, constancy of the interest rate means constancy of the somewhat higher profit rate.)

Trend 5 is of course verified, since the Harrod natural rate of balanced growth assumes from the beginning an unchanged K/Q ratio. In terms of the Ricardo-Marx-Solow model, even if the capital-output ratio *could* smoothly change, it will not have to in a situation where widening of K to match L^* means no diminishing returns and entails Q growing in full proportion to K.

Trend 6's constancy of the saving-income ratio is verified from the basic Harrod formula for the natural rate of balanced growth at the same compound interest rate per year: $s = $ constant $g \times$ constant K/Q.

Interdependence of trends   As mentioned in footnote 14, p. 724, the six trends are not all logically independent. We could have saved time by checking any two of the three trends 3, 4, and 5, knowing that their correctness would arithmetically guarantee the correctness of the remaining trend. Here is why. If property always gets the same fraction of output, say, one-fourth, and if the profit rate stays constant, then the process of capitalization of an income stream discussed in Chapter 30 shows that the value of the capital stock must be a determinate multiple of output. [I.e., K's fractional share of Q divided by the interest rate is equal to the capital-output ratio: $i(K/Q) \div i = K/Q$. Thus, if capital gets one fourth of 1,000-billion-dollar Q, and this property return of 250 billion is capitalized by dividing it through by $i = .07\frac{1}{2} = \frac{3}{40}$, then the value of capital is seen to be determinate at 3,333 billion dollars, or $3\frac{1}{3}$ times the value of output.]

Harrod's warranted rate of growth   The natural rate of growth is designed to cope with long-term problems of economic development. A few words can be said about a related tool designed more to explain cyclical instability than long-term trend.[8]

[8]These next two sections may be skipped.

What if society's actual saving fraction differs from that needed to keep the natural growth rate in nice balance? That is, suppose actual desired S/Q at full employment is greater, or less, than s given by $g(K/Q)$. Too high a schedule of saving, we saw in Part Two, will tend to lead to unemployment. Too low a saving schedule, relative to the investment schedule, was seen to produce an inflationary gap and tendency toward price inflation.

Very well. No longer is the natural growth rate g the one that the system will realize. Growth in balance has now become rather irrelevant. Still Harrod can ask this rather odd question:

Starting from enough unemployed resources so that the natural growth rate of labor and other resources provides no bottleneck or ceiling—starting from there, what rate of growth of output, W, if it could be achieved and maintained, would (through "the acceleration principle" of Chapter 14, page 246) lead to a large enough volume of investment to justify (via the multiplier analysis of Chapter 12) a continuance of its own growth rate W? The answering W is defined as the "warranted rate of growth."

In short, to get W, reinterpret the old Harrod relation $s = g(K/Q)$ and work it backward to solve for the growth rate of Q. Follow these steps: (1) Replace s by the actual desired saving ratio S/Q. (2) Replace the g specified by labor force and technological growth by the unknown warranted rate of growth W. (3) Provided that the capital-output ratio K/Q is a hard constant, let it stand.[9] (4) Solve for W by removing K/Q to the denominator under S/Q.

We go from the natural rate to the warranted rate thus: $S/Q = W(K/Q)$ replaces $s = g(K/Q)$, and

$$W = \frac{S/Q}{K/Q}$$

An example will help. With $g = .03$ and $K/Q = 3\frac{1}{3}$, Harrod needs $s = .10$ for his natural-growth process. But suppose people want to save $S/Q = .13\frac{1}{3} > .10$. This overthrift would lead to unemployment. But suppose somehow Harrod could start a faster expansion, of W per cent per year in Q, which can always get the labor it needs from the ranks of the unemployed, how

[9]Suppose an extra amount of Q, written as ΔQ, calls for an amount of extra capital ΔK that gives a $\Delta K/\Delta Q$ different from K/Q. Then we would have to replace the latter in the Harrod formula by the former, which is called the "*incremental* capital-output ratio" or the "accelerator coefficient." Those who like symbols should read the next footnote.

fast must it expand to generate enough I/Q to match $S/Q = .13\frac{1}{3}$? If every dollar of expanded Q always requires K to expand by $3\frac{1}{3}$ dollars, our answer is $W = .13\frac{1}{3}/3\frac{1}{3} = .04$. Any Q growth higher than $W = .04$ per year will generate $I/Q > .13\frac{1}{3}$, just as any Q growth less than $.04$ will generate $I/Q < .13\frac{1}{3}$.[10]

The warranted rate is an odd concept. It does not tell you what will in fact happen, but only what would—if it came to happen by design or by luck—have certain self-warranting properties. Such a growth rate of output, W, if it could somehow be established and maintained, warrants a level of investment just big enough to match the voluntary saving that its own income growth entails.

Cycles and instabilities   Two observations should be made about cyclical instabilities involved in the warranted rate of growth.

1. Once all the unemployed are back at work, the natural rate of growth g must set a ceiling against which the faster warranted rate of growth must collide. Thus W of 4 or 5 per cent per year and g of only 3 per cent per year ultimately means the Harrod warranted expansion will hit full employment. As was seen in Chapter 14 on business cycles, some writers[11] have constructed a theory of a collapse into recession based

upon a bouncing back of the system from its collision with the natural-rate employment ceiling.

2. The warranted rate of growth, even if originally established, will not persist after being disturbed. In the Harrod model it is definitely unstable. To see this, note that if the actual growth rate temporarily exceeds $W = 4$ per cent, this new income will be generating in desired investment *more* than the $13\frac{1}{3}$ ($= 4\% \times 3\frac{1}{3}$) per cent ratio of desired saving—thereby accelerating its own growth still faster above W. (Show that a *less* than 4 per cent initial growth rate will similarly create a deficiency of intended investment relative to the $13\frac{1}{3}$ per cent intended saving, thereby *de*celerating its own growth still further below W.)

Just as an unmanned bicycle, which is unstable if disturbed from the vertical, can be converted into a stable system by a steadying and compensating human hand, so can a Harrod-Domar growth path that would be unstable under laissez faire be made stable by compensating monetary and fiscal policies in a mixed economy.

NEOCLASSICAL DYNAMICS

The Ricardo-Marx-Solow model of smooth substitutability of labor for capital (i.e., of labor for a great variety of alternatively producible capital goods) has less need to work with Harrod-Domar concepts than those models which regard the capital-output ratio as a hard constant. However, it is useful to interpret the Harrod-Domar concepts for a neoclassical model like Fig. 37-2.

By a simple "neoclassical growth model" is meant one in which the state uses monetary policies to make sure that thriftiness does not lead to unemployment and abortive thrift: by making equity and loan funds available at lower interest and profit rates (and possibly by unorthodox credit policies that provide guarantees against risks and uncertainties) such a managed system can contrive deepening of capital as described earlier.[12] Alternatively, this neoclassical model can be

---

[10] Suppose the capital-output ratio K/Q is not precisely equal to the incremental capital-output ratio $\Delta K/\Delta Q$ where ΔQ means the annual change in Q or $Q_{t+1} - Q_t$, and $\Delta K =$ annual investment $= K_{t+1} - K_t$. Then we replace K/Q by $\Delta K/\Delta Q$ in the formula for the warranted rate. Economics aside, this can be seen from the obvious identity

$$\frac{\Delta K}{Q} \equiv \frac{\Delta Q}{Q} \frac{\Delta K}{\Delta Q}$$

which comes from multiplying the left-hand side by $1 \equiv \Delta Q/\Delta Q$ and rearranging terms. If investment matches voluntary saving, this is seen to be the same as $S/Q = W(\Delta K/\Delta Q)$.

The natural growth rate stems from the slightly different identity

$$\frac{\Delta K}{Q} \equiv \frac{\Delta K}{K} \frac{K}{Q}$$

where the left-hand side has merely been multiplied by $1 \equiv K/K$. Stipulating *balanced* natural growth, we require $g = \Delta K/K = \Delta Q/Q = \Delta L^*/L^*$. The last condition guarantees constancy of the K/Q ratio; and combining this last condition with the equilibrium requirement that maintained saving be equal to growth-induced investment, we convert the above identity into the already given natural-rate formula $s = g(K/Q)$.

[11] J. R. Hicks, *A Contribution to the Theory of the Trade Cycle* (Oxford University Press, Fair Lawn, N.J., 1950), gives a convenient summary of such nonlinear-cycle theories based on interacting accelerator-multiplier principles.

[12] This means that the variety of possible heterogeneous capital-goods processes is so great that any reduction of interest rate—even be it as little as from $i = .08$ to $i = .079$— will ultimately make it profitable to use some new pattern of known processes. E.g., at .079 the machine tools may be made a little more durable. In consequence, the factor-price frontier of Fig. 37-2(b) will look fairly smooth to the naked eye, even though a microscope will show that it contains little line segments that meet in corners. When we introduce realistic uncertainties into the model, one is first tempted to think that minute changes in interest rate will have negligible

interpreted as picturing the technology of an efficiently run collectivist society that never faces macroeconomic problems of unemployment or of inflation due to lack of proper effective demand.

In such a society, where whatever is withheld from consumption goes into capital formation, *any* rate of growth is essentially a "warranted rate of growth." This is because there is (1) no saving-investment problem, and (2) no hard constant for the capital-output ratio (or for the incremental capital-output ratio).

Here is an idealized example. Add a new supply of L to a system that has a certain K and has previously been producing a certain Q. This new L can be put to work with the given K *as rapidly* as we like. There will result a growth rate of Q that can be *as high* as the growth in L can produce. People can consume and can invest out of the new output *as much or little* as they like. Depending on *whatever* amount of capital formation they decide on, there will result a gradual accumulation of K with the K/L ratio being able to move *in any way* without causing trouble.

All the above is in sharp contrast to a model with fixed capital-output ratio, which calls for a specific W growth rate of Q. Contrast the Harrod case with the italicized words in the above paragraph!

Three sources of growth Neoclassical output growth can be decomposed into three separate sources: growth in labor or L, growth in capital or K, and technical innovation itself. Momentarily ignoring technical change, note that a 1 per cent per year growth rate in L together with a 1 per cent per year growth rate in K is assumed to cause output to grow also at a 1 per cent per year rate. (Resist the temptation to add 1 per cent to 1 per cent and come out with 2 per cent; L and K cooperate in production, each needing the other.)

Suppose L grows at 1 per cent per year and K at 5 per cent. It is tempting, but wrong, to guess that Q will then grow at 3 per cent, the simple average of 1 and 5. Why wrong? Because the two factors do not contribute equal shares to product: about three-fourths

of all product goes to labor as wages and only one-fourth of Q goes to property as its interest-profit share. This means L's growth rate should get 3 times the weight of K's; hence, the correct answer is that Q will grow at 2 per cent per year (= ³⁄₄ of 1% + ¼ of 5%).

Hence, output growth per year follows the law

$$\% \ Q \text{ growth} = \quad \tfrac{3}{4}(\% \ L \text{ growth}) \\ + \tfrac{1}{4}(\% \ K \text{ growth}) \\ + \text{T.C.}$$

where T.C. means technical changes that raise productivity by shifting the dd curve of Fig. 37-2; and where ³⁄₄ and ¼ would of course later be replaced by new fractions if the relative shares of the factors had later changed.

If we seek to explain *per capita* growth, matters are simpler still, since this enables us to get rid of L as a separate growth source. Now, using the fact that capital gets one-fourth share of output, we have simply

$$\% \ \frac{Q}{L} \text{ growth} = \tfrac{1}{4}\left(\% \ \frac{K}{L} \text{ growth}\right) + \text{t.c.}$$

This relation shows clearly how deepening of capital would raise the capital-output ratio if there were no technical improvements being made: output per capita grows only one-fourth as fast as capital per capita, reflecting one aspect of diminishing returns.

This relation now explains the meaning of Solow's conclusion—that more than half of the increased output recorded in historical statistics seems to be attributable to scientific advance rather than to thrift and capital formation. This means that the second term in the above relation—t.c. for per capita technical change—appears on statistical measurement to have been definitely bigger than the first term representing the investment contribution. When Solow tries to allow for the fact that new techniques get embodied in new capital goods, the relative importance of the first term rises; but apparently it still remains below 50 per cent. (Although the primacy of technical change seems corroborated by German or Japanese statistics, the importance of the capital factor does seem greater in Britain, Canada, and Russia.)

ALTERNATIVE THEORIES

Repudiation of aggregate production functions Professors Joan Robinson and Nicholas Kaldor of Cambridge University are skeptical that "capital" can be usefully measured as an aggregate, which together with labor produces aggregate output. This is certainly

---

effects. Actually, however, replacing certainty by probabilities smooths the small steps in a demand function into a continuous curve: a small change in i, long maintained, pushes some investment projects on the borderline of doubt into actual operation. See J. E. Meade, *A Neoclassical Growth Model* (Oxford University Press, Fair Lawn, N.J., 1961), for alternative interpretations in terms of a flexible aggregate of capital.

a healthy skepticism. They are more skeptical that the marginal productivities calculated from such an alleged production function can be used to explain wage and profit rates and the relative shares in NNP of labor and property. They go even further and doubt that economists can work with a detailed breakdown of numerous heterogeneous capital goods—machines of type A, B, C, . . .—to get quantitative results at all like the neoclassical case, in an actual realistic mixed economy of uncertainty and uneven growth.[13]

Dissenting voices Robinson and Kaldor by no means agree on what is to replace the aggregative analysis. Both incline, but in different degree, toward a macroeconomic theory of income distribution with the following property:

"Here is an economy with high property share and high growth. How wrong to think that it is the thrift of the rich (or anybody else) which *causes* that fast growth. The causation runs the other way: fast growth produces high profits, rather than vice versa."[14]

[13] Their works cited earlier can be contrasted by the advanced student in economics with the general neo-neoclassical viewpoint exposited in an advanced work like R. Dorfman, P. A. Samuelson, and R. M. Solow, *Linear Programming and Economic Analysis* (McGraw-Hill, New York, 1958). The latter makes the same supposition as was done here—that there are a great variety of alternative machines and processes known (or knowable) at any one time. If the interest rate changes even a little, say from .08 to .079 (as mentioned earlier), it will usually (but not inevitably!) pay to turn to a new blueprint that involves a slightly more durable machine. Hence, as already stated in the last footnote, the ff curve of Fig. 37-2(b) will look almost smooth to the naked eye, even though a microscope reveals it to consist of many short line segments that meet in corners. The simplified K fable thus does give some useful insight into a more realistic model, be it the U.S.S.R., the United States, or India.

[14] In long-run balanced growth, Robinson and Kaldor identify i as g/s_p, where saving out of wages is negligible and s_p is the average propensity of property income to be saved. This comes from matching the bracketed terms in the following identities: $I = (I/K)K = \{g\}K = I = S = s_p(iK) = \{s_p i\}K$. With the interest or profit rate known, if you believe in a constant capital-output ratio, K/Q, you can calculate property share in income as $i(K/Q)$. Kaldor also has a short-run theory of distribution: when I drops exogenously in the short run, Kaldor denies that this produces multiplier drops in Q and employment (as in Chapters 12 and 13); instead this depresses business demands, causing business to cut prices (relative to wages) until total profit, iK, has dropped enough to equate $s_p(iK)$ with lowered I. Mrs. Robinson disagrees with this new version of Say's Law and inevitable full employment,

This seems to say something more than does the familiar assertion that when a country like Japan or West Germany experiences a miracle of productivity growth, people find it easiest to be thrifty out of the increase in income and to be slow in renegotiating real wage rates commensurate with the recent rises in marginal productivities. It is beyond controversy that such induced thrift does further speed up capital formation and tends (in neoclassical fashion) to speed up growth still further, but that is another story.

Lifetime saving and the wealth-income ratio Professor Franco Modigliani of MIT has put forward an alternative theory that is quite at variance with those just above. Modigliani does not consider the constancy of the capital-output ratio a mere coincidence. He tries to explain it, not in terms of technological production or by induced innovation as in page 726's footnote 17, but in terms of people's psychological decisions about wealth, consuming, saving, and dissaving. He puts the greatest stress on lifetime patterns of saving for old-age retirement.

Here is an example. An adult works for about 40 years and lives in retirement for 20. To keep his consumption standards somewhat equal all his life, he consumes less than his income during the working years; he gradually builds up his wealth to a maximum just before retirement; then he gradually uses up capital and pension rights by his retirement consumption; at death he leaves little wealth.

When population is growing at an even percentage rate, the age distribution remains constant over time. This steady increase in population, combined with confidently expected rising real income, causes the average level of wealth of the people of all ages to remain constant in ratio to total income. Except for the public-debt and land part of wealth, Modigliani has supplied a reason for K/Q to be constant!

A test of Modigliani's theory, as against that of someone like Kaldor who thinks that businessmen will somehow be led to make innovation and investment decisions in order to keep the K/Q ratio from changing much, would be to perform the hypothetical experiment of juggling the public debt up or down and seeing whether the K/Q ratio finally does change enough to keep the wealth-income ratio fairly constant. This experiment is not to be recommended, but it does remind us of Chapter 19's assertion that

and most statistical analyses of profits in the mixed economy do too. (For more on Kaldor's 1955–1962 theories, cf. the 1964 6th edition of this book.)

a public debt can make the present generation want to do more consuming and less saving for its old age.

COMPENSATING FISCAL POLICY

Suppose it were true that monetary policy—because of balance-of-payments constraints, Hansen-like capital-output fixity, or other impotency—could make no effective change in private investment spending I. Then compensating fiscal policy would lead to results quite different from those given by laissez faire models of the simple Harrod and Kaldor type.

Whenever full-employment s was out of line with I/Q, the government would run a budgetary surplus or deficit just big enough to alter the effective s for society until it equaled I/Q. The effective "warranted rate of growth" could thereby be kept equal to any prescribed natural rate of full-employment growth.

Thus, in a year like 1968 when I/Q tended to exceed full-employment s, the rational thing for the government to do was to create a large budgetary surplus: to raise tax rates and lower people's disposable incomes and personal saving, to cut down on government use of resources and on transfers, or to do both. This surplus is, in effect, government saving: call it s_G and combine it with the private saving ratio s_{pr} to get $s = $ average (s_G, s_{pr}) as big as is needed to equal I/Q without inflation.

During the sluggish years of the early 1960's, the opposite fiscal policies would be designed to compensate: With $I/Q < s_{pr}$, a budget deficit creates government dissaving (or negative saving); then at full employment, $I/Q = s$, the average of s_{pr} and the government dissaving ratio.

In summary, laissez faire Harrodian discrepancies can lose their terror and relevance in a properly managed mixed economy.

THE EXPANDING UNIVERSE: A DIGRESSION

The late John von Neumann, a brilliant mathematician who helped build the hydrogen bomb and who founded the theory of games, described an economic model in which everything could be produced out of everything. If land and/or labor are no longer scarce limiting factors, then the law of diminishing returns no longer applies. All the fruits of production, above and beyond the costs of subsistence for horses, rabbits, looms, and comfortably living men, are plowed back into the system for growth of more horses, rabbits, looms, men.

In this system, which is like Smith's golden age

except that it definitely involves capital goods, there is a maximal rate of balanced growth. And it turns out that such a growth rate—call it g because of its resemblance to the Harrod natural rate of growth—is exactly equal to the interest rate i.

Because development theory, for countries like India and the United States, is preoccupied with the concept of "balanced growth," the Neumann model is of considerable interest. It is particularly relevant to the case where an industrial sector in a poor country finds it can get an unlimited supply of laborers from the rural sector at the same wage cost in terms of subsistence; needing little land, the industrial sector can "take off" and grow at a constant Neumann-percentage rate per year, provided it can produce the capital goods needed to match the new labor or can be helped by imports from foreign lenders, aiders, or exporters.

If there is technical change, the system can advance at a rate even faster than the Neumann rate; indeed, if the system can, so to speak, manufacture new inventions that make labor grow in efficiency at a steady percentage rate, it will then appear to an observer to be capable of even faster Neumann growth.

A simplest example of an expanding system would be the case of rabbits (or men) who produce 1.05 rabbits of output for each rabbit of input. The interest rate and the growth rate will obviously then be 5 per cent per period. Other examples are not quite so simple.

LEONTIEF'S INTERINDUSTRY INPUT-OUTPUT

The important interindustry tableau of Wassily Leontief is a modern-day realization of the eighteenth-century dream of the physiocratic economist, Francois Quesnay, who first envisaged the *Tableau Économique,* or circular flow of economic life. A score of nations—such as France, Norway, Egypt, the United States, the United Kingdom, and India—have computed input-output tables as an amplification of their national-income data and as a possible aid in development planning.[15]

[15] For additional discussion of theory and applications see Wassily Leontief, *The Structure of the American Economy, 1919–1929* (Harvard University Press, Cambridge, Mass., 1941; 2d ed.: *1919–1939,* Oxford University Press, Fair Lawn, N.J., 1951): or Wassily Leontief, *Input-Output Economics* (Oxford University Press, Fair Lawn, N.J., 1966). As part of the price that Leontief has to pay to make Walras's general equilibrium empirically measurable, he is forced to make the technical assumption that all factor proportions—to each other and to total output—are technologically *fixed* or con-

Leontief's input-output tableau x-rays the economy:

COLD-WAR INTERINDUSTRY FLOWS				
	AGRICULTURE	MANUFACTURING	HOUSEHOLD FINAL CONSUMPTIONS	GROSS TOTALS
AGRICULTURE		400	200	600
MANUFACTURING	200		600	800
HOUSEHOLD LABOR AND OTHER FACTORS	400	400	—	
GROSS TOTALS	600	800		1,400

All numbers in billions.

TABLE 37-2. Each industry appears twice, in a row and column: its row lists allocation of its total gross output as inputs for other industries and for final consumption; its column shows inputs needed to produce it.

The blue numbers show *gross* outputs, inclusive of amounts needed as intermediate inputs. To compute NNP without double counting, we add only the factor payments (or "value added") of the shaded row; or alternatively, only the final-consumption flows of the shaded column. (Fill in the proper NNP in the indicated blank, and check it two ways.)

Using agriculture and manufacturing as sample industries, Table 37-2 gives an oversimplified illustration of the table comprising several hundred industries that the government and Leontief have prepared for the American economy. Here is its general idea. Each industry is listed twice: in a *row* as an *output;* in a *column* as a needed *input.* In addition, the final consumption of households is treated as an extra column and their *labor* (or other primary factors of production supplied by households) as an extra row. These household figures are the numbers that enter into national income or net national product and are on the shaded part of the table. (Actually Leontief also includes government, foreign trade, investment, and other details.)

The *gross* value of agricultural output is shown by the blue $600 (billion) twice: at its row's right as the sum of all the places where farm output went—$400 as input to manufacturing plus $200 directly consumed by households as food—and at its column's bottom as the sum of the $200 cost it paid for manufacturing inputs (chemical fertilizers, etc.) and the $400 cost it paid for labor input (and other household factors).

Give a similar interpretation of the $800 *gross* total for manufacturing.

stant. (Back in Chapter 27's Appendix, page 532, we found reason to doubt that such an engineering assumption can be strictly realistic; but Leontief's clever statistical use of the fixed-coefficient case deserves notice here.)

The table also shows our old friend national income, or NNP. With no government or investment in the picture, NNP of 800 (billion) equals the sum of the third shaded column's final products; or alternatively NNP equals the sum of all factor-cost or values added shown in the shaded third row's wages. (NNP definitely does not include the intermediate purchases of one sector from another; the total in blue of $1,400 unquestionably involves double counting.)

This input-output table is more than a record of past history. How does Leontief or a planner hope to use it? *He hopes to use it to forecast the effects of changing consumption requirements.*

Thus, suppose Table 37-2 refers to a current cold-war situation where manufacturing employment and output have been swollen by military needs. (For dramatic effect we may think of peacetime goods, or "butter," as coming largely from the agricultural sector and military goods, or "guns," as coming largely from the manufacturing sector.)

Now suppose "peace breaks out." What will have to be planned for the new deployment of labor and other inputs if full employment is still to be maintained? Suppose we now want to double agriculture's final consumption, from the old brown $200 to new $400, also cutting the military manufacturing sector back from $600 to $400. Assuming fixed input-output coefficients, Leontief can solve linear equations for the new peacetime state and show that it *must* then be in the configuration given in

Input-output tableau helps a nation plan:

PEACETIME INPUT-OUTPUT FLOWS			HOUSEHOLD FINAL CONSUMPTIONS	GROSS TOTALS
	AGRICULTURE	MANUFACTURING		
AGRICULTURE		320	400	720
MANUFACTURING	240		400	640
HOUSEHOLD LABOR AND OTHER FACTORS	480	320	800	
GROSS TOTALS	720	640		1,360

All numbers in billions.

TABLE 37-3. End of cold war causes shift from guns to butter: agricultural final consumption goes up by 200 billion dollars, manufacturing down by same. Using fixed input-output coefficients from Table 37-2, Leontief calculates needed change in gross outputs shown here and resulting needed labor shifts and intermediate input changes. Same techniques help in development planning.

Table 37-3. Ten per cent of the workers (i.e., $^{80}/_{800}$) must be shifted from war work to peace work. Simi-

larly Leontief's tableau scheme can help plan for any development change in final-consumption goods.[16]

[16]All details aside, his key assumption is that $^{200}/_{600} = \frac{1}{3}$ of agriculture receipts will always be spent on manufacturing input, with the remaining $^{400}/_{600} = \frac{2}{3}$ always spent on labor input. Similarly, $^{400}/_{800} = \frac{1}{2}$ is the fraction that manufacturing will always spend on its needed agricultural input, the remainder $\frac{1}{2}$ being spent on needed labor input.

$$
\begin{array}{cc}
0 & 400 \\
200 & 0 \\
\hline
400 & 400 \\
\hline
600 & 800
\end{array}
\quad \rightarrow \quad
\begin{array}{cc}
0 & \frac{1}{2} \\
\frac{1}{3} & 0 \\
\frac{2}{3} & \frac{1}{2} \\
\hline
1 & 1
\end{array}
$$

Table 37-2 is repeated here in abbreviated form to show how one derives the gold fixed input-output coefficients needed for the transition to Table 37-3 or to any other situation envisaged by the planner. Now, if we call *gross outputs* of the two sectors X_A and X_M and their *final-consumption* amounts C_A and C_M, Leontief must finally allocate the total Xs thus:

$$X_A = C_A + \frac{1}{2} X_M \qquad X_M = C_M + \frac{1}{3} X_A$$

For the peacetime tableau of Table 37-3, this means

$$X_A = 400 + \frac{1}{2} X_M \qquad X_M = 400 + \frac{1}{3} X_A$$

These can be solved simultaneously by simple algebra to give $X_A = 720$, $X_M = 640$, from which all of Table 37-3 can be filled in using the gold fractions. Thus, we get the industries' labor requirements:

$$L_A = \frac{2}{3} X_A = 480 \qquad L_M = \frac{1}{2} X_M = 320$$

REMARK: To avoid simultaneous equations, Leontief can use a "multiplier" method. Each manufacture requires $\frac{1}{2}$ of agriculture as input, and each of these in turn requires $\frac{1}{3}$ of manufacture as its input; so *indirectly* each manufacture requires $\frac{1}{2} \times \frac{1}{3} = \frac{1}{6}$ of extra manufactures to produce itself. So $[1 + \frac{1}{6} + (\frac{1}{6})^2 + \ldots]$ adds up to 1.2, which is the needed expansion of new *gross* manufacture for each 1.0 expansion of *consumption* manufacture. Similarly, Leontief can calculate a multiplier for agriculture, showing how each billion-dollar change in its final consumption requires its *own* gross output to go up (coincidentally!) by 1.2 billion dollars. To compute what the shift of 200 billion dollars from guns to butter entails, Leontief must know how much gross agriculture and how much labor is needed to accommodate the 1.2 of manufacture that its own consumption expansion generated. The answer is not hard: The second column's gold manufacturing input requirements give the answers—$\frac{1}{2}$ of 1.2, or .6 in both cases. The reader should now be able to verify that when 1 new agriculture consumption entails 1.2 of its *own* gross output, the amounts needed for manufacturing and labor are $\frac{1}{3}(1.2) = .4$ and $\frac{2}{3}(1.2) = .8$. Given the knowledge of this paragraph's gold "own multipliers" and "cross multipliers" —the so-called "inverse matrix"—we perceive how Leontief is able to apply them to the $+200$ consumption shift to agriculture and -200 shift from manufacturing to get the changes needed to convert war Table 37-2 to peace Table 37-3.

SUMMARY TO APPENDIX

1 Schumpeter's stress on innovation, followed by competitive erosion of profit, is an important process of economic development.

2   If the capital-output ratio is an inflexible constant, neoclassical deepening of capital cannot be engineered by expansionist monetary policy.

3   The Harrod-Domar concept of the "natural rate of growth" g is determined by population growth and technical change. If K and Q are to grow at this balanced rate, the required fraction of income that has to be voluntarily saved is given by the Harrod condition,

$$s = g(K/Q)$$

4   The warranted rate of growth W will be higher than the natural rate g if the actual desired saving ratio S/Q exceeds the s needed by Harrod's condition. In the case where K/Q is constant for previous and for new changes,

$$W = \frac{S/Q}{K/Q}$$

If this W rate persisted, it would be self-warranting in the sense of coaxing out investment just large enough to match desired saving.

It will not come of its own accord or be stable against upward or downward disturbances. When $W > g$, a self-warranting expansion from a low trough would ultimately bump into the ceiling set by population and other bottlenecks, possibly bouncing back into recession.

A stubborn divergence of W from g could be controlled by budget surpluses or deficits, which augmented (or subtracted from) private saving enough to keep $W = g$, and which by a steadying hand would overcome Harrodian instability of income growth.

5   Where a neoclassical deepening of capital makes the K/Q ratio an accommodating variable, the Harrod conditions lose their terrors. Whatever people's thrift wants to make their private full-employment s be, a combination of monetary and fiscal policies can hope to induce the needed offsetting investment. Such fiscal and monetary policies can speed up capital formation and the technical changes embodied in, and stemming from, such new equipment. They can help the system grow faster than the natural growth of working population. They can stabilize the achievable rate of progress so that the system will be warranted in doing what comes naturally. But, even in a flexible neoclassical technology, laissez faire will not—in the absence of appropriate public monetary and fiscal policies—be led by an Invisible Hand to these ideal conditions.

6   The neoclassical model can parcel out the sources of Q growth into growth from more L, from more K, and from technical change. The last factor interacts with L through education and training and with K through embodiment in new machines. Still, technical change seems to have been historically primary in advanced nations.

7   Robinson and Kaldor agree in their suspicion of aggregates of so-called "capital" and in their doubts about smooth deepening of capital under capitalism; both look to factors of dynamic growth for determination of profit shares. (All this is still controversial.)

8   It is intellectually unsatisfying to explain some constancy trends by appeal to "coincidence" or to fortuitous canceling out of diverse tendencies of diminishing returns and technical change. So one can applaud the attempts to find mechanisms (induced invention, lifetime saving, etc.) that bring the constancies about. However, if like the present writer, you would not be much surprised to see K/Q fall in the future or drift in either direction, the wage share gradually rise, or the rate of profit sag or soar, you must beware of "overexplanations." If a thing may actually be a coincidence, you are not saying much by calling it that. But to *explain away* a coincidence which truly *is only* a coincidence, is worse than a banality; it is a scientific sin.

9   Leontief's tableau of interindustry flows gives a useful picture of the relations lying behind aggregate NNP data. By positing fixed input-output coefficients, a planner can use the

Leontief technique to program a shift from a war pattern of consumption to a peace pattern, or to achieve any other developmental target goal.

QUESTIONS FOR DISCUSSION

1 Contrast unemployment notions of Keynes with those of Schumpeter and Ricardo.

2 Why is g important for long trends? W for business cycles? Reread Chapter 14's acceleration principle.

3 Explain to yourself the basic idea of the two-way Leontief tableau.

Review your understanding of the following concepts:

innovation and deepening of capital
fixed versus variable K/Q ratio
natural versus warranted growth
$s = g(K/Q)$, $W = (S/Q)/(K/Q)$

% Q growth = % L growth + . . .
% Q/L growth = % K/L growth + t.c.
von Neumann model with $i = g$
input-output tableau

Problems of Economic Growth and Development

38

All the economic principles we have learned can now be brought to bear on perhaps one of the most challenging problems of the next quarter-century—the problem of underdeveloped economies.[1] There are about 4 billion people in the world, and at this moment half of them are hungry—literally hungry. Only someone who has been pursuing beauty or health on a temporary diet of less than 1,500 calories per day will know how food can fill one's dreams and every waking thought.

For conscience's sake, we are impelled to help. Besides, history teaches us that men do not always starve quietly.

DEFINING UNDERDEVELOPMENT

Writers used to speak of "backward" nations, which naturally irritated the people of those lands. To avoid offense the United Nations sometimes uses the roundabout expression "developing" nation. Today most people adopt the expression "underdeveloped" nation. What is meant by the term? Alternative definitions are given; most seem to involve the following:

An underdeveloped nation is simply one with real per capita income that is low relative to the present-day per capita incomes of such nations as Canada, the United States, Great Britain, and Western Europe generally. Optimistically, an underdeveloped nation is one regarded as being capable of substantial improvement in its income level.

Of course, every country is underdeveloped in the sense that it is not yet perfect and hence is capable of being

---

[1] Three useful anthologies on this subject are Theodore Morgan, George W. Betz, and N. K. Choudhry, *Readings in Economic Development* (Wadsworth Publishing Company, Belmont, Calif., 1963), A. N. Agarwala and S. P. Singh, *The Economics of Underdevelopment* (Oxford University Press, Fair Lawn, N.J., 1960), Bernard Okun and Richard W. Richardson, *Studies in Economic Development* (Holt, New York, 1961.)

Most countries fall in the underdeveloped category:

COUNTRIES GROUPED BY LEVEL OF ECONOMIC DEVELOPMENT

A. Highly developed
Australia
Belgium
Canada
Czechoslovakia
Denmark
Finland
France
Germany
Israel
Japan
Kuwait
Netherlands
New Zealand
Norway
Sweden
Switzerland
U.S.S.R.
United Kingdom
United States

B. Intermediate
Argentina
Austria
Bulgaria
Chile
Costa Rica
Cuba
Greece
Hungary
Ireland
Italy
Jamaica
Lebanon
Libya
Mexico
Panama
Poland
Portugal
Puerto Rico
Republic of South Africa
Rumania

Singapore
Spain
Uruguay
Venezuela
Yugoslavia

C. Underdeveloped
Africa:
Algeria
Angola
Cameroon
Chad
Congo
Dahomey
Ethiopia
Ghana
Guinea
Ivory Coast
Kenya
Liberia
Malagasy Republic
Malawi
Mali
Morocco
Mozambique
Niger
Nigeria
Rhodesia
Rwanda
Senegal
Sierra Leone
Sudan
Tanzania
Togo
Tunisia
Uganda
United Arab Republic
Upper Volta
Zambia

Americas:
Bolivia

Americas (continued):
Brazil
British West Indies
Colombia
Dominican Republic
Ecuador
El Salvador
Guatemala
Haiti
Honduras
Nicaragua
Paraguay
Peru

Asia:
Afghanistan
Burma
Cambodia
Ceylon
China
Formosa
India
Indonesia
Iran
Iraq
Jordan
Laos
Malaysia
Nepal
North Korea
Pakistan
Philippines
Saudi Arabia
South Korea
Syria
Thailand
Turkey
Vietnam
Yemen

Europe:
Albania

TABLE 38-1. (Sources: United Nations Statistical Office; Center for International Studies, MIT.)

improved still further. Even the so-called "advanced" countries were once underdeveloped by our definition and had to go through the process of development. Table 38-1 gives a picture of the relative stages of development of different countries.

About one-fifth of the world's population live in the highly developed group A with more than $1,500 per capita; just over one-eighth live in the intermediate group B; about two-thirds live in the underdeveloped group C.

About one-third of the world's population live behind the Iron Curtain. The Soviet Union and Czechoslovakia now fall in the highly developed group A; but just barely. As for the rest of the communist countries, how are their people divided among the groups? Recalling the vast population of China, we are not surprised to find two-thirds of the Iron Curtain peoples falling in the lowest group C. Little wonder, then, that economic development is a lively subject everywhere, in the East as well as in the West.

CHARACTERISTICS OF UNDERDEVELOPED ECONOMIES

To bring out the contrasts between advanced and underdeveloped economies, imagine that you are a typical twenty-one-year-old in one of the underdeveloped countries, be it Haiti, India, or Nigeria.

You are poor: even after making generous allowance for the goods that you both produce and consume, your annual income averages barely $100 per head, as against $3,500 per head of your fellow man in North America; perhaps you can find cold comfort in the thought that only 1 in 8 of the human race averages more than $1,200 per year. To each of your people who can read, there are three like you who are illiterate. Your life expectancy is only two-thirds that of the average man in the advanced country: already one or two of your brothers and sisters have died before reaching adulthood; and though your mother has had fewer children than your grandmother did, more of your brothers and sisters have lived to maturity, thanks to imported medical techniques—and you must compete with them for subsistence.

Most of your countrymen work on rural farms; few can be spared from food production for factories or service trades. You work with but one-sixtieth the horsepower of your prosperous North American fellow man. You know little of science, but much of folklore. Your methods and tools are primitive. Neither the discipline of markets nor the deliberations of planning commissions mean much to you. As a citizen in Asia, Africa, or Latin America, you and your fellows together constitute 70 per cent of the world population, but you must divide among you only 20 per cent of world income. You brood over the fact that the United States, with 6 per cent of the people, enjoys about 33 per cent of world income; and that Western Europe, with 10 per cent of the people, enjoys 25 per cent of world income.

URGENCY OF THE PROBLEM

There have always been differences between rich and poor. Why worry especially about the underdeveloped countries? Here are some reasons:

Differentials of nations' living standards are great and still growing:

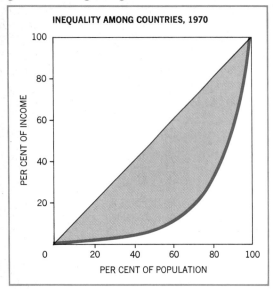

INEQUALITY AMONG COUNTRIES, 1970

PER CENT OF INCOME

PER CENT OF POPULATION

FIG. 38-1.   The poorest half of the nations receive only 8 per cent of the total income. The richest 6 per cent (and guess who that is) receive one-third of the total. Contrast this degree of nation inequality with the Lorenz charts of Chapter 6 depicting intranation inequality. (Source: Center for International Studies, MIT.)

Widening differentials   In contrast to the narrowing of income differentials within the advanced nations, the divergence between advanced and underdeveloped countries is probably now widening rather than narrowing. The United States and Western Europe have doubled their production per head since 1940. Many experts believe that living standards in India, Indonesia, and certain underdeveloped countries have improved little since then and may even have deteriorated in some regions.

Figure 38-1 shows how unequal is the geographical distribution of real incomes. Contrast this Lorenz curve of inequality among nations with Figs. 6-2, 6-3, 6-4, and 9-1, which show less glaring inequality within a country.

Ideological struggle   In the modern ideological war between the free and the communist worlds, both sides regard the underdeveloped regions as being torn between following the pattern of the mixed economy or following the pattern of socialism. Revolutionaries ceaselessly agitate in such lands, never failing to point out the poverty there, never failing to contrast it with our wealth, never failing to remind the people there of real and fancied evils of "colonialism." Cuba is a nearby example. Africa, Latin America, and Asia are cases in point.

Experience does not bear out the easy generalization, "Fill the stomachs of people, and they will refrain from going communistic." Men in utter misery often seem incapable of revolting; and the great revolutions of the past (such as the French and Russian) have often taken place at a time when some economic progress had already been achieved.

Nonetheless, to turn our backs on the problem of development is to court future disaster. Harvard's distinguished economic historian Alexander Gerschenkron has drawn the following important lesson from history:[2]

The Soviet government can be properly described as a product of the country's economic backwardness. Had serfdom been abolished by Catherine the Great or . . . in 1825, the peasant discontent, the driving force and the earnest of success of the Russian Revolution, would never have assumed disastrous proportions, while the economic development of the country would have proceeded in a much more gradual fashion. . . . The delayed industrial revolution was responsible for a political revolution in the course of which the power fell in the hands of a dictatorial government to which in the long run the vast majority of the population was opposed. . . . The paramount lesson of the twentieth century is that the problems of backward nations are not exclusively their own. They are just as much problems of the advanced countries. It is not only Russia but the whole world that pays the price for the failure to emancipate the Russian peasants

[2] Alexander Gerschenkron, *Economic Backwardness in Historical Perspective*, (The Belknap Press, Harvard University Press, Cambridge, Mass., 1962), pp. 28–30.

and to embark upon industrialization policies at an early time. Advanced countries cannot afford to ignore economic backwardness.

To reinforce this, tick off the advanced countries in Table 38-1. You cannot find a single one that had a successful proletarian revolution when its economy was strong.

Great expectations and "demonstration effects"   Within the underdeveloped countries, people are today acutely aware of their poverty and its contrasts with rich lands. They do not like it. What is more, they insist on doing something about it.

This was not always so: a century ago the Emperor of China sent a message to the Queen of England saying that his country neither needed nor desired economic improvement. Look at today's frantic efforts in China and mark the contrast. In the ancient formula,

$$\text{Happiness} = \frac{\text{material consumption}}{\text{desire}}$$

Thoreau's counsel to hold down the denominator now gives way to insistence on increasing the numerator of material real income.[3]

So nearly perfect are modern instruments of communication that people everywhere know about—and often envy—the comforts of modern Western life. No longer do they shrug their shoulders and accept their relative poverty as the divine will of Allah. Most important, this increased awareness comes at a time when the role of government is highly developed.

Today, when people want something done, they are likely to turn to government and to insist that programs be adopted toward the desired goal. They want to foreshorten history and get now what developed lands got late.

They want better health; land reform, the breaking up of landowners' holdings; better methods of land cultivation; industrialization; political rights as individuals. It is easy to see that men want these things for natural individualistic reasons. But economic welfare is not the only reason why men desire development. Modern peoples desire development also for reasons of *nationalism:* people want their country to be powerful, to be respected, and—let us face it—to be feared. Thus, the English and Dutch may have brought sanitation to their former colonies; they may have thereby increased people's life-spans and material well-being. But they did at the same time set up exclusive clubs whose front doors were barred to the native citizenry. "Freedom from contempt" is one Asian's way of describing his goal.

SUPERFICIAL THEORIES OF DEVELOPMENT

Geography   A look at Table 38-1 shows that all the advanced countries are in the temperate zones. Every tropical country is a poor one. Hence, the argument used to go, it is all a matter of *climate*.

[3] In affluent America or Sweden, particularly among high-income college students, there is a discernible trend away from materialism.

This sweeping explanation will not fit the facts. The first civilizations were in regions of the Mediterranean and Near East (or, if you will, in the Mayan regions of Central America). Greece was in her glory when Germans and Saxons were hunting wild boar.

Certainly, climate is an important factor, but it is not all-important. It does help not to have tropical heat and erosion from jungle floods. It does help not to have arctic snows. But one of the consequences of modern technology is that fevers can be checked by DDT. The bitter Oslo or Oxford cold can be offset by heating; and the humid heat of Texas need no longer inhibit the pace of body and mind.

The geographical distribution of *natural resources*—topsoil, rainfall, dammable water for irrigation and power, oil and ore deposits—is important. But in a world where trade is increasingly possible, grave deficiencies in this respect can be at least partially offset, as the examples of Denmark, Japan, Rhode Island, and Israel have shown.

Race[4] Throw a stone in the advanced countries and the skin you bruise is likely to be white. *Ergo*, the tale ran, prosperity is merely a matter of race.

No one has yet been able to find a causal link between a tendency toward albinism and productivity; the pioneers of Egyptian, Greek, Indian, and Roman cultures were generally not blond or tall. The most remarkable phenomenon of economic development in this last century and in this last decade has undoubtedly been the Japanese. Anthropologists cannot agree completely on how to classify *Homo sapiens* into Mongolian, Caucasian, and other categories.

A glance at history—at the Ethiopian and Berber cultures, at ancient China, primitive northwestern Europe, and flowering Near Eastern cultures—reveals that many factors have been dominant, and that the factor of race itself cannot be isolated as a discernible determinant of economic development.

Custom and culture Victoria's England or Coolidge's America came as close as any culture ever has to being a business culture. In the 1920s a biography of Jesus in terms of accounting virtues could be a best-seller. Hence, some have leaped to the theory that people must behave like the *Homo economicus* of the classical textbooks if a nation is to prosper.

This is a caricature. It provides a truth, and hides a more important truth.

Material progress does depend on replacement of a belief in magic and superstition by discernment of and belief in the cause-and-effect relations of engineering and science. If it is a nation's tradition to abhor manual work or work in general; if its people emphasize the hereafter as against this world; if they despise material prosperity; if they discourage ordinary honesty in contractual dealings with strangers; if their way of life puts a great premium on current consumption rather than provision for the future; if their government officials are corrupt and inefficient—all such cultural traits are not particularly conducive to economic development.

But putting stress on these noneconomic factors does not solve the problem of *explanation*. It poses new problems. Why did the brains that might have gone into business in

---

[4] See Chapter 40 for a deeper analysis of the economics of racial discrimination.

many countries go into science? Why did the anthropologists who stressed the unchangeable inertia of custom in Mexico go wrong in their predictions that penetration of the money psychology would be slow there?

We must not throw away seminal explanations merely because they turn out to be superficial and even wrong. But we must not overlook their superficialities and errors. Max Weber's celebrated emphasis on the "Protestant ethic" as both cause and effect of capitalistic development is a case in point. It did fit some facts: many of the advanced nations are Protestant. John Calvin and *some* Protestant theologians did break away from the Catholic Church's ancient edicts against interest. John D. Rockefeller, Sr., was both an avaricious profit maximizer and an ardent Baptist, who referred to his gains as "God's gold." Yet the "buts" that have to be applied to the Weber thesis are many and serious.

Northern Italy and Catholic Rhineland showed early development. You can find in eighteenth-century Japanese writings perfect passages of Weberian Protestantism. Jews, Chinese, and Basques have in many places played the role of the alienated stranger who pioneers in economic entrepreneurship. And if Weber seriously regards Benjamin Franklin—a prototype of the scientist, innovator, and business go-getter—as an other-worldly Protestant, biographers of that cynical deist tell us the name has almost lost its meaning. Modern statistical research on the Protestant and Catholic neighborhoods in German cities, upon which Weber originally rested part of his case, has found that correct statistical tabulation even belies Weber's own findings.

Whether or not Weber in some subtle sense was right, think how badly a crude belief in his theory would have served for prediction 20 years ago: The economies that have shown the greatest miracles of growth since 1950 have been Japan, Formosa, Thailand, Catholic France and Italy, largely Catholic West Germany, Israel, Austria, and atheistical Russia. Such predominantly Protestant countries as Canada, Britain, and the United States have done poorly in comparison.

All this proves nothing, because there is almost nothing to be proved.

RECENT CONCEPTS TO DESCRIBE DEVELOPMENT

For three decades economists have been intensely interested in economic development. While they have developed no unified theory that differs from the basic growth models introduced in the last chapter, they have added some special features to these models.

The following brief account represents a montage of the most important notions developed in the recent literature. It will pave the way for a systematic causal analysis in terms of the economic determinants of production: land and natural resources; labor (in quantity of man-hours and in quality of skills, training, and effort); capital formation; and finally, technological knowledge and innovation. The chapter ends with a brief discussion of modern development planning.

Preconditions for growth   Human history is long, and economic development is exceptional, being primarily the outcome of the last few centuries of Western history. During most of history, life was short, nasty, and brutish. A cruel Malthusian equilibrium prevailed in which deaths kept in balance with births.

In a few lucky places, warfare diminished. Superior production methods were applied to ample resources. A surplus over subsistence became possible. And usually wealth was so unequally divided among the aristocratic landowners and the bulk of the populace that the rich were able to abstain from consumption and to funnel savings into capital formation. Economic development could now take place.

The take-off   The more historians study the facts, the more gradual and evolutionary seems the process of growth. But revolution is always better drama and journalism than evolution is. So various economists like to use words such as "the take-off," "the spurt," and "the big push" to describe the period of accelerating growth. Thus, W. W. Rostow[5] develops stages of growth different from those of Marx and other writers described in the previous chapter. One of his stages is called the take-off, the obvious analogy being with an airplane, which can get off the ground only after it has attained a certain critical speed.

There is no purpose here in joining in the search to find out when each country had its take-off; England in the eighteenth century, Japan in the late nineteenth, the Congo in the 1990s. Nor shall we divide a country's development in stages as Shakespeare divides a man's life into various ages. Instead, we abandon strict chronology to stress the important economic *principles* that the take-off serves to dramatize.

Increasing returns, social overhead capital, and externalities   The last chapter's models of production proceeded for the most part in terms of the conventional economic principle of diminishing returns—referring to statical variations in labor applied to relatively fixed land, or to variations in the stock of capital goods applied to less rapidly expanding labor supply. Such a conventional model of production assumed that doubling all the factors together would, typically, exactly double total product—a principle referred to as "constant returns to scale" and serving as a background to the law of diminishing returns to a varying factor.

In dynamic economic development, however, the phenomenon of "*increasing* returns" is to be expected. Smith's *The Wealth of Nations* was in its day a manual of economic development: not for nothing did he encourage honesty and thrift. Smith stressed the advantage of *large-scale division of labor*. It is a case of the whole being bigger than the sum of its parts: if all factors together can be increased in size, product will grow *more* than proportionally. Each primitive region cannot develop the scale to achieve efficiency. A pile of enriched uranium suddenly goes active when it achieves a certain size. Similarly, the phenomenon of increasing returns can make it possible for dramatic spurts and accelerations to occur in economic development. (As we saw in Part Three, important areas of increasing returns cannot be left to the free play of competitive market forces; there is a case here for coordination, to prevent monopoly and to channel it into optimal patterns.)

MIT's Paul Rosenstein-Rodan introduced, three decades ago, an important related phenomenon. He spoke of the crucial importance of "social overhead capital." To develop, a private economy must have public roads, a railroad, irrigation projects and dams, public health spraying against malarial mosquitoes. All these involve bulky *indivisibilities* of the increasing-returns type. No small firm or family can profitably undertake them; nor can pioneering private enterprise hope to make a profit from them before the markets have been developed. They spread their benefits *socially*. Hence, it is argued, public,

---

[5] W. W. Rostow, *The Stages of Economic Growth: A Non-Communist Manifesto* (Cambridge University Press, New York, 1960). See Paul A. Samuelson, *Readings in Economics* (McGraw-Hill, New York, 1970, 6th ed.), for a strong critique of the Rostow theses by Simon Kuznets.

as well as private, responsibility is intrinsically involved in economic development from the beginning.

Another way of putting this, as in Chapter 8 and the Appendix of Chapter 23, is thus:

Often there are strong *"external* economies" involved in development. A county agent adviser can simultaneously benefit all the farmers in his region. A railroad can benefit all industry. A multiple-purpose dam has similar externalities. It should be obvious that one can find examples of externalities that do not involve increasing returns, and examples of increasing returns that are unrelated to social overhead capital or externalities. But it should be evident that there is often a strong interrelationship between these three notions—externalities, increasing returns, social overhead capital—which makes them worth being lumped together.

BALANCED GROWTH AND INDUSTRIALIZATION

In the development literature, there has often been a fascination with *balanced* growth. One would not want the skull to grow more rapidly than the skin of one's head. It is similarly argued that growth in a shoe factory should be accompanied by growth in a stocking factory and in a brewery, if what people want at a higher standard of living is shoes, socks, and beer.

For the world as a whole, the budgetary laws of Engel (which were reviewed on page 197) will impose some limited balance on consumption growth. Food will grow, but it will not keep pace with luxury items. Indeed, despite the emphasis on balanced growth, Colin Clark and other writers have long noted an apparent tendency for development to proceed in three stages; *agricultural* dominance first; then *manufacturing* dominance; and finally, as we all become affluent, a shift toward *services*. Supply and demand created these patterns in the old days of relatively free enterprise.

Is balanced growth inevitable or desirable for one region undergoing development? History suggests a negative answer:

America first developed by *specializing* in agricultural exports. Belgium early developed by specializing in glass and woolen production. The whole theory of comparative advantage, presented in Chapters 34 and 35, suggested that growth within a region does *not* best take place in balance.

This does remind us of an important issue, discussed on page 677, as to whether there is not an "infant-industry" and "young-economy" argument that can validly be used to criticize extreme specialization of a country along a few vulnerable lines of comparative advantage. If coffee demand and supply are volatile, and if *future* comparative advantage may lie in certain manufactures, a country like Brazil may be well advised to interfere with the market tendency to specialize in coffee production. But prudent diversification and truly balanced growth are by no means the same.

Industrialization versus agriculture   New Zealand, Denmark, Holland, Iowa, and Argentina are all regions where productivity in agriculture does not compare too unfavorably with productivity in industry. They are the exceptions. In most places, incomes in urban cities are almost double those in rural agriculture. And in the affluent nations large fractions of total resources are devoted to urban manufacture. Hence, many nations jump to the conclusion that industrialization is the *cause* rather than an *effect* of affluence.

One must be wary of making such an inference. As the saying goes, "Rich men smoke expensive cigars; but going out to buy an expensive cigar will not make you rich." Vanity seems to make each country want (1) an airline and (2) a steel mill. Analysis of present and future comparative advantage suggests that for most nations these are ornamental luxuries.

It simply is not true that the greatest productivity advances of the last century have been in industry rather than agriculture. (Recall Chapter 21's discussion of agriculture.) If India's five-year plan could increase the productivity of farming by 20 per cent, that would do more to release resources for production of comforts than would exclusive reliance on promoting industry.

The points made here are obvious. Yet they are often overlooked in political debate. But before leaving the subject, we should point to the germ of truth in the argument for pushing industrialization in order to speed development.

City and factory life tend to break up the cake of custom. People in close contact mutually stimulate each other. Hence, technical change is probably stimulated in the long run by subsidy to industrialization. Fortunately, there is often much "disguised unemployment" in rural areas, in the sense that several adult members of each family could move to the city or turn during off-harvest times to local industrial occupations without causing much loss of farm product.

CAPITAL NEEDS AND EFFICIENT RESOURCE ALLOCATION

To break out of a vicious circle of poverty and underdevelopment, capital formation is needed. But starving peasants cannot be expected to take much thought of the future. In past ages inequality of landownership probably helped solve the problem of social thrift, but in a ruthless way. Collectivist economies like China and Russia can by fiat impose the same ruthless abstention from current consumption.

Why cannot free economies do the same? Why cannot they use the fiscal measures discussed throughout this book to curb consumption and stimulate investment? An important reason lies in the realm of political science. Some of the developed countries are able to impose progressive income taxes and find that the taxes do get paid. In much of the world, this is probably not possible. Tax administration is primitive and inefficient. People simply will not cooperate. The problem is made worse where poverty is so great that public officials become corrupt.

As a substitute for taxation and coercion, many writers (such as Harvey Leibenstein) recommend that projects be favored which will produce incomes *for corporations and groups that can be counted on to do heavy investment.* They argue that this emphasis should be given even in some cases where there is an actual loss in current efficiency.

Planning, with or without resource pricing After 1930 Soviet Russia established a first, second, and third Five-Year Plan. Most nations today, including those neutral between East and West, have similar development plans. These set up quantitative goals. Alternative goals are scrutinized for their realism and compatibility. Comparisons are made, and finally a compromise set of aggregate targets is worked out.

These targets may be specified in general terms or in quite detailed terms. Thus, India will take into account her growth in labor force; her growth in capital resources from internal sources; the amount of capital she can import from America or the Soviet Union. She will canvass her need for dams and electric power; for fertilizer, steel mills, and machinery; etc. In the end a system of priorities will have to be worked out lest the demands on the system become so great as to produce galloping inflation, or as to produce so much expenditure on imports that the country will run out of foreign exchange and have to either devalue or ration severely by a system of austere import licensing.

Much of this planning will be in concrete physical terms. But much more has to be expressed in terms of rupees of *value*. More importantly, the planners will often find that the values quoted in the market place do not correspond to true national scarcities. Thus, in India people would starve if they were paid a zero wage; yet for many purposes labor is superabundant and ought to be regarded as almost a free factor of production. Capital goods, on the other hand, are truly scarce; charging fifty times as much for use of a tractor as for use of a man may be needed to do justice to the tractor's scarcity and superior productivity. Hence, some sophisticated planners (such as Jan Tinbergen, the noted Dutch economist and Nobel laureate) advocate applying corrected "shadow prices," or "accounting prices," to labor, capital, and imported goods for the purpose of getting a more rational valuation and allocation of scarce resources. That way growth can be maximized.

Capital-output ratios and screening of investment projects Poor countries are long on labor, short on capital. They are advised, therefore, to economize on the use of heavily durable and intensely roundabout capital projects. Often they are advised to concentrate as much as they can on activities that have a low "capital-output ratio." This advice is good. But it would be more accurate if expressed in terms of the investment concepts developed in Part Four. Each project should have calculated for it a percentage rate of return per annum: then a hydroelectric project that yields 20 per cent per annum ought to get done before a short-lived steam project that yields only 5 per cent per year—even if, to the superficial eye, the capital-output ratio of the steam plant seems smaller.[6]

We have described the general problem of underdevelopment, and surveyed the concepts used in this field. Now we can turn to the constructive task of analyzing in detail the four economic fundamentals: (1) population, (2) natural resources, (3) capital formation, and (4) technology.

POPULATION PROBLEMS

Mere growth in numbers does not necessarily mean development. Indeed, as writers since Malthus have warned, unbridled increase in numbers is likely to invoke the law of

[6]When experts shift from the capital-output ratio to the "marginal capital-output ratio," they can come out with the economists' correct yield procedures. Also, if capital will be less scarce 20 years from now—so that the correct interest rate society ought to use for its projects is 30 per cent this decade and 18 per cent next decade—a proper planning calculation will take this into account.

diminishing returns and to work against increases in per capita living standards. This can create problems. Thus we find many underdeveloped countries repeating the pattern of the eighteenth- and nineteenth-century economies: improved medical technology (e.g., sanitation and in our day cheap insecticides) first reduces the death rate; and with birth rates remaining high, population grows rapidly.

El Salvador, Java, and many other examples underline the twin lessons:

First, much of the increase in output made possible by technological advance may be spent on duplication of numbers.

Second, modern science, conquering disease faster than it promotes the food supply, may in the future keep people from dying from germs—only to threaten them with death from famine as they vie for insufficient food.

The grave question being asked by demographers is this:

Will birth rates fall in developing countries as they did in older countries? And before living standards actually deteriorate?

Improving human resources Since labor is an important factor of production, there is much constructive programming to be done in the manpower area. When planners draw up blueprints for hastening economic development, they write down the following specific manpower programs:

1. Control disease and push health and nutrition programs—both to make people happier and to make them more productive workers. Accordingly, do not look on hospitals and sewerage projects as luxuries but as vitally needed social overhead capital.

2. Educated people make more productive workers. Therefore budget for schools and other programs to reduce illiteracy. Beyond reading and writing, train people in new techniques of agriculture and industry. Send your best minds abroad to bring back knowledge of engineering and business. (But beware that they do not get drained off to the advanced nations!)

Disguised unemployment One important condition for promoting development is the better utilization of manpower. In poor countries, particularly rural ones, often a large part of the manpower pool does almost nothing because there is nothing for it to do. Such people may not be counted in the census of unemployment, but they can scarcely be called employed; they live with their kinfolk, and when a boom or a development plan comes along, sweeping them into productive city jobs, there is almost no reduction in the product back on the farm. The same phenomenon of disguised unemployment is met in advanced countries, both in the subsistence farming regions and in the city streets, where men eke out a bare existence doing door-to-door selling or begging and hustling whenever productive jobs are unavailable.

For a satisfactory solution to this underemployment and unemployment problem, governments sometimes find it desirable, along with manpower programs, to pursue expansionary fiscal and monetary policies like those in the advanced countries—even though these methods raise problems of inflation and of deficits in the balance of international payments.

NATURAL RESOURCES

Poor countries typically have been poorly endowed by nature, and such land and minerals as they do possess must be divided among dense populations. The romantic notion of overlooked geographical areas rich in resources has largely been exploded by geographers. Generally, people have *already* settled in the most productive regions.

True, geologists are still seeking and finding new hidden resources; and there are authenticated cases where control of malaria by DDT has reclaimed from the jungle hundreds of square miles of fertile Asian land. Balanced against these cheerful considerations is the fact that many underdeveloped countries are rapidly depleting their mines, their topsoil, and their irreplaceable natural resources.

Moreover, as was noted, many of the present-day resources of tropical countries are becoming obsolete in competition with scientific creation of *synthetic* substitutes from cheap substances found in abundance within the advanced countries. Thus nylon harmed the silk industry and impoverished millions; if synthetic rubber were to replace natural rubber completely, the Malaysian peninsula would find itself unable to maintain its standard of living, low as that is.

Economic geographers are agreed that further development must now largely come from discovery and better use of existing resources. Gone are the opportunities of a Columbus; and half-closing is the open door beckoning the poor of the older regions, begging them to migrate to the fertile prairies of North and South America or to the empty regions of Australia and New Zealand.

Of course, the quip still holds: "There's nothing wrong with any poor country that discovery of oil can't cure." The fact that primitive Kuwait falls, in Fig. 38-1, in the most prosperous category illustrates the point. Venezuela, Iraq, Saudi Arabia, Libya, Iran, Kuwait, and now Alaska, are cases where oil could help finance development.

Land reform Even without creating or finding new land, nations can make better use of the land they do have. The medieval village was divided into strips of land one could hardly turn around on, and each man might have to live off the produce of two or three such strips, frequently distant from each other. The same is still true in many parts of the world. It took from the thirteenth to the eighteenth century for the painful, and bitterly resented, *enclosure* movement in England to break up the common lands and to gather together into efficient larger-scale plots the land of the country. In the process many peasants were dispossessed and had to go to the city slums. The ruthless, and not altogether successful, "collectivization" of Russian agriculture in the 1920s provides an analogous case; China's collectivization program has encountered similar difficulties. The displacement of dust-bowl farmers during the 1930s by the tractor has been dramatically portrayed in John Steinbeck's best-seller *The Grapes of Wrath*. In many parts of the world, this same painful process of consolidating too small holdings is yet to be carried out.

At the other extreme, we see in many underdeveloped countries landholding of huge estates too large for efficiency. The tenant farmer has no incentive to improve the property, knowing that he can be dispossessed at any time and having learned from bitter experience that little of the fruit of his initiative will ever accrue to him. The landlord in turn has no incentive to improve the property, never knowing whether an irresponsible tenant will dissipate the costly resources placed at his disposal.[7]

As the Communists well know, the situation is explosive, and agitation for land reform signifies a ground swell of public sentiment not long to be denied. As more than one eminent agricultural economist has aptly said:

Successful reform that puts land in the hands of owners who can count on the fruits of their own enterprise has again and again and in country after country literally "turned sand into gold."

Anthropologists in Central America and elsewhere have noted to their surprise that peasant production management is often shrewd and rational, defying the inertia of custom and reacting to monetary incentives. And it is quite wrong to believe that tenant farming has never succeeded in making substantial productivity advance. So it is not all a one-sided story.

The problems of natural-resource development merge with the problem of improved technology and with the problem of improved capital-goods capacity for utilizing and discovering natural resources.

CAPITAL FORMATION

The fingers and brains of men in the underdeveloped countries are much like the fingers and brains of their more prosperous brethren; but men in the advanced nations work with a plentiful supply of capital goods built up over the years. To pile up net capital formation requires, as we have earlier seen, a sacrifice of current consumption. But there's the rub: underdeveloped countries are already so poor as to be near the minimum of subsistence; they feel that they cannot—in fact, they do not—save a very large share of their current national incomes.

Thus, in the advanced nations, from 10 to 20 per cent of income may go into capital formation; but in the underdeveloped nations, the rate of saving and investment may be less than 5 per cent.[8] Merely to provide for rapidly growing population, the primitive tools and housing now enjoyed can use up most of this saving. What is left, then, for development?

Until we learned how to prevent mass unemployment, many economists worried about *oversaving* **in** *advanced* **countries. But for** *underdeveloped* **countries the problem is often the classical one of** *undersaving:* **more precisely, the problem is the urgency of current consumption which competes for scarce resources—leading to underinvestment in productive instruments capable of increasing the nation's rate of economic progress.**

Qualitative distortion of investment   There is a further problem. Not only are saving and investment *quantitatively* low in these countries; equally serious is the fact that the

---

[7] We saw on page 544, Chapter 28, how inefficient systems of land tenancy can put society inside its production-possibility frontier.

[8] In countries going through civil disorders—like Malaya or the Congo—net saving could be negative. When the shackles of colonialism are first thrown off, a decline in income—happily temporary—often ensues.

qualitative composition of investment is often bad from the standpoint of national development. Thus, too much of the limited saving of India goes into hoarding of gold and jewelry, imported legally or illegally into the country and using up its scarce foreign exchange.

Many underdeveloped countries, like Brazil or Chile, suffer from chronic inflation; hence, there is a natural tendency for people to invest in real estate and in hoarding of inventory. When you can make 20 per cent on your money by hoarding goods, why seek an additional and problematical few per cent from manufacturing? Thus, no less than 55 per cent of Brazil's 1947 investment was in the form of construction. Observers are also struck with the fact that, in many of the poorest regions of the world, *luxury* apartment dwellings seem to mushroom, at the same time that industry is languishing for lack of new equipment.

Still another qualitative dissipation of the limited saving in an underdeveloped country comes from the frequent tendency of the wealthy to pile up their savings *abroad*, legally and illegally, thereby making them unavailable for internal development.

Capital from abroad   If there are so many obstacles to domestic-financed capital formation, why not rely more heavily on foreign sources? After all, did not England in the nineteenth century invest heavily in the United States, Canada, Australia, and Latin America? Did not France before 1914 invest heavily in Czarist Russia and Egypt? And did not Germany invest heavily in Eastern Europe? Does not economic theory tell us that a rich country which has used up all its own high-interest investment projects can benefit itself and at the same time benefit a poor country if only it will shift investment to the high-interest projects not yet exploited abroad?

Actually, prior to 1914 economic development did proceed in this natural fashion. Britain in her heyday saved about 15 per cent of her national income and invested fully half this amount abroad! If the United States were to match these percentages today, *every year* we should have to lend and invest privately abroad more than $100 billion, or many, many times the combined Marshall Plan and foreign-aid programs of the federal government, Export-Import Bank, International Bank, and all the rest.

For many reasons, we moderns cannot expect such great amounts of foreign investment. After all, was the pre-World War I pattern so natural, or was it perhaps the special result of fortuitous historical coincidences?

Thus, loans from Europe to the New World typically went together with migration of European peoples to those same new lands: Englishmen went along with their money, so to speak, to the American colonies, Canada, Australia, and other dominions; and notice that the same pattern of laws and customs prevailed in the capital-importing countries as in the capital-investing country.

Remember, too, that this antebellum world was an unbelievably cosmopolitan one. You could travel everywhere with no passport. You could migrate freely from country to country. You could expect low tariffs and no trade quotas. You knew the international gold standard would let you transfer capital from place to place at your slightest whim. You knew your property was safe abroad from government confiscation: back in those days few dreamed of questioning the sanctity of private property, and those nationalistic countries which did raise such questions could be easily intimidated by dispatching battleships for off-coast maneuvers. Finally, you could buy up—literally!—dictatorial governments in many backward countries and bribe them into giving you extremely favorable mining and other concessions.

If this sounds like an investor's paradise, be reminded that the historical facts were not really quite so rosy. Foreign investments often did go bankrupt, there being insufficient commercial demand for the railroads built across the plains of North America and elsewhere. Also, the people in the countries importing capital do not, from their historical utterances, seem to have been too happy over this investor's paradise. But the system did function. And often it did confer *mutual benefits* on both the advanced and backward areas. After dividends went abroad, a net increment of product due to the imported capital was left at home in the form of higher real wages.

Now all this is ancient history. This antebellum world is gone. Never was nationalism stronger than today. Never have borrower and lender been so in agreement: the underdeveloped countries are agreed not to sell to foreigners long-term rights in the development of their countries, no matter how advantageous the price; the developed countries are agreed it would be rash to buy bonds and stocks from backward countries in the old pattern.[9]

This does not mean we must rule out substantial foreign capital investment programs. But to be realistic, we must search out new instrumentalities for carrying them out. Often these will involve agreements between governments or various government guarantees of private ventures. Always foreign investment will have to take into account the rising tide of nationalism. Local management must be trained to take over ultimately; local sharing in ownership of branch plants is a modern necessity.

TECHNOLOGICAL CHANGE AND INNOVATIONS

In addition to the fundamental factors of population, natural resources, and capital formation, there is the vitally important fourth factor of technology. Here we can strike a cautiously optimistic note. Here the underdeveloped countries have one possible advantage. They can hope to benefit *by copying the more advanced technology of the developed nations.*

Imitating technology The new lands need not develop still unborn Newtons to discover the law of gravity: they can read about that law in any book. They need not go through the slow meandering climb of the Industrial Revolution: they can find in any machine catalogue wonders undreamed of by the great inventors of the past.

Japan, Germany, and Russia clearly illustrate all this in their historical developments. Japan joined the industrial race late: at the end of the nineteenth century she sent her students abroad and began to copy Western technology. Her government took an active and creative role in stimulating the pace of development, building railroads and utilities,

[9] Even in friendly Canada, citizens have resented the vast post-World War II investment by large United States corporations, and tax penalties were introduced in the 1960s.

and taxing heavily the newly created increments of land value resulting from the improvements in agriculture. A few energetic, wealthy families were permitted to develop vast industrial empires, while at the same time the general population was made to work, and work hard, in order to earn its living. Without relying on net foreign capital imports, Japan in a few decades had moved into the front rank both as a military power and as an industrial nation.

Only after the Revolution of 1848 did Germany really accelerate her industrialization. Through government aid to her universities, German scientists soon became preeminent in mathematics, physics, chemistry, and engineering. Fifty years ago, most American professors of these subjects—and of history, economics, and philology, too—went to Germany for their postgraduate degrees. German prowess in organic chemistry, optics, glass manufacture, and electrical equipment was unsurpassed until the two world wars set her back. Russia, too, illustrates the possibility of fast development through technological imitation, through study of Western techniques and practices.

Finally, the case of the United States itself provides an optimistic example to the rest of the world. Until Hitler made us a present in the 1930s of many of the best Continental scientists of all faiths, we could not honestly boast of having quite reached the very front rank in the field of pure science. Yet for a century our applied technology had admittedly been outstanding. Examine one by one the key inventions involving the automobile. Where did they originate? Mostly abroad. Nevertheless, Henry Ford and General Motors long outproduced the rest of the world. "Yankee ingenuity" is a phrase that *explains* nothing; but it does refer to a real phenomenon.

Interplay of technology and capital   It is all very well to speak of underdeveloped countries copying advanced technology. But have we not overlooked something important? Is not advanced technology embodied in the form of complex capital goods? And have we not already seen that those countries are short of capital? So how can we expect them to copy superior technology?

Certainly there is much truth in these suggestions. Technological change and capital investment do go hand in hand; often they are inseparable. All the same, we are right to treat them as analytically distinct—albeit related—processes. Here is one of many examples to show why:

Farming is inefficient in many backward countries. You see peasants breaking up the soil by the same primitive methods their ancestors were using back in the time of David and Solomon. Perhaps an ingenious light plow—something simple that would cost no more than a dollar and would pay for itself in the first month—can be found that will both lessen the total amount of capital needed and greatly increase output. This shows how technological innovation can often be capital-*saving* rather than capital-*using*.

Moreover, even in the poorest countries, some gross capital formation is always going on as things are wearing out and are being replaced. Why replace them with the same thing? Why let much of the economy's capital go into mere *duplicative projects*? Surely, it is much better to embody the newly available investment funds in the form of more efficient technological implements. Thus we see how the interrelated factors of capital formation and technology can be mutually reinforcing.

Entrepreneurship and innovation   Does this sound like an easy task for an underdeveloped economy? All that it must do to telescope into a few years the scores of years it took us to develop is this: Go abroad and copy more efficient methods; bring them back and put them into effect at home; then sit back and wait for the extra product to roll in.

Of course, it does not work quite this way. People in the underdeveloped countries know this from bitter experience. Yet the same illusion keeps cropping up among the people in the so-called "advanced" countries. Too often we think we can send a few technical experts on a short junket to a poor country; after surveying the field for a month or so, they can write up their recommendations for improvement, and then the neatly typed report they leave behind can be "implemented." In this way development will be solved.

Occasionally, in connection with particular technological processes, experts have indeed been able to work wonders in this facile way; thus, an American expert on leather tanning was sent out to Libya to advise on some of its difficulties, and in a short time he did diagnose the chemical troubles and come up with an effective cure.

Technologists soon discover, however, that this sort of quick miracle is exactly what cannot be accomplished in connection with the *development of a whole economy*. Indeed, the typical pattern is one of complete disillusionment: after spending several months surveying an underdeveloped country, the expert is thoroughly impressed with the thousands of cultural and economic barriers to progress, so much so that he comes back with a hopeless feeling of defeat. This thoroughly pessimistic conclusion is probably just as wrong in its way as was the opposite optimistic illusion.

Experience shows development is truly a hard and slow process—but not an impossible one. To hasten its evolution, spontaneous entrepreneurship and innovation must develop among the peoples directly involved. Remember, many cultures begin with a contempt for dirty, hard work—a contempt they often inherit from the colonial elite who used to rule over them. Often, too, they have a contempt for business—for money-grubbing and production. Gradually, they must develop for themselves, *within their own mixed cultural pattern,* a creative group of producers alert to trying out new ways, alert to consumer wants, responsive to pecuniary risk taking and rewards.

Why place the emphasis on creative innovation? Because it is by no means a cut and-dried task to adapt advanced foreign technology to an underdeveloped country's own use. Remember, the advanced technology was itself developed to meet the special conditions of the advanced countries. What are these conditions? High money wage rates; laborers scarce in number but replete with industrial skills; plentiful capital inherited from the past; mass production; and so forth. These conditions do not prevail in underdeveloped lands.

Time and time again, experience has shown us how easy it is to obtain a foreign loan to put up a model factory in Turkey or Burma. Often it is imported piece by piece from abroad and embodies the latest wrinkles of Western technology. Yet, with what result? With high production and sales in excess of costs, yielding a comfortable profit that can be plowed back into further industrialization? Only too rarely! Often such grandiose imported projects turn out to be extremely unprofitable. The factory that is an optimal investment for New York may in Ankara or Rangoon be a fiasco.

This task of creative innovation is not one for rugged individualism alone. The government can do much to set up extension services in every agricultural province for consulting with farmers on the best seeds, methods of cultivation, and implements. By sponsoring vocational schools and training courses in machine methods—and in bookkeeping, too— the government itself can innovate creatively. Somewhere between complete laissez faire and totalitarianism a developing nation must work out its destiny.

FIVE-YEAR PLANS

The advanced nations did not develop by means of a formal plan. Historically, England and the United States grew primarily in a spontaneous and unselfconscious fashion. And the same holds for the nations late to become industrialized, such as Japan at the end of the nineteenth century. As we have seen, though, the Soviet Union introduced successive five-year plans from the late 1920s onward.

Today all over the underdeveloped world, planning is a fashionable word. No country is too small or backward to have its five- or ten-year plan. Sometimes these are merely fancily worded documents that have little relationship to actual reality and performance. But sometimes they are carefully executed analyses which spell out in considerable detail programs for macroeconomic and microeconomic development. Here is a closer look at some of the elements involved in a good plan.

1. The plan is based upon the *initial resources* of the country, presupposing a careful inventory of present and future availability of manpower and domestic resources.

2. The plan sets up feasible *targets* or *goals* for the terminal date.

3. The plan sets out the *feasible policies* that permit achievement of the terminal goals from the initial resources, taking into account the intermediate economic resources that can be imported from abroad (through loans or gifts) and that can be produced at home out of the initial resources by the mechanism of domestic investment.

At the least, a plan will involve careful computation of the macroaggregates of gross national product: balance of saving and investment; allocation of resources between public and private sectors, between one region and another, between city and countryside. A good plan will not be so ambitious as to lead to inefficient galloping inflation, or so unambitious as to lead to stagnation and underemployment. Along with macroeconomic fiscal and monetary policies, it will take care that the resulting import demand does not exceed the available supply of foreign exchange, whether this is accomplished by the pricing system or by rationing. An ideal plan will provide for social overhead capital projects and be alert to the problems of externalities and indivisibilities.

Some plans will involve, at the microeconomic levels, no more than "indicative planning," merely keeping diverse industries acquainted with what is going to happen to the aggregates and to their own share of the total, but leaving to their pursuit of profit the resulting net response. Other plans will involve detailed allocation of inputs among different output uses, taking care to check the balance between inputs and outputs. They may or may not use the input-output techniques of general equilibrium developed by W. W. Leontief, which (as the last Appendix showed) give a detailed view of interindustry dollar and resource flows. The plan may or may not use the modern techniques of linear and nonlinear programming, in a form suitable for the giant electronic computer.

Often the plan will make mistakes. A crop failure due to bad weather may throw it out of kilter. Overambitious targets may produce foreign exchange shortages and rampant inflation. Sometimes the subsequent five-year plan will learn from the mistakes of its predecessors. Sometimes a situation goes from bad to worse. A cynic can find in the annals of the 1950s and 1960s countless examples of governmental and private bungling. But an optimist, looking at "miracles" of development in Thailand, Formosa, Korea, Puerto Rico, Israel, and El Salvador, can face the future with some confidence in the ability of nations to accelerate their own economic development.

SUMMARY

1 Most of the world consists of underdeveloped countries: countries with low per capita incomes relative to the most advanced economies; countries capable of improvement but now lagging behind the growth rates of the advanced nations. The increasing political self-consciousness of such countries, plus the eagerness of the communist ideology to help them "skip the capitalistic stage of development," reinforces our own self-interest in finding new sources of mutually advantageous trade—not new objects for imperialistic make-work programs. All this and altruism, too, make the development problem of major interest to us.

2 Geography and climate, race and custom, religion and business attitudes—each factor conditions economic development, but none does so in a simple and invariable way.

3 The phenomena of increasing returns, externalities, and social overhead capital provide some substance to notions of "take-offs," "spurts," and "big pushes." They suggest a scope for supplementation of competitive market forces. But they do not lead at all necessarily to any simple concept of "balanced growth."

4 The key to development lies in four fundamental factors: population, natural resources, capital formation (domestic or imported), and technology. *Population* causes sociological problems of explosive growth in numbers as death rates fall before birth rates fall; the Malthusian devil of diminishing returns stalks the underdeveloped realms. On the constructive economic agenda, improving the population's health, education, and technical training has high priority. The pool of "disguised unemployment" in country and city provides an important manpower source for extra product; the "brain drain" of talented men to developed countries provides an important threat.

5 Even in densely populated areas, discovery and better utilization of *natural resources* can help offset the law of diminishing returns. Land reform raises tremendous problems of transition. The process of capital formation—of investing in soil conservation, irrigation, drainage, and improvement—interacts with the natural-resource category, just as it does with population—through investing in people.

6 Rates of productive *capital formation* in underdeveloped countries are low because of (*a*) poverty, (*b*) lack of a bourgeois ethic stressing frugality and acquisitiveness, (*c*) qualitative distortion of saving outlets toward unproductive hoarding of precious objects and

idle inventory and toward luxurious real estate or money markets abroad, (*d*) emulation of consumption standards of advanced nations, and (*e*) nationalistic barriers to importing capital on terms acceptable to investors in the advanced countries.

7 *Technological change* interacts with, and is embodied in, new capital goods. Nevertheless, it is a distinct process, and one which offers much hope to underdeveloped nations inasmuch as they can copy from advanced nations. The experience of Japan, Russia, Germany, and the United States shows that the process of adapting to one's own fruitful uses the methods developed elsewhere is not easy. It takes a degree of *entrepreneurship* and creative innovation. One of development's most pressing tasks is to hasten internal growth of the scarce entrepreneurial and commercial spirit.

8 Five-year plans, involving feasible *targets* to be achieved out of *initial conditions* by suitable macroeconomic or microeconomic *intermediate programs,* occur widely.

QUESTIONS FOR DISCUSSION

1 Would you expect everyone to agree with the praise of material well-being expressed in the quotation at this chapter's beginning? A hippie? An affluent college senior?

2 Bertrand Russell is one of the greatest contemporary philosophers, logicians, and writers; yet the following words of his are agreed by competent historians to be wrong in asserting that the Industrial Revolution worsened living standards: "The industrial revolution caused unspeakable misery both in England and in America. I do not think any student of economic history can doubt that the average happiness in England in the early nineteenth century was lower than it had been a hundred years earlier; and this was due almost entirely to scientific technique." Actually, real incomes rose. Why the contrary notion?

3 Formulate your views on geography, race, culture, and development.

4 Briefly list the principal contrasts between life in America and in a typical underdeveloped country. Explain historically.

5 Delineate factors important in development; fit each into the outline involving the four main factors: population, ...

6 Is it fair for the advanced countries in the interest of conserving bird life to deprive poor countries of the DDT that prevents early death from malaria?

Review your understanding of the following concepts:

characteristics of underdevelopment
"take-off," "spurt," etc.
increasing returns, externalities
social overhead capital
capital-output ratio
balanced growth, diversification
disguised unemployment
planning, accounting "shadow prices"
population and natural resources

medical improvements without food
capital and technology
inequality, poverty, emulation,
   foreign lending, capital formation
entrepreneurship and planning
inflation and development
land reform
public and private responsibility
plans: goals, programs, initial states

Economic Inequality: Poverty, Affluence, and the Quality of Life

39

Ill fares the land,
to hastening ills a prey,
Where wealth accumulates,
and men decay.
OLIVER GOLDSMITH, *The Deserted Village*

Man does not live by GNP alone. Better a smaller social pie divided *equitably* among the populace, many ethical observers will say, than a larger one devoted to the vulgar objects of material display. Why seek what William James called the Bitch-Goddess of success, if the price of that striving is despoliation of man's environment and in the end the nonattainment of happiness and serenity?

The issues raised in this chapter go beyond the technicalities of narrow economic analysis. Yet they are issues that have come to the forefront of debate all over the world: in the affluent society of North America; in the advanced countries of Europe, which are going through a process which they sometimes ruefully call "Americanization"; in the Soviet society, which has finally achieved a standard of living that goes beyond the utilitarian items of consumption whose composition can be planned without an elaborate exploration of differentiated consumer tastes; and in the developing countries of the world, whose ancient cultural traditions of status—and in some cases even asceticism and otherworldliness—are challenged by the temptations of advanced technology.

ANALYSIS IN THE SERVICE OF CONTROVERSY

All of the present issues are controversial. They involve value judgments. They involve strong differences in tastes and convictions. Even though they go beyond economics, there is much that economic analysis can contribute to the elucidation of the issues. Thus, until you know the costs of alleviating inequality and poverty, how can you *rationally* determine how far to carry your campaign in that direction? And even if you believe that the ends justify the means, how in a complicated subject like economics can you be sure that the means you are using may not be calculated to produce exactly the *opposite* effect to the one you desire?

Will a very high minimum wage add to the well-being of the poorer workers? Or will the poor be the prime victims of this well-intentioned measure?

Will putting a low interest ceiling on small loans to consumers—say, 8 per cent per annum, which to many will not seem very low—help the needy and unlucky? Or will it play right into the hands of the lobbyists for the loan sharks? What are the debits as well as credits of comprehensive rent ceilings long maintained—and this means debits and credits, not for landlords as opposed to tenants, but for the low-income families of our growing population?

Many a social revolution—in the Middle East, in Latin America, in Africa—has aimed to help the workers and peasants, but during the transition has resulted in a lower standard of life for all the population.

The problems of social reform are not easy. If they were, many of those improvements which command a consensus among men of good will would have been made long ago. On the other hand, economic analysis can reveal how specious are many of the arguments for maintenance of the status quo. Despite what your grandfather's economic textbook used to say, a rich country can afford a large measure of redistributive taxation. The Roman Empire did not really fall, or even decline, because of an unbalanced budget or from planning by bungling bureaucrats.

In short, economic analysis is the indispensable handmaiden of those who seek social reforms and of those who wish to preserve and conserve the inherited order.

SINCE EDEN

Chapter 6 has already summarized the important facts about poverty and income inequality. Under laissez faire, income and wealth get distributed far from equally. The mixed economy has somewhat modified the inequality of distribution of the laissez faire regime, but the Lorenz curves of Figs. 6-3 and 9-1 show how considerable are the variations in economic well-being that still remain.

Chapter 6 also demonstrated how, in a growing economy, the numbers of those who fall below any fixed, absolute standard of poverty shrink. *As the whole nation becomes more affluent, our standards rise as to what we deem to constitute the minimum needed for a decent life.* We shall always have a lowest 20 per cent of the population with us. But in some decades of successful development a society will do better than in others in improving the lot of those at the bottom of the income pyramid. Thus the period of the 1920s was one of great advance in American GNP. But they were years in which there was probably a deterioration in the quality of American life as measured by the degree of income inequality. Ironically it was the war decade of the 1940s that raised the average income and reduced the dispersion around that average.

Some ask, "Why worry about the disparities of income within the United States when poverty here is as nothing in comparison with that abroad? A family on relief lives better in Cleveland than a workingman in Volgograd, and infinitely better than a peasant in India. Hunger in America still exists in some rural and ghetto pockets; but it represents largely malnutrition and *isolated* hunger, not the widespread famine that has characterized all history and still characterizes large parts of the globe."

The answer usually given by humanitarians is something like the following: "An affluent society can afford to provide a decent minimum for all its members. The fact that India is too poor to ensure good food and housing for most of her people may be an argument for a larger measure

of our foreign aid; but it is not a valid reason for our countenancing at home the glaring disparities that the market solution provides to the basic problems of WHAT, HOW, and FOR WHOM."

INEVITABLE LAWS OF THE DISMAL SCIENCE?

Vilfredo Pareto, the brilliant Italian economist and sociologist at the turn of the century, was one of the first to observe and describe statistically the extreme skewness of incomes. So impressed was he by the uniformity of inequality in diverse societies and diverse times that he enunciated an inevitable law of inequality. To vulgarize his view, "Essentially nothing can be done about inequality. The basic forces determining inequality are too strong and persistent to be affected by state intervention."

In this matter Pareto was essentially following in the tradition of most of the classical economists. The Reverend Malthus, Stockbroker Ricardo, and their popularizing disciples all thought that economics was the dismal science of unalterable distribution of income. The wages of labor, the rent of land, the profit of capital were determined by Economic Law, and not by Political Power. If labor unions or reform political parties tried to use the state to modify these facts of life, they would be ineffective in the end. All that they would accomplish in the attempt would be *to contrive a smaller social pie*, which would probably still get distributed in about the same way. Vexation and violence in trying to alter this would merely produce economic chaos and class warfare.

With some of this Karl Marx would have agreed. Marx was an admirer of David Ricardo the analyst. Marx agreed that *under capitalism* things could *not* become better for the workers and the peasants. The proletariat was bound to be exploited. In the more vulgar form of the Marxist doctrines, the immiserization of the working classes was inevitable. Under capitalism the rich would get richer and the poor poorer.[1] *Under capitalism*, that is! The logical corollary was to get rid of capitalism. Or rather, the scientific doctrines of dynamic socialism dictated that capitalism would decay of its own contradictions—as those rich got richer, as monopoly finance destroyed competition, and as the business cycle worsened and led to the ultimate capitalistic crisis and collapse. Hence while waiting for the inevitable revolution into socialism to take place, one could only try to hurry along this irreversible process.

THE WELFARE STATE

Ricardo and Marx turn out to have been wrong about the laws of motion of *politics*, as well as of economics. As every schoolboy now knows, the century since 1870 has been the century of state intervention in economic life. Gladstone and Disraeli in England and Bismarck in Germany began in Europe of the last century what Franklin Roosevelt and the Great Depression accelerated in America of this century—namely, the modern welfare state.

Voting class-interests   In retrospect there is nothing mysterious about this political process of using the state to change the distribution of income. The founding fathers of our

[1] Among Marxian scholars there is some disagreement over whether Marx actually meant that real wages would fall *absolutely* or only relatively. An absolute decline has, of course, greater shock value.

Constitution—particularly such Federalists as John Adams, James Madison, and Alexander Hamilton—were strong believers in the class struggle before Marx was born. They feared that the rights of property would be infringed if votes were given to all. Since the poor outnumber the rich, under universal suffrage the lower elements would legislate against the established wealthy. And that is why our Constitution provided checks and balances of limited government. That is why the suffrage was severely limited in the first half century after the American Revolution.

The same debate went on in Europe in the middle of the last century. Whigs like the historian Macaulay, although by no means reactionary in their own day, warned against the universal suffrage: Give votes to all and you must expect the instinct of self-interest—that *same* self-interest which Adam Smith counted on to work in the economic sphere of laissez faire—to lead to state interference with the inequality of incomes and property. And despite the prophecy by the revolutionaries of those days, that the privileged classes would *never* yield to the proletariat the right to vote, in country after country conscience and agitation led to widening of suffrage.

Less than a century after Bismarck and Gladstone introduced old-age pensions by the state, social security had become a function of the American federal government. Conservative, liberal, and radical parties may win and lose future elections, but the apparatus of the welfare state continues to grow: in Protestant Norway and Catholic Italy; in outlying Australia and the home counties of England; in free enterprise Switzerland and planned Sweden.

A century's progress Figure 39-1 provides a simplified summary of the laws of motion of economic and political development of the last century. The point A on the low curve shows that the lowest half of the population got much less than half of the total social product in 1870. By 1970 the total of GNP had grown mightily. If Pareto were right about the inevitability of the same relative share of product, the new division would be at A'. Real wages would have risen mightily—along with real incomes from property. But if the cruder forms of Marxism had been right, the system would have deteriorated to Z, with the poor reaching complete immiserization (and with a bloody revolution no doubt unavoidable).

Actually we have no accurate statistics of Lorenz curves for a century ago. What economic historians, such as Colin Clark and Simon Kuznets, do know is that there has been some slight reduction of Lorenz-curve inequality in modern as compared with less-developed nations, and in welfare states such as Sweden or Israel as compared with free enterprise societies such as Switzerland. So the best guess is to suppose a country like the United States or England or Japan is now at a point just above A'. The welfare state, through redistributive taxa-

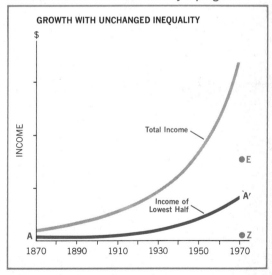

All classes have shared in century's progress:

FIG. 39-1. Lower half of population has had rising real incomes, as shown by AA'. Immiserization of workers, at Z, has turned out to be bad prophecy. But utopian equality, as at E, has also not occurred.

tion and through educational opportunity designed to lessen inequality of advantage, has moved the system somewhat toward greater equality. But note that the system is still a long way from the point *E* where both halves of the population get the same share of the total social product.

Is this a good or a bad thing? Apologists for the system say, "It is great; look at the doughnut and how it has grown." Critics of the system say: "It is not nearly enough; look at the hole in the doughnut." Displaced conservatives say, "It is a bad thing— un-American, unconstitutional; it won't work, but it is working too well for the long-run health of the system."

In the 1970s there is available an agreed-upon record of facts about real wage trends in the last century. Real wages have risen steadily and strongly in the last century. These laws of motion of capitalism are, as Chapter 37's analysis of technical change delineates, in line with what we should expect from the dynamic forces of supply and demand. Ford workers get real wages ten times what their great-grandfathers got because their productivity in Detroit enables that wage to be paid.

Even in the economic academies of Eastern Europe it is now agreed that the mixed economies of Western Europe and North America are likely in 1999 to have real wages several times those prevailing in the 1970s.

But these days, good is not good enough. Why be satisfied with existing relative inequalities? Why permit any hunger in the affluent society? Why not an all-out war on poverty? So declare critics of the existing order in increasing numbers.

EQUITY VERSUS EFFICIENCY

Even without the gift of prophecy, one can bet that the welfare state will long be with us. When a Nixon or an Eisenhower is elected in America, he consolidates rather than liquidates the economic reforms of his predecessors. The same pattern was seen abroad when socialist governments in Norway, Australia, or Britain were replaced by more conservative parties. The question naturally arises, therefore, Why not go all or much of the way toward equality of incomes? Why wait until 1999 to do what can be done *today* by a determined electorate?

Deadweight burdens   Figure 39-2 on the next page illustrates the opportunities and difficulties. How can one go from the present point *A* to the equality point *E*? If we make income taxes more steeply progressive, decisions to invest in risky ventures and to work hard at one's profession will be profoundly affected. If we freeze prices and rents or put floors on wages, we alter production and employment. Conservatives no doubt exaggerate the problems of distortion, but only romantics deny their reality.

Schematically, the heavy *ABZ* curve bends inward as a result of the deadweight cost, or burden, that is inevitably associated with strong state interference with the workings of the market mechanism. Indeed, experience has shown that in some cases the distortions due to interference can become so great that the attempt to help one social class at the expense of another can end hurting them all. (Thus the 1948 decision by Ludwig Erhard to end the rationing and price controls that were stifling the West German economy led to a dramatic movement—like that from B or inside A northeast to the *p-p frontier*—which much improved the lot of just about every income class.)

Argument and counterargument   Intentionally Fig. 39-2 presents a gloomily realistic picture of some of the difficulties. How might one react? First, some may say that the effort is still worth the cost, that greater equality is more important than greater affluence and is worth its cost. (And still others may demur, or reduce their aspirations.)

Second, one can mobilize the tools of economics to minimize the costs and distortions. Let the reader pencil in a new curve to lie between the solid ABZ and light AE. By skillful design of programs against poverty and inequality, the deadweight burden can definitely be lessened and society may move on such a new and better curve. Thus,[2] the subsidy of low-income housing may be a more efficient long-run solution to our urban problems than freezing rents by direct controls.

Redistributing social pie may reduce its total:

FIG. 39-2.   If outcome at A (under relative laissez faire) is to be shifted toward equality, deadweight loss or inefficiency may result. Instead of moving on the *p-p frontier* from A toward E, a movement along ABZ (or even southwest!) may be the result. The challenge is to develop tax and other programs that more closely approximate AE.

Outright confiscation   So far the problem seems to have been phrased as if there must always be clash between equity and efficiency. Even if the tradeoff is really there, the economist who keeps harping on the conflict may seem to act like an apologist for the status quo and an exponent of gradualism. But, actually, economic tools can cut both ways. A truly *revolutionary* policy—such as (1) confiscation of property of the wealthy, (2) a massive capital levy on the upper half of the income pyramid, or (3) steep wealth and inheritance taxation—might move one in the short run from the status quo at A toward the equality point E. Under a less revolutionary system, which respects the right of private property and protects it from expropriation without due process and, what is more important to its owners, without due compensation, complete efficiency of redistribution is indeed impossible. Paradoxically, it is a radical majority, which agrees with the 1848 definition of Proudhon that "all property is theft," that may have open to it a less distortive once-and-for-all redistribution from outright confiscation.

EXAMPLE: Abraham Lincoln freed the slaves in 1863. Rich slaveowners were simply disappropriated of their property. Czar Alexander II freed the serfs in 1867. But the former serf owners were given government bonds to compensate them. All the community, including the former serfs, had to work to pay off the principal and pay the interest on these bonds. Collecting these taxes inevitably involved a great deal of deadweight loss. In Fig. 39-2, the case of the United States may have more nearly approximated an AE movement, and the Russian case may have more nearly approximated an AB movement (as the Cuban revolution seems to have done).

---

[2]Chapter 40 deals further with urban problems. For those interested in theoretical demonstrations, Chapter 22's Appendix demonstrates some of the deadweight loss from rationing.

The example of confiscation illustrates that economic tools sometimes cut in the direction desired by conservatives, sometimes in the direction desired by revolutionaries. Experience and analysis also show that once-and-for-all confiscation can result in subsequent slower growth, unless the new order provides for efficient operation, maintenance, and growth of the capital which has changed ownership. *Capital will not automatically maintain itself, or be replaced, or be augmented along the most efficient lines without public or private entrepreneurship.*

CAUSES OF INEQUALITY

To alleviate inequality one must first diagnose its principal causes. Here are some of the important factors involved.

Differences in property wealth   The greatest disparities in income are due to differences in *wealth ownership.* After the father of William Randolph Hearst had discovered a mountain of silver, his children and grandchildren automatically moved to the top of the pyramid of wealth and power. The history of the greatest fortunes—associated with the names that can be read on the plaques of college buildings: the Mellons, Rockefellers, Vanderbilts, Gettys—shows that differences in personal abilities are dwarfed by differences in property owned.

Many of these differences in wealth were associated with plain luck in *discovery of natural resources.* Some were due in part to astuteness of exploration and productive innovation. Indeed, the new multimillionaire today is often someone like Edwin Land, who as a dropout from Harvard in the 1930s persevered in his research on polarizing materials, ending up with several hundreds of millions of wealth in Polaroid stock. The *Wall Street Journal* and the London *Financial Times* are replete with similar stories of wealth in one generation due to innovational skill or luck. Since capital gains are never taxed until they are realized by actual sale and since they are much more lightly taxed than ordinary income, it is simply not true that today's mixed economy prevents one from becoming a multimillionaire. Moreover, there are many loopholes in the tax laws that permit the retention and augmentation of initial wealth—special percentage depletion allowances for oil and other natural resources, tax-exempt municipal bond issues, stock options, capital-gains investments which escape all taxation at death, and so forth.

Differences in personal ability   Some of these may be *inherited:* within every family there are evident differences in physical and mental abilities, and between families one expects from the Mendelian theory of genetics that there will be some dispersion. Students tend to think of intelligence or IQ as the important variable; but when it comes to making money, such traits as energy, ambition, canniness, and flair can be just as important. (As Mark Twain said, "You don't have to be smart to make money. But you *do* have to know how to make money!")

While differences in inherited ability play some role, the common man if anything exaggerates them in comparison with the trained biologist and social psychologist. We all inherit from our environment as well as from our parents' genes. By the age of one, the affluent child of a serene and attentive mother already has a leg up in the race for economic status and success. By the time he is a six-year-old going to first grade in the suburbs, he already has an increased lead over the slum or rural six-year-old. And for the next 12 to 20 years, the scales are increasingly tipped toward them who already have.

Differences in education, training, and opportunity   The single most important factor working for reduced inequality in the last centuries has been the provision of public education. Here is the socialism that has subverted the ancient order of privilege, in which there was an infinite gulf between the educated upper classes and the illiterate masses.

As an educated man, John Stuart Mill could, in 1840, make the equivalent of 100,000 of today's dollars helping to run the East India Company (which in turn ran India). Perhaps it is not so remarkable that a man like Mill should receive an income twenty or thirty times that of the median man. But consider Charles Lamb, a lowborn cockney who also worked for the East India Company—as a clerk, and not a very hardworking one at that. Lamb too received several times the national average income. Why? Because he was *literate:* he could write, and add and subtract; scarcity of these skills made them command a handsome economic rent. The provision of schooling and the invention of the typewriter have done as much to emancipate women from the ancient domination of male chauvinists as all the hunger strikes of suffragettes or advanced plays of Ibsen and Shaw. (Indeed, Nora of Ibsen's *A Doll's House* could not have declared her independence if no careers were open to women.)

Class barriers to opportunity   We shall see in the next chapter's discussion of the economics of race how important the economic role of education and opportunity is. Modern economists have analyzed the problem of putting capital into people through education and training, in much the same way that one puts money capital into plant or equipment. To finish high school or medical school requires an investment that in the past those born poor simply could not afford. At the turn of this century only the affluent gentry sang the Whiffenpoof song at Yale; and even the state universities of the Middle West were the province of the privileged.

In a meritocracy, opportunities to pursue advanced education and training will be largely divorced from parental affluence. By fellowships and living allowances from the state and by partially repayable loans, those with the ability to benefit from education will be granted the opportunity. Nor will this be confined to professional training and advanced education: GNP is as much enhanced when several Appalachian high school dropouts are trained to program a computer or run a modern filing machine as when similar dollars are spent on a lawyer or a doctor. On-the-job training in welding, steamfitting, plumbing, and other vocational pursuits will involve great social payoff and also contribute toward the good society.

Graduates of Groton, Yale, and the Harvard Law or Business School show high earnings, as do Eton and Oxford graduates. Much of this may be the result of superior training and of selection standards that stress high personal ability. But historically part has represented differences in opportunity. The executive suites used to be full of Ivy League graduates who displayed no particular superiority over Big Ten graduates. As more objective standards become relevant for recruitment and promotion in an open society, the boardrooms of business and Cabinet offices of government will see more chaps who are not Episcopalian, whose eyes are not blue, and whose wives do not belong to the Daughters of the American Revolution.

Although public expenditure on education has been an important historical influence making for a more open society, it is, alas, not the case that all such expenditures work toward reducing inequality. For there is a great deal of evidence that much of state expenditure on higher education goes to *subsidize the middle classes* rather than the urban and rural poor. Calculations made for California, where college attendance is more widespread than anywhere else in the world, show that the families of students at state universities (and at community colleges, too) have incomes well above the median of the population at large. The same relative scarcity of working-class families in state universities is found in Britain, on the Continent, and in the developing world.

What can be done to prevent this outright subsidy to further inequality? First, more college students from the underprivileged classes can be actively recruited, even at the expense of scholarly standards at entrance. Second, funds can be diverted from higher education into vocational schooling. Third, if access to college education adds to earnings in later life—and statistics show this is indeed so—many argue that college students should be made to pay for the full costs of their extra education. I.e., tuition charges should be raised toward true costs, and repayable loans should be made available instead of scholarships (except in the case of the very poor). Does this seem inequitable? Adherents of equality reply that it is the present system, which taxes the poor as well as the rich to pay for state universities, which is inequitable. And certainly when we consider the high earnings of physicians, there is seen to be some merit in the argument. (The Harvard Business School has long substituted loans for fellowships, knowing that its graduates have high earnings in later life.)[3]

Difference in age and health Even if people were all born alike and subject to pretty much the same environment, some will suffer the vicissitudes of bad health. Cardiac disaster can strike anywhere. Neurosis and psychosis are not ailments that one can choose to have or not have. Alcohol and drugs take their toll in every stratum of society. And no one stays young and vigorous forever. Under laissez faire it has always been the aged who have been most subject to economic want.

A few years ago an English economist who was an enthusiast for the British Labor party spent a year at an American university. He was fascinated at Christmas to read the histories of the 100 neediest cases described in the *New York Times*. He found among them anguishing cases of mental and physical illnesses but finally concluded, "There is scarcely an instance where better *macroeconomic* policy of the fiscal and monetary type could do much to touch the problem."

Actually, he was wrong and had fallen into the trap of those who say that good health doesn't matter to those who are lucky enough to enjoy it. If he had visited America in

[3] An article by E. J. Mishan of the London School of Economics, reprinted in P. A. Samuelson, *Readings in Economics* (McGraw-Hill, New York, 1970, 6th ed.), argues that full-cost tuition cum loans will get rid of radical student activists and troublemakers, replacing them with a docile, vocational-minded student body. It is debatable whether this would (or should) happen, but it can hardly be doubted that a cadre of perpetual students at Continental and Latin American universities does make for political activity.

1932, he would have learned how important good macroeconomic policy is. For at that time, people from every social stratum were in desperate economic need because of the Great Depression.

The successful attainment of high employment has done more than any other single program to banish economic want and mitigate economic inequality. Differences in unemployment experienced have always been the single greatest cause of *economic variance within the working classes themselves.*

Moreover, if an observer were to follow a social welfare worker on her rounds in any typical week in the 1970s, he would find that every one of the health and personality problems encountered is exacerbated by the absence of money.

An alcoholic can be desperately unhappy. But if he is of independent means, his children need not go hungry on that account and his dependence upon a steady job is vitally lessened. In a lower-middle-class family, the onset of mental illness of a mother is a financial disaster in a way that is not true at the top of the income pyramid. Were it not for state-supported mental institutions, the vast bulk of the populace simply could not cope with the problem.

What inherited property has always provided for the privileged few, the modern welfare state in limited measure provides for the bulk of the populace. As we shall see, through *direct* public services and through *transfer*-payment programs, the modern mixed economy is in effect a gigantic *system of mutual insurance* against the worst economic disasters of life. "There but for the grace of God go I," each one of us thinks when he sees disaster strike some neighbor. And realizing we are all in the same boat, we troop to the polls every four years and vote upon ourselves the costs of the mutual-benefit programs that we call social security, Medicaid, and welfare. And, as we are about to discuss, some kind of income-maintenance plan, in the form of a negative income tax or the like, has moved to the top of the agenda for modern debate in the years just ahead.

DIRECT PROGRAMS FOR POVERTY AND INEQUALITY

Governments have always had some responsibility for the poor. Thus Elizabethan poor farms and Victorian orphanages have formed the targets of great novels of the past.

Private charity Years ago private charity had to play a significant if inadequate role: hand-me-downs for the poor, church missions and soup kitchens, handouts for beggars, and free medical clinics were part of the conscience money that the lucky paid to the unlucky.[4] Moreover, in an earlier time, the extended family system meant that each working generation took care of its parents in retirement: the institution of the baby-sitter was almost unknown because there was always a resident maiden aunt or grandmother. After you had settled in New York or Detroit, your cousins from Ireland, Poland, or Alabama could move in with you. Privacy is only a modern and middle-class privilege.

Private charity was never adequate (even though the situation would often have been

---

[4] See George Orwell, *Down and Out in Paris and London* (Berkley Publications, New York, 1966), for a moving account of what life was like among the derelicts of the 1930s.

frightful without it). Today, it is quite eclipsed in relative importance by the welfare functions of the state, of which the following are only a sample list.

Hospitals and asylums

Help *in kind* was the primary form that public assistance originally took. Not very long ago it was said, "Only the very rich and the very poor can afford adequate medical care." But that was of course an exaggeration except as applied to those who happened to be near a teaching hospital located in a slum, and who were not deterred by a demeaning means test from providing their bodies for medical experimentation and demonstration. As mentioned, poor farms and mental institutions are among the oldest of public agencies.

An argument still goes on in the modern welfare state. One school says, "Give people money and let them buy health services and the foods they need." The other school says, "If you give money for milk to the poor, they will spend it on beer. Your dollar goes farther in alleviating the rickets of malnourishment and the ravages of disease if you provide the services in kind. The dollar that a man earns may be *his* to spend, but the dollar that society makes available to him to meet particular deficiencies is a dollar that society has the right *paternalistically* to channel directly to its targets."

Neither side wins the argument. Whether in Sweden or America, whether at the national or local level of government, both forms of aid coexist.

Food allotments

After America rediscovered in the 1960s that there were indeed still many children and adults subject to hunger in this most affluent of societies, Presidents Kennedy, Johnson, and Nixon instituted a vast expansion of the food-stamp program. Under this program, families that qualify by virtue of their low incomes, receive stamps that permit them to get allotments of food at fractional or even zero cost. Since the Department of Agriculture is already supporting farm prices by the many loan and storage schemes described in Chapter 21, it seems only logical to have some of this unwanted market surplus go into the stomachs of hungry Americans as well as into the stomachs of hungry peoples from the underdeveloped parts of the world.

Unfortunately for the theory that grass-roots government is most sensitive to local needs, some of the greatest obstacles to the successful accomplishment of the food-stamp program come not from the scarcity of available supplies voted by Congress, nor from the pride or ignorance of the poor, nor from the physical problems of distribution by local stores and agencies. Rather it comes from the callous attitudes of the officials and voters in the poorest counties of the country, who work against the program by various acts of omission and commission.

Welfare assistance

In every county and city there exists some apparatus for help to the destitute. These programs involve some element of direct aid at the same time that they often involve some element of transfer of abstract purchasing power. Thus in a Northern city a welfare mother with three young children may be receiving a check of $300 per month. Some of this she may be free to spend as she wishes; but some part of it will be under the close supervision of the welfare worker assigned to her case, who lays down guidelines of how much can go for clothing, house furnishings, and so forth.

Because the minimum standards insisted upon by modern society have risen significantly, the cost of welfare programs has burgeoned in recent decades. Consequently there is great unease among the tax-paying citizenry over such programs. Thus a Gallup-like poll in 1970 would show that half the public think that welfare assistance is shot through with gross abuses. Anecdotes are told of mothers who spend hundreds of dollars fixing their teeth or buying color television sets with funds that ought to go for vitamin A drops for the baby. Illegitimate births among mothers on relief are not greeted with the same tolerance as are similar blessed events among starlets and the jet set.

Among informed professionals in the area of welfare and social psychology, there is a similar feeling of disquiet with the present apparatus of welfare assistance. It is indeed costly. And often inefficient. It puts a heavy psychological tax upon the recipients, and in some cases helps to create a caste of poor who must be taken care of in the same way that their parents were taken care of. A higher standard of sexual and other conduct is often demanded of those on relief than the critics themselves can, with all their advantages, live up to. Thus, in some states the father of a family on relief may find that the noblest thing he can do to enhance the well-being of his loved ones is to leave home and disappear. Only then can his wife and children continue to get the aid they desperately need. (And lest he should return at night, the social-service caseworker is often supposed to initiate surprise bed checks—a practice that strikes sensitive observers as despicable.)[5]

Welfare payments and economic inefficiency If a relief father were to be offered a job that paid him several hundred dollars, taking that job might in many states cost him several thousand dollars in the form of lost relief payments. Even a steady job at a minimum wage of $1.60 per hour might represent a net loss to him in terms of what is left over after *deductions* from his relief allotments.

Economically, the traditional system of welfare payments geared to need and earnings involves massive hidden costs in terms of *disincentive* effects. Literally billions of dollars of lost gross national product result from the disincentive structure of existing relief systems.

THE NEGATIVE INCOME TAX

Contemplating the great economic inefficiency of existing welfare programs to mitigate poverty and inequality, economists of quite varied political persuasions have come to agreement on the need for a basic reform in the modern welfare state. A New Frontiersman like James Tobin of Yale and a Goldwater and Nixon adviser like Milton Friedman agree that it will be both cheaper and more humane to replace or supplement the mess

---

[5] A changing list of programs, and names for programs, characterize the battle against poverty. Before his 1963 assassination, John Kennedy decided to initiate a special program for Appalachia, to alleviate rural and miners' poverty. Under Lyndon Johnson, the Office of Economic Opportunity (OEO) was set up, and manpower and labor market programs (the Job Corps, etc.) and Vista and Head Start programs were initiated. Under Nixon, these have been reshaped and coordinated with his proposed family-allowance plan.

that we call welfare assistance by a federal program that utilizes the efficient apparatus of the tax structure to attune incomes with needs.

Here is an idea whose time has come. Most economists have for some time favored it. Even President Nixon, in one of his early 1969 decisions, was persuaded to recommend to Congress a family-allowance program which embodied much of the philosophy and mechanisms of the negative income tax. Indeed, almost everything is good about the negative income tax except its name—which sounds so negative. So call it, if you like, the "incentive-guaranteed-income" plan.

How it works   The basic notion is simple. When I make $10,000 a year, I pay positive income taxes (as seen back in Chapter 9). When I earn an extra thousand dollars, I do pay extra taxes, but only in fractional amounts so that I am strongly motivated to earn more in order to have more.

Now consider a family below some defined poverty level—say, $4,000, in a typical year in the early 1970s, for a couple with two children. Below that level they are deemed to have no capacity to pay any taxes; and indeed under current philosophies of equity and ability to pay, our democracy feels that they should receive government aids. In short, these aids constitute a tax in reverse—a *negative* income tax.

But here is where incentives come in. It is a common mistake to think that only the unemployed are poor, or that only fatherless families are poor. Statistics show that much of poverty is among the *working* poor—people who simply cannot earn in the marketplace what is today considered a minimum-needed income. They, and their children, are deemed to merit government help.

Yet how can these aids be given them so as not to deter their efforts and incentives? Here is where the negative income tax provides a great improvement over those welfare programs which deprive people of all assistance the moment they get even a poor job. (And, of course, those on assistance know this very well and are thus deterred from trying to improve their position.) Just as the positive income tax is geared between $10,000 and $11,000 to leave people with an incentive to better themselves, the formula for the negative income tax is gauged to leave the poor with more income after they have used their own efforts to raise their private earnings by a thousand dollars, or even by a dollar. Even when their total tax is negative, their marginal tax rate is always a positive fraction less than unity.

Negative income tax blends compassion with incentives:

POSSIBLE FORMULA FOR NEGATIVE INCOME TAX		
PRIVATE EARNINGS	ALGEBRAIC TAX (+ if tax; − if aid received)	AFTER-TAX INCOME
$ 0	− $2,000	$2,000
1,000	− 1,500	2,500
2,000	− 1,000	3,000
3,000	− 500	3,500
4,000	0	4,000
5,000	+ 500	4,500

TABLE 39-1.   Here, a couple with two children is guaranteed at least $2,000 a year, but is left with incentive to work. (Verify this in last column.) The poverty line (shown in gold) could be raised as the nation gets wealthier, and, of course, the formula can be modified for families of varying sizes.

Possible formula   Table 39-1 illustrates how a typical negative income tax might work. What is shown there for a family with two children could be easily modified in the case of more or fewer family members. And of course, as the country grows richer and can afford to be more generous, the formula could be changed to begin at a higher level and to define a poverty level that is higher both in dollar terms and perhaps in terms of dollars of constant purchasing power.

The paramount advantages of the negative income tax are many.

1. It can replace much of present welfare assistance that destroys incentives.

2. It can help to equalize minimum levels of well-being over all the diverse regions of the United States.

3. It is less demeaning to the poor.

4. It could have various advantages of simple administration by the Revenue Service.[6]

GUARANTEED JOBS

The merits of the negative income tax are obvious. Criticisms of it are (1) that it will be costly and, like social security and Medicare, will grow increasingly in scope and cost; (2) that adequate benefits in New York City would be lavish in Mississippi and in rural areas generally; (3) that it can only supplement, not replace, existing welfare programs; (4) that it is niggardly in amount; and, most important of all to the man in the street, (5) that "people ought to have to work for their living, not be entitled to a guaranteed income handed to them on a silver platter."

Opinion polls report that many more people favor guaranteed *jobs* than guaranteed *incomes*. And some people have proposed that *the government be the employer of last resort:* anyone who cannot get a decent job from private industry should have the right to a job from the government.

The National Commission on Technology, Automation, and Economic Progress, consisting of prominent business, labor, and academic leaders, recommended in its 1966 Report to the government:

With the best of fiscal and monetary policies, there will always be those handicapped in the competition for jobs by lack of education, skill, experience, or because of discrimination. The needs of our society provide ample opportunities to fulfill the promise of the Employment Act of 1946: "a job for all those able, willing, and seeking to work." We recommend a program of public service employment, providing, in effect, that the Government be an employer of last resort, providing work for the "hard-core unemployed" in useful community enterprises.

If a program to guarantee jobs was as feasible as a program to guarantee minimum incomes, work for all would surely be the preferable alternative. It would be nice to screen out the lazy by having work available for all. But what if the government cannot devise useful, efficient, and satisfying tasks for the less employable part of the population? Digging holes and filling them up, or standing around in pointless and transparent idleness, can be destructive to personal and group morale. Hence, most economists recommend that macroeconomic policy be supplemented by manpower placement and training programs to achieve virtual full employment, but with the negative income tax providing minimal living standards for those who still cannot qualify for work.

---

[6]For more on the negative income tax, see the readings by James Tobin and Robert J. Lampman in P. A. Samuelson, *Readings, op. cit.,* and the article by Milton Friedman in Melvin Laird, ed., *The Republican Papers* (Anchor Books, Doubleday & Company, Inc., Garden City, N.Y., 1969).

THE QUALITY OF LIFE

This chapter has discussed the problems of inequality and of poverty. The quantity of gross national product cannot be appraised independently of its distribution. But even if inequality could be considerably reduced and poverty largely alleviated, there still remain important and vexing questions about the quality of life.

In the nineteenth century, moralists like Thomas Carlyle and John Ruskin declaimed against the acquisitive society. The poet Wordsworth expressed a common sentiment in the lines

> Give all thou canst; high Heaven rejects the lore
> Of nicely-calculated less or more.

And as a society becomes more comfortably situated, the more can it afford to indulge this distaste for a purely pecuniary motivation based on self-interest.

When scarcity ends Indeed we do not face squarely the philosophical issue if we make an era of greater altruism wait on the disappearance of scarcity. Marxians early had the notion of the ultimate "withering away of the state," after a transitory period of state capitalism and dictatorship of the proletariat. But such pie in the sky cannot appease the legitimate desire in the here and now of a Soviet citizen for greater political freedom. Similarly, there is no great virtue in paying lip service to unselfishness *after* there is superabundance. The test of sincerity of belief in a cause is how much you will sacrifice for it.

Galbraith was premature in proclaiming the end of scarcity at mid-century. But actually John Maynard Keynes had anticipated Galbraith by almost 30 years. In 1930 Keynes made the following prophecy with respect to the future:[7]

. . . suppose that a hundred years hence we are all of us . . . eight times better off . . . than we are today. . . . Assuming no important wars and no important increase in population, the *economic problem* may be solved. . . . This means that the economic problem is not—if we look into the future—*the permanent problem of the human race.*

Why, you may ask, is this so startling? It is startling because—if instead of looking into the future, we look into the past—we find that the economic problem, the struggle for subsistence, always has been hitherto the primary, most pressing problem of the human race—not only of the human race, but of the whole of the biological kingdom from the beginnings of life in its most primitive forms.

Thus we have been expressly evolved by nature—with all our impulses and deepest instincts —for the purpose of solving the economic problem. If the economic problem is solved, mankind will be deprived of its traditional purpose. . . . I think with dread of the readjustment of the habits and instincts of the ordinary man, bred into him for countless generations, which he may be asked to discard within a few decades.

To use the language of today—must we not expect a general "nervous breakdown"? . . . Thus for the first time since his creation man will be faced with his real, his permanent problem—how to use his freedom from pressing economic cares, how to occupy the leisure, which science and compound interest will have won for him, to live wisely and agreeably and well. . . .

[7] J. M. Keynes, "Economic Possibilities for Our Grandchildren," reprinted in his *Essays in Persuasion* (Macmillan, London, 1933) and also in P. A. Samuelson, *Readings, op. cit.*

There are changes in other spheres too which we must expect to come. When the accumulation of wealth is no longer of high social importance, there will be great changes in the code of morals. We shall be able to rid ourselves of many of the pseudo-moral principles which have hag-ridden us for two hundred years, by which we have exalted some of the most distasteful of human qualities into the position of the highest virtues. . . . The love of money as a possession—as distinguished from the love of money as a means to the enjoyments and realities of life—will be recognized for what it is, a somewhat disgusting morbidity, one of those semi-criminal, semi-pathological propensities which one hands over with a shudder to the specialists in mental disease.

But beware! the time for all this is not yet. For at least another hundred years we must pretend to ourselves and to every one that fair is foul and foul is fair; for foul is useful and fair is not. Avarice and usury and precaution must be our gods for a little longer still.

. . . in making preparations for our destiny . . . let us not overestimate the importance of the economic problem. . . . It should be a matter for specialists—like dentistry. If economists could manage to get themselves thought of as humble, competent people, on a level with dentists, that would be splendid!

This is indeed a passage of profound and prophetic insight. For one thing, despite the Great Depression, which had for a time set Keynes' time schedule behind, we are now right on target. In the 40 years since Keynes wrote, real output per head has grown at almost precisely the 2 per cent per annum rate that Keynes had prophesied.

For another thing, has not Keynes perhaps given a clue to the nature of the generation gap that is so prominent a feature of our time? In college youth, among offspring of affluence particularly, we can perhaps see the change in moral code that Keynes predicted would be the outcome of affluence. In view of modern psychiatric opinion that many of the young in the advanced nations are plagued by the problem of "existential vacuum," one of whose symptoms is a disquieting search for meaning and purpose in life, there is an almost uncanny clinical precision in Keynes' diagnosis that hitherto economic necessity has shaped man's very biological nature and provided him with that purpose. For what is more purposeful than filling your belly when it is empty? Tigers in the jungle do not Hamlet-like debate the meaning of meaning.

ONE FOOT IN AFFLUENCE

But we are not yet arrived at Utopia. In the meantime, in the here and now, what is it that economists must economize? This was the title of a provocative address given by the late Sir Dennis Robertson of Trinity College, Cambridge, on the occasion of the two-hundredth anniversary of the founding of Columbia University. What economists economize, said Robertson, is "love," for that is the scarcest commodity in the universe. We must make what we have go a long way. We must not waste this precious resource on petty problems which the mechanisms of the marketplace can handle.[8]

If the time is not yet when we can dispense with the economic system, still the time is long past when we can permit it to be master rather than good servant. We do still need the efficiency of our large corporations. But that is no reason for permitting a

[8] And yet, as was discussed in the Appendix to Chapter 25 dealing with game theory and with the problem of prisoners' dilemma, it is only in *special* social situations, where the checks and balances of competition happen to be available, that we can dispense with love and altruism if the good society is to be achieved.

military-industrial complex to be the arbiter of our national policy. We must be ungrateful recipients, and indeed bite the hand that helps to feed us. This is the privilege that the abundance of science and the Industrial Revolution has given us.

SUMMARY

1   Where economic inequality serves no economic purpose, ethical observers criticize its existence. And even where it does serve a function, such observers are willing to pay some price in terms of inefficiency for alleviating it. Now that a measure of affluence, above and beyond the minimum of subsistence, is available, the citizenry insists upon certain minimum living standards for all.

2   The view, associated with Pareto, that inequality is a universal constant which cannot be much affected by policy, is not consonant with historical experience. In the advanced countries, Lorenz curves of inequality show less disparity of living standards than they do in the underdeveloped regions. Coupling Smithian self-interest with universal suffrage has led, as the founding fathers predicted, to the modern welfare state with its multifarious social security programs of *mutual reinsurance.*

3   The laws of motion of capitalism, from Victorian laissez faire to the modern mixed economy, follow no simple formulas. Without substantial redistributive transfer expenditure by government, inequality of standards of life would presumably persist. But, provided educational opportunities prevail and monopolization of markets is thwarted, neither is there a valid iron law of ever-increasing polarization of wealth.

4   The major causes of inequality involve differences in (a) property ownership, (b) personal ability (attributable to both environment and heredity, (c) education, training, and opportunity, and (d) age and health. Decaying, but still with us in some degree, is the belief that it is the fault of the poor themselves if they are poor; and that private charity should be relied on to handle the cases of greatest distress.

5   For centuries public policy has provided asylums and hospitals, poor farms and old-people's homes, and various forms of ad hoc relief in times of famine and depression. But only in modern times has the positive role of government become dominant.

6   Cradle-to-grave social security and medical care are common among the mixed economies abroad. Only since the New Deal have social security and federally financed relief and welfare programs developed here. And only since the 1960s has there been a determined battle at the national level against poverty. Some form of the negative income tax—i.e., minimum-guaranteed-income-cum-incentives—seems the next item on the social agenda, providing as it does fewer difficulties than a program of jobs for all in which the government is the employer of last resort for hard-core unemployables.

7   As the problem of mere survival gradually recedes into the background (at least in the West), the problem of the *quality* of economic life begins to take precedence over the problem of mere quantity. How we shall use our new leisure and how we shall develop new codes of conduct are problems the future will pose.

QUESTIONS FOR DISCUSSION

1   From 1945 to 1970 inequality of incomes in the United States has not changed much. Is this an indictment of the system in your view? Or a symptom of the difficulty of a program for changing matters quickly in this sphere?

2   Do state and private colleges perpetuate inequality? What about the draft?

3   Why not jobs for all? What are next steps in your view (free medical care for all? . . .)?

4   Can you draw a graph of the tax structure both in the positive and the negative range of taxes? Is it the case that the more you earn the more you keep?

5   Was Keynes borrowing trouble in his worrying about the future? Cannot people be happy without working?

Review your understanding of the following concepts:

Pareto's laws   guaranteed jobs
Lorenz measures of inequality   end of scarcity
negative income tax   self-interest and altruism

Economic Problems of Race, Cities, and the Polluted Environment

40

Most of the world is nonwhite. But the white minority do control most of the economic power, and do enjoy a disproportionate standard of living. Within the most advanced economic society, the United States, the one in nine citizens who is black has long had to do with a measurably lower level of income and wealth. Along with these economic disadvantages have gone political and sociological deprivations that the modern conscience can no longer ignore.

Other minorities have also suffered from discrimination and lack of ordinary privilege. Americans of Mexican origin receive less-than-average incomes and have been the victims of prejudice in the Southwest and elsewhere. In recent decades our Eastern cities have been the mecca for a host of migrants from Puerto Rico, and for them the American melting pot has been slow to assimilate. Finally, the first inhabitants of this continent, the American Indians, have yet to receive their full share of the economic and social opportunities we boast of in our Fourth of July orations.

IMMIGRATION AND THE MELTING POT

Sometimes it is argued that such discrimination is nothing new or permanent. Three hundred years ago the settlers from Britain became the dominant elite. Anthropologists observe that every in-group is somewhat hostile to the outsider. Hence, when the potato famine of the 1840s sent hundreds of thousands of Irishmen to our shores, there was naturally resentment of these newcomers, particularly since they were often illiterate farmers. (Boston Brahmins are reminded of what is in the historical record, that many of *their* first ancestors in this country made their mark because they could not yet sign their names.)

As the tale goes, then came the Germans. Their strange language made them the butt of local humor: "No dogs or Germans need apply" was a frequent sign in lodging houses and in notices concerning job opportunities. But in time, as the society pages of Milwaukee and St. Louis newspapers will confirm, the children of German immigrants became part of the ruling elite. When you read Sinclair Lewis's novels about life on the main streets of Minnesota, you are reminded how the Scandinavians were regarded as boorish "Norskies," whereas today to have the name of Anderson or Olson is a positive advantage in the search for elective office. And so it has been with respect to the turn-of-the-century tide of immigration from Eastern and Southern Europe. A few Jews from Holland and Germany came to this land and prospered as merchants and investment bankers; a subsequent mass migration from Russia led, at first, to sweatshop conditions within a stone's throw of the Ellis Island point of entry; but gradually through the workings of the marvelous American melting pot, their grandchildren have come to occupy comfortable homes in Westchester or Los Angeles County. In the same way the descendants of the Italian immigrants who crowded into Boston's North End 60 years ago are now found throughout the greater Boston or San Francisco area. So runs the argument.

Of course, there is a measure of truth in this romanticized view of American history. But only a naïve sentimentalist would believe that this view of discrimination *as only temporary* applies here, or anywhere in the world. Nowhere is there a classless society free of prejudice and in which the laws of supply and demand operate in an even-handed way. It is the kernels of truth in the tales of successful integration of immigrant groups into the mainstream of American life which point up ironically the problems of American Negroes and Indians. The Sioux did not arrive here yesterday. And it is more than 100 years since slavery was abolished. Obviously the ancient timetable of gradual immigrant assimilation is not the relevant pattern for the student of the economics of race.

ECONOMICS OF SLAVERY

Little has been told in our history books about the black civilizations and cultures that were flourishing in Africa when the noble Teuton was still cowering over his primitive campfires in Northern Europe. We do know how the profit motive led to the slave trade: pursuing maximum profit—equating marginal revenues and costs, so to speak—merchants used bribery and force to abduct Africans in order to export and sell them in the New World. So long as a plentiful supply of replacement imports could be counted on, each slave was regarded as an exhaustible resource: just as a vein of copper can be worked to depletion, a slave could be worked to death without regard for natural reproduction or old-age incapacity. (The Spaniards had already found in South America that the native Indian population would not fruitfully produce and reproduce in captivity, instead dying out rapidly from disease and overwork.)

When conscience led to legal abolition of slave importation, around 1800, the economics rapidly adjusted.[1] The newer farmlands of the Mississippi afforded a high marginal-

---

[1] Illegal importation of slaves continued well into the last century, as pursuit of profit led to the same flouting of law that one sees in connection with traffic in narcotics. For that matter, illegal slavery is still a problem in the Middle East, as the United Nations commissions well know.

product to the owners of slaves. The older, depleted soils of the tidewater and border regions could no longer make such good economic use of slave manpower. Hence, the Invisible Hand of competition acted so that the tidewater regions came to specialize in the production and reproduction of slaves, for sale to the fertile lands westward.

Spontaneous decay of slavery? Among historians, most of whom knew even less of economics than they knew of the facts of history, a myth later grew up that slavery in the decades before the Civil War was becoming economically unprofitable. According to the myth, if Lincoln could have been a little more patient, the South's peculiar institution would have collapsed of its own weight. Economists, such as Yale's John Meyer and CCNY's Alfred Conrad, have convincingly utilized econometric analysis to show how unfounded this idea was. Quotations for slaves in the auction markets of Savannah and Charleston, taken in conjunction with the costs of food and of child-rearing in the tidewater, show that as high a competitive profit could be earned from the production of slaves as from the production of tobacco or cotton. (The intersection of ss supply and dd demand curves showed no signs of moving toward the vertical axis of zero slavery!)[2]

The tools of economic analysis tell us that labor productivity was rising mightily in the years before and after the Civil War. Why then should technological innovations have downgraded the marginal productivity of black hands and minds? If Swedes and Poles and Welshmen were needed for productive jobs in the northern mines and prairies of a century ago, and if supply and demand bid up their wages to far beyond levels in Europe and far beyond subsistence levels of reproduction, how could anyone but an economic illiterate have believed in the economic decay of slavery? Particularly when the records show that the artisans of the South, the carpenters and mechanics and not merely the farmhands, were largely black?

THE REVOLUTION DELAYED

After an abortive period of Reconstruction, Jim Crow legislation restored the black population to a caste system of peonage. The economic concept of "noncompeting groups" became applicable with a vengeance. Most of the well-paying jobs were simply unavailable to Negroes (and, deprived of education, they could not have qualified for them anyway). The existing supply of black workers had to be auctioned off along the demand schedules for the low-skill jobs that were open to them. Figure 40-1 shows how the economics of discriminatory exclusion works, whether it be in India in connection with the so-called "untouchable" castes, in Jim Crow America, or for that matter in the insurance and banking industries that still discriminate strongly in favor of native white Protestants of Anglo-Saxon origin.

Supply and demand for some favored employment are shown in Fig. 40-1(a). The supply

[2]Believers in this myth thought of it as kind of a benevolent development. But a close look at the economics of the situation shows that treating human beings as economic chattels will lead, in a situation where they have allegedly become "uneconomic," to genocide and extinction no less abhorrent than the genocide in the gas chambers of Hitler's Germany. During the decade of the 1920s, the horse became uneconomic on the farms of Indiana; and by 1930, through birth prevention and slaughter, the tractor had taken over and the workhorse had become extinct.

of privileged white labor is shown by SS. The demand curve for their labor, derived from their productive worth at the margin to the employers producing the important goods in industries from which blacks are excluded, is shown as *DD*. Equilibrium is at the high white wage shown at *E*. Meantime, what is happening on the plantation or in the enforced ghetto is shown in Fig. 40-1(b)? Working with inferior tools and being permitted to produce only certain limited goods that are not particularly desired by society, the demand curve for occupations open to blacks or untouchable castes is shown as *dd*. Their supply *ss* intersects *dd* at the low equilibrium *e*, where *their* market is just cleared. Note the discrepancy between the two equilibria.

Exclusion has discriminated against the earning power of the black workers. They are much worse off than the white workers. Such is the remorseless verdict of supply and demand if discrimination can be enforced by custom, law, or union collusion.

What would be the ideal situation in terms of both human equity and economic effi-

Racial discrimination exploits blacks and lowers total output:

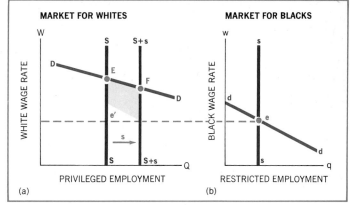

FIG. 40-1. Suppose blacks are excluded from good employment in (a) and must work in inferior employment (say, menial domestic service) in (b). Then white *DD* and *SS* intersect at high-wage *E*; and black *dd* and *ss* intersect in (b) at low-wage *e*. If all forms of discrimination and segregation were ended, all would go to highest-wage jobs, and blacks would go to (a), as shown by gold arrow of shifted supply there. New equilibrium with equal wages for all would come at *F*, where *SS + ss* intersects demand. The great gain in black wages would not be at the expense of an equal fall in white wages (which would fall, but only a little, because of the gentle action of diminishing returns). Ending discrimination necessarily increases total of product, so gainers (including now-better-off white capitalists!) always get more than losers lose. The gold shaded area under *EF* measures the gain in total GNP (because the area's lower boundary is drawn at the level of the productivity in (b) above *e*).

ciency? If we let the *ss* supply of Fig. 40-1(b) be added to the SS supply of Fig. 40-1(a), we would have the new light S + s curve of nondiscriminatory supply. Now at little expense to white wages, we would see a near doubling of black wages. Where would the extra wage income come from? It would *not* come primarily from an exaction by the blacks from the whites (even though justice might merit such a reparation if there were no other way to achieve equity). For the white workers receive pretty much the same wage as before, their only diminution coming from the weak operation of the law of diminishing returns, as shown by the slight drop along *DD*. The extra income for the blacks comes from the extra GNP that their higher productivity in their new employment brings as compared with their previous lower productivity enforced by discrimination. Instead of sweeping Milady's kitchen floor with an old broom, so to speak, now the Negro draws good pay working a modern computer-billing machine. Instead of cutting another ghetto resident's hair, the urban black now can hope to teach intermediate French at the state university. That is the implication of Fig. 40-1 *after* discrimination has vanished and the educational disadvantages that went with it have disappeared.[3]

---

[3]For emphasis, Fig. 40-1 is drawn with *dd* shown as below *DD* from the beginning, implying that after discrimination is removed all menial work disappears. It would be more realistic to redraw *dd* so that

CHANGES IN ATTITUDES

That day of nondiscrimination has not remotely arrived. By custom, it used to be rare for blacks to be given supervisory jobs in which they give orders to whites. And in many industries, white workers would not countenance working alongside black workers. Slowly, by the force of laws against discrimination and by education and by militant protest, this pattern of segregation has been loosening up a little. What happened long ago in the post office is beginning to happen at Monsanto Chemical and Litton Industries: both in the South and North, the good jobs are said to be, in principle, open to all races. Indeed, the phenomenon of "tokenism" has begun to develop: large corporations vie for a presentable black Harvard Business School graduate in order to be able to boast of an assistant vice-president who is a Negro.

Do the facts bear out a gradual improvement in the relative status of nonwhites as a whole? Only barely. In the stagnant 1950s, nonwhite family incomes averaged about half those of white families. In the thriving 1960s, this fraction climbed from one-half to about three-fifths. Progress? Yes, slow progress. But note that much of the improvement came from the swing of the business cycle from recessionary stagnation to brisker growth. Further progress from this factor can hardly be expected once unemployment as a whole has been brought down to minimum levels below 4 per cent.

Indeed, the 1969–1970 Nixon fight against inflation has sent the over-all unemployment rate up. And experience shows this tends to move nonwhites a bit back toward the old 50 per cent fraction.

IMPROVING EDUCATIONAL OPPORTUNITY

Illiterates—white or nonwhite—get low pay, have to do dirty work, and suffer much unemployment. To a degree, the same is true of those who dropped out of school after 8 years. And of course, college-trained people tend to draw higher salaries than high school graduates.

Since nonwhites receive less schooling than whites, this gives rise to racial differentials in income *beyond* those attributable to on-the-job discrimination. If Southern-rural and ghetto-urban schooling is of lower quality than that out in the white suburbs, the differentials become all the greater. Finally, if a black child comes from a home where no father is present, where no books line the shelves, and where the mother is hard-pressed to care for many children on a limited relief check, then already at the age of six the beginning student is under a handicap with respect to learning performance and educational achievement. From ages six to fourteen, the disparities in reading ability or arithmetical and verbal skills become all the greater—particularly if white teachers are relying on middle-class modes of instruction and tests of accomplishment. (A so-called "IQ test," which purports to measure "native general intelligence," is easier for a white if it uses familiar concepts like a bank check than if it were to ask "How long do you

---

it rises upward on the left asymptotically toward the vertical W axis. Then new nondiscriminatory equilibrium comes on a new third diagram, at intersection of horizontally-added SS and ss with horizontally-added DD and dd at an equilibrium just above F (but at a common wage lower than E).

cook chitlings?")[4] Discouraged by a curriculum that is meaningless to his life, the highly intelligent young black may become a "street hustler" rather than a Rhodes scholar; he sells numbers or pushes drugs rather than cracking the atom.

Very slowly, leading universities are recruiting black students. By law, public schools are becoming a bit less segregated—although the mere fact that nonwhites tend to be poor, and the poor tend to live together, leads to de facto segregation without any need for deliberate discrimination. Still we can expect nonwhites of the next generation to improve somewhat in opportunity and in economic status.

PROFESSIONAL AND ENTREPRENEURIAL OPPORTUNITY: "BLACK CAPITALISM"

In the past, few nonwhites have become engineers or vice-presidents of large corporations. A very few did become doctors, dentists, and lawyers—catering primarily to the "protected market" of black clients. Many more, particularly women, became teachers—again largely teaching black pupils.

Of course there have always been a few black millionaires from banks or insurance companies catering to black customers. But a census of nonwhite businesses will show a rather dismal picture: barber and hairdressing shops, laundries and dry cleaners, small restaurants and grocery stores—these, and real-estate operations in the ghetto, just about cover historic black capitalism.

What about the future? Can private enterprise *spontaneously* close the gap between the races in incomes and standards of life? Few believe this. Capital is scarce in the ghetto; credit is dear and hard to get. Risks are great, with bankruptcy and failures frequent. Because of riot and theft risk, insurance is many times more expensive and often simply unobtainable without government subsidy. Since inventories must be kept to a minimum to reduce risk, customer choice is limited. Because ghetto dwellers are poor, credit must often be granted and the price charged must be raised in order to cover risk of default. Even the prices in chain stores are found to be higher, and quality lower, in the ghetto than in the prosperous suburbs.

Many of the tools of Chapter 38 on economic development can be applied to understand the problems of the ghetto. It can be regarded as an underdeveloped area, but one operating with the great disadvantage of having to be contiguous with and compete with the most developed economy in the world. Just as the Malay peasants resent the Chinese entrepreneurs and the Kenyan natives resent the poor Indian traders in their midst, ghetto dwellers naturally resent the white merchants who run small stores

---

[4] It costs money to improve teaching and learning. The Coleman Report of 1966 alleged to prove statistically that more money spent on schooling to compensate for nonwhite disadvantage would improve things but little. (See James S. Coleman et al., *Equality of Educational Opportunity*, U.S. Government Printing Office, Washington, 1966.) However, statistical audit has cast doubt on the validity of the statistical methods used in the report. Similarly, a controversial article by Arthur Jensen in the Winter, 1969, *Harvard Educational Review* alleged that the average 15 per cent shortfall of black IQs in comparison with whites was substantially due to genetic factors and, hence, that it would be better to give nonwhites vocational and rote (rather than analytical) instruction. However, critics in great number have concluded that Jensen was *not able* to control properly for the differences in environment (nongenetic) factors, which operate to handicap nonwhites in preschool years.

in the inner city. These merchants tend to be regarded as "exploiters," who return at night to their comfortable suburban homes loaded with surplus value garnered from the poor.[5] Actual statistics on rate of return of such small-scale white businesses suggest that their rate of profitability is low relative to the labor and resources required. When they can, the sons of white merchants leave the ghetto for more profitable pastures elsewhere. And the slumlord is more likely to be a low-middle-class capitalist than a tycoon of high finance. (Some slum tenements are actually being abandoned by their owners as not netting their taxes.)

Can salvation come by replacing the small-scale white "exploiters" by a new group of small-scale black "exploiters"? There is in any case little likelihood of such a spontaneous flowering of black capitalism. Before the French Revolution, Marie Antoinette said, "Let them eat cake." It is as irrelevant and cruel today to quote to the 11 per cent nonwhite population Ben Franklin's adage, "Keep thy shop and thy shop will keep thee."

Subsidized black capitalism   If the ghetto is like an underdeveloped country, why not rely on all the devices that have been suggested to stimulate economic development? As Chapter 38 discussed, these include import of capital from the more developed economies, and also foreign aid in the form of welfare transfers or gifts of capital. Transmission of knowledge, skills, and business-management methods is also indicated along the lines of the international Point Four programs. And just as the best students are sent from Asia to the United States for higher education, so one can hope that some of the talented youth from the inner city will return, after their years in the Ivy League and the Yale Law School, to work on urban and race problems. Domestically, as well as internationally, one must worry about a "brain drain" of the best talents away from the sector most in need of development.

Specific programs could involve government subsidies (1) to bring industry to the ghetto and inner city itself, (2) to provide cheaper risk capital and lower insurance rates for black enterprise, and (3) to help develop basic business skills. Although President Nixon has advocated such measures, by 1970 comparatively little had yet been accomplished along these lines. More could be done by the use of the tax system to give special tax subsidies to activities that add to ghetto employment. Or, since transportation from the inner ghetto to factories on the city perimeter is often unavailable, and since the unemployed are unlikely to have cars, subsidies to commuter-bus services make sense.

For the most part though, the outlook for black capitalism has not improved much. Dr. Andrew F. Brimmer, an eminent black economist who is a Governor of the Federal Reserve Board in Washington, has warned in a 1969 speech against too much hope in this direction.

. . . my purpose today is not to demean small businesses which I feel do offer modest opportunities for some potential Negro enterprises. Rather, my purpose has been to point out some of the

---

[5] This helps explain the occurrence of some black anti-Semitism. However, careful studies in New York by Columbia researchers show that merchants are regarded as white exploiters, and suggest that if as many of them were Italians or Irish as are now Jews, there would presumably be anti-Italian and anti-Irish sentiment in the ghetto.

serious economic pitfalls of a strategy based upon separatism and segregation. Economic separatism has been tried in the past, and it has failed to provide genuine opportunity for Negro businessmen—and it certainly has failed to provide economic well-being for our Negro population. I am personally convinced that the most promising path of economic opportunity for Negroes lies in full participation in an integrated national economy. This holds for Negroes who want to be businessmen as well as for everyone else. The sooner we recognize this important lesson from the past, the quicker we can start to attack the real obstacles to the Negro's economic progress in the United States.

SEPARATISM VERSUS INTEGRATION

Economics cannot dictate values. Even if integration could lead to higher nonwhite living standards, blacks could decide to make the sacrifices required to lead their own lives. And many militant separatists, who believe in black nationalism, argue: "We will never get integration . . . only empty promises. Uncle Tomism never worked anyway. . . . Let us cultivate our own great historical past. Let us engage in African and American black studies. Let us realize black is indeed beautiful, and let us fraternize only with our own brothers and sisters. That way lies self-pride and power. And that way lies *ultimate* better economic well-being too."

Abstractly, one could analyze a model of complete "apartheid" following the South African design. But it is doubtful if this could ever yield to the black community 11 per cent of the total GNP, or give rise in this century to even one-half the white standard of life. Still, colonial countries have often been willing to throw off the colonial yoke even when that entailed a transitory drop in living standards for some years after liberation. And some sacrifice of economic well-being may be a cost to be willingly incurred in return for enhanced racial pride and integrity.

That some such economic cost will be exacted is suggested by Professor Arthur Lewis of Princeton, who was born in the black community of the West Indies and who has become one of the leading economists in the world. He believes:[6]

The black problem is that while we are 11 per cent of the population, we have only 2 per cent of the jobs at the top, 4 per cent of the jobs in the middle, and are forced into 16 per cent of the jobs at the bottom. . . . The measure of whether we are winning our battle is in how many of us rise to the middle and the top. When a so-called militant abuses a successful Afro-American for having, by virtue of extreme hard work and immense self-discipline, managed to get to the top in the outside world instead of devoting his energies to being—in the neighborhood—a social worker, or a night school teacher, or a semi-politician, such a critic is merely being absurd.

Nearly all of the top people are taken from a very small number of colleges. The breakthrough of the Afro-American into these colleges is, therefore, absolutely fundamental to the larger economic strategy of black power. . . . Let the clever young black go to a university to study engineering, medicine, chemistry, economics, law, agriculture, and other subjects which are going to be of value to him and his people. And let the clever whites go to college to read black novels, to learn Swahili, and to record the exploits of Negro heroes of the past: they are the ones to whom this will come as an eye-opener.

[6] See the article by W. Arthur Lewis (Sir Arthur Lewis) in P. A. Samuelson, *Readings in Economics* (McGraw-Hill, New York, 1970, 6th ed.).

A SOCIOLOGICAL REVOLUTION

Hitherto no economics textbook has grappled with the problems of the economics of race. And it ill becomes a white author to think that he can provide diagnoses and prognoses for a problem of this kind. But leaving the incomplete facts behind and venturing suggestive speculations, one can hazard certain crude guesses about the process.

All over the world there has been a rising tide of expectations. Burmese will not starve quietly while they see Europe and Japan prospering. The black community within America is no exception. They are not content to sing spirituals and hope for a better future. Economically, this ideological and political and sociological revolution can be expected to affect the supply of labor and, to use a technical term, its marginal-product.

Perhaps some clue is provided here to the puzzling rise in black youth unemployment. Twenty years ago, the percentage of black youth unemployment was *less* than that of whites! Few know this remarkable fact—remarkable because today we know ghetto youth unemployment to be double and triple that of white. Many partial explanations may be given for this: (1) World War II was favorable to black employment, and the war is ever farther away; (2) there has been a mass migration of blacks from the rural South to the ghettos, and quick absorption could be expected to be difficult; (3) because of the post–World War II baby boom, there has been a plethora of young people of all races, a condition which makes for lower wages and more unemployment; (4) since more young people are in college and school today, those who are not may be of lower average quality than used to be the case, and unemployment of people of lower skills has always been greater; and (5) finally, critics of the minimum-wage laws have long claimed that such laws hurt precisely those classes they purport to help: if a man or woman is not worth $1.60 per hour to some employer, even if he is worth $1.50 and is dying for a job, he is condemned to complete unemployment.[7]

Still, none of these explanations is by itself convincing, nor are all of them together sufficient to explain the quantitative rise in youth unemployment. Shrewd observers of the labor market have suggested there may also be *a change in the supply of labor.*

People, whether black or white, simply will not take dirty, low-paid jobs the way they used to. They would rather go without, live on relief, get training, hustle, look for a better job. So the census records higher unemployment at the same time that city factories lack hands and suburban housewives complain that no one will cut their lawns. Moreover, examine the graduating class of any inner-city high school. You will find in it hundreds of girls aspiring to be typists and secretaries rather than housemaids and beauticians. Aspirations have become elevated, but at the same time if one examines performance on standardized tests, only a few can type 50 words a minute or take dictation at 100 words a minute, as is required for successful employment. And so you have a measure of discontent and one explanation for unemployment.

If the cure for lack of skill is further training, this suggests that more resources must be provided by government to improve manpower training programs. And, on a more cheerful note, some of the difficulties noted would seem to be of a transitional character. When militancy has paid off so that it is not necessary to insist on one's rights at every

[7] See, for example, Milton Friedman's strong criticism of the minimum wage, in P. A. Samuelson, *Readings, op. cit.*, and some counterarguments there.

turn, the supply of labor and its marginal-product can cease to show the effects of a sociological revolution in process of taking place.

ECONOMICS OF GHETTO HOUSING

The environmental disadvantages of slum living and segregated schools, as we have seen, have a cumulative impact in handicapping the economic status of the nonwhite population. Blacks do not choose to live in smog and congestion in preference to suburban greenlands. Because of historic patterns of segregation, they face limited choice. Traditionally, racial covenants in real-estate deeds were used to keep neighborhoods restricted from minority occupation. After the courts had struck down such covenants, tacit discrimination by real-estate agencies and landlords pretty much continued the old pattern.

In the beginning bigotry was shameless. Later it became somewhat shamefaced. More and more people began to say: "*I* am not bigotted. But *others* are. And it is a well-known fact that property values go to pieces when Negroes get a toehold in a white neighborhood."

This becomes then what the Columbia sociologist Robert K. Merton calls a "self-fulfilling prophecy." If people believe in it and act on it, even if originally it were false, it may become true.

However, let us turn to the economic facts about race and real estate. If you tabulate bills of sale in two similar communities, but where one has had blacks move into it and the other has not, what would such a controlled experiment show? That is, of course, the relevant question, because it is obvious that many inner-city neighborhoods which are in economic decay will have falling prices anyway even if there are no racial intermixtures; and it is also well known that the black community tends to be confined to decaying neighborhoods which only poor people can afford.

A careful study of *matched* city neighborhoods, carried out under the auspices of the University of California[8] researchers and covering such diverse cities as Oakland and Detroit, Chicago and Portland, reveals:

It is a myth of the real-estate fraternity that desegregation of a neighborhood harms real-estate values. "Block busting," so-called, in fact if anything *raises* property values (as the block buster who spreads false rumors knows very well).

And why not when you come to think about it? Precisely because the black buyer and renter is discriminated against, his demand bids up the prices of those properties which may be available to him. Figure 40-2 on the next page illustrates the economics of housing discrimination in a fashion reminiscent of Fig. 40-1's analysis of job discrimination. When the real-estate market is split into two parts, and if the blacks are allotted less than their per capita share, the auction market bids up the rentals that can be exacted from them. After the barriers have been eliminated, rentals for similar accommodations become equalized—resulting in both a more equitable and a more efficient equilibrium.

---

[8]L. Laurenti, *Property Value and Race: Studies in Seven Cities* (University of California Press for Commission on Race and Housing, Berkeley and Los Angeles, 1960).

Discrimination raises rents to blacks:

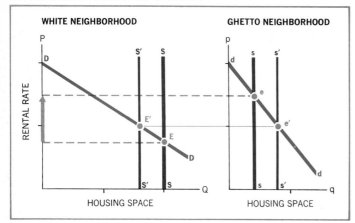

FIG. 40-2. Blue demand curves are drawn to be the same per capita. Without discrimination, rents would be at the common level *E'* and *e'* with same allocation of living space per capita. (In fact the markets could be combined in the absence of segregation, with everyone living at random.) But suppose under segregation blacks are given only half their per capita share of space. Then their *dd* intersects their allotted *ss* at high *e* rentals. Whites' *DD* intersects their unfairly swollen *SS* at low-level *E*. The gold arrow on the left measures the gap due to discrimination. (Though slumlords gain, landlords as a class actually lose!)

ECONOMICS OF URBAN BLIGHT

Discussion of housing segregation brings us to the general problem of urban decay. This topic heavily overlaps the economics of races and minorities, since the inner city is increasingly becoming the sole province of blacks, Puerto Ricans, Mexicans, and recent immigration groups. Metropolitan areas continue to grow, but it is the suburban areas around the old city limits which show the most rapid growth. Half a century ago urban sociologists, such as Robert Park of the University of Chicago, delineated *circular* patterns of city development. At the center is the downtown shopping district, the locale for luxury hotels, banks, and office buildings. Surrounding this nucleus is the tenderloin district of decay, where vice and vagrancy abound. Still further out come workingmen's flats and homes; and then finally you arrive at middle-class country. Farthest out of all are the estates, polo fields, and hunting acres of the very rich.

The circles fan out dynamically. As the middle classes move farther out, their old neighborhoods change. Mansions are broken up into rooming houses, and apartments that once housed 4 people come to house 10 or more. A new tenderloin or ghetto is born.

It is a mistake to think that this is an invariable pattern. A lakefront or river can modify the circular form. Or, as in Los Angeles, the ubiquity of the auto may destroy any real notion of a *center* to the city—which becomes, and perhaps should become, nothing but a concrete switchboard for the rerouting of freeway traffic. Manhattan and European capitals are also an exception, in that slum neighborhoods there are repeatedly reclaimed by the gold-coast clientele just through the force of dynamic competition. But still a general circular pattern can be discerned both here and abroad.

Experts tell us that it is *not* the case that slum and ghetto dwellers are worse housed as a whole than in the past. A count of the number of bathrooms per person, of rats, of hot-water versus cold-water flats, of outdoor privies versus indoor toilets, reveals that, whatever middle-class visitors may think of the inner city, conditions there are actually better now, on the average, than they used to be. This has not come about as the result of generosity or public programs so much as the result of the exodus of previous residents to the suburbs. Indeed, in a sense, inner-city dwellers are the *temporary beneficiaries* of buildings vacated by previous occupants and destined to be torn down soon as a result of the spontaneous growth of commercial activity in the city.

THE FEDERAL BULLDOZER

Ironically, the efforts by government to redevelop the inner city have in some measure served to help the middle class and to hurt the poor. When old tenement buildings are torn down and new developments put in their place, to the eye there has been an aesthetic improvement and an increase in space per person. But for whose benefit? For those tenants who lived in crowded quarters before? Only too rarely. Often the previous tenants are hard put to find quarters anywhere near so good as that which was torn down. And the new tenants who come in are young professional and white-collar couples who are childless and (most often) white. If a black family can pay $300 a month, it is free to live there. If . . . .

What can be done about this? Leave the slums to stew in their own juice, waiting for the Invisible Hand of perfect competition to rescue them? Deny governments the power to take land and buildings coercively under the right of eminent domain? Some urbanists have suggested just this. A more popular alternative, however, is to reshape the character of urban redevelopment programs along the following lines:

1. In rebuilding any neighborhood, responsibility should be assumed *in advance* for those who will become the victims of the new program. This involves rehousing of those displaced, either within the new development, or through location in as good housing elsewhere. This will cost money and require careful planning.

2. Massive apartment developments can themselves develop urban blight while their paint and mortar are scarcely dry. Such exceptional cases do not at all confirm the ancient canard, "You can get people out of the slums, but you can't get the slums out of the people." But it is a sad fact of modern life that life can be unsafe in the asphalt jungle and in open urban spaces after dark. Rent subsidies to people, so that they can fix up their own houses or take over and improve existing structures, have in many cases added more to the total of human happiness than have architectural cakeboxes on a grand scale. Here is a challenging field for creative research and public innovation.

THE POLLUTED ENVIRONMENT

One merely sees in the city in exaggerated degree a problem common to all modern life, namely, contamination of the general environment. The smog in Los Angeles is the sign in the skies of what is impending for cities elsewhere. Really clear days in New York, Paris, or Tokyo are almost completely a thing of the past.

Mark Twain said, "Man is the only species that feels shame—or has reason to." Certainly man is the only animal who has managed to pollute the atmosphere itself. Sulfur dioxide and particulates pollute the air of every city. The climate of the world changes as a result of what the Industrial Revolution has done to the concentration of carbon dioxide in the air. Some scientists believe that the irreversible accumulation of lead in the air we breathe will soon become a problem everywhere in the world. Strontium 90 and radioactive trace elements have been the consequence of atomic testing; and the threat of the ultimate-doomsday cobalt bomb which will end all human life forever is more than an old-wives' bogey tale. Even noise pollutes the urban environment.

External diseconomies   Here is a case of what we have met earlier under the heading of an "external diseconomy." The most pessimistic diagnosis of all is that ultimately the automobile is the prime cause of smog. Factories can be made to have high chimneys and to burn sulfur-free fuels. Strip mining of coal, which despoils the scenery, can be forbidden unless the topography is restored. Thermal contamination of rivers can be controlled by zoning ordinances and costly cooling towers. But to deprive each commuter of his natural right of driving to work each day in a box full of air is apparently more than any modern electorate will stand.

If the consumer will not willingly pay for the extra devices needed to limit air pollution, how can one expect the auto manufacturers to solve the problem? That is like expecting the cigarette companies to commit suicide voluntarily.

Is reliance on spontaneous business efforts futile in the solution of a problem like this? Experience gives a pessimistic answer. There has been one case, though, that offers a glimmer of hope. Detergents poured into our sewage systems were found to continue to foam and to contaminate the very water table into which all rivers and underground streams flow. Conservationists gave a great outcry. And, in this story with a happy ending, the trade association of the industry did sponsor chemical research that did come up with a complete solution to the problem. By industry self-regulation, every firm in the industry has adopted the new formulas, and we have heard nothing of this problem for many years. (But then along came the phosphate problem!)

Would that the contamination of wildlife by DDT, of which the late Rachel Carson wrote so eloquently, would as nicely disappear as a problem. Or that the perfect electric battery, or more plausibly a steam engine, could be developed to reverse the smog and carbon-monoxide effects of the internal-combustion engine.

GOVERNMENT LAWS, TAXES, AND PLANNING

Since no one profit maker has the incentive, or indeed the power, to solve problems involving "externalities," here is a clear case for some kind of public intervention. Thus, the threat of the California Legislature to ban all internal-combustion engines by 1975 may be an example of the action needed to galvanize Detroit into action. Or a heavy tax on fume-emitting vehicles or factories might be in order. Furthermore, the consumer has an important role to play. He must not curse Consolidated Edison for burning fuel oil with a heavy sulfur content, and then complain if there is added onto his utilities bill an extra charge to cover the removal of sulfur or finance the purchase of more expensive, sweeter fuels.

Examples of needed rules of the road are endless. Lake Erie is dead, killed by the sewage and fertilizers that have been allowed to pour into it. Not only must the cost of producing in the regions bordering on it be increased by the amount needed to decontaminate industrial and other wastes, but in addition, each farmer cannot be allowed to use the chemical fertilizers *he* deems best—since the residue of them flows into the brooks that empty into the rivers that empty into Lake Erie. Nor can farmers and firms be allowed to dig all the artesian wells they please, since the water table underlying much of the country can become dangerously low from unrestrained use.

HARD CHOICES AND THE ECOLOGY OF NATURE

Our trillion-dollar GNP may be, in part, an illusion. When we finally pay our way in terms of conservation and in preserving the environment, perhaps we shall have left for ordinary consumption only nine-tenths as much. Nor is it a question of *affording* the taxes to finance these expensive government programs. In a real sense we cannot afford *not* to have them.

And, as in all cases of public interest, there will be conflicts of interest. Shall Dade County be allowed to build a jet airport near the Everglades National Park if that threatens wildlife there? Shall the Disney Corporation be allowed to develop a winter skiing and recreation facility deep in the Sierras if that means disturbing the historic serenity of nature? Or to take a smaller example that points up the dilemma: Shall a small town near Boston, like Lincoln, Massachusetts, be permitted to remain an island of rural serenity if, by its remaining so, the teeming masses of Boston have their recreational activities limited, and are forced to huddle on the hot pavements and crowd a few adjacent beaches?

There can be no simple scientific resolution of these conflicts. The living, and those who will live, have their rights as against the historic past. But woe to a culture that destroys all its architectural glories and turns over its rural countryside to fried-chicken and hot-dog stands.

Modern economics teaches us that the curse of overpopulation is not simply that of Malthusian food shortage due to diminishing returns. It involves also the loss of privacy and uncrowded, pure living space. Modern technology has not solved all our economic problems and repealed the laws of scarcity. On the contrary, for the rest of the century, the social agenda will be crowded with these programs of the highest human priority.

SUMMARY

1   By accident of history, the minority of whites in the world have enjoyed the greatest affluence. Naked exploitation under slavery was not a self-curing process. And a century *after* slavery, inequality of opportunity and economic racial discrimination can be shown, by the tools of competitive supply and demand, to lead to loss of income by the underprivileged classes.

2   Economic progress of the nonwhite population has been slow. The analogy with earlier immigrant groups does not stand up to the facts of history. So long as substantial differences in educational and other opportunities remain, blacks, Puerto Ricans, American Mexicans, and Indians will inherit poverty from the environment itself. *Spontaneous* black capitalism seems as yet an empty promise. Compensatory spending to offset inequalities of environment seems indicated, and the needed costs should not be underestimated.

3   Segregated housing leads de facto to educational and other discrimination. Again, the tools of supply and demand show that segregation leads to higher rents for those discriminated against, so that partially black neighborhoods find their real-estate values rising relative to what they would otherwise have been—in contrast to the usual myths.

4 Blight in the urban environment is strongly correlated in the central city with racial problems. Urban redevelopment measures, unless carefully planned, can harm those who are already the worst victims of city blight.

5 Finally, urban blight is merely a dramatic case of the more general blight of the environment produced by the modern technological economy and growth of population. Smog and air pollution can change the climate; water pollution by sewage, industrial wastes, fertilizers, and detergents, and even by the heat thrown off from nuclear and nonnuclear power plants, has made a wasteland of our earthly inheritance. These "economic externalities and diseconomies" cannot be expected to be set aright by market competition and the pursuit of profit. They call for government zoning ordinances, fiats and prohibitions, planning and coordination, subsidies and penalties of taxation. We are not so affluent as our statistics of GNP would indicate, and much remains on the future social agenda.

QUESTIONS FOR DISCUSSION

1 What are comparative numbers of white, brown, black, and yellow peoples? How is real per capital GNP distributed geographically among them?

2 Discuss slavery as an economic problem, in actual history and as myth. Has there been any progress in the field of racial discrimination? Sketch changes you think are needed in the future. Even if all discrimination ceased in the future, show what reparations in the form of compensatory educational expenditures would be needed to remove inequalities of opportunities inherited from the past. Give pros and cons of integration, separatism, and militant black power. Of spontaneous versus subsidized black capitalism. Would college blacks today agree with the Brimmer and Lewis quotations?

3 Describe the overlap between segregated housing and economic opportunity. Between race and urban problems. Between urban blight and general environmental blight.

4 Banning of soft coal for city heating has actually improved the atmosphere of London and some other cities. Can you find other examples of progress? Of decay?

5 Look up "external diseconomies" in the Index and trace the pervasive influence in modern economics of this vital concept.

6 *Extra-credit problem:* Redraw Fig. 40-1 according to instructions of footnote 3. Better still, move (b) as follows: Line up w vertical axis to fall *on* (a)'s $S + s$ line, and flip-flop (b)'s horizontal axis so that it runs westward rather than eastward. As before, identify E and e (with e just below E). But contrast them with nondiscrimination intersection of DD and dd at F' just southeast of E and northeast of e. Shade the little triangle formed by e, E, and F' in gold. Can you deduce that it measures gain in national product from eliminating discrimination?

Review your understanding of the following concepts:

transient and lasting discrimination
wage differentials in divided markets
black capitalism
rent differentials in divided markets

circles of urban decay
disturbed ecology and environmental
 pollution
externalities and intervention

Problems of Growth and Price Stability in an Advanced Economy

41

Let the word go forth from this time and place, to friend and foe alike, that the torch has been passed to a new generation of Americans —born in this century, tempered by war, disciplined by a hard and bitter peace, proud of our ancient heritage. .
JOHN F. KENNEDY,
Inaugural Address

Economic development of backward countries has great popular interest. And so does the problem of how an advanced mixed economy can improve its growth performance without sacrificing stability and equity.

These are issues of intense public debate everywhere. In certain ways the problems of prospering nations are harder to analyze than those of a poor nation, which in the last analysis must primarily increase its productivity. Not even advanced treatises on economics are able to provide confident, conclusive answers to all the problems that impinge on an advanced economy.

Survey of contemporary history shows the predominant importance in the mixed economy of three related problems: economic growth; economic sluggishness and unemployment; and inflationary price creeps, of a "cost-push" type, different from older demand-pull inflation.

These issues dominate the scene in North America, Europe, and Japan. Under their headings would fall a problem like automation, already discussed in Chapter 18. And as will be seen here, the question of the degree to which post-World War II prosperity depends upon cold-war armaments can be tackled only in terms of the above larger categories; and the same is also true of an issue like "structural unemployment."

MEASURING ECONOMIC GROWTH

Growth is obviously a many-sided process. Although no single number can portray the varied dimensions of overall growth, we've seen that the real national product (net or gross) is perhaps the best single indicator. Because GNP and NNP tell largely the same story and GNP data are more commonly met with, this chapter will concentrate on GNP. But certain cautions are in order.

1. For some purposes, possibly such as war, the *absolute* magnitude of real GNP may count; but generally, in thinking about welfare, one of course wants to deflate GNP for population changes and concentrate on GNP *per capita.*

2. *Leisure* is one of the finest goods of life, but it is not registered in the GNP. Thus separate allowance is to be made for shortening of the workweek and work year and for degree of lifetime participation in the labor force.

3. A mere increase in the aggregate of GNP, if it were to be accompanied by a serious deterioration in its *distribution among people,* most people would deem no improvement at all. Many will feel that the problem of WHAT should never be divorced from the problem of FOR WHOM, i.e., from the problem of "equity." The previous two chapters dealt with these important issues.

4. *Quality improvements* in goods and services may not be registered accurately in GNP and price-level data, thereby tending to give them an overly pessimistic bias. Some rough allowance for this should be made. (The problem is peculiarly important if one compares a GNP made up of goods that people really want as compared with shoddy and undesired goods allocated to them in some kind of inefficiently run totalitarian society or advertising-dominated mobocracy.)

5. The measuring rod of money cannot gauge many of the important spiritual and *noneconomic aspects of human welfare.* (We saw in the previous chapters that the money value of large-finned cars and other material items in an "affluent society" may be indicators of nothing but money value; and that the denizens of smog-ridden cities are scarcely to be envied.)

Subject to these and other qualifications, we shall proceed to use real GNP (i.e., GNP that has been deflated for price-level changes) as the principal quantitative indicator of economic growth.

BRIEF HISTORY OF GROWTH

Economic growth has characterized the modern world. Nations have grown in population; in total production and employment; in real national product; in the standard of living that the typical family enjoys today, by comparison with what its grandparents enjoyed; in leisure hours off the job; in relief from the sweat and tedium that used to be man's lot in earning his subsistence. Any and all of these are aspects of economic growth. Each of these economic aspects can be loosely associated with the biological fact that people today live longer and enjoy more years free of sickness and pain.

The front flyleaf charts show the steady advancement in real GNP per capita of leading nations. While all such absolute comparisons are difficult, it will be noted that a century ago, Great Britain dropped from her position as the most opulent nation in the world because the United States rate of growth permitted us to surpass her. Today the United States, the U.S.S.R., and Japan are the three largest economies. Japan's recent sprint has been astounding. When one considers how different France and Germany have been in many of their governmental institutions, the similarity of their development is striking. The similar growth patterns of socialistic Sweden and individualistic Switzerland present the same paradox. (Space does not permit showing these or France on the flyleaf.)

Although the institutions of the mixed economy seem to have given citizens an advancing standard of living, the chart shows that the pace of growth has not been perfectly regular. World Wars I and II have left their mark. Moreover, just prior to World War I, in the veritable heyday of laissez faire, so to speak, a number of historians thought they could detect a leveling off in growth rates generally for the advanced countries. The Great Depression of the thirties also left its mark, particularly in the American case.

Post-World War II growth in the mixed economies does outstrip the best performances of historic capitalism. When people speak nostalgically of the good old days, they should be reminded that the good old days were not so good.

GROWTHMANSHIP

In the mid-twentieth century, preoccupation with development of poor regions and the challenge of Soviet growth rates have led to great concern over the questions: Is our own growth rate satisfactory? How can it be improved?

Many divergent answers are given. Here are a few important viewpoints:

Laissez faire   When Abraham Lincoln was asked how tall a man's legs should be, he replied, "Tall enough to reach the ground." Some firm believers in classical economics are definitely of the following belief:

However fast the citizenry want their economy to grow, as determined by their *day-to-day decisions* with respect to spending on present consumption and saving for the future, that is precisely how fast the economy ought to grow.

Thus, if in the last half of the 1950s the annual rate of growth of the real GNP fell from a 4 per cent to a $2\frac{1}{2}$ per cent rate, then that primarily indicates the desire of the citizenry to live well now and not to grow so fast.[1] It would be a mistake to do what America did in the 1960s—to adopt a deliberate faster-growth policy.

This is not a popular view today, but there is no reason why its adherents should not be given a fair and scientifically objective hearing.

No need for further growth   Ideologically removed from the above view, but somewhat allied in terms of complacency about growth, would be the belief of some that we are *already* so affluent a society as to have no great need for further growth.

"Why have a third and fourth monstrous car in each garage?" would represent only a slight caricature of this position. Intellectual observers abroad, who regard America as way out in front and as too materialistic anyway, are especially attracted to this view. Among youth, particularly children of the affluent, there are growing doubts about the importance of material things (as was observed in Chapter 39).

Full speed ahead   At the opposite extreme is the view of those who feel that the threat of the Soviet Union and our concern to keep neutrals from going communistic make GROWTH the No. 1 problem of the age.

[1] To be fair, libertarians and classicists have an answer to the gibe, "I suppose our loss of GNP from 1929 to 1935 was evidence that the American people did not *want* then to grow at all." They allege that, had the proper environment been provided for individualism by proper monetary and other policies, there would have been no Great Depression, and growth would *then* truly have reflected basic desires.

While some would be prepared to grant the government extraordinary powers in order to force the pace of economic growth, others of this persuasion would merely insist that government keep growth in mind in all its actions.

Stepping up growth by public and private measures   Most people think a mixed economy like ours should not be satisfied with its spontaneous post-World War II growth rate, but should take positive measures to increase it. Growth in their view is only one of many goals. But it is an important goal for the following reasons.

WHY GROW?

Advocacy of more growth has attracted odd bedfellows. Here is a brief recapitulation of the varied reasons given for additional growth:

1. The Soviet and Chinese challenge, military and/or economic
2. The struggle to impress the neutral nations, anxious for their own development, that a mixed economy provides the better choice
3. The Galbraithian belief that goods and services in the public sector are most needed by the people in the years ahead but that it will be politically easier for them to bring themselves to meet these needs out of *extra growth of GNP* rather than by taxing themselves more heavily within the existing GNP.
4. The belief that, even if more material goods are not themselves most important, nevertheless, *a society is happy when it is moving forward* and is unhappy when it is stagnating and beset by protectionist and other movements that thrive in such an environment

If the urge to speed up growth is not merely to reflect a desire of a minority to coerce the great majority into doing what they are not really keen about doing, its defense has to stress a line of reasoning something like this:

People exercise two kinds of choices, and each is a good thing. Every day *in the marketplace* they exercise buying and selling choices with their dollars, which in the context of growth means they make various saving and consuming decisions. But also, every year or at other intervals, the people in a democracy exercise their free choices *by means of the political ballot.*

In making the latter choices, they reveal that they are not really satisfied to let their own day-to-day market choices be decisive with respect to the growth rate. We deliberately, as a sizable majority, impose upon ourselves (and on the minority too!) the public policies designed to lead to a higher GNP and higher future consumption of the private and public type.

Valid as such an argument undoubtedly is, eternal vigilance is needed to ensure that it does not become a subterfuge for dominance by government, or by a minority, over individuals' desires.

HOW TO GROW

Let us assume that, from sources outside economics, faster growth is set as a major goal for America or any advanced nation. How does a mixed economy go about increasing its own rate of growth? The answers are by no means obvious. It is clear that a totalitarian society can by ruthless methods of coercion simply channel goods away from current consumption and into capital formation. But can a free society increase its own growth rate and still remain free?

Earlier chapters in Parts Two and Four show how, if at all, a mixed society can, in a democracy, hope to speed up the rate at which its real GNP rises. First, however, some ineffectual solutions ought to be noted.

Why not simply set up the target of 5 per cent growth rate per year? This is indeed easy to do, and as the next chapter indicates, many have done so. But just as one cannot increase his own stature merely by thinking about it, mere exhortation is not likely to accelerate growth. Only if a promotion campaign were really to change people's *fundamental propensities* to consume could much be hoped for here, and a careful scrutiny of exhortation campaigns suggests that they are more effective at selling one brand of soap than at making significant changes in people's *fundamental propensities*.

As we saw in our studies of production in Part Two and in the discussion of development of poorer countries in the last chapters,

There are certain factors that have to be changed if the rate of growth is to be improved:
  The quantity and quality of population and natural resources
  The stock of capital goods of all kinds
  Finally, the technological efficiency with which the different factor inputs combine to produce a larger output (i.e., scientific and technical knowledge must be improved)

These provide the clues for an effective program to stimulate growth.

EXPANDED PRIVATE AND PUBLIC RESEARCH

We can begin with the least controversial measure aimed at enhancing growth. All agree that expanded research—in pure science, applied science, development and engineering, administration and management, city planning—can pay high social dividends in terms of productivity. As was discussed on page 724, it has not been increased capital and labor so much as *increased technical productivity* that has been responsible for the historically achieved rates of growth. Having more people and more machines of the seventeenth-century variety would not be likely to take us far beyond the standards of living of the Mayflower Pilgrims. Obviously better machines—not simply new machines—are needed for progress.

Business firms do much research and can be urged to do more. However, there is no reason to think that management is so stupid as not to see for itself how much research is likely to be profitable *to it;* so unless some new *public* policies on research are added, we are unlikely to achieve greater progress here than is already the case.

This is where the government comes in. Since 1940 the government has been directly and indirectly supporting much of the scientific research done in this country. It could expand the level of its support. But how can nonmilitary research be justified as a legitimate function of government?

Recall from Chapter 8 that there is a prima facie case for public intervention whenever there are such economic "externalities" present as to make it unlikely that each entrepreneur, as he reckons *his private benefit and costs* in money, will thereby be truly reflecting the benefits and costs *to society* as a whole. Smoke nuisance was an example of an external diseconomy calling for public action. Similarly, research is an example of an "external economy" calling for public action, as the following soliloquy shows:

When I, as a prudent businessman, balance the dollar cost to me of an extra unit of research with the benefit that it can bring me, I shall realize that most of the results of my research will soon—or in the case of patents, eventually—serve to benefit all other producers in my industry and in society generally. The benefit to society as a whole, then, is likely to be much greater than to me; so I shall not be motivated to do all the research that society needs. Because of this externality, the government has a reason to subsidize research—by direct grants to universities, firms, and its own laboratories and by favorable tax treatment of research.

We can therefore deduce this corollary.

The single least controversial measure for inducing greater growth is promotion and subsidy of more research and development.

EXPANDED EDUCATION AND TRAINING

We saw earlier that just as machinery is capital to society, so too are people. Investing in equipment might yield society an interest return of, say, 10 or 15 per cent per annum. If investing in people, by providing more in the way of education, can step up their economic productivity greatly—and the record suggests that this is indeed true—then society ought likewise to spend more for education to promote growth. (All this is *in addition* to the various noneconomic civic and humanistic reasons for devoting resources to education.)

Enlarged public funds for *scholarships* are clearly called for. The case is also strong for enlarged funds to *lend* to students for training in lucrative callings, to be paid back by them out of the extra earnings their education makes possible. An important way to stimulate growth is for the government to increase its support of schools, colleges, universities, and vocational retraining institutes.

APPRAISING AND REDUCING STRUCTURAL UNEMPLOYMENT

In stressing the role of technical change and improved quality of the trained labor force, we are applying Chapter 37's analysis of the four factors that make the *potential product* of a nation grow: Output growth depends on inputs such as natural resources, labor, capital, and technical progress. Along with research stimulus to technical progress and an increase in the *quality* of labor, an increase in labor's *quantity* would also enhance real growth. But where quantity of labor is concerned, one must proceed with caution.

Few would want to emulate Dictator Mussolini's attempt to increase the birth rate merely for the purpose of enlarging the country's economic and military size. Nor would many want us to regress to a 45- or 50-hour week merely to increase our growth rate. Leisure is a correlative goal with tangible goods.[2] If fiscal and monetary policies do

---

[2] In an age where Saturday work has become rare and where summer and winter vacations are becoming more common, it is somewhat anomalous that youth from age 4 to 24 is now being urged to study and work harder than was ever before the case. Is one supposed to sprint while young in order to become rich enough to idle ever after?

their work well, so that people have a genuine choice between full employment at 40 hours a week or at 35 hours a week, and they opt for the latter, and for winter as well as summer vacations, then the resulting sacrifice in rate of potential growth will be a good thing and not to be regretted.

On the other hand, it was an unmitigated advantage in the mid-1960s to be able to increase our quantity of labor by being able to define full employment as a condition where $96\frac{1}{2}$ per cent of the labor force are employed, rather than where only 94 or 95 per cent are employed. This is an important point, because the upward drift of average unemployment rates in the 1950s was attributed by some to an increase in "structural unemployment." What does this term mean?

Structural unemployment is used in a sense which allegedly contrasts with ordinary unemployment. The latter can be created by having too little $C + I + G$ aggregate dollar spending and can be reduced by expansionary fiscal and monetary policies that swell total spending. Unlike ordinary unemployment, structural unemployment is supposed to consist of people who are *stranded in the wrong regions*—in distressed areas like the mining country of West Virginia, Pennsylvania, or Wales. It includes *youths who have dropped out of school;* the *uneducated* and the *illiterate;* the *unskilled, semiskilled, or the highly skilled in obsolete arts* like glass blowing or cigar rolling. It includes the *neurotic and rebellious* (and possibly the radical malcontents), who demand unrealistically high wages and contribute little net marginal-product to the employer. It includes the congenitally *low-IQ and poorly coordinated* populace, who used to be capable of getting menial jobs at low pay in a rural society, but who increasingly are thrown out of employment by minimum union-, legislature-, and company-promulgated wage floors. More doubtfully, it includes those who have quit one job and are taking their own sweet time in moving to a new one. More importantly, structural unemployment is supposed to include those who belong to *various minority groups:* females, the relatively aged, immigrants, nonwhites, and so forth.

Defining structural unemployment No one has been able to agree on the exact meaning of structural unemployment, but all are clear as to what it means in extreme instances. Thus, if brisk over-all spending results in only 2 per cent unemployment and prices are *not* being pushed upward by wage increases induced in a tight labor market, all would agree that so-called "structural unemployment" is low.

On the other hand, if unemployment is at 6 per cent, and every increase in aggregate dollar spending (whether brought about by a private-investment boom, or by expansionary macroeconomic policy) seems merely to result in a fast bidding up of wages of those *already* employed, with little effect on job opportunities for those who apparently have the wrong skills and talents in terms of what employers demand, then all will agree that structural unemployment appears to be high. This diagnosis will have been retroactively confirmed if, with no concomitant change in aggregate demand, a vigorous manpower program of reeducation and transportation subsidy leads to a marked reduction in unemployment, or if the same is accomplished by a reduction in minimum-wage and union-wage levels and by an increase in wage flexibility generally.

A case that is less clear is the following: Suppose aggregate demand has been sluggish year after year; the percentage unemployed rises; skills decay; employers prefer to get extra output by working their existing employees longer hours. Then suppose private industry or the government engineers a great increase in aggregate demand in a short time period. This is followed in the short run by a wage-price upward spiral. But in the longer run people get sucked out of the distressed areas into high-employment regions. They switch gradually from blue-collar to supervisory work. Their limited skills become valuable to an employer who now finds high-IQ workers hard to attract. Unemployment over a period of several years works its way down to below 4 per cent, and gradually down even to 3 per cent.

Which was originally present then? Structural unemployment or nonstructural? This is not an idle question: it deals with the actual history of our times, as surveying the 1920s, 1930s, 1940s, and 1950s will confirm. Experience here and abroad during the 1960s suggests this eclectic summary:

There is no hard-and-fast line between structural and nonstructural unemployment. The alleged hard core of the structurally unemployed is in fact a core made of ice and not of iron. The core of ice can be melted over a period of time by adequate effective demand, or it can become solidified from inadequate over-all demand. Specific measures for enhancing labor mobility, for retraining and relocating people, for improving employment exchanges and the organization of the labor market will by themselves help to melt the core of structural unemployment, but they are most needed and work most effectively when aggregate demand measures are also being vigorously promulgated.

All in all, as experience abroad so forcefully reminds us, there is no real opposition between the programs needed for structural and for nonstructural unemployment. Each is better than nothing. The two together will add up to more than the sum of each separately.[3]

The upshot for growth of the discussion of structural unemployment seems this: Increasing the fraction employed at what is defined as feasible full employment would be a powerful way of increasing the quantity of labor and would be conducive to growth. (Its social benefits would, of course, overshadow its mere growth benefits.)

FULL EMPLOYMENT AND REDUCING THE UNDERUTILIZATION GAP

In concentrating on the policies that can increase the rate of growth of our potential full-employment full-capacity GNP, we must not forget the less subtle contribution to

---

[3] The above formulation permits one to sidestep a notable 1961 debate between Chairman W. M. Martin of the Federal Reserve Board and Chairman W. W. Heller of President Kennedy's Council of Economic Advisers. Martin argued that much of the rising trend in unemployment had been due to an increase in structural unemployment. Heller argued that structural unemployment existed in 1953 or 1957, but that most of the subsequent *increase* in unemployment above 1957's 4 per cent level could not be attributed to a *genuine growth* in structural unemployment. He based this on study of statistical facts such as the following: High unemployment rates among, say, women, youths, or blue-collar workers have behaved in the years since 1957 almost exactly as they *had behaved in earlier years when over-all unemployment rates changed the way they have been changing since* 1957. Although many have tried to refute these statistics, no one seems to have presented a successful refutation except in one troublesome respect: Negro unemployment, particularly among youths, remained high relative to white unemployment. Why? Research is much needed here. See the debate between R. Solow and C. Killingsworth reproduced in P. A. Samuelson, *Readings in Economics* (McGraw-Hill, New York, 1970, 6th ed.).

growth that can come merely from *achieving a better record in reducing business-cycle unemployment.* Which decade showed by far the worst record of growth in American history? Of course it was the 1930s, when the Great Depression prevailed and there was no growth at all!

Those who used to speak more optimistically about 6 per cent targets for annual growth generally had in mind the improvements that would be possible if we could reduce unemployment down to minimal levels. This is a needed emphasis. It affirms the crucial importance—for the profit receivers as well as workers—of expansionary private and public policies that raise the $C + I + G$ equilibrium level of real NNP.

But a *return* to high employment is, in a sense, a once-and-for-all thing. From 1962 to 1966 our economy did sprint and achieve real growth of nearly 6 per cent per year! How? By getting rid of excess capacity and unemployment. While our *potential* GNP cannot grow at 6 per cent per year, our actual performance can temporarily do so, as it narrows the "gap" between our potential and actual performance. After we have succeeded in getting rid of this *gap*, our actual real GNP growth rate must revert to that of the potential GNP, which can be lifted above a 4 per cent rate only if the measures discussed in this chapter are successfully applied.

Fortunately, our potential GNP grows like compound interest. If we realize that potential, the generous profits and labor incomes that it will make available for reinvestment will reinforce its own rate of growth. (I put 96 cents in the bank and you put in only 93. Even if our sums compound at the same 4 per cent interest rate, if our heirs live long enough, mine will have thousands of dollars more than yours. And if my 96 cents, which corresponds to full—rather than partial—employment, should generate, an annual growth rate of $4\frac{1}{2}$ per cent whereas your 93 cents generates only 3 per cent,[4] my heirs will eventually end up millions of times as rich as yours. These are the elementary facts of compound interest applied to long-run growth.)

DEFENSE EXPENDITURE AND PROSPERITY: AN IMPORTANT DIGRESSION

Before leaving the problem of achieving and keeping full employment, we should examine what would happen if the Vietnam war (and the cold war generally) were to give way to a period of relaxed international tension. If America were to cut down drastically on her defense expenditures, would that confront her with a depression problem that has merely been suppressed by reliance on armament production?

The answer here is much like that given in Chapter 18 to the problem of some future acceleration of automation.

If there is a political will, our mixed economy can rather easily keep $C + I + G$ spending up to the level needed for full employment *without armament spending.*

[4] At high employment, attitudes of businessmen and labor toward increasing productivity may be better than in a soft-pressure stop-and-go economy with considerable idle manpower and capacity. If so, such attitudes enhance the growth contribution of full-employment policies. But, if the whip of fear that results from unemployment in a slack economy makes workers and management more efficient, then there is the possibility that the low-pressure economy *might* after a lag overtake the high-employment one. Yale's W. Fellner and H. Wallich hold the latter view; Yale's J. Tobin, the first.

There is nothing special about G spending on jet bombers, intercontinental missiles, and moon rockets[5] that leads to a larger multiplier support of the economy than would other kinds of G expenditure (as on pollution control, poverty relief, and urban blight). And the temporary increase in unemployment that would result from massive cutbacks in military expenditures could be offset by substantial tax reduction that would increase disposable incomes and lead to enhanced C to meet family demands. With cold-war expenditure no longer needed, our gigantic government expenditures abroad could be reduced and our international deficit would probably disappear almost overnight. With the dollar no longer overvalued, militant expansion of monetary and credit policy could stimulate capital formation (i.e., I) to utilize the resources released from armament production.

America's potential and actual growth rate, far from depending upon war preparations, would be markedly *increased* by an end to the cold war.

Is the story fully as optimistic as this? Yes. A laissez faire economy might face a crisis of some duration; but a mixed economy that has been using the tools of macroeconomics developed in the last 30 years need fear no such debacle.

There is but one possible flaw in the story. It lies inside the realm of politics, not economics. An economically illiterate electorate may less reluctantly use the tools of the new economics for war than for peace purposes. Any citizenry, any time and any place, that cannot *ideologically* stomach the political moves necessary to maintain healthy growth and high-capacity economic activity, can create *for itself* a problem of mass unemployment. But this is a quite different matter from that which critics of laissez faire (like Lenin and Rosa Luxemburg) faced at the turn of the century prior to the mixed economy.

PUBLICLY DETERMINED THRIFT

Now there remains capital formation as the final factor of importance for enhancing growth. While the unemployment gap is being narrowed, capital investment and consumption expenditures may be mutually reinforcing in expanding growth. But once full employment were assured, a determination to accelerate growth at any cost would involve trying to change the full-employment mix of resource use *away* from current private and public consumption and *toward* net capital formation for the future.

There is a most important way that a mixed economy can hope to increase its own

---

[5] Actually, expenditures on aerospace probably lead to fewer valuable research findings applicable to industry in general than did earlier military expenditure. It may cost $10 million to find a reliable control device that can be put into a match box; but to produce ordinary civilian products, there is no need to keep parts as light, small, and dependable as in traveling to the moon. Recent defense programs may have *used up* as much high-powered scientific and engineering resources as they have contributed to fruitful civilian uses.

If the cutback in military use of resources were not matched by an equivalent expansion in government programs for urban renewal, conservation, education, and medical care, the alternative pattern to full employment might (for reasons discussed on page 230) require a larger budgetary deficit (or a smaller surplus) than now prevails. Such a deficit would *not* be inflationary, since it comes into being only to offset the deflationary impact of the military cutback. But it might exacerbate the ideological problem of those congressmen and citizens who simply do not believe in any of the macroeconomic mechanisms that economic science has expounded.

rate of growth. This is the mechanism referred to earlier in several places, chiefly in Chapter 18 of Part Two and Chapter 30 of Part Four.

By properly blending its reliance on fiscal and monetary policy, the citizenry of a mixed economy can hope to shift the composition of its high-employment NNP more toward capital formation and away from current consumption.

By this device, it can hope to change its own growth rate. What exactly is the control mechanism involved?

First, recall from Part Two that Federal Reserve monetary policy can help to choke off investment spending and capital formation by making credit tight and very dear; alternatively, expansive monetary policy can hope to stimulate the rate of capital formation by making credit more easily available and interest rates lower. This whole process, by which a society undertakes more and more capital formation as interest rates become less and less and as credit becomes more widely available, was described in Chapters 30 and 37 as "deepening of capital."

As we saw, the process of deepening capital may not always be a smooth one under laissez faire; but let us review its operation in a managed mixed economy.

AUSTERE FISCAL POLICY COMBINED WITH EXPANSIONARY MONETARY POLICY

Assume that high employment is going to be maintained. (This could mean 97 per cent of all workers employed to allow for temporary switchings of jobs, or it could be any other agreed-upon percentage.) A fraction of such a high-employment output can be shifted away from consumption and toward capital formation by the following:

On the one hand, *monetary policy is to be expansionary,* making for a deepening of capital and much capital formation.

On the other hand, the tendency of such an increase in investment spending to create an inflationary gap is to be offset by an *austere fiscal policy* calling for high enough tax rates (and low enough government expenditure) to reduce people's disposable (after-tax) incomes enough to cause them to reduce their consumption enough to release resources for investment without inflation.

While the quantitative weight of taxes must be large in order to cut down on consumption, certain *qualitative* changes in taxes could stimulate investment directly. The 1962–1969 Kennedy investment tax credit, which Nixon terminated, provided a bribe to capital formation. Allowing faster depreciation also increases cash funds available for investment and increases the profit incentive for such investment; such measures have been liberalized here and abroad in the last decade.[6]

Reducing penalties for riskiness, by governmental insurance or unorthodox banking

---

[6] A problem with all such subsidies to investment is that they often confer benefits on those who would have invested anyway and even on those who can gain tax advantages without making *net* new investment. Such devices can come to be regarded as "tax loopholes," meaning by this not something illegal, but rather regulations created to confer benefits on special groups. Whether or not qualitative tax changes to promote investment directly are made, the program to stimulate investment would rely heavily on the healthy expansion across the board that a lower social rate of interest would make economical.

methods, can also stimulate net investment. Lightening the tax burden on the rich and thrifty and increasing it on the poor and relatively less thrifty may increase capital formation at the sacrifice of egalitarianism. (But is such a sacrifice of "equity" in the interests of faster growth ethically defensible?)

This doctrine of publicly induced shift in full-employment output away from consumption and toward capital formation does need two[7] objective qualifications.

Qualifications   First, Chapter 36 showed that our international payments deficit may make it impossible for us to push easy money militantly before we solve the problem of possible overvaluation of the dollar. Hence the postulated process of investment stimulus may not get off the ground until this international problem is overcome.

This hard fact, that America's balance of payments makes it difficult for her to realize domestic goals of high employment with high capital formation, underlines the basic error in a Leninist thesis that prosperity of the advanced nations depends upon imperialistic exploitation of the backward countries. If the cold war ended and made foreign military spending unnecessary and if America turned her back on foreign aid to the underdeveloped countries, our international payments deficit would be cured overnight and we would no longer fear drain of official gold. The Federal Reserve would be given back its freedom to employ monetary policy vigorously to keep employment full and domestic investment high. Whatever was the truth back in 1900 when Lenin was forming his theories, students and statesmen in the underdeveloped countries should be able to spot the error in a view that a modern mixed economy like America *needs colonies in order to avoid* unemployment and depression; if anything, the reverse is true today.

A second qualification was mentioned in the Appendix to Chapter 37. Some economists think that deepening of capital cannot be successfully achieved because the capital-output ratio is a stubborn constant. Here is a reprise of their arguments.

If you stimulate investment as was done in the plant-and-equipment booms of 1956–1957, 1965–1967, or 1968–1969, you will simply drive down to minimal levels the yield on further investment; and you will pay for it by reduced private capital formation in subsequent years. In the long run, investment will have to be held down to the requirements set by labor-force and technological growth. Be thankful for high consumption at full employment, because that is the *only* way you can maintain full employment.

A rebuttal might go along the following lines.

In examining a planned economy like that of the Soviet Union, one certainly feels that its product could be enhanced by faster accumulation of capital goods. If that is a fact of technology, why does not the same hold for us? Current capital goods have a yield before taxes as high as 15 per cent; therefore, goes this rebuttal, it is hard to believe that yields would drop to zero or below a minimal profit level (needed to offset risk) just because net capital formation is speeded up for a decade. Moreover, we advocates of enhanced investment for growth are willing, if it should prove necessary, to recommend nonconventional methods of credit expansion—guarantees and insurances against loss from risks, etc.—to engineer a deepening of capital.

[7] To forestall a third criticism by trade-unions that long fought to increase rather than decrease the community's final propensity to consume, one may add this reminder. The resulting increase in thriftiness is not permitted to abort itself as in the "paradox of thrift" discussed in Chapter 13. The shift away from consumption is not allowed to jeopardize the maintenance of full employment or any agreed-upon target level of high employment, for the tight budgetary surpluses will come into being only on condition that the credit-induced expansion in investment spending has *indeed succeeded* in taking place.

There remains a final difficulty with an optimistic synthesis that keeps the mixed economy at full employment and keeps it there with the desired mix of investment and consumption. This is the problem of "cost-push (or sellers') inflation."

A NEW COST-PUSH SELLERS' INFLATION?

No country in the world has been simultaneously enjoying (1) full employment, (2) free markets, and (3) stable price levels. Thus, from 1955 to 1958 our prices were generally rising: wholesale prices, farm prices, cost-of-living prices—in fact, all but staple prices. Everyone was disturbed about the month-after-month announcement of higher prices. But what was it due to? To excessive demand, like that of 1966's or 1968's conventional $C + I + G$ inflationary gap?

Turning to look at each industry, one found it hard to perceive excessive demand in 1957–1958. Autos were not selling well; and farm-equipment salesmen sang the blues. TV manufacturers took out the red ink as sales slumped and as people began to buy the low-profit cheap models. The steel industry operated often far below 80 per cent of capacity. And so it went in industry after industry.

Still, the price index continued to advance. Therefore some experts began to wonder whether this was not the case of "wage-push" rather than "demand-pull." Money wages were raised each year, and often by more than the growth of productivity. Nor did it seem to take many strikes to accomplish this. The wage-push happened outside the unionized industries, too. In the unionized sectors some observers said: "In pushing for higher wages, labor is pushing against an open door. The employers do not fight the increases the way they used to. They act as if they think that the Treasury and the Fed will keep aggregate demand high enough to buy the higher-cost output; so they grant the wage increases, and this sends up costs of production, which sends up the prices that firms charge for their goods. The result is a new kind of inflation. When the Fed and Treasury try to handle it by the usual weapons that affect demand, they create unemployment and a recession as in 1957–1958. From 1958 to 1963, wholesale prices were stable, but it seemed to require unemployment of more than 5 per cent to make this so."

Explanatory emphasis has shifted away from exclusive reliance on wage-push to more general cost-push. Thus, in 1959 the Joint Economic Committee of Congress reported research suggesting that the increase in steel prices during the 1950s was by itself responsible for a significant fraction of the increase in the wholesale price index. But the committee also found that profit margins stayed up in this administered-price industry, along with wage increases, and concluded that the pressure of nonlabor as well as labor costs was responsible. A. P. Lerner broadened the whole concept to that of *sellers' inflation:*

If all sellers, whether of labor or of property services or of goods, negotiate and determine their prices to try to get among them all *more* than 100 per cent of the total national product, then the result cannot help but be a frustrating upward push of the price level—a case of sellers' inflation.

Figure 41-1 shows how low unemployment rates—as in the post-1965 boom, when the average rate dropped below 4 per cent, reaching $3\frac{1}{3}$ per cent by 1968—are associated

Are full employment and price stability compatible?

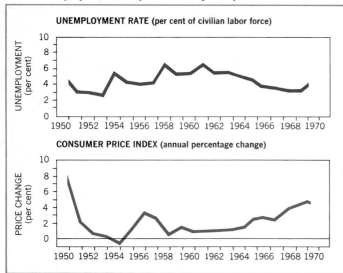

FIG. 41-1. From 1945 to 1960, each peak of the business cycle displayed higher unemployment, a disquieting trend. Fiscal and monetary policies were employed by the New Economics to end this stagnating. They could be used more extensively to raise employment, production, and real incomes were it not for the fear that the price level will be pushed up beyond a gentle creep. If an "incomes policy" could be found that would inhibit cost-push sellers' inflation, the ice block of structural unemployment could be melted by expanded aggregate demand, reinforced by retraining and relocation programs.

with a quickening of price inflation. By 1969 consumers' prices were rising at more than a 6 per cent annual rate; and the resulting acceleration of inflationary expectations was beginning to jeopardize the magnificent Methuselah of an economic expansion of the decade.

This same incompatibility of full employment with price stability can be observed in mixed economies all over the world: in Sweden and Switzerland; in Holland and France; in England and Belgium; and, to a lesser degree, in Japan, West Germany, and Italy. This important phenomenon calls for new analytical tools of description, interpretation, understanding, and prediction. The next section, which may be skipped in briefer courses, is a partial response to that need.

THE PHILLIPS-CURVE TRADEOFF BETWEEN FULL EMPLOYMENT AND INFLATION

To understand conventional "demand-pull" inflation is easy in an idealized model where wages cannot rise so long as there is still one unemployed worker to keep down the wage rate. And in the same idealized model where goods are all auctioned off in perfectly competitive markets, there could be no general price rises so long as there is spare capacity available to produce more output at (marginal) costs no higher than the ruling prices.

Simple demand-pull In such a model, begin with full employment, where the macro-economic managers have created just enough $C + I + G = MV$ spending to absorb all the full-employment output. If the managers now raise total spending by, say, 10 per cent, there will be more dollars of spending coming on the demand markets than can be supplied with goods at the previous equilibrium prices. We have engineered one of Chapter 13's so-called "inflationary gaps." Prices will then generally rise—ultimately by the 10 per cent needed to match the added $C + I + G$ spending. At the higher prices, employers will scramble to get more workers, bidding up wages ultimately also by 10 per cent (and thus leaving profits also higher by 10 per cent, but with all real or deflated wages being exactly the same as before).

In this first simplified model, demand has pulled up prices and wages.[8] Hence the name "demand-pull."

[8] Note that money wage rates have risen by 10 per cent more than productivity (which in our simple example has actually not changed at all) is rising. But that fact tells us nothing about the direction

Simple cost-push Now become more realistic. Drop the notion that labor gets auctioned off at a flexible wage rate. Go to the other extreme. Suppose that by union power or by the strong pressure of custom in the nonunionized areas, wage rates always rise by 5 per cent per year regardless of the amount of unemployment. And, since we are not trying to be entirely realistic, suppose that labor productivity always rises by exactly 3 per cent per year. Then if the employers can always administer their prices so as to keep the share of profit (or property return) unchanged—say, near the conventional one-fourth level—how will prices all rise? By arithmetic, we find that prices must rise by 2 per cent per year—which is the 5 per cent wage rise minus the 3 per cent productivity rise. The real wage rate also rises by only the 3 per cent productivity rise—since the 5 per cent money wage rise has the 2 per cent of price rise deflated out of it. The total *real* return to property owners has also risen by the 3 per cent change in average labor productivity—because the relative wage share stays at three-fourths.

Note that nothing at all has been said thus far about demand, about $C + I + G$ or MV total spending. In this extreme cost-push model, demand has nothing to do with prices—which get set exclusively by wages and productivity. Prices rise at 2 per cent per year whether there is peace or war, recession or prosperity, tight or loose Federal Reserve and fiscal policy, a Chapter 13 inflationary or deflationary gap. What then is the role of demand in this paradoxical extreme model of simple cost-push?

Under extreme cost-push, demand has *no* effect on prices, P. It became completely a theory of output, Q. Demand can still determine how total $PQ =$ NNP behaves at all times; for these are simply other names for total $C + I + G$ or MV spending (as we saw in Chapter 15's tautological "equation of exchange"). Let us examine the problems now created for the macroeconomic managers of fiscal and monetary policy.

If we began at full employment and money wage rates go up by 5 per cent instead of the 3 per cent of productivity growth, unless the macro managers engineer an increase in aggregate demand of 5 per cent—big enough to match the wage increase, which means big enough to finance the 2 per cent increase in P and the 3 per cent increase in Q—full employment will ebb away. (Perhaps the union leaders and oligopolists were counting on the managers to create the needed increase in aggregate demand.)

Thus, suppose the macro managers wrongly think they are facing old-fashioned demand-pull inflation when actually they are facing simple cost-push. Logically, they might decide to hold total NNP demand constant. What will happen? Output and employment will drop by 5 per cent a year! First 1 man out of 20 will be unemployed; then 2; . . . ; and if the irresistible force of cost-push meets the immovable object of macroeconomic policy, in the end the system will run down to literally nothing, with the last starving man losing his job and dying out. This is not a very tenable outcome, and perhaps the

---

of causation (which we know in this case definitely *not* to have been from wages as cause to prices as effect). Whenever prices are rising and the relative sharing of profits-to-wages is constant, as a matter of mere arithmetic money wage rates must be outstripping average labor productivity by the amount of the price rise, with real wages merely matching the productivity rise. But contrary to the confused arithmetic of conservative financial columnists, when real wages are thus advancing in line with average labor productivity, that does not mean that labor is "appropriating" or absorbing *all* the fruits of technological progress (which admittedly may have come from better machines and management methods as well as from greater worker effort or skill). It merely means that profit receivers and labor are *sharing* in progress on the same terms as before—say, at the historic fraction of about three-fourths for labor.

Real world falls between simple demand-pull and cost-push:

TRADEOFF BETWEEN INFLATION AND FULL EMPLOYMENT

FIG. 41-2.   If we move leftward toward full employ-ment, before we get there, wages and prices may tend to rise and keep rising. Most mixed economies face this dilemma—a cruel one, for it would be a bitter cost to pay for price stability to have to move rightward where the poor and nonwhite suffer high unemployment. (The right blue scale differs from the left black scale by the rate of productivity growth. If productivity growth attains a higher rate, shift everything blue down by that amount.)

macro managers will drop their stubbornness, with the result that they will create enough money spending to countenance the creeping inflation *indefinitely.*

Phillips tradeoff curve   It is too bad that the simple demand-pull model is not realistic, for under it the job of the macro managers would be the easy one of turning on or off the faucets of fiscal and monetary policy to keep employment just full but never overfull. Yet it is indeed fortunate that the nightmare of simple cost-push is also not realistic, for in simple cost-push there is simply no control of inflation or influence on it that the macro managers can contrive.

The real world is somewhere between the two extremes. The amount of unemployment does in some degree hold down the excess of money wage increase over productivity increase. Budget surpluses and open-market sales—all the weapons in Part Two's macro arsenal to control $C + I + G$ or MV total spending—can now have an effect on price and wage inflation.

Thus, when the Vietnam war caused a rise in spending that was not offset by determined tight-enough budgetary and Federal Reserve policy, there was a quickening in the rate of price inflation, a quickening that soon gave rise to wage increases that both reflected and aggravated the rise in the general price level. In some ways the macro managers are thrown into the most perplexing of all possible worlds. They are neither in the easy world of simple demand-pull nor the hopeless world of simple cost-push where they can do nothing about the rate of inflation. They are in the difficult world where the attempt to bring a 6 per cent rate of inflation down to 3 per cent may, at least in the short run, necessitate a retardation of real growth like that of early 1967 or 1968–1970, with rising unemploy-ment, ghetto unrest, and all the wastes of a growing gap between our achieved and potential GNP.

Professor A. W. Phillips, of the London School of Economics and the Australian National University, made a pioneering attempt to quantify the tradeoff relationship between unemployment and price-wage rises. Figure 41-2 pictures the typical down-ward-sloping Phillips curve, in which as you move leftward to reduce unemployment, then the higher becomes the rate of price and wage creep along the curve.

On the diagram's horizontal axis is the percentage of unemployment. On the black left-hand vertical scale is the algebraic percentage change per annum in average prices; on the right-hand blue scale is the accompanying percentage change in money wage rates per hour. These two scales differ only by the postulated amount of productivity increase per year (so that the price change of 2 per cent per year would correspond to a wage change of 5 per cent per year if productivity grew by 3 per cent per year and its fruits were shared in the same old proportions by labor and nonlabor).[9]

Be it noted that the MV and $C + I + G$ approaches to aggregate dollar spending are still applicable *offstage*, but one needs the information of the Phillips curve to translate the resulting product $P \times Q$ into its separate components. In simple demand-pull, the Phillips curve would be a vertical line at the minimal unemployment level: Q would then always correspond to full employment, and P would float in free labor markets to whatever level total money spending would determine. In simple cost-push the Phillips curve is a horizontal line, with no level of unemployment leading to price stability.[10]

The Phillips curve is a dramatic way of describing the dilemma for macro policy, even though it does not go much beyond description to give us "explanation." Thus, the problem is posed: how much can a mixed economy supplement macro policy so as to give itself a better Phillips curve? Better in what sense? Better in the sense that it permits us to enjoy a lower minimum level of unemployment at which the system can avoid undue price inflation.

Longer run   Before turning to the hard problems of policy, we should reemphasize that economics is not an exact science. The data will not really fit any one Phillips curve perfectly. More important still is the fact that the measured Phillips curves represent *short-term* relationships which will shift in the longer run. Thus, if Eisenhower runs a slack economy for many years of the fifties, that may kill off inflationary expectations and slow down wage demands. In short, much unemployment, long maintained, may gradually

[9] A higher rate of productivity growth will show itself in an equal downward shift of the blue curve and scale. Thus, with productivity growing at 4 per cent per year, a 5 per cent wage increase would correspond to only a 1 per cent annual price rise. A profit squeeze could be similarly shown.

[10] Note the difference between the realistic Phillips curve and the way it would look in the cases of simple demand-pull and simple cost-push. In simple cost-push, Fig. 41-3(a) shows the curve to be completely horizontal with no tradeoff possible. Figure 41-3(b) shows the curve becoming completely vertical in simple demand-pull, with no tradeoff being necessary. (Actually, in Fig. 41-3(a), if the macro managers insisted on boosting demand faster than the indicated wage rise, they would push the system to such minimal unemployment as to cause a frantic bidding up by employers of the market wage rate *above* the wage administered by the unions; and this gives rise to what in Scandinavia has been called the "wage drift," in which wages always run ahead of the minima set by collective bargaining. This means the horizontal curve really ceases to be horizontal when you move near to the vertical axis.)

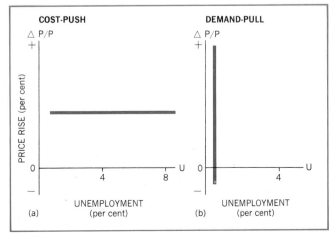

FIG. 41-3.

shift the short-term Phillips curve leftward. Then when a Kennedy comes along, he may be lucky enough to cash in on the Eisenhower "investment in sadism" by being able to engineer a long growth in $C + I + G$ before prices and wages misbehave badly. But by the same reasoning, after more than 100 months of uninterrupted expansion, and particularly as the result of Vietnam spending, continued low unemployment may shift the short-term Phillips curve rightward, making the policy problems of the 1970s that much harder.[11]

ARE GROWTH AND PRICE STABILITY OPPOSING GOALS?

Let us return from our analytical excursions to the pressing American problem of the modern mixed economy.

If consumer, wholesale, and general GNP prices all tend to creep upward when there is 4, 5, and even 6 per cent unemployment, what should the monetary and fiscal authorities do? Should they cut down on over-all demand (i.e., on $C + I + G$ or MV total spending),

[11]Some writers try to define a long-run curve from the systematic shiftings of the short-run curves (in much the same way that Fig. 20-5 was able to depict long-run Marshallian supply curves from systematically shifting short-run supply curves). The long-run Phillips curve tends to be twisted clockwise, as in Fig. 41-4(a). There is even one strong theory, suggested by W. Fellner and H. Wallich of Yale, M. Friedman of Chicago, and E. Phelps of Pennsylvania, which in effect says: "The Phillips tradeoff is based only on the *illusion* of *unanticipated* price-wage inflation. Once the system settles down to any constant rate of price-wage inflation, people will come to learn the fact and to expect it in the future. So you will then have just as much excess wage pressure over that constant rate as you had when prices were stable. There is really a 'natural rate of unemployment,' defined by a vertical long-run Phillips curve as shown in Fig. 41-4(b). If you temporarily bring unemployment below the natural rate, your short-term curves will twist upward indefinitely and your price rise will accelerate; if you temporarily bring unemployment above the natural rate (the Eisenhower rather than Kennedy pattern), the short-term curves will there twist downward indefinitely and your price rise will decelerate. In order for people to be adjusted to the rate of price change so that it will not be accelerating or decelerating, you have to be *on the long-run vertical line.*" These writers conclude: "Since you will be stuck with the natural rate of unemployment in the long run anyway, the macro managers should keep demand growing at only the rate of real growth of the system—say, 4 to 5 per cent per year so that Ps will be steady. To reduce unemployment's natural rate, policies other than macro fiscal and monetary measures are needed—such as repealing minimum-wage laws or restrictive union practices." Critics of this view say that by the time *their* proposed equilibrium is reached, the system may well have been torn apart by voter revolt, urban riots, and unemployment-induced hardships and dissatisfactions. And besides the data of experience are not yet available to judge whether Fig. 41-4(a) or 41-4(b) is the more realistic.

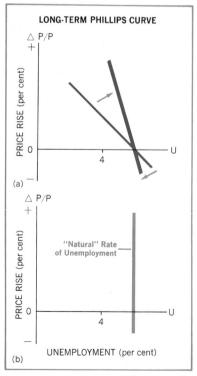

FIG. 41-4.

even though that means a further lowering of production and employment? Or should they increase total spending, even though that means some further increase in prices? There is no easy answer. Nevertheless, here are four different viewpoints:

Price stability at all costs Adherents of this view feel that a stable price level is itself so vital a social goal as to transcend other goals such as high employment and growth. Zealots would thus hold out unconditionally for price stability if it were a question of having to choose among such goals.

Most adherents of this view, however, are not such zealots. They take the more hopeful view that *in the long run* there is really no clash between price stability and growth or high employment. They claim that inflation today means depression tomorrow. They claim that only in an environment of stable prices will efficient business decisions be made. They claim that countenancing a little inflation will result in the *creep* of inflation inevitably becoming a *trot*, the trot inevitably becoming a *gallop*, and the gallop inevitably becoming a *runaway*. Why, then, let the whole process begin? Why not, so to speak, sacrifice a little of current output and employment as an investment in higher *future* growth and employment? So they argue.

Growth at all costs Former President Truman's economic adviser Leon Keyserling (and many on the left in England's Labor party) represents a view which is at first glance far removed from that outlined above. Keyserling believes in full employment and growth as primary goals and would give them great emphasis in any case; but he, and members of this camp generally, do have the optimistic hope that, by insisting on achieving growth, society will in fact end up with better-behaved prices.

The argument that growth brings price stability, which is a kind of cousin to the earlier argument that price stability brings growth, runs thus:

Higher output means downward pressure on prices, other things being equal.
Since workers tend to get *money* wages that increase at a fixed rate, by achieving a faster rate of growth of productivity, society can make this entail less price increases.
At high levels of capacity, the unit costs of businessmen get lower; therefore they can charge lower prices and still make good profits.
High employment and production make people efficient and venturesome.

Exponents of this view would, if necessary, make a short-run sacrifice of price stability as an investment in future growth and price stability.

Compromising between price stability and growth According to testimony before Congress, articles in learned journals, deliberations of the Commission on Money and Credit, and reports for the President's Commission on National Goals, there is a considerable body of professional opinion which rejects both of the above positions.

Many economists feel that absolute price stability may detract from high employment and growth in a modern mixed economy like that of America today. They believe that it would be necessary to engineer undue slackness into the economic structure if the gentle price creep were to be stopped entirely. They argue that a slow price creep, if matched by a similar creep in the mixed economies abroad, need not cause any balance-of-payments difficulties. (Some of them argue that the failure of the official indices to take proper account of quality improvements in goods means that the true rate of increase in prices is less than the apparent one by at least 1 per cent.)

What follows from such a diagnosis? Two realizations: first, that pushing full employment and maximal growth *to their absolute limits* would create such strains on prices as to make some compromising of goals necessary; second, that it will probably be necessary during some periods in the years ahead to tolerate *some degree of price creep* rather than sacrifice economic progress and reasonably high employment.

If acquiescence to price rises may be necessary at some times,[12] this fact raises one of the most vital and difficult queries of the modern age:

Will tolerance of a price creep and insistence on reasonably high employment and growth most of the time inevitably snowball into a runaway inflation? Considerable evidence of a somewhat optimistic type was gathered for the Commission on Money and Credit, and it suggested that the transition from a creep, to a trot, to a gallop, . . . was by no means inevitable. Nevertheless, it would be idle to deny that economic analysis and historical experience here and abroad are insufficient to permit one to make a definitive finding in the matter. The chronic rapidly trotting inflations of Chile and Brazil—where for decades prices advanced at a 20 to 60 per cent annual rate—provided an ominous specter for all mixed economies.

An "incomes policy"? Extensive study is needed to learn what changes can be made in the workings of our modern *institutions* to minimize the amount of price creep that has to be tolerated in the most feasible compromise: e.g., more vigorous antitrust activity in the administered-price area; changed legislation and attitudes toward trade-union attempts for higher money wage; presidential or congressional pressures in collective bargaining to uphold the consumer and national interest; and other policies yet unborn.

Britain, looking longingly at what it thought were the successful mechanisms whereby the Netherlands and Sweden brought united employers and unions together and determined a satisfactory rate of advance of wage rates and other income items, tried in the 1960s to develop an "incomes policy" that would make full employment and price stability compatible. But in 1966, Harold Wilson's Labor Government felt it had to impose a legal wage and price freeze.

WANTED, AN "INCOMES POLICY": WAGE-PRICE GUIDEPOSTS?

In the United States there are no united unions and employers who could possibly come together and agree on permissible wage-rate increases. Presidents Kennedy and Johnson did suggest wage-price guideposts of the following type:

[12]Charles L. Schultze, in research done for the Joint Economic Committee and for the nonprofit Committee for Economic Development (CED), has pointed out that an economy which has *sticky* prices as far as *downward* movements are concerned may end up with a more efficient configuration of relative microeconomic pricings if the average price level is permitted to *rise* a little rather than held constant. See P. A. Samuelson, *Readings, op. cit.*, for Sumner Slichter's defense of creeping inflation as a necessary and lesser evil.

Wage-price guideposts. **The average money-wage increase is to be no higher than the average national increase in physical productivity; but the increase in each industry is to be divorced from the increase in physical productivity in that industry itself, the difference to be taken up by price reductions to consumers of items with unusually high productivity growth (wheat? autos?) and by price increases to industries with unusually slow productivity growth (teaching?). Minor departures from the common wage increase are to be permitted primarily where an industry needs to raise wage rates to attract new labor entrants and where a declining industry needs to lower wages in order to expedite labor exit.**

These guideposts cannot be validly criticized as giving to labor all the fruits of technical progress; such a conclusion reflects merely bad arithmetic, which fails to recognize that an increase in wage rates in the same percentage as product means an increase of profits in that same percentage, not a zero increase in profits! These guideposts, however, do not have the force of law; and scowls by the President, when an industry like steel raises its prices before excess capacity has been reduced to a low level, cannot solve the dilemmas of full employment and price stability.

How did these guideposts work out? As expected, employers grumbled that they were slanted only against price increases. Unions grumbled that they were slanted only against wage increases. Many observers said they had no effect at all; or that if they had any effect, it was to make the suggested guidepost wage increase the minimum raise that the unions asked for in beginning their bargaining.

What about the actual facts? From 1961 to 1964, wages and prices were remarkably well behaved in the face of an unprecedented economic expansion. By 1965, 1966, and 1967, prices began to be pulled up by Vietnam spending, the Kennedy-Johnson tax cut, and a plant-and-equipment boom. Wages began to rise by more than the guidepost numbers; many statistical studies, however, found that wages were rising *less than could have been expected* from so high a profit environment and so tight a labor market.[13] Neither the United States, the United Kingdom, the Netherlands, nor Scandinavia has yet found an adequate "incomes" policy. After 1967 Johnson's guideposts were a dead letter, and Nixon formally has rejected them. Even if history decides that the guideposts have had some restraining influence, by 1967 enough experience has been acquired to confirm the expectations of modern economic analysis:

Wage-price guideposts, or other forms of "incomes policy," cannot be an adequate *substitute* for proper macroeconomic fiscal and monetary policies.[14] They can moderate somewhat the resulting inflation, or temporarily suppress its symptoms. But they cannot themselves take the place of *stabilizing policies of aggregate demand.* Beyond the short run, they—and actual legislated wage-price controls—become increasingly less effectual. And to the degree that they are effective, they become increasingly distortive of pricing and inequitable as between those who do and those who do not comply.

---

[13] E.g., George Perry, of Minnesota and Brookings, on the basis of multiple correlation analysis of pre-1962 patterns of wage change in relation to unemployment and profit trends, found that America's "Phillips curve" had apparently been shifted downward in 1962–1966 by the guidepost philosophy.
[14] See P. A. Samuelson, *Readings, op. cit.*, for debates on guideposts by Nixon adviser, Arthur F. Burns, and Kennedy-Johnson braintruster, Otto Eckstein of Harvard.

It would be nice if we could insist upon having complete price stability and maximal employment and growth, ruling out all compromises. But in an age of cold war and distressing conflicts of economic mechanisms, it may be that citizens of a modern mixed economy can find no shelters within which they can live with full security and without compromise.

CONCLUSION

One can expect mixed economies to show a considerable measure of growth in the future, as they have in the past. The United States, for example, should be able to grow at the rate of 4 per cent, even if we do not rouse ourselves but merely keep our system working reasonably well.

If we do rouse ourselves and do the things which can speed up growth, a rate of almost 5 per cent might be within our grasp. Admittedly, this is not the 6+ per cent rate which some proclaim, but that is no cause for despair.

Truly, it is a tremendous accomplishment if an economy can lift its annual growth rate by even $\frac{1}{2}$ per cent. That sounds small, but in terms of cumulative trends and absolute magnitudes, it would represent an important achievement.

The quantitative problem of growth in the Soviet Union and other communist economies will be discussed in the final chapter, along with a survey of alternative economic systems and ideologies.

SUMMARY

1   The best measure of growth is real GNP, qualified by data on leisure, population size, relative distribution, quality, and noneconomic factors. Attitudes toward the desirability of expediting growth vary, and in most places the citizenry in their *periodic political decision making* seem to want to step up the rate of growth beyond that implied by their *daily market decisions* on private saving and consuming.

2   Expanded *research and education* can accelerate growth. Attaining and maintaining *high employment levels* can also help. But for public policy to step up the rate of a nation's *capital formation*, when there has been no change in individual and corporate propensities to consume and save, requires the following:

(1) Low interest rates and *expansive* monetary policy designed to increase the net-capital-formation component of a high-employment national product; coupled with (2) a *restrictive fiscal policy* designed to eliminate the resulting inflationary tendencies by cutting down on disposable incomes and consumption (and also, possibly involving qualitative tax changes, such as accelerated depreciation, that grant subsidies and loopholes to investment spenders).

3   The essence of a cost-push mechanism is this: Is there a tendency for price levels to rise even when a sizable and undesirable level of unemployment persists? If there is such

a modern tendency, then policy decision (along a Phillips-curve tradeoff between full employment and inflation) becomes hard and compromises may be necessary. "Price stability is a prerequisite for growth." "Growth is a prerequisite for reasonable price stability." "New mechanisms for an incomes policy must coordinate free collective bargaining." "Some price creep may at times be the necessary compromise that must be made in the interest of growth and tolerably high employment." These are varying views, among which citizens and statesmen must today choose.

QUESTIONS FOR DISCUSSION

1   Evaluate the arguments that GNP growth is or is not a major goal.

2   Why are education, research, and high employment conducive to growth?

3   What tax changes favor growth? Do they clash with "equity" notions? How?

4   "High $C + I + G$, even to the point of over–full employment, will do more for the technically displaced, the aged, the illiterates, the geographically stranded, and the non-white workers than will any retraining programs or hour-shortening devices. How then can one speak of a clash between 'structural' and 'aggregate-demand' unemployment?" Appraise this.

5   "Cut down on consumption to promote growth? Are you mad? Only high C can give high I. I don't grasp this 'deepening of capital.'" Explain.

6   Size up the creeping-inflation problem. How would your vote on the creeping-inflation problem go? William Buckley's? SDS's?

7   "O.K., so Keynesian macroeconomics can restore prosperity by Vietnam spending. But why should we tolerate 'Keynesian-militarism'?" Evaluate this New-Left charge, showing that "Keynesian-welfarism" would be as legitimate an epithet.

8   *Extra-credit problem:* Write $PQ = WL + \text{Profit}$. Assuming $\text{Profit}/WL = c$, a constant, rewrite this as $P = W(L/Q)[1 + c] = [k]W/(Q/L)$. Interpret this to say "Price is proportional to wage rate and inversely proportional to (average) labor productivity: real wage grows at same rate as productivity, and so do real profits; when prices grow *from any cause,* their percentage increase equals money-W increase minus productivity increase." Set up a guidepost rule from this. For industries $i = 1, 2, \ldots$, write a like formula for P_i. If $(Q/L)_i$ grow at *different* rates, how will you modify your guidepost rules if (1) the *average* price level is to be constant, (2) interindustry wage structure remains about the same, and (3) relative profit shares do too?

Review your understanding of the following concepts:

real NNP or GNP, per capita	cost-push (sellers' inflation), demand-pull
managed tight-fiscal and	Phillips-curve tradeoff
easy-monetary policies	"incomes policy"
structural unemployment	dilemmas of goals

Alternative Economic Systems

42

THE CRISIS OF CAPITALISM?

After World War I, new governments were set up all over Europe. By 1925 an impartial observer might have said that the future of the capitalistic way of life appeared serene and assured. Yet within a half dozen years, country after country succumbed to dictatorship; totalitarian fascist governments covered the map of Europe. The depression decade of the 1930s finally ended in a great world war.

At the end of World War II, the outlook had changed. The world was divided into great blocs: Soviet Russia and her satellites of Eastern Europe stood within the Iron Curtain in an uneasy alliance with mainland China, and outside was the rest of the world. But nations outside the Iron Curtain were far from homogeneous. Labor-socialist governments were ruling in Britain, in Australia and New Zealand, and in all of Scandinavia. Various forms of dictatorship still lingered on in Spain, Portugal, Egypt, and Latin America. France, Japan, and Italy had within them noisy and articulate left-wing political parties. The awakening nations of Asia and Africa did not view the world with laissez faire–tinted glasses.

Only the United States and a few other nations remained as islands of declared capitalism in an increasingly collectivized world. But even here, the scene was drastically changed: almost unconsciously ours had become a mixed economy with both private and public initiative and control. The clock of history, sometimes, evolves so slowly that its moving hands are never *seen* to move. After the New Deal, American economic life was permanently changed. We had converged with Western Europe to the mixed economy.

Every news dispatch reminded us that the mixed-economy way of life was on trial. Not only did it have to perform adequately, but more than that, it was required to perform superlatively. Mass unemployment at home would have had disastrous repercussions upon our prestige abroad, to say nothing of the internal political unrest that a slump might involve. A faltering rate of our development and growth would have counted seriously against us. Most important is the image of itself that a society has—particularly its young people. And a quarter of a century ago a failure of nerve was becoming evident in the West.

THE NEW LOOK

Little wonder then that profound social philosophers, like Harvard's Joseph Schumpeter, thought they could foretell in the years after 1945 the displacement of capitalism by socialism. Even profound philosophers can turn out to be quite wrong. Following World War II, gradually the "New Economics" of the modern mixed economy, trumpeted by no ideology, began to take over. And it actually worked!

In West Germany there was a miracle of recovery and development. The same thing happened in the Netherlands, France, Italy, and the Common Market countries of Europe generally. Japan, by a mixture of private initiative and state planning, embarked on a sprint hardly ever before equaled in history. Israel—helped, to be sure, by gifts and loans from abroad—had her miracle decades. Even ancient problem economies, like Greece and Austria, were able to find in the mixed economy a path to rapid and sustained economic growth. Taiwan and Thailand both sprinted forward.

Something new has been born under the sun. The prophesied timetable of inevitability —savagery to feudalism, feudalism to capitalism, capitalism to socialism, socialism to communism—has for the moment begun to take on the appearance of a fable.

But fables and legends and aspirations have a hold on the minds of men. It is therefore worth reviewing, if only briefly, the traditional forms of alternative economic systems. These are of interest for their own sakes. They are also of interest as part of the intellectual history of the human race. And not least, they are of interest in disabusing our minds of the tyranny of certain facile generalizations which, like most facile generalizations, simply will not stand up to the hard facts of actual experience.

Thus, is it true that without free markets for goods and services, democratic freedoms and political civil rights cannot prevail? Many economic libertarians argue this: that *personal* liberties and *property* liberties are one and inseparable. But are they right?

At the other extreme, many advocates of socialism argue that "political democracy" is but a sham if the state does not get rid of "production for profit" and replace it by "production for use" and guarantee "fair shares" all around. But are they right?

And in particular, is the argument correct in the learned and persuasive book, *The Road to Serfdom* (1945), by Friedrich Hayek (of Austria, England, the United States, and Germany), that each step away from the market system and toward the social reforms of the welfare state, is *inevitably* a journey that must end in a totalitarian state with neither efficiency nor liberty? The opposing view, held by such evolutionists as Roosevelt, Churchill, and Nehru, is that gradual reforms are the only way to prevent a cataclysmic descent through revolution into a communist dictatorship. If the evolutionists are right, Hayek is quite wrong.

Let us review the troops.

A BOUQUET OF ISMS

Men have always had visions of a more perfect society: Plato's Republic, Sir Thomas More's Utopia, Marx's Dictatorship of the Proletariat, and so on without number. It is easy to look at concrete present-day imperfections and then to contrast them with the ideal features of a vaguely defined utopia. Beyond agreeing that the present order has faults, different schools of reform often have little in common.

At the one extreme are the anarchists, who believe in no government at all; at the other, the apologists for an all-powerful collectivized, totalitarian, communistic social order, where the first person singular is all but replaced by the first person plural. Within the field of socialism itself, we find subdivisions: Christian socialism, state and Marxian socialism, guild socialism, Fabian (evolutionary) socialism, and many others.

In the popular mind, socialists are characters who meet in a cellar lit by a candle thrust in an empty wine bottle to plot a bloody revolution, or at least to brew bombs sent in laundry parcels to government officials and capitalists. Or the term "socialist" is frequently used as a disparaging stereotype to discredit anyone who believes in social security, progressive taxation, bank-deposit insurance, or free love.

Whatever the strength of radical parties abroad, in America no third party has ever been able to develop in any strength.[1] The American Socialist party runs a candidate for the presidency—along with the Prohibition party—but gains only a negligible fraction of the vote. The Communist party never could gain any sizable vote, either under its own name or in disguise.

If we look at the picture in Europe, we find the names of almost all the parties have the word "socialism" in them. But this does not mean much: a party such as France's Radical Socialists turns out to be anything but radical, being one of the conservative parties. Even Hitler's fascistic party took the name of "National Socialism."

Often, however, the leading European reform parties can be characterized as "social democrats." For example, the Labor party in Britain, the German Social Democratic party, the ruling parties in much of Scandinavia—all these claim to be in favor of gradual, nonrevolutionary extension of socialism by peaceful and democratic methods.

It is clear, therefore, that we do not have to master all the thousand and one different "isms" in order to understand the world today. It is enough to understand something of (1) relative laissez faire, from which the mixed economy evolved, (2) socialism, (3) communism, and (4) fascism. There is no hard-and-fast boundary between these; it is a matter of degree. Moreover, we cannot even range these along a line, with fascism at the extreme right wing and communism at the extreme left wing. In some ways—although neither would admit it—communism and fascism have much in common. Anarchism of the New Left unites with Herbert Spencer's libertarianism in its contempt for the liberal state.

Capitalism, in the sense of undiluted laissez faire, died before Queen Victoria died.

---

[1] Theodore Roosevelt's 1912 Bull Moose party was primarily an offshoot of the Republican party. Old Bob La Follette's 1924 Progressive party was the most successful third party, yet was able to carry only his state, Wisconsin. Henry Wallace's 1948 Progressive party was an utter failure. George Wallace, catering to regionalism, bigotry, and conservatism, must pin his hopes for influence on an Electoral College stalemate and on increasing the bargaining power of the petty bourgeoisie and the privileged workers who fear loss of status.

And most of this book has been concerned with describing the mixed economy which buried it. So we may turn briefly to the others.

FASCISM

This is easier to characterize politically than economically. Be it in Hitler's Germany, Mussolini's Italy, Franco's Spain, Salazar's Portugal, Perón's Argentina, or the Greek junta, fascism was usually characterized by a one-man dictatorship, by one political party with all others abolished, by the disappearance of civil liberties of the type granted in our Bill of Rights. Fascistic movements are always highly nationalistic, sometimes with emphasis placed on a vaguely defined "master race" which exploits minority groups. In the words of Mussolini, fascists are urged to "live dangerously"—to value war and national power as ends in themselves. The individual is to be secondary to the state.

On the economic side, Mussolini's fascism happened to toy with the notion of a "syndicalist," or "corporate," state; each industry and group of workers was organized in a syndicate, and these were to meet and bargain and plan how the economy should be run. However, outside of Yugoslavia, this syndicalism has never come to much and has not been especially characteristic of other fascist regimes. Almost all of them are against free and militant trade-unionism; almost all give the central government great regulatory power over every sphere of economic life. Some work hand in glove with religious authorities; others are antichurch. The fascist mentality tends to be intolerant of opposition, romantic, and antirational, often with an especial appeal to youth. Usually capitalists and the lower middle classes contribute to the *initial* strength of fascist movements; but later, when the fascist movement begins to take on—as they sometimes do—revolutionary aspects, the capitalists may regret the Frankenstein's monster that they helped to create.

Their only consolation lies in the fact that one of the earmarks of a fascist regime is opposition to communism. Generally fascism sails into power by exaggerating the immediate likelihood of a Bolshevik revolution, and after it has come into power, the threat of communism is used as an excuse for the suppression of democratic processes.

SOCIALISM

In defining fascism, we were able to point to Nazi Germany or fascist Italy. Socialism cannot be so easily described. Of course, we can describe the Swedish socialist government or the British Labor party's program, but these do not present such dramatic contrasts with our system. They represent a middle way more like our own "mixed system" than that of Soviet Russia or China.

There are a few common elements that seem to characterize socialist philosophy:

1. *Government ownership of productive resources.* The role of private property is gradually to be lessened as key industries such as railroads, coal, and even steel are gradually nationalized. Unearned profits from increases in land value are also limited. (In West Germany and the United Kingdom, enthusiasm for nationalization has ebbed.)

2. *Planning.* Instead of permitting the free play of profit motives in a laissez faire market economy, coordinated planning is to be introduced. Sometimes the program of

"production for use rather than profit" is advocated; advertising expenditure on gadgets is to be reduced; workers and professional people are to develop instincts of craftsmanship and social service so that they will be guided by other motives than those of our "acquisitive society."

3. *Redistribution of income.* Inherited wealth and swollen incomes are to be reduced by militant use of government taxing powers. Social security benefits, free medical care, and cradle-to-grave welfare services provided by the collective purse are to increase the well-being of the less-privileged classes and guarantee minimum standards of living.

4. *Peaceful and democratic evolution.* Socialism, as distinct from communism, often advocates the *peaceful and gradual extension* of government ownership—revolution by *ballot* rather than by *bullet.* This aim is often more than a tactical move—rather, a deep philosophical tenet of faith.

British socialism   A brief look at British socialism will point up the modern issues. Just when Adam Smith's classical economics had won the day from its mercantilistic and feudal predecessors, English intellectual opinion began to move beyond laissez faire and toward socialism. A key case is that of John Stuart Mill, who was brought up by an eighteenth-century exponent of utilitarian individualism (his father, James Mill), but who had by the last half of the nineteenth century turned to a kind of socialism. Then early in the twentieth century, university and night school intellectuals were won to the Fabian doctrines of the *inevitability* of gradual socialism. And these socialist views of Bernard Shaw and Beatrice and Sidney Webb became pretty much the views of the trade-union movement.

All this was hidden until World War I. After that war, the Liberal party was ground away between the millstones of the Conservative and Labor parties. Only after World War II, did Labor really come into power. Its early goals included (1) vast extension of welfare services by the state—in which Conservative governments in large degree have acquiesced; (2) heavy redistributive income and estates taxation—in which to a degree the Conservatives also acquiesce; (3) extensive centralized planning, including stringent regulation of land use and zoning; and finally (4) initially a fairly sweeping program of nationalization, beginning with coal, power, and railroads and, in the doctrines of the left wing of the party, reaching beyond steel to many branches of wholesaling and distribution, engineering, and ordnance.

In the seventies, the Labor party finds itself quite divided and doubtful on how far to carry traditional socialism. This shows itself in debates over the extent to which nationalization should be pressed and the degree to which reliance should be placed on market mechanisms. At the intellectual level, now that so many of the goals set up years ago in *Fabian Essays* have been realized, there is much soul searching going on; and challenging new Fabian essays are hard to write. Is "mere New Dealism designed to make capitalism work well" adequate? And can the mixed economy command the idealistic enthusiasms that more sweeping reforms were historically able to fire? Has the improvement of living standards pushed the militant poor up into the contented middle classes? Has making society more fluid tended to drain off the bright son of poor parents to Oxbridge and the Establishment, alienating him from the radical trade-union tradition?

Nor is. this quandary unique to Britain. In Sweden, Norway, Denmark, Australia, and

New Zealand, the so-called "middle way" of moderate labor socialism has now been in or near power for a third of a century. Yet every one of these economies begins to look more and more like what the United States itself has become after three decades of administration by Roosevelt, Truman, Eisenhower, Kennedy, Johnson, and Nixon. With some exaggeration, John Kenneth Galbraith and Jan Tinbergen can point to a convergence, all over the globe, to a single modern industrial state.

French "indicative planning" Ideologically rather removed from traditional socialism is the remarkable development in France of planning by the state. Both before and after De Gaulle, many important industries are owned and run by the French government: railroads, electricity, and mines, for example. The tools of economics—marginal-cost pricing of power, benefit-cost analysis of the worthwhile program of investments in these state industries—deserve much of the credit for the remarkable rate of real growth in France during the 1950–1970 period. But that is not all.

Even private industry is brought into a comprehensive national plan. This involves, however, one important difference from the traditional planning of socialist societies. In the French mixed economy, participation in *Le Plan* is mostly voluntary. (But, as everywhere these days, what business firm dares get the authorities too angry at it—particularly when permission to go to the capital markets is controlled by government?)

Representatives of different industries sit down together in committees, presided over by the civil servants who serve the plan. Businessmen are given quantitative information on national goals for the years just ahead; and they respond with information on what these goals will mean for their own industries. In turn, these replies are made the basis for a *recalculation* of the aggregates and the details of the plan.

In the end, each industry learns that it can count on an expanding market. And as business firms in those industries proceed to meet these indicated goals, they do generate the production, income, and demand called for by the plan.

How has it all worked out? Apparently, remarkably well if we can judge by results. Almost too well to be credible, when one considers the informality of the arrangements and their quasi-voluntary nature. In the late 1960s, many an English reformer would have traded some of the "pie in the sky" of traditional socialism for some pragmatic fruits of indicative planning. A National Economic Development Council ("NEDDY") was set up to imitate the French methods, and Harold Wilson's Labor government set up a Ministry of Economic Affairs to promote such programs—as yet with little success.

Similarity must not conceal diversity. In Egypt and many countries recently released from colonialism, there has been widespread nationalization of industry; in the repeated examples of this process during the last decades, there have as yet been few cases where the result has been a rapid rate of real economic growth. Similarly, economies like Argentina, despite resources and technology that many a poor country would envy, stagnated under state controls introduced by dictator Perón. The dismal records of Ghana under Nkrumah and Indonesia under Sukarno show that the slogans of socialism under a great national leader will not suffice to solve the economic problems of WHAT, HOW, and FOR WHOM. Nkrumah, Sukarno, and Perón give one new respect for Lenin—and for Adam Smith too.

MARXIAN COMMUNISM AND SOVIET RUSSIA: HISTORY

Marxian communism represents a departure both from earlier utopian socialist movements and also from evolutionistic socialist movements of the last century. Karl Marx (1818–1883), who began as a student of Hegelian philosophy but ended up as the messiah of a new doctrine of "scientific socialism," worked in exile with his friend and financial sponsor Friedrich Engels to establish a whole new theory of economics and history. For three-quarters of a century after Karl Marx and Friedrich Engels issued their 1848 Communist Manifesto, numerous international socialist conferences were held; yet outside the British Museum, not much seemed to be accomplished.

In 1917, the big moment came. Czarist Russia was knocked out of the war by the Germans. Lenin, a follower of Marx, was transported in a sealed railroad car across Germany and into Russia. Aided by Trotsky, a one-time New Yorker, Lenin's Bolsheviks snatched power from the moderate Kerenski regime that had overthrown the monarchy. Preaching peace and promising land for the peasants and a dictatorship of the proletariat, the followers of the Red hammer and sickle gained adherents in the navy and army and forcibly took power.

There followed what John Reed (later buried in the Kremlin) called "ten days that shook the world." The meeting of the democratic Constituent Assembly, only few of whose elected representatives were pro-Bolshevik, was forbidden. An army was organized and trained by Trotsky, and successive towns were won over to the revolutionary forces—often by strategic capture of the water and power supply alone. Then followed a great civil war between the Red and White armies, the latter aided by Poland and Western powers. In the end, the officers of the White army ended up chiefly in Paris, driving taxicabs and drinking vodka to the memory of Czar Nicholas.

The revolution achieved   The world expected a Russian collapse; but the communist regime persisted—not without experiencing horrible famines, in which literally millions perished. Aristocrats and bourgeoisie were ruthlessly purged and liquidated. The Communist party was the only political party permitted; only a few per cent of the population could belong to this elite group; it elected the members of local "soviets" of factories and farms. These elected representatives to still higher soviets, until, at the very top, over all the federated Union Republics, stood the Council of People's Commissars of the Supreme Soviet of the U.S.S.R. (Union of Soviet Socialist Republics).

The Soviet leaders had no blueprint to guide them. Marx had confined himself largely to the *faults* of capitalism and had revealed very little about what the promised land was to be like. It was not even on the timetable that backward Russia, which had hardly emerged from feudalism into capitalism, should experience its revolution before the downfall of the top-heavy industrialized nations. During the 1920s, Lenin compromised with capitalistic enterprise in the NEP (New Economic Policy). But in 1928–1929, the first Five-Year Plan for industrialization of manufacturing and collectivization of agriculture was introduced. This was followed by a second Five-Year Plan.

Because of the rapid pace of capital formation, war preparedness, and the state of Russian technology, consumption was severely rationed throughout these years. Workers had ration cards that were honored at specific stores, but money continued to be used.

Excess money income could be spent only upon special goods at higher prices than on the basic ration. Real and money wages differed among occupations, with piece rates and incentive pay for high productivity becoming ever more dominant.

Stalin, one of Lenin's many lieutenants, finally won out in the struggle for power after Lenin's death in the early 1920s. Trotsky and other old-line revolutionaries were accused of plotting with foreign powers against the Soviet Union, and in the middle 1930s a tremendous purge of generals and officials culminated in the sensational Moscow trials—sensational because defendants vied with each other in avowing their own guilt. After the Chamberlain-Hitler appeasement pact, Nazi Germany and Soviet Russia in 1939 signed a nonaggression pact, which lasted until Hitler—flushed with his victory over Poland and France and lusting for the farmlands of the Ukraine—attacked Russia.

With fanatical patriotism and aided by United States lend-lease, the Russians traded their blood for the Germans' until few Germans were left in the Russian homeland. After the defeat of the Axis, the short-lived comradeship with the West flickered out, and the world stood in the shadow of the hydrogen bomb, with Russia trying to spread her influence over Europe and Asia and with the Atlantic nations and ourselves bent on stopping her on the one hand, and China threatening her on the other.

In the postwar period, Stalin's one-man rule became more and more paranoid, and his death in 1953 brought in the inevitable revulsion toward his regime. What seemed to be a thaw set in under the committee rule of Khrushchev, and sprigs of criticism began to push up their sprouts. But the Poles, Hungarians, and Leningrad students learned the hard way that winter was not quite over. Peaceful coexistence became the new official line, and was continued after Khrushchev's replacement by the committee rule of Brezhnev. Faced by the rivalry of China, Russia was in no mood to tolerate a free press and electorate in Czechoslovakia, much less dissident intellectuals at home.

THE SOVIET ECONOMY

So much for capsule history. How does the Soviet Union get the three basic problems decided: WHAT shall be produced, HOW, and FOR WHOM?

In broad outline,[2] the picture is this: *The state owns almost all factors of production:* factories, mines, and land. Workers generally earn their living *by wages;* they do have considerable choice of occupation, but a Soviet citizen does not have unlimited right to seek employment in any region and industry that happens to capture his fancy.

WHAT A political decision is made that defense and capital formation are to be pushed hard; what is left over is permitted to go to consumers' goods. While a Russian can indicate his preferences among different goods by the way he spends his income, any resulting shortages or gluts have been permitted only recently to result in the bidding up or down of consumer-goods prices, thereby automatically producing the positive or negative returns that serve to rechannel resources. So long as goods were very scarce, central planners

[2] F. D. Holzman, *Readings in the Soviet Economy* (Rand McNally, Chicago, 1962), is a useful reference. See also, in P. A. Samuelson, *Readings in Economics* (McGraw-Hill, New York, 1970, 6th ed.), articles by expert Abram Bergson of Harvard.

could decide that people would want so much of food, so much of shoes, and so much of various other necessities of life. Any and all of these were eagerly bought as they became available: if the local store or commissary had shoes not exactly your size, you were glad to take them a little large rather than do without.

Now that some of the comforts—and even luxuries—of life are beginning to become available, it is no longer enough to think of giving people merely what they "need," and centralized planning has become a little more difficult. These days certain goods will not get bought at all, and the planners have come to learn that they must cut back on them. Even advertising and selling have reared their heads in Russia! It is harder to learn what people want than what they do *not* want, and marketing surveys are still in their infancy. The Soviet commissars are not yet experienced in determining what people would want most *if* they had the choice; but they do find it useful to watch what Americans and others abroad like to consume and then later introduce such products: thus that rare comrade who gets a car will find it resembling our cars of the past; and experts tell us this imitative pattern, which is not at all irrational since it assumes that what one human being will like also will be sought by another, is becoming more common.

With respect to capital goods and military expenditure, *direct state decisions* are made. Industrialization is pushed hard: electrification, transportation, mining development, a big push in chemicals and fertilizers, collectivization of agriculture and crop patterns—*such matters are broadly determined by conscious political decision.*

How   Private enterprise is negligible in importance. Instead, the typical Soviet factory will be a state-owned *enterprise:* just as the president of General Motors owns little of its total stock, the manager or head of this state-owned enterprise has no ownership of its capital; but he does get better-than-average pay for his work, plus various travel expenses, auto transport, and other special privileges. This member of the Galbraithian "technostructure" may even get bonuses, and his chance of promotion to a bigger enterprise will depend upon how well his enterprise meets its quota. He gives orders much like any boss and expects his subordinates to obey them, just as he obeys orders from above. (To avoid penalties for failing to meet his quota, he may hoard steel and other materials rather than give them to some other enterprise; and many cases have been observed where bureaucrats will contrive to make it appear that their plant has been very productive, even if that means they must conceal its true potential efficiency. Ex-AMPLES: Enterprises may malinger so as to get a low quota that can be easily achieved or surpassed. Stories have been well told of a transportation enterprise which moved carloads of water back and forth in order to be able to say it had accomplished the target of so many physical ton-miles.)

In recent years, such meaningless physical quotas are beginning to be replaced by "profitability" criteria of performance that do involve *economic valuation* of diverse goods—a modest step in the direction of Western pricing methods.

The decision of how to combine various productive factors—land and labor, degree of mechanization—appears to depend on a mixture of purely technical considerations and adaptations to the scarcities of various economic resources. A continual process of trial and error goes on. The observer finds operations curiously uneven: on the one hand, he may see a military ballistic plant which has achieved a precision of ball bearings and gyroscopes rivaling the best in the world; on the other hand, he may find things being done in an almost unbelievably primitive way, with the quality of output practically worthless. (EXAMPLE: A Soviet farmwoman may be assigned 1 cow to take care of; on a mechanized Wisconsin dairy farm, a man and wife may take care of 50 cows, in addition to performing countless other daily chores.)

All Soviet economic life is a pyramid tapering upward. Above the individual enterprises in an industry and region will be a regional economic council. Above the regional councils will be a council of ministers; alongside the ministries will be the planners of the Gosplan. Experts tell us it is quite misleading to concentrate on the organizational charts of the process, for *there is a constantly changing mixture of centralization and decentralizing:* fiats, delegated responsibility, and initiative; carrots of reward and kicks or imprisonments as penalties.

Some things are very much the same everywhere. The head of an enterprise will, almost certainly, be a member of the Communist party. A successful bureaucrat there is something like a successful "organization man" here: he must be obedient but resourceful, both obsequious and arrogant, energetic and nonsentimental. The point is not that the worst types get ahead. The point is that ability does count on the average; but mere technical ability without the skill of getting along with people will not usually be enough either in Detroit or in Volgograd.

Experts also tell us that it is quite naïve to think that there is an elaborate formalized structure of planning, so that one could write a treatise on pure communistic economics that would equal in length a treatise on the general equilibrium of purely competitive market systems.

FOR WHOM   To a considerable degree the Russian economy works for the security of the state and for the future. How much the present generation of Russians consume of private goods is *not* primarily determined by their day-to-day spending and working decisions. True, they do earn wages (and a small amount of interest or lottery winnings on government bonds is also permitted). Moreover, wages are by no means equal, and certainly not higher for the needy and handicapped than for the energetic and educated. Skilled workers get much more than unskilled. Free trade-unions as we know them do not exist, but woe to the manager who gets all the workers against him. Piece rates and incentive systems are frequently used, and there is much exhortation toward working hard for the fatherland and for the "brotherhood of man." (Soviet novels often had for their plots the tale of how a good boy and girl foil the malingering of antisocial culprits and by use of a virtuous tractor overcome the recalcitrance of the stubborn soil. Boy meets girl here as everywhere, but the durable goods are much in evidence.)

Social classes as Marx and Engels knew them in 1848 may not exist in the Soviet Union, but there is a definite pattern of social and political stratification. A poor boy who is bright may become a physicist and live well. It is important for him to rank high in the exams that select the few who can go to college. (His way at the university is completely paid for, just as the comrade who puts the shot in the Olympics is paid to pursue that occupation.) After graduation he hopes to score well enough to be able to pursue the study of physics in Moscow, rather than be sent out as a technician and engineer to the Ural Mountains or some other distant post. As a well-paid professor he can look down on all but the top bureaucrats: he may have a car, a cottage in the country, and finely equipped laboratories. Of course, he cannot take it with him, but he can at least hope to give his son a good start in the stiff educational competition.

There are various economic devices by which the system ensures that it gets the FOR WHOM it desires—heavy emphasis on industrialization and military security.

For one thing, goods at every stage of production are subject to heavy taxation (the so-called "turnover tax," which contrasts with a tax on true value added). The resulting elevation of prices in relation to wages paid out ensures that the public will be able to consume only a part of all that it can produce, in quite the same way as our economy uses taxes to siphon resources away from private and into public channels. Macroeconomic equilibrium is needed there as here!

Another device is to set a much higher markup over costs for consumers' goods, ensuring that they generally are priced much higher in relation to some set of true economic costs than are military and capital goods. As a third device, certain consumers' goods, such as comfortable housing, are just not purchasable at any price for any but the few lucky persons of peculiar economic and political advantage.

By all such methods the Soviet authorities fight the battle against the price inflation that would burst out as workers try to spend their incomes on the limited supply of consumers' goods. To one who has studied modern economics, it is evident that these are devices by which their society determines FOR WHOM goods will be produced in accordance with *social* decision making.

NEW TRENDS IN IRON CURTAIN ECONOMICS?

Soviet economics is in a state of flux. In recent years intense debates have broken out concerning the use of some kind of pricing and profitability criteria that begin to approach a little the analytical tools of Western economics. Marxian concepts seem to be reserved for training of the young and for alleged explanation and denouncement of capitalistic economies. Among the high-level planners themselves, few words are squandered on such subjects. Instead, as in the much-debated writings of E. Liberman, there are attempts to get away from setting of crude quantitative goals expressed in physical units. There is to be emphasis on quality and on weighting items by their importance, setting for the plant manager the goal of maximizing something like a profitability magnitude. The hope is to get him to try new products and methods and economize on input requirements, rather than concentrate on establishing a low quota for his plant. Pilot experiments with markets are being planned.

Mathematical methods, such as the input-output analysis associated with W. W. Leontief of Harvard, have been released from Stalin's ban, and are debated as a possible tool for helping the planners allocate their available resources. More advanced methods, known in the West as linear and more general mathematical programming, have been developed by eminent Soviet mathematicians (Kantorowich, Pontryagin, . .); rates of discount, rather like the interest rates used in mixed economies to screen out less important capital projects, have been proposed in considerable variety. Although it cannot be said that they rely on the socialist game of a pricing system as described in Chapter 32's Appendix, there seems increasingly to be a pragmatic mixture of physical accounting and economic planning. And, remember, the pendulum oscillates between epochs of decentralization and of centralization.[3] Moreover, in the Satellite countries—Poland, Hungary, Czechoslovakia, . . .—the issues of pricing and planning are hotly debated.

This is not the place to describe the differences between Marxian and Western economics, nor the developments of either. But the back flyleaf of this book does give a sketch of the family tree of economic doctrines and ideas. Perhaps the widening gulf between the ideology of the Russians and the Chinese, despite the fact that both claim legitimate descent from Marx via Lenin, suggests that the Soviet is moving a small step toward reconciliation with the economic tools of modern analysis. This is not meant to suggest in the least that the Russians are turning to capitalistic enterprise systems or that mixed economies are veering down the road to serfdom and totalitarianism. Rather, the notions of scarcity, production, costs, substitution, and resource allocation have to be objectively regarded as fundamental in almost any economic system.

It is a mistake to think that most people in Eastern Europe are miserable there. While it is undoubtedly true that few citizens of the West would trade their degree of economic comfort and political freedom for life in the Soviet, it is also true that a Soviet citizen thinks that he is living in a paradise in comparison with life in Communist China, where family rights are much more restricted, industry is very much more primitive, comfort and living standards much lower, and the pressure on the individual to serve society infinitely greater. Remember, too, that life under the czars was no bed of roses for most classes; and to the eye of the traveler from impoverished Asia and Africa, the rising degree of Russian affluence must seem impressive.

COMPARATIVE ECONOMIC GROWTH

Today we know many facts about the Russian system. Teams of our economic experts pore over U.S.S.R. statistics, and while they often find the data incomplete and occasionally deliberately misleading, the experts are largely in agreement that it is possible to make an objective appraisal of the approximate dimensions of the Russian economy. No longer is there any excuse for the extreme views that the Soviets are so hopelessly inefficient that they cannot keep even one Model T Ford in good repair, or that they are giants 7 feet tall who will soon outstrip everyone else in productivity.

---

[3] Agricultural performance, as in the case of China, still seems to be remarkably bad on the Russian collective and state farms. These appear to be much too large for efficiency, averaging 7,000 and 22,000 acres of sown land, in contrast to the 400-acre average of our efficient commercial farms. Private farming is permitted in only minute degree, but the product of these private efforts seems to be many times higher per unit of input than on the collective and state farms. Uniform rules, ill-informed and subject to swings of fad and fashion, get imposed on everybody in a region. Supplies of tractor equipment, spare parts, fertilizers, and fungicides are quite limited, and optimal use is not made of them by the rural populace, who have little incentive to be efficient. Despite unfavorable weather, much-improved efficiency would seem technically feasible in the future.

The basic facts, as audited by numerous independent scholars here and abroad, seem to be these: In 1970 the Soviet gross national product was between two-thirds and one-third of ours in size, depending on whether one makes this difficult comparison by using dollar price weights or ruble price weights.[4] By splitting the difference for the purpose of a rough approximate calculation, one can give a reasonable estimate:

In the 1970s, as in the 1960s, U.S.S.R. real GNP is about one-half United States real GNP.

Since the Soviet Union's population is larger than the American and since she devotes a smaller fraction of her GNP to consumption, it follows that her real consumption per capita is an even smaller fraction of ours. This conclusion of the expert is well confirmed by casual observation of visitors to Russia.

But the issue that now dominates discussion and debate is not the comparative strengths of the two economies now, but rather whether one is growing so much faster than the other as to be able to narrow or close the gap in the decades ahead. This has led to the great game of what has been called "growthmanship." While it would be idle to deny that a great deal of nonsense has been talked about this subject and while the experts are the first to admit that their estimates are only approximations, there is a nucleus of objective economic fact that deserves impartial analysis.

Depending upon what years have been selected for comparison, one can say that America's real GNP has been growing at a long-term rate of between 4 and $4\frac{1}{2}$ per cent per year. Although there is often talk of a 6 per cent growth rate as a goal for the United States, a careful canvass of economic experts of all shades of political opinion will suggest that most do not really think this likely in the decades ahead. Figure 42-1 therefore extrapolated from 1970 a range of growth rates, varying from the reasonably optimistic to the reasonably pessimistic.

Estimates for the Soviet Union are more difficult. All seem to agree that her post-World War II growth rates started out considerably greater than ours as a percentage per year,[5] even though they have not surpassed the performance of such mixed economies as West Germany and Japan. Furthermore, many experts believe that it is easier for an economy that starts out from a lower level of productivity to show high initial percentage improvement. (After all, to go from zero to any positive level is an infinite jump.) They think that, as the Soviet Union reaches stages of development more comparable with ours and places greater emphasis on services, she is likely to show a retardation in her rate of growth and may lose the advantage of imitation of more advanced technologies.

[4]There is a technical index-number problem involved that need only be indicated. Here luxuries are fairly plentiful compared with necessities; the opposite is the case there, as can be illustrated by the fact that the ratio of auto prices to rye-bread price will there be many times the price ratio here. Result: If we calculate real GNPs for both places using their ruble price ratios, our numerous autos will show up with terrific weight and their GNP will be not much more than one-third ours. (Officially, these facts are denied; but their experts are probably in fairly close agreement privately.)

[5]In the 1960s we have not been the inferior performer. And it should be pointed out that, if our GNP is twice that of Russia, then to equal our *absolute* rate of growth her percentage rate would now have to be twice ours. Expert testimony before Congress and elsewhere estimates the following percentage annual growth rates for the Soviet Union: 1950–1958, 6.8; 1955–1960, $6\frac{1}{2}$; 1958–1963, 4.2; 1963–1964, 3; 1964–1970, $4\frac{1}{3}$–$6\frac{1}{3}$.

So they caution against blindly extrapolating the data of the recent past into the future.

While there is much that is persuasive in such arguments, there is also the fact that they may provide temptingly optimistic rationalizations to those who are wishful that America can stay ahead without effort. Moreover, the cases of Germany and other nations that are ahead of the Soviet Union in productivity, and yet seem to have hit a new rate of advance, warn us that such arguments of inevitable senility can, at least for a while, go into reverse. And although Marxians have in the past argued as if society were like a child, sure to go through certain inevitable stages of development, modern scholars know better than to be dogmatic about pronouncing on the *necessary* timeshape of industrial development. Consequently, in Fig. 42-1 the extrapolation for the Soviet Union shows a spread that can encompass both optimistic and pessimistic views.

It will be evident that the Soviet Union is unlikely to overtake our real GNP for a long time to come, and our per capita welfare level for a still longer time to come. In concluding any comparison of the growth patterns of the two systems, the economist ought to state two cautions:

War strength today cannot be measured by real GNP alone. Military analysts estimate that the U.S.S.R. now mounts about the same military effort as does the United States. Her real GNP may be half ours, but she devotes twice our fraction of the total to security purposes. Furthermore, once both parties have innumerable nuclear bombs and during the time period for which the U.S.S.R. enjoys a parity in the rocket and missile area, it is not necessarily the case that the United States, even by considerably increasing the fraction of her GNP spent on defense, could thereby gain decisive military advantage. Hence, for those concerned with the power struggle, any retained superiority in real GNP is not a sufficient condition for complacency or belligerence.

Recall, too, the fact that our two systems are on trial in the eyes of many uncommitted underdeveloped nations. Even if the United States stays well ahead of the U.S.S.R., were we to stagnate and she to show a vastly more rapid percentage rate of growth, that might tempt neutrals to imitate in the years ahead the totalitarian pattern of "full speed ahead"—suppression of democratic and personal freedom, and collectivist decision to cut down ruthlessly on current consumption in order to enlarge capital formation and development.

America leads Russia, but will the gap narrow?

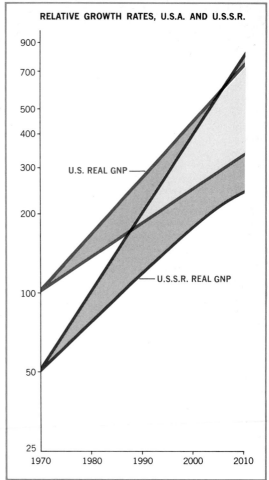

FIG. 42-1. The range of estimates shown here can make no claim to accuracy, but they do portray the nature of the Soviet challenge. (NOTE: All indices are based upon United States real GNP for 1970 = 100 and U.S.S.R. real GNP for 1970 = 50.) In the decade preceding 1970, the United States grew toward the top of the projected range of growth rates. The U.S.S.R., because of bad weather and crops and shortening of the workweek, seems to have moved lower down on its projected range of growth rates.

DIVERSITY ON THE LEFT

In the last part of the twentieth century the communist world no longer presents a monolithic front. The dominance of the Soviet Union is challenged by China, Yugoslavia, Rumania, and Albania. Hungary and Czechoslovakia, in the absence of Russian intervention, showed signs of divergence from the Moscow pattern. The two most interesting variants of communist development are, from the viewpoint of economics, the Yugoslav and Chinese alternatives.

Yugoslav decentralization   The communist resistance movement came to power under Tito after World War II. From 1945 to 1950 a program of planned development along conventional Stalinist lines worked out badly—both in terms of planning goals and in comparison with post–World War I similar years. Following the political break with the Russian COMINFORM in 1948, Yugoslavia undertook a new "separate path to socialism" involving "decentralization and popular participation." The experiment has excited much interest abroad, both for its own sake as an example of "participatory democracy" and as the only instance of a successful retreat from Soviet dominance.

In essence, Titoism involves a return to greater dependence on market pricing, on profitability criteria and incentives. It does not mean abandonment of socialism and one-party control, nor of central planning of macroeconomic goals. But it does mean that a factory may be run by its own workers in many sectors of the economy. Here is a sample case.

Twenty to one hundred workers in a factory form a workers' council. Nominally they elect their own managers. (They may even advertise for a trained executive!) They "borrow" their capital from the central pool. (Sometimes capital is "auctioned" off to the highest bidder.) *The firm can decide to produce what it thinks will sell.* It may import raw materials from abroad, sometimes even on foreign credit. It can cut costs in the hope that, after it has paid its income and land taxes, what is left over can go to the workers as bonus income or be plowed back into the enterprise.

How have things worked out? From 1950 to 1970 progress has been uneven, and there have been oscillations between centralization and decentralization. But the system has been viable, and growth under it has surpassed that of the earlier Stalinist period. Even if the cynicism expressed by insiders concerning the amount of power the workers themselves exercise is justified, this system of syndicalist structure presumably offers some countervailing influence to the power of the bureaucrats, those whom Milovan Djilas has called "the new class."

Maoist China   China is as far to the left of the U.S.S.R. as Yugoslavia is to the right. China and the U.S.S.R. each claim that the other has deviated from the legitimate Marx-Lenin line of communist development. (See the back flyleaf for the bifurcated genealogy.) Politically, the Chinese regard the Soviet doctrine of peaceful coexistence as heresy.

Economically, as befits a more primitive economy still in its early revolutionary years, the Chinese adhere to a more centralist policy. Collectivization of peasant agriculture has involved the usual drop in food output and decimation of the population. There has been the usual preoccupation with industrialization, with emphasis on heavy industry.

In 1958 a fair-minded observer of mainland China, India, and Pakistan might have expected China to show by far the greatest rate of real growth in the following dozen years. Under Chairman Mao the populace was mobilized for collective effort and sacrifice. It was even expected that steel could be produced in thousands of backyard furnaces. A "great leap forward" seemed to be in the offing.

Looking back from 1970, we see that reality differed from these expectations. India, under democracy, made uneven progress—depending on monsoon weather conditions and foreign aid. Pakistan, under military dictatorship and by dint of massive foreign aid to agriculture, was able to increase fertilizer and food production. China was notably successful in producing a uranium bomb, and then later a hydrogen bomb. But the increasing emphasis on ideological soundness and hostility toward technical experts led to a surprising degree of economic stagnation. Unlike the Russian statistics, which turned out under careful audit to have some tolerable relation to reality, the initial Chinese claims for production increases turned out in subsequent careful examination and cross-checking to be grossly inflated. A 1969 opinion by two Cornell experts tells a more sobering tale:[6]

The national product fell by roughly 15 per cent from 1958 to 1961. . . . Only by 1965 did the economy finally regain the 1958 level. . . . The Great Proletarian Cultural Revolution . . . led to a loss of 400,000 specialists who would have completed their training during 1967–68 had the schools not been closed. . . . Economism—i.e., efficiency, became one of the worst epithets. . . . Revolutionary mass enthusiasm replaced trained management. . . . Essentially, there has been no significant economic growth for the decade 1958–68.

A FINAL VIEW

We have studied the tools of economic analysis to understand how an economy works. Most of our chapters have been devoted to the mixed economy—not to the laissez faire dreamworld that never existed or to the utopia still unborn. And as that mixed economy changes, the tools to analyze it and its alternatives are ever in need of improvement.

There is a temptation for those living in the most prosperous part of the world to succumb to complacency, both about themselves and about their mixed economy. And indeed in our discussions of national-income determination, of microeconomic pricing, of growth and stabilization policies of the new economics, there has appeared to be tremendous progress in comparison with even so recent a date as 1929.

But at the same time, objective analysis of things as they are shows there remain many features of economic life which the concerned younger generation find ethically troublesome. What to them that monopoly is less prevalent in 1970 than in 1900—if it still is too much prevalent, and if no great diminution had taken place since 1945? What

[6] Letter to *New York Times*, June 17, 1969, by Professors Walter Galenson and Ta-Chung Liu. A more favorable view of these same events is expressed by Cambridge's Professor Joan Robinson: "Whatever disturbances there may have been in the course of the Cultural Revolution, economic development seems to have been running on. The harvest for 1968 is reported to be good once more; in some industries there have been setbacks due to disturbances, but in many there are claims of new technical advances, increased production, savings in costs and improvements in quality due to the simplified organization and high morale that the Cultural Revolution brought into the factories." (*The Cultural Revolution in China*, Penguin Books Ltd., London, 1969, p. 149.)

to them that the poor are less numerous and less poor than they used to be—if still there persist stubborn inequalities of economic opportunity, and no notable change in inequality of income since 1945? In their eyes how can a system be deemed satisfactory which still countenances racial discrimination and stratification? True, our modern economic world is better in many ways than the past. But more is now expected of it.

This raises unanswerable questions concerning the rate of improvement of the system. This has been a century of change in the mixed economy. But how fast is fast enough? How fast is too fast? You cannot expect a hungry mother in Appalachia to give the same answer to this question as a debutante from Sweet Briar. The role of value judgment can never be usurped by so-called "neutral science."

Beyond the internal questions of technical economics, there emerge basic political questions concerning the relationships between (1) *personal* freedoms—civil liberties and individual rights—and (2) *business or market* freedoms—property rights, freedom from price ceilings and floors, rationing, etc. Almost always those who wish to reform the workings of the system wish to turn to government for new programs and measures. Those concerned to conserve what they regard as valuable in our society counter them with the arguments: "In seeking *a better division* of the pie, you will *reduce the size* of the pie by creating distorting inefficiencies. But more important, *personal and property freedoms are one and inseparable.* Only in the Herbert Spencer laissez faire society that you find so repellant will men be free to speak their minds and choose their rulers."

Gradual economic reform need not lead to serfdom:

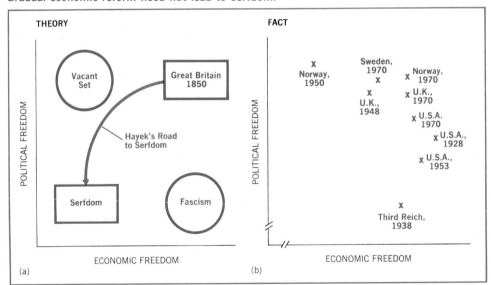

FIG. 42-2. In contrast to the libertarian view of Hayek, in (a) on the left, which holds that government modification of market laissez faire leads to political serfdom, observe the facts of history on the right. Since the 1953 witchhunting days of Senator Joseph McCarthy, political freedoms of American citizens have improved despite increased economic role of government. In Scandinavia or Britain, loss of business and property freedoms has involved no concomitant loss in personal liberties and no approach to a totalitarian pattern in which the citizenry enjoy neither form of freedom.

Here at the end of the book, after our major task of analyzing the economic world has been surveyed, perhaps we can relax the rigor of analysis and speculate about what has not yet been capable of scientific agreement.

What are the presumed relationships, suggested by experience and plausible reflection, between the state of individual freedoms and the interventions by government in the mixed economy?

Figure 42-2 suggests an eclectic alternative to the despairing extreme of a Hayek who says, Economic reform is the road to serfdom; and to the extreme of those who, like Sidney and Beatrice Webb, argued: Political democracy is nothing without the economic democracy that comes only with collective ownership of the means of production.

Speaking for myself, I read in the face of history the more optimistic message: One can have the best of both worlds—programmed improvement of the workings of the market economy along with those best things of life that aren't measured in gross national product—freedom to do one's own thing, freedom to criticize, and freedom to change.

QUESTIONS FOR DISCUSSION

1   Make a list of a number of "isms," describing each and its history.

2   Describe your own vision of Utopia. Does it differ from the present?

3   Compare and contrast fascism and communism. What is the relation of socialism and capitalism to each? To laissez faire and the mixed economy?

4   "The Russians claim they have 'industrial democracy.' This is clearly a different commodity from our political democracy. Even defenders of the Soviet Union will admit that expressions of opinion against the government or Communist party will not be tolerated. Free press—in our sense—is forbidden. Even if a majority of the Russian people were to prefer their form of government, no one should blind himself to its great differences from our own concepts of democracy and freedom." Discuss as objectively as you can.

5   Outline WHAT, HOW, and FOR WHOM in Russia.

6   What economic policies in the free world might predispose developing countries, like Ghana, Egypt, and Indonesia, to eschew the totalitarian path to development?

7   The U.S.S.R. is showing new interest in *input-output* and *linear programming* techniques. Review page 736's discussion of Leontief, and the samplings of linear programming on pages 17, 36, and 510.

8   Describe the problems of comparing growth rates in the United States and the U.S.S.R., in India and China, North and South Korea, East and West Germany.

Review your understanding of the following concepts:

laissez faire, mixed economy	centralized planning, Soviet style
anarchism; fascism, socialism, communism	Yugoslavian hybrid
	new U.S.S.R. pricing and profitability trends
nationalization of industry	economic freedoms, democracy
indicative planning, French style	comparative growth rates

Index

Slavery:
abolition of, 767
economics of, 781–782
Slichter, Sumner, 124, 131, 567n.
Sliding peg (see Crawling peg)
Small Business Administration, 80
Smith, Adam, 1, 3, 372, 463, 607n., 748, 765, 822
deer and beaver hunting, example, 713
Invisible Hand concept, 37, 39, 476, 482, 609–611, 712, 782
labor theory of value, 27–28, 34, 523, 613, 712–713, 717–718
paradox of value, 416–417
pinmaking, example, 49
taxation, canons of, 331, 332
theories analyzed, 712–716
The Wealth of Nations, 1, 712
Smith, Victor E., 17n.
Snow, C. P., 4
Social overhead capital, 748–749
Social security taxes, 158, 164
Social stratification, opportunity and, 116–118
Social wants, 149
public goods and, 150–151
Socialism, 710–711, 820–823
British, 822
capitalism and, 819
creeping, 145
elements of philosophy, 821–822
Fabian, 820, 822
government ownership in, 47–48, 144–145, 821
interest in, 580
Socialist parties, 820
Soil conservation, 392, 544
Solow, Robert M., 516–517, 735n., 802n.
economic theories analyzed, 718–721, 724, 733–734
South Africa, gold sales, 699n.
Soviet Union:
agriculture, 829n.
economic growth, 743, 745, 750–751, 796–797
compared with United States, 3, 829–831
prospects, 3, 830–831
rate, 830–831
economy, 711–712, 825–829
education in, 827–828
gold mining in, 700
history, 824–825
income inequality, 112n.
interest in, 580, 829
planning, 824–829

Soviet Union:
prices, 825, 828–830
taxes, 828
wages, 827
Space program, expenditures for, 804n.
Special Drawing Rights (SDRs), 305n., 629, 699, 703
Specialization, 46, 48–50
comparative advantage and, 645, 647, 650, 663, 665
economic growth and, 749
extent of market and, 463
interdependence and, 49–50
tariff and, 677
Speculation, 399–406
consumption stability and, 403
in foreign exchange, 701n.
prices and, 399–402
Spencer, Herbert, 710, 820, 834
Spending:
abstinence from, 47, 581, 587
budgetary patterns of, 196–198
income and, 17, 197–198
(See also Consumption schedule; Propensity to spend)
Spengler, Oswald, 712
Sprinkel, Beryl, 310
Stabilizers, built-in, 332–334, 349
Stalin, Josef, 825
Standard Oil Company, 501
Standards of living:
improvement, 107
income and, 106, 108–109
population and, 550–551
production and, 17
in United States, 108–109
Steinbeck, John, 753
Stigler, George J., 17n., 36, 505
Stock exchanges, 67–68, 72–76
crash of 1929, 72–73, 238
New York, 67–68, 72
as people's capitalism, 72
Stocks:
business activity and, 74
common (equities), 72–76, 86–88
convertible bonds and, 87
dividend versus bond yield, 73–74, 88
investment in, 72–76
mutual funds, 75
preferred, 87, 88
price-earnings multiple, 76
random-walk versus chartism, 76
speculation in, 75